THE IMPACT OF COLLECTIVE BARGAINING
ON MANAGEMENT

The Impact of
Collective Bargaining
On Management

By SUMNER H. SLICHTER

JAMES J. HEALY

E. ROBERT LIVERNASH

The Brookings Institution, *Washington, D.C.*

THE BROOKINGS INSTITUTION is an independent organization engaged in research and education in the social sciences. Its principal purposes are to aid in the development of sound public policies and to provide advanced training for students in the social sciences.

The Institution was founded December 8, 1927, as a consolidation of three antecedent organizations: the Institute for Government Research, 1916; the Institute of Economics, 1922; and the Robert Brookings Graduate School of Economics and Government, 1924.

The general administration of the Institution is the responsibility of a self-perpetuating Board of Trustees. In addition to this general responsibility the By-Laws provide that, "It is the function of the Trustees to make possible the conduct of scientific research and publication, under the most favorable conditions, and to safeguard the independence of the research staff in the pursuit of their studies and in the publication of the results of such studies. It is not a part of their function to determine, control, or influence the conduct of particular investigations or the conclusions reached." The immediate direction of the policies, program, and staff of the Institution is vested in the President, who is assisted by an advisory council, chosen from the professional staff of the Institution.

In publishing a study, the Institution presents it as a competent treatment of a subject worthy of public consideration. The interpretations and conclusions in such publications are those of the author or authors and do not necessarily reflect the views of other members of the Brookings staff or of the administrative officers of the Institution.

Foreword

THE BROOKINGS INSTITUTION in 1941 published a major study of *Union Policies and Industrial Management,* by Sumner H. Slichter. Because of changes in labor-management relations since that time Professor Slichter was invited to undertake a thoroughgoing revision of the original volume.

Professor Slichter enlisted the assistance of two of his Harvard University colleagues, James J. Healy and E. Robert Livernash, as co-authors. The three of them worked closely with a field staff of research assistants for nearly three years gathering new information firsthand from companies, unions, and other sources. The accumulated evidence revealed that, during the war and since, marked changes had occurred in the impact of union activities on industrial management. In scope and substance the authors have produced far more than a revision of the earlier book. They have produced a wholly new treatment of this important subject.

To the three authors and to those who worked closely with them Brookings wishes to record its gratitude for the contributions they have made. We deeply regret that Professor Slichter did not live to see the study in print. With characteristic tenacity, he continued his work on the volume during months of illness and several hospital confinements and completed it only two days before his death. Professors Livernash and Healy assumed responsibility for the final revisions of the manuscript. Virginia Haaga edited the manuscript, and Jean Kyle prepared the index.

The Institution is indebted to the Maurice and Laura Falk Foundation and to the Ford Foundation for financial support that has made this study possible.

ROBERT D. CALKINS
President

September 1960

vii

Authors' Preface

IN UNDERTAKING this study our objective was to discover as much as we could about what has happened and is happening in a significant number of union-management situations. To accomplish this, we talked directly and informally with many management and union representatives to learn in some detail their labor relations experiences. Although we outlined in a general way the topics we wished to investigate, ruling out any attempt to assess the broad economic impact of unions, we did not formulate any precise hypotheses for investigation. We followed Professor Slichter's characteristic approach of trying to acquire through extensive interviews a feeling for important developments in labor relations.

Over a period of three years of intensive field research approximately 650 individuals, representing 150 companies, 25 industry associations, and 40 unions, were interviewed. The companies were not selected on any sampling basis. We attempted to get elements of diversification: manufacturing and nonmanufacturing, various industries, large companies and small companies, and companies in various sections of the country. Considering the matter in retrospect, we probably overemphasized large manufacturing companies. However, what we were after was a significant sample of experience, and in this effort we were successful.

Our debt to the many individuals who assisted us is obvious from the approach we took. We thank sincerely the many company and union officials who spent many hours with us in reviewing their difficulties and accomplishments. Our thanks, however, must remain general because information was obtained in confidence, a confidence which we have endeavored to keep in spirit as well as in letter. We have attempted to conceal identities unless information was a matter of public record or very widely known. We hope that those who contributed will be compensated in some measure by the analysis we have been able to make.

In conducting the interviews and in the preparation of almost 800 memoranda, a substantial contribution was made by the research assistants on the staff of the project: Irwin Herrnstadt, now at Northeastern University, Thayne Robson, now at the University of California at Los Angeles, and Benson Soffer, now at the University of Pittsburgh. For a brief period Garth Mangum, now at Brigham Young University, joined the staff. An important participant in the project was its secretary, Miss Mary Watson, who handled competently the strenuous stenographic and clerical duties. Her sincere and enthusiastic interest contributed greatly to the spirit of the entire undertaking. Miss Florence Stinchfield assisted industriously in the typing of manuscript. The authors are deeply indebted to these individuals.

The project was initiated by Brookings Institution, whose financial support has been considerable. The authors thank the officers and staff of the Institution for their contribution and encouragement. We are also grateful for the assistance of the project's Advisory Committee: Robert D. Calkins, Ralph J. Watkins, David Kaplan, A. D. H. Kaplan, and George W. Taylor.

It is Sumner Slichter, our co-author, to whom the greatest credit must be given. It was he who provided the leadership and inspiration. During the four years devoted to field work and preparation of manuscript our research group spent many hours in stimulating discussion. Those associated with the project will always treasure the memory of working closely with him. At the time of his death the manuscript was substantially completed. Our sincere hope is that the book, which was Sumner Slichter's preoccupying concern during the final years of of his life, will be a fitting tribute to his lifelong interest in this field.

James J. Healy
F. Robert Livernash

Contents

1 / *Introduction*

THIS BOOK DEALS WITH some results of the most distinctive characteristic of the American system of industrial relations, the process of collective bargaining between labor and management. The terms of employment in the United States are determined, more than anything else, by the collective bargain and are embodied in agreements negotiated between employers and unions. These agreements are supplemented by laws, such as workmen's compensation laws, social security laws, wage and hour laws, and factory legislation, but the fact remains that the main immediate determinant of most conditions of employment is the labor-management agreement. With about 125,000 such agreements in force at any one time, the American workman is more richly endowed with self-determined rights than the workman of any other country, and American managements must conduct their operations within an elaborate framework of rules and policies imposed by collective agreements and trade unions.

Extent of Trade Unionism and Collective Bargaining

Although only a minority of the workers in American industry are union members, it is a large and strategic minority. Of the 64 million workers in 1958, about 47 million were nonprofessional and nonsupervisory employees. The others were self-employed, unpaid family workers, or professional employees. The 47 million nonprofessional and nonsupervisory employees constitute the potential trade union membership, and about 18 million of them, or 38 per cent, were organized. The great majority of these trade unionists (about 15 million) were concentrated among the 31 million "blue collar" workers—craftsmen, operatives, and service workers. Among the 13.6 million clerical and sales workers there were only about 2.5 million union members.

1

Although slightly less than half of the blue collar workers are organized, trade unions are dominant in nearly all of the large plants and enterprises of the country—those where technology is most advanced, where capital is used most abundantly, where the productivity of labor is highest, and where technological progress is most rapid. These are the plants and enterprises that by and large pay the highest wages and that take the lead in raising wages and setting wage patterns. In other words, trade union membership is concentrated and strongest where strength counts most of all. About two-thirds of the blue collar workers in manufacturing industries are organized, about four-fifths in mining and construction and in various forms of transportation, and a similarly high proportion in municipal utilities (gas and electric companies). Within the field of manufacturing virtually all of the workers in the needle trades and in the steel, automobile, rubber, paper, meat packing, farm equipment, airplane, and brewing industries are organized, as are a large proportion of workers in the electrical and electronic, printing, chemical, oil, shoe, and pharmaceutical industries.

The great unorganized areas in the labor force are workers in the textile industry (which employs a high percentage of women, is concentrated in rural southern communities, and consists of small enterprises generally paying low wages and having high costs), the women workers, the white collar workers, and the government employees.[1]

The 18 million trade union members are found in about 180 national unions and an undetermined number of independent local unions. The national unions vary greatly in size. There are several, including the teamsters, the automobile workers, and the steelworkers, with close to, or more than, a million members each, and several others, including the carpenters and machinists, each of which has considerably more than half a million members. There are also many small and obscure unions that do not make headlines but that are very powerful—for example, the pattern makers, the photoengravers, and the die sinkers. Most of the unions are affiliated with the AFL-CIO, but there are some important independent unions, such as the coal miners, the teamsters, the longshore and warehouse-

---

[1] There is considerable overlapping among the weakly organized groups. Thus, about four out of five trade unionists are male, but 64 per cent of the clerical workers (among whom unions are weak) are female. Even the several unions composed in the main of women (in the needle trades) are led by male officers.

men, the locomotive engineers. In 1956 the average membership of national unions affiliated with the American Federation of Labor and Congress of Industrial Organizations was 122,000; of unaffiliated national unions, 30,200. In the last 60 years there has been little change in the concentration of union membership in a few large unions. In 1900 the ten largest unions had 52.3 per cent of the membership; in 1920, 43.6 per cent; and in 1929, 44.5 per cent.[2] In 1958 the 10 largest unions had about 44 per cent of the members.[3]

Most of the trade union membership is of recent origin, though several unions are about a hundred years old, and many of them are fifty or more years old. But the great upsurge in union membership came with the vigorous encouragement by government of unionism and collective bargaining beginning in about 1932 or 1933.[4] At the bottom of the great depression in 1932, when public policy toward unions changed, membership was only about 2.9 million. By 1939 it had reached 9.0 million, and by the end of the war in 1945, 14.8 million. In 1958, as stated above, it was about 18 million. Many of the problems of union-management relations stem from the fact that much of the trade union membership and leadership is new.

The rapid growth of trade union membership from less than 3 million to 18 million was accomplished with a surprisingly small amount of social turmoil. In view of the strong traditional anti-union sentiment among American employers, the rather smooth transition to collective bargaining needs to be accounted for.

The unions themselves had little reason to cause trouble—they were having too much success in gaining members. Indeed, the ease with which members could be acquired stimulated inter-union competition and split the labor movement.

Why did not employers produce social turmoil by making a desperate fight to maintain their traditional nonunion plants? There were several reasons. One was that the encouragement of organization received strong backing from the law and public policy. A second was that the prestige and influence of employers was low because of the great depression of the thirties. A third influence was the overwhelming demand for production that was created by World

[2] Leo Wolman, *Ebb and Flow in Trade Unionism* (1936), pp. 16, 172-93.
[3] U. S. Bureau of Labor Statistics, *Directory of National and International Labor Unions in the United States, 1959*, Bulletin 1267, p. 10.
[4] Government encouragement of unionism began with the Norris-LaGuardia Act in 1932 and the National Industrial Recovery Act in 1933.

War II and that employers dared not resist. And finally, when the war was over, came the postwar boom with great opportunity for profits for the plants that were operating. For a combination of these reasons the shift from operation almost without unions to operation with collective bargaining in all the principal industries was made with extraordinarily little stress, strain, and turmoil.

Throughout this book three basic questions have been kept in mind: *what* has been the influence of unions and collective bargaining on management; *why* has the influence in each case been what it has; and *what effects* has union influence had on efficiency and production? The book is intended to influence management and unions by showing them the results of their behavior in the past, by making as clear as possible what results have followed certain policies under various conditions, and with what consequences. And since the fundamental purpose of every organization is to grow and prosper, the book is particularly concerned with the effect of unions and collective bargaining on this objective of business enterprise.

Scope and Purpose of This Study

The chapters that follow are an attempt to answer the question "How is the management of labor in American industry being affected by trade unions and collective bargaining?" Regardless of whether the employees of an enterprise are organized into unions, the same fundamental decisions must be made either by management or by some other organization. Decisions must be made, for example, concerning who is hired, promoted, transferred, laid off; wage scales must be set and often production standards, too; equipment must be selected, and, as technological developments take place, it must be replaced; production schedules must be set; discipline must be maintained and grievances settled; and work must sometimes be transferred from one plant to another.

All of these decisions and many others are affected by unions and by the labor-management contract. In addition to affecting the actual content of policies, trade unions have two other basic influences on industrial relations:

1. They alter the process of decision-making by management, either by direct restrictions on the process or by their indirect influence. Certain decisions may require mutual consent of

management and union; others may be made after consultation —as a matter of policy rather than of union right.

2. They affect the execution of management policies by subjecting the plant administration to organized scrutiny and criticism.

The book examines each of the three basic effects of unions upon management: their effect on the content of policy and practice, their effect on the decision-making process, and their effect on the execution of management policies. Most of the chapters focus on the content of policy and practice. The chapters that deal with the decision-making process are primarily Chapter 29, "Line and Staff Cooperation and the Position of Foremen," and Chapter 30, "Negotiation of Union-Management Contracts." Several chapters, such as Chapter 21, "Disciplinary Policies and Procedures," Chapter 22, "Wildcat Strikes and Union Pressure Tactics," and Chapters 23-26 on grievances, deal primarily with the problems of administering labor-management contracts. A few, among them Chapter 3, "The Control of Hiring," and Chapter 4, "Union Policies on Training and Apprenticeship," are concerned primarily with particular union policies. As a general rule, however, the influence of unions on the decision-making process and the administration of labor-management contracts is so intermingled with the influence of unions on the content of management policy, that the three aspects of union influence are best discussed simultaneously. This method of organization and approach explains why much of the discussion of the influence of unions on the decision-making process and on administration occurs in connection with the discussion of the effect of unions on the content of policy.

In addition, there are analyses of two situations that warrant special attention. One is the problem of high-cost plants, and the other is experience with schemes of union-management cooperation —arrangements under which the union actively assists management in cutting costs or raising output. Special chapters are devoted to each of these two topics.

The authors have not tried to describe what is typical industrial relations practice in American industry as there appears to be no feasible way of getting a representative sample. Material that is significant, rather than representative, has been sought. The varying experience of different companies with wildcat strikes, for example, with problems of automation, or with union time-study men have been of interest. And although no attempt was made to construct a representative sample of industrial relations practice, care was taken to obtain data from a variety of companies, large and small, and widely distributed geographically.

The emphasis of the book is on practice. The authors do not believe that the time is ripe to push very far with theories of the determinants of industrial relations—though the influence of certain determinants, such as the nature of the product and the nature of the market, is fairly obvious. But the factors involved in industrial relations are so numerous and occur in so many combinations and permutations that worthwhile theories are difficult to formulate. What is important is to know what is going on and to see that every industrial relations situation is more or less unique and must be explained as a whole. Particular stress is placed on the interrelationships between different parts of industrial relations policies. What may appear to be repetition in the book results from discussion of the same phenomena from different points of view.

While the scope of the book is broad, it makes no attempt to deal with the effects of unions and collective bargaining on the inter-industry wage structure, nor does it treat such economic issues as wage and price trends and distributive shares. Attention is concentrated on issues closely related to the day-to-day relations of unions and employers.

Whom is the book intended to help, and on what terms? To a limited extent it is intended to help *both* managements and trade unions—to help each party deal with the other with greater understanding and insight. But helping both sides can be the purpose of the book only up to a certain point because the objectives of unions and managements are sometimes in conflict. In cases of conflict, therefore, its orientation is provided by the goals of management. This does not mean that the purpose of the book is to show managements how to crush unions. The book accepts the widely-held view that workers are entitled to bargain with management through agents of their own choosing. It accepts the position that the terms of the employment contract should be set in the main through collective bargaining. The essential aim of the book is to analyze experience with collective bargaining for the purpose of helping business concerns grow and prosper in the kind of economic environment provided by the American trade union movement.

The impact of unions on management depends on many things—

on the nature of the union (its philosophy, its government, its traditions), on the nature of the management, including the kind of union-management relationship the company favors, and on personalities on each side. Some unions aspire to be pattern setters and pioneers; others are content to be followers; some are militant; others are easygoing; some are democratic; others are oligarchies or dictatorships, in which the rank and file have little to say. Industrial unions, because of their composition, pursue different policies from craft unions. Some managements are alert, aggressive, and highly systematic in their approach to every problem; others are weak and blundering and far from intelligent. Some managements are dominated by brilliant leaders, geniuses or near geniuses; others are made up of organization men among whom there is little originality or leadership. Variations in personalities among both union leaders and management are equally broad.

How to deal with the influences of these many differences on industrial relations poses a problem. Instead of trying to classify individuals, unions, and managements, which would have been cumbersome and not very enlightening, reports of a large variety of experiences were collected. They were obtained by going into the plants and finding out what happened and (if possible) why it happened. The emphasis has been on first-hand contact with the principals in the experiences described. The authors have tried to show the interplay of the multitude of influences that combine to make industrial relations what they are.

The importance of an inquiry into the impact of trade unions and collective bargaining on industrial relations is self-evident. The efficiency of American industry is at stake—the ability of managements to use resources of men and capital with reasonable freedom and effectiveness. Even more important issues are at stake because labor-management contracts and union policies represent by far the most detailed attempt to regulate men's lives that any organization has attempted, except a few religious groups.

Human history shows a continuing conflict between individuals and institutions. Institutions have a way of becoming inflexible, restrictive, and out-of-date. Individuals are constantly trying to assert themselves against the conformities imposed by institutions. A study of history supports the view that in this contest between man and his institutions the individual is slowly winning out, though he has not had an unbroken series of victories. The contest swings sometimes in favor of individuals and sometimes in favor of institutions. The most complete control of the group over the individual is found in primitive societies. Certainly modern man in western Europe and in America is more individualistic and more disposed to challenge authority than was medieval man. Collective bargaining represents an institutional arrangement, and there is always danger that the regimentation of men by institutions will be pushed too far. Our major objective is to deepen our understanding of collective bargaining experience as it has developed and changed during its recent unique growth.

2 / *Issues for Management in Industrial Relations*

WHEN A TRADE UNION becomes the bargaining representative for a group of employees, the management of the company is required sooner or later to make a number of important decisions pertaining to its relationship with the union. It is easier for the management to make the necessary adjustments if the concern is large enough to have an industrial relations staff headed by an executive of considerable stature, but the kind of decisions to be made are substantially the same whether the concern is large or small. Indeed, the development of wise personnel policies is likely to be more important in small concerns than in large ones since small concerns are dependent less on technology and more on personnel. Failure to balance the interests of the company and those of the union can be disastrous in the long run to both the company and the employees. If the company is to prosper, its relations with the union must promote efficient and economical operation.

This chapter examines the principal issues that a management must consider in working out a relationship with a union, particularly in administering a union-management contract. It discusses in a general way decisions that have been made in dealing with various problems; how they have been implemented is considered in a later chapter.

The fundamental issues for management in personnel and industrial relations that arise sooner or later in all unionized plants are of five principal types:

1. Decisions influencing fundamental management policies toward unions and collective bargaining,
2. Problems of adjusting to the presence of the union,
3. Policies dealing with the administration of union-management contracts,

9

4. Policies designed to adapt the structure of management to dealing with the union,

5. Procedural policies implementing management's basic labor policies.

Decisions Influencing Management Policies Toward Unions and Collective Bargaining

When employees want to deal with management through a union, the most fundamental question is how far management should be guided by definite policies. Every enterprise believes its actions to be guided by well-considered policies, whereas actually many policies are empty slogans that merely give the appearance of policy-guided action.

The conclusion that, in general, actions of management should be governed by policies does not exclude the possibility of some deliberate opportunism or experiment. Management is constantly being confronted with new and unusual situations, in which the wise choice may be to drift or to experiment. But there is a sharp contrast between drifting or experimenting for the purpose of developing policies, and opportunism that represents a failure to appreciate the need for policies. It is the latter sort of opportunism that has proved costly in many companies. The importance of policy development is discussed in Chapter 29.

A second basic policy question is "How important are industrial relations policies relative to other policies?" Some managements never face up squarely to this question, and yet if the short-run interests of the business owners in sales and profits are balanced against their long-run interests in low production costs, there must also be a good balance between the interest of the enterprise in quick and uninterrupted deliveries to customers and its interest in efficient operating methods. In a few industries, market considerations or the strong technological position of the company make costs of production of secondary importance. In many other industries, costs of production are of less *immediate* importance than are uninterrupted deliveries to customers. But in most industries, success depends in the long run on costs being competitive, and management's success in achieving competitive costs depends in large measure on industrial relations policies.

A few firms are in a position to dictate the nature of their relationship with the union; many small firms must take what conditions the union offers and get along as best they can; most firms, however, are more or less an equal match for the union, and the quality of their relationship with the union depends on the skill shown in negotiating and administering the agreement. The best goal for most firms is a stable relationship with the union on terms that permit the firm to be competitive and to adapt itself to changing conditions.

How can this goal of a stable and competitive relationship be achieved? Through the manner in which the company negotiates and administers the union-management contract. Here is where top management plays a decisive role. Top management may not conduct negotiations, and it may not participate directly in very many administrative decisions, but the kind of policies pursued in negotiation and administration are its responsibility. For example, only top management can decide that customers must wait and that large profits must be temporarily sacrificed to resist efforts by the union to saddle the company with wasteful working rules or featherbedding practices. Unless top management takes a firm position in advance against accepting uneconomic practices, subordinate officials will tolerate them rather than assume the responsibility of failing to meet production schedules.

A good job of negotiation and administration requires that a management representative be prepared to give almost unlimited time to these matters. Most managements are more interested in making and selling goods than in discussing grievances or the terms of contracts. Union representatives, however, often have almost unlimited time for these matters. Managements that are in a hurry to get back to making goods are likely to find that their haste is very expensive—that discussions are terminated only when management makes costly concessions. Hence, managements should be prepared, if possible, to negotiate with the unions through persons who are not responsible for day-to-day production. Large companies can afford to provide special personnel; small employers may need to economize the time of operating men by being represented by an association or a lawyer.

General Motors is an example of a top management that saw clearly from the start the importance of both good agreements and good administration of agreements. General Motors saw that the rise of unions threatened the freedom of management to run the plants and that this freedom would be gradually nibbled away unless the company was willing, if necessary, to take long and expensive strikes to protect it. Hence, top management made it clear to subordinate management and to the union that the company was prepared at any time to take strikes over certain rights or procedures that top management regarded as essential to efficient operations.[1]

Another important question for the company is, "What kind of a man shall head the industrial relations staff?" If top management is aware of the important long-run effects of industrial relations on labor costs, it will see that the staff is headed by a man of stature and resourcefulness who commands enough confidence to argue for minority points of view within management if necessary and to recommend innovations in policies. Furthermore, men of perception, ingenuity, and insight are needed to work out the best industrial relations procedures. For example, management, while doing freely what it has a right to do under the union-management contract, should rely on persuasion rather than on the assertion of rights, lest it build up in the union a demand for changes in the contract. Another example is the decision of the management of a multiplant company to shift consideration of fourth-step grievances from the central personnel office to the plant where the grievance originated with those immediately involved, the complaining workmen and the foreman, present at the hearing. The reasoning was that the participation of the people immediately involved keeps the grievance concrete and helps them to see what the union-management contract is and what it means. A representative of management said: "If you are going to have people accepting something, you have to bring them into the process of putting meaning into the contract."

Should multiplant companies negotiate a master contract with the union for all their plants or separate contracts for each plant? Opinions differ on this. Some companies prefer the simplicity of master contracts.[2] Others have taken long strikes rather than sign master

---

[1] Of course, the strong position of General Motors in the industry and the fact that it deals with millions of buyers rather than with two or three large customers helps the company treat industrial relations as important relative to sales, but in the main the success of General Motors in administering its contracts stems from top management's clear perception of the long-run importance of the issues involved.

[2] A study of 87 multiplant companies showed that 36 had master agreements, and 51 had individual plant agreements. Among the 36 companies with master contracts, 17 were with the United Automobile Workers, 8 with the United Steelworkers, 4 with

contracts. In several cases companies have gone through long strikes in order to get rid of master contracts. Particularly if a company is in several lines of business, with different plants making different products and facing different competitive conditions, there is a strong case for separate plant contracts rather than a master contract. There is also a case for separate plant contracts when plants are in labor markets with substantially differing wage scales. The important point, however, is that management should not make the decision without careful consideration of alternatives.

Problems of Adjusting to the Presence of the Union

The coming of a union is almost bound to create uncertainty in the minds of many officials and technicians as to the effect on their duties, authority, and relations with employees. These uncertainties are particularly pronounced in plants where managements use supervisors to fight the efforts of the union to organize the employees. The foremen may wonder where they stand in relation to the union they opposed. Recognition of the union may cause the foremen to feel that top management has let them down, in spite of the fact that recognition may be required by law. And recognition of the union may be interpreted by the foremen as evidence that top management is surrendering its right to run the plant.

As a general rule, foremen make the change from opposing the union to administering the union-management contract with surprising smoothness. But there are a few cases where the transition involves difficulties. There are plants where foremen fail to assert their authority in their own departments and allow many decisions pertaining to work assignments, rates, overtime, seniority questions that foremen usually make to be made by union stewards or committeemen. To avoid confusion in the minds of foremen and other superiors, top management at the beginning of its relationship with the union should make clear what it expects of subordinate and intermediate supervisors.[3]

The need to clarify what is expected of operating officers may persist in a few cases for years after the union has been recognized.

---

the United Rubber Workers, 4 with the International Union of Electrical Workers, and the remainder with miscellaneous unions.

[3] Sometimes there is a case for appeasement or opportunism, as was pointed out above.

An unusually astute and reflective management described the prob-lem as follows:

> The company came out of the war with an attitude on the part of second and third line management that you can't go forward and do things as long as you have unions. This raised a matter of delicate balance. Management mustn't try to defeat the unions and throw them out, but at the same time it must stand up for what is right and must sell lower management the idea that management must not pur-sue a policy of appeasement. This is a problem that has to be care-fully handled because a lot of resentment against the union has been built up in the first line supervision. The first line supervision has to be brought back to the feeling that the union has to be accepted but not allowed to interfere with management.

Important in adjusting to the presence of a union is to inform intermediate and front-line supervision of the company's labor poli-cies and the terms of the union-management contract. Some top managements have given out only incomplete information on these points, sometimes through oversight, but in a few cases deliberately. In a company manufacturing wire and cable the vice president made secret agreements with the unions, which no one was allowed to see—apparently because he did not wish it to be generally known that he had consented to a union shop.

As a general rule, top managements have found it advantageous to have all levels of supervision well informed about the company's labor policies and know the essential provisions (as distinguished from the technical details) of the union-management contract, as well as the principal changes made in the contract as a result of negotiations with the union.

Policies Dealing with the Administration of Union-Management Contracts

The administration of union-management contracts is bound to call for important policy decisions by top management.

Duration of Labor-Management Contracts

Most of the first labor-management contracts were for one year only. This was understandable since neither side knew what it was getting into and did not care to be bound for an extended period. A few agreements were terminable at any time on short notice, though as a general rule seasonal swings in business make a variable terminal date impracticable.[4] Experience with collective bargaining has led to a gradual lengthening of the term of contract. There are a few contracts that run for five years, notably those providing for pensions. For contracts pertaining to wages and working conditions, five years is too long, and most wage contracts now run for two or three years.[5] Employers as a rule prefer longer contract terms than do unions since the experience of most employers has been that, every time the contract is renewed, the employer has to make more concessions. But this may not always be true, in which case there may be interesting changes in the attitudes of both unions and employers toward the duration of contracts. As matters stand, the present willingness of unions to make contracts of two or three years' duration reflects their desire to reduce the burdens of negotiation and also to operate under the contract long enough to do a good job of administration.

If a contract is to run for two or three years or more, the union is likely to feel the need for some protection against a general drop in the purchasing power of money. The unions have not unanimously favored adjusting wages automatically with changes in the consumer price index, but the increases in living costs associated with the Korean War and later with the Near East crisis led many unions to insist on escalator clauses. Early in 1959, approximately 4.4 million employees were working under cost-of-living escalator clauses.

Management Policy Toward the Use of Economic Pressure

This is the most fundamental question that managements must face in administering union-management contracts. Newly-organized workers do not necessarily understand that their contract provides an orderly way of handling grievances and that they are expected to use the grievance machinery rather than resort to slowdowns, or wildcats, or threats of direct action. In some cases direct action may be part of

[4] A prominent exception are the union-management contracts in the railroad industry, which may be terminated on short notice.

[5] A report on "Changing Duration of Contracts" in *Labor Relations Reporter* (June 29, 1959), pp. 198, 225, found that among 1959 contracts half were for two years; 24 per cent for one year; 21 per cent for three years; and one per cent for more than three years. Considering numbers of workers covered, the three-year contracts would be a larger proportion since several of the largest contracts (railroads, steel, automobiles, aluminum) run for three years.

the bargaining over new production standards or rates—a refusal to do one's best until management revises an objectionable standard or rate. In still other cases direct action may be a carefully planned union tactic designed to stretch the meaning of the contract or to foster militance and antagonism toward the employer.

Managements have reacted in widely different ways to direct action. Some have tried secret deals or appeasement; some have refused to yield, but even in the case of wildcat strikes have imposed no discipline; some have tried to impose discipline. Experience with these and other policies is discussed in Chapter 22, "Wildcat Strikes and Union Pressure Tactics"; the only essential point to note here is that managements need carefully considered policies for dealing with different kinds of economic pressure under different conditions. Managements should not attempt to improvise or leave the decision to their junior members; when policies are improvised, the long-run interests of the firm are usually overlooked, and a policy of appeasement is followed more or less unintentionally. The reason is obvious. Subordinates are charged with getting out work on schedule. It is easier for them to make small concessions, of which higher-ups are not aware, than to permit production to be interrupted by wildcat strikes or slowdowns.

Preventing Usurpation of Authority by Union Representatives

Frequently union committeemen have assumed responsibilities that properly belong to the foreman. Sometimes the union committeeman is a better source of information than the foreman. Workers may go to the steward or committeeman with problems on production standards, incentive pay, seniority, or overtime because they get quick and well-informed answers from him. Some foremen have encouraged this to save themselves work, but its excessive use may lead to the committeeman's vetoing decisions of the foreman and, in fact, taking over in large part the running of some departments. Insistence by top management that production schedules be met regardless of conditions may threaten the authority of the foremen. Under these conditions, union committeemen, by threatening slowdowns or wildcat strikes, can control many decisions of foremen. During the war, in a plant that was a key supplier of transmissions for tanks it became the practice for piece rates to be approved by union stewards before being put into effect. The result, as might be expected, was great distortions in the rate structure.

Some managements have agreed to pay union committeemen for time allegedly spent on grievances but have neglected to enforce ordinary shop rules on the committeemen when they left their jobs and went into other departments. Sometimes managements neglected to negotiate restrictions on the activities of committeemen. As a result of these oversights, some managements found themselves with committeemen spending full time away from their jobs, roaming the shop at will, looking for grievances. In a plant making automobile axles efforts of management to limit the activities of committeemen was the principal issue in two long strikes.

Management Policies Toward Maintenance of Established Shop Practices

The legal right of managements to alter conditions of work that are not covered in the contract is in dispute. One view is that the contract implies that changes will not be made, without the consent of the employees, in major conditions of work not specifically covered by the contract. An opposing view, held by nearly all employers, is that the contract itself defines and measures the restraints on freedom to which management has consented, and that the management is free to do anything not specifically prohibited by the contract. In actual administration of the contract, management may behave in such a way that the issue is not raised, or at least not seriously pressed.

It is unwise for managements to neglect to make changes when technology, market conditions, or other conditions change. Failure to do so may lead the union to challenge management's right to make changes. But the attitude of the union toward changes in shop practices is largely within management's control. If management acts ruthlessly, unexpectedly, without consulting the union and without steps to alleviate hardship resulting from changes, union challenge can be expected. Some managers in the steel industry attribute the union's insistence on the controversial local-practice clause in the steel agreements to the abuse of managerial discretion in the past.[6]

Management Policies Toward Supplementary Agreements

The union-management contract is often supplemented by various kinds of special agreements. Some, between top management and the union, are written agreements, designed to clarify or to amplify (oc-

[6] The so-called local-practice clause in the steel agreement reads as follows: "The company shall have the right to change or eliminate any local working condition if, as a

casionally to modify) the terms of the principal agreement. Quite different are those sometimes made between foremen or other subordinate supervision and union representatives. They are of two kinds. One is designed to fill gaps in the general agreement. For example, the contract may provide that vacancies shall be filled on the basis of seniority provided the senior worker has the ability to do the job. If front line supervision and the union agree on what is meant by "ability to do the job," they are not nullifying or evading the contract—they are implementing it. Such agreements are inevitable and desirable, but it is important that they not bind the company until they are approved by central personnel.

The other kind of agreement between foremen and the union may nullify parts of the principal agreement between the union and the company or contradict important company policies. Supplementary agreements of this latter sort are virtually inevitable in plants where top management has failed to develop definite policies for dealing with the union or where it pursues a policy of appeasement—that is, plants where industrial relations policy is subordinated to sales policy or to maintaining production schedules. If first line and intermediate supervisors have no definite industrial relations policy to guide them, or if they cannot count on support from higher management when they refuse to yield to union demands and provoke threats of slowdowns, wildcat strikes, or other economic pressure, they have no alternative except to make supplementary agreements. In short, supplementary agreements are the natural way in which first line and intermediate supervision adapt themselves to the lack of adequate company industrial relations policies. In a plant manufacturing glassware, in which top management had no industrial relations policy, the foremen had entered into over a hundred oral agreements specifying crew sizes on new equipment (many of which became excessive) and otherwise restricting management. These agreements had grown up gradually, and the foremen were more interested in keeping them undetected than they were in making them known to top management. Until top management decided to get rid of most of them by taking a long strike on the issue, no one knew how many there were or just what provisions they contained.

---

result of action taken by management . . . the basis for the existence of the local working condition is changed or eliminated, thereby making it unnecessary to continue such local working condition; provided, however, that when such a change or elimination is made by the company any affected employee shall have recourse to the grievance procedure and arbitration, if necessary, to have the company justify its action."

A policy on supplementary agreements should be an integral part of general industrial relations policy. It should cover both the formal supplementary agreements between top management and the union and the agreements made by foremen and other subordinate supervisors. If agreements of the latter type are permitted at all, they should be in writing and subject to the approval of top management. Failure of top management to have a policy on supplementary agreements may mean that the union will obtain through the foremen concessions that it was denied when the principal contract was negotiated.

Management Policies on Uniform Administration of Contracts

Managements have a legal obligation not to discriminate on the basis of union membership or of activity in the union. Furthermore, arbitrators invariably hold that employees are entitled to uniform treatment and that an inequity exists when one employee is treated more generously or more harshly than another under similar circumstances. Discipline, for example, even though appropriate to the offense, is not permitted if management applied a different standard in other similar cases.

The many questions that must be settled in administering discipline cannot be decided in advance, but policies are needed to assure that discipline is administered uniformly and fairly. Fairness depends on the circumstances in each case, but it includes making clear the rules to be observed, giving the employee proper warning, and taking into account his record as well as the specific offense for which discipline is being imposed.

There are a few cases in which companies that usually follow the principle of uniformity make departures from it. They may go out of their way to avoid discharging men with long service who are within a few years of being eligible for pensions. Men having scarce skills also may receive special treatment. A Detroit company refused to discipline a group of toolmakers who resorted to the practice of going to the union hall during working hours to discuss their grievances. This happened at a time when toolmakers were scarce and when any toolmaker could find work quickly and easily. Discharging or even suspending the toolmakers would have hurt the company but not the workers.[7]

[7] In this case the company refrained from discipline but undertook to break up the group action by sending the leaders on the road to service equipment in the hands of customers.

Top Management Support of Decisions of Subordinates

What top management should do if it disagrees with the decisions of lower management should be determined by a carefully formulated policy. There are two possible dangers in such a situation. One, of course, is that lower management will feel demoralized if higher management agrees with some of the union's contentions and if it defends a position that lower management has told the union was unsound. Another danger is that the union will decide that the word of lower management does not carry much weight and will in the future insist on appealing over their heads to top management. The result would be a serious loss in management's ability to get things done.[8]

The need for top management to stand behind the policies of the firm and back up intermediate and lower management in executing these policies calls for a carefully considered policy toward strikes. No asset is as valuable to a company as a competent and dedicated management team. To preserve the high morale and esprit de corps of an efficient organization may require from time to time that top management accept the costs of long and expensive strikes. Managements should accept these costs if necessary without hesitation. Experience shows that there is nothing worse for morale than the abandonment of sound company policies in the face of threats, nor anything better for morale than willingness of superiors to stand behind subordinates when they are right.

When subordinate management makes mistakes and must be reversed, there are various ways to do it without producing ill effects. It is usually desirable that subordinate management be given an opportunity to change its own decisions; but most important is that higher management handle reversals so that the prestige and morale of lower management are not undermined.

Reorganizing Management to Deal with Union

The rapid rise of unions after 1933 led to an increase in the number of industrial staffs and growth in those already established. This is discussed in some detail in Chapter 29, "Line and Staff Coopera-

---

[8] The management of a plant making containers was demoralized by the willingness of the owner to overrule the decisions of the plant manager. The union soon learned that the owner could be counted on to reverse the manager's decisions in many cases.

tion and the Position of Foremen." Frequently the growth of industrial relations staffs was unplanned, and their success depended in considerable measure on personalities rather than on a carefully planned division of duties between industrial relations staffs and operating officers. If the personnel manager was strong and aggressive, he often took over a large part of the decision-making in the field of industrial relations. Frequently the operating people were glad to avoid the responsibility of handling labor matters. They did not know unions or the labor law and felt ill-prepared to decide labor issues, some of which were quite technical. With the passage of time, however, these haphazard arrangements have given way to more carefully worked out divisions of responsibility between operating staffs and industrial relations staffs.

Although the arrangements vary from company to company, personnel is usually responsible for the various employee services not directly connected with production (such as worker training, handling workmen's compensation claims, processing arbitration cases, and often conducting negotiations), and both personnel and operations participate in handling various problems connected with the administration of the union-management contract, with personnel giving advice and the operating men making the final decision. However, in a company manufacturing automotive parts, the usual relationship between the foremen and the personnel officers in discipline cases is reversed. Instead of the foreman's seeking the advice of personnel and then making the decision himself, the foreman files a complaint against the worker with a recommendation for discipline to the personnel director. Personnel investigates the case and makes a decision—subject to the approval of the plant manager. It is claimed that this system has not taken prestige away from the foremen.

Procedural Policies Implementing Management's Basic Labor Policies

Implementing the general labor policies of an enterprise involves questions and procedures that call for policy decisions. A few of the principal issues are: (1) how far should management go in consulting with the union; (2) how far should management go in building up the prestige of union officers and giving them responsibilities; (3)

how far should management go in acting jointly with the union; (4) how far should management go in acting independently of the union; (5) what should be the policy of management on submitting interpretation of the union-management contract to outsiders; and (6) what steps should management take to keep itself informed about what is happening in the administration of the union-management contract?

Consulting with the Union

Some managements have concluded that it is advisable to discuss plans rather freely with union representatives. They do not bargain with the union and do not feel any obligation to discuss plans with union representatives, but do so nevertheless. Some managements have set up regular weekly or monthly meetings between the plant manager or the personnel director and the union bargaining committee. A variety of problems are discussed—production schedules, technological changes, operating problems—with each side taking the initiative in bringing up matters for discussion.

Other managements fear that the practice of communicating their plans to the union will cause the latter to claim that management is obliged to consult it on innovations. They fear that the next step will be bargaining over management's right to make innovations. But there are advantages to management in discussing its plans with union representatives. Removing uncertainties in the minds of employees is often good for management as well as for the workers. Still another obvious advantage is that discussion of management's plans and problems sometimes evokes useful suggestions, and management may be led to modify its plans. Finally, such discussion is a good way of keeping union representatives informed about market conditions and the company's problems in meeting competition.

Management Support of Union Officers

Most union committeemen like to be active, and enjoy having responsibilities. Sometimes committeemen acquire responsibilities by stirring up grievances or by encouraging the appeal of grievances from department stewards to committeemen. But this kind of activity does not promote good administration of the labor-management contract. Some managements, therefore, go out of their way to give the committeemen work to do and responsibilities. In one company committeemen run the blood bank and administer the pension plan.

A company in the electrical equipment business makes an effort to support the local union leaders that the management likes. Two leaders who wanted to cause trouble were opposed by the company, but the needs of leaders who wanted recognition and status were satisfied. The policy of building up union leaders is obviously related closely to that of discussing management's plans and problems with them. Certainly if union leaders are able to report on management's plans to their members, their prestige with the rank and file is enhanced.

Joint Union-Management Action

Should management seek the help of the union in promoting safety, in reducing absenteeism, in getting shop rules observed, in cutting costs, and in improving technology?

The variation in managerial practice is wide. Some managements are opposed to seeking help from the union on the ground that such action would build up the prestige of the union. On the other hand, some weak managements go to great extremes in expecting the union to help them with their problems. The decision that best meets the needs of management depends on the general policy of the company toward the union, the nature of the problem, and the relative strength of the union and the employer. If it is the policy of the management to keep down the prestige of the union representatives, their help obviously should not be asked, but if management tries to help union leaders gain prestige and status, giving them jobs to do is a way of promoting their standing.

Much depends on the kind of help that is asked. Getting the union's help in promoting safety or a cleaner shop, in obtaining applicants for an apprenticeship course, or in reducing absenteeism is quite unobjectionable. Getting the union's help on matters of discipline raises more complicated issues. There is a difference between a union's refraining from obstructing management's efforts to impose proper discipline and aiding those efforts. Unions are often willing to refrain from protesting penalties that they believe have been justly imposed. They are often willing to warn members not to expect union help if they transgress shop rules, and unions may try to stop wildcat strikes that are preventing nonstriking members of the union from working. Some unions have been effective in breaking wildcat strikes against the employment or the promotion of Negroes. But managements that are so weak that they depend on union help to maintain discipline are likely to be in chronic trouble for many reasons, and they are not likely to get enough help from the union to get their shop rules well observed.[9] A few companies have embarked on a broad plan of union-management cooperation in which the help of the union is sought in developing ways of reducing costs and improving technology. To undertake such a program (assuming that the union is willing) involves a major policy decision. Experience with schemes of union-management cooperation are discussed in detail in Chapter 28.

Management-Employee Communications

Some unions believe that communications between management and employees should take place solely through the union. Efforts of management to communicate directly with the employees are regarded as "going over the head" of the union or its officers and are resented.

Managements cannot afford to accept as a matter of principle that they will communicate with their people only through the union. Managements should be in direct touch with employees and should not be dependent on intermediaries. But many managements never bothered to give their workers much information about the company and its affairs until unions became important. In recent years much more abundant information has been provided to employees, particularly information concerning the income statement and balance sheet (which has little interest to most workers), but little effort has been made to find out what questions the average employee would like to have answered and to answer them. For example, only a few companies give the employees an annual report on the industrial relations of the company. Most important of all, most managements lack arrangements for learning what the employees really think.

[9] Some managements report almost unbelievable lack of discipline among their employees. For example, an eastern railroad, which has been trying to build up rapid "piggy-back" service in competition with trucks, reports chronic lack of discipline among yard men. Yard men on the late night shift deliberately stall so as to create overtime work. From 2:30 to 4:30 or 5 A.M. they play cards, sleep, drink coffee, and swap stories, with the result that what little work is needed is pushed into the rush period around 5 A.M., when the incoming trains must be handled. In addition, the yard men will not work when it is raining or snowing, although they have proper apparel.

No two companies pursue the same policies on communicating with employees, but the policy in each case should deal with certain basic issues. It should include arrangements for determining the ever-changing subjects on which communication is needed—especially communication from employees to management. For example, changes in technology or prospective changes in technology or in production schedules create a demand for information. So do negotiations, though the two parties often agree that offers or counter-offers will not be divulged. The making of a new union-management contract creates a demand for explanation of the changes that have been made.

A policy on communicating with employees should cover the means of communication. Some methods are far better than others. It is important that management see that the union leaders know the facts about the company and its business that management would like to have the employees know, since the union leaders are likely to pass some of this information on to their members. In communicating with the rank and file word of mouth is usually better than the written word, and responses to questions are more effective than speeches or broadcasts. Hence, supplying foremen and other supervisors with facts and reports so that they come to be regarded as rich and ready sources of information is probably under most circumstances the best way to communicate with employees.

Contract Interpretation by Outsiders

One of the most dramatic developments in industrial relations in recent years has been the almost universal acceptance of arbitration clauses in union-management contracts. This development is discussed in Chapter 25. Today about nine out of ten union-management contracts contain arbitration clauses. There remains, however, a hard core of unions and employers that are opposed to submitting the interpretation of contracts to arbitration.

If there is an arbitration clause, management must decide what policy it will pursue about letting cases go to arbitration. A few companies are willing to submit to arbitration cases that they are bound to lose. This is true of a large rubber company that has many arbitration cases. More usual is the policy of screening cases carefully and letting go to arbitration only those cases that management is confident of winning. Settlements as a rule carry less weight as precedents than do decisions by the arbitrator. Management must balance the disadvantage of making some unfavorable settlements against that of getting some unfavorable precedents.

If management decides to keep out of arbitration all cases except those that it feels certain of winning, there must be some person or screening committee to review the grievances that the union is appealing to arbitration. The review should be made by someone who has not been involved in the cases at their earlier stages. In a multi-plant company making automotive parts the review is made by the personnel manager at the corporation level. He recently sent back for settlement five cases that the plant manager was ready to let go to arbitration. The personnel manager felt that the company was bound to lose the cases.

Sources of Information on Contract Administration

Planned stock taking should be a regular feature of every industrial relations program. An example of such a review is furnished by a large metalworking company that became concerned with the impact of unions on management—particularly on the attitudes of supervision and the ability of supervisors to put into effect the company programs. Surveys were made of several plants to find out whether some programs had been stopped by the unions. It was found that there had been no successful interference—that the planned changes in crew sizes, rates, and equipment had been executed. Some multiplant companies get a narrative industrial relations report from each plant each month. The emphasis is not on statistics (in fact, the inclusion of mere statistical information is discouraged) but on reports of significant events, developments, and attitudes.

The basic issues raised in this chapter are oriented toward the negotiation and, more particularly, the administration of contracts. The brief discussions here are in no sense complete, and the intent is to raise questions that underlie discussions in subsequent chapters.

3 / *The Control of Hiring*

FEW DECISIONS ARE MORE IMPORTANT to a business enterprise than the selection of its employees. The question of who gets hired is equally important to employees, to prospective employees, and often to the union. Hence, many unions exercise considerable control over hiring, the form of such control varying with the reasons for their interest. Union control of hiring in some industries has led to conflict between employers and unions with the result that government has intervened; in other industries there has been little such conflict, and many employers have willingly joined with the unions in violating the restrictions on hiring practices imposed by law.

Security for the union, virtually all unions in the United States feel, requires that hiring be limited to its members, or those willing to join the union, and that maintenance of good standing in the union be a condition of continued employment. This arrangement is known as the "union shop." Many unions, unable to obtain the union shop, have negotiated so-called "maintenance-of-membership agreements" with employers—though few unions are satisfied with the degree of security they give. They do not give the union any control over hiring but provide only that employees who are members of the union at a certain time or who later join the union shall, as a condition of employment, keep up their membership for the duration of the agreement or for some other specified period. A few unions have been willing to accept the so-called "agency shop" as a substitute for the union shop. The agency shop provides that all employees who elect not to become union members shall, as a condition of employment, pay the union a monthly service charge, usually equal to the regular union dues.[1]

[1] An agency-shop agreement has been negotiated between the Corn Products Refining Company and the Oil, Chemical, and Atomic Workers International Union and between the Atchison, Topeka and Sante Fe Railway and fifteen nonoperating unions.

Many unions want much more control over hiring than they obtain from the union shop, and some have succeeded in getting it. Often pressure for union influence in hiring comes from the business agent or other officers of the union, who gain power and prestige from being able to get jobs for friends. Some unions require that employers hire only members of the union (the closed shop); others demand that employers hire union members if available in preference to nonmembers (the preferential shop). Some unions that operate union, closed, or preferential shops also issue permit cards allowing nonmembers to work on union jobs in certain cases. Usually there is a charge for the permit card, and it is revocable at the will of the issuing union. Some unions go even further and demand that employers do their hiring through the union or through a union-controlled hiring hall.

In addition to the above, unions seek to impose various other specific controls on hiring. For example, some try to enforce racial discrimination; some seek to prevent it; a few unions insist that an employer hire a given ratio of older workers; the seniority rules of some unions impose restrictions on hiring, sometimes by requiring that vacancies be filled by promotion from within (if properly qualified employees are available) rather than from the outside and sometimes by requiring that vacancies be filled only by certain categories of workers.

Extent of Union Regulation of Hiring

No comprehensive statistics on the extent of the various controls over hiring exercised by unions are available, but the union shop is known to be by far the most prevalent. A survey of 1,716 union-management contracts in effect during all or part of 1954 shows that 1,035, or 60 per cent, provided for the union shop.[2] Most of the agreements studied covered a thousand or more workers, and most of them were negotiated with employers subject to the Taft-Hartley Act, which outlaws the closed shop. In plants where employment is not intermittent the union shop ordinarily gives the union adequate protection against discrimination by management, and the willingness of the employer to accept the union shop usually settles the issue of union security.

---

[2] Rose Theodore, "Union-Security Provisions in Agreements, 1954," *Monthly Labor Review* (June 1955), pp. 650-52.

The closed shop, though illegal in plants subject either to the Taft-Hartley Act or to the Railway Labor Act, is maintained in many small local enterprises not subject to either of these acts. Among the 1,716 agreements studied by the Bureau of Labor Statistics in 1954, the closed shop was found in only 87 agreements, or less than 5 per cent of those studied. Since the study was focused mainly on agreements subject to the Taft-Hartley Act, the proportion of closed-shop agreements is not to be regarded as representative. Furthermore, many enterprises subject to the Taft-Hartley Act, which nominally have the union shop, in fact have the closed shop either because the employer finds it advantageous or because the union is too strong for the employer and dictates the terms of the contract. The prohibition of the closed shop by the Taft-Hartley Act has important effects on union policy that will be discussed below.

Information on the extent of use of permit cards and the number of permit card holders in the United States is also lacking. Locals of over two dozen internationals have used the work permit at one time or another.[3] It is a means by which a union can meet a large temporary increase in the demand for labor without admitting the temporary workers into the union, where they would have a voice in determining union policies.

Immediately prior to World War II, the use of permit cards seems to have been diminishing. National unions opposed them, and the labor surpluses of the depression years were unfavorable to their use. Demands for labor during World War II, however, led to a vast increase in the use of permit cards. Cantonments, air fields, and other war installations were built in communities where the permanent body of construction workers was small. The locals sought to maintain the closed shop and at the same time prevent newcomers from taking over. They refused to accept new members but issued permit cards to allow the needed expansion in the working force. The asbestos workers had three times as many permit card workers as union members employed in their jurisdiction.[4] The labor shortages

---

[3] Among the unions are: the asbestos workers, the plumbers, the operating engineers, the food and tobacco workers, the brewers, the distillery workers, the stage hands, the seafarers, the maritime workers, the marine firemen, the hotel and restaurant workers, the pressmen, and the hod carriers. Constitutions of the following unions refer to permit cards, but it is not known whether the unions have used them: the Amalgamated Clothing Workers, the Carpenters, the Marble, Slate and Stone Polishers, the Bridge and Structural Iron Workers, the Pocketbook Workers, the International Longshoremen and Warehousemen, the Painters, and the Photo-engravers.

[4] Herbert J. Lahne, "The Union Work Permit," Political Science Quarterly (September 1951), p. 372.

in many skilled crafts during the postwar period encouraged the use of permit cards. Since 1947, however, there has been a great drop in their use because under the Taft-Hartley Act permit cards are illegal if used in a discriminatory manner; but use of them has by no means ceased.

The practice of requiring that hiring be done through the union or a union hiring hall is extensive and is growing, stimulated principally by three conditions: (1) the general scarcity of some types of skilled craftsmen, which has encouraged employers to turn to the unions for workers; (2) the increasing amount of construction work done in remote places where there is no adequate local supply of labor; and (3) the restrictions of the Taft-Hartley Act on the closed shop and of various state laws on the union shop. Unions seek to avoid the effects of such restrictions by requiring that hiring be done through the union.

The policy of discrimination against Negroes, and to some extent Puerto Ricans and Orientals, is well established in a large proportion of the craft unions. While union constitutions usually do not specifically prohibit the admission of Negroes, some unions as a matter of practice refuse to take them in. This refusal denies Negroes the opportunity to obtain employment where either the closed shop or union control of hiring is maintained. Sometimes discrimination takes the form of understandings with employers to restrict the hiring of nonwhites. In spite of much talk about civil rights and the establishment of a civil rights department in the AFL-CIO, and in spite of the industrial unions' fight against discrimination, the craft unions have done little in this direction. Most craft unions still keep their doors closed to Negroes, although in recent years the majority of them have eliminated such provisions from their constitutions. On December 4, 1958, the National Association for the Advancement of Colored People filed with the Civil Rights Department of the AFL-CIO specific charges of discrimination involving the boilermakers, the bricklayers, the carpenters, the electricians, the laborers, the machinists, the plasterers, and the plumbers.[5] Seven months later, in July 1959, the Labor Secretary of the NAACP wrote the AFL-CIO that no report on the discriminatory practices had been received.

Out-and-out agreements by employers not to hire Negroes are

[5] Herbert Hill, Labor Secretary of the NAACP, Memorandum to Boris Shishkin, Director, Civil Rights Department of the AFL-CIO (mimeo.).

unusual, though some important ones have been made on the railroads. Beginning about 1910, some of the running crafts began making agreements on the southern railroads limiting the percentage of Negro firemen or trainmen. On some divisions the proportion of Negro firemen was limited to 10 per cent.[6] The coming of the diesel locomotive increased the attractiveness of firemen's jobs and caused the Brotherhood of Locomotive Firemen and Enginemen to want all these jobs for its members. In 1941 the union entered into an agreement with twenty-two southeastern railroads which provided that (1) Negro firemen were ineligible for promotion to engineers, and (2) only "promotable" (white) men would henceforth be hired as firemen or assigned to new runs or to vacancies in existing runs.

The practical effect of the efforts of craft unions to enforce discrimination in most cases has been slight—mainly because discrimination was so well established before unions existed that unions added little to it. But with public support for discrimination gradually diminishing, the craft unions will gradually gain importance as endorsers of discriminatory practices unless they abandon their traditional policy.

Quite different from the attitude of most craft unions in this area has been that of most industrial unions. The mine workers, the steelworkers, the communication workers, the automobile workers, the oil workers, the electrical workers' industrial unions, the packinghouse workers, and the rubber workers have fought efforts of groups within the unions to keep Negroes out of their industries and out of the good jobs in the industries. The teamsters in St. Louis have fought and defeated wildcat strikes by white taxi drivers to keep out Negro drivers. There are about five hundred Negro cab drivers in St. Louis, all belonging to the teamsters' union. The contracts of the warehousemen's local in St. Louis (an affiliate of the teamsters) have a fair-employment clause that the union enforces. The United Automobile Workers and the United Rubber Workers Union have "Fair Employment Practices Departments," and many of the locals of the rubber workers' union have their own Fair Employment Practices Committees.[7]

[6] Charles Houston, General Counsel, Negro Railway Labor Executives Committee, Statement before a Special Subcommittee of the Committee on Education and Labor, Hearings on H.R. 4453 and Companion Bills, 81 Cong. 1 sess. (May 10-26, 1949), p. 132.
[7] Harry Fleischman and James Rorty, *We Open the Gates,* National Labor Service, New York (1958). This is a vivid account of some of labor's successes in fighting for equality.

Growth of Union Attempts to Control Hiring

Few American unions have had enough control of the labor market to limit the total number of people in that market, but there are a few exceptions. One such is Local 10 of the International Longshoremen's and Warehousemen's Union, which has five thousand members and controls the work of loading and discharging ships around San Francisco Bay. Hiring is done through a union-controlled hiring hall, and members of regular gangs can average between $6,000 and $7,000 a year. The union closed its rolls shortly after a postwar influx, but in the spring of 1958, in response to clamors for admission and to employers' pleas for a bigger labor pool, the local invited membership applications. It was immediately flooded with more than nine thousand of them. On the basis of physical fitness and experience the number of applicants was reduced to nine hundred. A joint committee of employers and union representatives undertook interviews with the nine hundred to determine their capability, and the applicants were required to pass comprehensive physical examinations.[8]

Control of membership by the ILWU and the dispatching practices agreed to by the parties have decasualized employment extensively in West Coast ports. This along with equal distribution of work among the membership over four-month periods have improved greatly the welfare of those employed.

Although few unions are in a position to adopt strong restrictive membership policies, most American trade unions have tried to protect their security by negotiating union-shop, closed-shop, or preferential-shop agreements. The notable exception is the railroad unions, which until about 1943 were opposed to the union shop or the closed shop and sought union security through strict enforcement of their seniority rules and through the need of railway employees for good representation in grievance cases. Indeed, the amendments to the Railway Labor Act, passed in 1934 largely as a result of union influence, made it a crime punishable by a heavy fine or a prison sentence for a railroad official to negotiate a closed-shop or union-shop agreement.[9] In 1943 an effort by the nonoperating

---

[8] "Dock Union Builds Itself a Hall," *Business Week* (March 14, 1959), pp. 116-17.

[9] The unions feared that the companies would negotiate closed-shop agreements with company-controlled unions and that such agreements might be used by some unions to defeat the jurisdictional claims of other unions.

standard railway organizations to obtain the union shop failed because the National Railway Labor Panel Emergency Board ruled that it was prohibited under the Railway Labor Act. In January 1951 the Act was amended to permit the union shop, and in July of that year the first union-shop contract with a major carrier was signed.[10]

A survey of union contracts by the Bureau of Labor Statistics in 1946 showed that about half of the workers were covered by either union-shop or closed-shop contracts—17 per cent by the former and 33 per cent by the latter.[11]

The proportion of union-shop or closed-shop contracts in 1946 would have been greater had it not been for World War II. Although wartime labor shortages put unions in a strong bargaining position, most unions adopted a no-strike pledge, and there was strong public hostility toward strikes. Disputes that unions and employers could not settle were usually referred to the War Labor Board. The Board, unwilling to force union membership on workers by government decree, but aware of the unions' need for security, worked out a compromise in the form of maintenance-of-membership contracts. The BLS survey of union contracts in 1946 showed that about 25 per cent of workers were covered by some form of maintenance-of-membership contract.

Since the end of the war, unions, with the help of a strong demand for labor, have been able to replace maintenance-of-membership contracts with contracts giving greater union security—usually union-shop agreements. Most unions were satisfied with these agreements, but their efforts to secure such controls were obstructed by a clash between public policy and union policy over the control of hiring. This conflict was reflected in the passage of the Taft-Hartley Act in 1947 outlawing closed-shop contracts and the so-called "right-to-work" laws in various states, which essentially outlawed all forms of union security.[12]

When the BLS surveyed union contracts in 1954, it found that the proportion of workers covered by maintenance-of-membership contracts had dropped from 25 per cent in 1946 to 17 per cent in

[10] American Federation of Labor, *Proceedings of the 71st Convention* (1952), p. 299.

[11] U. S. Bureau of Labor Statistics, *Extent of Collective Bargaining and Union Recognition, 1946*, Bulletin 909 (1947), p. 3.

[12] In 1960 nineteen states had so-called "right-to-work" laws in effect. They were: Alabama, Arizona, Arkansas, Florida, Georgia, Indiana, Iowa, Kansas, Mississippi, Nebraska, Nevada, North and South Carolina, North and South Dakota, Tennessee, Texas, Utah, and Virginia.

1954, but the proportion covered by union- and closed-shop contracts had risen from 50 per cent to about 65 per cent.[13] The Taft-Hartley Act, however, led to a sharp drop in the proportion of workers nominally covered by closed-shop contracts (from 33 per cent in 1946 to about 5 per cent in 1954) and to a sharp rise in the proportion nominally covered by union-shop contracts—from 17 per cent to about 60 per cent in the same year. The word "nominally" is used because, although the wording of many contracts was changed to conform to the law, actual practices often remained unchanged.

Determinants of Union Policies on Hiring

What explains union policies on hiring? Some of the policies, such as the demand for the union shop or the closed shop, reflect the general position of unions in the American environment and the peculiar need for union security. Some of these policies also reflect particular tendencies in trade union government—particularly the tendency for unions to be run by their officers. Others, such as the use of permit cards and union control of hiring, reflect peculiar conditions and problems in certain labor markets, especially markets characterized by intermittent employment and much casual labor. Some policies, such as the discrimination policies of the craft unions or the anti-discrimination policies of the industrial unions, reflect the natural reaction of different types of unions operating under different conditions to Negroes in the labor market.

Problem of Union Security

The strong and widespread emphasis on union security that is characteristic of American trade unions is a natural result of the conditions under which unions operate in this country. The American environment has produced strongly individualistic and highly competitive employers, who have been aggressively hostile to unions and who have been willing to go to great extremes in order to destroy them. In addition, the labor force in the United States is composed of strongly individualistic persons who have different racial and cultural backgrounds, who lack a tradition of class solidarity, and who are keenly interested in getting ahead. These influences have pro-

---

[13] Theodore, "Union-Security Provisions in Agreements, 1954," pp. 652-55.

duced business unionism—that is, unionism which has little or no interest in social reforms but which is frankly out to advance the selfish aims of its members. Furthermore, just as individual union members are eager to get ahead, so the several unions are in competition with one another. Over rivalry between the various business unions the national federation has only limited control. Hence, unions need arrangements to protect themselves and their members from the competition of other unions. Union security, therefore, is needed for three reasons—to protect the union from being undermined by employers, to protect it from so-called "free riders" (workers who accept the benefits of unionism without helping to pay for them), and to protect it from other unions.

The strong need of unions for security is a natural outgrowth of the individualistic outlook of American workers and of their keen desire to get ahead. The only kind of unionism that can attract such workers is "business unionism"—unionism devoted to furthering the narrow economic interests of its members. Business unionism appeals less to the workers' idealism than to their self-interest. In the pursuit of self-interest some employees remain outside the union and seek to enjoy free of cost the benefits of the union contract—in short, to be "free riders." The union shop protects the union against the self-interest of the "free riders."

The need of business unions for security is enhanced by the strongly individualistic and highly competitive American employers who are also a product of the American environment and who have been willing to go to great extremes to smash unions. The need of unions for security is also enhanced by the coercive methods by which many unions have acquired members. Often coercive organizing methods are simply the natural reaction of the union to coercive attempts by employers to keep workers unorganized. Be that as it may, members acquired by coercive methods may be ready to become "free riders."[14]

[14] Typical of many cases is the attempt of a union to organize a factory of the Paris Shoe Company in the Boston area. The union was able to gain the membership of only eleven or twelve cutters. Nevertheless, the union struck the plant and by picketing forced the company to accept a union-shop contract with a checkoff. The company required its three hundred employees to join the union and began withholding dues from workers' pay. This instance of coercive organizing, however, did not endure because some of the employees complained to the National Labor Relations Board, which ordered the return of all dues collected under the invalid contract. The teamsters' union has been particularly aggressive in the use of coercive organizing methods.

Control of Employment Opportunities and
Prevention of Labor Market Abuse

Although most unions find their interests sufficiently protected by
the union shop so that their inability to negotiate closed-shop contracts under the law is not a serious handicap to them, there is a
substantial minority of unions that have important reasons for preferring the closed shop. If employment in the industry is intermittent
or highly seasonal, as in building construction, the shipping industry,
and the needle trades, the closed shop may be used to protect the
workers who are permanently attached to the industry from transients
who seek to pick up a few days' or weeks' work during a period of
unemployment in their principal occupations. Furthermore, some
unions want the closed shop to protect the union wage scale from
being undercut or to eliminate abuses in the labor market. These
results may be achieved when the closed shop is supplemented with
the requirement that hiring be done through the union. Thus, for
many years unions in the needle trades wanted the closed shop and
hiring through the union in order to protect the union scale from
being undercut by workers who would accept less-than-scale wages in
order to obtain work. Today, conditions are very different and so,
as a result, are the hiring practices in the industry. Labor in the
needle trades has become exceedingly scarce. The employment offices
maintained by the Amalgamated Clothing Workers in Chicago, New
York, and Rochester have virtually ceased to function except for some
referral of unskilled workers like stock boys and some classes of operatives. Cutters, pressers, and tailors are so scarce that the union is glad
to have the employer find them anywhere. Some skilled workers are
being imported from Europe.[15]

Unions have also sought the closed shop and a requirement that
hiring be done through the union in order to prevent kickbacks and
the collection of various extortionate payments by foremen or others
working with representatives of employers. For example, in the shipping industry ship captains would agree to hire through certain
shipping masters or "crimps" who operated boarding houses. The

[15] Similar conditions prevail in the women's garment industry. In the women's garment industry in Boston up until eight or nine years ago employers were not allowed
to hire a worker until he first presented a working card from the union. In recent
years the shortage of labor in the industry has been such that the employer is allowed
to hire anyone he wishes without referral or notice to the union except for pressers
and cutters. All cutters and pressers are still hired through the union in Boston.

sailors would find it necessary to stay at these boarding houses in order to get employment. They were overcharged for everything they received and encouraged to go deeply into debt. The "crimp" who got the seaman his job would receive an advance on the seaman's wages to cover the debts.

Desire of Union Officers for Political Power

An important reason for the demand for the closed shop and for the requirement that hiring be done through the union has been the desire of local union officers for the power and, in some cases, the sources of extra income, that union control of hiring gave them. It is a characteristic of some American trade unions that they are oligarchies rather than democracies and that they are run almost entirely by the officers with little interest in union affairs being taken by the rank and file. The members of American unions have rarely been critical of their officers for seeking power, an attitude that has played into the hands of officers who wanted to build up political machines. Ability to get employment for one's friends has often been one of the most usual sources of political power in the craft unions.

Problem of Racial Discrimination

Unions cannot avoid taking a position either for or against racial discrimination in employment because such discrimination is an important characteristic of the American labor market. The principal discrimination is against Negroes, but there is also discrimination against Puerto Ricans, Mexicans, and Orientals. It is the result partly of the desire of the whites to avoid close association with members of other races and partly of the desire of the whites to keep the best jobs for themselves.

As was pointed out above, the craft unions generally have supported the practices of racial discrimination that were well established in the skilled trades and in many of the more attractive occupations before unions were established. However, as we have seen, the growing public sentiment against discrimination, as well as the passage of Fair Employment Practices Acts by some of the states (which apply to union admission rules as well as to employer hiring practices), have led various national unions to eliminate provisions from their constitutions denying membership to Negroes and other nonwhites.

As a general rule, however, the *practices* of craft unions toward Negroes have not changed. Most craft unions would stir up a revolt of the members if they opened their doors to Negroes.[16]

Quite different from the policy of the craft unions toward discrimination has been that of industrial unions. The industrial unions must face the fact that there are large numbers of nonwhites employed in the less desirable jobs in most industries. Hence, industrial unions cannot afford to support discrimination or even be neutral. Were they to adopt either policy, the unions would lose the prospect of organizing the nonwhites. The few industrial unions in the country before 1933 in coal mining and in the needle trades were opposed to discrimination. With the rise of new industrial unions after 1933 —in steel, automobile, rubber, electrical products, meat packing, electrical goods, chemicals, communications, agricultural implements, and aluminum—there developed a great increase in the opposition to discrimination in the trade union movement.

Problems and Consequences of Union Control of Hiring

The Union Shop

The union shop does not significantly narrow the employer's supply of labor, since he is not required to limit his hiring to men who have already joined the union. The only source of labor that he is denied are workers who are unwilling to join in order to gain employment. If the job is likely to be a lasting one, they will be ready to join the union, but if the job is expected to last only two or three months, many may be reluctant to pay the initiation fee of the union, which may be $50, $75, or even higher.

When the government permits unions and employers to negotiate union-shop contracts, it assumes the obligation of seeing that union

[16] For a comprehensive discussion of union policies toward Negroes see Herbert R. Northrup, *Organized Labor and the Negro* (1944).

Among the unions which recently removed the color bar from their constitutions are: International Association of Machinists, 1948; National Postal Transport Association, 1958; Order of Railroad Telegraphers, 1952; Railroad Yardmasters of North America, 1946; Switchmen's Union of North America, 1947; American Train Dispatchers Association, 1947.

The Brotherhood of Railway Trainmen in 1958 changed its constitution to permit Negro membership in those states prohibiting segregation in employment. The constitution of the Railway Mail Association excludes non-Caucasians, except Indians "except where state law forbids."

membership is open to employees on fair and reasonable terms—an obligation that the government has conspicuously failed to discharge. Section 8 (b) (5) of the Taft-Hartley Act makes it an unfair labor practice for an employer (pursuant to a union-shop contract) to require of employees as a condition of union membership "a fee in amount which the Board finds excessive or discriminatory under all the circumstances." As far as the actual effect of this section is concerned, it might as well not have been written. Congress failed to indicate any yardsticks to be used by the Board in deciding whether an initiation fee is excessive or not. Hence, the constitutionality of the section is often open to question.[17] The prevalence of the union shop in American industry makes initiation fees a matter of public concern, particularly in the construction industry, where many jobs are of short duration and initiation fees in many cities are fairly high.

Union-shop contracts raise the question of what shall be done about temporary or part-time help. If the union initiation fee is low, the temporary or part-time help may be required to join the union after a given period; if the initiation fee is substantial, such employees may be allowed to work under permit cards.

It is obviously unfair to require a worker to join the union before he has had an opportunity to demonstrate his competence for the job. The Taft-Hartley Act requires a waiting period of thirty days from the time of employment before a worker may be compelled to join. Unions complain that for some kinds of work (particularly in the construction industry) the thirty-day period is too long since the job may not last thirty days. This objection carries little weight for the simple reason that for many kinds of work thirty days are needed to determine the man's suitability.

The union shop is said to make for harmony in the plant and to minimize resentment that some workers are enjoying the benefits of the union contract without helping to pay the costs of securing and administering the contract. But proof is lacking that the net result of a union-shop contract is less friction. A union shop may simply change the kind of dissatisfaction from resentment by union mem-

[17] Congress undoubtedly has power to prescribe the conditions under which the union shop may be permitted in plants engaged in interstate commerce, but Congress does not have authority to delegate legislative power to the National Labor Relations Board, as it seems to have done with respect to union initiation fees. This part of the Taft-Hartley Act requires standards to guide the Board.

bers toward so-called free riders to resentment toward the union by workers forced to join against their will. Furthermore, today when many unions engage aggressively in political activities under the pretext that these are "educational," employees may object to the power of the union to tax them for the support of political or social causes in which they have little or no interest or to which they may even be opposed.[18] Unions have been quite outspoken in denouncing "free riders," but they have shown no concern about the problem of "forced riders" on political issues.

Unions claim that the union shop (or the closed shop) tends to discourage ill-grounded grievances. If a worker whose complaint the union refuses to handle may simply stop paying dues, the union feels compelled to process cases that have little or no merit. In fact, in the absence of a union shop or closed shop the union, it is said, may stir up grievances in order to keep the workers willing to continue paying dues. But it is easy to exaggerate the differences made by the union or closed shop. Unions, or union representatives, may find it advantageous to stir up grievances even in a union shop or a closed shop. The purpose may be to harass management into accepting interpretations of the agreement that the union wants; or the purpose may be to develop a militant attitude among the members to help the union in negotiating new contracts. Some union representatives may stir up grievances in union shops in an effort to advance their political fortunes within the union or to build up interest in it. Finally, elected stewards or committeemen may lack the independence to handle weak cases.

Before the Taft-Hartley Act limited the right of employers to discriminate among employees for the purpose of encouraging or discouraging membership in unions, the union shop (or the closed shop) was a powerful obstacle to democracy in trade unions. The union or the closed shop gave the union (or its leaders) the right to force the employer to discharge employees who violated union rules or incurred the displeasure of the union or its officers. This power was not frequently used, but it was probably important. It gave the "ins" in any union an effective way of dealing with critics and trouble makers, and the fact that union officers could take away a man's job undoubtedly discouraged dissent in many unions. The Taft-Hartley

---

[18] An examination of the process by which unions take positions on political issues shows that typically there is no real participation by the rank and file.

Act, by limiting the power of unions to deprive men of their jobs, might be expected to make unions more democratic, but this has not happened.

The Taft-Hartley Act drastically limited the ability of unions to use the union shop as a means of discipline. It forbade employers to discharge workers for nonmembership in a labor organization if the membership was denied or terminated for reasons other than failure to tender initiation fees and periodic dues. Even prior to Taft-Hartley other clauses in the agreement sometimes limited a union's right to compel the discharge of employees no longer in good standing in the union. Thus, the attempt of a local of the UAW in a Ford plant to obtain the discharge of two test drivers, expelled from the union on the ground that they worked too fast and produced too much, was denied by the umpire. The agreement between the company and the union provided that the union would "use its best efforts on behalf of the company both as to work and as to the conduct of its performance." The umpire held that this clause prevented the union from using the union shop to limit production.[19]

The Closed Shop

The requirement that an employer hire only union members, or only union members if they are available, might appear to restrict the labor supply seriously, and occasionally it has this effect. Often, however, the closed shop attracts workers into the union, and does not reduce the labor supply unless the union pursues a restrictive membership policy. It is true that sometimes the success of a union in gaining the closed shop may lead it to restrict membership. In that event it may be quite burdensome to employers since they are forced to pay considerable overtime at penalty rates and to hire the least desirable workers before the union is willing to open its doors to new members or, in some cases, to accept transfers from other locals of the same national union. An example of a closed union is the Newspaper and Mail Deliverers Union of New York, which for years has maintained an illegal closed shop in violation of the Taft-Hartley Act. Memberships in it are reported to have sold for as much as $5,000, although about $500 is said to be the usual price.[20]

[19] Harry Shulman, *Opinions of the Umpire, Ford Motor Company*, A-78 (March 29, 1944), p. 2.
[20] Fred J. Cook, "New York's Newspaper Strike," *The Nation* (January 3, 1959), p. 6.

Usually, however, the closed shop does not lead unions to restrict their membership. This is partly because most unions are dominated by their officers, and officers usually prefer a large membership. The major explanation is that unions cannot risk creating a supply of non-union labor, which might result from restrictive policies. But the closed shop, combined with a union policy of racial discrimination, may have the effect of excluding Negroes from certain trades or industries.

Is the combination of the closed shop and a restrictive membership policy illegal as a violation of fundamental constitutional rights? The question has usually arisen in connection with racial discrimination, and the courts have disagreed on the issue. In the well-known case of James v. Marinship Corporation, the California Supreme Court enjoined the operation of a closed shop by a local of the boilermakers' union that would not admit Negroes to membership. The court found that the arrangement violated the fifth, fourteenth, and fifteenth amendments to the Constitution.[21] Other courts, however, have taken a different view of the issue. Thus, in the case of Ross v. Ebert, in which two Negro bricklayers sought relief from the exclusion policies of the bricklayers' union, the Wisconsin Supreme Court held that the fourteenth amendment had not been violated since it applies only to actions by states, and the court held that the bricklayers' union, though the recipient of special encouragement from the state, was not an agency of the state.[22]

[21] 25 Calif. 2d 721 (1944). The union had set up an auxiliary union for Negroes, which they were forced to join. Two years later in William v. Brotherhood, 27 Calif. 2d 586 (1946), the California court reaffirmed its original position.

The fact that trade unions are given exclusive bargaining rights also raises as a matter of public policy the question of their right to exclude members. In Betts v. Easley (161 Kan. 459, 1946), the Kansas Supreme Court held that a labor organization may not act as the exclusive bargaining representative of a group of employees if it refuses membership to any employee in the bargaining unit because of race or religion. The Brotherhood of Railway Carmen had denied admission to about a hundred Negroes in the Argentine shops of the Santa Fe Railway.

The carmen's union added injury to insult by proposing to set up an auxiliary local of Negro employees, to which the Negroes would pay dues but which would have no voice in bargaining with the management. The union was restrained from acting as bargaining agent unless and until Negro members were given equality of privileges, participation, and full membership.

[22] 39 L.R.R.M. pp. 2233, 2238, and 2735-41. Likewise, in Oliphant v. Brotherhood of Locomotive Firemen and Enginemen, decided on September 27, 1957, the U. S. District Court of the Northern District of Ohio disagreed with the position taken by Kansas Supreme Court in Betts v. Easley. In the Oliphant case several Negro firemen sought a court order compelling the Brotherhood of Locomotive Firemen to admit them to membership. One question raised was whether the Railway Labor Act, in conferring

Permit Cards

A probable result of the closed shop or, since Taft-Hartley, an employment referral system is the permit card issued ordinarily to nonmembers of the union and permitting them to work on union-controlled jobs. For the permit card the nonmember pays a weekly or monthly fee that is usually higher than the regular union dues, although higher payment is illegal under Taft-Hartley.[23] A member of another local of an international union ordinarily does not need to obtain a permit card since he can usually transfer his membership. However, a few locals have refused to accept members of other locals of the same international and have insisted that these workers obtain permit cards.[24]

The most common use of permit cards is to enable a union that imposes a closed or union shop to meet large temporary increases in the demand for labor. For example, the demand for various construction crafts fluctuates violently in most localities. The construction of a large bridge or building will require temporarily in many places (especially in small nonindustrial communities) the employment of many more craftsmen than permanently live in the community. Were the union to expand its membership to meet the employer's need, the ultimate drop in demand for labor would leave the unions with far more members than there are union jobs available. By taking in new members the union would be jeopardizing the future employment security of its present members and also might cause the present members of the local to lose control of its affairs.

Permit cards are used by unions in some seasonal industries. The union members may assure themselves more or less steady year-round work by enforcing the closed shop and limiting union membership and by issuing permit cards to workers needed to meet the seasonal peaks. This was the practice in the food and tobacco workers and in the brewery workers until passage of the Taft-Hartley Act.

Although permit cards have a legitimate use, they give rise to many

---

exclusive bargaining rights on unions, made them government agents whose discriminatory membership policies would violate the fifth amendment. The Kansas court had answered this question "Yes." The federal court answered "No" in the Oliphant case.

[23] An exception is the asbestos workers, which traditionally allows permits free of charge when members are not available, though some locals insist on charging.

[24] Permit cards may also be issued during a probationary period while the qualifications of an applicant for membership are being investigated.

problems. For example, the use of permit cards may cause the union to fail to organize its territory. The permit card can be a lucrative source of revenue to a local and turn a local union into a sort of capitalist organization deriving revenue from selling access to union jobs. When Local 3 of the International Brotherhood of Electrical Workers was using permit cards on a !arge scale in New York in the early twenties, its books were closed, and repeated attempts by the permit-holders to join the local failed.[25] The Pittsburgh local of the Operating Engineers also closed its door to new members and met the employers' demand for men by issuing permit cards. The permit system in the Pittsburgh local was not dropped until the international ousted the local officers and set up a new local.[26] Local 403 of the Operating Engineers in New York issued permit cards and refused to take in new members. As a result the local was placed under international supervision.[27]

The permit card system is likely to lead to dual unionism and corruption. When the card holders, after repeated efforts, failed to gain admission to Local 3 of the International Brotherhood of Electrical Workers in New York, about a thousand of them formed a rival organization.[28] The rival union did not last long because Local 3 admitted most of the former's membership. But several years later the books of Local 3 were again closed, with more than five thousand membership applications on file.[29]

The use of permit cards by Local 403 of the Operating Engineers led to a dual organization of the permit holders.[30] At the 1932 convention of the stage hands, the president showed concern over dual organizations that were springing up, partly because permit men were unable to obtain work through IATSE locals.[31]

The permit card system easily becomes a source of favoritism and corruption. Many unions do not require a proper accounting of the money paid by permit card holders. Officers profiting from the issuance of permit cards may keep regular members of the union unem-

[25] New York Joint Legislative Committee on Housing, Transcript of Testimony (December 1921), pp. 4241, 4245, 4285, 4293, and 4297.
[26] The International Steam Engineer (October 1924), pp. 301-07.
[27] The International Engineer (July 1929), p. 53.
[28] New York Joint Legislative Committee on Housing, Transcript of Testimony (December 1921), p. 4240.
[29] William Haber, Industrial Relations in the Building Industry (1930), pp. 203-04.
[30] The International Engineer (July 1929), p. 53.
[31] International Alliance of Theatrical Stage Employees, Proceedings of the 31st Convention (1932), p. 38.

ployed while holders of permit cards are working. An investigation by the international office of the Operating Engineers showed that nonmembers worked on permit in Pittsburgh and Cleveland while members from the locals in those cities and also members of other locals walked the streets, and while employers complained that they could not hire real union members.[32] At Fort Devens four officials of Local 39 of the hod carriers' union, operating under a contract that provided that workers approved by the union might be hired, collected five dollars from each nonmember, but none of the sums collected were reported or recorded on the financial secretary's books as required by the laws of the international union.

The Senate subcommittee investigating welfare and pension plans turned up an interesting use of the work permit or "doby" in at least two locals of the pipe fitters. These locals are part of the plumbers' union, which in its national constitution forbids the use of permit cards. Local 102 at Knoxville, Tennessee, which had a membership of 2,356 persons when employment of plumbers, steamfitters, and steamfitter welders in the area reached as high as 25,000, began the practice of charging out-of-town members for a doby as far back as 1942. The rate was one dollar a week before 1952 and two dollars afterward. From 1943 to 1949 the subcommittee estimated doby income to have amounted to many thousands of dollars a week, and from 1949 on it fluctuated from $400 to $6,000 a week.

Sometime in 1951 or 1952 the international representative informed the local that collection of fees from members of sister locals had been forbidden by the international. As a result, the members on July 24, 1952, voted to remove the charge from the books but to require all out-of-town men to pay two dollars a week in advance for a "sick and welfare" fund. From that time on the doby collections were labeled as health and welfare contributions but carried on the local's books as local assessments. No benefits were ever paid from the sick and welfare fund. The Senate subcommittee estimated that at least $129,000 had been collected by this means from 1949 to 1955. The money was evidently spent through the local's general funds.

Local 211 of the plumbers' union at Houston, Texas also had a health and welfare fund financed by doby payments from 1951 to 1954. Approximately $90,000 was collected, of which about $38,000 was paid out in benefits to members of Local 211. No benefits were

[32] *The International Steam Engineer* (October 1924), p. 295.

paid to the individuals paying the doby. The practice was discontinued at the insistence of the international.[33]

In the case of Local 138 of the Operating Engineers, a permit system was used to keep political power in the local in the hands of the leaders. The local had 550 members, who had the right to vote in union affairs. It had approximately 700 additional members in two subsidiary locals (Local 138A and Local 138B), who were not allowed to vote. In addition, there were permit holders numbering 500 to 1,000. Union membership with voting privileges was available only to those whom the leaders favored. The permits were also used to give jobs to nonskilled favorites in preference to members. The local had a considerable number of "push button" jobs, on which engineers must appear to start a motor or watch it start and then leave, drawing a full day's pay. Bookies and race track men "worked" at these jobs, while members of many years' experience were unemployed.[34]

Many of the national unions have done little or nothing to regulate the use of permit cards. Other national unions have regulations that may or may not be enforced on the locals. Some unions, such as the plumbers mentioned above, prohibit the issuance of permit cards, though cases that have come before the National Labor Relations Board or that have been revealed by congressional investigations indicate that these prohibitions have not been strictly enforced by the national unions.

A second approach is that of the asbestos workers, which allows the use of permit cards but prohibits the charging of fees for them. But there has been some difficulty in enforcing this provision because a few locals and business agents have accepted "donations" or "gifts" from permit holders. In some cases the international stepped in and forced return of the money. When some of the permit workers could not be located, the money due them was turned over to the Red Cross. One local union official was expelled for repeated violations of this section of the asbestos workers' constitution, but cases before the National Labor Relations Board show that collections have not been completely stamped out.[35]

[33] *Welfare and Pension Plans Investigation,* Final Report of the Senate Committee on Labor and Public Welfare, S. Rept. 1734, 84 Cong. 2 sess. (April 1956), pp. 286-92.

[34] U. S. Senate, Hearings before the Select Committee on Improper Activities in the Labor or Management Field, 85 Cong. 2 sess. (January 21-24, 1958), Part 19, pp. 7755, 7788-89, 7796, 7825, 7827.

[35] International Association of Heat and Frost Insulators and Asbestos Workers, Local

The brewery workers provide that temporary employees may work upon payment of an amount equal to regular union dues, but after a given period the employee ceases to be "temporary" and must join the union. This arrangement greatly reduces the incentive for local unions to exclude temporary workers from membership.

Finally, some unions try to control the issuing of permit cards by requiring accounting for the money received. In some cases the national union requires that part of the fee be turned over to it.[36]

Requirement That Hiring Be Done Through the Union

Not all hiring that is done through unions is the result of union pressure. Some employers, especially small ones who have limited contact with the labor market through foremen and employees, find that hiring through the union is a convenient way of getting workers, especially when the employer's need for them suddenly exceeds the supply from his customary sources. However, employers sometimes complain that the most desirable men get jobs through the recommendations of friends so that the men sent out from the union office are likely to be the least desirable workers in the trade.

Union control of hiring raises important problems with respect to (1) the quality of the employment service; (2) the effect on equal opportunity of workers to gain employment; and (3) the effect on union democracy.

Employers ought to know their needs better than the union knows them. On the other hand, small employers generally lack adequate contacts with the labor market. There are great differences in the quality of employment service offered by unions and in the rules under which they operate. These differences probably account for the wide variety of opinion among employers as to the merits of these services. Some employers feel that the union does a good job of classifying its members on the basis of their experience and skill and

---

7, AFL, 92 NLRB No. 134, Sprinkman Corporation, NLRB Intermediate Report (May 1951).

[36] There has been some question whether the collection of fees for work permits violates the Federal Anti-Kickback Law of 1934—a statute that provides criminal penalties for any one who exacts monies for the right to work on a building or construction project financed in whole or in part by federal funds. The dominant view of the law is that it was intended to apply to the collection of kickbacks by employers and does not outlaw the collection of work permit fees. (Carbone et al., 56 Fed. Supp. 343 [1944]). Two states, Alabama and Texas, outlaw work permits. Under the Taft-Hartley Act, as interpreted in some court decisions, nonunion workers may be required to pay a nondiscriminatory fee for the use of union hiring halls.

that the union gives the employer broad latitude in rejecting men whom the employer does not find satisfactory. Other employers complain that the union employment service is unduly mechanical, and that employers are not given a reasonable chance to reject men who are not satisfactory. Large employers who have good contacts with the labor market are likely to do better on their own than by hiring through the union, but small employers with few labor market contacts may do better hiring through the union provided the union gives good service. The Pittsburgh Plate Glass Company complains that when an employer must make the union his employment agency, he has no opportunity to use modern or efficient methods of employee selection. The company also complains of the arbitrary fashion in which some unions create turnover in order to distribute employment opportunities broadly. In one sales and warehouse branch, where the company had permanent jobs for about 50 glaziers, it was compelled to accept the intermittent services of some 150 different individuals—three men rotating on each job. The union would send the company a glazier for one week, then take him away and send another glazier. Several weeks later, the company might get back the first glazier.[37]

In 1922 the employers in the men's clothing industry in Chicago, dissatisfied with the union employment service, unsuccessfully demanded that the control of hiring be returned to them. The union, however, did undertake a drastic reorganization and reform of its employment service in Chicago. It agreed to cooperate with the employers in drawing up regulations for sending workers to jobs and to organize an efficient employment service.[38] Bryce M. Stewart, head of the Canadian employment service, was engaged by the union to set up the Chicago employment exchange.[39]

Unless the members of a union are extremely vigilant in asserting

[37] Leland Hazard, Vice President and General Counsel of the Pittsburgh Plate Glass Company, Letter to the Honorable E. D. Thomas, Hearings on S. 249 before the Senate Committee on Labor and Public Welfare, 81 Cong. 1 sess. (1949), Part 6, pp. 3383-84.

[38] Amalgamated Clothing Workers, *Proceedings of the Fifth Biennial Convention* (1922), p. 139.

In 1926 the union organized an employment exchange in Rochester, N.Y. The union was concerned about the employers' practice of hiring workers at the factory gate instead of procuring them through the union. The employers objected to changing their procedure on the ground that the union employment service was not efficient. The Rochester Joint Board thereupon set up an efficient employment exchange modelled after the one in Chicago. *Proceedings of the Eighth Biennial Convention* (1928), p. 40.

[39] Amalgamated Clothing Workers, *Proceedings of the Sixth Biennial Convention* (1924), p. 88.

control over hiring (which is unlikely), union control of hiring means more power and influence for the union officers. If the members are not alert to prevent it, some union leaders will use control of hiring to strengthen their political machines by seeing that their favorites get the steadiest work and the most attractive jobs. William Wilkens testified before the McClellan Committee that the president and business manager of the Operating Engineers Local 138 "can tell you that you are going to eat oatmeal or you are going to eat steak every day of the year. . . . It is all according to if you are in favor or disfavor."[40]

Complaints to the National Labor Relations Board and to the courts illustrate vividly the severe hardships that union control of hiring may inflict on members of a local or others in the occupation who incur the ill-will of the powers-that-be in the union. Thus, 13 disgruntled members of plumbers' Local 60 of New Orleans filed charges against the union and 34 plumbing, heating, and air conditioning contractors alleging that they could not get work. The NLRB issued a complaint. A machinist named Gonzales, who was expelled by a machinists' local in San Francisco, was refused referral to jobs through the local's exclusive job referral system. The Supreme Court of the United States held that Gonzales could recover damages from the union for loss of wages and for mental suffering.[41]

In an attempt to prevent political abuses, some unions require that workers be sent to jobs in accordance with the duration of their unemployment. Unless this criterion is qualified by skill requirements, it may lead either to rejection by the employer of workers referred to him or to discharge because they cannot do the work.

The rules under which union hiring halls operate are a matter of joint concern to employers and unions, and they should be jointly negotiated. In a few cases (on the Pacific Coast waterfront, for example) this has been done. In the main, however, employers have left the important matter of rules to unilateral determination by unions. The rules should cover the right of employers to reject men sent by the union and also define the right of union members to refuse referrals. For example, some of the unemployed men may be temporary layoffs, looking for temporary work only; others may have no connection

[40] U. S. Senate, Hearings before the Select Committee on Improper Activities in the Labor or Management Field, 85 Cong. 2 sess. (January 21-24, 1958), Part 19, p. 7788.
[41] Gonzales v. Machinists' Union, decided by U. S. Supreme Court on May 26, 1958. Supreme Court Reporter, Vol. 78, p. 923.

with any employer. Some jobs are temporary, others are "permanent." And individual craftsmen within the same trade vary in their capacities, and jobs within the trade vary in their requirements. Thus, the man at the top of the list who is first referred to a job may not want it. It may involve too much travel time, or it may have prospects of being only a short job. The unemployed worker may have his eye on jobs which are expected to open up in a week or two and which promise a longer stretch of employment, perhaps enhanced by considerable overtime. What happens if he refuses to go out on a referral? Does he retain his position at the head of the list, does he go to the bottom of the list, or does he go down a given number of places on the list?

Union Control of Hiring on the Waterfront

The casual nature of employment in stevedoring makes the control of hiring on the waterfront a matter of great concern to both employers and employees, and the striking difference in policies pursued by different unions underlines the role of union politics in the control of hiring. On the Pacific coast the union has succeeded both in decasualizing employment and in assuming almost complete control of hiring. In the port of New York, on the other hand, the union strongly resisted efforts to decasualize employment with the result that a government body was created to control hiring in the port.

Efforts to decasualize waterfront employment were started by employers in Seattle in 1920. A central hiring hall to serve the entire port was set up, and a committee of four employers and four longshoremen was established to register the needed number of longshoremen and to decide which men should be eliminated from the labor force. The committee made a careful study of the work experience and qualifications of the men working on the waterfront, and the size of the force was cut from around 1,400 to 612. An effort was made to divide the work equally. Because the workers disliked employer-administered hiring halls the Seattle hiring hall is now jointly administered.

In San Francisco a major issue of the 1934 strike was the union demand for control of hiring. Hiring had been by "the shape up," by which the employers hired from among men who lined up in search of work. The strike was settled by an arbitration decision that nominally established jointly-operated hiring halls but provided that the dispatchers were to be elected by the union membership. This meant that in effect the union had won control of hiring. In 1936 there was another strike, in which the employers asked that neutral dispatchers, responsible to the joint employer-union labor relations committees, be substituted for dispatchers elected by the union. The employers lost this strike. Not only did the union retain full control of the dispatchers, but the settlement established union preference in employment.

Little change occurred in the operation of the hiring halls until after the passage of the Taft-Hartley Act in 1947. There was a strike in 1948 resulting in part from failure of the parties to agree on how the dispatchers were to be selected. Under the settlement there was no change in the operation of the hiring hall, and preference in employment for union members was continued. The latter provision was found by the NLRB in 1950 to be a violation of the Taft-Hartley Act. In 1951 the clause was changed to provide preference for longshoremen who were registered and available for employment on June 1, 1951. In effect this agreement confines hiring to union men, but two trial examiners of the NLRB have held that the present operation of the hiring hall does not conflict with the Taft-Hartley Act. At any rate, the union has succeeded in keeping the hiring system virtually unchanged and under union control in spite of the Taft-Hartley Act. As noted earlier in the chapter, this control has promoted stable employment and improved employee earnings. Greater security of the union has meant greater worker-employer cooperation in adapting to technological change.

Quite different has been the story in New York. Under the shape-up the hiring was done by a hiring boss who was an employee of the stevedore but who was also a key man in the union political machine. Although the shape-up resulted in an excessive number of longshoremen, it appealed to the union officers, partly because it was a source of graft for them, and partly because it helped them keep the men under control. The employers also liked the shape-up because it produced a large surplus labor pool and because they liked to deal with union officers who had the men well under control.

As a result of the recommendations of the New York State Crime Commission, a bi-state (New York and New Jersey) compact was passed creating a Waterfront Commission of New York Harbor to control hiring in the port of New York. The legislation was attacked in the New York legislature in 1949 and 1950 by both the International Longshoremen's Association and the New York Shipping Association, the latter being the employers' organization. Nevertheless, the legislation was passed, and the changes in hiring practices introduced by the Commission have gone far to decasualize employment on the New York waterfront. In 1952 there were 44,161 longshoremen in New York; in 1954, 33,551; in 1957, 26,629. In 1952, 8.7 per cent of all longshoremen employed in New York worked 2,000 hours or more, and 38.8 per cent worked under 100 hours. In 1957, 17.0 per cent worked 2,000 or more hours, and 14.7 per cent worked under 100 hours.[42]

Enforcement of Racial Discrimination

Should unions that bar Negroes or other nonwhites from membership be permitted to negotiate union-shop or closed-shop contracts or to represent as exclusive bargaining agents employees to whom they deny full membership? These questions remain to be faced squarely. The Taft-Hartley Act deals with the first question by providing that employers shall not discriminate against an employee for nonmembership in a union if he has reasonable grounds for believing that membership was not available to the employee on equal terms with other members. This provision prevents the union shop from barring the employment of Negroes or other workers whom certain craft unions will not admit. But the very fact that a union will not admit Negroes may discourage an employer from hiring them and thus narrow their employment opportunities. Are organizations entitled to the very substantial privileges and immunities granted them and their members by the Taft-Hartley Act unless the organizations are willing to open their doors to all qualified members of the community? And should unions be certified as the exclusive bargaining agents for employees whom they refuse to admit to membership? How can the National Labor Relations Board justify giving exclusive bargaining rights to organizations that practice racial discrimination? The Board has shown no interest in persuading unions to reform their membership rules. The constitutionality of procedures that force men to be represented through organizations that deny them membership is open to question.

[42] Vernon Johnson, "Decasualization of Employment on the New York Waterfront," *Industrial and Labor Relations Review* (July 1958) p. 535.

Most industrial unions find themselves involved willy-nilly in the struggle of the nonwhites for a chance to work at the best jobs in industry. Some of the industrial unions may not take the initiative in raising the issue of discrimination, but if it is raised by nonwhites themselves or by some outside body, such as the National Association for the Advancement of Colored People or the President's Committee on Government Contracts, the union cannot afford to be neutral. Unless it takes a stand against discrimination, it will find itself unable to organize the colored workers in industry. Furthermore, in industries where a large number of Negroes, Puerto Ricans, Mexicans, or Orientals are employed, the industrial unions must take an aggressive stand against discrimination or give up the prospect of organizing the nonwhites. Among the principal anti-discrimination steps taken by industrial unions are:

(1) Placing Negroes, Puerto Ricans, Latin Americans, Filipinos, and others through the union employment service without discrimination. Fifteen years ago there were scarcely any Negro or Puerto Rican clerks in New York retail stores. In recent years the employment office of District 65 of the Retail, Wholesale and Department Store Union placed 2,724 Negroes and 3,805 Puerto Ricans, Latin Americans, and Filipinos out of a total of 16,527 placements.

(2) Assisting Negroes and others to learn skilled trades. The Amalgamated Clothing Workers, in cooperation with the Urban League, arranged for a clothing manufacturer to lend six power machines to a social agency that undertook to train Negro applicants.

(3) Negotiating anti-discrimination hiring clauses. Anti-discrimination clauses are a common feature of the agreements of industrial unions. Typical of such a clause is the following from an agreement between the UAW and an automobile manufacturer: "Neither the company nor the union, in carrying out their obligations under the Agreement, shall discriminate in any manner whatsoever against any employee because of race, sex, political or religious affiliation or nationality." Although many of these clauses do not refer specifically to hiring, it is acknowledged that they are intended to apply to hiring, as well as to promotions, transfers, and the like.

(4) Helping to suppress wildcat strikes and other forms of protest when the company hires nonwhites for highly desirable jobs that some feel belong to whites alone. Of particular interest is the effectiveness of unions in handling wildcat strikes precipitated by the hir-

ing or promotion of Negroes. A threat by management to discipline leaders of wildcat strikes is extraordinarily effective if the union makes clear that it does not propose to defend strikers against company discipline.

Besides taking specific steps to prevent discrimination in hiring, many industrial unions try to carry out a general policy of anti-discrimination to make white members less prone to object to working with Negroes. The UAW collects one cent a month from each member to support a fair employment policies program. In 1949 the rubber workers' union created a Fair Practices Department to help local unions handle the various race relations problems that arise in the industry. The department is under the direct supervision of the general president, and it has an assistant director who devotes full time to it. The Fair Practices Department compiles data on every phase of civil rights, bias, and anti-discrimination laws; it keeps a record of local ordinances dealing with discrimination and of the records in this field of all members of Congress; it participates in panel discussions and work shops; it works with other departments of the union, particularly the Education Department and the Research and Contract Departments. The Packinghouse Workers have also worked actively with employers to reduce discrimination.

Seniority Rules as a Restriction on Hiring

Many union-management contracts carry a provision that jobs must be filled by promotion from within if properly qualified workers are available. This influence on hiring is a nominal one because most employers would ordinarily fill vacancies by promoting properly qualified men. But the method of hiring at the bottom and promoting within the organization does impose restrictions on the employees themselves. It means that a worker who leaves a job with one employer is likely to have to start at the bottom with a new employer. While there are many advantages for employees in such a provision, it also creates some problems for them. The employee who has worked up to a good job in an enterprise finds himself tied to this job. He may become tired of the community and want a change of scene. Or friction may develop between him and the management. Yet if he moves, he must begin at the bottom elsewhere at a big reduction in pay. A report issued by a special research committee of the

International Brotherhood of Papermakers discusses the problem created by seniority rules governing promotions.[43]

Public Policy on Union Control of Hiring

When Congress in 1935 decided to encourage unions and collective bargaining by passing the Wagner Act, it was careful to place little restraint on the right of unions to negotiate union-shop or closed-shop contracts. The Wagner Act was passed when unions were weak and limited in membership and when the country was deep in depression with one out of every five workers unemployed. Under the circumstances, Congress saw no need to disturb customary arrangements, such as the closed shop, that had existed for many years in the building trades and the printing trades and for a number of years in the needle trades. Although the Wagner Act made it an unfair labor practice for an employer "by discrimination in regard to hire or tenure of employment to encourage or discourage membership in any labor organization," it did permit employers to require membership in a union as a condition of employment, provided the union was representative of the employees in an appropriate bargaining unit and provided it was free from employer domination or interference.

The public policy of encouraging the formation of unions and the practice of collective bargaining led to spectacular gains in the membership and strength of unions, and the buyers' markets of the great depression were soon replaced with the sellers' markets of World War II. The closed shop operated in a highly unsatisfactory way in many places during the war and in the postwar boom. The unions insisted that all workers hired on various projects be union members, but they were often unable to supply workers in the numbers needed. In some cases the unions tried to meet the demand by admitting unqualified workers, after charging them a stiff initiation fee for memberships that were bound to be quite temporary. In other cases, the unions refused to expand their membership but issued permit cards allowing the holders to work on union jobs. Public dissatisfaction with unions and their operations was increased by the great increase in the number of strikes at the end of the war in 1945 and 1946. The

[43] International Brotherhood of Papermakers, *Labor Threat and Dissatisfaction* (June 15, 1944), pp. 447-50.

result was a widespread demand that the power of the unions be curbed, culminating in passage of the Taft-Hartley Act and some state legislation.

One of the principal curbs placed on unions by the Taft-Hartley Act was outlawing the closed shop. There was some sentiment in Congress for outlawing the union shop as well, but unions succeeded in persuading Congress to allow the union shop if the employees in the bargaining unit authorized it in an election held under government auspices. This turned out to be a satisfactory compromise from the union standpoint.[44] The National Labor Relations Board held many thousands of elections on the union-shop issue, and, to the surprise of many employers, the workers usually voted more than ten to one in favor of union-shop agreements. The strong worker vote in their favor undoubtedly helped unions to increase the number of union-shop agreements. As a result, the years immediately following the passage of the Taft-Hartley Act in 1947 saw a rapid expansion of such agreements.

The desire to curb the power of unions expressed itself also in state legislation, especially so-called "right-to-work" laws, which went further than the Taft-Hartley Act and outlawed almost all forms of union security. The first of these laws was passed by Florida in 1944. The year 1947 (the year with the greatest number of postwar strikes) saw eleven states pass right-to-work laws.[45] In 1951 Nevada passed a right-to-work law; in 1953, Alabama; in 1954, Mississippi and South Carolina; in 1955, Utah; in 1957, Indiana; and in 1958, Kansas. Delaware, New Hampshire, and Maine passed right-to-work laws in 1947 but repealed them later. Louisiana passed such a law in 1954 but repealed it in 1956.

The reaction of unions and employers to the attempts of the federal government to outlaw the closed shop and of some states to outlaw other forms of union security has varied with past practices and

[44] The encouragement of union-shop contracts offered by the Taft-Hartley Act does not seem to have been intended by Congress. The Act provided that union-shop contracts might be negotiated if they were authorized by a vote of the employees in an election conducted by the National Labor Relations Board. Congress apparently believed that in a large proportion of cases employees would reject the union shop, but the opposite proved to be the case. In 46,146 elections conducted between August 2, 1947 and October 22, 1951, when this part of the Taft-Hartley Act was repealed, the employees voted in favor of the union shop in 44,823 cases or in about 96.5 per cent of the polls. The total votes cast in favor of the union shop were 5,073,242, and the vote against it, 465,740—a ratio of more than ten to one in favor of the union shop.

[45] These states were: Arizona, Arkansas, Georgia, Iowa, Nebraska, North Carolina, North Dakota, South Dakota, Tennessee, Texas, and Virginia.

traditions in the particular occupation or industry. In industries where employment is not intermittent or highly seasonal, the unions have generally been satisfied to operate under the union-shop provisions of the Taft-Hartley Act. Quite different, however, has been the situation in industries where employment is intermittent or highly seasonal and where the closed shop and/or hiring through the union are traditional. In these industries (the building trades, the waterfront occupations, and some others) numerous special arrangements were adopted to avoid the limitations imposed by the law.

Sometimes the language has been noncommittal, such as an agreement to "employ union men insofar as permitted by law." Another device has been for the employer to agree to employ only workers who meet certain specifications that only union men could meet. Thus, the electrotypers in Philadelphia substituted for a closed-shop agreement an agreement that only persons recognized as "practical foundrymen" or "practical finishers" or "registered apprentices" should perform any operation in the foundry or finishing rooms. Practical foundryman or finisher was defined to mean one who had served at least six years at the business. This provision had the effect of limiting the work to previous members of the union. Union men in various trades have also made it plain that they would not work with nonunion men, and employers have avoided hiring nonunion men because they want to avoid friction. Some unions were led by the Taft-Hartley Act to place more emphasis on hiring through the union. A typical agreement is that of the pressmen's union with a New England press that provides for hiring through the union but gives the employer an opportunity to hire outside the union after reasonable notice if the union is unable to supply men.

Just as the unions and employers that have operated traditionally under the closed shop more or less disregarded the Taft-Hartley provisions against the closed shop, so the unions and employers that have operated under union shops have sometimes disregarded state prohibitions against union shops. A steel mill in a western state that passed a right-to-work law instructed employment interviewers to tell new employees: "The bargaining agent at this plant is the United Steelworkers of America. There is a union-shop provision in the contract which requires membership thirty days after first entering employment in the plant. However, there is a right-to-work law in this state which prevents the use of union membership as a requirement for employment." The interviewers then furnished a union membership application with no further comment about union membership unless asked. There was no noticeable trend away from union membership, but the international union protested this procedural change. The industrial relations staff was ordered to return to the procedure, that was followed before the right-to-work law was passed, of merely telling the employee about the union shop contract without informing him that the union-shop feature of the contract was not valid within the state. If the employee brings up the right-to-work law, the company representative admits that union membership is not necessary to hold a job.

In the nine years from August 21, 1947, when the Taft-Hartley Act became effective, until March 6, 1956, the National Labor Relations Board had a thousand or more cases in which unions or employers, or both, were charged with having an illegal closed shop or union security provision. However, all the Board did was to issue cease and desist orders against the continuation of the illegal practices and require that a notice to that effect be posted. However, in recent years the Board has imposed severe penalties. In one case it ordered a local of the plumbers' union to refund all dues and assessments collected during a six-month period from its members employed by the Brown-Olds Plumbing Company, where an illegal closed shop was maintained.

This decision showed unions and employers that maintenance of an illegal closed shop can be very expensive. It greatly increased the interest of unions in union-controlled hiring halls, which could offer to serve impartially both union and nonunion workers for the same fee. It is likely that the principal effect of the Taft-Hartley Act's outlawing of the closed shop will be to encourage the spread of union hiring halls.

4 / *Union Policies on Training and Apprenticeship*

WORKERS IN AMERICAN INDUSTRY may be classified in seven principal groups: common laborers, semi-skilled workers, skilled workers, technicians, professional workers, managers, and self-employed owners.[1] Unions are well represented in the first three groups and to some extent among the technicians but to only a very small extent among professional workers and the self-employed.[2]

Distinction Between Skilled and Other Workers

The differences between some of the classifications (for instance, between common laborer and semi-skilled worker, between semi-skilled worker and skilled worker, between skilled worker and technician, and between technician and professional worker) are partly matters of degree but partly also of custom. Furthermore, distinctions between succeeding grades of skill are much less clearly defined in the service and clerical occupations than in construction, manufacturing, mining, transportation, and communication.

Our concern in this chapter is with the policies of unions that directly affect the number and training of skilled workers. Skilled workers are distinguished from the semi-skilled below them and from the technicians above by: (1) knowledge, (2) mastery of technical skills, and (3) willingness and ability to assume responsibility, to

[1] This classification is more significant than the one used in the monthly labor force reports, which lump together without respect to skill clerical and kindred workers (which may include anyone from skilled stenographers to filing clerks), sales workers (ranging from insurance salesmen to clerks in ten-cent stores), and service workers (except in private households), a group with widely varying degrees of skills—for example, from cooks at hot dog stands to chefs in first class hotels.

[2] There are no unions composed exclusively of self-employed (such organizations would be trade associations), but some unions include self-employed persons among their members. Examples are the cigar makers, teamsters, barbers, musicians, and some of the building trades.

endure punishment, or to take risks.[3] Knowledge enables the skilled worker to know what to do as well as how to do it. This means that the properly trained skilled worker understands *why* he is doing what he does. His knowledge of what to do as well as how to do it enables him to work with little supervision. His mastery of technical skills must not be too specialized. If he is a manual worker, he is ordinarily able to use a variety of tools, to operate a variety of machines, and to work to close specifications. If he is an office worker, he knows the principal operations in running an office; if he is a salesman, he handles goods that have many features to present and that must be fitted to the customers' tastes. Finally, the skilled worker is one who can be trusted with responsibility, who can be asked to look out for the safety of others or for valuable goods, or who, in some occupations, is expected to take punishment or to assume risks (as in the case of prize fighters, lion tamers, and professional athletes generally).

The semi-skilled worker possesses only some of the qualities found in the skilled worker. In particular, the former does not have the skilled worker's knowledge of what to do, and his command of technical skills is more specialized (though within his area of specialization his technical skill may be high). He is not usually expected to assume as high a degree of responsibility as the skilled worker.

Above the skilled workers are the rapidly growing number of technicians, such as draftsmen, laboratory assistants, some camera men, sound effects men, radio and television engineers, flight engineers, most actors, most musicians, some expert salesmen, physical therapists, graduate nurses, dietitians. In general, the distinction between technicians and skilled workers turns on the relative importance of knowledge and technical skills in their work. The technical worker in general performs jobs in which the theoretical elements are more important to the manual skills than they are in the jobs done by the skilled workers. However, the manual skill as well as

---

[3] *The Dictionary of Occupational Titles,* which has been too much influenced by tradition, defines skilled occupations too narrowly as "craft or manual occupations that require predominantly a thorough and comprehensive knowledge of processes involved in the work, the exercise of considerable independent judgment, usually a high degree of manual dexterity, and, in some instances, extensive responsibility for valuable product or equipment." This definition by limiting skilled occupations to "craft or manual occupations" excludes many skilled office workers and sales people as well as jockeys, snake charmers, circus clowns, and others, who are not in crafts or manual work.

the knowledge required of the technician may exceed that required of the skilled workers.

The difference between the technicians and the professional workers is also a matter of degree—the emphasis in the professions being largely upon learning. The original learned professions were medicine, law, and theology. As knowledge and the importance of knowledge have increased, the number of professions has grown. Architecture is now regarded as a profession, as are engineering, military science, teaching, diplomacy, public administration, and the pursuit of the creative arts.

Number of Skilled Workers in the American Economy

The number of skilled workers in American industry is not known. The census of occupations shows the number of persons reported as craftsmen, foremen, and kindred workers and the number of craftsmen reported by the census is often taken to represent the number of skilled workers in American industry.[4] This assumption is not correct. In the first place, the census counts as craftsmen and kindred workers only persons engaged in the various mechanical crafts—those using tools or machines. Nonmanual workers, such as policemen, firemen, some salesmen, some office workers, most actors, circus performers, athletes, and many musicians, are not counted as skilled craftsmen by the census. Second, craftsmen and related workers as defined by the census do not include all skilled manual workers in industry—such as barbers, beauty parlor operators, embalmers, animal trainers, and many chefs. These workers are counted in the census simply as service workers. Third, many of the workers who are reported in the census as craftsmen are not really skilled since

[4] In the census of 1950 there were 59 general occupational classifications in the category "craftsmen, foremen, and kindred workers." Some of these classifications, such as "machinist," were quite general, and four of the categories were residual classifications—"inspectors not elsewhere classified," "foremen not elsewhere classified," "mechanics, repairmen, not elsewhere classified," and "craftsmen and kindred workers not elsewhere classified." Some of the census titles, such as "machinist" or "brick masons, stone masons, and tile setters," cover a variety of trades. The classification system remained virtually the same for the 1960 census.

Many categories which were separately counted in the census of 1950 were not counted in earlier censuses. Thus, in 1950 there were fifteen crafts counted separately that were not so counted in 1930—among them airplane mechanics, motion picture operators, heat treaters, radio mechanics, office machine repairmen, opticians, and bookbinders.

they do not have a comprehensive knowledge of the work or broad ability to do it. They are counted as skilled only because they happen to be employed in occupations that have traditionally been regarded as skilled. But many so-called "carpenters" are only saw and hammer men, many "painters" are just brush hands, and many "machinists" are merely machine hands able to do specialized work on only a few machines. Thus the census count omits many skilled workers and includes many workers who are not truly skilled. Since the two errors may rather closely offset each other, the *total* count of craftsmen may be more or less accidentally correct—though the number of craftsmen reported in the separate classifications is far from correct.[5] Since the census counts as skilled workers only members of certain traditional manual crafts and fails to include many members of new skilled occupations, its reports on the relative importance of skilled workers are not of much value. The census reports that about one-third of the male skilled craftsmen are in the building trades, about one-fourth in various mechanical trades, and about one-eighth in the metal working trades.[6]

The Growing Demand for Skilled Workers

Skilled workers form an increasing proportion of the labor force. Among males the proportion of craftsmen, foremen, and kindred workers to the male labor force increased from 12.6 per cent in 1900 to 19.0 per cent in 1950.[7] Male service workers outside private house-

[5] The importance of definitions is shown by a survey of skilled workers in the metal trades in New York State made recently by the Division of Research and Statistics of the New York State Department of Labor. The Department counted as skilled craftsmen those who were able to set up completely their own machines, read blueprints, and work to very close tolerances, but it counted these first-class machine hands separately from all-around machinists and toolmakers. As a result, the New York Division of Research and Statistics classified in March 1957 as machinists or toolmakers only about half as many persons as did the 1950 census.

[6] U. S. Department of Labor, Bureau of Apprenticeship and Training, *The Skilled Labor Force*, Technical Bulletin No. T-140 (April 1954), p. 28. The distribution of the male skilled workmen, as reported by the census, is as follows:

All occupation groups	7,879 thousand
Construction trades	2,660 "
Mechanic trades (specified)	2,058 "
Metal working trades	1,077 "
Printing trades	278 "
Other trades	931 "
Foremen and inspectors	875 "

[7] Gertrude Bancroft, *The American Labor Force—Its Growth and Changing Composition* (1958), p. 209.

holds, containing a large proportion of skilled workers, increased from 2.9 per cent of gainfully-employed males in 1900 to 6.0 per cent in 1950.[8] Between April 1950 and April 1958 craftsmen, foremen, and kindred workers increased from 12.8 per cent of the total labor force to 13.4 per cent.[9]

Behind the growing demand for skilled workers are rising per-capita incomes and changes in technology. Increased incomes enable people to demand more of the personal services (repair work of all kinds, for example, and entertainment) that skilled workers provide.[10] Technological change means many new kinds of apparatus and increasing quantities of old apparatus that must be installed and repaired. Some of it must be operated by skilled men. Many of the skilled crafts of today are not more than half a century old, and some are much less—airplane repairmen, hoistmen, heat treaters, forgemen, motion picture projectionists, and radio repairmen.

Within the craft labor force some crafts are growing, and others are shrinking. Among the rapidly growing occupations are auto mechanics, airplane mechanics, tool and die makers, and opticians. The declining occupations include blacksmiths, locomotive engineers, tailors, and shoe repairmen. The table on page 64 shows the number of male workers counted as craftsmen in some of the rapidly growing occupations and in some of the declining or stationary occupations. There are far fewer locomotive engineers and firemen than there were twenty or thirty years ago, and there have been startling decreases in the number of blacksmiths, tailors, and stonecutters. On the other hand, the number of tool and die makers; auto, airplane, and radio mechanics; office machine repairmen; excavators; and cranemen has increased dramatically.

In spite of the rapid growth in the number of craftsmen, the need has grown faster than the supply. This is shown by the fact that weekly hours of work reported by craftsmen, foremen, and kindred workers have consistently exceeded the number reported by all workers—and also the number reported by the operatives and kindred

---

[8] The same.

[9] U. S. Bureau of the Census, *Annual Report on the Labor Force 1950*, Series P-50, No. 31, p. 26, and *Monthly Report on the Labor Force: April 1958*, Series P-57, No. 190, p. 16.

[10] Rising per-capita incomes also increase the proportion of technical and professional workers in the labor force. Between 1940 and 1950, when the labor force as a whole increased by 25.2 per cent, the number of medical, dental, and testing technicians increased 125.6 per cent, radio operators 160.5 per cent, and professional workers 37.4 per cent.

Selected Changes in Skilled Labor Force
by Occupation, 1900-50[a]
(In thousands)

Occupation	1900	1910	1920	1930	1940	1950
	Workers in Some Rapidly Growing Crafts					
Opticians	–	–	–	–	12.2	19.8
Excavators	–	–	–	–	40.0	111.0
Cement masons	–	6.0	7.8	15.7	26.7	32.7
Heat treaters	–	–	–	–	10.9	18.3
Tool-die makers	–	9.3	55.1	78.8	96.9	157.0
Airplane mechanics	–	–	–	–	28.4	73.7
Radio mechanics	–	–	–	–	–	78.3
Office machine repairmen	–	–	–	–	–	16.3
Auto mechanics	–	–	–	394.2	441.8	677.6
Cranemen	–	–	–	60.9	80.2	106.9
Total	–	15.3	62.9	549.6	737.1	1,291.6
	Workers in Some Declining or Stationary Crafts					
Stonecutters	54.5	32.5	20.1	20.8	14.3	9.1
Plasterers	35.7	47.7	38.3	70.0	52.9	64.4
Painters	277.5	330.4	316.5	431.9	442.7	431.1
Paperhangers	22.0	25.6	18.7	28.3	30.0	22.5
Blacksmiths	–	233.0	195.3	124.4	62.7	44.9
Molders	–	120.9	123.7	94.4	87.6	63.6
Locomotive engineers	–	96.2	109.9	101.2	72.4	73.3
Locomotive firemen	–	88.8	106.3	80.2	48.8	56.0
Stationary engineers	–	231.0	242.1	256.1	200.1	218.1
Tailors	229.6	202.6	190.3	167.6	118.8	85.9
Furriers	–	–	–	–	17.2	12.9
Shoe repairers	–	68.9	78.0	75.6	65.7	58.9
Brickmasons	160.8	169.4	131.3	170.9	141.7	175.8
Total	780.1	1,647.0	1,570.5	1,621.4	1,354.9	1,316.5

[a] Data from U. S. Bureau of Apprenticeship, *The Skilled Labor Force*, Technical Bulletin No. T-140 (April 1954), Table IV, pp. 15-16.

workers. In fact, even in the recession of 1958, when overtime quite generally disappeared, the weekly hours reported by skilled craftsmen exceeded the weekly hours of other workers.[11]

[11] The following data, based on the monthly reports on the labor force of the Bureau of the Census (Series P-57), show the average weekly hours reported by several groups of workers.

	Craftsmen, Foremen and Kindred Workers	*All Workers*	*Operatives and Kindred Workers*
January 1956	41.5	40.9	40.8
January 1957	41.3	40.7	40.5
January 1958	40.4	39.9	39.1
February 1958	39.8	39.4	38.7

When a study was made of skilled metal workers in the state of New York in March 1957, it was found that about 4,800 additional craftsmen were being actively sought—one for every 17 already on the payroll. In the meantime employers were working craftsmen longer hours than their fellow employees—an average of 43.0 hours per week compared with 40.7 hours for all production workers in the same firms.[12]

The Growing Demands on Workers in the Skilled Crafts

Not only does industry require a growing proportion of professional workers, technicians, and skilled workers in the labor force, but in most occupations the demands for skill are increasing. Surgeons, engineers, and architects are tackling new and more difficult problems. The various kinds of skilled craftsmen must meet steadily stricter standards and growing responsibilities. They must work to closer tolerances, make more precise adjustments, install more intricate wiring and piping, make installations that meet stiffer standards of performance—greater and quicker ranges of temperature change, greater loads, greater charges, greater pressure—and they must know how to weld radically new alloys. They must assume responsibility for handling larger and more expensive pieces of apparatus and more costly materials. Some atomic energy piping may cost up to $1,000 per foot, and valves installed in atomic energy plants may cost fantastic amounts: one four-inch diameter valve costs $56,000.

Supply of Skilled Craftsmen

An addition to the skilled labor force of this country of around 500,000 is needed each year. Replacement needs alone are about 400,000 a year. The apprenticeable occupations account for about 5.5 million out of the 8.5 million skilled nonprofessional workers in the labor force. The U. S. Bureau of Apprenticeship estimates that about 250,000 persons a year leave apprenticeable occupations because of death, retirement, and shifts to other employment.[13] The

[12] Charles A. Pearce and Abraham J. Berman, "A Survey of Training Needs for Skilled Metal Trades Workers," *Monthly Labor Review* (August 1958), pp. 868-71.
[13] National Manpower Council, *A Policy for Skilled Manpower* (1954), p. 212. In the New York metal trades, where the average age of skilled craftsmen is 41 to 43 years (only slightly above the average for all production workers), the combined death and retirement rate is estimated at slightly above 2 per cent a year.
A survey of 31 key occupations in Bridgeport, Connecticut, by the Connecticut Labor

attrition rate in the other skilled occupations is probably equally high, making total annual losses of about 400,000. Needs resulting from expansion vary enormously from occupation to occupation. The remainder of this chapter will focus attention on union policies that affect the supply of craftsmen.

Formal training programs provide only a small proportion of the skilled workmen in occupations normally learned in industry. A survey in Bridgeport, Connecticut, showed that in 31 key occupations in-plant training was expected to provide only 1,326 of the 4,493 workers estimated to be needed by 1962.[14] In the metal trades of New York State only 19 per cent of the firms using tool and die makers, 11 per cent of those using all-around machinists, and only 8 per cent of those employing bench machinists, machine erectors, or mechanical instrument makers were training any workers in these skills.

Sources of Supply

There are seven principal sources of supply of skilled craftsmen:

IMMIGRATION. In recent years the importance of immigration as a source of skilled craftsmen has diminished. However, immigrants have been sought to meet special shortage problems since World War II. A few large companies, for example, are encouraging tool and die makers (especially among displaced persons) to emigrate from Canada, and emigration of skilled tailors from Italy has received special encouragement. In 1953 the number of immigrants counted as "craftsmen, foremen, or kindred workers" was 12,257. The highest figure since 1948 was 21,832 in the year 1950.[15]

FORMAL TRAINING IN TRADE OR VOCATIONAL SCHOOLS. Trade and vocational schools are an important source of supply of skilled workers

Department Security Division in cooperation with the Bureau of Employment Security of U. S. Department of Labor, indicated that replacement needs in these occupations in the five years from 1957 to 1962 will average about 2.3 per cent a year. *Skills for the Future* (September 1958), p. 21.

[14] Connecticut Labor Department, *Skills for the Future*, pp. 20-22. The 1,326 workers expected to be trained by 1962 would be well below the replacement needs of 1,694. Review of the current training programs indicated that Bridgeport industries expected to train about half of the 400 toolmakers, die makers, and die setters required in the next five years; a total of 340 inspectors will be required by 1962 with only 30 expected to complete in-plant training; only one job setter in five needed by 1962 will be trained under current programs.

[15] National Manpower Council, *A Policy for Skilled Manpower*, p. 213.

in a few occupations, particularly clerical and technical jobs. Few craftsmen come from trade or vocational schools ready to earn journeyman wages, largely because development of skill in manual work requires training on the job. The National Manpower Council estimated that no more than a thousand graduates of vocational schools enter the force of skilled craftsmen each year.[16] But perhaps ten times that number, according to reliable estimates, acquire enough basic knowledge and skill at vocational schools that after a year or two of practical experience, they can qualify as journeymen. A survey of over 1,200 apprentices graduated in 1950 from California apprenticeship programs showed that 7.2 per cent received credit in their apprenticeship courses for vocational school training.[17]

TRAINING IN THE ARMED SERVICES. Mechanization of the armed services has greatly increased their need for skilled craftsmen, and in recent years many workers have received training in the armed services—some at the technical level and some at the level of the skilled crafts. It is estimated that possibly half of the men entering the services receive some type of technical training.[18] But the military must train men for its own needs and under its own conditions. The great weakness of training in the armed services is that it is not continued long enough to give men a proper grounding in the trade. Hence, many who start technical training in the armed services do not pursue it after they return to civilian life. Since most people are in the service for a limited period of time, the military have tended to give highly-specialized training, whereas industry emphasizes broad training. But experience in the armed services helps workers move from farming to industry and away from depressed areas, and it helps Negroes overcome to some extent the effects of discriminatory practices in private industry. The California survey of 1950 apprentice graduates shows that 13.4 per cent received credit for trade experience or training in military service. The highest proportion was among electricians and linemen, of whom 28.8 per cent received such credit.[19]

[16] The same, p. 212.
[17] Division of Apprenticeship Standards, California Department of Industrial Relations, *Survey of Completed Apprentices* 1950), p. 20. Mill cabinet and mill men had the highest proportion receiving such credit—12 per cent. In the automotive trades it was 10.8 per cent.
[18] National Manpower Council, *A Policy for Skilled Manpower*, p. 122.
[19] California Department of Industrial Relations, *Survey of Completed Apprentices*, p. 20.

THE UNDERSTUDY-PROGRESSION METHOD. This is illustrated by the locomotive engineer, who learns his job by working as a fireman under
the supervision of an engineer, and by some of the job sequences in
the steel industry, the paper industry, and the printing industry,
where men move gradually up the job ladder. This method has the
important advantage of supplying skilled men on fairly short notice.
The supply is determined by the rate at which men move up the
ladder, and any increase in demand accelerates the movement upward.

PICKING UP THE TRADE. Acquiring skill by "picking it up" piece-
meal in various shops until one has learned enough to be considered
a journeyman, is the way most people learn a trade. It is a wasteful
way and produces poorly-trained workers. The number of workers
who enter the ranks of skilled craftsmen after "picking up" a knowledge varies from year to year with the demand. As vacancies open
up, more workers who have "picked up" their training get hired.
In years when the over-all number of skilled craftsmen is stable,
about one hundred thousand men enter the skilled crafts from un-
identified sources. These are men who have picked up a trade. Many
of them are not properly regarded as skilled craftsmen, though they
are fitted into jobs that skilled craftsmen ordinarily perform, and, in
time, some of them become competent craftsmen.

UPGRADING WITHIN PLANTS. Some large companies (such as the automobile companies) have sought to increase their supply of skilled
workers by upgrading helpers or especially skilled specialists through
special programs within the plants. These are similar to apprenticeship programs, but are shorter since the workers already have had
some experience in parts of the plant. The need for large additions
to the supply of skilled craftsmen on short notice during the war led
to a great increase in upgrading programs.

APPRENTICESHIP. This is the method by which a young man learns
a trade by working at each part of the trade under the close supervision of an expert. On-the-job training sometimes is supplemented
by class work. The U. S. Bureau of Apprenticeship estimated in
1956 that about 30,000 apprentices were graduated from registered
programs each year; in 1957 there were about 32,000. In each year

about 20,000 are graduated from unregistered programs.[20] In addition, a large proportion of the 20,000 apprentices who drop out in the third or fourth year of apprenticeship enter the skilled crafts. Among the latter have been many excellent apprentices who terminate their training in order to take jobs as journeymen. Consequently, about 70,000 to 80,000 persons a year enter the ranks of skilled craftsmen through formal apprenticeship programs.

During the period 1940 to 1958 there was a rapid growth in the number of apprentices in American industry, although its extent is not accurately known. The only figures on apprenticeship pertain to registered programs. The number of apprentices in training in registered programs increased from 17,300 on January 1, 1941, to 40,571 on January 1, 1945, 131,217 on January 1, 1947, and to 230,823 at the beginning of 1950. The number then dropped rapidly to 158,532 at the beginning of 1953, but had recovered to 188,137 on January 1, 1956. Since then there has been little change. Under the influence of the recession the number of registered apprentices dropped to 174,252 on June 30, 1959. The increase in apprentices in the registered courses undoubtedly overstates the true rate of growth because there has been a trend in many parts of industry toward registering previously unregistered programs. It is estimated that the registered courses now have about twice as many apprentices as the unregistered ones.[21]

Union Policies Toward Principal Sources
of Supply of Skilled Craftsmen

POLICIES ON IMMIGRATION. Unions in recent years have taken no strong stand for or against admitting skilled workers from abroad. They have not favored a general letting down of bars on immigration, but the sympathy of many union leaders for displaced persons and

---

[20] By registered programs is meant those registered either with state apprenticeship agencies, of which there are 21, or with the Bureau of Apprenticeship and Training in the U. S. Department of Labor. Registration is voluntary and requires certain basic standards, such as a sixteen-year age minimum for apprentices, a schedule of work processes, related classroom instruction, adequate supervision of apprentices, and the keeping of appropriate records. Unions usually exert their influence to have their apprenticeship programs registered. In recent years there has been a tendency in the Bureau to place less emphasis on registration and to be more flexible in accepting plans for registration.

[21] A competent government authority estimates that about four-fifths of the apprentices in the construction trades and about one-third in the metal trades are in registered programs.

refugees has led them to support somewhat more liberal immigration policies since the war than before. The Amalgamated Clothing Workers, cooperating with employers to break a production bottleneck, has gone even further by actively encouraging the immigration of skilled Italian tailors to the United States. Under the Refugee Relief Act more than 350 tailors from Italy migrated to the United States and found employment in the union's shops in New York and Rochester.[22] Early in 1957 the Men's Clothing Committee on Immigration was formed by the union and the Clothing Manufacturers' Association of the United States. Its purpose is to facilitate the immigration of skilled tailors into the United States under the Immigration and Nationality Act of 1952. The committee operates in all countries with quotas under the Act and up to May 1958 had petitioned for the admission of 500 skilled tailors, of whom 100 had been admitted.[23]

POLICIES ON TRADE OR VOCATIONAL SCHOOLS. The trade union movement generally has supported government aid to vocational schools. As long ago as 1917, Samuel Gompers was active in the support of the Smith-Hughes Act, which provides federal aid for vocational education. The trade union movement has supported appropriations under this Act as well as the George-Dean Act of 1937, which expanded such aid.

Most unions do not regard trade or vocational schools as a substitute for on-the-job training under apprenticeship programs but consider vocational training to be good preparation for apprenticeship, and unions quite generally try to include some school work (in shop mathematics, mechanical drawing, blueprint reading) as an integral part of apprentice training. In many cities unions and employers have cooperated with local boards of education to get vocational school training established.

Although craft unions as a rule do not believe that trades can be learned in vocational schools, they do not refuse admission to graduates of technical or vocational schools to whom employers are will-

---

[22] Amalgamated Clothing Workers, *Report of the General Executive Board and Proceedings of the Twentieth Biennial Convention* (May 1956), p. 88. Cooperating in the venture besides the union were the clothing manufacturers and contractors in the New York area, the National Catholic Welfare Conference, the Refugee Relief Program of the U. S. Department of State, and the Intergovernmental Committee for European Migration.

[23] Amalgamated Clothing Workers, *Report of the General Executive Board and Proceedings of the Twenty-first Biennial Convention* (May 1958), p. 51.

ing to pay the journeyman rate. For example, the machinists' union has taken in many airplanemechanics who are graduates of so-called aeronautical engineering schools.[24]

The International Ladies' Garment Workers Union has helped establish vocational schools to meet that industry's need for skilled workers and technicians. In New York the union, employers, and the Board of Education have established the High School of Fashion Industries and the Fashion Institute of Technology, and in Philadelphia a training program has been set up by the union, employers, the Board of Education, and the Pennsylvania State Employment Service. The courses sponsored by the ILGWU and the employers differ from many vocational courses in that they aim at turning out finished workmen. Most of the students are already working at the trade and are trying to qualify for better jobs.[25]

POLICIES ON ARMED SERVICES TRAINING. Unions usually give credit in apprenticeship courses for training in the armed services, the amount of such credit being determined by local joint apprenticeship committees. But unions have not emphasized the armed services as a source of well-trained skilled labor. This is to be expected, since it is the purpose of trade unions to represent not the interests of workers in general but those of their members.

POLICIES ON UNDERSTUDY-PROGRESSION. A survey of union attitudes shows little evidence of a definite union policy on this method. Some unions have objected to a helper working with a skilled worker since the helper would gradually learn the skilled job and become a potential strike breaker. The opposition of hosiery workers to the operation of two knitting machines by a knitter and one or two helpers is an example. Other unions have tried to exclude the understudy-progression method by forbidding helpers to use the tools of the particular trade. But where technological conditions make the

---

[24] The attitude of craft unions toward trade and vocational schools should not be confused with that of unions of technical workers. Since technical workers are the product of school courses to a much greater extent than are skilled craftsmen, their unions have not taken a stand against the use of trade and vocational schools as a source of technical workers.

[25] A good account of the interest of the International Ladies' Garment Workers Union in vocational education by Mark Starr, educational director of the union, "A Labor View of Vocational Education" appears in the I.U.D. Digest (Winter 1958), pp. 74-81.

understudy-progression method by far the best way of developing skilled men (as in parts of the railroad industry, the steel industry, and the paper industry), the unions accept it.

The principal concern of unions is that opportunities to move up the ladder be determined by seniority—for example, that the fireman with the longest service be given the first vacant locomotive engineer's job. Seniority problems arising in connection with promotions are discussed in Chapter 7. The fact that unions place great emphasis on promotion by seniority does not mean that they necessarily object to a qualifying examination.

POLICIES ON PICKING UP THE TRADE. A few unions, such as the Die Sinkers Conference and the Friendly Society of Engravers and Sketchmakers, rarely admit workers who have picked up the trade; they require a formal apprenticeship. The majority of craft unions, however, have been willing to accept as members men who have picked up the trade. Sometimes the local union may give an examination for competency—though in general the willingness of an employer to pay the worker the journeyman's rate makes him acceptable to the union. Unions know that by turning down applicants they would build up a force of hostile nonunion workers. A few local unions, as was pointed out in the previous chapter, pursue restrictive membership policies, but most locals maintain an open door. As a matter of fact, the great majority of skilled craftsmen in unions have picked up the trade—they have never completed an apprenticeship or other formal course of training.

POLICIES ON UPGRADING. Attitudes on such plans have been mixed. Established craft unions have opposed them except in times of war. During World War II there was extensive upgrading. In some industrial unions, such as the United Automobile Workers, upgrading has been fought by the skilled members (even though many of them are graduates of upgrading programs), and has been supported by the semi-skilled workers who hope to become craftsmen under such plans.

POLICIES ON APPRENTICESHIP PROGRAMS. The attitude of unions toward apprenticeship is also varied. Some unions are not interested because skill in their craft is acquired by the understudy-progression method, and some because they are industrial unions, and only a small proportion of their members are skilled craftsmen. There are about sixty national unions that are interested in apprenticeship programs in varying degrees.[26] The plumbers and the electricians are conspicuous for their great interest in apprenticeship, but there are other unions, especially in the building trades, that have well-developed programs. Union interest in apprenticeship is changing with changing technology and a growing demand for skilled workers. More and more unions see apprenticeship programs as a way of protecting and extending their jurisdiction and not, as is widely believed, as a means of keeping skilled labor scarce. The policies of the sixty-odd unions that concern themselves with apprenticeship are important factors in determining the supply of skilled craftsmen.

Policies of Unions on Apprenticeship

Traditional apprenticeship policies of unions, prevailing before the great depression of the thirties, had four principal aims:
1. To protect the journeymen's wage rate from being undercut.
2. To assure apprentices a good chance to learn the trade.
3. To assure apprentices a reasonable rate of pay.
4. To prevent the trade from being flooded with too many journeymen.

Union apprenticeship programs were fairly successful in accomplishing the first three of these objectives. Unions protected the journeymen's rate of pay by recognizing only two wage scales, one for journeymen and one for apprentices, by limiting the number of persons the employer could hire at the apprentice wage scale, and by requiring that those employed at the apprentice wage scale be genuine apprentices who were being given an opportunity to learn the trade through experience in all its branches. This opportunity was protected by rules requiring that they be given such experience and by limiting the time that they could be kept at any one kind of work. A few unions (the International Typographical Union, for

[26] The National Industrial Conference Board, in its *Handbook of Union Government, Structure, and Procedures* (1955), p. 59, found 42 out of 194 unions with provisions in their constitutions governing apprenticeship. These unions had about one-fourth of the membership of all the unions studied. In addition, a few local unions sponsored apprenticeship programs, though they were not mentioned in the national constitutions.

example) required apprentices to supplement their shop work with union-conducted correspondence courses. Negotiated wage scales gave them rates of pay properly related to their experience and to the journeymen rate.

These apprenticeship policies seem to have had virtually no effect on the number of journeymen. The number of apprentices has been small, but this has been due to the reluctance of most employers to train skilled workers rather than to union policies. Indeed non-union employers, who were free from union restrictions, have trained fewer apprentices than did union employers.[27] At any rate, as pointed out above, only a few trades have been in a position to control the number of journeymen by requiring that men serve an apprenticeship in order to receive the journeymen's wage.[28] In spite of the various obstacles to learning trades, the labor force in most crafts was augmented more or less constantly by workers who had picked up enough skill to command the union journeymen's rate from employers. Small towns and the farms have always provided a large supply of such men. As was explained above, the unions have no choice but to accept them since they would otherwise become a source of nonunion competition.

Many unions have joined with employers to set up joint apprenticeship committees. In August 1959, there were about six thousand joint committees, community-wide and in individual plants. There was great difference in the activity and interest shown by these committees. They helped select applicants; in some cases they saw that trainees moved from one employer to another if necessary to gain all-around experience at the trade; they reviewed the work of each apprentice and determined whether he had successfully completed each stage of the training and was ready to go on to the next stage. In many cases, joint committees handled personnel prob-

[27] Sumner H. Slichter, *Union Policies and Industrial Management* (1941), pp. 32-34.
[28] J. G. Meiner, head of the powerful Die Sinkers Conference, which has imposed a seven-year apprenticeship term and has insisted that all journeymen shall have served an apprenticeship, confesses that some unions, including his own, have overdone restrictions in training of skilled men. He says: "In a lot of crafts the journeymen were greedy. They bumped the apprentices out of jobs and the apprentices left the craft." "The New Labor Market," *Fortune* (July 1959), p. 199.
    In the Detroit tool and die industry the union converted the industry from a highly-specialized work force, made up partly of upgraded workers and partly of all-around skilled men, into a labor force where further entry was possible only through apprenticeship. By refusing to work with green hands the union was able to force many nonjourneymen with partial skills out of the industry.

lems of apprentices including disciplinary ones. Finally, many of the joint committees conducted graduation ceremonies. The establishment of local joint committees has been encouraged by the National Joint Committee on Apprenticeship that works closely with the Department of Labor in Washington.

Although the traditional apprenticeship policies of unions usually had little effect on the number of journeymen, the influence of most unions, contrary to popular impression, was to increase the number of apprentices. This influence was not usually due to deliberate union policy but rather to a natural desire of union members to give their sons and friends a chance to learn the trade. Since most employers were not particularly interested in training apprentices, the mild pressure that many unions exerted on employers to take on a few apprentices undoubtedly increased to some extent the scale of apprentice training.

Effects of the Depression and the War
on Union Apprenticeship Policies

The great depression of the thirties reduced the demand for labor of all kinds, including many types of skilled workers. As a result, the opportunities to learn skilled trades diminished, both because employers were less interested in training workers and because opportunities to "pick up" a knowledge of trades were scarce. It is true that there are a few trades in which the long-term upward trend in demand was so strong that the number in the trade was greater in 1940 than in 1930. The number of tool and die makers increased from 78,000 in 1930 to 96,900 in 1940; the number of automobile mechanics from 394,200 to 441,800; the number of sheet metal workers from 84,300 to 91,600; the number of photo-engravers and lithographers from 8,600 to 22,500.[29] But the total number of male skilled workers dropped from 6,200,000 in 1930 to 5,830,000 in 1940, and the proportion of male skilled workers to the total male nonfarm labor force dropped from 16.4 per cent in 1930 to 14.8 per cent in 1940. In the building trades, which were hard hit by the depression, carpenters decreased from 920,100 in 1930 to 766,100 in

[29] U. S. Bureau of Apprenticeship, *The Skilled Labor Force,* Table IV, pp. 15-16. There are no data that show what happened to the number of skilled men either at work or remaining in their craft as job seekers at the bottom of the depression in 1932 and 1933.

1940; the brickmasons from 170,900 to 141,700; the electricians from 277,500 to 227,100. The depression also accelerated the decline in some occupations that were decreasing in the long run anyway—for example, locomotive engineers and blacksmiths.

During the depression many unions negotiated agreements with their employers that no new apprentices would be trained for the time being. The net effect of these agreements on the number of apprentices trained was negligible—largely because employers had no desire to train them.[30]

In spite of the discouraging effect of the depression, the foundation was being laid for future apprentice training. In August 1934, when the depression was still in its depths, the Federal Committee on Apprenticeship was created under the NRA. In 1937 the Fitzgerald Act, which led to the present Bureau of Apprenticeship, was passed. Its aim was to encourage joint apprenticeship committees, and it received the support of both labor and management.

World War II greatly increased the need for skilled craftsmen and led to growth in all of the labor training methods. Since time was of the essence, heroic efforts were made to break down jobs into specialized operations that could be performed by semi-skilled workers, and there was a great expansion in all sorts of specialist training. But the training of skilled workers expanded also. Total skilled craftsmen in the labor force increased from six million in 1940 to eight million in 1950, and the proportion of the male labor force represented by the skilled craftsmen increased from 15.5 per cent to 19.0 per cent.[31] Many unions temporarily suspended their rules or agreements limiting the number of apprentices that could be trained. There was a considerable increase in the number of registered apprenticeship systems—from 760 at the end of 1940 to 5,820 at the middle of 1945. Group systems (applying to a number of enterprises) increased from 610 at the end of 1940 to 1,540 at the middle of 1945, and individual systems (applying to single enterprises or plants) from 150 at the end of 1940 to 4,280 at the middle

[30] In the glass industry, where apprenticeship is regulated by national agreements between the American Flint Glass Workers' Union and two associations (the Manufacturers of Pressed and Blown Glassware and the Glass Container Manufacturers' Institute), the employers in 1932-33 agreed to suspend indenturing in two craft groups. H. Ellsworth Steele, "An Evaluation of the American Flint Glass Workers' Apprenticeship Program," *Industrial and Labor Relations Review* (October 1951), p. 60.
[31] Gertrude Bancroft, *The American Labor Force* (1958), p. 209.

of 1945.[32] All of the group systems at the end of 1940 were joint systems, and at the middle of 1945, 1,520 out of the 1,540 were joint systems. Among the 4,280 individual systems in the middle of 1945, 740 were joint.

Effects of Demobilization on Union Apprenticeship Policies

Demobilization of the armed forces led to temporary adjustments and changes in traditional union apprenticeship policies. The most immediate need created by the demobilization was for a great expansion of apprenticeship training. This required suspension of rules pertaining to apprentice-journeymen ratios and age limits. Unions, as a rule, went much farther in suspending rules for veterans whose apprenticeship training had been interrupted by military service than for returning veterans who wanted to begin apprenticeship. Some unions had already suspended apprenticeship-journeymen ratios on account of the acute shortage of skilled labor during the war. Some unions (the American Flint Glass Workers, for example) exempted returning veteran apprentices from ratios limiting the number of apprentices, reduced their term of apprenticeship by one year, and increased the age limit for apprentices who were veterans.[33]

Postwar Changes in Union Policies on Apprenticeship

The postwar period has seen a considerable growth of interest in apprenticeship among unions and employers. The labor shortages and the U. S. Bureau of Apprenticeship were responsible. In the late summer of 1945 the International Brotherhood of Electrical Workers, estimating a shortage of 35,000 journeymen electricians, urged local unions to encourage the training of apprentices.[34] The next year the general president of the carpenters' union recommended that all local unions adopt training systems and apprenticeship standards. The structural iron workers amended their constitution to require local unions to try to set up joint apprenticeship

[32] U. S. Bureau of Apprenticeship, *Apprentice Statistics*, Technical Bulletin T-137 (April 1954), p. 10. The great majority, but not all, of these apprenticeship systems were active.

[33] Steele, "An Evaluation of the American Flint Glass Workers' Apprenticeship Program," p. 60.

[34] "Local Joint Training Committees Urged," *Journal of Electrical Workers and Operators* (September 1945), p. 273.

programs. The machinists at their 1948 and 1952 conventions gave extensive consideration to apprenticeship problems. The national officers of the plasterers' and cement finishers' union and of the lathers' union put pressure on local unions to establish joint apprenticeship programs. In 1948 President John F. Rooney of the plasterers and cement finishers, concerned about the advanced age of most plasterers, urged that each local joint apprenticeship committee determine the number of apprentices needed and have contractors hire them. Need was to be determined by volume of work, average age of journeymen, and loss of the latter from the trade.[35] An editorial in *Plastering Industries* (April 1948), seeking to clarify the confusion that had developed over the number of apprentices permitted, said both the plasterers and the lathers were ignoring prewar ratios. Local joint committees were to have complete authority to determine the number of apprentices needed; the only limits were to be manpower needs and the capacity to give adequate training. In some areas there were as many as one apprentice to every two journeymen.

Nevertheless, by 1951 concern was expressed that the numbers being trained were inadequate. The International Executive Council of the lathers' union, in a strongly-worded resolution, insisted that local unions seek additional apprentices.[36]

The growing interest of unions in apprenticeship training has encountered employer indifference in some industries, particularly in the metal trades. A survey made by the research department of the machinists' union in July 1953 among business agents, general chairmen, and grand lodge representatives showed that 23 (or 38 per cent) of the 60 replying found that a negative attitude on the part of employers was the most significant barrier to the training of skilled men. It was also the most frequently-mentioned obstacle.[37] In 83 per cent of the cases the respondents reported a shortage of skilled workers in their areas, and in half of these cases no program to relieve the shortage was under way.

More important than the growth of union interest in apprentice-

---

[35] William F. Patterson, "Apprenticeship Ratios," *Plastering Industries* (January 1948).
[36] *Plastering Industries* (November 1951).
[37] The second most frequently-mentioned barrier was the possibility of apprentices being drafted (mentioned in 16 cases); the third was the negative attitude of the union (mentioned in 6 cases); too low wages for apprentices were held to be the principal obstacle in 4 cases, and the union's seniority rules in one case. In 10 cases two or more causes were given.

ship has been the broadening of union thinking on the subject. A few unions, particularly at the national level, have been trying to attract the best possible persons into the apprenticeship program. As a general rule, there was never a dearth of young men, but in many localities the practice had been to reserve apprenticeship openings for sons and relatives of union men. Through emphasis on ceremonial graduations and apprenticeship contests, efforts have been made to attract a wider range of applicants, and screening procedures have been established to select the best candidates. An important objective has been to relate the number of apprentices to the projected future needs of the trade. The rise in the number of retirements resulting from negotiated pensions has provided an additional stimulus to the development of apprenticeship plans. Old ratios between numbers of apprentices and journeymen, which were without statistical justification, have been critically examined. Interest of unions in the quality of training has sharpened, and in a few cases has become quite sophisticated. Unions have become more concerned than ever that training be kept up to date and that it be fitted to the changing technology of industry. Finally, a few unions have come to see that giving good training to an adequate number of apprentices offers a way to protect their existing jurisdiction and to gain control over new types of work. For example, in 1952 a warning was issued that there would be no plastering industry if training were not expanded.[38] Substitute products already had seriously restricted employment. Unless new methods and materials were accepted, unions requiring shorter training periods would capture lathers' work. As late as 1954, it was said that productivity and employment opportunities could be greatly enhanced if more workers were adequately acquainted with new materials, equipment, and techniques. The problem was seen as requiring more apprentices and improvement of journeymen's skills.[39]

The upsurge of union interest in apprenticeship during the postwar years was due to a combination of circumstances—to the great shortage of skilled workers and the growing demand for them, to changes in technology that enhanced the need for new skills, and to the fact that the craft best able to supply skills was likely to get the work.

[38] *Plastering Industries* (July 1952).
[39] The same (April 1954).

The shortage of skilled workers was partly a result of reduced training during the long depression of the thirties and in some industries during the war. The rapidly-growing demand for skilled labor grew out of the postwar booms in construction, in capital goods, and in durable consumer goods, and the high level of demand for many forms of military goods due to the cold war and the Korean War. Had unions been disposed to try to keep skilled labor as scarce as possible, the postwar years might *appear* to have given them such an opportunity. But control of the market by unions was too limited to enable them to influence substantially the number of craftsmen who were trained. Restrictions on the number of apprentices in union-sponsored programs would simply have increased the number of men who got their training in other ways.[40]

The scarcity of skilled labor was enhanced by the rapid growth of work in heavy construction—new chemical plants, steel plants, oil refineries, aluminum plants, power plants, atomic energy plants— and by the more exacting demands steadily being made on skilled workers by technological developments.[41] Union leaders were impressed with the fact that the work on new jobs was likely to go to the organizations able to supply the men best capable of doing it. In some cases the availability of an adequate supply of skilled men was considered necessary to discourage the use of substitute materials.

To these reasons for the growing interest of unions in apprenticeship should be added the influence of the U. S. Bureau of Appren-

[40] Before the war, when skilled labor was still abundant, proposals that unions encourage apprenticeship training raised doubts in the minds of some members. When the 1940 convention of the International Association of Machinists was considering a resolution that the local unions cooperate in forming local joint apprenticeship committees and assist in the passage of state apprenticeship laws based on federal standards corresponding to IAM policies, one delegate declared that "the present propaganda" regarding a "shortage of skilled mechanics of all kinds" is leading the union "down a blind alley. . . . States, cities, schools, the government—they are all going to produce a flock of apprentices and you may rest assured that they are not going to be union apprentices. . . ." The delegates urged the convention to consider "what is going to happen five or six or eight years from now before being stampeded into any apprenticeship setup." (International Association of Machinists, *Proceedings of Twentieth Convention,* September 1940, pp. 204-07.) Another delegate expressed the view that government efforts to stimulate apprenticeship were just "a device to make, within two or three years, an abundance of cheap machinists who belong to our organization who will help drag down the conditions that we have built up." (The same, p. 206.) It is obvious that union members had little conception of how small a role apprenticeship played in determining the number of craftsmen.

[41] See above, p. 65.

ticeship, which by its ceaseless attempts to stimulate interest in apprenticeship and by the strong emphasis that it placed on joint union-employer programs greatly helped both unions and employers see the need for well-planned efforts to train skilled workers.

Influence of Unions on Apprenticeship Training

THE NUMBER OF APPRENTICES. Attention has already been called to the slight influence of apprenticeship training on the number of craftsmen. In the electrical construction industry, where the training of apprentices has been most highly developed, only about one-third of the journeymen have served an apprenticeship. The U. S. Bureau of Apprenticeship estimates that if apprenticeship in the construction trades continues at its present level, only about one-ninth of the need for skilled men will be met in this way.[42]

Unions have tended to increase the number of apprentices by helping interest employers in the establishment of training schemes. In addition, unions in the postwar years have suspended or repealed restrictions on numbers. William F. Patterson, in 1948 the director of the Bureau of Apprenticeship and Training, quotes John W. Jockel, secretary-treasurer of the Ohio State Building Trades Council, as follows:

> In the trade of bricklayers, stone masons, plasterers, tile layers, and terrazzo workers, there was previously a ratio of one apprentice to ten journeymen, but this ratio has now been done away with, and as many apprentices as can be trained are employed in the trades. We in Ohio realize that there is a shortage of skilled men, and as far as we are concerned there is no ratio. . . . We are encouraging our unions to put on as many boys as they can.[43]

In the construction industry a special effort was made to increase the number of training programs, rather than merely to expand existing programs.

The unions that have given most careful thought to the number of apprentices have favored basing it on estimates of the number of

[42] The Bureau estimates that additions of 2,138,400 to the skilled labor force in construction will be needed to replace losses from deaths and retirements and to meet increased demand between 1960 and 1970. Apprenticeship training on the present scale would provide only 240,610 journeymen.

[43] William F. Patterson, "Apprenticeship Ratios," *Occupations* (November 1948), p. 114.

journeymen who will be needed a few years later. It usually takes about four years to train an apprentice. No one can foresee whether business will be good or bad four or five years in the future. Hence, it is best to ignore the business cycle and to seek to start each year with enough apprentices to meet the estimated average need several years ahead. Allowance must also be made for dropouts.

ORGANIZATION OF TRAINING. Usually the best results are obtained when the programs are jointly sponsored by union and management. Joint sponsorship makes its greatest contribution when enterprises are small and are unable to give much attention to apprentice training. Under these conditions joint sponsorship usually results in better selection of apprentices, better quality of training, and better supervision during training. The most significant test of the desirability of joint arrangements is found in the percentage of completions. A study of 23,499 apprentice separations occurring in 23 states in 1949 and 1950 showed that separations caused by completion of the course were highest where the joint form of organization was used. Under the joint system, 66 per cent of separations were completions; under the others, only 38 per cent.[44]

In spite of the superiority of joint sponsorship of apprenticeship programs, nonjoint programs are in the great majority. At the middle of 1953, out of 50,220 registered apprenticeship systems, 7,830 were joint and 42,390 nonjoint.[45] Unions have strongly favored joint sponsorship of apprentice programs. Joint arrangements are most common in the construction industry, where the influence of unions on apprentice training has been strongest. Conversely, in the metal trades industry, where the influence of unions is weakest, joint arrangements are found in less than half of the cases. Joint sponsorship of apprentice training has been carried farthest in the electrical industry, where there is a national joint committee of twelve (six from the union and six from the employers' organization) operating with a full-time director. It is the policy of the national joint committee in the electrical industry to encourage the formation of local joint committees.

The Typographical Union has long had a national director of apprenticeship since it conducts its own apprenticeship course. A

[44] U. S. Bureau of Apprenticeship, *Apprentice Completion or Cancellation?*, Technical Bulletin T-130 (April 1951), p. 4.
[45] U. S. Bureau of Apprenticeship, *Apprentice Statistics*, p. 10.

notable development in the postwar era has been the creation by the plumbers' union of the post of director of training with the responsibility of promoting training in the industry.

SELECTION OF APPRENTICES. The importance of good selection is indicated by the fact that a study of 496 persons who discontinued apprenticeship training in 1951 and 1952 showed that nearly one-fifth (18 per cent) of the voluntary quits were attributable to dislike of the trade or inability to master the skills.[46] The traditional practice among local unions of showing strong preference for relatives and friends of persons already in the industry was acquiesced in by many employers. National union officers have stressed the importance of attracting the best possible applicants. The National Joint Committee on Apprenticeship in the Electrical Industry in particular has urged better selection of apprentices.

QUALITY OF TRAINING. The plumbers' union, through the creation of the post of director of training, and the electrical industry, through the National Joint Committee on Apprenticeship, have been leaders in improving the quality of training—both by providing materials for class study and by encouraging training of instructors. The plumbers' union has held several special conventions on apprenticeship in recent years, attended by local instructors. At the convention at Purdue University in 1959 there were 335 local instructors, local coordinators, and local business agents in attendance.

PROPORTION OF APPRENTICES COMPLETING TRAINING. Unions have been disturbed by the high proportion of apprentices failing to complete their training. Dropouts have been partly a result of the great demand for skilled men which has enabled third- or fourth-year apprentices to drop out and take jobs as journeymen. But dropouts in the early stages due to lack of interest in the work or lack of aptitude for it can be reduced by better selection. Unions are making increasing use of aptitude tests developed by state employment offices.[47] In the District of Columbia, for instance, aptitude tests for carpenter apprentices have cut failures substantially. On Miami

[46] John S. McCauley, "Employment Status of Former Apprentices in Early 1954," *Monthly Labor Review* (July 1954), p. 754.

[47] Arthur W. Motley, "Recent Trends in the Test Selection of Apprentices," *Monthly Labor Review* (October 1953), pp. 1068-70.

newspapers, the printing pressmen now require that each applicant be tested by the public employment service.[48] Tests are reported to have proven their value in selecting candidates in various trades.[49] In addition to aptitude tests it has been suggested that apprentices be urged to complete their training in the interests of long-term advantages.[50] William F. Patterson, when director of the Bureau of Apprenticeship, proposed that employers discuss the matter with apprentices and that "get-together meetings" of apprentices, journeymen, and management be held.[51] A public school official recommends better counseling and guidance to eliminate before they begin training those who are apt to fail or quit.[52] Union leaders also suggest competition among apprentices to stimulate interest.

RATE OF COMPENSATION OF APPRENTICES. With the average age of apprentices about five years higher than before the war, and with the customary age of marriage declining, the compensation of apprentices becomes more important than ever. It has two important effects—on the quality of the entrants into apprenticeship programs and on the rate of dropouts. As an editorial in *Machinery* puts it, "It is extremely difficult to keep young men interested in completing apprenticeship when their friends of similar age are getting much higher wages operating machines which they have learned to run in a day or two...."[53]

Unions have generally tended to increase the ratio of apprenticeship earnings to those of journeymen or semi-skilled workers. Thus, the pattern-makers of Chicago, who have operated an excellent apprenticeship training program since 1941, have raised the beginning rate for apprentices from 22.5 per cent of the journeymen's rate first to 31 per cent, then to 35 per cent, and finally, in 1953, to 40 per cent.[54]

[48] O. E. Craven, and L. A. Daniel, "Counseling Important in Selection of Trainees," *Employment Security Review* (April 1954), p. 15.
[49] U. S. Department of Labor, *Employment Security Review* (January 1952), p. 22; (May 1953), p. 3; and (April 1954), p. 15.
[50] Charles O. Herb, "Apprentices Safeguard the Future of Industry," *Machinery* (September 1952), p. 149.
[51] William F. Patterson, "Learn or Earn?" *American Machinist* (March 11, 1948), p. 234.
[52] James R. Warden, "The Apprentice Needs Guidance, Too!" *American Vocational Journal* (March 1954), p. 20.
[53] *Machinery* (November 1951), p. 23.
[54] U. S. Bureau of Apprenticeship, *Labor-Management Cooperation in Training Pattern Makers*, Technical Bulletin T-146 (June 1958), p. 12.

PROTECTION OF APPRENTICES AGAINST LAYOFF. Not long ago, Walter F. Simon, the director of apprenticeship for the state of Wisconsin, wrote, "If this country ever expects to have a stable apprenticeship system, some thought must be given to the problem of having a continuous supply of apprentices in training."[55] In the metal trades, where seniority usually determines layoffs, it has been common practice not to disturb the employment of apprentices during minor layoffs. But when there is a major layoff, the apprentices, having the least seniority, are the first to go, and the training program disintegrates. To avoid disruption of the programs some companies give apprentices leaves of absence during layoff periods. A few companies have handled layoffs of apprentices separately from those of journeymen, and the principle of equal division of work is applied to apprentices. An example is an agreement providing that in the event of a 20 per cent reduction in employment in the bargaining unit, the apprentices shall work three weeks on and one week off; if employment among journeymen is cut 35 per cent, apprentices shall work two weeks on and one week off; and if the employment is cut 50 per cent, apprentices shall work one week on and one week off. Thus, though the apprentices share in the loss of time, their connection with the employer is not broken, and their training continues.

Some Significant Apprenticeship Programs

Brief descriptions are given below of the apprenticeship programs developed by six unions—the operating engineers, the boilermakers, the machinists, the plumbers, the electricians, and the typographical union.

Operating Engineers' Program

The Operating Engineers' Union has shown a strong interest in apprenticeship training recently. Workers in each of the two principal branches of the trade (the stationary engineers and the hoisting and portable engineers of the construction industry) previously had "picked up" their knowledge of the trade. Many of the stationary engineers were upgraded firemen who had acquired licenses.

[55] Industrial Commission of Wisconsin, *Monthly Report on Apprenticeship* (February 1, 1958), p. 1.

Interest in formal apprenticeship began with Local 428 in Arizona. After success with a program for stationary engineers, the local in 1952 established a joint apprenticeship committee with the Arizona chapter of the Associated General Contractors. The program was financed by withholding one cent per hour from each operating engineer's pay, with the employers contributing an equal amount. The program was later adopted by the Western States Regional Conference of the union, and the 1956 convention of the union approved a national apprenticeship program.

Interest of the national union in apprenticeship received a strong stimulus from decisions of the National Labor Relations Board that the operating engineers are not a professional or skilled craft but a "service" calling. This view has led the NLRB to deny the engineers the privilege of carving out craft units from larger bodies of employers. Hence the national union is determined to develop training of uniform type on a national basis. Writing in the *International Operating Engineer* for February 1959, President Joseph J. Delaney said:

> We cannot grow unless we have the manpower with which to run more and more jobs. . . . We are faced with a great challenge. Will we meet it? . . .
> . . . This problem of apprenticeship is one of the most important to come before our union. The members of your General Executive Board are determined to develop plans and policies which will spell success.[56]

Boilermakers' Program

Two principal conditions have stimulated the interest of the boilermakers' union in training in the years following World War II. In the first place, the war brought into the union a large number of workers who had in-plant training on only one job.[57] These men, who were mostly beyond the apprenticeship age, needed an opportunity to broaden their skills. In the second place, there was a great expansion in the kind of work done by boilermakers. The boilermakers' union stresses the fact that new skills are being demanded. Atomic energy has created "a brand-new opportunity and a need for additional training of the skilled worker."[58] The union

[56] *The International Operating Engineer* (February 1959), pp. 3-4.
[57] *The Boilermakers Journal* (September 1945), p. 206.
[58] C. F. MacGowan, "Training Opportunity for Skills and Crafts," *Boilermakers-Blacksmiths Journal* (July 1956), p. 26.

also points out that standards of quality are rising. Twenty or twenty-five years ago, welds were examined on the surface. Today they are subjected to internal examination. Welds that might have been acceptable twenty or thirty years ago may not be so today. Standards of tightness have become more exacting. On an atomic energy job the permissible leakage of tolerance may be one drop in five years or longer. Handling materials through "slave" manipulators involves new skills. In order to keep up with new developments in the reactor boiler field, the union has obtained an access permit from the Atomic Energy Commission.

The general position of the boilermakers' union toward training of both apprentices and journeymen is that "the International Brotherhood of Boilermakers assumes a definite responsibility to educate and train our membership. . . . We hope to perform a definite service to employers of our members by providing higher trained men."[59] In order to implement the basic program of the union specific apprenticeship and training programs have been set up for various branches of the boilermakers' trade—the field erection and repair industry, the railroad industry, and others.

At the seventeenth annual convention of the union in September 1944, a committee was authorized to formulate a plan for apprenticeship and upgrading. In 1945 the committee submitted a report that gave standards of apprenticeship and procedures for upgrading single job mechanics and trainees and recommended that business agents and other representatives establish programs for upgrading specialized mechanics.[60] In April 1955 the boilermakers' union held a four-day joint labor-management conference of international officers, business managers, and representatives of contractors at the Town House Hotel in Kansas City. Much of the work of the conference was done by joint committees, which submitted recommendations to the entire conference. One of the committees dealt with apprenticeship training. It recommended that the president of the boilermakers' union appoint a subcommittee of three to work out details of a program for apprentice training and that the employers likewise appoint a subcommittee of three to work with the labor subcommittee. It was recommended that the training program not

[59] The same, p. 27.
[60] International Brotherhood of Boilermakers, Iron Ship Builders and Helpers of America, *Boilermakers' Apprenticeship and Training Procedures* (1945), p. 7.

exceed 6,000 hours. These recommendations were unanimously adopted.[61]

The Program and Policies of the Machinists

The strong traditions of decentralization in the machinists' union have led the organization at the national level to move at only a moderate pace in encouraging apprenticeship. Nevertheless, the national officers have shown growing interest in the problem, and A. J. Hayes, president of the union, served as a member of the Manpower Council, established at Columbia University under a grant from the Ford Foundation. The interest of the union in apprenticeship began to quicken in the early days of World War II, when the United States had not yet entered the war but was producing defense goods in rapidly-increasing quantities. At the twentieth convention in 1940, the union recommended that in granting defense contracts to machine and metal products producers the government require that employers have *bona fide* apprenticeship systems. A ratio of one apprentice to ten journeymen was recommended—a considerable increase over most existing ratios.[62] At the same convention the union recommended that local officers cooperate with the Federal Committee on Apprenticeship and apprenticeship councils to establish with employers local joint apprenticeship committees.

During the war the union, particularly the Executive Council, supported accelerated training and upgrading of semi-skilled workers under the auspices of joint union-management committees. Under these programs workers were to be given skills that would enable them to perform at least one job in addition to the one at which they worked. In return for supporting these upgrading programs the union sought to obtain the establishment of full-fledged joint apprenticeship programs. This policy was adopted by the Executive Council in May 1942.[63]

[61] *Boilermakers-Blacksmiths Journal* (May 1955), p. 104.
[62] International Association of Machinists, *Proceedings of the 20th Convention* (September 1940), p. 204.
[63] International Association of Machinists, *Officers Reports to the 21st Convention* (October-November 1945), pp. 21-24. The Officers' Report said that it was the policy of the union to "take and maintain the initiative to see that the needed number of apprentices within its jurisdiction are in training," but that the union was opposed to programs outside formal apprenticeship regulations, particularly some of the programs proposed by state and local boards of vocational education. (The same, pp. 26, 27, and 29.)

The end of the war saw renewed efforts on the part of the machinists to encourage apprenticeship training, in spite of the fact that employment in defense industries was dropping and also that the membership in the machinists' union was temporarily decreasing. Union thinking on these matters was influenced by the fact that the "depression years had prevented the training of an adequate number of apprentices" and that military requirements in the war had not only absorbed potential apprentices 18 to 26 years of age, but had taken a large proportion of the younger journeymen.[64] Apprentice recruits in the immediate postwar years were expected from two groups of workers—older union members who had obtained part of the skill in the trade through employment or training, and veterans, for whom maximum age limits of apprentices were to be relaxed. Both of these groups were to be allowed credit for prior experience.[65]

The twenty-first convention of the union in 1945 established a National Advisory Apprenticeship Committee, composed of two representatives from each Grand Lodge Vice Presidential area, to provide uniform apprentice standards for all divisions of the union.[66] In reporting to the twenty-second convention in 1948, the officers repeated the recommendation that it is "essential that greater immediate effort be made to establish apprenticeship programs in every establishment. . . ."[67] Particular attention was given to training for journeymen to enable them to learn new machines, techniques, and methods.[68] The convention declared its opposition to training outside of apprenticeship, and expressed special opposition to automobile mechanic schools approved by the Veterans Administration.[69]

At the twenty-third convention of the union in 1952 the officers reported that there were 950 joint councils in 2,300 establishments em-

[64] The same, p. 26; and the *Officers Reports to the 22nd Convention* (September 1948), pp. 47-48. It was feared that the end of the war would "find the ranks of skilled mechanics still further depleted and with neither apprentices in training or programs of apprenticeship established to make good the deficit."

[65] International Association of Machinists, *Officers Reports to the 21st Convention* (October-November 1945), pp. 27-28.

[66] International Association of Machinists, *Proceedings of the 21st Convention* (October-November 1945), p. 347. The committee issued a booklet as a guide to desirable standards.

[67] International Association of Machinists, *Officers Reports to the 22nd Convention* (September 1948), p. 49.

[68] The same, p. 47.

[69] International Association of Machinists, *Proceedings of the 22nd Convention* (September 1948), p. 201. These schools, according to the delegates, trained men who worked below the union scale.

ploying 5,000 apprentices.[70] The shortage of skilled mechanics caused by the Korean War led the union to support the government's campaign to stimulate training in various critical trades.[71] In the Korean War, unlike in World War II, the union opposed any "reduction of skill content" to remedy manpower shortages.[72] The twenty-third convention of the union adopted a manual on work schedules and related instruction for apprentices to guide committees in developing training programs.[73]

The railroads and the aircraft and guided missile industries have been problem areas for the machinists' union. Declining employment in the railroad shops and preference of managements for upgrading helpers have diminished the interest of railroad managements in apprenticeship plans. The twenty-third convention of the union advocated that the union negotiate its own apprentice plan for railway machinists in case the railway employees' department or system federation failed to provide for the establishment of a *bona fide* apprenticeship program.[74]

Managements in the airplane and missile industries have traditionally shown little interest in training skilled workers. In March 1957 the machinists' union joined with the automobile workers in launching a drive to induce managements in these industries to develop effective training programs for skilled workers. This program was announced by the IAM-UAW Joint Standing Committee.[75]

In spite of the efforts of the machinists' union to encourage apprentice training, the ratio of apprentices to journeymen in the union declined in the period 1947 to 1952. The latest available figures are not very recent, but a survey by the union shows a drop

[70] International Association of Machinists, "Officers Reports to the 23rd Convention," *Machinists Monthly Journal* (August 1952), p. 278.

[71] The same, p. 279. Of 32 occupations classified by the government as critical, 11 or a few more fell within the jurisdiction of the machinists' union. Of 21,480 apprentices in these trades in 1952, 15,955 were under the jurisdiction of the union. *Proceedings of the 23rd Convention* (1952), p. 262.

[72] International Association of Machinists, "Officers Reports to the 23rd Convention," *Machinists Monthly Journal* (August 1952), p. 278.

[73] International Association of Machinists, *Proceedings of the 23rd Convention* (1952), p. 262.

[74] The same, p. 142. The introduction of diesels seems to have raised the familiar problem of older men using their seniority to hold jobs that were destined soon to disappear. Younger men transferred to the new work and acquired skill on it. Later, as the old jobs went out of existence, the older men began to strive for the new jobs on the basis of seniority. See "Ten Ways to Train Maintainers for Diesel Locomotives," *Railway Age* (March 9, 1953), pp. 122-26.

[75] *The Machinist* (March 7, 1957), p. 3.

in the number of apprentices from 16,634 in 1947 to 10,707 in 1950 and 10,409 in 1952. The number of journeymen members dropped from 210,434 in 1947 to 206,696 in 1950 and increased to 257,568 in 1952.

The Plumbers' Program

The plumbers' union has a long tradition of interest in training both apprentices and journeymen. The demand for plumbers grew rapidly during the 1940's; their number increased from 210,800 in 1940 to 296,000 in 1950,[76] and the need for expanding apprentice training in the industry was evident. Martin J. Durkin, then the president of the United Association of Plumbers and Steamfitters, was disturbed by the large proportion of the members who had joined the union without having served an apprenticeship, and with the inadequacy of the training being received by the apprentices. The front and back covers of the union's journal of May 1952, carried a message on "Apprentice Training: The Keystone of Craftsmanship" from Mr. Durkin. He said:

> . . . currently the U.A. is taking into membership three journeymen for every one apprentice it actually trains to become a journeyman crafts-man; in time we shall be taking as new members men who are of poorer and poorer quality.

In the same announcement, Mr. Durkin said "in all too many instances there are no joint apprentice training committees actively engaged in training apprentices. . . . The training is not adequate for twentieth-century needs of our industry." Several months later in the union magazine, Mr. Durkin said:

> If the United Association is to continue guarding jealously its standing in the trade union movement of the United States and Canada as a craft organization of the highest calibre, then it must continue to develop its own journeyman members through its established apprenticeship train-ing. Furthermore, if the United Association is to maintain control over its trade jurisdiction, then it must be able to meet the demand for quali-fied journeymen of the plumbing and pipefitting industry at all times.[77]

In 1952 the plumbers' and steamfitters' union adopted a new policy, which provided for:

(1) National joint apprenticeship committees of five unions repre-

---

[76] U. S. Bureau of Apprenticeship, *The Skilled Labor Force*, pp. 15-16.

[77] *United Association Journal* (September 1952), back cover.

sentatives and five employer representatives to stimulate interest in apprenticeship throughout the industry. There are two national committees—one in plumbing and one in pipefitting.

(2) A training school for apprentice teachers. In 1952 the union invited the Heating, Piping and Air Conditioning Contractors National Association and the National Master Plumbers Association to join with it in the establishment of a training school for apprentice teachers to be held during vacation periods. The cost of establishing the program and the salaries of the faculty would be borne by the United Association and the employer associations, but the teacher-trainees would be expected to bear their own expenses or have them met by the local Joint Apprenticeship Committee.[78]

(3) The hiring of two members of the United Association—one a plumber and one a steamfitter—to help local unions in establishing apprenticeship programs. These men are known as coordinators of apprentice training. In the February 1953 issue of the *United Association Journal* it was reported that the two coordinators had been hired.[79] Two more coordinators were added in 1954, and in the summer of 1959 the number was increased to six. The effectiveness of the union's program is greatly enhanced by having men who devote full time to promoting apprenticeship. Efforts of the coordinators are far more effective in getting action than are resolutions passed by conventions recommending that local unions or their business agents try to negotiate apprenticeship programs.[80]

(4) Apprenticeship contests. In January 1954, Mr. Durkin announced that "as a first step toward increasing the number of new applicants in the building trades branch to be apprentices, the United Association has joined with the National Association of Plumbing Contractors and the Heating, Piping, and Air Conditioning Contractors National Association in establishing the Annual International

---

[78] The same.

[79] The same, front and back covers.

[80] The coordinators were practical men. One of them, Mr. Joseph Phillips, added in 1954, had been superintendent on a few large industrial projects for Robert Gordon Company and H. P. Refer Company, and had been field engineer for the Austin Company, and Project Coordinator on the United Airlines and the A. B. Dick Company projects. In August 1949 he was named Pipe Fitter Apprentice Coordinator for Local 597. Another coordinator, Mr. Robert Camp, had his own plumbing contracting business for three years and was Apprenticeship Specialist with the Engineering Extension Service of Texas A & M, from which position he took a leave of absence to help develop procedures and rules for the first International Apprenticeship Contest. *United Association Journal* (January 1955), p. 11.

Apprenticeship Contest." This annual contest is open to fifth-year apprentices who are members of the United Association and includes tests for pipefitter apprentices and for plumber apprentices. There is a written test and a "practical" or performance test. The contest begins at the local level, the winners becoming eligible for the state-wide or province-wide contest. The winners at this level are eligible for the final or international contests. Three prizes are awarded to pipefitter apprentices and three to plumber apprentices, the first prizes being $1,000 each; the second prizes, $500 each; and the third prizes, $250 each.[81] In 1958 five contractor associations offered side awards both in the main contests and in specialized competition.[82]

(5) Annual General Apprentice Conference. In August 1954 the union began holding conferences at which apprenticeship problems are discussed, with special attention to problems of training. They are held at Purdue University and last three to six days. The finals in the apprentice contests are held at the conferences. At the second annual general conference in August 1955, the Apprentice Teacher Training course for instructors was held six hours each day for six days. The size of the instructors' training course at the annual conference has grown each year. In 1954, 73 instructors attended; in 1955 there were 166; in 1956, 203; in 1957, 268; in 1958, 280 instructors representing more than 150 local unions; and in 1959, 335 instructors. In 1950 there were 90 apprentices at the Purdue conference.

(6) The negotiation in June 1953 of an educational fund to finance the apprentice agreement between Sprinkler Fitters Local Union 669 and the National Automatic Sprinkler and Fire Control Association. Local Union 669 is a nation-wide local of road men, who move from city to city as one job is completed and the next one begun. The apprentice agreement between Local 669 and the contractors' association became effective on July 1, 1951. The educational fund, negotiated two years later, calls for a contribution of $1\frac{1}{4}$ cents per hour per man. Arrangements were made with Pennsylvania State College to prepare correspondence courses for the academic portion of apprentice training. The Extension Department of the college grades the apprentices' work.

(7) The establishment in April 1956 of the Training Depart-

---

[81] The same (January 1954), front and back covers.
[82] The same (September 1958), pp. 15 and 33. The side awards were gold watches, gold pen and pencil sets, gold cuff links, and $50 savings bonds.

ment for Apprentices and Journeymen in the United Association "to assist local unions and the Joint Apprenticeship Committee in organizing and conducting apprentice training programs." It is provided that the coordinators shall "work with the officers and representatives of local unions and joint committees."[83] The director of training is Joseph T. Corcoran, a former principal of the Washburn Vocational School in Chicago, president of a UA local, and manager of a heating and air conditioning firm.

(8) The negotiation and establishment of a National Educational Trust Fund. This fund is supported by all contractors signing a national agreement. When it was started in 1956, the rate of contribution was 1.5 cents per hour for each journeyman and apprentice employed under the terms of the agreement. In 1959 this was increased to 2.5 cents per hour. The fund is managed by ten trustees—five from the United Association and five from the National Constructors Association. Its purpose is not to finance the apprentice activities of the national office of the union, but to promote local apprentice training on the basis of need. It is a grant-in-aid program similar to Federal aid to the states. Invaluable aid has been given to local unions needing help in buying training equipment.

There is no limit on the type of assistance that the trustees of the fund will approve as long as it is needed to improve the skills of the members of the plumbers' and steamfitters' union. The aim is to supplement but not supplant local financial support.

As a result in large part of the new apprenticeship policies of the plumbers' and steamfitters' union, at least 500 of the locals by 1958 had joint labor-management apprenticeship committees; 150 locals had established jointly-managed training funds supported by payroll contributions on covered work; and 10 locals had founded their own training schools for both apprentices and journeymen. In spite of the many steps taken by the union to encourage apprenticeship in the plumbing and steamfitting industries, there has been little change in the total number of apprentices. It was 22,398 on December 31, 1956, and 21,812 on June 30, 1959.[84] The union, however, did report an increase in the number of apprentices becoming journeymen plumbers or steamfitters in building construction from 1,803 in the year ended June 30, 1954, to 3,241 in the year ended

---

[83] The same (April 1956), back cover.
[84] Figures compiled by U. S. Bureau of Apprenticeship.

June 30, 1958.[85] The reason for the failure of union policies and programs to produce an increase in apprentices is not clear. Perhaps it is because there was already a fairly high ratio of apprentices to journeymen in the industry—about one apprentice to every ten journeymen.

Apprenticeship Program and Policies of the Electrical Industry

The most highly-developed arrangements for promoting apprenticeship on an industry-wide scale are found in the electrical industry. Employers joined with the International Brotherhood of Electrical Workers in 1941 to establish the National Joint Committee on Apprenticeship and Training in the Electrical Industry. It consists of six labor representatives and six employer representatives and is the outgrowth of a remarkable record of cooperation over the last thirty years between the union and the dominant contract group in the construction industry, the National Association of Electrical Contractors.

The program of the joint committee in the electrical industry is voluntary, and its success depends on its acceptance by local unions and local employer groups of individual employers. The effectiveness of the joint committee, however, is attributable largely to the fact that the committee operates through a full-time director, who was hired in 1952 and has an office in Washington, and a full-time expert staff. The joint committee sets policies, but the director must see that these policies are brought to the attention of local unions and local employer groups.

It is the objective of the national joint committee to establish local joint committees to carry out this program. In 1958 there were 397 active joint apprenticeship and training committees operating in 490 "wage areas."[86] The national joint committee believes that the local joint committees should operate, where possible, with the help of a full-time director. In 1958 there were 28 full-time local or regional directors, who supervised programs covering from 50 up to 1,200 apprentices. In addition, there were 37 part-time directors.

[85] *United Association Journal* (August 1958), back cover.
[86] A "wage area" means the geographical jurisdiction of a local union of the International Brotherhood of Electrical Workers in its collective bargaining with employers.

The policy of encouraging joint administration of apprenticeship programs has led to important changes in apprentice training. Before joint administration, apprentice training had been dominated by the local unions in some cities, and restrictive practices were followed. The philosophy of the joint program is that apprenticeship should be conducted in the interest of the industry—not in the interest primarily of either labor or employers.

The ratio of apprentices to journeymen varies considerably in the electrical contracting industry. In 1958 the ratio ranged from one apprentice to every 3.3 journeymen in North Dakota, to one to every 22.1 journeymen in Arkansas. For the country as a whole there was one apprentice to every 7.6 journeymen. In thirteen states there was no more than one apprentice for every ten journeymen. The national joint committee believes that the number of apprentices should be determined not by old-fashioned hit-or-miss methods but by a study of the number of journeymen who will be needed in the locality four or five years hence. The electric utilities and the chambers of commerce can usually supply predictions on the growth of industry in the locality during the next four or five years. The Kansas City joint committee paid a management consultant firm $8,000 to draw up estimates of the probable labor needs. In the country as a whole the use of electric energy is doubling every seven and a half years; a few years ago it was doubling every ten years. The director of the national joint committee admits that there is still some opposition to apprentices working while journeymen are idle, but the national committee is trying to get the local committees to make the need for journeymen four or five years hence determine the number of apprentices today.

In 1957 the manpower problem was discussed at all of the local meetings attended by the director or by other representatives of the national joint committee. An increase in manpower can be achieved through improved skills for a given number of men, as well as through an increase in the number of men. Many workers are limited in their production by the fact that they must wait for the foreman to tell them what to do next. If the skills of the present work force could be improved enough to increase their productive effort by one hour a day, the equivalent of 15,000 men would be added to the work force. Of course the efficiency of the work force depends in large part on the skill of foremen and superintendents. Most of the big and exacting jobs are now supervised by young men 26 to 30 years of age, who received their apprenticeship training not many years ago.

During the 1958 recession the national joint committee tried to discourage cutbacks in apprentice training. The committee pointed out that the recession was not reducing the need for apprentices several years hence when most of those in training will be finishing their apprenticeship.

The national joint committee stresses the importance of careful selection of apprentices and has developed a battery of tests, which are administered by the United States Employment Service. In some places the screening of apprenticeship candidates is carried on by professional university staffs. The importance of careful selection is indicated by the fact that a study of discontinuances of apprenticeship showed that almost one-fifth (18 per cent) were attributed to dislike of the trade or inability to master the skills.[87]

Although there are no definite figures on this, the national joint committee reports that drop-outs have been substantially lessened. During the year ended June 30, 1958, 69.5 per cent of all separations from the apprenticeship program were due to completion of the training. This proportion varied from a low of 24.7 per cent in Hawaii and 53.5 per cent in Region XI (Colorado, New Mexico, Utah, and Wyoming) to a high of 85.8 per cent in Region II (New York and New Jersey). It is a part of the program of the national joint committee to plug up the loopholes through which men become journeymen without completing apprenticeship. Potential drop-outs should be discovered during the original interview before applicants are accepted as apprentices.

Nearly all of the programs sponsored by joint apprenticeship committees in the electrical industry provide for 144 hours or more instruction in trade subjects each year. Most of the instruction is given in local public vocational, technical, or high schools. The majority of programs require apprentices to attend classes at night on their own time. About one-fifth of the apprentices are paid for attending classes. The national joint committee encourages giving credit for training received in the armed forces, the amount being determined by the local apprenticeship committees and varying with individuals. Much of the training given by the armed forces is of limited useful-

87 McCauley, "Employment Status of Former Apprentices in Early 1954," p. 754.

ness to men going into electrical construction work. For example, there is little that an airplane mechanic learns that will help him in electrical construction. But Signal Corps work is similar to outside construction work—transmission and distribution. The armed services, according to the staff of the national committee, are better in training people *how* to do certain things than they are in showing them *why* these things must be done. For men to work with a minimum of supervision, it is important that they know the why as well as the how.

The national joint committee stresses the importance of keeping standards up to date. In the electrical trade changing technology is introducing new skill requirements. National standards, developed by the committee in 1941, were revised in 1945, 1953, and 1957. About two-thirds of the local joint apprenticeship committees had revised their standards during the four years 1955 through 1958.[88] While the national joint committee had not previously originated any material, in 1958 it provided training material giving greater attention to the use of the electronic tube. The material is designed for home study by correspondence. It will help the industry in the small towns turn out apprentices with training nearly equivalent to that of apprentices trained in the large metropolitan centers. Material for a three-year course for outside electricians will cost the user $12.50. Equivalent material will be turned out for inside construction.

Apprenticeship Policies of the Typographical Union

One of the oldest and most highly-developed apprenticeship programs in the United States is that of the International Typographical Union—the oldest national union in the country. The union has high standards of craftsmanship and is seriously concerned: (1) that much of the work done by skilled compositors will be transferred to specialists who know only part of the trade, and (2) that the printing industry will be flooded with poorly-trained men who represent themselves as journeymen and who are willing to work below the union scale. The apprenticeship policy of the Typographical Union has reflected changing conditions and the changing problems of the

[88] As of the end of 1958, in nearly one-sixth of the cases, the latest revision of standards was made in 1950 or earlier.

union. It also reflects the prejudices and at times the shortsightedness of the union members or their leaders.

The depression of the thirties led the union to tighter limits on the number of apprentices. In 1939, influenced by high unemployment among its members, the union adopted a requirement that there be two journeymen (exclusive of the proprietor-member) instead of one before an apprentice could be hired. In addition, a new provision was introduced that five additional journeymen were necessary before a second apprentice could be hired, and that once four apprentices were employed, the ratio should be one apprentice to ten journeymen. In 1941 the latter stipulation was changed to one apprentice to ten "additional" journeymen. But local unions can, if they choose, demand fewer than four apprentices, regardless of the number of journeymen.[89] Some delegates at the national union convention urged tighter restrictions than those approved by the convention. It was pointed out to the delegates that some apprentices were necessary and that the number being admitted to the union failed to replace annual losses.

In the early forties efforts were made to reduce still further the ratio of apprentices to journeymen and even to bar all new apprentices. These proposals were rejected on the grounds that these ratios are maximums and that locals can provide fewer apprentices than the limits imposed by the General Laws.[90] With the end of World War II and with the coming of subsidized education for veterans, the union became concerned lest its training standards be disregarded and the market flooded with half-trained printers. The union held that training of veterans should be done under union apprenticeship standards, that union apprenticeship standards should govern training in nonunion shops, and that the union should determine whether or not the applicant was qualified for training. The

[89] International Typographical Union, *Proceedings of the 83rd Annual Convention* (1939), pp. 139-42, and *Proceedings of the 85th Annual Convention* (1941), p. 64.

[90] President Baker of the International Typographical Union cautioned, however, that with the average age of membership approaching fifty and with a declining number of apprentices there was a possibility that there would actually be insufficient replacements. International Typographical Union, *Proceedings of the 86th Convention* (1942), p. 26. President Baker suggested to the 1941 convention that a list of forty-year members not be printed in the union's journal since it would be "unwise to give undue publicity" to the fact that "a considerable percentage of the membership had passed the meridian of life." International Typographical Union, *Officers' Report to the 85th Convention* (1941), p. 15.

incorporation of union standards in government-supported training would have meant that shops would be limited to eight apprentices and that no apprentices would be permitted in shops where fewer than three journeymen were employed. The effort of the union to secure control over trade entry and training failed.[91]

The original position of the union was that the return of 10,700 ITU members from military service would provide more than enough craftsmen to satisfy the current needs of the industry, but the union seriously underestimated the postwar demand for printers. Furthermore, a large part of the membership wanted to reward returning veteran apprentices for military service. In 1946 in order to prevent a determined rank and file attempt to give veterans "priority" for time spent in military service, a substitute was offered that allowed the shortening of the apprenticeship term by one year by upgrading those apprentices who demonstrated special achievement.[92]

By 1948 the union reported that 1,580 apprentices had been upgraded within a twelve-month period (August 1946 to August 1947), and that approximately 1,600 new apprentices had been admitted, making a total of some 8,000 registered apprentices.[93] The union was also influenced in liberalizing apprenticeship requirements by the fact that thousands of men were learning the trade in nonunion shops. In 1955 the union made additional concessions to freer entrance to the trade. Apprentice upgrading of 24 months was permitted, replacing the previous 12-month period. Further, local unions, if they deemed it "necessary and advisable," were allowed to

[91] International Typographical Union, *Officers' Report to the 88th Convention* (1946), p. 25. The officers reported that "the administrators of the G.I. Bill of Rights have shown no inclination to favor organized shops, and as a result nonunion employers have taken advantage of the ignorance of the representatives of the Veterans Administration to obtain cheap labor under the guise of 'on the job training.'"

[92] International Typographical Union, *Proceedings of the 88th Convention* (1946), pp. 93-98. Later the rank and file by referendum established priority for military service.

[93] International Typographical Union, *Officers' Report to the 90th Convention* (1948), p. 44. The reports of the union on the number of apprentices paying dues differ somewhat from these figures. There was a rapid growth in the number of dues-paying apprentices from 3,627 in 1945 to 5,366 in 1947, and 6,303 in 1948—well below the 8,000 mentioned in the *Officers' Report* in 1948. *The Typographical Journal* (July 1958), p. 13s.

The number of dues-paying apprentices dropped in the depression of the thirties from 3,956 (or 5 per cent of the journeymen) in 1932 to 2,611 (or 3.5 per cent of the journeymen) in 1936. By 1939 it had increased to 4,835, or 6.5 per cent of the journeymen. It dropped during the war. In 1958, it was 6,808, or 6.6 per cent of the number of journeymen.

liberalize existing apprentice ratios making possible variations of the one-to-ten ratio required after the employment of four apprentices. One reason for the new regulations was to enable local unions to supply needed help for new processes.[94] Another reason for the change was to give assistance to local unions faced with critical manpower shortages. In considering the proper ratios, local unions were advised to take into account the rise in the number of retirements resulting from negotiated pensions.

At the one-hundredth convention of the union in 1958 the Committee on Apprentices and Supplemental Education urged that "every local union which has not complied with the provision of ITU laws to establish a joint apprenticeship committee do so at once."[95] But at the convention the committee placed particular stress upon the need for the training of journeymen. They said:

> The speed with which innovations, new methods, new processes and new machines are invading our trade emphasizes the gravity of the all-important problem of training to meet these rapidly changing conditions in the composing room. . . . Our members must be trained in the needed skills if we are to survive as a craft.[96]

General Influence of Unions on the Training of Skilled Workers

There are two principal ways of handling the training of skilled workmen in an economy like ours. One is the Wisconsin method, which treats apprenticeship as part of the state's educational system. The state assumes responsibility for training standards, and registered apprentices are expected to receive the quality of training that their indentures specify.

The other principal method of getting craftsmen trained is that sponsored by the U. S. Bureau of Apprenticeship and Training and best exemplified by joint apprenticeship committees. This method presupposes that there are unions in the community and that they are interested in apprenticeship. In the case of the joint committee method there is no close connection between the size of needs and

[94] *The Typographical Journal* (September 1955), p. 19s.
[95] *The Typographical Journal* (September 1958), p. 78s
[96] The same.

the adequacy of training facilities—no assurance that needs will produce training arrangements. Experience has shown that training arrangements are spotty and that they meet only a small fraction of the need—as is indicated by the small proportion of journeymen who have had apprenticeship training.

The need for skilled workers is growing rapidly, but few efforts are being made to meet that need. This is one of the great weaknesses of the American economy. It is unfortunate that most states, most unions, and most employers show so little interest in the matter.

The Crisis in Apprenticeship

There is no doubt that apprenticeship training in the United States now faces a crisis. Louis Ruthenburg, former president of the Servel Corporation, has written a strong article entitled "The Crisis in Apprentice Training."[97] The crisis is indicated first by the fact that apprenticeship training provides at present rates only one-ninth of the journeymen needed, so that most journeymen are literally forced to pick up a knowledge of the trade by haphazard methods, and second by the fact that in recent years there has been no increase in the number of apprentices. Earlier in this chapter attention was called to the failure of the number of apprentices to increase since 1956. In 1953 the number reached 160,258, and in 1956, a postwar peak of 188,137. Since 1956 the number has fallen off to 185,691 in 1957, 177,695 in 1958, and 174,252 on June 30, 1959.

What are the prospects that the volume of apprenticeship training can be greatly expanded in the United States within the next several years? They are not bright. The Bureau of Apprenticeship and Training has made heroic efforts to stir up interest in apprenticeship but with meager results. For example, in 1957 the Bureau, to test the potentialities of a national industry project, concentrated efforts in the foundry industry.[98] A committee from the industry, assisted by the Bureau's staff, contacted officials of a representative group of foundries, discussed training, and helped evaluate needs. The study showed that sharp increases were anticipated by 1960 in several key occupations, including a 30 per cent increase in the number of pattern makers. Nevertheless, the number of pattern maker apprentices in

---

[97] *Personnel Magazine* (July-August, 1959).
[98] John S. McCauley, "BAT and Community Apprenticeship Committees," *Journal of the American Society of Training Directors* (November 1958).

the United States, after rising from 870 on December 31, 1956, to 930 a year later, dropped to 653 on December 31, 1958, and to 638 on June 30, 1959. And among molders and coremakers the number of apprentices dropped from 1,028 on December 31, 1956, to 857 a year later, rose to 861 on December 31, 1958, and fell to 784 on June 30, 1959. Measured by the number of apprentices the attempt of the Bureau of Apprenticeship and Training to arouse interest in apprenticeship in the foundry industry was a complete failure.

In view of the disappointing record of the Bureau, any upsurge of interest in apprenticeship must come from the unions and the employers, and especially from the recently-founded Construction Industry Joint Conference. Each national union needs to agree on an apprentice quota, 50 per cent to 100 per cent larger than its present number of apprentices and undertake to meet it in the next five years. Responsibility for getting the several unions to set quotas and fulfill their agreements should be assumed by the joint committees. By making the attainment of targets a matter of agreement, the several national unions will be encouraged to undertake the necessary action.

5 / *Basic Concepts of Seniority*

IT IS DOUBTFUL whether any concept has been as influential, pervasive, and troublesome in collective bargaining as that of seniority. For our purposes, seniority will be defined simply as an employee's length of service with the company for which he works. In any given collective bargaining relationship, however, the word acquires special meanings through the language of the agreement, through practices followed in the daily administration of the contract, and not uncommonly through arbitration decisions.

It is the purpose of this chapter to develop an understanding of the growth in the use of seniority and of the more basic ground-rules that have been developed in applying the seniority principle. This will be done under the following headings: (1) The importance of seniority in labor relations, (2) General principles in the application of the seniority criterion, (3) Legal aspects of seniority, and (4) General implications of the use of seniority. This background will be helpful for the discussion of the applications of seniority in layoff procedures (Chapter 6) and in promotions (Chapter 7).

Importance of Seniority

For a number of reasons, seniority has become progressively more important during the past twenty years. First, there has been a growing belief among both managements and employees that for many purposes the long-service workers are entitled to greater security and superior benefits as a matter of equity. This is indicated by the increasing willingness of companies to make many concessions to protect the senior employees at a time of layoff.

Second, as a "basic regulatory mechanism" this criterion has the merit of objectivity. Therefore, it often prevails over subjective criteria that might be considered appropriate. From the union standpoint, its objectivity is compatible with internal political considerations, and it frees the union from the uncomfortable and unpopular judgments required by use of less tangible criteria. Management, too, either by default or by deliberate, rational policy, is insisting less on a high weighting of nonseniority factors.

Third, the last two decades have witnessed a dramatic rise in the number and types of benefit programs. Almost without exception, entitlement to these new benefits has been geared to seniority. In fact, this was occasionally a part of bargaining strategy; the new benefit was made more palatable cost-wise to management by limiting it to employees with long service. Subsequent negotiations often led to a reduction in the seniority requirement or, in the case of a few benefits, its complete elimination. It was not uncommon in the first contracts providing for payment for unworked holidays to limit payment to those with at least one, two, or even more years of service. This seniority requirement has now largely disappeared. However, because of the nature of nearly all new benefit programs, the element of seniority service still plays an important integral part.

Fourth, seniority has acquired added influence through the decisions of arbitrators. Oftentimes the discharge of an employee with long service has been set aside for this extenuating reason alone. In such cases the arbitrator would freely admit that the stated "cause" for discharge would have been a "just cause" if an individual with less seniority had been involved. Arbitrators sometimes have interpreted contract language so as to increase the influence of seniority.

Fifth, the enactment of certain laws, especially the Selective Service Act, has given added importance to seniority, as have the decisions of certain government agencies. There is no question that the decisions of the War Labor Board of World War II and, to a lesser extent, of the Wage Stabilization Board during the Korean War gave impetus to the extension of seniority arrangements. These wartime boards encouraged deferred-payment benefit plans in an effort to curb pressures for immediate wage increases, as will be noted in Chapters 13, 14, 15, and 16. They also extended the seniority criterion to such areas as shift preference and vacation preference.

The importance of seniority in labor relations today can perhaps best be shown by listing the areas in which it may affect an employee's status. For each of the categories given seniority may be a factor in only a few of the approximately 125,000 collective bargaining agreements now in effect in the United States. They are included only to show the various ways in which seniority may be a factor. How length of service is used in each category will be discussed more fully in later chapters. For example, the role length of service plays in layoffs and promotions will be considered at some length in Chapters 6 and 7. In Chapters 13 through 16 its use in the benefit programs developed through collective bargaining will be described. Its use in disciplinary procedures is covered in Chapter 21.

The list is undoubtedly incomplete. Its length and variety suggest that many other such arrangements may exist in practice or by contract. The listing is divided into two groups. The first includes those categories for which length of service determines an employee's status in relation to other employees. It is a criterion that helps resolve what might be a source of competition among employees. For example, employees vie with one another for promotional opportunities, for the limited jobs available at a time of work reduction, for desirable parking spaces, and the like. It will be convenient to identify this as "competitive status seniority."

The second category involves those benefits, rights, or privileges to which a man is entitled either explicitly, as in the case of severance pay, or implicitly, as in the case of partial protection from discharge, just because he has attained a certain number of years of service. The competitive aspect of seniority is of limited importance in this group. This will be identified as "benefit seniority."

Applications of Competitive Status Seniority

LAYOFFS AND RECALLS. It is in this area that the principle of seniority was first introduced and has been most widely extended. The general principles that the last person hired should be the first person laid off and that recalls from layoff should be in inverse order of layoff are expressed in nearly every current collective bargaining agreement in the manufacturing and transportation industries. Even in many highly seasonal industries, such as building construction and the needle trades, where the policy of equal distribution of work is more prevalent, the agreements sometimes adopt seniority as the guide in making permanent displacements.

PROMOTIONS. Within the past twenty years seniority has come to play an increasingly more important part in deciding who among several competing employees is entitled to fill a promotional vacancy.

Unions have succeeded in establishing as a minimum the principle that where ability is relatively equal, seniority shall govern. In many cases they have been able to assign even greater weight to the seniority criterion.

TRANSFERS. Sometimes the lateral, upward, or downward movements of employees on a temporary, day-to-day basis are governed, in part at least, by seniority. These are transfers occasioned by the absence of the regular job incumbents because of illness, vacation, leaves of absence, or other reasons; or they may be required by temporary production needs. While the seniority arrangements for such transfers vary greatly, where they do exist, they usually give the senior employee the preference for the available work and at the same time give him the privilege of rejecting the transfer; thus, the obligation of accepting transfer often falls on the least senior person. Generally, however, seniority plays a less important role in temporary transfers than in permanent transfers.

JOB OR WORK ASSIGNMENT. Claims to specific job assignments on the basis of seniority are closely related to layoffs, promotions, and transfers. Where seniority governs the distribution of work, serious problems may be created for management. The opportunity to match individual skills to the assignments involved becomes limited. The senior, more skilled employees may select only the easy work, leaving the less well-trained, junior employees to handle the difficult assignments. Or where there is an incentive system, the senior men may select only those assignments that allow the greatest opportunity for earnings. This is discussed more fully in Chapter 9.

A variant of this problem, which is more of an irritant than a serious cost matter to management, is "machine seniority." A senior worker may be given his choice of machine in a bank of identical or similar machines. In the winter he might select a machine which is in a warm part of the room; in the summer he might select that machine nearest to open windows or doors. Or he might select the machine nearest to the locker room, time clock, cafeteria, or rest room.

SHIFT PREFERENCE. Although evidence on this subject is limited, it is safe to conclude that there is increasing use of seniority as a basis for shift preference. Complications may arise over such questions as (1) the frequency with which applications for choice of shift may be made; (2) the scope of interchange, that is, the type of jobs to which workers may move when changing shifts; (3) the length of time a worker must remain on his shift before he may move after applying to do so; and (4) the length of time before shift preference balance must be restored following a layoff that disrupts preferences.

In agreeing to the use of seniority as a basis for shift selection, many companies have failed to consider its implications for managerial efficiency and flexibility. Although the considerations influencing employee preference vary a great deal, by and large the employees with longer service (who are likely to be older) will gravitate toward the daylight shifts leaving the newer (and therefore younger) employees to man the twilight or graveyard shifts. Some companies complain that the net result is an undesirable concentration of less experienced workers on the night shifts. One company reported that its best shift from the standpoint of output was the second one, from 4 p.m. to midnight. The day shift "is poor on quantity because the older employees work at a slower pace," and the third shift "is poor on both quality and quantity because the younger employees lack the experience of older workers."

Shift preference by seniority may also affect indirectly the scheduling decisions of management. A large brewing company found that its decision to change the starting times for a number of shifts had to be posted to permit employees to bid on the basis of seniority. After this process was completed, the least senior men were obliged to take any remaining vacancies. Thus, revising starting times invited considerable disruption. The company contention that seniority should not govern unless there were "competent replacements" for those changing shifts was rejected by an arbitrator.

SELECTION OF DAYS OFF. Related to shift preference is the use of seniority in a few contracts to determine the assignment of days off each week. For example, an agreement between a large news service organization and the Commercial Telegraphers' Union provides that employees shall have the right to choose days off on the basis of seniority, subject only to the requirement that the days selected be among those available as days off on the schedule prepared by the company.

OVERTIME DISTRIBUTION. The principle of equal distribution of overtime is probably more firmly established than is that of allocation of overtime opportunities on the basis of seniority. However, a few agreements provide for the distribution of overtime by seniority without any attempt at equalization. Sometimes, as in the case of transfers, the senior man is given preference for overtime, but he also has the right (denied to the least senior man) to refuse to work overtime. Some companies in the steel industry that have adopted the "local practice" clause in their contracts with the United Steelworkers have through practice committed themselves to this. To illustrate, if two or more employees have been doing the same work on a shift and a chance to "double over" on the next shift arises, it has been the practice and is obligatory under the contract to offer the overtime to the one with the longest service in the seniority unit.

VACATION PRIVILEGES. The status of an employee on the seniority roster may determine whether he will be granted vacation at the time of his choice. A typical clause is the following:

> Vacations will, as far as practicable, be granted for the period selected by the employee, but final allocation of vacation periods is left to the company in order to assure orderly operation of the plant. In the choice of vacation dates, departmental seniority shall prevail.

In some contracts, employees with long service are allowed to accumulate vacation credits beyond one year.

PARKING PRIVILEGES. The growing parking problem at many industrial plants has been handled in part by the use of seniority. One company assigned each employee a space according to his length of service, the most senior men having the most convenient spots. Because of the union's refusal to allow a time interval between the end of one shift and the start of the next, at any one shift two-thirds of the spots were vacant. The company estimated that seniority had tripled its necessary investment in parking space.[1]

Applications of Benefit Seniority

VACATIONS. The amount of vacation to which an employee is entitled is normally related to his length of service. The phrase "one-

---

[1] As a final illustration of "competitive status seniority" there should be mentioned the company in which senior employees had the right to punch out first at the time clock. Junior employees went to the end of the line.

for-one and two-for-five" (that is, one week of vacation for one year of service and two weeks of vacation after five years' service), which was the War Labor Board vacation formula, illustrates the tie-in between vacation benefit and seniority. The trend in this relationship during the past twenty years is discussed in Chapter 15.

PENSIONS. Service credits play an important part in the operation of pension plans throughout American industry. Seniority determines eligibility for pension plan coverage, the right to disability retirement, the creation of vested rights, and, in many instances, the amount of the pension benefit to be received. Very often it has been necessary to adjust existing seniority arrangements to meet the needs of pension plans. These developments are described in Chapter 13.

SEVERANCE PAY. The eligibility for and the amount of payment made under formal or *ad hoc* severance pay plans are correlated directly with service credits. Chapter 16 gives illustrations of the role of seniority in these plans.

HOLIDAYS. As stated above, many provisions for payment for unworked holidays formerly included a service requirement. Although this is less frequently the case today, many clauses limit payment to regular or so-called seniority employees and exclude part-time, temporary, or probationary employees.

SICK LEAVE PROVISIONS. Where paid sick leave is provided, it is customary to relate the eligibility and the amount of such payment to length of service. One such clause in an agreement between an aircraft engine company and its UAW local for salaried employees provides:

> Sick leave allowances within each calendar year . . . are contingent on the length of time during which an employee has been continuously within the Employer's employ as of the last day worked prior to absence.

Continuous Employment	Allowances
Less than one month	5 days
One month but less than six months	10 days
Six months but less than one year	15 days
One year or more	20 days

GROUP LIFE AND HOSPITALIZATION INSURANCE, HEALTH, AND WELFARE PLANS. The coverage of these plans is normally extended only to those persons who have completed a certain minimum period of service with the company. The service requirement is not necessarily the same as the probationary period designated in the agreement. Chapter 14 gives examples of this correlation between service and coverage.

PROFIT SHARING. Eligibility for and often the allocation of employee shares under profit-sharing plans are determined by length of service. Particularly, deferred types of profit sharing, comparable to pensions, use the seniority factor in allocating profits to individuals.

SUPPLEMENTARY UNEMPLOYMENT BENEFIT, EMPLOYMENT SECURITY, AND GUARANTEED ANNUAL WAGE PLANS. These plans, which are discussed in Chapter 16, rely upon the seniority criterion in several ways. For example, minimum service of one year is required for coverage under the SUB plans of the automobile industry. In others, such as the plans negotiated initially by the large can companies, three years' service is required to establish eligibility. In addition, under the automobile plans the rate of accrual of credits is related to seniority, as is the rate of cancellation of credits when benefits are drawn. Low-seniority workers surrender more accrued credits per benefit payment than do high-seniority employees.

INTRA-RANGE WAGE MOVEMENTS. As will be noted in Chapter 20, the past twenty years have seen a pronounced trend away from the use of rate ranges for merit recognition purposes and toward automatic progression based on length of service. In some cases, the retention of the merit criterion is limited to low-service employees. One labor agreement provides that "all persons with ten years or more seniority . . . shall automatically be entitled to the merit."

LENGTH-OF-SERVICE WAGE ADJUSTMENTS. In a very limited number of cases, special wage adjustments are given to long-service employees, thus creating personal rates for them rather than the established job rate. In one company, for example, as soon as an employee attains his fifth year of service he receives nine cents over and above the job rate; when he reaches eight years of service, he is given an additional four cents. Men doing the same work on single-rated jobs, therefore, get varying wage rates. Adjustments of this type are not always a heritage from pre-union days. In the case cited the practice originated in 1951, long after the company was unionized.

AUTOMATIC PROMOTION. In some instances the movement from one job classification to another is based entirely upon length of service. Admittedly, this arrangement is very similar to automatic progression within a rate range since the so-called classifications have little or no meaning in terms of job content. For example, one company promotes a man from a Second Class Laborer B job to a Second Class A job at the end of 4 months' service; from a Second Class A to a First Class B at the end of 8 months; and from a First Class B to a First Class A at the end of 12 months. But it is significant that, after the one year of service, this same company must automatically advance the Class A laborer to a still higher classification, or if it prefers to avoid an actual transfer, it must pay the laborer the higher rate or the rate of a process helper rather than the rate of any of the labor classes.

BONUSES. The payment of special bonuses, such as Christmas or "service anniversary" bonuses, is directly related to service with respect both to eligibility and to the amount of payment. For example, under the agreement between a large paper company and its union, the company is obligated to give a Christmas "gift" in the amount of $10 to those with six months to one year's mill seniority and $15 to those with one year's mill seniority.

LONG-SERVICE REWARDS. Long before unionization, companies had developed the practice of giving special recognition to long-service employees. While the service pin, service club, service watch, and other similar ceremonial or token gestures are well known, there are other less publicized policies that are more interesting, especially when their observance is continued by practice in a collective bargaining framework. Some companies unilaterally provide that employees upon attainment of a certain service level will no longer be required to punch a time clock. One company for many years before unionization and for a number of years after unionization automatically converted 25-year service employees from an hourly pay basis to a salary. Another company gives its employees one share of stock at the completion of each five years of service.

With collective bargaining, the wisdom of some of these long-service benefits is being reviewed anew. First, even though the labor agreement is silent on the subject of these benefits, there is a question whether the company may not have forfeited the right to discontinue such practices at its discretion. Extensive reliance by arbitrators on past practice means that what started as a unilateral grant may become a fixed obligation. This could be a serious problem since the number of high-service people in most long-established plants is rising steadily.

Second, the practices themselves often raise problems that affect the administration of the labor agreement or the collective bargaining demands. Excessive tardiness on the part of a long-service employee who does not have to punch a time clock, if tolerated, may be cited as proof of discrimination in a grievance involving discipline of another employee for tardiness. The salary method of payment gives rise to disparate treatment of employees when absences occur. A one-day absence due to illness would mean loss of pay to a less senior worker but not to a long-service employee on salary. Other similar consequences could be cited. The net effect in a unionized situation would be to make the company vulnerable to a demand for the extension of the "most favored employee treatment" to all employees or to those with a lower level of service.

PROTECTION FROM LOSS OF SENIORITY. It will be noted later in this chapter that the level of seniority itself may determine the loss of the seniority property right during periods of sustained absence from the job, because of either an extended layoff or a protracted illness. To illustrate, an agreement between a farm equipment company and the UAW provides that an employee will lose his seniority if he has been laid off by the company for a period of time equal to his seniority prior to layoff or for a period of three years, whichever is greater.

PROTECTION FROM DISCIPLINARY ACTION. It has already been observed that length of service may be a mitigating factor in determining the penalty for wrongdoing. Companies may recognize this in administering a disciplinary program, or they may be persuaded to this view by union arguments in the grievance procedure. The concept is given stature by numerous arbitration decisions, particularly when the discipline involves the loss of seniority and with it the many benefits and rights described above. In Chapter 21 it will be noted that consideration of length of service in administering discipline often makes the adoption of fixed penalties for stated rule violations unrealistic and untenable.

The foregoing list of areas in which competitive status seniority and benefit seniority apply, shows why seniority has become such an important consideration in the relations between unions and managements.

Parties to collective bargaining have not always made the sharp distinction suggested by these two categories. However, some contracts are careful to distinguish between the two uses of seniority, both in terminology and in application. For example, an electrical manufacturing company agreement with its union speaks of "job seniority" and "benefit seniority." The former applies to layoff, recall, transfer, and promotion and is carried by a worker only if he moves to a division of the company that is treated as part of the job seniority unit. "Benefit seniority," however, accompanies him wherever he may move within the company. Usually benefit seniority has the widest possible application and is unimpaired by movements of the employee within the company. This is often true even when an employee moves to another plant of the same company which is represented by a different bargaining unit. "Competitive status seniority" is less easily moved from one location to another within a company. This is understandable because the latter involves the rights of one employee *vis-à-vis* the rights of another employee. Many agreements purposely use the term "service" or "credited service" to describe the basis for benefit payments, as contrasted with "seniority," which is the criterion involved in relative ranking of employees for layoff, promotion, transfer, and recall purposes.

Given the substantial body of rights and benefits that flow from length of service, it is easy to understand why seniority has become a very valuable property right of the employee. It is deceptive because to the layman it appears to be a simple concept. It is anything but simple. In the negotiation and administration of the labor agreement there have been few issues as troublesome to the parties concerned. If one were to generalize on the trends in labor relations over the past twenty years, these conclusions on seniority would be reasonable:

(1) The basic principles and general ground rules of seniority have been resolved satisfactorily to both parties. Seldom are they a cause of serious bargaining difficulties or of grievances during the life of the contract.

(2) The question of which elements of the employment relationship shall be affected entirely or partially by the seniority factor is still a matter of some contention in many companies. It arises either as a bargaining issue or as a grievance involving deviation from past practice. Such elements as transfers, overtime preference, shift preference, job assignment (including machine seniority), and vacation preference have yielded more and more to the seniority influence. But its acceptance in all of these areas is by no means widespread. On the other hand, the use of the seniority principle to some degree for layoffs, recalls, and promotions and the use of the service factor for various benefit plans are no longer a point of contention.

(3) The *degree* to which seniority is to serve as a regulatory mechanism is also a source of continuing controversy, although as we shall see in the chapters on layoff and promotion, it is less and less a cause of grievances and seldom is considered a strike issue.

General Principles in the Application of the Seniority Criterion

A principal purpose of this chapter is to explore the first of the three trends mentioned above: stabilization over the years of the general ground rules of seniority. The following are to be considered: (1) definition and measurement of seniority or service, (2) acquisition of seniority, (3) loss of seniority, (4) use of superseniority, (5) effect of merger and succession on seniority rights, (6) seniority of employees outside the bargaining unit, and (7) special arrangements in administering seniority rosters.

In a multiplant company which has negotiated a master agreement, the basic regulations covering these seven questions are usually, but not always, incorporated in the master agreement. Benefit programs relying on benefit seniority are company-wide in most instances. Therefore, the definition of what constitutes continuous service for benefit seniority purposes and how such service is acquired and lost must be uniform throughout the company. Furthermore, variations from plant to plant would give rise to a justifiable charge of unequal treatment. Many of these concepts apply also to competitive status seniority and require reasonable uniformity. However, complete uniformity is not necessary in the definition and measurement of seniority. The latter is usually uniform for benefit seniority, but more often than not it is left to local determination in the case of competitive status seniority. The ways in which layoffs, promotions, work assignments, parking space allocation, and other items that we have identified with competitive status seniority usually are determined must take into consideration local plant conditions.

Definition and Measurement of Seniority

Up to this point the word seniority has been defined arbitrarily as an employee's length of continuous service with the company. This broad definition is reasonably accurate insofar as eligibility for benefit programs is concerned. It serves well in the application of benefit seniority. However, the definition may be entirely inadequate and misleading for those items involving the use of competitive status seniority to determine order of layoff, recall, promotion, and other preferential treatment. For these areas the definitions are almost too varied to enumerate.

A distinction should be made between the "unit" of seniority or its scope of application, and the measurement of, or ranking by, seniority. The need for this distinction will be recognized in Chapter 6 "Layoff and Work-Sharing Arrangements" and in Chapter 7 on the subject of "Promotions." For example, the phrase "departmental seniority" could have one or both of two meanings. It might mean that the least senior worker in a particular department will be the first laid off, yet ranking in the department might be based on total service with the company. In this sense, the term "departmental seniority" refers to the unit for purposes of applying seniority. Or the term may refer to the measurement of seniority; that is, the employees within the department will have their relative status determined by their length of service in the department. It could mean both if the measurement is based on the unit of application.

The scope of the seniority unit and the measurement of service vary according to the use to which the seniority criterion is being put. In the case of benefit seniority it is usually length of continuous service with the company. But where competitive job rights are at stake, there may well be one scope-measurement amalgam for temporary layoffs, another for permanent layoffs, another for promotions, and still others for different preferential treatments to be accorded senior employees. To illustrate, a broad unit is likely to apply in the case of layoffs, thus enhancing the chance of a senior man to be retained during a period of work curtailment. In the case of promotion a narrow unit is more likely to govern.

Furthermore, different units and measurements for applying seniority frequently are created for various stages of the layoff and promotion procedures. For example, a paper company agreement provides for job seniority, departmental seniority, division seniority, mill seniority, and finally company seniority in making layoffs.

A study of a number of contract changes over the past twenty years permits the following observations: the trend is toward the use of a single seniority date, usually the date of hire in the company or the plant, regardless of the units of seniority application. Ranking within any given unit by date of original hire in the company is becoming more prevalent. There are several reasons for these gradual changes.

First, the use of a single date for each employee prevents misunderstandings and reduces the chances of clerical errors possible when an employee has a number of different years of service for different seniority purposes.

Second, it is probably the best way to resolve a problem of human relations as well as of operating efficiency. If an employee is transferred to another department and the unit for applying seniority as well as for measurement of seniority is strictly on a departmental basis, he would start with zero seniority in the new department. He might have many years' service with the company, but his risk of layoff would be very great and his opportunities for promotion within the department very limited. Under these circumstances, there might well be a justifiable reluctance to accept permanent transfers, and operating efficiency as well as flexibility of the work force would be lessened. On the other hand, uniform measurement lets an employee carry with him his total company service for ranking purposes within the department. The new transferee might thus out-rank others who had been in the department for many years. The other employees would resent this change in their relative positions on the departmental seniority roster.

These undesirable consequences have led to compromise arrangements. One of two solutions was generally adopted: (1) Seniority was not transferred, but the transferee maintained residence in all departments where he had worked previously, based upon his length of service within each department; if laid off from the new department, he was privileged to return to a prior domicile on the basis of seniority. (2) To enable employees in the new department to adjust to the transfer of seniority, the transferee might have to wait one year, for example, to establish residence; he would then be allowed to carry with him his seniority from other departments and assume a new ranking on the basis of total company service. These compromises sometimes have proved less satisfactory than the use of a single seniority date.

Third, the single date for measurement purposes may have become more acceptable as the unit or scope of application, particularly for layoff purposes, became broader. A related reason is the growth in the benefit programs, which depend primarily upon date of original hire. These tended to highlight the differences. For example, it seemed incongruous for a man to get three weeks' vacation because of his fifteen years' company service and then be laid off because he had only two years' service in a given department. These benefit plans may well have influenced the measurement of seniority for competitive status purposes.

Agreement as to the date to be used for seniority computation by no means solved the problem of measurement. A number of subordinate problems arose, especially during the initial contracts, when the parties had neither their own experience nor that of others to rely upon. Nearly all of these have been resolved in recent years by new contract language. This explains in part the marked increase in the space devoted to seniority provisions in labor agreements. Among these problems were the following:

(1) Do periods of absence from work count toward total service

or not?[2] The answer has generally been that certain types of absences may count toward service, but time limits are ordinarily set beyond which the period of absence is not counted. For example, seniority may accumulate during layoffs of a certain duration or during the period of an approved leave of absence. However, some companies are reluctant to allow this, arguing that seniority should be based on time actually worked. In the 1955 negotiations of an electrical manufacturing company the union proposed that workers continue to accrue seniority while on layoff. The company was unwilling to grant the request, but finally agreed provided the union would allow a two-year cut-off on recall rights. The union promptly withdrew its demand. Another company has refused to permit union representatives on leave of absence for full-time union work to accumulate seniority. A top union official has said that this creates serious administrative problems for the union because the experienced union men are anxious to return to their company jobs to protect their seniority rights.

Where the date of initial hire is used in determining the relative status of an employee on the seniority roster, it is more likely that periods of absence due to layoffs, illness, or approved leaves will be counted in computing service. In some craft unions, particularly in the printing trades, absence has no effect on service accumulation. For example, it is traditional in the International Typographical Union that a man may be absent as long as he wants, provided he sees to it that his position is manned.

(2) How is the priority among employees with the same seniority date to be decided? This might appear to be a petty question, but it has been a source of numerous grievances, showing how concerned employees are with their relative seniority rights. For obvious reasons, most companies do not measure seniority in units of less than a day, and a few prefer to measure from the first day of the month nearest to the date of hire. Normally service credits are given in years, months, and days.

One company and union were confronted with a layoff grievance filed by a young lady who protested her layoff and the retention of another girl who had been hired on the same date. Both carried the same seniority date on the applicable roster. In deciding which

[2] It is well known, of course, that the Selective Service Act provided for retention as well as accumulation of service while an employee was in the Armed Services.

of the two to lay off, the company relied on the date of their medical examinations, when the decision to hire was made. The union argued that since seniority was not measured in fractions of a day, the company was obligated to toss a coin, thereby leaving to chance which of the two girls was to be laid off. The grievance was carried all the way to arbitration, and the union's contention was denied. A subsequent agreement contained a clause providing that the comparative seniority of employees with the same date of hire would be determined by the alphabetical order of their family names as recorded in the personnel record folder maintained in the industrial relations department. Thus an employee whose name began with "A" was considered to be senior to an employee with the letter "B." They even anticipated the problem of two people with the same seniority date as well as the same family name. They specified that in such an event the alphabetical order of their given names was to govern.

Thus far the discussion of measurement and definition of seniority and service has adopted the orthodox concept that seniority represents length of service, however it may be defined in the contract. Some interesting departures from this concept are to be found. A few attempts have been made to define seniority as more than a function of service date; such definitions might include various ability criteria. One variant of this is a "retention rating" system used by a large aircraft corporation for the engineers who are unionized. A man is assigned points according to his merit and ability plus one point for each month's service. The total points, which can go up to a maximum of 120, determine the man's position on the seniority roster for layoff and recall purposes.

An even more interesting approach to seniority measurement and definition is the Seniority Rating Sheet, which for many years has been part of the labor agreement between a rubber footwear manufacturer and its union. The entire rating sheet is reproduced here because it has special interest for the subsequent chapters dealing with the relative degree of influence of seniority and ability in layoffs and promotions.

Use of this rating sheet antedated the unionization of the company and had gained such wide acceptance that the union has never sought to do away with it entirely. Over the past twenty years of collective bargaining, seniority, as defined, has undergone a num-

SENIORITY RATING SHEET

Name .... Dept. .... No. ....

Present Job .... Date ....

Rated by .... Foreman   Checked by .... Supervisor

Approved by ....Superintendent

By ....Employment Dept.

I. LENGTH OF SERVICE

One point of credit allowed for each year of service.
Total Service .... Yrs. .... Mos. .... Days ....
FACTOR I TOTAL CREDIT ....

II. ATTENDANCE[a]

0-1 Absences	 4
2-3 Absences	 2
4-5 Absences	 1

III. QUANTITY

Day Workers

Above Average	 4
Average	 2

Bedaux Workers

80-Point Hour and Over	 4
70-79-Point Hour	 2

IV. QUALITY

A. To what degree is the product of the employee up to the dept's
accepted standard of quality
  1. Meets standard requirements   Yes 1
  2. Not more than occasionally below standard requirements   Yes 1
B. Workmanship
  1. Properly cares for tools, equipment and materials   Yes 1
FACTOR IV TOTAL CREDIT (Maximum—3)

V. VERSATILITY, ADAPTABILITY, SKILL

1. Satisfactorily performs two major jobs   Yes 1
2. Satisfactorily performs three major jobs   Yes 1
3. Has capacity to learn another major job   Yes 1
FACTOR V TOTAL CREDIT (Maximum—3)

VI. COOPERATION

1. Is this person always willing to carry out instructions and requirements of job?   Yes 1
2. Does this person notify Supervision regarding conditions that reasonably require attention?   Yes 1
3. Is this person one who does not offer excuses or alibis to avoid
accepting his proper responsibilities?   Yes 1
FACTOR VI TOTAL CREDIT (Maximum—3)
TOTAL CREDIT
(SENIORITY RATING)   ....

[a] Excusable absences, which are defined in the agreement, are not charged against the employee in making this rating.

ber of changes in the nonservice elements. The union has been successful in eliminating some factors (number of dependents, residence) and in revising downward the weighting of nonservice factors, especially the subjective elements. The program, however, is interesting in light of the tug-of-war between ability and seniority. In this company if one were to ask an employee what his seniority is, he might reply that he is a 26-point man, although his actual length of service may be only 12 years. Only after 17 years of service does the service factor automatically outweigh the nonservice factors, since the maximum points attainable under the latter total 17.

Ratings are made at six months' intervals and are made known to employees, who have the right to grieve their rating within a specified time. The periodic ratings are designed to eliminate the excessive influence of the most recent months as when employee ratings are made only for a contemplated layoff or promotion action. In the past ten years, during which more than 80,000 ratings have been made, only one protest was carried to arbitration.

The management likes the program because it frees employees from preoccupation with service dates alone. It helps handle the problem of absenteeism in a plant with a large number of women on the payroll. Both parties agree that it lessens the disagreements that arise if nonservice elements are not built into the seniority definition and are considered apart from service at those critical times when actions affecting the employees are imminent. In the words of a union spokesman, "when an employee is just about to be hit by a layoff or when he is pushing for a promotion to a vacancy, he usually has exaggerated ideas about his ability, attendance, etc. Supervision is no different. When either of these things are about to occur, they fit their judgments to meet whatever personal biases they may have. Under the seniority rating system we get away from the crisis evaluation of people."

To make a plan of this type work its administrators must have a lively interest in its success. Supervisors must have the training and the willingness to rate employees objectively. A pitfall characteristic of so many other merit-rating systems must be avoided—the tendency of a supervisor to be a "good guy" and to give everyone a high rating. The versatility criterion as well as length of service probably help management in administering the plan. Both parties assumed other obligations in its adoption. To apply Factor V on the rating sheet, for example, they have to decide by joint study or bargaining what are the major jobs in the plant.

There is no evidence of any trend toward the adoption of these unorthodox concepts of the definition and measurement of seniority. And it is significant that of the two illustrations given, one involved unionized engineers, for whom individual merit and ability are more acceptable criteria; the other involved a plan that in substance antedated collective bargaining. There has been a tendency to argue about seniority *versus* other criteria affecting employee status in which management is interested, and more often than not seniority has prevailed.

Acquisition of Seniority

Under most agreements an employee does not acquire any seniority until he has worked beyond the prescribed probationary period, at which time his original date of hire becomes his seniority date. In a few companies the acquisition of continuous service does not occur until after a period of employment that is longer than the probationary period.

In recent years there has been a reduction in the length of the probationary period. Six months' periods have given way to 30-, 60-, and 90-day periods in many instances, thus permitting an earlier acquisition of seniority rights. To some extent the growth of union shop provisions with the Taft-Hartley 30-day minimum period before membership becomes compulsory may explain the reduction in probationary periods.

The parties have learned through experience the necessity of defining more carefully the time credit to be given a probationer toward the satisfaction of his period. For example, if a new employee works intermittently for a company so that a total of 60 days are worked in a one-year period on eight different employment occasions, has he met the 60-day probationary requirement? Should periods of absence caused by layoff be treated differently from those caused by illness or personal reasons? One agreement resolves these questions by stating that if a probationary employee returns after losing ten days consecutively, he will start as a new employee. But if he is laid off, he will retain credit for time worked if recalled within six months. Another company and union have agreed that to become a seniority employee, a probationer must have been employed three months within the year following the date of hire or last rehire, whichever is later; layoff periods or leaves of absence for any reason are not to count toward the three months.

In the seasonal industries, such as the needle trades, millinery, and shoes, there is some reason to believe that the permanent employees prefer to maintain a longer probationary or temporary employee period. This is consistent with their job security interest. Since probationers and temporary employees are laid off first because they lack seniority, it enables the permanent or seniority jobholders to share work at a higher number of hours per week. If the period necessary to acquire seniority were less, more people would be entitled to share the available work, and the hours per person would be less. However, the desire of the regulars to secure for themselves the overtime opportunities in good times occasionally makes them want to limit the number of temporary employees.

In many companies, the "acquisition date of seniority" has probably not had the careful consideration it deserves. Stated differently, the purpose of the probationary period is often lost. Because of faulty administration and training, many foremen fail to watch carefully the performance of employees who are not yet permanent. They tend to allow a number of submarginal or marginal employees to remain beyond the critical point when they acquire seniority rights. These employees then automatically acquire protection from summary, unchallengeable dismissal. Too frequently the view of supervisors is that the "half-trained, partially incompetent present employee is better than any new, untried employee." Foremen need to be urged to drop marginal employees during the probationary period. Some companies require periodic employee appraisal reports from the foreman during each new employee's probationary period. Five days before the expiration of the period, a conference is held among the immediate supervisor, the department head, and a representative of the personnel department to decide whether the employee should be retained and given seniority status. While such procedures do not guarantee good selection, it is difficult to understand why so few companies have adopted them.

Loss of Seniority

The bases for losing seniority have become more standardized in labor agreements than any other aspect of seniority. Yet each has given rise to some administrative problems, leading to clarifying contract language in subsequent years. The principal reasons for the loss of seniority are the following:

QUITS. It might be assumed that a voluntary quit by an employee would be an easily understood and unambiguous action. This is not the case.

Sometimes an employee will quit or announce his intention of quitting in the heat of anger. Perhaps he resents the way the foreman has spoken to him or feels he has been treated unfairly. Yet within a day, the flow of adrenalin having decreased and impulse having yielded to reflection, he wants to return to work. Some arbitrators have held that on principle, whether or not an employee quits voluntarily is his own choice, and there is a time after which an employee who has said he is quitting may not change his mind. But if he changes his mind immediately, the quit will be set aside. Occasionally the union will seek contract language that will permit an employee to change his mind within a designated time, usually a day or two.[3]

Another situation involves management's conclusion that an employee has quit, although he himself has announced no such intent. Illustrative is the case of several employees who refused to work the scheduled hours and were told that under the circumstances they were considered to have quit. Adverse arbitration decisions have shown management that an essential element of a quit is the intention of the employee to leave voluntarily. Management's remedy in a situation such as this is the use of disciplinary procedures, not the unilateral conclusion that a quit, with the resultant loss of all seniority rights, has occurred. However, some agreements define a quit so as to cover this situation. For example, one company-union agreement provides that during a layoff if an employee refuses to accept a downgrading of one labor grade, he shall be considered a voluntary quit; similarly, on recall he must accept a job one grade below the one to which he is entitled or suffer the same consequences. Only if the demotion or recall in lieu of layoff involves a move of two or more grades, does he exercise an option without loss of seniority.

A re-examination of seniority rights in certain cases shows how serious is the loss of seniority. A new clause in a rubber company

---

[3] One company that acquiesced to such a union demand found that the clause was being used to circumvent the no-strike restriction. Groups of employees were "quitting" because of irritation over some action or other of the company, then changing their minds within the grace period allowed by the contract.

contract provides that, retroactive to January 1, 1946, all employees who return to work within one year of leaving the company will accumulate seniority for total time worked after having completed five additional consecutive years of service. However, it is specified that this restoration of service applies only to the determination of pension rights.

An indirect effect of the loss of seniority because of a voluntary resignation is the heightened interest among unions in special leave-of-absence arrangements during which seniority rights are protected. Most companies have reserved the right to approve or deny leave-of-absence requests based upon personal reasons within the employee's control, but they have accepted the obligation to grant leaves for sickness or disability. When absence because of pregnancy was found by many arbitrators to fall in the category of leave for voluntary reasons, a successful effort was made by many unions to force companies to grant maternity leave.

DISCHARGE. With very few exceptions there is an unqualified loss of seniority when an employee is discharged for just cause. In a few instances, where management subsequently has rehired discharged employees, the union has urged restoration of seniority. In one case, the union insisted on a contract clause providing for restoration of full seniority one year after the rehiring of a discharged employee. The result of this union achievement was almost inevitable: the company adopted the policy of never rehiring a dischargee.

FAILURE TO REPORT FOR WORK. This cause for loss of seniority may take one of three forms. First, it applies when an employee on layoff is notified to return to work within a specified period and fails to report. Procedural refinements, such as notification by registered mail to the employee's last known address, are common. If an employee can explain satisfactorily why he failed to report, a waiver of the loss may be sought or may be required by the contract. This leads to the question: what constitutes a satisfactory reason? Second, many contracts also provide that absence from work for a certain number of days without notification to the company and without a reasonable excuse will mean loss of all seniority rights. Third, overstaying a leave of absence is usually specified as a basis for seniority loss.

SUSTAINED PERIOD OF CONTINUOUS LAYOFF. This basis has undergone some interesting changes during the past twenty years. In earlier agreements the prevailing practice was to adopt an absolute maximum applicable to all employees. They provided that after one or, in some cases, two years of continuous unemployment, seniority was lost. The trend has been toward the correlation of the layoff time permitted before seniority loss with the length of service or seniority of those on layoff. For example, employees with from one to two years' service with the company will retain their seniority for two years; those with from two to five years will retain seniority for five years; and one contract states that those laid off with five years or more of service will retain and accrue their seniority rights indefinitely.

The liberalization of this arrangement has even led some companies to the complete elimination of, or a refusal to adopt, any cutoff times. One company spokesman said that "if a man is good enough to be laid off and not fired, he's good enough to be recalled." Liberalization in some instances has been prompted by the approach of the cutoff date in a protracted layoff. When this occurs, the union usually brings pressure for a special exception, but management itself may initiate action. One company that had a fixed two-year limit found that its 1953-54 layoff was extending beyond two years. The company went to the union and secured extension of the time to five years, with the company having the option to "clean house" at the end of two years. By "housecleaning" it was intended that the company would write to all employees on layoff to find out which of them were interested in retaining their seniority. If no interest was expressed, it reserved the right to terminate seniority.

The trend toward protection of recall rights and other rights flowing from seniority, even after very long or indefinite periods of unemployment, indicates a revision in management thinking. Many companies have concluded that their concern with the loss of skills during sustained layoff was exaggerated. Others yielded to union pressure because they were persuaded that the equities inherent in seniority outweighed the adverse effect on efficiency. Finally, some companies say they were willing to liberalize this part of the contract to forestall union pressure to broaden the seniority unit for layoff purposes. Adherence to narrow units, which the companies prefer, often means the layoff of people with long service.[4]

4 Some companies whose labor agreements provided for less liberal seniority cutoff periods found that in the case of protracted layoffs the union would bring considerable pressure to share the work when people were about to lose seniority. If the union was successful, laid off persons were recalled for a few weeks to share work with the senior

Use of Superseniority

Superseniority means the assignment of artificial and superior seniority dates to certain selected employees. The origin of this concept in the 1930's probably is attributable as much to managements as it is to unions. Confronted with growing union demands for seniority systems, many companies were anxious to exempt key employees from the impact of layoffs based on seniority. They argued that a "flying squadron" composed of men capable of performing a variety of duties was essential at the time of a general curtailment of the work force. From this bargaining table argument emerged the so-called "X" list, the "exempt employee" list, or the "flying squadron" list. In effect, these allegedly indispensable persons were accorded superseniority for layoff purposes.

At the same time, unions were troubled by the very real danger that their key representatives within the plant (stewards, local union officers, etc.) might be eliminated by layoffs if strict seniority dates were observed. They in turn sought superseniority or preferential seniority for these employees to insure that experienced union officialdom would not be disrupted by layoff. Occasionally the original arrangements for superseniority not only placed limits on the number to be given this privileged status, but also balanced the management and union groups. Thus, if thirty union officers were accorded preferential seniority, the company was entitled to give similar status to thirty key employees it designated for this privilege.

This equal-number approach resulted in some interesting controversies. The union designees were usually elected or appointed for fixed periods and were not replaced during that period except in case of death, retirement, or quits. On the other hand, some companies attempted to name their key personnel designees for each particular work curtailment. Who were considered the key personnel changed from one time to the next, depending, it was discovered, on whether their actual seniority date would protect them from layoff. If it did, they would be dropped from the list, and new persons would be added by the company to fill its quota. Inevitably this unintended advantage given to the company was protested by the union. It led to the requirement in some cases that the company

employees, thus protecting their seniority. They would then be laid off again and would start a new layoff period. To avoid this disruption, these companies often liberalized the protection of seniority during layoffs.

freeze its list, just as the union's was frozen. Substitutes or replacements could be designated only when a similar change was made on the union list. A second trend was the union's successful insistence that it be allowed to challenge the company's judgment concerning the composition of the "key" or "X" list. This demand arose from the belief that the designations were prompted less by the indispensability of such employees at the time of layoff than by considerations of favoritism.

During the past twenty years the use of superseniority for designated union representatives has become widespread. However, its use by management is far less prevalent. In the most recent analysis of contract clauses on this subject, the Bureau of Labor Statistics found that 590 agreements out of 1,347 studied provided for superseniority for union representatives; only 230 permitted this exception for key employees named by the company.[5] It is hard to understand why management has not insisted more on a *quid pro quo*. One company explained that careful use of the seniority clause at the time of layoff permits retention of employees with outstanding abilities and skills, and that it prefers this administrative discipline to the potentially irritating practice of maintaining a management superseniority list.[6]

One prevailing characteristic in these preferential treatment arrangements for union officials is that superseniority is applicable only to layoffs and recalls. Seldom does it extend to other uses of competitive status seniority, such as promotions, shift preference, and the like. There has been little or no pressure on the part of the unions to extend its application. This is understandable. What is a logical and tenable union position in the case of layoffs would have no merit in the case of promotions, for example. In fact, generally it would be a very unpopular and politically inept move if union

[5] Joseph W. Bloch and Robert Platt, "Layoff, Recall, and Work-Sharing Procedures— Part III," *Monthly Labor Review* (February 1957). Each of the agreements studied covered a thousand or more employees; the railroad and airline industries were not included in this study.

[6] In one interesting negotiation, the company industrial relations director put in a request for superseniority for all supervisors and apprentices. He intended that this be a bargaining device, expecting to withdraw the demand later in negotiations. Although his strategy was conveyed to top management people, they subsequently took the position that this was a reasonable demand and that they were going to insist on it, since the union enjoyed superseniority for its people. This company demand became the major issue in negotiations, and a strike was averted at the last minute only when the industrial relations director convinced management that it was not a strikeable issue.

officials were to try to exploit their superseniority position to gain promotional advantages over fellow union members.

Nevertheless, in a few agreements the original purpose of superseniority for union officers—preservation of administrative structure during layoffs—has been enlarged to include special job status rewards to these men. The Central States Area over-the-road agreement with the teamsters, for example, provides that "stewards shall be granted superseniority for all purposes, including layoff, rehire, bidding, and job preference, if requested by the local union within sixty (60) days after the effective date of this agreement." An industrial relations director of another company, which had enlarged the use of superseniority to include promotions and parking lot privileges, explained cynically, "It was a form of legal payoff. If we make big shots out of them, it keeps them happier." This is a regrettable development.

It would be interesting to know whether this special employment security for union officers provided by current agreements has encouraged employees whose actual seniority dates are relatively low to seek such positions. Evidence on this point is too slight to permit even a speculative judgment. If it has stimulated junior employees to seek union office, it would be equally interesting to know the extent of their success and the effect of their inexperience on the conduct of labor relations.[7]

Effect of Merger and Succession on Seniority Rights

In recent years there have been increasing numbers of consolidations of two plants of the same company or of two separate companies, which raise serious questions about the relative seniority of the employees affected.[8] By their very nature, they cannot be anticipated in detailed contract language, except where plants of the same company are under a master agreement with one union. The arrangements must be made when the details of the consolidation are known.

[7] Superseniority is sometimes granted to employees other than those mentioned in this section. In a relatively few agreements, student trainees, disabled employees, and disabled veterans may be accorded preferential status for layoff purposes. In one agreement the employees on the company basketball team were granted superseniority.

[8] For an excellent discussion of the problem see Mark L. Kahn, "Seniority Problems in Business Mergers," *Industrial and Labor Relations Review* (April 1955), pp. 361-78.

However, a few unions, such as the International Typographical Union and the railroad shop craft unions, have taken a strong position on the handling of conflicting seniority interests in the case of merger. Considerable internal discipline within the union is needed. In the railroad union agreements, employees are often allowed to follow the work with full seniority rights if their jobs can be identified in the merged organization. The ITU has had a long-standing policy that when two newspapers are merged, the seniority lists will be dovetailed. But when one paper buys another, the staff of the purchasing paper has priority over the staff of the purchased paper.[9] The Switchmen's Union has adopted the following policy:

> Where mergers or consolidations are effected in terminals or switching districts by two or more railroads, switchmen should be assigned to the merged work on basis of the engine hours worked by the respective lines in the respective terminals for a consistent period or periods prior to the merger or consolidation, the object being to preserve the equity of all switchmen in the rearrangement of any work covered by changes due to mergers or consolidations. . . .[10]

When a merger occurs, the conflict of interests is so great that mutually satisfactory arrangements between two unions or even two locals of the same union are difficult to achieve. Seldom does the company raise any serious obstacles, except to make known its concern for employee equities and its desire to retain experienced workers. Whether equitable dovetailing of seniority lists can be accomplished depends on a number of factors: (1) the disparity between the average seniority date level in one plant and that in the other plant; (2) the geographic distance involved, which affects greatly the probable number of transfers; (3) the economic climate, which may make the competing groups more or less concerned with the prospects of imminent layoffs; (4) the extent of centralized authority over the locals exercised by the national union or unions involved. Of these four factors, the last counts most. One cannot expect two rival locals to enter into a peace treaty. It is possible, however, to expect them to observe rules laid down in advance by the international union.

---

[9] Sumner H. Slichter, *Union Policies and Industrial Management* (1941), p. 157.
[10] Switchmen's Union of North America, Constitution, as revised June 11, 1951, Section 116b.

Seniority Rights of Employees Outside the Bargaining Unit

This concept involves three separate problems: (1) The rights of those employees who have never worked in one or more of the bargaining units of the company, as in the case of a supervisory or administrative employee hired directly into his nonbargaining unit position. Obviously his service with the company for the purpose of pensions and the like will start from the date of hire. But question arises as to his right to count his service with the company if he is cut back from his nonbargaining unit position. May he use this service as competitive status seniority to acquire a position in the bargaining unit? The answer to this question is invariably in the negative. In brief, a person who has never worked in the bargaining unit is seldom, if ever, allowed to exercise his service rights to the detriment of a member of the unit.

However, some managements have taken the initiative to assure that if such a person elects to go on an open position in the unit, his company service will be protected. One such agreement provides that "any employee now or hereafter employed by the Company outside the bargaining unit, and who is later transferred to a job classification in the bargaining unit, shall immediately receive his total seniority as his plant seniority." This type of clause is the exception. One company, troubled by the problem and with a typical inability to cope with it, observed, "Management has a heart, but the union won't let us take care of these people by putting them in the bargaining unit."

(2) A more prevalent problem involves the seniority rights of the employee who moves from a bargaining unit to a nonbargaining unit job. This problem arises most frequently in the case of advancement of employees to excluded supervisory positions. It is apparent that the service rights necessary to establish eligibility for benefit programs (benefit seniority) can be maintained by the company without regard to the union. The union's interest in the seniority rights of the supervisor, foreman, or other nonbargaining unit jobholder is based on the possible future exercise of those rights in such a way as to affect people within the bargaining unit. These issues develop: Does the person who leaves the unit for a supervisory position lose his accumulated seniority rights; or does he retain only the rights that he had at the time of the departure? If the latter, is this retention for a

limited or an indefinite period; or does he not only retain but also continue to accumulate seniority rights as a supervisor? Is such accumulation for a limited or an indefinite period? Assuming the retention and possible accumulation of seniority, in what way may these rights be exercised in relation to employees in the unit? If business curtailment forces a reduction in the number of supervisors or foremen, are those affected permitted to displace a less senior or the least senior man in the bargaining unit; or may the foreman return to the unit only if there is a vacancy? All of these questions have been the subject of considerable discussion in recent years. The great increase in promotions from the ranks caused by the expansion in employment during World War II and the Korean War and the subsequent inevitable cutbacks focused attention on these issues.

Most companies are anxious to allow employees who have been elevated to supervision the right to retain and accumulate seniority, although some express the view that once a man joins the management ranks, his security is entirely a responsibility of the company and he should not have to return to the bargaining unit later. This complacent view has embarrassed a few companies. One company's union contract, for example, had no provision on the subject. The company had never had a business retrenchment affecting supervision. Then came a severe business reversal, and many supervisors, some of whom were promoted from the bargaining unit, were out of luck. Managements should also consider that the degree of protection for supervisors has an important bearing on their selection of supervisors. If a man cannot be returned to the unit with seniority rights retained and if he proves to be a poor supervisor, a company is confronted with a dilemma: either keep an incompetent person on the supervisory staff or discharge him.

Unions, on the other hand, have mixed reactions. Their views range from the extreme position that once a man elects to leave the unit he should cease to have any rights to return to the unit, to the other extreme position, which coincides with that of management. This admixture of views in union circles is understandable. The union has as its immediate concern those currently within the unit and it does not wish them to be affected adversely by "outsiders." At the same time, a complete erasure of seniority rights would tend to discourage interest in promotion from the ranks to supervisory positions. In addition, as one union spokesman said, "the attitude of persons promoted will tend to be anti-union if we are responsible for the loss of their seniority, and this resentment could make it difficult for us."

The prevailing practice seems to be the retention of seniority rights. To a somewhat more limited extent, the continued accumulation of seniority for a specified or unlimited time is allowed. One company reported that one of its most serious differences with the union related to the union's attitude toward the accumulation of seniority by foremen. The union would not permit it. The company said it wanted to promote young men to be foremen. But these men felt they had not acquired enough seniority to take the promotion with the possibility that sometime in the future they might have to go back into the ranks with no more seniority than they had when they became foremen. The company observed that the higher union officials appreciated the merit of allowing accumulation of seniority, but the management could not get the union at the local level to budge from its position.

What is most surprising is management's failure to press for seniority protection for those elevated to management ranks. Very often this is not mentioned in the labor agreement.

(3) In a plant with more than one bargaining unit the seniority rights of an employee who moves from one unit to another often becomes an issue. As in each of the situations described above, the issue does not involve benefit seniority, which is not contested. But an entirely different attitude prevails when it comes to competitive status seniority. For example, in an aircraft company with two locals of the same international union, one representing production workers and the other salaried personnel, it is understood that an employee moving from one to the other starts with zero seniority in the new unit. In the new unit he must compete for status as a new employee, even though he may have many years of service with the company. The barriers erected within an enterprise between two or more bargaining units involving different and often competing international unions are even greater. Some companies have discovered that these barriers to the transference of competitive status seniority are an effective argument against "splinter movements." It can be pointed out to a disgruntled craft group that withdrawing from the industrial union may destroy the fluid job seniority rights of its members. Yet, as we shall see in Chapter 6, these fluid seniority rights

may encourage splinter movements if they involve displacement of craftsmen by bumping.[11]

Special Arrangements in Administering Seniority Rosters

It is generally agreed that the company should provide the union with a current seniority roster on a periodic basis. In addition, many unions have secured the weekly transmittal of all "personnel transactions." With these two lists in hand a union is able to check promotions, layoffs, recalls, transfers, and other transactions that might involve seniority rights. As one union leader stated, "the average fellow doesn't necessarily know when he's been given the business by the company; he doesn't always know his rights. So we have two girls in the union office check the rosters and transactions each week to tell us when a senior man has missed out on a job. Whenever we find a case, we talk with the man to see if he might not want to file a grievance. If we didn't do this, the company would throw past practice and the absence of a grievance in our face in some future case." Thus, insistence on records becomes an integral part of union vigilance in safeguarding seniority rights. In some instances the union's access to the records leads to the manufacture of grievances that would never have occurred to the employee involved.

The continuing, although diminishing, practice of some unions and companies of maintaining by explicit agreement separate rosters for male and female employees should be mentioned. This sex distinction, which usually was intended to restrict the competitive status seniority of women *vis-à-vis* men was widespread twenty years ago. While it has disappeared in most labor agreements, the Bureau of Labor Statistics study referred to earlier found in 1956 that about 8 per cent of the agreements provided for separate seniority lists for each sex. These agreements were most common in the food industries, where they appeared in one-fourth of the agreements, and in transportation equipment agreements.[12] Under these seniority rosters, men competed only with men, and women competed for status only with women. In a few agreements, race discrimination is still practiced by the maintenance of separate Negro and white seniority rosters.

[11] The legal implications of a craft severance from a plant-wide unit are discussed below.

[12] In these industries, the alleged noninterchangeability among occupational groups accounts for the separate seniority rosters for men and women.

Legal Aspects of Seniority[13]

Earlier in this chapter reference was made to seniority as an employee "property right." This fact, coupled with the dynamic nature of collective bargaining, raises some interesting legal questions that can affect the behavior of both unions and companies at the bargaining table. The purpose of this brief discussion is only to create an awareness that the decisions of the parties may have legal implications under some circumstances.

In any given contract the parties may adopt a method of seniority measurement or a system of seniority application that creates future expectancies on the part of the employees. For example, an employee with fifteen years' departmental and company seniority, the most senior man in the department, may feel that he is well protected from layoff under a strict departmental layoff unit arrangement. At least he is protected as long as there is any available work in the department that he is capable of performing. In the negotiation of a subsequent contract, the parties may revise the seniority system to permit plant-wide bumping on a restricted basis. The same employee now runs the risk of being bumped at the time of work curtailment by another employee with more than fifteen years' company seniority. In brief, his original property rights have been impaired by the later bargain.

Is this impairment construed by the courts as analogous to the confiscation of property without compensation by political units? In general, the answer is no. Although courts have termed seniority rights as "somewhat intangible," the majority of the court decisions on this subject have viewed seniority as a right that justifies use of equity's power. Nevertheless, they have usually held that the collective contract is the property of the union, and therefore the expectancies of employees under the agreement are subject to change by the union in its subsequent dealings with the employers. In the illustration cited, it is most unlikely that the employee whose so-called property rights were impaired would have any redress under the law.

A review of a number of court decisions on this subject justifies

[13] For a technical discussion of this subject, see *Harvard Law Review* (January 1952), *Notes:* "Duty of Union to Minority Groups in the Bargaining Unit," pp. 490-502; *Columbia Law Review* (February 1941), *Notes:* "Collective Bargaining Agreements: The Seniority Clause," pp. 304-17. See also Archibald Cox, *Labor Law, Cases and Materials* (1958), pp. 967-74.

the conclusion that the judicial view of the labor contract (as resembling legislation rather than the more orthodox private contract) and the reluctance of the courts to interfere with the internal operation of a union serve to give labor and management considerable freedom to modify seniority rights. The courts usually will interfere only if fraud is established, if procedural protections are ignored, and if arbitrary or discriminatory action is proved. The last basis was emphasized in the famous case, Steele *v.* Louisville and Nashville R.R., decided by the U. S. Supreme Court.[14] An agreement negotiated by the parties had restricted seriously the seniority rights of Negroes within the bargaining unit. The operation of the agreement was enjoined. The court reasoned as follows:

> We think that the Railway Labor Act imposes upon the statutory representative of a craft at least as exacting a duty to protect equally the interests of the members of the craft as the Constitution imposes upon a legislature to give equal protection to the interests of those for whom it legislates.

In the discussion of the definition and measurement of seniority, mention was made of the special problems that arise when two separate companies or two plants of the same company with different bargaining agents are merged. The dubious protection under the law of the seniority property rights of employees was highlighted in Britt *v.* Trailmobile Company.[15] Two plants, one of the trailer company and the other of its wholly-owned subsidiary, the Highland Body Company, were consolidated. Under a National Labor Relations Board ruling the two plants had been treated as one unit with separate AFL bargaining committees in each plant. With the consolidation, Highland employees were to go on the Trailmobile payroll, and understandably they claimed they should have seniority rights from the time they started with Highland Company. The trailer company employees, however, who outnumbered the Highland workers ten to one, insisted that the seniority of the transferees should start as of the date of transfer. It would mean the loss of many years of seniority for the Highland employees. The matter was referred to top AFL officials; they concluded that basic equities supported the Highland employees' views and that the seniority lists should be dovetailed. Whereupon the much larger trailer group voted to leave the AFL

[14] 323 U. S. 192, 204 (1944).
[15] 179 F. 2d 569 (6th Cir.), cert. denied, 340 U. S. 820 (1950).

and formed a CIO unit. The NLRB held an election, the CIO union was certified, and it promptly negotiated an agreement with the company, making the Highland employees' seniority start as of the time of transfer. The agreement was immediately challenged, but all efforts to have it set aside by the court failed.

The basis for the court judgments in the now-famous Trailmobile case was the conclusion that seniority arises only out of contract or statute. This view was affirmed in a unanimous decision of the United States Supreme Court in Aeronautical Lodge *v.* Campbell.[16] Justice Frankfurter said:

> In providing that a veteran shall be restored to the position he had before he entered the military service "without loss of seniority," Section 8 of the Act uses the term "seniority" without definition. It is thus apparent that Congress was not creating a system of seniority but recognizing its operation as part of the process of collective bargaining. We must therefore look to the conventional uses of the seniority system in the process of collective bargaining in order to determine the rights of seniority which the Selective Service Act guaranteed the veteran.
> Barring legislation not here involved, seniority rights derive their scope and significance from union contracts, confined as they almost exclusively are to unionized industry.

Apart from the legal significance of the Trailmobile Company case, it illustrates an important labor relations problem. Since seniority rights in many areas are used to resolve conflicting interests among individual employees or groups of employees, basic equities are likely to be recognized more at the higher levels of both the union and the company. Employees within a department or, as in the Trailmobile case, within an entire plant tend to be motivated by selfish interests. Department heads or plant managers, concerned as they are with efficient operations of their particular units, often find it difficult to take the broad view required by more recent seniority concepts. For example, a department head will be loathe to lose his more able people and to accept "outsiders" on the basis of seniority rights.

A question of some importance since enactment of the Taft-Hartley Act is the effect of the severance of craft members from the plant-wide unit on their accumulated seniority rights. For reasons stated

---

[16] 337 U. S. 521 (1949). In this case an employee protested his layoff on the ground that a contract negotiated while he was in military service, which granted union chairmen superseniority, should not be allowed to impair his competitive status rights.

above, the prevailing view is that while the employees involved retain their service with the company, what *rights* are to flow from such service will depend on the contract negotiated between the newly-created unit and the company. It is generally recognized that the severed group could not claim that its members had rights over members of the other unit. For example, they could not claim the right to bump into the other unit at the time of layoff. Similarly, the members of the larger plant-wide unit would have lost what seniority rights they had with respect to the craft group as a consequence of the severance. In the terms of one legal authority, "the walling-in accomplished by severance also walls out." The action of severance, therefore, in some respects may enhance and in other respects may diminish the job security rights created by the bargained seniority system.

General Implications of Seniority

Although some of the implications of the widespread and varied use of seniority will be discussed in succeeding chapters, several general observations should be made here.

(1) Numerous studies show that seniority has lessened the degree of mobility among industrial workers. Rights created by length of service strengthen attachment to a given employer. Clark Kerr, discussing what he terms the "Balkanization of labor markets," says, "the craft worker moves horizontally in the craft area, and the industrial worker vertically in the seniority area. Inter-occupational movement is reduced for the former and employer-to-employer movement for the latter. . . . Job rights protect but they also confine. Reduction of insecurity also brings reduction of independence."[17] In this same article Kerr observes, "The more secure are the 'in', the greater the penalty for being an 'out'." It is Kerr's conclusion that seniority rules probably reduce the freedom of the worker and retard his efficiency more than the craft rules "which are the customary target of criticism." The full social and economic implications of this development cannot be covered here.

(2) The effect of seniority rules on efficiency within a plant or an industry has not been studied enough to justify any firm conclusions.

[17] *Labor Mobility and Economic Opportunity, Essays* (1954), pp. 92-110. Other essays in this volume shed further light on the effect of seniority on labor mobility.

More thorough research should be done in this area. Many manage-ments are of the view that whatever loss in individual efficiency has occurred is offset by the gain in morale among employees. However, they are troubled by the inroads of the seniority criterion on the pro-motion of employees, and, more particularly, they are convinced that seniority rules impair the flexibility of assignments needed for effi-cient operation. Managements often have acceded too readily to the extension of the seniority principle. For example, the use of "in-stantaneous seniority" in making work assignments shows the ex-tremes to which the principle has been carried. When a company by practice or contract commitment is obligated to offer each and every open assignment in the course of the day to persons in the order of their seniority, inevitably efficiency and flexibility must suffer. This problem became so great in several companies that a showdown with the union was necessary to restrict or eliminate the costly practice.

(3) As it is defined, competitive status seniority inevitably creates serious internal problems for the union.[18] While seniority rules are designed to regulate and systematize competition among men for job rights, this fact does not relieve the union from pressure. The for-mulation of the rules themselves requires the compromise of a great variety of competitive interests among union members. Even in the use of benefit seniority there are competitive interests that cause difficulty for the union. In the 1959 negotiations in a farm equip-ment company the union was confronted by a sharp division be-tween junior and senior employees over the question of whether the vacation liberalization to be sought should be the addition of a fourth week for those with more than 25 years' service or the re-duction of the qualification for a third week from 15 years' to 10 years' service.

(4) A careful study is needed to determine the effect on younger people of the wide use of seniority. Undoubtedly it is great. It is known, for example, that some ambitious and able young workers avoid or leave jobs in certain companies or industries because they feel their chances for advancement are restricted by the seniority system. One international union president, an iconoclast among union leaders, said: "We have gone too far. Seniority has been over-emphasized. Of course job security for the long-service man is im-

---

[18] Leonard R. Sayles, "Seniority: An Internal Union Problem," *Harvard Business Review* (January-February 1952).

portant, but we're alienating young, ambitious people in the process. There must be some other formula, one which will afford the senior man income protection and at the same time will not stifle a young man's ambition." Management also expresses this concern. Unfortunately, its attitude is often one of defeatism, usually expressed in the phrase, "What can we do? We're helpless in the face of union demands."

(5) Seniority rights, because employees are sensitive about them, may easily become a cause for strike when negotiations break down. Perhaps it is for this reason that management concessions have been so extensive. The wise management will realize that attempts to discontinue costly seniority practices probably will mean a strike, and it should be prepared to face up to this. In fact, if management wants to have a long, bitter strike, all it has to do is promise seniority to the strikebreakers and tell the strikers their seniority will be lost unless they return by a certain date. Promises made to workers hired while a strike is in progress can prolong the strike disastrously.

(6) One of the most disturbing consequences of the seniority principle is its use during the past twenty years to impose unexpected restrictions upon the employer. Although a company may have insisted on the freedom to discipline and avoided the usual "just cause" qualifying phrase, it may find its efforts have been in vain. Arbitrators have held that seniority rights limit management's freedom to discharge. As will be noted in Chapter 10, management may discover that its freedom to subcontract is curbed even though the contract is silent on the subject. In part, this is because of the weight given to seniority by arbitrators. One industrial relations director has said, "It's bad enough to be saddled with the seniority rules we know about, but now we find seniority can be used to support almost any kind of restriction the union dreams up." There is enough experience by now to alert managements to the need for a clearer contractual and administrative understanding of the uses to which seniority will be put.

6 / Work-Sharing and Layoff Systems

THE ALLOCATION OF limited work opportunities has always been of great concern to unions. The seasonal and cyclical fluctuations that characterize many industries, and sometimes the secular decline in an industry, give rise to a series of basic questions: Who shall be entitled to the remaining available work? To what extent, if any, shall employees share in the available work before layoffs are effected? If work is to be shared, should this be done by reducing the number of hours worked per week or by rotating employees? If layoffs are to be made, what criteria should be used in selecting workers to be laid off? What unit of the enterprise should be adopted for initiating layoffs—the job, the department, the division, the plant, the company as a whole? If the unit chosen is narrow, to what extent should the senior man affected by the layoff be allowed to "bump" a junior man elsewhere? What advance notice, if any, should the company be required to give to the employees and/or the union before it may implement a work-sharing or layoff action? What distinction should be made between short-term, long-term, and permanent layoffs? These are typical of the questions that are the concern of this chapter.

Most unions have been opposed to giving employers a free hand in allocating limited work opportunities. In the study *Union Policies and Industrial Management,* Sumner H. Slichter cited these four reasons for such opposition: (1) favoritism is almost certain to result from unrestrained freedom of the employer, (2) efforts of individuals and groups to gain the favor of foremen injure shop morale, (3) concentration of the burden of unemployment on a few workers because they happen to be less efficient than others is harsh and inhuman, particularly since unemployment must be regarded as a social misfortune, and (4) at the time of layoff worker security is more important than management efficiency, and the threat of layoff should not be used as a means of stimulating efficiency.[1]

The most recent available survey shows that approximately 80 per cent of labor agreements provide for either work-sharing or layoff arrangements or a combination of both. Of the 20 per cent that made no such provision whatsoever, about four-fifths were concentrated in such nonmanufacturing industries as construction, transportation (other than railroad and airline), retail trade, and hotel and restaurant.[2]

Two characteristics of the industries mentioned, except for transportation, may explain the lack of such procedures in the agreements: (1) the attachment to a single employer is short-lived, as in the case of construction, and the union itself serves as the agent for distributing work opportunities;[3] or (2) there are a large number of part-time employees, as in retail trade, and hotel and restaurant businesses.

This chapter will cover (1) the general determinants of work-sharing and layoff systems, (2) union measures to protect regular or "seniority employees" from work reduction,[4] (3) work-sharing systems, (4) layoff systems, and (5) special problems in handling allocation of limited work opportunities.

Determinants of Work-Sharing and Layoff Systems

Methods of handling equal division of work and the layoff selection process vary considerably from industry to industry, company to

---

[1] Sumner H. Slichter, *Union Policies and Industrial Management* (1941), p. 99.

[2] Robert Platt, "Layoff, Recall, and Work-Sharing Procedures, Part I: Prevalence of Layoff and Work-Sharing Provisions; Forestalling and Minimizing Layoffs," *Monthly Labor Review* (December 1956), pp. 1385-93. This is the first of four articles in the *Review*, which will be referred to where relevant in this chapter. The reports are based on an analysis by the U. S. Bureau of Labor Statistics of 1,743 agreements in effect in 1954-55, each agreement covering a thousand or more workers. Manufacturing (involving 2.8 million employees) accounted for 1,182 of these. In appraising the data, three considerations should be kept in mind: (1) agreements covering large numbers of employees tend to be more detailed and specific, leaving few matters to *ad hoc* negotiations, (2) a statistical survey such as this cannot reflect the informal arrangements that modify or in some cases replace the formal agreement provisions, (3) in the case of multiplant situations, supplemental plant agreements are not included in the study.

[3] It is noteworthy that large building contractors who maintain a permanent work force enter into agreements with the union on the subject of layoff procedures. In the case of small employers, union control over layoff may well conflict with an employee's desire for freedom of movement from one employer to another.

[4] The term "seniority employees" refers to those who have begun to acquire seniority

company, and even from plant to plant within the same company. The necessity for adapting the systems to the needs of a particular plant contributes greatly to the complexity of the problem. A company and a union may be able to imitate what other parties have done in drafting a union security-checkoff clause or in formulating a vacation and holiday provision. But they are inviting trouble for themselves if they believe a layoff procedure clause can be borrowed from another contract and applied with similar success.

Variations in work-sharing and layoff provisions are due in part to: (1) the nature of business fluctuations, (2) technology and process, (3) the degree of product-mix, (4) job skills, (5) the method of wage payment, (6) wage structure considerations, (7) tradition, (8) employee benefit plans, (9) internal union considerations, and (10) the geographic proximity of plants. One or more of these determinants will be present in any given collective bargaining relationship.

Nature of Business Fluctuation

Where there is a high seasonality in business operations, as in the apparel industry, there is likely to be a greater interest in work-sharing programs. (See "Work-Sharing Systems" below.) Reliance on a seniority system to effect layoffs tends to concentrate the hardship on the same people year-in and year-out. The systems in the automobile industry take into account the annual model changeover periods, which lead to a temporary reduction in work. Even in nonseasonal industries, the systems may vary according to the type of layoff. Thus, seniority rights may play a more important part where there is a permanent elimination of jobs because of technological change.

Technology and Process

In some industries or plants the nature of the work may dictate the type of work-sharing or layoff system used. In a continuous operation, as in the glass or steel industry, flexibility is necessarily limited. For example, in the steel industry it is not possible to reduce economically the output of an open hearth. Instead, a cutback means the elimination of a whole open-hearth operation. This militates against work-sharing and encourages a direct layoff of excess employees.

---

as contrasted to part-time, temporary, or probationary employees. See Chapter 5 for a discussion of acquisition of seniority.

Degree of Product-Mix

In a plant devoted to the manufacture of one product only, a cut-back is likely to affect all jobs, even though the effect is seriatim in nature, given the sequence of operations. Under these circumstances, work-sharing on a plant-wide basis and, if necessary, layoffs are more easily effected. But where there is considerable product-mix, the cut-back is less likely to affect all jobs equally. In a typewriter company making portables as well as manual and electric standard machines, a cut in the production schedule for portables may affect only certain jobs. A large lithograph company pointed out that the variations in the different kinds of work resulted in an "activity index" of 45 per cent for one operation, while the index for another operation was 97 per cent. It emphasized that for this reason equal division of work had to be on a classification basis.

Sometimes the product-mix may facilitate use of a broader unit for layoff purposes. In the meat packing industry the continuous ups-and-downs for particular kinds of products provide a reasonably even flow of total work. This has led in some companies to the weekly guarantee of work and a system of plant-wide seniority rights.

Job Skills

Where the bargaining unit involves particular skills, such as a craft local in an industrial plant, straight seniority is often used for layoff purposes. On the other hand, where there is an industrial unit that embraces a number of jobs of different skills and also includes jobs of a skilled, semi-skilled, and unskilled nature, the layoff system will reflect this. Freedom to bump in lieu of layoff on the basis of seniority is more prevalent in semi-skilled and unskilled jobs. The skilled jobs are more sheltered from transfers in lieu of layoff and are more likely to share limited work on a job basis.

Method of Wage Payment

In a piece-rate industry the first step taken by management to meet a reduction in orders is usually to cut the production schedule rather than reduce hours or lay off people. In effect, this means a sharing of work. The labor costs for the company remain constant, and management is indifferent as to how many people hang around the shop with idle time on their hands. This may explain further the prevalence of equal division of work in the apparel industries, typically piece-work industries. Piece-work payment facilitates work-spreading because it minimizes employer objections. Under a day-rate system, employees are more inclined to take it easy when work-sharing is used. They want to make what work there is last longer. This often stimulates direct layoffs under the day-rate payment system.

Wage Structure Considerations

As important as protection from layoff is the protection of senior workers from drastic wage cuts resulting from transfers in lieu of layoff. The wider the wage spread in a given plant, the more likely is there to be a liberal bumping arrangement. The automobile industry is in the happy position of having a large percentage of its employees within a fifteen-cent wage spread. It can limit bumping and multiple displacements at the time of layoff. On the other hand, in the steel industry—with 32 labor grades—it would be impossible for the union to allow the company to bump back a labor grade 25 man to a labor grade 5 job. In large measure, bumping systems of the type described below under "Layoff Systems" developed more to protect wages than to protect job security.

Tradition

The influence of past practice has had a considerable effect on work-sharing and layoff systems. A large farm implement company has tried to rationalize the systems in effect in its various plants. Its efforts have failed simply because in the minds of employees whatever system has been used is right. They are suspicious of change. A container company and an aluminum company have had the same experience in their attempts to systematize layoff procedures.

An interesting, long-established layoff procedure is that followed by a certain shoe manufacturing concern. For years all workers with less than one year's service have been considered temporary employees by the company, although they all share work for reasonable periods of reduced activity. The large number of "temporary" employees insures little or no layoff for regular employees. The temporaries are laid off first. This means that the unit of layoff is narrow, and traditional criteria for layoff still prevail in the company:

layoff by department according to seniority, where such factors as ability and physical fitness are equal.

Employee Benefit Plans

The influence of unemployment compensation laws and privately-negotiated supplementary or income-security benefit programs on work-sharing and layoff systems is considerable. These influences will be discussed under "Work-Sharing Systems" and "Layoff Systems" below.

Internal Union Considerations

It is evident that the question of work-sharing and the layoff selection process involves serious political questions for the union. Can a union justify having one job or department on a short workweek while another job or department is on a regular workweek or is working overtime to meet business demands? If a layoff is necessary, to what extent can the union withstand pressures from laid off people who are senior to employees who are working? Or, conversely, can the union justify its insistence on extensive bumping rights when this means displacement of experienced junior people with inexperienced senior people?[5] These considerations may encourage or moderate union demands that seniority be placed above all other criteria, depending on the political stability of the union.

Geographic Proximity of Plants

In some instances it is difficult for a company and union to defend the layoff of senior employees from one plant while there are junior employees still working or new employees are being hired in another plant of the company a few miles away. This has led to the creation of special area-seniority systems, some of which are described in the section on "Layoff Systems" below.

In summary, each of these determinants may be important to the work-sharing and layoff systems described later in this chapter. Because no single influence dominates, it is understandable why the evolution of systems in a plant has taxed the ingenuity of parties in a collective bargaining relationship.

---

[5] One company spokesman observed, "The dirtiest trick we could pull on the union would be to grant its request for layoffs based on straight seniority applied plantwide. It would come close to wrecking the company, but it would wreck the union first."

Union Measures to Protect Regular or Seniority Employees from Work Reduction

In a variety of ways unions have sought to prevent work reduction or layoffs for regular employees. Sometimes these measures have been designed specifically to forestall work reduction; in other instances they have broader objectives but they nevertheless have the effect of restricting the employer's freedom to reduce the work or to lay off regular employees.

Specific Measures to Control Layoffs

Four union-imposed controls are most typical of this category. (1) By far the most common is the requirement that probationary and temporary employees be dropped before regular employees, as defined in the agreement, are subjected to a reduced work schedule or a layoff. Some agreements provide that those with less than a certain number of years of service be eliminated before there is any curtailment of schedule or of total size of the "regular" work force. This cutoff point (one or two years' service) is invariably higher than the defined probationary or temporary periods. In some agreements it is specified that no new employees may be hired when a layoff or work reduction is imminent.

(2) Another fairly common control device is the limitation or outright prohibition of subcontracting when slack business imperils a full work week or the job security of regular employees. This tie-in with layoff procedures is discussed at greater length in Chapter 10. A U. S. Bureau of Labor Statistics study found one hundred such agreements containing the following type of clause:

> The company agrees that it will not contract any work which is ordinarily or customarily done by its regular employees, if, as a result thereof, it would become necessary to lay off or reduce the rate of pay of any such employees.

These agreements are most prevalent in the apparel industry, where there is extensive subcontracting, and in the communication and utility industries.[6]

(3) In Chapter 8 we shall see that the employer's freedom to schedule overtime may depend on the availability of a full week's

[6] Platt, *Monthly Labor Review* (December 1956), p. 1391.

work for all regular employees. The BLS found that only thirty of the agreements studied limited the amount of overtime or prohibited any overtime in slack periods. It is surprising that any company would agree, except under unusual circumstances, not to schedule overtime while people were on layoff or before layoffs could be effected. One company which so committed itself found that in a final inspection department two hours' overtime were needed for one week to meet a shipment due-date, yet during one day of this week there was no work available for the approximately three hundred employees in other departments of the company. It found itself confronted with this dilemma: either miss the due-date and run the risks of a customer loss, or give three hundred people one full day's pay for the privilege of working the inspectors two hours' overtime. It chose the former alternative and made scheduling of reasonable overtime during periods of work curtailment a contract issue in the next negotiations.

(4) Union efforts to regularize employment by weekly guarantees have meant a minimum of work reduction in some instances. Such an effect, for example, has resulted from provisions (see Chapter 16) that persons scheduled for work during a given week shall be guaranteed a full week's work. A large steel company agreement provides that "after an employee, other than a part-time employee, is scheduled for a bi-weekly period according to the scheduling practices for his working area, he will not be laid off or required to work less than the normal 80 hours for such bi-weekly period."

Measures Indirectly Controlling Work Reduction Decisions

Some of the items mentioned above are not included in the agreement solely to restrict the employer's freedom to reduce the work week or to lay off employees. More often than not they apply during periods of peak production as well. For example, more than one-tenth of the agreements analyzed by the BLS contain some limitation on subcontracting.[7] And as we shall see in Chapter 10, even in the absence of any contractual limitation on a company's right to subcontract, arbitrators have sometimes found in more general clauses (recognition and seniority) an implicit restraint on such right while regular employees are out of work. Similarly, general overtime-

[7] The same, p. 1392.

limitation clauses, irrespective of economic conditions, affect layoff and work-sharing procedures. Almost 8 per cent of the agreements studied by the BLS contained clauses that either limited the amount of overtime allowable, called for union permission before overtime could be scheduled, or (in nineteen agreements covering 150,000 employees) prohibited the scheduling of *any* overtime. Twenty-seven contracts affecting 230,000 employees prohibited work on Saturday and/or Sunday. Finally, forty-four agreements either required union permission for, or prohibited the operation of, more than one shift.[8]

These direct and indirect restraints on management's freedom to adjust the work force and the work schedule to business conditions are too often overlooked in a discussion of layoff procedures. Some companies have compartmentalized their study of contract commitments to an alarming extent. A production manager of a pharmaceutical company summed it up well when he said: "We have no trouble with the union in cutting the work week to thirty-two hours or in laying off people on the basis of seniority and other factors. Our trouble is how we get to the damned point of doing these things. As long as any worker is doing one hour of overtime we can't cut hours or lay anyone off."

Work-Sharing Systems

The work reduction problem may be solved through equal division of work alone or by this means in conjunction with other measures such as layoffs.

In relatively few agreements—4 per cent of those studied by the BLS—is work sharing used exclusively, without any layoff procedure. The greatest concentration of these is in the apparel industries, where 90 per cent of the agreements had clauses of this type. This is attributable to the high seasonality of these industries. If layoffs were effected on the basis of seniority during the slow seasons, it would mean that some employees would work steadily while others would work intermittently year in and year out. Layoffs based on seniority would work a special hardship on the low-service members of the union.[9]

[8] The same, p. 1393.
[9] It is interesting that the frequency and concentration of work reduction programs in lieu of layoffs are about the same today as they were twenty years ago. See Slichter, *Union Policies and Industrial Management*, pp. 106-07.

However, even in the needle trades, there is often some provision made for layoffs when drastic work reductions occur due to causes other than seasonal fluctuations. The agreement between the Needle Trades Employers' Association and the International Ladies' Garment Workers Union, for example, provides that "in the event that equal division of work becomes unfeasible, then the seniority principle shall be used as a guide in making layoffs, by crafts or departments." In sharp contrast is the agreement of the Cap and Uniform Manufacturers of Chicago and the hatters' union, which states "there shall be no reduction in the regular working force at any time whatsoever, and all available work shall at all times be divided among the employees as above stated."

A few statistics will serve as a useful background for a discussion of the problems and significant developments in work-sharing arrangements. Of the 1,347 agreements found by the BLS in 1954-55 to contain layoff procedures, 356, or approximately one-fourth, provided for a reduction of hours as a means of forestalling layoff. Most of these (236) specified the level to which hours could be reduced before layoffs were made, the most common being 32 hours per week. Substantially fewer (96) specified not only the level of reduction but also the duration of the period of work-sharing.[10] For example, a textile machinery company's agreement with the United Steelworkers provides that work shall be shared equally by employees in their respective departments until the hours being shared average 32 per week for four consecutive weeks, at which time layoffs are to be effected to bring the work week back to 40 hours. In some agreements the union reserves the right to negotiate the question of work-sharing *versus* layoffs at the time of the work reduction.

The fact that 991 of the 1,347 agreements with layoff procedures made no provision for work-sharing does not mean that managements in those cases are unable to reduce hours before effecting a layoff. It is usually understood that this is a management right. For reasons given below, this right was tested in 1958 in a large number of cases. During the 1958 recession many companies instituted a four-day week or closed down operations entirely every other week. Some unions protested that, in the absence of an explicit contract provision for work-sharing, the companies were obligated to lay employees off on the basis of seniority and related criteria. In most instances the

[10] Platt, *Monthly Labor Review* (December 1956), p. 1393.

company's right was affirmed in arbitration. However, in a few significant cases it was held that past practice served to fetter a company's discretionary right to reduce hours before making layoffs. In a few steel plants the "local practice" clause was used in support of the union's position. A small electrical products company on a number of occasions prior to 1958 had given its employees a chance to vote whether they preferred work-sharing or layoffs. In each instance the employees had voted to reduce the work week to 32 hours for four or eight weeks rather than proceed to layoffs. In 1958 the company wanted to adopt a four-day week to meet a business curtailment. Again the employees voted, but this time the majority preferred layoffs. When the company claimed it was not bound by the vote and proceeded to put in the short workweek, a grievance was filed. Although the contract was silent, an arbitrator held that the company's past behavior created an obligation to abide by the majority wishes of the employees.

In recent years there is marked evidence of a growing desire on the part of unions to restrict management's freedom to reduce the work week or to adopt a rotational system of work-sharing. Whereas twenty years ago a substantial number of unions insisted on reasonable work-sharing before layoffs could be made, today the trend of union preference is more and more toward the restriction of work-sharing arrangements. Unions have always opposed work-sharing that was carried to the extent of "sharing misery," and for this reason a minimum cutoff point was put in many agreements. But the restrictions sought by unions in 1958 and 1959 were intended to go far beyond the usual controls. In some cases the union asked that layoffs be used exclusively without any work sharing. Early in 1958, for example, many plants of General Motors, Ford, and Chrysler went on a four-day work week. The agricultural implement companies either closed some plants for a week or two at a time or scheduled reduced work weeks. The United Automobile Workers promptly protested these reductions and asked that layoffs be made instead.

The principal reason for this shift in union thinking is the fact that the unemployment compensation benefits were liberalized and supplemented by privately-negotiated plans in 1955 and later years. The "share-the-work" principle has less ready acceptance, especially among junior employees, who reason that a 32-hour week provides little more remuneration than state unemployment compensation plus negotiated supplementary benefits during a layoff. Some employees doubt whether it is worth working four days a week for only slightly more than they would receive if they did no work at all.

Similarly, senior employees question the wisdom of sharing work with their juniors when the latter can get a reasonably good week's pay without working. This attitude of senior men is particularly pronounced under the type of supplementary unemployment benefit plan found in the automobile industry. Under this plan, which is described in Chapter 16, five cents an hour for each employee is allocated to the fund from which supplemental benefits are paid. The senior man understandably objects to this allocation to a fund from which he will receive little or no benefit because of his high seniority; he also objects to sharing work with those who can benefit from the fund.[11] Thus, internal pressures are built up within the union to resist the short work week or, as an alternative, to permit use of the funds if the work schedule falls below forty hours.

In the 1958-59 negotiations the unions made some progress toward the limitation of work-sharing. For example, an agricultural implement company agreement contained the following provision: ". . . the Company agrees that it will not schedule any employee to work less than four days in any calendar week in which he is scheduled to work if its purpose in departing from a five-day schedule is to reduce, or to avoid an increase in, inventory of finished products because of sales prospects. . . . No employee shall be scheduled to work such a four-day week for such purpose for more than four weeks at any one time, and an employee who has been scheduled to work from one to four four-day weeks for such purpose shall not again be scheduled to work a four-day week for such purpose unless at least 180 days have elapsed from the end of one such period to the beginning of the next such period." The Supplementary Unemployment Benefits administrator for the United States Steel Corporation reported late in 1958 that one of the unresolved problems that might have to go to arbitration was whether an employee was on "layoff" under the plan when he worked less than thirty-two hours a week.[12]

The issue implicit in the new trend of union thinking is an im-

[11] This attitude on the part of senior men is felt less strongly where supplementation is in the form of the individual account "income security" plans, such as those found in the glass industry.

[12] *Labor Relations Reporter* (December 3, 1958), p. 97.

portant one to management. A reduced workweek very often has many advantages over a reduction in work force. First, if the business curtailment is short-lived, the employer can keep an able, well-trained work force, segments of which might move to other jobs if laid off. Second, the short workweek for a limited period of time may be easier to apply than the layoff procedures described below. If an ill-advised layoff procedure, such as one based on straight seniority and with broad bumping rights, is prescribed, management's interest in the short workweek approach is greater. Third, the nature of some operations and the need to meet delivery dates may require a shorter work schedule for all employees. Use of the short workweek to preserve managerial flexibility may be at the cost of liberalizing the benefit plans to provide payments to employees working less than a normal workweek.

Layoff Systems

Up to this point in the discussion several components of a typical layoff procedure established under collective bargaining have been examined: (1) the observance of certain limitations to avoid or lessen the necessity of layoff, (2) the layoff of probationary, temporary, and, in some cases "seniority" employees with less than a certain number of years of service, and (3) if further curtailment is needed, a program of sharing available work by reducing weekly hours or by rotating employees. These are often the initial steps that an employer is expected to follow.

What procedures are to be followed if each of the foregoing steps has been taken and the business reduction, whether seasonal, cyclical, secular, or, in its most extreme form, permanent, requires still fewer or no man-hours of work for certain jobs? This section is concerned with this next step in the curtailment sequence: the procedure for laying off some employees who have acquired seniority while others are retained for the remaining work. Without doubt, the layoff selection process is one of the most complicated problems in collective bargaining.

A common error in analyzing the impact of unions on layoff and recall arrangements is the failure to think in terms of the total system. The emergence of complete and often complicated layoff

systems is one of the outstanding developments in collective bargaining during the past twenty years.

Formerly, in a typical manufacturing plant, for example, if five
fewer welders or ten fewer bench assemblers were needed, the employer would separate this number of employees from these particular jobs. He could rate workers readily by such criteria as seniority,
ability, physical fitness, marital status, number of dependents, and
place of residence. The five lowest welders and the ten lowest assemblers would then be separated from the payroll. It was a relatively simple process, and many managements took great pride in the
objectivity of the criteria used. This practice of laying off people
from a specific job to the street continued in the early days of unionization. Therefore, twenty years ago the typical layoff clause
would have only a few lines to the effect that "in making layoffs,
seniority will govern provided ability, family status, physical fitness
are approximately equal."

With the passage of time and as unions became stronger and more
secure, serious questions were raised about the equity of layoff by
criteria from job to street. Was it fair that the lowest welder be
dropped from the payroll when he had been in the department
longer then others? This led logically to the question whether it was
equitable for the lowest man in the department to be laid off if he
had more service than others elsewhere in the plant. The arguments
evoked by questions like these led to a transition from layoff by criteria to tailor-made layoff systems.

The nature of these systems will be the primary concern of this
section. The question now becomes what kind of seniority rights
does the *total* system provide? The BLS studies show the risks in
examining the components of a system on a statistical basis. They do
not indicate how layoffs are effected and at times are misleading.
For example, if a firm reports that it lays off workers on a straight
seniority basis, one might think that seniority rights were accorded
very high emphasis. In fact, the opposite could be true. If the layoff
is from the particular job to the street, the use of straight seniority
actually means that the seniority rights of an employee are rated
relatively low. On the other hand, a system based on both seniority
and ability, which allows the worker laid off from his job to bump
elsewhere in the department or plant, offers relatively greater seniority rights. As of today, seniority is probably the dominant cri-

terion in nearly all layoff systems, but the scope and significance of the seniority rights vary considerably from one system to another.

Some of the criticism that unions have forced management to consider seniority rights at the expense of such factors as ability and qualifications appears unjustified if the system is considered, rather than simple criteria. When managements, free from union restrictions, laid off workers from particular jobs to the street, they often retained incompetent people on the jobs unaffected by the work curtailment. Retention of an efficient work force was often considered less important than avoidance of a temporary increase in training costs.

The following discussion concerns two aspects of layoff systems: (1) the requirement of advance notice and/or consultation with the union before layoffs may be made, and (2) the significant developments in layoff systems.

Advance Notice of Layoff

Most unions have insisted that the employer give reasonable notice of his intention to lay off workers. Twenty to thirty years ago this was intended primarily to give employees time to look for another job and to save what resources they could for the layoff period.[13] With the growth of unemployment compensation, and, in some companies, the addition of supplementary benefit plans, these reasons have given way to others.

A number of companies have said that requiring advance notice when possible is a good discipline for management. A typical comment: "These days with complicated layoff formulas you have to plan as much as you can before the actual layoff. Otherwise you'll be in hot water. If you lay off the wrong man, you're stuck with back pay claims. We give three days' notice. During the three days the union and the employees help us catch any mistakes we've made in selecting people for layoff." The union interest is much the same. The unions point out that many headaches and grievances can be avoided by having this brief period for ironing out differences of opinion on application of the layoff system.

The crisis aspects of wholesale layoffs, which led to confusion, mistakes, misunderstandings, and inevitably many grievances, have

---

[13] Slichter, *Union Policies and Industrial Management*, p. 104.

largely disappeared. The latest study shows that more than half of the agreements with layoff procedures provide for advance notice. Most of these allow for emergency layoffs by such qualifying phrases as "wherever practical" or "if possible." Of the 707 agreements requiring notice, 204 required advance notice to the union only, 204 to both the union and the employees affected, and 299 required notice to the employees only. Nearly all specified the length of the notice, with two to five days being the most common.[14] Closely related to this requirement is the growing tendency of managements to confer with the union in advance of a scheduled layoff. This is usually a voluntary step, although a substantial number of agreements call for consultation with the union on whether hours shall be reduced or layoffs effected.

Many plant managers have said that a conference with the union to discuss the layoff plans and, more particularly, to explain the reasons for selecting certain employees has served to reduce grievances. The union is in a better position to explain to a senior worker, for example, why a junior employee has been retained. A plastics company reported that in 1958, when it had to cut its work force by eighty-five, a conference with the union eliminated by agreement several dozen employee transfers in lieu of layoff that would have resulted from strict adherence to the contract.

Significant Developments in Layoff Systems

A layoff system involves the interaction of three considerations: (1) the criteria to be used in selecting the employees to be laid off, (2) the unit to be chosen for layoff purposes, and (3) the right of an employee to bump another in lieu of layoff. No one of these is independent of the other.

The first layoff systems that developed under collective bargaining had a topsy-like growth, working from the typical administrative units of a company, such as the job, the department, the division, or the plant as a whole. Various combinations of seniority rights

---

[14] Rose Theodore, "Layoff, Recall, and Work Sharing Procedures, II: Union Participation in Layoff Procedures," *Monthly Labor Review* (January 1957), pp. 1-7. The required periods of notice in the 707 agreements ranged from one day to as high as 90 days. As might be expected, the high-notice periods were to be found largely in nonmanufacturing agreements, such as in the utilities and communications industries, where business fluctuations are less abrupt and the opportunity for advanced planning is greater.

emerged, depending on the interaction of the above three factors. For example, an agreement might provide that "in all cases of layoffs and rehiring the principle of straight seniority by departments shall be observed." As noted above, exclusive reliance on seniority would not necessarily mean that seniority rights were given great emphasis. The narrowness of the unit and the foreclosure of interdepartmental bumping limited seniority rights. A very different type of clause, using the traditional units, is one that defines seniority as total length of service with the company; departmental seniority is to be used for decreasing the working force, but an employee has the right to be transferred to any other department and replace an employee with less seniority, provided he has the necessary skill and ability to do the other employee's job. In some agreements workers with relatively low company service are laid off by department, those with five to ten years' service affected by a departmental layoff could bump within the division, while those with more than ten years' service could bump anywhere within the plant.

These few illustrations are given only to show the great variety of possible combinations in the use of the administrative units. In a number of instances a narrow unit, such as the department, was used for routine layoffs of indefinite duration, and a broader unit, such as the plant, was used for permanent layoffs caused by technological change.

The union's desire to increase the security of the most senior employees led it to request the widest possible unit, to permit the senior workers affected by a layoff to move anywhere in the plant to a job they were capable of performing. As an alternative, a union often sought liberal bumping rights if the units were narrow. Companies, on the other hand, usually preferred the narrower unit because it decreased costly bumping and movement by senior workers to jobs for which their qualifications were dubious. Adherence to the traditional units often produced unhappy results even for the party that secured acceptance of the unit it desired in the agreement.

If the union gained plant-wide seniority with extensive bumping privileges, it aroused the resentment of employees who were victims of constant displacement. This was particularly true when the senior worker was manifestly ill-equipped to do the job in question. In some extreme situations, even the senior bumper found his security to be short-lived. Sometimes within a matter of hours or days he too was bumped by a still more senior employee newly affected by the layoff.[15]

Selection of the seniority unit and the degree of bumping privileges usually depend on the characteristics of the enterprise and the bargaining unit. If there is great homogeneity in the work force, the unit is likely to be broad; if the units are narrow, the right to transfer in lieu of layoff will be greater. On the other hand, the more varied the skills required in an enterprise, the narrower the unit

[15] The following detailed case history is cited because it dramatizes the evils of the broad unit with relatively unrestricted bumping rights. It is the procedure followed until 1955 in a well-known automobile company. Under the layoff procedure in effect, a worker, if displaced either by the elimination of his job or by the transfer of another worker, could displace any worker with less or no seniority in the bargaining unit. There were no limits on bumping rights except that a man first had to be displaced, which was apparently not too difficult to arrange. A man could bump another employee with as little as one day's less seniority. Bumping rights were not confined to occupational groups but could be exercised plant-wide on as many as 950 different jobs. The way the company identified the various jobs (by letter code based on the job rate) made it almost impossible to determine by payroll records what an employee's actual experience had been. Sometimes very different jobs bore the same code, while very similar jobs carried different codes.

A man who exercised his bumping rights was allowed ten days "break-in or qualifying time" to demonstrate his ability to do the job. Until qualification was proved, the transferee was paid ten cents per hour below the day rate and was not made part of the incentive group. Also the worker originally on the job remained on it to train his replacement until the latter was qualified. The replacement could disqualify himself any time within the ten-day period and proceed to bump still another employee junior to him. To exert bumping rights an employee did not have to have any apparent qualifications or knowledge of the job in question. An inexperienced man could displace an experienced worker. For example, an elevator operator could bump an experienced assembler. While a foreman could disqualify a man, this right was not used frequently.

Still another feature of this chaotic layoff procedure was a thirty-day period allowed employees to exert their bumping rights. Stated differently, they could spend up to thirty days shopping around from one job to another. Movements were so frequent and numerous that the company had to hire three employees just to trace the bumpers. It was estimated that under this seniority system it cost the company more than $1500 to lay off eight people.

The above procedures led to complex strategies and connivances known as "scientific bumping." To manipulate the system to maximum advantage, workers would "buy" bumping rights for ten dollars and make deals with foremen. An integral part of the process was reciprocal relations with other employees. Men often walked around the plant for several days searching for desirable jobs held by workers with less seniority. In some instances deals were made with foremen so that a worker could be displaced and thus be eligible to bump, hopefully to a better job. Another stratagem was known as "hand-on-shoulder bumping." Assume five men, each with a different seniority standing. The most junior of the group would bump onto a job. He would then be bumped by the next senior man, who in turn would be bumped by the next senior man, etc. until the most senior man bumped onto the job. Then the remaining members of the group would repeat the process on another job and on successive jobs.

In the last two quarters of 1953 the company spent $1.5 million carrying two men on jobs at a time when it was trying to effect a sizeable layoff.

is likely to be, and the more restricted will be the bumping rights.

The use of a broad plant-wide layoff system *per se* need not be disruptive if there are strict limitations on bumping and if qualifications to perform the job at the time of the movement are insisted upon. Some companies join the union in preferring the wide unit if there are these safeguards. One of the leading packinghouses is proud of its plant-wide seniority plan, which antedated the union. Although the seniority unit for layoff purposes is the department or the division, the least senior man laid off from such a unit is then free to apply to the industrial relations departments for placement on a plant-wide basis if he has a certain length of service (one year under the company's agreement with one union; two years under its agreement with another union). This company admits that foremen occasionally protest the turnover resulting from plant-wide seniority, but for the most part the system has proved satisfactory. Because the pattern of movements becomes fixed—with customary seasonal variations—employees tend to become trained in advance by normal replacement arrangements; consequently, the cost of plant-wide movement at the time of layoff is minimal and, in the company's judgment, is more than offset by the gain in employee morale.

Another company in the same industry, with most of the same operations and with agreements with the same unions, is very much opposed to plant-wide seniority, except for rehiring to a vacancy. It argues that plant-wide seniority involves unreasonable training costs when employees move to jobs with which they are unfamiliar. In a few instances a union will speak openly against plant-wide seniority, although usually its opposition is based on use of the broad unit with considerable freedom to bump. One union leader representing employees in a number of dairies said that marked differences in occupations within three seniority units (yard and watchmen, plant employees, and drivers) made plant-wide seniority unrealistic.

On the other hand, adherence to the very narrow units has given rise to serious and obvious inequities. If the unit is as narrow as a job, occupation, or even a department, a man with considerable length of service may be laid off from the plant, while junior employees are retained on jobs that he is capable of doing. There is a growing recognition by many companies that the assumption of affinity among jobs within a given department or, conversely, of nonaffinity between those jobs within a department and those outside the department is not necessarily correct.

However, just as plant-wide seniority does not necessarily mean indiscriminate bumping rights, so too the narrowest seniority unit (job or occupational seniority) does not mean an almost complete absence of these rights. Again, other features of the total layoff procedure are important. For example, one plant of a large electrical manufacturing company has what is known as "code seniority." In effect, the unit is the occupational classification, and the person with the least seniority in that classification will be the first laid off. However, when notified of an impending layoff, an employee may assert seniority bumping rights within three days in lieu of accepting layoff. He may bump into an occupation in which he previously has worked and has acquired seniority; by definition this means he must have worked in the other occupational code at least thirty days. Experience has shown that employees are anxious to acquire seniority in a number of different codes, thereby increasing their bumping rights at the time of layoff. Even under this narrow unit approach, therefore, bumping is encouraged.[16]

While many unions and managements still adhere to the traditional administrative units, there has been a significant growth in the number of tailor-made systems based on the totality of seniority rights. In many ways the latter are less complex than those systems which pyramid rights by using the traditional units.

The following special unit forms and seniority arrangements are illustrative, but not necessarily typical of this trend.

THE LINE OF PROGRESSION UNIT. This unit is composed of a grouping of jobs in an orderly line of increasing skills. In a pulp mill, for example, one line of progression might consist of the least skilled job in the line, the Capper, next Second Helper, then First Helper, and finally, the highest job in the line, the Cook. Employees have three types of seniority, "job seniority" (length of service on a given job within the line of progression), "departmental seniority" (length of service in the line of progression), and "mill seniority." The phrase "departmental seniority" is misleading because it does not coincide with the administrative "department" but, as stated, represents the

---

[16] A subtle development in this plant's approach to the unit is worth noting. To facilitate transfers desired by management, the company broadened the job descriptions in many cases, thus diluting the narrow occupational character of the unit. In addition, a more recent agreement with the union permits bumping into "sequentially related codes" when a code is abolished, thus weakening the prior experience requirement. Finally, as a result of an arbitration ruling, it was held that when the company created new codes, men from related codes were privileged to bump into them.

given line of progression. Below the line of progression is a labor pool common to several lines of progression. Usually it is expected that an employee will move from the labor pool to a certain line of progression and then proceed systematically from one job rung of the ladder to the next. This upward movement is discussed more fully in Chapter 7. In the event of work curtailment in a given line, the movement downward is usually the reverse of the upward movement.

A variation of the progression line or promotional channel approach is the concept of the family tree of jobs. A senior man bumps first within his own job group; next, he may bump into successively lower job groups in his family tree, going eventually to the single labor pool. Although this system involves sequential bumping, a company normally is able to minimize employee transfers by planning the movements as far in advance as possible.

THE CONCEPT OF NONINTERCHANGEABLE OCCUPATIONAL GROUPS. This form of unit, coupled with a plant-wide general group, is fairly widespread in the local supplemental agreements of some automobile companies. The selection of these groups is the product of painstaking bargaining and is frequently reviewed. One such supplement, involving a parts plant of a large automobile company, will serve to illustrate. The agreement lists thirty-one noninterchangeable occupational groups, including such jobs as Machinist-Trainee, Toolmaker, Utility-Inspector, etc. All jobs not listed as in a noninterchangeable occupational group automatically are part of the departmental general group. In the event of a reduction in force in a given noninterchangeable group, the least senior man will be laid off from that group. He may then do one of two things: (1) He may replace an employee with less seniority in another noninterchangeable group within his own department, provided he has previously been in that group and has done the work satisfactorily; or (2) he may replace a junior employee, using plant-wide seniority as the guide in the so-called general group. A person laid off from one departmental general group may move to another departmental general group, plant-wide seniority permitting. Either a single job or several closely related jobs may be combined to form a single noninterchangeable group.

In addition, many local automobile agreements contain a number of "flow charts" showing the upward and downward movements permitted in the various divisions of the plant. The accompanying flow chart covering a number of noninterchangeable groupings is for the Assembly Division of one automobile company.

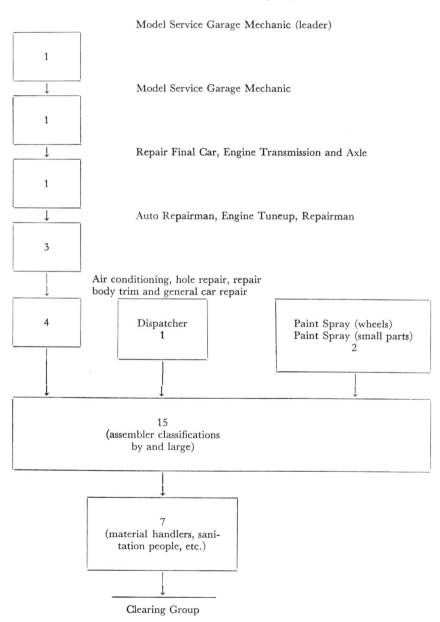

The figures in each box indicate the number of job classifications included in each occupational group. It will be noted that narrow groupings, that is, only one or a very few jobs, are characteristic of skilled production or specialized work, while the less-skilled jobs make up larger groups, e.g., assembler classifications. In the event of layoff, the usual procedure is to eliminate from the division employees lacking enough seniority to remain in the division. The vacated jobs are then filled by the company by reassigning employees to jobs in the boxes to which they have a right to transfer. It will be noted that this procedure is quite different from one which permits a series of downward bumps. The dislocations caused by layoff are minimized. In this illustrative flow chart, the jobs of Dispatcher and Paint Spray (wheels and small parts) are specialized or protected groups. The incumbents are free to bump out of these jobs in the direction indicated, but they cannot be bumped out of their jobs by others.

This system is built on several basic concepts: (1) a desire to avoid the costly features of chain bumping; (2) management's right to reassign employees to fill jobs vacated by layoffs; (3) the isolation of skilled and specialized jobs from bumping; and (4) the establishment of plant-wide or division-wide clearing groups to ensure that the least senior person will be the one eventually laid off.

ZONE SENIORITY. This involves the creation of a number of zones, each of which embraces a varying number of jobs considered by the parties to have similar skill and training requirements. It is not comparable to either the progression line or noninterchangeable flow chart types since workers may move on the basis of their seniority only to jobs within the zone; the least senior man in a zone can bump only into a labor pool to replace the least senior employee in the pool. Allowing replacement only of the least senior employee prevents a number of costly bumps. There is no progressive arrangement of zones or of jobs within the zone.

FLOAT-LINE SENIORITY. The float-line concept establishes a line of demarcation between less-skilled and more-skilled jobs in the plant, usually on the basis of a labor grade cutoff point. Therefore, a float-line might be established at labor grade 5, or at some other level agreed to by the parties. For jobs below the line, bumping rights are very broad; restricted bumping only is allowed among the jobs above the line. The significance of the float-line system, which varies in form from one situation to another, is that it establishes a difference between relatively free and relatively limited bumping rights.

In a large glass company this type of seniority was developed when the company met a union request for a guaranteed annual wage by promising to provide more security for senior workers by broadening the seniority base in layoffs.

The experience of an aluminum company shows the trend toward broadening the seniority rights of employees under a layoff system. For many years departmental seniority was the basis for layoffs, but it was provided that those with five or more years' service could bump employees with two years or less; those with ten or more years could bump employees with up to four years. This formula was developed as a compromise between the company's desire to adhere to department-to-street layoffs and the union's attempt to get a broader layoff unit. However, over the years it was found that workers were acquiring more and more seniority, and there were not many employees with less than four and very few with less than two years' seniority. Thus, the enhancement of seniority rights was gradually disappearing.

As a consequence, in 1956 the parties agreed to a new layoff system. A float line at a certain labor grade was adopted. Considerable freedom to bump, tantamount to chain-bumping, was granted for jobs below the line. This was allowed by the company in exchange for a distinction above the line between competitive and noncompetitive jobs. No bumping is allowed into noncompetitive jobs, and employees exercising bumping rights to competitive jobs must be presently qualified to do the work.

The float-line system in this company has satisfied, in part, the union's desire for more security for senior people; at the same time, it has largely met the company's desire for restricted bumping on key jobs. Arguments still arise over the meaning of the phrase "presently qualified." The union would like to have a trial period to determine whether a man is qualified, but the company has rejected this. Finally, it is of interest that the union joins the company in wanting to avoid chain or "railroad" bumping for competitive jobs above the line. It would prefer to have the company select the job and department to which a senior employee may bump.

AREA SENIORITY. Twenty years ago the idea of providing for employee seniority rights among several manufacturing plants of the same company in a fairly extensive geographic area was almost unknown. System-wide seniority protection was common in the railroad industry for many years, but in manufacturing it is new and still very limited. An electrical company in Cleveland has three separate plant locations under two separate divisions; these plants were integrated into one unit for layoff and recall purposes. A number of companies having plants near each other and the same union representing employees in each plant have developed an inter-plant seniority unit. They sometimes use a zone of comparable jobs to determine bumping rights between plants.

One of the most elaborate area programs is that adopted by the Ford Motor Company in 1951. This plan did not provide inter-plant bumping rights, but it established a preferential hiring policy and, therefore, it was part of a system enhancing seniority rights. It was started after the beginning of the Korean War, when there was a cutback in automobile production in some plants and an increase in war production in other nearby plants. At the union's request, a special conference was held to discuss the problem. Both parties agreed that it was uneconomical to lay off experienced workers while new, untrained people were being hired. Out of this developed the "Agreement Regarding Detroit Area Availability Lists."

Briefly, a worker laid off at one Ford plant in the Detroit area is to be given preference in any hiring at another Ford plant in the area. This preference is on the basis of his seniority with the company.[17] There has been no pressure to give inter-plant bumping

---

[17] All employees on layoff in the area are listed in order of seniority. If they are tradesmen, they are listed separately according to their skills. This agreement now covers every plant in Southern Michigan. Up to 1957, 27,000 workers were offered, and more than 21,000 accepted, jobs in other Ford plants. An employee who transfers under this plan has seniority rights in the second plant from his date of entry. He takes with him his accumulated pension and vacation credits from previous Ford service. If he transfers with his own job, then he retains his accumulated seniority. If he is on layoff from the second plant and returns to his original plant, then he adds his seniority credits from the second plant to credits he had at the first plant. In addition, the first plant can call the employee back if Ford needs him there, but the employee cannot go back at will, except, of course, if he is on layoff from the second plant. If the worker is offered a job within the "Hub" and he refuses it, he is not entitled to his Supplementary Unemployment Benefits. However, plants outside of the "Hub" are not part of the "availability" listings. Unless the worker has notified his local union or Ford offices that he wants a position elsewhere, he is not expected to give up his SUB benefits if he refuses a position that would increase his commuting distance and travel-

rights to these employees. To include inter-plant bumping rights would be anathema to the local unions in relatively new plants. A union official in one such plant observed: "We think it's a good idea to give a laid-off Ford worker from another plant a break in coming to work at our plant, but we'd never agree that he could exercise his seniority over us."

General Motors and the United Automobile Workers' Union adopted a similar understanding in the 1955 Master Agreement. They agreed that employees with seniority laid off from General Motors plants in a given community and filing application at the time of layoff are to be given preference in hiring at other plants. When employed, these workers are to have the status of temporary employees in the plants where they are hired.

As noted earlier, these various seniority systems—line of progression, noninterchangeable groups, zone, float line, and area seniority—illustrate the tailor-made arrangements that have emerged in the contract-development stage of many bargaining relationships. They reflect many of the conditions discussed above under "General Determinants of Work-Sharing and Layoff Systems." They are special systems by design, and some of the noteworthy elements in the design are: (1) By the nature of the units established and by the controls over bumping, a company is able to minimize training costs caused by transfers of senior workers at the time of layoffs. In each of these systems the companies have retained considerable flexibility. (2) The design has enabled the union to achieve its principal objective, namely, maximization of security for the most senior people; at the same time, bumping freedom among some jobs and limitations on bumping for other jobs can be explained in logical terms to the people affected. These special systems represent a constructive compromise of conflicting union-management interests that is often unattainable if traditional administrative units are retained.

Only brief mention will be made of recall procedures. Usually recall to work is roughly in inverse order of layoffs. However, the resumption of business activity seldom mirrors the sequence in the decline of business activity. Consequently deviations from the general principle of "inverse order" are permitted. Far more agreements

---

ing expense. Initially, four plants were part of the Detroit "Hub." This same understanding prevails in other areas where more than one Ford plant exists, for example, in Cleveland and in Buffalo.

qualify the seniority criterion by ability for recall than for layoffs.

Although the recall of employees has not created serious administrative problems for employers, there are several troublesome unanswered questions in a number of companies: (1) Are men on layoff obligated to accept a recall to any job offered? (2) What are the recall rights of employees whose separation was considered permanent and who were given severance pay? (3) Are recalls limited to vacancies, or may senior laid-off employees bump junior employees who have been recalled and later transferred? (4) Must laid-off workers be recalled before the company is privileged to work a department a full forty-hour week? (5) What is the effect of a recall for a few days on the operation of the "advance notice of layoff" requirement?

Most surprising is that many companies neglect to protect their flexibility in recalling employees. A substantial minority of agreements fail to mention the subject or specify "inverse order of layoff." In a number of these cases the union has succeeded in imposing on management unrealistic recall patterns.

Further Layoff Problems

Some of the problems involved in the handling of layoffs have been mentioned above. Other questions, however, warrant attention: (1) What distinction should be made between temporary layoffs and extended layoffs? (2) What are the layoff procedure problems in the case of a transfer or complete cessation of operations? (3) What is the relationship between work assignment practices and operation of the layoff procedure? (4) What policy should be adopted toward upward bumping? (5) What problems arise where there are different bargaining units within the same plant or company? (6) To what extent should a layoff procedure be allowed to serve as a substitute for discipline? (7) What are likely to be the effects of unemployment compensation and SUB plans on layoff procedures?

WHAT DISTINCTION SHOULD BE MADE BETWEEN TEMPORARY LAYOFFS AND EXTENDED LAYOFFS? In the typical manufacturing company there will be problems necessitating the layoff of employees from a particular department or division for a day or two, or for even as little as a few hours. Most agreements make a distinction between the procedures to be followed during periods of relatively brief work curtailment and those to be followed for protracted layoffs. Because the economic impact of a short-duration layoff is unlikely to be serious for an employee, most unions recognize that management needs more flexibility in effecting temporary layoffs. This flexibility may take one of two forms:

(1) A specific provision relieving management of any obligation to follow established layoff procedures if the contemplated layoff is to be for only a limited period. An illustrative clause is the following:

> Whenever an emergency occurs that makes it necessary for the company temporarily to curtail work operations, the seniority provisions of this agreement may be suspended among the affected employees for a period not to exceed seven (7) consecutive working days. The time limit herein stated may be increased by agreement between the parties.

In a large automobile company a temporary layoff for model changes only is defined as a layoff of not more than thirty working days, and a temporary layoff for any other reason is one that does not exceed twelve working days. In the case of a layoff, as defined, the company has the right to lay off employees as their work is completed, irrespective of group seniority. However, if employees are needed to form a skeleton crew during such a layoff, seniority employees are to be used "when practical."

(2) The second method for insuring flexibility at the time of short-duration layoffs is somewhat less liberal. It provides for layoffs on the basis of seniority, using a narrower unit of application than is required for extended layoffs. For example, layoffs of not more than five working days necessitated by temporary or emergency fluctuations are on the basis of seniority by occupation in the plant of an electrical manufacturing company. Furthermore, these provisions do not apply to any worker for more than two successive weeks or for more than ten days in any seven-month period. If the employee is not returned to work after five working days, he may replace a shorter-service employee in accordance with the permanent layoff provisions.

Although a distinction between temporary and extended layoffs is now made in most collective bargaining agreements, a few companies have neglected to secure this flexibility. As a result, they have found themselves held to cumbersome procedures even when the layoffs are for only a few hours. What has become known as "instantaneous" seniority has been a critical problem for an automobile company and for a plant of a large glass company.

If the union is grievance-minded, the impossibility of following the prescribed layoff procedure has led to many "rocking chair" payment grievances. In some instances, the distinctions provided by contracts leave unanswered a number of fundamental questions. If the temporary layoff must be for emergency reasons, what constitutes an emergency? If there is a machine failure attributable to faulty maintenance, is this a *bona fide* emergency? Another question is raised when management misjudges the length of the layoff. If the contract is silent on the matter, what are the rights of employees who were laid off irrespective of seniority on a temporary basis but whose layoff extends beyond the temporary period? A large aviation company was held responsible by an arbitrator for its poor judgment to the extent of $50,000 in back pay claims.

WHAT ARE THE LAYOFF PROCEDURE PROBLEMS IN THE CASE OF A TRANSFER OR A COMPLETE CESSATION OF OPERATIONS? Frequently the operations of an entire department are transferred from one plant to another; or a plant in one area is closed completely and its operations moved to a new plant in a different area. Either of these moves means the complete elimination of jobs and raises the question as to what job rights employees on the displaced jobs have. In the event of a job abolition caused by technological change, revision in method or layout, or discontinuance of a product line, it is customary to permit the displaced persons to exercise seniority rights on a broad unit basis. For example, in an automobile Master Agreement it is specified that "when changes in methods, products or policies would otherwise require the permanent laying off of employees, the seniority of the displaced employees shall become plant-wide."

Far more complicated, however, are the arrangements when the wholesale transfer of operations from one plant to another is involved. Some agreements establish general principles to guide the parties, as in the case of the following new sentence adopted in the 1955 agreement of one automobile company: "Any transfer of employees resulting from the review (by the corporation and the international union of transfer of major operations between plants which result in permanent release of seniority employees) shall be on the basis that all such employees shall be transferred with full seniority."

The purpose of the "review" mentioned in this clause is to give the parties an opportunity to negotiate an equitable solution.

In many ways the movement of employees from one plant to another creates far more internal difficulties for the union than for the company.[18] Inevitably the new local union will resent absorbing transferees with full seniority. Adoption of the above clause was said to be an attempt by the international union to override the parochial, selfish interests of the various local unions.

To illustrate the problem: In a Michigan community there were two plants of the same company, one new and one old, both with different locals. The seniority of the employees in the new plant was relatively low, while there were many high-seniority people in the old plant. Because of space problems, the company proposed shifting a small experimental tool room with seventeen long-service employees from the old to the new plant; it proposed also that the transferred employees retain their seniority. Immediately the local in the new plant resisted the move, arguing that the absorption of long-service people would alter detrimentally the relative seniority status of the members of its local. It also argued that job incumbents in the new plant would be deprived of the chance to advance to the transferred work opportunities. This resistance was countermanded by the international union representative involved, but the local was so resentful it took the issue to the floor of the next union convention. It was unsuccessful in having the international's ruling reversed.

The new contract addition described above still leaves to the parties the *ad hoc* determination of how employees are to be moved, but if they are transferred as a result of such determination, they are to have their full seniority rights. The company had no objection to this added guarantee, because it meant that the older, experienced employees could keep their seniority. Also, it was an important step toward strengthening the position of the international union.

A large multiplant glass company worked out an arrangement whereby workers who were transferred to new plants could retain their seniority and have a six months' grace period in which to decide whether to stay at the new plant or return to the old plant.

[18] For discussion of a similar problem, see "Effect of Merger and Succession on Seniority Rights" in Chapter 5, pp. 130-31.

Those who chose to move, but who were not transferred at the company's request, were to be given a preferential hiring right at the new plant and retain their former seniority. A large can company with a Master Agreement completely closed one plant and consolidated operations from two others into one new plant. Except for the employees in the closed plant, those who were willing to move were offered jobs in the new plant. However, competitive status seniority began only when they were hired at the new plant; no seniority credits were transferred. The right of hiring preference in new plants has become a standard feature in many agreements.

For the most part the discontinuance of jobs in one location and their transfer to another location has been handled by the preferential hiring procedure, whether a new or an old plant is involved in the new location. There is no discernible trend toward the full transfer of competitive status seniority credits for layoff and promotion purposes, largely because of the internal union problem. However, service credits for benefit purposes are usually preserved. In some cases, the plant to which the operations are being moved is organized by a different international union, making almost impossible the transfer of seniority rights.

Although both union and management show an interest in facilitating employee transfers when operations are transferred to another location, the fact is that very few employees avail themselves of the opportunity to move with their jobs.

A detailed case study has been made of the closing of a sizeable San Francisco automobile plant. The company and the union entered into a special agreement under which production workers were given the opportunity to transfer to the company's Los Angeles plant (450 miles distant) with retention of seniority rights. Because of the injection of the seniority element, both parties expected the long-service people to elect to transfer. At the time of this move (1954) the unemployment rate in the Bay area was high—an estimated 5 per cent. Of the approximately 1,450 persons eligible to transfer, only 315 actually made the move, and seniority standing did not seem to be as important an influence in their decision as were other factors.[19] Experience has been similar in other transfer cases.

[19] Margaret S. Gordon and Ann H. McCorry, *Plant Relocation and Job Security: A Case Study*, Institute of Industrial Relations, University of California, Reprint No. 981 (1957).

When operations are terminated entirely, union pressure to preserve transfer rights and competitive status seniority is likely to be less than its insistence upon income security protection. The growth of severance pay plans, as described in Chapter 16, is indicative of the union concern with the large numbers of employees unwilling to move to a new location.

WHAT IS THE RELATIONSHIP BETWEEN WORK ASSIGNMENT PRACTICES AND OPERATION OF THE LAYOFF PROCEDURE? The way jobs are described and assignments made may affect the operation of a layoff procedure. If a job is so constituted as to embrace a variety of different duties and if assignments are made so as to create employee specialization on a given duty, trouble in the form of inefficiencies or grievances may arise at the time of a layoff.

For example, one of the skilled jobs in a large machinery company some years ago was that of Photographer Senior. The incumbents did the necessary general photographing work for company brochures, public relations, and parts manuals. It was decided to purchase graphic arts equipment instead of having this specialized work done outside the plant. Several experienced Graphic Arts Cameramen were hired, and they were put in the job of Photographer Senior, although the skills of general photographic camera work are quite different from those of graphic arts camera work. Over the years the Photographer Senior incumbents specialized in one or the other of the two basic duties. When it was decided to curtail the general photographic work, the men affected had no experience in graphic arts work. Yet the junior man in the classification, a graphic arts cameraman, had to be the first laid off even though six months would be needed to train the senior photographer in this work.

Where ability to do the available work is a criterion and it is not built into the unit by a system of promotional channels and progression lines, many companies have adopted the policy of giving the senior men in the unit an opportunity to become familiar with other jobs by filling in for absentees. Normally the assignments are at management's request, and therefore the senior man suffers no loss of pay if he moves to a lower-rated job. This policy has two advantages for management: it enhances the security of the senior man, and it makes for a more flexible work force. On the other hand, it has the possible disadvantage of being interpreted as a commitment to the senior man when a promotion is to be made.

WHAT POLICY SHOULD BE ADOPTED TOWARD UPWARD BUMPING? Most agreements specify that transfers in lieu of layoff shall be to equal or lesser paying jobs. However, because of either poor contract language or deliberate policy, some procedures permit or even require upward bumping under certain circumstances. Interestingly, this occurs when prior experience is the criterion for assignment to a specific job. It may be that an employee in a lesser-paying job sought a downward transfer because the work was easier; or experience on the higher-paid job may have been acquired on a casual replacement basis at management's request. Whatever the reasons, the results at the time of layoff are often anomalous. The person who enjoys this unusual windfall at the time of expected adversity will probably be the most junior employee in a given occupation in which work is being curtailed. While he moves to a higher paid job, there remain on his former job senior people who have had similar experience. Thus the senior persons in a job may be placed at a relative disadvantage by the seniority system designed to protect them.

Occasionally the upward movement of junior employees at the time of layoff is entirely unexpected. For example, in one automobile assembly plant this occurred because of the combined right of the company to make re-assignments required by layoffs and the reluctance of senior (and, therefore, older) employees to move to the more highly-paced line jobs. Accordingly, the company sometimes was forced to upgrade the least senior people in the readjustment of personnel to meet layoff situations.

WHAT PROBLEMS ARISE WHEN THERE ARE DIFFERENT BARGAINING UNITS WITHIN THE SAME PLANT OR COMPANY? If there are two or more bargaining units within a plant whose relationship with each other is unfriendly and competitive, the layoff and transfer problem may be a difficult one. Refusal by one unit to permit bumpbacks from the other unit may subtract considerably from the rights of the senior man, particularly if the impact of a work curtailment is concentrated in one unit. Sometimes the combination of a broad seniority unit and indiscriminate bumping rights has actually encouraged a splinter movement leading to two bargaining units. Skilled employees who felt vulnerable to displacement by less skilled senior employees were usually the ones initiating such a move. Their purpose was to restrain bumping by revising the structure of the bargaining unit.

TO WHAT EXTENT SHOULD A LAYOFF PROCEDURE BE ALLOWED TO SERVE AS A SUBSTITUTE FOR DISCIPLINE? Surprisingly often supervision uses a layoff to "get rid of a guy" who is considered an inferior employee. Yet this same employee has never been given a disciplinary warning for poor work, and, in some instances, he may have been moved systematically to the top rate of his job classification. This means one thing: The supervisor has been derelict in using the constructive measures of discipline, and he is exploiting the "ability" criterion in layoff to punish the man.

In a 1959 cutback a paper company laid off a senior top-rated Machinist "C" man under a clause that read, "seniority shall be the determining factor in layoffs, demotions, and re-employment. . . . In instances where the oldest man in service is not selected for benefits of this section, satisfactory explanation shall be made by the company to the union." The company explained to the union that the quality of this man's work was inferior. It went so far as to say that it had no intention of recalling him no matter how business improved in the future. In effect, the company was discharging the employee under the guise of applying layoff criteria.

Sometimes the approach is more subtle. The industrial relations manager of a tractor plant reported that foremen attempt to "get men out of their hair" by devious use of the seniority system. "They try to unload guys when there's a reduction," even though this means passing them on to someone else under the transfer in lieu of layoff provision. Sometimes the procedures taken are not under the "deviation from seniority" provisions of the master agreement, but represent instead an exploiting of the seniority rules. For example, maintenance may lay off men by trade. If fifteen men have to be dropped, supervision can distribute the reductions as it sees fit among the various crafts, and by this process get at the man or men whom it wants to dump.[20]

These subversions of the layoff procedure are risky for manage-

[20] The following example was given: "Suppose Maintenance wants to eliminate 15 men because of a drop in volume. They decide to reduce 2 Electricians, 1 Millwright, and so on. They then say, 'Who's the next Millwright? Oh boy, it's the guy we wanted to get rid of! Let's lay off more Millwrights.' "

ment. Probably too few managements are aware of their use by department heads and foremen. In effect, it means that foremen are not facing up to their responsibilities in meting out discipline in a forthright manner. A long-run consequence may be union insistence upon straight seniority in the layoff procedure.

WHAT WILL BE THE EFFECT OF UNEMPLOYMENT COMPENSATION AND SUB PLANS ON LAYOFF PROCEDURES? The influence of these plans on union attitudes toward work-sharing has already been discussed. Other considerations are:

(1) Will the plans result in an increase of waivers of downward transfers in lieu of layoff on the part of senior employees? Frequently the mistake is made of comparing the benefit levels under the SUB plans with the earnings of an employee in his present job. Under most layoff procedures this is not a proper comparison. The choice for the worker rests between the level of benefits geared to his present job earnings and his rate of pay if he exercises his bumping privileges. If a considerable demotion must be taken in lieu of layoff, the employee may prefer to be unemployed. Obviously other variables, such as fringe benefit coverage during layoffs, the probable duration of layoff, and social pressures, will enter into this decision.

From the standpoint of both the union and the company, the use of waivers encouraged by SUB creates several problems. For the union, there is a risk that the employee exercising his waiver right may jeopardize his claim for unemployment compensation. It could be construed by the state administrative bodies as a refusal to accept work. This has given rise to a new, somewhat devious, arrangement incorporated in some local seniority agreements. Employees are given the right to be placed in lower rated jobs at the time of a layoff only if they have applied for such jobs. Failure to apply is considered evidence of no interest in demotion in lieu of layoff. Under this system it is reasoned that the employee takes the layoff without any actual rejection of alternative employment opportunities.

The companies are even more concerned with this problem. The shorter the contemplated layoff, the greater is the likelihood of use of the waiver (or nonapplication) right. Many employees the company would prefer to retain may elect to take the leisure time. This is particularly serious for the automobile companies during model changeover periods, though they have found that their best interests are served by granting waiver rights at least to skilled employees. At a time of work curtailment, skilled workers resented demotions to less attractive jobs and were disposed to lose their seniority rather than accept such assignments. They left the firm when told they had to accept such work in lieu of layoff. This led to a company concession that skilled employees should be privileged to decline demotion to certain jobs without a loss of seniority.

(2) The development of SUB programs of various types has given rise to a new term in labor relations: *Juniority*. It is a term coined by a large glass company in its discussions with the union on the subject of the demand for a guaranteed annual wage. Elements of "juniority," implying superior advantages to junior employees, are already beginning to creep into layoff arrangements. It is not unreasonable to speculate that the continued quest for security in the form of income protection at the time of job insecurity (see Chapter 16) has already had some interesting repercussions, and these may develop further. One company and union had a foretaste of this possible trend when it decided to handle a special four to six weeks' layoff by asking for volunteers. Approximately seventy-five such volunteers for layoff were needed, and surprisingly, the invitation to be laid off was oversubscribed. This did not mean that the volunteers necessarily wanted to loaf. Many of them had very good reasons for wanting the temporary layoff, such as doing repair work around the house, fixing up a summer camp, visiting a sick relative, etc. The parties had to decide which of the volunteers were entitled to the layoff. They based the selection on seniority: the most senior had the first claim to the layoff.

Entitlement to an enforced, but perhaps desired, vacation by layoff conceivably could be a right that senior employees may claim in the future. This observation is not by way of prediction. Rather, it is an invitation to managements and unions alike to anticipate the policy and procedural decisions that will be necessary if the present emphasis on seniority is reversed by programs that encourage juniority.

7 / Promotion Policies and Procedures

THE SELECTION OF employees for advancement has been regarded by management as one of its most important responsibilities and prerogatives. While most companies recognized very early in their collective bargaining relationship the legitimacy of union interest in layoff procedures, they were much more reluctant to treat promotion arrangements as a proper subject for collective bargaining. In the initial agreements between companies and unions, promotion was not treated as a negotiable matter. Instead, the typical collective bargaining agreement specified in the management rights clause that decisions on promotion rested exclusively with the company. The only implicit concession to the union was its right to grieve against discrimination, favoritism, or nepotism in promotions. The difficulty of carrying the burden of proof on these grounds made it almost impossible for the union to justify the claim of a disgruntled, by-passed employee.

The unions themselves did not assign high priority to promotion policies and procedures in their initial collective bargaining demands. In part this was because of their preoccupation with more pressing needs, such as wage improvements, protection of employees from arbitrary disciplinary action, development of employment tenure through seniority, and the like. But it was also because many unions twenty or thirty years ago were inclined to the view that promotion decisions were primarily a management function and that the union's principal role was to prevent discrimination and caprice in the exercise of this right.[1] This attitude was prevalent particularly in the skilled trades or craft unions and, for a short while, in the

[1] The railroad unions are a notable exception. At a very early date they succeeded in establishing progression lines for advancement, and seniority was the principal criterion.

178

newly-formed and relatively weak unions in the mass-production in-dustries.[2]

However, within the past twenty years the resistance of manage-ment and the early reticence of unions have undergone a gradual and remarkable change through the influence of collective bargaining. Unions have become more assertive, particularly where members seeking advancement far outnumber available opportunities for pro-motion or where management abused its early freedom to select in-dividuals for promotion. Companies have regarded as a direct chal-lenge to management's basic rights union efforts to make criteria for promotion within the bargaining unit a matter of collective bargain-ing. Yet by a variety of overt and sometimes subtle influences, the collective bargaining process now effectively limits management's freedom to promote employees.

Promotions have become an important issue in labor-management negotiations and in the administration of the labor agreement. In its periodic report on collective bargaining provisions, the Bureau of Labor Statistics presents the essential issues for negotiation as fol-lows:

Negotiations between labor and management on a promotion program generally center on the following questions: (1) Shall the employer have the right to promote solely as he sees fit, and, collaterally, must he promote from within or may he hire from the outside; (2) if not, what qualifications or factors shall govern the selection of an employee for promotion; and, on the basis of such standards, who shall finally deter-mine the best qualified employee. In brief, the issue lies between organ-ized labor's desire to extend seniority to cover promotions (so that length of service rather than special qualifications for the job would determine who is promoted . . .), and management's effort to control the assignment of men to jobs on the basis of competence rather than the length of service.[3]

[2] It is interesting that union concern with management's promotion decisions is less pronounced in the organizations of skilled employees. In craft unions the prescribed movement to the journeyman status via apprenticeship, as described in Chapter 4, makes promotion an academic issue. The union controls "promotion" by defining journeyman requirements. But it is noteworthy that the historic view of skilled trades unions still prevails in the newly-organized professional engineers' unions. For example, they are reluctant to impose contractual restrictions on management's freedom to select people for promotion within the bargaining unit. It is likely that the relative shortage of engineers has maximized promotional opportunity and lessened the de-gree of competition among members for promotion. Therefore, promotion has not been a serious bargaining issue. However, another explanation is the acknowledgment by professional people of the importance of the ability factor.

[3] U. S. Bureau of Labor Statistics, *Collective Bargaining Provisions: Promotion, Trans-fer, and Assignment*, Bulletin 908-07 (1948), p. 2.

No less important than the negotiation issues are the administrative problems arising under labor agreements. The decisions that managements have made in administering the agreement and in acting on promotion grievances, as well as the decisions of arbitrators, have been more responsible for union gains than the contract language itself.

This chapter will describe the impact of collective bargaining on promotion policies and procedures under the following headings: (1) a summary of the more significant developments during the past twenty years, (2) the meaning of promotion, (3) promotion procedures, and (4) criteria for promotion.

Significant Developments

In the conduct of industrial relationships during the past twenty years there have been several important developments, each influencing management's handling of promotions within the bargaining unit: (1) the enlargement of contract rules governing promotion, (2) the growth in the use of seniority as a criterion in promotions, (3) the development of techniques by management for the measurement of employee ability, (4) the establishment and improvement of tailor-made plans for handling promotions, (5) the gradual reduction in promotion grievances, and (6) the considerable influence of arbitrators in formulating promotion procedures and policies.

CRITERIA GOVERNING PROMOTION. Increasingly the rules governing the criteria and procedures to be used in promoting employees are being incorporated in the collective bargaining agreement. The first step in this process was the negotiation of standards for promotion and adoption of the principle that current employees should be given preference for advancement before new employees were hired. However, in these early stages management still retained considerable freedom by insisting on standards that were to its liking and specifying that its judgment as to ability and qualifications was final and could not be challenged in the grievance procedure. The second step typically was union success in making management's judgment a proper subject for grievance. Next, as new contracts were negotiated, the standards were often changed, or the weight to be assigned to the promotion criteria were revised; invariably these changes represented gains for the unions. Finally, in more recent years unions have succeeded in the negotiation of what they consider procedural improvements, such as job posting arrangements, broadening the promotional unit, and, in a few instances, provision for trial periods.

SENIORITY AS A CRITERION IN PROMOTIONS. The evidence shows that seniority has become a more influential criterion for deciding which employee is to be promoted. This development was first discernible in the rulings of the War Labor Board in dispute cases. In a policy-making case in 1942 the Board ruled that "in filling vacancies and making promotions, where qualifications are equal, seniority shall prevail." In its accompanying opinion the Board pointed out that "promotion is basically a managerial function and that seniority is one of the factors, but not the controlling factor, to be taken into account in the selection of employees for promotion."[4] However, three years later in another case the Board directed that seniority was to determine promotions as well as layoffs and rehiring, provided the employees were qualified to do the work.[5]

While the increased emphasis on seniority has been brought about occasionally through changes in contract language, usually it is the result of a change in management behavior. Although management once felt that promotion decisions were one of its most important prerogatives, it is now coming to realize that proper use of the seniority criterion in these decisions is not necessarily incompatible with efficiency and employee morale. This is not to say that American management has decided that seniority alone is the proper criterion; nor is management uniformly satisfied with the amount of emphasis on seniority in making promotions that has evolved over the years. Many companies are troubled by its consequences.

MEASUREMENTS OF EMPLOYEE ABILITY. By making management's promotion decisions subject to the grievance procedure, the union has stimulated most companies to consider more carefully what they mean by "ability," "qualifications," and other nonseniority criteria. As noted later in this chapter, a variety of personnel pro-

[4] Golden Belt Mfg. Co., Case No. 151, *Termination Report, National War Labor Board,* Vol. 1, U. S. Department of Labor, pp. 145-46.
[5] Ball Brothers Co., Case No. 111-5901-D, *Termination Report* (cited in note 4), p. 146.

cedures have been adopted to help management arrive at sound judgments and defend that judgment before the union and, if necessary, an outside arbitrator. Merit-rating programs, foremen training, use of special tests, and pre-planning for promotion are examples of these efforts.

TAILOR-MADE PROMOTION PLANS. As with layoff procedures, there is impressive evidence that arrangements for promotions within the bargaining unit have become more and more tailor-made. Although the agreement usually specifies the general criteria, in the administering of the system fairly elaborate procedures have been developed in many cases to minimize friction and promote the interests of both employer and employees. This is normally true where the total relationship has matured to the point of accommodation. However, where the relationship has not matured to this point, the attitude of one or both parties is often suspicious and legalistic and there is disagreement over the meaning of such words as "ability," "qualified," and "aptitude."

The language of the agreement itself does not determine the way promotions are made. Different companies, and even different plants under the same master agreement, interpret the language differently. "Seniority" may mean the length of service in a narrow unit in one case, in a much broader unit in another. "Ability" may acquire special meaning because of a special system for measuring ability. Promotional ladders, bidding systems, informal distinctions between skilled and semi-skilled or unskilled jobs, and other *supra* contract arrangements add to and sometimes alter substantively what seems to be conveyed by contract language. These are often the result of grievance dispositions by the parties or a response to the *dicta* and judgment of an arbitrator. In some cases, what appears to be a modification of contract rights and obligations is a function of an aggressive union-weak management or a weak union-strong management situation. For the most part, however, the evolution of promotional arrangements irrespective of contract indicates a sophistication not present in the initial stages of collective bargaining.

REDUCTION IN PROMOTION GRIEVANCES. There have been relatively few grievances arising from management's promotion decisions in recent years, although when promotions first became subject to collective bargaining, there were many grievances.[6] The highly subjective question of ability was particularly susceptible to challenge and offered a fertile area for the union intent on making grievances. In part, the reduction in promotion grievances may be explained by the workable arrangements developed by the parties over the years. In part, it is because management deliberately promotes the senior employee either because it minimizes the importance of its conviction or because it is unsure of its own position. In some cases the union may have sufficient faith in the fairness of a company to be unwilling to challenge its promotional decisions. Sometimes the union deliberately avoids this issue and seeks to discourage the claim of a by-passed senior employee because to do otherwise would only antagonize another union member.

However, it cannot be said that the subject of employee promotion has yielded to adjustment over the years to the same extent as layoffs, discipline, job evaluation, and many others. While grievances have undoubtedly decreased in many companies, there are some companies where this remains a dominant grievance issue. Furthermore, the degree of union control over promotions is often found to be a critical bargaining issue.

A grievance-prone union may challenge any and all promotions of junior employees. For example, in a multi-plant automobile company it was found that more than one-third of the grievances filed on promotions occurred in four of its more than forty plants. In these plants a grievance was always filed if the top seniority employee was not selected. But in these same four plants the number of grievances filed on nearly every other subject—discipline, foremen working, equal distribution of overtime—was abnormally high. The volume of promotion grievances was symptomatic of a more basic relationship problem.

Generally, however, promotions are less productive of grievances than one might expect. This may or may not be a healthy trend. If it reflects a truly satisfactory mutual approach to promotion decisions, it is undoubtedly healthy. On the other hand, if the low grievance rate reflects management or union default. as it clearly does in some instances, it could be an unhealthy situation.

[6] Information on the frequency of grievances is from an unpublished study tentatively entitled: "The Role of Ability in Determining Employee Status," Division of Research, Harvard University, Graduate School of Business Administration. There is no doubt that persistent grievances in the early stages of a relationship brought about more emphasis on seniority.

INFLUENCE OF ARBITRATORS IN PROMOTION POLICIES. Although grievances on this subject are not numerous, there is reason to believe that
the grievance process, through the decisions of arbitrators and umpires, has played an unusually important role in the formulating
of promotional procedures and policies. In discussing "Criteria for
Promotions" below we shall examine in detail the extent of this
influence. Wisdom of hindsight has prompted many managements
to wonder whether they have given too much authority to arbitrators in this area. A recurrent complaint is that outside neutrals have
been too quick to substitute their judgment for that of management
and in some cases have almost rewritten the agreement. Typical of
these complaints is the following comment of one industrial relations
manager:

> The Umpire, by his interpretation of this provision has practically
> eliminated management from the picture by ruling that management
> has not promoted fairly until he has given the seniority employee an
> opportunity to try out on the job. If this practice is followed, it is
> necessary to disqualify the employee if unsatisfactory, which is always
> difficult to accomplish. This section has worked considerable hardship,
> especially in making group leaders. Some foremen have advised that
> they have held off making group leaders knowing that they would be
> required to take the seniority man furnished by the Union.

The Meaning of Promotion

At least five separate considerations are involved in determining
the meaning of promotion as far as collective bargaining is concerned:
(1) a definition of what constitutes a promotion within the bargaining
unit, (2) determination of when an opportunity for promotion exists,
(3) the reluctance of employees to seek or accept promotions under
some circumstances, (4) the distinction between a temporary and a
permanent promotional opportunity, and (5) the limitation of union
interest to promotions *within* the bargaining unit.

DEFINITION OF PROMOTION. It is usually assumed that promotion
means advancement to a position carrying a higher rate of pay. This
definition is expressed or implied in most collective bargaining
agreements. To an employee, however, a promotion often means a
movement to a preferred position, and this is not necessarily associated with an immediate increase in pay. Preference may be for a

lateral or even a downward transfer for a number of reasons: (1) a belief that employment security on the less remunerative job will be greater—a consideration that is sometimes more pronounced among older employees, who reason that they should seek duties commensurate with their declining physical capabilities, (2) a desire for a position with better working conditions, (3) an interest in a job with greater prestige value or greater responsibility in the opinion of the particular employee, and (4) greater potential advancement in a lesser job on the promotional ladder than one can anticipate on the present job.

Occasionally what might appear to be economically undesirable is an employee's attempt to be "promoted" to a lower-rated job because it affords an opportunity for greater total earnings through incentive payments. One company reported that there were "abuses" when its Job Continuity Plan was first installed because people in a higher labor grade bid for lower positions since the latter had looser incentives and involved lighter work. Another economic incentive for what superficially appears to be a downward bid is the enhanced opportunity for overtime earnings on a lower paying job, although in a few cases employees will bid on lower paying positions to avoid overtime.

To avoid such unorthodox ideas of promotion, some parties have defined promotion as a movement involving an increase in rate of pay. Others have developed understandings that workers are not to bid laterally or downward. However, in a few instances the unions have secured acceptance of a broad definition of promotion that includes movement to any job of the employee's preference. In the absence of restrictive contract language, the "bid" system for filling vacancies has encouraged the unorthodox approach to promotions and has made it difficult for management to refuse the claim of a senior applicant. Inability to define promotion in its narrowest sense in contract negotiations has led some companies to resist posting of vacancies and bidding for such job openings. In general, a reference only to "promotions" without specifying what is meant by the term, creates problems for management. Employee movements within the average company, especially laterally, are usually quite frequent. If management has to observe the promotion criteria in effecting the numerous horizontal moves, its flexibility and efficiency may be seriously impaired. In one company the union insisted that even transfer to a different assignment within the same classification constituted a promotion since working conditions or some other aspect of the assignment might appeal to one or more employees.[7]

DETERMINATION OF EXISTENCE OF OPPORTUNITY FOR PROMOTION. Typically it is understood that there is a promotional opportunity if a company decides a certain job needs to be filled. In nearly all cases this decision rests exclusively with management. In other words, the union seldom can force a company to acknowledge the existence of or to fill a promotional vacancy. However, either unwittingly or deliberately, some companies have created a legitimate union claim that certain employees had to be promoted even though no clear vacancy existed. This risk occurs, for example, in craft jobs where there are three or more separate job classifications for each craft, as in the case of Welder A, Welder B, and Welder C. In deciding the complement of men for each one of these jobs, the orthodox management approach is to determine from the nature of the work-flow how many "A" men are needed, how many "B" men, etc. This may be described as the job-approach. However, in some companies poor administration or deliberate policy results in the use of the man-approach or a mixture of the job- and the man-approach. That is, if a "C" employee has demonstrated his capacity to do "B" work, he is given the "B" rating regardless of the content of the work assignment. One company reported that in theory it does not raise a worker automatically from a "C" to a "B" classification unless there is an opening that he can demonstrate his ability to fill. It found, however, that in actual practice foremen were yielding to pressure and advancing workers to higher classifications even when there had been no change in their work assignment or their work content. What was theoretically a job promotion avenue had, in effect, become a merit increase avenue within the broad rate range of several job classes. A grievance may arise, therefore, over whether an employee is entitled to an advancement even though no vacancy exists.

A variant of this same problem arises from the development of fixed crew sizes or manning complements through past practice. Even though there may be no formal agreement on the subject, the union often will insist that the management's right to alter crew size has

[7] In one plant of a large glass company, the development of instantaneous seniority coupled with an inadequate definition of what constituted a vacancy created serious difficulties for management.

been limited by custom. In spite of changed conditions that would justify a lesser crew, the union resists any such move. The steel industry discovered that retention of an unnecessarily large crew in some operations was viewed by the union as a fixed basis for advancement as well as employment opportunity. Again, faulty administration or the adoption of a broad past-practice clause may restrict management's right to determine whether a promotional vacancy exists.

EMPLOYEE ATTITUDE TOWARD PROMOTION. Promotional opportunities do not invariably attract employees. Some persons simply do not want the added responsibilities of a higher paying job, or they recognize their own limitations and do not aspire to better positions. In some plants the compression of wage structures, in large part the result of union policy, has served to deter interest in self-advancement. Employees feel that the slight gain in pay is not worth the added responsibility or effort. One company with a "mono-rate" structure found it necessary to force junior employees to take vacancies demanding higher job requirements because senior men were not interested. With this type of wage structure senior workers bid for less demanding jobs because there is little or no wage reduction involved.

TEMPORARY VS. PERMANENT PROMOTION. Normally the parties treat as promotions the filling of those vacancies which are relatively permanent as contrasted with those of short duration. This distinction often was not anticipated in the early provisions on this subject with the unhappy result that cumbersome procedures were forced upon the company when it wanted to fill vacancies of one or a few days' duration. Most managements have been successful in establishing the principle that they must have relative freedom in filling temporary vacancies occasioned by absenteeism, vacations, illness, or short leaves of absence. However, by unilateral company policy or by joint understanding between the parties, even this action has been influenced by the arrangements for filling permanent vacancies. It has been recognized that the experience acquired by employees during brief assignments on more demanding jobs helps them to qualify later for promotions, or, it enables a foreman to become familiar with an employee's ability to do various jobs. Thus, it is often the practice either to give senior workers the first opportunity to fill temporary vacancies or at least to rotate these assignments among eligible persons. It is interesting that union grievance claims protesting the promotion of a junior employee over a senior employee on the basis of superior ability have had the subtle effect of limiting management freedom in filling temporary vacancies. It has been argued successfully in some instances that the junior employee was given an unfair advantage, or that the senior man was discriminated against in the granting of temporary promotions.

Managements have found themselves confronted by this dilemma. If they do not use the seniority principle in filling temporary vacancies, they risk long-run difficulties; on the other hand, observance of seniority in filling these brief vacancies may involve short-run operating difficulties and costly dislocations. There is a natural tendency for the foremen and supervisors, who are under immediate pressure to get production out, to try to avoid the short-run headaches. This, in turn, has led some companies to decide that as a matter of policy they will require foremen to offer the temporary opening to the senior man first and, if he refuses the opportunity, to proceed down the list in the order of seniority. This is a time-consuming process, but it protects the company against a possible union complaint in the future that a by-passed senior man did not have a fair opportunity to acquire experience on the higher job.

LIMITATION OF UNION INTEREST. Finally, it is usually understood that promotions falling within the purview of collective bargaining are those involving upward movement *within* the bargaining unit. Most unions have not tried to restrict management in its selection of supervisory personnel outside the bargaining unit.

Promotion Procedures and Patterns

Because of the growing tendency to develop tailor-made arrangements for promotions, it is difficult, if not impossible, to describe typical procedures. The following considerations, however, have confronted nearly all parties in the evolution of promotion systems: (1) promotion from within as contrasted with hiring from the outside; (2) selection systems; (3) development of a system of priorities for considering employees for promotion.

Promotion from Within

The principle is generally recognized that persons within the bargaining unit will be given preference for advancement to vacancies before new employees are hired. However, some companies retain the right to hire rather than promote and tend to exercise this right particularly in the filling of specialized jobs. To do this, they usually have to demonstrate that no present employees are qualified or that the new hire has outstanding skills and aptitudes. Unions are quick to protest the hiring of new workers if there are even partially qualified employees within the unit. Some have argued that the preference principle means that in the absence of a qualified person, the senior employee is entitled to be given a trial or to be trained for the vacancy before anyone else is hired. This more extreme position has been resisted successfully.

Selection Systems

This term applies to the pre-promotion steps followed by the company and, in certain cases, the employees. There are four distinct approaches: (1) the employer-selection system, (2) the job-posting and bid system, (3) the application system, and (4) the union notification—union suggestion system. To only a limited extent does our evidence permit analysis of the rationale behind the adoption of any one of these systems.

THE EMPLOYER-SELECTION SYSTEM. Under this arrangement the employer selects the employee to be promoted, and his decision may then be challenged by the union. No practice of posting the open job, of accepting bids, or of reviewing existing applications is followed. Very often the selection process used by the employer does not deserve to be called a "system." A surprising number of employers make last-minute selections without any pre-planning. This lack of system is likely to give rise to grievances when the senior employee is by-passed for promotion. Some companies admit that failure to pre-plan often prompts them to select the senior man even though he may not be the best qualified for the vacancy. Lacking a well thought out arrangement, they realize the vulnerability of their hasty selection of a junior man.

However, one of the significant effects of collective bargaining on many managements has been the recognition that advance thought must be given to promotion moves. This is done by (1) training foremen to develop potential promotion charts, based on periodic review of existing skills and abilities, (2) systematically trying out employees on higher-rated jobs during absences for sickness, vacations, and the like, and recording comments on their aptitude, (3) requiring supervision to make regular reports as to probable future vacancies, thereby increasing the time for consideration. In some companies, preplanning means that an employee knows he is slated to move to a certain job. Therefore, he is less likely to be disturbed if he is not selected for other openings arising in the meantime.

THE JOB-POSTING AND BID SYSTEM. Unions have frequently tried in negotiations to require management to post vacancies and to allow interested employees to bid for the openings. They argue that this gives them a better opportunity to police the agreement, and that it affords employees a chance to express their desire for the position. Some companies have refused to adopt job posting or have acceded reluctantly and with misgiving. They feel that posting encourages the transfer of workers from one line of skill to another, that it tempts persons manifestly unqualified to bid for the openings, and that it delays the filling of vacancies. Underlying the opposition of many managements to the bid system is the belief that it represents an abdication of management rights.

One company official said that the employer-selection system gave management a strategic advantage; if notices of vacancies are posted, management has to disprove an applicant's ability, whereas with an employer-selection system the union must disprove the ability of the company's choice. One industrial relations director observed that "the bidding system tends to crystallize the arguments in the event the top senior man is not given the job." It has also been claimed that the bid arrangement that accompanies posting enables the union to "rig" the response in one of two ways: (1) the union can put pressure on junior employees to refrain from bidding, thus leaving only the senior man as the applicant; it is then extremely difficult for the company to turn down the senior employee's bid even though there are doubts as to his qualifications; or (2) the union can encourage mass bidding on the theory that the administrative burden of reviewing all the bids will force management to select the senior employee or at least will provide ammunition in the event a junior employee is chosen. There is little evidence to show that these union tactics are used extensively.

Some companies feel that these defects can be remedied by the manner in which jobs are posted. For example, if the posting is limited to the department or section where the vacancy occurs and the initial bid opportunity is offered only to employees in the narrow unit, indiscriminate bidding is less likely to occur. Others are willing to accept job bidding only for certain jobs, reserving the right to make outright selection for most jobs. To illustrate, one company, strongly opposed to posting, permits a certain type of job bidding for upgraders, feeling that management is here engaged in a talent search and that the posting assists this effort. It is interesting that one division of this multiplant company has posted jobs for many years, although it was not required to do so by the local agreement until recently.

It would be wrong to conclude that job posting inevitably produces the results described above. Some employers prefer the posting system, but only under one or more of the following conditions: (1) the unit for posting and within which promotions are made is narrow; (2) the company has successfully avoided the promoting of employees with doubtful qualifications, thus discouraging indiscriminate bidding; (3) the union itself has actively discouraged unqualified employees from bidding; and (4) there is a limitation on "chain posting and bidding," that is, the filling of one job does not require the posting of the job vacated by the successful bidder, and so on. One industrial relations director of a company that uses job posting in one plant and the application system in two of its plants said that he preferred the bidding system if it had proper safeguards. It is his view that foremen tend to keep workers too long on the same job; some employees don't exercise the special initiative required under an application system and, consequently, fail to acquire new skills by exposure to new work. The bidding system stimulates movement, which is desirable for the company in developing a well-rounded work force.

APPLICATION SYSTEM. This is a relatively new system that has been quite successful from management's standpoint. It is an arrangement

with the union whereby employees may file a request for consideration for a specified number of jobs. These requests are reviewed as
job vacancies occur. A large rubber company for many years had a
plant-wide bidding system on transfers and promotions; any vacant
job could be bid upon by postings at plant gates with the result that
employees signed up almost indiscriminately for vacant jobs. This
arrangement was dropped in recent negotiations, the union having
been persuaded that the scope of internal movement it permitted was
disruptive. In its place, an application system was introduced giving
employees the right to apply for future openings on four jobs and
requiring that applications be on file at least seven days in advance
of the vacancy. Employees are likely to be more objective about their
own qualifications under some sort of application system than when
bidding for a currently posted vacancy.

UNION NOTIFICATION—UNION SUGGESTION SYSTEM. This is used infrequently and usually represents a compromise when the union wants,
and the employer resists, a job posting and bid system. For example,
a large automobile company, which refused repeatedly to grant job
posting until a recent contract was negotiated, did, however, follow
the practice of notifying the union committeemen of job openings in
their jurisdiction. In some cases the union would then post the openings in selected locations, and later give the plant or department
head the names of applicants together with the committeeman's
recommendation. This procedure had political appeal for the committeeman, and it served to restrict wholesale bids. Usually the committeeman preferred to have a constituent secure the job; therefore,
he did not post the notice outside his own area of jurisdiction. This
system did not prove entirely satisfactory. A survey for one year
(1953) showed that in 13 of the 50-odd plants the union always submitted the name of the top seniority employee. In 10 plants the
union always filed grievances if the person chosen was not on the
list submitted by the union. In 9 plants, even if the employee selected was on the list, the union invariably processed a grievance
if he was not the most senior employee on that list.

Development of a Priority System for Considering Employees

In an effort to reconcile the two sometimes conflicting factors of
seniority and ability, the labor-management agreement usually es-

tablishes a system of priorities or of limitations in deciding who is entitled to be considered for promotion. The operation of the selection systems described above is influenced greatly by the seniority unit. The unit chosen may be one or more of several forms. Basically, two general types of units prevail:

(1) Most frequently the unit for promotion is derived from the existing organizational structure of the plant. It may be a section, a department, a division, or in very rare instances, the plant as a whole. Where an established unit is used, it is usually narrower for promotion purposes than the unit chosen for effecting layoffs. A company will seek to have the department serve as the unit or, if possible, even the more limited section within a department.

There are several reasons for this preference. Jobs within a section or department are more likely to be similar, and therefore employees considered first for promotion will already have some familiarity with the work to be performed in the open job. Also employees within the department usually fill temporary vacancies and so may have had actual experience on the job to be filled. Finally, the more narrow the unit, the greater is the probability that the judgment of only one or a few supervisors will be involved in deciding relative abilities of the applicants under consideration. The department foreman or the section supervisor will have an intimate knowledge of *both* the employees *and* the work to be done. Where there are several grades of the same classification, the employer may succeed in having the classification serve as the unit. The agreement in such a case will provide, for example, that "upgrading shall be made on the basis of seniority, and the most senior employee in the next lower labor grade in the same classification in the department shall be assigned to the open or newly-created job provided the employee can do the work."

One might expect that with the narrower unit there would be less rigid standards of ability. However, the sheer numbers of employees in broader seniority units may prevent a careful appraisal of ability.

The principal disadvantage in the use of a standard unit is that one of the basic assumptions is invalid. It is not necessarily true that a department embraces jobs of similar skills or that the progression line from the least paying job to the highest paying job is a logical one. Very often incumbents of the lesser jobs could not possibly meet the standards of a vacant job. When this occurs, it is to management's advantage to move outside department boundaries for eligible applicants or to hire from outside the company, a move that is often damaging to the morale of the employees within a department. Conversely, in some plants the similarity in pay among jobs within a department makes strict use of the department unit unjust to employees.

(2) Recognizing the limitations of established plant organization units, some companies unilaterally or jointly with the union have developed special job groupings. These groupings may contain jobs from a number of different departments, or if the departments are large, certain jobs within a department. In addition to job grouping, a well-defined system of progression is recognized. It has been noted in an earlier chapter that similar zone, district, or grouping units were devised for layoffs and recalls, but the so-called flow charts for layoff are sometimes quite different from the tailor-made promotional channels.

These are not necessarily a product of agreement. One large automobile corporation has a brief, concise promotion clause in its master agreement: "In the advancement of employees to higher paid jobs, when ability, merit and capacity are equal, employees with the longest seniority will be given preference." Although most of the detailed seniority arrangements are left to local plant supplemental agreements, even these agreements are silent on the subject of the promotional districts. In fact, the company avoids diagramming the groups. The promotional districts are based on traditional groups of related jobs and are followed except in rare cases. The paper industry for many years has followed a system of promotion in accordance with job sequence ladders.

Several important administrative problems have arisen where the concepts of zone or group seniority and promotional ladders have been combined.

Since each successive rung of the ladder is intended to be a logical training ground for the next rung, it is important that a man who enters a given job sequence have the capacity to learn the more difficult jobs in the ladder. If a man starts at the bottom job and can progress only to the fourth or fifth job, where he is frozen by his own limitations, he is depriving another worker of the chance to acquire training and experience at this particular level. More often, however, the company makes every effort to have the more limited person move upward by providing closer supervision and training. This may mean, however, that top jobs in the sequence are held by somewhat incompetent persons.

A number of administrative policies have been adopted to meet this problem. First, a company may be more careful to hire able new employees so that the one entering at the bottom step is more likely to go through the entire sequence. A steel plant reported that it now places a great deal of emphasis on selection in the lowest jobs in the chain. To illustrate, for this reason extreme care is taken in selecting the cleaner-laborers since first helpers are selected from this group. However, this plant—one of several plants of the same company—was limited by layoff and recall arrangements in its ability to select carefully for the first steps of the promotional channel. Under an interplant availability agreement, it is obligated to absorb workers on the recall list before new persons are hired. Thus, it may have to take men laid off from other plants into the cleaner-laborer classification who are not and will not be able to move successfully through the established promotional lines.

Second, some companies have reserved the right to assign men from the general labor pool to a given job sequence without regard to seniority of the men in the pool. In effect, this means that common laborers have no seniority for promotion purposes. Management also can hire from the outside directly to the bottom rung.

Third, if movement of a senior man to the first step of a job sequence is under consideration, the company may adopt more stringent ability standards. These will include some appraisal of future promotability to jobs in the sequence above the lesser job currently being filled. It is not easy to develop criteria for potential promotability, especially since the nature of job sequence is to provide systematic training en route for the acquisition of higher skills. Even the need for formal educational training in the higher levels cannot be used successfully in all cases to bar a man, because the union may argue that the senior applicant can seek such training through night school or extension courses. Nevertheless, the concept of promotability as a criterion is used and has been sustained by arbitrators where job sequences and job requirements are well defined.

Fourth, trial periods frequently determine whether the senior man is qualified to do the work on the next higher job. One company and union have a two-week trial period, which by practice is often extended another two weeks if more time is needed. If the worker fails, he is penalized by being assigned not to his former job but to a lower one on the promotional ladder. In a few cases, he may be sent to the bottom rung. The penalty approach may deter the obvious misfits from seeking promotion; but it has the unfortunate effect of causing those who probably could qualify to view the possibility of advancement as too great a risk and thus to avoid the promotional opportunity. As a result the penalty is used sparingly. In a large paper plant only eight to ten men have had to take demotions during the past five years.

The trial period, which will be discussed more fully below, is not always enough to determine an employee's qualification. Three handicaps are noted by companies that have job sequence arrangements: (1) supervision is not always sufficiently alert to the performance of a man during the trial—as in the case of the probationary period at the time of hire, there is a tendency to let the man "slip by"; (2) if the trial results in disqualification, the union may question its fairness, especially if the assignments on the job are variable and cover a range of skills; and (3) in the case of a crew setup, effectiveness of the trial period is sometimes handicapped by the crew's attitude toward the employee being tested. A crew may help a mediocre but popular worker and may make it difficult for a good but unpopular one.

Fifth, most companies have found that use of built-in training opportunities is essential for successful operation of a promotional ladder. Each worker is given some exposure to the higher jobs by filling in temporarily during absences.

Finally, a few companies have met the problem of the clogged ladder by deliberately broadening the unit, as was done in some steel plants, for example. Lateral transfers could then be effected which would permit upward movement of able persons on the lower jobs.

A similar clogging of the ladder occurs when employees are disinclined to seek promotion to the next step, for any one of a number of reasons. It may be lack of initiative, or fear of the difficulty of the work at the next higher rung. Another reason often mentioned is the fact that the rate differential between one step and the next step is too slight to compensate for the added responsibilities involved.

To cope with this lack of interest in promotion, some countermeasures have been tried with varying degrees of success. A program of in-plant training may be developed to encourage worker promotion. If a man shows no desire for upward movement, the supervisor and the union representative will talk with him and try to determine the reasons for his disinterest. Some agreements provide that the senior qualified worker *must* take the promotion or be penalized. One steel company, for example, will permit a refusal of promotion without penalty only if there are obvious physical reasons why a man should be frozen in his present assignment. Otherwise, a refusal will result in his being dropped to the bottom rung of the promotional ladder and losing his job sequence seniority.

The emergence of special groupings of jobs and of rather formalized promotional sequences is often a response to the pressure for seniority by the union. But these programs tend to build into the priority unit itself a consideration of ability and qualification factors. Two comments on the development and application of these units should be made. In the first place, the grouping of jobs for this purpose is no easy task. It is accomplished over a long period of time by small labor-management committees, not at the bargaining table during the negotiation of a new contract. Even if management itself had the exclusive right to determine the nature of job groupings and the format of promotional channels, there is considerable evidence that the task would be formidable. Some companies freely admit that they cannot secure an understanding among their own foremen and department heads on the most desirable promotion procedure.

Second, actual administration of promotions does not conform in all instances to the established groups. For example, sometimes the unit is narrowed without serious protest from employees or union. If the unit includes departments under several foremen, the foreman in whose department the vacancy occurs tends to select an applicant from his own department, even though senior men in the unit from other departments are interested in the job. It is understandable that a foreman would be inclined to prefer a worker with whom he is familiar. It is less easy to understand why action of this type does not produce more grievances. There are several possible explanations. The union may be convinced that management has been reasonably fair in its promotion decisions; or departure from the accepted unit may be recognized as the most practical course in a given situation. Also, as mentoned above, a union steward or committeeman for the area in which the vacancy occurs may prefer to have one of his constituents receive the promotion instead of a senior qualified worker from another area. He may forestall a grievance by promising on his part to give his fellow steward similar cooperation in the future. However, a union more prone to file grievances will quickly challenge any deviation from the established unit.

In general, there has been little union pressure to broaden the seniority unit for promotion purposes. The security-of-employment motive, which prompts the drive for plant-wide seniority in the case of layoffs, is lacking in promotions. Instead, what might be called the "propinquity theory" militates against use of a broad unit. In the smaller units there is a desire to keep the "foreigners" out when it comes to advancement opportunities. Employees share with the foreman the view that members of the "family" should be given first consideration.

Criteria for Promotions

Nearly all of the grievances on promotions relate to the question of whether the criteria for making promotions have been applied fairly. Very few grievances stem from alleged failure by the company to follow procedures, such as posting, trial periods, and adherence to the unit. Moreover, there is often a sharp difference between what one would expect to happen under certain contract language and what actually happens in daily administration of the clause.

To understand the relative importance of the criteria of seniority and personal ability, a number of influences must be analyzed: (1) the contract language adopted by the parties, (2) the influence of grievance procedure and arbitration on the criteria for promotion, (3) the pattern of operations and skills within a plant or among plants, (4) management's administrative procedures, (5) the locus of decision-making, and (6) the relationship between the parties.

Contract Language Adopted by the Parties

Rarely does one find a contract clause in which seniority is the exclusive criterion for deciding on promotions. In a small plant of a large glass company seniority is the only factor specified, and if the senior man is not qualified for promotion, he must be trained until he is qualified. However, nearly all companies have insisted that at least some minimum qualifications be required. The two most common clauses are the following:

(1) "The most senior employee in the applicable unit will be promoted if he is qualified for the job." This may be considered a "weak" clause as far as the ability criterion is concerned, but it is not necessarily inadequate from the point of view of management. Adoption of such language in some agreements may have been a reluctant decision at the bargaining table. Yet it is sometimes accepted willingly because it reflects management's general practice prior to unionization; or it may be acceptable because management controls the seniority unit to be used; or there is a well-developed promotion ladder system and job training program. Finally, it is sometimes agreed to because of the nature of the skill requirements on most jobs.

The phrase "qualified for the job" means that the senior man must be able to meet the minimum recognized standards for the job. Thus, the senior person who applies, or bids, or is chosen (depending on the selection procedure) need not be the best qualified of those under consideration. Generally it is understood that a person who has had some satisfactory prior experience in temporary vacancies is automatically qualified for the job. However, the phrase can prove troublesome in several respects. Disagreements can arise on the factual question of whether a worker is or is not qualified. In the absence of proved, prior performance, what tests or criteria should be used? Does the phrase mean qualified at the time of his assignment to the vacancy, or is it enough if an employee's record establishes a *prima facie* case that he can become qualified in a relatively short period of time? Does the term mean qualified only for the job opening at hand, or, where there are promotional channels, does it also mean qualified to progress at a reasonable rate through the promotional hierarchy?

(2) "Ability, skill and competency being relatively equal, seniority shall govern in the applicable unit." This clause and the many variants of it are intended to give the senior man the promotion unless it can be shown that a junior man possesses superior ability. Unlike the first typical clause described, this one is designed theoretically to permit selection of the *best* man for the opening. In the hope that repetition will give such factors greater emphasis, some companies have tried to incorporate a series of words all related to the general concept of ability. Frequently the words are synonymous or nearly so, and subtle differences become meaningless. Thus, one clause adopted

at management's urging after many reversals under arbitration of its promotion decisions, read: "ability, experience, background, skill, capability, competency, reliability and aptitude being approximately equal, seniority shall govern." (This company found that the impressive array of words did not solve its promotion grievances.) It is true that some of the broad ability criteria specified in an agreement may have a substantive effect. For example, the words "general work record" were intended in one agreement to permit consideration of absenteeism, prior discipline notations, and willingness to work overtime, criteria which had been disallowed by an arbitrator under the prior clause.

This second type of clause offers more fertile breeding ground for complaints and disagreement than the first. Although many companies consider it the stronger of the two clauses from management's standpoint, other influences justify some speculation as to whether the choice of words adds materially to the weight of the ability factor. Under this clause, if a company is to select a junior employee from among those applying or being considered, it faces the administrative task of comparing abilities of different men. The greater the number of senior persons by-passed, the more difficult is the company's task. The union can rig a buckshot grievance, signed by all the more senior applicants claiming that their ability was equal or approximately equal to that of the promoted junior man. A recurrent problem of interpretation is whether the words ability *et al* refer to the individual's attributes in relationship to the specific job opening or whether they refer to his over-all desirability as an employee.

In a few contracts the parties themselves try to define ability. However, as in the case of "just cause" terminology for disciplinary action, unions usually prefer to retain the looser, undefined term, which leaves them free to challenge a company decision on two fronts: Was the concept of ability fairly defined by management, and if so, was it applied properly to the facts of the given case? But efforts to dispel ambiguities in the contract are not always successful. One contract, for example, was amended to define "ability" as the "capacity in management's judgment of the senior employee to meet the normal job requirements within a five (5) day trial period." This definition, in effect, meant a return to the first generic clause type described above; and in subsequent application other irritating questions arose, such as the soundness of management's judgment and whether the five-day trial period was to be given automatically to the senior employee.

Influence of Grievance Procedure and Arbitration
on the Criteria for Promotion

A review of management's decisions could be expected to produce useful (although not necessarily satisfactory to both parties) guideposts. In the initial stages of a collective bargaining relationship, the resolution of what was meant by "qualified" or "approximately equal ability" was more likely to be reached by arbitration than by the parties themselves. This was due in part to a lack of maturity in bargaining and in administering labor relations matters. Also, the average union representative is not disposed to reject the claim of a senior man that he is qualified to do a higher job or is as able as the promoted junior employee. Except in cases of obvious physical handicap, the self-appraisal of a senior man is accepted by the union. To discourage a claim involves a judgment decision the union is reluctant to make. If a union representative errs as a grievance processor, it is likely to be in favor of the senior employee. There is less hesitancy if tangible guideposts are established by arbitrators.

Sometimes management's decisions favoring the junior employee are disposed of readily, regardless of the stage of the parties' relationship. Evidence disclosed in the grievance discussion may convince the aggrieved that his claim is without merit; or the company may give the union assurance that the senior employee will be given first chance in the next promotion, a commitment that often has embarrassing consequences for management. It may result in the introduction of trial periods contrary to the company's intention. The harassment of supervision by grievances may mean the adoption of practices which go beyond the contract or which subtract from rights under the contract. For example, one company in a foreman training program emphasized the need for consultation with the union. It found later that several of its foremen were consistently conferring with the union steward and securing advance agreement on all promotions. The practice came to the attention of management when a new foreman made a promotion without the concurrence of the steward; the union argued that the practice was so firmly established that promotions had to be a product of joint deliberation and not of a management decision subject to challenge.

Occasionally the tendency to negotiate out grievances for the sake of settlement detracts in the long run from the original intent of contract language. One industrial relations director observed that contract law, insofar as labor relations are concerned, should contain a new secondary rule for contract interpretations: "Interpretation by Expediency." To illustrate, the head of an automobile tool and die plant said that the union had consistently pushed for seniority as a basis for selecting leaders, and reluctantly the company had engaged in horsetrading. In order to promote some of the employees the company wanted, it was necessary occasionally to accept the more senior, less able men the union wanted.

The settlement of grievances short of arbitration sometimes results in the legislation of additional principles for implementing contract language. Or, if it is concluded in grievance discussions that present language is inadequate, the company may adopt supplementary policy criteria. One company was asked by the union to define what was meant by "ability to do the work." It responded with a list of five factors which were not negotiated, but which served thereafter as guides: educational background, experience (relative), attitude, physical ability to perform the job, and sincerity of interest in the promotion. Some parties have legislated the principle that where the variation between abilities is slight and the variation between seniority ranking of the competing employees is great, the senior man will at least be given a chance to try out on the job. In some other instances, particularly in promotion grievances involving the skilled jobs, the parties have agreed that a formal testing procedure will decide relative abilities.

Interpretation by arbitration rulings, however, has been the principal method of "adding meat to the bones of the contract," or in the words of one disgruntled employer "of performing plastic surgery on the language of the promotion clause." Without trying to catalogue the many guideposts arbitrators have developed, we describe below some findings of principle that have gained widespread acceptance:

(1) In a significant number of cases, arbitrators have proceeded as if the burden of proving the superior ability of the junior employee were on the company, though theoretically the union, as the complaining party, would be expected to prove that the bypassed senior man was qualified or had approximately equal ability. This has far-reaching consequences. It puts the company in the position of having

to prove outstanding ability on the part of the junior man, even though this is not required by contract language. The industrial relations department may demand from the foreman a great deal of tangible evidence as to superior ability before it is willing to carry a case to arbitration. Eventually the foreman may reach the conclusion that advancing a junior man is not worth all the fuss and bother.

Arbitrators do not always transfer the burden of proof to the company. They are more likely to do so in layoff cases where relative abilities and qualifications are the issue. Yet it is done frequently enough in promotion cases to justify comment.

(2) The "head and shoulders" doctrine, which was originated by an umpire in the automobile industry has been adopted by many arbitrators. Under a clause providing that "in the advancement of employees to higher paid jobs, when ability, merit and capacity are equal, employees with the longest seniority will be given preference," the umpire suggested the following procedure:

(a) An outstanding employee, "head and shoulders" above others in ability, merit and capacity, is entitled to promotion irrespective of seniority considerations. If necessary, management should have no difficulty in pointing out the factors that account for his superior qualifications.
(b) When such an outstanding employee is not available, management may select employees whose "ability, merit and capacity" are adjudged by management to be approximately equal. The individual in the group with greatest seniority may then be selected for the promotion. . . .

The "head and shoulders" principle is probably practiced by many managements even though it is not spelled out. There is much to be said for deciding close cases on the basis of seniority, because seniority is objective and what is objective is good for employee morale. The "head and shoulders" concept has proven itself practicable to both companies and unions. Generally, both parties can agree on the ten best men for the job, for example. The selection of the most senior employee among the ten is then acceptable to the union and company.

(3) In general, arbitrators have been more disposed to accept management's judgment on ability in the promotion of employees to key jobs because the element of ability is considered more important on this type of job. The difficulty of measuring ability for key jobs is

often recognized by the arbitrator, and less stringent standards are imposed on a company.

(4) In promotions to semi-skilled jobs and even noncritical jobs of some skill, arbitrators have been disposed to offset slight differences of ability with substantial differences in seniority. Thus, even if a company shows that the abilities of the junior and senior employee were not equal, seniority is often allowed to prevail.

(5) Where management has a reasonable and well-developed policy for measuring ability and where its policy has been applied without union protest over the years, the arbitrator will accept it as a guide. For example, in some utility companies written tests are used to determine the relative abilities of workers interested in advancement. Even though these formal tests are not agreed to by the union, the arbitrator will confirm their use in implementing the agreement.

(6) Many companies complain that arbitrators are unwilling to accept as persuasive evidence of inferior ability anything except demonstrated inability to perform the job. Whether this conclusion is justified is very questionable on the basis of available evidence; but the view is so widely held that it has conditioned management behavior. Often this inference is derived from an arbitrator's conclusion that actual experience on the job is the best possible evidence of a man's ability or lack of it.

The role arbitration has played in developing these and other more specific interpretations of the promotion clause has had a significant effect on many relationships. One multiplant company reported that there used to be many grievances on this subject; now they are infrequent because of the body of precedent established by arbitration decisions. A large automobile company said that its rules for promotion have been staked out by 75-80 umpire decisions on which the company relies as a basis for foreman training on promotional policy. On the other hand, as observed earlier in this chapter, there are many managements which deplore the extent to which arbitrators have made law and policy in this area. They feel that arbitrators have made it difficult for management to make promotions as much as they would like to on the basis of ability.

The Pattern of Operations and Skills

Regardless of the contract language, a company may in actual practice place little or no emphasis on the ability factor. This may follow from a rational appraisal of the skills involved. If the level of responsibility, experience, and job knowledge required is fairly low, ability will be interpreted in one way; if the jobs are highly skilled, ability will assume more importance as a criterion. A coal operating company said that in considering ability it looked only to the safety factor; if there was reason to believe a senior man might be a safety risk, he would be by-passed. Otherwise, the senior man was automatically chosen. The vice president in charge of industrial relations of an automobile company said that for the great bulk of jobs, ability, merit, and capacity were roughly equal anyway, and therefore seniority generally governed. The view was often expressed that with machine-paced jobs or with automated operations, where much of the work involved watching and correcting the machines, differences in ability could not be measured adequately. In the words of one employer:

> As the company grew from 5,000 to 30,000 people, it became impossible for supervisors to adequately judge people's ability. There were many claims that via favoritism, relatives and friends were being promoted. We gave in to the pressure and instituted a straight seniority system. I don't think ability matters much in the first five labor grades. The skill needs get stiffer above that though, and it's at these higher levels that we sometimes by-pass a senior man. For example, if a job requires some imagination and ingenuity the supervisor is in the best position to judge whether or not the senior man has it. . . .[8]

For very skilled jobs management usually places much more emphasis on ability, even to the point of requiring special tests or proof of a certain number of years of training and experience. In summary, the ability criterion is less important in the low-skill jobs. If statistics show a high percentage of promotions of top seniority employees, it does not necessarily follow that the ability criterion has been neglected. It may mean only that in many cases the senior employees were the most qualified or that the ability criterion was considered unimportant.

Management's Administrative Procedures

The very fact that the criterion of ability is uncertain in meaning and susceptible to subjective application makes the influence of man-

---

[8] Neil W. Chamberlain, "Management, on the Importance of Ability in Promotions," *Sourcebook on Labor* (1958), p. 677. The other observations by management in this article are equally interesting.

agement personnel procedures of great importance. It is the company through one or more of its representatives that decides who is to be promoted; it is the company that exercises judgment as to basic qualifications and relative abilities. One would expect, therefore, that management would take the initiative in developing procedures to give full force and effect to the contract language. Surprisingly, this is not always the case. As a consequence, the language of the agreement acquires interpretation from other influences, with results that are not always satisfactory to management. There is a high correlation between lack of good administrative practices and the number of complaints that the ability criterion in the promotion clause has been emasculated over the years. It would be wrong to infer from this conclusion that the mere existence of personnel practices insures minimum challenge of management decisions. Sometimes the policy is ill-conceived or is poorly administered with the result that other influences prevail.

Among the various practices adopted by some companies, the following have had a significant effect on the interpretation and application of promotion criteria:

FOREMAN TRAINING. Because the foreman plays the most important role in deciding who is to be promoted, the subject of promotions is an integral part of foreman training. If the company itself has developed criteria for measuring ability or if grievance disposition and umpire rulings have established guides, these are made known to the foreman. One large company, which has expressed satisfaction with the role ability plays in conjunction with seniority, reports that it emphasizes the foreman's system of choosing the man for promotion. This is prompted by the discovery that the outside arbitrator is more concerned with whether the foreman tried to consider all the relevant factors and was not obviously prejudiced. Thus, in working with the foremen, the company covers such topics as the scope of selection, the steps and criteria to be followed, and the choice of criteria for different kinds of cases. Job requirements are determined first, and then criteria are developed on the basis of these; finally, the men under consideration are evaluated in terms of the criteria for the specific jobs to be filled rather than for jobs in general.

Most companies that attach a great deal of importance to foreman training realize that they must see that the foremen do not follow the path of least resistance by using seniority as the principal criterion in the interest of harmony with the union. They try to forestall the gradual erosion of the ability consideration by watching the administration of the clause. However, a few companies fail to go beyond the initial training step and admit that they do not know whether the foremen are promoting qualified or the most able men. It is assumed that by and large they will for their own protection. Whether this assumption is justified or not cannot be determined.

DEVELOPMENT OF DEFINITIONS AND MEASUREMENTS OF ABILITY. Divergent views among management representatives at all levels as to what constitutes ability, the fact that the concept of ability applicable to one type of job may not be appropriate for another type of job, and the inevitable inclusion of subjective concepts (attitude, cooperation, etc.)—all of these are obstacles to a systematic definition and measurement of ability. Nevertheless, it has been tried by a number of companies with varying degrees of success.

Some companies use elaborate merit or ability rating schemes. One of the plants of a large automobile corporation relies on the "critical incident" technique, a system of giving employees a red or a blue mark for a particularly praiseworthy (or the reverse) action. The plant personnel director is satisfied that it is an effective program, and, except for a concern that it may be used in disciplinary cases, the union has recognized it as an acceptable guide in promotions. A dairy company worked out a system for rating bidders for route vacancies. The union claims that this grew out of its dissatisfaction with the company's prior reliance on the unsubstantiated opinions of foremen. It even takes credit for suggesting the factors to be used: sales records, collection records, and a miscellaneous category covering accidents, customer complaints, or any other item in the man's record which is "particularly good or bad." A numerical weighting system is applied. As mentioned above, a number of companies use formal tests to determine qualification or relative abilities for promotion to particular jobs.

Formal merit rating programs are by no means the answer to management's problem of defining and measuring employee ability for promotion purposes. In fact, it is fair to conclude from the evidence that where the merit rating system is most elaborate, there is more likely to be a breakdown in administration and a greater opportunity for union attack on management's judgment. For example, one such plan rated a man on six factors (quality, quantity, adaptability, job knowledge, dependability, and attitude) and provided for no less than eight possible scores for each factor. Inevitably the differences between scores were slight, and individual ratings were difficult to defend. One company reported:

> We have discontinued our employee rating system. Constant attacks by the union against the rating principle itself, together with an unflagging pressure through the grievance procedure against the raters (supervisors) to "prove" their distinctions, nullified all attempts to get judicious ratings.[9]

This problem is discussed in Chapter 20 in connection with the use of merit rate ranges in the wage structure. Most managements have learned that an elaborate system is not the answer; it may complicate further the use of the ability criterion.

One company recently installed what it calls an Employee Qualification Index. To insure that qualifications of employees would not be overlooked in promoting workers, the company had each employee fill out a questionnaire showing all his experience, education, and training outside the plant that would apply to various job skills. The company does not use the EQI's as part of its defense in handling grievances, but it has found that the index is an important aid in promoting qualified people. The company states that it was "amazed to learn how many people under its very nose had experience and skills it never knew about."

EMPLOYEE TRAINING PROGRAMS. Although not a company practice which lends meaning to the terms of the contract, the development of special training programs for certain jobs can remove much of the uncertainty in applying the ability criterion. These programs may be worked out unilaterally by the company or jointly with the union. This has been done for such skilled jobs as production mechanic, machine repairman, and the like. A large firm in the electronics industry and its union have agreed to a joint upgrading program designed to enhance promotional opportunities; by its very nature it will provide employee ability guides.

[9] National Industrial Conference Board, *Appraisal of Job Performance*, Studies in Personnel Policy, No. 121 (1951), p. 15.

The Locus of Decision-Making

Who makes the final decision to promote one person rather than another depends on a number of factors, such as the breadth of the priority unit, the availability of qualified persons within the unit, and company policy. If the seniority unit extends beyond the jurisdiction of one foreman and if applicants must be considered who work under different foremen, the decision may rest with a general foreman, department head, or division manager. Whoever makes the decision is expected to confer with the various immediate supervisors to secure their judgments on the capabilities of the employees involved.

Typically, the decision to promote is a "line" function. There is some reason to believe that the immediate supervisor or foreman is more likely to give greater weight to seniority than to ability, even when he is convinced that the senior man has markedly less ability than a junior applicant. Management representatives in the higher echelons whose advice as to relative abilities is sought are more inclined to emphasize differences in ability. The reasons for this are not difficult to understand. The immediate supervisor is subjected more directly to dual pressures.

On one hand, the supervisor is expected by management to operate an efficient unit, and the harmony of employees working under him as well as a low grievance rate are often considered in appraising his supervisory ability. In reviewing the records of one company, it was found that grievances concerning promotion had been filed at one time or another by employees under all except six foremen who had held their supervisory positions for three years or more. But it was then found that these six had never promoted other than the senior person who had applied for an opening under a limited unit bid system. The company was not aware of this until the research investigations were conducted.

On the other hand, the first-line supervisor is exposed to the pressure of the union steward and seeks to avoid decisions that will incur his resentment or displeasure. The net result is decision-making that influences and often alters the contract language.

Because of a heavy grievance load or adverse arbitration verdicts, the staff of the industrial relations or personnel department of a plant may play an important part in the decision. Theoretically they are called on for advice, but actually they often decide who is to be promoted. In one automobile stamping plant, the labor relations supervisor runs the entire promotion system. Evidence shows that the best arrangement is one in which the immediate supervisor makes recommendations, as he does in discharge cases. His recommendations are then reviewed by personnel, and together they arrive at a promotion decision they feel is consistent with the labor-management agreement.

The Relationship Between Parties

The relative influences of seniority and ability may depend on the relationship between the parties. If the union is very weak and the company very strong, the company may give great weight to differences in ability, however slight such differences are. One hosiery company said it very rarely promotes on the basis of seniority but it also said that "you'd never know there was a union in the shop." Other companies said that they have practically given up trying to use the ability factor to promote an employee out of seniority, because of pressure tactics used by the union. If the relationship is one of mutual trust, the company will normally use the ability criterion where it is meaningful and readily apparent. The union, in turn, will usually accept management's judgment, recognizing that its by-passing of senior employees was probably justifiable.

In summary, unions have greatly affected management's freedom to promote whomever it chooses. Union challenges of promotion decisions are no longer limited to the narrow bases of favoritism and discrimination. They have succeeded in introducing procedural arrangements and criteria for promotion that reduce management's freedom. Many of these have helped to improve employee morale. But there is reason to conclude that the most able junior man is frequently prevented from advancement because of union insistence on the seniority criterion or because management has failed to exercise its rights wisely under the labor-management agreement. More often than not it is management's remissness rather than unrealistic union-imposed controls that has been responsible for the growing use of seniority instead of ability as the principal promotion criterion.

8 / *Work Scheduling*

WHEN A UNION IS CERTIFIED or recognized as the sole collective bargaining agent by a company, one of its acknowledged responsibilities is to bargain hours of employment. It might be inferred from this and from a casual inspection of the terms of agreements that a union's impact on work-scheduling is limited to a definition of the workday and workweek. This is not the case. Collective bargaining in the past twenty years has introduced many indirect, devious, and subtle influences on scheduling.

For example, the meaning of scheduled work has been revised in the past two decades. If 8 hours of work are scheduled during a day or 40 hours during a week, does this schedule mean by contract definition that all of these hours are to be devoted to the production of goods or the performance of services? The answer is almost certainly no, because of idle time periods within the work schedule that are treated as work periods. Rest periods, lunch periods, wash-up time, holidays with pay, travel time, and many other nonproductive periods have acquired through collective bargaining the status of "work" time. In Chapter 15, "Employee Benefits," the scope of these new arrangements will be discussed in some detail.[1]

The present chapter is concerned with four principal subjects: (1) The nature and scope of the conflict between the needs of industry and the interests of workers, (2) union measures to deal with this conflict, (3) control of the use of leisure, and (4) implications of union policy.

---

[1] The readjustments of schedule required by equal-division-of-work provisions at the time of work curtailment have been discussed in Chapter 6. The impact of guaranteed annual wage and supplementary unemployment benefit programs on the scheduling of work is treated in Chapter 16.

Nature and Scope of the Conflict

Quite apart from any union influences, managements do not always have complete freedom to decide how work is to be scheduled. Sometimes the range of managerial discretion is surprisingly narrow. Influences beyond management's direct control and beyond the union's ability to regulate are constantly at work. Large groups of workers are called upon to work unusual hours on a regular basis or from time to time even though both the employer and the union would prefer an orthodox schedule.

Influences Outside of Collective Bargaining

The origin and often the form of union interest in the scheduling of work become much more meaningful if the variety of factors that influence scheduling are understood. Among the several work scheduling determinants other than collective bargaining, the following will illustrate the problems encountered by managements and unions in their efforts to systematize or regularize the hours of work.

HABITS OF CONSUMING PUBLIC. To a considerable extent the hours that some people work are determined by the buying or use habits of the ultimate consumer. This is the case particularly in the service industries. For example, a local transit company must operate at peak capacity during the early hours of the morning and the late hours of the afternoon to handle the large volume of passengers going to and from their work. The "spread" of the workday for some transit employees may be 12 to 14 hours, but during the relatively slow hours of 10:00 A.M. to 4:00 P.M. there will not be enough demand to justify full use of equipment. Therefore, many employees must be available at widely separated periods of the day, and yet the intervening time-off periods are often too short to permit the employees to go home or to engage in other pursuits to their liking. These employees, in effect, are committed to their work for 12 to 14 hours but actually work a lesser number of hours each day. We shall see later in this chapter how union pressures to limit the spread or to provide proper compensation for the off-hours have stimulated transit company efforts to mold consumer habits. To illustrate, publicity campaigns are undertaken to persuade the housewife to do her in-town shopping between 10:00 A.M. and 4:00 P.M.

Other branches of the transportation industry have similar scheduling problems because of the nature of consumer demand. In scheduling daily passenger train runs there must be some accommodation to the peak period demand. Airline companies must plan their scheduling to respond as effectively as possible to the Friday afternoon and Sunday night traffic volume. It is obvious that the incidence of layovers away from home for airline pilots, stewardesses, and flight engineers is high on weekends. Having completed an East Coast-West Coast flight on Friday evening, New York-based personnel may have to remain on the West Coast until Sunday or Monday before there is a scheduled return flight for them to operate. As in the case of local transit companies, the railroads and airlines have tried with little success to revamp passenger habits. The adoption of "family fare plans," applicable during the slow days of the week, was designed in part to regularize passenger use and thereby to reduce erratic or "bunched" scheduling. Nearly all transportation companies are confronted not only with daily and weekly scheduling problems but also with seasonal or emergency problems. These influences are discussed below.

The schedules of department stores, variety stores, food marts, and other retail establishments are a reflection of the buying public's desire for convenient opportunities to shop. Restaurants, hotels, the entertainment business all must maintain unusual schedules of work to satisfy the public. For many years the milk industry was reluctant to discontinue daily delivery of milk to homes, although this frequency of service involved costly scheduling problems. It was believed that consumer insistence on fresh milk required daily delivery. In recent years this fetish has been greatly modified, thanks in part to improved refrigeration methods. But to no small extent union pressures helped bring about every-other-day milk delivery although the principal union involved—the Teamsters—did not advocate this rescheduling of service.

These few illustrations, which could easily be added to and enlarged upon, show how the habits of the buying public dictate the hours of work of large segments of our working population. In fact, the very nature of work schedules observed by millions of people in our economy almost forces the adoption of different work schedules for millions of other people.

NATURE OF THE PRODUCT OR SERVICE. In many cases what may be considered an unorthodox schedule results from the characteristics of the product being made or the service being rendered. It is not easy to draw a sharp distinction between this determinant and the influence of the buying public.

Illustrative of the product factor are the following. Some printing companies that print weekly or monthly periodicals must gear their schedules to the regular release date of the publications. A large company in Philadelphia, which prints *Life* magazine, must schedule two long shifts of 12 hours each on Monday and Tuesday to insure delivery of the product to all newsstands and to subscribers by Thursday and Friday. On Wednesday, Thursday, and Friday three short shifts of 8 hours each are worked. Newspaper publishers, although able to regularize their scheduling of work to a great extent, must adopt special schedules for morning, afternoon, and Sunday editions. The gathering of news, the make-up of the paper, the printing, and the distribution of the final product may involve different "odd-hour" scheduling for the various employees involved in each step of the process.

For many years large bakeries have felt it necessary to follow irregular scheduling to satisfy two considerations: the fact that 50 per cent of all bakery sales in supermarkets occur on two days of the week (a consumer-habit influence) and the requirement that the product be fresh. One plant found it necessary to run three shifts two days a week, two shifts on two days, and one shift on two days. If perishable products are involved, special scheduling often becomes necessary. Delivery of fruits and vegetables to local markets until fairly recent years, after refrigerated cars were introduced, required night-time schedules.

Periodic changes in product style sometimes create irregularities in work hours not only for the immediate manufacturer but also for the suppliers who are affected. This is true especially in the automobile industry, where major or minor design changes occur each year. During the changeover period short work schedules are characteristic of the prime producers and the automotive parts suppliers. Immediately after the changeover, with the introduction of the new models, long work schedules may be in effect. In some manufacturing industries the product is of such a specialized nature that the enterprise might be considered a job shop. Large items are made to order, and a fixed delivery date is specified. Manufacturers of large turbine equipment, locomotives, and complicated machines fall in this category. Unless advance orders are substantial, the work schedule may reflect the irregularity of orders. It is obvious that in a product market of this type, production for inventory is not a good way of regularizing schedule.

NATURE OF THE PROCESS. In some of our most important industries the very nature of the process involved calls for a continuous, round-the-clock operation, week after week. Ceasing operation on days or at hours normally considered periods of leisure by the rest of the community is not feasible. In the steel industry, coke ovens, blast furnaces, and open hearths, including the blooming mills, must be operated continuously. The process and technology make it pro-hibitively expensive to start and stop the equipment. The same is true in the glass industry because of the long time required to heat and cool the furnaces. Employees in these industries are expected to work on Saturdays and Sundays on a staggered basis. Thus, in one steel company 40 per cent of the employees work on a 6- or 7-week, rotating shift schedule. A Wednesday-through-Sunday schedule might be their regular workweek for $1\frac{1}{2}$ months; then they would change to a new regular workweek.

NATURE OF THE CAPITAL INVESTMENT. Similar to the case of industries where process is the determining factor, resulting in continuous or semi-continuous operation, is that of enterprises with unusually high capital investment per employee. High investment leads to the desire to reduce unit overhead costs by maximum utilization of equipment. To a certain extent this is true of some parts of the steel industry, where the process alone does not dictate continuous operations. The paper industry's interest in continuous operation is motivated by this cost consideration as well as by the considerable cost involved in shutting down for the week end. Using second and third shifts for a five-day week is another way of lowering overhead costs per unit.

SEASONAL INFLUENCES. Erratic scheduling may be caused in many in-dustries by seasonal factors. Again, these factors are sometimes related to natural or carefully cultivated consumer habits and tastes. Thus, a department store usually has to adopt special work schedules dur-ing the pre-Christmas and pre-Easter seasons. An airline serving Florida or Cape Cod has to schedule special flights during the winter and summer months respectively. In the entertainment-sports field, seasonal influences are considerable. Somewhat different from the seasonal influences related to customer preference are those in which the processing can and must be performed only at certain times of the year. Canning factories usually are scheduled for 24-hour-a-day operation during the harvesting season. Meat packers traditionally have found it necessary to correlate the kill and processing operations with the flow of livestock, which is somewhat seasonal in nature.

NATURE OF THE JOB. In a few enterprises the work to be done in certain occupations prevents any definite scheduling or requires what may be called unorthodox scheduling. Typical of the former are insurance agencies. While agents may be scheduled for specific reporting times or training times at the agency office one or two days a week, the rest of their activity is unscheduled. They are expected to utilize the most effective times available to sell policies and to collect premiums. In some areas the agent will find it desirable to visit homes only in the evening; or he may work a few hours during the day and a few hours at night. The absence of any fixed work scheduling, a natural characteristic of the work to be done, is invariably accompanied by a method of payment based upon performance rather than upon hours of work. Also typical of unorthodox scheduling related to certain jobs are the cases of watchmen and guards, and of maintenance men who can work on machines only when they are not in operation.

INFLUENCE OF WEATHER AND EMERGENCIES. In a number of industries the unpredictable weather element subverts the best efforts to adhere to a regular work schedule. The operation of airlines is an excellent illustration. In spite of use of the most detailed statistical analyses of past weather behavior in making flight schedules for winter and summer months and in spite of remarkable control systems to overcome weather situations, actual flight times are still subject to considerable weather influence. The variation of tail winds, the need to bypass storm centers, the inability to take off or to land because of low ceilings—all of these may disrupt the planned monthly schedule for the operating crews. The inability to schedule work systematically on outside building construction is almost entirely due to the variability of weather.

The handling of emergencies may be an inherent function of some types of enterprise. An electrical utility company or a telephone company must have sufficient flexibility of scheduling to allow for expeditious repair of breakdowns. Adherence to a rigid schedule would entail neglect of an essential purpose of the enterprise or would require maintenance of additional manpower on a continuous basis, which would be unreasonably expensive. In other companies the emergency or Act-of-God occurrence is infrequent but no less disruptive of scheduling. A major power failure, the breakdown of essential equipment, or the inability to secure necessary parts or raw materials because of a strike or transportation breakdown may force a hasty revision of schedule.

The possibility of an emergency influences scheduling. A company will often work long hours to build up inventory in anticipation of a strike. The payment of overtime is considered a reasonable investment to insure continued delivery to customers while a strike is in progress. Or, if a strike is probable in an industry, customer desire to stockpile in advance may force the industry to work longer hours. In the spring of 1959 the orders for steel were very heavy because the users of steel wanted to protect themselves in the event of a steel strike.

INFLUENCE OF LAW. The freedom to schedule work has been circumscribed in absolute terms or has been affected to a very great extent by local, state, and federal law. The Fair Labor Standards Act, requiring payment at the rate of time and one-half for hours of work in excess of 40 a week, serves as the model for the weekly overtime provisions in most collective bargaining agreements. The Walsh-Healy Act, which extends overtime pay requirements to hours in excess of 8 a day for work on government contracts, has resulted in the adoption of a similar requirement in most labor contracts. The pervasive effect of these two laws both on the terms of labor agreements and, more important, on the scheduling of work has been considerable.

In some cases existing laws are more specific and absolute in controlling the hours of work. A number of state laws prohibit the employment of women during certain nighttime hours. Federal regulations limit the number of flight hours a pilot may work in the course of a day or a month. State or local blue laws prohibit the opening of some enterprises on Sunday. The observance of a few stated holidays by complete shutdown of other than public-service enterprises is required in certain states. A more subtle effect of the law on work scheduling is to be found in the requirement that employees be paid within a certain time following performance of the work. When a pay day falls within a holiday week many companies have found it necessary to schedule Saturday or daily overtime work for the payroll department to insure compliance with the law. The growing prevalence of laws allowing limited time off on election days requires adjustment of work schedules.

GENERAL ECONOMIC DETERMINANTS. Applicable to nearly all enterprises are the influences on work scheduling of general fluctuations in the entire economy or of fluctuations affecting an industry or an enterprise. A cyclical downturn, the inability of a firm to meet competition, or the gradual decline of an industry will cause schedule adjustments: overtime will be discontinued, second and third shifts may be dropped, and the regular workweek may be reduced. The reverse will be true if the demands for the firm's or industry's product or services are unusually high.

INFLUENCE OF TECHNOLOGY. It has already been pointed out that continuous operations are more likely where the investment in capital equipment is great. Improved technology, however, may have a more immediate effect on work scheduling. Technology may be used for the deliberate purpose of regularizing the hours of work and of counteracting the factors described above that make for erratic scheduling.

One large bakery, troubled by the costs associated with the concentration of work in a few days each week, installed a freezing plant, which cut costs substantially by putting the baking of bread on the same basis as "making nuts and bolts." The freezer permitted elimination of night work, irregular starting times, and payments for overtime and idle time. Labor costs inherent in erratic scheduling were responsible in large measure for the investment in the freezer. Another large supermarket bakery plant has installed a freezer at a cost of $100,000 for the storage of cakes. Although production in quantity resulted in savings in material costs, the principal reason for the investment was the savings effected by more regularized production. This same bakery is now studying the possibility of advance preparation of dough. If this is successful, doughs can be made early in the week for baking later in the week. In the transportation industry improved technology has increased the opportunity to follow a more predictable schedule.

PERSONNEL CONSIDERATIONS. A recital of the factors other than collective bargaining that influence work scheduling would be incomplete without some mention of the personnel problems that help to determine the schedule. Regardless of whether a union represents the employees, the typical management today is mindful of the adverse effects of unrealistic scheduling and of the favorable personnel effects of a reasonable work schedule. Long hours of work over a sustained period frequently result in lower efficiency and higher absenteeism. The decision to add a second or a third shift may be affected by the knowledge that the labor market would provide only marginal employees for these less desirable hours. When the labor market is tight, the attractiveness of reasonable hours of work often helps a company's employment problem. Insurance companies, banks, colleges, and other establishments that rely heavily on women for office work emphasize the desirable work schedule. However, some manufacturing companies highlight the opportunity for overtime work, hoping to attract ambitious employees whose take-home pay will be increased by hours of work beyond 8 a day or 40 a week.

This listing of eleven determinants could be enlarged upon. They are adequate to show why work scheduling is a source of controversy in labor-management relations and why it is so difficult to negotiate and administer the terms of an agreement on hours of work. These influences are not always entirely beyond management's control; some managements have exaggerated the extent of their subservience.

Management's Scheduling Problems

In a few cases the extension of collective bargaining to a complete or almost complete product or service market has probably increased the independence of the individual enterprise from the pressure of competition in deciding what its work schedule will be. In still other cases the scheduling nightmare is the direct result of management's own attempt to create new buying habits and thereby improve its competitive position. Department stores, for example, have probably done as much to mold consumer buying habits as they have to exploit the more natural, existing habits. The same is true of automobile manufacturers, who have created an annual preoccupation with new styles.

But by and large, a regular 8:00 A.M. to 5:00 P.M. schedule, Monday through Friday, on a permanent basis is not possible in most of American industry. The eleven factors suggest that there is a range of scheduling complexities. Many companies, mostly in manufacturing, are able to fix regular and orthodox hours for the employees.[2] But even these companies face occasional shifts in the volume of business or experience emergencies. When this happens, the problem of scheduling individuals arises. With reasonable orthodox regularity, the scheduling problem is less serious for these companies. The problems that do arise border on issues of work assignment.

Next are companies with continuous operations, such as steel, oil, and chemical firms. They must arrange special schedules for groups of employees to give them a semblance of regularity in their work-life. But such schedules cannot allow only for daytime work and cannot avoid week end work. Moreover, for these companies the continuous nature of operations may create aggravating problems in assigning individuals. For example, if no one is on layoff and members of the group have already worked 8 hours, who is to cover for absentees on the succeeding shift?

Even more complex are the problems of companies in the airline and railroad industries. For several of the reasons mentioned above, it is difficult, if not impossible, for them to maintain regular and orthodox hours for their employees.

Perhaps the greatest absence of fixed work scheduling is to be found where casual employment exists. Attachment to an employee may be so brief that the schedule is determined on a day-by-day or week-by-week basis.

In any discussion of management's scheduling problems it is important to recognize the close relationship between scheduling and the manning of jobs. The simplest illustration of this is the alternative available to many companies of working the existing complement of employees overtime or hiring more employees to handle the extra work. In some instances scheduling limitations force over-manning, as in the case of the airlines. A more recent example is that of the oil industry and its trend toward contract maintenance. For

[2] The term "orthodox" as used in this chapter means daytime, Monday-through-Friday hours.

many years the companies were over-manned with maintenance employees because they had to be certain of an adequate work force to handle the periodic turnarounds. Normal maintenance needs were far less than peak-force needs. An oil company could not easily hire extra persons for maintenance turnaround because of the expectation of steady employment by normal factory workers. As a consequence, there has been a clear trend toward the contracting out of this work to outside groups. The building trades crafts do not have as strong a resistance to irregular scheduling and are willing to take on job assignments that may last only a short time. In effect, the scheduling problems of oil companies have led to solutions that in turn create subcontracting issues with their industrial union of the type described in Chapter 10.

Union and Employee Interests

Union interest, as we shall see throughout this chapter, is often at odds with the practical considerations that influence management's scheduling decisions. At least six, sometimes conflicting, factors help to explain union and employee interest: (1) a desire for leisure time, (2) health considerations, (3) personal convenience, (4) additional money, (5) job security, and (6) increased job opportunities.

It is emphasized that these desires of employees are by no means consistent from one group to another or from one period of time to another. To illustrate, while employees generally are interested in a shorter workweek, they are often equally anxious to avail themselves of overtime work opportunities because of the premium pay involved. The very success of the union in achieving the shorter workweek with penalty payments for hours scheduled beyond a certain number has often stimulated employees to want longer hours and to compete for the privilege of working longer hours. Employees in an industry suffering from a cyclical or secular decline will want a short week with no reduction in take-home pay. Scheduling becomes an issue in combating unemployment.

The conflict of interest between leisure and added income is sometimes heightened by the time factor. Employees who normally are eager to work all available overtime will suddenly become convinced of the sanctity of the regular work schedule when asked or ordered to work overtime during the hunting or fishing season or during summer months. The employee who is plagued at the moment by installment plan obligations or unexpected drains on his income will find the remunerations of an irregular schedule far more desirable than the convenience and planned leisure permitted by a predictable, orthodox schedule. The dichotomy of employee preference does not permit generalizations, but it can be explained rationally in terms of time and the circumstances of each individual.

Sometimes the interests of employees are not compatible with those of the union as an institution. Many employees would prefer to have added work handled by overtime scheduling than by the addition of a second shift or by the employment of more persons for the existing shift. The union, in turn, may favor greater employment, either to rationalize its traditional argument for a shorter workweek or to gain institutional strength through more members. One of the difficult tasks of union leadership is the reconciliation of the short-run, occasionally shortsighted, desires of its members with the long-run goals and interests of the union and its membership.

As a consequence, anomalous situations arise. Employers who have yielded reluctantly to a reduced schedule of work and have agreed to the payment of premiums for overtime, call-in, or other scheduling irregularities are often confronted by union grievances on behalf of those who want to enjoy the gains of these irregularities. This is an irritant to many employers. Sophisticated employers have learned to recognize that the union's attitude in negotiations does not necessarily reflect its attitude in the processing of a particular grievance.

In summary, the conflict of interests in scheduling is considerable. What a company might want or need to do because of one or more of the eleven determinants described does not coincide with union and employee desires, explained in terms of the six factors listed. The further conflict arising between union long-term and employee short-term interests serves to heighten the problem for the employer.

Union Measures to Deal with the Conflict

It is difficult to classify the many ways in which unions have affected the scheduling of work. Some union policies and achievements are concerned directly with this subject. Others, however, involve very different matters, yet have a significant influence on how work is scheduled. The influences, therefore, are both *direct* and *indirect*.

Direct Measures

The *direct* measures, in general, seek to accomplish three objectives: to limit departure from normality, to make departure from normality a function of joint agreement, and finally, to penalize the use of abnormal arrangements by premium pay requirements. The concept of normality has been fairly stable in the past twenty years. In the discussion that follows, these direct measures will be considered: (1) definition of the regular workweek, (2) definition of the regular workday, (3) control of starting and quitting times, (4) scheduling and manning of shifts, (5) penalty payments for irregular work scheduling.

DEFINITION OF THE REGULAR WORKWEEK. Although the labor movement in the United States is associated traditionally with the drive for the shorter workweek, there has been little change in the length of the workweek within the past twenty years, during which union membership reached an all-time peak. This is not surprising since it is a period in which there was no major depression. On the contrary, the pressures on the economy during World War II and the Korean War and the great pent-up consumer demands in the years following led to unusually high employment. In fact, over the past twenty years the average number of hours worked per week in manufacturing industries has been in excess of 40. Under these circumstances the labor movement as a whole made no concerted drive for the shorter workweek.[3]

The fact that the standard workweek has not been reduced does not mean that the union drive for more leisure time has not progressed. In these twenty years the preference has been to secure more leisure time in the form of more liberal vacations and holidays. In effect, the total number of hours worked regularly on an annual basis has declined.

In some specific industries, however, changes have been made in the regular workweek. Either conditions peculiar to the industry have resulted in the adoption of a workweek of less than 40 hours, or industries that traditionally have been on a longer workweek have been forced by collective bargaining to conform to the nationally-recognized norm.

Illustrative of the first group is the lithographic industry. The

[3] For a further discussion of this subject and of the growth of premium pay arrangements, see Chapter 15, "Employee Benefits."

Amalgamated Lithographers led the drive in the commercial printing industry to secure a shorter workweek as a means of maintaining
jobs in the face of technological change. In 1946 the union was able
to gain a 36 1/4-hour week in many segments of the industry, and in
1954 there was a further drop to 35 hours a week. In the 1955 convention the delegates unanimously rejected the use of a guaranteed
annual wage as a substitute for, or as a supplement to, their shorter
workweek approach.

In the baking industry there has been similar union preoccupation
with the effects of rapid mechanization over the past twenty years.
In 1955 the major demand on the West Coast was for a reduction in
the workweek to 35 hours although the union made pensions and
insurance the key issues for bakeries elsewhere in the nation. By
1956 this campaign was successful, and as of 1960 the 35-hour workweek was fairly standard throughout the entire industry. In large segments of the rubber, men's clothing, and construction industries a
36-hour workweek was gained by collective bargaining some years
ago.

Typical of those industries that customarily had long workweeks
and recently reduced the week to a level closer to 40 hours are the
trucking and railroad industries. A Midwest over-the-road agreement
provided for the gradual reduction of hours in some localities from
60 to 40 per week with an offsetting increase in basic wages to protect take-home pay.

A 40-hour workweek standard became the principal goal of a
number of railroad brotherhoods in late 1948. For thirty years the
railroad employees had been on a regular schedule of six 8-hour days
a week. In 1944 the carriers had granted a 2.4-cent wage increase in
lieu of overtime for hours in excess of 40. In 1948 sixteen nonoperating railway labor organizations demanded a 40-hour week with time
and one-half for Saturday work and double time for Sunday work.
The carriers countered that a large amount of Saturday and Sunday
work was unavoidable and that penalty payments could not reduce
the need for work on these days. They also said that the union demands would force them to get more employees to make up for the
man-hours lost.[4]

An Emergency Board set up to review the controversy pointed out
in its report to the President that

---

[4] This consequence may have been hoped for by the unions since there had been a
shrinkage of employment in the industry.

forty basic work hours per week with time and a half for overtime is the prevailing practice in American industry. . . . To a large degree it is an established working condition in many transportation industries, including airlines, pipelines, local transit, over-the-road busses and motor trucking. . . . It is in effect in innumerable continuous production industries. . . . The railroads now stand out as a striking exception.[5]

The Board recommended that a workweek of five 8-hour days be established with time and one-half for hours worked in excess of 8 a day and 40 a week. It also recommended that two consecutive days off, Saturday and Sunday wherever possible, be given in every 7 days. Basic rates were to be increased by 20 per cent to provide the same take-home pay for 40 hours' work as had been received under the 48-hour schedule. No punitive pay for Saturday and Sunday work as such was recommended.[6]

The Board's recommendations were adopted for the most part. In a similar proceeding this new concept of a regular workweek was extended to the operating groups.[7] The 40-hour week is now in effect throughout most of the railroad industry. As recently as July 1960 a successful strike was called by the Brotherhood of Railroad Trainmen on the Long Island Railroad to secure the 5-day week.

At the present time most employees in American industry enjoy a regular workweek of 40 hours, with penalty payments assured for hours worked in excess of this number. The exceptions are mainly in the hotel and service industries and, to a lesser extent, in transportation. Some collective bargaining agreements provide for a variable "regular" workweek. The variation may be a function of seasonal requirements, as in the case of a food company whose agreement allows a 48-hour "exempt" week at straight time when the preparation, cooking, or freezing of perishables is being conducted. In the hotel industry the variation may be a matter of occupation, with dining room employees on a 44- or 48-hour straight time week while others are on a 40-hour week. Sometimes the variable workweek depends on the geographical location of the work. For example, in the maritime industry a 48-hour week prevails for work done in port, but a 56-hour week prevails for work at sea.[8]

[5] *Report to the President*, Emergency Board 66, National Mediation Board Case A-2953, December 17, 1948, pp. 11-12.
[6] The concept of punitive pay for work on "abnormal days" is discussed below in the section on "Penalty Pay."
[7] *Report to the President*, Emergency Board 81, N. M. B. Case A-3290, June 15, 1950.
[8] Harry P. Cohany and Dena G. Weiss, "Hours of Work and Overtime Provisions in Union Contracts," *Monthly Labor Review* (February 1958), pp. 134-35.

DEFINITION OF THE REGULAR WORKDAY. The spread of the 40-hour week as a norm gained considerable impetus through the enactment of the Fair Labor Standards Act in 1938. Collective bargaining was responsible largely for the extension of this norm to industries not subject to the Act, such as transportation and intra-state operations. To a greater extent unions have been responsible for the fixing of daily schedule standards. FLSA was silent on this subject, and the Walsh-Healy Act prescribed daily overtime after 8 hours for companies doing work under government contracts. Inevitably, however, both provided a basis for the extension of the 8-hour day norm. By 1958 this norm was found in 85 per cent of the agreements studied by the BLS.[9] In the ladies' garment industry a 7-hour day had been secured through collective bargaining. The Pacific Coast longshoremen had gained a 6-hour day. The shorter workday was also prevalent in the rubber and men's clothing industries.

In summary, the 8-hour day and the 5-day, 40-hour week represent "normality" in American industry. The following sections are concerned largely with the departures from this legal or contract-prescribed normality and union efforts to control such departures. Although the workweek and workday standard has been stable for many years, there is reason to believe that it may become a critical bargaining issue in the future. The 1958 recession and the unemployment in some industries in 1960 prompted a number of unions to warn management that the shorter workweek is likely to be a principal union goal in the decade of the '60's. Having now increased leisure time through liberalization of vacations and holidays, they are likely to seek additional leisure through the shorter workweek.

CONTROL OF STARTING AND QUITTING TIMES. Many labor agreements specify the starting and quitting times for each shift and permit changes in these times only where such changes are dictated by sound business reasons. A few agreements provide that the management will discuss the changes with the union before they are made effective. However, where the scheduling of work is inherently unorthodox or irregular, unusual controls and arrangements may emerge. For example, in some bakery establishments the timing of technical sequences makes it difficult to have well-defined shifts. Bakery workers often cannot have regular starting hours because whenever management changes the volume of production or the type

[9] The same, p. 136.

of product, there is a change in the number of hours the bakery must run.

As a result, unions in the baking industry have tried successfully to place an absolute maximum on the hours of work per day. In one large bakery the union limits the number of hours any employee may work to 10 within a 24-hour period. This means that if 11 hours of work are needed, the company must add a second shift. In this particular case the impact on scheduling is aggravated by a companion clause providing that if a second shift is added, the employees on it will be guaranteed at least a full 8 hours' pay. Thus, if 11 hours of work are needed, the company must pay for two 8-hour shifts, or 16 hours.

The trucking industry, which is also in the category of enterprises with unorthodox irregularity of schedule, is confronted by increased demands from the union for a definite starting time. The union has proposed the imposition of penalties if an employer uses irregular starting hours. In the opinion of some employers, such a penalty would be enough to drive a few companies out of business; it is claimed that they have no control over the specific time they start operations because they service other employers with irregular trucking needs. Although the penalty approach has been resisted for the most part, New York employers must now pay a penalty if the starting time falls outside the 7:00-9:00 A.M. period. The union objective in this situation is not to obtain more money but to regularize starting times for the personal convenience of drivers.

For many years a powerful longshore group in an East Coast port has refused to work after 11:00 P.M., thus often delaying the dispatch of ships. Although personal convenience may be a reason for this arbitrary refusal to work, it is more likely to be a result of the inherent casualness of employment in this industry. By setting this limit, the employees are able to force a partially loaded or unloaded ship to remain over for another day, thus improving the chances of increasing the total number of hours worked.

In the interest of additional pay, one union has deliberately insisted that an unnecessarily early starting time be maintained. A fish processing union succeeded in establishing a 6:00 A.M. starting time for the warehouse handlers. However, the fish boats normally arrive at the dock at 6:00 A.M., and the auctioning of the catch is not completed until 8:00 A.M. During this two-hour interval there is nothing for the warehouse handlers to do. In effect, they are paid for idle time. The monetary gain from this arbitrary starting time is compounded by the payment of time and one-half after 8 hours on the job.

The costly direct control of starting and quitting times described above is not typical of industry in general. It is generally limited to those industries in which irregularity of operation is necessarily great or in which casual employment tempts workers to maximize income or job security by exploiting schedule irregularities.

In some industries the union is willing to accommodate management if rigid starting and quitting times are harming the company's competitive position. For example, an agreement between a milk drivers' union and small retail dairies provided that no driver could work more than 9 hours a day; retail trucks "must be off the street" by 6:00 P.M., and no retail deliveries could be made before 8:00 A.M. In the winter (November to April) no loading was allowed before 7:00 A.M., and in the summer (April to November) no loading before 6:30 A.M. was permitted. In its negotiations with large retailers the union was persuaded to accept 7:00 A.M. as the starting time for deliveries. Within a few months the union discovered that this disparity in starting times placed the small retailers at a great competitive disadvantage. The one-hour advantage of the larger companies enabled their drivers to attract customers by promising earlier and prompter deliveries. The union succeeded in setting back the starting time for the large retailers to 8:00 A.M., thus removing the advantage the latter had enjoyed. The 6:00 P.M. quitting time in this contract has also been administered flexibly in the interest of the small dairies. When the union discovered that the large dairies, with more customers per unit of area, were able to handle the deliveries more easily within the prescribed time limits, it entered into an agreement that the 6:00 P.M. deadline could be ignored on the following basis:

> . . . a salesman will not discontinue the performance of his regular duties at the "off the street hour" if delayed by conditions beyond the employer's control or because of unusual collection problems.

SCHEDULING AND MANNING OF SHIFTS. Under most agreements the company is free to add to or subtract from the number of shifts it operates. In only a few situations can evidence be found of successful union pressure to curb the addition of more shifts. In a mill of a large steel company the union was effective in opposing the addition of a fourth crew when more than 15 turns were operated, although this was customary in other plants of the same company. The men had a strong preference for overtime work and the resultant earnings. Until recent years the company was unsuccessful in breaking down this opposition. In some companies it is required that extra shifts be dropped when there is a reduction in work volume.

Shift differentials have as their principal purpose the compensation of employees for having to work disagreeable hours. Unions seldom try to increase the penalty pay for nighttime hours to the extent of discouraging the addition of shifts. The noteworthy exceptions are in industries that have concentrated much of their work scheduling in the night hours. The bakery workers' union, for example, has tried unsuccessfuly to get the prevalent night work eliminated. After unsuccessful efforts to accomplish this by direct restriction, the union tried to use night-shift differentials to persuade the employer to allocate more of his employment to daytime hours and less to nighttime. In some localities this union succeeded in negotiating shift differentials as high as 25 to 27 cents an hour for hours between 6:00 P.M. and 6:00 A.M. in a genuine desire to discourage night work. This use of differentials as a penalty measure has not achieved the desired result. The large bakeries have been willing to pay the high price for night work in the interest of customer requirements, but, what is more interesting, the employees, whose resentment of working at night prompted the union action, now find the temptation of the high differentials too great to be resisted. If anything, the union's approach has backfired; now employees prefer the night work to the day work.

Nevertheless, the gradual increase in night shift differentials over recent years, regardless of purpose, has become a significant element in management's decision whether to handle greater work volume by adding a second or third shift or by using present personnel on an overtime premium basis. In this decision the cost consideration is obviously not limited to overtime premiums *versus* shift differentials. As we shall see, the use of overtime has hidden costs due to absenteeism and decreased efficiency; the addition of shifts has hidden costs due to the nature of the workforce attracted to night work, the fringe benefit commitments, and the added costs of more supervision.

Where pressures of the type described among the eleven factors discussed earlier do not make it essential or desirable to schedule

additional shifts on a continuing basis, both unions and managements seem to prefer the use of overtime to the addition of more
scheduled shifts.

In a few special cases unions have been instrumental in forcing the
addition of shifts even when management preferred to use overtime.
These are generally situations where the union has secured an absolute limit on the number of hours an employee may work per day,
as in the case cited above of the 10-hour day for bakery workers. For
very different reasons a steelworkers' local union in a saw manufacturing company, which operated under the Scanlon Plan, urged that
the workforce in a newly-acquired plant be divided between two
shifts so that the machinery could be utilized more effectively.

PENALTY PAYMENTS FOR IRREGULAR WORK SCHEDULING. The requirement that premium rates be paid for work performed after a certain
number of hours, or at times that represent a departure from the
normal schedule, has grown considerably in the past twenty years. It
is probably the most prevalent union measure to cope with the conflict described earlier in this chapter.

These penalty payments take many forms. The commonest form
is the payment of time and one-half for hours worked after 8 a day
and 40 a week. A restriction against the pyramiding of daily and
weekly overtime invariably accompanies the payment provision. This
pattern has remained the same for the past twenty years, consistent
with the relative stability in the definitions of the regular workweek
and workday. In the final section of this chapter attention will be
given to some of the policy questions that arise in connection with
overtime payments.

The present section will make note of the emergence during recent years of special penalty payment arrangements other than normal daily and weekly overtime. One of these is the growing recognition by union agreement that usually Saturdays and certainly Sundays are considered days of rest in our society. As a consequence,
more and more agreements now require premium pay for any work
performed on these days, regardless of whether the employees have
worked a full 40 hours during the week. The premium payment required is greater for Sunday than for Saturday. The trend is toward
double time for any work performed on Sunday. The same has occurred with respect to premiums for the sixth and seventh days of
work.

A BLS survey of 1,736 agreements in 1958 showed that over 90 per cent provided for time and one-half or double time, or a variable premium, for work done on one or both of the days outside the normal workweek.[10] As might be expected, these arrangements were most common in manufacturing industries, particularly those with noncontinuous operations.

However, since 1955 even those industries with continuous operations, where some employees are regularly expected to work Saturdays and Sundays on a staggered basis throughout the year, have yielded to union pressure to pay premiums. This became a critical issue in the 1956 steel negotiations. Prior to negotiations in that year, President David McDonald said, "This year shall be a breakthrough year on the subject of week-end premium pay." He said it was not the union's desire to put a penalty on the company so that its members could work and make extra money on the week end; "instead, it's an age-old desire of the steelworkers—even before the union—to spend some time with the family, go to church, and live like first-class American citizens on these days."[11] The steel companies countered that the union demand for time and one-half for Saturday and double time for Sunday would be nothing more than a penalty on the companies and a reward to employees because such a premium could not alter the necessity to work on these days.

In the 1956 strike settlement a Sunday premium of 10 per cent (an average of 25 cents per hour) was agreed upon for 1956, 20 per cent for 1957, and 25 per cent for 1958. In the 1959 negotiations the union asked for a liberalization of Sunday overtime, but in the settlement of the 116-day strike on January 4, 1960, no change was made in the 1956 premium provision.

Our information is inadequate to appraise the effect of premiums on scheduling in the continuous-operation industries, such as steel. The effect is probably slight. The premium serves mostly to compensate the employees who must work on Sunday, the traditional day of rest in most of American industry.

Another widely-adopted penalty approach is call-in pay arrangements. These provide an employee with a minimum number of hours of work or pay if he reports for his regular shift in the absence

[10] Rose Theodore, "Premium Pay for Weekend Work in Major Contracts," *Monthly Labor Review* (April 1959), pp. 379-88. See Chapter 15, "Employee Benefits," for a more detailed summary of this study.
[11] *Steel Labor* (May 1956), p. 3.

of advance notice not to come in. Similar arrangements apply to emergency call-in when employees are asked without prior notice to work during hours outside their regular shift. The following clause illustrates the type of contract provision that has become prevalent in recent years.

> Employees who report for work in their regular and usual way, unless notified not to report, and who are sent home without being given work shall receive four (4) hours pay for reporting. Employees who thus report for work shall be guaranteed four (4) hours of work, or the equivalent pay thereof, in the event they are not sent home when they report for work. They may, however, be offered a minimum of four (4) hours of employment on that day at other work within their ability to perform, in which event they shall perform such work at the classified hourly rate in effect for the classification at which they were scheduled or for which they were notified to report, or forfeit call-in pay.
>
> This section shall not apply in the event of strikes, work stoppages in connection with labor disputes, failure of utilities, fire, flood, or acts of God beyond the control of the Company which make it impossible for the Company to supply work.

In some instances the call-in guarantee is for a full 8-hours' pay.

Most managements recognize the fairness of giving some reporting pay to employees who report for work in accordance with instructions and then find no work available. Controversy in negotiating and administering these provisions arises over such matters as what constitutes advance notice. If a key machine breaks down two hours before the start of the day shift and employees are hastily telephoned and told not to come in, is this sufficient advance notice? What is the status of an employee who cannot be reached by telephone? Is the company relieved of its obligations if it resorts to other general communication media, such as the radio? In addition, the question of what is meant by "Acts of God" is recurrent in grievances arising under this type of provision. In the opinion of some union leaders the Lord is used too often as the scapegoat for the human failings of management. These matters may be of very great cost significance when a major breakdown affects the work available to large groups of employees.

Most managements agree that call-in or reporting pay provisions have forced them to be more careful in the scheduling of employees. Supervision must analyze carefully the need for employees well in advance of their reporting time. These penalty provisions have also been an incentive for better preventive maintenance. On the other hand, it has been discovered that there are numerous abuses of call-in by employees. Some illustrations of these are given in Chapter 9, "Work Assignment and Jurisdiction."

Indirect Measures

These five direct measures are important in their influence on scheduling. Also important and perhaps more troublesome from the employer's standpoint are the indirect influences that affect his scheduling decisions. Among these are the following: (1) local practice and past practice provisions, (2) time counted as work time, (3) vacations, and (4) seniority. In addition, in this section we will consider (5) individual employee control over the length of the workday.

LOCAL PRACTICE AND PAST PRACTICE PROVISIONS. Without realizing it, many managements have limited their scheduling freedom by adopting local practice or past practice clauses. One company had always followed the procedure of discussing and reaching an understanding with the union before altering the daily or weekly schedule. It found that this became a contract obligation under the past practice clause. Scheduling difficulties were one reason cited in management's drive to eliminate the local practice clause in the 1959 steel negotiations. For example, a plant of one steel company was committed to schedule all people in a department for overtime before any overtime could be worked.

TIME COUNTED AS WORK TIME. The considerable growth in idle time periods of the type described in Chapter 15 gives rise to special scheduling problems. By contract definition, holidays, wash-up time, rest periods, and the like may be counted as time worked. This automatically increases the entitlement to overtime for work outside the regular day or week.

Where the law or collective bargaining imposes absolute restrictions on the length of the work schedule, these credited times become especially significant. The most dramatic illustration of this is found in the airline industry. As noted earlier, under a government formula developed in the mid-thirties a limit of 85 hours of flying a month was established for pilots and co-pilots. In an excellent study of industrial relations in this industry, John Baitsell reached the following conclusion concerning the effects of collective bargaining:

> In the scheduling area, the findings revealed a proliferation of work rules which were making it increasingly difficult for airline administrators to obtain a full month's flying from a flight crew member. Under most of these work rules, flight crew members received credit for flight time, although they did not actually fly during that time. The four types of work rules which stood out in this study were flight credit for one-half of the time spent deadheading; for scheduled or actual time, whichever was greater, on a leg-by-leg basis; for guaranteed time under the on-duty ratios; and for guaranteed time under the trip time ratios. The justifications for or against these work rules may be argued in terms of featherbedding or establishing minimum working conditions. The fact remains that airline administrators have lost flexibility in the scheduling of flight crew members and have had to hire extra men because they have not been able to get as much actual flight time from their flight crew members.[12]

VACATIONS. Liberalization of vacations has created new scheduling problems for management. Although some companies are able to effect complete plant shutdowns of one or two weeks a year to handle vacations, they still must adjust schedules because of absence of persons whose seniority entitles them to three or four weeks' vacation. Very often overtime work is necessary in anticipation of the shutdown, and it is needed to cover the absences of those who take their extra vacation allowance at other times of the year. In continuous operations, such as steel, glass, and transportation, extra workers are needed to cover vacation absences.

The multiple influences of weather, law, and collective bargaining on scheduling are best illustrated by another example from the airlines. On the last day of July 1959, Mohawk Airlines had to cancel 21 scheduled flights because the available pilots ran out of flying time. The legal maximum of 85 flight hours, the crediting of nonflight time as flight time under the agreement, the unusual fog conditions on Mohawk routes in July 1959 that forced pilots to use up flight time circling fog-bound airports, and the fact that many of the line's 112 pilots were on vacation combined to force this cancellation of scheduled flights.[13]

SENIORITY. Because the influence of seniority on scheduling is discussed in Chapters 6 and 16, only brief mention will be made here.

---

[12] John M. Baitsell, "Industrial Relations in the Airline Industry," Harvard University, Graduate School of Business Administration, unpub. thesis (May 1960), p. 341.

[13] *New York Herald Tribune* (August 1, 1959).

In the event of temporary work expansion, many companies prefer to work overtime rather than increase employment on a given shift or add a second shift. Seniority regulations under the agreement and the added cost involved in laying off people are the reasons for this preference.

The growth of shift preference arrangements based on seniority is a factor in management's decision whether to continue the operation of a second or third shift. Very often the nighttime shifts must be manned by inexperienced, junior employees, or, as some employers have observed, there is an excessive concentration of older employees on the daytime shift. In either case, the manning imbalance created by this requirement may be sufficiently detrimental to efficiency to justify the use of overtime rather than extra shifts.

Employee Control over Length of Workday

Control of scheduling by employees cannot be considered a union measure, either direct or indirect, but it deserves mention. It has been found that by subtle methods employees may be able to control the length of their workday despite explicit starting and quitting times established in the labor agreement.

The chance for employees to control their workday is greatest under incentive systems when they pace their own output and adhere to set production goals. In Akron rubber plants it is estimated that most incentive employees finish their daily production quota at least an hour and a half before the end of their 6-hour shift; the rest of the time they loaf. In an automobile parts company the employees were able to fill their quotas in 6 hours instead of 8; production became so regulated that nearly all employees made $2.74 an hour in 6 hours of working time even though the wage structure provided for base rate differentials of from 35 to 40 cents per hour. After a long strike a new agreement, incorporating the tenet of a fair day's work for a fair day's pay and discontinuing the standards system, was negotiated. The company reported that its productivity has increased and, more relevant to the present discussion, its equipment is being utilized much nearer to the 8-hour norm.

A forge plant of a large automobile company reported that the crews were usually all dressed and ready to leave at least a half hour before the established quitting time; again this stopping of work at an early hour reflected the pegging of production to attain a fixed level of earnings. In this case, however, the men claim the adherence to quota is justified by the heat and heavy work; the hammer crews say they make up production by working hard in the morning when they are still fresh and are not overheated.

One metal trades company, which subsequently adopted the Scanlon Plan, was convinced that employee efficiency was high under the existing incentive system. The employees asked management if they could go home whenever they chose, provided they maintained their prior level of production. The permission was granted, and much to the amazement and consternation of the employer, nearly everyone completed his production quota by 1:00 P.M. and went home two hours ahead of the normal quitting time. The immediate reaction of the employer: "They've been gypping me all these years and I never knew it." In these and similar instances the employees succeeded in establishing their own quitting time within the span of the 8-hour "work" day. The evidence available warrants the conclusion that there is a fairly high correlation between these occurrences and the existence of what is described in Chapter 17 as a demoralized incentive system.

To a somewhat lesser extent workers paid on a day-rate basis have developed methods of controlling their hours of actual work within the scheduled workday. A forge shop found that the workers in the Heat Treat, Machining, and Inspection Departments were working only 5 hours for 8 hours' pay. Output restrictions were described as a "creeping paralysis that became progressively worse." In some longshore operations the crews establish their own arbitrary production pegs. For example, in one port the crews decided unilaterally that they would not handle more than two cars a day of certain commodities.

The evolution of these work-limitation arrangements by day workers is often attributable to the existence of a strong, militant union group on the one hand and a weak employer or employer group on the other hand. There is no question that the combined elements of intense competition and what might be described as "time vulnerability" explain the union's ability to extract reluctant acceptance of costly scheduling practices from stevedoring employers. This one-sided power sometimes produces very unusual arrangements.

A large port grain elevator operator, conscious that his competitors were unable to use their loading and unloading facilities to full capacity because of daily schedule and/or work limitations, entered into a special program with his union. He "decasualized" longshore employment by hiring two crews on a full-time basis. The scheduling was set up as follows: on one day the first crew worked 4 hours and was relieved by the second crew, which worked 8 hours; the next day the first crew came in and worked 8 hours and was relieved by the second crew, which worked 4 hours. But each crew was automatically paid 12 hours' wages a day. In effect, this employer paid a considerable amount to insure a full work schedule. On occasion, he purposely ignored quitting times as an inducement to get the work out. For example, if especially heavy loads came in before a scheduled holiday he would tell the employees, "I don't care how many hours you work; when you get the work done you can knock off for the rest of the day." In his words, "the men would work like hell so they could finish before quitting time and leave early to enjoy the holiday."

A somewhat different type of employee control over scheduling is the deliberate restriction of output by employees to "make" overtime. In the yards of one railroad it was found that the carmen and inspectors on the 12 midnight to 8:00 A.M. shift delayed work so they could go into overtime hours. The men did little or nothing from 2:00 to 4:00 A.M. and took prolonged lunch or coffee breaks to require overtime scheduling. In a case such as this, which is illustrative of many situations, management itself is at fault in not enforcing the fair day's work principle.

In some instances the union is an active party in "making" overtime. The policy of restricting union membership in a closed-shop industry may be for this purpose. In an East Coast city one of the printing crafts has restricted the supply of labor to insure that there will be ample overtime at high rates of pay for its members. Because of the labor shortage, the companies organized cannot expand. The Die Sinkers Conference undoubtedly restricts trade entry by vigorous apprentice controls with this motive in mind. For this to be achieved, a closed shop is necessary.

In summary, by direct or indirect measures, unions have affected substantively management's freedom to schedule work. If these measures do not always reflect a union desire to resolve the conflict between employers' felt needs and the employees' desire for "normal" lives, it is because the union recognizes that extra payment for abnormal scheduling is sometimes more popular than the achievement of normality. Or, it is a practical recognition that a completely "normal" work life cannot be secured, given the pressures on industry, and that under these circumstances employees are at least entitled to some added reward for their sacrifice of personal convenience.

Control of the Use of Leisure

Where unions have been successful in securing more leisure time for employees through regularization of the workweek or workday and through liberalization of vacations and holidays, the question arises: Who is to control the use of their leisure time? More specific questions are the following: If work becomes necessary during hours outside the regularly scheduled workday or workweek, may the employer require people to work, or is it purely voluntary with the employees? Are vacations to be scheduled when employees want them even though their preferences conflict with employer scheduling needs? If work is necessary on holidays, is it to be voluntary or compulsory?

Where the performance of normal overtime work is voluntary under the agreement, it has been found that employees are usually willing and often anxious to do this work. However, in a surprising number of cases the voluntary aspect of overtime was exploited by groups of workers or by the union to extract special concessions from the employer. The withholding of overtime became a pressure tactic of the type described in Chapter 22.

Because of scheduling pressures noted earlier in this chapter, automobile parts plants have been vulnerable to employee control of leisure. In one such plant refusal to work overtime was used to win looser standards for incentive workers and to gain reduced workloads for hourly workers. In another, employees refused to work overtime until management agreed to call in an unnecessary number of men. In the automotive tool and die shops for many years this tactic was used to win merit increases, control transfers, and the like. Voluntary overtime became a strike issue in 1953 in the Detroit tool and die industry. A clause stating "in no case shall overtime be compulsory" was replaced by a provision that "although overtime work is not compulsory, the union will not restrict overtime in any manner and employees will cooperate when requested by the management to perform overtime work."

Even where the contract permits the employer to control the use of leisure by making reasonable overtime compulsory, pressure tactics may still be used. Employees who are scheduled to work the extra hours may suddenly become "ill" or offer other excuses. However, the problem is mitigated somewhat under this type of provision by making disciplinary action more likely.

To a considerable extent agreements are silent on the question of whether reasonable overtime shall be voluntary or compulsory. They are limited to a definition of the regular workweek and workday. Inevitably the issue of control of leisure has arisen under some of these contracts and has been referred to arbitration. Most arbitrators have held that group refusal to work overtime is an assault on the no-strike, no-work stoppage clauses. But when it comes to the refusal of individuals to work overtime, the guides provided by arbitrators have been vague and sometimes contradictory. Two classic rulings under agreements that merely defined the regular work schedule illustrate the problem. In one case the arbitrator held as follows:

> It may be urged that an employer's business requires some flexibility in scheduling overtime and that he needs the assurance that longer hours will be worked by all the employees. Employers wishing to retain such flexibility as a matter of right conclude contracts which protect them in such situations. Such contracts usually contain provisions affirmatively setting forth the right of the company to schedule overtime work, or they contain provisions that overtime will be required of the employees after the amount has been specifically arranged with the union. In the absence of such affirmative provisions, it must be held that work in excess of 8 hours in a day or 40 hours in a week is solely within the discretion of the employee.[14]

In another case a second arbitrator adopted the basic premise that some overtime work is necessary from time to time in almost any manufacturing enterprise. He noted that there were degrees of necessity and said:

> Given this premise, there is logic in the view that management starts with the inherent right to require overtime work. And it follows, as the Company argues, that this right not only to schedule but also to require overtime work can be lost only by some fairly concrete language to that effect in the labor agreement. Certainly the more basic the right peculiar to one party or another the more specific must be the clause in an agreement if that right is to be erased.

It was his opinion that the clause defining the regular schedule was

[14] Connecticut River Mills, *Labor Arbitration Report*, Vol. 6 (1947) p. 1019.

not specific enough to destroy the basic right of management to expect performance of reasonable overtime work.[15]

There appears to be a trend toward the adoption of the compulsory
overtime principle. Most managements, however, have learned to use
this principle as a last resort only. Rather than assert their right to
control leisure, they rely on worker cooperation. The usual practice
is first to locate workers who want to work the extra hours. Only if
this voluntary approach fails is the company's right to assign men to
work overtime exercised.

The scheduling of vacations also involves the control of leisure.
Under most agreements employees are not free to take their vacations whenever they like. The employer retains the right to schedule
vacations at times that are consistent with the needs of the business,
although the principle of meeting employee preference wherever
possible is recognized. The use of vacation leisure is most serious in
continuous operations where a mill cannot be shut down without
considerable cost. In one paper company agreement there was a
provision that no more than 6 per cent of the workforce in any department could be on vacation at one time. In its effort to increase
the number of vacations that could be taken during the summer
months, the union agreed to allow the management to hire a large
number of college student trainees.

In the plant of a large automobile company management wanted
to institute a 3-week vacation shutdown as part of a production
stabilization plan. The UAW opposed the idea, ostensibly because
such a shutdown would deny workers a choice of time off. However,
behind the UAW's opposition was the fear that a precedent might
be established that would deny men unemployment compensation
during changeover periods. It is interesting that some UAW contracts call for vacation pay but no vacations as such. The custom is
to take one's "vacation" during layoff (usually at the time of changeover), and collect both unemployment compensation and vacation
pay. Under the national agreement of this company vacations must
be scheduled between May 15 and December 30, but usually they are
concentrated in the two changeover months of July and August.
Sometimes this has created problems of securing replacements and
of shifting personnel.

A problem is likely to develop over the control of vacation leisure

---

[15] General Electric Co., *Labor Arbitration Report*, Vol. 31 (1959), p. 403.

time in the future as vacation allowances become more liberal and as more people become eligible for longer vacations. Unions are interested in provisions that allow an employee to carry over part of his vacation credits to a succeeding year, thus permitting him to take 4 or 5 weeks off at a time. This is a direct result of the desire for long trips, travel to Europe, etc. Although up to now management has succeeded in controlling the time when leisure is granted, the competition for control will become an issue. If unions secure concessions, scheduling and manning problems will be aggravated.

Holidays always create scheduling difficulties. In one steel plant the position has been taken and upheld in arbitration that work on a holiday is voluntary. But operation needs have caused the company to schedule skeleton crews, the selection of which has involved numerous grievances.

Implications of Union Policy

In a book such as this it is impossible to describe the thousands of scheduling arrangements that have evolved under collective bargaining in American industry. As in the case of seniority arrangements, this is a subject that even the parties can handle only by general statements of principle in the basic agreement. In multiplant companies under a master agreement, local supplements are used to develop the skeletal concepts. Understandably the grievance procedure and arbitration are relied upon extensively for the development of scheduling guides. Innumerable special situations arise that cannot be anticipated in contract negotiations.

For this reason it is difficult to generalize concerning the impact of union policy. We know that it has been considerable. In a few instances, where direct controls have been imposed, the union may exercise a strong veto power over scheduling decisions. This is true where the agreement expressly forbids any work beyond a specified number of hours or during certain hours of the day. It may also occur where the union requires that any schedules deviating from the normal be agreed to by the union.

In most cases the union's impact has been to add considerably to the cost of irregularity and unorthodoxy in scheduling. Undoubtedly the original union proponents of overtime and special premium payments were sincere in arguing that such payments would have the salutary effect of regularizing the work schedule. They hoped that the added costs of working employees for extra hours or at abnormal hours would be a strong incentive to management to add shifts or otherwise rearrange schedules so that work outside the norm could be avoided. A lesser consideration in their campaign was the argument that *if* such work was necessary, the employee was entitled to special payment for the inconvenience and the irregularity of the hours. Seldom were premium payments advocated on the ground that they offered greater earnings opportunity for employees.

The fact is that these payments are viewed by employees primarily as an excellent opportunity to increase their take-home pay. Only when the irregular work is excessive on any given occasion or when it becomes a schedule pattern day in and day out, does resistance arise. The following sampling of comments reflects the dominant attitude. The die sinkers in a forge shop are said to "just love overtime and Saturday work because of the high earnings involved." A large drug company experienced a strike in which one of the issues was the subcontracting of work, which deprived maintenance men of Saturday overtime work. A paper company found that, in spite of what it considered to be a "grueling" 56-hour weekly schedule in a newly-acquired plant, the workers still wanted Sunday work because of the large **overtime earnings**. In fact, some employees resented the establishment of a 6-day schedule.[16] The earnings opportunity theory is sometimes deliberately fostered by management in promoting overtime as a substitute for basic wage increases. One well-known company admits freely that it has scheduled week-end overtime in part to offset the fact that its machinist and tool and die rates were below the area average, a differential that had led to unrest among the craftsmen. The New York plant of a large chemical company says that while it has low base rates, the high overtime of a 56-hour weekly schedule provides "good earnings relative to the area." One of the most extreme cases of the use of overtime as a revenue measure is to be found among Pacific Coast longshoremen. In their 1959 agreement with the Pacific Maritime Association they gained a guarantee of 8 hours of work, which had to be provided between 8 A.M. and 6 P.M. However, overtime is paid after 6 hours of work.

[16] There are notable exceptions. Some employees for health or family reasons or because they are holding two jobs dislike overtime or irregular call-in at any price. Where the Scanlon Plan is in effect (see Chapter 28), there is union and employee opposition to overtime and other premiums because of their adverse effect on bonus levels.

The straight time rate for longshoremen is $2.74 an hour, and the overtime rate is $4.11 an hour. The average hourly earnings have been $3.70, showing clearly the significance of overtime in take-home pay.

The conclusions stated should not be interpreted to mean that employees necessarily want to work overtime or at irregular hours. Instead, the evidence seems to indicate that the prevailing premium pay arrangements are a satisfactory—perhaps more than adequate—supply price to induce people to give up leisure time and personal convenience. If the overtime is excessive or if it falls on days when the preference for leisure is very high, the supply price exacted is likely to be greater. Undoubtedly this accounts for the growth in double-time payments on Sunday and after a certain number of hours of overtime and the use of triple-time payment for work on holidays.

An important consequence of the attractiveness of premium pay work is the competition among employees for such work. This has led unions to seek from management a commitment that, wherever possible, overtime will be shared equally. The right to be called in at irregular hours is often claimed by those with the greatest seniority. Administering these systems for allocating irregular work opportunities has become a difficult problem for many companies and is a significant source of grievances.

Except in rare cases management has retained considerable freedom in scheduling work to meet normal or unexpected business needs. But collective bargaining has imposed a stiff price for this freedom, either in the form of requiring the employment of additional workers or in the form of premium payments. This price has been an incentive to many managements to avoid irregular scheduling wherever possible.

9 / Work Assignment and Jurisdiction

IN THE CONSTRUCTION of a metal ceiling edged with metal molding, which employees should be allowed to put on the molding: the sheet metal workers or the carpenters, each represented by separate unions? If construction work is to be done in Madison, Wisconsin, by a contractor from Chicago, Illinois, to what extent must he use Madison craftsmen rather than members of his Chicago crew, even though they are all members of the same building trades unions? In a large machine shop, may a punch press operator be required to clean around his machine if no reference to such activity is made in his job description? May this same operator make minor machine repairs and adjustments, or must this work be done only by a machinist, an electrician, or a millwright, all of whom may be in the same union? May a foreman or nonworking supervisor pitch in to correct a production bottleneck by working briefly with the employees? May he make a simple adjustment on a machine? If there is a shortage of crane operators because of illness on a given day, may the employer freely transfer to the vacancy an employee who is classified as a floorman?

These are illustrative of the situations to be explored in this chapter. They raise one or the other of two basic questions: Who is entitled to do the work, and who is obligated to do the work? The former is the more important of the two as a source of labor-management disputes and will be discussed first in this chapter. The second issue, the obligation to perform certain work assignments, will be taken up next. Most of the determinants of work assignment problems discussed in the opening section are relevant to the second issue. Moreover, the determination of who is entitled to do the work often answers indirectly the question of who is obligated to do the work. In these discussions we are concerned with the *nature* of the work to be done rather than the *volume* of work. Therefore, problems of workload, equal-division-of-work, layoffs, overtime opportunities—all of which are related primarily to changes in work volume—are considered separately in Chapters 6 and 8. The question of management's freedom to subcontract work, although it may involve the nature as well as the volume of work, is taken up in Chapter 10.

Who Is Entitled to Do the Work?

Disagreement over work assignment and jurisdiction has been extensive on the American industrial scene. In at least one industry, building construction, it has been the principal cause of costly work stoppages. In many unionized firms it is a source of numerous grievances. One authority in the field has said that "disputes over work assignments are the outward manifestation of a great variety of problems; they are akin to the one-eighth of the iceberg that is visible. The complexities beneath the surface have almost infinite variety."[1] There is considerable truth to this statement, and it suggests the difficulty of trying to analyze systematically the nature of the problem. One can understand the varying forms of disagreement, the conflict of interests, and the blend of contributing factors only by studying a number of different actual situations.

There are three general types of situations: First, those in which the conflict of interests is between two or more unions claiming jurisdiction over the work to be done; second, those in which the conflict involves bargaining-unit employees *vis-à-vis* nonbargaining-unit employees; and third, the numerous situations in which the disagreement over work assignments is intra-union in nature.

From these classifications it might be assumed that the conflict of interests is only between unions or between groups of employees. Nothing could be further from the truth, because the employer's interest is very much at stake. The employer is seldom indifferent to the question of who is to do certain work; and in fact, the determination of work assignment in the first instance is considered by most managements as one of their essential rights. But it is the exercise of this right, the assignment of work to certain individuals or groups,

[1] John T. Dunlop, "Jurisdictional Disputes: 10 Types," *The Constructor* (July 1953), p. 166.

which generates the three types of conflicts mentioned above. These, in turn, become issues in dispute between the union and management. Thus, several layers of conflict are involved.

There are several possible combinations of conflicts of interest. The interest of one union, as an institution, *vis-à-vis* that of a competing union may force management into the front line of the battle in self-protection. Or the interest of the union as an institution and that of management may be the same and in conflict with the interest of a group of employees who feel their proprietary right in certain work has been abrogated. Or the interest of a single union and its members may be in direct conflict with that of the employer, as when work claimed by the union is assigned to employees outside the bargaining unit. Still another possible combination is a conflict of interest between the union and some of its members, on the one hand, and the employer and some groups of union members on the other hand.

Determinants of Work Assignment Problems

The following ten influences warrant special attention: (1) the tradition of the American labor movement, (2) technology and methods, (3) skill and craftsmanship, (4) job security, (5) job descriptions, (6) internal union and management politics, (7) management policy and practice, (8) method of wage payment, (9) impact of legislation, and (10) climate of labor relations.

THE TRADITION OF THE AMERICAN LABOR MOVEMENT. The concept of exclusive jurisdiction was fundamental in the growth of the American labor movement. The loose structure of the Knights of Labor demonstrated to the founders of the American Federation of Labor that uncontrolled competition within the labor movement itself was harmful to growth. Therefore, competition among unions was limited by a definition in their charters of the scope of their exclusive jurisdiction. At the same time, however, charters were issued along craft lines. Thus, the combined factors of exclusive jurisdiction and organization by craft both reflected and heightened job consciousness. Each organization zealously watched its fellow national unions to be certain that the defined boundaries were observed.

Because of still another factor, rapid changes in technology, the boundaries often became less and less distinct, leaving an indefinite no-man's land where a jurisdictional battle raged. For example, the use of wood in building construction has diminished over the years, yet the carpenters' union remains a potent force among the building trades unions. This has been achieved only through militance on the part of the union in establishing jurisdictional control over work on many substitute materials.

The craft structure has prevailed in several industries and has heightened the conflict of interests among employees who are members of different unions. Working side by side on the same job site, each group of employees with its own union affiliation and loyalty is prone to adopt broad interpretations of jurisdiction insofar as its own group is concerned and to interpret narrowly the jurisdictional rights of the group's competitors. The building trades, printing trades, entertainment, and railroad industries are important segments of American industry in which organization is by craft. Inevitably, there is likely to be intense job consciousness with attendant quarrels over which group is entitled to do what work. It is not alone employee interest that is involved. The institutional interest of each national union is no less great; at times the acquisitive interest of the union may be stronger and more militantly expressed than that of its members.

This same problem exists in many other industries. For example, in those normally identified with industrial unions, such as automobile, glass, electrical, steel, rubber, and airframe and aircraft engines, it is not uncommon to have some craft splinter groups. Whenever a company has some of its employees organized by one union and some by another, the competitive spirit of the two or more organizations will be a breeding ground for work assignment disagreements. In fact, there is reason to believe that the craft union philosophy in this area is making its influence felt even in those industrial unions that represent both production and maintenance employees. Commenting on the problem, one CIO union official observed: "We are caught between the maelstrom of skilled trades unrest and the rigid views of AFL craft unions. We are tied by the position of the AFL craft people."

Another characteristic of the American labor movement which contributes to the competition for work jurisdiction is the presence within the movement of unions that are semi-industrial or semi-craft in nature, for example, the International Association of Machinists, the International Brotherhood of Boiler Makers, the International Brotherhood of Electrical Workers, and the United Brotherhood of Carpenters and Joiners. Each of these unions is prepared to assert jurisdictional claims over work identified with a craft (Journeymen Machinists, Boilermakers, Electricians, and Carpenters) as well as over work identified with an industry (airframe, electronics, shipbuilding, furniture, etc.). As we shall see in Chapter 10, controversies over work jurisdiction may develop between the craft and industrial segments within the same union, as in the case of a construction branch of the International Brotherhood of Electrical Workers competing with one of its industrial union branches over "repair and improvement" work in an automobile company. The pliability of union structure has created problems of work jurisdiction and assignment not only within the labor movement but within the framework of union-management relations.

In formulating the terms of the AFL-CIO merger agreement, the drafters recognized the need to modify the older AFL concept of exclusive jurisdiction. The new standard adopted in Article III, Section 4 of the AFL-CIO Constitution substitutes the doctrine of "established bargaining relationship" for that of exclusive jurisdiction. In effect, the jurisdiction actually being exercised by an affiliate national union at the time of the merger was considered inviolate; thus, the status quo was preserved. It is acknowledged that in the constitutional principles of the new merged body there is an effort to control competition within the labor movement, not only by the doctrines of the "integrity of affiliates" and "established collective bargaining relationships," but also by the establishment of special voluntary agreements to curb raiding and to resolve interunion disputes. Nevertheless, the existing structure of the labor movement continues to give rise to many work assignment conflicts.[2]

TECHNOLOGY AND METHODS. Where the methods of performing work are reasonably stable and where there is little or no change in technology, there are less likely to be frequent disagreements over work

[2] An excellent discussion of the background and nature of the AFL-CIO Constitution on this subject is contained in John T. Dunlop "Structural Changes in the Labor Movement and Industrial Relations System," *Proceedings, Industrial Relations Research Association* (December 1956), pp. 12-32. See also Arthur J. Goldberg, *AFL-CIO, Labor United* (1956), pp. 143-44, 228-31.

assignments. The scope of employee job duties is fixed by habit, if not by specific description. But once the existing makeup of jobs is altered by methods changes, by combining operations, or for any other reason, conflict may develop. In an economy such as ours, industries in which technology is stable are rare. New methods and materials used in building construction have made craft jurisdictional lines more difficult to define; new printing processes have destroyed the traditional alignment of crafts in that industry.

In recent years one of the most interesting illustrations of the impact of technology on work assignments is in the television industry. In 1950 it was reported that CBS had 81 contracts with 40 local and 20 international unions. "Keeping the jurisdiction lines untangled and everyone happy requires the wisdom of a Solomon, the agility of a tightrope walker."[3] Although the jurisdictional controversies in this industry were less than had been anticipated because of a series of constructive interunion compromises, the technical changes since the beginning of television have continued to jar the formerly accepted work-jurisdiction lines. The recent development of video tape has revived jurisdictional contentions.

The critical issue in the 1958 negotiations between the airlines and two of their unions, the Air Line Pilots Association and the Flight Engineers, was the question of who was to be the third man in the cockpit of a jet plane, a pilot or a flight engineer. Confronted by an emergency board report deemed partially unfavorable to its jurisdictional interests, the flight engineers were prepared to engage in a strike rather than yield any jurisdiction to the pilots. Some airlines finally settled the problem by establishing a four-man crew, thus meeting the desires of both organizations. One industry spokesman observed, "We jumped ungracefully from the pot into the frying pan. We resolved the work assignment issue by committing ourselves to a costly make-work arrangement."

Still another illustration is that of an electrical manufacturing concern having contracts in one plant with two unions, the International Brotherhood of Electrical Workers and the International Association of Machinists. For a number of years the IBEW mechanics had been sharpening cutting tools on grinders. However, when carbide tip tools were adopted, which could not be sharpened on the regular grinders, the company gave the work of sharpening

---

[3] *Business Week* (September 16, 1950), p. 123.

them to the IAM machinists. The IBEW mechanics promptly filed a grievance, claiming that this work belonged to them by practice and tradition. To resolve the problem, the management modified the old grinders so they could be used to sharpen carbide tools, thus allowing the mechanics to retain the work.

These few examples of the influence of changed technology involved companies with multi-bargaining unit arrangements. However, the influence is felt also where there is only one union in a given work establishment; or its impact may be confined to one union within a multi-unit structure. In these situations, the greater sensitivity to changed job duties is more likely to be found among the skilled trades.

SKILL AND CRAFTSMANSHIP. The higher the skill required on a job, the greater is likely to be job consciousness and pride in the job level. Therefore, regardless of whether the employees on the skilled jobs are members of one union or different unions, there will be found among them a strong acquisitive/protective interest and, often at the same time, an equally strong exclusion/selective interest.

Work assignment problems will be more pronounced among the skilled trades employees in an industrial union than among the semi-skilled. To illustrate, in a large steel plant there have been many grievances arising from jurisdictional disputes between the craftsmen of central maintenance and the assigned maintenance crews in the various departments. All of these employees are in the same union. The craftsmen fear that the company will make combination workmen out of them, e.g., if a job requires a boilermaker, a rigger, and a welder, the company might require one person to do the whole job. The men want to remain specialists in their trade or craft and resist any management effort to have them do work that could be construed as outside their job classification. Thus, a boilermaker may file a grievance claiming he should not be required to operate power-driven tractors, loaders, winches, etc. At the same time, however, these same craftsmen will grieve what they consider to be encroachments on their special work domain by members of the assigned maintenance crews or by their fellow craftsmen in central maintenance.

The preoccupation with work assignment among skilled workers is understandable. The introduction of work elements alien to the basic skill threatens the dignity and worth of the job in their opinion, and in the long run this could jeopardize the high rate for the job. By the same token, subtraction of work elements inherent in the job skill could lead to the same results.

In this connection it should be emphasized that the so-called incidental tasks are the principal cause of work assignment difficulties in large companies. The question of who is entitled to perform or who is obligated to do the fringe tasks not easily identifiable with any given craft continues to be a source of discontent among maintenance crew members.

JOB SECURITY. It is not true, as one might assume, that work jurisdiction problems disappear during periods of full employment. Even when nearly all members of a given craft who want jobs are employed, they continue to guard against poaching on their work domain. Nor is concern over what one is entitled to do much less among the jobholders in an industrial union environment. The security of full employment is not enough to erase the influence of other factors. For example, the skilled trades in the automobile industry did not seem to be less interested in job jurisdiction when there was an acute shortage of craftsmen in 1953, 1954, and 1955. To some extent the desire for more overtime opportunities is enough to maintain the interest.

There is evidence, however, that the proprietary interest in scope of job duties is likely to be expressed more forcibly when work opportunities are slackening; at the same time, the selective, pick-and-choose interest of the type discussed below is likely to be at its weakest. A classic illustration involves a group of storekeepers in a company who were assigned over a period of a week to help take annual inventory. They promptly filed a grievance protesting this assignment on the ground that it was not in their job description. In the arbitration decision, the arbitrator noted that the descriptions were fixed by agreement and that taking inventory could not be considered properly as part of the job. One year later, at a time when layoffs were being made, the company put several nonbargaining-unit office employees on the inventory assignment and was promptly confronted with a grievance from the same storekeepers. The gist of their novel complaint this time was that the company, having offered them the work in the past, should have extended the same invitation again before using other employees.

Although this is an extreme example, it confirms the general view that the concern with work jurisdiction probably will be greatest and certainly most widespread when job opportunities are low. A large rubber company reports that it had a notable increase in work assignment grievances whenever hours were cut back or layoffs became necessary.

JOB DESCRIPTIONS. It is well known that one of the refinements in labor relations and personnel policy during the past twenty years has been the development of a classification system and job descriptions. Few companies ever entered into these programs of classification and description with the thought that they would limit their right to assign work or that they would lead to unrest among employees concerning work assignments. Yet in a surprising number of cases these have been the consequences. Even though a written job description ends with the standard phrase, "and such other duties as may be required from time to time," this did not forestall grievances when work duties were subtracted or added. The company suddenly had the burden of proving that its assignment of certain duties to one job, or conversely its assignment of those duties to another job, was consistent with the written descriptions.

Perhaps unwittingly some companies have made union acquiescence a prerequisite for changes in methods and resultant changes in assignment. A large special instrument company agreed with its union that job descriptions as now written could be changed only with the consent of the union. For example, a process change clerk had as one of her duties taking engineering orders that arrived on her desk to the departments affected and on the job site replacing the obsolete blueprints with new ones. In this process, she had to locate the prints, a time-consuming activity that often led to the manufacture of a number of parts under the old blueprint after the revised one had been released. To avoid this costly delay it was decided that an employee on the job (an expeditor) would be responsible for physically substituting the new prints for the old on receipt of instructions sent to him by messenger from the process change clerk. The efficiency of this new procedure was proved beyond any doubt. It was also shown that no clerks had been laid off because of the reassignment of functions. However, an arbitrator held that the change had the effect of removing from the clerk's job several fundamental job duties and constituted a unilateral revision in the clerk's description in violation of the agreement. This meant that the change in method and in assignment had to be approved by the union before it could be implemented.

Problems stemming from job descriptions are occasionally inherent in the way the descriptions are written. More often, however, they are the result of management's failure to make it clear that, in agreeing to a set of descriptions, it is not yielding its right to change methods in the interest of efficiency. Most arbitrators recognize this to be a fundamental right of management, but unthinkingly some managements themselves modify this right. To illustrate, one company over a period of years entered into a number of grievance settlements on work assignment jurisdictional issues. The import of these commitments was that so long as a certain duty was being performed, it would be done only by incumbents of a given job. Thereafter, when changes in operation were contemplated that would require a rearrangement of duties, the company found itself seriously limited. The company reports that it had to "pay for the right to change operations" in subsequent negotiations.[4]

INTERNAL UNION AND MANAGEMENT POLITICS. At times political considerations contribute to the prevalence of work assignment complaints. It has been found that a supervisor in the shop will seek the favor of those working directly with him by giving them maintenance duties that rightfully belong to the craftsmen in the maintenance department. In the building trades, where business agents are ordinarily elected for relatively short terms, a frequent charge in hotly-contested campaigns is that the incumbent has been too lax in pushing jurisdictional claims. As a result, during these campaigns, an agent may try to change jurisdictional lines that have been taken for granted in the locality. Or a new business agent, trying to fulfill election promises, may try to extend jurisdiction. This leads to prompt retaliation by other crafts and sometimes interruption of work on existing projects.[5]

Inevitably the exploitation of work assignment as a political issue will be found chiefly where other factors have made it an important

---

[4] The use of job descriptions is discussed more fully in Chapter 19.
[5] Dunlop, "Jurisdictional Disputes," pp. 165-73.

issue to most voting members, as in the case of the craft unions. But in recent years the large industrial unions with an articulate and discontented skilled trades minority (the UAW, for example) have faced problems of work jurisdiction.

MANAGEMENT POLICY AND PRACTICE. In many ways management can control the extent to which its assignment practices will result in discontent among employees or among its bargaining units. Since tradition and habits play such a compelling part in the creation of work empires, it is essential for management to guard against haphazard work assignments. Management may invite trouble for itself in two different ways: First, it may lack a basic policy on methods of making work assignments or, second, if it has such a policy, it may fail to provide for periodic review to insure that the policy is being observed.

In either event, a company may discover that a poorly-conceived practice has developed, to which it is wedded by union insistence. This may have very unusual and costly consequences. In one company, which had job descriptions and which had undergone an expansion in workforce over the years, it was found that foremen had adopted the practice of assigning specialists to handle very limited segments of the total job. In effect, separate job assignments within a job were developed, without any system of rotation to insure training on the total job. Top management woke up to what had happened when there was a business curtailment. It found it could not effect layoffs from certain jobs because there was no single individual capable of doing all phases of the job without lengthy further training. The danger of an inadequate policy, and more particularly, of poor administration of a work-assignment policy, has been referred to in the chapters on layoff and promotion procedures.

Management has discovered that in some departments the union steward plays a more active role in determining work assignments than does the foreman. An aggressive steward or committeeman may browbeat an ineffective supervisor by threatening to file a grievance if he makes an assignment to certain job incumbents. To avoid this risk and believing it better to have union concurrence, the foreman may yield to the wishes of the union representative. Without top management knowing it, supervision may be turning over to the union a basic management responsibility.

Some companies that report very few grievances on this subject say that they impress each supervisor with the need to use care in making assignments. A union leader in the building trades says that in his opinion "jurisdictional disputes are at least as much the fault of the employer as the crafts. If the superintendent on the job happens to be a carpenter, he will lean toward the carpenters. Actually the crafts are doing more in working together to avoid disputes than contractors do in properly assigning work." There is a considerable body of evidence to show that in this industry management has aggravated the problem by defaulting in one of two other ways. Either it fails to exercise its prerogative to assign work out of fear of a jurisdictional dispute, or, if it does assign work to one craft, it may vacillate as soon as a strong protest is received from another craft. This subject will be developed more fully below. Efficiency or the lack of it in managerial administration may also account for the number of grievances involving the issue of foremen doing bargaining unit work. This is also discussed below.

METHOD OF WAGE PAYMENT. The evidence shows that an incentive payment system sometimes aggravates the problem of work assignments. The workers tend to fight over easy jobs and do their best to avoid those assignments that do not yield easy earnings.

In a study of a large shoe company four different ways of assigning piecework were found: (1) Some foremen made assignments by trying to match the work to the capacities and abilities of individuals. If a certain style shoe was hard to cut, the most able cutter got the assignment. Naturally this method gave rise to charges of discrimination. (2) Some workers used a system known as "passing the buck." A stick was actually used and was passed to the next man when it was his turn to take the next rack of shoes. This meant exactly equal and random distribution of the work as it came along. There was no matching of skills, and the speed of a whole group depended on the slow man. (3) In some departments where the foremen were weak, the employees fought for the work. A few individuals were allowed to get all the gravy jobs while others got the poorer work. Under this system it was found that some kinds of shoes were constantly delayed. If a difficult style came along, nobody would take the work. In a situation such as this the union steward may take control eventually. He may settle quarrels among employees by assigning the work. (4) In other departments seniority determined the assignment. Seniority practices ranged from simple procedures where the senior man had first choice to very elaborate assignment systems.[6]

Even on day-rate jobs there is a tendency for senior people to use their status to avoid the hard jobs. Mechanics in garages will try to get the easy cars to work on, leaving to juniors the old ones. By and large, however, disagreement over work assignments is likely to be more prevalent where a piece-rate or incentive system is used.

These illustrations point up the two sides of the coin. Where seniority is used to give certain employees entitlement to desirable work, it creates an obligation for junior employees to do the less desirable work.

IMPACT OF LEGISLATION. The most important statute affecting jurisdictional problems is the Taft-Hartley Law, which includes jurisdictional strikes among the concerted activities considered unfair labor practices. In addition, its prohibition of the secondary boycott limits, at least theoretically, reliance on this device to enforce a jurisdictional interest. As will be seen below, the law's greatest effect has been to stimulate efforts by competing unions in the building trades to work out with the construction industry the necessary machinery for settling jurisdictional conflicts.

In one respect, the law may have encouraged preoccupation with work assignment questions. By making it easier for craft groups to carve out separate bargaining units from what had been an all-inclusive industrial union, the law may have made the proprietary interest in work boundaries a more substantive issue in certain cases. On one hand, an industrial union, confronted with the possibility of a carve-out by the craftsmen, would become especially attentive to their interests; this would include their need for sanctity of job scope. On the other hand, if the carve-out was sought and was successful, the resultant multi-unit setup would establish sharper demarcation of work jurisdiction. This possible effect of the Taft-Hartley Law is conjectural, but it is interesting that many firms have

[6] On one occasion the company found that a serious bottleneck had developed among the fancy stitchers although there were enough experienced workers. It found that the foreman had agreed to a written document listing the style numbers to be done according to seniority. Then a product-mix shift took place. The style numbers assigned to senior fancy stitchers became more prevalent. As a result the senior workers were very busy, while the junior fancy stitchers were idle.

joined with their large single-unit industrial unions in resisting carve-out attempts by the crafts. They cite as one compelling reason for doing so the probable increase in work assignment controversies if the attempts were successful. It is interesting, however, that many employers who are preoccupied with the rights of minorities in discussing the union-shop issue are disposed to take a dim view of minority group interests when a bargaining unit carve-out is attempted.

CLIMATE OF LABOR RELATIONS. A listing of the various factors influencing the form and intensity of work-assignment disagreements would be incomplete without some discussion of the general influence of labor and personnel relations within a company. One company reported that more often than not complaints about improper assignments could be attributed to other more serious disturbances. The grievances on misassignment were an effective way of retaliating at management.

One union leader said that in too many instances misassignment cases were deliberately contrived by predatory employees who found them a convenient way to collect pay for time not worked. He agreed readily that these employees had been abusing their right not to work outside their trades. In fact, the phrase "rocking chair pay" was used by some employees who engaged in the "misassignment grievance racket." The practice was to allow oneself to be assigned to work of another trade, perform this work willingly, and then tell the man whose work has been "taken." The latter then filed a grievance that he should be compensated for work that belonged to him. The concept of fair play among employees followed this creed: "If I do your job, I will tell you, then you grieve for pay. I have my pay and you will have the same if you win your grievance." In some instances the racket was so refined that the employees purposely invited misassignment. For example, an electrician called in on Saturday would complete his job and tell his foreman, "I want something else to do." The foreman would oblige by letting him paint; on Monday the electrician would tell the painter, and a claim would be filed by the latter.

These are not typical cases and probably belong in the category of "horrible examples." But where the relation between the parties is poor, it is commonly found that work assignment grievances are high. Charges of misassignment of fringe duties among employees within a bargaining unit and of foremen working offer an easy and effective way of expressing discontent.

Inter-Union Work Assignment Problems

It has been pointed out that rivalry among unions for work jurisdiction is most pronounced in industries with a high degree of craft organization. The building and construction industry has been selected for detailed description. In addition several illustrations of inter-union controversy in manufacturing and service enterprises will be discussed, together with the methods of settlement in each case.

BUILDING AND CONSTRUCTION INDUSTRY.[7] This industry is organized on a craft basis by nineteen international unions affiliated with the Building and Construction Trades Department; each has its "exclusive" jurisdiction over some phase of building construction work. The industry itself has unusual characteristics that help to explain why it has been the storm-center of jurisdictional strife.

First, by its very nature construction work is performed on new job sites. In addition, the sequential nature of the various operations, from the time piles are driven or excavation is started to the time the structure is completed, means that one craft is often moving in to start work as another is leaving after completing its part of the total job. This constant changing of the composition of crews prevents the development of the stable, continuing relationships that are characteristic of most industrial plants. There are few opportunities for inter-group or inter-craft relationships that might militate against work-assignment controversy.

Second, this is an industry in which changes in design, materials, and methods have been of an almost infinite variety. The following illustrations will show how these changes contribute substantively to the problem by upsetting the usual allocation of work: For many years the coppersmiths (Sheet Metal Workers Union) made in their

[7] In this description there has been considerable reliance on the following documents:

    (a) John T. Dunlop, "Jurisdictional Disputes: 10 Types," *The Constructor* (July 1953), pp. 165-73.

    (b) 1956 Report, National Joint Board (January 11, 1957).

    (c) Brief field by National Joint Board, N.L.R.B., Docket No. 5-CD-14.

    (d) Bureau of National Affairs, *Construction Labor Report* (September 18, 1957).

    (e) Proceedings of Conference, *The Resolution of Jurisdictional Disputes in the Building Trades and Economic Prospects for the Industry, 1957-1958*, University of Michigan-Wayne State University (June 28, 1957).

shops the pipes and coils to be installed in breweries. Within recent years these copper pipes have been made in factories according
to specifications. When this change first occurred, the plumbers and
steamfitters said the installation of such pipes was their work right
because the pipes differed in no way from other types of pipes they
installed. But the Sheet Metal Workers said that "tradition" required assignment of the work to them. A Midwest contractor had
always used carpenters to install a standard acoustical ceiling. He
then found a way to use a spray gun to blow on a surface which
looked like plaster. When the carpenters were allowed to continue
the finishing of the ceiling, the plasterers claimed jurisdiction and
struck the project.

Third, on the average a craft works on a project for a short period
of time. For this reason, when a dispute over work assignment arises,
there is a natural desire to have it decided then and there; moreover,
the aggrieved union is quite aware that the contractor may have
agreed to a penalty payment if the work is not completed by a given
date. The result is hasty resort to economic pressure through a work
stoppage. In this situation there is no effective remedy once the work
has been done.

Fourth, the mobility of contractors as well as some of the craftsmen often results in the import of work-assignment practices that are
foreign to the particular locality and constitute a break from tradition. This produces conflict over jurisdiction.

Finally, project supervisors in this industry are usually members
of a union, and sometimes their identification with a particular craft
may lead to favoritism toward that craft in assigning borderline
work.

These and other characteristics of the industry (the bidding for
work, the frequent conflict between the general contractor and the
specialty contractor, and the nature of the union organization structure) all combine to make the construction industry a center for
wasteful, frivolous jurisdictional disputes. Although unions must
shoulder considerable responsibility for these disputes because of
their tendency to place parochial interests above industry and public
interests, their behavior must be judged in the context of the total
characteristics of the industry and the political science of the union
movement.

One of the most important developments within the past two
decades has been the constructive effort by the building industry

and its many unions to reduce the number of jurisdictional work stoppages. Anxious to avoid having jurisdictional disputes reviewed by the National Labor Relations Board, the member unions of the Building and Construction Trades Department and a group of national contractors' associations, including the Associated General Contractors, Inc. and eight national specialty contractors' associations, entered into an historic agreement which became operative on May 1, 1948: *Plan for Settling Jurisdictional Disputes Nationally and Locally.*

This unusual agreement, amended several times since 1948, represents a departure from the extreme views traditionally adhered to by a craft union and the reverse, but equally extreme, position implicit in the Taft-Hartley Law. The AFL unions had always taken the position that they alone should determine jurisdiction, and most of the early, unsuccessful efforts to establish machinery for resolution of disputes were based upon this tenet. The 1948 Agreement created a National Joint Board composed of an impartial chairman, four labor members appointed by the Building and Construction Trades Department, and four employer members. In recognition of the occasional conflict between general contractors and specialty contractors, it was provided that there would be two employer representatives from each of these two categories. It is not the purpose of this summary to convey the details of the implementing agreement or of the Board's operation. Article III, Section 3 of the Agreement provides that:

> It shall be the duty of the Joint Board to consider and decide cases of jurisdictional disputes in the building and construction industry, which disputes are referred to it by any of the International Unions involved in the dispute, or an employer directly affected by the dispute on the work in which he is engaged; or by a participating organization representing such employer.

Two procedural rules involved in the Board's operation are note-worthy because they reflect the accommodation of the machinery to the special problems and characteristics of an industry. First, the contractor has the obligation to make the initial assignment of work. A request for a decision in a particular case need not wait until the disputed work is started, but the work must be assigned before a dispute will be considered. The Board discovered that years of unrestrained union pressure on jurisdictional issues had caused employers to default on their basic right and obligation to make work assignments. In the words of the first Board Chairman, Professor John T. Dunlop:

> I repeat what I have often told contractor groups: The making of work assignments is as vital a part of managing a project as providing for the scheduling of materials and inspection. The making of decisions on work assignments requires considerable care, planning, and attention to the relevant decisions and agreements and to area practice determined on a factual basis. Jurisdictional problems will no more take care of themselves on a project than will the smooth flow of materials. Both require careful planning.

By painstaking education, the Board is gradually making it customary for the contractor to make the work assignment. This has been and continues to be a difficult task. The industry is composed of many contractors, and not only is the total number of such contractors increasing, but there is a high turnover among them. Thus, the job of educating them to the basic obligation to make the initial assignment is a continuing one.

Second, a decision rendered by the Board applies to a particular job only. It is because conditions vary widely among disputes that prior decisions of the Board cannot always be used as precedents. This does not mean, however, that a series of similar decisions for a given community does not acquire the status of a recognized jurisdictional pattern. In deciding a given case the Board must be governed first and foremost by a decision or agreement of record. If the disputed work is not covered by any such agreement, it may apply one of two other standards, area practice or national trade practice. Many of these agreements result in an allocation of work jurisdiction along geographical lines. The carpenters, for example, might be recognized as having the right to perform a certain type of work west of the Mississippi, but the machinists would have jurisdiction of such work east of the Mississippi.

In its twelve years of operation, the Joint Board has made slow but steady progress toward the resolution of jurisdictional disputes. It has purposely chosen the painstaking approach of developing long-range bases for settlement, and given the difficulty of the problems, its results have been remarkable. Putting out the immediate jurisdictional fire has been subordinated to the less dramatic, but more meaningful, goal of effective fire prevention. The decisions issued in hundreds of individual cases are gradually providing the basis for resolving many disputes without reference to the Board. Less well known, yet far more significant, is the fact that within twelve years' time the Board assisted in the successful mediation of thirty-five National Agreements between national unions on some of the most troublesome disputed work issues. The philosophy of Joint Board Chairman Dunlop, who resigned in 1957, and his associates was that a

> jurisdictional dispute is better solved by national agreement than by a decision. . . . No man is wise enough to write words that another (particularly the thousands of business agents all over the country) cannot misinterpret or which do not contain loopholes. In the event of an agreement in good faith, the two international unions, at least, are trying to make it work rather than to pick it to pieces. An agreement usually avoids the unhappy consequence in which one of the parties feels it has lost.

In summary, the construction industry and its unions—which face many of the factors that are likely to maximize jurisdictional and work assignment friction—are joined in an earnest effort to reduce this area of controversy. Dunlop had reason to conclude in his report on July 25, 1957, that "the record of the past 10 years shows that any dispute, no matter how bitter and complex and no matter how ancient, can be settled by persistent, imaginative and determined effort." The Board has succeeded in changing the method of solving questions of jurisdiction throughout the construction industry.

MANUFACTURING AND SERVICE ENTERPRISES. It has already been mentioned that many plants in the United States have more than one union representing its employees. The scope of work to be controlled by any one union is not always susceptible to precise definition. Therefore, over a period of time almost any employer is likely to assign work to one union that will invite an immediate protest from another of the bargaining agents. In some cases the employer will want to see that the work is given to one particular unit; in others his attitude may be one of indifference. In the latter event, if he is uncertain to which unit the work should be allocated, he may confer in advance with the competing units hoping that they will work out a mutually satisfactory agreement.

For example, in the paper industry it is not uncommon to have some of the employees represented by the United Papermakers and

Paperworkers and others by the Brotherhood of Pulp, Sulphite, and Papermill Workers. Historically, these two organizations have been very successful in resolving amicably their jurisdictional differences. When an employer was in doubt about where a newly-created job belonged, he often discussed the matter with the local representatives, who, failing to agree, would refer it to the national headquarters for resolution. Occasionally joint committees were established by the international presidents to determine in which unit a work assignment in an organized plant should fall.

However, if a settlement satisfactory to the competing unions and to the employer is not reached, or, if the employer starts with a firm conviction that the work should go to a certain job and unit, it is obvious that he must make the assignment as he sees fit. His decision may give rise to a grievance filed under the agreement with the bypassed union. It is seldom realized that some inter-union jurisdictional questions are decided by arbitrators in American industry. Usually these are controversies in which the real dispute is between unions and not between a union and the employer. The employer is the defendant in the proceedings only because he has exercised the right of management to assign work. For example, in one such arbitration case, the management opened with the assertion that it did not care what verdict the arbitrator rendered. Its only witnesses were officials of the union to whose members the work assignment had been made.

Illustrative of these types of cases is the following. A large glass company had assigned colmonoy process work, a relatively new process in the industry, to its mold makers, who were represented by the American Flint Glass Workers' Union. The United Glass and Ceramic Workers of North America, the organization representing many other employees, protested that this work should have been assigned to welders under its jurisdiction. A grievance was filed, and the case was carried to arbitration. At the start of the hearing, an international representative of the American Flint Glass Workers requested leave to intervene in support of the company's position. The rival union, which had initiated the proceedings, protested such intervention on the ground that the Flint Glass Workers' Union was not party to the dispute and could not be because only the agreement between the subject company and the United Glass Workers was involved.

The arbitrator denied the request for intervention, pointing out that if any party could intervene in an arbitration merely by showing that it might be affected in some way by the decision, many interveners might present themselves. For example, in a contention between a senior employee and a junior employee over layoff or promotion the successful jobholder could present himself as a party to the dispute. Another important factor in the arbitrator's ruling was the finding that a joinder of the parties to avoid multiplicity of overlapping arbitrations was not called for because the agreement between the company and the Flint Glass Workers contained no arbitration clause. As it developed, the intervention interest was met by the company's adopting as its own witnesses those men who would have testified for the Flint Glass Workers. The arbitrator found that, although the new process is sometimes called "spray welding" in the industry, it is not treated as a type of welding in the standard handbooks of the craft. He found that this process had a closer kinship with moldmaking than with welding. The union grievance was denied.[8]

A somewhat different approach to the resolution of an interjurisdictional conflict by arbitration is to be found in the case of a limestone company. The company had installed a new machine, the first of its type in the industry, which was to be used in preparing the limestone for market. The machine was intended to replace the so-called "jenny lind" machines, which had been operated by members of the International Association of Marble, Slate and Stone Polishers, Rubbers and Sawyers, Tile and Marble Setters Helpers, Marble Mosaic and Terrazzo Workers Helpers Union. In addition, the new surfacer machine was expected to reduce the amount of work done on its carborundum machines, which used a "drum" motion to improve surfacing with abrasives. Traditionally the carborundum machines had been considered within the jurisdiction of the Journeymen Stonecutters. Both union organizations sought jurisdiction over the work to be done on the new machine. Evidently the company did not proceed to make an assignment in this case. Instead, an unusual stipulation was agreed to by all three parties. The question to be decided was which organization had jurisdiction over the new surfacing machine, and as part of the stipulation it was agreed that "the Presidents of both International Unions and their locals and

[8] Bureau of National Affairs, *Labor Arbitration Reports* (1957), pp. 353-55.

the Company involved" would "abide unconditionally by the decision of the arbitrator;" moreover, the cost of the arbitration was to be borne equally by all three parties.[9]

The procedure followed in this case is more important than the verdict, which gave jurisdiction to the union that had represented the "jenny lind" jobholders. It suggests the wisdom and desirability of management insisting on a joinder in arbitration proceedings where it is indifferent to the outcome and where the contract with each union organization contains an arbitration clause. By so doing it was spared the costly proceedings faced by one company when a contention by a union protesting work assignment was upheld in arbitration, only to have the company's observance of the first arbitration ruling challenged by the other union through the arbitration procedure. Fortunately for the company, the second arbitrator confirmed the first finding and did not place the company in the hazardous position of being in violation of an arbitrator's ruling.

These are only a few of the cases that might be cited to show the extent to which the arbitration process under labor agreements has become a variant of the Jurisdictional Disputes Board's activity in the building and construction industry. In a few cases the employer refuses to become party to the controversy, as in a case decided by President George Meany of the AFL-CIO. As impartial arbitrator, he decided whether program directors of the Radio and Television Directors Guild were privileged to issue certain types of instructions to members of the technical crew, a practice protested by the technical directors, who are members of the National Association of Broadcast Employees and Technicians. Although the question arose under contracts between these organizations and the National Broadcasting Company, the company remained aloof from the proceedings.[10]

In summary, there is no evidence of serious concern over the interunion jurisdictional conflicts in American industry arising from management work assignments, except in those industries organized along refined craft lines with nebulous distinctions among the several crafts. Even in these industries, such as building and construction, remarkable progress is being made in using neutral review and anticipatory agreements between potential rivals. Elsewhere in American industry, the arbitration process has served well to handle these

[9] The same, pp. 802-04.
[10] The same (1958), pp. 420-24.

problems where they arise in multi-bargaining-unit companies. In most manufacturing industries, inter-union work jurisdiction claims are a source of more trouble in company decisions to subcontract, particularly in the "grey" area of maintenance and construction work. This problem is discussed in the next chapter.

Bargaining-Unit vs. Nonbargaining-Unit Work Assignment Issues

It is not hard to understand why employees and their unions are concerned when work they identify, rightly or wrongly, as belonging to their bargaining unit is given to workers outside the unit. This is discussed at some length in the chapter on subcontracting. Two problem areas warrant discussion in dealing with work assignment: the assignment of bargaining-unit work to nonsupervisory, non-bargaining-unit personnel, and the issue of foremen working.

NONSUPERVISORY, NONBARGAINING-UNIT WORK ASSIGNMENT. Very often the work jurisdiction lines between some bargaining-unit jobs and excluded jobs of a nonsupervisory nature are indistinct. This is true particularly when the bargaining coverage extends to jobs of a technical and research nature where the union employees work closely with laboratory heads, engineers, draftsmen, and others who are excluded from the bargaining unit. The semi-creative nature of their work is such that the covered and excluded employees are sometimes doing the same work.

A case in point is that of a large aircraft engine company with a UAW local covering technical and salaried employees. During the immediate postwar period, when the shortage of professional engineers became acute, it was decided to assign the work of writing up experimental engineering orders to one of the top skilled technical workers, thereby relieving the excluded engineers from some of this skilled, but nonprofessional work. The assignment never became exclusively that of the technical jobholders; they were expected to do this work if and when the engineers were too busy on other, more important duties. Thus for many years both the covered and excluded employees did this same work in varying proportions from time to time as part of their total duties. This practice resulted in a serious controversy in 1958, when the company suffered from recession cutbacks. Arguing in part that the engineers were now free to handle the experimental orders without interfering with their professional duties, the company withdrew this assignment from the technicians at the same time it effected the layoff of a number of technicians. A grievance was promptly filed by the bargaining-unit members claiming that by practice they had acquired a vested interest in the work.

In this case it is clear that the work in question had fallen into a no-man's land category as a result of assignment practices pursued by management; it was not identifiable either as bargaining-unit or as nonbargaining-unit work. It is also evident that at a time of work curtailment a reassignment was made favoring the nonbargaining-unit people.

The hazards of overlapping work assignments such as this are apparent. Sometimes the hazard arises not because of any deliberate policy of management, but rather because of the gradual admixture of duties effected by the employees themselves without management's knowledge. Managements are often surprised to discover that employees have for years assumed responsibilities and duties in addition to those assigned simply because they were ambitious or because the nonsupervisory, nonunit people with whom they worked were quite willing to share part of their jobs. As noted above, this accidental, subtle change in "assignment" is most common where the covered and excluded groups work together, and it is not always disclosed by a claim for a rate adjustment on the ground that one's job has changed. But if layoffs are threatened by the elimination of "assignments by gradual acquisition," a vested rights claim is almost certain to be filed. With the predicted growth of organization among technical and research personnel, this problem of deliberate or subtle fusion of bargaining-unit and nonbargaining-unit assignments may become more important.

THE ISSUE OF FOREMEN WORKING. The great majority of labor-management agreements now restrict the right of a foreman excluded from the bargaining unit to perform work within the unit. These restrictive clauses usually provide for exceptions in specific circumstances. For example, a foreman may be permitted to perform work if he is training new employees, or he may be allowed to do work in testing the efficacy of a new process. In a large automobile company, a foreman is allowed to do production work to test the reasonableness of a standard and to determine the extent of an alleged slow-down. Usually foremen are also allowed to do bargaining-unit work when an emergency arises. The issue of whether or not a *bona fide* supervisor or foreman should do production or maintenance work is no longer a matter for serious contention. Most companies feel that their supervisors should not do bargaining-unit work but should spend all their time on supervisory duties.

Agreement on the general principle, however, has not eliminated the question of foremen working as a cause of frequent disputes in the administration of the contract. In three assembly plants of one automobile company it was found that in 1956 foremen-working grievances accounted for 34.8 per cent, 24.9 per cent, and 19.7 per cent of the total grievance volume. The blame in this as well as in other companies must be assigned to both parties.

Management may subscribe sincerely to the tenet that foremen should not do bargaining-unit work, but at the same time management judges a foreman by the quality and quantity of his performance. Therefore, when a bottleneck arises for one reason or another, a foreman often finds it difficult to stand idly by; he is tempted to move in and help a worker out to insure prompt resumption of production. The fact that many foremen have been promoted from within makes it unnatural for them to refrain from doing any production work, particularly in the early period of their advancement. In a true sense they are "firehorses" who cannot avoid applying their production knowledge by actually doing the work themselves. One employer reports that he has some foremen who virtually cannot be kept from doing some work, and in extreme cases they will get on the line and work a half day or more. It is obvious that managements cannot expect to avoid grievances if their supervisors and foremen are not trained to—or refuse to—observe the restrictions agreed to in the labor contract.

Employees and unions in turn have also been responsible in many instances for the disproportionate role played by "foremen-working" grievances in the application of the agreement. This type of complaint lends itself well to an harassment campaign against management. Sometimes if a foreman so much as picks up a tool, a grievance will be entered. One case was cited of a foreman who carried a jack for ten feet, and a formal grievance was filed that he was working in violation of the agreement. What is even worse, union committeemen have sometimes invented false claims of foremen working and bolstered their claims by having worker witnesses testify to the manufactured charge. Part of the difficulty may be that a resolution of these grievances in favor of the aggrieved employees often means a money payoff. A cease-and-desist order by an arbitrator is used initially, but if there is any evidence that this is a repetitive occurrence, he will award damages to employees deprived of work or will award a money payoff as a penalty on the employer. The money payoff invites abuse, particularly where the decision must be based on testimony of the "Yes, you did; no, I didn't" variety. One employee in a manufacturing company who had been given a one-day disciplinary suspension for some rule infraction boasted to his fellow workers that he would quickly get back the money he lost. And he did just that, by winning a false claim that his foreman had worked.

One company tended to encourage this type of "rocking-chair-payment" grievance by its method of disposing of them. Given the problem of determining credibility, the company decided it was best not to have grievances of this type go to arbitration. Therefore, it settled the grievance in the later stages of the procedure by splitting the amount of time claimed.[11] If a grievance alleged that the foreman had worked a total of two hours, the company would offer to settle by paying the aggrieved employee for one hour. The results were inevitable. Over a period of time the claims soon rose to three, four, and finally eight hours before the company realized the consequences of its compromise approach to grievance settlement.

In this as in so many other significant grievance problems, the high or low volume of complaints is often symptomatic of the general climate of labor relations. Harassment of the employer with this weapon does not necessarily mean that the foreman-working issue is a serious problem; this difficult-to-prove-or-disprove type of question may be exploited in order to achieve an entirely different goal. Sometimes the prevalence or relative absence of this type of grievance can be explained by the personalities involved. If the foreman is well liked by the employees, if his relationship with the stew-

[11] For obvious reasons, this kind of grievance is seldom settled in the first stage of the grievance procedure.

ard or committeeman is good, he might work a great deal and never be challenged. On the other hand, if he is disliked or if he scoffs at a union representative's protest, he is likely to invite a grievance for the most trivial performance of bargaining-unit work.

Before leaving this subject, it might be well to raise the question whether management's ready acceptance of the union position that foremen should do no bargaining-unit work is wise or defensible. One cannot challenge the conclusion of many companies that to be a good supervisor a man must attend first and foremost to his supervisory and administrative duties. But this is a far cry from acquiescence in a policy that precludes the foreman from doing any work on the jobs under his supervision. He might well prove to be a more able supervisor and command greater respect from those working under him if he were to try his hand now and then on the various jobs. It must be remembered that the union policy grew out of fear that if foremen worked, bargaining-unit members might lose their jobs. It does not follow that to allay this fear management must put a complete ban on foremen working except for training or emergency purposes. Yet this is precisely what most managements have done. Ironically the unions themselves often challenge a foreman's judgment as to the performance of an employee on a machine or work assignment in a promotion, layoff, or disciplinary case. They seek to discredit his judgment on employee ability by claiming that a foreman can scarcely be expected to have a reliable judgment when he himself has never done the work in question. In brief, it is probable that management has gone too far in agreeing to an unrealistic barrier between supervisory duties and any direct participation in the duties being supervised.

Intra-Union Work Assignment Problems

Public interest and even the interest of scholars in the field of labor relations have centered around the more dramatic inter-union jurisdictional squabbles. This is understandable because often these disputes have involved strikes and have been the most critical issues in a few industries. But there has been a consequent neglect of the manifold jurisdictional and work-assignment problems that give rise to grievances, verbal complaints, and contract issues in situations where there is no contest between unions. Day in and day out, management's decisions to revise work assignments on a temporary or semi-permanent basis are the cause of controversies.

Those who conclude that the solution of jurisdictional conflicts in the building trades industry lies in the creation of "one big union" to replace the present craft breakdown would do well to examine the jurisdictional problems faced by managements of plants or companies having only one union. What may be described as a security and sometimes an acquisitive interest on the one hand and a selective-exclusion interest on the other hand are interests of individuals, not just of power groups or power institutions. The unions may appear to have these interests, particularly the acquisitive interest, to a greater extent because they vocalize them so effectively and because they sometimes initiate forceful action to achieve their jurisdictional goals. But in the last analysis it is the individual whose psychological makeup sets in motion action in one form or another that affects management's method and occasionally freedom of making work assignments. Stated differently, there is some currency to the facile notion that power hungry and grasping union leaders "create" jurisdictional controversies. This may be true in some situations, but it is more accurate to say that unions themselves may trace their origin, in part, to concern by individuals with the scope of their duties. A secretary in an office who is asked to assume a number of unpleasant tasks while a portion of her more responsible and challenging duties are given to someone else will feel resentful. This could lead easily to interest in a union organization.

Therefore, even in establishments with one union there are individual and small group job proprietary interests that create problems not only for the company in making work assignments but also for the union leadership, to which these interests appear as dangerously divisive and factional. There is substantial evidence to support the conclusion that industrial unions are becoming more jurisdiction conscious. A form of classification jurisdiction is emerging and, not unexpectedly, it is manifesting itself most among the skilled trades groups included within the industrial union. In a study made of one steel plant organized by the United Steelworkers of America, it was found that in the course of one year there were more than fifty jurisdictional disputes and almost twenty-five work stoppages on this issue alone.

The difficulties for union and management alike are shown by the way in which the parties in a large automobile concern have handled the problem of maintenance work on automated equipment. The company established its first automated stamping plant in 1950 and concluded that it would be much more efficient to have a separate "automation department" composed of conventional skilled trades people, who would be classified under the generic title "automation equipment maker and maintenance man." This would constitute a new classification with its own rate and would embrace such trades as tinsmith, electrician, welder, machine repairman, die maker and toolmaker. Thus within the automation maintenance department, the men who formerly had been in separate trades were expected to work interchangeably and cross orthodox trade lines. At the time this plan was conceived and implemented, the UAW had not been certified at the plant. Nevertheless, when the union became the bargaining agent, no attempt was made to set aside the new, inclusive automation maintenance job. It is pertinent that as part of the over-all move, the company also created a new production classification known as "automation tender" with a five-cents-an-hour increase to replace the existing heavy press operator classification with no change in job duties. There can be little doubt that this latter move was designed, in part, to instill in the production workers satisfaction with the program that would override any possible dissatisfaction on the part of the craft groups whose separate, orthodox identities were being destroyed. In part, job evaluation considerations were involved. Over the years the company found that it could train a non-journeyman to become a competent all-around "automation equipment maker and maintenance man." By early 1956 there were more than a hundred men in this classification. Seventy-three were journeymen electricians, die makers, machine repairmen, millwrights, welders, and machinists. But some thirty to forty others had no skilled trades background; some of these men had been oilers, one was a farm manager. Yet all of the men were earning the equivalent of the tool and die rate in the general classification. The company's innovation at this plant could be described as a complete success.

The company hoped to repeat this success when it opened a new stamping plant in another city in 1955, a plant described as the "Utopia of automation." A single UAW unit was established for collective bargaining purposes, and the company proposed the same arrangement, i.e., a separate automation department with a generic maintenance classification and a five-cent increase for nonskilled production workers reclassified from heavy press operators to automation tenders. Two developments gave the company and the union their first warnings that this unorthodox departure from craft lines, dictated by new technology and regard for efficient maintenance methods, had uneasy acceptance. First, the skilled people refused to accept the classification "automation equipment maker and maintenance man." One union leader explained that "the skilled trades representatives abhor the word 'automation' in the title; it symbolizes the destruction of old craft lines." Therefore, although it was agreed that the craftsmen would become part of a separate automation department and would cross trade lines in their work, they were to retain the titles of their respective crafts. Second, in the vote on the settlement it was evident that the nonskilled production people, who represented a majority of the local union members, outvoted the skilled trades people, who were lukewarm toward the whole arrangement. It was the appeal of the five-cent increase that insured acceptance of the settlement. Unlike the first plant, the men in the automation department at this plant have a skilled trades background. The retention of the craft titles militated against recruitment of competent, nonskilled men.

The company's next effort was to inaugurate the special department in one of its other stamping plants that had been automated earlier. It hoped that the appeal to heavy press people of the five-cent increase would offset any resentment toward the idea by craftsmen. But it failed to appreciate a significant difference in union structure in this plant. Although part of the same local industrial union, the skilled people belonged to a separate unit within the local; they had their own officers, and on a proposal such as this they voted separately. The leaders of the skilled group opposed the automation equipment maker and maintenance classification, even though the tool and die rate range for it would have meant an increase for some of the trades people involved. Their principal objection was that the proposed interchangeability among the trades would mean a dilution of skills.

The net result was that the production employees voted for the plan because of the five-cent increase, but the skilled groups rejected it. The parent local or the international union could have intervened, yet chose not to do so in spite of the fact that the rejection meant an annual loss of more than a quarter of a million dollars for the production employees. A representative of the heavy press operators explained, "The matter is out of our hands. We like the five-cent increase, but the international is leaning over backward not to offend the skilled workers." The recent loss of the pattern makers to the Pattern Makers League and a threat by the tool and die unit to break away undoubtedly explains the caution of the international on any action that might alienate the member craft employees.

Although internal union political considerations are the principal reason for the UAW's resistance to an extension of the plan, the union tries to rationalize its position on other grounds. For example, it claims that no one man can ever become a truly qualified repairman capable of handling all problems that might arise on the automated equipment; in effect, some union spokesmen deny the validity of a new super-trade classification. There is some evidence that the pressure to increase compartmentalization of skilled trades within the UAW, a pressure that has had steadily growing success, is not viewed unanimously as a desirable trend among top UAW officials. But there has been a political capitulation by the officers to the craft identification interests of the skilled group minority within the union.[12]

Meanwhile, what are the consequences of this classification jurisdiction position insofar as the management is concerned? Perhaps the best way to show its effect is to appraise the benefits resulting from the work assignment freedom enjoyed in the two stamping plants where the plan was adopted. These plants report that the savings were substantial and more than offset the cost of granting the five-cent increase to production people. The automation department manager at one plant said his costs would rise from 20 per cent to 25 per cent if he had to use the various trades on a separatist basis; the manager at the second plant estimated that the costs would be

---

[12] Some of these union officials make a distinction between large and small plants. In the smaller plants with fewer craftsmen, they feel there is a more legitimate reason for broadening the scope of work assignments. In smaller plants the unions admit the desirability of having broader craft definitions. Obviously it is very difficult to write standard craft definitions that will apply to both large and small plants.

50 per cent higher. The principal cost saving derived from the plan was in avoiding waiting time, where one or more tradesmen stand idly by while another performs his specific craft job.

This one experience shows the complexities of the work-jurisdiction problem of the company dealing with just one union. The partial success of this company in achieving adjustment by the skilled trades groups to the new technology is not typical of most industrial union situations. Even this limited degree of success is seldom secured. One is more apt to hear of the situation described by a manager of this same company, who reported that five men were sent to install a thermostat in his office. While one of the men worked, the others "just sat around." An aluminum company reports that there is a constant struggle for efficiency in the face of craft traditions, even with a single bargaining agent. An example is the problem of getting pipefitters to do welding. In this case management says it prefers to argue these matters out with the union rather than attempt to formulate a written rule in the agreement. Its theory is that such a rule might turn out to be a still greater restriction.

A steel company states that it has made some progress in achieving greater flexibility in the use of maintenance people and has succeeded in reducing the size of the crew. But the 1956-57 layoff problem led to a setback. The number of maintenance grievances increased; laid off craftsmen claimed jurisdiction of work being performed by employees still on the payroll. An aircraft company claims that within one of its bargaining units the craft lines are so strict and narrow that on any given job the company will have to have workers from a dozen different crafts before the job can be done.

A number of parties have developed contract language or special machinery to minimize the number of work assignment problems involving contention among the skilled craft groups within the union. A union representative in a chemical company acknowledges that jurisdictional disputes between the two bargaining units in the company are less serious than disputes arising within his own local union among the skilled trades. The most serious problem was the company's practice of assigning to tradesmen some work outside their craft. To minimize the frequency of such hassles the parties in 1955 negotiated a new clause acknowledging that "the interest of both parties is best served by having men of certain skill doing work normally requiring such training." However, the agreement goes on to say that "this shall not be interpreted to restrict men of one skill from doing incidental work of another classification necessary for the performance of the job." The agreement gives examples of how this "incidental clause and the assignment of work thereunder" shall be applied. In the assignment of a millwright to move equipment, incidental work is identified as removal of and replacement of a door to gain necessary clearance. When a machinist is assigned to check or repair gear train, incidental work would be the removal of guards to gain access to the gear case.

Some contrast may be made between the work assignment problems arising in an industrial plant and those within a craft-union environment. The prime need in an industrial unit is flexibility, and so the definition of jobs within a large manufacturing plant is often vague on day-to-day assignments. One union official in the automobile industry observed logically that it was almost impossible to say what the duties of a millwright were supposed to be. Those duties may vary from day to day and, if a shop committeeman is bent on causing trouble for management, it is easy for him to do so. Some companies have tried to avoid a large volume of work assignment complaints by entering into fairly rigid jurisdictional agreements, particularly on maintenance and other semi-craft work. They have found that these attempts to establish sharp lines of demarcation serve only to aggravate work assignment problems. As a consequence, one company with an industrial union says it would prefer to "run in an open field," having tried creating assignment lines that became targets for attack instead of effective regulatory divisors in making working assignments.

Who Is Obligated to Do the Work?

Unwillingness by employees to perform certain tasks is a much less serious problem than their claim that tasks belonging to them have been given to others in violation of the contract. This does not mean that employees or the unions that represent them are reconciled to the logic of work assignments in all instances. Rather, it is a recognition that, except when safety and health are involved, the employer's assignment of work should be observed first, and if there is a question concerning the propriety of the assignment, it should be the subject of a grievance. Most arbitrators have sustained a company's right to discipline employees for refusal to comply with reasonable orders on the grounds that they may refuse to comply only if there is a clear showing that the task would jeopardize their safety or health.

Where these problems have arisen in the day-to-day conduct of a plant, it has been for one of several reasons. First, in some instances the management has given the impression to employees that they will be required to do certain work only under special circumstances. Illustrating this situation is the case of the cleanup of a lathe used in a package machinery company by both testers and assemblers. The lathe could be operated by incumbents of either of these two job classifications. Complaints were made to supervision that those using the lathe were leaving the machine filled with debris. This led the foreman to post a notice on the machine that anyone using it had the responsibility of cleaning it. After the posting of the notice if an assembler wanted to use the machine and found it dirty, and if the foreman could not find who last used the lathe, who was to clean it? The assembler might well say, "Why should I clean it? I didn't use it last, and you yourself said the last user had this responsibility. It's up to you to find out who used it last and make him do it." In one such instance the foreman asked three people (an assembler, a sweeper, and a protesting shop steward) to do the job. Each refused on the ground that it was an assignment contrary to the company's own posted notice. At this point the foreman said he would do it himself, and he was told that if he did he would be guilty of performance of work within the bargaining unit in violation of the agreement.

Second, there are occasions when unwritten seniority practices lead to refusal to perform certain assignments. Many companies have discovered that their supervisors have adopted the practice of offering assignments to senior men first; if they refuse, the next in order of seniority are asked. This procedure continues until someone accepts the work. If no one accepts it, the junior man is then obligated to take the assignment. In other words, the refusal of assignments develops as a privilege of the senior employees. Usually this causes no difficulty, but if a company feels it needs a certain worker on a given job because of his skill, it may find that its attempts to transfer him are frustrated by a claim that reassignment is contrary to seniority practice.

Loss of transfer rights may go even further. One company in effect lost the right to transfer. Over-manned jobs required layoff and bumping procedures. Under-manned jobs were filled by promotion through posting and bidding. A complex "daisy chain" was required to get workers from one assembly assignment to another. Direct transfer was not allowed.

Third, it has already been pointed out that many union representatives succeed in being more authoritative than is supervision. By sea-lawyer tactics and by allusions to job descriptions, they often advise employees that they are not required to do work assigned to them, and they force supervision to yield. If refusals of this type are tolerated, a supervisor may find he is no longer in charge of his department. In effect, he has turned the reins over to the union representative.

Fourth, in some instances a refusal to accept additional or different work assignments takes the form of concerted action or pressure tactics of the type described in Chapter 22. Usually this refusal is symptomatic of a relationship problem that goes beyond the legitimacy of the given work assignment.

Fifth, sometimes the refusal to do certain work is a result of contract restrictions sought by the union. The refusal by the teamsters to have truck drivers load or unload trucks has become an important issue in some parts of the country.

The fact that refusal to perform work assigned is a relatively minor problem in American industry is only partially attributable to management's care in making work assignments. Management is indeed exercising greater care in making assignments, but also important has been union and management promotion of the view that the wise procedure for protest is through the grievance machinery, not through outright refusal to do the work.

Management's freedom to assign work has been curtailed to a considerable extent by union rules and practices. The acquisitive interest of unions and of their members in the assignment of work has proved more troublesome than the selective-exclusion interest. The desire to broaden entitlement to work by the individual or by the group has been stronger than the desire to avoid enlargement of jurisdiction.

Union-imposed rules have often tried to substitute orderly assignment procedures for the haphazard ones that were followed when management was left to its own initiative. But there is evidence that often these rules have been carried too far. Managerial flexibility and efficiency have been impaired in two ways: by the necessity of observing work assignment jurisdictions that have led to inefficient utilization of manpower, and by harassment resulting from frequent grievances over who is entitled or, to a lesser extent, obligated to do the work.

In an impressive number of cases, management itself is to blame for its predicament. Poor judgment in assigning work has often led to the development of costly practices. Sometimes management has not been definite as to what it considers a desirable work assignment policy. As a consequence, some managements have become enmeshed by default in a lot of needless rules and restrictions. Work assignment remains an area of conflict in labor relations in the United States, although there is evidence of gradual adjustment, as in the building construction industry.

10 / *Subcontracting*

HISTORICALLY, AMERICAN BUSINESS enterprise has been free to decide the extent to which it would subcontract some of its work to other enterprises. These decisions were considered an inherent management function not affected by the presence or absence of a union. A review of the management literature on the subject discloses little or no attention to the influence of collective bargaining.[1]

However, the research undertaken for this study justifies the conclusion that union policy and actions are playing a progressively greater part in influencing management's decision to subcontract or to move work from one plant to another plant. Subcontracting is a relatively new issue, and it remains one of the most difficult areas in labor relations. Unlike many other subjects considered in this volume that have moved from the contract development to the adjustment stage, subcontracting and, to a lesser extent, work movement within a company are still a source of considerable conflict. It is the purpose of this chapter to analyze the bases and extent of union interest in this subject and the ways in which the freedom traditionally exercised by management has been limited or conditioned by the collective bargaining process.[2] This will be done under the following

[1] James W. Culliton, *Make or Buy* (Division of Research, Harvard University Graduate School of Business Administration, December 1942). Carter C. Higgins, "Make-or-Buy Re-Examined," *Harvard Business Review* (March-April 1955), pp. 109-19. "Make It or Buy It. Which Pays Off?" *Business Week* (July 3, 1954), p. 106. A typical list of major factors influencing a manufacturer's decision includes the following as reasons for buying or subcontracting: inadequate volume to justify capital and inventory investment, inadequate plant space, benefit of outside suppliers' specialized ability, demand variation, lack of skilled personnel, quicker delivery, higher quality, and lower cost. Reasons for making rather than subcontracting are the following: integration of plant operations, transportation delivery and expense, unreliability of suppliers, complexity of parts requiring direct supervision, overhead considerations, secrecy, higher quality, and lower cost.

[2] Principal attention is given to subcontracting rather than movement of work from one plant to another within the same company since the former is the more serious problem. The seniority problems involved in work movement were discussed in Chapter 5.

four headings: (1) general statement of the problem, (2) determinants of union interest, (3) nature of union influence and control, and (4) role of arbitration in defining the scope of management's rights.

It is recognized that public policy in the field of labor relations may affect the freedom of management to relocate work or to subcontract. For example, under the Wagner Act and the Taft-Hartley Law a decision to relocate in an effort to escape unionism could be considered a violation of the law. The Labor-Management Reporting and Disclosure Act of 1959 makes special reference to subcontracting in Section 704. The Walsh-Healy Act, requiring observance of certain wage standards for government contract work, may well affect a decision to subcontract work. The Air Force, in the interest of relieving distressed areas, may require the subcontracting of work as a condition of contract-grant. While these and other legal or administrative requirements deserve mention, they are not within the purview of this chapter.

General Statement of the Problem

It probably would be impossible to find a completely integrated enterprise in the United States. Actually every producing unit buys from a number of other producing units. A steel mill, for example, engaged in the manufacture of a basic product, is the buyer of raw materials, machinery, transportation, and construction services from other enterprises. In the clothing industry, particularly the women's garment industry, reliance on contracting shops has been extensive. Companies in the aircraft engine and airframe industries operate as prime contractors, farming out a considerable amount of the work. A large tire company reports that it has always subcontracted a wide range of production and maintenance items; the contracts range from the installation of new tire molds to the replacement of fluorescent tubes. Perhaps the automobile industry is the classic illustration of reliance on outside suppliers. Each company in this industry buys extensively such component parts as carburetors, tires, batteries, bumpers, glass, and many other parts that go into the completed automobile. In some instances, companies will both make and buy at the same time, as in the case of metal-working plants that use stampings. A survey of 355 such companies shows that 49.8 per cent of them both make and buy the stampings they need, 20.6 per cent buy all the stampings required, and 28.2 per cent make all the stampings they use.[3] Even in a service industry, such as a department store, a portion of the service rendered may be purchased from another enterprise. The goods bought from a store may be delivered by another company. The meals served on an airplane are likely to be prepared by an enterprise under contract to the airline.

It is also important to understand that most of these purchased parts or materials or services are made to the specification of the buyer. In fact, the buyer may even undertake to train the supplier in making a given part. He may send specialists to the supplier firm to handle difficult problems, and it is not uncommon for the customer to advance necessary moneys for equipment purchases.[4] Furthermore, the history of enterprises shows that there is constant experimenting to determine which materials or parts should be bought and which made.

By and large unions have understood and have accepted these economic facts of life. Many unions operate without raising questions about the routine procurement or subcontracting decisions of management. For example, there is no indication that the UAW has tried to restrict by contract terms the extensive purchase of component parts by automobile companies. Usually the problem becomes most critical when there is a change in the accepted way of doing things. If a company has always performed certain work in one of its plants and then decides to subcontract the work to another company or to move it to another plant, conflict is likely to develop. On the one hand, management regards its rights as very broad, holding that it has the right to subcontract at any time, even operations that traditionally have been integrated. On the other hand, the union maintains that the jobs and work for which it bargained when it was recognized as the collective bargaining agent and entered into an agreement belong to the union. Because of these sharply disparate views, the problem has proved to be a serious one.

There is a discernible trend toward union control over some forms of subcontracting, and it seems likely to continue. More and more managements are being called on to defend their actions, and under

[3] Higgins, "Make-or-Buy Re-Examined," p. 110.

[4] In this connection it is interesting that automotive parts companies confronted with labor difficulties and a threatened strike may be advised how to handle the problem by the labor relations experts of the automobile companies that buy from them.

a growing number of labor agreements their actions are subject to grievance review, including arbitration. The implications to management of a more intense and resolute union interest in its decisions to subcontract or to move work are of considerable importance.

Determinants of Union Interest

In a discussion of the various reasons for union interest, several considerations should be kept in mind. First, the form of the subcontracting may affect greatly the union reaction. As noted above, a company's adherence to long-established make-or-buy practice is not likely to provoke union resistance. But there are three things an employer may do that can create conflict. (1) He may send work that has been identified with the plant and the bargaining unit jobs to be performed outside. For example, a maker of carton containers, who had always had printing work done in a separate department of the plant, decided it would be more efficient to give this work to a company specializing in printing. It meant the elimination of a number of jobs and led to a union complaint that the company was subverting the terms of the agreement. (2) The subcontracted work may require the outside enterprise to enter the premises of the company with its own employees. This is illustrated by the use of a cleaning firm to wash windows and to handle general janitorial tasks or by the use of a catering service to operate the cafeteria. A more common illustration is the use of an outside building contractor to handle plant alterations and repairs. Very often in the purchase of new machinery, such as IBM computers, complicated packaging machines, elevators, and the like, the purchase agreement provides for the servicing of the machine by the supplier. Therefore, outside service representatives may be working within the plant along with maintenance employees of the company. During the war years and during special emergencies, such as the collapse of a bridge or extensive flood damage, the railroad carriers brought in outside contractors to expedite track maintenance and repair work. (3) Finally, the subcontracting may change the status of existing employees, converting them from employees to independent contractors. This has happened in some jobs in the newspaper industry, for example.

Of these three possibilities, union interest, particularly at the local level, is likely to be most intense in the last two. The very proximity of outside employees tends to dramatize the competition for work opportunity. Implicit in each of the situations described is a clear-cut change in the established practice. But a persistent source of grievance on the subject of subcontracting and work movement is disagreement as to what constitutes established practice.

A second consideration in considering union interest is the need to make a clear distinction between the attitude of the local union and that of the international parent body. The UAW, for example, is interested in the employment of UAW members; the locals are interested in specific jobs. Therefore, if a company decides to buy a part it has customarily made, the loss of jobs will cause the local union to resist the move. The international will be less concerned provided the supplier plant is under contract with the union. If the international opposes subcontracting too strongly, it will be taking a stand against part of its own membership. To illustrate, one union urged more extensive subcontracting of work under large government contracts in the interest of relieving the plight of small companies and their employees. Yet a local of the same international union protested the subcontracting of such work. However, when the work is going to members of a rival organization, the international may be just as militant in resisting a decision to subcontract.

A third important background fact is that many outside contracts involve work usually performed by maintenance people. In general, craft personnel have a high sense of work ownership, and they are more likely to seize on the issue of subcontracting than are the semi-skilled industrial employees. The problem here is somewhat similar to the work assignment issues involving craft jobs that were discussed in Chapter 9. But the problem is aggravated by the difficulty of defining work. In some companies maintenance men acknowledge management's right to use outside contractors for major construction projects, but they challenge management's interpretation of what constitutes major construction. Where major construction leaves off and minor construction or maintenance work begins is a difficult matter to define.

It is commonly thought that the union's interest in restricting the freedom of management to subcontract work is based solely on a desire to maximize work opportunities for its members. Actually the motives are far more complex. Union interest is chiefly: (1) to protect normal employment opportunities for its members, (2) to preserve the particular union's jurisdiction and strength, (3) to enlarge work opportunities of its members, (4) to combat escape from unionism, and (5) to protect union standards against competition. These motives are not mutually exclusive. In any given situation one or more may be present.

TO PROTECT NORMAL EMPLOYMENT OPPORTUNITIES FOR ITS MEMBERS. This is by far the most common basis for union interest. It is understandable that local unions, and to a greater or lesser extent the parent international union, want their members to be given work opportunities before available work that they can do is given to an outside contractor. It is believed that subcontracting at the expense of layoffs, normal work week reductions, and decrease of pay for regular employees should be avoided.

In a very informative study on this general subject, one company spokesman is quoted as follows:

> We have been in a period of a full employment economy ever since the war, and under these conditions we are not pressed to use our best judgment. Now this slowdown we're going through may encourage us to sit down and ask the question "Could we do this cheaper ourselves?" We have had terrific layoffs in the last months with the exception of one division. Workers who never complained about contracting suddenly file grievances. Stability of employment is a big factor. We have the same tests, but they are applied differently. With full employment, the employee "heat" does not exist.[5]

One might expect to find that the union and the employer have a common interest in protecting normal employment opportunities for existing employees of a company. However, this is not always the case. A shift in make-or-buy and subcontracting decisions by management is not used extensively as a device for stabilizing employment. The deterrents may be other than the lack of qualifications of regular employees to do certain work or the lack of equipment and facilities to perform specialized jobs. In the automobile industry it was found that companies felt obligated to hold rather closely to their ratio of outside purchases even in a recession. They did so out of

---

[5] Margaret K. Chandler and Leonard R. Sayles, *Contracting-Out: A Study of Management Decision Making*, Monograph, Graduate School of Business, Columbia University (1959), p. 27.

concern for future relationship with suppliers. In the study cited above an inquiry was made into the willingness to contract out maintenance and construction work during layoff periods. On the basis of their interviews the authors concluded that "while great stress is placed on unemployment as a factor in contracting out decisions, it would appear that, to some extent, lip service, rather than fealty, is paid to this variable. Actual practice seems to diverge sharply from such platitudes as, 'Of course, we would never contract out with men on lay-off.' . . . The surprising lack of influence of employment level is partially due to the fact that almost one-half of the firms could not interchange craft and production workers."[6]

In a few situations the union desire to maintain a stable workforce has led to the encouragement of subcontracting. For example, in one company in the airframe industry both parties recalled the effect of the cutback at the end of World War II, when the industry had to reduce its workforce from a wartime peak of 1,346,000 workers to approximately 159,000 in 1946. It was recognized that subcontracting was much more desirable than the constant confusion of hiring and laying off caused by the ups and downs of airframe orders. Maintenance of a stable workforce below that required for maximum capacity output was preferred by both the union and the company.

TO PRESERVE THE PARTICULAR UNION'S JURISDICTION AND STRENGTH. Closely related to the objective of protecting employment opportunities is that of maintaining the union's institutional security when it seems to be threatened by management's subcontracting and work movement policies. This happens most often when the work being subcontracted goes to employees under the jurisdiction of another union or to unorganized employees. The contracting out of maintenance and construction work, or in some instances, as we shall see, the failure to contract out such work, is an irritant to the rival unions affected. The Chandler-Sayles report observes:

> Inevitably wrapped up in the decision is the traditional struggle over jurisdiction between craft and industrial unions. It is clear that this is not simply a dispute over principle or status. The stakes are high: the very large number of jobs in American industry involved in the maintenance and construction of equipment and facilities. Current economic trends point to growing difficulties in this area. Automation, techno-

[6] The same.

logical improvements of all kinds, are eliminating industrial union jobs. . . . The skilled machinist, repairman and technician is the workman of the future, and these are the types of members-workers most likely to be found in the ranks of the craft union and the specialized contractor. At present the craft groups seem to be regaining some of the ground lost during the heyday of industrial unionism. The attendant loss of membership on the part of industrial unions has increased their pressure on other available sources of work within the industrial plants.[7]

This problem in the construction-maintenance area is aggravated further by the fact that the "outsiders" come into a plant. Sometimes they work side by side with industrial union craft members. The pay differential favoring the outside building trades craftsmen increases the hostility of the insiders toward them. The net result is that management is in the middle with rival union groups quarreling over its subcontracting decisions.

The jurisdictional implications of subcontracting decisions sometimes put the employer in an extremely difficult position. In such cases, the pressure on the employer may originate as much, if not more, from the "outside" contractor's union as from the employer's own union. In recent years the automobile industry has been plagued by a struggle on the part of the building trades unions to assume exclusive jurisdiction over construction work being performed in part by members of the United Automobile Workers and in part by the employees of outside contractors. The Teamsters Union played an important role in this inter-union struggle resulting from the necessary subcontracting of construction work.

To illustrate, a large automobile company was installing machinery and equipment in its Detroit plant, which had been stripped completely to permit retooling for defense work. Assigned to the work were sixty-six of its own skilled craftsmen plus the building trades craftsmen employed by subcontractors. No difficulty arose until the outside employees outnumbered the UAW craftsmen. At this point a delegation from the AFL Detroit Construction Trade Union Council demanded that the entire job be turned over to AFL union employees. A picket line was put up to force compliance with this demand. The company's own sixty-six union men on the job went through the line and continued to work; in addition the company imported 285 skilled union craftsmen who were about to be laid off from a plant in New York State. An injunction to stop the picketing

[7] The same, p. 5.

was secured. Subsequently an agreement was reached between the UAW and the AFL construction unions to allow sixty-six UAW people to remain on the job. The company refused to honor this agreement on the ground that this work was the property of the company to allot as it desired. It asserted that it had a moral obligation to give work to its own people if they could handle it. This is a classic illustration of outside union pressure to compel subcontracting and of management insistence on subcontracting only to the extent that its own employees are unavailable or cannot do the special work.

In many other situations the industrial union is the grievant. In one city the building trade unions complained that members of the United Steelworkers of America had chased them off a construction project of a U. S. Steel Corporation mill. The steelworkers struck for one day, after which the company decided to keep the outside craftsmen off the project. The local Building Trades Council and the contractors who were to have done the $12-million construction job then filed a series of damage suits in the local courts.[8]

The conflict is not necessarily limited to different unions. It may arise within the same union, as in the case of craft unions that have both industrial and craft-type locals. In one unusual situation the maintenance electricians of an automobile engine plant were in a local of the International Brotherhood of Electrical Workers that also included outside construction craftsmen. Within this local there was a continuing argument as to whether the construction work to be done at the automobile plant belonged to the outside or the inside people. The business agent was in the unenviable position of being forced to represent and argue both sides of the question. This anomalous situation was resolved to some extent by including the inside employees in a newly-formed IBEW production and maintenance local.

A very different form of subcontracting that affects union jurisdictional interest is the conversion of collective bargaining members into independent contractors. In some instances this is a device of employers to counteract unionization. An oil distributing firm reported that when its drivers were showing interest in organization, it made arrangements to sell the equipment to the employees and to

[8] *New York Times* (February 19, 1959), p. 18.

enter into an independent contractor relationship with each of them; its efforts were successful.

This type of conversion, however, is not prompted solely or even largely by a firm's desire to escape unionization. A development in the newspaper industry shows how individual contractorships may emerge, replacing the employer-employee relationship within the framework of collective bargaining. For many years a well-known newspaper was distributed to newsstand and sheet salesmen through 26 independent contractors; distribution in rural areas was accomplished through some 100 so-called Tube Distributors who were also independent contractors. However, a different arrangement was followed for home deliveries in the city and suburban areas: in this territory there were 58 zone and area managers who were employees of the company in the circulation department and who were part of the bargaining unit represented by the Newspaper Guild. These 58 managers covered certain prescribed areas and were in charge of the actual delivery of the newspaper to homes by approximately 3,000 newsboys. The newsboys in turn were considered by the company to be in the status of independent contractors. There is no question that the Guild was the exclusive bargaining agent for the zone and area managers. One of the assistant home delivery managers, a member of the union, asked if he could change his status and enter into a dealership contract with the company. It was his belief that personal initiative would bring him higher earnings if he were "on his own." After exploring the feasibility of such a contract, the company decided that the employee's proposal had merit and would result in a more effective circulation system; it would stimulate sales through the profit incentive. Accordingly, it entered into an independent dealership contract with this one employee. No publicity was given to the action, but as one employee manager said: "In the newspaper business you have a lot of scuttlebut going along the grapevine, and as soon as I heard one man had signed up, I made a beeline for the circulation director's office to see what kind of a deal I could work out for myself." Within three months the entire operation had been converted from an employee basis to an independent-contractor basis. There is no question that the employees preferred the change. In brief, the conversion, considered advantageous by these union members, had cost the union 58 members. The employee interests were incompatible with the institutional interests of the union. This is not an isolated instance. Inevitably the union must protest the action, not out of regard for the employees who have enthusiastically changed their status, but because of concern for its own loss of institutional strength.

TO ENLARGE WORK OPPORTUNITIES OF ITS MEMBERS. Some unions take the position that before any subcontracting is done, the regular employees should have an opportunity for overtime work. This is found especially among industrial unions with respect to the maintenance or skilled craftsmen. One union leader explained that, in part, it was hoped that an opportunity for overtime premium rates would reduce the skilled craftsmen's dissatisfaction with the compression of the wage structure over the years. In a few cases a union will view an overloaded shop, even though it is temporary, as a reason for expanding the work force, and it will resist subcontracting in favor of new hiring.

TO COMBAT ESCAPE FROM UNIONIZATION. In certain industries in the past this was the primary reason for union interference with subcontracting or work relocation. In the garment industry special restrictions were imposed to curb the subcontracting of work to non-union shops and to prevent runaway shops, those located in outlying areas difficult for unions to police. This motive was also important in the issues raised by the union in the very competitive automotive parts industry. The various measures taken by unions to implement their policies are discussed in detail below under "Nature of Union Influence and Control." The threat of runaway work has sometimes been met by requiring the parent, unionized plant to give its employees priority in work opportunities. Some unions have insisted that the outside work be handled only by union members. To illustrate, a refining company agreed with its union to the following:

> All contract jobs including cost plus contracts in areas for which the Union has bargaining jurisdiction as defined in Article I, shall be performed by members of a bona-fide labor organization when more than three employees are engaged in such work by any one contractor. The Company shall have 4 days to enforce compliance with this Article.

One company admitted freely that when the teamsters' union tried to organize its truck drivers it decided to discontinue its own trucking operations and to contract the work to an outside common carrier. Its equipment was sold or leased to the carrier. Although the outside contractor was organized by the teamsters, the company decided it was preferable not to have to deal directly with this union. After three years' experience with the arrangement, the company resumed its own trucking and recognized the Teamsters Union as the bargaining agent for its forty-odd drivers. The company found that the disadvantages in dealing with the union were far outweighed by the advantages and cost savings that it could realize from doing its own trucking.

TO PROTECT UNION STANDARDS AGAINST COMPETITION. This motive is closely related to the preceding one. Extensive union controls over subcontracting in the clothing industry were prompted by the union's desire that its hard-won standards should not be undermined. The Federal Trade Commission, in dismissing a complaint in which three garment unions and three employer associations were charged with restricting competition because of contract limitations on subcontracts, observed that the activities of the unions in securing these provisions were reasonably related to the advancement of labor well-being. They were designed to eliminate the possibility of substandard labor conditions in runaway shops and in outside shops, the latter being in reality agents of the manufacturer; and to make the manufacturers assume some responsibility for labor conditions in the subcontractor shops.

These last two bases for union interest in subcontracting are most likely to be found in industries composed of a large number of relatively small producing units with low capital requirements. Competition, mobility, and the mortality rate are usually high. In effect, through this and other controls, the union tries to establish an industry discipline that the industry itself is incapable of developing on its own. To accomplish this goal, a union must have considerable strength. The achievements of the International Ladies' Garment Workers Union and the Amalgamated Clothing Workers are far beyond those of the weaker unions in the textile and shoe industries, for example.[9]

[9] The teamsters' union and building trades unions are other notable illustrations of unions that have developed controls to prevent competition that would injure wage standards. The teamsters have succeeded in controlling the gypsy owner-operated trucks. By disciplining their members, the building trades have discouraged them from doing work on their own at less than union rates.

Nature of Union Influence and Control

The methods by which unions have sought to influence management's decision to subcontract or re-locate work are varied. They may be explicit—either specific restraints in the contract or limitations developed through arbitration—or they may result indirectly from contract provisions that were not intended primarily to restrict subcontracting decisions, such as guaranteed annual wage arrangements, supplementary unemployment benefits, and severance pay commitments. They may be implicit in the sense that managements tend to adopt a policy of greater restraint to prevent the union from making an issue over subcontracting. In this as in other areas discussed in this volume, it has been found that the mere existence of a union often affects management's behavior as much as do limitations imposed in the agreement.

Four general approaches to the problem are followed by the union, (1) cooperation, (2) indirect union controls, (3) control by contract provision, and (4) use of grievance procedure and arbitration. Some methods employed by unions are designed to encourage managements to do certain things, while others are designed to discourage certain action. In this section the first three of these general approaches will be discussed. The fourth will be discussed separately in the final section of this chapter.

Cooperation

In some situations the union does not try to limit or to restrict the company's freedom to farm out work. Instead it tries to make it more attractive for the company to have the work done by its own employees than by outsiders. As far back as the early 1920's, shortly after the return of the railroads to private operation, one of the principal issues between the shopcraft unions and the carriers was the "contracting out" of repair work to nonunion shops. The railroads argued that this was necessary to get equipment repaired in time and to save money. The unions contended that it was simply a device to evade union standards. On several important railroads a union-management cooperation program designed to increase output and reduce costs was developed gradually. This appealed to some union leaders as a means of discouraging the contracting out of work.[10]

A policy of cooperation is followed currently in a large pen company. The company and its two unions have adopted the Scanlon Plan (discussed in Chapter 28) with the result that the tool room's one hundred employees have increased output considerably. There is little need to purchase tools from the outside as was necessary in the past because of capacity limitations. More important, as a result of the tool room's becoming competitive with outside suppliers, management has installed new equipment and has returned to the tool room a large amount of subcontract work. The same results were achieved in the screw machine department of another plant where the Scanlon Plan was in effect. Confronted with the problem of inadequate capacity, the parties found that the Scanlon Plan helped them to do more of their own work and at the time of a cutback they were even able to bring in outside work.

In a large printing plant a joint union-management committee under the Scanlon Plan reviewed cost conditions in the hope that improved management would bring about the return of subcontracted work. The farming-out of work seemed indefensible to men who were working irregularly. It was discovered that in estimating costs for price quotations, the company was using studies of average cost per hour that included the cost of idle equipment; yet the equipment was idle because management was farming out press work to offset shops. It was a vicious circle, and the union urged management to buy modern, speedier presses to enable the company to be competitive. On one occasion the printing of a workbook for a history text was returned to the plant chiefly because a pressroom machinist invented a device to perforate the workbook pages while they were being run off the press.

Union-management cooperation designed to make the company more competitive and to reduce the likelihood of subcontracting need not be of a formalized character. In the negotiation of basic wages a company may state that increased labor cost will force it to rely on an outside supplier for certain parts or assemblies. The union's willingness to moderate its demands in response to this warning is a form of cooperation. In one instance the company threatened to engage in further subcontracting in view of the serious pegging of

---

[10] A detailed description of these formal union-management cooperation programs is presented in Chapter 28.

production in the plastic molding department, which was pushing its costs above those of suppliers. The union's reaction was to co-operate with management to raise worker effort and productivity.

Indirect Union Controls

Some unions have succeeded in limiting by a variety of indirect controls, the opportunity of companies to subcontract work or to exercise freely their purchase decision. The International Brother-hood of Electrical Workers policy, which prohibited members from installing other than approved, union-made materials, illustrates one such control. The drive for the closed shop by construction unions was directed in part toward this goal. In some communities unions have succeeded in securing licensing laws that have the effect of limiting the number of contractors eligible to perform certain work. Finally, in the building trades it is understood that a general con-tractor may not have even one nonunion subcontractor no matter how large the total job and how insignificant the role of that one subcontractor. These are indirect controls, yet they have a significant effect on management decision-making.

Sometimes the unions meet the subcontracting problem by organ-izing the suppliers whose low labor costs encourage subcontracting. For example, a business agent of a large local in a plant manufactur-ing electrical products conducted an intensive organization cam-paign of tool and die, machine, and plastic molding shops in the area. He said his main purpose was to eliminate two types of threats to his local and its members: subcontracting and product market compe-tition. Organizational campaigns are used more extensively as a de-vice to combat the movement of work. For example, the Upholster-ers' Union carries on periodic organizing drives among the smaller, nonunion companies. The union recognizes that its chances of being certified in many of these shops are negligible, but the campaigns have an important salutary effect for the unionized members of the industry. Threatened with organization, the small shops raise wages voluntarily, thus narrowing their labor cost advantage over the un-ionized shops.

Control by Contract Provision

Most commonly, union interest in this issue is found in the great variety of limitations and controls incorporated in labor agreements or in memoranda of understanding. The extent of the restrictions re-flects the underlying union motivation and the union's bargaining strength vis-à-vis the employer. These provisions may be classified gen-erally in four categories: (1) consultation and information, (2) regula-tion based on specific criteria, (3) veto power, and (4) prohibition.

CONSULTATION AND INFORMATION. In 1949 a large automobile com-pany decided to discontinue a centralized maintenance department that had serviced a number of plants in the area and to establish separate maintenance units in the various operating divisions or buildings. In addition, a separate construction section was to be cre-ated to function within a stated geographic area. In implementing this change, the company advised the union by letter of its criteria for subcontracting maintenance and construction work. The con-struction section was to do

> all construction work which it is feasible for the company to do, con-sistent with equipment and manpower skills available, with the limita-tion that outside contractors may be called upon when the volume of work required exceeds the capacity of the Construction Section.

In addition it was specified that subcontractors would be used where

> peculiar skills are involved, where specialized equipment not available at the company is required, or where for other reasons economies can be realized because specialized contractors can better perform the work in question.

Further, the company said it might also contract out work when the volume of construction work precluded the possibility of its comple-tion within the necessary time limits. Finally, the company promised to continue the practice of informing union representatives of its reasons for letting contracts, but it asserted that it retained the right to make the final determination as to whether work should be done by the company or by outside contractors. The company offered as-surance that, in exercising this right, it would keep the interests of its own personnel in mind.

It is noteworthy that the company committed itself voluntarily to certain criteria in this letter. However, it limited its obligation to giving information to the union. In the same year the union suc-ceeded in having incorporated in the national agreement a clause stating that it was the policy of the company to utilize fully its seniority employees on maintenance and construction work in accordance with its letter to the union. This clause has continued unchanged since 1949.

The union in this case has filed many protests on the company's subcontracting of work, but the policy letter has been interpreted by arbitrators to mean that the company is required only to give "careful consideration" to employees before subcontracting and to give pertinent information to the union. Union efforts to strengthen the clause in negotiations have been unsuccessful. In one of the plants an extensive renovation job was planned, including the installation of automatic equipment, reconstruction of buildings, construction of special ovens, and the like. The company contracted with an engineering firm for the design and execution of the job and so notified the union. The union protested vigorously, arguing that its craft employees, such as electricians, could do part of the job and that its members could handle the work on overtime and still do it cheaper than the outsider. The engineering firm refused to perform the job on this basis because it was guaranteeing a working operation. Over the years the union has become reconciled to the position that outside contractors may be used if none of its people are laid off. But occasionally under this clause there may be layoffs of craftsmen at the very time outside contractors and their crews are working.

In a large rubber company there had been no contractual language regarding subcontracting until 1952. Few grievances were generated, and the company awarded contracts for a wide range of projects with little limitation. In the spring of 1952 subcontracting became a critical issue because of a dispute over the construction of elevator shafting. The contract for walling in certain elevator shafts had been awarded to an outside contractor. The fracas that followed was referred to by the parties in such terms as "a hell of a mess" and "a riot over a subcontract." As a result both parties entered negotiations with a desire to formulate a policy statement that would facilitate an orderly handling of subcontracting work. The union initially sought a very restrictive clause that would foreclose performance by outside contractors of work normally done by employees of the engineering division. This proposal was rejected. In three succeeding proposals the union moderated the degree of limitation to be imposed upon management. Management's counter-proposals, which took the form largely of an agreement to advise the union when outside contractors had been engaged to do work within the plant, were rejected by the union. This became one of two critical issues (the other being control of wildcat strikes) in the strike that followed the breakdown of negotiations. During the strike the company submitted three proposals to the union, stating its willingness to put into the agreement any one that the union selected:

It is agreed that every effort shall be made when we have people on the inactive list to schedule mechanical or maintenance work with our own maintenance people before work is let out to outside contractors wherever possible and practical. If such work is to be let out, the committeeman of the department and the chairman of the division shall be so notified and the matter discussed in full. It is further agreed that any dispute which arises as the result of the operation of the above paragraph shall be subject to the full grievance procedure, including arbitration.

or

The company will explain in full to the union committee of the mechanical shops involved before the letting of outside contracts for work that could be done in the maintenance shops were it not for the fact that time, expense, or facilities prevent the maintenance shop from performing the work.

or

It is the policy of the company that work normally performed by employees of the Engineering Division generally will not be contracted to others when the employees normally assigned to that work are being offered less than a normal work week but a contract once let will be carried to completion. It is understood that the company will contract work to others when it believes that the work involves or requires unusual or specialized skills, patented processes, special equipment beyond normal shop capacity, or a guarantee of completion date, or when the application of business practices indicate that other reasons exist making it desirable to contract such work.

The union chose the second of these three alternatives, and it was incorporated into the agreement with very little prior discussion about its meaning. In effect, it was deliberately vague and ambiguous because both parties were reluctant to commit themselves to specific criteria; in addition, the adoption of a vague clause was dictated by the more compelling desire to end a strike. In the words of an Arbitration Board called upon subsequently to resolve a subcontracting issue under the new language, the "effect of their (the parties) doing so was to 'pass the buck' on the question to the Board of Arbitration."[11]

After 1952 a number of cases involving this clause went to arbitration. The ground rules specified in arbitration were equally vague. In one of the first cases, the Arbitration Board observed that in reconciling the conflict of principle between the responsibility of management for the efficient conduct of the enterprise on the one hand and the integrity of the bargaining unit on the other hand, it had to decide what was fair and reasonable in the circumstances of each case:

> Some of the questions that are likely to present themselves in such cases are the following: What is the nature of the work involved? How closely related is it to the production process? Are the skills needed to perform it present in the bargaining unit? Are there compelling technical or economic considerations that justify its being performed by outside contractors? What is the effect on bargaining unit employees in terms of loss of jobs? Is there a practice in existence for this or related work to be done on contract? These and other questions that may logically present themselves in the context of particular cases must be weighed in each instance to determine the specific question.

In the 1954 negotiations the company proposed that the clause be eliminated on the ground that it had actually increased rather than reduced misunderstandings about subcontracting; the union, in turn, wanted to strengthen the clause to require union approval before work could be subcontracted. The final settlement made no change in existing language.

In 1957 this same company was confronted in negotiations with a more insistent demand by the union that no work should be subcontracted without union approval.[12] In support of its position the union cited several cases that surprised and disturbed top management. In some of the cases outside contractors were brought in to

[11] In all fairness, however, it should be pointed out that on this subject it is almost impossible to write a definitive, unambiguous clause. Vague language is usually not a mere bargaining stratagem. This matter is discussed further below.

[12] This was part of a broader union campaign on the subject, undoubtedly reflecting the growing concern of industrial unions with craft union inroads on construction and maintenance work. In the May 1956 issue of the *United Rubber Workers Journal* it was stated: "the local unions are urged to negotiate adequate provisions in their agreements to protect the right of their members to carry on all the work which they are able to perform unless otherwise agreed by the local union."

do the work while employees of the company who could have done the work were on layoff. In one case the plant manager brought the outside contractor in to do the work even though his own people could have done it more cheaply. His reason was that his own maintenance budget was already used up, and the cost of work done by an outsider was charged instead to special projects. The company reiterated its intention not to subcontract any work that could be done in the plant within the limits of time, expense, and facilities. This intention was stated in a letter that probably has the status of a contract commitment. As part of the understanding, the company obligation to inform the union was clarified.

Three basic lessons may be learned from the foregoing, which is similar to the experiences of other parties. First, it is important to note that where a simple requirement of keeping the union informed of management's decisions is adopted, the unions usually try to get more specific limitations on management's freedom through either arbitration or subsequent negotiations. Putting something into the contract usually invites broadening the reach of the clause. Second, the adoption of ambiguous clauses is somewhat characteristic of this particular subject. Because they are either unable or unwilling to draft language to cope with probable subcontracting contingencies, the parties tend to adopt loose statements of principle and then let the arbitration procedure put flesh on the contract bones. Third, internal administrative practices of management may determine the extent of union concern with subcontracting decisions. In the case cited it is evident that abuse of its stated policy intentions by management provided the union with effective ammunition in insisting on more firm commitments than those afforded by the existing clause.

REGULATION BASED ON SPECIFIC CRITERIA. The regulations adopted in some agreements take many forms and have a varying impact upon management flexibility. In some instances the form of the regulation reflects the characteristics of the industry. In others, the control is designed to correct a particularly difficult situation facing the union.

One of the most stringent forms of control has developed in both the men's and women's garment industries. Subcontracting has always been used extensively in these industries. The union has not tried to prohibit this practice, but has succeeded in policing subcontracting practices in the interests of its members in the manufacturer's unit as well as those in the subcontracting unit. Protection of standards, equalization of work opportunities, and the avoidance of runaway shops are the principal motives. Two illustrations highlight the extent of the regulatory measures in effect.

The agreement of the National Dress Manufacturers' Association and the New York Joint Board of Dress and Waistmakers, International Ladies' Garment Workers Union provides that an association member must confine his production to his inside shop and to his previously designated contractors who are actually needed. In turn, contractors must work only for association members who have designated them and must not sell to anyone else. Before an employer member may designate additional contractors, he must get the approval of the joint Union-Association Administrative Board. Such approval will be given only if he can show that his designated contractors are fully employed and more are needed to handle an increased volume of business. Furthermore, an employer may change contractors only with Board approval, and only if specific reasons are shown, such as product change, poor workmanship, and late deliveries. When there is insufficient work, an association member must divide it among his inside shop and his subcontractors on the basis of the number of machine operators employed. Under no circumstances may an employer deal with a nonunion or undesignated contractor. Violation of any of these arrangements results in forfeiture of all rights under the agreement and the assessment of damages large enough to offset any advantages derived from improper dealings.

These encroachments by the union on what are usually considered prerogatives of management are a direct outgrowth of the dog-eat-dog competition characteristic of the industry. Too frequently employees in both the prime contractor and subcontractor shops were victimized by this ruthless competition. Although managements today say they are constrained by the collective bargaining agreement, which provides also for the registration of contractors, union inspection of books, etc., they accept the restrictions as justified.

A somewhat similar set of restrictions is to be found in the men's clothing industry. The Agreement between the New York Clothing

Manufacturers' Exchange, Inc. and the Amalgamated Clothing Workers of America provides that a manufacturer who uses contractors shall deal with only those who employ members of the union in good standing and who are registered. This agreement also contains a provision that no manufacturer may move his shop or factory from its present location to any place where the public carrier fare is more than the going New York subway fare or establish any new shop in addition to those he operates without the mutual consent of the parties.

In some companies unions have imposed less refined, but nevertheless effective, controls as a result of the complaint that the company was using runaway shop tactics or escaping union standards. A Detroit automotive parts company, organized by the UAW, opened a new plant in a rural area of Michigan in 1941. Some work was transferred to the unorganized plant, where an independent union was eventually formed. The parent plant union raised a vigorous protest that this was a runaway shop and voiced its charges effectively before the National Defense Mediation Board. In defense of its good faith, the company agreed to a contract provision which it later regretted for many years. It agreed that all employees of its Detroit plant who were covered by the contract on November 1, 1941 would have preferential seniority over the employees of its outside Michigan plant. If any jobs were discontinued, or if any loss of work caused a layoff in the Detroit plant in excess of two weeks and involved more than twenty-five employees, the company would transfer enough work from the outside plant to compensate for the loss. It was also agreed that if the movement of work to Detroit proved "impracticable through unforeseen conditions that may arise," the parties would negotiate a proper procedure. Between 1941 and 1950 this clause proved to be a source of constant conflict, and an arbitrator added to the company's difficulties by taking a dim view of its interpretation of what was "impracticable." The elimination of the clause was a critical issue in a protracted strike in 1950, and it was removed only in exchange for the granting of a liberal severance pay arrangement.

In many cases the union seeks assurance of normal employment for regular employees before subcontracting is permitted, although these contractual guarantees are sometimes qualified by other criteria, such as past practice and the availability of equipment and facilities.

A cork company's contract with the teamsters' union provides that employees on the seniority list will not be laid off on account of the use of outside equipment, not in accordance with past practice, if the employer has appropriate equipment to do the work. A foundry company has agreed with the steelworkers that outside contractors not covered by the contract will not be permitted to perform work now done by the production employees if the latter would be displaced thereby. A textile mill agreed with its union that no work done in the plant shall be given out unless the mill is filled to capacity on its normal shift operations. It was agreed also that when work is subcontracted, it must be to a mill having a contract with the union. However, this clause did not prevent the company from laying off people in a department that was eliminated by the transfer of work from the parent plant to a newly-acquired plant. The arbitrator held that the clause was limited to subcontracting and did not bar the company from transferring work among its own plants.

An automotive parts company has agreed not to remove any machinery, tools, or work from the plant, including manufactured parts such as tools, machine repair, or tool designing, or contract with outside vendors to perform any work in the plant if such removal or contracting would cause a reduction of hours below the "normal work week for any of its employees." This clause, like so many others, originated some years ago during War Labor Board days and has continued unchanged since then. Although somewhat ambiguous, the provision has not been the source of much trouble. In the company's opinion it was intended originally to cover outside contracting of heavy construction work, major electrical installations, and similar work for which the company lacked the necessary equipment or could not perform economically itself. It has been used primarily for this purpose. A furniture company's agreement with the Upholsterers' International Union provides that the employer will send out no contract work unless all its workers are fully employed. It was understood, however, that this limitation did not apply to those articles of furniture that the company had traditionally had made for it by outside contractors. The union filed a grievance under this agreement claiming that the subcontracting of certain tables, admittedly not of a type theretofore sent outside, was improper because the employees had been on a 44-hour week for a long time and were reduced to 40 hours while the work was being subcontracted. An arbitrator denied the grievance, saying that the phrase "fully employed" contemplated a normal workweek of 40 hours.

A similar situation developed in the case of an electrical utility company under its agreement with the International Brotherhood of Electrical Workers. The agreement provided as follows:

> It shall be the company policy that all its usual and customary work shall be done by its regular forces, and so to manage, control, and allocate its work, seasonal and climatic conditions permitting, as to reduce to a minimum layoffs and reductions of its forces. To that end the company will endeavor in good faith not to contract out work usually and customarily done by its regular employees at a time when such work can be performed by them. However, nothing herein contained shall restrict the company's right to contract out work at its discretion, so long as that right is not exercised to effect discrimination against employees.

This clause follows the pattern of ambiguity which, as already noted, is typical of subcontracting provisions. For a long period the employees of this company were working as much as 48 and 56 hours a week, and at the same time some of the work was being performed by outside contractors. A grievance was filed when the work schedule for regulars was changed from 48 to 40. The union argued that the work could be done by its members at no greater cost even though overtime rates would be paid, and if the company wanted to avoid overtime, it should add to the crew size. The company countered that it had developed an "ideal model" of a permanent working force. If it were to add employees, they probably would be laid off later; the cost of training new employees with no assurable future with the company would be a poor investment. The issue went to arbitration, and the grievance was denied on the ground that the clause was intended to prevent layoffs not to assure take home pay.

A metal processing company under its agreement with the Oil Workers' International Union agreed to two provisions affecting its right to subcontract work. First, it promised to make every reasonable effort to use its available working force and equipment to avoid having work performed by outside contractors. Second, it agreed not to contract work that would require employees to be laid off or to be reduced in rate of pay, or would prevent the re-employment of those who had been laid off not longer than one year.[13] In the course of one year the company entered into two outside contracts, one for the demolition of a stack and the construction of a new one, the other for the erection of a new plant to process waste acid material. The union argued that laborers on the layoff-recall list who were rapidly reaching the one year limitation should be used on these projects. The company said this request was unrealistic because it could not get an outside contractor to take these jobs if he had to use other than his own laborers. Furthermore, it was argued that during negotiations the union had said its concern was with the contracting out of regular work, not of special construction work of this type. The company's position was sustained on the ground that parties to an agreement on tin-smelting work would not be thinking of construction jobs when they wrote the agreement.[14]

---

[13] This part of the subcontract regulation is based on the loss of seniority after one year's layoff. See Chapter 5.

[14] A very interesting clause negotiated between a milk drivers' local and one of the many milk companies with which it negotiates illustrates several points mentioned earlier in this chapter: (1) willingness of unions to accept the status quo, (2) concern for institutional protection, and (3) union resentment of conversion of employees to independent contractors. The clause is of sufficient interest to quote in its entirety:

To the extent that duties which are necessary to the processing and packaging of products handled by the company are being performed on the effective date of this contract by those employed within covered categories, the continued performance of such duties shall be maintained to that extent by such members of Local 380, but not necessarily in the manner being performed on the effective date of this contract.

The company, through negotiations with the union, may effect a cessation of the processing or packaging of a product which is to be continued in distribution by the company provided that no lack-of-work layoff, demotion, or declassification occurs. A resulting excess of personnel may be dissipated through attrition. Approval by the union shall not be unreasonably withheld, but failure to receive the concurrence of the union will permit the company to submit the following question to arbitration:

With full consideration of all the circumstances, shall the company be empowered to eliminate either processing or packaging of the product which is to be continued in distribution by the company?

The status quo shall be observed until the decision by arbitration.

The company may, without negotiations, effect a cessation of the processing or packaging of a product by arranging with other contractual employers of Local 380 the processing and packaging of the product which is to be continued in distribution by the company.

Such duties which are necessary to distribution to the point of sales shall be fulfilled by those employed within covered categories; and provided further, that the company may neither sell, lease, give or otherwise dispose of a route or plant operation directly or indirectly to an employee, a combination of employees, or an entity controlled by its employees without the written approval of the union nor shall the company convey a route or plant operation to any other entity except one which is or shall become a contractual employer of Local 380. If the company fails to find a purchaser from among the contractual employers of Local 380 or from among those agreeing to be subject to this contract, then the company may abandon the territory. In this event

In most of the provisions cited above the union's control over subcontracting was intended to safeguard the normal employment opportunities of the entire workforce represented by it. In some instances, the union's bargaining demands have been limited to the protection of certain types of work from the intrusion of subcontracting. An industrial union's agreement with a large rubber company provides that the right to subcontract in the engineering departments will exist only if the craftsmen are working 48 hours per week. This has caused considerable difficulty for the company because of the admixture of craft skills required on the work performed. It might be that plumbers and masons would be working 48 hours per week but not carpenters, yet a given subcontract could involve all three crafts. The following provision which appears in an agreement between a grain product company and its union illustrates the regulatory policy of selective control:

No job shall be let to Outside Contractors, other than major construction and major repair; and fabrication installation and use of patented or highly specialized equipment and the following specific exceptions:

1. Brick Layers
2. Boiler Makers
3. Roofers
4. Elevator Service Men
5. Exterminators
6. Cement Sprayers
7. Sewer Cleaners
8. Scale Men
9. Telephone Men
10. Office Equipment Repair Men
11. Refrigerator Repair Men

Mechanical workers shall be scheduled on a forty-eight (48) hour or more week as long as an Outside Contractor is in the Plant doing work of a mechanical nature except for permissible contract work set forth above.

The Workmen's Committee will be notified ten (10) days in advance of

---

abandonment of territory will enable the company to dispose of its accounts within the territory burdened by no restrictions.

The company's right to reduce its work force through mechanization or automation or through the application of any other item within this agreement shall be maintained. The company's right to go out of business; to abandon territory; and to abandon the processing or packaging of a product withdrawn from distribution shall not be impaired by the effect of this item.

all jobs to be let to Outside Contractors of a mechanical nature. The company and the union will then meet to discuss the nature of the work involved in the contracts. If the union believes the job of which it has been notified is one that does not fall within the above definition, it will so notify the company in writing within five (5) working days. However, the company may proceed to let the contract. The union may thereafter and within ten (10) days refer the matter to arbitration, and if it is determined by arbitration that the contract was erroneously let under the provision of this section, Employees in the mechanical department will receive the opportunity to work forty-eight (48) hours per week for the same period of time as the contractor involved was in the plant, or if no work is available will receive forty-eight (48) hours' pay per week for said period. Any mechanical Employee claiming compensation under this section must have been available for work at the time in question.

No Employee of any craft, which craft is being utilized by an Outside Contractor, shall be laid off as long as the Outside Contractor is in the plant doing work that Employees in such craft are able to do.

This summary of a number of regulatory arrangements is intended only to illustrate the extent to which unions have successfully made an issue of subcontracting or work movement in negotiations. It should not be thought that these clauses are contrary to the basic policy of management. On the contrary, the criteria in the first instance are often nothing more than a formalization of management policy in the absence of any contractual restriction. But for several reasons incorporating existing policy in the agreement has an important impact on management behavior. First, management's flexibility in handling borderline cases is reduced. Second, each decision is subject to review through the grievance machinery, and internal discipline in administering policy must be maintained or a decision may be reversed at considerable cost. Third, recognition in bargaining of the union's valid interest in subcontracting policy establishes a basis for the gradual refinement and tightening of controls in future bargains.

VETO POWER. In a few known instances the union has succeeded in requiring advance approval before subcontracting may be undertaken. Provisions of this type are to be found in some teamster agreements. However, the union's contractual right to exercise an *ad hoc* veto, or, by consequence of such right, to join actively in the make-or-buy and subcontract decision-making process, is very infrequent.

PROHIBITION. In very few cases have unions succeeded in securing by negotiation an absolute ban on a company's right to subcontract work. They have been most successful in prohibiting some forms of contracting through arbitration rulings and in the absence of *any* explicit provisions on the subject. This method is discussed below. An agreement on complete prohibition is to be found, not unexpectedly, in a branch of the clothing industry. As early as 1928 the Agreement between the Furriers Joint Council of New York and the Employers' Association provided that "no inside or outside contracting in any shape, manner or form shall be permitted." It is interesting that this unqualified foreclosure has been strengthened over the years by the adoption of more severe enforcement provisions.

Originally the first offense had involved a maximum fine of $150, the second offense meant three months' suspension from the Association. In 1941 the Conference Committee clarified the disciplinary measures by ruling that an employer found guilty of substantial violation of the contracting provision shall pay the labor cost of the work done on the garment. This mandate against any and all contracting is policed efficiently by the union. In 1950 a New York company was accused of having muskrat coats, jackets, and capes made outside by contractors. The Impartial Chairman found the accusation to be valid. A penalty of $150 plus $9,850 was imposed. The firm refused to comply. On a motion to confirm the award the company argued among other points that the contract clause was in violation of the Sherman and Clayton Antitrust Acts and the Taft-Hartley Act, and that the payment of awards to the Conference Committee was illegal. The New York Supreme Court denied the company's claims, noting parenthetically that the payments were applied by the Committee to whatever welfare, charitable, philanthropic, and humanitarian purposes the employer and union representatives of the Committee jointly agreed upon.

However, it is safe to say that no national union could support an absolute ban on management's subcontracting rights. Union policymakers at the national level must reconcile their possibly conflicting objectives of maintaining standards or of organizing the unorganized. Nearly all unions have discovered that an inexorable insistence upon standards may inhibit their ability to organize workers.

Role of Arbitration in Defining Scope
of Management's Rights

As stated earlier in this chapter, the role of arbitration in the evolution of subcontracting controls during the past twenty years has been
so unusual and so influential as to require separate discussion. Many
arbitrators have, in effect, legislated the question of whether or not
management's complete freedom to decide this policy issue is circumscribed by the terms of the agreement. In so legislating, the outside neutrals have developed an often conflicting array of guideposts.

For at least two reasons, the influence of arbitrators in this field
is understandable. First, when the parties to the agreement try to
negotiate a clause governing management's subcontracting rights,
they often resort to the deliberate use of ambiguous language, or the
nature of the subject makes ambiguity unavoidable. Second, in many
instances one or the other of the parties will demand a provision covering the subject. Management may seek to incorporate in the standard
management rights clause a phrase affirming (the word "clarifying" is
the strategic term) its freedom to subcontract; or the union may request a regulatory or restrictive provision. Yet nothing is incorporated
in the final agreement because neither party is prepared to treat this as
a strike issue. The phenomena of deliberate ambiguity and deliberate
avoidance of the issue may be explained by the sensitivity of the subject. To the union, jobs are at stake; to the company, prerogatives are
at stake. A union, on the one hand, often fears that a regulatory
clause short of outright prohibition will highlight areas in which
management is free to subcontract and will arouse unnecessary concern on the part of its members. A company, in turn, may retreat from
its position lest it provoke the union to counter with demand for a restrictive clause. In effect each party often would prefer to take its
chances on arbitration when a problem arises. Thus, if a gap exists in
the agreement, it is often because there has been no meeting of minds
at the close of negotiations. The union feels that even without a regulatory clause management's rights to subcontract are restricted, while
management considers that with the contract as written it retains the
full right to subcontract. In Chapter 8, "Work Scheduling," it was
noted that the question of the voluntary or compulsory nature of overtime work was similarly ignored in the contract.

Under these circumstances, what may appear to be an unwarranted arrogation of authority by an arbitrator has sometimes been the result of the strategy of the parties in negotiation or the ambiguity of language on this subject. Nevertheless, legislating the void in the agreement has been carried to an extreme by a few arbitrators. Three aspects of the role of arbitration deserve comment: (1) the arbitrability of the issue in the absence of an explicit clause on the subject; (2) the reliance on the recognition clause and other provisions; and (3) the appraisal of relevant criteria.

Arbitrability

Even though the contract is silent on the subject of subcontracting or work movement, many arbitrators have held that the propriety of a company action is an arbitrable issue. The prevailing doctrine is that the union is entitled to be heard on the merits of an issue if it can establish a *prima facie* case that the interpretation of some contract provision is involved. In the subcontracting issue the union can usually point to the recognition clause or seniority provisions to support its right to be heard.

Reliance on the Recognition Clause and Other Provisions

As stated above, some unions have succeeded in securing controls through arbitration that they probably would never have gained by direct negotiation of the issue of subcontracting. This is because a few arbitrators feel that the recognition clause must be interpreted to cover *work* as well as the *employees* and that once the company recognizes the union as representing designated employees for the duration of the contract, management must have agreed to a status quo of work for the employees in the bargaining unit. A contrary view, they claim, would permit gradual erosion of the bargaining unit. In addition to relying on the recognition clause, these arbitrators also refer to the layoff provisions and to the "total spirit" of the instrument.

Two almost identical cases illustrate the sharp difference of opinion among arbitrators. Both cases involved companies that had operated their own plant cafeterias for a number of years. In recent years, however, each company had told its union in contract negotiations that operation of the cafeteria was uneconomical and that it was unreasonable to expect the company to pay factory wages to cafeteria workers.

Both companies finally decided to turn operation of the cafeteria over to an independent contractor. The applicable agreements contained no reference whatsoever to subcontracting.

In one company the independent contractor offered employment to those who had been furloughed, but at rates lower than those they had been receiving. The union advised against acceptance of employment or separation pay, sponsored a boycott of the cafeteria, and filed a grievance protesting the company action. The arbitrator upheld the union and awarded back pay to those who had not accepted severance. He relied entirely on the recognition clause and the totality of the agreement, saying:

> The failure to incorporate into the Agreement an express prohibition against a contract such as we find in this case is not sufficient to authorize such a contract. "The law has outgrown its primitive stage of formalism when the precise word was the sovereign talisman, and every slip was fatal. It takes a broader view today. A promise may be lacking, and yet the whole writing may be 'instinct with an obligation,' imperfectly expressed." These well chosen words of Cardozo, J. in Wood v. Duff-Gordon, 22 N.Y. 88,91 are just as apposite today as they were when written in 1917.

He found that the cafeteria operation was an essential and integral part of the plant operation because of the remoteness of the plant from other food sources. This finding is interesting in the light of the effectiveness of the boycott. Even more interesting is that the company introduced evidence that it had once shut down its print shop and subcontracted the work, but the arbitrator discounted this precedent, saying the print jobs had been removed entirely from the plant, whereas the cafeteria jobs remained in the plant.

In the second company only four employees were affected by the transfer of cafeteria operations to an outside catering service, but they suffered a wage reduction in going to other jobs in the plant. Here too the union filed a grievance, which was carried to arbitration. The union relied entirely on the recognition and seniority clauses, while the company defended its action as a proper exercise of a management right. The arbitrator dismissed the union grievance saying in part:

> In the opinion of the undersigned the right of a company to subcontract work for sound, justifiable business reasons is such an inherent and integral part of the conduct of a business enterprise that it requires more than a Recognition Clause to erase or even subtract from that

right. A Recognition Clause of the type relied upon by the union in the instant proceeding merely says that the company recognizes the union as the bargaining agent for its employees *if it decides to have employees* on the jobs included in the bargaining unit. The Clause does not give jurisdiction over the work *per se*. Starting from one extreme, it would be impossible for the union to argue that the company had to have a cafeteria manned by union employees; Paragraph 11 of the Agreement obviously anticipates the possibility and thereby confirms the right that the company may eliminate an entire department. Thus, the company could have announced that it was discontinuing the cafeteria and the union would have no claim other than seeing to it that the seniority rights of employees affected by this decision were protected. Moving to the other extreme, the company could not offer any sound defense if it decided to operate the cafeteria with its own employees, but arbitrarily or unjustifiedly gave the work to some of its employees outside the acknowledged bargaining unit; this would be a blatant violation of the Recognition Clause.

These two cases point up sharply the disparate views held by arbitrators. The majority of arbitrators have not read control and restriction into the recognition clause. But those who have subscribed to this theory have caused a serious impairment of a right that management believed it had unless it was specifically contracted away. A large aluminum company reports that very early in its relationship with the union an arbitrator decided that the recognition clause covered work as well as employees. As a result its right to subcontract now is severely circumscribed. In the company's judgment a new clause, possibly at the cost of a strike, is needed to regain this right. A metal trades company in its agreement with the UAW made no provision to restrict subcontracting. On one occasion the employer hired an independent contractor to do the regular weekend work (washing the exterior surfaces of machines) of a type performed by employees within the unit. None of the regular employees was laid off and none worked less than a normal 40 hour week. The company wanted to have the machines cleaned regularly when they were not in operation, and it believed the members of its own crew would not want to work overtime every weekend; it also concluded that the work could be done more reasonably by an outsider. Interestingly, the subcontractor hired people who worked during the week in other departments of the same company. Relying entirely on the recognition and overtime clauses, the arbitrator upheld the union claim that this subcontracting was a violation of the agreement. He said that to permit the right if economy was the primary motive could ultimately nullify the contract. A distinction was made between "on-premise" and "off-premise" subcontracting.

In summary, American management seems to be confronted with a formidable dilemma in retaining its traditional right to decide what its make-or-buy or its subcontracting policy will be. On the one hand, reliance on a management rights clause or the doctrine of management's reserved rights is tenuous, given the disposition of some arbitrators to subordinate these considerations to other, less explicit clauses in the agreement. On the other hand, the bargaining of a contract clause on this subject either impairs management's freedom to subcontract or, in the case of a mild clause, paves the way for more limiting demands by the union.

The Appraisal of Relevant Criteria

Arbitrators who find in the recognition clause and other provisions a restraint on management's right to subcontract do not automatically prohibit subcontracting. They develop accompanying criteria to determine whether the decision in a particular situation is justified. The greatest usefulness of these criteria is that they can be relied upon to support almost any position. The inconsistency among arbitrators, already illustrated in the discussion of the recognition clause doctrine, is present to an equal degree in the guideposts they employ to judge the merits of a given case. Among the most commonly-used criteria are the following: (1) good faith, (2) proof of sound business justification, (3) performance of subcontracted work on the premises, (4) *bona fides* of independent contractor, (5) extent of harm to members of the bargaining unit.

GOOD FAITH. Most arbitrators are in agreement on this criterion. If it can be shown by the union that the employer action was not in good faith but was a deliberate attempt to undermine or impair the bargaining unit or to circumvent contract commitments, the grievance is likely to be sustained. But to prove bad faith is difficult, and in most situations the employer is able to point to some honorable motive.

PROOF OF SOUND BUSINESS JUSTIFICATION. The freedom to contract is usually acknowledged if the employer can demonstrate that costly equipment would have to be purchased if he were to undertake the work himself or that his own employees lack the skill necessary to do the work. Because most unions are realistic enough to recognize these as justifiable reasons for contracting out work, few grievances and arbitrations arise where these circumstances exist. The criterion of "sound business justification" in its broader sense, however, is a cause of considerable conflict and has led to inconsistent arbitration rulings. Is it proper for a company to subcontract work to effect economies? A newspaper company under an agreement with the Newspaper Guild proposed to drop nine janitors and have their work done by an outside cleaning and maintenance company. It argued that by so doing the company would save over $10,000, which might make the difference between profit and loss. The arbitrator found the savings figures to be exaggerated and dismissed economy in any event as a proper justification for subcontracting. He adhered to the somewhat inflexible rule that stability of the bargaining unit was the controlling factor. In a drug manufacturing company the layoff of two people from the Service Department was contemplated as the result of the company's having engaged an independent contractor to do the office cleaning. Economy and efficiency were given as reasons for the action. The arbitrator sustained the union grievance, observing that it was reasonable to assume that during the term of the agreement, work in the categories required by the company would be performed by those of its employees who were covered by the agreement. Relying solely on the recognition and seniority clauses, he said:

> Any other holding would render the substance of the collective agreement a nullity and without force and effect . . . the deliberate subcontracting of work intended to deprive the employees of the company who are now covered by the collective bargaining agreement between the company and the union, of work in the categories fixed by this agreement, would be in violation of the spirit, intent, and purpose of such collective agreement since inherent in the agreement there is an obligation on the part of the company to avoid depriving the employees covered by this agreement of the work in the categories covered by the collective agreement between the company and the union. . . .

> Economy alone can never be a sufficient reason to warrant laying off employees with years of seniority and replacing them with new people doing the same work under substantially similar conditions under the guise of an outside contracting arrangement.

In other cases, however, arbitrators have held that economies dictated by the efficient conduct of business did justify the decision of a company to subcontract part of its work in the absence of a contract clause to the contrary.

PERFORMANCE OF SUBCONTRACT WORK ON THE PREMISES. This criterion has been emphasized by some arbitrators. In one case involving the use by an oil company of an outside crew to lay and connect a water line, it was held that even though the contract was silent on the subject of subcontracting, the company erred in giving this work to an outsider. A principal reason was that this work was done on the premises and was of the same type as that normally performed by the regular crew. On-the-premise work does not, however, militate against the right to subcontract in the opinion of most arbitrators. On the contrary, this criterion usually yields to other considerations, particularly in the case of maintenance and construction work, which perforce must be done on the premises but for which the employer lacks properly-qualified employees or needed equipment.

BONA FIDES OF INDEPENDENT CONTRACTORS. In cases involving a change of status of existing employees to that of independent contractors, arbitrators have often inquired into and considered as determinative the actual independence of the workers affected by the change. Where it has been concluded that the change to "independents" has been in name only and where the company has retained control over the work method or procedures and can terminate the relationship at will, arbitrators have sometimes held that this was a subterfuge to avoid bargaining with the union.

EXTENT OF HARM TO MEMBERS OF THE BARGAINING UNIT. This is the most common criterion adopted by arbitrators in the absence of a contract provision on the subject. If present employees are laid off *because* of the decision of a concern to give some work to outsiders, or if present employees are on layoff while outsiders are performing work in the plant, an arbitrator may find management's decision to be in violation of the spirit of the agreement. This view seldom extends to situations where the exercise of management's rights deprives employees of theoretical *supra*-contract advantages, such as overtime opportunity, promotions, and the like. Furthermore, past practice is an important influence in the application of this criterion. An orthodox make-or-buy decision implemented at the time of a work recession and attendant layoff is seldom set aside by an arbitrator if it conforms with the recognized practice of the enterprise.

These criteria are not always serviceable as guides to management because their adoption by arbitrators is inconsistent and, in many instances, seems to border on caprice. Many managements have learned that the best way to exercise the right to subcontract and to reach efficient make-or-buy decisions under conditions of collective bargaining is by deliberate attention to the interests of employees together with the other needs of the enterprise. Where these interests are in conflict and where the institutional interests of a union challenge the goals of efficiency established by a firm, the best recourse of the enterprise is to face up to the issue. Resolution of the problem by arbitration is not likely to produce results consistent with the interests of either unions or managements.

One of the most thoughtful discussions of the problem has been presented by Professor Archibald Cox.[15] He points out that

> ideally the parties should write the answer into the contract, for the choice is theirs, but often the difference of opinion is too deep and too enduring for either party to express in writing even its temporary acceptance of the position of the other. . . . Sometimes the sphere (of joint government) is expressly delineated with all the rest reserved as management prerogatives but as often as not the impossibility of making an explicit compromise, coupled with the impossibility of not reaching an agreement, results in a more or less ambiguous silence. The task of finding where the boundaries would have been drawn if the parties who signed the contract had drawn them explicitly is then a problem of interpretation within the jurisdiction of the arbitrator. . . .

Professor Cox goes on to say that seldom is the interpreter left wholly without guidance. The presence of even a vague management rights clause suggests to him that the boundaries are narrower than under a contract without it. Where the arbitrator's authority is limited to interpretation and application of the contract, narrower boundaries are implied. Under these circumstances it is doubtful if subcontracting should be placed in the realm of joint government on the tenuous basis of a recognition or seniority clause unless the facts show management's decision was not made in good faith.

In summary, subcontracting remains an area of conflict in labor relations. Where adjustment has been achieved by the adoption of

[15] Archibald Cox, "The Legal Nature of Collective Bargaining Agreements," *Michigan Law Review* (November 1958), pp. 1-35.

workable contract language, it has usually had the effect of limiting management's flexibility to a considerable extent. Seldom has explicit language been adopted affirming management's right to subcontract without challenge from the union. The trend has been in the opposite direction. Where parties have been unable to agree and have chosen to maintain an "ambiguous silence," the arbitration process has played an unusual semi-legislative, semi-interpretive role in determining management's rights. Even where some seemingly innocuous language on the subject has been adopted, the arbitration process has played an important part in defining rights. Some feel that managements must retain the unrestricted right to subcontract and to move work not only in the interest of efficiency but also as a way of restraining union power. Others recognize a legitimate interest of unions in this area because of the impact of such management decisions on employees. Whichever view prevails, it is likely that this subject will gradually move to the adjustment stage in labor relations as have many other subjects discussed in this study.

11 / *Make-Work Rules and Policies*

THIS CHAPTER DEALS with cases of unions deliberately limiting the output of certain groups of employees for the purpose of increasing the number of jobs. There are many cases in which unions dispute with employers over the rate of work, but we are not concerned here with honest disagreement over the proper speed or method of work. We are concerned rather with the relatively few cases in which the union tries to force the employer to hire unnecessary labor. In practice there may be a few borderline cases, but usually, where the union is out to create unneeded jobs, the purpose is clear.

Six principal questions relate to the make-work rules and practices of trade unions:

1. What are the principal kinds of make-work rules and practices?
2. How extensive is the practice of forcing employers to hire unnecessary workers? Is it increasing?
3. For what reasons and under what conditions do unions force make-work rules and practices on employers?
4. What are the principal effects of make-work rules and practices—do they really make more jobs?
5. Why do not unions engage more extensively in make-work rules and practices?
6. What success have employers had in persuading unions to abandon make-work rules and practices?

Principal Kinds of Make-Work Rules and Practices

Make-work rules do not usually begin as attempts by unions to force employers to hire an excessive number of workers. There may have been agreement between union and management as to the desirable size of crews, or management may have made the decision unilaterally. Then if technological changes reduce the number of workers needed, it is natural for the union to resist the employer's effort to dispense with the unneeded employees. The result is a make-work policy. For example, the railroads operated steam locomotives with an engineer and a fireman. When diesel locomotives eliminated the need for firemen, the firemen, of course, fought to keep their jobs. Technological change and the struggle of the men to keep their jobs bring into existence a make-work policy.

The forms taken by make-work rules depend in large part on the technology of the industry and the methods of production. Although there are an almost indefinite number, the following eleven varieties include most of the make-work practices:

Limits on the Amount of Load That May Be Handled

The milk drivers' union in Chicago and other places limits the number of units that drivers may handle. Such limits may start out as perfectly reasonable means of protecting against overwork, but as shortcuts and improvements in equipment are developed, they become ways of keeping a growing number of unnecessary jobs in existence. The longshoremen's regulation of sling loads began as a safety measure, but in some ports (Boston, for example) it has become a make-work rule. In Hawaii the employers' association, although resisting considerable pressure from the union over a number of years, agreed to pay longshoremen West Coast rates. However, it has firmly refused to accept limits on sling loads as the West Coast employers have.

Restrictions on Duties of Workers in Given Occupations

Some locals of the teamsters' union discourage or prohibit drivers from assisting helpers in unloading their trucks—a policy pursued by teamsters' Local 107 in Philadelphia. The driver is idle part of the time, and the number of helpers needed is increased. As is pointed out in Chapters 9 and 19, job descriptions under job evaluation plans are sometimes given a make-work interpretation. The unions may contend that the descriptions do not just identify the several jobs. They also limit what the workers may be required to do and specify duties that may not be added even though they do not change the skill or responsibility required by the job. For example, changes in the process of cutting tools may give a machine-tender time for additional duties between loading and unloading a machine. The right of the employer to give him additional simple duties may be challenged. Usually such a challenge would not be upheld, but some employers have acquiesced in the view that job descriptions limit the work that may be required of employees.

The railroad brotherhoods have gone to unbelievable extremes in restricting duties, taking the position that every item of work *belongs* to some employee. If that employee is deprived of the opportunity to do the work, he is entitled to compensation first. In addition, the one who does the work is entitled to compensation. In many instances the amount of compensation given to both is a day's pay. The result is that two days' pay may be given as compensation for a trivial amount of work.[1]

The most efficient use of manpower on the docks in the San Francisco Bay area has been limited in the past by the unwillingness of the men to shift between ships and the docks. Traditionally the men have tried to enforce equal division of work by refusing to shift from ship to dock work or from one ship to another, even for the same employer. In the summer of 1959 the employers agreed to guarantee eight hours' work or pay for men called to work, the previous guarantee having been four hours. In return for the eight-hour guarantee, the union agreed that employers were to be free to shift men between ships and docks.[2]

[1] For example, an agreement separating yard and road duties was interpreted to mean that the yard employee was entitled to an extra day's pay for a few minutes' work on the road—and a road employee was entitled to a minimum day for not doing the work. (*Railway Age*, March 24, 1958, p. 23.) A road engineer recently got an extra day's pay at yard rates for moving his engine the length of 40 cars in a freight yard. (The same, p. 30.) A railroad in the era of steam had negotiated an "arbitrary" providing that the fireman should get two hours' pay for "firing his locomotive." A fireman demanded two hours' extra pay for pushing a button to start his diesel and he was awarded the pay. A conductor on a western railroad picked up a U. S. stamped envelope from a box at an industrial spur. He carried it several miles down the line. Several conductors did this. Each conductor claimed—and got—an extra day's pay at baggagemen's rates for every day he carried a letter five miles. (The same, p. 31.) Rules requiring that starting time limited to certain hours have compelled railroads to use two crews instead of one under certain circumstances.

[2] The union admits that there may be some difficulty in carrying out this agreement. In this industry of traditions and family firms the union and the employers have many in their ranks who are happiest doing things "the old way." But it is believed that the more progressive firms will benefit from the removal of restrictive working rules.

Requirement That the Work Be Done Twice

This is found occasionally in the building trades, where it arises from a conflict of jurisdictional claims. Local 3 of the International Brotherhood of Electrical Workers in New York has insisted on rewiring apparatus that has come wired from the manufacturer, even though the employees of the manufacturer are members of the same international union. By far the best-known instance of such a requirement is the famous "bogus" rule of the International Typographical Union. This rule provides that when plates or papier-mâché matrices are exchanged, as is frequently done when the same advertisement is run in two or more papers, the copy be reset, read, and corrected within a stipulated period. The time limit within which borrowed or purchased matter must be reset varies with local agreements. Not originally a make-work rule, it dates back to a time when compositors were paid by the piece. Since the most lucrative piece-work jobs as a rule were the advertisements, the use of plates and matrices threatened to reduce the pay of the compositors, who introduced the rule to protect their earnings. The copy to be reset is known as "bogus."

The rule was kept in spite of the gradual disappearance of piece-work. Its net cost to newspapers is limited by the need to have enough men in the composing room to meet the peak demand, which usually comes shortly before the paper goes to press. Hence, the resetting may be done in time when the men would otherwise be waiting for work.[3]

---

[3] It is customary to include a reproduction time limit in the bogus rules. A survey by the American Newspaper Publishers' Association shows that among 321 contracts in February 1958 the time limits were as follows:

Less than one week	40
One week	49
More than one week but less than two weeks	30
Two weeks but less than 30 days	47
30 days	123
45 days or longer	25
No time limit specified	7

In the large cities the time limit is shorter than in towns and small cities, where it is usually 30 days. In New York it is 7 days; Chicago, 7 days; Cleveland, 5 days: Boston, 3 days; Philadelphia, 8 days; Los Angeles, one week.

The meaning of the time limit varies widely. In a very few cases bogus not reset within the time limit is automatically cancelled. In other cases extra help must be hired after the time limit has expired. Many of the newspapers in the larger cities put on extras or substitutes when reproduction has exceeded the time specified in the contract.

There has been a tendency for the reproduction time to be increased, thus reducing

Although the bogus rule is primarily a make-work one, it is also used for bargaining purposes by the union. In some cities where there is a bogus rule bogus is not being reset. In a large proportion of the cases the employer has paid for the exemption by wage increases or a guarantee of a given number of jobs. The union in busy times may threaten the publisher that he will have to reset all of the back bogus if he does not grant certain concessions. An arbitration award in New York City held that several advertisements of grocery chains, chain stores, and factory branch stores were "national" ads and, therefore, exempt from the resetting requirement. In negotiations in 1959 the union sought unsuccessfully to get the employers to agree to a reversal of this ruling.

Requirement That Unnecessary Work Be Done

Scattered instances of this sort of thing are found in the building trades. Haber and Levinson mention that until recently the plasterers' union of Chicago required three coats of plaster to be used in homes even though the building code required only two.[4] The most important example of enforcement of unnecessary work is the requirement of excessive venting in plumbing. This is the result not of a union rule but of the building code, and the contractors must share with the unions the blame for getting the excessive requirements in the code.[5]

Limits on the Number of Machines a Worker May Operate or Tend

The best-known cases of this sort of restriction have been in the cotton and wool textile and the hosiery industries. The make-work rules in the textile industry are good examples of ones that were originally not make-work but became such through technological change. Piece rates were originally set on the assumption that workers could tend a given number of machines. As improvements were made in the equipment, in the quality of raw material, and in main-

---

the burden of the rule on the employer. In 1940, 30 days or more were allowed in 37.9 per cent of the contracts; in 1958, 30 days or more were allowed in 46.1 per cent of the contracts. Contracts allowing less than one week dropped from 18.3 per cent in 1940 to 12.4 per cent in 1958. For 1940 figures see Sumner H. Slichter, *Union Policies and Industrial Management* (1941), p. 183.

[4] William Haber and Harold M. Levinson, *Labor Relations and Productivity in the Building Trades* (1956), p. 181.

[5] As Haber and Levinson point out, unduly strict plumbing codes were adopted in some cities before unions became important. The same.

tenance practices, it became feasible for spinners to handle more spinning sides and weavers to handle more looms. The unions more or less successfully resisted the efforts of management to increase work loads until the early 1950's. The nonunion mills in the South were able to increase the work load as conditions changed. As wages came closer and closer to equality, the higher work load gradually became the principal competitive advantage enjoyed by the southern mills and undoubtedly accelerated the drop in the number of jobs in the union plants.

The hosiery workers' union has long had a rule prohibiting knitters from operating more than one machine. It grew out of a fear of the knitters that employers, by operating machines in pairs with a knitter and a helper, would build up a reservoir of trained helpers eager to step into the knitters' jobs—a potential source of strike breakers. The rule against two-machine operation has tended to prevent the use of helpers in knitting machine operation—though changes in the quality of product demanded, and other factors have also contributed to, this result. This rule also was an influence in encouraging equipment manufacturers to increase the number of sections to a machine. Since the union has now virtually disappeared from the hosiery industry, its rules are no longer of practical significance.

The operating engineers, who claim jurisdiction over all machines and engines used in construction regardless of motive power, assert control over all sorts of small apparatus, such as mortar and plaster mixers, small compressors, welding machines, and small hoists, as well as cranes, shovels, bulldozers, and the like. The various locals enforce rules regulating the employment of men to tend these various machines. The rules vary, but in many cases they are quite wasteful since they require an engineer for every two or every three of the small machines—in a few cases, an engineer for every machine.[6] Indeed, the engineers may require that an engineer turn the power on and off—even though it is purchased from an electric power company, and all that is required is to push a button or turn a switch.

Requirement of Excessive Crews

Closely related to unreasonable limits on the number of machines a crew may run is the requirement of excessive crews on machines.

[6] The same, p. 176.

Some unions, such as the printing pressmen, the longshoremen, the musicians, and the stage hands, customarily negotiate agreements specifying the size of the crew that will be used either on certain equipment or in certain operations. The crew sizes, of course, may not be excessive. Sometimes (as is the case in some agreements of the printing pressmen) the union's objective is to prevent overwork or to promote safety. But in a vast majority of cases where crew sizes are negotiated the size of crew is excessive—often flagrantly so. There is a temptation when the union is negotiating in this area to press for an extra man or two, and in some negotiations, if the employer is not in a strong bargaining position, he concedes. Once an excessive crew has been established, eliminating unneeded workers becomes extremely difficult. Furthermore, on new equipment that is expected to yield large gains in productivity, the pressure on the employer to agree to excessive crews is exceptionally strong, as is the temptation for him to yield somewhat.

The musicians' union in some cities requires a minimum size of band or orchestra in theaters or in hotels and dance halls. In the case of dance halls, the size of the hall may determine the minimum size of orchestra permitted. By far the most ambitious attempts to require excessive crews have been made by the running crafts on the railroads. It was a desire of their members for promotion that first caused these unions to press for excessive crews. Later their interest in make-work rules was stimulated by the decline in railroad employment and by the technological changes that threatened the jobs of some employees, especially the firemen.

The railroad running crafts have made a few attempts to negotiate excessive crew requirements, but they have relied chiefly on legislation. They have sought two types of laws—full-crew laws and train limit laws. The full-crew laws vary in content, most of them providing that train crews shall consist of an engineer, a fireman, a conductor, and a specified number of brakemen. The latter may vary with the length of the train. Some of the laws regulate only the number of brakemen. Some states do not prescribe the minimum size of train crews but authorize state commissions to require as many men as, in the judgment of the commission, are needed for safe and efficient operation.

In 1959 seventeen states had full-crew laws in effect.[7] Pennsylvania

[7] The states are: Arizona, Arkansas, California, Indiana, Maine, Massachusetts, Mississippi, Nebraska, Nevada, New York, North Dakota, Ohio, Oregon, South Carolina, Texas, Washington, and Wisconsin.

had a full-crew law on the books, but it had been held unconstitutional by the state supreme court in 1939.[8] Six states (Connecticut, Maryland, New Jersey, Pennsylvania, Rhode Island, and West Virginia) had authorized the state public utility commission to prescribe minimum crew sizes. Unsuccessful attempts were made by the railroad brotherhoods to get Congress to pass a full-crew law in 1932 and 1935. In 1946 and 1947, the railroad brotherhoods tried unsuccessfully to negotiate minimum crew sizes for all classes of road service, yard service, and special service.[9]

Variations in the size of the crews from state to state dramatize the anomaly of the full-crew laws. Great Northern's fast transcontinental freight, No. 401, runs from St. Paul-Minneapolis to the North Dakota state line with two brakemen. At Breckinridge, Minnesota, the last division point in Minnesota, the train picks up a third brakeman because North Dakota has a full-crew law. When it reaches the Montana border, the third brakeman is dropped, and all through the mountains of Montana and Idaho, No. 401 operates with two brakemen. Then when it reaches the Washington border the train takes on a third brakeman, since Washington also is a full-crew state.[10] Some of the laws require no larger crews than the roads had previously been using. Furthermore, the laws authorizing state commissions to prescribe minimum crews have resulted in little or no increase in the size of crews. Somewhat more than half of the laws, however, have compelled increases. Texas, Nebraska, Wisconsin, and Mississippi require five men on all trains no matter how short; Washington requires not less than six men on any freight train of 25 or more cars. New York requires a crew of five on most trains, but a crew of six on passenger trains of six or more cars. One of the most drastic laws was the California law of 1911, amended by referendum vote on November 2, 1948. The original law required all freight trains of 49 cars or less to be manned by a crew of five with additional brakemen depending on the length of trains and grades. Long freight trains in California sometimes had as many as seven or eight brakemen.

The plea of the unions has been that the full-crew laws were legitimate safety regulations, but none of the state utility commissions,

---

[8] Pennsylvania Railroad v. Driscoll, 330 Pennsylvania 97; 198 Atlantic 130.
[9] Conductors' and Trainmen's Forty-Hour Week and Rules Case. Carriers Exhibit B (1950), pp. 351 and 416.
[10] Jay Edgerton in the Minneapolis Star and Tribune (May 26, 1958).

with the safety factor as a guide, established crews as large as those provided in many state laws. When California repealed the full-crew law that had resulted in as many as seven or eight brakemen on a train, the public utilities commission, using its authority to require as many brakemen as safety requires, set the number only as high as three on some operations in California. During World War II, Joseph B. Eastman, Director of the Office of Defense Transportation, tried to get an agreement between railroads on the one hand and the conductors and trainmen on the other to eliminate unnecessary train-men, but nothing came of this effort.

Full-crew laws make jobs for conductors and brakemen, but not for engineers and firemen. Hence, the running craft unions have sought legislation limiting the length of trains, especially freight trains. Such legislation would make jobs for members of all four running crafts. Again the argument has been that safety requires that the length of freight trains be limited—though the best judgment seems to be that safety is promoted by fewer and longer trains rather than shorter and more numerous trains. In any case, only four states, Arizona, Louisi-ana, Oklahoma, and Nevada, were persuaded to pass train limit laws. Each limited freight trains to 70 cars, exclusive of the caboose. At-tempts to get Congress to pass train limit laws in 1934, 1935, and 1937 were unsuccessful. On September 11, 1942, the Interstate Com-merce Commission issued Service Order No. 85, which suspended for the duration of the emergency the then-existing state train limit laws on the ground that those laws wasted men and material. In the 1946 and 1947 wage disputes, labor organizations tried to limit trains by collective bargaining. They proposed that the maximum length of any freight train should not exceed 3,000 feet or 70 cars, and that the maximum length of any passenger train should not exceed 1,200 feet or 14 cars.[11] On June 18, 1945, the United States Supreme Court held the Arizona train limit law to be unconstitutional on the ground that it had no reasonable relationship to safety and was an undue burden on interstate commerce.[12] No train limit laws are now en-forced.

The introduction of diesel locomotives raised the question whether or not the fireman's job was necessary. The first diesel elec-

[11] *Conductors' and Trainmen's Forty-Hour Week and Rules Case.* Carriers Exhibit B, pp. 352 and 417.
[12] Southern Pacific Company *v.* Arizona, 325 US 761.

tric locomotives were operated only in yard service. They had been designed for one-man operation, and this fact was used as a selling point. Some of the full-crew laws, which specifically state that each train must have one engineer and one fireman, preserve the firemen's jobs. The State of New York, however, in 1936 passed special legislation to preserve firemen's jobs.[13]

The second use of the diesel was in passenger service, beginning in about 1934. The first trains were operated with only an engineer in the cab, but the firemen immediately demanded that a fireman be added. This was agreed to by various roads, and in February 1937, the so-called National Diesel Agreement was negotiated providing for a fireman on all diesel electrics with a weight on the drivers of more than 90,000 pounds. The limit of 90,000 pounds prevented application of the agreement to Budd one-car units.

The next step was the use of diesels in road freight service. In this service trains were often operated with as many as four diesel units controlled from the front unit by a single crew. The firemen demanded that an additional fireman be placed on each unit. The engineers asked that the additional man come from the ranks of the engineers. The two brotherhoods, unable to agree on a joint demand, pressed separate rival ones. These demands were eventually heard by an Emergency Board appointed under the Railway Labor Act on February 20, 1943. The engineers modified their request to provide for one additional man, designated an assistant engineer and placed on single and multiple-unit assemblies up to and including four units. The firemen also modified their request to one additional fireman on multiple-unit assemblies up to four units.

The Board found that with crews of only an engineer and fireman, the fireman was not at all times in the cab where he could check signals with the engineer. Part of the time the fireman was in the engine room checking on the heating and lighting apparatus for which he was responsible. The Board decided that on high-speed main-line through passenger trains safety demanded the presence of a fireman in the cab at all times while the train was in motion. The Board added that if compliance with this requirement called for the

[13] The New York law states: "No person . . . shall operate . . . on any railroad within this state any fuel electric engine unless said engine shall be manned with a crew of not less than one engineer and one fireman or helper." *New York Consolidated Laws* (1936), Chap. 777.

services of an additional man in the engine room, the man should be added, but the carriers were left to work out the problem as they saw fit. The Board held that on freight trains no additional man was needed because the head brakeman rode in the diesel and customarily watched signals while the fireman was in control of the engine room. The Board also held that a third man was not needed on yard engines or on single unit local freight and passenger locomotives. The Board concluded that when an additional operating man was required on diesel locomotives he should be from the ranks of the firemen.

The firemen had also asked that a fireman be required on all locomotives regardless of size or type of power, but the Board refused to modify the terms of the Diesel Agreement of 1937, under which firemen were not required on locomotives having a weight on the drivers of less than 90,000 pounds.

The Board's findings with respect to the use of firemen on diesels were accepted reluctantly, but both the engineers and the firemen continued their efforts to get a third man on diesel locomotives. They did this by serving notice on individual railroads requesting the employment of an additional man. Again the dispute went to an Emergency Board. On April 11, 1949, the Board recommended against the employment of an additional engineer. On September 19, 1949, the Board issued a report denying the request of the firemen for the employment of an additional man. The engineers did not strike, but the firemen struck four major railroad systems on May 10, 1950. The strike was settled on May 16 by the firemen's withdrawal of their demand for a second fireman on multiple-unit diesel locomotives and by the railroads' agreeing to arbitrate the union's charge that certain practices in connection with the operation of diesels violated existing contracts.

A strong position against excessive crews on diesels has recently been taken by the two principal Canadian railroads. A strike precipitated by the refusal of the Canadian Pacific to hire firemen to replace existing firemen on diesels in freight and yard service was settled by the appointment of a Royal Commission, which early in 1958 reached the unanimous decision that firemen are superfluous on diesels in freight and yard service. The firemen's union struck against the effort of the Canadian Pacific to put into effect the recommendations of the Royal Commission. The railroad undermined the will of the firemen to strike by agreeing not to lay off any firemen with several years seniority. In view of the company's position the firemen were striking not to promote their own interests but to protect workers not yet hired. A similar agreement was signed May 1, 1959 between the firemen and the Canadian National Railways. Job and seniority rights of presently employed firemen are protected, but the long-range result will be the elimination of firemen from freight and yard service. In England the British unions and the Transport Commission have negotiated an agreement under which most diesel electric locomotives will be manned by only one man.[14]

Even if the minimum crew established by a rule or a law is right under most circumstances, it is likely to be wrong under others, and it is also likely to become obsolete. The agreement between the union and the stevedores in the port of Boston contains several pages setting forth the minimum size of gangs under various conditions. For general cargo there is a minimum of twenty men, but for special types of cargo the union has agreed to use a smaller number of men or to permit a different proportion of men. The crews have been increased under union pressure by about four men since the early thirties. The union justifies this increase on the ground that the type of cargo has changed from heavy, bulky freight to lighter, more delicate goods that require more careful handling, but employers insist that the size of crews is excessive. For small vessels, especially, the minimum of twenty men is prohibitive.[15]

An interesting example of a law that changing conditions have converted into a make-work law with union support is the full-time station agent law of Minnesota passed in 1903. The law provides that any railroad point that has gross receipts of $8,000 a year must have a full-time station agent. In practice this means that sixteen cars of corn shipped to Chicago during the busy season call for the station to be maintained the year around. Attempts to repeal the $8,000 law in the Minnesota legislature failed in the House after passing the

[14] *The Economist* (December 28, 1957), p. 1146.
[15] A small boat brought potatoes from Nova Scotia expecting to load the potatoes directly onto trucks without the use of longshoremen. The shipper had been assured by the teamsters that this would be possible, but when the boat arrived the teamsters did not back up the shipper. He was forced to take a crew of 21 men, 2 clerks, and a gate keeper. The ship was so small that only 4 men could work at a time in the hatch. The shipper proposed to the longshoremen that he accept a crew of 15 men every two weeks to unload his potato boat. The union refused, and he was forced to give up shipping potatoes to Boston by boat

Senate.[16] A station agent from western Minnesota was a member of the House. In Iowa some of the roads have "dualized" stations where traffic is light—that is, one agent tends two stations by staying part of the day at each one. Dualization has been accomplished over the opposition of the Order of Railroad Telegraphers.

The theater is unusually susceptible to featherbedding because attendance at performances can be so easily affected by picketing. Hence, the theaters are heavily loaded with unnecessary stage hands, extra musicians, and unneeded help of various kinds receiving pay for doing little or nothing. The cost of this unnecessary labor has gone far to destroy the commercial theater in many cities. When the Broadway success "The Solid Gold Cadillac" came to Minneapolis, the road company carried with it a motion picture machine operator to operate a movie projector for four minutes per performance. But the company was served with notice that it must have a local operator at $125 per week.[17]

Featherbedding by the musicians' union, under the leadership of its recent president James C. Petrillo, led in 1946 to the passage of the Lea Act that made it unlawful to compel a licensee under the Federal Communications Act (1) to employ or pay for more employees than are needed; (2) to refrain from carrying educational programs with unpaid performers on a noncommercial basis; and (3) to interfere with the production or use of records. As a result of this Act the employment of unwanted staff musicians is no longer a problem in broadcasting.

Prohibiting Use of Modern Equipment or Tools

An outstanding example is the restriction placed by some locals of the painters' union on the use of the spray gun—a restriction that seems to be disappearing. An alleged restriction is the limit placed by most painters' locals on the width of the brush that may be used in applying oil paint—usually four or five inches. But the extensive field investigations of Haber and Levinson among both union and nonunion contractors led them to the conclusion that the rule is not in fact restrictive.[18] The longshoremen of Boston refuse to use pallets, though it is estimated that about one-third of the general

[16] Jay Edgerton in the *Minneapolis Star and Tribune* (May 28, 1958).
[17] The same (June 10, 1958).
[18] *Labor Relations and Productivity in the Building Trades*, p. 164.

cargo coming into the port of Boston could advantageously be handled on them. In 1948 the musicians forbade their members to cut records on the ground that the use of records by disc jockeys and juke boxes caused unemployment. The ban was soon lifted under an agreement by which the companies agreed to establish a union performance fund to provide employment for instrumental musicians.

Enforcement of Less Efficient Methods of Work

In handling lumber at Boston the gangs in each hatch are divided into numbered pairs—No. 1, No. 2, No. 3—each pair making up sling loads of lumber. But each pair must wait its turn—so that if No. 3 has a sling load ready to come out before the others, it has to wait until pairs 1 and 2 complete their sling loads, and their lumber is removed. Some building construction unions have restricted the doing of work in shops where it can be done more efficiently—though postwar labor shortages seem to have reduced these restrictions. Much of the opposition to certain types of technological change discussed in Chapter 12 is due to their labor-displacing effect. Business concerns fight progress no less than do trade unions when progress brings market shifts.

Requirement of Excessive Relief Time

Compelling the employer to give excessive relief time is a way of forcing inflation of the labor force. An automobile company that was struggling to hold its own in competition with the big three and that was no match in bargaining with an aggressive local union was giving 43 minutes a day for rest, preparation, clean-up, and relief in contrast with the industry average of 24 minutes.

Idle time at full pay was more or less inadvertently provided by a mistake in negotiating a contract covering workers processing frozen fish fillets for a large chain store on the Boston Fish Pier. The contract was negotiated by company lawyers who were not familiar with operating conditions. It provided for a working day of eight hours to start at six in the morning. But the fish boats reach the dock about six, and the catch is then auctioned. Until the auction is completed, the fillet processors have little or nothing to do. The company has tried to change the uneconomic rule, but the union replies: "You made it yourself."

Requirement of Unneeded Standby Crews

The musicians require the use of local standby bands or orchestras when traveling or out-of-town bands and orchestras are used or of standby musicians when mechanical music is used. In an aviation engine plant the automobile workers' union requires that a plant maintenance man stand by doing nothing while repairmen from machine vendors are in the plant making repairs that the employer is entitled to have them make on equipment.

Enforcement of Loose Production Standards or Limits on Speed or on Daily Output

These are probably the most widespread form of make-work rule or practice, and yet they did not normally originate as such. Furthermore, the enforcement of limits on output often did not begin as a union policy, but rather as simply an attempt by the workers to protect themselves against a speed-up and (if there is an incentive method of payment) against rate cuts. Sometimes the basis for a union policy of enforcing loose production standards starts with poor standard setting or rate setting by management. Even if the original setting of standards was good, looseness may develop as materials and equipment are improved and as better methods of work are developed, unless management is alert to the need of making small changes in standards as methods and conditions change. The problems of operating standards and incentives and keeping them up to date are discussed in Chapter 17 on "Wage Incentives" and in Chapter 18 on "Measured Daywork." During the war many companies were lax in setting rates or standards or yielded readily to pressure for more liberal rates or for looser standards. Many agreements between unions and employers provide that the job may not be retimed unless there are changes in methods or conditions that warrant altering rates or production standards by a given amount or percentage.

In the steel industry the right of management to reduce excessive crews has been limited by the so-called "local practice clause" added to the agreement between the United Steelworkers and the principal steel companies in 1947. The agreement requires the maintenance of local practices that were in effect in 1947 unless change is required by technological innovations. There are conflicting views concerning the effect of the rule. Some managers believe that it has greatly handicapped management in its efforts to reduce excessive crew sizes and to correct mistakes that were made during the war and at other times. Others feel that it has also stimulated plant managements to look for opportunities to make technological changes since excessive crews can not be reduced unless such changes occur. And though the rule does not apply to practices that have developed since 1947, it has made management more aware of the wastefulness of loose practices and has stimulated management to guard against the development of them. The balance of opinion seems to be that the net effect of the rule is bad, and in the negotiations of 1959 the companies made a strong but unsuccessful effort to have it amended.

Whatever may be the original reason for the loose rates or standards, the condition is bound sooner or later to involve the union and to force the union to defend them against efforts of management to tighten them. This means that the union may become involved in pursuing a make-work policy even though it never intended to. The difficulty is that once pegging of production has gone on for some time, pegs cannot usually be eliminated without reducing the number of men needed. Even though the union had no part in pegging production or in insisting that standards or rates be loosely set, it is likely to be called upon to defend some of its members against the threatened loss of jobs that would follow from getting greater output per manhour.

Reluctance to face the political difficulties of the period of transition has led some local unions to refuse to abandon their support of make-work practices until the plant was on the verge of going out of business. A few such cases will be discussed in Chapter 17, "Wage Incentives," and in Chapter 27 on "Problems and Policies in High-Cost Plants."

Extent of the Practice of Requiring Employers to Hire Unnecessary Workers

Creating unnecessary jobs is the equivalent of destroying the usefulness of part of the labor force. In measuring the extent of make-work practices, rules, and policies, therefore, one should ask how many workers they in effect render useless. The number is considerable and undoubtedly greater than might be assumed from superficial impressions since many make-work activities are obscure and affect only small groups. There is evidence that much useless labor is required in the entertainment industries, in the operation of railroad trains (though not in other parts of the railroad industry), that small amounts are required in building construction and printing, and that significant amounts are required in manufacturing as a result of the opposition of unions to tightening loose standards. But the responsibility for wasting labor cannot be attributed solely to the unions. It falls on customers too, especially in the construction industry. In 1953 and in 1955 in strikes in Texas by the operating engineers for make-work practices the contractors' position was undermined by the oil companies and the chemical companies that insisted on their facilities being completed in a hurry.

The loss of output from deliberately restrictive practices cannot be estimated with any accuracy. It is certainly far less than the output lost from unemployment, which leads to a loss of effective demand. Is it equal to the time lost because of sickness, which in an average year runs about a million man-years? There is no satisfactory answer to that question because there is no agreement as to what rate of work is reasonably to be expected. It is likely that the loss of production from deliberate make-work practices is considerably less than a million man-years per year.

It should be observed that managements do not remain passive in the face of restrictive practices. Years may be required, but most (not all) restrictive practices are eventually discontinued or their application substantially narrowed. Technological change is the most effective, but there are other weapons against them. Arbitrators are hostile to restrictions and seek to limit their scope.[19] Of course, while old restrictive practices are being eliminated, new ones are being introduced.

Are make-work rules and policies on balance growing or diminishing in extent and importance? If one compares the present with the great depression of the thirties, when unions were smaller and weaker than they are today, one must conclude that make-work rules and policies have increased considerably in extent. On the other

[19] The importance of make-work rules and practices cannot be measured merely by the number of unneeded jobs in existence. Sometimes the make-work rule or practice has no visible effect because it forces abandonment of the activities to which make-work rules apply—as when the full-crew laws force railroads to abandon passenger trains that cannot afford to carry a crew of five.

hand, if one compares the present with 1947 or 1948, there has been on balance a drop in their extent and severity.[20]

The progress that has been made in reducing make-work practices in manufacturing represents in the main the partial correction of their abnormally rapid growth between 1937 and 1947. This period included several years just prior to the war, when new unions were being established in many plants and when many managements, unfamiliar with unions, were suddenly compelled to deal with them. It included the period of war, when new unions continued to grow up, when the pressure for uninterrupted production was exceptionally strong, and when the government was attempting to enforce a policy of wage stabilization. It included the immediate postwar years, when accumulated demand was abnormally large and when enterprises were eagerly attempting to re-establish connections with old customers and, in many instances, get established in new parts of the market.

All of these conditions combined to produce deterioration of rate and standard setting practices in many plants. Hence the period 1937 to 1947 bequeathed to American industry a body of loosely set rates and standards. About 1947 the tide turned, and management after management began the slow and difficult task of putting its house in order—reforming the rate structure and the classification of jobs. The many problems involved in this process are set forth in detail in Chapter 17, on "Wage Incentives," Chapter 18, "Measured Daywork," Chapter 19, "Evaluated Rate Structures," and Chapter 20, "Wage Structure Considerations." These chapters are an analysis from the technical point of view of the many management administrative improvements introduced in American plants mainly by collective bargaining.

What is the long-term trend in make-work practices? Has recent progress in getting rid of these practices been simply an interruption of a long-term tendency for them to grow in extent and severity? No one knows the answer to these questions, but the best evidence is that

[20] In the case of the railroads the efforts of the running crafts to get new full-crew laws or a national train limit law have failed. One burdensome full-crew law, the California law, was amended by a referendum vote in 1948 to eliminate the requirement of more than two brakemen except where ordered by the State Public Utilities Commission for reasons of safety. Considerably earlier two full-crew laws were repealed, and in 1939 the Pennsylvania law was held unconstitutional. New Jersey, which had passed a full-crew law in 1913, repealed it in 1917, but gave the Board of Public Utility Commissioners authority to compel the railroads to employ enough men in the operation of trains. Maryland repealed a full-crew law in 1922 and authorized the Public Service Commission to regulate the size of train crews.

lasting progress is being made by managements toward eliminating them. In the manufacturing field, where the most important make-work practices are the result, not of union initiative, but of union resistance to management's efforts to correct mistakes in setting rates or standards, pressure of competition is forcing some employers to take strikes to force the abandonment of make-work practices. Managements are gradually learning the vital importance of doing a good job in setting standards and rates, of having proper time studies made, and of refusing to bargain over the results of the studies. In some non-manufacturing fields, such as building construction and West Coast ports, there has also been progress towards correction of make-work practices.

Reasons Why Unions Force Make-Work Rules and Practices on Employers

Four principal conditions stimulate the interest of unions in make-work practices: (1) shrinking employment in the industry (because of either contracting markets or technological change); (2) intermittent employment; (3) union success in negotiating unusually high rates of pay and attractive conditions of work; and (4) conditions that enable a substantial proportion of the union's membership to benefit from make-work practices.

The railroad running crafts are the principal example of unions that have been led by shrinking markets to restrict production. House-to-house milk delivery is another example. Intermittent employment has produced an interest in make-work practices in the entertainment industries (musicians, stage hands, Hollywood studios), longshore work, and building construction. When intermittent employment causes union members to lose their jobs at short intervals and to seek new ones, the men become interested in forcing the employer to take on more men than he would otherwise hire or in making each job last a little longer than it otherwise would. And whenever a union for any reason is successful in negotiating unusually favorable rates on jobs, it is likely to be under strong pressure from its members to increase the number of these jobs, and it may press hard for make-work rules. The success of the unions in the Hollywood motion picture industry in negotiating high rates gave them an incentive to negotiate make-work rules.

Make-work practices have small attraction for unions when they affect only a small fraction of the members in a bargaining unit. Only when a large proportion of the union members in the bargaining unit would gain from a make-work practice can the union afford to make a strong effort to force its adoption. In trades where employment is intermittent and employers are frequently required to hire new gangs or crews, every member of the union finds that his chance of being hired is improved by make-work practices. The seniority system of the railroad running crafts causes all members to benefit from make-work rules. The addition of a few jobs does not merely benefit the men who get those jobs—it affects the runs held by all the members and enables a considerable proportion of them to hold better runs than they otherwise would. Hence, make-work rules readily command broad support among the running crafts.[21]

The ability of unions to impose make-work rules or practices depends in the main on two conditions—the extent of the union's control of the market and the ability (or willingness) of the the employer to stand shutdowns. Control of the market means that the union is able to impose the make-work rule on all competitors alike, thereby putting no employer at a disadvantage. A large proportion of the industries in which make-work practices are found are those in which markets are local and the product is perishable; if it is not produced today, it will not be produced at all. Examples are the entertainment industries, the water front, building construction, railroad service, and bus and street car service. Stoppages hurt employers most when the business lost during the shutdown is in large part a permanent loss that cannot be recovered later. Some manufacturers whose customers are mainly other manufacturers in highly competitive industries operating with small inventories fear the permanent loss of customers (or at least the loss of a considerable part of the customers' business) through failure to make deliveries.[22] Most manufacturers,

[21] On the other hand, the various jobs in railroad shops fall into a few groups and do not vary in individual attractiveness as do the various runs in train service. Hence, the shop crafts have far less incentive than the running crafts to press for make-work practices. Another reason why the shop crafts, in contrast to the running crafts, have shown little interest in make-work rules is that the craftsmen in the shops (machinists, boilermakers, blacksmiths, electricians, sheet metal workers) can readily pursue their trades in other industries when railroad employment drops.

[22] The automotive parts industry is the best example. The manufacturers in this industry service the highly competitive automobile manufacturers, who maintain only small inventories of most parts. Automotive parts makers fear that failure to meet delivery schedules will cause their customers to shift part of their business permanently elsewhere.

however, do not suffer a permanent loss of customers from strikes and are also able to make up part of the business not handled during the strike. On the other hand, in the amusement and some service industries, business not done during a stoppage is permanently lost. And if the completion of a building is delayed for a month or two by a strike, the rental income that is lost is not recovered later.

Principal Effects of Make-Work Rules and Practices

Make-work rules are intended to create employment opportunities for the groups imposing them, but they may have the opposite effect. Perhaps the safest generalization is that make-work rules stimulate technological change. Processes will be altered so that output will no longer be restricted.

A question of some interest is how restriction of output affects wages and costs. Must the union choose between imposing costs in the form of make-work rules and in the form of higher wages? Do costs imposed on employers in the form of make-work rules limit the ability of the union to impose costs in other forms, such as higher wages?

Much of the cost of make-work practices is undoubtedly paid by the workers rather than by the employer. Their wages are less than they otherwise would be. But the view that the higher costs of make-work rules come entirely out of wages overlooks the fact that the strength of a union's willingness to fight (and, therefore, its ability to impose higher labor costs upon employers) depends upon how many things the members of a union desire and how strongly they desire them. A union may become interested in establishing some make-work rules or practices without diminishing its interest in getting wage increases comparable to those being gained by other unions in the community, the industry, or related industries. In this event the union's interest in make-work practices simply means that the union has increased its total demands, that greater concessions are needed by employers to avert a strike, or to settle it if one occurs. Of course, the resistance of employers to union demands grows at an increasing rate as the demands increase. While an increase in union demands produces settlements more favorable to the union, the additional gain achieved by the union will ordinarily be less than the rise in the union's demands.[23] Hence, though the demand for make-work practices may limit the union's ability to raise wages, the cost of these practices will not be met entirely by the employees in the form of a slower rise in wages. In most instances make-work practices mean some extra cost to the employer.[24]

Factors Limiting Make-Work Rules and Practices

The reason why only a minority of unions pursue make-work policies to any great extent is that only a small minority would benefit even temporarily from such policies. Suppose that through various make-work devices a union were able to increase the number of jobs available to its members by 10 per cent. Let us assume first that the union members were virtually all employed. In that case the additional jobs would help them only temporarily—if at all. If the employer had no idle equipment, the make-work rules might force the employer to resort to more overtime, which might benefit a large proportion of the union members. The employer, however, would seek to avoid the overtime by adding another shift or buying additional equipment. Hence, the ultimate effect of the make-work rule would be to enlarge the work force and incidentally the union membership. But the real beneficiaries of the make-work rule would be the new employees—not the men who supported the make-work policy.

Let us assume a different state of conditions—that about 10 per cent of the union members are unemployed. This volume of unemployment would handicap the union seriously in compelling the employers to accept make-work practices. Let us assume, however, that the union succeeds and that the increase in the number of jobs

[23] What is under discussion are the effects of a *shift* in the union's demand schedule and the elasticity of the employer's resistance schedule. It is assumed that the shift in the union's demand schedule produces no shift in the employer's resistance schedule. Perhaps this assumption of the independence of the schedules is unrealistic. Certainly there are instances in which the determination of a union to insist on more may so alarm employers as to produce a shift in the employer's resistance schedule. The rise in the employer's willingness to resist demands may be so great that the union ends up getting less rather than more.

[24] It is possible to analyze the effects of make-work rules or practices on output in static terms using the concepts of the elasticity of demand and the elasticity of substitution, but in view of the fact that the principal effect of restrictions on output is to set employers hunting harder than ever for opportunities to change technology, an analysis in static terms is not worthwhile.

absorbs the unemployed members of the union. It still remains true, however, that only a small minority of the union members gain from the make-work policy.

Unions cannot ordinarily afford to press hard for conditions that would benefit only a small part of their members. That is why they must concentrate on such issues as wages, hours, and various fringe benefits that benefit all or most of the members.[25] In order for most of the members of a union to gain from make-work policies, either employment in the industry must be intermittent or the seniority system must be such that a few extra jobs enable a large proportion of the workers to move into better positions—as in the case of the train service employees on the railroads.

Efforts by Employers to Eliminate Make-Work Rules and Practices

A discussion of the success of employers in getting rid of make-work rules and practices should distinguish between the imposition of formal rules, such as the bogus rule in the printing industry or excessive crews, and make-work practices that are the result of lax or weak management rather than of an agreement between the union and the employer.

Little progress has been made by employers in getting rid of formal restrictive rules, but considerable progress has been made in getting rid of restrictive practices allowed by lax management. Most notable is the success of the Canadian railroads in starting the gradual elimination of unneeded firemen from diesel locomotives in yard and freight service. This result was accomplished only by going to arbitration.

Several obstacles have impeded employers in getting rid of formal make-work rules. One is that employers who are too weak to resist the imposition of make-work rules in the first instance are usually too weak to negotiate a relaxation or termination of the rules. A second reason is that many make-work rules are imposed in industries where markets are local and where the union is able to apply

---

[25] Some unions have found difficulty in arousing enthusiasm for pension demands since many younger members attach little importance to pension rights. But employers need pensions as an instrument of personnel policy, and unions do not encounter serious opposition to moderate pension demands.

the rule to all competitors alike. Hence, many managements lack a strong incentive to press for the elimination or relaxation of the rules. A third reason is that the resistance of the union is likely to be strong.[26] Unless markets are expanding rather rapidly, the immediate effect of the abandonment of make-work rules will be a drop in the number of jobs. When markets are expanding, unions are strong enough to resist any demand for relaxation of make-work rules.

There have been a few instances, it is true, in which unions have welcomed expanding markets or labor shortages as opportunities to get rid of make-work rules or practices that were limiting the earnings of union members or were handicapping some union plants in meeting competition. During World War I, for example, the flint glass workers' union took advantage of the labor shortages to agree to the elimination of limits on production in many (though not all) departments of the industry.[27] But such cases of union foresight are rare, and only a few developed during World War II and the period of acute labor shortage that followed.

Although little progress has been made in getting rid of formal make-work rules, considerable progress has been made in eliminating make-work *practices*—substituting tight, carefully engineered standards for loose ones and ending the restriction of output that accompanied loose standards. Management is able to make progress in tightening standards because it can deal with a few jobs at a time and because it can frequently raise productivity without displacing workers. Thus the resistance encountered by management is much less than the opposition aroused by an attempt to change a rule in such a way as to eliminate a number of unneeded jobs. But even when the elimination of make-work practices took the form of tightening production standards, often nothing was done until the plight of the plant had become desperate and the jobs of all the employees were in jeopardy. In some cases the plant was on the verge of being closed, or the work was being moved away; in other cases the practices had become so burdensome that management took a long and costly strike in order to get rid of them. In one case the management succeeded in convincing the union that abandonment of wasteful practices was

---

[26] The 1960 decision of the Supreme Court in the case of the Order of Railroad Telegraphers *v*. Chicago and N.W.R.Co. (80 S. Ct. 761) may serve to strengthen union resistance. Bargaining the discontinuance of jobs appears to have been made mandatory. The precise implications of the decision remain to be determined.

[27] Slichter, *Union Policies and Industrial Management*, p. 390.

necessary for the workers to keep their high rates of pay. Management was able to agree to protect the workers against layoffs by bringing in work from other plants. Some cases, where make-work practices have been abandoned, will be discussed in some detail in Chapter 27, "Problems and Policies in High-Cost Plants," and in Chapter 28, "Union-Management Cooperation."

12 / Union Policies Toward Technological Change

BETWEEN 1930 and 1956 technological research in American industry, measured by the number of scientists and engineers devoting full time to it, increased five-fold and, measured by the ratio of research expenditures to the gross national product, about thirteen-fold. Research and development expenditures, which in the fiscal year 1958-59 were about $11 billion, were larger than the cumulative total for all years prior to the end of World War II. Never have men made such large and systematic efforts to change the technology of industry, and never has technology been in a state of such rapid flux.

Our interest is in all the interactions between this rapid technological change and union policies. Particularly we are concerned with how union policies affect the adjustment to change—do these policies facilitate the adjustment to change; do they tend to reduce the social cost of change by making the actual rate of change correspond more closely to the optimum rate?

Developments in Technology

Technological change has meant an increase of 93 per cent in output per man-hour in all private industry between 1929 and 1957, and of nearly 35 per cent between 1947 and 1957.[1] There are few industries in which productivity has not increased considerably. A recent study of 17 manufacturing industries showed that only one (glass containers) had a gain in productivity between 1947 and 1957 of less than 5 per cent, 6 of the 17 had gains in excess of 50 per cent, and 10 had gains in excess of 40 per cent. In railroading the increase in output per man-hour was over 46 per cent between 1949 and 1957, and in

[1] Solomon Fabricant, *Basic Facts on Productivity Change*, National Bureau of Economic Research, Occasional Paper 63 (1959), p. 45.

mining the increases ranged from 7.9 per cent in iron ore mining to
66.9 per cent in bituminous coal.[2]

Technological change affects every aspect of industry—power, raw
materials, methods of communication, and the variety and quality of
products. Many developments—atomic power, plastics, computers, jet
planes, industrial diamonds—are quite dramatic and may be the basis
for important new industries. The vast majority of technological
changes are small and produce only limited immediate effects, but
the variety of changes is immense. They include such broad groups
as (1) the substitution of power-driven equipment for hand labor
—earth moving equipment for the pick and shovel—and machines for
tools; (2) the use of faster, more adaptable, and often larger equipment—faster and sometimes larger locomotives, trucks, papermaking
machines, machine tools, sewing machines, printing presses, turbines,
airplanes; (3) the improvement of cutting tools, speeding up machine
operations; (4) the use of automatic controls, signals, automatic stops
or shifts; (5) the growing use of moving conveyors and the development of automatic machine loading and unloading equipment; (6)
the substitution of continuous processes for a succession of starts and
stops; (7) the use of machines to replace the brain—computing machines of various sorts and machines with memories; and (8) the substitution of factory production for on-the-job fabrication and production—pre-fabrication and pre-packaging.

The above list is not exhaustive but is simply a reminder of the
many kinds of technological changes.

Reaction of Unions to Technological Changes

Many important *general* effects of technological change, however,
have little effect on union policies toward *specific* changes.[3] For example, technological innovation, by adding to the number of investment opportunities, increases the demand for labor and tends to
sustain employment at a high level. But this general consequence of
technological change does not affect the policies of unions toward

[2] U. S. Bureau of Labor Statistics, "Indexes of Output per Man-Hour for Selected
Industries, 1919 to 1958" (April 1959) (mimeo.).

[3] But the general effect of technological change upon the demand for skilled labor
has stimulated interest of some unions (especially the plumbers, the boilermakers, the
electricians, the operating engineers, and the machinists) in the spread and improvement
of apprentice training. See Chapter 4.

technological changes that may be affecting jobs of a particular craft or group of workmen. Technological change also has the general effect of increasing the demand for skilled labor. It has created new occupations (airplane pilot, for example), and it has greatly increased the proportion of skilled craftsmen (pattern makers, tool and die makers, boilermakers, steamfitters, welders) in the total labor force.[4] The development of new models or new products seems to require an unusually high proportion of skilled men, and so also does the maintenance and repair of equipment and structures. The amount of plant and equipment to be kept in repair has been growing faster than the total labor force.[5]

Toward many important technological changes there is no union policy for the simple reason that the change occurs in another industry beyond the reach of the union most affected by it. Examples are the automobile and airplane industries which limit job opportunities in the railroad industry; television, which has destroyed many jobs in the moving picture industry; new paper products (milk bottles, towels, napkins), that have limited jobs in the glass industry and the textile industry; and technological developments in the gas and oil industries, that have limited the demand for coal. Toward many other technological changes there is no union policy simply because the change is too small to arouse much interest.

Union policies toward technological changes are of five principal types: (1) willing acceptance; (2) opposition—as when the union strikes against the change or forbids its members to use it; (3) competition—attempting to keep the old method in use in competition with the new, perhaps by accepting wage cuts on the old jobs; (4) encouragement—taking the initiative in urging employers to adopt new methods or otherwise encouraging employers to make technological changes; and (5) adjustment. This last may take many different forms, but it is essentially a policy of doing what can be done to help the workers immediately affected use it to the best possible advantage and suffer the least possible harm from it.

These five policies are not necessarily mutually exclusive. A union

[4] Data on the growing proportion of the labor force falling in the category of craftsmen are given in Chapter 4, "Union Policies on Training and Apprenticeship," pp. 62-65.

[5] Between 1929 and 1956 the amount of physical plant and equipment per worker increased about 25 per cent. This is based on the estimate of stocks of privately owned plant and equipment expressed in constant prices in Joint Economic Committee, *Productivity, Prices, and Incomes*, Joint Committee Print, 85 Cong. 1 sess. (1957), p. 93.

may be trying to limit the use of a new method (the policy of opposition or of competition) while seeking to control the jobs in the new method (the policy of adjustment). Furthermore, the policies blend into one another so that it is not always easy to say where one ends and another begins. This is true, for example, of the policy of opposition and the policy of competition; it is also true of the policies of willing acceptance and encouragement.

Determinants of Union Policies Toward Technological Change

Four principal conditions determine the policies adopted by unions toward technological change: (1) the nature of the union; (2) the condition of the industry or the enterprise; (3) the nature of the technological change itself; and (4) the stage of development of the technological change and of union policy toward it.

NATURE OF THE UNION. The principal distinction is between craft unions and industrial unions. A policy of opposition, when it occurs, is usually pursued by craft unions. Industrial unions, on the other hand, generally find that technological changes affect such a small fraction of their membership or affect different parts of the union in such different ways that the union does not find it advisable to oppose the change. Indeed, a change that hurts some members of an industrial union may help other members. Industrial unions, therefore, are likely to pursue a policy of adjustment toward technological change.

Industrial unions are usually less interested than craft unions in the question of who shall hold the jobs on the new process—the men who worked on the old process or other workers. The reason is obvious. Since the industrial union covers all men in the plant, the workers on the new process remain within the bargaining unit, but a craft union may have to fight to prevent the employer from giving work on the new process to men who are outside its jurisdiction—either because they belong to another craft or because they are not craftsmen at all.

CONDITION OF THE INDUSTRY, THE ENTERPRISE, OR OCCUPATION. The important question here is whether the industry, the enterprise, or the occupation is facing stiff competition and whether it is expanding or contracting. Many of the instances in which unions have gone out of their way to encourage technological change have been in areas where there is serious competition and where employment would be increased if better equipment and methods were used. The carpenters, for example, by readily accepting new power-driven tools and new materials (plywood and dry wall), have gained employment at the expense of the bricklayers and the plasterers, and the plasterers, by accepting the plaster gun, have tried to meet the competition of dry wall. In expanding industries and enterprises unions are likely to concentrate on negotiating the best possible rates on the new jobs created by technological changes. If the industry or the enterprise is contracting, the union's course of action becomes more complex and less predictable.

The problems of the workers displaced by the technological change are likely to have considerable effect on the policy choices of the union. If the union believes that the technological change will have no effect upon the rate at which the industry or the enterprise contracts, it may try to limit displacements through make-work rules of one kind or other. This has been the reaction of some of the railroad unions to technological changes in that industry of declining employment. On the other hand, if the union believes that the decline of the industry may be retarded by technological change, the union may positively encourage this change. It must be confessed, however, that experience gives no reliable guide as to whether a specific union will react to technological change by accepting it, as the carpenters have done, or by adopting make-work policies, as some of the railroad unions have done.

The widely-held notion that unions are more willing to accept technological changes when business is good and less willing when business is depressed is an oversimplification. For example, the painters refused to handle the spray gun when business was good, but when the depression struck many locals accepted the gun on some types of work because it helped them to get work that otherwise would have gone to nonunion workers.

NATURE OF THE TECHNOLOGICAL CHANGE. This is the most important determinant of union policies toward technological changes. Three factors are of utmost importance to the unions: (1) the effect of the change on the number of jobs on the process or in the bargaining unit; (2) the effect on the *degree* of skill and responsibility of the employees; and (3) the effect on the *kind* of skill or other qualifications required to do the work.

The effect of a technological change on the number of jobs is obviously important. If the change has the *immediate* effect of greatly reducing the number of jobs, the union may decide simply to oppose it. Since union policy tends to reflect the interest of all persons in the bargaining unit, the effect of the technological change on the number of jobs in the *bargaining unit* is usually more important than its effect on the number of jobs on the *process* or in *a particular department* directly affected by the technological change. In other words, the fact that a technological change may greatly reduce the number of jobs in one department does not necessarily mean that a local union covering the entire plant will make an important issue of the matter.

Some technological changes affect the *degree* of skill and responsibility required without substantially altering the general *kind* of skill. A technological innovation may require more or less the traditional skills and knowledge plus some additional ones (the effect of diesel locomotives upon the skill and knowledge required of locomotive engineers is an example), or it may require little or no new knowledge or skill and only part of the traditional ones. On the other hand, other technological changes may change the *kind* of skill and qualifications needed. Changes of the latter type may transfer the work to a new craft or perhaps precipitate a conflict between two crafts over which one shall do the work. The automobile truck, replacing the horse-drawn vehicle, is an example of a technological change of this second type. So also is welding. Many technological developments in the building trades modify skill requirements sufficiently to produce a conflict between crafts over the new jobs.

It is obvious that the several principal characteristics of technological change may occur in a variety of combinations and that union policies toward any given change will depend in large measure on what combination of effects are produced. The following table classifies technological changes with respect to their effects on the number of jobs in the bargaining unit, on the *degree* of skill, and on the *kind* of skill and other qualifications required. There are other variables not covered by the table, but the three selected are the ones of greatest interest to unions. In subsequent discussions it will be convenient to refer to the 18 types of technological change by the numbers given them in the table.

Effect on Level of Skill and Responsibility

Effect on Number of Jobs	Kind of skill or responsibility slightly changed			Kind of skill or responsibility significantly changed		
	Degree of skill greatly increased	Degree of skill little changed	Degree of skill greatly reduced	Degree of skill greatly increased	Degree of skill little changed	Degree of skill greatly reduced
Number increased	1	2	3	10	11	12
Number little changed	4	5	6	13	14	15
Number greatly diminished	7	8	9	16	17	18

STAGE OF DEVELOPMENT OF THE TECHNOLOGICAL CHANGE AND OF UNION POLICY TOWARD IT. There are many cases of unions changing their policy toward a technological change—perhaps opposing it in the beginning and then shifting to a policy of adjustment. An example is the policy of the painters' union toward spray painting. The original opposition may be a more or less instinctive reaction, or it may be based on the fact that the new technological change at the beginning had so many imperfections that a policy of opposition seemed feasible. But as the new process or new equipment is perfected and becomes well established in the industry, the union may have no choice but to cease opposing it and to adjust itself to the change as best it can.

The five principal policies that unions pursue toward technological change are examined below.

The Policy of Willing Acceptance

The most usual policy of unions toward technological change is willing acceptance. This happens in the numerous cases in which the technological change makes little difference in the kind and degree of skill required and has little immediate effect on the number of jobs. But the gain in productivity from the change may make it attractive by giving labor improved opportunity to bargain for wage increases. Unions may be led by favorable bargaining opportunities to accept willingly technological changes that involve a mixture of advantages and disadvantages. Thus, the bargaining advantages that accompany a change requiring greater skill may lead to willing acceptance even though it greatly reduces the number of jobs.

How does the policy of willing acceptance differ from the policy of encouragement? The difference is in the degree of initiative shown by the union. In the case of willing acceptance the union leaves the initiative to the employer and simply acquiesces rather completely in accepting the changes. In the case of the policy of encouragement the union plays an active role in suggesting specific technological changes.

Almost innumerable examples of the policy of willing acceptance can be given. Most of the multitude of technological changes in the building trades have been accepted by the unions affected without bargaining over conditions. The carpenters' union, for example, has offered no resistance to new tools (the portable power saw is the most important), or to the use of plywood and other forms of sheathing; and the lathers' and plasterers' unions, having to meet the competition of plasterboard, have readily accepted large perforated sheets of gypsum or rock lath as substitutes for wood lath or prepared plaster mixes.

A conspicuous example of acquiescence in technological change is that of the United Mine Workers. Although the industry has not been an expanding one, the union has given the employers a free hand in making technological changes. The rank and file would probably block many changes or attach special conditions to their acceptance if they had their way.[6] John L. Lewis, the head of the union until 1960, preferred to give the employer a free hand to raise productivity and then compel him to pass on the gains of productivity in the form of higher wages. The policy is so sensible that it requires no special justification, but two possible reasons for it come to mind. One is that the nature of coal mining is such that it is better to have a few men engaged in it at high wages than a larger number at lower wages. A second is that the competition of oil and gas makes high productivity essential if coal miners' wages are to be high.

[6] Evidence in support of the above statements is found in the large number of resolutions from locals offered at the national conventions of the union. Few of these resolutions are ever considered by the conventions, but they are published in a separate volume. At the 1952 convention there were 1,806 resolutions concerning wage rates, manning, and seniority changes—most of them directly or indirectly caused by mechanization. At the 1956 convention there were 1,387 resolutions.

Policy of Opposition to Technological Change

The policy of outright and uncompromising opposition to technological change is not rare, but it is pursued in only a small proportion of cases. One reason for its limited use is that most unions
know that the policy is not likely to be successful over an extended
period. Another reason is that there are few technological changes
that do not hold promise of *some* benefit to the workers. Hence,
bargaining for the potential benefit may be more advantageous to
the union than uncompromising opposition. Consider technological
changes of type 9, which reduce greatly both the number of jobs
and also the skill requirements. One might expect that in these
cases the union would pursue a policy of opposition, but this is not
necessarily true. An industrial union is likely to find too small a proportion of its members affected by a technological change to justify
it in pursuing a policy of opposition. Furthermore, even when a
technological change reduces greatly both the number of jobs and
the skill required, it does raise output per man-hour. Hence the
union may believe that more is to be gained by bargaining over
rates on the new jobs or over the complement of men on the new
machines than by trying to keep out the technological change.

There are, however, a few cases in which the union or some part
of it simply refuses to use the new apparatus. Some locals of the
painters' union refuse to use the spray gun; but some of these locals
have limited the refusal to certain types of work. Another case of
refusal to use apparatus comes from the waterfront in Boston, where
the longshoremen refuse to handle cargo on pallets. Boston is the
only important port where this is the case, and the refusal there
seems to be due to circumstances at the port of Boston and to the
peculiar character of the Boston longshoremen's local, which creates
a strong interest in make-work rules.[7] In December 1958 the International Longshoremen's Association in New York refused to load
twenty-seven big Connex containers carrying a total of 1,437 bags
of army Christmas mail. The union objected to the containers because their use deprived the longshoremen of many hours of work.

---

[7] It is estimated that about one-third of the general cargo, including bulk cargo, coming into the port of Boston could be handled advantageously on pallets. The strong
emphasis that the Boston longshoremen place upon make-work rules seems attributable
in part to the fact that a large proportion of the local hold other jobs. They are, therefore, quite indifferent to the effect of the make-work rules on handling costs and hence
on the amount of work coming through the port.

The army requested the containers because the mail was destined for Mediterranean ports noted for extremely high rates of pierside theft and pilferage.[8]

Sometimes the opposition of the union takes the form of a refusal to use the new equipment efficiently. In a plant in central Illinois about 300 hand polishers resisted the use of automatic polishing machines, which management introduced in an attempt to make the plant competitive. The automatic machines were constantly breaking down, and failed to produce at the expected rate. As work was lost, the number of hand polishers declined. After four or five years there were only 35 hand polishers left. A little later the operation was completely shut down.

In some places the teamsters' union has undertaken to limit the practice of "piggybacking"—the carrying of trucks on railway flat cars. Two business agents of Local 25 in Boston persuaded drivers of the New England Transportation Company (a subsidiary of the New Haven Railroad) not to deliver trailers to the railroad units for piggyback loading. In July 1952 the railroad obtained a restraining order against this restriction by the union.[9]

In Chicago and St. Louis the Meat Cutters and Butcher Workmen have prevented the chain stores from handling pre-cut and pre-packaged meats, and they have imposed similar restrictions in Philadelphia.

The compositors' union has restricted the use of the teletypesetter by requiring that the machine be operated only by one of the two categories of workers recognized by the union—journeyman printer or apprentice. The employers argue that there is a tremendous difference in skills required of a tape puncher, which are those of a clerk-typist, and the skills of a compositor. The average girl, anxious to make good on the tape, does a better job operating the teletypesetter than does the average skilled printer. This fact, together with the lower wage paid girls, has caused the work to go to special composition shops. Many newspapers make limited use of the teletypesetter because they prefer to reset long feature stories or syndicated columns taken from tapes or direct wire service. But the teletypesetter

[8] *New York Times* (December 6, 1958), p. 46. The union later withdrew its objection and allowed the containers to be loaded, but apparently an informal agreement was reached with the union leaders that the use of the containers would be limited.

[9] A final decree against the union was granted in 1953, and this decree was upheld by the Supreme Judicial Court in 1954.

is advantageous for stock-market quotations and baseball box scores. The agreement between the Typographical Union and the Boston Herald-Traveler Corporation limits the use of pre-punched material from wire services to an average of 12 columns for the morning paper and 8 columns for the evening paper. But this limitation is not in fact restrictive because the Boston papers do not ordinarily use as many columns of pre-punched materials as are allowed.

The Typographical Union has restricted the use of the newer, automatic typesetter. The agreement between Typographical Local 16 in Chicago and the Dow-Jones Company (*Wall Street Journal*) restricts the use of this machine to stock-market quotations.

Union efforts to require the use of skilled men on apparatus that does not demand their skill may amount to a refusal to use the apparatus. Thus, the insistence of the compositors that jobs on photosetters go to journeymen or apprentices has caused much of the work to go to nonunion shops in which skilled compositors are not employed.

Although industrial unions cannot as a rule afford to take a strong stand against technological changes that affect only a small part of the work force, these unions may oppose changes that affect the entire membership or a large part of it. Opposition of an industrial union in the paper industry delayed for some time the execution of a company plan to consolidate the operations of two small pulp mills in one large modern mill. The new mill was to employ considerably fewer men than the old mills. The plan was not carried out until there had been a change in the operating officials and a strike.

An industrial union in a small, high-cost metal refinery in Montana struck against a plan of the company to modernize the mill. New machinery was installed that required a smaller crew, and the payroll was cut in half. At the same time, total production was increased. The local union staged a wildcat strike in an attempt to prevent the reductions in force. In this case the local was simply giving vent to emotion rather than protecting the true interests of its members. The company had to make the changes in order to make the plant worth operating. The international union understood the problem but was not willing to come out in favor of modernizing plant and equipment. After the one-month wildcat strike, the union took the grievance to arbitration contesting the company's right to assign the work. The company won the case. The international union was apparently happy that management made the changes because it realized that the choice was between fewer jobs and no jobs.

How unions can implement a policy of opposition to technological change depends on circumstances and on the terms of the agreement between the union and the employer. The union may try to negotiate a rule that new apparatus may be installed only with union consent. This does not mean that the union is determined to oppose the introduction of technological changes, but it undoubtedly puts the union in a position to force the employer to pay a high price in terms of concessions for the privilege of making changes. Some locals of the Typographical Union have forced employers to agree that the union must give its consent to all technological changes in the composing room. An agreement in 1954 between Typographical Local 6 and the New York newspapers provided that the introduction of new equipment should be subject to joint determination under collective bargaining, putting the union in an excellent position to block technological development if it so desires. Typographical Local 10, in Louisville, has the same provision in its agreement.

A local of the steelworkers in a New Jersey plant making paper cups claimed that management had no right, without union consent, to make changes in the stamping operation which eliminated one girl from each press. Management contended that there was nothing in the agreement prohibiting it from making technological changes. Management was willing to pay five cents an hour more on the new job, but the union insisted that this amount was inadequate. Management agreed to arbitrate the amount of the increase, but declined to submit to arbitration its right to make technological changes. When the union tried to argue the latter question before the arbitrator, the company refused to discuss the point and said that it would not observe the decision if the arbitrator ruled on the point. The arbitrator did not rule on the point and held that the five-cent increase offered by the company for the changed job was adequate.

If the use of the new equipment or process requires new rates or changes in seniority rules, the union may block the installation by refusing to negotiate on them. The men's clothing workers' union in the Boston market has resisted the introduction of section work and the replacement of some hand operations by machine operations by refusing to agree to rates and, in some cases, where the leaders have agreed to new rates, by wildcat strikes. The railway clerks on a western railroad recently blocked (for the time being at least) the plans of the management for centralization of data processing by demanding the right to determine just what work could be put on machines and by demanding unrelated rule changes.[10]

In some situations the union may resort to contract violations to block technological changes—especially if it is militant as a matter of policy or if the employer's behavior has been arbitrary. The union may encourage its members to refuse to handle the new process or to refuse to do overtime. Organized refusals to accept job assignments or do overtime are a violation of the terms and the spirit of most agreements—even of agreements that give workmen as individuals the right to do these things. However, the employer may be unwilling to arouse the antagonism that would be created by his imposing discipline to assert his rights.[11]

Policy of Competition

Sometimes unions seek to meet a technological change by actively trying to compete with it either by pushing an old method or by encouraging the use of an alternative one. The policy of competition is, of course, a form of the policy of opposition, but it is convenient to consider it separately. The policy of competition is pursued when there are some kinds of work on which the new process has little superiority or on which the new process is less costly but the old process produces superior quality. An example are the efforts of the lathers' and plasterers' unions, in cooperation with their contractors, in a few cities to advertise the alleged deficiencies of dry wall.[12] The Typographical Union is said to be making some effort to compete with the teletypesetter by encouraging the use of the Brewer key-

[10] In this case the union may have hurt itself because the management shifted its efforts to streamlining data processing on a decentralized basis. This was done within the framework of the existing agreement, which does not provide special protection for those adversely affected.

[11] A dangerous amount of emotion may be aroused if the workers become convinced that the employer is trying to monopolize the gains of a technological change by insisting that the men do the work at unreasonably low rates.

[12] William Haber and Harold M. Levinson, *Labor Relations and Productivity in the Building Trades* (1956), p. 119. The campaigns seem to have had little or no effect.

board. The Brewer keyboard permits a regular linotype operator to perforate teletypesetter tape without learning a new keyboard.[13] Originally the ITU felt that the linotype could outproduce the teletypesetter, though the reasons why are not clear.[14]

Policy of Encouragement of Technological Change

Unions undertake to encourage technological change fairly frequently. This policy usually is followed when the union is worried about the ability of an industry or a plant to hold its own in competition. Examples are found in the needle trades, the plastering industry, the railroad shops, the trucking industry, and the printing industry. In addition, a few unions encourage technological change because the wage systems under which they operate make this advantageous. The policy of encouragement may be contrasted with the policy of competition. The former involves the union's support of *new* technological methods to help it compete for work; while the latter involves the union's support of *old* methods to help it compete with new methods.

In the needle trades the profit margins of most employers are small, and the mortality rate among enterprises in the industry is high. The unions can do little about the high mortality rates, but in a few cases they have special reasons to help employers who are in trouble. Both the International Ladies' Garment Workers Union and the Amalgamated Clothing Workers have engineering departments. It is not the principal purpose of the union engineering departments to help employers make technological changes, and the departments could not begin to give help to all of the employers who need it. Nevertheless, when the union has special reason to assist the employer, the engineering department may suggest technological changes and may help the employer to make them.[15]

The plasterers' union at the national level has encouraged its locals

[13] "The Brewer Keyboard," *The Bulletin* (May 1955), p. 1. Forty of these Brewer keyboards are in use in 27 cities.

[14] See International Typographical Union, *Officers Reports and Proceedings of the 89th Session* (August 16-22, 1947), pp. 5, 6.

[15] The work of the industrial engineering departments is discussed in Chapter 28 on "Union-Management Cooperation." The uses of the departments are various. They are frequently called in to help improve the methods and operations of employers who have recently been organized by the union. Often these employers are quite inefficient but remained in business prior to being organized by paying less than the union scale. Once they are organized and compelled to pay the union scale, they can survive only by improving their efficiency. The industrial engineering departments help some important

to use the experimental plaster gun in the hope that it will help them hold their own in competition with dry wall.[16] Estimates of the proportion of newly built homes in the low to moderately low price brackets ($15,000 or below) using dry wall vary, but there is agreement that the proportion is half or more.[17] When work is declining, unions are usually unwilling to encourage the use of labor-saving equipment, but the situation of the plasterers' union is exceptional. Boys are reluctant to learn the plasterer's trade—with the result that recent years have seen a chronic shortage of plasterers.[18] Competition between over-the-road trucking and the railroads has led the Central States Conference of Teamsters to encourage the use of sleeper-cab operations. To do this the Conference waived first-in and first-out seniority rules and seniority bidding for sleeper-cab jobs. The sleeper-cab trucks are operated by two men, who alternately work four hours and rest four hours.[19]

In a Kentucky railroad shop the union goes out of its way to encourage improvements in methods in order to bring more work into the shop. The superintendent says that the men are well aware that they are competing for the work against outside contractors and workers elsewhere, either of whom might get it. As a result of the efficiency of the shop, more and more work has been concentrated there. Suggestions are handled by a committee of seven supervisors

---

employers who have operating problems that threaten the job security of the employees —though in industries such as the needle trades where the business mortality rate is high, the industrial engineering departments can help only a small proportion of the marginal firms.

The principal reasons for the industrial engineering departments of the needle trades unions seem to be that the vast majority of the employers are too small to have their own industrial engineering departments and that the unions cannot afford to let piece-rate problems in the various plants be settled by uncontrolled bargaining. This method would create too much unevenness in piece rates and would force some employers out of business.

[16] Haber and Levinson, *Labor Relations and Productivity in the Building Trades*, pp. 113-19.

[17] The same, p. 118.

[18] The number of plasterers, which was 47,700 in 1910 and 70,000 in 1930, was 52,900 in 1940, and 64,400 in 1950. U. S. Bureau of Apprenticeship, *The Skilled Labor Force* Technical Bulletin No. T—140 (April 1954), p. 15.

[19] The reference was specifically to the Los Angeles to Chicago run and the Los Angeles to North Bergen (N.J.) run. Under the current Central States over-the-road contract, two-man operations cannot be used on runs of less than 340 miles with a 680-mile round trip. Furthermore, sleeper cabs cannot be used on the same route where an employer has established relay or through runs unless to move an overflow or unusual freight load.

and seven local craft chairmen, which meets every week to consider suggestions and to make recommendations to the shop superintendent.

The rivalry between letterpress printing and offset printing has led both the pressmen's union and the lithographers' union to encourage technological change. The printing pressmen have encouraged their employers to add offset equipment in order to meet the competition of the lithographers, and the lithographers have offered to join with their employers in encouraging technological research. Early in 1958 the lithographers named a director of technology to consult with manufacturers on how new machinery and processes could be brought into the industry. Behind this action is the desire of the lithographers to compete with the printing pressmen for jobs on the new equipment. The number of so-called "combination" shops, that is shops doing both letterpress and offset work, has been growing rapidly—from about 3,700 in 1951 to 8,800 in 1956. Most of this growth resulted from the acquisition of offset equipment by letterpress shops where the pressmen are already established. The pressmen in many cases have smaller manning crews and lower wage scales than do the lithographers.

Where the compensation of the employees is related to the profits of the company or to the efficiency of operations, the unions are likely to encourage technological change. In a prosperous New England textile company a profit-sharing plan led the union to encourage the employer to buy specially designed looms from Germany. At the suggestion of the union president, one of the best loom fixers was sent to Germany to help design the loom. The union president admitted that work assignments on the new looms would be larger, but he added that with the new looms the company "would be able to beat the pants off of their competition." Business had been expanding, and the union president thought that the released workers could be absorbed without difficulty.

The various unions in shops operating under the Scanlon Plan (discussed in Chapter 28) show great initiative in encouraging technological changes and other improvements. In these cases the men increase their earnings by cutting payrolls below a given percentage of sales since most of the gains (usually three-fourths) go to the workers in the form of a bonus.

Sometimes a union accepts a technological change willingly without asking for special conditions because the change helps the union deal with certain problems—or so the union leaders believe. The union may not go out of its way to encourage the change, but it may be quite ready to negotiate conditions favorable to the operation of the new equipment. Hence union policy may be considered a form of encouragement of the change. An example is the policy of the Central States Conference of Teamsters toward the "piggybacking" operations of railroads. The conference has been willing to negotiate contracts to handle trucks in connection with "piggybacking" because the leaders believed that the "piggybacking" would divert traffic from "gypsies," owner-operated trucks that undercut union truckers. The union trucker who seeks to avoid having idle equipment frequently has excess freight as the result of fluctuations in shipments. This excess freight is usually subcontracted to gypsies. By allowing it to be "piggybacked," the union deprives the gypsies of an important source of income.

The teamsters' union saw an opportunity to gain members by encouraging the McLean interests in an experiment of hauling trucks between the North and the South by specially built vessels— "fishbacking." The company agreed to accept for shipment only union-driven trucks and to permit trucks to be delivered to their destination only by teamster union drivers.[20]

The Glass Bottle Blowers' Association at its convention in 1957 passed a resolution that its officers and members "continue to support and further emphasize the need for new or expanded capital improvement programs, thus protecting our job opportunities and preserving the position of our industry in our expanding economy."

[20] Each of the eight ships intended to operate between Gulf ports and the East is to have a capacity of 200 trailers. *Business Week* (November 9, 1957), pp. 104-08, reports the following:

Lift-on—lift-off by dockside cranes has been used for boxcars (sea train) for a number of years. McLean, whose Pan-Atlantic Steamship subsidiary was supported by Hoffa, has used a more flexible system with cranes on board the ship, and with truck trailers as the basic shipping container. Cargo can be loaded for 20 cents a ton, as compared to $4-$5 a ton with palletized cargo. Apparently, the longshoremen maintain the minimum crew size. ("The cranes can completely unload and reload a full cargo in 8 to 10 hours with only two 15-man longshore crews working a bit longer than one shift.") On the other hand, at maximum efficiency, "it will be a day or two slower than over-the-road transportation. To balance this, it will be able to charge between 5 per cent and 25 per cent less for the haul, depending on the type of cargo." McLean's pricing policy does not seem so aggressive as to drive out road transport in view of the disadvantage of slowness. However, prices may be cut further as the operation expands. (Pan Atlantic . . . six-ship fleet should gross . . . almost as much as the entire East Coast Gulf shipping industry grosses now.)

In a strong editorial President Minton of the union explained why the failure of some companies in the industry to recognize the need for technological improvement jeopardized the employment opportunities of the union's members.[21]

An interesting example of union encouragement of technological change is furnished by the International Longshoremen's and Warehousemen's Union of San Francisco in connection with the introduction of new methods of cargo handling, particularly through large containers. The union is favorably disposed toward the changes because it believes that they will help it hold work and also recover work that has been lost to other carriers. But the union wants to know what gain in productivity occurs (which involves the unsolved problems of measuring the output of the port), and it has the problem of how to distribute its share of the gains among union members without distorting the hourly wages of longshoremen in comparison with rates paid other workers of comparable skill in the industry.

In August 1959, as part of a Memorandum of Understanding, the Pacific Maritime Association and the union adopted the following section on the subject of mechanization:

> Mechanization and the utilization of labor saving devices have been a subject of discussion between the parties since 1957. During the course of the 1959 negotiations the following items were agreed to on this subject.
>
> To allow a certain amount of time (not more than one year) for the parties to further study and gain factual experience:
>
> (1) of actual changes made by labor saving machinery, changed methods of operation, or proposed changes in working rules and contract restrictions, resulting in reduced manpower or manhours with the same or greater productivity for an operation;
>
> (2) of savings to the employer because of such changes;
>
> (3) of a proper share of such savings to be funded as hereinafter provided; and
>
> (4) of the manner of distributing such fund to the fully registered work force:
>
> A) PMA proposes to create a coastwise fund for the fully registered work force, through contributions by the Employers to be accumulated during the first ensuing contract year, in the amount of one million five hundred thousand dollars. This amount, in addition to "buying time" for necessary study and experience, represents a recognition by the Employers that savings accrue as a result of mechanization and changed methods of operation, and a recognition by the Union that no addi-

---

[21] *Glass Horizons* (December 1957), pp. 14-16.

tional payment is due for changes made or to be made prior to June 15, 1960. This payment shall constitute a part of the consideration for renewal of the contract, and shall be distributed to the fully registered work force in a manner to be determined. (Tax and legal problems to be resolved.)

B) It is the purpose and intent of the parties, during the course and as the result of this study period, to achieve and meet the following aims and objectives:

1. To guarantee the fully registered work force a share in the savings effected by labor saving machinery, changed methods of operation, or changes in working rules and contract restrictions resulting in reduced manpower or manhours with the same or greater productivity for an operation.

2. To maintain the 1958 fully registered work force, with allowance for normal attrition.

3. To create a coastwise fund for that work force through contributions by the Employers, such contributions to come from savings described in paragraph B) 1. hereof.

4. To provide that this fund will be separate from contractual wages, pensions, welfare and vacations.

5. To guarantee the PMA the right to make changes, and remove restrictions along with protection against reprisals for making such changes, and enforcement under the contract of such changes if and when made.

During the ensuing year, in addition to making of such study, the following agreements shall be in effect:

    a. PMA will accumulate the one million five hundred thousand dollar fund as provided in A) hereof.

    b. PMA shall be free to make such changes as are deemed necessary under Section 14 of the present Longshore contract, and Section 25 of the present Clerks' contract, restricted however by the observance of rules prohibiting individual speed-up and unsafe operations. The load agreement shall continue.

Except for changes in operations made hereafter by introducing labor saving devices in addition to those already used and practiced by him in the past, the Employer shall not invoke the provisions of Section 14 of the Longshore Agreement or Section 25 of the Clerks' Master Agreement during the ensuing year. Nor shall the Employer seek a reduction of gang sizes or number of clerks, elimination of multiple handling, or other existing contract or working rule restrictions with relation to operations now existing, except during future annual review negotiations or by mutual agreement.

    c. The parties will continue negotiations on the matters outlined in this proposal for a period of not to exceed one year for the purpose of determining a basis for converting the above fund and Employer contributions thereto to a continuing basis which will meet the aims and objectives set forth herein. Such negotiations shall not exclude tonnage taxes, manhour assessments, or any other basis of conversion, nor exclude conversion of present contributions for welfare, pensions and vacancies.

d. The parties shall continue to operate in accordance with the terms of the contract and working rules, with mutual agreement against reprisals and for enforcement of the contracts, working rules, and the provisions of this agreement.

Policy of Adjustment to Technological Change

The essence of the policy of adjustment to technological change is an effort by the union to control the use of the new equipment, process, or materials. Even if the technological change presents no special opportunities or problems to the union, some negotiations over conditions of employment may occur. If there is a job evaluation plan in the plant, the new jobs will have to be evaluated and slotted into the job evaluation schemes. Agreements on rate of pay may be necessary, and in some cases standards of production will have to be set.

Our concern with the policy of adjustment is not with the normal and almost routine negotiations that accompany technological changes. Rather it is with the efforts of unions to deal with extraordinary opportunities or special problems presented by technological changes. Technological changes produce opportunities for unions when they bring great increases in productivity. In such cases the union may have an opportunity to gain wage increases on new jobs. Problems are produced, of course, when large numbers of men are displaced or the skill required is changed. In such cases the union may want to bargain over what will be done to minimize the adverse effect on some workers. Since no two technological changes are alike, implementing the policy of adjustment means negotiating tailor-made agreements on a wide variety of issues such as, who is to do the work; what will be the rate of pay; what is to be done about the displaced workers; will they be given severance pay or special compensation? In a few cases the union may threaten a policy of opposition unless the employer agrees to certain minimum conditions, but as a rule opposition is not a feasible alternative to the policy of adjustment.

The form a policy of adjustment takes depends on the objectives sought by the union and on conditions in the particular plant or industry.

CASES IN WHICH THE PRINCIPAL ISSUE IS WHO SHALL DO THE WORK. This question arises in any of four principal kinds of situations:

(1) When technological change alters significantly the kind of skill or responsibility required without a marked reduction in the degree of skill and responsibility—as in types 10, 11, 13, 14, 16, or 17 in the table on page 348.

(2) When technological change creates seniority problems by transferring the work from one seniority unit to another.

(3) When technological change makes reorganization of the work desirable.

(4) When technological change greatly reduces the degree of skill or responsibility required, as in types 3, 6, 9, 12, 15, or 18.

(1) When a technological change alters the *kind* of skill needed (without diminishing the general *level* of skill or responsibility needed), other crafts that have the skill needed on the new process may claim the work. But the craft that originally did the work may also claim the right to operate the new process. For example, the introduction or proposed introduction of teletypesetters and the photo-composition machine into composing rooms has set off disputes between the Typographical Union and the employers, between the Typographical Union and photoengravers and the pressmen, and between the pressmen and the lithographers. The Typographical Union claims jurisdiction over all composition regardless of the process. The dispute is over where composition ends and other processes begin. The claims of the locals of the Typographical Union have varied from city to city, but they involved disputes over who should handle the products emanating from the photo-composition machines. Prolonged negotiations in various cities failed to produce settlements, and as a result employers were operating without signing contracts.

At its convention in 1955 the Typographical Union amended Article VII of its general laws pertaining to machines to make clear the extent of its jurisdictional claims. To enforce its jurisdictional claim the union established a new process training center at union headquarters in Indianapolis to train instructors in the new processes for local training centers.

Controversy developed between the pilots' union and the flight engineers as to whether the third man in the crew should be a pilot or a flight engineer. The flight engineers struck the United Air Lines in 1955 over this issue. The pilots ignored the engineers' picket lines and helped the company win the strike. Strikes by the flight engineers on Eastern Airlines and by the pilots on American Airlines were settled by agreements to add a fourth man to jet crews—making a crew of three pilots and a flight engineer.[22]

In the case of multi-craft unions, technological changes may produce severe disputes even within the union. The introduction of new types of presses in the printing industry has led to contests among different groups in the Printing Pressmen's Union for jobs. The introduction of the web press into the newspaper industry in the nineties and into the book and job industry later produced claims for jobs on the new presses from the newspaper pressmen, from the pressmen in the book and job industry, whose jobs on the flatbeds were dwindling, and from the feeders and assistants, who claimed the helpers' jobs on the new presses.[23]

Claiming jurisdiction over certain work does not get it for the union unless the union can supply men who are able to do the work. Hence, when technological developments change the *kind* of skill required (as in technological changes of types 10, 11, 13, 14, 16, or 17), the union may set up schools to give members an opportunity to learn how to operate the new equipment. The pressmen's union maintains such a school at Pressmen's Home, Tennessee. The training programs of the Typographical Union has been mentioned, and it was pointed out in Chapter 4 that the electricians, the boilermakers, and the plumbers have all established classes for journeymen members to learn the latest techniques.

(2) Technological changes may transfer work from one seniority

[22] British Overseas Air Corporation operates jets with a crew of four—captain, co-pilot, navigator, and flight engineer officer. British European Airways began operating Comets in April 1960, with a crew of three—captain, second pilot, and third pilot. All three will be trained to operate the service panel.

[23] An excellent account of these contests is given by Elizabeth Faulkner Baker in her *Printers and Technology* (1957), Chap. XI, "Union Status of Webpress Printers."

district to another. For example, the introduction of centralized electronic data processing equipment in the accounting and statistical departments of railroad operations not only diminishes the number of clerical jobs, but transfers jobs from line of road to large central offices. This means that the work is transferred from some seniority districts to others, and the problem of seniority rights of the workers involved may become very complicated. This sort of problem is discussed in Chapter 6 on "Work-Sharing and Layoff Systems."

Sometimes technological change produces such serious internal conflicts that the union is unable to take a position. This was the case with a union in a paper company that was building a large new pulp mill to take over the work done by two smaller mills. The management proposed a number of different plans for determining who was to work in the new mill, which, because of its efficiency, would require a considerably smaller force than the two old mills. The union was unwilling to agree to any of these plans. Furthermore, the split among union members was so serious that the union was unwilling and unable to propose a plan of its own. The various plans were finally submitted to an arbitrator, who decided the issue.

(3) There are technological changes that make reorganization of the work desirable. The repairing of various kinds of specialized equipment can frequently be done best by men who are skilled craftsmen, who become familiar with the new equipment, and who do not confine their work rigidly within traditional craft lines. In the automobile, oil, and other industries, management wants to train maintenance men in a diversity of skills. For example, "automation equipment repairman," is a job title used by one automobile company. Attempts to create all-round or specialized mechanics have met with considerable opposition because of traditional craft distinctions. This problem is far from resolved in American industry and is of increasing importance.

(4) Technological changes that greatly reduce the degree of skill or responsibility required present a problem for the union for which there is usually no satisfactory solution. Shall the union try to force employers to use skilled workers at journeymen rates on jobs that do not require their skill? Or shall it consent to rates on the new jobs that are commensurate with the new skill needed and try to persuade employers to man these jobs with journeymen and persuade

journeymen to accept them? Or shall the employer use workers of much less skill than journeymen at below the journeyman rate and try to bring them into the union?

None of the three alternatives is practicable or satisfactory from the union's point of view. If the new work must be done in shops that the union controls, the union may force the employer to use journeymen on it. But if the work can be done outside the shop, the union's effort to compel payment of the journeyman's scale will simply force the work out of the union shops—as the Typographical Union found when it demanded the compositor's scale for operators of justifying typewriters. Since the machines can be operated by women, who earn far less than compositors, the union's demand for control of the work caused much of it to go to nonunion shops.

The second alternative, having the work done by journeymen at less than the journeyman's scale, simply is impracticable; journeymen would not accept the jobs. The third alternative, letting the work be done by workers of less skill than those used on the old process and trying to bring them into the union, is feasible provided it is an industrial union and is prepared as a matter of union policy to take all occupations regardless of skill. But this alternative is not satisfactory to craft unions because admitting semi-skilled or un-skilled workers would introduce a new element into the union. Skilled workers are not likely to be willing to grant a voice in their affairs to semi-skilled or unskilled workers.

The decision of the Typographical Union to demand that the justifying typewriter be operated by journeymen compositors at journeymen's rates meant in effect that the union was content not to seek control of most of these jobs. For, as the union undoubtedly knew, its policy meant that union members would not hold the jobs.

The lithographers' union, confronted with a similar problem (a technological change of type 3), reached the same result by a different method. The question confronting the lithographers was whether to assert jurisdiction over semi-skilled and unskilled workers manufac-turing pre-sensitized plates in the Minnesota Mining and Manufac-turing Company. The union is nominally an industrial one, but as a matter of fact it is composed in the main of skilled workers and at several of the largest lithographing plants has given up jurisdiction of the unskilled workers. At any rate, the convention in 1955 refused to assert jurisdiction over the plate workers at Minnesota Mining and

Manufacturing. To have done so would have involved the lithographers in jurisdictional disputes with the chemical workers. In addition, as Vice President Martin Grayson said: ". . . if you want to go into organizing that type of coating operators, I believe you have to change the basic characteristics of your organization."[24]

CASES IN WHICH THE UNION IS PRINCIPALLY INTERESTED IN WAGE ADJUSTMENTS. If the technological change increases the degree of skill required or at least does not diminish the degree of skill (as in changes of types 1, 2, 4, 5, 7, 8, 10, 11, 13, 14, 16, and 17), the union may see an opportunity for wage increases for its members. In these cases the policy of adjustment will take the form, in part at least, of negotiations over wages. The union is in a particularly strong position to push the wage issue in changes of types 1 and 10, which increase both the degree of skill required and the number of jobs, and it is also in a strong bargaining position over wages when the skill requirements are not changed but the number of jobs is increased (types 2 and 11), or when skill is increased and the number of jobs changed but little (types 4 and 13). But even when there is little or no change in the degree of skill required and little or no change in the number of jobs, the union is in a moderately good position to bargain over wages because the technological change increases productivity.

A few unions (such as the airplane pilots and the locomotive engineers) expect technological changes to raise the productivity of their members and have constructed their wage scales so that faster and larger planes and more powerful locomotives will automatically produce wage increases. In other cases it is necessary for the union to negotiate new rates for new jobs.

If the new jobs require greater skill or responsibility, the union may be content to negotiate new rates to provide proper compensation for the additional skill and responsibility. But if the technological change saves the employer substantial amounts without raising the skill or responsibility required, the union will try to get some of the gains for the workers on the new job even though the new rates raise them relative to other workers of similar skill and responsibility.

In a new automated stamping plant of an automobile company, the

[24] Amalgamated Lithographers of America, *Proceedings of the Thirteenth Convention* (1955), p. 146.

union succeeded in negotiating an extra five cents an hour for the heavy press operators. Its position was: "We're all for automation, but we want you guys to pay." No change in the job duties required the change in pay, but the management wanted to establish a new automation maintenance department, in which traditional craft lines would not be observed. The bargain was that the union would accept the automation maintenance department, and the company would give a five-cent increase to heavy press operators.[25]

The pulp and sulphite workers find that technological changes usually do not reduce the number of people in the mill but often increase the skill needed by the workers. Since the union generally faces no displacement problem, it concentrates on trying to make technological changes yield wage increases. In order to get these increases the union encourages the creation of new and specialized classifications in connection with the technological changes.

When a technological change reduces the skill required on the operation, the union may strive hard to get an agreement that men operating new equipment requiring less skill than old processes shall receive the same rates as workers on old processes. Thus, the New England bakery workers tried unsuccessfully several years ago to get an agreement that men displaced by machines would continue to get their old rates even if transferred to lower-paying jobs.

A strike occurred in 1957 in the Westclox Division of the General Time Corporation over the refusal of the company to arbitrate issues arising from changes that made unnecessary the "escapers," who make final adjustments on watches and clocks at the end of the assembly process. The company offered to place the "escapers" at new jobs at a lower salary, paying them for six months one-half the difference between the rates on their old jobs and the new jobs; but the union demanded that the workers be paid their old rate while working on the new jobs.[26]

When a company introduces a technological change that obviously means large savings to the enterprise, it is difficult for management to refuse to share the gains. The resulting injury to morale can be costly. But if technological changes are permitted to raise substantially the wages of the workers immediately affected, regardless of the

---

[25] In the new department the craftsmen kept their old craft titles, but they did not observe craft lines rigidly in doing repair work. Chapter 9, "Work Assignment and Jurisdiction," describes this situation in some detail.

[26] *Wall Street Journal* (July 23, 1957), p. 14.

effect of technology on skill or responsibility, wage inequities will be created.[27] Revolutionary changes are occurring because of the handling of cargo on the waterfront in enormous aluminum containers.[28] Use of the huge boxes has been retarded by opposition of the longshoremen on the East Coast. In the 1959 New York negotiations with the longshoremen it was agreed to keep the same crew size (20 men and a foreman) and allow free use of containers. However, the parties agreed to arbitrate the matter of the payment to be made for loss of employment caused by containers. (This loss takes the form of fewer crews and fewer extras.) As of September 1960 no arbitration decision had been rendered. On the Pacific Coast the International Longshoremen's and Warehousemen's Union proposes to deal with the tendency of the containers and other technological changes to introduce inequities into the wage structure by pooling the gains from more efficient methods of cargo handling. The fund would be for the benefit of qualified registered men of all ports, and contributions would come from employers on the basis of their individual gains. The scheme requires the development of objective measures of improved output applicable to individual operations.

CASES OF DISPLACEMENT OF UNION MEMBERS BY NEW TECHNIQUES. A principal concern of the Brotherhood of Railway Clerks is that the introduction of electronic data processing equipment on the railways shall not *immediately* affect the number of persons employed. The union does not try to make work permanently by requiring an excessive complement of men. Rather, its position is that the necessary reduction of forces should come from resignation, retirement, death, or discharge for cause and that special provision should be made for employees furloughed as a result of technological changes. The introduction of electronic data processing equipment requires new jobs

---

[27] Chapter 19, "Evaluated Wage Structures," discusses the upward bias in wage structures introduced by technological changes even under job evaluation plans and the resulting need after a period of years for extensive revisions of job evaluation plans.

[28] The big boxes are 10 feet 6 inches long, 7 feet 6 inches wide, and 7 feet 4 inches high. The boxes are loaded into the ships' holds by means of the vessels' cargo booms and winches. They are used to ship high value goods, especially consumer goods. Not only do the containers save much labor, but they prevent breakage and pilferage and lead to drastic cuts in insurance rates. The United Cargo Corporation, which had been using the boxes on shipments to South Africa, in the summer of 1959 extended the service to Europe. In shipments averaging $350,000 each month, the company had not a single claim for loss from pilferage, damage, or contamination.

with new duties, and these raise questions of the rate of pay, the opportunity of qualified employees to learn the new jobs, and above all, the determination of which employees shall be entitled to the new jobs—in other words, how the new jobs will affect seniority rights of the members. Union acceptance of a proposed change depends on its success in negotiating agreements on accompanying problems.

CASES IN WHICH THE UNION WANTS TO INCREASE THE NUMBER OF JOBS ON THE NEW PROCESS. There are various possible reasons for this. The union's interest may be to give more employment to the displaced persons. But if the jobs on the new technique are attractive, possibly because they are well paid or because they are clean and easy, their very attractiveness may spur the union to try to make as many of them as possible. Indeed, make-work rules, as we have seen in Chapter 11, are likely to spring up in any situation where the jobs are unusually attractive. The experience of Hollywood is an example. The employer who pays above the market risks pressure from the union for make-work rules. But the strongest pressure for making the new technique produce as many jobs as possible occurs when the new process or new apparatus simultaneously makes jobs more attractive but diminishes their number. Introduction of the diesel made the fireman's job far more attractive because it is cleaner and the work is less onerous. At the same time, the diesel and other factors decreased the number of firemen's jobs. Hence, the union, composed of white workers, is trying to deprive Negro firemen of their jobs.

The interest of the union in seeing that the new technique provides the maximum possible number of jobs may be stimulated by decreasing employment in the industry or occupation. The Brotherhood of Maintenance of Way Employees has had to face the tendency of extensive technological change to accelerate the loss of jobs coming from other causes, such as the abandonment of branch lines and the use of single tracks with central traffic control instead of double tracks or double tracks with central traffic control in place of three or four tracks. In the last thirty years the number of employees engaged in maintenance-of-way work has been reduced by more than half. The union has considered various methods of dealing with the problem but has put none of them into effect. An employment stabilization movement in May 1950 proposed, among other things, agreements by the railroads that the average number of employees in each major class of maintenance-of-way work in each calendar year after 1950 would not fall below the number required to maintain the same ratio to the total of all employees of the carrier as prevailed on the average during the ten years 1940 to 1949.[29] In 1955 the convention of Maintenance of Way Employees went on record in favor of a shorter work week with reduction of weekly earnings to alleviate unemployment.[30] In January 1956, the Grand Lodge and system officers of the union authorized an independent analysis by economists of the job instability faced by its membership.[31] The result was an able and searching analysis of the employment problem in maintenance-of-way work done under the direction of Professor William Haber and published by the Brotherhood.[32]

CASES WHERE THE UNION HELPS DISPLACED WORKERS FIND OTHER EMPLOYMENT. If the amount of displacement is uncertain and if there is a good chance that it will be small because the industry is a growing one, the main concern of the union may be to help displaced workers find other jobs, and to obtain severance pay for them. The strike of over 1,300 technicians, camera men, radio and television engineers, all members of the International Brotherhood of Electrical Workers, against the Columbia Broadcasting System in New York, Chicago, Los Angeles, and four other major cities in April 1958 is an illustration. The principal issue in the strike was provision of some job security for the men expected to be displaced by the introduction of "video tape" in place of the TV tapes.[33] The strike was settled after twelve days with provisions for severance pay—up to eight weeks' pay for temporary economic layoff for workers with five years' service and thirteen weeks' pay for anyone, no matter how short the term of service, for layoff or dismissal due to the automated processes.[34]

[29] Brotherhood of Maintenance of Way Employees, "Employment Stabilization Movement, 1950, Handbook of Conference Material for Use of General Chairmen," pp. 16 and 17 (mimeo.).

[30] Brotherhood of Maintenance of Way Employees, *Proceedings of the 32nd Regular Convention* (June 1955), p. 800.

[31] Brotherhood of Maintenance of Way Employees, *Proceedings of the Meeting of Grand Lodge and System Officers* (January 5-7, 1956), pp. 73-88.

[32] The title of the study is *Maintenance of Way Work on United States Railroads.*

[33] The tape recording of moving images that can be instantly played back eliminates the slow and costly process of developing and printing films. The scene caught by the camera and the accompanying sound are broken down into electronic components and registered on a magnetic tape. On playback the electronic components re-create the original scene and sound.

[34] The growing significance of severance pay plans is discussed in Chapter 16.

Consequences of Union Policies Toward Technological Change

Going back in union history one can find a few cases where unions were destroyed largely because they were unable or unwilling to adapt themselves to technological changes. The window glass workers' union, which ceased to exist about 1928, is the principal example. However, no national union in recent years has destroyed itself fighting technological change.

Nor is there record of any union in recent years being able to prevent technological change by opposing it—though many unions have retarded certain changes temporarily and locally. Union wage policies appear to have been partly responsible for stimulating technological change under some circumstances and may have affected the distribution of gains. Three principal effects have been produced by union policies toward technological changes:

(1) They have tended to give to the holders of jobs on the new machines or new processes somewhat higher wages relative to other workers in the same plant—in other words, they have tended to introduce distortions in the wage structure of the plant.

(2) They have tended to a slight extent to cause the new techniques to be operated with excessive crews and under make-work rules.

(3) They have considerably eased the hardship of displacement, partly by forcing managements to do advance planning in the introduction of technological changes, partly by encouraging more gradual introduction of technological changes and partly by giving displaced workmen an opportunity to qualify for other jobs.

13 / *Pension Plans*

THE DISCUSSION of pension plans has been divided into three parts: (1) the impact of unions and collective bargaining on the establishment, the revision, and the characteristics of plans, (2) negotiation issues, and (3) administrative problems.[1]

Impact of Unions and Collective Bargaining

Unions and collective bargaining have had an important influence on the establishment and spread of pension plans, although social and economic trends and conditions, management policies, and government actions have also been significant.

Establishment of Plans

The pioneer plans were initiated by companies. A few hundred plans, covering about four million employees, were in existence in 1940,[2] and were created by leading companies as an important element in the expanding field of personnel and employee relations. Unions were tardy even in endorsing Social Security. It was not until 1932 that President William Green of the AFL gave up his opposition to state intervention to create unemployment compensation and old-age pensions. Also industry pension plans had become associated in union thinking with employer paternalism and hence were subject to suspicion. The discretionary and nonfunded character of early plans frequently warranted criticism. Furthermore, unions faced

[1] Particular reference within the extensive pension literature is made to John J. Corson and John W. McConnell in *Economic Needs of Older People* (1956), Chaps. 9, 10, and 11.

[2] Alfred M. Skolnik and Joseph Zisman, "Growth in Employee–Benefit Plans," *Social Security Bulletin* (March 1958), p. 10.

problems with their own benefit programs.[3] Union pension plans were particularly hard hit in the years 1929-32, the Iron Workers, Locomotive Engineers, Granite Cutters, Electrical Workers, and others having had severe financial problems with their plans.[4]

The burst of pension plans during World War II increased coverage from 3.8 million in 1940 to 5.9 million in 1945.[5] The immediate causes of this rapid growth were clarification of the tax status of funded plans, war-time financial prosperity, war-time taxes, and war-time stabilization regulations.

The 1942 Internal Revenue Code, specifically section 165 (a) and related provisions, clarified the right of companies to deduct for tax purposes contributions to trust funds for plans that qualify under Treasury Department regulations. The new tax law encouraged, and to some extent required, soundly financed plans. The war, with its very high tax rates and financial prosperity, offered employers a chance to start at government expense on funding past service, the cost dimension of pensions that most troubled employers. War conditions and war taxes stimulated the introduction of pension plans to a considerable extent. Pension costs and funding are such that, if an employer felt that sooner or later a pension plan would be created, he was likely to introduce it at once if the immediate cost increase could be absorbed. Also Treasury-approved plans were not curtailed by War Labor Board regulations. Along with other employee benefits, pension plans were encouraged since general wage increases were difficult to obtain.[6]

Behind the immediate causes of this sudden increase in plans were: (1) the community-wide desire for security growing out of the depression and related changes in political, social, and economic outlook, (2) the growing proportion of older workers in the labor force, (3) the interest in security aroused by the passage of the Social Security Act, as well as the direct assistance it provided and its limitations in the size of payments (particularly for executives), (4) the significant growth and spread of the personnel point of view

[3] A brief review of union benefit plans is to be found in Abraham Weiss, "Union Welfare Plans," in *The House of Labor,* Hardman and Neufeld, eds. (1951), Chap. 22.
[4] Murray Webb Latimer, *Trade Union Pension Systems* (1932), Chap. V.
[5] Skolnik and Zisman, "Growth in Employee–Benefit Plans," p. 10.
[6] As Corson and McConnell point out *(Economic Needs of Older People,* p. 291), some authorities do not attribute more than minor influence in the expanded number of plans to the 1942 Revenue Code provisions and excess-profits taxes, but it is difficult to believe that tax considerations were not decidedly important within the totality of war-time influences. ·

within industry, partially a response to the union movement, and (5) the indirect influence of unions discussed below.

Though unions were not very active in seeking pension plans during the war, they were indirectly magnifying the pension problem for employers. Since seniority was widely accepted as the basic criterion in layoff procedures, and discharge could be only for cause, employers were faced with the dilemma of what to do with older employees. They could not be eased out under the watchful eye of the union, nor were there enough "elevator jobs" for all the older workers. Except for new or rapidly growing companies, the prospect was for a progressive rise in the average age of the employee group. As a result there was the increasing problem of those older employees whose work fell modestly short of standards in both quality and quantity because of their physical impairments. Pensions offered a practical exit from employment and protected efficiency since they tended to counter the trend toward a rising average age.

Employers looked with favor on pension plans since they help maintain efficiency, in addition to their benefits from a humanitarian point of view. While concerned with the cost of pensions, managements commonly expressed the view that they were a "good idea." An added indirect influence was the fact that many companies, in view of the low maximum pensions provided under Social Security, had created pension plans primarily for executives. To be nondiscriminatory under tax regulations executive plans covered all salaried employees, or all employees earning in excess of the maximum level applicable to taxes and benefits under Social Security. As may now be the case with major medical plans, some companies created a double standard by not extending company pensions to blue collar workers. Such a double standard does not survive easily under collective bargaining.

Major direct union influence began in the period 1945 to 1950, during which pension coverage increased from 5.9 to 9.0 million.[7] The pension dispute in the coal industry, the fact-finding report and strike in steel, and pension negotiations in the automobile and other major industries during this period involved considerable social strain, but culminated in very significant, negotiated pattern plans. Negotiated plans attained a leading position in the economy.

While both the International Ladies' Garment Workers and the Amalgamated Clothing Workers negotiated pension plans prior to the United Mine Workers, it was the negotiation in 1946 between

[7] Skolnik and Zisman, "Growth in Employee–Benefit Plans." p. 10.

John L. Lewis and E. J. Krug, negotiating for the government, that put the unions dramatically in the forefront of the pension picture. The miners' plan providing $100 a month plus Social Security, with the union tax on coal, challenged all the unions. As unions sought negotiated pensions, a major dispute developed over the legal question as to whether employers, if requested, were required by law to bargain on the pension issue. The National Labor Relations Board decision in the Inland Steel case, upheld by the United States Supreme Court in 1949, brought pensions within the scope of compulsory bargaining.

A dramatic event in 1949 was the presidential fact-finding board's report on steel. The board recommended against a wage increase, but strongly endorsed pension and welfare benefits as appropriate costs of doing business. A noncontributory pension plan was advocated, drawing an analogy between provision for pensions and depreciation reserves. A strike followed, primarily over the issue of employee contributions. While this strike was in progress, Ford and the United Automobile Workers concluded an agreement for a noncontributory pension of $100 per month, including Social Security, for employees with thirty years of service. The year 1949 thus became the pension year, and pattern plans were created in the automobile, steel, rubber, and other industries. Once these pattern plans were established, unions pushed for pensions on a broad front. Coverage grew from 9.0 million in 1950 to 15.2 million in 1956.[8]

One aspect of union influence should be particularly noted. The negotiation by unions of multiemployer plans with joint union-management trustee control brought private pension plan coverage to industries with casual employment and to some industries with many small employers—construction, maritime, printing, clothing, mining, trucking, upholstering, and others.

This development was not easy to foresee, and it remains a limited one. Clark Kerr, speaking with other distinguished individuals at a National Industrial Conference Board conference in New York in November 1949, said: "Pensions, unlike wages and hours, cannot readily be taken from the highways to the byways of collective bargaining."[9] To a remarkable extent, however, unions have succeeded in bringing pensions to the byways. The craft unions, though initially hesitant to endorse the idea of pensions, have been ingenious in pro-

[8] The same.
[9] National Industrial Conference Board, *Handbook on Pensions,* Studies in Personnel Policy, No. 103, p. 84.

moting area, regional, and national plans that bring private coverage to industries, such as those noted above, in which it would be very difficult and expensive for employers to establish plans on an individual company basis.

On the other hand, private pensions have not been brought to all the byways, and this is a significant limitation on their social contribution. Various types of benefit programs were estimated in 1956 to cover the following percentages of the wage and salary labor force:[10]

Life insurance and death benefits	62.8
Accidental death and dismemberment	30.6
Hospitalization	62.8
Surgical	58.6
Medical	40.0
Major medical expense	6.4
Supplementary unemployment benefits	4.1
Temporary disability (including formal sick leave)	51.5
Retirement	31.1

Among major well-established benefit programs the relatively low coverage of pensions is obvious. This is no doubt primarily attributable to their relatively high cost and to the long-term nature and uncertainty of this cost, particularly for small companies, as compared with other benefits. However, pension coverage for union employees is clearly greater than for nonunion. The Bureau of Labor Statistics estimates that slightly over 50 per cent of unionized employees have such coverage.[11] At the end of 1957 about 10 million of the approximately 17 million employees covered by private pensions were unionized. In part the high coverage of union employees is explained by concentration of union membership in large companies, which tend to have pension plans; in part it is attributable to the negotiation of plans with multiemployer associations; and, in part, it reflects the widespread union drive for pensions.

Unions have not been able to carry pensions to all the byways, however. Where unions bargain on an individual company basis, rather than with employer associations, their success is related to size of company. For example, a study made in 1953 of "Pension Plans Negotiated by the UAW-CIO" by J. Perham Stanley indicated that for plants of 1,000 employees and above there were 100 "plans" and

---

[10] Skolnik and Zisman, "Growth in Employee–Benefit Plans," p. 5.
[11] U. S. Bureau of Labor Statistics, *Digest of One-Hundred Selected Pension Plans Under Collective Bargaining, Winter 1957-1958,* Bulletin No. 1232 (May 1958).

88 "no-plans," but for plants with from 100 to 1,000 employees there were 153 "plans" and 907 "no-plans."[12] While coverage among both large and small plants has increased since 1953, the same distribution no doubt remains.

It seems reasonable to conclude that unions have contributed substantially to the rapid spread of pensions. Employers, however, initiated the move toward pensions and cannot be cast in the role of antagonists even though they are concerned about costs. As indicated above, broad social influences are important, as are tax considerations. Further analysis would show differences among industries in the degree to which pensions have developed. Most large companies, union or nonunion, now have plans.

The impact of pension reserves on the economy, while definitely important, is as yet still in its infancy. A report published in *Business Week* showing a projection by Vito Natrella, of the Securities and Exchange Commission, indicates that fund assets will grow from the $25 billion level of 1955 to over $75 billion in 1965.[13] The one-billion-dollar common stock purchases by pension funds in 1957 was equal to about 30 per cent of all new stock issues, and pension funds were the largest net purchasers of common stock in that year. As indicated below, control of pension-fund investment could become a major negotiation issue.

Revision of Plans

Union influence in the revision of pension plans has been particularly significant. Pension plans were revised frequently during the war and immediate postwar years, when union influence was not directly important. These amendments may be followed in the various surveys by Bankers Trust.[14] Revision usually took the form of liberalization of benefits; but they were made with considerable reluctance and only after a considerable lag behind wage and price level changes. The union push for pensions was partially a response to inadequate benefits under established plans and to inadequate Social Security benefits.

Company-designed pension plans did not lend themselves to ade-

---

[12] *Monthly Labor Review* (January 1954), p. 15.
[13] "The Startling Impact of Private Pension Funds," *Business Week* (January 31, 1959), p. 88.
[14] Particularly: *106 Retirement Plans 1944-45* (1946); *289 Retirement Plans* (1948); *A Study of Industrial Retirement Plans* (1950): *A Study of Industrial Retirement Plans* (1953), Bankers Trust Company, New York, N.Y.

quate revision with rising wage levels because they were almost uniformly built upon a percentage benefit formula tied to "career" earnings. Modifications in a limited number of plans based benefits upon "final" earnings, but these final earnings were ten- or five-year averages.[15]

Percentage plans, particularly when based on career earnings, do not work well over a period of rising money wages. A formula that is quite adequate when drawn up may produce totally inadequate benefits in relation to the wage and price level at the time of retirement. It takes relatively few years of steady wage increases to reduce substantially the intended level of benefits. On the other hand, if such plans are revised to correct for low past earnings, they are too high relative to present earnings.

Union influence led to the establishment of the dollar formula for either a minimum pension coupled with a percentage plan or the entire pension. If pension payments are divorced either wholly or in part from past earnings and if revisions are made frequently, retirement income of workers will not decline significantly relative to wages and prices.[16]

On the other hand, a frequently-revised benefit formula does not fit well with traditional attitudes toward funding pensions. According to traditional thinking pensions were earned and funded year by

[15] For those not familiar with pension terminology, a percentage plan operates as follows: For example, a benefit formula may provide a monthly pension of 1 per cent of monthly earnings for each year of credited service. Credited service begins after eligibility requirements are met, which might, for example, be five years of service and age 30. Eligibility thus restricts the maximum possible number of years of pension credit. Eligible years from age 30 to 65 would establish 35 years of credited service. Ignoring the complication of past service, 35 years of credited service calls for a pension of 35 per cent of earnings. If earnings are "career" earnings and wages have been rising for 35 years, 35 per cent of 35-year average earnings (or even a ten- or five-year average) is much less than 35 per cent of earnings in the year of retirement. Percentage plans usually are in addition to, but integrated with, Social Security.

[16] Again for those not familiar with pension terminology, the first dollar formula plans were inclusive of Social Security. A benefit formula might be a pension amount of $4 a month for each year of service to a maximum of $100 a month or to a maximum of 25 years of service. Note that eligibility requirements are not needed since the maximum pension can be limited by a maximum number of years of service and the pension amount is divorced from earnings in particular years. With the disappearance of the Social Security "offset," the dollar amount in the pension formula was correspondingly reduced. Such a dollar formula might be a company pension amount of $2.50 a month per year of service, with or without a maximum, to which Social Security is added. If the dollar formula is used for a minimum pension and is combined with a percentage formula, then the plan becomes more complex. Effective modification of the minimum is, however, very important. If there is a wide spread in earnings among employees, a union may favor use of the dollar formula only as a minimum.

year; and the pension due on retirement is the sum of the pensions earned year by year. A dollar benefit formula revised upward requires additional funds to cover credited service prior to the date of revision. Revision creates a recurring problem of refunding to cover past service. There has not been enough recognition of union influ ence toward continuous revision and the significance of the dollar formula in this process. By forcing a break with tradition on financ ing and promoting the dollar formula, unions have been influential in creating more realistic pensions. Much of the lag has been taken out of adjustment of pensions to rising wages.

The newly-devised five-year pension contracts represented a victory for employers since they kept pensions from being revised every year. However, revision every five years represents a break with past practice. Union influence was responsible for making pensions fluid, and conservative financing must "overfund" a plan to keep it in shape for future revision. Equity investment provides a partial hedge against inflation and the consequent revision of pension plans.

An even greater break with tradition has been the revision of pensions of those already retired. This has been a feature of almost all major pattern negotiations. As one employer remarked, "we now find ourselves bargaining with the union with respect to pensions for those who are no longer in our employ." A fundamental notion of funding a pension is to charge the pension cost against production as the pension is earned. If the employee has already retired, and the pension is revised, funding has truly lost its moorings.

Revisions in the last several years have generally increased the pensions of workers already retired by a smaller amount than pensions of workers to be retired. In the 1958 negotiations with Ford and in subsequent bargaining, the United Automobile Workers agreed not to request pension revision in the future for those already retired. So far as is known, this marks the first time a union has made such an agreement. As pension plans continue in existence, and the number of pensioners grows relative to the number of current employees, revision for those already retired becomes an increasingly serious cost problem. Cost considerations will force a choice between total revision, including those already retired, and revision limited to those to be retired in the future.

There has been very little interest shown in devising a pension formula which provides automatic revision or which could be presumed not to require revision. There are a few pension plans with a cost-of-living escalator clause. The 1957–58 BLS *Digest* reports one such plan between the National Lock Company and the United Automobile Workers. This is a percentage plan with a ten-year average earnings base adjusted by the BLS cost-of-living index. The Retail Clerks signed a contract in 1959 with a thousand California supermarkets for adjustments in pension payments with changes in the consumer price index.[17]

The most interesting deviation from traditional pension plans has been secured by the Air Line Pilots Association. The Board of Directors of the Pilots Association made a special study of pensions in 1952-53 and endorsed a combined program of fixed benefits and variable annuities[18] in roughly equal proportions. Both types of plans, separately or in combination, have been negotiated with most airline companies. A few companies had previously-existing traditional fixed-benefit plans. The pilots also accepted the principle of employee contributions, and under most programs the pilots contribute to both the fixed-benefit and the variable-annuity plans. Most plans provide for retirement at age 60, with special provision for early retirement at age 50 or 45. The fact that pilots must continue to pass rigorous physical examinations limits the usefulness of the usual pension plan since early retirement may be required. It is interesting that the pilots have elected to use variable annuities with approximately 100 per cent equity investment to help meet their particular retirement problem. The Tennessee Valley Authority has also established, with union agreement, an optional and supplementary variable annuity plan, but interest in the variable annuity has not been strong among organized TVA employees.

What course pension revision would have taken in the absence of union influence is speculative. But the pattern of regular revision, the dollar-benefit formula, and the forced breaks with financial tradition lend weight to the opinion that unions have had a decided influence in establishing a policy of frequent pension revision. Their influence on the level of real pension benefits is discussed in the next section.

Characteristics of Plans

Surveys of plans created during the war and up to 1949 show

[17] *Wall Street Journal* (June 23, 1959), p. 12.
[18] The benefit under a variable annuity depends on the value of the pension fund. Appreciation in the value of equity investments increases the amount of the pension.

characteristics which may be attributed in major part to the policy of management.[19] The present characteristics of negotiated plans may be studied in a 1957–58 BLS *Digest*.[20] While the characteristics of negotiated plans cannot be attributed unqualifiedly to unions, collective bargaining has certainly altered these characteristics.

The following aspects of plans will be considered: (1) financing and funding, (2) benefit formula and level, (3) eligibility, (4) retirement policies and dates, and (5) vesting.

FINANCING AND FUNDING. The most significant financing issue relates to employee contributions. Union opinion has been strongly against employee contributions, but many employer-designed plans were also noncontributory. A table in the 1950 Bankers Trust survey (page 11) shows the percentage of noncontributory plans according to year of adoption from 1943 to 1949-50. For the entire period 46 per cent of 333 plans were noncontributory. The proportion of contributory plans increased after the war and constituted 70 per cent of plans adopted in 1947, 67 per cent in 1948, and 65 per cent in 1949. After the war a larger proportion of newly-designed employer plans were contributory.

None of the early negotiated pattern plans were contributory, and of the 100 plans covered in the 1957–58 BLS *Digest* only 14 were contributory. In some of these the contributory feature applied only to a supplementary benefit. Clearly most negotiated plans have been noncontributory. Although 1949 witnessed the steel strike over employee contributions, they ceased to be an issue thereafter.

Employers offer strong arguments for employee contributions. Perhaps the most persuasive of these is that employees will be more appreciative of the cost of increasing benefits if they contribute to the fund. Other arguments in favor of contributions can be made, such as the value of employee savings for those who leave or die; but arguments in favor of employee contributions have been spiked in no small degree by the personal income tax consideration. It is quite possible that the issue of contributions might have taken on major

[19] Bankers Trust Company surveys in 1946, 1948, and 1950 have been used for this purpose. The 1950 survey, *A Study of Industrial Retirement Plans*, contrasts plans adopted by employers, 217 plans covering about 1,500,000 employees, with 11 pattern negotiated plans, also covering about 1,500,000 employees. The 1950 survey is estimated by Bankers Trust to include 35 to 40 per cent of private plan coverage.

[20] *Digest of One-Hundred Selected Pension Plans*, cited in note 11 above. This survey is estimated to cover 3.3 million employees, about one-third of total union coverage under pension plans.

proportions had it not been for the unintended income tax reper-
cussion.[21]

There has been little argument related to the funding issue. There
have been a few instances, such as the Chrysler strike in 1950, where
employers did not want to fund and the union did. Most plans, however, whether designed by employers or negotiated have been funded.
Only six of the *Digest* plans are not funded. Both employers and
unions have overwhelmingly favored a funded plan. Two kinds of
negotiating situations should be distinguished.

In the first type, unions negotiate with particular companies. In
this situation the primary issue is the level of benefits, but all characteristics of the plan are spelled out in the pension agreement. With
the level of benefits already determined, unions have been willing to
accept a provision to the effect that the plan will be funded by the
employer and maintained on an actuarially sound basis. Under this
provision decisions on funding and on investments have been made
by companies. Some companies have funded rapidly, while others
have funded slowly. Different methods of funding produce in effect
different degrees of funding. The companies have decided among
the alternatives presented by the actuaries, and this has not been an
issue between company and union. Appropriate investment policy
for pension reserves has likewise been a company decision, and companies have followed a variety of investment policies. Some unions,
such as the UAW, have voiced a strong desire for joint administration of investment, but to date companies have resisted such demands. This subject will be discussed further under negotiation
issues.

In the second type of situation, where unions bargain with a multiemployer association and establish an area, regional, or national plan
with joint trustee administration, the crucial issue for negotiation is
the rate of employer contribution. If both a contribution rate and a
benefit level are established, one or the other will require adjustment
in the light of experience.[22] With benefits appropriate for a given

---

[21] While employees pay income tax at retirement on pensions from employer contributions, this tax is remote and is not a meaningful offset to the gain from creating
pensions from dollars not reduced by the personal income tax amount.

[22] A traditional distinction among pension plans has been between those with fixed
benefits (uncertain costs) and those with fixed contributions (uncertain benefits). Since
actual costs depend on actual mortality experience, interest earnings, and employee
turnover, it is not possible to fix both contribution rate and benefits. This distinction has
lost much of its original significance because pension revision has become commonplace.

contribution rate to be determined by joint trustees, serious arguments might develop over funding and investment decisions.

While there are a host of questions raised by the use of the union-
management joint trustee device, some of which are discussed in
connection with welfare plans, neither funding nor investment
appears to have created major issues. In the first place, it might be
expected that unions in bargaining or trustee deliberations would
push for an unrealistic level of benefits relative to contribution rate
with resulting inadequate funding. Such was the case when the
welfare fund of the United Mine Workers' Union was established. It
was not established on an actuarial basis. It was obvious that the initial contribution rate was inadequate and that benefits would force
a higher rate.[23] The coal plans, partly because of inadequate initial
planning and partly because of the economic problems in the industry, have gone through a series of crises. The anthracite plan was
forced in 1954 to cut benefits from $100 to $50 a month. But coal has
been an exception, and such problems have been found in only a
small minority of plans. The typical course has been for management
and union trustees to agree on an actuary and follow his advice. In
some cases management and union have each chosen an actuary and
differences have been resolved by the two actuaries. But unions have
favored funding and have been realistic in building pension reserves.

There also appears to have been little argument to date over investment policy in these plans. A few unions have urged unwise
investment policies; the refusal of some to invest in equities has
been severely criticized. The Amalgamated Clothing Workers, for
example, has restricted its investments to government bonds. But
most funds have relied on expert financial advice just as they have
on actuarial advice. Also unions have commonly not voted proxies
for common stock. With the future growth of pension reserves both
funding and investment questions are likely to attain greater significance. Also there are questions as to the desirability of industry
or regional plans as opposed to company plans. These questions will
be discussed briefly under negotiation issues.

The treatment of funding and investment decisions has necessarily been greatly restricted relative to its complexities, but the

---

[23] For experience under the plan see Robert J. Myers, "Experience of the UMWA
Welfare and Retirement Fund," *Industrial and Labor Relations Review* (October 1956),
pp. 93-100. In recent years the bituminous fund has benefited greatly from technological change and the resulting increase in tons produced per employee.

major point is that unions and management, with a few exceptions in each category, have been guided to date by experts in these fields.

BENEFIT FORMULA AND LEVEL. As noted previously, in almost all employer-designed pension plans benefits are established as a percentage of earnings. For example, the benefit might be 1 per cent of earnings (career or final average) per year of credited service plus Social Security. The meaning of the particular percentage used depends on the related eligibility requirements. The stricter the eligibility requirements (5 years of service compared with 3 years, and/or a minimum age of 35 compared with 25), the lower the actual maximum pension benefit. Plans are tailored to employee groups of varying age and service characteristics by various combinations of percentage figures and eligibility requirements. Benefits are independent of Social Security.

Percentage plans are complex in character. Individual pensions vary directly with the level of individual employee earnings and length of service. Benefit varies, as previously noted, in an unintended fashion with wage trends and with changes in Social Security benefits.

Unions reacted against such plans at a time of marked increase in money wage levels. They sought simple dollar plans, under which an employee would know where he stood. President John L. Lewis created a sensation with a plan for the United Mine Workers paying $100 a month plus Social Security at age 62 (later reduced to 60) for those who had been members of the union for twenty or more years. This plan raised many questions of a financial and legal character; it was applied not to employees generally but to union members. It was negotiated with the government in 1946, but not applied until 1948 because of the opposition of operators after the mines were returned to private ownership.

The pattern plan in the automobile industry provided for $100 a month (including Social Security) for employees at age 65, with 30 and later 25 years of service, scaled down for lesser years of service. The Social Security offset plus the 30-year service requirement enabled the union to come out with a $100 plan without excessive cost. Steel also established a minimum of $100 a month minus Social Security for 25 years of service, combined with a percentage plan.

Negotiated pattern plans called for either (1) flat dollar amounts per month for all who qualify (a minority of the plans), (2) monthly dollar benefit amounts per year of service with a maximum number of years of service (the most common dollar formula), or (3) a combination of a percentage formula with a dollar minimum per year of service to a given maximum. Overwhelmingly in the early negotiated plans the Social Security benefit was included in the benefit provided by the plan.

By 1957-58, however, 14 per cent of the negotiated plans were percentage plans, according to the BLS *Digest*. In some cases, it would appear, the unions favored the percentage principle; in others, the plans were sufficiently liberal to induce the unions to accept them even though they opposed percentage plans in principle. The *Digest* further shows 49 per cent of the plans as dollar formula plans and 37 per cent as combinations of dollar and percentage. It would appear that employers who strongly favor percentage plans have been able to retain them through combination plans incorporating a high dollar minimum. While unions have been particularly interested in the minimum pension in combination plans, they have frequently favored the combination plan too when the employee group had considerable diversity in skill and earnings. Many employers have not objected to converting to or establishing dollar formula plans for production workers, often supplemented by percentage plans for salaried and executive groups.

The Social Security offset has disappeared. Early employer plans never had it; negotiated plans began with the offset, but have been converted by revised monthly dollar payments to private plus Social Security, or the Social Security amount to be deducted has been frozen, as in the steel industry.

It is doubtful that any devious strategy was involved in this change. Social Security remained static from 1939 until the wave of revisions in coverage and benefit amounts in 1950, 1952, and 1954. In the initial plans in autos and steel the unions wanted the UMW's $100 figure and accepted the Social Security deduction to get it. The deduction seemed reasonable while Social Security benefits remained static. However, as Social Security was revised upward, the unions could not sit by and see their members get no benefits from the revisions. A device that automatically reduced the dollar amount of private pension benefits as Social Security was gradually liberalized soon disappeared. Private plans are now firmly established as an addition to Social Security for those fortunate enough to be covered by private plans.[24]

A disability benefit has been incorporated into 70 of the 100 plans surveyed by the BLS. Disability provisions were extremely rare in employer-designed plans. Such a provision has been resisted by employers (but clearly not too strenuously) because it has a highly uncertain cost. Insured plans rarely contain total disability benefits. Union influence was primarily responsible for the inclusion of total disability benefits and for gradual liberalization of the amount of benefit and eligibility requirements for these benefits.

Employer-designed plans tended to incorporate retirement options, such as joint and survivor. The early pattern plans rarely contained these options. Unions may not have been seeking the "frills" in their drive for simplicity, and employers were probably not averse to any omissions. Options, however, have been coming back. The joint and survivor option is in 43 of the 100 BLS plans. A level-benefit option with early retirement (to fill the gap prior to the receipt of Social Security) is found in 20 plans. Options on an actuarial basis cost nothing, and it is difficult to see why the way should not be opened for individual choice with variations in circumstances.[25]

Considerable thought has been given to the question whether unions have modified the level of real pension benefits. It has already been pointed out that unions have been an important influence in obtaining effective and frequent revision of plans. But have they in the process raised the level of real benefits?

An informed answer to this does not appear possible, as the following questions will indicate: How should percentage plans be appraised? Should they be viewed in terms of their intended benefit level by applying the formula to hypothetical or present wage levels, or should such plans be analyzed in terms of their actual benefits with an estimated lag, such as that created by the upward trend in wages in recent years? How should the changes in Social Security be interpreted? Should allowance be made for possible future liberalizations of Social Security? Suppose, for example, a typical 1946 percentage plan is compared with a typical 1956 dollar plan. The 1946 plan is

---

[24] An interesting question is whether the offset of unemployment benefits in the calculation of supplementary unemployment benefits will experience the same change as did the Social Security offset in pensions. This question is discussed in Chapter 16.

[25] Options, such as joint and survivor, period certain, cash refund, level income, and others, have benefits reduced in amount to maintain an actuarial cost equal to the employee's pension. Joint and survivor to protect husband and wife and level income for early retirement without Social Security are particularly important.

likely to appear superior to the 1956 plan viewed prospectively on the assumption of stable future wage levels. The superiority is in no small part attributable to liberalization of Social Security, which the designers of the 1946 plan could not have foreseen. The 1946 plan is likely to appear inferior to the 1956 plan if comparison is made on the basis of actual yield. This result is because of the rapid rise in wage levels and the consequent unintended decrease in the real yield of the 1946 plan.

Depending on how the comparison is made, the older percentage plans can be made to look either superior or inferior to the current dollar plans. Important variables, such as the changes in Social Security and the rise in money wages, were not within the knowledge of the designers of the earlier plans, and so no valid comparison can be made between the two types.

Suffice it to say that intentions, as indicated by the results of the bargaining, appear to have changed very little if at all. The objective of providing total retirement pay (with Social Security included) of one-half the full-pay level has been little altered over the years. Some of the early plans coupled with today's improved Social Security benefits are very good ones. Most plans, both old and new, provide, with Social Security, about one-half pay; and about one-fourth of the negotiated plans in the *Digest* (not the average negotiated plan) provide more than this amount. The rough conclusion is warranted that negotiated plans have maintained the level of real benefits indicated above, but have not gone beyond it except in a minority of instances. The plans that have gone above the half-pay level may be setting the stage for a future negotiation issue.

ELIGIBILITY PROVISIONS. It has already been pointed out that under percentage plans eligibility requirements influence the amount and distribution of pensions. One feature of changing to a dollar plan (assuming no employee contributions) is substantially to remove the requirement for eligibility provisions. A plan, for example, with a benefit amount of $2.25 or $2.50 per month per year of service to a maximum of 25 or 30 years limits pensions by the maximum years of service rather than by entrance age or service requirement. Eligibility requirements are therefore not found in many negotiated plans because they use the dollar benefit formula.

With respect to percentage plans, the trend has been toward liberalization of eligibility requirements. This has in some degree liberalized the average benefit amount. Negotiated percentage and combination plans frequently contain only a one- or two-year service requirement, which is a considerable reduction from early employer-designed plans. With dollar plans the maximum credited service has moved in both directions. At first the maximum years were reduced with the total pension ($100 a month) held constant. The recent trend has been to liberalize plans by counting more service at the given monthly benefit rate. The 1955 negotiations in the automobile industry removed the maximum altogether.

A short maximum number of years of service tends to equalize pensions since nearly all employees attain maximum service credit. Liberalizing the maximum years, or eliminating the maximum, tends to make actual pensions vary among those retiring in accordance with actual years of service. This greater variability with years of service has developed with both dollar and percentage plans. Pensions under percentage plans also vary, of course, with the level of employee earnings.

RETIREMENT POLICIES AND DATES. An important question to be considered is that of compulsory as opposed to voluntary retirement. Three questions may be raised: First, have unions significantly altered employer policy and practice? Second, assuming that unions prefer voluntary retirement, is negotiated compulsory or automatic retirement a sufficient problem for them to create a future major issue? Third, assuming that employers prefer compulsory retirement, is negotiated voluntary retirement a sufficient problem for employers to create a future major issue?

The difficulty in discussing the first question is that employer practice under employer designed plans is not precisely known.[26] Employer-designed plans were commonly written to provide for retirement at age 65, with provision for continued employment after age 65 only with employer consent or at employer invitation. All such plans can be called compulsory retirement plans and are so called by most writers. Practice varied under such plans. Some employers practiced substantially automatic retirement at age 65 by making excep-

[26] There is no problem with the term "automatic retirement," which means retirement without exception at the stipulated age. The term "voluntary retirement" is also reasonably clear in that choice of retirement or continued employment rests essentially with the employee. "Compulsory retirement," however, while giving control to the employer, has been associated with varying practices.

tions only very rarely. But some employers made many exceptions, thus approaching the practice of voluntary retirement. Labor shortages caused many employers to try to retain employees eligible to retire. In other words, employer policy varied, and it is not known what was the predominant practice. In principle, however, retirement was under the control of the employer.

Policy and practice under negotiated plans can be reasonably well established from the BLS *Digest*. About half of the 100 plans provide for voluntary retirement. Almost all joint-trustee, multiemployer plans (39 in total) have voluntary retirement. Again about half of these 39 plans are in industries with casual employment, in which compulsory or automatic retirement would have limited applicability since unsatisfactory employees need not be hired. A high proportion of single-employer plans have automatic retirement features. A common pattern is voluntary retirement at age 65 and automatic at 68.

Do the above facts with respect to negotiated plans appear to indicate a change in employer policy and practice? There has been a clear change in written policy. Employer discretion has largely disappeared. Employers have gone along with voluntary retirement or unions have accepted automatic retirement. How much change this represents in actual practice is not known.

The second question asked whether the acceptance of automatic retirement created a problem for unions. The answer appears to be in the negative. The compromise on voluntary retirement at 65 and automatic at 68 is a constructive one. Where automatic retirement at 65 has been negotiated, if unions strongly desire change, employers can move to the 65-68 position without serious difficulty.

While union leaders commonly favor voluntary retirement, membership opinion is divided. Older employees favor voluntary retirement. Younger employees favor automatic retirement to increase promotion opportunities. Union leaders are not in a position to push strongly for voluntary retirement because the issue might split the membership. It is not difficult to see why a number of unions have accepted a compromise on the question.

The third question asked whether the acceptance of voluntary retirement created a problem for employers. The answer may also be negative. Examination of the actual pattern of retirement in a very few but large plans that have voluntary retirement indicates that employees are in fact retiring in the great majority of cases at ages 65, 66, and 67. Experience to date does not indicate that employees remaining after age 65 are a major problem for employers. Some early fear was not borne out by experience. Since delayed retirement reduces pension cost, there is this offset to any reduction in employee efficiency.

Employee pressure is no doubt a factor in retirement experience under voluntary provisions. Many older employees are not eager to retire, but there appears to be considerable feeling among younger employees that men eligible to retire should not continue to hold jobs. This feeling is accentuated if any employees are on layoff.

What conclusions can be stated? The following appear warranted: (1) Employer discretion under older type compulsory retirement provisions has largely disappeared. Selective retirement is resisted by unions and not regarded as practical by employers. (2) There has been a clear increase in the *principle* of voluntary retirement. (3) Many unions have accepted automatic retirement though commonly at age 68 with voluntary at age 65. (4) The actual statistical incidence of compulsory retirement may have increased or decreased. Majority practice under employer-designed plans is not known. (5) From limited evidence, orderly retirement appears to be taking place under voluntary provisions. Employers do not appear to have a major problem with employees remaining at work beyond the age range of 65 to 68. (6) The great majority of multiemployer plans provide for voluntary retirement, but employees are not permanently attached to employers in most such industries. (7) There does not appear to be any reason to expect major future conflict over this issue.

It has already been noted that unions pushed for and obtained total disability retirement. Disability provisions continue to be liberalized. Employer concern led to tight definitions of "total and permanent" disability, and so administrative problems have not developed. Scattered data indicate considerable variation in the incidence of total disability, but at least in most situations cost experience has not so far indicated an extreme burden. It is difficult to see how pension plans could have continued to operate ignoring the problem of total disability.

Except for the issues discussed, there have been only insignificant differences between employer-designed and negotiated plans with respect to employment policies and dates. Normal retirement date rarely deviates from age 65. Social Security continues to anchor this point in pension planning.[27] Early retirement continues to be allowed at about age 60 or 55 and has been made voluntary in some negotiated plans. Early retirement, however, remains essentially a provision for those forced to retire because of poor health who are not totally and permanently disabled.

Early retirement is not attractive. The private pension is cut almost in half for retirement at age 60, and there is no Social Security benefit. Some plans do not cut by the full actuarial amount, but cost limitations are such that early retirement benefits are necessarily small. It is possible to have a level benefit option for those retiring early, under which money available is used primarily to take the place of Social Security benefits prior to age 65. Such options were common in employer-designed plans. Their frequent absence from negotiated plans is puzzling.

VESTING.[28] Employer-designed plans usually have vesting provisions. The Bankers Trust survey in 1950 indicated, for example, that 75 per cent of the 1943-47 plans provided for vesting as did 80 per cent of the 1948-50 plans (page 10). None of the early pattern negotiated plans, however, had vesting (page 112). Any explanation of this initial difference is speculative. Possibly employers were afraid to provide an opening wedge for what they considered to be a potentially high-cost feature. In subsequent years pattern plans, through union influence, have introduced and liberalized vesting. A BLS study of 300 negotiated plans in late 1958 indicated that 162 of 174 single employer plans were vested, but only 12 of 69 multiemployer plans.[29] In a 1952 study of 300 negotiated plans only 25 per cent were found to have vesting provisions. Full deferred vesting at age 40 or 45 with 10 or 15 years of service predominated in 1958.

The cost of vesting depends on labor turnover. When pension

[27] Provision in 1958 for retirement of women under Social Security at age 62 does not appear to have created a problem in pension planning. A partial explanation is the actuarial reduction in Social Security benefit for retirement at age 62.

[28] Vesting gives to the employee rights to the employer contributions made on his behalf on termination of employment prior to retirement. The rights are vested in whole (full vesting) or in part (partial vesting) when various age and service requirements are met. The right is not, except in rare instances, a right to "cash," but is a right to a pension based upon service to termination of employment if and when the employee reaches the retirement age.

[29] W. W. Kolodrubetz, "Vesting Provisions in Pension Plans," *Monthly Labor Review* (July 1959), pp. 743-50.

costs are calculated, the usual procedure is to assume that all employees (discounted for mortality) remain employed until retirement.
When a plan is in operation, if an employee leaves employment
under the plan without a vested right, previous contributions made
on his behalf revert to the fund. Future payments required are reduced by the amount of such refunds.

To clarify the cost aspects of vesting, consider two hypothetical
extreme cases. In plan one there are 1,000 female employees all un-
married and under age 40. This plan would have a calculated cost as
of a given year. Assume, however, that none of these employees remain to retirement. Marriage takes them all out of employment
prior to age 65. The plan would never pay any pensions, and the
turnover refunds would in essence cancel required contributions. To
grant vesting in this case would be highly expensive. In plan two
there are 1,000 male employees all under age 40 and with the same
age distribution as the females. Assume, however, that all of these
employees remain to retirement. Mortality considerations aside, the
stated cost of the two plans would be the same, but it would actually
cost nothing to grant unrestricted vesting under the latter illustration.

While the above illustrations are highly artificial and oversimplified, they bring out the fact that the actual cost of vesting depends on
the labor-turnover characteristics of the employee group. Since turnover rates decline with increased age and length of service, it is not
an unreasonable burden for a plan to vest at a point where loss of a
vested right would be serious to the employee in building up pension
credit in a different employment. Vesting at about age 40 with ten
years of service, for example, is not a major cost burden for most employee groups.

The degree to which failure to vest restricts mobility is open to
debate. Mobility is low in any event for older and longer-service employees. The importance of the seniority criterion also tends to limit
mobility. In such circumstances there is a strong argument for not
decreasing such mobility as exists. Considerable weight should be
given to the great loss suffered by an older and longer-service employee who may be compelled by circumstances to leave employment
under a private plan without a vested right. A related consideration
is the reluctance of employers to hire older employees who have no

chance to earn a reasonable pension. Vesting would reduce this reluctance.

There is no question as to the need for reasonable restrictions on
vesting in the light of cost considerations. The point at issue is the
opposition of some companies and unions for institutional reasons.
Some companies are disinclined to give vesting to those "disloyal"
individuals who quit. Some companies particularly dislike to vest for
those few older and longer-service employees who have been discharged. Some unions oppose vesting for analogous reasons.

Jointly-trusteed pension plans in most cases do not vest. For example, from the BLS *Digest* the following plans, among others, do
not vest: Bakery and Confectionery Workers (national plan); Clothing Workers (national plan); Ladies' Garment Workers (New York
Cloak Joint Board and Dress Joint Board); Hatters, Cap and Millinery Workers (industry plan); Carpenters (lumber industry, Southern California); Furniture Workers (national plan); Upholsterers
(national plan); Typographers, Local 6 (New York City publishers);
United Mine Workers (bituminous coal); Carpenters (construction
industry, New York, N.Y.); Electrical, IBEW (national plan); and
Teamsters (Central States, Southeast, and Southwest areas). Of 39
union plans listed in the *Digest,* only the following nine vest: Team-
sters-Brewers Board of Trade (New York, N.Y.); Textile Workers
(TWUA)-Textile industry, dyeing and printing, various employers;
Lithographers, Local 17-Employing Lithographers of San Francisco,
and other employers; Automobile Workers-Automotive Tool and
Die Association (Detroit); Machinists, District 9-Various employers
(St. Louis area); Plumbers, Local 130-Plumbing Contractors (Chi-
cago); Teamsters (Western Conference)-Trucking, other industries;
Retail Clerks-Food Employers Council (Southern California); and
Retail, Wholesale and Department Store Union, Local 1199-Retail
Drug Industry (New York, N.Y.). All of these latter plans provide for
"deferred full" vesting when employment is "terminated for any
reason."

It appears, therefore, that many important plans designed in major
part by unions do not vest. Cost is not the reason. The reason is that
interest in protecting the union as an institution is placed ahead of
the interest of the individual employee. Consider the present situation in the baking industry. The Bakery and Confectionery Work-

ers, expelled from the AFL-CIO, provide pensions in the national plan only for members of the union. The new bakery union, The American Bakery and Confectionery Workers, is handicapped in its drive for membership by the question whether pension funds will be lost for those who transfer to the new union. While the illustration goes beyond the question of vesting, the vesting issue is involved in the problem. Failure to vest cannot be defended as a device to hold employees to a union or to a company.

Multiemployer industry type plans do provide pensions so long as the employee remains in the industry, or its covered part, and, in some plans, in the union. In one sense such plans do not need to vest. But various circumstances force a small number of employees out of an industry and union, and a few want to leave. In this sense vesting is as desirable in a multiemployer as in a single employer plan.

The subject of vesting shows divided practice among both unions and employers. Bargaining issues have been created where a union wants to vest but an employer does not. In these circumstances vesting is becoming more prevalent. But employers have not made an issue of vesting if the union is opposed. Where there is agreement not to vest, clearly important in some major plans, a few individual employees must bear a high personal cost in being forced or in wanting to leave the protection of the plan. Credit must go to employers and unions that provide reasonable vesting for termination for any reason.

Negotiation Issues

Interviews that were conducted over the past three years have indicated that pensions only infrequently have created major issues in negotiation. Perhaps a partial explanation is that many of the companies interviewed had a sufficiently favorable financial position to maintain good pension plans. However, the companies also included a few that did not have pension plans. The unions up to that time had accepted the inability of these companies to introduce pensions. There have, of course, been some pension strikes, such as the steel strike in 1949 over employee contributions and the Chrysler strike in 1950 over funding, though this latter strike rapidly acquired a wide range of issues. Strikes in the rubber industry in 1959 involved pensions as one issue, but it is impossible to state whether or not strikes would have taken place had pensions been the only issue. The pension issue in the rubber strikes was unusual in that a proposal to change from a percentage plan with a dollar minimum to a dollar formula for the entire pension came as a company proposal. The proposed dollar formula presented a difficult issue for the union since the proposal, while increasing some pensions, would also reduce the pensions of some employees. While unions have generally sought the dollar formula, where the wage spread is large, both managements and unions have frequently favored a dollar minimum combined with a percentage plan. Also most plans have retained the basic type of benefit formula originally negotiated. So far as is known, rubber is unique in changing, for some companies, from a well-established combination plan to a dollar formula. The change was made in the strike settlements, which provided alternatively for partial application of the previously-existing plans. However, it remains evident that pensions have only infrequently led to serious controversy in negotiation.

Why have pension issues not created more frequent controversy? In no small part this can be explained by the fact that managements regard pensions as desirable, and, having a pension plan, they want it to be a good one. A pension plan which cannot be viewed with pride, and under which employees resist retirement, can be worse than no plan. There is not much point in maintaining a poor plan. Consequently, frequent revision during a period of rapidly rising money wages has been regarded as inevitable. Naturally there have been questions with respect to the inflation issue, but, granted that inflation is taking place, there is not much argument that pensions have to keep pace.

An additional major reason for lack of conflict is that, as has been indicated above, negotiation and experience have not created notable issue areas. Normal retirement at age 65 has been fixed by Social Security. Full employment has been an important factor in minimizing controversy over this issue. Union policy during the early 1930's supported a lower retirement age, but they have come to accept the low pensions and high cost of early retirement. Benefit formulas have been worked out to the satisfaction of both parties. Employers have not made a strong issue of employee contributions in the light of the personal income tax. Lack of vesting also raises some questions but has not been a major negotiating issue. The varied solutions to compulsory retirement, though not equally satisfactory to both parties in all cases, have been the source of only modest conflict.

One issue, not mentioned so far, was encountered in a number of situations. This was the resentment of employers at being forced into a large industry-area plan. There have been at least two major strikes over this issue. The number of strikes does not measure the intensity of reaction; there would have been more except that employers have felt in most cases that they couldn't win them.

Various discussions of the West Coast teamsters' plan brought out these points: (1) conviction, based on actuarial study, that an already-established company plan was superior in benefits and lower in cost than the proposed teamster plan (as of 1957), (2) dislike of a plan that embodied many diversities so that some companies would in effect be subsidizing other companies, (3) dislike by employers of an employer trustee arrangement in which the employer trustees could not be effective bargaining representatives (all employers in eleven states dealing with the teamsters are not a coherent bargaining unit), and (4) various administrative questions and objections.

Basic questions on the joint-trustee mechanism will be discussed in connection with health and welfare plans. Putting aside general questions of this type, there are both advantages and disadvantages to an industry or area pension plan. The larger coverage of such plans reduces risk and cost up to a point. Small plans have particularly high administrative costs. Industry and area plans have the special advantage of bringing coverage to industries with casual employment and small companies. In some industries they appear to be the only feasible approach. On the other hand, industry plans have disadvantages. They cannot be designed to fit the particular needs of the employees of a particular company. Past service credit, for example, may be poorly related to the situation in a particular company. Cost may be high in view of the average age in a particular company. Such differences are inherent in an industry plan, but should companies be forced into such a plan in lieu of providing equivalent benefits through their own plans? Some unions, perhaps particularly the teamsters, have been very reluctant to allow alternative plans. Clearly conflict can continue over the nature and application of some of these plans, but the plans and their administration are still sufficiently new to make judgment premature.

Finally, pension funds will continue to grow in size. An anticipated growth from $25 billion to over $75 billion from 1955 to 1965 was noted above. The use of these funds could become an area of very serious conflict. Unions that have negotiated plans with particular companies protest against being frozen out of the area of investment decisions. Companies under some joint plans protest against union control of funds. As funds grow in size, so will the protests.

Behind questions of who controls the funds are questions relating to the use of such funds. It is not difficult to find instances of questionable investment decisions. A union pension fund buys the union hiring hall, and the union pays a comfortable rent to the fund. A company fund buys a company warehouse, and the company thus acquires capital, a congenial landlord, and a comfortable rent. Behind, and more important than, particular investment decisions lies the possibility of using funds to control companies for business or union reasons. Finally, some unions are interested in using funds for social purposes, such as slum clearance.

The immense financial power implicit in the future growth of funds is bound to raise questions, regardless of who controls the funds. Many funds, of course, give control to financial trustees, but some self-administered plans place control of investment decisions in the hands of corporate or joint union-management trustees. Protecting the interests of the beneficiaries of the trust should, of course, be the exclusive guiding principle in the use of funds. Making investments for business reasons, for union reasons, or for social purposes is a highly questionable procedure and may ultimately necessitate some form of controlled trusteeship.

A report on pension funds and economic freedom finds no "clear and present danger" in the administration of funds.[30] The evidence is strong that most companies shun "own-company" investments and the use of funds for control purposes. The conclusion is that unions also have not used their potential power. Trust companies have taken steps to avoid becoming involved in control of companies. A few company and union situations, however, present sharp contrasts. Cases that clearly involve improper action are perhaps less important than cases resulting from carefully developed policy. For example, the Savings and Profit-Sharing Pension Fund of Sears, Roebuck and Company Employees with its "pass-through" of voting

[30] Robert Tilove, *Pension Funds and Economic Freedom*, a Report to the Fund for the Republic, New York, N.Y. (April 1959).

rights to employee beneficiaries challenges existing concepts particularly by its outstanding success.[31] The Sears fund up to 1940 was
invested entirely in company stock; at the end of 1957 75 per cent
of the fund was invested in Sears common stock.[32] While it can be
argued that the very philosophy of a profit-sharing fund warrants
heavy investment in company stock, the risk taken by employees on
their retirement income raises a serious question as to the wisdom
of low diversification of investment. A comparable question is raised
by the policy of the International Ladies' Garment Workers Union.
As David Dubinsky states, "We prefer to invest our money in projects that not only yield a fair return, but are socially useful. New
cooperative housing has, therefore, been one of our major sources
for investment. It is gratifying to know that our investments help
to promote a cleaner and happier community."[33] Again a strong
argument can be advanced for this union philosophy. Agreement
must be expressed, however, with the Air Line Pilots Association:
"Retirement plans should ideally be limited to the performance of
one function; to meet the need of an income after a pilot's working
life is over. All other considerations should be secondary. The retirement plan should not be a tool for the payment of severance pay,
furlough pay, disability pay, or any other form of welfare benefits.
It should be used for one and only one purpose. Any extraneous
features attached to it can only serve to make more difficult the
attainment of the primary aim. The acceptance of deferred wages
in lieu of a current wage increase is a sound and proper objective
for the Air Line Pilots Association."[34] Socially oriented investments
may well become an important future issue. The question may then
be put as follows: Assuming satisfactory return on investment, is it
appropriate for companies and unions to use investment of retirement
trust funds for purposes other than providing retirement income for
the beneficiaries?

Administrative Problems

As indicated above, pensions have not been a significant grievance
area. Company after company reports substantially no grievances

[31] The same, pp. 60-66.
[32] The same, p. 61.
[33] David Dubinsky, "The Problems of Success," *New York Times* (May 17, 1959), Section 10, p. 17.
[34] Advisory Committee to President on Retirement Problems, *Air Line Pilots Association Negotiator's Guide to Pilot Retirement* (July 1, 1953), p. 6.

over plans. Joint committees created under some single employer plans have generally found little to do. Administrative issues with joint committees under multiemployer plans are discussed in connection with welfare plans.

A notable exception to the above rule is one airframe company that has numerous pension grievances. There have been continuous arguments over years of employee credit and other factual considerations. The slightest opportunity for variation in interpretation of the plan produces grievances. And pensions have not been the only subject of wholesale grievances. The parties dispute all manner of issues. In other words, if relationships are poor, even pensions can produce a flow of grievances.

One particular administrative issue should be mentioned. Companies have attempted compulsory retirement even when the pension agreement and contract were silent on this issue. Arbitrators have not normally upheld compulsory retirement in the absence of specific provision. Seniority and other contract clauses have been interpreted as not allowing automatic or compulsory retirement.

After ten years of pension negotiation and administration, most early "viewing with alarm" appears to have been unnecessary. One early criticism, voiced by many, is worth recall. Various individuals argued against private pension plans in view of the existence of an expanded and liberalized Social Security program. A combined and permanent government-private pension system, nevertheless, has been created. This retains the deficiency implied in the early criticism. Some employees are fortunate enough to be covered by both Social Security and a private plan, but the majority of employees do not enjoy the benefit of a private supplement to Social Security.

14 / Health and Welfare Plans

WHERE BACKGROUND INFLUENCES behind health and welfare plans are similar to those of pension plans, they will not be described in any detail. Also because most plans, both negotiated and employer-designed, are conventional in character, their various features can be discussed in general terms.

Health and welfare plans have been established by negotiation in two ways. The method prevailing in negotiation between a single company and the associated union or unions has been the establishment of a specific benefit package. The package contains, in varying degrees and amounts, life insurance, accidental death and dismemberment, accident and sickness payments, and hospital, surgical, and medical benefits. It may also contain other special benefits. The point to be emphasized is that actual benefits, including amount and eligibility, are negotiated directly and specifically between the parties. A special agreement may be used, or the plans may be included in detail or by reference in the regular agreement. Administration of the program parallels the administration of other phases of the labor agreement and is subject to challenge through the grievance machinery. Cost, with or without employee contributions, is met by the employer and depends on experience.

The second method has been to create a joint union-management trust fund.[1] Multiemployer plans are of this character. In accordance with the Taft-Hartley law an equal number of employer and union trustees is selected, and provision is made for a neutral to break deadlocks. The trustees usually determine the types and amounts of benefits. A significant proportion of organized employees is covered by multiemployer plans. The most extensive recent study by the Bureau of Labor Statistics of 300 negotiated benefit plans[2]

[1] A small number of trust plans are administered directly by the union. Plans in operation January 1, 1946, were allowed to continue under the Taft-Hartley law.

[2] U. S. Bureau of Labor Statistics, *Analysis of Health and Insurance Plans under Col-*

includes about 100 such plans, which cover two-fifths of the workers. Most, but not all, trusteed plans are conventional in character, purchasing insurance and/or providing limited service benefits, such as Blue Cross and Blue Shield. Employee contributions toward the cost of benefits are practically unknown under these plans.

The trustee mechanism raises unique negotiation and administration issues. Often negotiation is restricted almost exclusively to the employer contribution rate. A trust agreement or declaration is created, under which the trustees are given broad responsibility in determining the character of the benefit plans. Introducing the trust mechanism separate from the labor agreement raises questions as to what decisions should be made by the parties and specified in the labor agreement, and what should be the scope and form of the responsibility of trustees. Furthermore, jointly-administered plans vary in the degree to which trustees delegate responsibility to the administrator. While our research has not been sufficient to explore the novel issues of the trust mechanism in detail, some pertinent questions can be posed.

Note should be taken first of the distinction between conventional health and welfare plans and pioneering plans. The term "conventional plan" is used to describe the typical group insurance approach. Departure from convention is of two types: The first is the development of self-insurance, the direct payment of conventional benefits. The second departure is the development of more or less comprehensive medical service facilities. Direct provision of comprehensive medical service is the most advanced frontier of health and welfare plans. Departure from convention is found primarily among trusteed plans. Some unions have pushed vigorously for comprehensive medical service programs, which are likely to become increasingly important.

Health and welfare plans will be discussed in this chapter in accordance with the following outline: (1) the impact of unions and collective bargaining on the establishment, the revision, and the characteristics of plans, (2) negotiation issues, and (3) administrative problems.

---

lective Bargaining, Late 1955, Bulletin 1221 (November 1957). This study of 300 plans, each covering 1,000 or more workers, appears reasonably representative of the status of negotiated plans. It covers almost five million workers or over 40 per cent of all workers covered by such plans under collective bargaining. This study will be referred to as the 1955 BLS study.

The Impact of Collective Bargaining

There has been an amazing growth in protection through group insurance—life, sickness and accident, hospitalization, surgical, and medical—and through group service and benefit plans, primarily Blue Cross and Blue Shield.[3] Employers, unions, and all members of the community have been actively interested in developing these benefits.

Establishment of Health and Welfare Plans

Ordinary life insurance and group life have a long history. The first group life contracts were written in 1911, the first group contracts for temporary disability in 1914, group hospital expense insurance began in 1935-37, surgical contracts in 1936-38, medical in 1940, and major medical in 1950.[4] By 1941 there were hospital service plans in 65 communities, and medical society plans developed in 1939-40.[5] In the decade 1942-52 hospital coverage increased from 20 million to 92 million persons, surgical from 8 million to 73 million, and medical, principally for hospitalized illness, from 3 million to 36 million.[6] In 1956, it has been estimated, life insurance and death benefits covered 62.8 per cent, accidental death and dismemberment 30.6 per cent, hospitalization 62.8 per cent, surgical 58.6 per cent, medical 40.0 per cent, major medical 6.4 per cent, and temporary disability 51.5 per cent of the wage and salary force.[7]

Employers clearly took the initiative in establishing benefit plans, and their interest was more widespread than in the case of pension plans. Employers were more reluctant to begin pension plans because of their long-term cost implications and because of large past-service obligations. Insurance benefits in contrast were short-term in character and could be discontinued if an emergency arose. Also benefit plans were significant to all employees. Interest in pensions has always been weak among younger employees. Hospitalization, surgical, and medical plans were desired by employees of all ages.

[3] The history and scope of coverage is discussed by Margaret C. Klem and Margaret F. McKiever in *Management and Union Health and Medical Programs,* U. S. Public Health Service (June 1953).

[4] The same, p. 11.

[5] The same, pp. 11-13.

[6] The same, p. 8.

[7] Alfred M. Skolnik and Joseph Zisman, "Growth in Employee-Benefit Plans," *Social Security Bulletin* (March 1958), p. 10.

Benefit plans became an integral part of personnel programs much more widely than did pensions.

Union interest in benefit programs became significant during World War II, which marked the beginning of "fringe benefit" bargaining on a broad scale. As Dunlop has noted, "The inflationary pressures under the wage-stabilization program shifted during 1944 and 1945 toward 'fringe' items, as other forms of wage increases were exhausted under the stabilized limits."[8] Union interest in bargaining benefit plans developed as a phase of bargaining "fringe" benefits. Interest in benefit plans was less marked than interest in vacation and holiday pay and shift premiums, but the degree of union interest and influence was significant.

The request of unions to negotiate benefit plans did not provoke the same degree of employer opposition as in the case of pension plans. The War Labor Board met very little opposition to its policy of requesting joint union-management applications for approval of new or modified benefit programs, and these were presented in increasing numbers toward the close of the stabilization period. On the other hand, the legal obligation to bargain benefit plans, if so requested by a union, was not established until the Court of Appeals for the First Circuit upheld the National Labor Relations Board in 1949 in the W. W. Cross case.[9]

It appears that negotiation of benefit plans gradually supplanted unilateral determination of benefits, although the process can not be described precisely. Benefit plans during World War II were frequently not included in the labor agreement, but many employers discussed such programs with unions and filed joint applications with unions to the War Labor Board for introduction and modification of plans. During the postwar years formal negotiation of plans increased rapidly and was legally required in 1949 by the W. W. Cross case.

Various BLS studies[10] indicate the growth of benefit plans under collective bargaining. Estimated coverage in 1945 was one-half million, in 1948 it was three million, in 1950 about seven million, and in 1954 over eleven million (about 70 per cent of all workers under contract). The trend is clear and also the high degree of coverage

[8] John T. Dunlop, "An Appraisal of Wage Stabilization Policies," *Problems and Policies of Dispute Settlement and Wage Stabilization during World War II*, U. S. Bureau of Labor Statistics, Bulletin 1009 (1950), p. 167.

[9] W. W. Cross & Company, 77 NLRB 1126, enforced 174 F. 2d 875 (C.A.I.).

[10] Noted in the preface to the BLS 1955 study.

among organized workers. The growth from 1945 to 1950 in contract coverage resulted both from bringing established plans within the scope of the contract and from the development of new plans.

Union influence in the establishment of benefit plans might be judged to have been somewhat less important than with pensions. Some interesting coverage estimates were made by the Senate Subcommittee on Welfare and Pension Funds in their final report.[11] The subcommittee estimated that 60 per cent of those covered by pension plans were under bargained plans, while 40 per cent of welfare-benefit coverage was bargained. These percentages, however, should not be confused with the fact that about one-half of the organized workers have pensions, compared with one-quarter of all workers, and about three-quarters of the organized workers have welfare benefits compared with about one-half of all workers.

As with pensions, it is impossible to attach specific weight to union influence in the establishment of plans. Again, however, their unique contribution in obtaining coverage for casual and other employees under multiemployer plans deserves special mention.

Revision of Plans

As with pensions, the belief is that union influence has been particularly important in bringing about rapid and continuous revision of plans. In fact, the continuous revision of plans greatly complicates study of trends and characteristics.

This revision, as with pensions, has generally been a process of keeping up with inflation. No study has been made of changes in the real level of previously-established benefits. The scope and character of benefits has broadened, however, as unions have pushed for a "bigger" package. Employers also continue to take the initiative. In one field—major medical—employers are pushing ahead with very good plans for salaried and executive groups. Major medical[12] has not as yet been strongly endorsed by unions. Unions have ex-

[11] Senate Committee on Labor and Public Welfare, *Welfare and Pension Plans Investigation*, S. Rept. 1734, 84 Cong. 2 sess. (1956), p. 12. A summary of conclusions, including statistics quoted, is to be found in the *Monthly Labor Review* (July 1956), p. 812.

[12] Major medical may be distinguished from ordinary medical and surgical insurance by (1) a deductible amount (small medical expenses are paid by the individual or by regular medical plans), (2) co-insurance (over-use or abuse is curtailed by requiring the individual to pay a fraction, for example, 20 per cent, of medical bills above the deductible amount), and (3) a high maximum of, for example, $10,000. The obvious purpose and effect of major medical is to provide coverage for serious illness.

pressed a fear that major medical would be used as a substitute for the more ordinary insurance rather than as an addition to it. A very logical case can be made for the desirability of substituting major medical for ordinary plans since the need for insurance coverage increases markedly with the seriousness and total expense of the illness. However, under major medical insurance fewer employees receive benefit payments, and it appears difficult for unions to endorse a change under which a smaller number of employees will receive larger benefits.

Characteristics of Plans

No known study has been made to determine whether or not there is a "pattern" difference between employer-designed and negotiated conventional plans. Robert Tilove has suggested union influence toward more uniform benefits for employees rather than gradation by wage level.[13] This seems logical and would be comparable to union influence on the character of pension benefit formulas.

Among conventional plans, unions have maintained pressure on important issues of the moment. In the first instance, this was the development of the package for active workers. The latest development for active workers has been the incorporation of medical benefits to cover office and home medical care.

The 1955 BLS study of 300 plans shows a pattern of almost complete coverage of active workers with respect to life insurance, and hospital and surgical benefits. There is some lag in sickness and accident benefits, which are not found in 61 of 300 plans. The largest deficiency is in medical benefits, which are not found in 107 of the 300 plans.

In the second instance, unions pushed for coverage for dependents, which is now very widespread. Only one of 279 plans does not provide hospitalization for dependents, 16 plans do not provide surgical, and 134 do not provide medical. Life insurance for dependents is uncommon, and sickness and accident coverage for dependents is nonexistent.

The latest coverage frontier has been for retired workers and their dependents. The 1955 BLS study indicated that 146 plans extended life insurance to retired workers, 67 hospital benefits, 58

[13] Robert Tilove, "Recent Trends in Health and Welfare Plans," *Proceedings of Third Annual Conference on Labor*, New York University, Emanuel Stein, ed. (1950), p. 153.

surgical benefits, and 35 medical benefits. A total of 56 plans extended one or more benefits to dependents of retired workers.

There is a hidden cost in the extension of group insurance to retired workers and their dependents. Mortality rates are high in this group. Pension plans are new at the present time, and the proportion of pensioners to active workers will increase substantially in the future. Group insurance rates will necessarily rise markedly.

Union influence has also worked toward the elimination of employee contributions. The 1955 study shows that in about half the plans, covering half the workers, the employer paid all for active workers. In almost all plans where payment for the active worker was shared, payment for dependents was also shared. Out of 162 plans in which the employer paid all for active workers, there were 107 where the employer paid all for dependents. Under trusteed multiemployer plans the employer generally pays all.

There was no noticeable upward trend between 1954 and 1958 in the proportion of plans in which the employer paid all for active workers.[14] There was a slight tendency for employers to pick up more of the tabs, or a larger fraction of them, for dependents, retired workers, and dependents of retired workers.

Complete employer financing, except for multiemployer plans, is decidedly less common for health and welfare benefits than for pensions. The personal income tax consideration is less significant. Many employers have so far maintained a strong position on retaining employee contributions. Major pattern plans call for employee contributions. Employer assumption of all insurance costs as part of the 1959 steel settlement is an important change in prevailing practice.

Union influence on conventional plans thus has been, in addition to liberalizing existing benefits, one of broadening and deepening the benefit package. The package has been enlarged for active workers and for dependents and is beginning to be available to retired workers. Union influence, however, appears particularly important with respect to multiemployer plans under joint-trustee control. Some 7.5 per cent of all welfare plan coverage is within this joint-trustee framework.[15] It is within this framework that nonconventional plans have developed. While most joint-trustee plans are conven-

[14] Trends for 1954-58 may be found in "Changes in Selected Health and Insurance Plans, 1954 to 1958," *Monthly Labor Review* (November 1958), p. 1243.
[15] Estimate by Senate Committee on Labor and Public Welfare, *Welfare and Pension Plans Investigation*, S. Rept. 1734, 84 Cong. 2 sess. (1956), p. 14.

tional in character, there has been considerable union influence toward self-insurance and a significant amount of such influence toward comprehensive direct-service plans.

The trend toward self-insurance is interesting. It has not been unusual for a plan to start out buying insurance and then after several years of experience embark on self-insurance. This was the history of the National Maritime Union plan, of the International Brotherhood of Electrical Workers Health and Welfare Fund, Local 103 (Greater Boston), and of the Retail Drug Employees Union, Local 1199 (Greater New York City).[16] It was also the history of the Marine Cooks and Stewards and Pacific Maritime Association Plan.[17] In the 1952 survey of 401 union welfare plans in the state of New York it was found that about 300 were insured and 100 self-administered (not insured).[18]

There are advantages and disadvantages to self-insurance. Multi-employer plans by their very nature must establish special facilities and staff for administration whether or not the plan is insured. The increase in administrative cost is likely to be small in establishing self-insurance. A substantial saving may appear to be possible if the increase in administrative cost is compared with the insurance company's "retention." But retention is a complex concept and includes an amount for taxes, commission, contingency reserve, administrative costs, and profit. Clearly a close analysis is required to determine whether or not a meaningful saving is actually to be realized. Without insurance a plan must establish its own reserve, and the nature of the reserve is decidedly different from that required by multiemployer plans which purchase insurance. Even a careful comparative study of cost may not give adequate weight to the difference in the nature of the risk involved when insurance is not utilized,[19] and, of course, a worker has no opportunity to convert to an individual policy if he leaves the coverage of an uninsured group plan.

[16] Paul L. Poston, "The Administration of Joint Union-Employer Health and Welfare Plans," unpublished thesis, Graduate School of Business Administration, Harvard University, 1959, Chap. III.

[17] George Elner, "Marine Cooks and Stewards—Pacific Maritime Association Plan for Direct Payment of Welfare Benefits," *Proceedings of Health and Welfare Conference*, University of California (July 21-26, 1958), pp. 49-51.

[18] Adelbert G. Straub, Jr., *Whose Welfare? A Report on Union and Employer Welfare Plans in New York*, State of New York, Insurance Department (1954), pp. 172-74. Only 250 of 8,456 employer health and welfare plans were not insured (p. 119).

[19] Self-administration of pension plans does not involve catastrophe risk, as is the case with life insurance.

A second reason sometimes given for self-insurance is the desire to establish a liberal claims policy, but payment of claims is not necessarily closely supervised by an insurance company under an insured plan. Insured cost is based on experience, and claims are administered primarily by the employer or trustees.

It is not possible to assess adequately the trend toward self-insurance. On the one hand, some insurance charges, particularly commissions, appear high with respect to group plans, and self-insurance may be regarded as constructive competition. On the other hand, self-insurance may deprive employees of adequate protection and may represent escape from the desirable and necessary legal regulation under which insurance companies must operate. As the New York study states: "These self-administered benefits, while they were fewer in number, present the major problem since they are not subject to any type of government regulation. Over 390,000 union members covered by self-administered plans do not have the protection of state regulation and supervision afforded to members of insured plans."[20] While six states have passed laws with respect to trusteed plans (1955 Washington, 1956 New York, 1957 Wisconsin, 1957 Connecticut, 1957 California, 1958 Massachusetts) they are predominantly disclosure laws with a minimum of regulatory controls.

More interesting and more significant than union influence toward self-insurance has been the development of direct service programs. These plans have been classified as follows: (1) group I—diagnostic services (such as the Health Institute of the United Automobile Workers, Detroit), (2) group II—medical care for ambulatory patients (such as the American Federation of Labor Medical Service Plan in Philadelphia or the Sidney Hillman Health Center in New York), (3) group III—medical services at center and hospital (such as the New York Hotel Trades Council and Hotel Association Health Center, Inc., New York), (4) group IV—medical services at center, home, and hospital (such as Moving Picture Machine Operators Union, Local 306 in New York, which contracts for comprehensive medical services through the Health Insurance Plan of greater New York), and (5) group V—medical services at center, home, and hospital; dental care and hospitalization (such as the Labor Health Institute, St. Louis, Local 688 of the Teamsters).[21]

[20] Straub, *Whose Welfare?* p. 70.
[21] The above classification and illustrations are from Klem and McKiever, *Management and Union Health and Medical Programs*, pp. 69-70.

A brief description of various service plans can only roughly indicate their actual and potential contribution. For example, the International Ladies' Garment Workers Union in 1958 had 13 health centers and 6 mobile units with 486 physicians, 42 nurses, and 222 technical and other personnel. Capital invested in medical facilities amounted to $8.5 million, and 133,386 individual patients received medical services.[22] Amounts and types of care provided by the following plans, among others, are described in the Public Health Service study: the Health Institute of the United Automobile Workers, Detroit; the Union Health Center, ILGWU, Boston; AFL Medical Service Plan of Philadelphia, a multiunion plan; Sidney Hillman Medical Center, Philadelphia, Amalgamated Clothing Workers; Sidney Hillman Health Center of New York, Amalgamated Clothing Workers; Union Health Center, ILGWU, New York; Motion Picture Machine Operators Union, Local 306, contract with Health Insurance Plan of Greater New York; and the Labor Health Institute, St. Louis, Local 688, Teamsters.[23]

The medical service features of the Welfare and Retirement Fund of the United Mine Workers of America should be given special mention. Not only is it a very large plan with approximately one million members, but it also has had special opportunity along with difficult challenges and problems. The hazardous industry, inadequate medical facilities in rural communities, and unsanitary living conditions combine with unemployment and severe competition among mines to create difficult problems for entire communities.[24] Not that conditions are universally bad, the larger mines have more adequate medical facilities and living conditions, but the total picture is one that definitely calls for a special medical service.

The program is under the professional direction of the fund's executive medical officer. The staff of about 2,700 includes 200 doctors. During 1955 and 1956 a chain of 10 Memorial Hospitals was opened in Kentucky, West Virginia, and Virginia at a cost of approximately $35 million. These hospitals have a little over 1,000 beds.

[22] "Picture of a Union . . . the ILGWU," *New York Times* (May 17, 1959), Section 10, p. 11. See also Adolph Held, *Health and Welfare Funds in the Needle Trades,* International Ladies' Garment Workers Union (January 1951).

[23] Klem and McKiever, *Management and Union Health and Medical Programs,* pp. 69ff.

[24] Report of the Coal Mines Administration, *A Medical Survey of the Bituminous-Coal Industry,* U. S. Government Printing Office (1947).

They were not expected to care for more than a fraction of total patients. Their purpose, which in itself has created fear and uncertainty in the medical profession, was to elevate the standards of medical care in the area.[25]

A wide variety of medical services is available to those eligible, which include, according to established regulations, pensioners, unemployed, dependents, and employed miners. An outstanding part of the program has been rehabilitation. As of 1956 some 317,000 beneficiaries had received corrective treatment. In 1956 some 97,000 miners received such assistance, and 6,500 returned to work in the mining industry, 15,500 found work in other industries, and 5,800 were self-employed.[26]

In 1957 the fund limited payment to physicians whose services were "necessary and essential" in providing authorized benefits. This created serious controversy with the American Medical Association, whose traditional position has been one of free choice of doctor and determination by the doctor of the amount and type of care required. A subsequent change in the position of the AMA is noted. The medical directors of the fund have pointed to improved experience under their supervision, with continued availability of a wide choice of physicians, no deprivation of benefits, and decreased cost with declines in both hospital admission rates and days in the hospital.[27]

The general challenge of direct medical service is summarized by Louis B. Laplace, M.D., president of the Philadelphia County Medical Society, in *Philadelphia Medicine* (April 7, 1951).

> A visit to the Hillman Medical Center is an impressive experience. The building is spectacular with its ultra-modern design based on the latest concepts of hospital construction. The equipment is more elaborate and complete than I have seen in any institution of comparable size. The most important feature to us, however, is its function. . . .
>
> Here is a very challenging situation. Patients of a low-income group receive medical care costing far more than they could possibly afford on the usual fee-for-service basis. Compare this with the types of medical care which are available to them otherwise: attendance at a hos-

[25] William H. Potter, "Experiment in Elevating Standards of Medical Care, The Coal Country Controversy," *Harvard Medical Alumni Bulletin* (July 1958).

[26] United Mine Workers of America Welfare and Retirement Fund, *Annual Report* (1957), p. 12.

[27] United Mine Workers of America Welfare and Retirement Fund, *Annual Report* (1958).

pital clinic, obtaining the favor of reduced fees by consultants, or entirely foregoing consultant and laboratory studies which might be vitally necessary. The advantages to the patient therefore are obvious. Even the possibility that the patient may not appreciate the service because it is free is unlikely because of the impressive surroundings and his feeling that it is his own organization.

From the doctor's standpoint, there likewise appears to be no valid criticism. The staff physicians are, of course, employees of the union, but their status differs in no essential respect from that of physicians employed in industry, insurance and even in some hospitals. Little if any income is diverted from private physicians since this patient group can scarcely afford laboratory and consultant services.

The most significant feature to us of this situation is the fact that if all the advances of medical science are thus made available at no cost to members of a union, what will be the effect on all the other people in the low and middle income groups who also want medical care of comparable quality as part of their employment benefits, or at least without the unpredictable and often financially disastrous features of fee-for-service payment, especially fee at the time of service payment? The eventual effect can scarcely be doubted. The demand for more complete medical care on an insurance plan, paid by the employer, by some organization, or by the patient himself will increase until, in one way or another, it has been met. There will always be some who will pay on the conventional fee-for-service basis, but increasing taxation is inevitably reducing the number of those who can or prefer to do so.

This is our great opportunity to direct the further development of medical care programs into forms which will combine the best service to patients and the most satisfactory conditions for the doctor. What the Hillman Medical Center has done for its union workers will have to be done, appropriately modified to the circumstances of individual groups, for millions of others. Let us see that it is done right. . . .[28]

Significant for the future development of direct service plans is the action taken at the 1959 Annual Convention of the American Medical Association. A policy change at the convention, a new definition of "free choice" of doctor, allows cooperation with closed panel plans. Action was based on a report of the approximately 150 prepaid group practice plans in operation. Such plans covered some 5.5 million of the 123 million persons with some form of voluntary health insurance. The survey committee reported favorably on the quality of care being received. Lack of free choice of doctor in the traditional sense, they said, does not necessarily result in inferior

[28] Klem and McKiever, *Management and Union Health and Medical Programs*, p. 109.

care. Extensive facilities and early diagnosis through the practice of preventive medicine, combined with low cost, frequently means superior medical services.[29]

In contrast to the social challenge of union influence in the direction of comprehensive medical service programs, malpractice in the administration of health and welfare funds must also be noted. While the Senate Subcommittee on Welfare and Pension Funds and other investigating bodies have emphasized that most plans are honestly and responsibly administered, clearly a significant minority of joint trustee plans are not. In the New York investigation in 1954, Sol Gelb as Special Counsel, assisted by a staff of 32 lawyers, accountants, and professional investigators, examined closely 162 union welfare plans. Of these 162 plans, 37 were subject to some criticism, and serious abuses were found in 34.[30]

Listing the various malpractices illustrates the dual character of the problem, that is, the distinction between "serious abuse" and "some criticism": (1) union and fund officials or their relatives acting as agents or brokers, (2) "kickbacks" to officials, (3) "gifts" to officials, (4) excessive salary payments, (5) larger benefits to union and fund officials than to the general membership, (6) nepotism, (7) failure to collect contributions, (8) excessive restrictions on eligibility, (9) too extensive powers conferred on trustees, (10) fund assets held by union officials in their own names, (11) infrequent meetings of trustees, (12) lack of minutes of trustees' meetings, (13) laxity of employer trustees, (14) failure to invest funds, (15) failure to record transactions, (16) disbursements without countersigned checks, (17) absence of expense vouchers, (18) financing of strike benefits, (19) erecting or renovating union headquarters, (20) subsidizing a union cafeteria, (21) purchasing real property of little worth, (22) excessive management fees and commissions to insurance agents and brokers, (23) trustee payments disproportionate to services rendered, and (24) various excessive charges.[31] While existing and new laws can and should correct serious abuse, malpractice, which falls under the more modest but significant heading of "some criticism," can be only partially corrected by law and by supervision of national unions under ethical practice codes. Professional trustee management is a

---

[29] "AMA About-Face," *Wall Street Journal* (June 11, 1959), p. 1.
[30] Straub, *Whose Welfare?*, p. 129.
[31] The same, pp. 129-32.

prime necessity for efficient administration of multiemployer welfare plans. Such management is related to questions raised in the following sections.

Negotiation Issues

Negotiation of specific benefit provisions in conventional plans between individual companies and unions has involved a host of small issues in the evolution of the plans, but rarely a major issue. Each new feature of a plan has been in some degree controversial until quite widely accepted. As with pensions, however, employers want good plans and take considerable pride in programs that have been established. They have not been happy with the growing cost of the package, but individual additions have rarely been strike issues.

Major strikes may arise in the future over the employee contribution question. Where employers have strongly desired to retain employee contributions, the matter has not so far been an important strike issue for unions. The breadth of this question, however, cutting across all types of welfare programs, makes it a greater potential issue than are various new or modified characteristics of specific plans. The 1959 steel strike settlement, however, points toward elimination of employee contributions.

The question of union participation in administering individual company conventional plans is not likely to be a major issue. Some unions have stated frankly that they want no direct part in administration. Union and employee interest in the administration of individual company benefit plans appears to be adequately protected by challenge through the grievance procedure.

One of the most interesting questions for the future is what attitude large companies will take on the issue of converting conventional plans into direct-service programs or introducing direct-service programs in addition to conventional plans. At least some of the large industrial unions are clearly interested in direct-service progams. The United Automobile Workers and the United Steelworkers appear to be interested. As was the case with pensions, the greatly expanded direct-service program of the United Mine Workers is a challenge to all unions.

Direct-service programs by industrial unions will call for the creation of joint trustee arrangements similar to those in multiemployer plans. Unions will want at least joint control of such programs. The prestige associated with owning and operating medical centers and hospitals would be one aspect of union motivation. There is even a question as to whether such medical programs cannot be at least partially exempt from the joint trustee requirements of the Taft-Hartley law. For example, the Labor Health Institute in St. Louis appears to be run fundamentally by the union. The Institute is incorporated and controlled by its members. The Board of Directors has members representing employers and the community, but membership control would appear to be in the hands of Local 688 of the Teamsters. This arrangement has been upheld by the courts on the ground that the Institute is an entity separate and apart from the union.[32] But whatever the legal arrangement, negotiated direct-service programs are not likely to be administered directly by companies.

The above potential developments would give a reverse turn to historical events. Various companies have created comprehensive medical care programs for employees. Some such programs continue in operation, for example, the medical program of the Endicott-Johnson Corporation,[33] but most companies have abandoned direct-service programs. Employee and union criticism of paternalism implicit in the provision of comprehensive employee benefits by corporations has led to the abandonment of such programs by most companies. How will companies react in the future to union proposals for joint trustee control, or independent union control, of comprehensive medical care programs? This remains an open question but increases the significance of the negotiation issues raised by the joint-trustee mechanism.

The negotiation issues of the joint-trustee mechanism raise some unique and complex questions. The questions involve (1) the powers, duties, and responsibilities of trustees relative to those of the parties, (2) the powers, duties, and responsibilities of the trustees relative to those of the administrator, and (3) the protection of the rights and interests of the employee beneficiaries. In creating and modifying benefit plans the fundamental responsibility of the parties should be preserved and the interests of employees as beneficiaries

[32] Klem and McKiever, *Management and Union Health and Medical Programs*, pp. 192-94.
[33] The same, pp. 3-4.

protected. However, the trust form can divorce the parties in negoti-ation from essential elements of responsibility. The trustees in turn can delegate broad responsibility to the administrator. Formal ar-rangements are not necessarily indicative of substance, but the trus-tee device is a questionable arrangement to introduce as an adminis-trative mechanism in the collective bargaining process. The prob-lems created can be explored only briefly.

A review of thirty-seven agreements and declarations of trust showed wide variation in their content.[34] There appeared, however, to be a strong temptation to give to trustees broad and somewhat vague powers. In parallel fashion there appeared to be a strong temptation to include only minimum provisions in the labor agree-ment itself. A labor agreement was likely only to recognize the exist-ence of a health and welfare trust and to require a stated employer contribution. A labor agreement and the associated declaration of trust could be read without discovering answers to such questions as the following: (1) By what procedure are the trustees to be selected? (2) What use may the trustees make of trust funds? It would almost appear in some cases that trustees could donate funds to charity. (3) Under what circumstances and by whom may the trust be termi-nated? Only one of 37 trust agreements specified how the trust could be terminated, by action of the parties to the collective bargain-ing agreement.[35] (4) What duties and responsibilities may the trus-tees delegate to the trust fund administrator and what responsibili-ties may not be delegated? Can the trustees in effect escape responsi-bility by delegation to the administrator? (5) What are the limita-tions on the character of investments that the trustees may make? (6) Must the trustees make rules and regulations for the administration of benefit plans to be made available to employees and to provide an employee appeal procedure?

The above questions could be elaborated but they serve to illus-trate two basic problems: (1) What powers, duties, and responsibil-ities should be retained by the parties and incorporated in the labor agreement? (2) To what degree should the powers, duties, and re-sponsibilities of the trustees be spelled out in the declaration of trust? Dogmatic answers to these questions cannot be given, but it

[34] Poston, "The Administration of Joint Union-Employer Health and Welfare Plans," p. 91
[35] The same, p. 93.

would seem appropriate for the parties to retain basic control in the labor contract and to specify in the trust instrument in reasonable detail the duties of trustees. Consider, for example, the question of by what procedure employer and union trustees should be appointed. The provision that there be a given number of employer trustees may conceal the process of appointment by a minority of employers or even selection by the union. Selection of employer trustees by the union has been alleged in some teamster plans. Lack of a provision for termination of the trust can create confusion when there is a change in union certification and representation. This problem has been raised by the expulsion of the Bakery and Confectionery Workers from AFL-CIO and the creation of the American Bakery and Confectionery Workers Union. It appears desirable as a minimum that the labor contract should provide a method of selecting trustees, a means of terminating the trust, specification of types and forms of benefits to be provided, and provisions for contributions to the trust.

It also appears desirable to include in the trust instrument a carefully drawn section on the responsibilities of trustees. Trustees should not be able to delegate basic policy and administrative decisions to a fund administrator. Laxity on the part of trustees, particularly employer trustees, was found to be a major weakness in the administration of plans in the New York investigation.[36] It should particularly be required that rules and regulations for the operation of plans be drawn up and made available to employees.

The argument can be made that the questions that have been raised are not very important in some circumstances. Frequently employer and union representatives negotiate a labor agreement, then negotiate a trust agreement, and subsequently take off their hats as negotiators, put on trustee hats, and administer the trust. Since the same individuals remain in control, it can be argued that it is not very important what provisions are contained in what instrument or whether only very general provisions are drawn. There is merit to this argument in that there is no necessary connection between what appear to be poorly drawn instruments and poor administration. On the other hand, bargaining units do not always parallel welfare fund coverage, and circumstances change. The coverage, for example, of an eleven-state teamster welfare plan has no parallel

[36] Straub, *Whose Welfare?*, pp. 57ff.

bargaining mechanism bringing together all employers with team-ster contracts in that area.

One criticism that can be made of many welfare plans is that the units are too small to create minimum administrative expense and minimum risk. High administrative expense, and assignment of a relatively large percentage of the insurance premium dollar for com-missions, were found in small plans by the New York study. "Inte-gration of those small plans, located in the same geographical areas and affiliated with the same international union, is advisable in the interest of providing a reasonable level of benefits for members of these plans."[37] While many local union officials and employer repre-sentatives serve without compensation in administering such plans, some units may be retained almost as a make-work or prestige ar-rangement. Welfare units have grown in scope and will continue to be enlarged to attain greater efficiency, frequently making advisable a departure from customary bargaining units. The separation of wel-fare units from bargaining units enhances the importance of ade-quate arrangements for the administration of such plans.

The purpose of the above discussion relating to the trustee mecha-nism has not been to give conclusive answers, but to raise questions. The trust mechanism requires special adaptation to the collective bargaining process, which can be either accomplished by the parties or required by legislation. With the growing scope and importance of trusteed welfare plans these questions require careful consideration by the parties to minimize required legislation.

Administrative Problems

Sickness and accident, hospital and surgical, and medical payments have their administrative problems, but they are not strongly union-oriented. Sickness, accident, and medical benefits are susceptible to employee abuse. Surgical and hospital benefits are modestly suscepti-ble to overuse, particularly hospital benefits. Costs have increased in part because of increased utilization, and increased contributions have frequently brought less net gain to employees than was planned in negotiation.

It is not possible to assess the validity of these various criti-

[37] The same, p. 134.

cisms. As Odin W. Anderson of the Health Information Foundation has stated: "The problems of increased cost because of both utilization and increases in unit costs—not to mention increases in costs accompanying expanded benefits—are very hard to explain to the public when premiums have to be examined and increased periodically. Voluntary health insurance is prone to avoid the issue by going on the defensive and blaming increasing costs on 'abuse' and 'overuse' and presumably unwarranted inflation of unit cost of services. There is then fear that voluntary health insurance is pricing itself out of the market. Sad to say, no real examination has been made as to what extent the increased utilization is warranted or to what degree increased unit costs are inherent and justified in our hospital economy and in physicians' services for some time to come."[38]

There is, of course, some employee abuse and some overuse. Every personnel officer can list particular instances of abuse. Recovery from sickness or accident can be delayed for personal reasons. One plant in a cold climate customarily had the experience in winter of having letters published in the union paper saying "enjoying Florida climate, wish you were here" from employees being compensated under the sickness and accident plan. Or a visit to a home might indicate that a married woman had decided to get the spring housecleaning done before showing enough recovery to return to work.

As a basic administrative device, reliance must be placed on statements by doctors. Doctors perhaps do not wish to offend patients by refusing to give permission to remain away from work, and their honest professional judgment can differ from the lay opinion of the personnel officer. Again it is very difficult to know how legitimate are sarcastic remarks about the availability of a "doctor's excuse" for two dollars.

These reports of abuse, however, simply indicate a difficult administrative problem, and they are not all one-sided. Some employees return to work too soon after an illness or accident. Growing statistical data provide some norms for recovery periods. Investigations can be made when abuse is suspected. But utilization of health services does not lend itself to clear-cut determinations. To some extent the risks are not insurable under conservative determination of predictable risks.

[38] Odin W. Anderson, "Issues in Voluntary Health Insurance," Industrial Relations Research Association, *Proceedings of the Tenth Annual Meeting* (September 5-7, 1957), p. 120.

Considering the nature of the problem, it is interesting to discover that almost never do grievances arise in significant number on the administration of benefit plans. This may imply reasonably lenient administration of plans and only a modest degree of abuse. At times, nevertheless, a plant is discovered in which abuse is widespread.

One company negotiated a sickness and accident plan with payment from the first day of sickness (as well as accident). In addition, it provided for fractional payment for the first and second day of sickness. Payment for the first day was one-third the normal rate, the second day two-thirds the rate, and the third and subsequent days were at the full rate. However, the rate was applied retroactively so that employees staying out three days obtained the full rate for all three days. With no sickness waiting period, and with a premium for staying out at least three days, utilization was extremely high. In one plant the problem was particularly bad, and local union officials assisted the employees. It was reported that blanks of a signed doctor's statement were available in the union office. It was necessary only to fill in the employee's name. The national union and the company intervened and were successful in eliminating the worst of the abuses.

This one case was the only instance coming to our attention of large-scale abuse. It was normal, however, for multiplant companies to have, from time to time, particular problem plants in which utilization rates increased and required special administration for a temporary period.

Where union-management relations were decidedly poor, significant numbers of benefit grievances might be brought, but only as part of a generally poor grievance record. Even with high grievance rates, benefits were not normally among the most frequent causes of grievances. In the overwhelming majority of union-management relationships, benefit grievances were insignificant. As initially stated, the administrative problems do not appear to be particularly union-oriented.

Mention should be made of the fact that trusteed plans in industries with casual employment have novel and difficult administrative problems. It is necessary to work out, for example, rather complex eligibility standards. One state-wide building construction plan with nine craft unions had an hours-of-employment eligibility requirement that was applied on the alternative tests of the last three, six, and twelve months. The trustees of this plan had employed an industrial engineering firm to study their record-keeping and administrative problems. They had continuously made progress in improving their administration. But with good administrative procedures, claims and payments varied directly with the degree of unemployment. Casual employment creates a very difficult administrative problem.

One tentative conclusion with respect to the administrative mechanism under trusteed plans, implied in the discussion of negotiation issues, was that such plans fell into two different patterns. Under some plans the joint-trustees clearly assume major administrative responsibility, and the administrator operates under well-defined procedures. The administrator's job in such an administrative organization, while a significant one, is not a policy-making job nor one that carries responsibility for major decisions. Under such plans the trustees meet frequently, are well acquainted with what is going on, develop well-defined policies and procedures, and clearly have good control over the plan. Under other plans the trustees meet infrequently, and the administrator comes close to running the plan on his own. For the infrequent trustee meetings he makes out the agenda and makes recommendations that are usually adopted by the trustees.

These two different administrative patterns, with contrasting concepts of the relative roles of the trustees and the administrator, cannot be coupled automatically with good administration where the trustees assume major responsibility and poor administration where the administrator plays the major role. On the other hand, the belief is that a comprehensive study would support the conclusion that better organization calls for the trustees to exercise major responsibility, and this is also the intent of the Taft-Hartley Law.

With so much criticism of the administration of trusteed plans, of which note has already been taken, it should be emphasized that most joint plans appear to be improving in their administrative efficiency. The joint character of the trustee board might be expected to carry over bargaining animosities to administration, and to deadlock many issues. This was frequently the early history of such relationships. But experience has tended to improve the functioning of the boards that have come to our attention, and relatively few questions are deadlocked and arbitrated. In some situations joint experience in welfare administration has improved union-management relations in an area or an industry. Joint administration appeared to be operating successfully in a higher proportion of instances in 1958 than in the early 1950's, when many such trustee arrangements were established.

Broadly speaking the administrative problems of all forms of benefit plans do not create union-management controversy. Neither unions nor managements want to deny employees the benefits that the plans provide. Neither wants to encourage abuse. Some degree of abuse is primarily a social cost of providing benefits.

15 / Employee Benefits

MAJOR EMPLOYEE BENEFITS[1] include: (1) pay for time not worked, (2) premium pay for time worked, (3) pension and welfare plans, and (4) provision for legally required benefits. Legally required benefits, primarily social security and unemployment and workmen's compensation, will not be considered here even though certain elements of union-management negotiation and administration are involved. Pension and health and welfare plans have been given separate treatment in Chapters 13 and 14; severance pay and supplementary unemployment benefits are discussed in Chapter 16. This chapter will be devoted chiefly to pay for time not worked, premium pay for time worked, and other miscellaneous benefits. The final section of the chapter will consider selected negotiation and administration issues.

Detailed analysis of benefit plans and payment practices was not made in connection with this study. Competent surveys are continuously being made by the Bureau of Labor Statistics, the National Industrial Conference Board, the U. S. Chamber of Commerce, and by many industry associations. Also many of the more difficult administrative problems related to benefit provisions are indirect rather than direct in character. The direct payment of benefits is normally governed by fairly objective contract clauses clearly specifying the amount of benefit and the eligibility requirements.[2] With such clauses direct grievances are not likely to be particularly troublesome although factual disputes as well as some questions of interpretation arise. More difficult are the indirect problems, chiefly in the areas of work scheduling and work assignment. These latter problems were discussed in Chapters 8 and 9.

[1] The term "fringe benefits," though widely used in labor relations parlance, purposely has been dropped here as inappropriate. Payments that aggregate 20 per cent of total payrolls are decidedly more than incidental.
[2] There are special administrative problems associated with health and medical programs, but they are more employee- than union-oriented.

The primary concern of this chapter is the advancing frontier in negotiation. Unions continuously have pushed for new and more liberal plans and provisions. Clearly union influence has been important in creating a substantial structure of benefits.

The Total Benefit Package

The elaboration and liberalization of benefits of all types has taken place on a large scale in the past twenty years. Probably the most fundamental influence in this development was the changed social attitudes growing out of the great depression. The desire for security took on new meaning. Also government regulation of wages during World War II had a unique influence. As a result of such regulation benefits were easier to obtain than wage increases. This was the result both of their lesser inflationary impact, as contrasted with wage increases, and of the sympathetic view toward such benefits held by many public members of the National and Regional War Labor Boards. Finally, both management and union attitudes were changing. With the development and spread of improved personnel policies, management began to introduce various benefit programs, and unions took an increasing interest in them. Union attitude shifted from limited interest to strong endorsement. Development of the package has witnessed some variation in the emphasis on different types of benefits over the years.

Premium pay for excessive or undesirable hours has a long history. Historically penalty pay has been an integral part of the drive for shorter hours. Union influence in these areas has extended over many years. Overtime after 40 hours for nonexempt employees was made compulsory prior to the war by the Fair Labor Standards Act. In addition. the Walsh-Healy Act had both direct and indirect influence in establishing and spreading daily overtime after 8 hours.

But collective bargaining during and after the war greatly elaborated the premium pay structure. Unions became increasingly interested in additional and special compensation rather than in penalty payments. Union interest in shorter hours, and the related prohibition of long hours of work, no doubt varies with the extent of unemployment. The war not only eliminated the fear of unemployment but added an unpatriotic aspect to resisting overtime work. In such a setting overtime and premium pay became a decidedly important source of added wage income. Overtime for worked holidays, for the sixth and seventh day, for Saturday and Sunday as such, as well as basic daily and weekly overtime, developed rapidly under war and postwar conditions of employment. Also during the war there was considerable extension of shift premiums to rotating as well as fixed shifts.

The union policy of premium pay for long or undesirable hours has undergone considerable change. In fact it is difficult to say just what is the union position on this issue because the desire for special and added payment considerably blunts the traditional goal of prevention. In effect, what started as a protective tariff has become a revenue measure.

While premium pay has been elaborated and has undergone a change in character, decidedly more novel has been the introduction, extension, and liberalization of paid vacations and holidays. The principle of payment of vacations and holidays for production employees was widely established and extended during World War II and the early postwar years. Steady liberalization of provisions has continued.

Employee welfare and pension plans were in a sense the third round of benefits, developing into a major movement subsequent to premium pay and pay for vacations and holidays. These benefits have also been subject to continuous liberalization. Even more recently, private supplementary unemployment compensation has been established on a considerable scale, and severance pay may well become increasingly important in the future, as developed in Chapter 16.

The speed and extent of development of the total package brings forth continuously from employers the questions: When will it end? How far will it go? While these questions are not susceptible to specific answer, brief speculation may provide some perspective.

Economic progress can mean higher real wages, more leisure, or greater employee benefits. There is nothing new in translating progress into wages and leisure. During these past years, however, instead of shorter hours, paid vacations and holidays have been the order of the day.[3] Paid leisure in these forms has been more attractive than shorter hours once the 40-hour workweek was attained. Since the average employee in 1956 received two weeks vacation and six or seven

[3] A drive for shorter hours could be revived by a period of sustained unemployment.

paid holidays, paid time off was equivalent, on an average, to about a 2½-hour reduction in the workweek.[4] This is, in other words, a new form of a long term development.

Promotion of welfare benefits represents a change in point of view and reflects the cost advantages of group provision of such benefits by employers. Both employers and unions have abandoned the code of individualism, which calls for "putting it in the pay envelope." In a limited sense paternalism has been revived with unions actively seeking added benefits. Along with this there are the advantages of the "group insurance" approach and the tax advantage to the individual of not receiving directly income that would subsequently be spent for such benefits.

Bargaining today takes place on all three fronts: wages (including premium type benefits), paid leisure (some direct reduction of hours), and welfare benefits. The introduction of paid leisure and other benefits during the last twenty years has been associated with a rising total cost, increasing from a negligible amount to roughly 20 per cent or more of payroll. Will the decade of the 1960's witness a continued increase in this proportion, or will it level off?

The U. S. Chamber of Commerce survey of benefits showed an average outlay of 21.8 per cent of payroll in 1957 for 1,020 companies,[5] as compared with 20.3 per cent in 1955 for 1,000 companies.[6] For 102 identical companies the biennial years from 1947 to 1957 have shown a trend in percentages as follows: 15, 16.9, 18.7, 19.6, 21.7, and 23.7.[7] For these identical companies during the same ten years the package has grown by almost 1 per cent of payroll each year. While not a large sample, the belief is that it is a fairly good approximation of average experience. It does not appear that the trend has leveled off. On the other hand, novelty in type of payment or benefit becomes increasingly difficult, though by no means impossible, to achieve. Balance could possibly develop in coming years with the cost of the package as a percentage of payroll remaining constant. This would imply a growth in benefit costs at least equal to that of wage costs. Many benefit provisions are geared directly to

[4] National Industrial Conference Board, *Time Off With Pay*, Studies in Personnel Policy, No. 156 (1957), p. 10.

[5] Chamber of Commerce of the United States, *Fringe Benefits 1957* (1958), p. 9.

[6] Chamber of Commerce of the United States, *Fringe Benefits 1955* (1956), p. 6.

[7] *Fringe Benefits 1957*, p. 5.

wages, others must be revised to maintain their real wage equivalent.

With a rising standard of living, a balanced sharing of gains cannot be expected in the near future. Both leisure and benefits are likely to remain attractive relative to wages. With the more complete package now developed, it will be very interesting to see whether the 1960's bring a decline in the rate of growth. This would seem the most that might reasonably be anticipated.

Pay for Time Not Worked

Pay for time not worked can be divided between time at work and time away from work. Pay for lunch and rest periods, as well as wash-up, travel, and other such factors, has grown in frequency and complexity, but these practices will not be discussed here. Time off with pay consists primarily of vacations and holidays but also includes military training time, voting time, and personal time for jury duty, death in the family, and other needs.

Vacations

As is well known, paid vacations have been expanded greatly in American industry. The Department of Labor estimated that only about one-fourth of the organized workers had paid vacations in 1940, and rarely was the maximum in excess of one week.[8] In 1957 only 8 per cent of 1,813 agreements each covering over 1,000 workers did not provide vacations, and in the majority of the agreements the maximum was three or more weeks of vacation.

Paid vacations existed in 1940. The importance of the World War II period in establishing and spreading vacations can easily obscure the significance of earlier provisions. A National Industrial Conference Board study,[9] while pointing to the fact that 99 per cent of 276 companies studied in 1956 had paid vacations for hourly employees, makes reference to their study of 2,700 companies in 1939, in which 46 per cent had paid vacations for hourly employees—a higher

[8] Data on vacation provisions of union contracts used in this section, unless otherwise noted, are from *Paid Vacation Provisions in Major Union Contracts, 1957*, Bulletin No. 1233, U. S. Bureau of Labor Statistics (June 1958). This comprehensive study of vacation practice covers about 8 million workers and includes virtually all agreements in the United States involving 1,000 or more workers, exclusive of railroad and airline agreements, which are not maintained in Bureau files.
[9] *Time Off With Pay*, p. 8.

percentage of all workers enjoying vacations than the BLS estimated for organized employees.[10] In other words, leading companies had incorporated the idea of paid vacations for hourly employees, typically one week, in their personnel policies. Morale, productivity, and labor turnover might well be favorably affected by granting vacations.

During World War II under War Labor Board regulations unions took an increasing interest in employee benefits, particularly as general wage increases became more difficult to obtain. While the Board granted vacation and other benefits only if warranted by prevailing practice, this was a somewhat flexible concept. In voluntary cases in which an employer and union had agreed upon a vacation provision, board members were frequently inclined to grant approval without applying strictly the prevailing practice standard. Stricter standards tended to be applied in dispute cases, but voluntary approvals were continuously expanding existing practice. In addition there was considerable feeling that employee benefits were not strongly inflationary, were important in improving worker welfare, and were something of a safety valve in the difficult process of restraining wage increases. In this setting the Board increasingly allowed one week of vacation for one year of service, and two weeks for five, a formula which became almost standard.

The BLS studies indicated that 61 per cent of 1,314 agreements in 1949 that had vacation provisions had a maximum vacation of two weeks, only 6 per cent had a one-week maximum, and 33 per cent had over two weeks. By 1952, in 951 agreements 2 per cent had a one-week maximum, 48 per cent two weeks, 46 per cent three weeks, and 4 per cent four weeks. In 1957, of 1,529 agreements, 1 per cent had "less than two weeks" as a maximum, and 15 per cent had two and two and one-half weeks. By 1957, 64 per cent had three and three and one-half weeks, and 20 per cent had four or more weeks. The introduction and spread of a longer maximum vacation period has so far been a continuous process, and four weeks was the 1959 frontier.[11]

Reducing service requirements has also been important. In 1957, 20 per cent of the plans required less than one year of service for

[10] It would appear from the data that many of the early introductions of vacation provisions in union contracts served to bring already-established vacation practices under contract rather than to establish the practice. Impressions from War Labor Board experience are that this point was decidedly significant for insurance programs but less important for vacations.

[11] "Little vacations" are also on the horizon with one or more "floating" paid holidays to create long weekends when a regular holiday falls on Tuesday or Thursday.

one week, and 60 per cent granted the second week for three or less years of service (about 20 per cent gave two weeks for one year). The third week predominantly required 15 years (in some cases it had been introduced on this basis, in others reduced from 25 years), but almost 25 per cent of agreements required only 10 or less years of service. Two-thirds of the four week plans required 25 years, while about 25 per cent required 20 or fewer years. Four agreements gave four weeks for five years.

So far the discussion has applied to plans with benefits graduated by length of service and has dealt with the broad outline of such plans. Vacation plans show basic similarities along with complex differences. More than 400 different detailed patterns were found by the Bureau among 1,515 graduated plans, but half the workers were covered by 12 principal patterns. The two related patterns of 1 for 1, 2 for 5, and 3 for 15, along with 1 for 1, $1\frac{1}{2}$ for 3, 2 for 5, $2\frac{1}{2}$ for 10, and 3 for 15, were found in 338 agreements covering more than 2 million workers.

This large number of particular vacation patterns involves variation by industry and union. High-wage industries appear definitely to have more liberal vacation provisions than do lower-wage industries. There also appear to be differences according to region and size of company.[12] These generalizations do not entirely explain all differences in liberality. For example, special explanation would probably be required for petroleum, utilities, printing, transportation (without reference to airlines and railroads), and some other particular industries with liberal plans analyzed in the BLS study. However, the question of why differences in liberality exist can only be raised and not analyzed in detail. One difficulty is that the BLS study, since it includes only those agreements covering 1,000 or more employees, has more extensive representation of some industries than others.

Differences among plans, in addition to the distinction between graduated and nongraduated plans discussed below, reflect industry differences which can be associated directly with level of pay, some significant differences in objectives, and a great deal of minor "product differentiation." The most important difference in objective is in relative emphasis upon lower service requirements rather than more liberal maximum vacations. Emphasis, for example, by the printing

---

[12] Size-of-company and regional differences (as well as industry) are to be found in the National Industrial Conference Board study, *Time Off With Pay*, Table 39, p. 43. Industry differences are to be found in the BLS study (Bulletin No. 1233), Table 3, p. 9.

unions has been to lower service requirements (2 or 3 weeks for 1 year and 3 weeks for 5 years or less) rather than to introduce the fourth week. The teamsters also have sought and obtained short service requirements. The high cost of reducing service requirements must be given great weight in comparisons among unions, but there also appear to be differences in objectives not associated with bargaining power and ability to pay. Seniority discriminations appear less prominent in the older unions.

While the great majority of union agreements with single companies provide for graduated plans (only 4 of the Bureau's 1,218 single-employer agreements had a uniform plan), a substantial minority of multiemployer agreements have a uniform or ratio-to-work plan.

The BLS study included 595 multiemployer agreements, of which 144 had no vacation provisions. Since multiemployer contracts are commonly found in seasonal and casual industries and trades, such as construction, maritime, entertainment, coal mining, and clothing, the relative scarcity of vacation provisions is understandable. Vacation time as such is less important to the employees in these industries. Interestingly enough, however, vacation plans in these industries were widely developed in 1957, and 330 multiemployer agreements provided for graduated plans.

The characteristics of the remaining 121 plans cannot be stated precisely since detailed provisions were not written into many of these agreements. Frequently only a contribution rate was negotiated (consolidated, or not consolidated, with a health and welfare plan), and trustees or the union determined the nature of the plan. Only two agreements (in anthracite and bituminous coal mining) provided specifically for a uniform payment to all eligible workers. Thirty-four agreements were specific ratio-to-work plans. Local supplements in the women's coat and suit industry under which vacations were provided varied a good deal but appeared to place a minimum of emphasis on length of service and a maximum emphasis on percentage of earnings.[13] The construction industry appeared frequently to use a ratio-to-work approach. In this industry, where seniority is used less and is administratively very complex, there is considerable logic in making vacation pay proportionate to the degree of attachment to the industry during the year.

In other words, casual and seasonal industries had vacation plans

[13] *Monthly Labor Review* (November 1957), p. 1347.

in a large proportion of cases. Frequently they were operated along with health and welfare plans. Some significant plans, as in the clothing industry, were operated by the union since they were established prior to the Taft-Hartley law and did not have to operate under a joint trustee arrangement. Most such plans were administered by trustees. Casual employment and mortality of firms have led to the development of union or joint-trustee plans, and the employment characteristics of the industries have led frequently to plans with a minimum emphasis upon seniority. Seniority may, however, become more important in those industries influenced by pension plans and legal hiring arrangements.

Of the agreements that contained provisions for scheduling vacations, more than half required that they be taken at the time of a plant closing. This type of provision was not found outside of manufacturing (all but nine of the plant-closing provisions were in manufacturing). About three-fourths of manufacturing plants with scheduling arrangements provided for closing the plant. While no data are known to indicate a trend, it is suspected that longer vacations make it increasingly desirable for a company to close down its plant if possible. Individual scheduling of vacations as the plans become more liberal makes the maintenance of production schedules difficult. However, plant shutdowns create problems for the union since some employees are not eligible for vacation pay and there are variations among states as to eligibility for unemployment compensation.

Some contracts provided for two vacation periods, but individual vacations were usually allowed only during the summer months. A few agreements prohibited split vacations, and about a comparable number required them. Only 47 of 1,664 agreements with paid vacations permitted accumulation of vacation credit from year to year. Carry-over from year to year could conceivably become an important issue.

More than three-fourths of the agreements had provision for pay for terminated employees. The typical provision was for pay for the amount of vacation earned up to the time of termination. Some agreements excluded discharge for cause.

Allowance for holidays within the vacation period was found in about two-thirds of the contracts. Some provided for extra vacation time and some for extra pay in such cases.

Some 200 of the 1,664 agreements provided for vacations for part-time or seasonal employees. Nearly half of these agreements were in steel, telephone, and retail trade.

Pay for vacations is based on the principle of no loss in normal take-home pay. The usual method of payment was to multiply stipulated normal hours or average hours by the hourly rate or average hourly earnings. About one-fifth of the 1,372 agreements in the BLS study that specified the base for vacation pay used the alternative method of a percentage of annual earnings. Rarely under the hourly rate method did calculation of vacation pay include overtime and in only a minority of agreements were shift premiums included. However, where the percentage method was used, more than half appeared to use total pay.

Half of the agreements contained no provision for pay in lieu of vacation. Of the half that covered this point, somewhat more than half provided for such pay while the remainder prohibited it. Vacation plans in seasonal and casual trades tended to emphasize receipt of vacation pay rather than time off for vacation.

Paid Holidays

The practice of paying for holidays for hourly employees[14] was more definitely a creation of the World War II period than was the case with paid vacations. The National Industrial Conference Board found only 14 per cent of 2,700 companies providing paid holidays for hourly employees in 1939.[15] In 1946 in a sample of 240 companies the Board found that 40 per cent granted paid holidays.

The same influences noted in the question of vacations were brought to bear on the War Labor Board. The standard of prevailing practice was not strictly applied, and toward the end of the stabilization period approval of six paid holidays a year was almost automatic except in dispute cases.

The first extensive study by the Bureau of Labor Statistics in this area was for the year 1950. A survey of 2,316 labor agreements showed that almost three-fourths granted paid holidays.[16] The immediate postwar years thus saw considerable spread in the prevalence of paid holidays. Almost 60 per cent of the 1,701 agreements with holiday provisions provided for 6 each year. About 10 per cent provided for 7 days and the proportions providing for fewer than 3 days and for 4, 5, 8, and 9 days were all under 10 per cent.

[14] Paid holidays and vacations for salaried workers developed during World War I and were well established by 1939.
[15] *Time Off With Pay*, p. 8.
[16] Irving Rubenstein and Rose Theodore, "Holiday Provisions in Union Agreements, 1950," *Monthly Labor Review* (January 1951), p. 24.

An important landmark in the spread of paid holidays noted above was the 1947 pattern settlements in major industries. The "second round" postwar pattern was commonly 11½ cents an hour in wages and 6 paid holidays (costing about 3½ cents an hour) for a total of 15 cents. The major exception was in steel, in which the full amount was taken in wages, and holidays were delayed until 1952.

The second extensive BLS study was made in 1952–53.[17] An analysis of 1,709 agreements showed that 89 per cent provided for paid holidays. At this date about 55 per cent of the agreements granting paid holidays provided for 6 such holidays, and the number with 7 holidays appears to have grown very modestly, to about 12 per cent.

The third substantial BLS study was for 1958.[18] This was a study of 1,736 major collective bargaining agreements, each covering 1,000 or more workers, which was an almost complete sample of such contracts exclusive of airlines and railroads. While not strictly comparable with the earlier studies, since this study was restricted to major agreements, it is probably reasonably comparable as far as broad trends are concerned.

About 90 per cent of these 1,736 agreements provided for paid holidays. In other words, there had been little change in the prevalence of paid holidays since 1952. In 1958 virtually all agreements in manufacturing had paid holidays, while 25 per cent of nonmanufacturing agreements did not have such provisions. The fact that many construction industry contracts did not have paid holidays accounted for most of this difference, and this was probably the case also in 1952.

There was a marked shift in the number of paid holidays between 1952 and 1958. In 1958 over 40 per cent of the contracts provided for 7 days; contracts with provision for 6 paid holidays had declined to about 20 per cent. Negotiations in 1955 and 1956 very frequently added the seventh paid holiday. Future years will no doubt witness the further spread of the seventh paid holiday. Also almost 20 per cent of agreements provided for eight paid holidays. Eight paid holidays in 1958 were somewhat more prevalent than were 7 paid holidays in 1952.

[17] Abraham Weiss and Dena G. Wolk, "Holiday Provisions in Union Agreements in 1952-1953," *Monthly Labor Review* (February 1954), p. 128.
[18] Dena G. Weiss and Henry S. Rosenbloom, "Paid Holidays in Major Contracts, 1958," *Monthly Labor Review* (January 1959), p. 26.

Work on a paid holiday is well established as requiring premium pay. The three BLS studies previously quoted all found double time to be the most common rate of pay, but there has been some liberalization of this. Agreements calling for double time (either as such or straight time plus holiday pay) dropped from 66 per cent of the total in 1950 to 38 per cent in 1958. Provisions for double time and one-half grew from under 20 per cent in 1950 to about 30 per cent in 1958; triple time grew from about 5 to 20 per cent.

Other Time Off with Pay

Increasingly companies have granted time off in the summer for military training. The Conference Board reported 'that the percentage increased from 60 to 85 between 1950 and 1956.[19] In 1956 about half the companies gave supplementary pay. According to the Conference Board, unions became increasingly vocal on this issue when participation in reserve training became mandatory under the Reserve Forces Act of 1955.

Twenty-seven states in 1956 had laws requiring employers to allow time off to vote. These laws differed considerably, and the question of pay for time lost was confused and conflicting. In some states pay deductions were forbidden, in some allowed, and in some the law was silent. Courts reacted differently with respect to pay requirements. Frequently companies appear to have followed required practice, and there does not seem to have been any significant drive to liberalize legal requirements through negotiation.

While a majority of companies in 1956 appeared to give time off with pay for jury duty and about one-third for death in the family, other personal time off with pay was given only by a small proportion of companies. Office workers paid on a salary basis, however, commonly did not receive salary deductions. Personal time off was the one remaining area where office workers had a substantial advantage over plant workers.

Time off for jury duty and death in the family were about the only kinds of personal paid time for employees in which unions took a substantial interest. The entire area of personal time off with pay, however, was the only one in which the Conference Board found more liberal practice among nonunion than among union companies. The general question of union influence will be discussed below.

[19] *Time Off With Pay*, p. 25.

Premium Pay for Time Worked

The term premium pay will be used here to cover overtime pay, shift differentials, and premium pay for work on specific days.

The length of the workweek resumed its long-term decline in the years after World War II,[20] though manufacturing was little affected by this decline. While hours of work in manufacturing varied with economic activity, the standard 40-hour (5 day) week was well established before World War II and had not been reduced by 1960. A BLS survey of wages and related benefits for 19 labor markets in 1957-58[21] found only 10 per cent of the plant workers on a less than 40-hour schedule. Provisions in union contracts for workweeks of less than 40 hours are discussed below.

The decline in the average workweek in all industry (to about 44 hours in 1956) was significantly influenced by a drop of about 10 hours in agriculture between 1940 and 1956 to about 47 hours in 1956.[22] Outside agriculture the downward trend was resumed in trade and service industries and in transportation and communication. Census estimates indicate a decline for all nonagricultural industries of 1.4 hours between 1947 and 1956.[23]

The purpose of this very brief discussion is to take note of the fact that bargaining over the basic workweek during the last twenty years has been quite limited and predominantly has been in industries where the 40-hour week had not previously been achieved. Unions generally have not tried to push below 40 hours in manufacturing, mining, and construction. Notable bargaining gains have been made in transportation. The 40-hour basic week has been extended on the railroads and in trucking. Worked hours have been reduced in shipping, and an elaborate overtime structure has been created.

The 40-hour week, the expansion of trade and service employment, and the growing participation of older married women in the labor force has given rise to some increase in part-time employees and to dual job holding.[24] In nonagricultural industries those employed 1 to 14 hours increased from 3.2 per cent of total workers in

---

[20] Joseph S. Zeisel, "The Workweek in American Industry 1850-1956," *Monthly Labor Review* (January 1958), pp. 23-29.

[21] U. S. Bureau of Labor Statistics, *Wages and Related Benefits in 19 Labor Markets, 1957-58*, Bulletin 1224-20 (February 1959), p. 39.

[22] Zeisel, "The Workweek in American Industry," p. 24.

[23] The same, p. 25.

[24] The same, p. 28.

these industries in 1940 to 4.5 per cent in 1956; for agriculture the increase was from 2.1 per cent to 6.3 per cent. Limited Census studies cited by the BLS indicate that some 3.6 million persons, 5.3 per cent of the total employed, held more than one job in July 1957, as compared with 1.8 million persons and 3 per cent in July 1950. Extra jobs held in trade and service appear to have tripled between 1950 and 1956, from 350,000 to over a million.

Dual job holding is particularly interesting as it raises some questions as to the desire for a shorter workweek. Interest in extra earnings is not simply the result of low pay. The proportion of dual job-holders among professional and technical workers was as high as for all nonfarm labor, and the proportion among craftsmen was higher than among operatives and service workers.

Work Schedules and Overtime Premiums

The Bureau of Labor Statistics study of hours of work and overtime provisions in major union agreements in effect in late 1956 and 1957 is the basis for the following discussion.[25] Some did not provide schedules because such schedules were in local supplements, and some made provision for overtime without specifying a schedule. Of the 1,508 major agreements with schedules, 1,266 established a 40-hour workweek. Only 126 fixed the normal schedule below 40, though this is known to understate somewhat the proportion of provisions for less than 40 because local agreements were not included in the study.[26] Local agreements for rubber workers in Akron specified the 36-hour week. Some local agreements in men's clothing provided for less than 40 hours. The agreements in the study calling for less than 40 hours applied to approximately 588,000 workers, about 10 per cent of all workers in contracts with schedules. About half of the workers with less than 40 hours were in the apparel industries, and 2 out of 3 of the remaining workers were divided between construction and printing. Of 132 construction agreements with schedules, 18 were for less than 40 hours, and one was in excess of 40. Of

[25] Harry P. Cohany and Dena G. Weiss, "Hours of Work and Overtime Provisions in Union Contracts," *Monthly Labor Review* (February 1958), pp. 133-41. This study covers 1,813 contracts in effect in late 1956 and 1957. Each contract covers over 1,000 employees for a total coverage of over 8 million workers. Railroads and airlines are excluded. Local supplements are not covered.

[26] The situations leading to workweeks of less than 40 hours are discussed in Chapter 8, "Work Scheduling."

36 printing agreements, 17 provided for workweeks of less than 40 hours.

Of equal importance is the small number of agreements calling for more than 40 hours. Five agreements fell in the class of over 40 and under 48, 14 were for 48 hours, 6 for over 48, 21 varied by occupation, and 20 varied by season. Fifty agreements were not within these classifications. Of 86 agreements in retail trade, 11 had no schedule, 67 were for 40 hours, 1 was for 48, 2 varied by occupation, and 1 by season. Of 516 nonmanufacturing agreements with schedules, 405 were for 40 hours, 10 were for 48 hours, 17 varied by occupation, and 2 varied by season. There were 37 "other" nonmanufacturing agreements, which included varied schedules in transportation and variation by location and duty in maritime, with 40 hours in port and 56 at sea.

Overtime after 8 hours in the day (and 40 in the week) was the predominant practice. An 8-hour day was standard in 85 per cent of agreements with schedules. The ladies garment industry with a 7-hour day and the 6-hour day for Pacific Coast longshoremen were major exceptions.

One out of eight agreements (scattered widely) provided premium rates for all hours outside the regular schedule. About three-fourths of major agreements in printing fell in this category. As previously noted, premium pay was common for paid holidays. Observed holidays normally counted as days worked for payment of weekly overtime.

Premium pay for particular days (Saturday, Sunday, sixth day, and seventh day) is widely prevalent, but available studies do not show its historical development. A 1958 BLS study of 1,736 major agreements[27] analyzes the status of this pay practice and may be compared in outline with a 1952 BLS study of 1,674 selected agreements.[28] The 1958 study indicated that 90 per cent of major agreements gave some type of premium for one or more of these days. Seventy-five per cent specified Sunday, 57 per cent Saturday, 35 per cent the sixth day, and 35 per cent the seventh day. This represented a modest increase since 1952. In all except 113 of 987 contracts with a Saturday premium,

[27] Rose Theodore, "Premium Pay for Weekend Work in Major Contracts," *Monthly Labor Review* (April 1959), pp. 379-88. This study of virtually all agreements with 1,000 or more workers exclusive of railroads and airlines covers 7.8 million workers.
[28] Joseph W. Block and William Poschell, "Premium Pay for Weekend Work, 1952," *Monthly Labor Review* (September 1953), pp. 933-39.

typically time and one-half, there were no work requirement qualifications. Only 87 of 1,300 agreements with Sunday premium, typically double time, were qualified. About two-fifths of the sixth- and seventh-day provisions required that the employee work the full weekly schedule to qualify. Qualifying requirements were usually subject to an excusable absence clause and counted holidays as days worked. There was some reduction in the proportion of contracts with qualifying clauses between 1952 and 1958.

Just how significant the coverage is cannot be determined. Sixth- and seventh-day provisions can be, on the one hand, supplementary to Saturday and Sunday provisions in the same contract. The Saturday and Sunday clause applies to workers with a Monday to Friday workweek, and the sixth- and seventh-day clauses to other workers. About two-thirds of the sixth- and seventh-day provisions were of this character. On the other hand, sixth- and seventh-day clauses standing alone, and with their more common qualifying provisions, are a somewhat weaker form of protection than Saturday and Sunday "as such" provisions. But the more fundamental question is the significance of gaps in coverage. In many cases lack of coverage indicates only that the clause is not needed. On the other hand, a clause may be only window dressing. It is impossible to check workweek employment practices against coverage.

The 1958 BLS study separates out clauses applying to regularly scheduled work. Sunday premium for regularly scheduled work was found in 14 per cent of the contracts. Less than 3 per cent of the contracts had a similar provision for Saturday work. The 1952 BLS study did not distinguish between regularly scheduled work and workdays not regularly scheduled. The presumption is that there was little premium pay for regularly scheduled work in 1952. The practice was introduced in steel and meat packing in 1956. In 1958 steel paid time and one-quarter for regularly scheduled Sunday work, and meat packing paid one and three-tenths. Telephone contracts paid time and one-half, and some paper contracts paid double time. All such premiums are, of course, a regular addition to weekly wages for employees whose regular schedule includes Sunday.

Shift Differentials

Shift differentials have not usually carried the high penalty rates associated with overtime and Saturday and Sunday premiums. While overtime became so common during the war and postwar years that it came to be considered as much desirable as undesirable work, the rate, nevertheless, tends to restrict normally-scheduled work to non-penalty hours. Shift premiums, on the other hand, are additional wages for less desirable but regularly scheduled hours. About the only exception has been penalty payment for night work in the baking industry, penalties which to date have had very limited effect in actually reducing night work.

The 1958 study of shift differentials made by the BLS[29] may be compared with a similar study in 1952[30] and with the broad outlines of a 1943 survey. In manufacturing, provision for shift differentials was found in about 50 per cent of the agreements studied in 1943; this figure increased to 81 per cent in 1952 and to 87 per cent in 1958. By 1952 it appeared that substantially all manufacturing industries that worked shifts provided for such payment. There is no data for nonmanufacturing for 1943. As of both 1952 and 1958 about 60 per cent of nonmanufacturing agreements provided for shift differentials. Again this appeared to cover the large proportion of those working shifts. There were, however, 63 of 614 nonmanufacturing agreements in 1958 that provided for shift operations or nightwork and made no provision for a shift differential. Detailed investigation would be required to determine the significance of this and other nonmanufacturing data.

Shift differentials were most commonly stated in cents per hour (in about 60 per cent of the agreements in 1958), though a considerable number were in percentage terms (about 17 per cent in 1958). Some contracts, particularly third shift, provided for more hours of pay than of work, a time differential. For example, 8 hours of pay might be given for 7 hours of work. Some contracts had unique provisions based on work practices in particular industries. The median cent-per-hour differential increased from 5 cents to 8 cents for the second shift and from $7\frac{1}{2}$ cents to 12 cents for the third shift between 1952 and 1958. Both shift practices and payments varied greatly among industries, and payment provisions will not be given in detail here. Payment of shift differentials has been extended

[29] John N. Gentry, "Shift Provisions in Major Union Contracts, 1958," *Monthly Labor Review* (March 1959), p. 271.

[30] Morton Levine and James Nix, "Shift Operations and Differentials in Union Contracts, 1952," *Monthly Labor Review* (November 1952), p. 495.

throughout most industries using shifts, and pay is adjusted with wage increases.

Miscellaneous Benefits

To give some idea of prevailing practice with respect to incidental benefits, and those benefits that have not been discussed, a partial listing of practice is given below. Data are for hourly workers in 1954 and are taken from the National Industrial Conference Board.[31] Items are noted which would not be included in most benefit surveys as a reminder of the increasing variety of payments and services included in labor cost.

The following list was elaborated deliberately to include at least some minor benefits. Educational and recreational activities could have been extended. There is obviously no clear way to distinguish between some items that are usually called company personnel activities rather than benefits. A few of the practices noted warrant brief comment.

Sick leave plans were not discussed in connection with health and welfare plans. Most organized employees are covered by sickness and accident insurance rather than a sick leave plan. On the other hand, unions in public utilities frequently negotiate sick leave. There are also some such provisions in agreements in retail trade, in agreements with office and professional workers, and in a few agreements with production workers in manufacturing.

Our interview material deals with sick leave in only two instances. The fact that a definite amount of sick leave was allowed appeared to create a suspiciously higher incidence of sickness under paid sick leave than under sickness and accident insurance. The problem of absenteeism was likely to be particularly acute at both the beginning and end of the allowance period. Any attempt to discipline for this type of absenteeism ran into the problem of doctor's excuses. In one company statements of certain doctors became an accepted joke in arbitration on both sides of the table. Though evidence is too scanty to support generalization, there is the suspicion that paid sick leave is more difficult to administer than sickness and accident insurance.

[31] *Personnel Practices in Factory and Office* (5th ed.), Studies in Personnel Policy, No. 145 (1954).

Survey of Fringe Benefit Practices

	Number of companies surveyed for item noted	Per cent giving benefit or service
Paid rest periods—men	438	55.8
Paid rest periods—women	438	65.1
Paid lunch periods—1st shift	438	21.7
Paid lunch periods—2nd shift	302	36.8
Paid lunch periods—3rd shift	215	46.5
Granting wage advances (usually with restrictions)	495	82.8
Pay guarantee—emergency work	438	71.5
Reporting pay	438	67.4
Supper allowance	438	22.6
Treatment of injuries in plant (paid time)	495	93.3
Waiting time—paid time	495	90.1
Preparing reports—paid time	495	80.4
Checking equipment—paid time	495	78.8
Grievance meetings—paid time	495	67.9
Attend company training—paid time	495	65.1
Wash up at closing time	495	60.0
Wash up (lunch) paid time	495	51.9
Company medical exam—paid time	495	58.4
Making ready—paid time	495	54.1
Union negotiation—paid time	495	47.1
Arbitration—paid time	495	31.5
Compensation hearing—paid time	495	29.5
Tuition refunds	519	29.9
Coffee breaks—paid time	519	65.3
Subsidized cafeteria	519	47.1
Christmas party	519	36.6
Picnics—entire cost	519	51.8
Free legal advice	519	17.3
Required uniforms—pay laundering	201	56.7

Profit sharing was noted to be in effect in a minority of companies. Most plans are of the deferred type, amounting primarily to a particular method of financing a pension plan. In a special study of profit sharing by the National Industrial Conference Board[32] a brief

[32] *Sharing Profits with Employees,* Studies in Personnel Policy, No. 162 (1957).

Survey of Fringe Benefit Practices (Continued)

	Number of companies surveyed for item noted	Per cent giving benefit or service
Required uniforms—pay cost	201	77.6
Clothes changing—paid time	495	32.1
Payment for military training	313	44.5
Pay time off—marriage	438	8.4
Pay time off—death immediate family	438	28.1
Pay time off—jury duty	438	37.0
Pay time off—family illness	438	10.5
Pay time off—trial witness	438	12.3
Pay time off—medical or dental appointment	438	11.4
Paid sick leave plan	495	13.5
Supplement workmen's compensation	495	13.7
Profit sharing plan	438	11.2
Length of service bonus	438	6.4
Military leave bonus	438	30.1
Year-end or Christmas bonus	438	34.0
Employer contribution—savings plan	438	6.6
Company loan plan—formal	519	14.2
Company loan plan—informal	519	82.3
Credit union	519	45.9
Loan—home purchase	519	6.4
Severance pay	519	16.3
Guaranteed wages or employment	1,529	2.4
Company owned housing	519	7.1
Transportation assistance—buses	519	2.5
Parking space	519	91.1
Company pay for required clothes and accessories	444	74.5
Sale of company products	519	50.3
Sale of noncompany products	519	53.8

chapter is devoted to unions and profit sharing. The traditional opposition to such plans by unions is reported.[33] It is also interesting that of the 204 companies with active plans only 88 had a union agreement. Of the 88, only 15 reported that the plan had been

[33] It is doubtful whether the demand of the United Automobile Workers for profit sharing in 1958 was anything other than a temporary public relations and bargaining strategy.

negotiated with the union. Profit sharing appears without much question to be company motivated. On the other hand, by company report, local union officials favored the plan in 44 cases and were enthusiastic in 15.

Significant interviewing was done in only one company with a direct profit sharing plan. While this plan was initiated about 1940 without union enthusiasm, it has become an important area of well-developed union-management cooperation. It has encouraged active employee and union interest in efficient operation of the company. The broad subject of union-management cooperation is treated in Chapter 28.

Dismissal or severance pay plans are discussed in Chapter 16. The negotiation of such plans is heavily concentrated. Of 1,693 contracts studied by the BLS, 266 contained dismissal pay provisions. Of these 266, 114 were negotiated by three unions: the United Steelworkers, the Communications Workers, and the International Brotherhood of Electrical Workers.[34] Two final pay practices should be noted, reporting and call-in pay. Reporting pay is well established. In 1953 a BLS study[35] found reporting pay provisions in 80 per cent of 1,737 agreements. In manufacturing agreements the percentage was 90, and in many nonmanufacturing industries the guarantee is not needed. The most common guarantee was for 4 hours of work or pay. Reporting pay provides compensation for reporting to work as scheduled in the absence of notice not to report. Its purpose is to encourage adequate notice that an employee will not be required for regular work on a given day. Call-in or call-back pay is more complex, and no major study of the practice is known. A 1953 BLS study of 190 selected agreements[36] found varying provisions in the contracts, ranging from regular rate to double time and requiring from 2 to 4 hours of guarantee. Call-in or call-back pay applies to emergency or special work outside of a regular shift. It is subject to abuse, and problems arise related to calling in an improper employee. Some questions are similar to those involved in equal division of overtime and are discussed in the chapters on work scheduling and assignment.

[34] "Dismissal Pay Provisions in Major Bargaining Agreements," *Monthly Labor Review* (June 1957), p. 707.

[35] Dena G. Weiss and Cordy Hammond, "Reporting and Call-Back Pay in Collective Bargaining Agreements," *Monthly Labor Review* (December 1954), p. 1335.

[36] The same, p. 1338.

Negotiation and Administration

Unions have spearheaded the liberalization of major benefits, particularly vacations, paid holidays, and overtime and premium pay. They are working increasingly for liberalization of sickness, medical, and pension plans, as is pointed out above.

Penalty premium pay beyond the framework required by law, and the sponsorship of such laws, has grown out of the traditional union desire for a shorter workweek and day. Premium pay protects the established normal workweek and workday although penalty payment makes the work attractive for many and confuses union objectives.

The drive for paid vacations and holidays has been characterized by the achievement of temporary goals and the establishment of new goals. The National Industrial Conference Board's brief discussion of "union status" with respect to paid time off is particularly pertinent.[37] The Board takes note of strong union patterns but finds that nonunion companies both lag and lead.

> For example, a three-week maximum vacation has been a major union goal during the past few years. A much larger proportion of unionized companies report a three-week maximum than nonunionized companies. The nonunion companies include a much higher proportion of companies granting a maximum vacation of only two weeks or one week, or no vacation. But they also include a slightly higher proportion of companies granting a maximum of four weeks or more than unionized companies.

> Regarding holidays, a similar picture shows up, though not so clearly. Unions have concentrated on gaining six paid holidays, where they previously had less than this number, and on adding a seventh or eighth holiday where they already had six holidays. This is reflected in the fact that a larger proportion of unionized companies grant six, seven, or eight holidays than do nonunionized companies. But, as in the case of vacations, the nonunion companies both lag and lead unionized companies; a higher proportion grant fewer than six holidays, or report no holidays at all; and a slightly higher proportion report nine or more holidays.

> As to time off for personal reasons as jury duty, death in the family or military training, the nonunion companies lead the unionized companies. . . .

It is not known whether a larger sample of union and nonunion companies, refined to correct for differences in industry practice and

[37] *Time Off With Pay*, p. 46.

size of company, would lead to the same conclusions.[38] There is reason to believe, however, that unions would show a significantly higher proportion of benefits on the "frontier" of the moment, whatever it might be. It is also to be expected that a minority of nonunion companies would be ahead of the unionized companies, just as in particular instances with respect to pension and welfare benefits and with respect to wages.

Much of the thinking about employee benefits has been cast in competitive terms derived from a negotiating context. Government regulation also was built on the concept of prevailing practice, but this competitive measurement has remained. Unionized or not, a company acts, on the basis of continuously revised surveys, according to the prevailing industry or area pattern.

While studies tend to show that more liberal benefit packages are associated with relatively high-wage industries and firms, there is reason to believe that most benefits are more directly comparable across industry lines than are wages and that unions gradually adopt earlier goals that prevail throughout broad industry segments. Major companies regardless of industry must match the most liberal benefits unions have achieved. Smaller companies within the jurisdiction of the union are brought along, frequently with a modest lag. Nonunion companies with a strong desire to remain nonunion are likely to keep well up in the procession and even to lead if financially able. Union and nonunion companies are likely to keep fairly close together within the central pattern but with some union companies advancing more rapidly to new standards and some nonunion companies lagging behind.

Whether or not this picture of interaction is precisely accurate, the strong union drive of recent years has probably produced a more rapid advance in benefits throughout the economy than would have been the case in the absence of a broad union movement. While studies tend to indicate that unions have had little general effect on real wages, they may well have altered the form of the total real gain.

Another interesting aspect of this development has been the degree to which factory workers have closed the gap between themselves and

[38] Surveys rarely distinguish between union and nonunion practice. The BLS tends to study union practice, but most other surveys cover total practice. No organizations making surveys appear interested in highlighting differences between union and nonunion practice, and so information on these differences is decidedly fragmentary.

office workers. Adequate data are not available, but clearly the differences in benefits between the two groups are considerably reduced. To some degree union plant workers have become pattern setters for the office group. This would seem to be another indication of the importance of the union drive in the speed with which benefits have developed.

It also appears that nonunion segments of an industry where there is sharp union-nonunion competition have a significant cost advantage in less liberal benefits. For example, one of the major labor cost differentials between organized Northern textiles and unorganized Southern textiles has been the benefit package. While the union segment in hosiery has largely disintegrated, one of the last actions of association bargaining was to abandon the pension plan. In some of the incompletely-organized segments of the apparel industry benefit costs are a serious competitive disadvantage for organized plants.

A related consideration is the reportedly strong desire of the International Ladies' Garment Workers Union for gains in employee benefits. According to some of the union officials wage gains tend to be washed out in subsequent piece-rate negotiation. The benefit package, however, is permanent and decidedly less subject to erosion.

It is interesting to speculate on whether or not negotiation of benefits has been a factor in the desire of employers for longer-term contracts, and for long-term contracts with deferred or formula wage increases. There is logic to the contention that long-term contracts were in part a means of allowing the employer to escape from annual negotiation of benefits. This was only partially successful where wage reopening was allowed. Wage gains at reopenings in steel have at times clearly reflected equivalent gains in automobile benefits. Subsequently the benefits were also attained in steel. Steel companies have paid twice for benefit settlements. In other words, to avoid the indirect purchase of benefits it may be necessary to have a long-term contract not subject to wage reopening.

The role of employee benefits in negotiation requires more thorough study. At times increased benefits appear as an inexpensive alternative to wage increases. At times they appear as an expensive addition to a pattern wage adjustment. In part benefit bargaining may be more closely adapted to differences in ability to pay than are wages. At the same time, benefits acquire an independent pattern of prevailing practice. Once a new frontier is created, a broad pattern is usually quickly established. Standardization of major benefits appears at least in some respects to spread among industries with very different wage levels.

Administration of major benefits has not constituted a major operating problem. Grievances and arbitrations arise, but they are usually not recurring, large-scale grievances. Issues arise over eligibility and sometimes over pay. If a new vacation clause is written, some grievances will arise until adequate interpretation of the clause is worked out, at which time the rate of grievances will fall to a nominal level. Benefit provisions can be based on fairly objective administrative criteria as contrasted with the less definite "fair and reasonable" criteria, and with a few exceptions they are not intimately tied to operating efficiency.

In a somewhat broader vein, benefits have been interpreted increasingly as accrued wages or earned rights. Qualifications tend to be washed out. If six paid holidays are negotiated, this is equivalent to six days' pay. Whether the holiday falls on Saturday, Sunday, or within a vacation, it is to be paid. Improper call-in is typically a wage loss. Union influence has clearly been in the direction of close identification of benefits with accrued compensation.

As mentioned earlier and as discussed in Chapters 8 and 9, overtime, shift, and call-in payments have intensified grievances on work scheduling and work assignment. Premium pay may intensify assignment and scheduling grievances by making money grievances out of them. The problem, however, is not one of the premium *per se.* Vacation and holiday grievances are increasingly infrequent and largely routine. Layoffs in 1958 brought a novel problem in holiday pay to the fore. It was not clear in some contracts whether an employee on extended layoff was or was not entitled to holiday pay. Though an employee might have been in the middle of a six-month layoff, some arbitrators held that such an employee under particular contracts had worked his last scheduled day before the holiday and so was entitled to pay. This is carrying the accrued right to a considerable extreme, and illustrates the point that contract language can be drafted to meet a problem. The contrast with legislating a "fair and reasonable" production standard is an important administrative distinction.

16 / *Income Security and Severance Pay Plans*

INCOME SECURITY PLANS did not become a critical issue in collective bargaining in the United States until the mid-1950's, except in a few special situations. In part, this was because other issues were given a higher priority. Probably the most important reason, however, was the belief held by many unions that a guarantee of income and certainly of employment was beyond the capacity of the individual firm and therefore could not be achieved at the bargaining table. Even on the governmental front, unions were followers rather than leaders in the drive for social security legislation during the great depression of the 1930's. The traditional reluctance of the older craft unions to rely on government was coupled with a proud view that they could take care of their own members during periods of unemployment.

Several developments changed income security from a relatively quiescent issue to an extremely active one in the 1950's. Inadequacy of unemployment compensation under the various state laws, the successful use of the funding principle in pension plans, the adoption of employment security plans by a few unorganized companies, and the temporary satisfaction of other bargaining demands led many unions to give income security and severance pay plans special attention.

This chapter is devoted to a discussion of the tailor-made plans worked out at the bargaining table in recent years to reduce the insecurity caused by various forms of unemployment.[1] Two major areas will be examined: the development of and special problems relating to income security plans, such as supplementary unemployment benefits (SUB), and the growth, significance, and administrative problems of severance pay plans. Of the two, greater attention will

[1] The benefit programs designed for loss of income through retirement and disability have been treated separately in Chapters 13 and 14.

be given to severance pay. The administrative problems for managements and unions created by SUB and variant income security plans have been neither many nor serious. Severance pay plans, on the other hand, are likely to be a critical issue for the future, and they pose numerous difficult problems. It is not the purpose of this chapter to consider basic public policy on unemployment compensation, except to the extent that doing so will assist in understanding the origin of, and problems involved in, privately negotiated plans.

In the discussion that follows one very significant fact emerges to explain the growing capacity of American managements and unions to develop private programs to supplement inadequate governmental measures and to fill gaps left by existing laws. It is the willingness of unions to bargain for *income* security rather than *employment* security. This attitude is most important to management, and it is evidence of a basic conservatism in the American labor movement. By choosing income security as the goal, unions avoid the necessity of bargaining over such essential management decisions as production schedules, capital improvement plans, and plant location. By and large, management has retained its freedom to make these decisions.

Income Security Plans

Interest in the concept of guaranteed employment or a guaranteed annual wage has always been high in this country. However, until recent years this interest was stimulated more by the initiative shown by a few individual firms than by the efforts of unions. The so-called "Big Three" of the guaranteed annual wage plans—Procter & Gamble Company (1923), George A. Hormel & Company (1931), and the Nunn-Bush Shoe Company (1932)—were management-inspired and were not the product of collective bargaining.[2] Furthermore, the interest was primarily academic. The pioneering efforts of a few enlightened managements and the very few plans worked out

---

[2] Procter & Gamble officials maintained from the start that this was not a proper subject for collective bargaining. In both Hormel and Nunn-Bush the local union committees have played a fairly important role in employment stabilization efforts to implement the guaranteed wage principle. One of the earliest bargained plans was between the ILGWU and the Cleveland garment manufacturers. They agreed in 1921 to guarantee employees forty weeks' employment per year. This plan was dropped in the depression years.

through collective bargaining did not become the pattern for much of American industry. In a BLS study in 1940 it was reported that only 14 of the 7,000 agreements on file contained provision for such plans, and these covered a total of only 5,000 employees.[3] It is probable that the earlier plans had a greater chance of adoption in the unorganized companies. Some managements turned to job security programs as a way to discourage employee interest in unions. Most unionized companies in turn feared that these programs if bargained collectively would lead to union control over scheduling and other matters considered to be exclusively management functions.

The significance of the earlier plans should not be underestimated. Much was learned from the experience of those that succeeded, and probably even more was learned from the experience of those that failed.[4] However, this section is concerned with the new programs produced by collective bargaining. They may be classified under the following three headings: weekly employment guarantees, supplementary unemployment benefit and security account plans, and special guarantee programs of recent origin. In the discussion of each only minimal attention will be given to the bargaining table arguments for and against adoption of these security measures. After a brief description of the typical plans, primary emphasis will be on the more important implications of these plans for managements and unions.

Weekly Employment Guarantee

The assurance that employees who start a week's work will be given a full week's work or pay therefor was probably the first step toward income security under collective bargaining. However, even this somewhat mild form of guarantee did not become a critical

[3] *Monthly Labor Review* (August 1940), pp. 283-89.
[4] Among the hundreds of books and articles on the earlier plans, the following are of special interest: Joseph L. Snider, *The Guarantee of Work and Wages* (1947); A. D. H. Kaplan, *The Guarantee of Annual Wages* (1947); J. Chernick and G. C. Hellickson, *Guaranteed Annual Wages* (1945); *Guaranteed Wages, Report to the President by the Advisory Board*, U. S. Office of War Mobilization and Reconversion (1947). The last study, prepared under the direction of Murray Latimer, was undertaken at the request of the President pursuant to a recommendation of the War Labor Board. The steelworkers' union had demanded wage guarantees from the "big steel" companies in 1943 on the basis of anticipated unemployment after the war. The WLB held that the demand as submitted would "subject the industry to such serious financial risks . . . as to be unworkable." The Board said that "the present state of the country's information on this subject" was inadequate.

union demand. Its adoption was limited to a few industries, such as meat packing and sugar refining, although a number of agreements in other industries also included such provisions.

Illustrative of the weekly guarantee is the clause in the master agreement of a large meat packing company. The company guarantees to each regular full-time hourly paid employee pay equivalent to 36 hours at his regular rate for each period of Monday through Friday provided the employee is present and available for work each day. The protection does not apply to those who are normally hired on a day-by-day basis, as in the case of snow-shovelers, unloaders, and the like. Hours of absence are deducted from the 36-hour guarantee.

While the principle of the weekly guarantee is uncomplicated, it gives rise to myriad administrative problems in its application. Among the questions which arise and which must be answered by the parties are the following: (1) May the company credit overtime toward the guarantee? (2) Are call-in payments required elsewhere in the agreement which exceed the hours actually worked on such call-in to be credited? (3) Does the guarantee apply in a holiday week? (4) What special arrangements are needed for shift employees or for others who work on jobs regularly performed on six or seven days a week? (5) What protection, if any, is given to those employees who are hired after the first of the payroll week, particularly regular employees who are recalled under the seniority provisions of the agreement? (6) Is the guarantee applicable when acts of God occur which make it impossible for the company to provide work, as in the case of a power failure caused by a tornado, or which make it impossible for the employee to report for work, as in the case of a serious snowstorm? (7) How much advance notice not to report for work at the beginning of the new payroll week must be given to relieve the company of its obligation? (8) Is a company free to reassign employees to any other work, without regard to the limitations described in Chapter 9, if work on the employee's regular job ends during the workweek?

For the most part unions and managements that have adopted the weekly guarantee have resolved these and other problems over the years. Those who have adopted the principle more recently have learned from the experience of others. As a consequence, the administration of such plans has become stabilized, and relatively few grievance and arbitration cases arise in applying the weekly guarantees.

Weekly guarantees undoubtedly were given some impetus by the accelerated union drive for the guaranteed annual wage in the mid-1950's. Where supplementary unemployment benefits or income security plans of the type described below were unattainable, unions often settled for the lesser guarantee. For example, the Radio Manufacturing Company and its UAW local agreed in 1955 that each hourly employee who started work on Monday of any week would receive forty hours' pay for the week even if he worked fewer hours and was given insufficient notice not to report.[5] This plan, like many others, was a compromise following company rejection of the union's more ambitious annual wage proposal.

Many companies, without realizing it, have committed themselves to a variant of the weekly, or in some instances, longer guarantee. This has been done by the agreement to give advance layoff notice.[6] The guarantees of work or pay implicit in such notices have created more administrative problems than the explicit weekly guarantees. In the 1958-59 recession many grievances arose as a consequence of the layoff notice clauses. For example, a firm which had agreed to give one week's layoff notice and which was also committed to the recall of senior laid-off employees when work was available, recalled a number of employees for three days' special work. The union contended that these employees were entitled to five days' work or pay before they could be laid off again. The major New York newspaper publishers in their contracts with the various printing trades unions agreed that regular jobholders would not be laid off until the end of the regular "fiscal week." A strike by the deliverers' union in December 1958 prompted the publishers to suspend publication. The nonstriking unions demanded pay for the remainder of the fiscal week under the layoff notice clause. Arbitration cases involving these demands were decided against the unions in 1960.

Most managements committed to weekly or, in rare cases, monthly guarantees have said that their adoption has led to more careful scheduling of work and manpower. Pre-planning of schedules has become an important management function. Some companies stated that an unexpected consequence has been the development of a more

[5] Bureau of National Affairs, *The Guaranteed Annual Wage*, Operations Manual (1955), p. 77. The UAW's over-all income security proposal in 1955 provided for a forty-hour weekly guarantee in addition to the annual guarantee. This guarantee was not to be credited against an employer's maximum liability; it was to be handled on a pay-as-you-go basis, the same as call-in pay.
[6] These notices are discussed in some detail in Chapter 6.

versatile work force because of reassignment of workers to varying tasks in the course of a week. Only a few criticized the work or pay guarantees on the ground that they led to make-work practices, and in these cases there was evidence that pre-planning efforts had been inadequate.

Supplementary Unemployment Benefit and Security Account Plans

By far the most significant development in recent years has been the adoption of SUB and other similar plans as a compromise resulting from the vigorous union drive for the guaranteed annual wage. As noted earlier, the steelworkers during the war years made the guaranteed annual wage one of their principal demands. But it was not until the early 1950's that an all-out campaign to achieve this goal was launched, and then it was undertaken largely by the UAW and the USW, both industrial unions in basic or heavy goods industries.[7] An intensive educational program was begun in 1953 and 1954, while the five-year automobile agreements negotiated in 1950 were in effect, to demonstrate why the annual and weekly guarantee of wages was to be given top priority in the 1955 negotiations. It was one of the most carefully prepared and best publicized union campaigns in labor relations history. It left no doubt in the minds of most automobile management representatives that this was viewed by the union as a strikeable issue. The Ford Motor Company, although reluctant to embark on a variant of the guaranteed annual wage, nevertheless decided to prepare for the forthcoming 1955 negotiations by planning a program that conformed to its own ideas of what an income security agreement should be. The mandatory tests it adopted and the preparation for these critical negotiations were no less painstaking than the union's. They are outlined in Chapter 30, "The Negotiation of Union-Management Contracts."

Briefly, the Ford Motor Company concluded that if it were to accept the doctrine of income security in collective bargaining, five requirements would have to be met: (1) the payments during periods

---

[7] Most of the earlier plans had been limited to the consumers' goods industries. The UAW, troubled by the seasonal layoffs during the model changeover period, felt that management could do a better job of stabilizing employment. It is interesting that this issue arose when employment levels nationally were and had been very high. One union leader explained that this was the most propitious time, since "the cost of securing employee income seemed less formidable to most managements."

of unemployment must supplement state unemployment compensation payments, and entitlement must be governed by state regulations; (2) the benefits should not be of such amount as to destroy the incentive to work; (3) the company's liability must be limited; (4) the plan must insure that the interests of senior employees will not be jeopardized because funds have been exhausted by payments to junior laid-off employees; and (5) before management would agree to any supplementary benefit plan the union must agree to grant the company flexibility in the operation of the enterprise.

The concept of supplementary unemployment benefits began with the historic agreement negotiated between the Ford Motor Company and the UAW in June 1955. The SUB plans characteristic of the automobile industry, and later the steel and can industries, were soon followed by other plans that provided some degree of income security. Two years after the negotiation of the Ford agreement more than two million employees, or 4 per cent of the private labor force, were covered by such plans. Employee coverage by some form of income guarantee had increased twentyfold in these two years.[8]

In the discussion of supplementary unemployment benefits, two subjects will be examined: the basic types of plans negotiated and the experience under them and the implication of such plans for managements and unions.

TYPES OF PLANS. Two basic plans have been negotiated, the *funded* or insurance plans and the *individual trust account* or savings arrangement. The first and prototype funded plans were those adopted in the automobile, can, and agricultural implement companies in 1955. Many of these were liberalized in subsequent negotiations as to duration and level of benefits. Briefly, each company agreed to pay five cents per employee hour into a master trust fund, out of which benefits were to be paid.[9] The company payment was to continue until maximum funding was reached. This maximum, redetermined on a monthly basis, was fixed at approximately $400 per covered employee in the case of the Ford Motor Company.

Entitlement to benefits from the trust fund was geared closely to

[8] Alfred M. Skolnik and Joseph Zisman, "Growth in Employee-Benefit Plans," *Social Security Bulletin* (March 1958), p. 5.
[9] In Continental Can Company and in the 1956 steel plans three cents per hour worked was paid into the trust fund. However, the companies remained liable for an additional two cents if it was needed to pay the benefits.

that under the state unemployment compensation laws, including the customary one-week waiting period. The employee was to receive from the fund the difference between his state benefits plus other earnings and a fixed percentage of his weekly after-tax straight time earnings; this percentage was fixed at 65 per cent in the 1958 automobile negotiations. A laid-off employee was eligible for supplementation of income if he had one year's seniority and qualified for unemployment compensation. The automobile plans allowed a maximum benefit payment of $30 per week and in the 1958 negotiations increased the maximum duration for receipt of benefits from 26 to 39 weeks unless the state maximum was less than 39. The steel industry funded plan agreed to in 1956 established two years' seniority for eligibility, but it was somewhat more liberal than the automobile plans in other respects. The benefit maximum was $25 per week plus $2 per dependent up to four dependents. But the steel plan allowed a maximum duration for benefit payments of 52 weeks, and when state compensation was exhausted, the weekly benefit maximum from the private fund became $47.50. The actual amount of benefits any person could draw depended on three variables: the number of credits accumulated (so many for each week worked), the level of the fund, and the employee's seniority.

It is evident from this capsule description of the prevalent funding plans that the five criteria established by the Ford Motor Company have been met in large part. Invariably the funds are administered by a company-appointed trustee. The plans themselves are usually administered by a company representative, whose decisions are subject to the grievance procedure.

The second basic type of plan, *the individual trust account,* originated in the flat glass industry in September 1955. The plans of the Pittsburgh Plate Glass Company and the Libbey-Owens-Ford Glass Company provided for a company contribution of five cents an hour to a trust account set up in the name of each individual employee. The account could go to a maximum of $600; thereafter the company contribution was to be used to increase the employee's vacation pay. Employees were entitled to draw from the account when they were laid off for at least one full pay period or when they were out because of injury or sickness for two full pay periods. The benefits drawn per pay period were at the discretion of the employee within a prescribed range: a maximum of 10 per cent of the balance in his Security Benefit Account or $30, whichever is smaller, and a minimum of $15 or the balance in his account, whichever is smaller. Unlike the automobile plans, there is no tie-in whatsoever with state unemployment compensation arrangements. Moneys credited to an employee's account were to be paid to him in the event of termination or retirement or to his estate in the event of death.

Probably the most important difference between the master trust fund and the individual trust account plans is that in the latter the money contributed by the company belongs to each individual employee and becomes his security "kitty"; whereas in the master trust funds, no such personal identification exists. Another initial distinction of some importance was that the individual accounts were used to provide income security for illness and injury as well as unemployment for lack of work, while the over-all trust funds were limited to unemployment benefits only.[10]

Many variations of these two basic types of plans may now be found throughout American industry, and, as is to be expected, they reflect the conditions peculiar to certain companies and industries. One of the most interesting is the 1956 agreement between the National Maritime Union and the Atlantic and Gulf Coast shipping operators. The plan covers 35,000 workers of many different companies, each company paying 25 cents per day per worker into a pooled central fund. As amended in 1958, the plan calls for the payment of benefits in flat amounts, irrespective of state unemployment compensation and prior earnings: $25 a week if unemployment compensation is received and $40 if it is not received. The duration of benefits depends on the reason for unemployment: 13 weeks for disability, 3 weeks when a ship is laid-up, lost, or sold, 2 weeks for involvement in legal proceedings, 4 weeks while waiting to re-ship after vacation, etc. In a small textile plant which had a profit-sharing plan for many years, union pressure for supplementary unemployment benefits was met by amending the plan to permit payment for this purpose out of profits.[11]

At the time of this writing there was little available information on the operation of the plans. There is no doubt that they played an

---

[10] In the section on "Severance Pay Plans" in this chapter it will be noted that this initial difference has become less clearcut as a result of recent negotiations. The automobile SUB funds may now be used to provide severance pay.

[11] For a description of these and other plans, see Bureau of National Affairs, *Supplemental Unemployment Benefit Plans*, Operations Manual (1956).

important part during the 1958 recession. A report on SUB plans issued by the AFL-CIO in December 1958 said that the large volume
of unemployment placed a heavy drain on the funds, and, as was to
be expected, the newest plans were forced to reduce benefits either in
weekly amount or in duration when the finances fell below a certain
point.[12] But the older plans—in the steel, auto, and container industries—were able to "weather the recession without much cutback in
benefits." The steelworkers' union at its September 1958 convention
reported that in May 1958, the month of highest unemployment,
83,000 members out of 200,000 unemployed were collecting benefits.[13] In the period September 1957 to May 1958 nearly $45 million
was paid in benefits to the steelworkers. The average benefits in the
period April-June 1958 were between $22 and $24 per week, almost
three-quarters of the average amount received from state compensation. The United Automobile Workers in 1959 reported that its unemployed members in the United States and Canada had received
more than $108 million in supplemental benefits. Contributions by
employers to the various UAW-negotiated funds totaled about $265
million, and reserves in mid-1959, in spite of the substantial recession, were approximately $180 million. Walter Reuther, president
of the UAW, observed that the three years' experience with SUB was
"a conclusive demonstration of their practicability and of the great
value of the protection they provide."[14]

In spite of the relative newness of these plans and the extensive use
to which they were put in the 1958 recession, very few serious administrative problems have arisen. The careful draftsmanship of the
original plans explains this in part. As noted earlier, the plans were
the end result of many months of study. The tie-in with state unemployment compensation administrative decisions also eliminated
many routine problems for the parties in the case of the automobile
and steel plans. Finally, many managements developed a careful allocation of responsibilities to assure effective administration of all
phases of the plan.[15] Commenting on the experience during the recession, the AFL-CIO *Collective Bargaining Report* said "the plans

[12] AFL-CIO, Department of Research, *Collective Bargaining Report* (December 1958).
[13] The figure would have been over 100,000 had it not been for legal obstacles that
prevented operation of the plan in Ohio and Indiana.
[14] *Business Week* (August 22, 1959), p. 85.
[15] For example, see W. C. Hampton, "Administering an SUB Plan: The Ford Experience." *Personnel* (July-August 1957), pp. 76-83.

have worked fairly smoothly, with not many hitches or grievances. . . ."[16] Most company spokesmen agree that the problems have been relatively minor.[17]

IMPLICATIONS OF SUB AND SECURITY ACCOUNT PLANS FOR UNIONS AND MANAGEMENTS. Although the administrative problems are few, a number of questions on the impact of these plans will be raised and tentative answers suggested.

What internal problems, if any, are created for the union? There is considerable evidence that the adoption of the master trust fund plan by the UAW created some dissension within the ranks of its members. Many senior employees as well as the highly skilled workers felt that the five cents contributed by the company for each hour they worked would never inure to their benefit. They believed their chances of layoff were slight and would have preferred a wage increase rather than a company payment in their behalf which would never be used or which would go principally to junior or semiskilled employees. As a consequence, the desires of the skilled trades were given special attention by the union in the 1958 negotiations. This problem was far less prevalent where individual security accounts were negotiated. Regardless of seniority or skill status, each employee considered the account a contingency reserve for his personal use. Even if it was used infrequently for unemployment or illness, it remained a personal savings account available to him if he left the company.

What effect will the plans have on layoff and seniority arrangements? This subject has been explored in Chapters 5 and 6. There is already evidence that these consequences are being felt: (1) Downward bumping in lieu of layoff which entails a substantial reduction in earnings is resisted by many employees. They argue logically under SUB and, to a somewhat lesser extent, under the individual account plans that if the benefits available are nearly as much as the reduced earnings, there is little purpose in working. Contract changes are being made to give the employee the option of refusing a downward transfer of any depth. (2) There is considerable union pressure to

[16] December 1958, p. 74. See also *Labor Relations Reporter* (December 1, 1958), p. 97, comments by C. H. Sunderland, U. S. Steel Corporation SUB Administrator.

[17] The greatest problem for managements and unions alike under the plans that are integrated with state compensation laws has been in the few cases where the states have disallowed the integration. This problem is being resolved gradually.

prevent the sharing of work by use of the short workweek. Senior employees particularly resent the sharing process under SUB on the theory that junior employees have supplementary benefits available to them during layoffs. Two steps have been taken to meet this problem: restrictions on the use of the short workweek have been written into the contract, or the plans have been liberalized to provide for payment of benefits in a short workweek.

Do SUB and security account plans provide incentive to management to stabilize employment? The UAW convention in March 1953 said that the "primary goal of a guaranteed annual wage plan should be to stimulate management to provide steady full-time employment, week by week, the year around." None of the plans described above constitutes a guarantee of annual wages, and only to a very limited extent do they provide the stimulus sought by the union. Under the master trust fund plan the company contribution ceases when maximum funding is achieved. Therefore, it might be expected that a company would do everything possible to avoid layoffs that would lower the fund. But it is doubtful if the five cents per hour cost creates a strong incentive. As will be noted below, most managements also realize that when maximum funding is achieved for any length of time, the unions will seek to liberalize the benefits or otherwise provide for a continuation of the five-cent cost commitment. In the case of the individual account plans the incentive is even less because the companies were committed to the payment of five cents an hour in another form when account maxima were reached.

Will the plans make employees prefer idleness to work? Except where downward bumping in lieu of layoff is considerable, it is not likely that the plans will encourage idleness. The level of benefits in 1959 was fairly modest in relation to take-home pay. In a few scattered instances mentioned in Chapter 5 there was evidence of an emerging "juniority" concept, where senior men sought the chance to be laid off for personal reasons; undoubtedly the improved layoff benefits explain this preference. But there is no trend in this direction. If unions succeed in bringing the level of benefits, with or without unemployment compensation, close to 100 per cent of former earnings, a drastic revision in seniority layoff arrangements would be required.[18]

[18] Sumner H. Slichter, "SUB Plans—Their Economic Impact," *Management Record*, NICB (February 1956), p. 46. When a man is on layoff, the level of benefits will often

Are SUB and other similar plans a stopgap pending liberalization of state unemployment compensation laws? One of the compelling reasons for the adoption of SUB was the woeful inadequacy of state benefits. Although state benefit rates were increased by an average of 20 per cent from 1950 to 1955, wages increased at a much faster rate. In 1955 the average state benefit was $24 per week at a time when the average factory worker was earning $80. Some managements took the view that by integrating SUB with state unemployment compensation, subsequent liberalization of state laws would gradually eliminate the supplement and, consequently, the employer's cost commitment. This is most improbable. The same view was held when pension plans were formulated in the late 1940's. What developed thereafter has been described in Chapter 13. In the first place, liberalization of state benefit levels is not likely to keep pace with wage increases. Benefit duration has been extended by many states, but this has led to a similar extension in the duration of SUB payments. Second, even if higher state benefit levels were to reduce the demands on SUB funds or on individual security accounts, there are many other security uses to which these funds could be diverted. As noted earlier, the more recent plans provide for payment from the fund for various forms of unemployment, such as injury and illness. The funding concept has also stimulated interest in severance pay plans. Having committed themselves to this cost, employers will be expected to continue the commitment, either by liberalizing existing plans or by converting the commitment to other uses, such as vacations, short workweek, basic wages, and the like.[19]

These income security plans represent one of the most important

---

determine his willingness to seek other work. But is it logical to expect a man on temporary layoff to hunt diligently for other work and represent himself as willing to accept a new permanent position? Given his seniority rights, he knows he will return to his former employer when recalls are made.

[19] The extension of unemployment compensation to 39 weeks by various states, and by the temporary federal program, highlights certain problems. Added protection for persistent and long-term unemployment is desirable, though not a solution for this problem, but extended duration may not be appropriate for the growing number of secondary family employees and for those with marginal attachment to the labor force. All federal and state programs bearing on unemployment require integrated review. Out of such review unemployment compensation might be refined to apply differently to various types of unemployment. (See Industrial Relations Research Association, *Annual Proceedings*, 1958, for a discussion of these issues.) Private SUB and severance pay plans require integration of purpose and mechanism both with public plans and with other private benefit plans. This point is developed throughout this chapter, but note should be taken of the fact that the future character of private plans will depend in some degree on the future development of public programs, although private plans are not expected to decline in total significance.

recent products of collective bargaining. Although the coverage of two million persons was accomplished in a short time, there is little evidence that the plans are being extended rapidly throughout the economy. Many of the craft unions have shown no serious interest in SUB or similar plans. They continue to emphasize basic wage increases in bargaining. Even in some noncraft unions, the protection against layoff provided so many employees by seniority has resulted in limited interest in unemployment benefits. For these reasons, the stabilizing influence of the plans on the economy as a whole has been less than one might expect.

Special Guarantee Programs of Recent Origin

A discussion of income security plans would be incomplete without some recognition of the isolated, but significant, guarantee arrangements worked out in collective bargaining in recent years. Many of these are far more ambitious than the SUB or security account programs.

In the period 1952–55, Local 688 of the Teamsters' Union in St. Louis, with a membership of 10,000 in food processing and manufacturing, warehousing, and distribution, succeeded in negotiating an annual wage plan with 75 firms. These firms employed more than 5,000 employees, approximately 3,000 of whom were given the annual guarantee protection. Briefly, the plans call for a guarantee of 2,000 hours' pay, exclusive of overtime, for whatever number of employees were agreed upon in negotiation. In the case of a company planning to expand, the coverage approached 100 per cent of employees. More commonly, the coverage applied to the most senior 60 per cent of those on the plant-wide seniority roster. Thus, the principal issue in bargaining was over the number of employees to be covered. The plan itself is remarkably simple, and it is doubtful if the employers affected gave very careful thought to its implications. One employer, for example, said he did not know whether he would be obligated to pay the balance of the guarantee in the event his plant burned down.[20] The plan leaves unanswered the extent of the employer's obligation when a laid-off employee receiving guarantee pay has secured other employment.

Although large-scale layoffs have not occurred that would test the

[20] Bureau of National Affairs, *The Guaranteed Annual Wage*, p. 26.

operation of the St. Louis teamsters' plan, there is evidence that it has already had unexpected consequences. As stated above, coverage is based on plant-wide seniority, but layoffs are on a departmental basis. Thus, a man with low departmental seniority but high plant-wide seniority would be subjected to layoff and would be entitled to 2,000 hours' pay. In this case the company may avoid laying him off by transferring him to another department with full rate protection, a choice naturally preferred by the employer. It has meant that in companies which had operated on a segregated basis, with only Negroes employed in some departments and only whites in others, the pattern of segregation has been broken down by the desire to avoid payment to laid-off employees.[21] As yet there is no evidence to determine whether the limited coverage feature increases instability of employment for the employees not covered. This might be expected because of the desire of employers to be certain there is enough work left for the covered workers. If this were to happen, internal frictions might develop within the union.

Other plans providing for annual guarantees were negotiated by the sugar refining industry and the Packinghouse Workers and Longshoremen's Association in 1951 and 1952. The basic guarantee is 2,000 hours of work or pay at the regular rate to employees with one or more years' service. Only eight hours of work a day is credited toward the 2,000 hours, but these may be overtime hours if the work is on Saturday and Sunday. A special exemption is allowed the companies when sugar is unavailable due to labor dispute, major breakdown, or other reasons beyond the company control. Payments required under the plan are made at the end of the year. It is important to note that in the plants where the plan has worked most successfully from management's standpoint, there has been considerable flexibility in making plant-wide transfers of employees. In other plants, however, the very practices caused by the former short and irregular workweek schedule—such as crew requirements and limited work assignments—have been continued at union insistence and have made the guarantees costly to the employer.

In summary, income security arrangements in one form or another are becoming more common in American labor relations. Their extension is likely to be slow and gradual. In their more moderate forms, the problems they create are not formidable, but as

[21] The same, p. 27.

they are liberalized, they may affect drastically some of the stabilized arrangements discussed elsewhere in this volume.

Severance Pay Plans

Most severance pay arrangements were designed originally to provide some income security to the employee whose job at a given employment location was eliminated permanently.[22] This might have been for one or more of several reasons: the complete discontinuance of an enterprise, the merger of one manufacturing or service unit with another, the movement of a plant from one location to another, the discontinuance of a department or product-line, or the introduction of a technological or methods change. In each of these circumstances it was expected that the affected employees would have no opportunity for return to their regular work. The rationale of severance payment from the union standpoint was relatively simple at the beginning of such plans. The union's position was the following: that an employee with long service whose job was permanently eliminated was entitled to have his living expenses covered while he was in the process of finding and getting started in new employment. The amounts paid were usually modest and relatively long service was required to qualify for payments.

Although elimination of the job remains the principal basis for severance payment, it is interesting to note that over the years severance payments have come to apply to temporary layoffs where recall is anticipated, to forced retirements because of age or health reasons, and even to dismissals for incompetence. With the growth of pension arrangements described in Chapter 13, and with the extension of unemployment benefit programs of the type discussed at the beginning of this chapter, it is probable that severance pay plans that have acquired a multipurpose coverage will revert to their original purpose except in those establishments where the adoption of a more complete security package is not feasible.

With rare exceptions, payments are related to length of service and vary considerably in amount from one bargaining situation to

[22] The term "severance pay" is used in this discussion, but these plans are also identified by such terms as "dismissal compensation," "separation allowances," or "termination pay." Payments in lieu of a required layoff notice are not considered within the scope of this section.

another. Except for newly-bargained plans only incidental attention will be given below to the mechanics of severance pay systems. The discussion will cover instead the history and extent of severance pay plans; an analysis of the interest in and prevalence of severance pay plans; and significant administrative problems.

History and Extent of Severance Pay Plans

Most of the plans in effect prior to 1940 were the product of employer personnel policies and were unrelated to collective bargaining. Over five hundred firms paid some form of dismissal compensation on their own initiative before 1940. Nearly all of these plans developed in the period 1920–40 and were attributable largely to the growing preoccupation with good personnel practices that began in the 1920's and to the impact of the depression and the growth of trade unions in the 1930's. Most of these companies fell in one or more of five categories: (1) they were large companies, (2) they employed many white collar workers, (3) they dealt directly with the public, (4) their labor cost was a relatively small part of total cost, or (5) their business was largely in noncompetitive markets. Furthermore, in many instances the "plans" were nothing more than layoff-notice payments. It is interesting that in this twenty-year period the number of formal dismissal programs designed to cover all contingencies, such as discharge and retirement, instead of just special labor displacement situations, increased slightly.[23]

One of the earliest severance pay plans developed through collective bargaining was in the clothing industry in Chicago. A drastic change in job requirements at Hart, Schaffner and Marx occurred in 1926 because of the demand for popular priced suits and a change in cutting methods, and it became necessary to displace 236 cutters. Under a plan worked out by the company and the Amalgamated Clothing Workers each displaced cutter received $500, the money being contributed by the company and by the remaining cutters, who temporarily gave up their unemployment insurance rights. As early as 1925 the ILGWU and the New York Dress Manufacturers' Association had agreed that if the employer gave proper notice to the union at the start of a season of his intention to install labor-

[23] For an informative account of the growth of severance pay arrangements in the United States, see Everett D. Hawkins, *Dismissal Compensation* (1940).

saving devices, he could make such installation, but employees displaced were to receive not less than two weeks' wages. In addition, periodic reorganizations of the work force complement could be effected because of permanent curtailment of business. However, pattern makers and cutters laid off as a result of any reorganization were to be given from one to four weeks' wages, the exact amount to be based on their length of service.[24]

In the men's and women's clothing industry the seasonality and high business mortality rate led to the use of the equal-division-of-work principle rather than layoffs by seniority. Inevitably some employees demanded that part of the force be dropped to make work for the rest when business was curtailed over a long period. Severance pay helped to encourage voluntary resignations and to cushion the blow of forced layoffs.[25]

Probably the most significant of the early plans introduced by collective bargaining was in the railroad industry. The depression of the early 1930's accelerated interest by the Interstate Commerce Commission and financially-pressed carriers in the consolidation of operations. The Emergency Railroad Transportation Act of 1933, which created a Federal Coordinator of Transportation, had as its principal purpose to prevent unnecessary duplication of railroad services and facilities. In response to a vigorous campaign by the Railway Labor Executives' Association, Congress included in the Act a provision that railroad workers employed during the month of May 1933 should not be dismissed or put in a worse situation as a result of mergers effected under the law. This restriction did much to emasculate the law. It was evident that savings of hundreds of millions of dollars annually by car pooling, joint use of terminal facilities and shops, mergers, and consolidations could be accomplished only by a reduction in railroad employment.

After a year's experience under the law, the Coordinator recommended to Congress that the employment-freeze provision be modified in exchange for some form of dismissal compensation program. However, the railroad unions were successful in resisting any change. It was not until 1936, when the possibility arose that the 1933 Act might not be extended, that the unions urged adoption of a generous dismissal compensation law.

[24] The same, pp. 153-55.
[25] Sumner H. Slichter, *Union Policies and Industrial Management* (1941), pp. 114-15.

Both the Federal Coordinator and President Roosevelt urged the unions and managements to try to work out a joint agreement, arguing that voluntary action by them would probably yield a better program than would congressional action. On May 21, 1936 the parties finally reached a compromise settlement in what is known as the Washington Job Protection Agreement. Among other things, it provided that an employee displaced because of consolidation would receive 60 per cent of his average monthly pay, the duration of payment depending on his length of service. For example, a person with one year but less than two years of service was entitled to 6 months' pay. The schedule called for 60 months' pay for those with fifteen or more years' service. It was also provided that even if an employee was retained at his regular pay, he could elect to resign at the time of the consolidation and receive a lump sum based on length of service. This resignation allowance was substantially less than the forced displacement allowance.[26]

The Washington Agreement has been reaffirmed by public policy. In 1938 the ICC imposed a similar severance payment plan as a condition of its approval of a merger involving a carrier not under the Agreement. Its action was sustained by the United States Supreme Court. In 1940 the Interstate Commerce Act was amended to require the ICC to provide protection in merger actions so that no railroad employee would be in a "worse condition" for four years or a period equal to his prior service if less than four years. The agreement, which applied originally to mergers only, was extended by public policy to cover displacements caused by abandonment of a railroad line. This occurred in 1944, when the ICC imposed employee protection conditions in approving the abandonment of a line by the Chicago, Burlington and Quincy Railroad.[27] Neither the Washington Agreement nor the "Burlington formula" covers displacements caused by technological improvements.

With the railroad formula in mind, Congress in 1943 amended the 1934 Communications Act to allow for merger of domestic telegraph carriers with the requirement that dismissal pay be given to workers whose jobs were terminated thereby. The amendment guaranteed employment for at least four years after a merger to those

[26] Employees transferred as a result of a consolidation were to be reimbursed for moving expenses and any property loss.

[27] Hawkins, *Dismissal Compensation*, pp. 157-75. See also William Haber, *Maintenance of Way Employment on U. S. Railroads* (1957), pp. 161-63.

with a minimum service date, and those who were displaced because of the merger were to receive one month's wages for each year worked.

During the war years, in spite of conditions of full employment, there was some increased interest on the part of the unions in severance pay plans. This was partly a reflection of the general movement toward employee benefits while wage increases were restricted. In a few companies the plans negotiated in wartime were prompted by the prospect of dislocation at the end of hostilities. The War Labor Board generally approved voluntarily-negotiated severance pay plans even though they were not supported by prevailing practice in the industry and area. However, in nearly every instance the Board denied union requests for severance pay in dispute cases on the ground that such plans should be the product of voluntary agreement or appropriate legislation. The abnormal wartime payrolls in some industries, such as aircraft, and the prospect of inevitable sharp cutbacks at the end of the war stimulated union interest but at the same time strengthened employer resistance to these plans. The one significant exception to the WLB's policy in dispute cases was its directive issued in 1944 in a group of steel company cases. Recognizing that after the war the steel companies might close down old plants and facilities and concentrate production in the more efficient, modern plants built during the war, the Board directed the parties to negotiate a severance pay agreement appropriate to each plant or company. When the parties failed to reach an agreement, the Board on December 28, 1945 ordered adoption of a plan for employees permanently displaced by the closing down of plants and facilities after the war. It provided for a minimum of four weeks' pay for those with ten or more years of service.[28]

Since 1944 there has been a slow but steady rise in the number of negotiated severance pay plans. Three studies by the Bureau of Labor Statistics provide the most complete available information on this trend.[29] In 1944 only 5 per cent of the agreements studied by the BLS contained severance pay provisions, and only a few industries, particularly newspaper publishing and railroad transportation, had adopted the principle of severance pay to any considerable extent. By

[28] National War Labor Board, *The Termination Report*, Vol. I, pp. 391-94.
[29] U. S. Bureau of Labor Statistics, *Dismissal Pay Provisions in Union Agreements* (December 1944), Bulletin No. 808; *Labor-Management Contract Provisions, 1949-50*, Bulletin No. 1022; *Collective Bargaining Clauses: Dismissal Pay, 1955-56*, Bulletin No. 1216. Agreements in the railroad and airline industries are excluded from these studies.

1944 the American Newspaper Guild had succeeded in making this a contract condition in over 90 per cent of its agreements, and the International Typographical Union had secured such provisions in 79 newspaper and 90 commercial printing agreements. These two union groups accounted for two-thirds of the agreements with such clauses in 1944. The only other notable concentration (approximately one-sixth of the agreements) was in agreements of the now-defunct United Office and Professional Workers of America.

The 1949 study was based on an analysis of 2,137 agreements, of which 1,584 were in manufacturing industries. Of this total, only 168 or 8 per cent provided for severance pay. Again there was a marked concentration of agreements by industry. Almost 75 per cent of the agreements studied in the communication industry, 60 per cent of those in the rubber industry, 50 per cent of those in the printing and publishing industry and 12 per cent of the iron and steel industry agreements contained such provisions.

The most recent study undertaken by the BLS covered 1,693 agreements effective in 1955-56. Of this total, 1,142 were in manufacturing and 551 in nonmanufacturing industries. In 266 or 16 per cent of the agreements analyzed, there were severance pay provisions. These 266 agreements covered more than $1\frac{3}{4}$ million employees. Three industry groups accounted for half of all the severance pay clauses: communications, primary metals, and electrical machinery. One hundred and fourteen of the 266 agreements were negotiated by three unions, the United Steelworkers of America, the Communications Workers of America, and the International Brotherhood of Electrical Workers. It would be wrong to infer from this concentration that the earlier severance pay plans in the rubber industry and in the newspaper and publishing industry had disappeared. The 1955-56 BLS survey shows 5 rubber industry agreements, covering 55,000 employees, with these clauses. Only 7 printing and publishing agreements were included in the survey.[30]

From 1944 to 1956 the proportion of agreements containing such provisions increased from 5 per cent to 16 per cent. The BLS describes this as "a relatively slow growth . . . as contrasted with the rapid spread of such practices as pension plans and health and in-

[30] The 1955-56 BLS study was of "*major* collective bargaining agreements," defined as agreements covering a thousand or more employees. This explains the differences in industry concentration between this study and earlier studies.

surance coverage." It is evident that union concern with pensions,
health and welfare programs, and, as has been noted in this chapter,
with supplementary unemployment benefit programs had high priority in this 12-year period. Furthermore, the enactment of unemployment compensation laws lessened somewhat the need for severance pay.

But it is reasonable to predict that the next survey made of severance pay provisions will reveal a substantial further increase in the
number of these clauses. There are three reasons for this prediction.

First, in recent years many union leaders have announced that
severance pay will be given considerable attention in future negotiations. For example, early in 1958 the Oil, Chemical and Atomic
Workers said that a principal demand would be a severance pay plan
with a base of two weeks' pay. Its proposal is described as a "radical
new approach" designed to meet the special problem of those in the
40 to 65 age bracket, who are too old to get new jobs easily and too
young to draw a reasonable pension. The union hopes to secure a
graduated severance pay scale based not on service but on the age
of the displaced employee. The union explained that "it had not
focused on severance pay in the past because it was fighting for more
pressing matters."[31] The IUE has insisted that severance pay be an
integral part of its employment security program to be negotiated
with the leading electrical product manufacturers. The presidents
of the automobile workers' union and the machinists' union announced after a joint contract policy conference in August 1959 that
severance and relocation pay clauses would be a number one demand
on the aircraft, missile, and related electronics industries in 1960.
They said this protection was needed because of the movement of
the industries inland and because of the shift in emphasis from aircraft to missiles.

Second, although often some time elapses between the publicizing
of union intentions and their partial or complete fruition at the
bargaining table, evidence indicates that a considerable number of
severance pay programs were adopted in the 1958, 1959, and 1960
negotiations. There has been a break-through on at least three new
highly- or moderately-organized industrial fronts. In the 1958 automobile negotiations, severance pay arrangements were integrated
with the supplementary unemployment benefit programs. In the

[31] Industrial Relations Counselors Service, *Current News* (February 27, 1958), p. 35.

same year the International Ladies' Garment Workers Union was successful in securing widespread acceptance of a severance pay plan to begin in 1960. The oil workers' union has had notable success in getting a plan adopted in several segments of the oil and chemical industry. The agreements negotiated between Philco and the IUE in 1959 provided another unique feature, inclusion of severance pay as an integral part of the pension plan.[32] In 1959 an arbitrator ruled that severance pay should be granted to crew members of American ships when their vessels are transferred to foreign registry. The nature of some of these more recent plans will be described below.

Third, the 1950's have seen a rise in the number of plant relocations and company mergers. Also there has been a rapid growth in the use of automated equipment. These developments result in permanent dislocation of workers and stimulate union interest in income security measures.

In summary, except for the fairly early achievements of some unions in the railroad, garment, steel, and newspaper industries, unions have been slow to press for special pay provisions for the permanently separated employee. Cyclical or seasonal unemployment, the hardships of personal and family sickness, and the insecurity of old age have been of greater concern in collective bargaining during the past twenty years. Although the growth of severance pay plans has been less than spectacular in this period, there is persuasive evidence that these plans are now becoming a widely-accepted part of the enlarged comprehensive security packages sought at the bargaining table.

Analysis of Severance Pay Plan Interest and Prevalence

A review of the history of severance pay plans in labor-management relations in the United States gives rise to a number of interesting questions. Why, for example, has there been a long-standing interest in these plans on the part of the American Newspaper Guild and, until recently, relatively little or no interest on the part of the UAW? Why did this become a critical bargaining issue in the railroad industry? Why is it probable that a concerted drive for such provisions in the labor contracts will be under way in many newly-organized industries? Why has there been no concerted effort to

[32] AFL-CIO, Industrial Union Department, *Fact Sheet* (May 1959), p. 2.

force the adoption of these plans by some unions that might have been expected to show a keen interest in them, such as the United Mine Workers or the Hosiery Workers? Is the intensity of competition in these industries so great that the unions cannot hope to obtain severance pay?

An understanding of the conditions giving rise to union demands for severance pay will also help to explain the nature and scope of the arrangements adopted. One or several of the following seven influences are likely to account for the concentration of these plans in particular industries in the past and for their future rapid extension to many other industries. More often than not these influences operate in combination.

FREQUENCY OF BUSINESS MORTALITY AND MIGRATION. In an industry with a high rate of business mortality the union, if it is strong, is likely to show a keen interest in economic security for the permanently-displaced employee. The dress industry is illustrative. A relatively low capital investment requirement permits easy entrance into, and intense competition often causes prompt exit of firms out of, the industry. The ILGWU as early as the 1920's showed an interest in the payment of employees whose jobs were eliminated abruptly by a cessation of operation. This gave way temporarily to efforts by the union to correct the basic causes of high business mortality, such as the insistence on union-approved, sound cost accounting methods in exchange for the availability of union employees. But the continued high rate of business demise, either because of receivership or because of migration to low-cost areas, has led the union to insist on a severance program.

In 1958 as part of its strike settlement the ILGWU obtained severance pay benefits, which were to apply to an estimated 475,000 employees in the industry. Under this plan employers contributed .5 of 1 per cent of payroll to a fund to accumulate until 1960. In that year and thereafter the fund is to be used along with current contributions to pay severance benefits to workers whose employers go out of business or move elsewhere. It is expected that the benefits will provide one week's pay for each year of employee service, but whether this can be done is uncertain.

The northern textile industry, which experienced extensive liquidation or exodus to the South in the past decade, soon found severance pay an important union demand. The movement of plants or of jobs in the automobile and electrical industries, as a result of decentralization programs, helped explain the interest of the UAW, IUE, and IBEW in these plans. The IUE-General Electric Conference Board in 1958 observed that the union had contracts covering 150,000 employees that provided for some form of severance or termination pay. It noted that the G. E. Master Agreement provided for severance pay only when the entire plant is shut down, but the union considered this coverage inadequate. In arguing for a higher benefit and more inclusive plan the IUE claimed termination pay not only would provide an income during readjustment, but it would help prevent plant shutdowns, relocations, and unnecessary dismissals by making it expensive to terminate employees. This view seems unjustified. The cost of severance pay may well affect the timing of decisions to relocate, but it is not likely to be the determining factor in decisions whether or not to relocate.

In October 1957 the AFL-CIO *Collective Bargaining Report* emphasized the need for a series of policies to cope with the "stepped-up tempo of plant movement." It stated, "In the past, most unions have sought to ease the effects of plant moves largely by meeting each situation as it arose and by attempting at the time to negotiate measures to minimize the blow to workers. Now increased effort will be devoted to writing protection into agreements long before any plant move may be contemplated." One of the principal measures suggested for meeting this problem was a liberal severance pay plan.

Plant closures and migration have become such serious problems in the hat industry in recent years that the union has tried to secure clauses in the contract prohibiting *any* transfer of work. In 1953-54 an eleven-month strike occurred over one management's right to move work from an existing location to new plants. The company involved, the Hat Corporation of America, would not grant a prohibiting clause but did agree to "center" its operations in Norwalk, Connecticut, and to give severance pay to workers displaced by any discontinuance of operations who preferred the allowance to other jobs with the company.

It has become increasingly evident that the offer of jobs in a new location to employees affected adversely by a partial or complete movement of operations is not enough to forestall severance pay demands. Unions usually insist on the right of employees to follow their jobs if they so desire, and some have been successful in securing payment by the company of all moving costs. But the trend is toward arrangements that give employees a choice between moving and accepting severance pay. This recognizes the understandable reluctance of employees, many with long service, to break their community ties.

FREQUENCY OF MERGERS. Formal mergers or consolidation of the operations of several companies in the same industry frequently cause job elimination and accentuate the need for protecting displaced workers. The extensive cost-saving coordination program in the railroad industry described above gave rise to the Washington Job Protection Agreement. The early emergence of severance pay plans in Newspaper Guild agreements is explained in part by the many mergers in this industry in the past two decades. In a contract survey in 1949 it was found that 201 of the 202 Guild contracts in effect in December 1949 contained severance pay provisions. Some other unions in the newspaper industry have made demands for severance pay or have adjusted other contract devices to meet the merger problem. For example, the "bogus work" system of the ITU described in Chapter 11 has been used as a kind of severance pay plan. By not keeping up with the inflow of bogus it is possible to create work for the compositors who cannot find other jobs when newspapers merge. In Columbus, Ohio, no bogus was set for eighteen months to provide a work-cushion for men who would become surplus in the merger of the *Ohio State Journal* and the *Columbus Dispatch*.

The general increase in mergers in recent years has led more and more unions to fear the consequences of complete job elimination. The Industrial Union Department of the AFL-CIO cites this trend as a basic reason for revived interest in severance pay over and above the security provided by unemployment compensation and supplementary unemployment benefits.

THE SHRINKING INDUSTRY. Some industries threatened by competitive products or services face gradual but inevitable business decline and loss of job opportunities. If highly organized, they are almost certain to be confronted with severance pay demands by the union. One of the earliest formal agreements for severance benefits was adopted in 1936 between the National Organization of Masters, Mates and Pilots of America, the Marine Engineers' Beneficial Association, and the Seamen's Union of America and the four ferry lines operating in the San Francisco Bay. The ferryboatmen, represented by the unions, became convinced that the opening of the San Francisco-Oakland and the Golden Gate Bridges would result in gradual elimination of their jobs.[33]

The secular decline in the transit industry explains the interest of local transit unions in severance arrangements. The Newspaper Guild Director of Organization said in 1953 that "because the newspaper industry is a shrinking industry, economy dismissals are one of the Guild's major problems."[34]

EXTENSIVE TECHNOLOGICAL CHANGE. In 1933 the Cigarmakers' Union, by then an almost defunct organization because of its historical policy of opposition to technological change, proposed as part of the Code for Fair Competition in the industry a tax of 4.66 cents on each 1,000 cigars made by machinery to allow payment of $10 a week for 52 weeks to the cigar maker displaced by machinery.[35] Although this machinery-based tax proposal, quite obviously aimed at deterring further mechanization, was unsuccessful, it was imitated by other unions as the tempo of technological change and resulting elimination of jobs increased in other industries.

In railroads the Brotherhood of Railway Clerks was moved to insist on extension of the 1936 Washington Agreement principles to cover technological displacements not caused by a consolidation or an abandonment. In February 1956 an agreement between the clerks and the Chesapeake and Ohio applied the 1936 Agreement to "all employees adversely affected by their work being placed in the (Univac) Computer Center."[36] The clerks have also negotiated severance pay benefits to cover job losses due to the introduction of electronic data computers on the Baltimore and Ohio, the Illinois Central, the Boston and Maine, and other carriers. In 1956 in the meat packing industry the union succeeded in getting severance pay

[33] Hawkins, *Dismissal Compensation*, pp. 175-82.
[34] *The Guild Reporter* (May 8, 1953), p. 2.
[35] Hawkins, *Dismissal Compensation*, p. 147.
[36] Haber, *Maintenance of Way Employment*, pp. 187-219.

coverage extended to include displacement due to technological change; the plan negotiated in 1949 had covered only that due to department or plant closing.[37]

One of the critical issues in the 1958 strike of the IBEW against CBS radio and television facilities in seven cities was the union demand for severance pay for the people whose jobs were threatened by the introduction of new processes, such as video tape, automatic transmitting facilities, and the like. The strike settlement agreement provided for 13 weeks' severance pay to anyone, regardless of length of service, who was laid off or dismissed because of automated processes. In a new contract (1957) between the Retail, Wholesale and Department Store Union and the Charleston, S.C., plant of American Tobacco Company displaced workers were given a choice between severance pay of from one to seven weeks and top preference in rehiring for two years. Between 150 and 200 employees were displaced because of new technology.[38] Early in 1958 the Hatters, Cap and Millinery Workers Union negotiated a severance pay plan with the Hat Corporation of America to provide benefits to workers "automated" out of their jobs.

SEVERANCE PAY IN LIEU OF OTHER CONTRACT PROVISIONS. In some instances there is reason to believe that the severance pay program is a substitute for other more direct ways of handling problems of employee security and status. Mergers are part of the reason why the Newspaper Guild insists on such clauses, but equally important is the relative absence of seniority arrangements for effecting layoffs in newspaper staffs. In exchange for the high degree of freedom newspaper managements have retained in determining who is to be laid off, the union has been able to extract a dismissal pay provision.

This also explains the broad scope of many of the American Newspaper Guild severance pay plans. Pay is usually given to those who resign or who are dismissed for any reason except gross misconduct,

[37] Plant closing in the meat packing industry, especially in Chicago, became a serious problem at an early date. In 1953 Swift and Company closed its Chicago hog slaughter operations and later its small stock (calves, lamb and sheep) operations; in mid-1959 it closed its cattle slaughter facilities. In 1955 Wilson closed all of its Chicago slaughter plants. In July 1959 all Chicago livestock slaughtering operations of Armour and Company came to a halt, causing displacement of 2,000 of Armour's 3,000 Chicago employees.

[38] IUD Fact Sheet (October 31, 1957).

neglect of duty, or similar offenses. The Guild constitution requires that no local may negotiate a contract without severance pay unless the international executive board gives specific permission.[39]

In recent years the locals have been urged by the collective bargaining committee to eliminate any qualifications at all in severance pay clauses. The Guild stresses the importance of what it calls "genuine" severance pay, that is, a fully vested right and property of the employee whether he resigns or is dismissed.[40] A survey of 146 guild contracts in 1953 revealed that 27 were entirely free from qualifications that would modify severance payments. Eleven allowed nonpayment when the employee had failed to maintain good standing in the Guild or when he deliberately provoked his own discharge in order to obtain severance pay. Of the 146 contracts, 123 provided for severance payments on death, 63 on retirement, and 42 on resignation.[41]

In some instances severance pay has been adopted in lieu of a restriction on the subcontracting of work sought by the union. In 1950 the Transport Workers' Union struck American Airlines for ten days to secure a prohibition against the contracting out of work and to get severance pay. The union was given the latter but failed to gain any limitation on subcontracting. In the New York hotel industry noncontractual severance payments are often made on an *ad hoc* basis when the smaller hotels decide to subcontract the food operation.

In the northern cotton textile and woolen and worsted industries a separation payment plan was adopted in 1952 as a substitute for a regular pension program. The industries felt they could not afford the vesting, funding, or assumption of past service credits called for in a pension plan. Yet the instability of the industry, the frequency of mill closures, and the high average age of the work force made an unfunded plan without past credits meaningless for most workers. Under most of the 1951 agreements provision was made for "retirement-separation" pay for employees with 15 years of service who retired voluntarily at the age of 65. One week's pay was given for each year of service, up to a maximum of 20, and was payable in a lump

[39] *American Newspaper Guild Manual*, Twenty-Second Convention (June-July 1955), pp. 71, 97-98.
[40] *American Newspaper Guild Convention Proceedings* (1955), p. 116.
[41] *The Guild Reporter* (June 1953), p. 5.

sum. To qualify, a worker had to have an average of 1,000 hours employment for each year of service.[42]

In 1950 a Midwest milk drivers' union negotiated a retirement fund program under which both employees and employer made deposits in individual employee accounts. Only employees in good standing in the union were eligible to participate. If a person severed his employment, either voluntarily or because of disability or retirement, he could receive the sums credited to his account during his years of active participation in the program. If a worker died, his beneficiary received the credited amount. This plan evolved when it was discovered that because the work was arduous, many drivers left the industry before the age of 65. The usual kind of pension program seemed unsuitable for this reason and also because it failed to take care of other risks and contingencies that the workers faced. In effect, a severance or separation pay program was developed as a substitute for the more common pension arrangement.

One of the difficulties in administering this type of program is to prevent indiscriminate withdrawal of funds for purposes other than those for which they were intended while at the same time making certain that the funds were available for *bona fide* purposes. A number of safeguards were introduced to handle this problem. First, a person who left the industry voluntarily was required to wait six months before the payment was made unless the Fund Committee decided an earlier payment was justified. Second, to discourage quits motivated by a desire to use the available fund, the parties decided that if a person's account exceeded $300, the sum was to be payable in monthly installments of $75. Finally, if a person had used his separation fund and re-entered the industry, he had to re-establish eligibility with six months of employment before he could again be covered by the plan.

In some cases, severance pay, rather than being a substitute for other clauses, minimizes union reliance on standard clauses. For example, in the radio and TV industries, severance pay is usually provided and is used to compensate employees who quit or are discharged. A union spokesman for the various performing guilds explains that in this type of operation separation is considered more desirable than forced retention through the protest of a discharge.

[42] B. Yabroff and A. J. Herlihy, "History of Work Stoppages in Textile Industries," *Monthly Labor Review* (April 1953), p. 11.

Because there are employees at radio or TV stations, relationships are highly personal. Employees must get along well with each other, and if animosities develop, it is wise for the offending person to move to another job rather than to protest a discharge. In the judgment of this spokesman it is often "futile" for the union to win a discharge arbitration case because the victory leaves in its wake insurmountable relationship problems. Under these circumstances the union seeks a fairly liberal severance pay program, thus allowing the employer to discharge or to invite resignation without employee or union challenge. This helps to explain the emphasis on severance pay by the Newspaper Guild as well.

In some instances the pressure for severance pay may be influenced by the scope of the seniority unit used for layoff purposes. These units have been described in Chapter 6. If the management insists on a narrow unit, it may mean that long-service employees will be vulnerable to layoff, and the union will seek some dismissal pay arrangement. This has prompted some companies to agree to a broader unit for seniority application where permanent displacement is involved.

INFLUENCE OF RELATED BENEFIT PLANS. The significant growth in employee benefit programs, such as those described in Chapters 13 and 14 or the income security arrangements described earlier in this chapter, has contributed to union interest and union success in securing severance pay. It has done this in two ways.

First, success in bargaining for the security of employees at the time of retirement, of sickness, and of cyclical and seasonal temporary unemployment has helped to bring into sharp focus the remaining uncovered areas of insecurity. One of these is the permanent displacement of workers due to plant liquidation, to mergers or migration, or to technological elimination of jobs. A decade or more of preoccupation with employment and income security measures in bargaining has stimulated a desire to perfect the total package. Up until recently pensions, sickness and accident insurance, and supplementary unemployment benefits have had priority. Union interest is now turning to areas of insecurity felt to be covered inadequately by existing programs. The format of many new severance pay plans shows careful integration with other parts of the benefit structure.

In this connection it should be noted that unions do not consider unemployment compensation, supplemented by privately-negotiated plans, an adequate answer to the problem of the permanently displaced employee. The latter has little or no chance for recall and consequently loses the many cumulative rights associated with seniority. By the permanence of his separation from a given employer, he is put on notice that he must seek employment elsewhere. In some cases this may mean a geographic move, particularly where the job loss occurs in a depressed industrial area, such as the New England textile or shoe communities. It may mean the loss of opportunity to use specialized skills acquired and applied over a long period of time; sometimes the termination forces the employee to learn new skills at some cost, or, as an alternative, to move to a lesser paid, unskilled or semi-skilled job.

In brief, the economic hardships occasioned by irrevocable separation for reasons beyond the employee's control are deemed to be much greater than the temporary layoffs, for which unemployment compensation and SUB were intended. Severance pay is intended to compensate a man for the loss of accumulated rights. It follows that most union leaders consider a separate, special protection apart from unemployment benefits a requisite part of any security package.

In securing this protection, union leadership may be confronted with internal political problems. A good severance pay plan must provide by far the largest compensation to long-service, older employees. They are the ones who lose more accumulated rights and for whom the hardship of permanent job loss is greatest. In some unions the older workers may lack enough votes to compel pursuit of a properly designed plan.

Second, the formulation of other benefit plans has often provided a natural basis for extension of coverage to include special severance payments. As we shall see in the illustrations below, the creation of SUB in 1955 and thereafter gave considerable impetus to an increase in the number of contingencies covered. The fund machinery lends itself well to union justification for, and employer acceptance of, a more complete security package. The growth of the funding device in recent years has had a remarkable influence. Its acceptance for pensions and for health and welfare programs, as noted in Chapters 13 and 14, has led to its adoption for other purposes. The present and probable potential growth in severance pay arrangements, as well as in supplementary unemployment benefit plans, is attributable in large measure to the funding principle, which has gained widespread acceptance.

Union accomplishment on other fronts in the fight for income security is not the only reason for the extension of severance pay plans, but it is an important contributing factor. The stimulus afforded by related benefit plans is illustrated by the following developments.

As stated above, the Oil, Chemical and Atomic Workers Union announced in 1957 that a mandatory goal for locals was to be a severance plan based on *age* and *service* to eliminate surplus refinery workers, especially those too old for re-employment elsewhere and too young for pensions.

A variant of this proposal was secured in an agreement in 1957 with the Standard Oil Company of Ohio. Under this negotiated plan that portion of severance pay to be based on company service is 75 per cent of a week's base pay for each year of service after the first two years. This would apply to employees through 57 years of age, after which the allowance would decline until it reached zero at age 65, when the employee would be entitled to a full pension. That portion of severance pay based on age would begin at age 51 and would increase in amount to age 58, when it would start declining until it reached zero at age 65. For example, under the plan a man who is permanently severed at age 58 and who has 25 years of service and a weekly base pay of $100, would receive $1,725 for service and $4,800 for age, or a total of $6,525, the equivalent of full pay for about 15 months. A younger or older man would receive proportionately less. An employee is qualified who is permanently terminated for any of the following reasons: elimination of jobs, consolidation of departments or divisions, mergers, abandonment of plants, or technological changes.[43] The extent of private plans for separation payment among oil companies undoubtedly facilitated this new achievement by the union.

Another major development showing the influence of related benefit plans in the adoption of severance pay are the automobile settlements of 1958. Although the drains on the accumulated SUB funds were somewhat heavy because of the 1957-58 recession, the funds were still in good condition due to the built-in restrictions adopted in 1955. At the same time, the UAW became increasingly

[43] *OCAW Union News* (November 6, 1957).

concerned as it approached the 1958 negotiations with the insecurities created by plant movement, complete plant shutdowns, and automation.

The 1958 automobile agreements added the separation pay principle as an integral part of the SUB. The essential features of the Ford plan, for example, are the following: to be eligible an employee must have at least two years' service at the time of layoff, and he must have been on layoff for one year before he can apply, although the company may permit earlier application if his prospects for re-employment appear negligible. Those who are eligible for any retirement benefit other than a deferred vested benefit are not eligible for separation payment. The payments to these employees are to be made out of the SUB trust fund and will be made only if the trust fund position is equal to or in excess of 13 per cent. The nature of the trust fund has been explained earlier in this chapter. If the fund is below 13 per cent, the application will be placed on file and will be paid at a later time when the fund position is improved. A man will be entitled to lump sum payments varying from 40 hours' pay for those with 2 to 3 years' service on a graduated basis to a maximum of 1,200 hours' pay for those with 30 or more years' service. However, the payment will be reduced by the amount the employee has received in the form of SUB payments after the last day he worked, and payment will vary with the level of the trust fund. Finally, it is provided that the seniority of an applicant who accepts separation payment will be considered broken as of the date the payment is made. If he is rehired subsequently, there will be no reinstatement of his seniority.

In seeking this innovation in the automobile industry the union hoped that it would serve as a pattern for the auto parts industry, where plant closures, migration, and mergers were even more numerous. It has had considerable success in extending this formula.

As early as 1955 the individual-account approach to supplementary unemployment benefits of the type negotiated in the glass industry automatically permitted use of the account for terminations. These agreements, as noted earlier in this chapter, permit an employee to withdraw the balance left in his account if he is terminated for any reason. The money set aside by the company is vested in him and acquires the form of severance pay when complete termination takes place.

Undoubtedly the future extension and form of severance pay plans will be similarly shaped by other elements in the over-all security benefit program. Unlike the older plans, which often occupied no clearly-defined niche and whose use was sought in contingencies such as routine layoffs, retirement, and the like, the new plans are part of a coordinated, multipurpose benefit structure.

AD HOC SEVERANCE PAY ARRANGEMENTS. Although our interest is primarily in the adoption of formal, contractual arrangements, the very considerable number of *ad hoc* severance payments made by managements to handle a particular problem or grievance should not be overlooked. The number of companies that have actually paid severance to one or more employees at one time or another far exceeds the total of formal plans reported by the BLS or other surveys. Many illustrations may be given. A company wishing to introduce a new machine may voluntarily offer a cash severance payment to those displaced directly or indirectly by the machine. Although not obligated to do so, the company makes this offer to lessen the resistance of employees and the union. Many companies have avoided disputes over the contracting out of work, such as building maintenance, cafeteria operation, and the like, by agreeing with the union to give a money settlement to those whose jobs are eliminated.

Frequently a discharge grievance is settled to the satisfaction of the union and the aggrieved by a lump-sum settlement. This occurs most often in hardship discharge cases where both the union and the company agree that it would be better for plant morale for the employee to be discharged even though his service is considerable.

In a number of cases the *ad hoc* severance payment has much broader application. Several companies closing all or a substantial part of their operations and moving them to another location may grant such payment even though not required to do so by the labor agreement.

Severance Pay Plan Administrative Problems

Normally a severance pay plan, by its very terms, is used only infrequently. Therefore, as one might expect, the grievances or administrative problems involved in such a plan are not a significant source of trouble in labor relations. The few principal problem areas are (1) the determination of when a layoff is permanent, (2) the cause of the permanent layoff, (3) the relationship between severance payment and seniority rights or alternative employment rights, and (4) the effect of unemployment compensation regulations on the application of severance pay plans.

DETERMINING WHEN A LAYOFF IS PERMANENT. Many of the earlier agreements providing for severance pay specified that it was to apply only when the termination of employment for stated reasons was permanent. Illustrative of these clauses is the agreement of a large steel company with the United Steelworkers of America. It provides that "if the Company shall close permanently a plant or discontinue permanently a department of a plant or a substantial portion thereof, each Employee whose employment shall be terminated by the Company as a result thereof and who at the time shall have a length of continuous service with the Company of 3 years or more shall be entitled to a severance allowance."

Under a clause such as this the question of when the closing of a plant or department is permanent may arise. For example, a department of the Bethlehem Steel Company devoted exclusively to the production of projectiles for the armed forces was shut down because of a lack of orders. Some employees were transferred to other jobs, and some were laid off. The question arose whether an indefinite shutdown such as this was permanent within the meaning of the agreement. The union emphasized that the shutdown could extend beyond two years, after which time the laid off employees would lose all their seniority under another contract provision. Proceeding on the basis that this was a factual question, the arbitrator held that the department appeared to be in a "sort of 'stand-by' status—held in readiness by the Company for a resumption of active operations whenever new orders for projectiles should be received." He observed further that the severance pay provisions were not written to apply to all layoffs of more than two years' duration.[44] Accordingly, he denied the union claim for severance pay.

Under this language, which is generally characteristic of steel industry severance pay provisions, the question of what constitutes a permanent shutdown has been a persistently vexatious issue. In general, severance pay has been denied when operations were cut to

[44] Bureau of National Affairs, *Labor Arbitration Reports*, Vol. 23 (January 5, 1955), pp. 618-20.

meet business conditions, when existing facilities were replaced, and when more efficient equipment was installed.

Although there have been numerous arbitration decisions on this subject in steel, there remains the troublesome problem of when a gradual cutback in operations becomes a permanent shutdown. To illustrate, a rolling mill of one company was cut back to one turn in the fall of 1947, and the mill was finally closed completely in 1948. Were the workers laid off by the cutback the victims of the first stages of a shutdown? When do marginal mills, used only when capacity is inadequate to meet demand, become shutdown facilities whose employees are entitled to severance pay? Arbitrators have not succeeded in resolving conclusively the ambiguities in contract language. In contrast to the Bethlehem Steel case cited above is that resulting from the closing of Republic Steel's Spaulding Mines concentration mill. In the latter case, the arbitrator agreed that the question of "permanency" is a factual matter, but he held that the mere statement by management of its future plans and expectations was not enough. He concluded that a "permanent" shutdown had occurred when equipment had been shut down for an indefinite period and there was no real likelihood of its being reactivated.[45]

CAUSE OF PERMANENT LAYOFF. Many agreements limit entitlement to severance pay to certain types of layoff. The limitation may be in the form of the rare exception, as in the case of the Newspaper Guild agreements, which provide for liberal use of severance pay. For example, many of these agreements call for payment of a severance allowance "if an employee is discharged for reasons other than gross neglect of duty or gross misconduct." Although the severance payment system has enhanced the freedom of the employer to discharge in this industry in the sense that grievances on discharges are relatively infrequent, there often arises the question whether the cause for discharge was "gross neglect of duty or gross misconduct." In effect, the nature of the discharge rather than the justification for the discharge becomes a matter of paramount concern for the parties.

A review of many arbitration decisions involving this union and various publishing companies justifies the conclusion that the single

[45] *Basic Steel Arbitration Information Bulletin*, Case No. 767 (July 13, 1952), pp. 3989-91.

exception in an otherwise broad coverage plan has been construed liberally. Arbitrators seem to be guided by the concept of liberality of severance pay in exchange for freedom for the employer in discharging employees, although this is seldom stated explicitly as a basis for their decisions. Thus, an employee who was discharged for continued tardiness and absenteeism over a five-year period in disregard of repeated warnings was found to be guilty of neglect of duty but not of "gross" neglect. He was considered eligible for severance pay.[46] An advertising solicitor of a newspaper company, who had a history of drinking and had been suspended for intoxication, was finally discharged for reporting to work an hour after consuming four or five martinis and for making "incoherent" remarks at a business meeting. His discharge was not contested by the union, but his entitlement to severance pay did become an issue. The arbitrator concluded that this was not "gross misconduct" within the meaning of the contract as claimed by the employer.[47]

The restriction under many severance pay clauses is expressed in a positive, but more limiting manner, as in the case of the General Electric Company agreement with the IUE, which provides for severance pay only when the entire plant is closed. Under these and similar clauses, many questions may arise as to whether the cause of the layoff was such that discharged workers were eligible for severance pay. The union in a steel fabricating company sought severance pay for those employees laid off by the transfer of operations to an improved, technologically superior new mill. It was held that the action of the employer was a replacement of old facilities rather than a discontinuance of operations, and severance pay was denied under the agreement.[48] This illustration is very similar to those involving determination of when a layoff is permanent.

Extremely limiting clauses are to be found in the agreements between motion picture and related industry companies and such organizations as the Studio Projectionists, the Film Technicians, and Motion Picture Studio Cinetechnicians. For example, one such contract provides that persons laid off shall be granted dismissal pay only if layoff is not occasioned by "voluntary resignation, physical incapacity, epidemic, fire, action of the elements, strike, walk-outs,

[46] The Evening News Association (*Detroit News*) and American Newspaper Guild, Local 22, 25 LA 912-14.
[47] Post Publishing Company and American Newspaper Guild, 24 LA 173-78.
[48] 18 LA 267-68.

labor dispute, governmental order, court order or order of any other legally constituted body, act of God, public enemy, war, riot, civil commotion, or for any cause or causes beyond the control of the Producer whether of the same or any other nature." Yet in spite of these restrictions on entitlement to severance pay, questions arise inevitably. For example, is a decline in customer demand for the color process or for the printing of film negatives, prompting the discontinuance of a company's laboratories in these fields, something which is beyond the control of the Producer?

SEVERANCE PAYMENT AND SENIORITY RIGHTS. There are two fairly common administrative questions in the operation of a severance pay plan that arise unless the governing agreement is quite specific.

The first is whether the employee laid off permanently from his job is obligated to exercise his seniority rights before he is entitled to severance pay for termination of the employer-employee relationship. It has already been noted earlier in this chapter that the breadth of the seniority unit for rights of transfer in lieu of layoff may affect interest in severance pay. Thus, if the unit is extremely narrow by contract design, the vulnerability to complete separation of a senior employee is greater, as is the union's interest in severance pay.

But even if the unit is broad, entitling an employee to avoid layoff by bumping an employee on another, often less desirable job, the existence of severance pay arrangements may create the question whether the right to bump becomes an obligation.

For example, a severance pay agreement in the textile industry, adopted as a substitute for a pension trust fund, provided that employees with 15 or more years of service, who were displaced for technological reasons, because of movement of plant or equipment, or other similar reasons, would qualify for payment. A loom fixer was removed from his job because of the movement of looms from the plant under agreement with the union. The company sought to assign this man to an available position as a weaver, a lower-rated job to which he was entitled by right of seniority. The employee protested such assignment on the ground that he preferred to receive severance pay. The company argued that he was not eligible. He had not been displaced since he was assigned to a job to which he had a contractual right. A refusal of the assignment would be tantamount to a voluntary quit, and the severance pay plan excluded temporary layoffs, discharge for just cause, or quits. In this case the arbitrator rejected the company position on two separate grounds. First, the contract terms assumed that the exercise of a seniority right was not obligatory upon an employee, that entitlement to severance was destroyed only if the displaced employee accepted other employment. Second, he held that the employer's interpretation would give employees with lesser seniority rights greater freedom of choice than employees with longer service, an untenable effect of seniority.[49]

As might be expected, Newspaper Guild agreements have been interpreted liberally on this subject. For example, a sports reporter who refused to accept a transfer to the job of rewrite man at the same rate of pay was considered eligible by an arbitrator for severance pay even though he was discharged because of this refusal. It is significant that neither the union nor the reporter grieved his discharge in spite of 17 years' service.[50] They were more interested in his entitlement to severance than in the merits of his discharge.

In general, it has been concluded that the "rights" of seniority do not create an "obligation" that must be exercised before severance pay may be received by an employee. But there have been some important exceptions to this prevailing view. A company with an agreement with the American Communications Association, an independent union, decided to transfer its plant from various locations in New York City to one centralized plant in Stamford, Connecticut, approximately 33 miles away. A number of employees, reluctant to move or commute to Stamford, sought severance pay under an agreement clause providing for such payment in the event of "force reduction furlough." Their claim was denied by an arbitrator on the ground that there were no enforced or involuntary layoffs.

In some steel industry severance pay plans, it is provided that "in lieu of severance allowance, the company may offer an eligible employee a job in at least the same job class for which he is qualified, in the same general locality. The employee shall have the option of either accepting such new employment or requesting his severance allowance." These agreements provide further that an employee otherwise eligible for severance allowance who is entitled by seniority to a job in at least the same job class in another part of the plant

[49] 25 LA 587-94.
[50] 23 LA 231-38.

shall *not* be entitled to severance allowance whether he accepts or rejects the transfer.

These two provisions may appear to be incongruous, but, as applied by the steel companies and as interpreted by arbitrators, they are not. They mean that an employee who is offered gratuitously a job in the same job class as that from which he was displaced may elect the job or severance pay; but the employee who is entitled by seniority to a job in at least the same job class becomes ineligible for severance pay. This means that those whose seniority rights entitle them only to a lower labor grade job and who otherwise qualify not only get a job but also receive a severance allowance, according to numerous arbitration decisions on the subject. The results seem to be unusual, even to the parties who negotiated the language.

It may be that the extension of severance pay to employed men in this industry is a consequence of the narrow seniority units. When a unit shutdown is effected, the narrowness of seniority units forces considerable vertical downgrading and limits horizontal transfers. Severance pay thus acquires a new purpose. It not only reimburses the person whose employment status is destroyed; it also compensates the person whose status is injured by downgrading. In the steel industry job seniority is generally based on service in a particular department or mill. If the job seniority unit closes down, there is little opportunity to bump on a plantwide basis in one's job class. More often a worker displaced from his job is out on the street or is downgraded to a lesser job or to the labor pool. In the steel industry income loss because of downgrading has become as important a basis for severance payment as is complete loss of job.

A second, but distinct, question is that of retention of seniority and, therefore, recall rights by those who have been granted and have accepted severance pay. If termination pay is given only on the assumption that an employee will never be re-employed, and if acceptance of it assumes an irrevocable break in the employer-employee relationship, it would be assumed that all seniority rights were ended. This is the case when the agreement provides expressly that the receipt of severance pay ends all seniority privileges, for example the 1958 automobile agreements. But many contracts fail to relate the termination pay clause to the provision for seniority loss, or they neglect to make any provision for seniority loss. The resultant problems for companies with liberal severance pay are considerable. An employee whose job is considered permanently erased by a technological change or the closing of a department may receive severance pay in a considerable amount and then claim recall rights when there is an unexpected revival of business.[51]

Companies and unions alike have often been guilty of negligence in failing to specify the effect of severance payment on retention of seniority rights.

UNEMPLOYMENT COMPENSATION AND SEVERANCE PAY. The issue of whether payments disqualify the recipient from state unemployment compensation benefits has been a critical problem in many areas, particularly in the case of agreements with a liberal basis for payment. In many ways the problem is similar to the integration of SUB plans with state unemployment compensation.

The latest figures issued by the U. S. Bureau of Employment Security show that in eighteen states the receipt of severance pay disqualified the recipient or was used as an offset for unemployment benefits.[52] In 1957 a Missouri Court of Appeals ruled that a severance payment granted under an American Newspaper Guild contract barred the employee from receiving unemployment benefits for the number of weeks the payment covered. The Guild argued that severance pay was more than compensation for a layoff; it was designed also to compensate for the loss of important rights. In its statement to the Court, the Guild pointed out that severance payment was given even if the severed employee found a job with another employer immediately after his layoff. Nevertheless the Missouri Court was unpersuaded by these arguments. The Supreme Court of the State of California issued a similar ruling in 1956.[53]

[51] A related question that arises occasionally is that of how many times an employee is entitled to receive severance pay. If receipt of payment is not accompanied by a break in seniority, the employee may be recalled and "severed" again within a relatively short period of time. Some agreements provide for this through various limitations. For example, one agreement states: "An employee who accepts severance pay shall not be eligible again for severance pay until he has accrued one more year of service. Any employee who accepts severance pay in preference to displacing a junior employee shall be placed at the bottom of the seniority list, for the purposes of recall, but may retain his seniority, for the purposes of recall, if he refuses to accept severance pay."

[52] The states disqualifying a person from receiving unemployment compensation while receiving severance pay are Alabama, Arizona, Arkansas, Connecticut, Montana, North Carolina, and West Virginia. Weekly benefits are reduced by the amount of severance payment in California, Indiana, Maine, Minnesota, Missouri, Nebraska, New Hampshire, Ohio, Oregon, Pennsylvania, and Virginia.

[53] "Severance Pay in Industry," *IUD Digest* (Spring 1958), pp. 133-40.

It is possible that public policy in this regard will undergo a change or at least a careful review because of the growth of SUB plans. It is disconcerting that administrators have given very little thought to the role of severance pay in relationship to unemployment compensation. An inquiry of one such official produced the following rationale for the disallowance of compensation when dismissal pay was granted under a union contract: "to the extent that dismissal payments are included in taxable wages for contribution purposes, claimants receiving such payments are not unemployed for the weeks concerned." The suggestion that severance payments could be considered compensation for the loss of accumulated job rights was new to this administrator. He viewed such payment as a wage payment to a worker during a readjustment period.

The more recently negotiated severance pay plans have benefited from the experience of the earlier ones. For example, the 1958 automobile plan, described briefly earlier in this chapter, deals directly or indirectly with each of these problem areas. In other situations, older plans are being revised to eliminate these controversial issues. The concept of severance payment is likely to receive more attention in collective bargaining in the immediate future, and it is unlikely that the adoption of such plans will create more than minor administrative difficulties.

17 / Wage Incentives

THIS AND THE FOLLOWING chapter deal with the variables affecting employee efficiency and union-management relations in companies and plants employing wage incentives and measured daywork.[1] The marks of success of such programs are both good efficiency and good union-management relations.

This and the next chapter are organized under the following twelve interrelated topics: (1) experience with wage incentives, (2) demoralized incentive plans, (3) revised incentive plans, (4) efficient incentive plans, (5) the piece-rate industries, (6) wage incentive provisions in contracts, (7) technology and method of pay, (8) replacement of incentives by measured daywork, (9) administration of measured daywork, (10) union time-study representatives, (11) management policy and production standards, (12) union policy and production standards. The first six are covered in this chapter, and the remainder in the next.

World War II, postwar prosperity, and differences in union and management behavior have given rise to very mixed experience with wage incentives. Some incentive plans have become quite demoralized, not infrequently damaging seriously the competitive position of plants and companies. This latter point is covered in Chapter 27, on the problems of high-cost plants. For this and other reasons some companies and unions have turned to union-management cooperation. Cooperation utilizing plant-wide incentives, such as the Scanlon Plan, is of particular interest, and is discussed in Chapter 28. More frequently traditional incentive plans have been revised or in some cases abandoned. When abandoned, the usual substitute has been

---

[1] The term "measured daywork" is used to indicate pay by the hour in association with some type of control of worker efficiency by means of production standards. It is not used in its early sense of paying workers one of several hourly rates depending on their average performance over a period of time. Today this latter form of payment is very rare; only one plant was encountered that used it. The longer term "daywork associated with work measurement" is more accurate but needlessly cumbersome. A popular term frequently used is "a fair-day's-work program."

measured daywork or a fair-day's-work program. Technological advances have to some extent diminished the need for incentives or at least opened up a wider area of choice as between incentives and daywork. While some incentive plans have become demoralized, others have continued to operate successfully. Some daywork plants have introduced incentive plans. Where incentives are used, there has been a considerable trend toward broad coverage of all employees in the plant. Such broad coverage has frequently created some questionable applications of incentive wages.

Neither incentives nor measured daywork automatically produce the results sought. There are at least the following important variables: (1) management policy and practice, (2) union policy and practice, (3) the character of union-management relations, (4) the influence of particular technology and the frequency and degree of change, (5) community environment, and (6) employee attitudes.

One might assume that with good administration and receptive employee attitudes, either method of pay would work quite successfully. But the problem is more complex than that. For example, consider five plants of the same company organized by the same international union. Two are incentive plants, and three are measured daywork plants. The most efficient plant among the five and the least efficient, separated by a wide margin, are incentive plants. The best daywork plant is almost as efficient as the top incentive plant. The poorest daywork plant is above the poorest incentive plant but by a modest margin. Questions about comparing relative efficiency arise because of differences in technology. Better labor relations are associated with higher efficiency, but it is hard to say which is the cause and which is effect. Community environments vary as do employee attitudes. Some management opinion in each plant favors the method of pay which it does not have. The majority opinion of management in the company referred to above now favors daywork. Clearly the relative success of the two methods in any plant will depend on at least the variables mentioned, and these variables will be considered in this chapter and the next.

Finally, method of pay and production standards (the crucial administrative problems under both incentive and daywork systems) are important for three primary reasons. In the first place, there is no question that efficiency varies significantly among plants and companies and over time in the same plants and companies, thus affecting competitive standing to a major degree. Plants are being abandoned because of high cost associated with poor efficiency. Collective bargaining creates an environment that definitely influences worker efficiency. In the second place, the attitudes of both managements and unions are confused—an indication of the difficulty of the problems involved. Finally, the area is important because there is considerable union-management conflict over production standards and, generally speaking, little adjustment. Emotions run high. Serious strikes have been caused basically by this issue. There is a challenge to both unions and managements to develop improved working relationships in this area.

Experience with Wage Incentives

Experience with wage incentives over the past twenty years has been affected by drastic changes in the environment in which they have operated. World War II brought extreme pressure for increased production as well as a host of regulations and controls. In the postwar years pressure for production continued with long-sustained prosperity and inflation. On the other hand, as the years brought more adequate capacity, cost competition became increasingly severe. Technological changes were also having their influence, altering the character and content of work performed. Finally, the spread of collective bargaining was challenging management's exclusive control of production. Experience with incentives will be sketched in broad terms as viewed by management and labor.

Management's attitude toward incentives in about 1940 was possibly somewhat as follows: incentive compensation is desirable in plants where output is measureable and jobs sufficiently standardized. In some industries, notably the processing ones, incentive plans were recognized as virtually impossible. Within that large segment of manufacturing where incentive compensation appeared feasible, there was a reasonably clear distinction between particular jobs that could be placed on incentive and those that could not. Coverage in some plants and industries might thus be a relatively large proportion of the work force and in others a small one. While recognizing the desirability of giving as large a proportion of the work force as possible the opportunity for incentive earnings, limited coverage was not considered an injustice since the prevailing view was that incentive pay required incentive effort as contrasted with daywork effort. There appeared to be at this time very little questioning of the fundamental desirability of applying wage incentives or of the effort philosophy on which incentives were based. The questions were those of technical applicability.

Union attitude in 1940 was divided. The unions in the traditional piece-rate industries tended to favor or accept this method of pay, though a few of these unions, the women's garment workers' union and the cloth hat and cap workers' union, had for a time opposed piecework.[2] But except for the unions in the piecework industries, there was considerable union opposition to incentives and all the appurtenances of scientific management associated with them. While the "speed-up" had special meaning in the textile industry, there was a general fear of excessive and unreasonable work requirements. This was a valid fear, particularly in view of working conditions imposed during and following the 1932 depression. Unions also resisted the practice of pitting one worker against another under an incentive plan, and the threat of unemployment added impetus to their opposition. On the other hand, unions such as the rubber workers, machinists, steelworkers, and others continued to adapt to incentive payment plans in most cases. The suspicion is that unions frequently did not feel strong enough to fight management on the issue, particularly since some employees favored the plans. Nevertheless, this attitude of potential if not active opposition is an important background consideration.[3]

A significant and quite unique instance of union opposition was that of the new United Automobile Workers Union, which secured the elimination of incentives in the major automobile companies. It had very limited success, however, in achieving this goal in auto parts companies, where the union lost some important early strikes on the issue. This contrast points up the fact that the automobile companies, with their particular production conditions, were one of the first management groups to question the incentive philosophy, and as a result bargaining on this issue did not in fact involve any great divergence of views.

World War II changed the earlier conditions under which incen-

[2] See Sumner H. Slichter, *Union Policies and Industrial Management* (1941), Chap. X, "Union Attitudes Toward Basic Systems of Wage Payment," p. 282.
[3] Early union attitude is portrayed in the able study by Milton J. Nadworny, *Scientific Management and the Unions, 1900-1932* (1955).

tive plans operated. Intensive pressure to increase production was the dominant characteristic of this period. In addition to patriotic motivation, there was direct compulsion from the government to maintain and expand production. Government agencies encouraged the use of incentives to increase production and to stretch manpower. Companies adopted or expanded incentive plans. Unions went along partly for patriotic reasons and partly because other avenues of securing wage increases were severely limited.

A study by the New England War Labor Board of 302 incentives installations in that region up to July 1944 showed, based on reports after three months of operation, an average incentive yield of 15 per cent, a 14 per cent reduction in unit labor cost, and a consequent 29 per cent (approximately) increase in production.[4]

But incentive plans also began to show distorted results. Drastic changes in products and methods, long runs of standardized items, exhortations to workers to increase production, reinforced guarantees that production standards would not be tightened, production standards manipulated to give hidden wage increases, grievances with slowdowns and wildcats to force concessions, shortage of trained time-study engineers, direct pressure by the armed services, relaxed worker discipline, absenteeism and production difficulties, cost-plus and excess profits—all contributed to distorted wage structures and the demoralization of some of the wage incentive plans.

At the end of World War II the condition of the incentive plan in one plant of a national company can be deduced from this episode. As the last war vehicle went down the assembly line it was accompanied by a large worker placard bearing the legend "end of Gravy Train." In a plant of another company the practice grew up during the war of not instituting new production standards without union consent. This practice was made compulsory by a Regional War Labor Board whose decision was upheld by the National Board. Coupled with slowdowns and wildcat strikes it produced extremely loose standards and high earnings. The company felt that it was caught in an impossible situation because of the critical nature of the war prod-

[4] An unpublished study by E. R. Livernash and others at the New England War Labor Board. It also showed 49 per cent of the plans to be individual incentives, 37 per cent group (largely extensions to indirect workers), 10 per cent plant-wide, and 4 per cent combination. More than half of the individual plans had "past performance" standards rather than time study, indicating the haste with which plans were put in. The averages noted in the text also cover up wide variations in results; three plans fell in the 60-65 per cent yield category after only three months of operation.

uct being manufactured. At the end of the war this company faced a competitive situation that forced a revision of standards. In this case the revision was accomplished and a good union-management relationship evolved.

Postwar prosperity continued many of the conditions of the war. The pressure for sales tended to submerge other management objectives. But demoralized and distorted wage incentive plans became more of a burden on cost and labor relations as competition stiffened. Some incentive plans were abandoned, or they were not introduced in new plants. Technological change contributed to this course of action by developing production conditions under which there was less compulsion to use incentives. In one community an auto parts company went through a two-month strike to abandon a plan while, at about the same date, a machine-tool company took a six-months strike to install a plan. More generally, however, plans were being revised by various means and in various degrees. Some plans were revised by the gradual displacement of "old" incentives by "new" incentives. In some cases management forced revision without union consent at considerable cost in grievances and unrest. On the other hand, some plans operated in satisfactory fashion throughout the war and postwar period.

As of 1958 there was thus a very mixed picture in the wage incentive field. There were extreme differences in the success with which wage incentives were operating in different companies and in different plants in the same company. For example, a survey of 100 companies[5] indicated that 60 were satisfied with their incentive plans, and 40 were not. These differences heighten the interest in and significance of the major variables noted above.

There have also been a few specific developments of which note should be taken. In the first place, plans have been simplified. Almost all (except for piecework) are standard hour or standard minute plans with the full amount of production over standard paid as bonus. Unions have succeeded in obtaining revision of gain-sharing plans and fractional premiums. Managements also have favored simple plans. Piece rates have been displaced to an important extent by standard hour systems. In the steel industry, for example, the multiplicity of plans is being displaced by standard hour incentives. In the second place, small group plans are growing in fre-

[5] *Factory Management and Maintenance* (May 1955).

quency relative to individual plans. Technology appears to have promoted this change as has extended coverage. In the third place, coverage has been extended to indirect groups and to less standardized production not covered previously. Employee and union pressure, as well as some influence of technology, are creating increasingly a situation in which the choice is an incentive plan for all factory employees or none. Finally, there has been a great deal of dilution of incentive. Wage increases have frequently not been added to or factored into base rates but have been paid as an hourly "add on." There have been various reasons for this practice. Wage increases during World War II and later were frequently thought of as temporary. It would be easier to remove them later if they were not built into the incentive structure. Under some systems it was difficult to incorporate incentive earnings, or at least it was difficult to avoid a magnified wage increase. There were other reasons, but an important consideration was growing lack of confidence in incentives. Since incentives were "running away," there was no point in adding to the problem. As a result, it is not uncommon today to find incentive workers receiving half their pay in the form of a cents-per-hour extra payment. One reason for incentive revision has been to remove the dilution by incorporating "add-on" wage payments into the system.

With the variations in experience it is not surprising that both managements and unions have varying views on incentive plans. In one unusual case management, much against its will and only in the face of a strike threat, discontinued its incentive plan. To its surprise both total unit cost and unit labor cost were lower without the incentive. Subsequently the union tried to negotiate the plan back in, but management refused to go along. While some managements have abandoned incentive plans, a larger number are dissatisfied and would like to do so but see no way of accomplishing this objective on terms acceptable to both union and management. Some managements remain convinced of the fundamental desirability of incentives, even with a technology and process that builds in considerable control of production.[6]

Some unions, for example, the steelworkers, are dropping their resistance to incentives. A number of unions are taking an increasing interest in procedures for setting standards and are strengthening

[6] This point is discussed in Chapter 18 in the section on technology.

staff departments in this area.[7] They apparently are convinced that they must continue to live with incentives, and some local unions have found incentives to be a rich source of indirect wage increases. As a result local unions frequently resist the removal of incentive plans. On the other hand, there remains a dominant tone of union opposition and a pronounced reluctance to accept "engineering principles." There is no clearly-defined trend or simple resolution of problems.

Demoralized Incentive Plans

The term "demoralized wage incentive plan" means more than just a poorly-functioning plan. It implies: (1) substantial inequities in earnings and effort. A mixture of tight and loose standards is both cause and effect in perpetuating a multitude of grievances over standards and a distorted wage structure; (2) a growing average incentive yield or bonus. The most dramatic figure found was a plan with a 60-point hour base, designed for an 80-point hour yield, which had, as of 1955, a 300-point hour average yield. This figure, of course, indicates only payment results and not a high level of effort; (3) a declining average level of effort. Workers appear to take the gains of looser standards partly in increased earnings and partly in increased leisure. Informal quotas are met in 7 or 6, or, allegedly in one case, in 4 of the 8 working hours; (4) a high proportion of "off-standard" payment and time. Incentive workers in one multiplant company averaged 40 per cent off-standard time for all plants. This may involve many factors, but an important element is abuse of various types of guarantees.

The above may be described as the technical or semi-technical characteristics of a demoralized plan. The relative importance of the four characteristics varies in different situations, as does the degree of demoralization.

Some illustrations of varying degrees of demoralization are given below. One example is that of a rubber products company with about

[7] In addition to the Amalgamated Clothing Workers and Ladies' Garment Workers, who have long had technical departments, such unions as the rubber workers, the automobile workers, the machinists, the upholsterers. and others are creating and expanding staff engineering departments.

twenty plants having incentive plans. With expected earnings or yield equal to 100, earnings in the plants in fact ranged from 107 to 150. There was a rather even and broad scattering of plants within this range, and all plants were above the theoretical norm. All of the plants were organized by the same international union. The variations in yield noted above did not correspond with variations in effort; the best effort levels were in the lower-yield plants.

In some of the lower-yield plants the incentive operated very well. Examination of data on the lowest-yield plant indicated a perfectly satisfactory incentive system and good union-management relations. The grievance rate was modest, slowdowns were rare, wildcats were essentially nonexistent, make-up costs were low, there was consistent meeting of schedules, etc. On the other hand, among the entire group of plants there was a remarkable correlation between man-hours lost in wildcat strikes and the size of the incentive yield, and union-management relations were reported as poor in the high-yield plants. Significant variation in labor cost was obvious.

The above example begins to bring into focus variation in (1) management policy and practice, (2) union policy and practice, (3) the character of union-management relations, and (4) employee attitudes. Serious demoralization typically involves not only poor union-management relations and a high rate of grievances but continuous use of wildcats and slowdowns. Management loses control of standards. Engineered standards are grossly distorted by bargaining. Other examples illustrate variations of this situation.

CASE A. In one plant of a large auto parts company expediency on the part of the company and aggressive union tactics had resulted in a high proportion of poor standards and a badly administered incentive system. The workers had complete control of production. There was an evaluated base-rate structure which provided for wage differentials in base rates for incentive jobs of about 40 cents an hour. This base-rate structure had been completely nullified by control of production and by the bargaining of production standards. Every incentive worker, and it was a large group, aimed at earning $2.74 per hour, day in and day out, and week in and week out. Deviation in earnings was slight. It was reported that quotas could be made easily in 6 of the 8 working hours.

There were also in this plan numerous special types of earnings guarantees that were subject to manipulation. Foremen were reported to spend about 75 per cent of every day arguing with employees and union representatives over standards and their application. Clearly the system had become something of a nightmare although the technology appeared suitable for an incentive system.

In this case the incentive system was abandoned. The company, convinced that incentive was rarely desirable in a union environment, demanded that it be eliminated in a 1955 negotiation. The union would not agree although no cut in earnings was proposed. The plan was eliminated as a consequence of a two-month strike. Several months after the strike, but before daywork production standards were introduced, worker efficiency had increased modestly. Machine down time had dropped; power consumption and output per day had increased. While one cannot separate the impact of the strike from the elimination of the incentive, the atmosphere appeared to be one of relief to be rid of the system.

CASE B. In contrast with the above is the example of an electric products plant, whose primary characteristic was poor management. Possibly its plan should not be called demoralized, though extreme earning inequities and a very high average incentive yield were present.

The company established this plant in a section of the country where it had not previously operated. It hired foremen and other supervisory personnel from the community, none of whom were familiar with the product or the methods. Piece rates were used, and standards were set largely by foremen on the basis of performance. No adequate time study was made in the plant. Earnings and costs increased, and a very distorted wage structure developed. Earnings of 200 per cent and 300 per cent on base rates were not uncommon. Clearly demoralization in this case was predominantly in inequities in earnings and effort and in high average yield. Worker performance, other than poor quality, was not a major problem.

Employees in this plant accepted an incentive pace although subsequently there was further improvement in worker efficiency (over several years) under daywork. But employee efficiency was good regardless of the system.

The union was not militant. There were no wildcat strikes and few slowdowns. Grievances were very numerous, but the inequities were great. A new and more aggressive union won representation rights in 1952. In the first negotiation with this union the company demanded abolition of incentive and a substantial cut in earnings. Labor cost had become too high for their product to be competitive. A long and bitter strike ended in the company's favor.

The experience with daywork in this plant will be considered in the next chapter, but new local management by 1957 had achieved an efficient and peaceful plant. The chief union steward, a man with many years of union experience in various parts of the country, was well satisfied with local management though critical of some corporate policies in negotiation.

A second similar case will not be presented in detail, but factors distinguishing it from the first one will be outlined. In this case management gradually relaxed production standards in order to get along with the union. There were no wildcats, but there were large numbers of grievances. This was not a problem of inability to set standards, but a definite top management policy of "giving a little" on grievances. The belief was that good union-management relations could best be maintained by this practice. The incentive plan was finally negotiated out, and a Scanlon Plan was substituted. The high level of earnings created under the earlier incentive plan presents a problem in a changing product market that is growing more competitive.

CASE C. This is an example of extreme militancy on the part of the local union. The incentive yield in one plant of a flat glass company had grown to such an extent that average earnings had increased somewhat more through incentive gains than through negotiated increases in wages.

Standards were adequate during the war years, but after the war new products and methods required that standard data be revised. This was never done. Almost all standards were grieved, and time studies were demanded. Bargaining would start with the union demanding about half of what the company proposed for a standard. Slowdowns and wildcats were frequent and severe. Both manning and production standards were negotiated in a tense atmosphere. A strong local union president exercised clear control over all workers.

Methods changes that had looked favorable on paper became marginal when finally in operation.

Indirect worker incentive plans were put in to correct daywork inequities. A gain by one group of employees would create inequities for other employees. The management was whipsawed between direct and indirect, and among various direct groups.

An industrial engineer was critical of top corporate policy. With a heavy demand for product and an over-all favorable economic climate, local union leaders knew that the company would yield considerably rather than take any loss in production. Industrial engineering in setting standards had become a farce, and the plant appeared in 1956 to be facing a tough future competitive problem.

CASE D. This is a one-plant company in the machine tool industry with a long history of union-management conflict. While conflict related to many matters, job evaluation and wage incentives were major sources of discontent. The wage incentive plan as originally introduced had a normal incentive yield of 20 per cent, but in the postwar period it increased to 75 per cent. The workers shared very differently in the growing yield. The increase, in other words, was very uneven as among jobs. Where grievances were pushed and where opportunities for grievances arose through technological change, standards became loose; where workers were less aggressive or where no technological changes occurred, tighter standards survived. In this particular case the general level of incentive earnings was held back relative to those of day workers since lower wage increases were negotiated for incentive workers. In spite of this, inequities developed between day workers and incentive workers.

Union-management relations deteriorated culminating in a fairly lengthy strike in 1951. With a change in top management and some changes in union leadership, the strike appears in retrospect to have been a turning point in union-management relations. There was a much more cooperative attitude on both sides in the period following the strike. In this improved relationship the company undertook to negotiate a complete revision of its incentive plan, which will be considered below. The revision was accomplished with very few grievances and not a single arbitration. With a very modest increase in average incentive earnings there was a greater than 30 per cent increase in worker efficiency.

CASE E. This case cites two examples to give emphasis to the difficult problem of union and worker acceptance of drastic unfavorable change.

In one foundry of a national company, incentive earnings had grown to some 62 cents an hour above the level other companies were paying for comparable work. The company retained outside consultants, who reported a looseness of about 25 per cent on the average in current standards. Armed with information on competitive earnings and on work standards, the company informed the local union that a correction in both standards and base rates was imperative. The union opposed. The employees, of course, were being asked to accept a cut in earnings, a higher level of effort, and a reduction in the number of jobs. The union was reported to feel that the plant was a big money-maker. The company presented a demand to drop the incentive plan saying that the plant would have to shut down rather than continue to operate at a loss. After fruitless negotiations the plant was closed, causing great suffering to the local community. After a lapse of about one year, and after various forms of community intervention, the plant was reopened with a dramatic increase in efficiency and by negotiation with the same group of union officials.

In another case, which had an unfortunate outcome, the management proposed a complete retiming of jobs and a revision of the incentive plan. Costs were high and the level of effort low. The alternative to a drastic revision was reported to be to close the plant. In a union meeting to take the final vote on the management proposal the leading local union officials advocated acceptance, but an opposition faction contended that the company would not close the plant. In the end 40 per cent voted to accept, and 60 per cent were opposed. The plant was closed.

Other cases could be cited, but the above are enough to indicate the problem. No attempt is made to estimate how many incentive plans are demoralized to a substantial degree, how many only slightly, and how many operate well. Such an estimate would require a very comprehensive study. However, there appear to be a substantial number of demoralized plans, more than the authors would have expected prior to their research.

In conclusion, three points should be emphasized:

(1) The above consideration of major variables has been illustrative only. Managements and unions have difficult policy problems, chiefly in the administration of production standards. The last two sections in Chapter 18 are devoted to this topic. Variations in community environment and in employee attitudes are revealed most clearly in comparing successful with demoralized plans, but there are some differences in employee attitudes in the above examples.

(2) In no aspect of our study is the contrast between the "short-run" and the "long-run" more important. The establishment or revision of a single production standard on a particular day is of little consequence for costs and profits. The path of least resistance for management is obviously to give in a little, loosen the standard a bit, and avoid trouble with the union. Over the years, however, there is no surer way to develop a high-cost plant and poor labor relations.

(3) Substantial demoralization of an incentive plan results in an unstable situation. It leads eventually to abandonment, revision, or catastrophe. Abandonment or revision may be reasonably smooth or it may be accompanied by major difficulties.

Revised Incentive Plans

Incentive plans have been revised under varying circumstances by varying methods, to varying degrees, and with varying results. The following have been singled out for discussion: (1) broad revision in crisis situations, (2) broad revision in noncrisis situations, (3) gradual replacement of old by new incentives, and (4) revision by management without union consent. Some revisions make definite improvements in administrative procedures and techniques; some do not. There are included in addition (5) broad extension of incentive coverage and (6) revision by imposition of a limit on earnings.

Broad Revision in Crisis Situations

Of the instances of over-all revision coming to our attention, most were situations in which the alternative was closing the plant, discontinuing the manufacture of certain items, or a serious loss of business to competitors and a consequent decline in the number of jobs. It is difficult to negotiate over-all revision unless a company is faced with serious economic problems. Five examples are outlined below.

CASE A. In a noncompetitive auto parts plant, management proposed to abolish piece rates and to establish measured daywork. The proposal would have meant a 33 per cent reduction in earnings. Part of the proposal was an offer to construct an entirely new plant with the most modern equipment. With new plant and equipment and a lower wage scale the plant was expected to be competitive.

The union presented the proposal to the membership, but the vote by the rank and file was in the negative. The management thereupon decided to abandon the plant but on a short-run basis made a pattern offer to the union equal to the union's initial demand. While there was no statement to the union that the plant would be closed, union officials expected that result and did not accept the pattern offer. They countered with an offer of a wage reduction with retention and revision of the incentive.

An agreement was arrived at that cut piece rates by varying amounts in different departments. Most reductions amounted to about 15 to 20 per cent, but in some departments they were more and in some less. The cut in piece rates was a first step. Base rates for incentive jobs were equalized at a single figure, thus wiping out an existing 35-cent spread. On the new base rate, new production standards were to be set to provide normal incentive earnings of 30 per cent.

A crew of potential time-study people was recruited from the hourly and clerical staff and given training in time study. A broad revision of standards was undertaken, though the work was not completed in all departments at the time of our last interview. There was some tendency for earnings to go above the normal under the new system as employees strove to maintain former earnings.

There are some interesting aspects to this case. The union could not persuade its members to accept a deep cut in earnings and abolishment of incentive to save the plant. Management did not try to promote its initial proposal after the first negative vote. On union initiative a wage cut and revision of the incentive plan was worked out, though the revision does not show any definite improvement in the administration of standards. It did, however, cut costs, improve worker efficiency, and remove some of the existing inequities. Whether it represents the start of improved relations and further progress remains to be seen.

CASE B. The home plant of a heavy equipment producer had high costs and was in a poor competitive position. A program for a completely new job evaluation plan and a new wage incentive system was presented to the union. While the union-management relations were good, the international officials of the union were not convinced that the program was necessary, and no progress was made in negotiation. Meanwhile, various company officials, including the president, gave extensive explanations of the program to the employees and their wives, and the character of negotiations gradually changed. The international withdrew, and local officials agreed to the company proposals, giving the company broad initiative to apply job evaluation and revise incentives.

Perhaps this should be called a semi-crisis situation. The company as a whole was not in financial difficulty. While a firm decision had been made to reduce costs of operation or close the plant, when the union and employees responded favorably, the company did not feel compelled to rush revision. Newly-developed standard data were used by agreement with the union. Study and revision were carried out department by department. Union time-study representatives were selected and trained. Three years after the negotiation about 80 per cent of the standards had been revised, and employee efficiency had increased significantly. This revision holds out substantial promise of a permanent improvement in wage structure and incentive administration. It has done more than cut costs.

CASE C. This case, involving two plants of a reasonably large automobile parts company, started far from auspiciously. Initial negotiations proved fruitless. The company decided, therefore, to discontinue a major high-cost product in one plant. A new plant was built to replace the second one and some equipment moved to the new plant. After facing the loss of jobs, the union was willing to negotiate revisions in incentive standards. Business expanded to fill the new plant as well as the two original plants. Union-management relations improved. Union time-study stewards worked constructively in the revision of standards. Earnings were not cut, but efficiency was considerably improved. Administration of incentives has improved, but inequities in earnings among departments remain.

CASE D. Success in this case has been decidedly limited. Local union officials were convinced by an international union officer that a drastic revision of the incentive system was necessary for the home plant of an automobile parts company to continue in operation. A large reduction of earnings as well as tightened standards were involved. The program was substantially, but not completely, carried through during a contract year. Cost reduction was achieved, but the plant appeared still to face a difficult competitive situation. Employee acceptance, however, was at best only partially accomplished. The local union leadership, which went along with the revision, has been largely displaced; thirteen of fifteen committeemen have been defeated in union elections. The international union official who encouraged acceptance has probably lost all influence over the local. The new, anti-reform committee has been militant in trying to negotiate looser standards in grievances and has led one legal strike.

This strike was of two weeks' duration and ended in a union victory. The company agreed to halt the program for revision of standards, since it produces mostly for one customer only and feared loss of business if the strike continued. Labor-management relations were unsettled after the union victory, and the future of the plant remains uncertain.

CASE E. A company in the farm equipment industry with a very demoralized incentive plan became involved in a strike in the majority of its plants, although the major cause of the strike was not the incentive issue. The union with representation rights in these plants tried to break the wage pattern as a weapon against a rival union that was trying to organize the plants. The union underestimated company resistance, partly because it didn't recognize the need to improve efficiency and was severely defeated in a long strike.

The agreement ending the strike was on the company's terms and included a complete revision of wage structure and incentives. While former incentive earnings were guaranteed to incumbent employees a very complete revision of the system was carried out over a two-year period. The company greatly improved its time study and incentive procedures, costs were reduced, and employee efficiency increased. These were the result, however, of the defeat of the union in a predominantly union-motivated strike. The union has now lost representation rights to the rival it was trying to outdo in negotiations.

Broad Revision in Noncrisis Situations

In two of the following three cases the outcome of incentive revision has been an improvement in union-management relations along with improved efficiency.

CASE A. This is a one-plant company in the machine tool industry with a long history of union-management conflict. The poor relationship culminated in a serious strike which, with changes in management and union leadership, was a turning point in union-management relations. The most important change was that of president of the company. No special contract changes led to the changed relationship, although subsequently contract changes were made. The union gained, for example, a union-shop clause, and management gained, among other things, a revised incentive plan. The real change was an increase in cooperative consultation and a far different attitude in day-to-day contract administration. Formal grievances declined, and arbitrations became rare.

In this new atmosphere, following a revision of their job evaluation plan, a revised incentive was proposed. Advance agreement was not asked. A standard data approach (MTM in essence) was used, and departments were studied in turn.

The use of standard data forced a close study of job content in the modification.[8] Job set-up was worked out step by step. One of the difficulties in the earlier operation of incentive was that job set-up was rarely specified in detail, and older workers, who knew the tricks of the trade, were better able to make out on set-up times than newer employees. The new procedures for set-up and for operation were worked out with employee cooperation. New standards were put in only after all job analysis for a department had been completed, and a final meeting had been held with the employees of the department to explain them.

[8] The significance of standard data is discussed in the final sections on production standards in Chapter 18

Could this procedure be considered one of bargaining standards? In one sense it could, since union officials initialed the data sheets after each department was completed. In a more fundamental sense, however, it was not. Management consulted with workers and the union and paid attention to their suggestions, but each and every standard was not bargained. Standard time values were being applied and not distorted. Formal grievances were not entertained in these meetings but could be brought subsequently.

In fact very few grievances were ever brought, and there were no arbitrations. This was in sharp contrast to the operation of the earlier plan, in which both grievances and arbitrations were numerous. There was a 30-per cent increase in worker efficiency following this revision and an increase in employee earnings of about 5 per cent. Some workers were not able to attain their former earning levels, and there was no guarantee of former earnings. The increase in worker efficiency came in substantial part from improved knowledge on the part of the workers of proper job set-up and operation. The union retained the right to request a time study in grievance cases, but the right was almost never exercised. Fundamental improvements have been made in this case. Standards are no longer bargained, and standard data have now for several years created consistency in standards among jobs and stability in requirements of effort over time.

CASE B. This is a small company managed by one man only, the president. He fought unions bitterly in the late 1930's. A company union was established, but it was ordered discontinued. A friendly union was invited to avoid the risk of a "radical" union, but it finally lost out to the "radical" union. The former president of the "friendly" union was made personnel manager.

Union-management relations were in a state of turmoil until the late 1950's. Management fought bitterly to preserve its rights as it viewed them. But strikes, wildcat and legal, harassment tactics including slowdowns, and low morale gradually eroded production standards. Management took a strike at almost every negotiation, and continuously fought the union. This uncompromising stand did not make for efficiency and was very costly.

About two years after a new president, the son of the former president, took over, and after two years of continuing the former policies, an opportunity came to expand the business. The president questioned whether it would be advisable to put additional capital in the business, since costs were high, though wages were only average. He decided to have a frank talk with the top union official in the area, a step his father never would have taken.

The talk resulted in no commitment, but both agreed to try to improve union-management relations as well as plant and worker efficiency. The new business was undertaken, and a consulting firm helped create a completely new plant layout and revised production standards. Extensive new equipment was installed, and employment was gradually doubled and then tripled.

Completely new standards covering about 95 per cent of the work force were established in less than a year. Union time-study stewards were appointed under a joint selection process and trained. While time study rather than standard data continued to be basic in setting standards, bargaining over standards was substantially eliminated. Worker efficiency, costs, and profits substantially improved.

In this case it is not certain that a superior standards technique as such has been established. What is very clear is that a new relationship has virtually eliminated grievances, improved efficiency, and created an atmosphere for efficient administration of the incentive plan.

No contract changes were made in this case. There were provisions in the contract which the union waived, as for example, when in adjusting workers to the new layout and plant and equipment, seniority provisions were at times set aside. In fact, the contract became much less important. Consultation between union and management increased, and management was decentralized. Foremen were increasingly more important, and the positions were eagerly sought. Communication on all levels increased. This drastic change, accompanied as it was by growth, far from creating unrest, led to improved relations.

CASE C. In the heavy-equipment division of one company relations of management with the machinists had been good for many years. While in need of revision, the incentive plan was not at all seriously demoralized. Yield had increased somewhat, and there were some loose standards primarily as a result of failure to adjust adequately to technological change over the period from 1930 to 1947. For example, lathe operators operated four machines. After restudy under the revised standards, they operated six to thirteen lathes, depending on the nature of the work.

This wage incentive plan was successfully revised in 1947. Standard data were developed that are still in use and that in 1957 were checked against MTM. The incentive yield held steady from 1947 to 1957. Worker efficiency has been high, and there have been few grievances. The only problem in 1957 was whether to extend the incentive to maintenance and other workers. The union favored it, but the company did not feel this could be done satisfactorily.

Almost all revisions coming to our attention that were negotiated in a noncrisis situation brought an improvement in administration as well as in efficiency. On logical grounds one might expect to find many such revisions, but in fact they appear to be rare and to require exceptional leadership. Only a few crisis revisions bring a permanent improvement in administration.

Gradual Replacement of Old by New Incentives

The outstanding example of revision of incentive plans over a period of time is in the basic steel industry.[9] In no other incentive industry coming to our attention has there been a general pattern of incentive revision. Also, outside of the steel industry, very few cases of this general approach have been found. Without reference to any particular company, developments in basic steel were as follows:

In the war and early postwar years, the incentive picture in steel could at least be described as confused, types of plans being very mixed—tonnage plans, piece rates, and various incentives—and with mixed results. Both the union and the companies, however, were concerned, in the early postwar years, with the cooperative wage study to be discussed in Chapter 19.

The new hourly wage structure in steel had three effects on incentive payment: (1) it raised the level of pay for hourly workers relative to incentive workers, substantially removing an inequity that was a source of employee discontent; (2) it "submerged" some incentive plans, thus reducing incentive coverage, and lowered the incentive yield of the remaining plans when calculated on the new

---

[9] Incentive revision in basic steel is discussed in Jack Stieber, *The Steel Industry Wage Structure* (1959).

hourly guaranteed rates; and (3) it brought to attention variations in earnings among incentive jobs relative to the newly-created guaranteed minimum rates.

The inequity program originally contemplated carrying negotiations to basic principles of incentive compensation. This was not fruitful in most cases and shows the fundamental difficulty of reducing the concept of a fair day's work to objective contract language. The parties agreed on the term "equitable incentive compensation" and left it open for continuing definition through application and arbitration. They also agreed on procedures for introducing new incentive plans and conditions under which they should be introduced. The companies had the obligation to introduce new incentive plans for old operative plans in the event of technological change. Plans could also be revised by mutual consent, and the companies had the right to introduce plans to extend the coverage.

General wage increases following the cooperative wage study usually provided for a general cents-per-hour wage increase and for widening the wage differential among labor classes, thus in effect preserving percentage wage differentials. The amount by which wages were increased in widening the differential usually was not incorporated into the old incentive plans; it was incorporated into new plans, as these plans were usually allowed-hour plans based on the new standard hourly rates. The average percentage incentive yield of the old incentive plans thus declined modestly with wage increases over the postwar years facilitating the introduction of new plans. New plans could not cut incentive earnings for equivalent effort. While this guarantee required the creation of some out-of-line differentials, the number and amount of these guarantees did not usually constitute a serious problem.

As of 1958, for example, about half of the incentive workers in a steel plant might be under old plans and half under new plans. The new wage and incentive structure is gradually replacing the older types of plans and wage relationships. Insofar as the incentive plans relate to commonly accepted incentive jobs, the new plans are usually considered technically superior to the plans they replaced. Obviously there is some variation in the quality of the new plans, but in examining statistically the earnings of workers in two companies under old and new plans, the variation in yield among jobs is much less under the new plans.

There are some differences in incentive concepts within the industry. In a few instances companies have shifted, where they could, to an equipment utilization incentive concept. Under this approach all direct workers in a machine crew, if the equipment is being operated at 100 per cent of practical capacity, receive a normal incentive bonus, say 30 per cent, for hours worked, regardless of their effort input. Indirect workers receive, for example, 15 per cent under a half-pay formula. This differs from the more traditional work-load approach of most companies, under which employees receive incentive compensation only for the hours they spend actually working at an incentive pace. Machine time as such receives no incentive compensation. However, the work-load philosophy has frequently been modified to equalize incentive bonus for a crew by a formula based on a crew average and by incentive compensation for "attention" time as distinct from "idle" time. The union has sought to modify or abandon the work-load philosophy.

The union has also had an important influence in extending incentive coverage to more and more employees. Coverage has grown from the 40 to 50 per cent level after the cooperative wage study to about 65 per cent for the industry and to about 80 per cent in some companies.

Revision of an incentive system by the gradual replacement of old plans seems to be a most desirable approach. It requires agreement on a new wage and incentive structure that will gradually displace an older structure. The displacement process requires limitation in the application of wage increases to the old structure relative to the new one. This process is too slow in a crisis situation and not good if the old structure is seriously distorted. Agreements to revise by this procedure are not common. The interesting fact is that so many revisions seem to require compelling circumstances before they are attempted.

Management Revision Without Union Consent

Quantitatively there has probably been more incentive revision falling in this category than in any other. This can probably also be said of revision of daywork production standards. Except for dramatic cases, however, examples do not readily come to light. Also, although it may be known that standards have been tightened, there is usually no way to judge how extensive this process has been.

One case of incentive revision is particularly worthy of note although it represents an unusual situation. In about 1950 a company manufacturing heavy equipment began to improve its standard-setting procedure and created a new corporate standards department. Prior to this time there had in reality been very little corporate control of incentive administration. Administration of the incentive systems, including the establishment and revision of standards, had been carried out at the plant level. The new department at once set up a training program to help create more consistent standards.

It proved impossible to negotiate provisions for the revision of standards. On the other hand, the incentive plans in the various plants were in such bad shape that the company considered revision imperative for future competitive survival. It took advantage of a rather broad clause in the contract giving the company the right to revise standards and began a program of extensive revision. They did this deliberately, recognizing that a period of employee unrest and union resistance would follow. Incentive grievances were so numerous that both the grievance and the arbitration procedures bogged down. The company also created and maintained a policy of discipline for wildcat strikes while operating under a five-year contract.

It took approximately four years to revise the bulk of the former standards. At the end of this period the company was reasonably well satisfied with about 85 per cent of their standards. In several plants standards appear to have been tightened about 30 per cent. The aftermath of unrest was a contributing factor to a strike at the conclusion of the contract. The parties were able, however, to agree on procedures for establishing future standards. In making this agreement the company gave up its broad right to revise standards, and the union recognized the right of the company to give full weight to past technological change if revision is called for because of newly-instituted methods changes. Under the new contract union-management relations have improved, although problem plants remain. This improvement was possible in no small part because incentive revision had been substantially accomplished.

The general significance of this type of revision cannot be appraised. It is not unusual for management to admit that it has been taking some "water" out of production standards when it gets a chance. Union officials, particularly international officials, recognize that companies in some cases must tighten standards. As competition has become more intense, partial revision of this sort has been quite widespread.

One brief reference is made to revision of daywork standards. An extensive survey of production standards in a company showed under-utilization of man-hours. Over a period of years the company has achieved very close to a 1 per cent increase per year in output per man-hour by revising job content. This has been accomplished almost without challenge, due partly to the fact that the union has agreed to the company's right to utilize a full 60 minutes of work per hour apart from recognized allowances.

Broad Extension of Incentive Coverage

As has been noted, incentive coverage in the steel industry is being extended rapidly to a point where a high percentage of all production employees will be under an incentive plan.

Management representatives in various steel companies expressed different views as to the wisdom of this extension. Some felt that efficiency gains made it worthwhile. Others questioned particular plans but felt that broad coverage was essential to the continued use of incentives. Still others were critical of extension, saying that the cost of extension had been far in excess of any gain in efficiency.

The Steelworkers Union has been a major influence in bringing about the extended coverage. A frequent cause for wildcat strikes has been to obtain incentive coverage. An editorial in a local union paper asked how long the daywork employees must remain second-class citizens and be excluded from the "profit sharing wage incentive plan."

Why has the union demanded the spread of incentive payment? While an answer can only be speculative, some points are worth considering. In the first place, as workers are more and more assisted by machines and as machines take over substantial parts of the heavy work, there may well be less objection on the part of workers to incentive. To an important extent it is the machine that gets the speed-up treatment rather than the worker. In the second place, and related to the first point, getting good production from equipment is less a matter of heavy physical effort than it is one of good teamwork and coordination. There are situations where heavy and fast work is required under difficult working conditions, but in many ways technology has broken down the relationship between degree of worker effort and quantity of production. In the third place, the points already mentioned make it very difficult to distinguish incentive from nonincentive jobs by the character of the work performed. To some extent a reverse relationship is developing. Many traditionally nonincentive jobs have a higher degree of manual work and a volume of output that is more dependent on worker effort than do incentive jobs. While it may be very difficult to develop direct-measurement incentives for these jobs since work is not standardized, efficiency on the job is clearly related to individual skill and effort. Finally, with the completion of the Cooperative Wage Study, the union in steel has had experience with the concept of equity of compensation among jobs. To some extent there may be a feeling that differences in earnings between jobs with incentive compensation and those without makes equitable classification of jobs meaningless.[10]

To illustrate the labor cost aspect of extension of coverage, the position of management in one steel company—not one of the better-known companies—will be considered briefly. This company, while it had not extended incentives to coke ovens and blast furnaces, had almost complete coverage outside of these departments. To improve the competitive position of the company, management proposed: (1) to eliminate incentives entirely in approximately 200 occupational classifications, such as janitors, timekeepers, various inspectors, some maintenance workers, etc., (2) to revise incentive plans for certain indirect service groups to a total of nearly 300 occupational classifications by creating "half-pay" plans rather than full incentive earnings, and (3) to convert a few of their incentive plans to very low incentive-yield plans. While to a limited extent this proposal by management may be regarded as a bargaining position taken in opposition to the union's demand for extending incentives to coke ovens and blast furnaces, it indicates quite clearly that this management, on its own initiative, would never have developed and applied incentives over the wide range of jobs now covered, nor would it have created the equality of yields that the plans now have. No changes were in fact negotiated.

While specific reference has been made only to the steel industry,

---

[10] For example, if there is no incentive coverage in coke ovens and blast furnaces, the maintenance men assigned to these departments can argue rightfully that they are as much entitled to incentive payments as are maintenance men assigned to departments that are covered by incentive.

the union aim in incentive industries and plants is quite frequently for full coverage of all employees in the bargaining unit. There are a few exceptions. In one unusual case the union took a strong stand against incentives in general, and as a result ignored the question and allowed the company to determine their scope unilaterally.

For a variety of reasons, it appears increasingly difficult to limit incentive coverage. To have or not have incentives is much more an "all or nothing" decision than it was some years ago. Selective coverage appears to be an increasingly unstable situation, but extensive coverage almost inevitably means some incentive pay for negligible improvement in worker efficiency.

Revision by Limiting Earnings

Only three cases of limitation of incentive earnings were discovered, but it would not be surprising if this method of using incentive attained greater importance in the future. One large company, for example, has agreed at the request of the union on a 25 per cent limit on incentive earnings for reasons discussed below. Incentive earnings were not revised. Rather, if average incentive earnings on a job were more than 25 per cent above base, the base rate would be increased so that the actual average earnings became the limit. In only one plant of the multiplant operation was it necessary to make adjustments in some base rates. This appears to be a good indication of the fact that incentive was operating satisfactorily in plants other than the one in which revisions in base rates were made. In at least one plant the incentive system has operated very successfully for many years. While the plant with base-rate revisions did not have an entirely satisfactory incentive plan, it was not in extreme difficulty competitively. Adoption of the limit was a policy decision by the company rather than the result of either excessive pressure by the union or serious difficulties in incentive administration.

The fundamental question raised by the limit concerns the effect on worker efficiency and on the administration of the plan. The head of industrial engineering in the company, who favored the change, reasoned that minimizing the pressures for distortion would have, on balance, favorable effects. In other words, standards would not deteriorate, and where they were loose they could be improved. Manipulation of reported time with respect to guarantees would decline, and adjustment to technological change would be facilitated. The pressures toward demoralization might well be significantly reduced.

The above arguments are quite radical in relation to the "textbook theory" of incentives. In this theory the imposition of a limit destroys the whole notion of unfettered individual response. Furthermore, the "maximum" becomes the "minimum," and standards deteriorate. The arguments for the limit start from a recognition of practical operating difficulties and were advanced, in this case, by a company that, on the whole, has maintained incentive plans that operate well.

Will standards improve or deteriorate? Where a standard is now loose, there is, under a limit, no possibility of increasing a superior earnings position. The opportunity to improve earnings gradually through loose standards is eliminated. Also group pressure to hold back and not to exploit a standard in higher earnings is out of the picture.

In one incentive plan in a different company, for example, some departments are clearly recognized as high-earnings departments. The time-study people cooperate in setting new standards to continue the vested interest of the group in an abnormally high incentive yield. It takes twenty or more years of seniority to bid into these favored departments. Any tightening of standards would reduce earnings and would be very difficult to achieve. These higher earnings are not realized through any great effort but rather by a poorer level of standards.

If the above kind of vested interest can be removed, more consistent standards can be applied and loose standards tightened since a reasonable opportunity for maximum earnings will be preserved. Preserving high past earnings, which is certainly not unusual in administering incentive plans, would be removed from the pressures under which the time-study man operates.

Much the same kind of argument can be advanced for minimizing abuse of guarantees through whipsawing the incentive system. Employees can build up earnings by working the easy jobs on incentive and the difficult jobs on guarantees. In many plans which guarantee either average incentive earnings or some fraction of such earnings, the guarantees rise with the yield.

The real test is in worker and union reaction to technological change. Incentive demoralization has developed as standards became gradually looser with technological change and as employees gained both in leisure and in earnings. Removing the earnings factor may reduce both resistance to technological change and pressure for loose standards. On the other hand, the leisure factor is still influential. One company, however, with ten years' experience with a limit reports that the effort level was maintained; a second company with several years of experience considers a limit to be a necessity in any incentive system.

A strong argument has been made that control of an incentive is often lost on the factory floor. Jobs are short-cut and not performed as the standards specify. The foreman "looks the other way" when workers "gyp" the time-study man on revised standards. A new foreman soon gives up trying to suggest new methods because of the problems involved in carrying them through. Many opportunities for small improvements are lost.

If a limit can facilitate adaptation to technological change, and even encourage improvements, the argument for it is very strong indeed. A contrary argument, however, can also be advanced. Time-study people, freed from the risk of high earnings, may not exercise the care that is required in an unlimited system.

A limited incentive is a compromise between measured daywork and ordinary incentive.[11] A decline in worker efficiency means a decline in earnings. Supervision has the assistance offered by an incentive system. On the other hand, there is no reward for very outstanding performers. Performance and manning would approximate the level inherent in the limit. Can this system minimize the difficulties in an incentive system while preserving some of its positive advantages? It is clear that there are strong arguments on both sides of this question.

From the point of view of some unions there seem to be real advantages in negotiating for a limit. The rubber workers might be cited as a case in point. The union's view of inequities in earnings and effort is broader than that of any one company since it is interested in the tire plants of all the companies. With such a complex picture how is it possible to begin a general inequity program?

[11] As will be seen from the discussion of measured daywork in Chapter 18, the arguments for that method are in part parallel to the arguments for an incentive limit.

Limited incentive might be, from the point of view of the union, a very good way of getting started.

Efficient Incentive Plans

While examples of efficient plans will not be outlined here, comment will be made on the characteristics of such plans in relation to the variables already noted: (1) management policies and practices, (2) union policies and practices, (3) union-management relations, (4) character of the particular technology, (5) community environment, and (6) employee attitudes.

Technology as it relates to the choice of incentive or daywork is discussed in Chapter 18. A point of reference will be machine control of output as contrasted with worker control. As the proportion of machine time increases, the scope for incentive is reduced. Also as the flow of production is regulated by conveyor or process, the need for incentives is decreased. But under these conditions it is also true that incentives can be applied with a higher degree of reliability. Some efficient incentive plans have been aided by the character of the technology and the nature of the manufacturing process.

An incentive plan is also helped by stable technology. The manufacturing industries where the value of incentive plans is most frequently questioned appear to have had continuous and significant technological change. Those industries where incentive payment is taken for granted appear to have had relatively stable technology.

Community environment may or may not be an important variable. Almost all multiplant companies, regardless of method of pay, feel that variation among communities is significant. Smaller and more rural communities tend to have a climate favorable to a high worker efficiency, superior union-management relations, and cooperative employee attitudes. Clearly there are exceptions, and our study was predominantly in the larger industrial areas. This commonly-held opinion, however, may well be justified by experience. And, whatever may be the cause, employee attitudes are more receptive to incentive in some plant environments than in others.

The most significant variables are union and management policy and practice. Management policy is of primary importance. Consider, for example, one multiplant company that operates some forty incentive plants in many different sections of the country. It deals with several international unions and faces the usual variation in the characteristics of local unions and local union-management relations. Incentive coverage is extensive, in excess of 90 per cent of factory employees, and a direct measurement incentive for maintenance employees has been in effect for many years. The financial position of the company is the best in the industry.

The incentive yield in this company has remained normal with no upward creep. The level of incentive effort as measured by their data was slightly better in 1958 than in 1940. Performance relative to production standards has not deteriorated. While plants vary somewhat, the system is obviously a successful one.

A number of features in the policy and practice in this company stand out: (1) extensive emphasis on incentive administration, (2) a good technical base for incentive, and (3) a minimum of negotiation in establishing standards. In addition there is a refusal to yield to pressure tactics. These are characteristic of efficient incentive plans.

There are three important characteristics in the administration of incentive plans that are typical of the successful ones. First, strong top management support for the industrial engineering department; second, an adequate central and plant engineering staff; third, continuous control of incentive on the factory floor. These three combine to create a situation very different from that in the demoralized plans. Furthermore, in the plants with efficient incentive plans there is no expectation that the incentive plan will run itself or can be run with a minimum staff. Also there is no underestimation of the problem of control on the factory floor. The statement often heard that foremen have an easier task under an incentive plan than under daywork is highly questionable. Perhaps in the short view this is true, but it is doubtful that this is true if the incentive plan is to operate well over the years. Supervisors must see that work is performed in accordance with specifications, maintain quality, report small changes in methods, cooperate in setting standards, and administer allowances and guarantees. There is little point in refined standards if guarantees and allowances are given with superficial investigation.

A good technical plan cannot be separated from good administration. Philip Carrol's discussion of management errors—failure to plan, failure to specify, and failure to follow up—is very pertinent.[12] Also his emphasis on standard data seems warranted. A high proportion of the incentive plans that operate well use predetermined times, thus making continuous time study unnecessary. Also a good technical system is inseparable from good plant layout, good scheduling, and other characteristics of good production management.

The use of standard data means a minimum of negotiation of standards. If a standard data system is accepted by the union, this is in essence an agreement not to negotiate individual standards. There is further discussion of this question in Chapter 18. Unions frequently object to standard data, but it was observed that efficient incentive plans tend to be standard data systems.

Both management and union policy are involved in the question of pressure tactics. Pressure tactics, particularly wildcat strikes and slowdowns, are the subject of Chapter 22, and the subject will not be developed at length at this point. It is clear, however, that extreme demoralization has been commonly associated with the use of pressure tactics. The following example will illustrate the problem.

In a modernization program in one department of a mill an investment of $40 million was made over a four-year period. This called for a revision of standards, but there was no attempt to adjust standards for past technological change. There was thus no attempt to cut earnings. Slowdowns cost the company $15.4 million in conversion costs with unbalanced operations and 499,200 tons of lost product. Stoppages cost $1.3 million in conversion costs and 42,600 tons. The slowdowns were all resistance to revised standards, but some of the stoppages were not. There was a period of about four years during which technological change was producing no operating benefits but considerable loss. There is a very great temptation to depart from engineered standards in the face of this kind of operating problem. The log-jam in this case was ultimately broken by a technical arbitration.

Continuous pressure for small changes is perhaps more insidious than for major technological change. But, in either event, yielding to pressure makes quite impossible any rational method of setting standards.

A good many plants with good incentive operation have had no

[12] Philip Carrol, *Better Wage Incentives* (1957).

problem with wildcats or organized and systematized slowdowns. Union leaders and management are increasingly reducing the threat of wildcats and other pressure tactics. This fact alone helps assure the future success of revised incentives. Incentives may at the moment be discounted too heavily in some situations because of the past history of labor relations.

Union policy is important apart from pressure tactics. Unions, particularly local unions, differ in the degree to which they accept orderly incentive administration. In some instances unions accept it because they are passive or weak. In one case this was clearly true. A bad defeat in a strike had so weakened the union that no grievances of any type were brought. In other situations unions accept orderly administration because of confidence in the reasonableness of management decisions. Confidence in management decisions on standards was enhanced in some plants by the opportunity to review grievances through union time-study representatives. Union time-study representatives are discussed in Chapter 18.

Weaknesses in incentive plans have been treated in some detail here because of the belief that the advantages of incentive often have not been sufficiently qualified in the light of actual experience. On the other hand, as is pointed out, in particular cases incentive plans work very well. New incentives continue to be introduced. A machinery company with most of its plants on measured daywork introduced incentives in a newly-acquired plant. Daywork performance was measured at 55 per cent of standard and was brought to 125 per cent of standard under incentive. Companies that have maintained healthy incentive operations, however, have clearly held to firm administrative policies and increasingly have adopted standard data systems.

The Piece-Rate Industries

It has not been feasible to study the piece-rate industries in detail. Only a few interviews have been possible, and reports of both existing practices and problems within an industry have not been uniform. The purpose of this section is to distinguish the piece-rate from incentive industries rather than to explore them in detail.

The advantages and disadvantages of piecework to workers, employers, and unions remain substantially as discussed in *Union Policies and Industrial Management*.[13] Establishment and administration of piece rates, while having many facets, are a central focus of competition within these industries.

It is tempting to argue that intense price competition in the product market—resulting from many small firms, low capital per worker, stable and common technology—dictates the use of piece rates. Product-price competition translates into piece-price competition. Labor cost is the strategic cost element in competition. Small companies with unstable sales can control labor costs by piece rates. Piece rates are in some degree substitutes for refined management methods. However, certainty in labor costs for the company means uncertainty in employee earnings. Piece-rate bargaining gives the union some opportunity to maneuver, but profit margins are small, and there is the constant threat of nonunion (and union) competition. Frequent style and product changes bring continuous piece-price setting.

The unions in these industries strive to control competition, and some succeed reasonably well. Some do not. Those unions achieving a reasonable degree of control by this very fact create a condition favorable to union-management cooperation. Employers and unions within the industry have a mutual interest in preserving competitive stability. Unions that do not achieve control create a condition perpetuating conflict between union and nonunion segments of the industry, making cooperative union-management relations difficult and threatening the disintegration of the union segment.

The unions in the needle trades are frequently cited for their cooperative relations with employers and for their stabilization programs.[14] Both the Amalgamated Clothing Workers and the Ladies' Garment Workers have maintained a relatively high degree of control, using somewhat different approaches, in their respective indus-

[13] Sumner H. Slichter, *Union Policies and Industrial Management* (1941). The basic discussion is contained in Chapters X and XI, but Chapter XII on competition between union and nonunion plants is directly relevant, as is the discussion of cooperation in the Cleveland Women's Garment Industry, the subject of Chapter XIV.

[14] The experience of these and other unions is discussed in Slichter, *Union Policies*. For a short statement with respect to the ILGWU see Theresa Wolfson, "The Role of the ILGWU in Stabilizing the Women's Garment Industry," *Industrial and Labor Relations Review* (October 1950), p. 33.

tries. Control is not uniform in different branches of their industries. The Hosiery Workers, while maintaining cooperation and control[15] in varying degrees over the years, has now substantially disintegrated under the impact of nonunion competition. At no time have the shoe unions been able to introduce stabilization beyond the boundaries of a particular shoe center. With about half the industry unorganized, bargaining is highly competitive among shoe centers and sharply limited by nonunion conditions. Peace and harmony are difficult to achieve in such a competitive setting. Even more difficult has been the struggle and decline of such textile centers as New Bedford and other New England communities.

Bargaining in all of the piece-rate industries has been preoccupied with the wage level and rates.[16] It is labor cost, not worker efficiency, that is being bargained. The instability of sales and the difficulty of planning ahead make worker efficiency a less important factor in overhead per unit (larger and better-managed concerns are an exception).

The piece-rate industries do not develop "demoralized" incentive plans in the fashion previously discussed. With quite stable technology, long experience guides both union and management in estimating the earning potential of particular piece rates. In periods of prosperity piece rates will be bargained upward not only by general wage adjustments but through the perpetual bargaining of rates for new styles and products. In periods of increased competitive pressure, piece rates are bargained down. Manipulation of grade systems, relating piece rates to product price, and "extras" are part and parcel of this bargaining process.

The above statements do not imply that there are not significant variations in worker efficiency in different piece-rate plants within an industry. These variations relate in part to differences in quality of product and shop conditions. They also relate, however, to differences in the accepted work pace. Various sociological studies have pointed out that employee groups develop a concept of a fair day's work, which is enforced by the group with greater or lesser stringency. But little study has been made of the question why one work

[15] The piece-rate system and its administration are well presented in Thomas Kennedy, *Effective Labor Arbitration* (1948).

[16] An able presentation of competitive pressure is to be found in George P. Shultz, *Pressures on Wage Decisions* (1951).

group has a much higher concept of a fair day's work than another. In one shoe community, for example, the accepted daily quota in the cutting rooms was reported to vary over a range of 100 per cent. But bargaining is not with respect to efficiency, even though efficiency is of concern to some managements. Bargaining is to establish labor cost.

Consider very briefly the New York market of the ILGWU. One estimate was that 100,000 piece rates are set each year, 80 per cent by bargaining and 20 per cent by arbitration. Union control is substantial. In most industries management sets production standards (or piece rates) subject to union protest. Here, however, specific price lists are established by bargaining. For the market, divided into its branches, the union has master price lists by price lines. These lists, however, are guides, not binding rates, and rates are bargained shop by shop, subject to the arbitration system prevailing in the market.

It is not clear to what extent there is deviation from the established prices. In a pessimistic mood a union official will report that control has broken down widely even within New York, quite apart from outlying regions. In an optimistic mood, particularly since the strike in 1958, the system of control is described as reasonably healthy. But with the gradual invasion of section work into the New York market, in response to competitive pressure outside New York, there is no doubt that the control system has been weakened. Variations in the degree of section work create complex problems. Also, different business agents appear to pay varying degrees of attention to the official prices. Internal problems indicate continued competitive pressure. Without the union, such pressure would obviously be much greater. Clearly the piece-rate industries have special problems.

Wage Incentive Provisions in Contracts

There is great variation in the extent and significance of contract provisions on wage incentives. A few contracts are completely silent on the subject, although this does not imply absence of union influence. A few contracts have extensive provisions. One contract has a wage payment section of 64 pages, about half of which is devoted directly to the operation of the incentive plan with an added section of 4 pages devoted to allowance rules. Throughout this contract, which is in excess of 250 pages, are to be found indirect influences of the system of payment. Short provisions may also be deceptive. A provision such as, "the company shall maintain the existing incentive system," may bring within the contract company manuals, standard procedures, and comprehensive rate books. The effect of provisions may be to reinforce management rights or to restrict management. Simple words may carry extensive historical and technical meaning. It is not possible here to develop the complexities of contract provisions. This section is limited to some general observations on the nature of the provisions and their significance.

Contract provisions may be divided into (1) general provisions, (2) provisions establishing the major characteristics of a plan, and (3) provisions establishing detailed rules and regulations for the setting of new and revised standards and for the operation of the plan. This indicates the different kinds of provisions, though classification of any particular contract clause is necessarily somewhat arbitrary.

General provisions of the contract may prohibit or limit incentive payments or, on the other hand, may allow extension or discontinuance. Conditions governing extension or discontinuance may be spelled out. Basic rights and obligations are established by these provisions.

Provisions on the major characteristics of plans will specify its type (allowed hour, etc.) and its relation to the wage structure (guaranteed base rates with a normal yield of 25 per cent), and may specify rights to revise standards, obligations to guarantee some level of earnings for abnormal conditions, and the general level of effort required (equitable incentive compensation, fair and reasonable, etc.).

The above kinds of provisions are supplemented by detailed operational rules. Guarantees and allowances may be spelled out in detail as to type and as to method of administration. Guarantees provide pay for "off-standard" time, while allowances give added earned time for nonstandard conditions. There is no question that unions have succeeded in liberalizing guarantees and allowances. Any type of handicap may be made subject to a guarantee or allowance: waiting time, faulty material, inadequately operating machine, etc.

Guarantees are susceptible to abuse and manipulation. Ratchet techniques are particularly disturbing—building up high incentive earnings by selected products or distribution of time that generated the high earnings. The fundamental problem is to determine what are standard conditions and what are not. As hazardous conditions fade into undesirable conditions, so faulty material fades into less than perfect material. Poor leather or poor glass can grow to become a substantial part of all material processed.

Not only have guarantees been multiplied in character and application, but compensation is increasingly at average earnings rather than base rate or fractional earnings. If the average is of hours on incentive work, rather than total hours, manipulation of production and reports is encouraged.

Guarantees and allowances, on the one hand, and standard setting procedures, on the other, are the major subjects that are elaborated in contracts. Almost all contracts restrict the revision of standards to new or changed jobs, and changes are specified in terms of methods, materials, etc. While these clauses read very similarly, some are more restrictive than others. Going beyond this basic procedural regulation, some contracts specify the use of standard data, and some prohibit it. Some contracts require the use of time study, and some limit its use by requiring the use of comparable standards. Some contracts prohibit the use of cameras for job study.

Most contracts allow complete resetting of a standard when a job is changed, but some do not. In the latter case elements of the job that have not themselves been changed must have their established times carried forward into the new standard. The use of comparable standards or a new time study can become extremely complex. For example, part of one contract reads (out of context):

> In the event there is no operation performed by a method identical with that used on the changed or new operation at the same work station, group of machines or group operation in the same department of the same Works, and
> (1) There is a similar operation with a time-study at such work station, group of machines or group operation, and
> (2) Such operation has elemental descriptions and break-off points which are adequately clear and complete, and
> (3) Such operation is not "unavailable" within the meaning of Subsection A (2) above, and
> (4) Such operation does not contain apparent distortions such as percentage or flat money or time additions, apparent inflated performance rating or other factors used to produce a higher inaccurate piecework price, except that timestudies on group assembly

operations identified in Exhibit "L" for this purpose, will not be rejected for comparison use under this Sub-section (4), the piece-work price will be established as follows:

(a) The piecework price shall be based on an elemental compari-son with the timestudy of the comparable operation, on the same basis as in Sub-section A above.

(b) In the event there is in existence more than one particular operation timestudied and priced to which comparisons could be made under this Sub-section, the Company shall use the most recent eligible operation timestudied for the comparison except that if such operation is not available for comparison under the provisions of Section 10 A (2) of this Article, the piecework price shall be established under Sub-section D.

(c) Where no timestudy exists for the operation being compared or conforms to the requirements of this Sub-section, no com-parison shall be made, and the operation to be priced shall be run on a no-price basis and a piecework price will be estab-lished under Sub-section D.

(d) When a piecework price is to be established by elemental com-parison under Sub-section (a) above, the piecework price of the operation being used for comparison will be applied to the operation being priced until a piecework price is established.

(e) The performance of either a changed operation or new opera-tion during the period involved in determining a proper new piecework price under either Sub-section A or B of this Article shall not, as such, be construed to be a handicap situation under Section 3 of Article XIII of this Contract.

(f) In the event no comparison is made, for the reasons set forth in Sub-section A or B above, the operations to be priced shall be run on a no-price basis and a piecework price established under the procedures of Sub-section D below.

Another common provision prohibits a new standard unless there has been "substantial" change in a job or unless the standard time will be adjusted by as much as some specified percentage.

It is not feasible to examine contract clauses as to their substantive significance or their equity. But detailed provisions, particularly on guarantees and allowances, offer unlimited opportunities for chal-lenge. Picking a short clause at random from a contract: "The pieces produced during the taking of a time study shall be inspected in the normal way in accordance with inspection requirements. If there is more than the normal amount of rejects, a new time study will be taken." Any time study could be challenged on the basis of this clause (unless no work had been rejected), and it might well be easier to take a new time study than to decide what are "normal rejects." In intent, however, the clause has an obviously equitable base.

Administration of incentive plans can lead to intricacies and manifold grievances. On the other hand, incentives can operate with a high degree of mutual trust. Fundamentally, however, a "fair" production standard cannot be legislated, and elaborate contract provisions usually reflect union-management controversy in incentive administration.

18 / *Measured Daywork*

THIS CHAPTER CONTINUES the development of the variables in method of compensation that influence worker efficiency. Emphasis in this chapter is on measured daywork.[1] The following topics are discussed: (1) technology and method of pay, (2) replacement of incentive by measured daywork, (3) administration of measured daywork, (4) union time-study representatives, (5) management policy and production standards, and (6) union policy and production standards.

Technology and Method of Pay

Developing technology is clearly modifying the union-management environment with respect to the performance of work and influencing choice of method of pay.[2] Technology also creates wide variation in the work environment among industries and plants. The relationship between technology and method of pay should not be oversimplified, however.

The obvious effect of advancing technology is toward more work by machine and less by the individual worker. But the fact that the machine "does the work" does not necessarily mean that the worker no longer controls the rate of production. A man operating a rheostat to control a slitting machine has no burden of physical effort, he does not work physically in pace with the machine, but he can run the machine at varying speeds. On the other hand, some machines are completely automatic and determine the rate of production when they are running. Some machines are "semi-automatic" with varying degrees and kinds of work requirements. But in spite of

---

[1] As earlier noted, the term is used to indicate pay by the hour associated with direct or indirect control of worker efficiency through the use of production standards.

[2] John T. Dunlop, *Industrial Relations Systems* (1958) creates a significant interpretive frame of reference with respect to environmental influences.

these qualifications, technological advance has increased the effort burden carried by the machine and has brought a higher degree of automatic production.

The production process, as well as the degree and type of mechanization, must be taken into account. Production process derives as much from the economics of the industry or plant as from machine technology. Line production, symbolized by the conveyor, provides a much higher degree of built-in production control than does a functional or job-shop process. Wide variations exist among industries and plants in process patterns. Flow of production can be simple or complex and more or less controlled by means of built-in work requirements. A conveyor, for example, does not necessarily imply built-in control of work. Workers may take work from a conveyor and put it back on the conveyor but work at their individual pace. All the conveyor does is move the material. On the other hand, a particular pace at each station on the conveyor may be required, or a serious "snafu" will develop. For example, workers on an automobile assembly line can create an involved tie-up.

Technology and process combine to create varying degrees of control over rate of production and varying degrees of association between physical effort required and rate of production. A relatively high degree of control of production diminishes the scope and need for incentive and makes for relative ease of administration under a measured daywork system. This does not imply fixed labor cost. One highly controlled production line may be manned much more intensively than another. There can be serious disagreement over production standards and manning. In one such comparison, with conveyor control, man hours were found to be more than three times as great in one plant as in another with comparable product and method. But once standards are set and the line manned, there is limited scope for incentive and a high degree of control of pace.

In the basic process of manufacturing plate glass (not fabricating), for example, there is a high degree of mechanical control of production. Through mixing materials, through the tank, and through grinding and polishing, the product moves in a highly automatic fashion. It is very difficult to see how incentive could have an important influence. Employees have almost no opportunity to exert positive control over the rate of production. They can, of course, exert a negative influence by bringing about a breakdown in the functioning of the line. Incentive systems appear to have been inherited from an earlier technology. It can be argued, however, that incentive helps in securing consent to a mechanical increase in the speed of the line without a proportionate increase in manning.

The other dimension, association of physical pace to rate of production, may be illustrated by the situation in a shoe factory. If more shoes are scheduled for production and the number of men and machines is fixed, workers work harder in direct proportion to the increase in output. Each machine is paced by the worker. In a steel mill, with the number of men and machines fixed, an increase in production has much less direct relation to an increase in physical effort. Operating a given piece of equipment at capacity requires only slightly more effort than does operating below capacity. Although there are exceptions to this rule in some jobs and phases of jobs, the incentive pace in a steel mill does not mean the same thing in terms of continuous incentive effort as it does where workers pace the machine or line.

Another example is that of a can plant, in which the production lines are highly mechanized and automatic. The "line" operates as one large machine that turns out cans automatically at an extremely rapid rate. The "production" workers do not determine plant efficiency. Maintenance, material handling, and shipping employees are much more important for plant efficiency than are operators on the line. Minimizing downtime on the lines (maintenance work) is of critical significance, and shipping and material handling are important. For incentive to have meaning, it would have to apply to maintenance work, which is not repetitive or standardized. Employees whose work is very difficult to include under direct incentive plans are becoming a larger proportion of the work force and more critical in determining plant efficiency. Technological advances are making maintenance workers the critical work group.

Technology and process have combined to reduce the need for incentives in many instances and in some virtually to outmode their use. Throughout the metalworking industries, for example, there has been a decided increase in automatic machines quite apart from the dramatic but limited use of transfer mechanisms. Technology has changed the character of incentive. As operators manipulate controls rather than do the work, incentive pay to maintain high equipment utilization is not pay for added effort, although it may be use-

ful in maintaining low cost per unit of output. In one plant a minority of workers on "push-button" equipment clearly had the most
desirable incentive jobs in the plant, and very high seniority was
needed to get one of them. Mixtures of job types create problems,
but their main effect is to spread incentive to all types of work if
incentive is used at all.

It would be wrong to conclude, however, that technology and
process are usually decisive in determining whether incentive or daywork is used. The influences discussed in many situations are much
better described as permissive rather than controlling. In an able
study of twelve plants,[3] some on measured daywork and some on
incentive, there was no clear relationship between technology and the
use of incentive. Level of mechanization was not controlling, nor was
process. In some highly controlled and mechanized situations incentive was used. In some poorly controlled and slightly mechanized situations measured daywork was used.

Clearly worker motivation remains a consideration. Some managements want incentive as an aid to supervision and to encourage a
higher degree of worker effort and cooperation even with a highly
controlled technology and process. A number of companies with high
control through conveyor strongly favor incentive. Other companies,
even on worker-paced assembly with little conveyor or line control,
prefer measured daywork.

Union-management relations have definitely been decisive in some
situations. Some managements are convinced that "with unions in
the picture" incentives are more of a handicap than a help. Some
managements question incentive as a long-term motivating influence
and even its "deadening" effect on supervision. Some managements
prefer measured daywork because they believe that, through supervisors who are not spending all their time haggling over incentive, it
encourages more rapid technological change, and facilitates employee
acceptance of the change.

It seems clear that changes in technology and process have, over
the years, created a larger number of work environments in which
there is a realistic choice as to method of pay. There is a higher degree of built-in control of production. However, publicity on auto-

[3] Robert B. McKersie, "Incentives and Daywork: A Comparative Analysis of Wage
Payment Systems," unpub. thesis, Harvard University Graduate School of Business
Administration (May 1959).

mation has greatly exaggerated the possibility of a push-button factory. When one plant in an industry, which has caused much discussion of automation, can use more than three times the man-hours per unit of product (with comparable product and process) than a second plant, worker efficiency has certainly not been removed as a significant competitive variable.

Replacement of Incentive by Measured Daywork

As was true with the revision of incentive plans, abandonment of incentive, it has been found, has taken place under various conditions, and experience with worker efficiency under measured daywork has not been uniform. Again most of the plants and companies that gave up incentive did so because their costs were not competitive and they faced serious economic difficulties. In other words, a high degree of incentive demoralization and consequent high cost sometimes led to revision and sometimes to abandonment of incentive. When daywork was adopted, management favored this over incentive revision. Sometimes feasibility determined the course of action. Sometimes it was easier to negotiate abandonment than revision. Also discovered were cases in which incentive was replaced by measured daywork as a policy choice and was not forced by high cost. Discussion will consequently be divided into (1) crisis abandonment of incentive and (2) policy abandonment of incentive though the distinction is one of degree rather than of a difference in type.

It is doubtful that there has been a significant shift to daywork from incentive. One study, a doctoral thesis, discovered approximately 60 plants which had replaced incentive by measured daywork since 1953.[4] No quantitative statement can be made from our present study. However, companies that have not used incentive in new plants are probably more numerous than are those that have changed from incentive to daywork. While some companies have in-

---

[4] Harry F. Evarts, "Management Problems in the Removal of Wage Incentive Plans," unpub. thesis, Harvard University, Graduate School of Business Administration (December 1958). Evarts discovered 60 instances of removal of incentive by a limited questionnaire survey. He studied 14 plants in detail. Of the 14 studied, 6 increased payroll and 4 decreased payroll when the plan was removed. In the period immediately following removal productivity tended to be unchanged though it dropped in 3 instances. He concluded that in his 14 cases the plants were "at least as efficient and in many cases more efficient" (p. 257) after adjustment to daywork.

troduced incentive, the rate of incentive introductions has probably declined.

Crisis Abandonment of Incentive

Three examples will be discussed briefly. In two situations there has been a clear increase in worker efficiency (one a very marked increase), and in one the change in worker efficiency has been small, but output per worker has increased very notably through a revision in methods.

CASE A. This example is of a large single plant operation in heavy industry with an assembly line process. Because of high cost the company felt compelled to abandon the incentive. Earnings were above those of leading competitors, and worker efficiency was very low. The incentive was meaningless except as a bonus to employees. Manning had been negotiated under the pressure of a refined slowdown technique. Production was subject to worker control at a key point and flowed in a trickle until manning grievances were resolved to the union's satisfaction. Superficially union-management relations appeared to be above average because there was no record of strikes and formal grievances were not excessive.

Negotiation to remove the incentive and decrease earnings by eliminating incentive pay resulted in a strike. The union ultimately agreed to the company proposal under the influence of international officials. Most local union officials who argued for acceptance, secured by a close vote, were subsequently defeated in union elections.

The cut in cost through eliminating incentive was not adequate. After about two years, and with a change in management, a program of engineered standards was begun. In one relatively short period, data showed a more than 200 per cent increase in output per worker. Subsequently there was further improvement. Clearly this case illustrates extreme demoralization of the incentive plan rather than superior performance under daywork.

CASE B. This example (a continuation of Case B under "Demoralized Incentive Plans" in Chapter 17) relates to one plant of a small multiplant company in the electrical products industry. It has machining and assembly operations in the plant. As pointed out above, worker efficiency was not notably low in this plant. Neither wildcats nor slowdowns had been a problem. Bargaining piece rates had created high cost and many inequities. Incentive had been eliminated after a serious strike with a newly certified union that had won representation rights from the established union.

Over five years from 1952 to 1957 worker efficiency improved consistently under measured daywork. Changes in management after the strike led to a good industrial engineering department and to the appointment of a new and capable labor relations director. These personnel changes were brought about by a new plant manager who took a particularly active interest in labor relations. The union was not "knocked out" by the strike. It continued as an active local with able local leadership and good membership support.

A mixed system of measured daywork was used involving ultimate standards as goals for supervisors in improving departmental efficiency and explicit minimum standards for employees where feasible. Most jobs in the plant were worker-paced. Workers appeared to accept willingly a consistently high level of performance. Standards grievances were not frequent and were resolved amicably.

Discussion with local union officials and observation in the plant led to the conclusion that new management leadership in this plant had completely changed its complexion. Management was particularly pleased with improvement in quality of product and completely sold on daywork, although, as noted, most jobs were worker-paced.

CASE C. This case, which is a continuation of Case A under "Demoralized Incentive Plans," will be discussed very briefly. The plant is in the automobile parts industry and is characterized more by machine operations than by assembly. As noted earlier, the incentive plan was eliminated after a two-month strike. Worker efficiency increased slightly.

Although worker efficiency has not increased much, drastic changes in methods have been made over a period of three years. Management feels that it would have been impossible to make such a drastic change if incentive had continued. It has not been difficult to increase output to the capacity of new equipment, but no important attempt has been made to increase the level of worker effort.

Policy Abandonment of Incentive

Two cases illustrating this type will be described. One is that of a multiplant company.

CASE A. This is the main plant of a company in the paper industry. In addition to making paper it manufactures a variety of paper products. It had used incentive for many years; the yield was modest, and there were no serious problems in its operation. Union-management relations were good. Abandoning incentive was an experiment in labor efficiency and labor relations.

The question of giving up incentive came up for consideration by top management primarily because of dissatisfaction with the quality of product. The consensus of management was that it would be easier to improve quality and reduce related costs without incentive. There was also a belief that labor relations would be improved if it were dropped since most grievances arose because of incentive compensation. It was also felt that resistance to technological change would be diminished. The primary question concerned labor efficiency. There were many worker-paced jobs on which incentive seemed quite important in maintaining efficiency, but it was decided to make the experiment and give up incentive.

In the conversion to daywork, employees were guaranteed their present earnings, but wage increases were applied to a competitive day-rate structure, which gradually submerged the guarantees. There were no serious tensions in negotiating the abandonment as both parties favored the change. There was, however, a large negative employee vote indicating a reluctance to give up incentive earnings.

Daywork production standards were used primarily as a guide for supervision, but they were known and openly discussed. Production standards were not used rigorously as a condition of employment, but they did set a level of expected performance.

Worker efficiency under incentive and under daywork cannot be compared precisely. There was a complete review and revision of standards. The new standards under daywork were roughly comparable in average level to incentive standards adjusted upward to correspond with expected performance rather than a base rate level.

There had been in 1957 five years of experience under the daywork system. Actual performance was charted, department by department, relative to standard. Standards were revised with technological change. Worker efficiency averaged about at the level of the new standards, but with irregularities according to variation in business and production conditions. The trend over the five years was one of improvement.

Differences in performance by departments were very interesting. Certain departments had individual operations that were worker-paced in character. In these departments there was an initial drop in worker performance that was anticipated. Over the years these departments returned to the former incentive pace. There were variations among these departments but no net disadvantage resulted from giving up incentive. Machine-type departments were performing better without incentive and in a few cases were substantially above standard.

This company concluded definitely that adjustment of workers to technological change was much easier without incentive. In some departments standards advanced sharply with technological change. There was almost no lag in increases in output with these technological changes. From a level-of-effort point of view one might argue that this case shows no gain and no loss through dropping incentive, but a demoralized incentive plan was not involved. There has been a substantial gain in quality of product. Improved quality has reduced costs, overshadowing any change in performance. There has also been an improvement in labor relations, which the company attributes to dropping incentive, and a definite conclusion that resistance to technological change has been greatly reduced.

CASE B. This example is of a large company that has abandoned its incentive policy. In about 1952, after many years of widespread use of incentives, the policy was given up. There have been some conversions from incentive to daywork, and the newest plants have not used incentive. In 1957 there were about 25,000 employees on measured daywork and an equal number under incentive.

This company, because of its size, has had diverse experience. It can point to plants with good incentive operations and to plants with poor incentive operations. It can also point to plants with very satisfactory measured daywork operations as well as plants with less satisfactory measured daywork. There are differences in the character of local unions, differences in the quality of management, differences in employee attitudes, differences in community atmosphere, differences in process and technology, and differences in production problems. Differences in labor relations are particularly important, and they are not static. Nevertheless, top production and labor relations officials favor a policy of measured daywork. Progress in introducing technological change, in labor efficiency, and in labor relations has been very marked under measured daywork. It is significant that a large company with diverse production conditions has seen fit to abandon an incentive policy.

Administration of Measured Daywork

The obvious distinction between incentive and measured daywork is the absence of money motivation in "getting out the work." While it has been demonstrated that an incentive plan can become so demoralized that its removal will not lead to a decline in employee effort, without demoralization of incentive the assumption would be that effort would decline unless an adequate substitute for the desire to maintain incentive earnings were found. The problem would presumably be somewhat less critical if machine time were relatively high per unit of product and if the manufacturing process had built-in control of the flow of work.

Under measured daywork, line and staff officials must assume direct responsibility for employee efficiency. This calls for the direct or indirect imposition of work standards. It also means some change in the nature of the foreman's job and an increased ratio of supervisory personnel to workers. However, the foreman's job is in fact very different under incentive than under daywork. This fundamental difference must be clearly understood.

Under incentive the foreman can, and perhaps must, become preoccupied with supporting, servicing, and controlling the incentive. Checking work steps and quality, giving allowances for nonstandard conditions, administering guarantees, assisting in establishing new and revised standards, and handling questions and grievances on these complex administrative rules relative to work flow and work distribution create an environment in which the foreman tends to lose direct contact with the level of employee effort as long as it is above the required minimum. Effort above the minimum is essentially voluntary. Except in the case of a clearly demonstrated concerted slowdown, discipline for inadequate effort is contrary to the incentive concept.

But perhaps more significant than losing direct contact with the level of worker effort is the temptation to preserve the status quo.

Searching for improved work methods, for improved layout, for improved flow of work is not particularly rewarding. Under an incentive plan the foreman is (1) preoccupied with the task of servicing the incentive, (2) operating under a system where effort above the minimum is voluntary with the employee, and (3) considerably motivated to leave well enough alone and not to become a crusader for improved methods.[5]

Under daywork the foreman must assume direct responsibility for employee effort, and he has no "assist" from money motivation. On the other hand, he has more time to devote to this task because he is free from the responsibility of administering an incentive plan and there is increased scope for improving employee efficiency. Greater output can be obtained by simplifying the job, by improvements in methods, and by better work flow. Increases that can't be accomplished directly through better employee effort may possibly be accomplished indirectly by more efficient utilization of existing employee effort. Some foremen are more effective leaders than others under any system, but under daywork they have a direct challenge to maintain and improve employee efficiency. Before the role of production standards in the administration of daywork is examined, the terminology of standards will be examined briefly.

Production standards are referred to as "low task," "average task," and "high task." They also may be labeled as "ultimate" or "attainable." Low, average, and high task signify different relationships among base rate, expected incentive earnings, and the production standard. These differences need not be explored, and they are far from clear in practice since they involve judgments with respect to normal incentive effort. But introducing the concept of normal effort and its varied translation into standards raises the question of the real differences in the level of effort required.

Ultimate as distinct from attainable standards differ in their treatment of allowances for nonstandard conditions. Attainable standards require that allowances be built into the standards for lack of line balance and normal delays and also that special allowances be made for poor material and temporary production hindrances. They are attainable in the sense that they are adjusted to actual operating conditions and do not assume ideal conditions. Ultimate standards

[5] Motivation of employees and supervision under plant-wide incentives, such as the Scanlon Plan, is in sharp contrast with these points. See Chapter 28 on "Union-Management Cooperation."

make no allowance for nonstandard conditions and represent a goal that is aimed at, not necessarily with the expectation that it will be realized.

The distinction between task levels is less directly pertinent to this discussion than is the distinction between ultimate and attainable. However, differences in actual task level reflect differences in normal pace which tend to become institutionalized. A union industrial engineer contrasted three companies in the same industry, all using daywork, by estimating that "normal" was 20 per cent lower in "B" than in "A" and 20 per cent lower in "C" than in "B." In each case the normal was accepted. Changing from a lower to a higher normal is obviously a most difficult undertaking, and standards under measured daywork may deliberately be set quite high to avoid the necessity for such a change.

A good performance under ultimate standards requires eliminating nonstandard conditions as well as maintaining reasonable employee effort. Performing well under attainable standards depends on employee performance since nonstandard conditions are discounted in the standard. Incentive plans use attainable standards, but most, though not all, daywork systems use ultimate standards. The use of ultimate standards puts the responsibility on management to try to remove hindrances to production.

There are three distinct variables in administering daywork.[6] First, the standards used may be either ultimate or attainable and may vary in the level of effort required. Second, the standards may be explicit or not, that is, they may or may not be announced to employees. Finally, discipline may be direct or indirect, that is, directly related to the standard or without reference to the standard. Various combinations among these variables are possible, but two different combinations are most common: (1) attainable standards explicitly made known, with direct discipline for failure to meet standard, and (2) ultimate standards not made known to employees and with indirect discipline.

The concept of measured daywork is sometimes limited to the first combination noted above. This is a forthright kind of system under which meeting the standard is in effect a condition of continued employment. It places emphasis on the pace of the worker, gears man-

---

[6] We are indebted to Robert B. McKersie ("Incentives and Daywork") for this precise distinction among systems.

ning to standards, and does not anticipate that employees will produce above standard. If coupled with a fairly high normal task level.
it can create a very efficient plant. On the other hand, it throws pro
duction standards directly into the union-management arena, and
disputes over standards or grievances and disputes over discipline
based on standards cannot be avoided.

Companies using the second combination frequently state that they
do not have measured daywork and do not use standards except for
cost and other management purposes. Some companies have a fair-
day's-work approach without required performance standards. On the
other hand, the system may be labeled measured daywork, but with
supervision trying to operate as closely as possible to the goal set by
standards. Discipline for inadequate effort, given less emphasis than
improved methods, is usually indirect in character. Discipline will be
for such offenses as taking too much time off from the job, loafing,
interfering with production, not maintaining a reasonable pace, and
so forth. Standards do not become a matter for the union-management dispute because discipline is never based on standards.

Some remarkable improvements have been made under a fair-
day's-work approach. One large plant began such a program after
abandoning a demoralized incentive plan. Local union-management
relations were poor and after three years of the new program could
hardly be described as good. But plant efficiency has been definitely
increased. A smaller work force produces 40 per cent more output
than was produced three years ago. How much worker effort has improved is impossible to say. By far the major sources of improvement
have been new methods and better management. Methods changes
have been extensive, including a completely revised plant layout.
Investigation by management of proposed discipline under a fair-
day's-work concept has more often than not found the difficulty to lie
with management, that is, delays and hindrances beyond the control
of the employee have been the cause of inadequate employee performance. Continued attention to eliminating and minimizing delays and hindrances have improved work flow and labor efficiency.
The continuous revision of standards with new and changed methods has been so extensive that it is not possible to say whether the
effort level has been shifted upward. Employees have accepted methods changes with growing confidence that management is not engaging in a "speed-up" program. The management is convinced that

the extensive changes could not have been made in the former incentive environment.

Measured daywork systems do not fall readily into the two combinations noted. Systems are not unmixed, and practice may vary among plants in multiplant companies. A company need not announce standards, but it may not refuse to state a standard if requested. In some plants of such a company few standards may be known while in others many are known. As for discipline a company may usually, but not always, use indirect discipline. Again, in such a company, some plants will discipline directly on the basis of the standard quite frequently whereas in other plants almost never. While systems are frequently not unmixed, there appear to be some noteworthy trends.

Ultimate standards appear to be far more common than are attainable standards. Attainable standards may be used where there is a strong belief in direct discipline. Ultimate standards with a high task level, however, have various advantages. For example, they serve to emphasize the drag of nonstandard conditions on the efficiency of performance. A high task level maintains high performance goals in the department. There is no problem of the minimum becoming the maximum. And there is considerable advantage in using standards as goals rather than as requirements.

There appears to be a clear trend toward indirect discipline. This is partly because it is conceived to be a more intelligent form of discipline. The cause of poor performance must be found and discipline based on this cause. Such a search frequently uncovers management deficiencies. It increases the range of discipline. A 90-per cent performer is as much subject to discipline for loafing as is an 80-per cent performer. And indirect discipline is favored partly to maintain a higher degree of management control in establishing standards. Indirect discipline provides no opportunity for a direct standard challenge. Even when a standard is challenged, the response of management is likely to be to restudy and revise the job rather than engage in a direct contest over the appropriateness of the standard. Direct discipline appears to be practiced extensively only when largely uncontested by a local union.

It is believed that there is some trend away from making standards known to employees, although the practice is mixed. Some companies want to operate a system with an openly-known goal. They have no fear of the minimum becoming the maximum because they would be quite satisfied to operate a plant at 100 per cent of standard. They feel that it is impractical to keep standards secret and they avoid challenge by indirect discipline. Companies that do not make known their standards appear to do so primarily to avoid negotiation and challenge. They maintain further that there is no reason to announce standards since they are not used for discipline. Standards are nothing more than a system of internal management control. It is not clear how difficult it will be to keep them secret nor how important it is to do so.

Emphasis so far has been on the advantages of daywork systems, but experience with daywork is not uniform. There are unquestion-ably demoralized daywork systems, but they are more difficult to dis-cover. Poor incentive plans are more obvious. However, one plant with a daywork system developed most of the difficulties of a poor incentive plan. Pressure on first line supervision to maintain good performance in the department, without the right to require stand-ard performance from employees, led the foremen to try to beat the system. The foremen protested tight standards, jealously guarded any loose standards, did not report small changes in methods, and acted, in the small group studied, just like incentive workers out to beat an incentive plan. On paper, department performance was satisfactory, but workers were completing their day's work in much less than eight hours.

In a study[7] of 12 plants of 5 companies, the author ranked the plants on employee efficiency and found incentive and daywork plants spread throughout the range. However, in this study the top three plants were daywork. Clearly daywork plants can be more efficient than incentive plants. It is difficult to find plants sufficiently comparable in product and methods to make a valid direct com-parison, but in the few cases where a comparison was possible the daywork plant had a decided advantage. However, the reverse can also be found. A few tentative conclusions are suggested:

(1) Methods changes are easier to make under daywork than under incentive. Every plant coming to our attention that had changed from incentive to daywork appeared to have had this experience. This was true for major changes as well as small changes. Even at some sacrifice in the level of worker effort, long-run competitive

[7] The same.

standing in many situations might be enhanced if management would concentrate on discovering improved methods.

(2) Management appeared to have greater freedom in establishing standards under daywork than under incentive in both a formal and in informal sense. From a formal point of view it was decidedly more common to find under incentive than under daywork extensive contract provisions limiting management in establishing standards and determining allowances and guarantees. This may be only temporary, and more such contract provisions may develop in daywork plants. From an informal point of view, and regardless of contract language, particular standards seemed to be challenged much more frequently under incentive than under daywork. In part this results from the removal of the earnings factor in standards under daywork, and also from the tendency to use standards indirectly so as not to provoke challenge.

(3) Good labor relations are easier to attain under daywork than under incentive. Of course neither type has a monopoly on good labor relations. Very cooperative relations can be found in some incentive and piecework plants and disturbed relations in daywork plants. Any plant trying to raise the task level will face a temporary period of employee and union unrest. But since many variables affect employee earnings under incentive, good labor relations appear more difficult to attain and maintain under incentive than daywork.

(4) The level of worker efficiency under both incentive and daywork is subject to wide variation. Each system has its particular administrative problems, and neither produces automatic results. Policy of management is crucial under each system, but other variables are important too.

Some management situations were found in which control of worker effort appeared relatively easy. In small plants in small communities with more passive local unions and considerable labor surplus, management usually can require a fairly high effort level. Management dominated in the determination of worker effort. New employees were not retained unless they produced in satisfactory fashion, but they accepted established levels of effort, and extensive discipline was not required.

With less passive employees and local unions, it was more of a challenge to management to maintain a good effort level by acceptance and consent. Some managements met this challenge, and a good effort level became institutionalized. In other situations the effort level deteriorated. A primary consideration appeared to be the character and ability of first-line supervision. But first-line supervision acts in response to the attitudes and policies of higher management. Long-term success called for a sincere attitude of reasonableness coupled with firmness.

Under daywork each first-line supervisor must know each of his workers and get from him performance commensurate with his individual capacity. If in turn top management is equally sympathetic with first-line supervision, the basis for a system of consent is being established. If, on the other hand, top management drives for results and criticizes a foreman for low performance in his department without understanding the particular problems involved, daywork can deteriorate.[8] Daywork requires a high degree of consent to the effort level being maintained. Discipline is negative, peripheral, and secondary. Some managements secure this consent. Some do not. In some union situations consent is clearly more difficult to achieve than in others. Obviously there is no blueprint for success, but some managements have created a superior work environment by giving up incentive. On the other hand, as was pointed out in Chapter 17, some managements have maintained very good incentive operations.

A close study of incentive and daywork plans that operate well would probably reveal considerable similarity in management leadership and employee and union consent. Incentive plans have the advantage of assisting supervision; but they may also invite control and manipulation that counteract this advantage. Neither system, therefore, can be assumed to give automatic results.

Union Time-Study Representatives

Managements want unilateral control of production standards and are frequently hostile to the idea of union time-study representatives. They feel that use of union time-study representatives is a step toward, if not the endorsement of, joint determination of standards.

Unions themselves frequently have not looked with favor on union time-study representatives, possibly because of hostility toward industrial engineering. Unions want no compromise with the principle of

[8] For discussion of this point see the section on the position of foremen in Chapter 29.

bargaining standards. Use of such representatives appears to be an endorsement of engineering principles. Industrial unions, however, such as the automobile workers and rubber workers, have accepted industrial engineering as a defensive move. At the national level engineering appears to be a growing staff function. At the local level a few unions have proposed time-study representatives or have agreed to such a proposal by management.

The use and formal recognition of union time-study representatives is thus not common. When it is proposed by one party, it is likely to be turned down by the other party. There may be a good many local plant situations where one or more regular stewards or representatives specialize in standards cases, but they are not formally-recognized trained stewards or representatives. Our study has indicated, nevertheless, a small number of instances where a formal system prevails and where it is working to the mutual satisfaction of both parties.

The following discussion does not deal with the function of national union engineering staff members who at times assist local unions on standards problems or grievances. It deals rather with four plants in which local managements and local unions have agreed on a procedure for utilizing locally selected and trained union time-study representatives. Two of the plants use measured daywork, and two plants use incentive. The plants will not be considered individually. While there were differences in administrative practices, all four had instituted formal procedural arrangements. These particular plants are thus to be distinguished from those with informal arrangements where the companies have agreed simply to train union time-study representatives but have not worked out other procedures.

The formal arrangements in these four plants had the following characteristics and results in common: (1) Both management and union participated in the selection of the individuals to be trained, (2) basic training was received outside the company, (3) management gave special and restricted recognition to the union representatives, (4) the union protected the representatives from easy dismissal, (5) management did not relinquish responsibility for establishing standards, (6) union representatives did not assume responsibility for standards, (7) union representatives had open access to time-study and other data, (8) union representatives conducted themselves in a professional manner, (9) most standards grievances were resolved by management and union industrial engineers (though not necessarily directly), and (10) union time-study representatives had strong support from the rank and file.

The first two points do not require extended discussion. Management usually used tests in selecting from a list submitted by the union and also reviewed carefully the previous experience of the men. The union either appointed or elected the representatives. Basic training, usually at a university, was never very extensive. Subsequent experience and informal company training was of more importance.

The third and fourth points were decidedly important. They should be understood in relation to the seventh and eighth points. Union representatives cannot be expected to act professionally unless they have unrestricted access to data. In this sense management gave special recognition to union time-study representatives, though it was restricted. Access to data and to the plant was made to depend on professional conduct. Whatever the form of the limitation,[9] this restriction by management appeared to strengthen the position of the union time study representatives since recognition continued only so long as it was not abused. Also the union protected its representatives from ready dismissal. In two plants where the representatives were appointed by local union officials they could be dismissed only by a three-fourths vote of the membership. Where elected, the representatives had three-year terms with staggered election dates in one case and indefinite terms subject to removal in the second case.

In all four of these plants it was recognized that the jobs of time-study representatives required maximum freedom from temporary political pressure. Both parties endorsed the idea of professional conduct, and safeguards were jointly agreed upon. It is believed that this joint protection from political pressure was of major significance in bringing about mutual satisfaction with results achieved in these plants.

Points five and six deserve emphasis. Management definitely did not give up its right and responsibility to set standards in these plants, nor did the union have any desire for joint endorsement. A specialized protest mechanism existed. It was expected that griev-

---

[9] In two plants the limitation was contained in a letter of understanding between the company and union giving the company the right to refuse recognition, and in two other cases it was in a local contract.

ances would be resolved within an industrial engineering reference. There was mutual respect between union and management industrial engineers. To be sure, the management was in no position to indulge in high-handed practices. On the other hand, management was possibly less subject to serious challenge in these plants than in many if not most plants without such representatives. Four plants are not enough for broad generalization, but the indication is that management may gain rather than lose freedom by providing opportunity for close professional scrutiny of its actions.

The character of the grievance procedure with respect to standards was not uniform in these plants. In the measured daywork plants the union time-study representatives carried a heavy burden of investigation. Individual employees and regular union representatives called on them to investigate potential grievances. A lengthy discussion with one such representative indicated that he took these investigations very seriously. He took the position that he did not want to endorse a grievance unless he was convinced that it warranted strong support. This meant that he endorsed very few grievances. How could he retain rank and file support by this approach? In the first place, he had established a strong reputation for integrity. In the second place, when he endorsed a grievance, there was a definite probability of adjustment. Finally, he frequently found that the job was not being operated as established and detailed by industrial engineering. He might almost be considered to be in league with the company industrial engineering staff in controlling line management. If jobs were being operated as specified by the industrial engineers, they were usually satisfactory to the employees involved.

In the above grievance procedure regular union representatives carried the ball, sometimes against the advice of the union time-study representative. The union time-study representative acted in an advisory capacity. But because in fact he commanded the respect of both management and union standards were not an important cause of grievances. Formal grievances were few in number because an informal union investigation satisfied most employees. The situation in the second measured daywork plant was substantially the same, and interestingly in this plant the only important area with low formal grievance activity was production standards.

In both incentive plants the time-study representatives functioned more nearly in a union "line" capacity in processing incentive grievances. Again the union time-study representatives did not want to be forced to defend poor grievances. Again they maintained the respect of both the management and the rank and file. Local union officials and other representatives seemed to want to delegate this function to the union time-study representatives. In one plant the same men had been re-elected throughout the postwar years.

This section in essence represents a challenge. A meeting of minds is particularly hard to achieve in the area of production standards. It appears that there is no way to legislate fair and reasonable standards in the contract. It may, however, be possible to achieve mutual understanding by creating appropriate procedural checks and balances. At least in the four plants noted both management and union were satisfied with the level of effort and with the method of resolving grievances. It may be that many managements and unions are giving inadequate attention to the potential advantage of a carefully established procedure for union time-study representatives. Emphasis should be placed, however, on the distinguishing characteristics of the systems used in these plants. In contrast, in one plant with union time-study representatives, but with no procedural checks and balances, the union time-study men were the most aggressive bargainers in the plant.

Management Policy and Production Standards

The competitive importance of production standards deserves primary emphasis. The president of one large company reported that worker performance was 65 per cent of standard in 1948, 94 per cent of standard in 1951 and, in 1954, 10 per cent above standard which, in turn, was 10 per cent tighter than in 1951. A smaller company had five plants. One plant, the most recently built and most modern, developed severe labor relations difficulties and low worker efficiency. Important customers were lost, and work was diverted to other plants. The company came close to selling the plant. A change in labor relations and a dramatic increase in efficiency made this plant the best among the five. Instances of improvement in labor efficiency of as much as 50 per cent have not been uncommon in our study. Poor labor efficiency as a cause of high cost stands out in the cases discussed in Chapter 27. Among major companies in leading manufacturing industries there is variation in financial position corresponding with, and partially caused by, variation in labor efficiency.

Labor efficiency has also become of greater relative importance in determining labor and total cost. Wage standardization over the area of product competition has spread considerably during the past twenty years. While wage-rate competition is still very important in particular industries, the growth of wage standardization has increased the relative importance of labor efficiency as a determinant of labor cost. Labor efficiency is also important in determining total unit cost. While to some extent labor efficiency and labor cost is a consideration separate from capital cost, it should be emphasized that labor efficiency is frequently very important in determining capital cost per unit of product. Increased capital investment per worker can be a most significant cost factor in labor efficiency. For example, consider the cost significance of low labor efficiency, which continuously held a plant down to 6o per cent of capacity compared with a neighboring plant with substantially identical technology, which never dropped below 9o per cent of capacity.

Management policy on production standards is: (1) to establish and to maintain over time a satisfactorily high level of labor efficiency, (2) to establish and maintain consistency in production standards among jobs, and (3) to give appropriate allowance for nonstandard operating conditions either in standards or in the application of standards. It is not possible to consider the technical implementation of these policies. Comment is restricted to some labor relations implications of production standard policy.

Clearly it is most important in the administration of production standards to prevent deterioration in standards and the creation of vested interests in loose standards either for an entire plant or for particular jobs. The connection between labor efficiency and labor relations is a fascinating field for observation and speculation. Logically it might be expected that a fairly high task level, creating a strong competitive position for a plant, would lead to serious union-management conflict. While the possibility of conflict cannot be ruled out, observation tends to support the view, when reasonably qualified, that the reverse is true. It is the demoralized incentive plans and the poor daywork plans that are associated with union-management conflict. Efficient plants tend to have satisfactory to good union-management relations.

The phrase "when reasonably qualified" is important because the term "good labor relations" is a complex concept. Also an inefficient plant can be a peaceful plant because management accepts inefficiency. One such, within a multiplant corporate structure, was considered for many years to be a model labor relations plant. The present corporate vice-president of production was then plant manager in a rival plant and continuously had the low grievance rate in the peaceful plant pointed out to him. High cost in the peaceful plant forced a change in plant management, and the reason for peace in the plant was quickly discovered. The reverse situation can also be found. If a high grievance rate is taken as evidence of poor labor relations, then some poor labor relations plants are efficient plants. One such plant has very interesting grievance statistics. A very small group of employees, divided into two rival union factions, brought all the grievances. (Some employees are no doubt grievance-prone just as others are accident-prone.) While the labor relations director did not have an easy job, plant efficiency was good. However, with some exceptions, efficient plants tend to be good labor relations plants although both factors are probably joint products of more fundamental considerations.

To maintain good production standard administration, management must refuse to yield to pressure and must keep up with technological change. Since a separate chapter is devoted to wildcat strikes and pressure tactics, this point need not be explored. Clearly, however, yielding to pressure has been a major cause of deteriorated standards. Keeping up with job changes, particularly so-called creeping changes, requires an adequate industrial engineering staff. In many plants the staff is simply not adequate to check job changes. While the necessity for adequate staff is no doubt generally recognized, it is still probably the greatest single weakness of standards systems. If standards are not changed promptly with job changes, vested interests are created. Many grievances stem from arguments over "picking up" past changes when a job is finally studied and timed.

A weakness related to inadequate staff is concentration on establishing standards rather than on job analysis and methods study. Where staff is adequate to engage in a thorough study of a job before setting a standard, challenge is much less likely to occur. While the technique for setting standards is criticized a great deal, the primary need is to apply techniques constructively and not to introduce standards hurriedly.

It is probably easier to maintain stability and consistency of standards under daywork than under incentive. Management has greater freedom of method in establishing standards. (Standard data are prohibited under some incentive contracts; cameras are frequently taboo under incentive.) There is less time pressure in establishing standards under daywork. Management can postpone establishing standards until a job is standardized and operating satisfactorily with less serious consequences under daywork than under incentive. The problem under daywork is more to make the standard effective than to establish it, but the opportunity under daywork to maintain greater stability and consistency in standards deserves mention.

Increasingly management is turning to standard data to maintain stability and consistency. While such systems are subject to criticism and have their limitations, there is no question that they make for stability from year to year and consistency among jobs. Particularly interesting are data systems developed internally (charted data), although predetermined time values (such as MTM and Work Factor) appear to have received more attention in the literature. Clearly "home grown" standard data systems can be developed only with an adequate staff even if the long-run effect is to save time in establishing standards.

A point worthy of emphasis is that standard data systems force a careful study of methods. The temptation under time-study procedures is merely to time the job rather than to give it close analysis prior to timing. Standard data require and give emphasis to methods study; they contribute to more satisfactory standards independently of the existence of constant times for job elements.

Standard data facilitate centralized control of standards within multiplant companies. With or without a standard data system (but with some degree of development of comparative data) centralized control of standards has been developed and strengthened over recent years. This has no doubt contributed to stability and consistency of standards.

Both standard data and central control reduce bargaining over standards. Failure to bargain standards, for whatever reason, meets with union opposition. For example, in 1958 the UAW issued a particularly strong statement against standard data. The upholsterers' union has also recently taken a firm stand against data systems, particularly MTM. Can management continue to use and develop such systems in the face of union opposition?

Under daywork with indirect discipline management has considerable opportunity to maintain whatever standards system it wishes. Under incentive, standard data have been prohibited in some contracts. Time study has also been restricted by requiring the use of comparable data from existing or similar standards thus freezing established relationships between earnings and effort, whether or not they are appropriate. These types of restrictions under incentive have been important in decisions to give up incentive. Union attitude toward standard data is important and is discussed in the next section. It is a highly questionable practice, however, for management to compromise by agreeing to inferior standard setting procedures.

Note should be taken of differences in policy with respect to arbitrating or not arbitrating standards. Usually standards are arbitrated and this is in accordance with the wishes of both parties. There have been at least a few instances where an arbitrator with industrial engineering experience has been required. This management proposal has been accepted in a number of cases coming to our attention. Where standards are not arbitrated, usually both parties prefer that they not be. Where parties disagree as to policy, it appears usually to be a case of union opposition to a management desire for arbitration. Historically the reverse was true. Management refused to arbitrate standards.

Of all the policy issues faced by management on standards the most important is the determination to keep them adjusted to technological and other methods changes. Standards appear to become loose, and inconsistency to develop, by creeping change more often than by having been set poorly in the first instance. Not keeping up with change is analogous to yielding to pressure tactics. In the short run it makes little difference if a few standards are not adjusted or are reduced a bit under pressure. Over the years, however, the entire system deteriorates.

Keeping up with change requires continuous effort on the factory floor and top management support in maintaining an adequate staff. The point does not require elaboration but is obviously of first importance. More subtle is inertia and resistance to change. While evidence suggests that change is easier to bring about under daywork, there is some degree of resistance and inertia in all organizations. Unions tend to increase resistance to change by being a potential source of trouble if existing routines are disturbed.

Union Policy and Production Standards

This section emphasizes production standards, inadequate attention to which is a hazardous long-run weakness. Once vested interests in loose standards are created, management faces strong resistance to upward revision.

While interviews with union officials have not been extensive enough to warrant generalization, no international union official interviewed has failed to be concerned with low-efficiency plants. Discussions have usually involved frank statements that weak managements, by giving continuous concessions in standards and creating high-cost plants have done no more of a favor for unions than they have for their companies. This is not to say that such officials would be in a position to negotiate substantial increases in the effort level in particular plants, but it does indicate a high degree of appreciation of the realities of competition and of tolerance toward efficiency levels maintained by successful plants and companies.

In the case of some union officials in the large industrial unions the above view represents a change from an earlier attitude. As the industrial unions have become more secure in their industries and as particular officers have had more experience at the international level, problem plants appear to be no more attractive in the eyes of the union than of management. This growing attitude is a favorable influence for the future.

Attitude toward standards is essentially a local union consideration and defies simple explanation. At one extreme are locals using pressure tactics in open or subtle fashion, challenging standards extensively, and developing a vested interest in control, conflict, and inefficiency. Such locals have frequently succeeded in driving efficiency to a low level. It is under such situations that incentive plans appear to have lost substantially all vestige of their original purpose.

Evarts reported local union opposition to removal of incentive in almost every one of the 14 plants studied even if an increased wage level was proposed by management.[10] If a local union has achieved high average earnings, comfortable production quotas, and bargaining relations to increase earnings and reduce effort, no change is likely to be desired. National union officials are not in a position to endorse giving up incentive while perpetuating or increasing the level of effort. Regardless of the level of effort, upward revision is resisted. As a result, most incentive revisions and abandonments are in "crisis" situations. An unhappy stalemate continues until competition forces action upon the parties. Persuasion then may prove effective, or a strike may be required.

Other local unions run a system of control of production but institutionalized at a satisfactory level of output. For example, a local union representing hammer crews in a forge shop completely controlled production. They standardized the day's piecework earnings with a fixed differential by size of hammer but accepted competitive piece prices through negotiation. They turned out whatever was required to make a day's pay, no more and no less, but were described by management as reasonable in accepting competitive prices and in adjusting the effort level accordingly. A second local union in this plant drove continuously for lower and lower levels of output. Conflict with this second local culminated in an extremely serious strike.

On the other hand, local unions, and they are by no means all weak locals, accept a good effort level with only a small and reasonable amount of challenge. Frequently plants are started on an efficient basis and remain so, and standards never become a pervasive issue. While variables noted earlier in this chapter influence the degree of dominance of the effort level by management, strong managements have reached agreement with strong locals on a good effort level.

Some of the most interesting cases are those of negotiated agreements involving acceptance of standard data. These cases show an evolution similar to that in the acceptance of job evaluation and a stable internal wage rate structure. In these cases the union relinquishes the right to protest basic time values though reserving the right to checks by time-study. In one such case in a machine-tool plant, the time-study check had not been used in several years.

[10] Harry F. Evarts, "Management Problems in the Removal of Wage Incentive Plans," unpub. thesis, Harvard University, Graduate School of Business Administration (December 1958).

The analogy with job evaluation is close. Prior to acceptance of stability, wage rates or standards were protested almost indiscriminately. Protest was something of a game frequently bringing a reward if management was weak. After stability was accepted, adequate proof was required if a protest was made.

The question is whether there is the same degree of mutual interest in stability of standards as was found with internal wage rates. The steel industry, which successfully negotiated evaluation, was unable to negotiate standards on an industrial engineering basis. The union would seem to be interested in removing inequities in incentive earnings, but this represents more an interest in wages than in effort equalization. Of course, the difficulty should not be overlooked of negotiating principles for standards short of the elaborate detail of standard data.

There is some evidence that unions are moving toward a greater acceptance of industrial engineering principles and stability of production standards at a competitive effort level. In 1958, however, conflict tended to be greater in the area of production standards than in many other facets of contract administration.

19 / *Evaluated Rate Structures*

THE OUTSTANDING ASPECT of the establishment and modification of wage rates for particular jobs is the extent to which controversy has been eliminated. Rational wage structures have been created and considerable agreement achieved on policies of wage administration. Wage administration procedure has also been definitely improved. Before and during World War II, as well as during the early postwar years, individual job rates produced a high volume of grievances as well as important issues in negotiation. In 1958, as will be shown below, only infrequently was this area of contract administration and negotiation an important issue between the parties.

The situation described above pertains where job evaluation is not used as much as where it is. Stable wage relationships have been established under collective bargaining partly by freezing job rates for the term of the contract except for new and changed jobs. Wage rates for new and changed jobs produce grievances, with or without job evaluation, but administrative resolution of differences primarily through formal or informal job content comparison, has in large measure supplanted bargaining for what the traffic will bear. Grievances have been reduced in number, restricted in scope, and controlled by agreement on method of resolution.

Plant and company wage structures take different forms, reflecting the use of job evaluation, labor grade job classification,[1] and individual job rates. Simple wage structures typically had individually negotiated job rates: a particular wage rate or rate range was negotiated for each job or occupation. Many slightly complex job structures used individual job rates, and a few very complex ones retained a job rate form. A minority of complex wage structures were

---

[1] The term "job classification" has two meanings in the literature; the classification of *jobs* by *labor grades* and the classification of *individual employees* by appropriate *job title*. The first meaning, slotting jobs into labor grades, is involved above. The second meaning, slotting individuals into jobs, is discussed later in this chapter.

simplified and adjusted by informal classification of jobs into labor grades. Under such a system wage rates or rate ranges were established for a predetermined number of labor grades or classes. Jobs were then classified without the formal use of a job evaluation plan into the various labor grades or classes. Finally, a large proportion of the complex wage structures have been evaluated by means of a formal plan.[2] No statistics are known to be available distinguishing among these types of wage structures, but, with some notable exceptions, such as the automobile and meat packing industries, job evaluation is very commonly used with complex job structures.

There were also various mixed approaches which do not fall directly into the types of wage structures noted above. One association of some seventy plants and the certified union classified all jobs into five predetermined labor grades and then jointly developed an evaluation plan that was used only for new and changed jobs. These parties have not had an arbitration on job rates in more than ten years. In some cases the company uses evaluation as a guide, but the accepted system is job classification or individual job rates. In one novel case with individual job rates the company used evaluation but allowed itself a six-cent spread, within which it reached agreement on the job rate with the union.

Evaluated structures are discussed under the following headings: (1) development of job evaluation, (2) job evaluation in basic steel and West Coast paper, (3) introduction of job evaluation, and (4) some issues in evaluation administration. Labor grade job classification and individual job rates are discussed in Chapter 20.

Development of Job Evaluation

Job evaluation has developed primarily through management initiative. Unions, with the exception of the steelworkers in recent

[2] There are three steps in evaluating jobs: job description, point rating (or ranking) jobs in terms of job factors or characteristics, and attaching wage rates to jobs grouped into labor grades. Job descriptions may be brief or fairly detailed; duties and responsibilities are described to facilitate analysis by job factors or characteristics. Point rating jobs by job factors is the primary distinguishing characteristic of evaluation. Job factors fall under the general headings of skill, responsibility, working conditions, and physical effort. Specific factors vary in name and number in different plans. A point scoring system is normally used which calls for weighting the factors, and jobs are scored factor by factor. Point totals create an hierarchy of jobs, which are grouped in ascending order by systematic point ranges, and wage rates or ranges are established for the labor grades thus created.

years, have usually opposed it in principle. In fact, however, most unions have gone along with, and participated in, evaluation programs. In a large proportion of cases where management wants to introduce job evaluation, union acceptance has been secured, though sometimes only after several years of delay. However, in a minority of instances, evaluation proposals have been flatly rejected. Where evaluation has been introduced, the plan used generally has been developed or selected by management, but unions influence the timing, the method, and the character of the introduction. In some instances, particularly with the steelworkers, the plan was selected by the union, at times with management having a strong preference for a different plan. Unions have usually achieved a significant degree of formal or informal participation in the introduction and administration of plans, which, no doubt, modified the particular placement of jobs. The degree of this influence cannot be measured.

There have been a variety of reasons for management interest in evaluation. Of course, the primary direct purpose was to develop an equitable and simplified job rate structure. In case after case the existence of a more or less chaotic wage structure was given as the basic reason for introducing job evaluation. Job evaluation, through job description, job analysis, and job rating by factors, creates an hierarchy of jobs according to skill and responsibility requirements, and according to physical effort and working conditions. Grouping jobs by labor grades or classes usually simplifies the rate structure by establishing only a relatively small number of grades and related wage rates. A simplified rational wage structure is created based on factor analysis of job content.

Job evaluation has developed as a part of the expansion and definition of the staff functions of personnel and industrial engineering. It is one phase of the growth of management by policy. It centralizes control over the determination of individual job rates. It calls for specialists in job analysis to determine wage rates. Establishing and modifying job rates is thus subject to specialized administrative procedure under an evaluation policy. Also in large companies where job evaluation is not formally used, a wage rate department will nevertheless exist and will operate in much the same way as in companies formally using evaluation.

While pioneering work was done earlier, job evaluation developed in the late 1930's. By 1940 the National Industrial Conference

Board reported in a survey of personnel practices[3] that 13.3 per cent of 2,700 companies surveyed had "job evaluation by points and/or ranking." Historically job evaluation developed out of (1) civil service classification, (2) job analysis for time study purposes, (3) job descriptions to be used in the selection and hiring of employees, and (4) salary standardization and classification practices in the 1920's. Earliest applications of job evaluation on a significant scale were in the years 1935 to 1940, when they were stimulated by the growth of the union movement, particularly of industrial unions.

Various industry groups were particularly important in influencing the adoption and spread of job evaluation. Groups such as the American Management Association and Industrial Relations Counselors early saw the significance of job evaluation as a device both to improve company wage structures and wage administration and to maintain management control of the wage structure under collective bargaining. Industry associations, most notably the National Metal Trades Association, took the lead in directing the introduction of job evaluation.

Just as all personnel activities were directly and indirectly stimulated by the expanding union movement, job evaluation was used by management partly to deter or prevent unionization, partly to rationalize its wage scales prior to unionization and establish principles and practices for future wage administration, and partly to stabilize the wage structure and eliminate continuous bargaining over particular rates after unionization.

Both stability and orderly change have been achieved by job evaluation. An evaluated wage structure agreed to by a union holds rate relationships constant unless job content changes. With changes in job content, a frame of reference has been set up for use in the grievance procedure and in arbitration. Job evaluation thus leads to better administrative practices as well as to a more equitable wage structure.

Government regulation of wages during World War II gave a decided stimulus to both wage and salary evaluation. This stimulus was threefold: (1) General Order 31 placed a premium on rate ranges. Individuals could be compensated within a given rate range subject only to general regulation, as contrasted with the freezing of

[3] National Industrial Conference Board, *Personnel Activities in American Business,* Studies in Personnel Policy, No. 20 (1940), p. 9.

individual wage rates. The increased flexibility inherent in rate-range regulation undoubtedly encouraged the spread of wage and salary evaluation in order to develop appropriate rate ranges. (2) In the face of rather rigid control over general wage increases, an increase for a substantial number of employees could be obtained through the introduction of job evaluation. The Regional War Labor Boards tended to follow liberal policies in the introduction of job evaluation. Frequently the general level of evaluated rates was allowed to reflect an average increase for the structure as a whole in order to minimize the "red circle" rates and smooth the transition to the new rate structure.[4] When, for example, a five-cent average increase could be obtained by introducing job evaluation, even though employees shared unequally in the increase and a few employees received no increase at all, the process of evaluation was artificially stimulated. Unions sometimes went along only because the added money outweighed the unrest created by unequal increases. (3) In dispute cases the War Labor Board frequently was confronted with a broad issue of wage-rate inequities. While the Board did not normally order job evaluation as such (the Southern California Airframe Industry was an exception), it frequently required the parties to bargain out inequities within the framework of an order setting up certain guides and controls. It was out of such an order that the steel industry evaluation program was developed. In meat packing, while evaluation was not used, fairly similar results were achieved through bargaining the classification of jobs. Board orders in dispute cases involving inequities seem to have stimulated formal or informal evaluation, and inequity cases were probably encouraged in order to obtain an inequity fund from the Board to supplement allowed general wage increases.

World War II was a period when job evaluation spread rapidly. The spread of unionism, wage controls, and the many job content changes associated with conversion to war production and simplified civilian production, greatly encouraged its use. Internal wage structure problems continued to be important in the immediate postwar years. To some degree reconversion to civilian production kept alive job-rate problems, but, more important, additional time was needed

---

[4] An individual does not have his wage rate cut if his new evaluated rate is less than his existing rate, but his rate is personalized or "red circled." New and promoted employees receive only the evaluated rate and usually general wage increases are applied only to evaluated rates thus wiping out "red circles."

to negotiate acceptable wage structures and for unions to accept stability of internal rate relationships. As the postwar years went by, internal wage-rate relationships became a progressively less acute labor-management problem. In considerable part this meant that job evaluation became an accepted approach to job-rate problems.

The influence of job evaluation principles spread beyond the scope of formal plans. It is found almost universally in labor contracts that grievances on job rates can be brought only if job content changes. In earlier contracts, while wages were frozen for the term of the contract, this frequently precluded only general wage adjustments, and job-rate inequity grievances of all types were brought continuously during the term of the contract. Accepting stable job rates for the term of the contract, unless job content changes, is, in effect, an evaluation principle which has found general acceptance. Again, for new and changed jobs, an informal evaluation approach is almost universal. Such jobs are in-lined by a job content comparison, though the structure is also influenced by prevailing rates.[5]

Special mention should be made of union attitudes toward job evaluation. With only a few exceptions, like the steelworkers, the official union position has been one of opposition.[6] This grew out of distrust and suspicion of the technique and the use of job evaluation by management to reduce the scope and degree of bargaining on individual wage rates. But, as indicated in this section, the official position has not been controlling except in a minority of instances. The UAW has refused to accept job evaluation in important instances, as have the Packinghouse Workers and other unions, but usually unions "go along" with management proposals for evaluation. A number of points bear on this seeming inconsistency between official opposition and actual acceptance.

In part, unions have been bought off. Objection was not strong enough to turn down evaluation if an increase in the rate structure was also involved. Raising the rate structure corrects inequities by a process of differential wage increases. Only a small number of jobs

---

[5] See George W. Taylor and Frank C. Pierson, eds., *New Concepts in Wage Determination* (1957), Part II, especially Chapters 5 and 6. The present chapter cannot explore the relation of wage forces to job evaluation.

[6] A good summary of union attitudes is to be found in William Gomberg, "Trade Unions and Industrial Engineering," *Handbook of Industrial Engineering and Management*, Ireson and Grant, eds. (1955). See also *What's Wrong with Job Evaluation?*, International Association of Machinists (1954).

are reduced in rate, and only a small number of individuals must accept "red circle" rates. Since an important source of union objection to job evaluation has been unwillingness to accept job-rate reductions, an accompanying wage increase minimized the objection. The extensive wage increases of the period under consideration thus created opportunities for the introduction of job evaluation.

In part, unions became willing to accept less bargaining over individual job rates. This change in union attitude was very important and is illustrated in the next section. Unions found that job evaluation did not freeze them out of a reasonable voice in influencing the wage structure, and continuous wage grievances became a union problem. Particularly when accompanied by formal or informal joint participation in the evaluation process, the technique became acceptable.

The official union position is usually still one of opposition. One union official said that as vice president of the union he was opposed to job evaluation, but as an individual he thought it was a good thing in many instances. Clearly union practice indicates a far higher degree of acceptance of and tolerance for evaluation than do official pronouncements.

This brief sketch of the development of evaluation and the achievement of stability with orderly change cannot portray at all adequately the magnitude of the accomplishment involved. The following section will illustrate by two specific cases the very general statements of this section.

Job Evaluation in Basic Steel and West Coast Paper

Basic Steel

Subject to some qualification the development of job evaluation in basic steel offers a good illustration of the general changes that have taken place.[7] A statement in 1947 by R. Conrad Cooper, then assistant vice president, industrial relations, currently executive vice president, industrial relations, United States Steel Corporation, quoted by Stieber most concisely describes the early problem:

[7] The discussion of basic steel leans heavily on research and writing by Jack Stieber. The quotations included are from "The Development, Impact, and Administration of the Steel Industry Wage Rate Inequity Program," unpub. thesis, Harvard University (November 1955). See also Jack Stieber, *The Steel Industry Wage Structure* (1959).

Thus the principal ingredients of the wage rate situation of 10 years ago were: a body of specific rates emerging from differing backgrounds in various localities; a new union striving for position; employees possessed of a new device by which to explore real or imaginary wage rate grievances; no fixed wage scale in the agreements; a specified right to challenge the equity of any particular rate; and no agreed yardstick by which to judge the equity of a rate once challenged; and no terminal point for the settlement of such differences.[8]

Only brief development of a few points is feasible here. The original 1937 agreement between U. S. Steel and the Steelworkers Organizing Committee contained only the following sentence on wage rate inequalities: "Where alleged inequalities in wage rates prevail, the matter may be taken up for local plant adjustment, and settlement made on a mutually satisfactory basis." Contrast this with the detailed, approximately sixty-page, manual now part of the contract between the parties and the extensive additional job descriptions and data.

The 1941 contract made reference to job evaluation principles to be used by management and allowed grievances over new and changed jobs to go to arbitration and other alleged inequities to go to the fourth step of the grievance procedure. The 1942 agreement dropped the reference to job evaluation, continued the arbitration and grievance procedure, and established a joint commission to study wage inequities. (The joint commission referred to is in U. S. Steel, but such commissions were established in various contracts.)

Establishment of the joint commissions showed a desire to make progress with a difficult problem. The union's growing concern with numerous grievances was well illustrated by a passage from a 1947 Steelworker Training Conference quoted by Stieber.[9]

McDonald: Why did we get into the business of adjusting wage inequities in the first place? Remember those thousands and thousands of inequity grievances which you had arise? They were driving you insane—That is how we got started and why we got started, because of the trouble which existed. Our people were at one another's throats, as it were, on this business of inequities. One machinist would say, "Look at Joe over there. He is getting a buck and a half and I am getting $1.40." There was veritable hell going on.

[8] R. Conrad Cooper, "A Fair Day's Work for a Fair Day's Pay," address before the American Management Association (October 3, 1947), Stieber thesis, p. 19.

[9] Transcript of Steelworker Training Conference for District Wage Inequity Committee Representatives (June 26, 1947). pp. 12-13 and 467, Stieber thesis, p. 26.

Malloy: They were mostly organized by the fact that we urged the people to give rise to these grievances on wages and inequalities and later created a problem for ourselves that was almost impossible of solution by the time we got everybody of the opinion that all they had to do to get a raise was to join the union. Everybody used to say: "Well, I haven't got anything out of this yet. I don't know why I should pay dues." That was really the big problem that we had to face.

The 1942 joint commission, however, could not reach agreement. According to Stieber, negotiation broke down on issues of scope, method, and cost. The union wanted equal pay for equal work within the industry; the companies were looking at inequities primarily within particular plants. The union opposed job evaluation; the companies wanted to use industrial engineering methods. The union wanted a sizeable fund to eliminate inequities; the companies wanted a balanced payroll approach. The same issues carried over into the 1944 War Labor Board case.

The inequity issue in the 1944 WLB steel case became of major importance when it became clear that the Board did not intend to break the "little steel" wage formula and grant a general wage increase. In this setting the Board met the issues noted above by (1) ruling against the union on the demand for equal pay for equal work within the industry but allowing the parties to take into account rate relationships existing in the industry in classifying jobs within each plant and company, (2) not ordering job evaluation but rather negotiated classification of jobs in the smallest practical grouping of jobs with substantially equivalent content, and (3) limiting each company's cost to a maximum of five cents per hour.

The Directive Order of the Board in November 1944, while raising many questions, provided a framework for negotiation. Negotiations continued to January 1947 with various interim agreements. In these negotiations the union agreed to an evaluation approach worked out by the companies. Behind this agreement was extensive work by the companies. Twelve major steel companies became charter members of a Cooperative Wage Study begun in Pittsburgh in 1943. A tailor-made plan was worked out with factors and weights that caused a minimum disruption of the historical wage structure existing in the industry. This was undoubtedly one reason why the union was willing to accept it. Another reason was the extreme difficulty of the administrative task if evaluation were not used. The most novel feature of the plan was the relatively heavy weight given to the responsibility factor.

The companies ultimately agreed to a single industry wage structure except for the southern differential, which was eliminated in later negotiations. With minor exceptions, and with recognition of differences in job content, a uniform day rate and incentive guarantee wage structure was created throughout the basic steel industry as organized by the steelworkers.

The 1947 agreement barred grievances on alleged inequities once the standard hourly scale went into effect. On new jobs or on jobs that were changed to the extent of one full class or more a new description and classification were required. The proposed description and classification were submitted to the plant grievance committee. If agreement was not obtained, a grievance could be filed and carried to arbitration. The only basis for a grievance was improper classification under the Cooperative Wage Study Manual.

The steel industry inequity program, carried out by corporate and plant joint committees, represents a remarkable administrative accomplishment. The union accepted evaluation principles in the form of the CWS Manual. In fact the manual has become identified with the Steelworkers Union and has been advocated by the union in almost all of its contractual relationships. While in some cases the union has agreed to a different evaluation approach, there appear to be more instances in which managements have agreed to the manual though preferring a different plan.

Acceptance of the manual and standard hourly rate scale, while involving some very real problems of employee reaction to the placement of jobs, was facilitated in basic steel because it did not affect incentive earning relationships, except for submerging some incentive plans,[10] and because it was worked out to fit closely the existing wage structure.

This close correspondence with the existing wage structure, with its heavy weight on responsibility, may well have a bearing on the continued acceptability of the plan. Whether it is because of the nature of the plan, or because of the nature of technological change, or

[10] Incentive earnings in basic steel plants varied considerably from job to job. The new standard hourly rates were above incentive earnings on some jobs, and thus some incentive plans were "submerged." "New" incentive plans, based on the new hourly scale, have now replaced "old" incentives to a considerable extent.

both, job changes in steel have almost never reduced the value of a job. If experience under the plan had been different, the union might well have taken a different attitude.

The union clearly was as interested in removing differentials among plants and companies within the industry as in revising job-rate relationships within the plants. The union also was interested in a wage increase. Had the WLB not made a direct increase impossible, the entire program might at least have been delayed. Much of the money ultimately obtained raised the day rates and reduced the differential between incentive and nonincentive workers, an inequity aggravated by wartime production conditions.

Emphasis should be placed upon the thread of common experience in the steel story as well as its importance as a particular development in a major industry. Beginning with a new union, an unplanned wage structure, frequent wage-rate grievances, and no principles for the resolution of grievances, there was developed a stable wage structure with orderly grievance processing. This was the general picture in many situations when job evaluation was introduced although the particulars of each case vary widely.

West Coast Paper

The development of job evaluation by the Pacific Coast Association of Pulp and Paper Manufacturers, the International Brotherhood of Pulp, Sulphite and Paper Mill Workers, and the International Brotherhood of Paper Makers has many unique features.[11] It was developed out of experience of the parties to fit their particular needs and desires.

At the time of the first Association contract in 1934 a uniform base or common labor rate was set for all mills; those paid less were brought up to the minimum rate. Also a Joint Classification Committee was created to equalize all job rates among mills. As in steel, the problem was one of equalization among mills as well as of inequities within particular mills.

While the first agreement established the principle of a uniform wage structure, the classification of jobs by job titles proved to be of

[11] This section leans heavily on *Industrial Job Analysis*, 6th ed., J. M. Tedford, Job Analyst for the Pacific Coast Association of Pulp and Paper Manufacturers, Approved by Colonel Alexander R. Heron, Representing Management, Mr. Bart L. Tidland, Representing Labor, *Post-Record*, Camas, Washington (1956).

only limited applicability. Classification, however, established the principle of removing inequities while adhering to established structural relationships. As Tedford states;

> Adherence to the prevailing wage trends and differentials is basic. There is no better guide to acceptable and sound values. However, due to outside pressures and influences, certain job fields that are common to other industries may experience exceptions to the prevailing pattern. This may represent a temporary or faulty tendency, or it may be an indication that our own pattern is faulty and needs correction. This points to the fact that one industry can hardly set a permanent wage pattern for a job field which has a parallel in other industries. It is fortunate for our own industry from the standpoint of rate simplicity that there are but few job fields which have counterparts elsewhere.
>
> The prevailing complex wage structure has developed over a long period of years out of many individual rate decisions, and it is only natural that some rates after having been set have become ill-related through improper setting and subsequent changes in the jobs themselves. It may seem a paradox that we must use a faulty structure as a guide in order to develop an improved one with the inequalities largely eliminated. But apparently there is no other guide and a wage structure of a widely diversified industry such as ours covering a wide area (the entire Coast) and a large number of plants (thirty-four paper, pulp and board mills) has offered a laboratory for research which likely has no parallel.[12]

In 1936 a program of research and development was begun to develop a more systematic job analysis approach. The concept of a "step" was used as a basic unit of measurement. This has been carried forward since that time. Evaluation points and the various credit tables equate one point to one step, and labor grades are referred to as being a given number of wage steps above the base rate.

In the process of research, again quoting Tedford, "charts and tables were made, fitted, destroyed or revised over and over again until something workable began to evolve." A nine-factor point system, with groups according to skill, responsibility, and working conditions, was created.

"Complaint" jobs were analyzed. In 1937 some 451 jobs were jointly analyzed. In 1938-39 study continued, but wage activity was at a minimum. In 1940 complaints again accumulated, and 461 jobs

---

[12] The same, pp. 5-6.

were analyzed. In 1941 a joint general analysis of 3,500 jobs was made, but for a variety of reasons the unions did not accept the over-all analysis approach. With this refusal agreement was reached that analysis would apply only to jobs that had changed materially or to new jobs. Unchanged jobs could not be grieved. Analysis applied only to new and changed jobs from 1941 to 1948.

In 1948 the freeze on old jobs was removed. The "Job Analysis Board of Directors" was also created supplementing the "Job Analysis Board" and the "Joint Plant Job Analysis Committee." In subsequent years, particularly in 1950 and 1951, a large number of jobs were analyzed, so that as of 1957 a large proportion of jobs coming under the program had been analyzed.

A number of points warrant emphasis in this sketch of developments. The plan clearly grew out of experience and went into effect gradually over many years. Even in 1957 not all jobs had been analyzed. Rates for mechanical crafts and rates on newsprint machines were excluded from the program by contract, although these jobs have a systematized structure. Craft rates have an A plus Mechanic class, an A, B, and C Mechanic class, and a D (Helper) classification. A procedure for qualification by test is provided in the contract. Newsprint rates vary each month by speed of machine in accordance with this phase of the Paper Makers scale. While most other jobs have been analyzed, as mentioned, some have not. If official analysis is requested, the results (upward or downward) are binding on the parties.

Joint union-management administration has been developed. Job evaluation appears to be an area that lends itself to joint action. Tedford says in the introduction to his *Industrial Job Analysis:*

> It is quite evident to those who have made the surveys and resultant applications that any plan—no matter how closely it follows other accepted principles—unless jointly developed, has little chance of finding root enough for substantial growth in a country whose labor policy grants an equality of bargaining power.

In introducing and administering job evaluation, managements and unions frequently employ joint committees or procedures, but joint action means different things in different situations. Rarely has joint authority and responsibility been carried to the degree it has in this case. The joint administration operates as a policy formulation agency and as specialized grievance machinery. (A union and a management analyst go to a plant as a step in handling grievances not resolved by the local joint committee.) The parties have demonstrated a high ability to resolve differences with a minimum of outside help. In the entire history of the relationship only a few arbitrations on any subject have been held.

Finally, the job evaluation plan itself has one very unique characteristic. Mention has been made of the nine job factors under three broad headings. Attention has not been given, however, to "job features." The credit tables are constructed in terms of "job features"— loads, items, feet, pounds, speed, width, batches, dumps, fills, etc.— which in turn are related to factors and points or steps above base. Job features are worked out by job fields (related job groups) so that, in effect, several job evaluation sub-plans are built into one over-all plan. Some job fields have been measured so objectively that rating is virtually automatic, other fields have a more general type of evaluation approach. Of most importance is the fact that the application of the plan to different fields can be separately studied and revised with a minimum of disturbance to other job fields. This principle is in accord with the notion of adaptation to change endorsed by the parties and probably reflects a wage environment somewhat different from that in basic steel.

Introduction of Job Evaluation

These examples, while highlighting the accommodation in union-management relations implicit in the development of job evaluation, also raise questions as to the nature of job evaluation and its administration. Some of these questions will be considered in this and the following section.

In each of the examples in the previous section the particular job evaluation plan used was developed by the parties to fit the unique technological and wage environment of each industry. The particular administrative machinery was also evolved to fit the particular needs and desires of the parties in each case. In basic steel and West Coast paper the plans and the administrative machinery were tailor-made perhaps to an unusual degree; however, quite generally, job evaluation appears to have worked best when it was well adapted to its particular environment.

What is involved in adapting a plan to its environment? What is meant by a tailor-made plan? Job evaluation plans look so similar, and superficially are so similar, that it is difficult to appreciate their differences. There are, however, two distinct dimensions of difference: (1) differences in the degree to which plans have been operationally adapted to the job structure, and (2) differences in the degree to which joint administration has developed. Job evaluation plans that were working well showed a good wage and job fit, and the administrative mechanism had been adjusted to the needs and desires of the parties.

Operational fit can best be made clear through examples of the introduction of plans. In these introductions, adaptations to the job structure hinged upon creating operational distinctions among jobs and operational definition of factors and degrees of factors. If words were not given real job meaning, administration was more susceptible to continuous argument. These concepts will be considered again after a brief discussion of selected aspects of three introductions.

First, is a small single-plant company with about 350 employees. This metal trades company and its local of the International Union of Electrical Workers had had over the years an unhappy experience with job evaluation. The National Electrical Manufacturers' plan (the plan that became more widely known as the National Metal Trades' Plan) was installed in 1943 by outside consultants. Its introduction was chiefly in order to evade the wage freeze. As applied it had many difficulties in job definitions and was in reality neither understood nor accepted. From 1943 to 1953 wage grievances were extreme in number and were bargained out in such fashion that wage distortions accumulated. In 1953 the plan was a real headache for both the company and the union and was the major area of disagreement between the parties.

In 1953 the union asked for a complete revision of the evaluation plan. The company agreed, and a joint committee was established to work out the review. Real progress was made in the job description phase of the work. Descriptions were simplified but were kept operational in character. Being a small company with job shop production conditions, too minute differentiation in job definition had, in the past, and would, in the future, create problems with variations in product and transfer of employees among jobs. Where job differentiation was retained in the new descriptions, the distinctions were clearly operational. For example, while work on a multiple spindle drill press was distinguished as a separate job from work on a single spindle, all work that could be performed on a given machine was kept within the definition of a single job. In fact, many jobs were defined in terms of all work that could be performed on a given machine or group of machines. Previous difficulties led the joint committee to both simplicity and operational precision of the new definitions in view of the frequently necessary transfer of employees.

The review at first bogged down on rating the 130 jobs. The NMTA plan was again being used. The committee began rating the jobs factor by factor putting an "x" beside each job rating that was in dispute. After they had rated the jobs on four factors, a halt was called as they had "x's" beside 85 per cent of all ratings. Rating against a manual with general degree definitions simply was not working in spite of a sincere effort to resolve a difficult problem.

The parties then began to simplify and tailor the plan. Under the plan each of the eleven factors had 5 degrees. They kept 5 degrees on one factor, used 4 degrees on a second factor, cut all other factors to 3 degrees, divided all points by 5, wrote their own degree definitions in terms understood by foremen and union representatives, and agreed on bench-mark jobs to illustrate and peg degree definitions. Reducing the number of degrees for some factors reduced the amount of job distinction attempted and placed major weight on one factor. Reducing the point spread helped to eliminate minor arguments. Writing new degree definitions and developing bench-mark comparison jobs were fundamental improvements. Agreement on a job-comparison framework paved the way for general agreement.

The rating subsequently went smoothly with better than 85 per cent agreement. Disagreements were resolved by restudy of particular jobs with insignificant resort to arbitration. The plan was carried through to single job rates with a three-step progression to job rate. Jobs in the lowest three labor grades progressed to job rate in six months, the middle four labor grades in 12 months, and the jobs in the top three grades in 24 months with apprentice rates below the job rates where appropriate.

Since the parties had had grievance difficulty in the past, their agreement provided for an annual general review of all jobs for which it was requested. After the first year, 12 jobs were reviewed, after the second year 4, and none since that time. The union's attitude toward the plan was indicated by its advocating use of the plan

by other locals. The most troublesome area of union-management relations was successfully resolved by realistic adaptation of the plan
to the job structure.

One phase of the introduction of a second plan will be discussed
briefly. This is a case of a seventy-plant association with a uniform
wage structure and five labor grades. Evaluation was used only with
respect to new and changed jobs. A point plan had been developed
on the basis of bench-mark job comparison. The company and union
had agreed upon the point ratings for each factor for each of 39
bench-mark jobs. On any new or changed job the basic rating principle was clearly stated and agreed to. The job in question was compared with bench-mark jobs factor by factor. Whatever bench-mark
job the job in question most nearly resembled on any factor determined the points on the factor.

This example brings out in very direct fashion the principle of
grounding and pegging word definitions of factors by the use of
bench-mark jobs. Also involved was the selection of enough bench-
mark jobs to cover the various types of jobs found within the wage
structure. All of the different "families" of jobs had their particular
bench-mark reference jobs. This plan was particularly interesting
because it had worked well from 1947 to 1957 without a single arbitration case.

The third introduction involves the United Steelworkers and a
large company outside of basic steel. Job evaluation was not introduced until 1957. For many years the company and the union had
been unable to agree on a program of evaluation. The union had insisted on using the plan worked out in basic steel. The company was
convinced that the basic steel manual would not work well with its
job structure. The company also feared that if the steel manual were
used, the temptation would be strong for the union to carry over job
descriptions and labor grade placement of similar jobs from basic
steel to this company. In other words, the company insisted on tailor-
ing its own plan to fit its own wage structure.

Progress in negotiation became possible only after certain international union officials, strongly committed to the steel manual, withdrew from the negotiations. It then became possible to start the program without a manual. Job descriptions were written by the company and reviewed by the union. It was agreed that the existence of

the job description did not mean that job content could not be changed by the company. If job content was found in the future to differ from the job description, the description was to be revised. Job content governed the job description and not the reverse.

After job descriptions were completed, job factors were agreed upon. Jobs were then ranked factor by factor by joint committees. Ranking jobs by factors, with no points and no manual, meant a minimum of difference of opinion since it was almost impossible to infer wage results from the rank lists. In other words, the factors were used to establish rank lists of jobs rather than bench-mark jobs.

The rank lists were converted into points and a manual by a complex process of fitting them mathematically to existing wage rates. The company and the union agreed on the principle of best fit. Whatever weights for the factors and spread of points produced the best fit to the existing structure was to constitute the manual and the point scoring for the jobs. Specific points for jobs were thus not negotiated. A very good statistical fit and thus a minimum of disturbance to existing relationships was achieved. It is interesting to note that the factor weights that produced the best fit differed substantially from those used in the basic steel plan, although the latter had originally been developed by a similar process of best fit to the steel structure.

In the process of attaching wage rates to jobs and working out labor grades, a minority of jobs were treated as exceptions and given special wage consideration. Some jobs, while reasonably evaluated, were changed so drastically in promotional and wage status that both parties wanted to upgrade the jobs. The exception principle was openly used without undermining the plan. Exception jobs had no standing in grievances and arbitration of new and changed jobs.

The basic administrative principle adopted for new and changed jobs was to fit such jobs into the rank lists originally developed. To date the administration of the plan has involved an insignificant amount of controversy.

This example shows strong initiative and leadership on the part of the company. While the company wanted to work out job evaluation jointly with the union, it firmly refused to act until the union agreed to start fresh and not copy the plan in basic steel. The company also insisted on the ranking approach, making the manual the result and not the beginning of evaluation. Results appeared to justify the company position that a tailor-made plan was needed both to develop appropriate factor weights and to create rank lists for future administration. Factor weights did differ significantly from those in steel, and the job rank lists required for the manual provided a firm jointly-agreed administrative reference for new and changed jobs.

Omitting for the moment the administrative mechanism to be used by the parties, which is discussed below, operational fit must be achieved (1) at the job description level, (2) at the factor definition level, and (3) at the level of the choice of factors and their weights. Each point will be discussed briefly.

Job descriptions do not flow automatically from looking at the work performed by employees. A "job" is an arbitrary concept. Specific tasks of employees can be organized into a smaller number of broadly defined jobs or a larger number of more specifically defined jobs.[13] Much administrative difficulty has developed from inappropriate job description or from failure to maintain consistency between work performed and the job description. The next section considers two administrative problems growing out of inappropriate job descriptions or related administrative difficulties: (1) the job classification of individual employees, and (2) the job description and work assignment. Jobs must be defined to the mutual satisfaction of the parties to avoid continuous problems in employee classification, work assignment, and transfer.

Operational fit at the factor definition level has been illustrated by the two basic approaches that are used, bench-mark jobs and ranking. Neither method is superior, and actually most plans use both, but with emphasis on one or the other. Those emphasizing either method work well. The important differences among plans are in the degree to which definitions are well or poorly "grounded" by reference to actual jobs, by either ranking or bench-mark jobs. If the administration of a plan depended too much on "words in a manual," there was usually friction in administration. Words must be translated into agreed-upon job relations by reference to particular jobs. Most plans had become more firmly grounded over the years by development through administration; some plans had not. The related

<hr>

[13] A major objection to job evaluation by the International Association of Machinists is its use to dilute skill by breaking down the journeyman machinist job into many machine operation jobs. As can be seen, this result doe' not flow from job evaluation as such.

administrative problem, discussed in the next section, is the rating of new and changed jobs. The better-grounded factor definitions gave a better basis for handling grievances.

Good fit at the level of choice of evaluation factors and relative weights is very complex for brief discussion. Choice of specific evaluation factors may well be less important than the relative weight given to each factor. Weights evolve by ranking or scoring jobs in the process of creating the job evaluation skeleton. The effective weight of a factor depends largely on the point spread utilized in scoring and the distribution of jobs within this spread, rather than on the maximum points allowed.

It may be assumed that a plan that has a good initial statistical wage fit will have created factors and weights that will work well for future job changes. If working conditions require a considerable range of points and job dispersion to get a good initial wage fit, future job changes will also probably involve working conditions as an important job consideration. If working conditions are substantially uniform on all jobs and can be virtually eliminated from consideration in initial fit, they are not likely to be important in future job changes. If it takes a heavy weight on responsibility to get good initial fit, as it does in some industries, future technological change is likely to continue these conditions. This assumption as to the future validity of good initial fit cannot be proven, and logical objections are easily raised, but experience seems to justify it. Again, however, plans frequently require major revision after about ten years because of major changes in the technological and wage environment and because of compromise with technological change in wage administration.

Finally, wage fit involves applying factors and weights somewhat independently to different groups of related jobs. No plan of which we are aware formally recognizes various "job fields" as specifically as does West Coast paper. But most plans group jobs into general fields. For example, one company using the metal trades plan said "we grouped our jobs into eight different types: assembly, machine operation, processing, testing, inspection, trades, maintenance, and general service," and then explained its bench-mark approach to each field.

Good statistical fit at the level of choice of factors and weights is required because the relative importance of different factors in distinguishing among jobs varies by industry in the light of its particular technology. It varies too in the historical evolution of particular industry wage structures. To work well, a plan must be adapted to the technology of its jobs and to the historical wage structure of the industry.

In addition to good operational fit job evaluation requires an administrative mechanism suited to the needs and desires of the parties. There is a considerable range of variation from essentially unilateral to joint administration of job evaluation plans, although it is not clear what proportion of plans fall in each category or which are the more successful. Two plans that have been followed over a considerable period of years appear casually to be administered in about the same way. They are both National Metal Trades plans and involve different locals of the same international union. Neither plan provides for joint administration by contract. In both cases the company runs the plan, with the union having the right to grieve through the regular grievance procedure. In both cases the plan runs smoothly and gives rise to very few grievances. In fact, however, the plans have two very different histories and are administered quite differently. In one case the plan was introduced prior to unionization and has had very able management administration. The union has at times been critical of it, but has never brought many grievances, and has, in general, simply gone along with the plan, playing a very minor role in its administration. In the other case the plan was introduced after unionization, had a turbulent early history, was extensively revised by the parties. Today it has a high degree of informal joint consultation and administration, although none of this joint action is embodied in formal arrangement. To distinguish substance from contract language is so difficult that, as has been pointed out, it is impossible to generalize.

Most of the plans that have been of primary interest in connection with this study, however, have had an important degree of joint action. It seems reasonable that unions will usually accept a plan only if they understand it enough to be convinced of its equity and have no fear of arbitrary action by management. Mutual acceptance of the basic rating principle of the plan—initial ranking of jobs by factors, or points by factors for an ample number of bench-mark jobs —was an outstanding feature in a number of plans that appeared to be particularly successful.

There was great variation, however, in both management and union attitudes. Some managements had a particular fear of joint action though more with respect to formal contract provisions than informal consultation. The management's desire to eliminate a joint evaluation committee was a key issue in one long strike. In a second case management was extremely dissatisfied with a joint committee and wanted to eliminate it.[14] On the other hand, some managements were convinced of the wisdom of a joint approach. One management official who had introduced job evaluation on a plant-by-plant basis in a large multiplant company strongly favored them even though relations between the company and the various local unions were far from uniform.

Some unions wanted no part of joint responsibility although they accepted job evaluation. On the other hand, some unions accepted job evaluation only when convinced that their interests were adequately protected by joint administrative arrangements.

Administrative arrangements are important, but no particular mechanism appears superior to others. Agreement on particular administrative machinery depends on the attitudes of the parties, the kind of relationship that has developed, and on the scope of the bargaining unit. In some cases both parties wanted close joint administration. In others both avoided a joint approach. In some cases administrative procedures were spelled out in great detail in the contract or in a supplement to it. In others simple reference to the plan was made in the contract, and informal procedures were followed. More formal arrangements appeared desirable in larger bargaining units. Successful operation required satisfactory administrative arrangements, good administration within whatever arrangements were established, good operational fit, and mutual acceptance of basic principles.

Some Issues in Evaluation Administration

While job evaluation was normally well-established and operating with considerable success, this was not always the case. Problem areas of considerable importance were noted as follows: (1) the job classi-

[14] It may well be true that the difficulties encountered in a poorly operating plan, whatever their cause, are magnified by the existence of joint administrative machinery.

fication of individual employees, (2) the job description and work assignment, (3) job rating and technological change, and (4) wholesale inequity grievances. These problems do not arise because of job evaluation, but they may not be resolved by job evaluation. Poor design of an evaluation plan, lax administration of a plan, or failure to establish or agree on principles of administration may create or exaggerate the problems.

Job Classification of Individual Employees

The point has been made that the concept of a job is somewhat arbitrary and that jobs should be defined to create a good operational fit. There are various ramifications to this statement. In the first place, the job descriptions as written may not have good distinguishing characteristics. This point can be made quite independently of the question whether jobs have been too narrowly or too broadly conceived.

In one chemical plant, for example, a very high proportion of job distinctions were based on work of "average" difficulty and work of "above average" and "below average" difficulty. The job classification of individuals in this plant had become hopelessly confused, and the large number of employee classification grievances presented an extremely difficult problem.

In a second plant, a metal trades type of plant, brief and ambiguous descriptions had been written deliberately to avoid debate in the joint installation of a plan. In retrospect it appears that both the company and the union felt it would be advantageous to themselves not to face up to the issue of the continuing classification of individuals. Over some ten years there was a continuous employee classification battle. At times the union was successful in upgrading a high proportion of employees. At times the company downgraded on a broad scale. In 1955 joint administration of evaluation was a major issue in a long strike. Since the strike job descriptions have been rewritten more satisfactorily.

In the second place, jobs may be too narrowly or too broadly conceived. When evaluation is used, the primary problem is a too narrow subdivision of work,[15] and administration of the plan is extremely complex.

---

[15] Under negotiated individual job rates the problem is frequently an overly inclusive job title, as discussed in Chapter 20.

In one company, again with a metal trades type of wage structure, all machine operation jobs were subdivided into four, five, and six classes of the A, B, C, D, E type. In practice it was not clear whether these classifications were of men or of jobs. Classification was supposed to be based on the type of work actually performed. Individual employees, however, were upgraded partly as a reward for longer service, and they retained a particular classification regardless of work actually performed. On the other hand, the number of employees granted the higher classifications was restricted by the volume of work presumed to warrant the pay. Actually the type of work required varied constantly with the product mix, and the evaluation system was too complex for the particular operating conditions. Consistency in work and classification was impossible to maintain.

Relations between this company and the machinists' union were deteriorating badly in 1957. The company tried to claim the exclusive right to classify employees by refusing to arbitrate grievances over employee classification. This position was not upheld in arbitration. In negotiation between the parties no agreement could be reached to revise the descriptions and plan. So long as these conditions continue, the plant will remain in a turmoil.

There are some production situations, airframe manufacturing being a notable case in point, where variation in the volume and methods of work make classification of individuals very difficult. In airframe manufacturing extreme swings in employment have necessitated widespread upgrading and downgrading of individuals. Also, at different stages in the production of a given model, there is considerable change in the work cycle of individual employees. Job content is less specialized in the beginning stages of the production of a model; in later stages employees are downgraded as the scope of their job duties is reduced. A good argument was presented by union officials that many grievances could be avoided by more inclusive job definitions and consequent greater stability in the job classification of individual employees.

Discussion so far has been concerned with poorly written job descriptions and with questions as to the appropriate scope of job content. But classification problems may develop not so much from the job descriptions or the scope of jobs, but from laxity in wage administration. New work is performed, but new descriptions are not written. Jobs are modified, but descriptions are not revised. The work assignment of employees is changed, but the employees are not re-classified. If misclassification is not promptly corrected, vested inter ests are created. One company that had many job and employee changes conducted an employee audit every two months. Misclassi-fication was usually found in 2 to 4 per cent of the cases. In one audit it reached 10 per cent. Even with a much lower percentage and with a less difficult administrative task, the cumulative effect of misclas-sification can seriously disrupt an evaluation plan. Lax administra-tion was primarily responsible for the problems discussed below.

Job Description and Work Assignment[16]

What is the contractual meaning and status of a job description? One company has established by agreement and practice that the job description has no official status in determining either job content or work assignment. The description is in no sense a negotiated agree-ment with the union as to the content of a job. It is a written state-ment of the major duties and responsibilities of the job as it is in fact being performed. If job content or work assignment has been modi-fied and does not correspond in certain essentials with the descrip-tion as written, the description is wrong and must be rewritten to conform with the work assigned and performed. The revised job de-scription is subject to re-analysis as to rate of pay under the plan, and the pay is in turn open to the grievance procedure.

While companies quite generally adhere to the view that a job description is not a restriction on the right to modify job content, nor a limitation on job assignment, cases have been found where in practice management has lost considerable flexibility in the use of manpower. In a plant of one company, for example, the major grievance area and major administrative problem was a refusal to do work except that defined as the employee's regular job. By custom and practice, initially by outright refusal to do work not called for in the job description, employees acquired the right to refuse other as-signment. A new plant manager in assigning work out of classifica-tion when other employees were absent brought on a mass of griev-ances. Every employee filed a grievance when so assigned and even a separate grievance for each day of the assignment. There were no

<hr/>

[16] This section and the previous one are closely related to the discussion in Chapter 9, "Work Assignment and Jurisdiction." This chapter is limited to the evaluation context.

outright refusals to do the work and no disputes as to rate of pay. In this plant, workers had been granted a special right to overtime—no employee worked overtime in a department unless all employees in the department were offered overtime. There was also an issue on size of crews. This plant, not in basic steel, had a local working practice clause. In the first six months of 1957 grievances were filed at a rate of 50 grievances per 100 employees per year. None involving these issues were settled, and a number awaited arbitration. How would these issues fare in arbitration with a general management rights clause, a local working practice clause, and no specific contract language on any of the points at issue? It is not at all unlikely that management will be found to have "fettered its rights" in some respects by its past actions.

In a plant of a different company employees were not assigned incidental tasks unless these were specifically included in their job descriptions. Employees had successfully refused such work. In the evaluation agreement and in arbitration the company's right to assign incidental work had been clearly established. Direct refusal, at times supported by wildcat strikes, appeared to have accomplished a worker objective which would not have been supported had the grievance procedure been used and a case carried to arbitration.

Questions of employee classification, work assignment, revision of job description, and re-evaluation of a modified or new job become confused if changes in job content or assignment are not reviewed and action taken within a reasonable time. One company made no audit of employee classifications and job descriptions over a period of years. In 1951 they began to strengthen their wage administration staff and in 1953 undertook an audit of all jobs. The results of the audit became a serious issue between the company and the union. Leading cases went to arbitration to determine the proper classification of individual employees.

No general statements should be made about results without adequate reference to the particular contract provisions and their history. It is enough to state that: (1) Under certain circumstances the arbitrator held that the company had lost its right to rewrite the job description and downgrade the job. (2) Under certain circumstances the company could not set up a new job and assign the work to employees put on the new job if it had previously been included by practice within a different job description. This was of particular significance in preventing certain specific work from being "carved out" of a general craft definition though the work was not specifically included within it, i.e., electricians continued to replace light bulbs and carpenters to repair wooden pallets. (3) Under certain circumstances the company had the right to rewrite descriptions, downgrade jobs, and reclassify individuals as well as to establish new jobs and reassign work. With the contract ambiguous or silent on the point, the arbitrator worked to establish guide lines to reconcile stability and certainty for the employees with the desirability of having descriptions, work assignments, and pay consistent with job duties.

The important point is not the difficulty of establishing guide lines. It is that failure to revise descriptions and wage rates with changes in job content and work assignment created a major issue. It led to detailed decisional rules that complicated the administration of the wage structure and restricted the assignment of work while perpetuating some questionable rates of pay.

Job descriptions as related to rates of pay, work assignments, and classification of individuals have come to have a somewhat different status in different union-management situations. While management has generally retained the right to determine and modify job content, certain job rights have at times been associated with a job description. At issue is not the reasonableness of the restrictions on management action, but the laxity in wage administration that has led—by custom and practice, by arbitration, and by negotiation—to questions of what work shall be performed and by whom. Wage administration at the level of the job description bears upon these related subjects, and serious problems have been created by a lack of policy or by administrative neglect in the wage area.

Job Rating and Technological Change

Two points will be considered with respect to job rating and technological change. The first relates to the design of the plan and the resolution of grievances. Plans that have high grievance rates and poor resolution of grievances appear to be poorly conceived in that they lack adequate agreement on rank lists of jobs or benchmark jobs. Word definitions of factors then provoke continuous debate in bargaining new and changed jobs. Of course it is not possible to say why agreement has not been achieved. Poor relations between the parties may have blocked agreement, or a poorly designed plan may have given rise to tension and conflict. A few examples of bargaining relationships that produced wholesale grievances are discussed later in this chapter. Clearly a primary consideration in the development and administration of a successful evaluation plan is sincere agreement between the parties on the principle of a stable wage structure with orderly and rational consideration of new and changed jobs.

The second point is the question why well designed and well accepted plans work as well as they do in the light of continuous technological change. Rates of pay for new and changed jobs and the job classification of individual employees constitute the major administrative tasks under job evaluation, and most grievances focus on these issues. As noted above, in a small number of relationships almost all job changes lead to serious grievances. Usually, however, the proportion of such jobs grieved is not unduly high, and, more importantly, grievances are resolved without serious difficulty.

A major reason why job changes do not usually produce a large number of serious grievances is that only a small proportion of the jobs appear in fact to be downgraded. It has already been noted that industrial engineers in the steel industry have a hard time even citing an example of a job that has gone down in grade. There are a few such examples where the only change in the job was in improved working conditions. In another industry with a plan covering about 40 plants, job changes (as distinct from new jobs which can usually be established to provide promotion opportunities) during a seven-year period showed 778 jobs graded up, 237 unchanged in grade, and 78 graded down. In still a different industry, a large multiplant company with 5,000 to 6,000 job changes a year reported that an insignificant proportion were downgraded. Even with the introduction of considerable automatic equipment job consolidation typically upgraded the job. In a single-plant company during a two-year period with slightly over 100 changed jobs only 4 went down in grade. In another company in one year there were 84 new jobs (61 were entirely new and provided promotion opportunities, 23 new jobs grew out of old jobs and in all cases were upgraded). This company had 60 changed jobs, of which 31 were upgraded, 26 unchanged in grade, and 3 lowered in grade. In addition there were 27 jobs upgraded in negotiation and 11 in arbitration which the company did not regard as true job changes.

The above evidence tends to support a statement by Martin Segal, who examined the records of 12 plants only some of which used job evaluation:

> In view of the large number of technological changes simplifying particular jobs, or eliminating some skill or duties from their performance, it would appear that reduction of hourly or base rates of workers affected by change would be a frequent phenomenon. In most of the examined plants, however, reductions in rates were extremely rare.[17]

Segal found no obvious difference in reaction to technological change in plants using job evaluation from those not using it.

More evidence is needed to establish definitely that only a small proportion of jobs are in fact downgraded. However, the evidence available, including considerable oral testimony not supported by statistical records, points that way. Assuming that only a small proportion of jobs are downgraded, the question remains as to why this is true.

There are a number of considerations relevant to this question. First, there may be more technological change which does not reduce skill, or which increases it, than is commonly assumed. Mechanization has greatly reduced the common labor category by creating semi-skilled jobs. Much highly skilled specialized maintenance work also has been created. Second, responsibility frequently increases with technological change. Some industry wage structures reflect considerable upgrading of jobs because of added responsibility. Operating larger, faster, and more complex machines has had this effect, for example, in steel, in paper, and in printing. In steel, which gives heavy weight to responsibility, industrial engineers appear satisfied, for the most part, that changed jobs are realistically evaluated under the plan. The upgrading influence of responsibility may or may not be entirely legitimate on the basis of skill required, but it has had this impact quite apart from job evaluation. Third, much technological change results in new jobs as distinct from changed jobs. The administrative distinctions involved can at times be very diffi-

[17] Martin Segal, "Some Economic Aspects of Adjustment to Technological Change," unpub. thesis, Harvard University (1953), p. 279.

cult. New jobs, almost regardless of the nature of the technological change, usually can be set up to allow promotion opportunity. Finally, bargaining in the administration of job evaluation leaves some jobs unchanged in grade, or even increased, which should, if evaluation were applied strictly, be downgraded. There is an upward bias in administration.

It is very difficult to appraise the degree of upward bias in the administration of job evaluation. Some over-rated jobs will be found in any plant. In one company, for example, in its first move toward automation, the operator jobs were blown up in description and rated several labor grades above the appropriate one. The head of the wage administration department came close to resigning. Many companies earmark over-rated jobs, and the union agrees that these jobs may not be used for comparison in grievances and arbitration. Some companies are satisfied to hold simplified jobs unchanged in grade to facilitate acceptance of technological change.

The degree of compromise in the administration of job evaluation does not appear to be particularly serious in the short run.[18] In most situations the parties accept the plan and its principles. The union may try to do as well as it can for the employees while still living with the plan. Arbitration provides a degree of balance that checks extreme distortion. It would be utopian if technological change did not cause some differences of opinion, some compromise, and some favorable wage-rate positions for employees.

Because normal administration of job evaluation leads to compromise in wage-rate adjustment to technological change, and because both the technological and the wage environments can change considerably over a period of years, destroying the original statistical fit of the plan, basic revisions in the plans will be required from time to time.

A number of job evaluation plans have had extensive revision after a period of years or have been replaced by new plans. In such revisions jobs can be adjusted to technological change by red circle rates and relative upward job movement, and, as noted above, factor weights and applications can be redesigned. Consider the following example.

One company and union agreed in 1957 that revision of their

---

[18] Compromise in the administration of job evaluation is clearly less serious than compromise in establishing production standards.

evaluation plan would be desirable. According to the chief union negotiator, changed jobs that "fitted into the old patterns" could be slotted in with no trouble. But the plan was more than ten years old, and there were new jobs that could not be properly related to the existing structure. A group of old jobs had top rating on working conditions, but now there was a completely new department that ought to be placed above the maximum. For all of the factors there were jobs that "didn't fit," and some changes had been made that were not recognized in the past. Compromise on some jobs needed to be corrected. This kind of evolution will continue in the future and will call for redesign of plans and new adjustment to changed environments.

Wholesale Inequity Grievances

Modest compromise with technological change is to be contrasted with the minority of situations in which serious grievances were brought on practically every new and changed job and bargained out with minimum regard for evaluation principles. Such situations also involved frequent grievances on the classification of individuals and related considerations. At times grievances on wage structure matters were a phase of generally poor union-management relations; at times wage structure problems appeared as a special problem area with otherwise satisfactory relations.

In one company job evaluation had been dominated by an extreme bargaining approach during and since its introduction. Relations between the company and union had been neither particularly good nor particularly bad. The union went along with the evaluation program but was not seriously interested in creating a stable relationship. It sought the highest possible initial rating for each job. The company was not enthusiastic about the initial introduction but bargained out job placement to the best of its ability. Administration over the years continued this kind of approach with grievances on new and changed jobs being brought at almost every opportunity. While the plan had not broken down, clearly there had not been a meeting of minds nor genuine acceptance of a stable structure.

In two cases job evaluation had been introduced by a joint committee, which remained as a special vehicle for wage administration. The committee became a focal point of conflict between company and union. In both of these cases relationships were generally poor. It is doubtful if any particular area of contract administration or negotiation could be labeled as a primary source of difficulty. Job evaluation stood out only because a joint committee to review job and wage changes was not appropriate in this atmosphere. Joint review of jobs simply assured that all changes led to serious grievances.

In a fourth example, relations between the company and union were definitely above average, but job rates acquired and retained a bargaining flavor. Production standards had this same flavor before a plant-wide incentive plan was substituted for a traditional incentive plan. Behind the bargaining atmosphere was a management policy of yielding somewhat on small issues.[19] But the plan in 1957 had a high proportion of distorted job relationships. Management felt increasingly that the job rate structure must be stabilized and bargaining curtailed. Management planned in the next negotiation to propose a complete revision of the existing plan.

It would be most unusual if there were not a few job evaluation plans that existed in name far more than in fact. It should be remembered that technical considerations are less important than basic attitudes and principles.

In summary of this chapter five conclusions may be noted:

(1) The major conclusion, stated at the beginning of the chapter, is that a high degree of satisfactory resolution of problems relating to the negotiation and administration of individual job rates has been achieved. This implies a high degree of acceptance of job evaluation, although it also is true of nonevaluated structures discussed in Chapter 20. This conclusion should perhaps be qualified by noting that poor wage incentive plans have destroyed underlying wage relationships in some situations. Clearly, however, the area of individual job rates substantially has lost its earlier turbulence.

(2) Minimum administrative difficulties arose when the particular application was tailor-made. This was discussed in terms of operational fit at the level of the job description, at the level of factor definition and application, and at the level of choice and weighting

---

[19] This approach resembled somewhat the expressed satisfaction with a bargaining method of establishing incentive earnings and job rates in the Libbey-Owens-Ford Glass Company and the Glass Workers (CIO) as outlined in the National Planning Association study by Frederick H. Harbison and King Carr, *Causes of Industrial Peace*, Clinton Golden and Virginia Parker, eds. (1955), pp. 82 ff.

of factors. A tailor-made plan also involved an appropriate administrative mechanism.

(3) While administrative problems grow largely out of poor
design and poor operational fit, they also arise from lax administration and from a low degree of acceptance of evaluation principles.

(4) Upward bias in adaptation to technological change and
changed environments will require basic revisions of plans from time
to time.

(5) The final conclusion is that a minority of cases were found
where job evaluation existed more in name than in fact, but that
these instances should not obscure the major conclusion that unions
and managements had resolved substantially individual job-rate
problems.

20 \ *Wage Structure Considerations*

DEVELOPMENTS OVER THE past twenty years do not indicate a consistent trend toward resolution of the difficult issue of employee efficiency, which was discussed in Chapters 17 and 18 on wage incentives and measured daywork. At least in many companies, as competition has stiffened, the issue has become more acute in recent years than earlier. There has, nevertheless, been considerable extension of and refinement in industrial engineering practices, and there is some evidence of increased union acceptance of industrial engineering principles.

Unions strengthened considerably the ability of employees to challenge management's decision on required effort. While there has always been some employee control over pace of work,[1] unions made possible direct challenge of production standards and strengthened indirect resistance to management authority by achieving greater job security for employees. Prior to unionization even some large companies did not bother with production standards. Foremen established the work pace and had the authority to insist on performance. In response to union challenge some managements considerably weakened their competitive position. Some managements, on the other hand, maintained employee efficiency. While the issue of employee efficiency, as noted, cannot be said to have been resolved, the focus has been sharpened by the refinement and spread of industrial engineering practices.

Variation in level of production standards, performance, and manning among competitive plants has a definite influence on wage structure. While economics and labor relations textbooks always refer to employee efficiency as a consideration in labor cost, varia-

---

[1] For example, see the classic studies: S. B. Mathewson, *Restriction of Output among Unorganized Workers* (1931); and F. J. Roethlisberger and William J. Dickson. *Management and the Worker* (1939).

tion in wage level receives primary attention. Perhaps relative neglect of the former was justified under nonunion conditions when the employer dominated in the establishment of performance standards. Certainly, however, under collective bargaining relative performance levels must be given at least equal emphasis with relative wage levels as a determinant of cost. It is not valid to assume that incentive performance is consistently superior to daywork performance nor that two incentive or two daywork plants with comparable products and methods will have approximately equal employee efficiency. With growing standardization of wage levels within many industries, variation in performance levels among plants is increasingly important as a determinant of differences in labor and total unit costs. These variations correspond with differences in employer and union policies and practices.

Chapter 19 on evaluated rate structures indicated a consistent trend toward resolving the issue of wage-rate determination for individual jobs. The spread and acceptance of job evaluation have brought considerable stability to what was formerly a rather turbulent grievance area. While certain continuing issues were noted in the administration of evaluation plans, these issues did not often constitute serious problems. Job evaluation is also important with respect to other wage structure considerations. It has helped to draw a sharp distinction between payment for the job and payment to the individual employees on the job. It has in some instances been used directly to secure wage standardization within an industry. Even where it is not so used, it has sharpened the distinction between payment for the job and the general level of wages in a plant. Wage surveys of prevailing rates of pay for key jobs have become standard practice in wage administration, have been refined by making wage-rate comparisons based upon job descriptions, and have forced policy decisions as to the general level of wages in a plant relative to prevailing wage rates. Wage level negotiation has been undertaken in the light of an increasingly refined and comprehensive knowledge of comparative wage rates.

A number of wage matters remain for consideration in this chapter. The first two subjects concern experience with plant and company wage structures which are not based on job evaluation: labor grade job classification, essentially an informal type of job evaluation, and individual job rates. Labor grade job classification has been used as a substitute for job evaluation usually because particular unions opposed any formal evaluation plan. In most such cases formal job evaluation was not in 1958 an issue between the parties; management was satisfied with the more informal procedure. The major question for discussion is whether or not labor grade job classification raised issues between the parties distinct from those arising under job evaluation.

Individual job rates are found primarily where wage structures are not sufficiently complex to warrant the use of either labor grade job classification or job evaluation. They also were found in some modestly complex wage structures, and in a few quite complex structures. Again the existence of negotiated individual job rates in 1958 was usually in itself not an issue between the parties. Where management strongly desired a more formal wage procedure, it was usually able to negotiate such a procedure. As with labor grade job classification, the primary question for discussion is whether or not negotiated job rates create issues in wage administration distinctly different from those arising under job evaluation.

Mention should again be made that wage administration under collective bargaining, regardless of the procedures employed, has developed the common characteristic of freezing job rates for the term of the contract except for new or changed jobs. This was not always true, and the more hectic wage administration of earlier years was associated with the right to grieve any job rate regarded as inequitable. Stability was greatly increased by restricting the right to grieve. Where job evaluation has not been agreed upon, negotiating a new contract may involve "inequity" negotiations with respect to the wage rates for a larger or smaller number of protested job rates.

The third topic to be discussed is union influence on individual employee compensation. It has already been mentioned that job evaluation draws a sharp distinction between payment for the job and payment to the individual. In some instances job evaluation is applied by using single rates for labor grades rather than rate ranges. If single rates are used, all employees on each job, in the absence of wage incentive compensation, receive the same pay. Variation in payment to individual employees has been eliminated. If rate ranges, minimum and maximum wage rates for each labor grade, are used, there must be a policy to determine compensation of individual employees within the appropriate rate range.

The fourth topic to be discussed in the chapter is intra-industry wage structure. In our study no attempt was made to consider inter-industry wage structure, nor was there a systematic study of intra-industry wage structures. Discussion of the latter topic is therefore limited in scope. This is not a survey of wage structures in a variety of industries nor a critique of wage theory.[2] On the other hand, discussion of the competitive position of particular plants and companies frequently touched upon union wage policy within an industry. It became clear that wage-rate standardization, pattern wage adjustments, and pattern deviation showed complex differences among industries. In some respects union wage policies reduced wage-rate competition within an industry, while in others they sharpened such competition. The object of the discussion of intra-industry wage structure in this chapter is to raise questions as to the competitive impact of various union wage policies within industries and the nature of the conflicts that develop between management and union interests.

Finally the chapter contains some brief comments on occupational wage structure. A good deal has been written on the subject of narrowing occupational differentials. Discussion in this chapter takes note of a few types of unpublicized special adjustments for skilled workers.

Labor Grade Job Classification

As noted in Chapter 19, the term "job classification" has more than one meaning and application. It refers most commonly to job classification of individual employees. It is the employees who are being classified, and under all methods of wage administration the job title and description of each employee must be determined. Issues created in the classification of individual employees have been discussed in Chapter 19. A second application of the term is the classification of jobs by labor grades. An appropriate number of

---

[2] Melvin W. Reder, "Wage Determination in Theory and Practice," Chapter III, *A Decade of Industrial Relations Research, 1946-1956*, Neil W. Chamberlain, Frank C. Pierson, and Theresa Wolfson, eds. (1958), discusses research pertinent to theories of wage structure. Lloyd G. Reynolds and Cynthia H. Taft, *The Evolution of Wage Structure* (1956), describes various wage structures and analyzes union influence thereon.

labor grades with attached wage rates or rate ranges is established, and all jobs are classified into the various labor grades without formal application of a job evaluation plan.

A system of labor grade job classification, for example, was created throughout much of the meat packing industry. The War Labor Board in both basic steel and meat packing was presented with the problem of a complex admixture of intra-plant and inter-plant wage inequities. The unions in both industries sought wage standardization throughout the industry and removal of intra-plant inequities. The War Labor Board dealt with these problems in meat packing both in the 1942 and in the 1943-44 "big packer" cases. In the second case guide lines for negotiated resolution were established. A specially created Meat Packing Commission supervised the carrying out of the decision. The unions were opposed to formal job evaluation, and the parties, working with the Commission, adopted a job classification plan with initially some 25 labor grades. The number of labor grades was subsequently reduced to about 14. Jobs were classified into these labor grades on a plant-by-plant basis giving weight to intra-plant and inter-plant comparisons. The final result was in essence similar to that in basic steel. A high degree of wage-rate standardization was created within the meat packing industry and the intra-plant inequity issue substantially resolved. After 1948 wage inequity grievances and arbitrations have been modest in number. The wage inequity issue in meat packing was resolved by the mechanism of job classification to substantially the same degree as in basic steel by job evaluation.

Labor grade job classification is not common in industry; both job evaluation and individual job rates are more frequently encountered. Labor grade job classification usually indicates union opposition to a formal job evaluation plan, but quite frequently companies use job evaluation as a unilateral guide in the classification of jobs. The distinction between job evaluation and job classification may be more a difference in nomenclature than in actual wage administration.

An important question is whether the absence of a formal evaluation plan indicates particularly serious problems in wage administration between the parties. Logic might suggest that since job classification is less formal than job evaluation, it is therefore more open to controversy than the latter. Also since job classification commonly indicates union opposition to job evaluation, it might mean inability to agree on guiding principles in wage administration. In a few instances this might be so, but a general conclusion of this nature is not valid.

Job classification shows the same types of wage administration problems as job evaluation: (1) difficulties in the job classification of individual employees, (2) problems with job descriptions and work assignments, (3) challenges of the classification of new and changed jobs with changing products and technology, and, in few cases, (4) wholesale inequity claims. One large company, not in meat packing but using job classification, had a particularly difficult wage administration problem. Only since 1955 had the parties begun to resolve issues that created wholesale wage administration grievances. In this union-management relationship inability to agree on job evaluation was an indication of inability to agree on basic principles of wage administration, but absence of a formal job evaluation plan was not the primary cause of grievances. Laxity in wage administration and refusal by the union to accept stable wage relationships among jobs were the important sources of difficulty. In contrast to this company other companies using job classification could be cited in which wage administration grievances were not acute. For example, interviews in meat packing did not reveal any peculiar pattern of wage administration problems.

An agreed-upon labor grade job classification program can create stability in wage-rate administration by substantially the same procedure as job evaluation. Agreement on the classification of key jobs creates in essence an evaluation framework. Grievances on new and changed jobs are resolved by comparison with key jobs. Relatively good wage administration with job evaluation was found to require well written job descriptions, good operational fit in the determination of the scope of job content, and agreement on key jobs or rank lists of jobs to give meaning to factors and weights. Although operating without job factors and weights, good wage administration can be achieved under job classification when the parties accept the objective of equitable wage-rate relationships. Although only a few instances of job classification were studied, there was no general indication of particularly acute wage administration issues or problems.

Individual Job Rates

Individual job rates constitute the normal form of wage structure for craft and other structures having only a few job rates and are also found in relatively simple industrial structures. In oil refineries and utilities, for example, while job evaluation is sometimes used, individual job rates appear to be more common. Transportation and mining have individual job rates. Some complex manufacturing wage structures retain negotiated job rates.

Individual job rates found in industrial and other wage structures have elements of job classification and informal evaluation. Such wage structures were frequently simplified by establishing identical wage rates for closely comparable jobs. Another method of informal classification was the continuing use of broad occupational titles under which a variety of more narrowly defined jobs were included. For example, in automobile assembly the two categories of light and heavy assembly covered a large proportion of all assembly jobs and employees. Degrees of skill in many industries have been indicated by "A," "B," and "C" categories for various jobs. In other words, the very definitions of occupations and jobs contain elements of classification, and the negotiation of job rates involves patterns of related jobs. Establishing job rates by negotiation necessarily utilizes an informal evaluation procedure.

Before job evaluation was used, wage structures had various deficiencies. Procedural deficiencies were the loose use of job titles without job descriptions and the decentralized determination of job rates. What was essentially the same job might be called by different titles in different departments and paid different rates. Definitely different jobs could also be included within the same job title and paid the same rate. In the absence of a careful system of wage administration, job titles could be used so poorly as to fail to make clear wage distinctions and also to involve inconsistent payment for related, comparable, and identical jobs. Complex structures also contained large numbers of particular wage rates with many small wage differentials that were impossible to justify.

Systems of individual job rates have over the years been corrected and improved even though no formal plan of evaluation or labor grade classification has been adopted. The wage administration officials in an oil refinery, for example, had experimented with various evaluation plans but saw no merit in any of them. Individual job rates in the refinery were based on carefully developed job descriptions. The wage structure had been given as much study and attention as if evaluation had been applied. Promotion progressions and job relationships were in no sense haphazard. The wage administration departments in the automobile companies have complete knowledge of the wage structure in the plants and perform a wage control and wage setting function comparable with the job they would carry out if an evaluation plan were being administered. Also some companies with negotiated job rates use job evaluation as a unilateral guide.

There have been improvements in wage administration, in other words, regardless of the system used for establishing wage rates. On the other hand, individual job wage structures are not necessarily identical with the structures that would result from evaluation. To some extent the following deficiencies of earlier structures continue to exist: (1) job rate structures use broad occupational titles that fail to make sufficient wage distinctions; (2) job structures in limited instances perpetuate many small wage differentials that would have been eliminated under a system of labor grades; (3) individual job rate structures appear to be somewhat less adaptable to technological change than are evaluated structures. The use of broad titles and the absence of formal evaluation principles appeared to perpetuate established wage relationships through custom and tradition to a somewhat greater degree than with evaluation.

An extreme example of the use of broad titles was found in one automobile plant that had a single job rate at which almost every employee was paid. Apparently the historical influence of a socialistic group of workers was responsible for this concept of identical payment. In 1958 there were a few special rates for skilled jobs, but otherwise all employees were paid at the same rate.

Without question this single rate caused problems. New and inexperienced employees were given the difficult and unpleasant jobs. Advancement by seniority was to the simpler jobs. The wage structure provided no basis for allocation of workers to more onerous or more skilled jobs. Since the rate was high, creating a high plant average there was no opportunity to break away from the uniform rate.

The entire wage structure in the automobile industry raises a question of this sort. Many varied assembly jobs are lumped together with a very minimum of discrimination in wage rate. This entire wage structure may possibly reflect today the impact of the famous Ford five-dollar daily wage. The five-dollar per day payment, along with its associated six and seven dollars per day, must have greatly compressed the rate structure. The plan seems also to have reflected a very minimum of occupational distinction. Such rate discriminations as were made were generally differences in pay for different individuals rather than for different jobs. The high concentration today of employees paid at one of three hourly rates with five-cent spreads may well reflect this historical influence.

Job evaluation as usually applied would increase the number of wage distinctions within the automobile wage structure. One company spent a considerable amount of money to work out an evaluation plan. It would have broken up many of the present broad job categories but encountered the unqualified opposition of the union.

It cannot be said, however, that the present wage structure in the automobile industry has so far presented a particularly serious problem either to the companies or to the union except for the somewhat unique problem of the skilled rates in Detroit. Wage-rate grievances are limited to new and changed jobs. In the absence of evaluation principles the union is in no way committed as to the position it takes on new and changed jobs. The union can resist downgrading of simplified jobs and can press for favorable rates on new jobs, such as that of automation operator, which it feels will offer more extensive employment in the future. But rates for new and changed jobs are negotiated on the basis of job comparisons. The number of grievances in this area does not appear to have been particularly large, nor their resolution very difficult. However, the absence of agreed-upon evaluation principles, combined with agreement not to arbitrate new and changed jobs, seems to have led at times to a more serious impasse over a job-rate grievance than in many other industries and relationships. While evaluation would modify the automobile wage structure, substantial stability has been achieved, and the structure appears reasonably well adapted to the needs and desires of the parties.

Broad occupational titles usually accompany journeyman rates in the skilled trades. Only a few crafts, such as the printing pressmen, have developed a system of rates with advancing technology. The compositors, on the other hand, have held quite strictly to a single journeyman rate. How much justification there is for a single rate applied to hand compositors, machine compositors, machinists, and other subgroups is open to question. While some wage distinctions are made within craft groups, the nature of the union and the labor market tend toward a single rate. Technology, however, appears to be creating more and more specialists within the crafts. One local of the operating engineers has experimented with the internal use of job evaluation. Heavy construction also appears to involve greater diversity of skills among many of the crafts than does home construction and repair work. Strong tradition becomes attached to craft training and craft rate structures, but technology and markets may require revisions to maintain equity among members and control of employment opportunities.

There are still a few industrial wage structures with large numbers of job rates and many small wage differentials. Before World War II this type of wage structure was typically associated with complex job structures. The fact that only a few such now remain indicates considerable wage structure progress. But some companies still have large numbers of particular job rates. The plate glass companies, for example, have many bargained job rates with small differentials. Redevelopment of job evaluation seems desirable here. Several large automobile parts companies also have wage structures that seem somewhat disorganized.

Companies and unions did not necessarily express dissatisfaction with these structures. One auto parts company and the UAW had gone through what was called a blackboard evaluation plan. They negotiated job rates department by department. They used no system of either labor grades or evaluation factors. They perpetuated many small and varied wage distinctions. New and changed jobs were fitted into the existing pattern of departmental rates. A second large company followed the same procedure and had a similar history. Each of these companies expressed satisfaction with its rate structure, but there continued to be more wage bargaining over small differentials in these companies than in most of the ones that had simplified their rate structure. Many small wage differentials are a fertile ground for wage grievances though the fact that grievances have been restricted to new and changed jobs gives considerable stability to all wage structures.

No proof can be given that individual job rate structures are more firmly bound by custom and tradition and less susceptible to technological adaptation than evaluated and classified structures, but there is a strong suspicion that this is true. Related jobs in a craft group, for example, tend to show a quite unique degree of stability. In the printing trades the various journeyman rates for the different crafts have usually advanced by about the same amount. Substantial parity has been maintained among the railroad crafts. While there are differences in local patterns in construction, there is again considerable retention of historical cents-per-hour relationships.

Craft union rivalry and independence, combined with bargaining mechanisms in which related crafts must all settle with a single employer bargaining group, tend to freeze cents-per-hour rate relationships. Bargaining on the railroads is an extreme example of this situation. It is almost impossible for this complex bargaining mechanism to produce anything except equality in adjustment for all of the crafts. This tends toward a continuous narrowing of percentage differentials among related crafts and locks a given craft into its relative position regardless of the impact of technology upon the particular craft.

Customary rate relationships appear stronger among related crafts than among jobs within an industrial structure. In industrial structures special adjustments, as for skilled workers, can and have been negotiated. All industrial structures also have the built-in adjustment mechanism of establishing rates for new and changed jobs. It is probable, however, that individual job rates are more closely related to job title than are evaluated rates. Also the use of broad and general titles containing many narrowly-defined jobs may perpetuate existing wage relationships. The question is one of degree, but custom and tradition seem stronger at least within some job rate structures than within evaluated structures. It should be noted that some craft and personal rate relationships in transportation have been peculiarly disturbed by payment on a mileage basis. Rate relationships among the fireman-engineer categories on the railroads are an outstanding example. Mileage pay has produced very different earnings for different types of train service. Yard service, freight service, and passenger service, along with discriminations as to speed and type of train create personal and occupational inequities in earnings. Mileage pay in trucking has somewhat the same result, and differential earnings among pilots may well become an increasingly difficult problem. Both the operating crafts on the railroads and the pilots have developed extremely complex payment formulas that function as built-in annual improvement factors with technological change, but also can create various inequities. Such payment formulas are highly resistant to any form of basic modification.

It should also be noted that the most disorganized wage structures coming to our attention were in plants using incentives. Earnings in many incentive plants have lost their intended relation to base rates. Grievances arise out of arguments over base rates and over production standards. Incentive revision in such plants requires the reestablishment of base rate relationships.

Complex industrial wage structures have been largely eliminated. Many wage structures were initially fertile fields for grievances. Put on the defensive, management developed and adopted job evaluation. Where job evaluation was not desired or could not be negotiated, labor grade job classification was sometimes used. Where job classification in a formal sense has not been adopted, evaluation and classification principles have been applied to job rate structures. In 1958 job rate structures were generally satisfactory to the parties, and grievances were not excessive nor difficult to resolve. Some negotiated job rate structures raised questions of the application of very inclusive job titles, of inability to adapt to technological change, and, in a few cases, of large numbers of small wage differentials. But the only possible general conclusion is that all forms of plant and company rate structures have been substantially rationalized over the years and wage administration considerably improved.

Individual Employee Compensation

The influence of unions has clearly been one of minimizing and eliminating judgment-based differences in pay for individuals employed on the same job. One avenue of influence has been toward the establishment of systems of single job rates rather than rate ranges. A second influence has been toward automatic or nearly automatic wage progression to the maximum within rate-range systems.

The majority of job evaluation plans created rate ranges for non-incentive workers, that is, minimum and maximum wage rates for each labor grade. Most managements favored rate ranges to permit payment on the basis of merit. Unions accepted rate ranges to secure maximum job rates higher than the alternative single rates would be. War Labor Board regulations allowed a choice of rate ranges or single rates at the mid-point of the rate range. Many job evaluation plans were established during the period of wage regulation.

Some evaluation plans, on the other hand, created single-rate systems. Basic steel is an example. Individual job rates are frequently single rates, particularly in the crafts.[3] The automobile industry, except for maintenance jobs, has established single rates. For industry generally both single rates and rate ranges are important.[4]

While unions have accepted rate ranges to secure higher wage levels, they have also exerted a direct and an indirect influence toward eliminating the ranges. An exception is the engineering unions, which endorse the principle of merit payment and favor rate ranges.[5] Arguments with management relate to the amount of the merit kitty and to the criteria and methods to be used to measure and determine merit. There appear to be wide differences in point of view among the engineering unions on measuring and applying merit principles. But the existence of the unions, and the impossibility of developing objective merit criteria, have encouraged the management practice of equal treatment to employees. In the 1958

[3] Single-rate systems have elements of wage distinction among individuals based on ability and seniority. Job distinctions, for example, may be made in machine operation jobs of the Class A, Class B, or Class C type. Wage administration varies in its procedures for classifying individual employees among these A, B, C categories, but reflects distinctions based on ability and seniority.

[4] Some idea of the relative prevalence of single rates and rate ranges may be obtained from Otto Holiberg, "Wage Formalization in Major Labor Markets, 1951-52," *Monthly Labor Review* (January 1953), pp. 22-29. The study covers more than ten million workers in forty major labor markets. A distinction is made between "formal wage structures" and "individual wage structures," and the former are divided into rate-range and single-rate types. Formal wage structures indicate pay by the job and are not limited to evaluated structures. Individual wage structures pay individuals in a random way without a formal job-wage structure. Percentages are based on total employment in office or plant according to predominant type of payment for time-rated workers. For all industry individual rates apply typically to less than 20 per cent of production workers. Rate ranges and single rates appear about equally important in the figures for formal rate structures for production workers in all industry, but variations among labor markets are large. Including incentive workers in the totals and classifying by predominant method of pay for time workers raise questions as to the detailed meaning of the figures.

[5] Richard E. Walton, "The Impact of the Professional Engineering Union Upon Management Policies and Practices," unpub. thesis, Harvard University, Graduate School of Business Administration (April 1959).

recession some companies reduced their engineering departments. Supervisors selected engineers to be laid off on the basis of relative efficiency. Almost invariably the poorer engineers were found to have participated regularly and completely in the merit-increase programs. In other words, the path of least resistance was equality of treatment. Even with unions that favored compensation by merit, automatic systems tended to develop.

Where managements have accepted or originally proposed single rates, they were undoubtedly influenced by a desire to avoid the problems of administering a rate-range system. It is difficult or impossible to develop a satisfactory measurement of relative ability, and without such a measurement, it is difficult to defend a judgment rating against charges of discrimination.

Where rate ranges have been established, union influence has been toward automatic and rapid advance of all employees to the maximum rate. This has led in some instances to the negotiation of automatic progression plans. It was not uncommon for the War Labor Board to allow, or order, automatic progression to the midpoint of the rate range with merit to govern from there to the maximum. Also progression plans to the maximum have been worked out. In chain grocery stores, for example, length-of-service progression schedules to the maximum are common. The Newspaper Guild also has negotiated detailed progression schedules.

While it is not difficult to find a considerable number of formal progression plans, the major question relates to informal custom and practice. Companies retain the merit principle, but by establishing periodic review of individual employees not at the maxmum, and developing the practice of granting "a nickel" at each review, an informal, semi-automatic progression plan is created.

The rate-range and merit concepts have undergone gradual change. Initially the expectation of the "average" employee was to be paid at the middle of the range. This was gradually changed so that the maximum became the expected rate. All employees expected to reach the maximum. The remaining question was how long this would take. Rather frequent review, with grievances entered when a merit increase was withheld, frequently meant rapid progress to the maximum.

One company recently proposed automatic progression. The union opposed the plan because it would admittedly slow down the time taken for an employee to reach the maximum. In this company employees not at the maximum had been reviewed every 16 weeks (those at maximum were reviewed once a year), and at the time of our interview 87 per cent of the employees were at the top of their rate ranges.

The evolution is such that the maximum rate develops into the normal job rate to be attained within a reasonable period of time by all employees who continue in the job. The idea of an employee having his personal rate reduced because his performance has deteriorated is not consistent with this new thinking. Satisfactory rather than superior performance calls for the maximum rate.

Some companies retain the original merit concept. Two of these will be discussed briefly. In one small company automatic progression prevailed through the lower three rates within the range. Length of progression time varied with the average training time required by jobs in the labor grade. Above the mid-point of the rate range there were three merit wage levels. A specific score on a merit rating plan was required for each of the three merit wage levels. Production standards were used to measure employee performance, and employee efficiency ratings had heavy weight in the merit scoring. An employee could lose his merit standing and drop down or out of the merit rate range. The union accepted this plan but negotiated a perpetual "grandfather" clause: all employees of ten or more years of service had to receive at least the lowest merit wage rate. In terestingly, this clause did not weaken the system. In 1957 at the time of the interview not a single ten-year employee required protection under the clause. Older employees had maintained good efficiency levels.

In a second large company, payment within the entire rate range was based on merit. There were five rates within each rate range, and each rate had an associated range of performance. A normal distribution of employees tended to prevail with average earnings at the mid-point. In times of rapid expansion of employment, the average remained below the mid-point. With layoffs the average rose above the mid-point as, on the average, the longer-service employees performed at levels above the shorter service employees. Individual employees were rarely reduced in rate, though this action was taken if an employee continued over a considerable period of time to fall below expected performance for his position within the rate range.

This system was maintained in the company over union objection, though the objection seems to have diminished over the years. Only two companies were discovered that followed a formal merit program using measured employee efficiency.

The primary question is thus how much of a merit concept remains in the administration of most rate-range systems. A categorical answer to this question cannot be given. Formal merit rating plans tied directly to employee compensation seem to be very rare. The administration of production standards is also rarely tied to wage steps within the range. Measured daywork is typically administered without direct connection to level of pay. Except for rate-range advancement in the probationary and learning period, very little appears to be left of the original merit concept. Some companies argue, however, that they retain considerable control over merit increases, that they distribute such increases on an incentive-like basis, and that they do not accept the maximum as the job rate. But where data were available, a considerable concentration of employees at the maximum was found, and most companies admitted quite automatic advancement practices.

Unions appear to have been very influential in removing ability and performance judgments as a factor in individual pay for job performance. Managements have not developed objective merit criteria because there are serious objections to such systems. Unions have been assisted by labor shortages and lack of strong desire by management to prevent the maximum rate from becoming the job rate. They have also been aided by management use of merit funds in a budgetary way, giving merit increases liberally when they wanted to raise average wages and withholding them to reduce average wages. But defending a merit system against grievances has not, it seems, appeared to be worthwhile. The path of least resistance has been to develop automatic or nearly automatic increases.

Intra-Industry Wage Structure

Wage standardization within an industry or local product market is the most widely heralded union wage policy. Short of wage standardization unions have applied pattern settlements within an industry or segment of an industry thus tending to freeze competitive wage relationships. They have also practiced, to greater or lesser extent, pattern deviation. Mixtures and degrees of standardization, pattern following, and pattern deviation have in some instances reduced wage-rate competition and in some instances increased such competition. Results have been partly intended and partly accidental.

The extremely complex character of product competition, and limited knowledge of the functioning of competition in a wide variety of industries, restrict discussion to an attempt to highlight certain issues between unions and managements that appear to constitute present and future problems for the parties.

Wage Standardization

Wage standardization requires substantial union organization throughout an industry with reasonably homogeneous product and process, or throughout a self-contained competitive segment of an industry. Mention should be made of the many environmental variations that are significant in this connection: national as contrasted with local product markets, large-scale as contrasted with small-scale operating units, large multiunit companies as contrasted with small companies, locational stability as contrasted with locational fluidity, industries with many diverse products as contrasted with industries with fairly simple product structures, various degrees of price competition in product markets, hourly method of pay contrasted with piece rates, some form of industry bargaining contrasted with local bargaining, single union representation as contrasted with rival union representation, complex variations in union jurisdiction relative to product markets, differences in organizational structure and bargaining control within unions, and so forth.

Where environmental influences have been favorable, unions have made progress in achieving wage standardization. From 1900 to 1915 the railroad brotherhoods pushed forward toward national agreements.[6] Standardized wages were achieved under federal operation during World War I and have been maintained in large measure.[7] Considerable standardization has been achieved in maritime wages in spite of union rivalries.[8] The Air Line Pilots apply a wage for-

[6] Chapter XXX in Selig Perlman and Philip Taft, *History of Labor in the United States, 1896-1932* (1935), summarizes these developments.
[7] The details of the development of the wage structure are to be found in Reynolds and Taft, *The Evolution of Wage Structure* (1956), Chapter 2.
[8] See Joseph P. Goldberg, *The Maritime Story* (1958).

mula, with differences based on type of equipment, in almost identical fashion to the various commercial airlines.

Certainly one of the most dramatic changes in the intra-industry
wage structure in recent years has been in over-the-road trucking
and local cartage. The drive toward wage uniformity was associated
with a change in bargaining by the Teamsters Union from local to
state-wide and conference units. A Central States Drivers Council
was established in 1936. In 1945 the union set out to organize in
the South. By 1955 the union had established a uniform over-the-
road contract in 23 central, southwestern, and southeastern states.
Local cartage followed over-the-road trucking. In 1955 a local cartage contract for the 12 Central States took the place of 200 local
contracts covering about 14,000 employees. In 1958 the local cartage
contract was extended to 23 states. A Western Conference strike was
settled in September 1958, when firms employing long-haul drivers,
formerly under 35 contracts, signed a single contract. According to
Business Week,[9] this three-year contract opens the way for a master
contract covering the 11 western states by 1961. Short-haul drivers
will also be brought to parity with long-haul by May 1, 1960. *Business Week* speaks of this agreement as an important step toward a
master contract for all western drivers, short- and long-haul, and
eventual national trucking agreements. Wage uniformity is least developed in the eastern states. However, the New England Freight
Agreements cover private, common, and contract carriers in three
states. The rates are internally uniform but lower than in the Midwest.

The trend toward wage standardization in trucking has obviously
gone far and is likely to continue. In this process the long-term
contract has been used by the union as a device for the progressive
elimination of differentials. Particularly in local cartage, great dispersion in wage rates has been eliminated. In process there has been
forced association of employers, although employer associations do
not appear to match the union in cohesion. An important question
for the future is whether the very large number of small employers
in this industry will become effective bargaining groups.

Unions have a very difficult task in small firm, national product
markets. Locational advantages of the New York market have helped
the International Ladies' Garment Workers Union in its stabiliza-

---

[9] *Business Week* (September 27, 1958), p. 139.

tion program,[10] but the union has had difficulties with Pennsylvania shops and internally in New York City. In men's clothing standardization is primarily within city markets. Differentials among markets exist and appear to have been narrowed most effectively by the NRA Clothing Code rather than by the union.[11] The unionized segment of the hosiery industry achieved standardization by means of a basic piece price scale with various extras for nonuniform conditions,[12] but the unionized segment of the industry had almost disappeared by 1958. Unionized cotton textiles achieved, with WLB assistance, considerable standardization of occupational wage guarantees at the close of World War II through the extension of the so-called New Bedford scale.[13] Again by 1958 the union segment of the industry had declined drastically.

Standardization tends to be the wage policy pursued within local product markets. Craft unions notably follow such a policy. Wage distinctions may be made if the jurisdiction of the union covers more than one product market, such as newspaper compared with book and job printing or if there are differences such as in the class of a hotel or theatre. However, organized local construction, local service, and some types of local manufacturing tend to develop association bargaining and local wage standardization.

The degree of wage standardization within manufacturing is difficult to appraise because of lack of detailed knowledge of the multitude of product markets involved. Unions in large-scale manufacturing industries tend to seek standardization at least in the central segment of such industries. A few unions have carried out formal standardization programs, as in basic steel and meat packing. Some unions have achieved indirectly, through competitive negotiation, considerable standardization, such as in automobiles.[14] Some unions, like the paper unions, have a mixed approach. In paper there is virtually complete standardization in the West, a large amount of it in

[10] The program is discussed in Theresa Wolfson, "The Role of the ILGWU in Stabilizing the Women's Garment Industry," *Industrial and Labor Relations Review* (October 1950), pp. 33-43.

[11] Elton Rayack, "The Impact of Unionism on Wages in the Men's Clothing Industry, 1911-1956," *Power in Industrial Relations: Its Use and Abuse*, Industrial Relations Research Association (May 2-3, 1958), p. 685.

[12] Thomas Kennedy, *Effective Labor Arbitration* (1948).

[13] Reynolds and Taft, *Evolution of Wage Structure*, Chapter IV

[14] H. M. Douty, "Wages in the Motor Vehicle Industry, 1957," *Monthly Labor Review* (November 1957), pp. 1321-29, portrays the high degree of standardization that has been achieved.

the South, and some in the Northwest, but major deviation in scale in fine-writing paper plants is found in New England.[15] On the other hand, product diversification is so great in industries such as rubber, chemicals, auto parts, machinery, and others that there is little standardization. For example, in nonelectrical machinery, a statistical study[16] indicates that "interplant differences in pay levels were quite substantial." This is an instance of not one industry but many industries, organized by various unions. Yet there may be hidden elements of standardization such as in textile machinery as organized by the steelworkers. It is usually possible to find elements of standardization within highly diversified industries.

While the degree to which intra-industry wage standardization in all industry has grown over the last twenty or so years is not known, certainly it is considerable. Formal programs of standardization, such as basic steel and meat packing, are important, but inequity comparisons and negotiations are no doubt more important. Even industries with diverse products, such as auto parts (which is discussed in connection with pattern following and deviation) show fairly small occupational spreads for regional averages in important occupations under refined analysis.[17] Large auto parts companies producing a substantial proportion of total product would probably exhibit considerably smaller differentials than the industry as a whole. Oral testimony is to the effect that differentials within the industry have narrowed significantly.

The large firm is a particular target for standardization either through corporation-wide or through plant-by-plant negotiation. For example, though unionization would not normally be looked upon as very strong in oil refining, and negotiation is usually on a plant basis, oral testimony indicates virtual elimination of differentials within the industry. Economic conditions in the country have also contributed toward standardization. The wartime labor shortages and the inequity type of governmental wage regulation used directly stimulated standardization, and private as well as public wage surveys were numerous. While unions spearhead the removal of differ-

[15] See Chapters V and VI by Robert M. MacDonald in Reynolds and Taft, *Evolution of the Wage Structure.*
[16] Morris H. Rice, "Wages and Related Practices in the Machinery Industries, 1957-58," *Monthly Labor Review* (September 1958), p. 991.
[17] Toivo P. Kanninen and James F. Walker, "Wages in Motor Vehicle Parts Manufacture, 1957," *Monthly Labor Review* (February 1958), p. 164.

entials, the desire to avoid unionization can also be important. Wage standardization, while to some degree taking wages out of competition, rarely equalizes labor cost within the area of standardization and of course does not reach to other aspects of product and process competition. Standardization in the piece-rate industries comes closest to the goal of labor-cost equalization but meets various obstacles. Standardization of day rates allows variation in labor cost with or without incentive payment. Finally, the area of standardization is rarely complete. This may lead to union-nonunion competition, competition within a union, or competition among unions.

A number of issues will be discussed briefly: (1) the growing scope of wage standardization in local product markets, partially the result of the changing character of many of these markets, (2) noncompetitive products caught in an inappropriate standardization program, (3) significant variation in process or technology with consequent internal strain on wage standardization, (4) price, wage, and product competition in a standardization program, and (5) competition with union or nonunion firms beyond the area of standardization. The above issues are not unique to industries with wage standardization programs but are highlighted because of standardization.

One of the most interesting questions for the future is the degree to which standardization may develop among what have been considered to be local product markets. There are signs pointing toward broader concepts of standardization. In part, the competitive character of local product markets is changing. Greater speed and flexibility in trucking transportation broaden local markets, and such products as bread and milk, for example, can be shipped over longer distances. The large company, operating in many local markets, is a target for corporate bargaining and wage standardization. In 1958 one large milk company signed an area-wide contract with the Teamsters covering operations in several southwestern states, although bargaining had previously been on a local association basis for many years. As Dunlop points out, "intermediate bodies between the national union office and the local union have come to play an increasing role in the life of the national union and in the negotiation or administration of collective bargaining contracts."[18] Bargain-

[18] John T. Dunlop, "Structural Changes in the American Labor Movement and Industrial Relations System," *Proceedings Industrial Relations Research Association* (December 1956), p. 27.

ing power is in some cases going above the local union. Standardization is thus going beyond local markets both to meet broader competitive elements and also simply to achieve equality in compensation over and beyond the competitive scope of a product market.
The Teamsters Union has already standardized local cartage to a
considerable extent, and they are moving in this direction in other
markets. The effect of their example is of considerable importance.

The teamsters will certainly move toward standardization among
warehouses through that division of the union. There are some competitive reasons for this potential drive. An improved system of
highways, the growth of the trucking industry, and the relocation
of industry in the suburbs are factors that appear to be giving greater
choice in the use and location of warehouses. There is a growing
geographical area within which there is warehouse competition. A
high-wage warehouse in the center of a city organized by one teamster local may be losing business to a lower-wage warehouse some
miles distant organized by a different teamster local. But beyond
competitive considerations warehouse wage diversity is an attractive
negotiating target.

A more difficult situation is faced by the teamsters in the milk
industry. Again the area of competition is increasing. Milk moves
over greater distances, and local markets are less distinct entities
than formerly. Large dairy companies operate in many cities, and
increasingly the union is bargaining with the same companies in
city after city. The large chain food stores are also a target for
standardization.

It is difficult to visualize wage standardization in the milk industry except on a high base-rate and low commission basis. Such a
system of payment affects employment adversely in the home delivery of milk. Large loads, encouraged by commission payment,
maintain better the cost position of home as contrasted with store
delivery. Commissions can also increase somewhat the cost of store
delivery. Teamster locals that have retained high commissions and
low base rates, and a higher proportion of home-delivered milk, are
not strong advocates of state-wide or broader wage standardization.
Such locals appear, however, to be in the minority. The broadening
of the area of competition and the desire to negotiate with large
companies on a more than local basis are leading to changes in bargaining units and to enlarged areas of wage standardization.

Baking is another industry undergoing change in this respect. The large bakery is displacing the small one, and the large company is becoming more important in each local market. The ability to keep bread fresh for a longer period of time, and the advantages of the increasingly mechanized bakery, are bringing about this change. More and more the bakery union has been bargaining with the same representatives of large companies in city after city. Local bargaining in the industry is becoming national bargaining although its form retains a local character. Although the union is now divided and engulfed in internal difficulties, a form of "national demands" is likely to continue under national and regional organization and to be increasingly effective in standardizing wages over a broader area.

Retail food is distributed predominantly through chain stores, and here a form of pattern bargaining by areas seems to predominate. Oral testimony indicates that regional and national differentials have narrowed, and bargaining is likely to move toward broader units.

Construction still remains an industry with predominantly local bargaining, but some broader bargaining units of an area, state, and regional character have developed.[19] McCaffree attributes this trend to (1) increased contractor mobility and market competition, (2) government construction, (3) union bargaining power, and (4) convenience factors. As in other cases that have been noted, the local market is changing. Improved highways, mobile construction equipment, and an increased number of equipment rental firms, have expanded the area over which a contractor can operate. Large government projects have undoubtedly had considerable effect at least in certain areas. McCaffree's point on bargaining power is particularly interesting. He argues convincingly that extending the agreement weakens the association of employers and increases union bargaining power.

A factor not mentioned by McCaffree is the influence of health and welfare plans. A reasonably broad unit is required for these plans, and even the units now existing are frequently too small, have high administrative costs, and face administrative difficulties inherent in the considerable mobility of workers. Bargaining by means

[19] Kenneth M. McCaffree, "Regional Labor Agreements in the Construction Industry," *Industrial and Labor Relations Review* (July 1956), pp. 595-606.

of area, state, and national units for health and welfare plans—and this point is not restricted to construction—may well encourage broader general bargaining through new working relationships. The agreements in pipeline and highway construction deserve more than mention, but they appear to have disturbed local wage patterns.

There is considerable evidence of a breakdown in local product markets. There is also evidence of structural change within unions. Bargaining with large firms, and in local markets influenced to a great extent by large firms, seems to call for various types and forms of broader bargaining units. This does not necessarily mean an all-out drive for wage standardization, but it is likely to increase the degree of wage standardization. It at least raises a question as to how much local autonomy in bargaining will survive these changes. Changes in the scope of bargaining at least temporarily intensify conflict between unions and management.

Some noncompetitive products are likely to be caught within an inappropriate area of standardizaton. Some paper container plants organized by the steelworkers are in serious competitive difficulty because of a basic steel wage level higher than that in the paper industry. Some fabricated aluminum products with basic aluminum wages are having increasing competitive difficulties. Diversity of product and its associated problems are more common in industries without wage standardization, but when they exist within a wage standardization program, they are likely to create very serious negotiation issues. Wage standardization may limit or reduce product diversification within a company.

Process and technological differences are more difficult to define than product competition, but they exist. Bituminous coal, for example, not many years ago was a piece-rate industry. In 1958, with mechanical loading, tonnage rates were insignificant, and mechanical loading has created great differences among mines in output per man hour. Technology and day-rate payment have increased the spread in labor cost per ton and aggravated the problem of the marginal mine. Coal strikes in Kentucky and Tennessee in 1959 to secure the full coal wage increase may well close certain mines permanently.[20] Differences in technology may not logically be an ap-

[20] In September 1959 the strike appeared to be unsuccessful. Many small mines were operating on a nonunion basis and paying well below the standard scale. See "Stalemate in the Coal Fields," *Business Week* (September 19, 1959), p. 53.

propriate basis for wage concession, but this is an interesting union policy question. Wage standardization is not likely to be associated with wide differences in technology, but where it exists it clearly creates severe internal strain.

Price, wage, and product competition within a standardization program will not be discussed in any detail but should be recognized. Standardization within an industry such as women's clothing has a continuous enforcement problem. Such a program can almost never be based on identical piece rates. Piece rates vary with price line, with variation in product and methods, and with variation in "conditions." Compromise is made between equalization of earning opportunity and equalization of labor cost. Competitive advantage continues to be sought by employers. Cost concessions interest employees in enlarging job and earning opportunities. Even when a union can maintain organization throughout most of a product market, price and wage competition can continue internally. Firms in industries with a high degree of price competition, and related product competition, continue to try to escape from wage standardization. Where price competition is not too severe, wage standardization has been maintained without much internal strain; but with considerable price competition, employer associations tend to be weak, and wage standardization is continuously threatened.

Competition with union or nonunion firms beyond the area of standardization represents an extension of the forces noted above but involves a limit to the standardization program. Union and nonunion competition has been discussed earlier.[21] More recent examples in hosiery and northern cotton textiles show that the problem is a continuing one. The union segment of the hosiery industry, operating under a standardized piece rate agreement, made concessions to nonunion competition from time to time, but was unable to survive. High labor cost in union firms was too great a handicap in view of the overcapacity that developed after World War II. A few unionized mills continue in existence, but the association no longer exists, and bargaining is on a company-by-company basis. Northern cotton textiles achieved considerable wage standardization at the close of World War II but again could not meet the competition when overcapacity developed subsequently. The union

[21] Sumner H. Slichter, *Union Policies and Industrial Management* (1941), Chapter XII.

made concessions in work loads and wages,[22] but the organized seg-ment of the industry has rapidly declined.

As previously noted, a formal wage standardization program was carried out in meat packing. This covers the plants of the large and medium-sized packers with the exception of a few plants where con-cessions have been made. But many small packers, usually producing for an intra-state market, appear not to be covered. Some of these plants are unionized, and some are not. In the case of meat packing an overwhelming proportion of production is within the area of wage standardization, but low wages outside of the standardized area, particularly in the South, were an important issue in a 1959 meat packing strike.

Standardization thus gives rise to various types of competitive problems. The geographic or organizational limits may not cover the entire area of product competition. Product, process, and price com-petition within the orbit of standardization may create instability. Industries with standardization programs merge into those discussed below, which show considerable wage diversity but contain elements of wage uniformity. The central segment of large firms in most in-dustries tends to have fairly comparable wage levels. Geographical differentials have been narrowed and eliminated by the union drive for wage uniformity. Wage uniformity, while on the whole tending to produce rational wage structures, can be unrealistic in certain applications. Serious negotiating issues can arise if such is the case.

Pattern Following and Deviation

Many industries, particularly those with great diversity of product, have traditional types of interplant and intercompany wage differ-entials. There will be wage differentials between large and small companies and plants, differences between large city and small city locations, differences among sections of the country, and competitive differences within and among particular product groups within a broadly defined industry. Also if piece rate or incentive payment is widespread, there will be differences among plants in incentive yield, and differences between incentive and nonincentive plants and

[22] Wage and fringe differentials are summarized in *New England Textiles and the New England Economy*, a report by the New England Governors' Textile Committee (March 1958), Chapter IV, pp. 1-22.

occupations. Rubber products, electrical products, steel fabrication, and auto parts are illustrative.

It is within industries such as those noted above that union influence is most difficult to describe and analyze. Elements of wage standardization, pattern following, and pattern deviation are all to be found. In addition union jurisdiction is mixed. For example, there are many fabricating and assembly type plants with fairly similar machine operation and assembly occupational structures. These plants may be organized by the steelworkers, the machinists, the auto workers, the electrical workers, or other unions almost regardless of their product competition and classification. One multiplant electrical product manufacturer has several IUE plants and one steelworker plant. The steelworker plant has presented unique problems of pattern conflict. Many companies have substantial product diversification and hence compete in different product markets. The plants of such a company may be organized by several major unions with union representation corresponding only partially with product differences. Let us look briefly at a few of these diversified industries.

The rubber industry, as viewed from union data on average earnings, has considerable wage diversity. To some extent this reflects characteristic differences in incentive earnings. To some extent diversity is related to product. If comparison is narrowed to tire plants of major companies, diversity still exists. There is, however, a definite tendency for earnings to be at a level higher than those outside of tires. In tires there is an industry wage level with a few "high-paying" and a few "low-paying" plants. The highs and lows do not conform to any geographical wage pattern, although the historical influences of both Akron and Detroit can be observed. Differences in earnings and effort on particular jobs would show, it is believed, a great deal more dispersion than plant averages. There are at least some instances where jobs show extreme variation in earnings and effort among plants.

Intra-plant and inter-plant inequities within tire companies are such that some type of standardization program may develop within the industry. The union has negotiated with two companies a maximum limit on incentive earnings. This could conceivably be the beginning of a broader program though most of the companies are strongly opposed to an incentive limit. Some type of incentive revision appears to be necessary if a wage standardization program is to be successful. In steel, however, the standard hour day rate system became the basis for "new incentives," which are gradually replacing "old incentives." A comparable approach would be possible in rubber tires.

The fundamental complexity in rubber, however, is the extreme diversity in product apart from tires. This requires, from the point of view of each major company, diversity in wage level among plants. It is impossible to say, however, to what extent actual differences are planned in the light of the competitive factors associated with various products and to what extent differences are the unplanned result of variation in incentive yield. Even with an original planned differential relative to tire plants and in line with competitive conditions in a particular product market, pattern wage and fringe adjustments may develop a high cost plant. Companies outside the major group in some instances report that they settle for about half the wage adjustment of the major companies and do not maintain the same employee benefit levels. A few unorganized plants maintain an even lower wage position.

To choose an isolated case, consider briefly a sole and heel plant, one of the big-four plants. It started operations in 1937. In 1940 it had a wage level that required upward adjustment to meet the federal minimum wage. As a result of applying the pattern over the years it is currently paying the highest wages in this branch of the industry. In 1955 it gave a 12-cent pattern increase, while a large competitor outside the big-four pattern gave 2 cents. In addition this competitor had decidedly lower benefit costs than plants of the major companies.

The problems facing the union and companies in the rubber industry appear to be (1) reconciling earning differentials between tires and other rubber products, (2) locking all plants of the big companies within the pattern but deviating considerably from the pattern for companies outside of the large company group, (3) historically high wages in particular locations, (4) unwarranted differences in earnings and cost associated with incentive administration. Routine bargaining will not resolve these problems.

A good description of wage dispersion in auto parts is in a Bureau of Labor Statistics study, which notes that "the influence of such variables as product, size of community, size of establishment, and geographic location on wage structure is suggested by the foregoing data."[23] This study, however, necessarily deals with regional and other averages.

Plant averages for 178 auto parts plants in an industry association survey showed a geographical gradation outward from Detroit, a clear size-of-city differential, and a good deal of variation that statistically appeared random but indicated product and incentive influences.

There are certain auto parts companies and plants for which the union demands that the level of earnings shall at least match the level of the major automobile companies. In some of these plants earning levels are above the automobile scale. Cases of this latter type appear usually to involve relatively high incentive earnings not infrequently associated with somewhat demoralized incentive plans. On the other hand, some auto parts plants retain a lower level of earnings than parts plants of the automobile companies and also lower than the major auto parts companies.

In the auto parts industry competition exists among similar auto parts companies (such companies can vary their product mix a great deal) and between all of these companies and the parts plants of the major automobile companies. In any one bargaining year the pattern established in automobile plants is more or less completely extended throughout auto parts. Levinson's study[24] indicated a fairly high proportion of employees typically covered by a prevailing pattern, but a significant portion of plants did not make pattern adjustments. He found somewhat greater deviations from the pattern after 1950.

Looking only at pattern adjustments is not enough. Oral testimony of an over-all narrowing of differentials over the years indicates that local bargaining must have been of a pattern plus character at certain times. This is particularly true of the effect of local bargaining on the incentive earning level. On the other hand, pattern following tends to freeze existing competitive relations, and pattern deviation usually improves competitive standing.

In the auto parts industry as a whole it may be assumed that gradually narrowing wage differentials have greatly increased the importance of differences in the level of work efficiency, compared with

[23] Toivo P. Kanninen and James F. Walker, "Wages in Motor Vehicle Parts Manufacture, 1957," *Monthly Labor Review* (February 1958), p. 163.

[24] Harold M. Levinson, "Pattern Bargaining by the United Automobile Workers," *Power in Industrial Relations: Its Use and Abuse,* Industrial Relations Research Association (May 2-3, 1958).

wage differentials, as an element in competitive labor cost. The industry also has enough competitive coherence to create a high degree of pattern following and frozen competitive wage differentials. High-cost plants are locked in an unfavorable competitive position by the compulsion of pattern following. In at least some cases auto parts companies have built or acquired new plants as the only feasible way of extricating themselves from such a situation. Long strikes are difficult if not impossible in parts plants. There is also the opposite situation where the pattern enables a company to maintain a favorable competitive situation. The evidence of increasing pattern deviation is encouraging. In a number of both large and small companies the union has worked out with the company a program to improve its competitive situation. Again simple pattern bargaining with emergency deviations will not resolve problems.

Steel fabricating seems to have greater wage dispersion than auto parts plants and a lower degree of pattern following. The policy of the steelworkers toward the steel fabricators has changed considerably in the direction of greater flexibility. In 1946 the union made the same demands on all companies with which it had contracts and struck most of them when negotiations broke down in basic steel. The strike with fabricators continued after the settlement in basic steel. A strong drive was undertaken to achieve the basic steel settlement with all fabricators. This led to a change in policy. The fabricating plants are now kept at work during any basic steel strike. Negotiations follow the steel settlement, and Seltzer's study[25] shows a low degree of conformity to the terms of the basic steel settlement and a diminishing degree of conformity from 1946 to 1950. Seltzer's study also shows marked variation in the absolute wage level of the various companies. In 1950 only 20 per cent of the fabricators were paying the same minimum as U. S. Steel, and 65 per cent had lower minimums.

There are both a parallel and a difference between auto parts and steel fabrication. There is not the direct competition between basic steel and steel fabrication that there is between automobile companies and auto parts. There is less competitive coherence among steel fabricators than among auto parts companies. Steel fabricators break down into many more self-contained product groups. There is thus a lower degree of wage standardization among fabricators

[25] George Seltzer, *Pattern Bargaining and the United Steelworkers*, University of Chicago, Industrial Relations Center (1951).

than in auto parts and greater flexibility in settlements. On the other hand, there is union pressure to upgrade plants to the basic steel level and to obtain the pattern settlements in basic steel. Steel fabricators can be found who have a basic steel wage level (or an even higher one) and who are locked into the basic steel pattern by their particular history of bargaining. There are also some for whom the steel pattern is competitively satisfactory, and some who appear to make below pattern settlements of a satisfactory character. The results of individual company bargaining greatly influence competitive position.

No attempt will be made to consider similar industries such as chemical and electrical products. Each industry, however, has its unique competitive characteristics and differences in union behavior. The most flexible union is the machinists', which perhaps is fortunate in not having a dominant relationship with a particular industry with an established union pattern. At times, however, competitive negotiation among lodges in the same industry, such as with airline mechanics, has been highly disturbed.

Many interesting wage structure studies remain to be done. This chapter does not pretend to reflect an adequate study of intra-industry wage structures. It is possible, however, to emphasize either the degree to which unions are "rationalizing" industry wage structures or the degree to which they create particular problems. The major purpose has been to illustrate how standardization, pattern following, and pattern deviation both reduce and increase competitive pressures in particular situations. Clearly also the problems in some industries are very complex. Standardization and patterns have their negative characteristics. There appears to be a growing need for intelligent flexibility.

Occupational Differentials

Various studies, which will not be reported in detail, show that occupational differentials have narrowed.[26] Special mention should

---

[26] For example, Harry Ober, "Occupational Wage Differentials, 1907-1947," *Monthly Labor Review* (August 1948), pp. 127-34; Harry M. Douty, "Union Impact on Wage Structure," *Proceedings of the Sixth Annual Meeting*, Industrial Relations Research Association (1953), p. 62; Toivo P. Kanninen, "Occupational Wage Relationship in Manufacturing, 1952-1953," *Monthly Labor Review* (November 1953), p. 1171; and Reynolds and Taft, *Evolution of Wage Structure.*

be made, however, of the slowing down of this narrowing process by the early fifties and the creation of reasonably stable differentials.[27] This has been due partly to an increasing tendency to grant special increases for skilled workers.

This section will take note only briefly of some points that are not adequately covered by the general statistical studies. Of considerable interest is the question of how much influence the proportion of skilled workers to unskilled and semiskilled has had in the differences in the pattern of narrowing. At least a superficial case can be made that occupational narrowing within industrial units has been less where the proportion of skilled workers is high. The outstanding example since World War II of an industry where narrowing has been slight is basic steel, in which the proportion of skilled workers is quite high. Again the large proportion of skilled workers in the automobile industry may be the reason this union led in the reversal of the trend, creating the special increase for skilled workers. There is no proof of this relationship, but it looks significant. If it is valid, the trend in many industries toward a growing proportion of skilled workers should be watched with interest for its future wage effect.

In a number of instances companies were encountered in the study in which special increases had been given to skilled workers though not emphasized in settlements. For example, in meat packing, while there have been only a few wage adjustments that have widened the labor grade spread, indicative of the relatively small proportion of skilled workers, there have been unpublicized instances of upgrading within the labor grade structure. With no change in formal structure skilled jobs have been upgraded. This same type of adjustment has been noted with respect to a number of job evaluation plans.

There have also been local wage settlements in major industries, supplementing national adjustments, which have given special increases to skilled workers. In one year in rubber there was a double increase in skilled rates. A round of local settlements increased skilled rates, and then a national settlement gave an added special increase. A number of instances have been noted where local adjustments have increased skilled rates to levels prevailing in the area.

Rate ranges frequently exist for skilled workers where there are single rates for production workers. Special merit increases have

[27] Noted by Reynolds and Taft, *Evolution of Wage Structure*, for example, p. 325.

been given to skilled workers thus raising the entire level of skilled rates. One case was found where a general merit increase to all skilled employees was an off-the-record part of the acceptance of a pattern increase. The importance of merit increases in increasing skilled rates is not known, but it may well be quite significant.

The introduction of job evaluation and extensive revisions in evaluation have commonly resulted in an increase in the skill differential. Frequently an important objective in introducing job evaluation has been to give a relative increase to skilled jobs.

One of the major factors in narrowing differentials has been the growing earnings yield under incentives and the percentage character of this yield. Granting wage increases to incentive workers as an hourly "add-on" without incorporation into the incentive structure has limited the narrowing of differentials. Revision of incentive plans has corrected some unintended narrowing.

None of the above points is intended to dispute statistical findings of narrowed differentials. They do indicate, however, that general wage settlements do not indicate the total character of wage adjustments. Forces operating to preserve differentials are frequently of an indirect and special character.

21 / Disciplinary Policies and Procedures

FEW AREAS OF personnel policy have been more significantly affected by collective bargaining than management's administration of employee discipline. The origin of a union in many enterprises can be traced to a belief on the part of employees that the company had been arbitrary, discriminatory, or capricious in meting out discipline. There have been foremen who acted like little czars in administering discipline and companies that imposed the most extremely personal rules upon employees.[1] To a great extent the development of constructive personnel practices eliminated some of the abuses of "autocratic discipline." But labor unions must be given much credit for initiating directly or indirectly less draconic systems of discipline.

Even where there was little evidence of such irresponsible behavior on the part of management, the union seeking to organize employees often impressed upon employees the protection offered by collective bargaining against unfair disciplinary treatment. It is a mistake to feel that a union's contribution is limited to periodic contract improvements; it has a great influence on disciplinary policies and actions. This is felt on almost a daily basis during the life of an agreement, either because of the silent presence of the union or because the union has been quick to prosecute grievances relating to allegedly unfair discipline. In many instances the union has helped the company solve difficult problems of employee misbehavior. Sometimes the admonitions of fellow employees are more effective than those of a company spokesman in persuading an employee to observe reasonable rules and regulations.

The principal results of union influence on disciplinary procedures and policies have been the following:

[1] For example, see "1857 Store Working Rules" as reprinted in G. P. Shultz and J. R. Coleman, *Labor Problems: Cases and Readings* (1959), p. 114.

(1) The desirability of a forthright disciplinary policy is now appreciated by management. In the absence of such a policy the supervisor is in an untenable position. To secure reasonable performance or conduct he must constantly nag or "ride" employees, a frustrating procedure for both. Everyone is much happier when definitive, predictable action is taken instead of periodic, temperamental discipline-by-nagging. Both collective bargaining and improved personnel practices are to be credited with this change.

(2) Management has learned the wisdom of developing reasonable rules and regulations to govern the conduct of employees and of making these standards of behavior known to all employees. Unions have argued persuasively that employees are entitled to know what is expected of them before discipline is applied.

(3) In administering its rules and regulations, management has been stimulated to seek more uniformity of application. It has discovered that a reasonable code of conduct may be ineffective if it is applied erratically throughout the plant. For example, the tolerance of a foreman in one department in applying a no-smoking rule may become the defense of an employee against the discipline imposed by another foreman for violation of the rule. This has prompted many companies to undertake extensive foreman-training programs on disciplinary procedures.

(4) Greater care in investigating the facts surrounding any given case of employee misbehavior has been a product of union pressures. The prospect of grievance review of a disciplinary action puts the employer on notice that he must have evidence to support his charge against an employee. In the final analysis, the employer carries the burden of proving that the action was for just and proper cause under the terms of the agreement. A reversal of management's judgment because of inadequate investigation of the facts, particularly in suspension and discharge cases, may result in financial liability and damage to employee and supervisory morale.

(5) The union must be credited with the development of more orderly and sophisticated procedures in the administration of discipline. The concept of progressive discipline for less serious infractions, giving the employee an opportunity and motivation to correct his behavior by a system of warnings and other lesser penalties short of discharge, is typical of these procedures. The careful maintenance of records and restraints on the use of outright discharge are also illustrative.

(6) Collective bargaining has been influential in molding management's entire philosophy of discipline. When to discipline and to terminate employment was the exclusive and unchallenged right of management, there was a temptation to use it arbitrarily and often unjustly. The absence of avenues open to the employee for appeal and redress permitted the negative, punishment concept of discipline to flourish. Unions have helped many companies to recognize that management through imposed discipline is less efficient than the process of management through constructive training in self-discipline.

(7) Finally, and perhaps most important, some managements have learned that experiences with employee discipline provide a significant tool for the improvement of management. This effect will be evident throughout the discussion but will be covered separately in the final section of this chapter. Management may learn from the study of discipline cases that its selection policy, its use of the probationary period, its training system, its appraisal of performance, and/ or its quality of supervision are the real causes of difficulty.

By and large, the effects of unions on the formulation and administration of disciplinary programs have been salutary. Few companies today will deny this fact. Nevertheless, in some respects collective bargaining has substituted new problems for those that accompanied the unrestricted control of discipline by management. For example, while the influence generally has been to improve the procedures, there are a limited number of situations in which the presence of a union has served to delay adoption of proper procedures. During the war years some companies were loathe to follow firm, systematic policies because of union resistance. In addition, the grievance review arrangements have been found by some companies to invite challenges of company action in nearly every instance of discipline. Union policy, sometimes nurtured or encouraged by arbitration findings, makes discipline an easy avenue for the harassment of management. In a few instances it has been found that unions have weakened disciplinary procedures. These companies have given up trying to discipline because of reverses experienced under union pressure. However, such instances are infrequent and usually reflect a weak management-strong union relationship.

This chapter will try to analyze the accomplishments in techniques and processes as well as the principal problems caused by collective bargaining under the following topics: (1) general disciplinary procedures, (2) special disciplinary procedures and problems, (3) the administration of discipline, (4) grievance review of disciplinary cases, (5) special problems of discipline, and (6) discipline as a management tool.

General Disciplinary Procedures

Only to a limited extent does the language of the labor agreement deal with disciplinary procedures. In many instances the sole reference to the subject is in the management rights clause, which lists among other things, the right of the company to discipline employees for "just and proper cause." Typical of such clauses is the following:

> The management and the operation of the works and plants of the Company, including the direction and disposition of the working forces, the right to hire, rehire, transfer, discipline, suspend or discharge for proper cause, employees of the Company, and the right to relieve employees from duty because of lack of work or for other legitimate reasons, are vested exclusively in the Management of the Company. The Company in the exercise of its rights, shall observe the provisions of this Agreement.

However, there has been a discernible trend during the past decade toward the incorporation in the labor agreement of additional references to the disciplinary procedure to be followed by management. The more important of these are the following:

ADVANCE NOTICE OF DISCIPLINARY ACTION. Some agreements now specify that before imposing a disciplinary penalty of discharge, which is based on an accumulation of written warning notices, the company will notify the employee concerned several days or even one week in advance. In such cases the proposed action may become the subject of immediate grievance discussions, but the imposition of penalty need not be delayed pending the final outcome of the grievance discussions. It will be noted that the advance notice requirement applies only to actions based on accumulated written warnings, as in the cases of excessive absenteeism or poor quality work. It is not required where the alleged misbehavior is so critical as to warrant immediate, decisive action, as in cases of theft or fighting on company premises.

NOTIFICATION TO UNION REPRESENTATIVES. This requirement may take several forms. Some contracts now provide that any matter of record of a disciplinary nature must be communicated to the local union office. In others it is provided that whenever a formal action is taken, such as a written warning, suspension, or discharge, it is to be done only when a union representative, either steward or committeeman, is present.

LIMITATION ON USE OF WARNINGS. One union, troubled by the recital of oral warnings allegedly given to employees prior to more drastic action, succeeded in securing a clause that no warning or derogatory notation on any employee's record could be used for disciplinary purposes against an employee unless he had received a written notice at the time the warning was issued or the notation was made. In the union's opinion this new clause prevented the company from the *ex post facto* building up of a case against an employee and voided the use of the "little black book" maintained by many supervisors.

In only a few agreements is there a detailed statement of rules and regulations the violation of which may result in disciplinary action. Occasionally, by contract provision, there is recognition that employees are expected to observe the rules and regulations formulated by management. Illustrative is the simple statement in the agreement between a retail food chain and the Teamsters Union to the effect that "employees shall comply with all reasonable shop rules when the same shall be made known to them."

The relative absence of any practice to agree formally on the rules and regulations is understandable. The union, although it may occasionally voice a protest that it had nothing to do with the formulation of rules, implying that it should have had a say, usually prefers to remain aloof. By leaving to management the sole responsibility for developing plant rules, the union acquires greater flexibility in appealing a given disciplinary case. It can argue not only that a penalty was too severe or that the facts of the case show no misbehavior, but it also can argue that the rule allegedly violated is an unreasonable one. A more basic reason is union recognition that the establishment of rules is essentially a management task, and union involvement could be unpleasant and unpopular. Union approval of a set of rules is frequently interpreted by employees as a pro-management gesture. This is the case especially when the company cites the union as a co-author of the regulations in an effort to secure compliance. Sometimes when the union gives formal agreement to a list of rules and a penalty system, it is held to be prejudging a given case against the employee. The principal exception to this is a formal agreement that violations of the no strike, work stoppage, or slowdown clause are to result in disciplinary action.

Managements in turn are in less agreement on the question of whether rules should be a product of joint bargaining. Some believe that if the union subscribes to a given set of regulations, there is a greater chance for effective discipline; the union's endorsement of the regulations can be emphasized to employees. Others take the opposite view, arguing that it impairs the company's ability to adopt new rules and regulations as conditions warrant them. One company negotiated with the union a definitive list of rules, but through an oversight failed to include insubordination as a type of misconduct. When the company sought to discipline an employee for refusing to obey the order of a foreman, the union protested on the ground that no discipline could be imposed in the absence of a rule covering the offense.

To an even lesser extent degrees of penalties are prescribed in the collective bargaining agreement. By indirect reference the agreement may acknowledge the use of warning notices, suspensions, and discharge. But very seldom is there agreement that a certain penalty is appropriate for a given offense or a number of offenses.

In summary, the labor agreement does little to illuminate the nature of disciplinary programs and procedures. The agreement's principal purposes are to require that discipline be imposed only for just and proper cause, and to afford the employee an opportunity to grieve against a disciplinary action that he considers unfair.[2] The development of programs and procedures has remained a management function. However, as we shall see, the impact of the right to appeal from management's decisions has had a profound effect on policies and procedures and on the administration of discipline. The basic ingredients of a program are the development of

[2] This right is denied probationary employees in nearly all agreements, although there is some slight evidence that unions have succeeded in securing protection for these employees as well. For example, a number of agreements now require that the unions have the right to "discuss" the discipline of a probationary employee with the employer.

a philosophy toward discipline, the adoption of reasonable rules of conduct, and the establishment either formally or informally of a system of penalties for infraction of rules.

Philosophy of Discipline

Enlightened management is disposed to accept the tenet that "effective discipline is that training which makes punishment unnecessary." It proceeds on the assumption that an employee is entitled to know what is expected of him, and in most instances is to be given an opportunity to mend his ways before complete termination is effected. Collective bargaining and improved personnel policy have resulted in the widespread adoption of a corrective disciplinary policy. One company official observed that "the development of systematic procedures to enforce discipline has proven more effective than the old method of allowing a man 'to ride' and then suddenly discharging him. Now employees become worried over an initial reprimand, since they know the steps that are coming if their conduct persists." This same spokesman added that collective bargaining has not meant a lack of discipline, but development of better techniques by management to handle discipline.

As early as 1943 the American Management Association in a special report on the subject made the following observation:

> Until human nature attains greater perfection, the fullest measure of individual freedom of action can be realized only within the framework of an *expressed* discipline. In the social situation, this takes the form of laws; in industry it is manifest in standards. Firmness in securing conformity in both instances is wholly consistent with our democratic approach. But the requirements must be fair, the reasons behind them must be clear, and, insofar as possible, they must be arrived at cooperatively. This is the road to self-discipline; this is the aim of a wise leadership.[3]

Most companies now recognize that discipline is a negative concept, that one cannot manage a company by discipline alone. Punishment becomes a last resort and is reserved primarily for that mi-

[3] "Constructive Discipline in Industry," American Management Association, Special Research Report, No. 3 (1943), p. 36. See also, Ordway Tead, "The New Discipline," *Human Nature and Management: The Application of Psychology to Executive Leadership* (1953), pp. 270-79.

nority of employees who fail to respond to the incentives for self-discipline.

An essential ingredient, however, in any management philosophy of discipline is firmness in applying its rules and regulations. In some companies it has been found that warnings and, to a lesser extent, brief suspensions are given frequently to the same employee, but there is a reluctance to face up to the final action of discharge. An employee may have dozens of warnings on his record. In the long run this reliance on the petty penalty without a systematic movement toward more extreme action subverts the purpose of a good disciplinary program. A large multiplant company stated that it had learned three things, in part because of collective bargaining: (1) to evaluate misconduct objectively; (2) to apply less than discharge as a corrective measure; and (3) to move on to discharge when it became necessary. Firmness is no less essential than fairness in a good disciplinary program.

Reasonable Rules of Conduct

Nearly all companies have learned, sometimes through union pressure or through an adverse arbitration decision, that it cannot always be assumed that employees know what is expected of them. For this reason most companies prepare regulations or codes of acceptable behavior and advise the employees that infractions of these rules may result in some form of discipline. These may be made known through an employee handbook, which is distributed at the time of initial employment and for which the employee signs as evidence that he has knowledge of the regulations available; or they may be made known by a posting procedure. In addition, whenever there is a change in the regulations, new rules are adopted, or a decision is made to apply an existing rule more rigidly, the company is expected to make its action known to all employees.

To illustrate, a rubber footwear company had established a no-smoking rule in certain areas of its plant. Although the rule had been in existence for many years, it was not applied during the war years. The company had relaxed its application in the interest of maintaining a stable work force during a period of tight labor. Immediately after the war it enforced the rule and disciplined several persons for smoking in restricted areas. The company action was reversed on the theory that its own action had made the rule inoperative, and the employees were entitled to sufficient advance notice that it was to be revived and enforced.

System of Penalties

Formalized penalty systems based on types of infractions or their frequency are less common than is the adoption of rules and regulations. The desirability of a uniform penalty arrangement has been impressed often on management by both unions and arbitrators. For example, there are many instances where discipline for absenteeism has been set aside voluntarily by management when it discovered that another employee with an equally bad record had not been similarly disciplined. However, a rigid penalty system is often criticized because it is not flexible enough to take account of special circumstances in a given case. One company had an explicit rule that discharge would be a mandatory penalty for theft. When confronted with the discovery that an employee with thirty years' service and an unblemished record was leaving the plant with a company wrench, the company felt it had to discharge him, although it would have preferred another course of action. It felt that departure from its announced penalty would create a precedent that the union would exploit in the future. The union, in turn, was quick to plead the special consideration of service and prior record as a basis for making an exception in this case.

The pressures for uniform treatment and for a policy of reasonableness in a given case create serious administrative dilemmas for management. In general the penalties adopted for violation of rules are more a matter of *ad hoc* administrative discretion than a prescribed scale of penalties. Nevertheless the nature of the rules themselves may affect the degree of discretion in selecting penalties. Some rules are recognized by everyone to be rigid rules, such as a no-smoking mandate in a chemical company. It is understood and expected that violation of such a rule calls for immediate discharge. On the other hand, a regulation as to quality or quantity of work calls for a more flexible application of penalties. The penalty is not implicit in the rule itself. Furthermore, the approach to discipline necessarily will reflect the special problems and customs peculiar to the plant involved. Some plants, because of the nature of their operations, will place special emphasis on safety rules. A plant with a liberal sick leave program will be concerned with absenteeism. It is for this reason that in multiplant companies, rules and regulations and the penalties for violations are usually plant-oriented.

Because of the philosophy of discipline that has gained currency in the past twenty years, nearly all companies have adopted some form of progressive discipline. Its use is limited to the moderate or minor infraction of rules. For example, the pattern of discipline in one company follows these steps: (1) friendly inquiry and warning with explanation of reason actions cannot be allowed, (2) stronger verbal warning, (3) formal reprimand in writing, (4) reprimand accompanied by suspension, (5) further suspension, (6) discharge. When managements adopt progressive discipline, unions usually insist on its observance.

In some companies one or more of the above steps may be omitted. For example, there is a growing doubt in some management circles about the wisdom of using any disciplinary layoffs or suspensions. It is contended that the penalty layoff of a few days is no more effective than the additional warnings, the last of which puts the employee on notice that the next offense will mean almost certain discharge. Some employees actually welcome the few days' suspension, especially if it occurs during the hunting or fishing season or during the World Series. It is also pointed out that the brief suspension creates operating difficulties for the company, since a replacement must be secured to fill the vacancy. Or if a replacement is not secured, the suspension may work a hardship on the employees who are expected to absorb the duties of the absent miscreant. One supervisor is reported to have said, "The fellow you lay off is often glad to take the time off, and in the meantime you've lost the services of one of your regular hands. And if he isn't glad for the loaf, he's sore at you when he is allowed to come back."[4] One company has avoided the use of suspension, adding one or two more formal warnings in the sequence. The union's attempt to upset this established procedure through arbitration has been unsuccessful. Adherence to the sequence also varies from company to company. A few require almost inexorable movement from one step to the next. A large leather company, for example, has a

[4] Paul Pigors and Charles Myers, *Personnel Administration* (1947), p. 202.

"three strike" system that has been applied so consistently that the union accepts it as established practice. Under it a man is automatically discharged when the third strike, i.e., report of misconduct, appears on his record. On the other extreme, a few companies eliminate any semblance of a systematic procedure by permitting numerous formal warnings to accumulate before the next more severe penalty is imposed. This is evidence of an administrative breakdown that will be discussed more fully in the section on administration of discipline.

Where movement from the lesser to the more severe penalty is rigid, there is likely to be a forgiveness period. Thus, if a man has received a formal reprimand and a year passes with no further misconduct report on his record, the reprimand is removed from his record. Occasionally the original reprimand form is returned to him to be destroyed, thereby dramatizing the value of sustained good behavior. An agreement between a metal manufacturing concern and the UAW provides that when disciplinary action is taken by the company, only the preceding twelve months' record of an employee will be given consideration in that action. The formalization of forgiveness procedures can often be traced to an arbitrator's verdict which dismissed an old warning as too outdated to contribute to current "just cause" for discharge. If the progressive discipline is observed loosely, the forgiveness concept is less likely to be found. One such company argues that there should be no statute of limitations, that it is a matter of judgment whether warnings given a few years ago should be counted today.

The following plant notice of a large electrical manufacturing company illustrates a disciplinary procedure which combines a statement of rules, a prescription of penalties, and the use of progressive discipline.

> In a Plant community such as ours, there are certain regulations which govern the conduct of employees on Company property, just as there are regulations covering citizens in the community in which you live. These regulations—which are an aid to maintaining safe and desirable working conditions for everyone—are posted for general information and to assure uniform administration of disciplinary action if ever it is necessary. These regulations are divided into three main groups, depending upon the disciplinary action which must be taken. For violation of any plant rule, a written report must be completed promptly by employee's supervisor.

A. A violation of any of the following regulations by an employee is considered inexcusable and will result in immediate discharge:

1. Deliberate damage to Company property or to the property of other employees.
2. Stealing.
3. Fighting.
4. Carrying concealed weapons or any other violation of criminal laws.
5. Immoral conduct or indecency.
6. Willful hampering of production or failure to carry out definite instructions or assignments.
7. Gross insubordination.
8. Falsification of records.
9. Hiding, concealing or the misappropriation of Company property or the property of other employees.
10. Gambling or conducting gambling activities.
11. Sleeping on the job.
12. Punching clock card of another employee.

B. The violation of any of the following rules by an employee is considered a serious misconduct. The first violation of any of these rules will be punishable by three days off without pay. The second violation of any of these regulations will result in release.

1. Careless waste of materials or abuse of tools and equipment.
2. Possessing intoxicants or drugs in the plant or reporting to work under the influence of intoxicants or drugs.
3. Insubordination.
4. Playing of pranks or "horseplay."
5. Unauthorized selling, soliciting or canvassing.
6. Disorderly conduct.
7. Producing or concealing defective work through obvious carelessness or negligence.
8. Abusive or threatening language.
9. Excessive absence from work or habitual tardiness.

C. The violation of any of the following regulations by an employee is considered misconduct and is not to be tolerated. The first offense will bring a reprimand. The second offense will be punishable by three days off without pay. Any further offense may result in release.

1. Absence from work area without permission or satisfactory excuse.
2. Loitering.
3. Leaving job or work area before end of shift.
4. Failure to report personal injury.
5. Smoking in prohibited areas.

6. Posting unauthorized notices, defacing walls, or tampering with bulletin boards.
7. Wage attachments.
8. Improper parking or improper operation of cars on Company property.
9. Unreported absence or absence without justifiable cause.

Special Disciplinary Procedures and Problems

In the preceding section the more general procedures for handling disciplinary problems have been discussed. They are used in the great majority of cases of rules infractions. An interesting phenomenon during the past decade has been the development of special arrangements for specific disciplinary problems. Sometimes the special procedures are designed because of the intrinsic nature of the problem; more often it is because of the seriousness of the problem, and the "new or tailor-made approach" dramatizes the need for action and helps enlist union support for disciplinary measures. Three such problem areas will be discussed in this section: inefficiency or failure to meet production standards, absenteeism and wildcat strikes and slowdowns.

Inefficiency or Failure to Meet Production Standards

Inefficiency in the performance of work is not always a product of willful neglect. It may result from faulty appraisal by management of the employee's capacity to absorb the responsibilities of a given job. For example, if a girl is transferred to a job requiring considerable dexterity and is found inefficient because of a lack of dexterity, or if a man is transferred to a fireman's position and is disposed to panic when an emergency arises, discipline for inefficiency does not seem appropriate. Accordingly it has become the practice of many managements to transfer such employees, usually through demotion, until they are placed in a job to which they are suited. Only after reasonable efforts to fit the employee to available positions have failed is termination used. The company's efforts to relocate an employee are usually correlated with his length of service. In some cases an employee is rendered unfit for the work normally performed because of drastic technological changes. The use of transfer and demotion prior to discharge is a substitute for the customary suspension steps, which would serve no purpose where the inefficiency is beyond the control of the employee.

Under some circumstances a different approach is used where failure to meet production standards is involved. In Chapters 18 and 24 mention is made of those agreements that exclude disputes on standards from arbitration. There has been an increase in the use of discipline under measured daywork in an effort to secure efficiency. However, while some companies discipline for repeated failure to meet standards, it is the growing practice of many companies to avoid disciplining for failure to meet measured daywork standards as such on the theory that to do so might put the standards themselves on trial. Instead, where performance below standard level persists, the discipline is based on neglect of job, as in excessive loitering, failure to follow instructions, or leaving the job early. This approach to discipline on production standards has resulted in better supervision according to some companies; foremen are more concerned with its causes than they are with the mere fact of poor performance. With attention focussed on the causes, it is more likely that the disciplinary action will have a remedial effect. This approach provides an excellent illustration of discipline as a management tool.

A few companies do not insist on any absolute level of efficiency. The criterion of discipline is the relationship between a man's capabilities and his performance rather than failure to meet standard. If an employee is doing his best and is attentive to his job, he will not be disciplined even though he is producing at only 70 per cent of standard. On the other hand, an employee who is capable of performing at the rate of 110 per cent and is producing only 90 per cent might be disciplined. In effect, continuous effort on the job is required, and only failure to give such effort is deemed a proper cause for discipline.

Absenteeism

This problem is encountered in nearly every company in American industry, and it has proved to be one of the most difficult to handle by disciplinary measures. It is generally understood that discipline of a progressive type will be imposed for "excessive absenteeism," but what constitutes excessive absenteeism is not easily defined. One employee may be absent 20 days in the course of the year, but if the absences are primarily because of a lengthy illness, it is unreasonable to impose discipline; another employee may be absent only 15 days, but this total could be considered excessive if there are not good reasons for the absence. The problem, therefore, is more than one of simple measurement; it involves the difficult administrative task of determining the reasons for absence. Most companies cannot probe into the *bona fides* of the reasons offered by employees.

When the absenteeism problem becomes critical, many companies have tried to work out special procedures with the union. One company developed a five-step procedure that the union agreed to; unfortunately failure of the foremen to apply the agreement consistently resulted in a breakdown of the procedure. A new one was developed and has worked well, although the union officials fear that management's present tendency to be too strict in granting time off in the form of leaves of absence may affect the union's willingness to cooperate. When approved time off is denied, employees may take it anyway. As a result, they are pushed into the upper stages of the absentee procedure, even though they are not the chronic absentees for whom the system was devised. Another company believes that it has solved the problem by working with the union. Its absentee rate is now less than one per cent. The parties have defined "chronic absenteeism" as more than ten days a year of absences, and the union, at its request, is given regularly a list of employees who are absent frequently; the union talks to them in an effort to persuade them to improve attendance.

Very mechanistic programs to cope with absenteeism have been tried but with indifferent success. The more mechanical the disciplinary formula, the more vulnerable to attack it is likely to be. An electrical products firm, confronted with an annual cost of $120,000 attributable to absence and lateness, decided to take drastic measures after the more conventional controls failed. Employees who were absent were given a one point penalty; those who were late were given a half-point penalty on each occasion. Five steps were involved. In the first three, no excuses were accepted by management. Only in the last two steps would management consider whether the cause of absence or lateness was reasonable and waive the imposition of penalty points. After the accumulation of a certain number of points an employee was subject to automatic discharge. The union protested the system on two grounds: first, it was not the product of negotiations, and the company was obligated to bargain about working conditions; second, the plan itself was improper. An arbitrator concluded that under the management rights clause the company could set up an absentee control system without bargaining with the union. But he did find that the company plan was unreasonable. For example, the failure to consider excuses for absence and lateness on the first three occasions discriminated against those who had good excuses for their first absences and poor excuses for their last two.

A special program of progressive discipline combined with purposeful enlistment of the union's help are the most frequent arrangements for coping with the absentee problem. Some unions have special reason to be concerned with the problem. For example, a large aircraft engine company agreement has a liberal twenty days' sick leave provision; no formal evidence of illness is required for entitlement to the sickness pay. It was found that the absenteeism rate was becoming alarmingly high, particularly toward the end of the calendar year when the unused days were about to expire and again at the beginning of a calendar year when a new quota of twenty days became available. It was obvious that many employees were exploiting this allowance for reasons other than illness. The company threatened to press for a withdrawal or modification of the sick leave program at the next negotiations unless absenteeism was corrected. The union promptly started a campaign through its monthly newspaper urging employees to use the allowance only for real illness, pointing out that the misuse by a few could jeopardize a valuable program for the many. In addition, a system of progressive discipline consisting of two formal warnings, a three-day suspension, and finally, discharge was agreed upon. With the help of an arbitrator, certain tests were adopted to determine whether days of claimed illness should be counted in measuring excessive absenteeism, such as the scatter of the absences, the pattern of absences (Monday and Friday), the holding of dual jobs, and so on. Finally, the union has emphasized that fraudulent claim for sick pay will result properly in immediate discharge and that the union will not prosecute a grievance where fraudulence on the part of the employee is obvious. Improvement has followed these steps.

Discipline for Illegal Work Stoppages and Slowdowns

This subject is of such importance and the developments during the past twenty years have been of such significance that a separate chapter will be devoted to the problem. Many companies have learned that the most effective way to control this type of interruption to production is vigorous enforcement through discipline of the no-strike, no-slowdown restriction. Because suspensions and discharges of large numbers of people could affect drastically the operation of a company, many managements were reluctant to use stringent measures. Often only mild warning notices were used. The net result was greater indulgence by employees in this illegal behavior, particularly when the company yielded on the issue that gave rise to the walkout or slowdown. To no small extent, sales departments of companies contributed to the breakdown of discipline because of their desire to meet promised delivery dates.

The tightening of discipline, either through more effective use of general procedures or through the development of specially-designed procedures, often with official union support, has done much to correct this chaotic situation. Methods for handling this problem will be discussed in detail in Chapter 22.

The Administration of Discipline

Most managements have learned that no matter how well conceived are the procedural aspects of a disciplinary program, they mean very little if its daily administration and application are ineffective. Often the more detailed and rigid procedures of the type described early in this chapter are adopted deliberately to solve the administrative problem. It is often believed that if rules are spelled out, if the penalty for each type of infraction is specified, and if there is an "inflexible progression of penalties leading to discharge," the administration of the program becomes automatic. This is not always the result. On the contrary, the more inflexibility and built-in administration contemplated by such a program, the greater are the chances of a breakdown.

In a large ball-bearing company, management officials were surprised and dismayed to learn that the elaborateness of procedure had been the very cause of its undoing at the hands of foremen. The procedure called for automatic discharge for any offense if two formal warnings and a warning-suspension appeared on an employee's record. A long-service employee with such a record had been discharged when he was found to have been loitering in an area removed from his work location. The union protested the action, not because the offense was unproved, but because it denied that automatic discharge was inevitable under these circumstances. It used witness after witness with similar records, who testified that after the second or third disciplinary measure—the second written reprimand or the reprimand-suspension—they had committed infractions and were admonished only verbally by their foremen. It was discovered that the foremen, realizing the grave consequences of the next offense and reluctant to lose an otherwise able employee, often concealed the infraction by keeping it off the employee's record. Faulty administration had destroyed what top management thought was an ironclad system.

Among the principal problems of administration are the following: (1) unwillingness to face up to disciplinary action; (2) failure to apply discipline in a reasonably uniform manner; (3) inadequate investigation of circumstances surrounding the infraction; (4) locus of discipline action authority; and (5) deportment of management personnel.

Unwillingness to Face up to Disciplinary Action

Imposition of discipline is a disagreeable task, unless the foreman is of a particularly aggressive nature. Very often the foreman is so anxious to maintain the good will of his employees and the union representative in his department that he will back away from enforcement of rules. One industrial relations manager cited the case of a foreman, angry and determined, who came to the Labor Relations Department to find out what punishment he could mete out to a difficult employee. He was told that a penalty was appropriate, but when he called in the employee, who had brought his union committeeman with him, the foreman backed down. He explained later that "the committeeman talked me out of it."

Another case involved an automatic screw machine operator who transferred in lieu of layoff to a chucking machine job; he was disqualified because he did not know the job, and management found a lathe for him to run. When he was recalled finally to his screw machine job, he ran scrap for seven days, let his tools get dull, and jammed the machine. An expensive salvage job was required as a result. Yet the foreman only reprimanded the man, and the union promptly filed a grievance claiming that a loose spindle had caused the scrap and damage. When asked why he had tolerated a bad situation for so long and had used only mild discipline, the foreman complained bitterly: "I never should have disciplined the man at all. All I'm getting now is questions, questions. I should have put him on a lathe or some simple machine."

In another case a foreman admitted frankly that he did not want to reprimand his men for fear they would "give him a rough time"; he explained that they might refuse to work overtime, for example, and he did not want to order them to work overtime. It has been found that some foremen will try to get rid of undesirable employees through the devious use of the seniority system rather than resort to discipline. In the words of an industrial relations manager, "They try to unload guys when there's a reduction, even though this means passing the problem on to someone else." If during a period of work reduction the maintenance department wants to eliminate fifteen men, it may be decided to lay off two electricians, one millwright, and so on; then, discovering that the next millwright on the seniority roster is someone they would like to get rid of, they exercise their right to lay off men by trade and lay off two instead of one millwright. This problem was discussed in Chapter 6.

The foreman is reluctant to face up to discipline in part because he must justify his actions to the steward and to higher union officers as well as to his own superiors, who review his decision in the grievance machinery. In part, the possibility of being overruled by higher management or by arbitration may discourage the foreman from positive action. The possible consequences of his action may seem so formidable that a foreman will forego discipline even though the occasion may fully warrant it. Any operations man has difficulty in making a decision that might shut the plant down. Improper management policy often explains the lack of firmness by foremen in applying discipline. If management impresses on its supervisors that absence of trouble is the mark of a good supervisor, the typical foreman is likely to avoid the provocation caused by disciplinary measures.

Sometimes without realizing it top management engenders in foremen the feeling that they will not be backed up in their disciplinary decisions. As a result the foremen see little purpose in facing up to disciplinary action. In one electrical products company the industrial relations director acquired considerable authority; he developed the practice of working out settlements of discipline and other grievances with the union business agent without consulting the operating people affected. The stewards soon became aware that they could readily get a foreman's decision reversed by going over his head. Ostensibly there is an atmosphere of "peace and harmony" at the top level, but as a consequence discipline has suffered. Line management believes it has been sold down the river, and foremen report that they have given up trying to correct excessive loafing and absenteeism. Many supervisors have quit in disgust, making for a high turnover among foremen. Others, because of their frustration, develop an anti-union attitude and, either out of conscious intent or anger, try to get even with the union by actions that violate the agreement, which they feel is rigged against them anyway. These actions are promptly reversed by top management, thus reenforcing the foremen's conviction that the deck is stacked in favor of the union. A vicious cycle has been created.

Another explanation given by several managements is that unless the foreman is of a particularly aggressive nature, imposing disciplinary action is a disagreeable task at best. He may, therefore, sometimes use the union as an excuse for not imposing discipline.

The risks involved in avoiding discipline where it is needed are considerable. If, for example, a foreman has not enforced a rule for a long period, he is almost certain to encounter trouble when conditions deteriorate to the point where enforcement becomes absolutely necessary. The annals of arbitration decisions are replete with rulings to the effect that failure to apply a rule negates enforceability of the rule. In effect, management must start all over again to re-establish the regulation, and before punitive action for infractions can be sustained, advance notice and warnings must be given.

Lack of Uniformity in Discipline

The effectiveness of many disciplinary systems may be impaired because of this defect. The lack of uniformity may be found in disparate treatment among individuals, or it may be related to the time dimension. It is emphasized that consistency of application is difficult, if not impossible, to achieve if there are no carefully thought out policies or standards to be used in the detailed problem areas. For example, unless a plant-wide approach to absenteeism is developed, it is very probable that discipline for this offense will be inconsistent among departments.

Typical of the situations leading to lack of uniformity among employees are the following: (1) If the authority to discipline rests entirely with supervision, there is always the possibility that one foreman by temperament may be easygoing while another may take an almost draconic approach to discipline. (2) Consideration of the length-of-service factor may result in a more tolerant attitude toward senior employees and a stricter application of discipline to junior employees. (3) The degree of skill of the employees may influence the use of discipline. Very often a company will show forbearance toward the highly skilled, indispensible employee, but it will proceed with dispatch in imposing discipline upon employees whose lesser skills make them more expendable. (4) The number of employees involved may be a criterion that leads to variation in treatment. To illustrate, an electrical manufacturing plant was experiencing a slowdown on a refrigerator door assembly line. After repeated warnings to all members of the line, it finally suspended two persons on a certain day who seemed to be causing the bottleneck. On subsequent days, the output of the line was even lower, but no discipline was imposed. Management's explanation was simple: "It is one thing to suspend one or two persons, but if members of the entire line—numbering some fifteen persons—were suspended, it could have the effect of shutting down the entire plant." (5) A distinction usually exists in the minds of supervision between the employee who is also a union official and the employee who has no official status in the union. Very often the former enjoys greater immunity because of his status. This is either because the company wants to maintain a good relationship with the union as a whole or because the company fears that action in the case of a union official will be discredited on the ground that it is revengeful in nature. This matter will be discussed more fully under the section on special problems of discipline. (6) Varying production pressures from one department to another may influence the administration of discipline.

Lack of uniformity may also be in the form of movement from loose to tight to loose application of rules and imposition of penalties over a period of time. This vacillation may be a function of several things: (1) State of the labor market. Nearly all companies acknowledge that during World War II and the Korean crisis there was a relaxation of discipline. Attempts after these periods to restore higher standards of employee behavior often met union resistance. (2) Economic health of the enterprise. One company that relied heavily on government cost-plus contracts permitted absenteeism to reach an alarming rate. Employees would work all available Saturday and Sunday overtime when premium rates applied but would be absent during one or two of the week days, when straight time rates were paid. Indifference to costs resulted in tolerance of this practice. When government contracts were fewer and cost considerations became important, the company quickly changed its approach toward absenteeism. Inevitably the transition was a difficult one, and nearly every case involving discipline for absenteeism became the subject of a grievance. The pressure for production at the beginning of a new model year in the automobile industry creates a temptation to be more tolerant of employee misbehavior. (3) Change in management personnel. The replacement of a lax management by a more strict-minded management usually produces a stiffening of disciplinary measures. Time and patience may be required before the poor habits inherited from the past can be corrected. (4) Change in union administration. A union leadership bent on challenging every exercise of discipline by management and given to the use of harassment tactics in response to discipline may cause management to back down. Replacement of such leadership by a more moderate, amenable element may lead to the revival of constructive discipline.

It should not be inferred from the foregoing discussion that lack of uniformity occasioned by one or more of the above factors necessarily militates against management's discipline action in a given case. Length of service or the risk of closing an entire plant if many are disciplined may justify variation of treatment in the eyes of the union or an arbitrator. Similarly changes in policy from one period to the next may be countenanced if adequate preparatory steps are taken. But the principle of reasonable uniformity is one to which management has learned or is learning to be alert. A union does not hesitate to plead unfair treatment if there is evidence that this principle has not been followed.

Inadequate Investigation

Discipline is often the product of emotionalism and anger of the moment. What is a trivial offense may loom large in the mind of the supervisor at the time of its occurrence. The experience of many companies in handling disciplinary grievances has taught them the need for careful investigation of the facts before final action is taken. The precautions are greater where the penalty contemplated is more severe. In effect a company now must proceed in discipline with the expectation that its action will be subjected to the most searching examination by the union and an outside arbitrator.

To illustrate, in some companies twenty years ago if a foreman found an employee sleeping on the job, he would arouse him and impose a suspension or discharge penalty. Today foremen are often instructed to leave the sleeping man undisturbed and seek out other witnesses to the offense. Only then is the man awakened and confronted with his wrongdoing. Whenever corroboration of employee misconduct can be secured it is done in anticipation of later requirement of proof.

An essential part of any investigation is to give the employee affected full opportunity to explain his actions. One company representative states: "If the employee has no explanation, this fact is important, particularly if an explanation is later offered by the union in processing the case. A belated explanation is not as persuasive as a prompt one. . . . Any explanation by the employee should be investigated. Find out if he is telling the truth. Even if the explanation provides no real excuse, or perhaps even sounds silly, it is a mistake not to investigate it. The foreman should take the initiative. He should ask the employee point blank if he has an explanation and if so, what it is."[5]

Many companies also require foremen to make detailed reports of each incident leading to suspension or discharge within 24 or 48 hours of the occurrence; sometimes it is standard procedure to have these reports notarized. Again the company is motivated by a desire to have the strongest possible case in the event of a union challenge. The written report prepared at the time is important evidence if there is conflict of testimony in an arbitration hearing, and it is also helpful in refreshing the memory of the principals involved who may be called upon to serve as witnesses.

To insure adequate investigation of all the facts some companies no longer permit immediate discharge of an employee no matter what the offense. Instead, the foreman has the authority to suspend the employee and to instruct him to leave the plant at once. The employee is advised that he will be notified within 48 hours of the final disposition of his case. During the intervening period a full investigation of the facts can be made, and the case can be reviewed at length by the foreman, his superiors, and staff representatives from the labor relations department. If it is concluded that discharge is in order, the employee is notified by registered letter over the foreman's signature, and the action is made effective as of the day of initial suspension. If the investigation discloses mitigating circumstances, the employee may be reinstated with retroactive pay, or a penalty short of discharge may be imposed. Companies that have adopted this administrative control are convinced of its salutary effect.

Several illustrative cases may highlight the advantages of such investigation. A night foreman of one company summarily discharged an employee who had entered the general foreman's office, opened the files, and removed the overtime allocation schedule for the week. When asked by the foreman, "What in hell are you doing?" the employee replied, "I have a right to see these sheets." Following the discharge a grievance was filed promptly. The night foreman was forced to retract the action and suffered a blow to his

[5] Harry D. Garrett, General Motors Corporation, "Management's Responsibility for Maintaining Discipline," speech before the 60th Convention, National Metal Trades Association (October 30, 1959).

prestige when he learned that the employee had asked for and had been given permission by the general foreman to examine the documents. In still another case, a foreman who had discharged an employee for threatening him with a hammer was overruled by management when it was proved that the foreman himself had provoked the gesture by making disparaging remarks concerning the fidelity of the employee's wife. In each of these instances the morale of employees and supervision would have been better served if investigation had preceded the extreme action of discharge.

A further advantage in the opinion of some companies using this policy is that it permits greater care in specifying the cause of discharge. A hastily prepared statement of the cause may foreclose the company from enlarging the basis later on. For example, one company employing the "suspension pending investigation" technique suspended an employee for gross insubordination. The employee had on his record two written reprimands and one three-day disciplinary layoff. In the course of investigating the insubordination charge, an assistant foreman commented casually to the labor relations representative, "I'm not surprised; he was fired from another company for the same reason." This information was investigated and found to be true. It led to an examination of the employee's application form, which disclosed that he had falsified his prior work history presumably to conceal this episode. The employee was sent a formal letter of discharge on the basis of "gross insubordination, falsification of employment application, and other misconduct of record." In one company a foreman cannot discharge a worker without the signature of an official of the company. Interestingly, this is a contract requirement which also provides that the higher official must investigate the discharge of discipline before the foreman can put it into effect. In the company's judgment this has improved personnel relations considerably because the foreman is constrained from venting his personal feelings on a given individual knowing that his action must be reviewed by his superiors.

Locus of Discipline Action Authority

Largely because of the problems discussed above, there has been a definite trend away from assigning exclusive disciplinary authority to foremen. It is impossible to say with certainty how much authority to impose suspension or discharge the foreman formerly had; it probably was more a theoretical than an actual authority. But certainly his authority has been lessened through the impact of collective bargaining, at least insofar as the imposition of more severe penalties is concerned. The decision to penalize an employee is shared with higher management representatives in either a line or a staff capacity or both. It is true that management's recent concern with the status of foremen has led to some renewed efforts to enhance their authority, including the area of discipline. However, the evidence does not indicate that decentralization has occurred. In effect a cyclical change in locus of authority can be traced at least in management's theoretical adjustment to collective bargaining. Prior to unionization authority to discipline rested primarily with the foremen and operating personnel. In the early days of unionization the specialists in labor relations matters, who had a monopoly of expertise in the field, tended to absorb this function. More recently the doctrine that discipline is an operation, not a staff, function is gaining currency.

An official of a steel company expressed the view that a labor relations man can make a better decision about discipline than can a production man who is responsible for discipline. This view was shared by the industrial relations manager of an automobile plant, who deplored the decision of management to re-transfer the responsibility for discipline from the labor relations staff to the foremen after a "big training program to get supervision to handle discipline." The net effect was a sharp reduction in the number of disciplinary cases and a slackening of discipline, presumably attributable to refusal by foremen to face up to the problem. It is claimed that foremen prefer to "pass the buck." In one plant of this company there were approximately 500 disciplinary cases per month when the industrial relations office meted out discipline; during the first month in which foremen reassumed authority for discipline there were only about 100 cases, and thereafter the average number fell to 45 to 50 cases per month.[6] It is an interesting phenomenon that a higher percentage of the smaller number of cases are now grieved by the affected employees.

In still another plant of the same automobile company, the new policy of decentralization of authority resulted in a drop of cases from 300 to 100 per month; as foremen gained experience, the

[6] When the foremen initiated a recommendation for action and industrial relations had the job of carrying it out, the foremen exercised their right freely.

number increased, but never to the level that prevailed when staff personnel handled discipline. Even with the new policy, however, the foremen take care of only the simplest problems. In nearly all cases the foremen consult with the industrial relations department. In a large paper company discipline is handled by a supervisor, but he is expected to check with the personnel office to insure conformity of his action with existing practices before making a final decision. If the foreman and the staff representative disagree, the mill manager has the final decision. A metal container company, after discovering that operating men do not realize adequately the importance of protecting the company's interest by proper imposition of discipline, solved the problem by developing closer cooperation between industrial relations and plant managers.

There is some evidence that excessive influence by the personnel or industrial relations staff in disciplinary matters has had a harmful effect. Undoubtedly this led to the decentralization efforts in the automobile company referred to above. The same problem arose in the case of the electrical products company that was cited earlier as an illustration of why foremen became unwilling to face up to disciplinary action.[7]

In general it is felt that the immediate supervisor should play a very active role in initiating and applying disciplinary action. In the extreme case of discharge and in the special cases of offense mentioned below it is desirable that the supervisor confer with the industrial relations or personnel staff before taking action. However, it is valuable for the employee affected to know that his supervisor concurs in the action taken. Many companies have found it best always to convey disciplinary action over the signature of the immediate supervisor except where the offense involved is construed as an assault on broad company rules, as noted below.

The nature of some offenses tends to place them beyond the authority of first line supervision. For example, in one automobile plant, six categories of discipline are handled exclusively by industrial relations: (1) garnishment, (2) theft, (3) work stoppages, (4) immoral acts, (5) union representation, and (6) fraud in unemployment compensation. Special disciplinary problems, such as misconduct on the picket line, are handled by centralized authority. Use

[7] p. 643.

of the type of offense as a criterion for the locus of disciplinary authority is very logical. On the one hand, rules relating to employee efficiency are properly a function of work supervision and should be judged by the immediate supervisor. On the other hand, illegal work stoppages, even though participated in by only a small group of employees are considered to be actions challenging the entire company and become the immediate concern of the central labor relations staff.

Deportment of Managerial Personnel

The discipline of employees within the bargaining unit may not be sustained if management is inattentive to the conduct and behavior of its own representatives. Stated differently, the administration of discipline within management circles may have a direct effect on administration of discipline under the labor agreement. For example, in a case involving the use of obscene and profane language by a union chief steward in his discussions with supervision, the union's principal defense was evidence to show that a "climate" for such language had been established by supervision. The discharge of an employee for soliciting on company property was reversed when it was proved that management personnel was equally guilty of selling tickets for raffles and testimonial dinners or of interesting employees in the real estate services or automobile agency of a relative. The frequent practice of a night shift supervisor of reading comic books and paperback pocket editions while on duty rendered ineffective his disciplinary action against employees loitering on the job. The fairly common offer of a foreman to take bets on an important baseball game or prizefight was used effectively to show why his discipline of an employee for gambling put him in the untenable position of operating under a double standard.

The behavior of supervision not only affects the success or failure of disciplinary action when subjected to review in the grievance procedure, it also motivates employees to observe or ignore company rules and regulations in the first instance.

Grievance Review of Disciplinary Cases

Many of the procedures and techniques referred to in the earlier sections of this chapter have resulted from the review of disciplinary cases in the various grievance steps. The percentage of disciplinary cases grieved is fairly high if the penalty involved is suspension or discharge. One company reports that out of 25 discipline cases, the union usually appeals all but 2 or 3. In a troublesome plant of a large automobile company it is reported that since 1953, 80 per cent of the cases appealed to the umpire have been disciplinary cases. In a recent year about 25 per cent of all arbitration appointments made by the Federal Mediation and Conciliation Service were in discharge matters. In 1954 the American Arbitration Association reported that of the 1,728 grievances it had handled in that year at the arbitration level, more than one fourth (26.4 per cent) involved discipline. If one were to judge the condition of labor relations in a given enterprise solely by the number of aggrieved discipline cases, the conclusion might well be unwarranted. One must consider a number of factors before concluding that discipline is a serious problem area in labor relations.

First, it is necessary to know the incidence rate of disciplinary actions. A formal oral reprimand or a written warning is often a discipline "of record," and these may be numerous. It would be more useful to know what percentage of total disciplinary actions become the subject of a grievance.

Second, one should know the level of settlement of these grievances. Discipline is an intensely personal matter. Very often an employee, in the interest of self defense and pride, is hasty in protesting a formal reprimand or a penalty. When the facts are reviewed, either he or the union is more disposed to recognize the justice of the action. Similarly an immediate supervisor, no less motivated than the employee by the desire to defend his initial action, may be persuaded to the view that he acted unjustly and in haste. Thus many disciplinary grievances are resolved before the final appeal step.

Third, some grievances entertained by the union and carried to the ultimate appeal level are a function of the inherent political nature of the union institution. Not infrequently a union may prosecute a grievance of this type through the arbitration level, even though the leadership recognizes that the employee claim lacks merit. This is most often true of discharge cases. One union leader acknowledged that he usually carried a discharge case to arbitration on the theory that an employee subjected to such an extreme penalty was "entitled to his day in court" no matter how the union leadership felt.

Fourth, it is important to know what percentage of the various types of disciplinary action result in formal grievances. The available information indicates that the probability of appeal is correlated with the seriouness of the penalty. The percentage of written warnings grieved is likely to be small, while the percentage of discharges appealed is likely to be very high. This is understandable in view of the import of discharge in modern industrial society. Because of the benefits that flow from seniority and attachment to one employer, the loss of job means much more today than it did twenty or thirty years ago. All available avenues of appeal are likely to be used no matter how tenuous the case.

Fifth, and perhaps most important, the very question whether a person has been guilty of wrongdoing and should be punished in one manner or another involves subjective and emotional judgment. It is a natural arena for honest differences of opinion, and sometimes these differences arise not alone between the union and the company. They frequently arise within union and within company circles. The subjective nature of disciplinary decisions provides a fertile basis for disagreement and grievances.

Sixth, arbitration is used extensively in the review of disciplinary decisions because it serves as a valuable balance-wheel in an area where resolution by power pressures and constant legislation could be disruptive. The contractual criterion of "just cause" is purposely ambiguous. It is an expression of general intent and nothing more. The parties recognize that the problem of resolving by specific agreement the bases for each and every possible disciplinary action and the appropriate penalties for such action would be insurmountable. They also recognize that such resolution is not always or even often attainable in the grievance review of a given case. Inevitably, arbitration becomes a natural, final appeal when the merits of a disciplinary action are in doubt.

Seventh, the number of grievances arising from disciplinary action may be symptomatic of an unrelated problem. One company reports that in 1958 it found that contrary to past experience there were few disciplinary actions that were not made the subject of formal grievances. It concluded that this phenomenon was not because discipline *per se* had become a problem, but rather because the insecurity caused by the 1958 recession and the desire of the union to generate employee support in the forthcoming 1959 negotiations led the union to exploit this "natural" area for grievances.

Whatever the complex of reasons in a given situation, the number of disciplinary grievances as a percentage of disciplinary actions is likely to be high. Because the most important direct gain secured by the union has been the right of the employee to grieve when he believes he has been disciplined unjustly, it is appropriate to review the operation of the grievance procedure in disciplinary cases. Two subjects are involved, the need for expeditious handling and the influence of the arbitration process.

Need for Expeditious Handling

Both the union and the company normally are anxious to process disciplinary cases, particularly discharge actions, as rapidly as possible. The hardship of such action for the employee and the accumulated liability of potential back pay for the employer dictate special treatment. In addition, some discharges are inflammatory in their effect. It is not uncommon for the discharge of an employee to be accompanied by an illegal walkout by sympathetic employees. Emotions are assuaged somewhat by putting in motion the appeal procedures. Most contracts provide that a grievance involving a disciplinary action must be filed within a few days of its occurrence. Thereafter the parties, in accordance with either the contract agreement or accepted practice, will give priority to discharge grievances in the various steps of the machinery. Sometimes the early steps are waived entirely. If settlement is not reached short of the umpire or arbitration level, it is usually agreed that the pending discharge cases will be the first heard by the neutral.

The Arbitration Process

The arbitration process itself has contributed many, sometimes conflicting, guides to the parties. It is interesting to note that the decisions most often collated for use in foreman training and steward training programs are those involving matters of discipline. The Ford Motor Company, for example, has prepared a digest of representative decisions by the umpire "to be used as a Guide in the imposition of disciplinary penalties." It is not the purpose of this section to summarize the views of arbitrators on procedural matters in discipline or on how particular misconduct cases are to be handled.[8] It should be noted, however, that the judgment of neutrals has had a very great influence on management.

Two elements in the process are of considerable importance to the parties in the arbitration of disciplinary cases: the scope of the arbitrator's authority and the procedures required by the arbitrator.

An arbitrator's authority in deciding a discharge or disciplinary case, as any other type of case, is determined by the applicable contract language and/or the stipulation of the issue. In the early agreement of a large automobile company it was provided that the umpire "shall have the power only to adjudge the guilt or innocence of the employee involved." As recently as 1955 the contract was amended to give to the umpire for the first time authority to make some retroactive pay adjustments in disciplinary cases. In the agreement of a steel company a similar limitation is placed on the authority of the arbitrator. The arbitrator can only make a decision with respect to the guilt or innocence of the employee; if he is guilty, the company penalty automatically applies; if he is innocent, the employee is reinstated with full back pay. Restrictions of this type are not frequent. Usually the arbitrator has the authority to modify a company's disciplinary action and to award back pay. The more restrictive clause sometimes results in the arbitrator's reinstating an employee where he might otherwise have modified the penalty.

Some agreements impose limitations of another type. For example, the agreement of a large insurance company provides that the arbitrator shall have no authority to substitute his judgment for that of the employer as to the reasonableness of any rule or regulation of the employer; his role is limited to deciding whether the facts established by the employer justify the action of the company within the reasonable exercise of managerial discretion. The arbitrator, however, does have the authority to determine whether the rule or regulation upon which the employer relies had been effective prior to the grievance.[9]

[8] A valuable study of arbitration is Orme W. Phelps, *Discipline and Discharge in the Unionized Firm* (1959). This study presents an interesting statistical analysis of penalties involving incompetence, unreliability, troublemaking, insubordination, dishonesty and disloyalty, immorality, strikes and slowdown, and "improper acts."

[9] See Chapters 25 and 26 for additional comment on the arbitrator's authority in discipline cases.

The manner in which back pay is to be computed if the arbitrator reverses a discharge or suspension and modifies the penalty is also covered in the contract in a few agreements. In these cases, it is usually provided that moneys earned by the employee through other employment are to be deducted. The question should be raised whether the parties might give more consideration to the back pay issue. Not uncommonly an award by an arbitrator that calls for retroactive payment gives rise to the issue of the computation in another grievance. Are overtime hours to be included? If so, at the premium rate of pay? Are incentive earnings based on extra effort to be included, or is the employee to be reimbursed at his regular day or base rate? Do the moneys earned elsewhere include those received from jobs on which the employee was "moonlighting"? If there is delay in processing the appeal resulting from action of the dischargee or the union, should this period be excluded in the computation? These and similar questions arise frequently. They are seldom covered by contract language.

The prevailing view among arbitrators is that in disciplinary cases, unlike nearly all other grievances that go to arbitration, the company has the burden of going forward and the burden of proof. This procedural requirement occasionally is to be found in the agreement itself. Placing the onus on the company to prove that its action was for just cause is responsible, in part, for the great care now exercised by companies in investigating and recording all facts relating to discipline. The best statement of this arbitration requirement is to be found in a study of arbitration awards of the New York State Board of Mediation for the period 1937-46:

> In the absence of any special controlling clause in the contract, the general rules of forensic proof would seem to apply. The burden of proof lies with the party who asserts the affirmative of the issue. The person who asserts the affirmative is ordinarily seeking to bring about a change of circumstances. Consequently, under the most usual type of clause where provision is made that discharge may occur only for just cause, the employer is seeking to bring about a change of circumstances in that he wishes to remove an employee from his job. The employer, therefore, would appear to have the burden of proof. This analysis may be complicated by the fact that the arbitration takes place after the discharge has been effected. Thus, seemingly, the Union is attempting to bring about a change of circumstances by having the discharged employee restored to his job. But if the issue is the justifiability of the

discharge, the arbitrator may be concerned as of a point in time before the discharge, leaving the affirmative burden with the employer....[10]

Available evidence indicates that management's disciplinary decisions have not fared well at the hands of arbitrators. A study of 1,055 discharge cases reported in the Bureau of National Affairs *Labor Arbitration Reports* for the period January 1942 through March 1956 revealed that management was sustained in 41 per cent of the cases; the penalty was revoked in 25.2 per cent and reduced in 33.8 per cent of the cases. However, it is significant that this same study shows an improvement in the management arbitration record over the years. In the 762 cases decided between 1942 and 1951 management was sustained in 39.4 per cent of the cases; but in those cases reported from 1951 to 1956, totalling 293, the percentage of management verdicts was 45.4.[11] These data are not to be interpreted as evidence that management's discharge actions are ill-founded in the majority of cases. As the researchers emphasize, the sample does not allow any such authoritative conclusion. For example, the very fact that an appeal to arbitration was made could indicate that the merits of the action were delicately balanced. Nevertheless, this record of management reversals dramatizes the extent to which arbitration continues to influence the conduct of disciplinary programs.

Two other aspects of this fourteen-year survey are of special interest. First, it is significant that management's most favorable record was in discharges for incompetency and/or inefficiency (44.5 per cent). This somewhat elusive cause for discharge was proven to the satisfaction of arbitrators more often than those causes identified with violation of plant rules. Second, a review of the 1,055 discharge cases discloses that the following principles were found to govern:

1. Policies must be both known and reasonable.
2. Violation of policies must be proven, and the burden of proof rests on the employer.

[10] State of New York, Department of Labor, Division of Research and Statistics, *Discharge for Cause*, Special Bulletin No. 221 (1948), p. 14. The same observations are usually applicable to cases involving warning notices and suspensions.
[11] J. Fred Holly, "The Arbitration of Discharge Cases: A Case Study," *Critical Issues in Labor Arbitration*, Bureau of National Affairs (1957), pp. 1-17.

3. The application of rules and policies must be consistent:
   a. Employees cannot be singled out for discipline.
   b. Past practice may be a controlling consideration.
4. Where employees are held to a standard, that standard must be reasonable.
5. The training provided employees must be adequate.
6. The job rights of employees must be protected from arbitrary, capricious or discriminatory action.
7. Actions must be impersonal and based on fact.
8. Where the contract speaks, it speaks with authority.[12]

It is apparent that this listing is consistent with and confirms the developments described earlier in the use of disciplinary measures under collective bargaining.

Another interesting and revealing study for American management is the report of the consequences of arbitration verdicts where reinstatement of the discharged employee is required. In a study of discharge arbitration cases for the period 1950-55 it was found that more than half of those discharged were in "junior status," defined as having five years or less seniority. Further, the majority of the 207 discharged and reinstated grievants were discharged for "overt and dramatic types of misbehavior." It was found that

> if a similar distribution of all discharged employees were made, including those *not* reinstated, the proportions would be somewhat different. Nevertheless, it seems evident that the drastic and shocking episode, such as a fight, an illegal strike or an act of defiance, puts the greatest strain on the employment relationship. Quieter problems like absenteeism and poor workmanship do not produce a crisis in the shop, do not mobilize emotions, and are more likely to be resolved without resort to the sanction of discharge. It may be that the modern theory of corrective discipline, which emphasizes patient educational effort with the delinquent employee, is widely accepted in industry insofar as the less dramatic offenses are concerned. . . .[13]

This study, which was concerned primarily with what happens after reinstatement, found that about two-thirds of the reinstated employees proved satisfactory in the opinion of management. Sixty per cent made normal occupational progress and 70 per cent presented no further disciplinary problems. Nevertheless, only 39 per

---

[12] The same, p. 16. See also Phelps' study, pp. 137-143.
[13] Arthur M. Ross, "The Arbitration of Discharge Cases: What Happens After Reinstatement," *Critical Issues in Labor Arbitration*, Bureau of National Affairs (1957), pp. 21-56.

cent of the employers were willing to acknowledge that reinstatement was a proper verdict.[14] This study does not imply that the wisdom of arbitrators is superior to that of management. The inferences derived are more modest: (1) that managements tend to act more hastily and less advisedly in cases that seem to involve overt gestures of misbehavior, and (2) that arbitration decisions adverse to management do not always have the dire consequences predicted. There is little evidence to show that supervisory morale and plant efficiency have suffered in the long run because of the reinstatement of discharged employees by arbitrators.

One final comment concerning the review process: Many companies are recognizing the import of rulings by Division of Employment Security Boards in the arbitration of discharge cases. State laws provide in effect that no benefits shall be paid to an individual for unemployment caused by discharge "shown to the satisfaction of the director to be attributable solely to deliberate misconduct in wilful disregard of the employing unit's interest."[15] In many instances a discharge grievance is being processed simultaneously under the contract and, in effect, under the employment security law if the director has rejected a benefit claim. The decisions in the appeal steps under the law, either at the Review Examiner or Board of Review levels, can have an important evidential effect in the arbitration procedure.

Special Problems of Discipline

Although the growth of sophisticated and orderly procedures for handling discipline has been an impressive development since 1940, there remain several problem areas that call for at least brief mention.

Most unions and managements have yet to work out a mutually acceptable approach to so-called hardship cases. These are cases in which the employee's usefulness to the company becomes seriously limited for reasons that are largely or entirely beyond the control of the employee. Some cases of progressive alcoholism fall in this category. More frequent are those of employees who develop an organic illness that either causes excessive absenteeism or renders the

[14] The same, p. 43.
[15] Massachusetts Employment Security Law, Section 25.

employee unfit to do the available work. They may have consider-able service yet not be entitled to disability retirement. The re-medial measures of progressive discipline are inapplicable, yet some companies carefully follow the steps of warning and suspension to protect themselves when final separation is effected by discharge. Even the use of discharge, which usually connotes separation for wrongdoing, seems an inappropriate type of action. Many unions and companies state that while cases of this type are infrequent, they are by far the most difficult to handle.

The discipline of elected union representatives is cited by a num-ber of companies as constituting its most serious problem in ad-ministering discipline. Very often the behavior that suggests a need for disciplinary measures is identifiable both with the person's role as an employee and with his role as a union representative. For example, the use of abusive language to a foreman, which would dictate some action if committed by a regular employee, may be tolerated in the case of a steward or committeeman. This is especial-ly likely if its use occurred during a discussion of a grievance. Some companies admit that they lean over backward to avoid disciplin-ing a union representative lest the action be construed as an anti-union gesture. It is fair to say that a double standard often exists that favors the union representative. One industrial relations di-rector commented that "when the discharge of a union steward is suggested, we spend twice as much time discussing, investigating, documenting as we do on a routine case, and then we usually end up giving him another chance."

In some plants it was discovered that a complete breakdown of discipline had occurred. Employees were contemptuous of super-visory orders and openly disregarded rules and regulations. In a few cases the absence of any semblance of law and order became so serious that those employees not disposed to adopt the prevailing bad habits preferred to quit their jobs. Where discipline has de-generated so completely, one may expect to find several contributing causes. (1) It may reflect a breakdown in other aspects of the rela-tionship. One company said that the absence of effective discipline in several of its departments was attributable to a demoralized standards system of the type described in Chapter 17. (2) The fore-men may not be facing up to the problem. (3) The disciplinary system may not be progressive. Too often there is an overindulgence in warnings which lose their effectiveness when employees learn that the supervisor is not likely to impose more stringent measures. (4) There may be an absence of well thought out policies for handling special disciplinary problems, as in the case of wildcat strikes or slowdowns. (5) Occasionally the breakdown may be traced to a history of overbargaining on discipline in the short-run interest of washing out grievances. Excessive compromising in the grievance process can undermine what may have been a good disciplinary program.

Discipline as a Management Tool

As noted earlier in the chapter, one of the most important potential consequences of disciplinary experience under collective bargaining is its diagnostic value for management. The concept of "corrective discipline" is usually thought of in terms of a specific case. Yet by some few companies it is also thought of as "corrective discipline" for management, as a way of detecting shortcomings in personnel practices and in the supervision of people. The inability or failure of an employee to meet company standards of conduct or performance may be more the company's fault than the employee's.

It is unfortunate that so few companies have discovered the lessons to be learned from disciplinary problems. If hiring and selection procedures are weak, should the employee who is hired under such procedures be discharged for failing to meet company standards of behavior, without any regard for correcting the real problem? Why was he hired in the first instance? In one company a number of female assemblers were discharged for "poor quality" work. Only after many such painful actions was it discovered by the company that the work involved required women with a certain calibre of eyesight. In a bus company several drivers were discharged because of "incompetency," the justification for which was the number of accidents in which they were involved. In these instances was the fault the employees' or the management's? If careful selection techniques, including tests for eyesight or accident-proneness, had been used these disciplinary measures, harmful to employees and costly to the companies, might never have occurred.

Sometimes weakness in training methods is at the root of a disciplinary problem. Failure by an employee to conform to certain regulations or to do acceptable quantity-quality work may be less his fault than that of those responsible for his training on the job. In other cases the need for discipline and punishment may be symptomatic of inferior or inadequate supervision. The deportment of managerial personnel, as stated earlier, may set a poor example for employees. A foreman may be remiss in applying disciplinary policy; or he may be violating the very rules which he expects employees to observe. Some companies have discovered that "poor" employees were retained beyond the probationary period because they were needed. Later, when the labor market condition eased, these employees were discharged on one pretext or another, although their "poorness" had not become more serious.

In several cases it was found that a periodic appraisal system of management was at fault. Employees who were rated as having done "good" or "very good" work were discharged later for poor work. In effect, the merit-rating system had misled employees into believing that their work was commendable. When confronted with the ratings they had given, foremen explained that they had not thought these ratings "meant very much."

In summary, it is found that many companies, having responded to union pressure to develop a policy and program of corrective discipline for employees, would do well to extend the concept of corrective discipline to management as well. In a discipline case some managements have learned much by asking first "what have we done wrong" instead of concentrating only on the wrongdoing of the employee.

22 / Wildcat Strikes and Union Pressure Tactics

WILDCAT STRIKES, that is, strikes in violation of contract, and other union pressure tactics have not been sufficiently recognized as a distinct and important aspect of the development and evolution of union-management relations. Day-to-day union-management relations have involved more than the peaceful adjustment of grievances because the existence of a grievance procedure with arbitration as its final step has not guaranteed that this procedure would be used. In some cases, the grievance procedure has been ignored and direct action taken in its place. In others, grievances have been filed, but the processing of grievances has been supplemented effectively and frequently through pressure on management. The objective may have been to obtain concessions beyond the scope of the contract, to liberalize the interpretation of the contract, or simply to obtain favorable grievance decisions under existing principles of contract interpretation.

An open question is whether the use of force, direct and indirect, in contract administration has not been more significant than have strikes over the negotiation of contracts. Actually no accurate measurement of such influence can be made, but it is clear that certain plants and companies have become noncompetitive not through concessions granted in negotiation but through the cumulative effect of concessions granted in contract administration. This is one area where the importance of pressure tactics has not been recognized. It has also not been adequately recognized that such tactics are associated with a particular phase in the evolution of union-management relations over the last twenty years.

Too frequently wildcat strikes have been looked upon simply as an abnormal reaction of a small group of workers to unusual provocation by management or to some other incident arising in a given plant. All wildcats can be interpreted in this way if they are analyzed as individual incidents. A group of workers become aroused, lose their heads, and walk off the job. There are many cases of wildcats and other pressure tactics, and some brief illustrations are given below.

In one plant a man was selected as a trainee foreman. He had an excellent record but had had a fight with the union steward that never was put in his record, where it would become a factor in the selection process. When first put on the floor he had a loud argument with the union steward. He ignored advice to walk away to allow a cooling off period, and there was subsequently an incident of "bodily contact," the facts being in dispute. The rumor went through the plant that a foreman slugged the steward, and a considerable number of employees walked out. In another plant fifteen power truck operators stayed out because they felt the union committeeman was monopolizing the overtime. An investigation of one wildcat involving sixty employees revealed the fact that one employee wanted time off to go fishing, but, not wanting others to make money while he fished, he instigated a wildcat. A move to clamp down on absenteeism during deer season led to a well-timed, large-scale wildcat in one company over a very different formal grievance. At the cost of a formal reprimand most employees got in several days of hunting.

This chapter is not concerned with wildcat strikes as individual incidents. It is concerned with such strikes and other pressure tactics as a pattern of behavior in the evolution of union-management relations since about 1940 and in particular companies and plants as this behavior relates to company and union policy and practice. The chapter will deal first with the general meaning and extent of such tactics. This will be followed by a section on a definition and illustration of pressure tactics. In subsequent sections the significance of pressure tactics, the development of management policy, and the development of union policy will be discussed.

Meaning and Extent of Pressure Tactics

It is clear that the use of force in contract administration over the past twenty years has been related to the evolution of union-management relations within a changing economic environment.

Evolution of Union-Management Relations

A general evolution of union-management relations has been associated with changed management and union policy and practice toward the use of direct action in contract administration. There is, however, variation among industries, companies, and unions. A particularly harsh management may provoke wildcats. A very weak management may invite wildcats. Militant and aggressive local union leaders may use pressure. Local union officials may have great respect for their contract and shun pressure. New locals may have experienced guidance in establishing initial relationships with a company, or inexperienced local leaders may drift into a direct-action approach. But these variations fall within a larger pattern that stands out distinctly in the results of our study and show three overlapping stages of development: an organizing stage, a contract-development stage, and an adjustment and accommodation stage.[1] Pressure tactics are far more a characteristic of the first two stages than of the third. This evolution will first be described in broad terms.

The conflicts over organization and recognition, and the hostility that remained after legal recognition was achieved, had a direct carry-over to the administration of contracts. Many union officials felt that force was the only language management could understand. Management in many cases reacted by restraining and restricting the union, only partially accepting unionism as a permanent institution. As the organizing stage moved into and overlapped with the contract development stage, union aggression to obtain contract concessions and containment by management continued.

Almost any account of union-management contracts shows the contract development stage and its merging into the accommodation stage. Consider, for example, the transition from the simple 1937 agreement between United States Steel and the Steel Workers' Organizing Committee to today's contract. Such a transition could hardly take place without considerable conflict in administration as well as in negotiation.

As the years have gone by, to a greater and greater extent the non-

---

[1] This classification of stages and the related discussion, though not identical with Professor Benjamin M. Selekman's development and use of types of union-management relationships, owes much to it. See, for example, "Part I. Frameworks for Study of Cases in Labor Relations," B. M. Selekman, Sylvia K. Selekman, and S. H. Fuller, *Problems in Labor Relations,* 2nd ed. (1958), p. 1-11.

economic phases of labor contracts have become more stable both in language and in interpretation. There has been increasing accommodation in specific contract provisions, and pressure tactics have declined.

It so happens that the organizing and contract development stages, during which a relatively high degree of conflict in contract administration might be expected, have coincided in time with economic expansion, war, and super-prosperity. Resistance by management was low. With sales pressure maximizing production, with cost-plus sales contracts, with the ability to pass on cost increases to consumers, many managements gave in to pressure without adequate consideration of the longer-run consequences. Because of the pressure of military needs, it was imperative to settle grievances without risking a plant shut-down during World War II. Pressure for production continued after the war. A typical report is the following:

> When the union says, "If that's the way you are going to look at it, we'll shut the place down," management informs industrial relations: "We've got to have production. Don't let them shut us down. Give it to them."

As economic conditions have changed in the postwar period, and as adjustment has increased in union-management relations, more and more managements have taken a firm position against wildcat strikes and pressure tactics. At the same time union officials have found by experience that high-cost plants and direct-action plants are a problem for the union as well as for management. The higher officials in unions particularly have modified their views. Changing policies of managements and of unions, generally during the years 1948 to about 1952, have cut down dramatically on wildcat strikes and pressure tactics.

To avoid oversimplifying, some qualifications must be noted. First, the definition of "legal" and "illegal" strikes has been refined over the years. Contracts before World War II rarely contained arbitration provisions. By 1960 almost all contracts had such provisions. This dramatic change is discussed in Chapter 25. Without arbitration as the terminal step in the grievance procedure, and without refinement of the no-strike clause, the distinction between "legal" and "illegal" strikes was far from clear. While this distinction was made in a few relationships before World War II, an important change is the almost unconscious use today of a sharp distinction between contract administration and contract negotiation and between strikes allowed and those prohibited by contract. The turbulent union-management relations in the 1930's lacked such refinements.

Second, reference is generally to the newer as distinct from the older unions and relationships. This does not always hold, but respect for contract has been somewhat more firmly established for many years by the older unions. President George P. Berry's stern action in breaking the New York Pressmen's strike in 1923, though the issues were far more complex than in an ordinary wildcat, is a rather extreme example.[2] In particular industries where newer CIO unions and older AFL unions both have recognition, companies frequently reported a different attitude in bringing grievances, in appeals to arbitration, and in the use of direct action by the CIO locals compared with AFL locals. Greater militancy in administration of contracts, more extensive grass-roots "democracy" in the new unions, less guidance and supervision by the national unions in establishing locals, less control of locals by nationals, unionism operating in large integrated plants, and difference in the skill composition of the work forces are possible explanations. In the older unions instances are found where the national pays half of the salaries of some local officials and establishes appointed rather than elected stewards.

There are exceptions to this, however. Some plants organized by the older unions have had a turbulent history. There are direct-action locals in most unions, and in manufacturing industry variations among locals within each union appear more important than variations among national unions. Even railroad operating crafts kept one freight yard in a tangle for months by an exaggerated application of rules. Some building projects have been plagued by direct action, though jurisdiction is a special problem. Rules may be enforced by older unions unilaterally. Nevertheless, a qualified statement can be made that the older unions and older bargaining relationships have been less involved in the pressure-tactic problem portrayed in this chapter than have the new unions in automobiles, in steel, in rubber, and in other industries.

Third, the incidence of pressure tactics is probably related to the power position of locals and the vulnerability of managements. Pipe-

[2] Selig Perlman and Philip Taft, *History of Labor in the United States, 1896-1932,* (1935), pp. 456-60.

line industries and plants with small inventories, companies and industries particularly sensitive to loss of business if delivery to customers is interrupted, and large integrated operations where strategic work groups can shut down a large plant may well have faced a
higher incidence of pressure tactics than did other industries.
Greater power on the union side and greater loss on the management
side may have affected incidence. The difficulty here is that posses-
sion of power is not synonymous with its use and some managements
have acted more firmly than others in the same industry. A weak
management in any plant or industry may invite wildcats.

Finally, the concept of accommodation and adjustment portrayed
is limited. The belief is that adjustment has been marked in certain
aspects of contract administration. The area of seniority has lost
much of its early turbulence. Some layoff clauses are applied almost
mechanically. Wage rates for particular jobs are now substantially
stabilized. Discipline is less controversial than formerly. Arbitration
is firmly established. Less adjustment has been achieved in the area
of production standards. It is not contended that accommodation has
been reached as to economic demands. It can be argued that union-
management conflict shifts from one frontier to another without
making permanent progress. Since new issues are continuously
brought into collective bargaining, the concept of an advancing
frontier has validity. But in the noneconomic aspects of contract
negotiation and administration, the belief is that there has been a
real advance in adjustment, accommodation, and stability. Contract
administration in 1958 was far less turbulent than in 1938 or 1948.

Extent of Wildcat Strikes and Pressure Tactics

While a few statistics will be given later in this chapter, it is not
possible to describe the extent of wildcat strikes in quantitative
terms.[3] It is equally impossible to measure other forms of pressure
tactics. At the same time the significance of the problem cannot be
appreciated without some indication of its dimension.

[3] A systematic study of wildcats in all the companies interviewed was not attempted,
but enough statistics were collected to indicate the need for caution in their use. Many
companies made no attempt to keep records of lost man-hours. Companies that kept
records had different concepts of what constituted lost time. Also local management
might adjust a record to avoid criticism. One wildcat was quietly settled because of an
imminent visit of top union and company officials. Neither the local union nor the local
management wished to be caught with a wildcat in process.

Major companies in the following industries will be cited to indicate in a general way the extent of the problem: automobile manufacturing, automotive parts, agricultural machinery, meat packing, rubber tires and other rubber products, plate glass, electrical manufacturing, and basic steel.

There is hardly a company in the group that has not had some difficulty with organized pressure tactics. A very few companies adopted policies that substantially eliminated the problem before World War II. At the end of the war union-management relations in many plants were very hectic. Some were beginning to solve these problems by the end of the war or shortly thereafter. It is probably correct to say that by about 1952 wholesale pressure tactics were a thing of the past for a large majority of the companies. By 1960 only a few companies were having major problems of this sort, although a larger number still had a few plants where relationships were not stabilized. Subtle pressures continued in a larger number.

It may be true that a sample of large companies in industries that were focal points in the organization of industrial unions overstates the existence of conflict in contract administration. In one relatively small city, the center of an agricultural region and not a highly unionized section of the country, twelve companies were studied. These twelve unionized manufacturing companies (chemical, machinery, a railroad shop, automotive parts, electrical products, hosiery, shoes, and garments) represented about 80 per cent of the manufacturing employment in the city. In only three of the plants had there been a serious wildcat strike problem. In three more plants there had been some difficulties. Six plants had no history of such a problem. By 1958 the three problem plants had resolved their contract administration problems.

From all the interviews conducted for this study it appears that solution of this problem has been an important phase in the evolution of union-management relations. However, while pressure tactics are still significant, more serious in 1960 are the high costs and inefficient practices inherited from the period before such tactics were brought under control.

Definition of Pressure Tactics

Pressure tactics include wildcat strikes, threats to strike, slow-downs, various contract clauses and working practices, the indirect use of legal strikes, and flooding the grievance procedure.[4] Each will be discussed briefly and illustrated.

WILDCAT STRIKES. The simplest type of pressure tactic is a strike by a smaller or larger number of employees in violation of the contract. An extreme example is that of one major appliance plant in the electrical industry in which there was never any resort to the grievance procedure before striking. Management learned that a grievance existed only when a group of employees walked off the job. At this point the labor relations manager for the company went to the union office and negotiated with respect to the grievance. When a satisfactory settlement was reached, the men returned to work.

THREATS TO STRIKE. Closely related to an actual wildcat is an open or implied threat to strike. In a plant of one steel company there was an extremely low rate of formal grievances. There were also very few actual wildcats. This is a particularly interesting example because on paper union-management relations appeared to be very good. However, a very strong local union official always got favorable action on particular grievances, presented orally and not through the usual grievance procedure, by pointing out that the workers would take direct action if a favorable decision were not obtained. This situation came to light within the corporate structure only after a new manager took over the plant because of the high costs that had developed.

SLOWDOWNS. A slowdown is a very effective pressure tactic. Almost all companies have at least some difficulty with slowdowns, and in some cases it is extreme. In one automobile plant, with every new model, production standards and manning were established by means of a plant-wide slowdown. Only a very low level of production could be obtained while grievances on manning and standards for new models remained open. When all grievances were resolved, production rose to the scheduled level. Again these grievances were presented orally and were recorded only partially in the grievance procedure.

[4] Strikes in cases of jurisdictional disputes are not included nor are various partial strike tactics sometimes used at the time of contract expiration.

In another case a modernization program brought continuous slowdowns over a period of about five years. As new equipment was put in, it was operated substantially below capacity. A new machine introduced in early 1953 had a capacity of 89.9 tons per hour. During 1953 it actually produced at 50.5 tons per hour, which was 10.2 tons per hour below the level with the old machine in 1952. In 1954 production on the new machine was 60 tons per hour, or roughly the same as in 1952. An arbitration award and negotiation finally substantially eliminated slowdowns on this and other equipment in 1955. Unbalanced production and increased cost were the only result of a very large increased investment during a five-year period.

Slowdowns are usually associated with production standard and manning grievances. Such grievances frequently involve prospective earnings under a wage incentive plan. Some slowdowns are extreme in form and easily detected, though responsibility for the slowdown may be far from clear. Others are mild and their organized nature is open to question. A particular slowdown may last for months. Because of these characteristics several management officials have commented, "Give me a good clean wildcat any day."

Slowdowns can involve problems for union leadership comparable to those for management. Local union leadership may disclaim responsibility in discussion with international officials. Stewards may disclaim responsibility to higher local officials, and, of course, leadership may be outside of the current union officials. In one company the international union official was convinced that a plant slowdown was not being led by the local union officials and so testified privately and in arbitration. In a subsequent arbitration a local union official through a slip of the tongue commented, "that was when we were running a big slowdown."

CONTRACT CLAUSES AND WORKING PRACTICES. Various contract clauses, or practices not specifically covered by contract, may be used as pressure tactics. Refusal to accept temporary transfer and refusal to work overtime are two such tactics found in a number of cases. The creation of excess overtime work is another such practice. Quite apart from contract provisions there are many ways in which employees may refuse to cooperate in production until some grievance is settled satisfactorily. Creating strategic bottlenecks or special problems is one such device. In a broadcasting studio literal and deliberate adherence to all established rules brought production almost to a standstill. On one of the airlines some workers discovered that they could park a plane in a hangar in such fashion that it took at least an hour and a half to get it out again. Changing route tags on customer baggage, as was done on an airline at one terminal, comes close to sabotage from the passenger point of view. Causing various types of machine breakdown is a common tactic. The use of a contract clause is illustrated below.

One company had very bad union-management relations with a bargaining unit in its plant. The local union president ran the unit and was contemptuous of management. He called the foremen "floor walkers with flashlights," a job description encountered in several situations. The plant manager and plant superintendent were lumped together as "worthless overhead" who served no useful purpose and whose salaries should be applied to the workers' wages.

While this company and union had "nothing but trouble" over "everything you could think of," the chief mechanism of difficulty was a contract clause requiring union approval for all temporary transfers. This clause was negotiated to meet a particular problem. The union claimed management abuse in transferring workers from high-temperature inside work to outside work in cold weather. Management denied abuse and agreed to a mutual consent clause on temporary transfer. The clause, however, was general in form and was interpreted in arbitration to apply to all temporary transfers. To bring pressure on management during the processing of a serious grievance the union allowed no temporary transfers, thus disrupting production. This situation ultimately led to a long and serious strike, in which the union lost representation rights to a rival union.

In another company one of the actions which most undermined first line supervision was refusal by an employee of an assignment other than his regular one. This was allowed under a contract clause written for a special situation but given general applicability in arbitration. The union used the clause as an economic weapon to retaliate for grievances and supervisory action. When a worker was absent, another worker would refuse to fill the job. While union-management relations were never particularly bad in this company and have improved over the years, this practice was more than a minor annoyance until resolved indirectly by arbitration. It was banned by interpretation in arbitration of a revised no-strike clause. In a number of companies refusal to work overtime has been used as a pressure tactic particularly where the contract was silent on the point. For example, in 1955 one company added to the contract a provision that an employee must work overtime except for good personal reasons. Prior to this change, working overtime had been voluntary by custom and practice and was used in connection with processing grievances. In this situation the company felt the addition to the contract was a very important one, although concerted refusal to work overtime would normally be regarded as a contract violation even if the contract were silent on the point.

To list all of the ways in which a contract (or working practices) may be used for pressure purposes is not possible. One 1957 contract was discovered that had thirty-seven mutual consent provisions. While union-management relations in this company were quite good, at various times one or another of these clauses would be invoked against the management as an aid in processing unrelated grievances. Various practices, particularly ones relating to job assignments, grow up in the absence of contract provisions and are used indirectly to obtain some type of favorable action.

Two other pressure tactics should be noted: the indirect use of a legal strike or strike threat, and flooding the grievance procedure.

LEGAL STRIKES USED INDIRECTLY. A relatively small proportion of contracts allow strikes during their term in lieu of arbitration of certain issues. One company has recently written into its contract a confinement of issues provision that illustrates the problem. It is now provided by contract that "no grievance, complaint, issue or matter other than the strikeable issue involved will be discussed or negotiated." While a company and union may be in real agreement to allow strikes during the term of the contract over important matters that neither wants to arbitrate, such a clause becomes a pressure tactic if used indirectly in connection with nonstrikeable issues.

One company official, not associated with the automobile industry, said that management had initially refused a union request for a general arbitration clause, and had reserved certain matters for company determination, giving the union the right to strike. He felt that this was one of the worst labor relations mistakes the company had ever made. In this official's view it would be well worth "ten cents an hour" to get rid of this opportunity to strike during the term of the contract, but the union would never buy it at that figure.

There are definite differences of opinion among management officials in several companies having this type of provision in the contract. Some favor retention of the clause, some favor its elimination. One of the common arguments for elimination is the extreme difficulty of actually restricting the right to strike to strikeable issues. Under some contracts strikeable issue grievances may be kept active indefinitely as a continuing strike threat.

FLOODING THE GRIEVANCE PROCEDURE. "Flooding the grievance procedure" is included within the scope of pressure tactics even though such a concept cannot be defined precisely and is usually complex as to its nature and causes. There is a point, however, where a grievance procedure ceases to function in a normal manner. When the number of grievances is extremely large and almost all of them are appealed up to the step prior to arbitration, with many being carried to arbitration, normal resolution of grievances becomes almost impossible. The investigation process, the resolution process, and some-times the arbitration process break down. Compromises, trading of grievances, and wholesale methods of clearing the docket may be used by a union to obtain a larger absolute number of concessions than would be realized without the pressure of numbers. Also the continuous high rate of grievances is in itself a type of harassment. Detailed discussion of considerations influencing the functioning of the grievance procedure will be found in Chapters 23 and 24, but deliberate manipulation of the grievance procedure must be recognized at this point as an important pressure tactic.

Significance of Pressure Tactics

The significance of pressure tactics can be viewed in terms of motivating influences from the point of view of the union and the employees. It can also be viewed in terms of the effects upon management. Their significance in a broader frame of reference, the evolution of union-management relations, has already been noted. Whyte's *Pattern for Industrial Peace* shows the relation of pressure tactics to the changing character of union-management relations in a particular plant.[5]

Union and Employee Motivating Influences

While pressure tactics can and should be related to the evolution of union-management relations in general, and in particular companies, a more specific motivation is the obtaining of more favorable grievance decisions, initially or through modifications and reversals at higher stages in the grievance procedure. These grievances may be routine in character or may relate to the extension of the contract to new areas or principles of application. Dissension over grievance decisions may be associated with very strict management decisions or with very aggressively-pursued objectives of unions and employees. Personality clashes between union and management officials may accentuate and perpetuate hostility. Political instability in a local union may be important in contributing to direct action. Whatever the associated circumstances, where pressure tactics are used, employees and union officials find that management policy allows them to pay off and not result in severe discipline.

Organizational hostility should be illustrated at least briefly. In one company recognition of the union came in 1941, after four years of violent organizational struggle. Upon recognition, in the words of a company labor relations executive,

> the union went wild. A good part of this was a rebellion against being pushed around by the foremen. This was particularly meaningful since the company had no industrial engineering department and no objective production standards. Foremen set the production requirements. This situation readily developed into work stoppages and reversals by top supervision of lower supervision to get men to go back to work.

In this company there were approximately 800 work stoppages in the first four years of the relationship. At this point the management negotiated, with definite union agreement, the basis for management discipline for stoppages as well as other stronger management rights. Substantial improvement followed, but wildcats continued on a diminished though significant scale for some years because of management's inconsistency in applying discipline.

[5] William Foote Whyte, *Pattern for Industrial Peace* (1951). The story of change in Inland Steel Container Corporation from conflict to cooperation has many of the characteristics associated with developing adjustment and accommodation.

The president of one large industrial union put the matter of organizational hostility very well indeed:

> The early and intense management opposition to unionism was a primary cause of sit-down and wildcat stoppages in the 1930's. Once this pattern of response was established, it became characteristic as a mode of behavior. In one company it required four years after the company was organized before management recognized the union by signing a contract. The contract was won after a nine-week strike. The only weapon the union had was the strike. It was this that produced results. Consequently, the habit was developed that force alone achieved ends. After the first contract was won, the people failed to see any change in the situation that disproved the tactical correctness of using force.

This union president went on to say that wildcat strikes could not always be explained adequately by early management opposition, particularly their persistence over the years. Speaking about sit-downs, walkouts, mass absenteeism, and organized illness at one company, he stated that

> over the years most of these were settled by a company concession which got the men back to work without considering discipline as a solution in spite of the no-strike clause.

It is not necessary to elaborate the simple fact that if pressure tactics pay off in favorable initial grievance decisions, in modifications and reversals of decisions, and in concessions beyond the scope of the contract, they are almost certain to be used. Where a contract provision is general in character as, for example, discipline for "just cause" or "fair and equitable" production standards or job rates—and important parts of a contract usually are general because of the nature of the problem—refusal to accept initial management decisions may create a continuing pressure-tactic problem.

It is impossible to generalize here as to what is cause and what is effect. Hostility over grievance decisions and the use of direct action may come from overly-harsh management decisions or overly-aggressive union objectives. One management official described his company's early action, for example, as an effort to write clever contracts and administer them in a clever way. The company tried to be tough and oppose the union at every opportunity. Under such circumstances the union felt that the only way to deal with the company was in a tough fashion. This company made real progress in reducing wildcats by fair settlements of grievances. On the other hand, when unions and employees are unduly aggressive in seeking their objectives, high costs have resulted. Again wildcats may be common where company policies are incomplete or vacillating.

Another question regarding pressure tactics on which generalization is not particularly fruitful is whether union officials are leading the employees or being pushed by them. No doubt it varies in different situations, but it appears that employees and union officials have a common attitude on pressure tactics, though there may be differences in degree of influence. In a few instances ideologically radical union leadership appeared responsible for pressure tactics.

Another consideration bearing on pressure tactics is instability within a local union, which the following account (using fictitious names) illustrates: There are three groups in the local—the Smith group, a group following Jones, the secretary-treasurer, who is an old IWW member and does not believe in a written agreement, and a left-wing group following Avery, the business agent. Avery is called a communist by the Smith group. Last year Jones signed the agreement with an "X" to show that he does not believe in written agreements. Avery assented to the agreement in negotiations but played a role in getting the rank and file to reject the contract. Jones believes in wildcat strikes. In his judgment they speak the only language management can understand. The management in this company was trying to convince the men that wildcat strikes no longer paid, but instability within the union and lack of management discipline were perpetuating wildcats.

Attention is given to political instability in the chapters on grievances. Just as grievances can be influenced significantly by political considerations, so can pressure tactics. On the other hand, a one-man local may also use pressure tactics. In one plant a strong union leader using pressure tactics outlasted sixteen plant managers. The plant was finally abandoned because of high costs attributable in part to concessions granted under pressure.

There are thus a variety of specific motivational influences within the union-management environment. Primarily direct action is used to gain concessions. A management that is harsh, weak, or inconsistent may be at fault. Equally important is union attitude. Local union leadership shows varying degrees of militancy, aggressiveness, and reasonableness in the acceptance of management decisions.

Workers in particular industries, plants, and departments may well be more prone to direct action than are others because of the degree of their strategic power. Especially within a given plant, strategically located work groups appear more prone to direct action than are other groups. Whatever the initial cause, direct action creates hostility that perpetuates conflict.

These more specific motivational influences have tended to diminish and disappear as an integral part of the evolution of union-management relations. As the noneconomic clauses in contracts acquired stability through agreement and acceptance, a basic source of conflict disappeared. Along with this, lasting principles of interpretation developed, frequently with important guide lines established by arbitration. Grievance settlements became more routine in character, though differences in opinion continued to be normal. Companies supplemented the contract provisions by personnel and labor relations policies. Unions acquired security, gained their most pressing noneconomic objectives, and no longer felt the need for militancy in contract administration. Leaders on both sides acquired experience, and administrators of a professional character developed. Companies developed, and unions accepted, policies in disciplining for pressure tactics. This evolution has, of course, taken place to varying degrees in different companies.

Effects on Management

No precise appraisal can be made of the effects of pressure tactics on management. Some companies by taking an early and firm position against such tactics, and by developing good employee and labor relations policies, have had no serious problem. The foresight of such companies is in sharp contrast with more typical early relationships. Some local unions have not engaged in such practices to any important extent, with the result that management has not suffered. Some companies have had very slight difficulties. On the other hand, a significant number of companies and plants faced a serious loss in competitive position through high costs and inefficiencies acquired as a result of the cumulative effects of long-continued concessions.[6]

Most important is an appreciation of the longer-term cumulative

[6] Discussion in this section is closely connected with that in Chapter 27 on management and union problems and policies in high-cost plants.

results. For example, the history of lost man-hours in one company was as follows:

Year	Man-Hours Lost (in thousands)
1948	190
1949	339
1950	188
1951	456
1952	1,000
1953	337
1954	66
1955 and after	not significant

The increasing trend and the drastic losses in 1952 brought a change in policy in 1953 which brought an end to the problem. In 1954 somewhat stiffer penalties, along with growing acceptance (the policy was at no time opposed by the international union), greatly reduced the lost man-hours. Since 1955 there has been no significant problem. There was a legacy, however, of many poor production standards, excess manpower, and some inefficient practices in manpower utilization.

Another example in a multiplant company also shows a difference between two industrial unions with roughly equal employee representation. Union A actively practiced a direct action policy; with Union B wildcats were a serious problem only in certain plants. The figures given below are of the number of strikes, both legal and wildcat, but legal strikes are overwhelmingly outnumbered by wildcats. Man-hour figures are not given as they are distorted by legal contract-negotiation strikes.

Year	Number of Strikes	
	Union A	Union B
1945	130	20
1946	97	16
1947	97	15
1948	172	25
1949	173	23
1950	177	32
1951	118	40
1952	80	34
1953	6	11
1954	2	4
1955 and after	Not significant	

Again the imposition of disciplinary policies, which came after a long strike by the more militant union in 1952, while not completely effective immediately, resolved the problem after one year. There still remained, however, a difficult period with many grievances. Issues were transferred to the grievance procedure, and a high grievance rate resulted. After policy resolution of certain key issues there has been an improvement in union-management relations. Considerable tension remains, however, in some plants.

The most extreme situation was discovered in a large company. On a large group of comparable operations, without any great differences in technology, man-hours required per unit of comparable product were almost four times as great as in the plants of the two strongest competitors. This loss of efficiency developed less from stoppages than from a mass slowdown tactic. In this company there was also an extreme plant-wide bumping system based on seniority, and it added materially to production costs. In one short period of less than a year, during which these problems were partially resolved, there was an increase in worker efficiency of more than 200 per cent.

In another company, after a wildcat was converted into a major strike by company resistance, revised production standards were largely responsible for a 50 per cent increase in output per man-hour. This can be viewed only as a case of cumulative deterioration over a period of years. Other examples could be cited showing similar improvement.

A final example will be given of the impact of slowdowns in one plant. A large modernization program involving an investment of approximately $50 million over five years necessitated a wholesale revision of production standards. Slowdowns and stoppages cost the company $16.7 million in added outside conversion cost of product plus a direct loss of 541,800 tons of product. Slowdowns accounted for $15.4 million of the conversion costs and 499,200 tons of product. Stoppages accounted for the remaining losses. There was no benefit from this large investment in lower labor cost nor any improved output per hour until the end of the five-year period, at which time the problem was substantially resolved by a key arbitration, which in itself cost the parties $35 thousand.

It is worker efficiency and its effect on labor cost that bring out sharply the contrast between short-run and longer-run effects. For example, in one plant a wildcat developed because the company took one man off of what had been, prior to technological change, a two-man job. The loss to the company in production, which came at a time when the company could sell every unit it could produce, would have paid the wages of two men for some 3,000 years. From a short-run point of view a given concession may have a totally insignificant effect on profit and labor cost, whereas the cost of a wildcat may be quite significant. On the other hand, the cumulative longer-run effect over a period of five or ten years of a policy of yielding to threats and wildcats has created such situations as have been noted earlier.

Many issues which catch the headlines in labor relations, and to a considerable extent the emphasis in textbooks, are from a competitive point of view less important than matters bearing directly on worker efficiency, such as production standards, practices affecting the utilization of labor, and, more generally, discipline. These areas, however, are usually the ones affected by pressure tactics. Illustrations have been given concerning production standards. Various manpower utilization practices will be noted briefly.

In a division of one company most stoppages were over demands which the workers could not get under the contract. Refusal to work outside of the regular job assignment was one such concession. In various ways contract provisions and arbitration decisions had been undermined by concessions. Refusal to work overtime was common in a number of companies. A variation in one plant was a provision that no employee in a department could work overtime unless all employees in the department were called in. Again in this plant there was a refusal to work outside the scope of the regular job classification. More generally, seniority practices of an extreme and costly character may grow up through concessions in administration.

The most intangible effect, but a very important one, is the loss in authority and prestige of first line supervision that comes with the gradual deterioration of disciplinary policy. Time after time a story was told of declining morale among first line supervision as union officials "run the shop" by force and threats.

Cumulative concessions are not found in an atmosphere of good union-management relations, and the uphill battle to correct a legacy of low worker efficiency and other costly situations is almost certain to create difficulties and unrest. Not infrequently a serious strike has been a turning point in both efficiency and union-management relations. The most favorable situation is one of relatively good worker efficiency, well developed management policies and administration, and an absence of pressure tactics.

Management Policy

A few companies since first becoming unionized have had firm disciplinary policies with respect to wildcat strikes. Where this has been the case, the top management of the company has seen the long-run difficulties of not having such a policy in terms of (1) the possible deterioration of the competitive position of the company, (2) the need for consistent application and interpretation both of the labor contract and of personnel and industrial engineering policies, and (3) the relation of such a policy to the character of union-management relations. In other words, when wildcat strikes and pressure tactics were viewed in this broad perspective by management, discipline in case of wildcats became a major corporate policy invariably applied regardless of short-run losses in production and sales.

Discipline for wildcats is thus not just one phase of a general disciplinary policy. It has a much more important position in total corporate policy. Regular disciplinary policy has few completely rigid and inflexible penalties. Progressive discipline to correct the behavior of individual employees quite properly has a fairly high degree of flexibility in application. A few rigid penalties remain as, for example, for some safety rule violations. But to put discipline for wildcats and yielding to pressure within the area of flexible policy, with each case considered on its own merits, is a dangerous policy.

An argument can be made that the severity of discipline for wildcats should be adjusted to the degree of provocation in the particular situation. One company with such a policy has a good record of negligible lost time. This company has been able, it appears, to maintain a consistent policy with some flexibility. The danger, however, is that the flexibility will be of the wrong type, bending with production necessities. Most companies are inflexible in the application of disciplinary penalties for strikes in violation of contract when the policy is truly endorsed by top management.

A division in one large company was still having considerable difficulty with a very high grievance rate and some difficulty with wildcats and slowdowns. They had tightened up on discipline for wildcats. In point of fact the very high rate of grievances was partly a reaction against the new policy on wildcats. There was a question, however, as to how effective this policy would prove to be. Indus trial relations in this division felt that it was necessary "to be practical" on the matter of discipline for wildcats. At a time of year when competition between companies was intense, the sales and production "necessities" of the situation took precedence over "desirable" labor relations policy. In the off season it was practical to have a consistent policy but not in the busy season. In the busy season it was necessary to keep the men at work. While there was a good appreciation of the broad significance of wildcats and pressure tactics by the labor relations staff, it is doubtful whether the top management of the company understood it well enough to give unqualified support to this labor relations policy. In another company one plant adopted a firm policy during the 1958 recession. It remains to be seen whether this policy will survive during business revival and high capacity operations. The question again is the degree of top management support.

In another large company there has been considerable variation among divisions in the development and application of policy. Some divisions have a wildcat problem of significant proportions while others do not. Divisional decentralization gives to each division responsibility for contract administration and consequent policy formation, although a uniform labor contract applies to all divisions. This raises an interesting question as to the appropriateness of decentralization of administrative policy under these circumstances. Some large companies under master contracts centralize basic contract administration policies, and some do not. While there are good general arguments for decentralized management responsibility, there are definite difficulties if a master contract is being interpreted and applied.

A final example of a lack of corporate policy is that reported by an official of an international union. This union official pointed out that a particular company in an important manufacturing industry was now the only remaining major company that did not have a corporate policy on discipline for wildcats. A regional official of the union said that two plants of this company were the only ones in his jurisdiction where "it was hopeless to try to maintain respect for the contract."

The specific nature of the disciplinary policy followed is undoubtedly less important than the stature of that policy and its consistent application. In the interest of consistency most such company policies are quite mechanical in application, and, as was pointed out above, do not take provocation into account. Redress for management failures is available through the grievance procedure. Discipline is for breach of contract. Barring matters of individual health and safety, which are usually protected by state law and sometimes by contract, this seems essentially a correct position.

Most company policies distinguish between leaders, followers, and sympathizers. Some company policies are more severe in initial penalty than others. A typical procedure is to issue a written warning for initial participation, a one- (or two-) week suspension for participation in a second wildcat, and discharge for a third offense. Leaders are usually suspended for at least two weeks (or discharged) for the first offense, and sympathizers are not disciplined. As mentioned above, initial discipline for followers is sometimes more severe than a written warning—a one- (or two-) week disciplinary layoff.

There is frequently great difficulty in determining, and proving in arbitration, the fact of leadership. For this reason some companies discipline only for direct participation and do not make a distinction between leaders and followers. Since either approach is effective, difference in policy is not of major importance.

The question of policy as it relates to those who sympathize is somewhat more difficult. One company started with a policy of a two-week suspension for leaders on first offense, a one-week suspension for followers, and no penalty for those who walked out in sympathy. In introducing this policy with the concurrence of the international union there was considerable difficulty in some plants with a pattern of sympathetic behavior. The entire plant would stay out while the one-week penalties were being served.

This policy met a crucial test in one plant. The plant was behind schedule on delivery for an important government contract when a small wildcat developed. The consequences of the entire plant being down in sympathetic reaction almost broke the consistency of company policy. The view that prevailed, however, was to modify the policy to a four-week suspension for leaders and two weeks for followers. With the more severe penalties no sympathetic reaction developed. Several companies favor relatively severe initial penalties for direct participants to prevent sympathetic walkouts.

On the other hand, in one plant of a different company, all wildcats were converted by local union leadership into plant walkouts. There was no way to distinguish between followers and sympathizers, and for a time the company policy broke down since management was not willing to suspend the entire plant. Later, however, the company backed off to a written warning for the first offense, and, through interviews with all employees in small groups, made it clear that it was prepared to impose stiffer penalties later. This general policy was quite effective. Another company has carried out discipline for large groups by a relay type of action. Sympathetic reaction, however, is typically only a temporary problem. Again, the specific nature of the policy can be varied a good deal without weakening its effectiveness if it is consistent and takes precedence over production considerations.

A disciplinary policy for slowdowns is both more difficult and more controversial than that for wildcats. The usual policy is one of discipline comparable with that for wildcats for clear-cut, deliberate slowdown. The primary difficulty is in distinguishing between workers deliberately engaging in a slowdown, and those caught unintentionally in the consequences. This difficulty is greater if the slowdown is mild in character rather than obvious. The most effective management device in investigating the facts of a slowdown appears to be intensive (and sometimes on a large scale) industrial engineering observation of employee performance. Frequently the observation will in itself break the slowdown. If not, it can usually provide the basis for discipline.

As deliberate slowdown merges into what might be regarded as normal employee reaction to change, there is some question as to how effective and appropriate disciplinary measures are. Also, production above standard is regarded in some companies under incentive as voluntary on the employee's part even to the extent of not allowing discipline for clear cases of deliberate slowdown.

Management must rely to a considerable degree on working with employees to minimize slowdowns and their consequences. Discipline, because of the nature of the problem, plays a more modest role in dealing with slowdowns than with wildcats, but for extreme problem cases and plants parallel policies are followed in the two cases.

Discipline is usually not appropriate in the first instance for pressure tactics based on established contract clauses or established work practices. The first requirement is a change in the clause or practice by negotiation or announcement, as the case requires. These changes are frequently hard to achieve. Negotiated change may be possible only by means of a strike, and the issue may not warrant the cost of a strike. Generalization is not feasible, as particular clauses and practices must be viewed in their particular environments. Discipline, however, is appropriate only after a change in contract or policy.

While it has been made clear that the purpose of a management policy of discipline for wildcats and other pressure tactics is broad in scope, some elaboration of the impact on labor relations of such a policy is appropriate. Quite apart from cost considerations, a rather dramatic change in union-management relations frequently follows the introduction of such a policy.

It is not uncommon, for example, in new plants for pressure tactics to be used for a period by inexperienced union leaders and employees. In one such plant, operating under an inherited master contract, the employees raised a wide variety of issues as grievances. A grievance was anything that did not suit the employees and had very little relationship to a well-developed contract. The contract, including the no-strike clause, was almost meaningless. The plant production manager was inexperienced in labor relations, and the labor relations manager appeared weak and tried to maintain peace by making concessions. After two years of turbulent plant relations a new labor relations director came into the plant.

At the first reasonable opportunity discipline was invoked for a wildcat. Seven employees were discharged, and ten were given a thirty-day suspension. Some union officials were included among those disciplined. The disciplinary penalties were not bargained down and were substantially upheld in arbitration. This incident marked a turning point in the entire character of union-management relations in the plant.

Many similar union-management relationships could be cited. After adequate notice and discussion with union officials, discipline was imposed. The change brought about by the first such discipline was dramatic in character since employees had been conditioned, sometimes over many years, to a good deal of harsh talking by management but not much disciplinary action. Once management's ability to stand firm had been demonstrated and accepted, then the grievance procedure began to function as it should, and contract interpretation and application developed under rational principles.

An early decision in hosiery by an impartial chairman, Professor George W. Taylor, states very well the union-management principles involved.[7] Two employees had been discharged, and a number of other employees struck in violation of the contract in protest over the discharges. The company in turn discharged those who struck. The impartial chairman reinstated the two employees initially discharged, finding an absence of just cause, but upheld the discharge of those who struck with a forcefully worded opinion. The parties had agreed on a no-strike clause, on a grievance procedure, and on a system of arbitration. All of these related provisions would fail if strikes in violation of contract were condoned. A rational system for the adjudication of disputes could not operate if pressure were used.

Discipline for wildcats is in a sense a negative type of company policy. While it is usually necessary to have such a policy and to deal firmly with pressure tactics, a more positive contribution is the development of healthy union-management relations. Just being firm, while necessary, is not the ultimate objective. Several companies, for example, along with adopting a firmer policy on wildcats have revitalized their entire labor relations program, beginning with the grievance procedure. A firm policy on the part of management will serve to bolster the morale of the foremen but, at the same time, management cannot manage effectively by relying heavily on discipline in any of its forms. Positive leadership is needed.

Union Policy

The announced policy of unions has quite generally been one of respect for contracts. As time has gone by, bringing a greater degree of accommodation in union-management relations, practice has more and more conformed with stated policy. International union officials

[7] Thomas Kennedy, *Effective Labor Arbitration* (1948), pp. 149-50.

in particular appear quite generally to oppose strikes in violation of contract.

A union, however, has no true authority to enforce consistently a policy of respect for contract. The international officials of a union may all be opposed to wildcat strikes but be in a difficult position to do anything effective with a local union whose elected officials believe that force is desirable and proper. One company, for example, has an acute problem plant where both wildcats and slowdowns are frequent and severe. Most of the grievances causing the difficulties arise over wage incentive production standards and manning.

One such dispute arose a month after a contract had been signed. The contract provided that if the management and union could not agree on a new rate after a reasonable period of time, the management, with notice to the union, would install the new rate and the union might grieve. When management installed these particular protested rates, 200 men walked out. This shut down the entire plant, throwing 5,000 employees out of work. The management appealed to the international president of the union just before the time the 200 men had threatened to walk out.

The international president immediately telephoned the local union president in an effort to prevent the walkout. This appeal was not effective. After the walkout the international president sent what the management described as "the most strongly worded telegram we have ever seen" instructing the workers to get back on the job. The strike continued throughout the week. As soon as possible the international president came to the community, arranged a mass meeting at a football field, and, in management's words, "laid his political head on the block" by giving the workers a severe dressing down. Thereafter the men began to return to work.

A closer look at this problem plant, however, shows very clearly that the workers have gained dramatically in higher incentive earnings and lower work standards by their militancy. They have won concession after concession by strikes, slowdowns, and threats. The local union president is openly militant and is undoubtedly supported by the workers. The international president thus not only chastised the employees for their action but also put himself in the awkward position of appearing to oppose the benefits the workers gained thereby.

In another multiplant company the international union was trying to eliminate wildcats. To a considerable degree this action again put the international officials in conflict with the local union officials. In one incident in this company a local union official had been discharged, and a wildcat was called to revoke the discharge. An international official called a mass meeting. Everyone expected an order to go back to work. But since the international official knew the strike was instigated and led by local officials he told the employees that they should stay out as long as they wanted, but that the people who were keeping them out would be responsible for negotiating the terms under which they returned. There was to be no negotiating help from the international. This approach put the heat on the local leaders, who then broke the wildcat. Again, however, the basic problem of the international was that pressure paid off, and local officials were supported by the employee group.

Contrast these incidents with a problem plant of a different company. In this case management, international union officials, and local officials reached an understanding to abolish wildcats. The management announced a disciplinary policy for wildcats. At the same time the regional director of the international union wrote a strong letter, which the company posted. The letter was to the effect that employees should not expect grievance representation if they walked out. They would be entirely on their own, and the company would be within its rights to impose discipline. Local union officials endorsed the international letter. A minority faction tested the policy with one walkout. Discipline was imposed and not grieved. This change in 1953 ended wildcats in the plant and union-management relations began to improve.

Most unions are in a position where they can be effective in preventing wildcats only if they are acting in support of management policy. The difficulties of the United Rubber Workers in trying to control wildcats unilaterally during World War II showed this very clearly. President Dalrymple obtained authority from the convention to penalize those who engaged in illegitimate stoppages. Although an attempt was made to carry out this policy by expulsion from the union and by fines, it broke down primarily because of lack of management support. Management in particular cases resisted discharging workers expelled from the union and resisted the collection of fines. There were also instances where union members were penalized, but equally guilty nonunion employees received no penalty. The union was forced to abandon a unilateral attempt to control wildcats.

There are, of course, similar problems within a local union. The majority of officers and stewards may be opposed to wildcats, but an elected minority may condone or encourage such action. Informal leaders who are not officials of the union and, in fact, may be in an opposition political group can encourage stoppages to embarrass those in office. The reverse situation occurred in one plant. Informal leaders became disgusted with the use of wildcats by local union officials. Resentment grew because of loss of pay through participation in wildcats. At the next election the union leaders were defeated.

Considering the difficulties of international officials (and local officials) in many situations, it is quite understandable that management frequently encounters resistance from union officials who are asked to intervene. A vice president of one union was quite bitter about one of his experiences. He had intervened, ordered the employees to go back to work, and informed the local officials that they could not get concessions by striking. Immediately thereafter local management made important concessions to get the men to go back to work. In another situation in which management was appealing for help, they were advised to "keep the lines shut down until the men know you are serious, but don't come crying to me for help." This was a plant in which management had been making concessions because of force and threats for many years.

Unions are criticized by management for not insisting on respect for a contract. It is no doubt true that in years past a significant proportion of international officials felt that force was necessary in contract administration. As of today, most international officials clearly do not take this view. While the attitude of the majority of local union officials who are under more immediate pressure from the rank and file can only be surmised, it seems clear that enforcement is a problem in only a minority of locals. Management criticism, however, is in large part misdirected. Maintenance of respect for a contract must rest primarily on management policy, since this is where authority rests, rather than on union policy. At the same time, unions can assist management, and this is the trend. A local union that does not respect its contract is essentially as much of a "problem child" for the international union as it is for the management.

This chapter is closely related to many others in this book since it involves the administration of all parts of the contract. Before the research none of the authors had appreciated the full significance, particularly historically, of the problem of force in contract administration. Distinctions on this point cannot be made between small and large companies; however, there may well have been a difference based on the strength of a company's financial and competitive position. There have also been some differences among international unions as noted, but most union differences were local in character. Of greatest interest, however, have been the clear relation of the use of pressure to the historical development of union-management relations and the changed character of union-management relations in particular companies when pressure tactics are controlled by company policy with union agreement.

23 / The Problem of Grievances

THE ARRANGEMENTS FOR handling grievances have been well described as the heart of union-management contracts. They are the heart because their effectiveness determines in large measure how well the terms of the contract are observed.

Role of Unions in Adjusting Grievances

It is extremely difficult for management to operate a grievance procedure effectively in nonunion plants. In these plants a few individuals may voice complaints or suggest changes, but in general the employees are not heard from, and their complaints rarely go beyond the foremen.[1] Attempts to set up arrangements for handling grievances in plants where there are no unions have generally failed. Many managements have tried it, some by establishing employee representation plans to handle grievances. The employee committees were intended to be safety valves—to prevent the building up of discontent by giving workers a regular and management-approved procedure for bringing their problems to the attention of supervision. A high proportion of them failed. Usually the representation committee was active for a few months, but after a while the employees made less and less use of their committees. Often the meetings with management became purely social affairs, and in many instances the plans ceased to operate.[2] Of the employee representa-

[1] An exception to this generalization is an eastern scientific instrument manufacturer whose employees have asserted their interests and have questioned almost every job description in the job evaluation plan. Because the workers speak out on their own behalf, unions have not been able to organize them. The workers do not feel the need of a union. Several similar exceptions are known to the authors.

[2] The National Industrial Conference Board found that of 715 employee representation plans started prior to 1932, 389 were abandoned during the 13-year period from 1919 to 1932. *Collective Bargaining through Employee Representation* (1933), Table I, p. 16. Of considerable interest is the following observation in the report of the NICB on the activity of employee councils. The report states: "At first they served primarily as grievance boards. The mechanics of the system permitted the employee who harbored a real or fancied grievance to bring it before the council through his representative and

tion plans that survived, most remained in existence only because management went out of its way to stimulate interest in them.

Trade unions change all this. They give the workers machinery for presenting complaints to management, and they protect workers who make complaints from being victimized. Furthermore, unions negotiate contracts that impose obligations on management, thus creating the basis for grievances. Finally, the union itself may be the source of grievances. It may be interested as an organization in enforcing certain parts of the agreement that do not interest the employees. Or the union may seek to enforce an interpretation of the agreement different from that accepted by the workers in the plant. In a few cases the union may stir up grievances as a matter of union policy to harass management or to foster interest in the union. And political rivalries within the union may produce grievances.

Our interest in grievances relates to eight principal topics: (1) the nature of grievances, (2) statistics on grievances, (3) variations in grievance rates, (4) determinants of grievance rates, (5) variations in formal grievance procedures, (6) deviations from formal grievance procedures, (7) the step at which grievances are settled, and (8) the grievance procedure and union-management adjustment.

The first four topics are discussed in this chapter, the other four in the next chapter.

The Nature of Grievances

Fairness and reasonableness on the part of both management and union do not assure that the grievance rate will be low—although

---

secure an unprejudiced hearing. But after a time these matters were disposed of, conditions that may have led to them were corrected, and cases for adjustment by the council steadily diminished. This was the critical period in the council's existence. If nothing of a constructive character was provided to occupy the council's attention, it was likely to drift into disuse ending in abandonment. When, however, its possibilities for bringing management and working force together in united effort for the success of the enterprise were realized, the works council usually made for itself a permanent place in the company organization. As grievances claimed a diminishing share of the council's attention, they were replaced by subjects affecting the operating efficiency of the plant and the general welfare of the employees." The same, pp. 13, 14.

The Conference Board's explanation that the activity of many employee representation plans diminished because the employee councils cleaned up grievances may be questioned. Experience with unions shows that new sources of grievance are constantly arising. A more likely reason for the decline in grievance activity is that the unorganized workers gradually became timid about bringing complaints and that the foremen were increasingly successful in discouraging them.

they assist in the speedy and unemotional settlement of cases. An important reason is that most grievances relate to matters on which reasonable men easily differ. Furthermore, the nature of many grievances is such that unions have a wide choice in the number of grievances they bring; the grievance rate is very much within the control of the union.

Grievances should be distinguished from complaints. Any behavior of the employer that an employee or the union does not like (what he has done or what he has failed to do) may be the basis for a complaint. Some complaints are also grievances. The essence of a grievance is a charge that the union-management contract has been violated. It should be emphasized that the union has great latitude in charging contract violations on almost any complaint. Therefore, it follows that some grievances discussed in the grievance procedure may not be arbitrable. This subject is discussed in the chapter on the arbitration procedure.

Grievances are usually thought of as involving charges by employees or the union against the employers, but occasionally employers have grievances against employees and the union. The latter are rare, however, since management as a rule is able to act on its own interpretations of the union-management contract.

Grievances may be divided into five main groups:

(1) Cases arising out of plain violations of the agreement by the employer. No dispute over the meaning of the agreement or over facts is involved—the employer for some reason (ignorance, carelessness, or some other reason) has simply violated the agreement.

(2) Cases arising essentially out of disagreements over facts, as when a worker is discharged for an offense that he denies having committed. Another example is a charge that an employer altered the working hours of a chef in a cafeteria for the sole purpose of avoiding payment of overtime, in violation of a prohibition in the agreement. The umpire upheld the employer, finding that avoiding payment of overtime was only one of several reasons for changing the chef's working hours. Some agreements prohibit managements from changing "established practices" except under certain conditions. Hence, there may be differences as to what is the established practice in a given department or plant.

(3) Cases in which the essential issue is the meaning of the agreement between the union and the employer. These include cases

where the scope of the agreement is in dispute. Even plainly written agreements may give rise to a multitude of disputes over what the agreement means in specific situations. Included in this group are grievances that arise from omissions in the agreement. For example, an agreement may contain no provision against the employer's contracting out work, but include a wage scale for various occupations. Does inclusion of the wage scale mean that the employer is prohibited from contracting out work done by the crafts for which the agreement includes a wage scale? Must a plant with a tool and die shop and a wage scale for its tool and die workers do all of its own tool and die work? May it abolish its tool and die shop and contract out all of its tool and die work? The job evaluation plan in a plant contains descriptions of the various jobs. Are the descriptions merely a means of identifying the various jobs, or are they a complete and limiting definition of the duties that go with the job? If some duties are added to a job, must the job be re-evaluated? An agreement specifies rates of pay for overtime but is silent on the obligation of employees to work overtime. May the employer require them to do so? The agreement provides that employees who report for work at their regularly scheduled time are guaranteed four hours pay unless the employer has given them a certain number of hours' notice not to come in, or unless he has been prevented from giving work by "an act of God." What is an act of God?

Not infrequently the ambiguities in the union-management contract are deliberate; the language is purposely indefinite because it is all the negotiators can agree to. Making a section of the agreement ambiguous may represent a decision by the negotiators to "pass the buck" to those charged with administering the agreement.

(4) Cases involving the method of applying the agreement. For example, an agreement provides that overtime shall be divided equally among the employees who do a given kind of work. But the agreement does not say during how long a period management must make an equal division of overtime.

(5) Cases involving differences of opinion as to the reasonableness or fairness of various actions. Cases of this sort give the union great discretion in influencing the grievance rate. The union, while admitting that a worker was at fault, may contend that the discipline imposed is too severe. Or workers may complain that a standard is too high or a piece rate too low. In a plant making electrical goods,

production standards may be changed whenever there is a "significant" change in the time required to do the job. There is no agreement on the meaning of "significant," but there is an informal understanding that it means 3 per cent or more. There may be a difference over the evaluation of a newly-created job and of the rate that it should pay. An airline agrees that it will not contract out services unless it is uneconomic or impracticable for the company to do the work. Differences of opinion may easily develop over what is uneconomic or impracticable. In the absence of express provisions in the agreement, does management have the right to impose discipline for failure to meet standards on measured daywork? Under a step rate system based on production, may management reduce the hourly wage of a man who has earned a given rate for good production and then dropped back to a lower level of output?

A common cause for grievance under seniority rules is whether a given worker who would like to be promoted to a vacancy has "sufficient ability" to do the job. What is meant by "sufficient" ability? Is it ability to do the job at once, ability to attain a satisfactory level of output within a week, a month, or some other period, or ability to learn the job? Differences over these issues may go on for years and produce many grievances.

Statistics on Grievances

Many companies keep statistics of grievances—some fairly elaborate ones. A typical detailed compilation will show the grievance rate (grievances in relation to man-hours worked) by plants (or departments); the number of grievances by principal subjects (such as seniority cases, incentive cases, or discipline cases); the proportion of grievances settled at various steps in the grievance procedure; and, in some instances, the proportion of cases settled in favor of the union, the proportion settled in favor of the company, and the proportion compromised. Some companies make periodic reviews of their grievance statistics and try to interpret the figures. This is particularly helpful to managements in preparing for contract negotiations, since it may indicate changes needed in the contract.

Grievance figures can be useful in showing where investigations should be made of union-management relations and in suggesting problems for study. But grievance figures can be very misleading unless one is well aware of the way in which the particular figures are compiled, what they include, what they omit, and what circumstances lie behind them.

Among the limitations of grievance figures are the following:

1. Cases settled orally at the department level between the foreman and steward or committeeman without being reduced to writing are not uniformly classified. Often these cases are not counted at all because no record is made of them. The cases settled orally vary considerably in importance among departments and companies. Where the relations between the union steward and foreman are unusually good, nearly all cases may be settled orally, and the written grievance rate will be low. But in some departments or plants, it may be the practice to put in writing cases that are settled orally, in which case they will appear in the figures on grievances. A steward may try to build up a record of settling cases by insisting that settlements be put in writing. In some cases the union may as a matter of policy instruct its stewards to get settlements in writing. Sometimes supervisors may try to protect themselves by putting them in writing.

2. In a few cases the filing of grievances may not necessarily mean a real complaint. The purpose may be to safeguard the rights of the employees if it is later decided that a real complaint exists. In a steel company for three or four years every wage incentive was questioned. In another steel operation the men had 60 days to question new incentive rates. As 60 days was sometimes too short a period to enable the employee to test the incentive, a grievance was often filed to protect the right to protest. In connection with disputes pertaining to job evaluation, a union automatically filed a grievance whenever a new evaluation was made. In one plant this was done to protect the worker's claim to retroactive pay in case he wished later to challenge the evaluation. The grievances were taken to the third step in the grievance procedure before the union decided whether or not it had a real issue. Changes made in the contract in 1955 to protect the workers' claims to retroactive pay stopped this procedure.

3. When an issue simultaneously affects a number of workers, some unions count the issue as only one grievance since only one question is involved. Others may file separate grievances for each individual affected. Occasionally a union may file a separate case for each day the employer operates in the way that the union challenges. In one company many hundreds of grievances arose over a single issue, namely whether the job descriptions in a job evaluation plan limited the right of the company to assign duties to workers not specifically covered by the job description.

4. If plant or department supervisors gain the impression that grievance rates will be used as a measure of managerial performance,
they will see to it that the grievance statistics show the kind of results that top management desires.

5. The proportion of grievances settled at different stages of the grievance procedure may represent different policies by the union or the
employer. For example, the union under some circumstances may
instruct its shop stewards to settle no grievance at the first stage.
Some politically-ambitious committeemen may object if the department stewards settle cases before they get a chance at them. In one
plant the chairman of the grievance committee, who dominated the
committee, was anxious to be in on as many settlements as possible.
Consequently, he discouraged the settling of cases before the third
step, at which he represented the men.

6. Since grievance rates are the result of a wide variety of conditions,
they cannot be interpreted correctly until the conditions behind
them have been carefully explored. For example, a low grievance
rate does not necessarily mean that relations between the union and
management are good, although it usually has that meaning. But it
may also mean that union representation is weak, and the union is
doing a poor job of policing the agreement. Or a low rate may
mean that union representation is strong and is carefully screening
grievances and refusing to handle weak cases. Nor does a high grievance rate necessarily represent bad relations; it may mean simply
that the union follows the policy of doing the best it can to argue,
with little or no screening, every case that a member brings up.

Variations in Grievance Rates

Grievance rates vary greatly over time, and they vary between
unions (if there are several in the same plant), between departments
and plants of the same company, between companies, and between
occupational groups. In view of the shortcomings of grievance
figures, the real variations in grievance rates may be very different
from those indicated by the figures. Nevertheless, to one familiar
with the conditions in the plants involved, variations in the rates
will provide useful clues to the determinants of grievances. In view
of the lack of standardization in methods of reporting grievances,
only the roughest idea of a typical grievance rate can be suggested.
But a rate of about 10 to 20 grievances per 100 employees per year,
if grievances are written at the first step, is frequently encountered.

Variations Over Periods of Time

It is not unusual, especially among fairly new unions, for a bulge in grievance rates to occur just before periods of contract negotiation. Sometimes the true origin of these grievances is with the rank and file of the union, sometimes with the leaders. The rank and file may stir up certain types of grievances to remind the union negotiators and the management that the men are dissatisfied with certain clauses. The leaders may stir up grievances in order to improve the solidarity of the union and to strengthen their bargaining position. The practice of stirring up grievances as a negotiating tactic tends to disappear as unions grow older and as relations with the employer become more stable.[3]

Union election campaigns frequently produce a rise in grievance rates and, if new local leaders take office, the high rate sometimes continues after the election. A large manufacturer of rubber goods reports a 400 to 500 per cent jump in the grievance rate at one plant after a new union representative came in. In a western steel mill grievances rise sharply after a new grievance man is elected while he pays off his campaign debts. An aluminum manufacturer notes that grievances vary with business conditions, tending to rise in bad years. Important changes in the union-management contract may produce an increase in grievances until the meaning of the changes has been worked out and the methods of applying the contract to plant conditions determined. An increase in the grievance rate in some companies followed new contracts in the automobile industry in 1955. In 1954 the union in one plant decided on a deliberate program to test the new industrial relations director by filing many grievances and refusing to settle with the foremen.

The interest of unions in certain problems rises and falls, and some employers have noted that there have been waves of grievances of certain types. A meat packer, for example, noted a wave of seniority grievances soon after recognition of the union, then a wave relating to wage inequities, and finally one relating to work standards. The efforts of a maker of rubber goods to tighten up on production standards that had been allowed to become loose during the

[3] In the plant of an airplane manufacturer there was a tendency for grievances to decline during periods of negotiation because of the preoccupation of local union officers with negotiations.

war and to change from the Bedaux system of incentives to a standard hour plan led temporarily to bad relations and enough grievances to produce a one-week strike.

Variations Between Occupational Groups

Some companies report a much lower grievance rate among the crafts (who usually do repair and maintenance work) than among production workers. The crafts as a rule are on daywork rather than incentives or standards of production, and they are less affected by layoffs and changes in methods of production than are the production workers. Those three sources of grievances, therefore, usually affect the crafts much less than they do the production workers. But there are some plants (especially in the steel industry) where the desire of the crafts to be put on incentives has produced a concentration of grievances among the craftsmen. And the crafts often have grievances growing out of their jurisdictional claims.

Variations Among Unions

Unions pursue different policies toward grievances. In general the newer industrial unions are much more aggressive than the older AFL unions in stirring up grievances. The older unions as a rule assert more national influence over the affairs of new locals and discourage local political factionalism. The newer unions give the locals more autonomy. This has usually meant greater influence in rank and file and more factional rivalries. The result has been higher grievance rates in the new CIO unions than in the old AFL unions. A multiplant manufacturer of electrical goods, dealing in different plants with recently organized locals of the International Association of Machinists, the International Brotherhood of Electrical Workers, the International Union of Electrical Workers, and the United Electrical Workers, found far lower grievance rates in the plants represented by the first two unions than in those represented by the last two. During 1955, for example, the grievance rate in plants represented by the machinists was 2.2 per 100 employees; in plants represented by the International Brotherhood of Electrical Workers, 5.7; in plants represented by the International Union of Electrical Workers, 11.4; and in plants represented by the United Electrical Workers, 12.3.

A meat packer reports that in 1954 grievance rates per 100 employees were 16.0 in plants represented by the United Packinghouse Workers of America (CIO); 6.8 in plants represented by an independent union; and 2.0 in plants represented by the old AFL union, the Amalgamated Meat Cutters and Butcher Workmen of North America.[4] A large manufacturer of electrical equipment contrasts its relations with the IBEW, which are good in all plants, with those with the IUE, which are less satisfactory but which have recently been improving. The industrial relations director of a container manufacturer with many plants points out that in his company differences between local unions are greater than differences between nationals—although the older unions from the former AFL that have recently come into some of the company's plants have lower grievance rates than the steelworkers' union from the old CIO. But the industrial relations director did not find fault with the steelworkers—in fact, he commended, on the whole, its handling of grievances.

Variations Among Plants

Differences in grievance rates in different plants of the same company represented by the same national union may be remarkably wide. Among 9 plants in a company represented by the International Union of Electrical Workers, the rate for the year 1955 varied from a low of 1 per 100 employees (in a fairly large plant) to 55.4 per 100 in a somewhat smaller plant. Among 14 plants in a steel manufacturing company, the rate averaged about 15 grievances per million man-hours, with a range from no grievances to 35 or 40 per million man-hours in 2 or 3 plants. A manufacturer of window glass reports that one plant has more grievances than all its others combined.

Determinants of Grievance Rates

The most striking finding from a review of grievance rates in many plants is that the satisfaction of individual workmen has rela-

---

[4] These differences in grievance rates are also reflected in the arbitration experience of the several unions. The CIO, with 25 plants in the company, had 129 arbitrations between 1943 and 1955. In only 4 plants were there no arbitrations. The meat cutters and butcher workmen (AFL), with 13 plants, had 13 arbitrations. In 9 AFL plants out of 13 there were no arbitrations. The independent union, with 16 plants, had 59 arbitrations. In 4 plants the independent had no arbitrations.

The company was upheld in two-thirds of the arbitrations, the union in one-third.

tively little to do with the grievance rate. The chief determinants appear to be organizational and institutional conditions. An exceptionally low grievance rate does not necessarily mean that employees are satisfied with conditions, and an exceptionally high rate does not mean that they are very dissatisfied. When very low or very high grievance rates are found, they are usually associated with one or more of the following conditions: (1) The state of relations between the union and the employer, (2) the experience of the union and the employer in dealing with each other, (3) the personalities of key union and company representatives, (4) methods of plant operation, especially methods of wage payment, (5) changes in operating methods or conditions, (6) union policies, (7) union politics, (8) grievance adjustment procedures, and (9) management policies.

Of the several influences on the grievance rate, grievance adjustment procedures and management policies are of the greatest importance because they have most to do with determining the results of filing grievances. If the employees find that they get good results from filing grievances, they will file a great many; if filing grievances does not pay off, few will be filed. Let us examine each of the principal determinants of grievance rates.

Union-Employer Relations

In the first chapter it was pointed out that management and unions have adjusted to each other in widely differing degrees. In some cases the two have achieved about the kind of relationship that each desires, and in many instances this relationship is one that tends to minimize grievances and facilitate their settlement. In other cases, the two sides are in disagreement over important issues and thus fail to achieve harmonious relations.[5] Relations may be good in some departments but bad in others, and in multiplant companies there may be great differences among plants.

In general, friendly relations make for a low grievance rate and bad relations for a high grievance rate. Good relations make for low rates because employees are less inclined to raise technicalities and do not bring cases for the purpose of arousing militancy among the

[5] The state of relations between the union and management reflects many of the specific influences (such as union policies or management policies) that determine the grievance rate. However, it is useful to consider this factor as a separate influence on the grievance rate, because the state of relations is not entirely the result of other conditions that directly affect grievances.

union members or harassing management; also employees are better able to settle their complaints orally with foremen. Bad relations produce high grievance rates for the opposite reasons. The union stirs up grievances to strengthen the solidarity of the union and to harass management; and foremen are less willing to settle cases, so a larger proportion are reduced to writing and appealed.

A low grievance rate does not always mean, however, that relations are good, and a high rate does not necessarily mean that they are bad. Sometimes a low grievance rate accompanies bad union-management relations. This is the situation in one plant of a large machine tool maker. This manufacturer recently defeated the machinists' union in a long strike. The company has an incentive system, and such systems often lead to a good many grievances. Too, it has had extensive layoffs, which also often produce a bulge in grievances. Nevertheless, grievances in this company are few, partly because relations between many old-time employees and supervisors are good, but mainly because the management is tough and the defeat of the union in the strike has left the union too weak to do an effective job of challenging the foremen. A low grievance rate may also indicate only that many grievances are not adjusted through the formal grievance procedure.

Just as low grievance rates do not invariably mean good relations or good conditions, so high grievance rates do not invariably mean bad relations. A high grievance rate may accompany good relations because the union does not screen cases or because the particular operating conditions produce a good many problems and differences of opinion. Where the parties are judicious and are experienced in dealing with each other, these problems and differences may produce grievances without producing bad relations. A fairly high grievance rate may accompany good relations simply because an unusually large proportion of cases reach the written stage and hence get counted because of company or union policy. For example, technological or managerial changes may be producing a number of problems that need to be resolved above the foreman-shop steward level.

Degree of Experience of the Parties

Sometimes the most significant determinant of the grievance rate is the amount of experience union and management have had in dealing with each other. One side or both may take unreasonable positions simply because they do not know what is reasonable. The result is certain to be more grievances. When a union is new, it may lack leaders who are willing and able to distinguish between complaints that charge violations of the union-management contract and those that do not. In the new stamping plant of an automobile company the inexperienced leaders of the new local union wrote up grievances for anyone who had a complaint regardless of whether a violation of the contract was involved; and the management, which lacked a settled labor policy, allowed these complaints to be handled through the regular grievance procedure. Eventually a change in local management led to new policies with grievances being screened on the basis of whether or not they charged violations of the agreement. Screening of 180 grievances that had reached the third step led management to conclude that only 18 had merit. All but these 18 were denied. At the first review board meeting under new management 14 out of 32 grievances on the agenda were withdrawn. But it was necessary for management to take a firm stand under threat of a wildcat strike to convince the union that it would not yield to pressure.

In a New England rubber company because of inexperience the union complained about all problems that came to its attention. As a result, much time was spent in arguing whether the worker had a grievance under the contract. When all the union shop stewards are inexperienced and have not yet had the opportunity to win acceptance from the rank and file, they do not have the inclination or the ability to go very far in screening the complaints of the workers. The national union helped to correct this by conducting courses on how to handle grievances and, at the same time, stressed the importance of living up to the contract.

Personalities of Management and Local Union Officials

Often policies are less a decision of a group than an expression of the personality of a strong individual. In those cases industrial relations are being molded more by personalities than by policies.

The industrial relations manager of a company with some sixty operating units says that problem plants usually reflect faults on both sides. The company had to ask the union to remove a district director in Ohio who was causing a considerable amount of trouble.

Plant managers have been transferred because of their inability to deal effectively with the union. Often they make good with a fresh start. Many dramatic examples can be given of drastic changes in labor relations and hence in grievance activity following changes in management. In an important machine tool manufacturing company the retirement of the president and his replacement by his son resulted in new policies and in a great improvement in union-management relations. Changes in top management (the vice president in charge of operations and the general superintendent) in a large meat packing company produced new industrial relations policies. In a plant making containers, grievances were affected by the ignorance and weakness of the local union president, who was not able to inform employees when they did not have a case. A manufacturer of electrical equipment, where there was a shift from the United Electrical Workers to the International Union of Electrical Workers, says that the local IUE leadership is less aggressive than was the UE leadership. In a steel mill that had no grievances from 1948 through 1955 the cause seems to have been a weak manager, who was always ready to yield under union pressure, and a strong union chief committeeman, who used walkouts and slowdowns to force concessions from management. The chief steward was a master at using the slowdown. A high grievance rate in an eastern plate glass plant seems to have been due in considerable measure (though not entirely) to a tough local union president. On the other hand, part of the explanation of the lowest grievance rate among the plants of the same company (in a plant in the Middle West) seems to have been the local union president, who had been in office (until recently defeated) for ten years.

Methods of Plant Operation

The use of wage incentive plans introduces a source of grievances that does not exist under ordinary daywork. Every piece rate or every production standard used to determine bonus payments is likely to be challenged. Furthermore, when straight daywork is paid but employees are expected to meet standards of production, new standards are likely to be questioned. Piecework and bonus plans produce differences in the earnings of different individuals or groups that may be regarded as inequities and so give rise to grievances.

Some companies that have installed plans to enlist organized cooperation from unions in increasing production and reducing costs report a low rate of grievances. A maker of automobile parts with 700 employees reports that in the first eleven months of operation under a plan of organized cooperation know as the Scanlon Plan (to be discussed in Chapter 28), there was not a single written grievance. In this company cooperation with management was stimulated by fear of the workers that the company might not be able to remain in business. The workers themselves have assumed much of the responsibility of seeing that each member of the force works at a proper pace and does not waste time away from the job, thus reducing the need for management to impose discipline and cutting the possibility of grievances over discipline. The interest of the workers in getting as large a bonus as possible has led them to discourage individuals from claiming wage inequities.

Changes in Methods of Operation

Change is likely to be viewed with suspicion if not fear, and new conditions may be regarded as unreasonable simply because they differ from those the workers are used to. Periods of change in methods of operation thus are likely to produce grievances. In an airplane manufacturing plant grievances have been produced by changes in job specialization as production rises and falls. When it rises, men are specialized to a greater extent; when it declines, duties are added to many jobs. Either change produces an increase in grievances because workers question what they are supposed to do. Where specialization is reduced, they may argue that the added duties require a re-evaluation of the job. In the same plant the Korean War brought a large number of grievances based on the charge that foremen were doing work belonging to men in the bargaining unit. The large numbers of inexperienced employees and changes in the interior construction of planes made it necessary for foremen to help assemblers who were learning the work. Although the foremen's work represented instruction, it was protested in grievances. In a paper mill the engineer who ran the railroad from the pulp wood yard to the mill demanded a re-evaluation of his job when a second locomotive was added for use when the first locomotive was out of repair.

Technological changes and changes in managerial methods and policies raise questions as to the application of the union-management contract under new conditions. Such questions are particularly likely to arise, of course, in plants where wages are based on productivity. A large manufacturer of cans that has been tightening up production standards and rates reports that standards are the second most frequent general cause of grievances, in spite of the fact that 99 per cent of the standards are accepted. Even under daywork, however, changes that produce new jobs or change the content of jobs raise questions as to rates of pay. And changes that require transfers, promotions, or layoffs are likely to raise issues that produce grievances. Companies that find their costs out of line with costs of competitors and take steps to correct this are likely to make many changes that produce grievances.

Union Policy

There are three principal policies toward grievances—a policy of fostering grievances, a policy of neither encouraging nor discouraging the raising of grievances, and a policy of discouraging the bringing of grievances. In view of the many possibilities for differences over the precise meaning of agreements or over the precise way in which agreements should be applied, and in view of the many cases in which the issue is one of the fairness or reasonableness of management's action, the volume of grievances is very much determined by union policy. The union, if it wants, can tell its stewards and committeemen to seek out and thereby bring far more cases than the employees would if left to make their own decisions. Or the union can screen complaints carefully either at the beginning or at later stages. If the union is disinclined to push weak cases, members will be discouraged from bringing them. The union can thus make the grievance rate high or low, with no necessary relationship to employee satisfaction.[6]

---

[6] Do unions in general tend to mirror the state of mind of the employees or run counter to it? In other words, when employees are contented, do unions let well enough alone, or do they try to stir up grievances? When dissatisfaction is rife, do unions try to raise the grievance rate? The answers to these questions are not known. Unions apparently are often content to represent the employees without changing their attitudes, but instances in which unions either try to stir up discontent or to eliminate discontent and the use of pressure tactics are not infrequent. Newly organized employees often learn to live under union-management contracts through persuasion by the union to avoid the use of pressure tactics. (See the discussion of this topic in Chapter 22.)

A wide variety of conditions influence the policy that unions choose to pursue with respect to grievances. In some plants a low grievance rate may simply reflect the fact that the union is inactive, with no local or regional leadership to stir it up and no causes to move it to action. The union shop sometimes leads to inactivity because both the national and local officers feel no need to stimulate interest in the organization. Among the plants of a maker of electrical goods with an average grievance rate of 10.5 per 100 employees in 1955 one plant had a grievance rate of 2.4 per 100. Asked for an explanation, the central personnel office of the company said that the local union is completely ineffective. The international has made no effort to stimulate the interest of the members in the union.

In general, as was pointed out above, the newer CIO unions have been more aggressive in pushing grievances than have the older AFL unions. Some newer unions have pushed grievances in order to win the support of the members by showing them what the union can do for them; the better-established AFL unions have felt less need of demonstrating their effectiveness. Some Communist-led unions tried to harass management as part of a policy of building a spirit of revolt among the workers. Some unions have been led to be aggressive in fostering grievances by the simple discovery that it works— that management, inexperienced in dealing with unions and impressed by union pressure, will yield. Thus the union can impose on management its ideas of what the agreement should mean or of what is fair or reasonable. In some cases, aggressive union grievance activity may be a natural response to similar activity by management. In one case the employer was convinced that the union was running a sort of contest among the stewards to see which one could produce the most grievances.

In some instances, when the national officers of a union believe that relations between the local and the company are too friendly, they send in a national representative to stir things up. The steelworkers sent a national representative into the southern operations of a steel company because the national believed that relations between the local and the management were too close. Since the national representative has come in, there have been a large number of grievances. The automobile workers sent a representative to change the policies of a local in an eastern stamping plant that had come under the domination of an aggressive local industrial relations manager. The latter was alleged to have controlled the local through a block of displaced persons to whom he had given jobs in the plant.

A high grievance rate may be produced when a strong union in a plant with incentives determines to reject time studies and to drive for the best rate it can get on each new or changed job, regardless of the effect on the rate structure. In the Cleveland plant of a large manufacturer of automobile parts there were 40 to 50 grievances, practically all time study cases, at every meeting of the grievance committee. The company finally took a nine-week strike in order to get rid of the incentive system.

The policy of not encouraging grievances, which is found in many unions, may result from a variety of conditions. In a few instances the union may discourage grievances in order to help management reduce costs and remain competitive with rival companies paying lower wages. In other cases, the union may be discouraged from carrying cases beyond the oral stage (where no record of the cases are made) because the management has a firm policy of settling on liberal terms at the oral stage all the cases that it is prepared to concede, and is adamant in refusing concessions (even to the point of going to arbitration) on all cases where it feels the union position is weak. Finally in some plants the union may be discouraged from bringing grievances simply because management is quite definitely in control, is unyielding, and is unwilling to consent to arbitration.

At the plant of a manufacturer of electrical goods it is the policy of the union (IBEW) to take up to the third step grievances that employees feel strongly about. But grievances are not written before the third step. Hence, although there may be many grievances handled, they do not appear in the statistics. For all of the company's unionized plants in 1955 the grievance rate was 10.5 per 100 employees; in this plant it was 5.3.[7] The willingness of the union to handle all cases up to a certain step has resulted in its simultaneously presenting two conflicting grievances. For example, it presented two claims to a vacant job, one on behalf of the most senior employee to bid for the job, who claimed it by virtue of his seniority, and the other on behalf of the most junior bidder, who claimed the job on

[7] After the second step the union business agent talks over the grievance with the personnel supervisor, and if the employee has no case, the business agent will try to dissuade the employee from taking his case higher.

the basis of ability gained through more experience at this particular work.

The policy of the union toward technological and managerial changes has much to do with the grievance rate. In the eastern plant of an electric storage battery manufacturer, the union's policy of strongly resisting changes was abandoned when a new plant manager (in whom the union had confidence) succeeded in convincing it that reductions in costs were needed to keep the plant competitive. The result was a great drop in the number of grievances. In this plant the fact that the union was given an opportunity to work with management in constructing a job evaluation plan has tended to reduce grievances on this subject. When a worker complains of the classification of his job, a union official hands the employee the job evaluation manual and says: "We studied your job carefully and came up with an answer that you think is wrong. Why don't you take this manual, study it, and rate your job?" In most cases rating of his job by the employee ends his grievance.

Union Politics and the Nature of Union Government

Since union policy has much to do with grievance rates, so does the union political system. Some of the older unions have adopted the practice of having the shop stewards in many new locals appointed either by the local union executive committee or by the union business agent or the union national representative. In new IBEW locals in the plants of a large manufacturer of electrical goods, for example, the stewards are appointed by the international representative. The international picks good men and gets rid of poor men.[8] In the local unions of the newer national unions (especially the national unions formed since 1933) the stewards are nearly always elected by their constituents. Elected stewards may mean more grievances than appointed ones since they may seek to win support by urging workers to make claims, and since the elected stewards may be less disposed to tell workers with weak cases that their claims stand little chance.[9] When stewards are elected, the term of the election may

[8] The company does not think that the method of appointment results in a disadvantage to the rank and file.
[9] But management policy has much to do with the behavior of stewards. If management stands firm against weak claims, stewards will learn not to disappoint workers by helping them to make claims that they are pretty certain to lose.

affect the union policy toward grievances. The California Metal Trades, which deals with both the boilermakers' and the machinists' unions, attributes the lower grievance rate among the boilermakers to the fact that the business agents of the boilermakers are elected for four years, and those of the machinists for one year. The boiler-maker representatives are more inclined to tell their members when they are wrong.

Political conditions at the top of the local, such as rivalries for the presidency or for places on the union grievance committee (the committeemen are usually one stage above the stewards), affect grievance activity. A very stable situation at the Illinois plant of a plate glass manufacturer, where the union president had held office for ten years, seems to account in part for the fact that this plant had the lowest grievance rate among the company's eight plate glass plants. In an elevator construction company, the director of industrial relations thinks that the key determinant of the grievance rate is the local leadership. Among the engineers in the New York offices (members of the UAW) the former officers of the local conducted a "hate company" campaign. They dug up a larger number of grievances. But conditions changed when the officers were replaced by a more reasonable group of leaders, who won election by opposing the campaign.

The older national unions as a general rule have developed stronger influence with their local unions than have the newer ones. The influence of the national is usually toward orderly handling of grievances. A large manufacturer of cans contrasts the steelworkers' union and the machinists as to administrative control. The machinists have a national vice president who looks after their locals in the can plants. If there are difficulties, he goes in quickly and establishes order. There is no comparable control by the steelworkers.

Rivalries between unions are likely to start the leaders of the rival unions seeking to gain the favor of the workers by stimulating grievances.[10] The plant with by far the highest grievance rate of many in a company manufacturing electrical equipment (55.4 per 100 employees against an average of 10.5 per 100 for all plants) was one with keen rivalry between the IUE and the UE. The IUE had displaced the UE as bargaining representative of the workers, but the leaders

---

[10] The leaders of a union that is seeking bargaining rights may try to stir up grievances that the recognized union cannot settle.

of the local UE remained in the plant and were anxious to persuade the workers to switch their membership back.

When a man is elected president of a local union by a small margin, his position on grievances is likely to be affected, at least until he improves his political position. In a can manufacturing company the man elected president of a local by a small margin in June 1956 told management that he was aware of the responsibilities that went with the job but hoped that management saw his problems and would be patient. The former president of the local was an ignorant chap who said "No" to management because he was afraid to say "Yes."

Grievance Adjustment Procedure

Grievance rates are affected by the arrangements for handling grievances. A high ratio of union representatives to employees, payment to stewards and committeemen, and absence of time limitations and other controls on the activity of representatives encourage a high grievance rate. This subject is further discussed in Chapter 24. With loose controls, stewards and committeemen can find ways of spending virtually all of their time away from their jobs on grievances. Furthermore, a certain amount of competition is stirred up for these jobs, which encourages the stewards and committeemen to find grievances.

Some concerns in the automobile and automotive parts industries have full-time committeemen paid by the companies. This arrangement is generally believed to foster grievances. The full-time committee jobs are regarded as attractive by many employees, and rivalry for them causes workers to hunt for grievances. The industrial relations manager of a plant of an automobile manufacturer said: "Full-time committeemen give management a lot more grievances than there would otherwise be. All that the committeeman has to do is to walk around the plant and look for grievances. He is virtually invited to produce them." An automobile parts manufacturer attributes difficulties in one of its several plants to the existence of a full-time union shop committee paid by the company and with freedom to roam around the shop, to talk with any employee, and to check up on the operations of the plant and the work of the supervisors. The management believes that the committee has stirred up many grievances that otherwise would not have arisen. The aggressive action of the committee resulted in the abdication of supervision by the foremen. In 1955 the company took a nine-week strike in order (among other things) to limit the authority of the committee and succeeded in getting two restrictions placed on the activity of the members: an employee must request the presence of a committee-man, and the committeeman must get the foreman's permission before he is allowed in any department of the plant.[11] A large manufacturer of farm equipment was able in 1955 to negotiate changes in the grievance procedure that greatly reduced the opportunity for activity by union committeemen.[12] The grievance procedure was reduced from three steps to two. In the first the grievance is considered by the employee with or without his department steward and a general foreman or other representative designated by management; in the second the grievance is considered by a committee of union and management representatives. The committeeman may be called in by the steward at step one, but he no longer handles grievances as an individual at a middle step in the procedure.

Management Policies and Methods

Management policy is an important determinant of the grievance rate because it largely determines how worthwhile it is for the union to bring grievances. Management policy affects both the number of grievances and the ways in which grievances are settled. This discussion will relate to the effect of management policy on the number of grievances.

Sometimes management adopts policies that are intended to reduce grievances; often the effect is unintended and indirect, though nonetheless important. So immense is the variety of management policies or the forms of management behavior that the effects of only

[11] The company believes that it must get rid of the full-time union committee, but it regarded the restrictions imposed on the activities of the committeemen after the 1955 strike as a big step forward. The company was surprised that up to March 6, 1956, the grievance load had not declined since the restrictions were imposed. The company's surprise seems unwarranted. With 50 to 70 shop stewards under the committeemen, there is no reason to expect the restrictions to reduce the number of grievances as long as the committeemen want many grievances.

[12] A minority view is expressed by the able manager of industrial relations of an automotive parts manufacturer that operates with full-time committeemen selected by a strong local of the UAW. Full-time committeemen are less disrupting to operations than part-time committeemen who are frequently called away from their jobs. The full-time committeemen are also kept busy on useful welfare work of various kinds. They welcome these responsibilities.

a few of the most important can be discussed. The following have been selected for discussion:

a. Taking a firm stand but refusing to back it up in the face of union threats of wildcat strikes, slowdowns, refusal to work overtime, and other forms of economic pressure,
b. taking a firm stand and holding to it in the face of actual or threatened economic pressure,
c. taking a carefully analyzed, reasonable stand but yielding in the face of actual or threatened pressure,
d. taking a carefully analyzed, reasonable stand, arguing strongly for it, and not abandoning it in the face of arguments or economic pressure,
e. seeking to avoid differences by consulting with the union before making changes; then taking a stand and not abandoning it in response to pressure, and
f. seeking to operate outside the agreement.

The first two types of management policy are most likely to be found in the early stages of the union-employer relationship, and they tend to disappear as the parties gain experience, for the simple reason that they do not work well. Furthermore, the last of these six policies is likely to be temporary. If it works at all, its success is likely to be due to the personality of some manager who commands great confidence among the workers and whose ways of doing things are not challenged by them.

POLICY (A). This policy calls for taking a firm stand but refusing to back it up in the face of actual or threatened economic pressure by the union. It is surprising how many managements follow this practice. A firm stand is one that resolves most doubts in favor of the company, imposes discipline or production standards that most people would regard as quite stiff, and interprets the agreement in a legalistic way that favors the company. These types of behavior are found most frequently in the early years of a union-management relationship—especially in companies that were strongly anti-union before they were organized and that have strong fears of unions. But strong opposition to unions and fear of them does not assure that the company will take a firm stand when the union threatens slow-downs, wildcat strikes, or other forms of economic pressure. The company may give in later because it is making large profits or because the management fears that an interruption to production will cause the loss of important customers. But domiration of industrial relations policy by the sales department usually does not last for many years because managements gradually learn that it is expensive to yield to union pressures. Hence the policy of being tough but yielding ordinarily does not last, but has persisted in some relationships for a surprisingly long period.

An example of this type of policy is provided by a large chemical company. The company for several years after being organized had no industrial relations experts. Top management had an excessive fear of the union's power and doubted its ability to deal with the union. When unilateral action provoked grievances and threats, a vice president was rushed to the plant to persuade the local management to yield. When the union discovered that protests and threats worked, it did not hesitate to use them further. The situation was later changed when the company hired a highly competent industrial relations executive who insisted that the company weigh all aspects of problems carefully before taking a stand and that, having taken a position, it refuse to yield to pressure.

POLICY (B). Under this policy management takes a firm stand and holds to it in the face of actual or threatened economic pressure. A large meat packer is an example. The fight against the union, which had gone on for years before the company was organized, did not cease when the union was recognized and a union-management contract was signed. Management continued to raise technicalities in interpretation. Foremen regarded it as their duty to fight the union at every opportunity.[13]

A firm policy, not backed up by a strong stand, is bound to produce many grievances, but the effect of a tough policy and a tough stand cannot be predicted. Firm positions taken by management tend to provoke many protests and grievances; but the refusal of management to listen to arguments or to yield to threats discourages workers from making complaints that they strongly feel.

Management may take a tough and unyielding position because

---

[13] The following example shows the extremes to which management pushed its interpretation of the contract. The health and accident plan provided that an employee was not entitled to sickness and accident compensation if he was out on personal leave of absence. An employee took such leave to have a tooth pulled. Returning from the doctor's office he slipped and broke a leg. He was denied sickness and accident compensation because he was out on personal leave of absence. The incident stirred up the entire plant

it fears that the union through bargaining up rates on individual jobs, introducing uneconomic shop practices, or preventing improvements in methods will make the company noncompetitive.[14] A source of grievances over a job classification in a factory making receiving tubes was the extreme cost consciousness of management. Because of competitive pressures management was reluctant to upgrade new and changed jobs. More and more duties were added to jobs as a result of technological change and management policy, but management resisted appropriate reclassifications. Indeed, managment contended in some instances that the job had simply become less specialized rather than more exacting.

POLICY (C). Here management takes a carefully-analyzed, reasonable stand but yields in the face of actual or threatened pressure. A policy of yielding to strike threats encourages protests and complaints even when management takes a reasonable stand. Whether the complaints show up in the grievance statistics depends on the stage at which they are settled. If management yields at the first stage so that the complaint is settled orally, it does not ordinarily show up in the grievance figures. But if the yielding occurs at a level or two above the foreman, the complaints encouraged by management's soft policy show up as grievances. In such cases the policy of appeasement produces a high grievance rate. The coke plant of a large company in New Jersey is an example. This has been a very profitable plant, and local management has been unwilling to take a strike or even a firm position. When the men struck against a disciplinary layoff, the management withdrew the discipline in order to get the men back to work. The company's manager of industrial relations at the national level was not even informed of the incident. The division manager and the division director of industrial relations make no effort to change conditions.[15] A steel mill went from 1948 to 1955

---

[14] The reverse effects of competitive pressure should be noted. In some cases competitive pressure may lead a company to take a tough stand and hold to it firmly; in other cases competition may lead the company to yield to union threats. Which effect is produced depends on the nature of the competition. When competition is a matter of costs and prices, it encourages a firm stand in support of tough conditions. But when competition is in large part a matter of service and continuity of deliveries is important in holding customers, it tends to produce a policy of appeasement—as the experience of the automotive parts industry shows.

[15] But in 1953 the company did take a three-months strike and as a result got some improvement in the highly restrictive terms of its union contract.

without a written grievance because the local management pursued a policy of appeasement. Top management in Pittsburgh was not aware of this and considered the plant a model of union-management relations.

POLICY (D). Under this policy the company takes a carefully-analyzed, reasonable stand and holds to it firmly in the face of arguments or economic pressure. This policy does not mean that the management will not listen to arguments and will not change its stand if convinced that the stand was based upon an erroneous view of the facts or that the logic of its stand is faulty. But there is a vital difference between listening to arguments and yielding to economic pressure, such as slowdowns, refusal to work overtime, and wildcat strikes. The policy of being fair but firm usually produces a low grievance rate— or at least a lower rate than does a policy of yielding in the face of threats.

At the chemical company described above as originally pursuing a policy of toughness combined with yielding, it was necessary for the new director of industrial relations to threaten to resign if top management reversed the stand he took with the union.[16] A steel producer pursues a "fair but firm" policy by referring all grievances that reach the written stage to a review board at the national personnel office, which considers carefully the foreman's answer. Unless the review board feels that chances of winning the case before arbitration are at least 80-20, the matter is referred back to the plant management and the foreman for reconsideration. But once the foreman's stand is taken, he is backed up at all stages. One effect of this careful review and screening has been greatly to reduce the number of grievances.

A manufacturer of cans limited disputes over standards of production by careful staff work plus the policy of waiting for important technological changes before introducing new standards. The new manager of a plant that had had a bad grievance record improved the situation by treating the employees fairly and liberally. He did this in the expectation that the employees would respond by working with management to raise productivity and by not resisting changes if their nature and the reasons for them had been explained to the

---

[16] A reversal occurred soon after the new director of industrial relations began his duties. It did not happen again.

union well in advance. The confidence of the manager in the workers turned out to be justified. The success of his policy was due to his obvious sincerity, to his warm and outgoing personality, which helped convince men of his sincerity, and to the fact that as a supervisor in the assembly department of the plant he was well known to the employees.

POLICY (E). Managements following this policy seek to avoid differences by consulting with the union before making changes, then take a stand and do not abandon it in response to pressure. This policy is the same as Policy (D) with consultation added.

Some managements fear that the practice of informing or consulting the union about changes will be regarded as an invitation to veto their decisions and will eventually limit management's freedom of action. Such was the view of the management of a battery manufacturer which, up until several years ago, avoided advance disclosure of plans to the union. The long-term trend, however, seems to be for managements to give unions advance information on plans and to consult with union officers on problems. Although union officers ordinarily and quite properly refuse to share responsibility for changed management practices or policies, they are usually willing to offer advice. The policy of informing and consulting with union leaders tends to reduce the number of grievances because it eliminates fears and uncertainties and because it helps management work out plans and procedures that are satisfactory to the workers. The battery manufacturer referred to aggravated its difficulties by avoiding advance discussion with the union. Abandonment of this policy of reticence by a new management, in conjunction with other more important changes in management policy, improved relations greatly, and led to a drop in the number of grievances. The new plant manager expressed the view that many of the grievances could have been avoided had the management explained the reasons for its actions to the union beforehand.

A manufacturer of valves found a great contrast between the majority of the plants of the company, where the men were kept well informed, and one of the plants, in which management failed to explain what industrial engineers and time-study men were doing. In the latter plant lack of information led to unfounded rumors, ferment, and dissatisfaction. The director of industrial relations at the company level expressed the view that uncertainty due to lack of information was the real underlying cause for most grievances in the trouble-ridden plant.

The personnel supervisor in one of the plants of a manufacturer of electrical equipment is convinced that his policy of close consultation with the union has eliminated many grievances and has enabled management to secure employee acceptance of many changes. In 1955 the rate of grievances reaching the written stage, was 5.3 per 100 employees compared with an average of 10.5 per 100 employees in the 20 unionized plants of the company. Only three grievances reached the fourth step between 1946 and 1956. The plant personnel supervisor consults with the business agent of the union before making any major decision. In addition the local plant management holds monthly meetings with the union's local executive board. Before an important change is made in any department, the union steward is told of it insofar as it affects the employees. The management believes that informing the stewards gives them a feeling of importance and prepares them to answer the workers' questions.

POLICY (F). Management here seeks to operate outside the agreement. One of the important accomplishments of trade unions has been the acceleration of the inevitable long-run shift from personal management to management based on rules and policies. But in a few rare cases personal management survives even under a trade union agreement. Sometimes this happens without stirring up an unusual number of grievances based on the agreement. An example is in one of the twenty union plants of a maker of electrical goods. This plant specializes in developing new products that are later moved to other plants. The manager feels that he should operate without restrictions from the union, and he runs the plant largely outside the terms of the contract. At the fourth step in the grievance procedure, at which a representative of central personnel sits in, the representative from central personnel frequently has to argue against the stand of the local manager. In spite of the fact that the union has a militant tradition, the grievance rate is about average—in 1955 it was 9.4 per 100 employees compared with an average of 10.5 per 100 employees for all plants. The people have confidence in the manager, and this enables him to do things the workers would not tolerate from other managers.

This analysis makes it plain that the grievance rate is largely a product of the behavior of organizations and institutions. Hence, an explanation of the grievance rate requires an exploration of all of the complex variables discussed in the chapter. The next chapter will consider the formal grievance adjustment procedures worked out by the parties and the problems involved in the operation of these procedures.

24 / Adjustment of Grievances

HOW ARE GRIEVANCES actually handled in industry? What are the usual steps in disposing of grievances? How does the machinery actually work, and what conditions determine how it works? What are the trends in the development of machinery for handling grievances? What are some of the principal problems that have arisen in handling grievances? These are some of the principal questions that are examined in the present chapter, which focuses attention on the actual operation of arrangements for handling grievances.

Grievances were classified in the previous chapter into five types: (1) plain violation of the agreement, (2) disagreement over facts, (3) disagreement over the meaning of the agreement, (4) disagreement over the method of applying the agreement, and (5) disagreement over the reasonableness or fairness of various measures. While a particular grievance may not fall readily into a single category, the distinction among issues of fact, issues of language, and issues in the determination of reasonableness and fairness in applying necessarily general language is important. It should also be clear that the seriousness of grievances, particularly of the last three types, varies with the degree of mutual understanding that has been achieved. Some parties have succeeded in reaching a high degree of mutual understanding in many substantive areas, thus minimizing so-called policy grievances. In other cases a large proportion of grievances involve serious disputes with a low degree of mutual understanding, and the machinery functions poorly. Also in some relationships a large proportion of complaints are converted into charges of contract violation and become grievances. In other words, the mechanics of the grievance procedure is in many respects subordinate to considerations already discussed.

Variations in Formal Grievance Procedures

In a broad sense the formal grievance procedures found in various labor agreements are very similar. Since they are appeal procedures, there are always several steps involved. Usually there are two lower steps and one or two higher steps followed by arbitration. The lower steps are the first line supervision step and one appeal. The one appeal may be to line or staff or to both line and staff, but in any case there is close association with operating officials and conditions. Those involved in lower-step discussions may be: one or more employees, foremen, general foremen, superintendents, labor relations representatives, stewards, committeemen, chief stewards, district committeemen, and similar company and union officials. Grievances involving established policy and precedent are expected to be settled at the lower steps. The one or two higher steps in the grievance procedure allow appeal to top management officials, line, or staff, or both, and to higher local and international union officials frequently through use of union or joint union-management grievance committee arrangements. The higher steps are usually required for grievances calling for a new policy or precedent and also for a few grievances too "hot" for lower-step settlement.

While formal grievance procedures are very similar in their fundamental characteristics, there is a high degree of individuality in each contract and wide variation in details. In the first place, the parties may be content with a very minimum of formal provisions, requiring a fraction of a page in a contract, or they may want very detailed formal provisions running to several pages. Second, the nature and size of the bargaining unit and company, as well as the preferences of the parties, give rise to various degrees of complexity in the appeal procedure. For example, there are two-step, three-step, four-step, five-step, and six-step procedures. It does not follow that large companies always have complex appeal procedures and small companies simple procedures. For example, one very large company has a two-step procedure plus arbitration, and many small companies match each level of supervision with a separate grievance step. Third, representation at each level on both the company and union side varies widely. On the union side there may be a steward and chief steward arrangement with or without a grievance committee, a full-time or part-time committeeman system of one representative for a stated number of employees, a combination of the above systems, a business agent arrangement, and so forth. Various union officials function at quite different levels under different procedures. Union or joint union-management committees may be very important in a procedure, or there may not be any at all. On the management side representation may be predominantly line or staff, or various combinations of the two, with considerable variation in the responsibility of particular officials. Fourth, procedural provisions may be extensively developed or largely lacking. Time intervals, written grievances and answers, minutes of meetings, special procedures for special grievances, and similar provisions are found in various forms. Finally, there is variaton in what might be called regulations and privileges of union representatives, such as payment for time spent handling grievances, allowed time, reporting provisions, seniority standing, overtime representation and payment, and so forth.

Many of the variations in formal grievance procedures noted above represent adaptations to particular bargaining units and to the particular organizational structures of the companies and unions involved. On the other hand, some variations are more general in character and warrant comment. General differences in formal procedures will be discussed briefly under four topics: (1) the degree of formality, (2) the character of representation, (3) the regulation of grievance activity, and (4) special grievance procedures.

Degree of Formality

There has been a distinct trend toward more formality in grievance procedures in recent years, particularly in industrial units. Broadly speaking this trend reflects the gradual elaboration of the grievance section of the contract in the light of experience. But, in particular, formality has been increased by a requirement that grievances be written, frequently at the first step of the grievance procedure, stating the specific nature of the grievance and the contract section allegedly violated. Written answers at each step are also required. Some parties conduct quite formal hearings and develop rather elaborate records at the step before arbitration.

Time limits for the consideration of grievances at each step have also been incorporated increasingly into formal grievance procedures. The initial demand for such limits came chiefly from unions to prevent delay and stalling and consequently to avoid employee unrest. Management also was interested in avoiding delay, and over the years time limits became at least as much a management as a union demand. Time limits created a systematic procedure, as grievances not appealed within the limits were formally closed on the basis of the last answer given. Management particularly wanted to avoid the cumulation of retroactive costs associated with discharge, layoff, and similar actions. Unions too wanted particularly to avoid delay in cases of major employee hardship. It should be mentioned, however, that where relations between the parties are good, exceptions to time limits are not uncommon. An orderly procedure is maintained, but extensions are allowed, for example, when time for further investigation is requested. Where relations between the parties are less good, time limits may be rigidly applied.

Rarely do procedures in industrial units, however, acquire the formality of the system of charges and hearings in the railroad industry. Railroad grievance procedure will not be discussed, but the functioning of the adjustment boards is reviewed in Chapter 25. In many relationships the nature of employment conditions, as well as the structure of the union, perpetuate informal procedures. If employees are not attached to a particular employer and both the jobs themselves and the conditions giving rise to grievances are temporary, on-the-spot settlement of grievances is common. The construction industry and the waterfront are illustrative. The business agent and job steward structure of such unions is adapted to these conditions. If the grievance is not resolved, direct action in stopping a job is traditional in some relationships. However, there is some trend toward more formal procedures. The Teamsters Union in the Central Conference has created an elaborate procedure for over-the-road trucking under the master contract. Local union officials report a substantial decline in direct action. Brief observation and study of this procedure showed increasing use of established precedent in resolving grievances. Though only superficial investigation has been possible, various association bargaining relationships with craft unions have indicated the growth of effective local market grievance mechanisms. Employment conditions in many craft markets, however, tend to make the operation of formal procedures quite difficult.

Company and union officials are torn between the desire to avoid formality and the desire to avoid inconsistent, improper, or inadequate oral settlements. The desire to avoid formality is based at least in part on a belief that a formal written grievance with an issue clearly drawn is more difficult to resolve than an oral disagreement in which the issue is perhaps less sharply stated. There may well be greater flexibility on both sides in reaching a satisfactory settlement if the grievance is not reduced to writing. Parties with a strong desire to avoid formality usually do not require that grievances be written until about the third step of the procedure and sometimes not at all. On the other hand, the growing complexity of substantive contract provisions and the importance to higher union and management officials of consistent and appropriate lower-step settlements have led increasingly to a requirement that grievances be written at the first step. The major distinction between complaints and grievances in many relationships is that complaints are oral and grievances written. An interesting variation in some contracts is to provide for both an oral and a written stage for the first step. Thus, while grievance procedures still vary widely in formality, the trend has been toward more formal procedures.

Formality, while it has disadvantages, also has one important advantage: writing a grievance at the first step and requiring a written answer at that step encourages the clarification of the issue, the dropping of complaints with inadequate substance, and more thorough investigation before a written answer is given. While writing grievances at the first step cannot guarantee satisfactory consideration of grievances at that step, it encourages more adequate consideration. Some companies have substantially improved the functioning of the grievance procedure by attaching great importance to the first-step answer. This point will be developed below and in Chapter 29.

Character of Representation

The character of union and management representation in the grievance procedure varies widely, and no attempt will be made to describe all the differences. The organizational structure of unions leads to differences in representation. In some unions the international representatives play a much more important role in contract administration than they do in others. Differences in the structure of local unions also lead to differences in representation. Within companies a major difference is in the role played by line as contrasted with staff, a subject developed in Chapter 29. Representation is also a phase of the grievance procedure in which the informal may deviate considerably from the formal procedure. Some procedures also are written without specifying the particular representatives of the union and management at some of the steps.

A few grievance procedures define the union and management representatives at each step as including the representatives at all lower steps. Most grievance procedures do not formally carry up the lower representatives, but it is customary in actual practice for representatives at each lower step to be involved in the consideration of grievances at the higher steps. In other words, those involved in grievance discussions can be distingushed from the official representatives at each step, and practice differs in the degree to which representatives at lower steps participate at high steps. In fact the question of who should properly be involved at each step appears to be less well thought out in many procedures than is the question of official representation at each step. The view of the authors is that it is in general advisable to carry up lower representatives to higher steps insofar as this is practical. All too frequently the complaint of foremen and stewards is that they have little or no knowledge of what happens to grievances at higher steps or that they are inadequately or tardily informed as to the reasons for dispositions. More careful consideration should be given to this question.

Grievance procedures also differ widely in the use of union or joint union-management grievance committees. A union grievance committee frequently meets with several representatives of management, so that the distinction between a union grievance committee and a joint committee is not particularly important. Many grievance procedures use committees at one or more higher steps, while smaller or different committees function at lower steps. Higher step grievance consideration by a committee makes for balanced representation. Both lower and higher union and management representatives can be involved, as can both local and international union representatives and both line and staff management representatives.

The trend in the use of committees has been toward regular rather than *ad hoc* meetings. Management opinion is divided on the advisability of committees. Where union-management relations are reasonably good, management usually favors regular committee meetings. Such meetings almost invariably take on functions beyond the formal consideration of particular grievances. Both the union and management air general complaints, management presents company prospects and problems, and informal consultation frequently takes place. It was clear in a number of union-management relationships that the consideration of grievances was decidedly subordinate to the more general exchange of views that took place. On the other hand, where relations are not as good, regular committee meetings have stimulated a conflict, and management has sought to restrict the number of meetings or abandon them altogether. Clearly the significance and character of regular grievance committee meetings vary widely in different union-management situations.

Regulation of Grievance Activity

Some managements have been lax in establishing routine regulations for union representatives. The problem arises primarily, though not exclusively, out of the practice of company payment to union stewards or committeemen for time spent handling grievances. A few unions, most notably the United Steelworkers, have not sought such pay from the company. Their preference has been for the union to compensate its representatives for time lost. Most contracts, however, require the company to compensate union representatives for lost time. Companies have agreed to such provisions in the interest of expeditious handling of grievances. Frequently the contract does not limit the amount of time union representatives may spend handling grievances, although there may be limitations, such as maximum hours per week, "reasonable" time, or payment may be restricted to meetings called by management. If the contract does not specify any such limit, and particularly if it does not require supervisory approval to leave the job and to enter other departments, union representatives "roam the plant looking for grievances." Furthermore, working representatives may simply loaf at company expense, making it difficult to maintain production schedules.

Behavior is determined only partially by contract provisions, but the major issue in one quite long strike was stricter contract controls over union representatives, and they are an issue in many relationships. A few companies, unable to negotiate limitations on hours for part-time union representatives, have changed over to a smaller number of full-time union committeemen. At least one company went to considerable expense to provide comfortable offices for full-time union committeemen in the hope of encouraging them to stay in the office. This approach also minimizes interruptions to production.

It is very difficult to assess the significance of the relative number of lower union representatives, payment to them, and formal controls over their activities. Extreme differences clearly are important. In one large company for many years there was one union representative for every 25 employees, but only one foreman for every 200 to 250 employees. Some managements have refused to match each foreman with a union representative, and the ratio of foremen to employees is substantially higher than that of union representatives to employees. If working union representatives roam a plant under substantially no control, not only may they stir up grievances but they may create production difficulties for foremen and exert a demoralizing influence. On the other hand, in one plant no grievance investigation or discussion was allowed during working hours. This rule was strictly enforced, and normal grievance activity was clearly curtailed.

Except for major variations, however, assessment of differences is most difficult. Where relations are poor and the grievance procedure dramatizes the conflict, management frequently appears to find fault with the mechanics of the procedure to the exclusion of more fundamental problems. In Chapter 23 an example was noted in which a management took a long strike to gain contract controls over the activities of union representatives only to find that grievance activity did not decline under the new controls. Where relations are good, management may never have thought of writing into the contract controls over the activities of union representatives. Abuse of rights is not a problem, and normal shop courtesy prevails in requesting time to investigate a grievance. It is thus very easy to emphasize mechanical and legislative deficiencies in the functioning of the grievance procedure when they are only symptomatic of more important problems. At the same time reasonable controls are appropriate to the orderly functioning of the grievance procedure.

Special Grievance Procedures

Special grievance procedures, and modifications of the regular procedure for particular kinds of grievances, have been an important development. While only occasionally spelled out in the contract, a common practice is to expedite discharge, suspension, and layoff cases either by filing such grievances at about the third step or advancing such grievances rapidly to that step. Priority in docketing for arbitration in these cases may also be allowed. Under a few procedures other types of grievances also are initiated at an advanced step. Grievances affecting employees in more than one department, and policy grievances variously defined, may be initiated at the third step.

It is an interesting question whether contracts should more generally specify at what step various types of grievances should be initiated. The argument against this is that all types of grievances should be considered at the first step even though appeal to a higher step is expected. A growing number of contracts, however, allow general grievances to be initiated at about the third step.

An interesting development is the increase in the number of parties that either formally or in effect have special procedures for grievances on production standards and job evaluation, that is, grievances with an industrial engineering orientation. Joint committees established under a job evaluation plan frequently operate a specialized grievance procedure. Where there are union time-study representatives, they, together with company industrial engineers, may handle production standard grievances. In some companies the management representative on industrial engineering cases is an industrial engineer. In others it is considered poor policy to require industrial engineers to negotiate. Some specialized procedures for industrial engineering cases appear to work very well and clearly warrant investigation. As is pointed out in Chapter 25, the trend is toward special arbitration of such cases.

If a contract permits strikes over some nonarbitrable issues, a special grievance procedure is usually created, bringing in higher representatives of the union and management at an early step. While many contracts make no provision for specialized procedures, and no distinction among types of cases, grievance procedures are being refined increasingly in these respects.

Deviations from the Formal Grievance Procedures

It is well known that the behavior of people and organizations often differs greatly from the pattern provided for in constitutions, organization charts, and rules and regulations. Grievance handling practices are no exception to this rule. They often differ in important respects from those spelled out in the union-management contract. Changes in procedures go on indefinitely as individuals and conditions change.

In a few extreme cases the actual grievance procedure bears no resemblance to that in the contract. For example, one company had several plants in the same city, in which the employees were represented by one local union. The contract provided for four steps prior to arbitration, for time intervals between steps, and for grievances to be written at the first step. The actual procedure, however, was quite different. In fact, a union steward would telephone the union business agent, a full-time representative of the local union, and the business agent would visit the plant and talk with the union steward. The business agent subsequently would appear at the labor relations office of the company, with or without an appointment, and hold a preliminary discussion with a labor relations representative of the company. The result of this conversation usually would be to set a time for a grievance meeting one or two days in the future. Before the meeting the labor relations department would investigate the grievance. Attendance at the meeting would vary. If the grievance was relatively unimportant, the assistant vice-president for production might not be present, but usually was. The first meeting rarely brought a settlement, and one or more subsequent meetings brought either a settlement or the attendance of the vice-president for production, which led to settlement or arbitration. The succession of meetings, bearing no resemblance to the steps in the contract or to the time intervals, had the general effect of securing the attendance of the vice-president for production for the settlement of an extremely high proportion of cases. The provision for writing grievances was never followed.

In one plant of a steel company the official grievance procedure was used for relatively unimportant grievances. On important ones the union steward contacted the president of the local union. The latter, who had no official function in the grievance procedure, made an appointment with the plant manager. All important grievances were resolved orally by the plant manager and the president of the local union. The same man had been president of the local since its inception many years earlier. In rare cases the grievance would be placed in the grievance procedure and carried to arbitration. The plant had an extremely low official grievance rate.

The most common deviations from the grievance procedure are the skipping of steps, the consolidation of steps, and the introduction of new steps. Where the procedure requires that all grievances be initiated at the first step, important ones may actually be initiated at the third step. Reluctance of higher management or higher union officials to trust supervisors, foremen, and stewards to dispose of cases satisfactorily has led to the skipping of the first step or two of the grievance procedure in some cases. In an airplane manufacturing plant the local union president, who again had no official status in the grievance procedure, interceded at step two and in effect created a final step prior to arbitration.

Consolidation of steps occurs because in some cases the intermediate steps really add little to the adjustment machinery. In a paper mill the second, third, and fourth steps were consolidated into one because the men representing the company at those stages were in large part the same ones who had already heard the case and had made a decision, from which the union had appealed.

When a new step has been added to the formal grievance procedure, it has usually been just before the appeal to arbitration in an effort to avoid some of the uncertainties and cost of arbitration. In the plant of one airplane manufacturer, the accumulation of 100 cases set for arbitration led the director of industrial relations for the company to sit down with the union president and his business agents and to settle all of these cases. At the third step, where the 100 grievances were not settled, they were in the hands of the plant industrial relations committee, consisting of four elected business agents and representatives of management.

In an aluminum producing company, no backlog of cases developed, but only a small proportion of the cases appealed to arbitration were ever tried. The union and employer set up an informal step between the third step and arbitration, and the cases were settled there.

A screening step, just before arbitration, has developed in a large automobile company. It has been kept because it works and saves both sides time and money. The screening is done by the experts on the staffs of the union and the company to handle those cases that do go to arbitration. The union staff visits the locals to discuss some cases. After the screening process some cases are withdrawn on the ground that the issue has already been decided by the umpire; and some are referred back to the plants for further consideration, perhaps with the suggestion that specific aspects be considered that may have been overlooked.

There are plants in which a screening step just before arbitration has weakened plant discipline because it has led to the overruling of plant officials. Furthermore, in a few cases the added screening step has been used by the unions to keep cases unsettled which the union was unwilling to withdraw and also unwilling to arbitrate. Where there is no required order or procedure in docketing for arbitration, it may be expedient politically to hold weak cases in the backlog and take no action on them.

Deviations from grievance procedures specified in the contract usually indicate deficiencies in labor relations policy of management and union. In some instances the procedure in the contract is unnecessarily elaborate, as where each level of supervision is matched with a separate grievance step. The obvious remedy is to revise the contract procedure. An informal screening step prior to arbitration does not necessarily indicate poor policy. Most deviations, however, represent an effort to sabotage an appropriate procedure and thus indicate basic policy deficiencies.

Step at Which Grievances Are Settled

Statistics indicating at what step grievances are settled should be interpreted carefully. One large company and the union settle a very large proportion of grievances at the first and second steps. The second step in this procedure, however, is at the level of the plant manager and plant industrial relations director. In the following discussion the first two steps are used to indicate first line supervision and one appeal to a level below the plant manager and plant industrial relations director. The level of the plant manager and plant industrial relations director is considered to be a crucial higher step though not necessarily in large organizations the step immediately prior to arbitration.

One often hears the opinion that grievances should be settled as near the point of origin as possible, namely by the worker's immediate supervisor at the first step. However, routine grievances—minor discipline, for example—frequently require one appeal for settlement. Complaints that can be settled by the immediate supervisor often do not become formal grievances. Union stewards or first-level committeemen are not considered to be fulfilling their jobs if they don't take at least one appeal above the immediate supervisor. Technical grievances often require one appeal for adequate discussion and explanation. A grievance procedure that settles a large proportion of routine grievances at the first two steps is functioning very well. Grievances involving interpretation of the contract or applications of the contract to several departments or perhaps the entire plant obviously cannot be settled at the lower steps. Such grievances might concern, for example, management's right to require employees to work overtime, or its right to contract out work. The higher steps are appropriate for settlement of such policy questions. It has already been pointed out that some contracts permit discussion of these plant-wide issues to be started at the top. If not started at the top, discussion is bound to move there. The company's views may be presented to the union by the plant manager or the director of industrial relations, but management's position on these general issues will probably be made by top management—the president or executive vice-president or the administrative committee, if there is one.

With these exceptions, it is desirable to settle as large a proportion of grievances as possible at the lower steps. The reasons, generally inadequately stated, have been listed as follows by a division director of labor relations in a large company: (1) to maintain the authority and status of first line supervision, (2) to prevent the grievance from changing in character, and (3) to gain meaningful employee acceptance. The complex problem of maintaining the authority and status of first line supervision is discussed in some detail in Chapter 29. Substantially enlarging the authority of the foremen is not a feasible solution. Of great significance is the development of a satisfactory labor relations policy at the operating level to create first-step settlements that are acceptable in the light of policy and practice.

Many grievances change in character as they move through the grievance procedure—a fact not always realized. A production standard grievance on the factory floor has real significance to the employee and to the operating management. It involves the basic question of how much work the employee should do in a given time. As such a grievance advances up the grievance procedure, it loses its operating flavor and content. It becomes a "paper grievance" on the way the job was timed, on whether the proper allowances were given, and on other technical questions. Other types of grievances change in character as they are appealed. This point is in turn related to the third point—securing meaningful employee acceptance. Discussion and settlement of a large proportion of grievances in their operating environment by those most immediately concerned in the outcome go much farther to create a satisfactory employee relations environment than do higher-step settlements. A top-step settlement of an individual employee grievance, no matter which side wins, creates no meeting of minds of those most immediately concerned. Reflection on these reasons for seeking a high proportion of lower-step settlements shows the importance of the goal.

Consider briefly the functioning of the grievance procedure in three different plants of the same company under the same master contract with an international union. In the first plant, with from 5,000 to 9,000 employees, the grievance procedure functioned very satisfactorily. Statistics on grievances covering a four-year period have been consolidated. There were no significant differences among the years. The grievance rate was somewhat high, but not significantly so in the light of circumstances. Grievances were written at the first step (first line supervision) and averaged 22 grievances per 100 employees per year for the four years. The plant was a new one, having operated for less than six months prior to the period surveyed. It grew from 5,000 to 9,000 employees over the first three of the four years. A new and growing plant with inexperienced local union leadership is expected to have a fairly high grievance rate. The pattern of settlement is of primary interest. Of 6,747 grievances over the four years, 51.2 per cent were settled at the first step (immediate supervisor), 37.1 per cent were settled at the second step (labor relations supervisor), 10.3 per cent were settled at the third step (labor relations director, plant manager, and union grievance committee), and 1.4 per cent were arbitrated. A clear pattern of settling most grievances at the lower steps was established.

For the other plants of the company statistics will be given for only one year, but the pattern has been similar in recent years. The grievance rate in the second plant with grievances again written at the first step was 49.8 grievances per 100 employees per year. There can be no question that the grievance rate was very high in this plant although again the pattern of settlement is of primary interest. What was happening in this plant can best be seen by considering the number of denials. Of 710 grievances denied at the first step, 689 were appealed to the second. Of 638 grievances denied at the second step, 617 were appealed to the third. Of 228 grievances denied at the third step, 162 were carried to arbitration. In the third plant the grievance rate was 34 per 100 employees per year. Of 1,242 grievances denied at the first step, 1,079 were appealed to the second. Of 531 denied at the second, 381 were appealed to the third. Of 210 denied at the third step, 143 were carried to arbitration. In both of these plants the company granted, wholly or in part, 60 to 65 per cent of all grievances, and denials at lower steps were reversed in a high proportion of cases at later steps. The chances of favorable action on routine grievances at the third step were so good in the last two plants that the union would have been negligent if it did not appeal unfavorable lower-step decisions. In the first plant the number of modifications of decisions on appeal was very low.

The difference between a pattern of settlement at the lower steps and a pattern of constant appeal to the top has been made clear in the examples. The reasons for differences in patterns will be explored briefly. It will be recognized at once that most of the determinants of grievance rates discussed in Chapter 23 apply, sometimes with a different emphasis, to patterns of settlement. The state of relations between the parties, the degree of experience of the parties, the personalities of key union and company representatives, changes in operating methods or conditions, union policies, union politics, some features of the grievance procedure, and management policies are all pertinent, and the earlier discussion need not be repeated to introduce small differences in emphasis. Conditions that produce instability within the union or management or both and lead to a high grievance rate are also likely to mean that most grievances will be brought to the top.

As with grievance rates, caution is required in judging the significance of a particular pattern of settlement. It is easy to get a pattern of settlement in the lower steps if decisions unfavorable to employees and the union are rare. It is easy to get low-step settlements if the union is weak. More important, sometimes top plant management, line or staff, does not really want a pattern of settlement at lower steps. Real grievance decisions are made only at the top. Denials at lower steps are only trial balloons—a way of playing it safe. It is generally recognized that real decisions are made only when a grievance reaches a key man at the top. The same situation may exist on the union side. While this is frustrating to lower management and to lower union representatives, it does not necessarily indicate inconsistent or poor management policy or highly disturbed union-management relations. It is amusing, however, to hear a top company official complain vigorously because lower management can't settle grievances and he must spend an inordinate amount of time on them, when it is perfectly clear that the real trouble is that the executive in question would no more give up the personal privilege of making the decisions than he would stop complaining about the consequences. Such situations, however, should be distinguished from that in plants where policy is inadequately developed and not made effective at lower levels with the result that lower-level decisions are inconsistent and of poor quality. An effective pattern of lower-step settlements must rest on a high proportion of good decisions at the first step. This question of the importance of policy and of "right" first-step decisions is developed in Chapter 29.

The Grievance Procedure and Union-Management Adjustment

As was pointed out in Chapter 22, there has been a considerable growth in union-management adjustment in contract administration. The large growth in union membership after 1932 and the consequent spread of collective bargaining created successive and overlapping stages that might be described as an organizing stage, a contract development stage, and an adjustment stage. Wildcat strikes and pressure tactics in contract administration were more characteristic of the first two than of the third stage. Increasingly in the postwar years managements developed and unions accepted employee discipline for participation in wildcat strikes. Use of pressure tactics as a substitute for, or as a supplement to, the grievance procedure declined. A closely related development was the change from very limited to almost universal acceptance of arbitration as the terminal step in the grievance procedure.

Equally important and related to the decline in pressure tactics and the growth of arbitration is the process of union-management adjustment that has been reflected in the increasing stability of contract language and its interpretation. Union-management relations, in resolving day-to-day problems, have gone through the contract development stage into the adjustment stage. This process of adjustment takes place in many substantive areas, and hence is referred to in many chapters of this book. The development of layoff systems and of job evaluation plans is an example. Early lack of agreement on the principles and practice of layoff gave rise to many grievances. But by 1960 in many relationships the procedure of layoff was almost mechanical. During the war and early postwar years disagreement over wage rates for particular jobs caused many grievances and considerable conflict. By 1960 formal or informal job evaluation had created stable job rates with an orderly procedure for establishing rates for new and changed jobs in most union-management relationships. The process of adjustment is less marked in some substantive areas, such as production standards and manning. In the concluding chapter an attempt will be made to indicate the areas where adjustment appears to be reasonably well developed and those where it is less so. But on balance, even with wide diversity in the results of collective bargaining in different companies and plants, there appears to have been a considerable growth in union-management adjustment in contract administration.

The process of adjustment has not necessarily reduced the average grievance rate in collective bargaining relationships, although it might be expected that this would be the result. In some cases there has been a drop in both grievance and arbitration activity, but in others where adjustment has clearly taken place, there is no evidence of a declining trend in grievances. In several large multiplant companies statistics show fluctuations in the grievance rate over the years as well as some extremely large bulges in grievances associated with the development and resolution of important issues, but there is no evidence of a trend. Also obvious are great variations among plants in multiplant companies and diverse experience over time.

It is believed, however, that the process of adjustment has reduced the degree of conflict in contract administration. Looking back in most relationships, as previously noted, large segments of the contract have shown little change over recent years. Interpretations and applications of these elements of the contract have been refined, and there has been an increasing meeting of minds with respect to these substantive areas. As policy and precedent were established, more and more grievances became routine in character.

The above discussion ignores the significant variation among companies and plants. It is in particular relationships that the various determinants of grievance activity find their full expression. The processing of grievances reflects the wide range of considerations that bear upon contract administration. The grievance procedure reflects the degree of adjustment between the parties, and in turn facilitates the process of adjustment and the development of policy. Use of the grievance process calls for communication within managements and unions and between them. The deliberate goal of improving the functioning of the grievance procedure can carry forward the process of adjustment.

The consequences of grievance adjustment arrangements extend far beyond the prevention or correction of injustice in individual cases. First, the status that unions and collective bargaining confer upon the worker, the respect that they help him acquire, are the result not only of the rights that he gains through the union-management contract, but of the fact that he has at his disposal arrangements by which he can assert the rights given him under the agreement. Second, the fact that there are arrangements by which representatives of unions can argue with management over specific management decisions in a wide variety of cases, particularly cases in which the reasonableness of management's decision is in question, makes for more carefully considered decisions and, in general, for better management. Finally, the grievance procedure amplifies and develops the meaning of the contract and reflects the degree of adjustment between the parties. Specific applications of the contract in grievance settlements and in arbitration create and develop procedures, rights, and obligations. Contract clauses take on meaning in the light of practiced policy. Adjustment between the parties moves forward, or fails to progress, both at the level of negotiation and in contract administration. These broad effects of grievance adjustment arrangements cannot be measured, but they are of outstanding importance.

25 / The Grievance Arbitration Process

IN THIS CHAPTER and the next we are concerned primarily with the arbitration of grievances that arise under the terms of an existing agreement. These are grievances that have been processed through the steps described in Chapters 23 and 24 and have not been resolved by the parties themselves. A clear distinction exists between the grievance arbitration process and the use of arbitration to decide what provisions shall be put into an agreement. The latter use will not be considered in these chapters.[1]

Twenty-five years ago the arbitration process as a method for settling grievances arising under labor-management agreements was relatively unknown. Although we have no reliable studies of the use of arbitration prior to 1940, it is estimated that fewer than 8 to 10 per cent of the agreements in effect in the early 1930's provided for arbitration as the final step of the grievance procedure.[2] By 1944 the U. S. Bureau of Labor Statistics found arbitration provisions in 73 per cent of the agreements. This had increased to 83 per cent in 1949 and to 89 per cent in 1952.[3] At the present time from 90 to 95 per cent of an estimated 125,000 collective bargaining agreements contain such clauses.

An analysis of union constitutions shows that one-fifth of 130 constitutions contain either an official endorsement of grievance arbitra-

[1] These chapters will not deal with the legal aspects of arbitration, although interest in this subject was sharpened by the Supreme Court's decision in the *Lincoln Mills* case (1947). For an excellent discussion of this subject, see articles by Benjamin Aaron, David Feller, and Archibald Cox in Bureau of National Affairs, *Arbitration and the Law* (1959).

[2] The lack of surveys undoubtedly is due to the infrequent use of the process. Special reports are available for the few industries in which the process gained early acceptance —apparel, printing, and coal. It is interesting that in Sumner H. Slichter's *Union Policies and Industrial Management* (1941), there is no reference to arbitration in the index.

[3] E. M. Moore, and J. Nix, "Arbitration Provisions in Collective Agreements, 1952," *Monthly Labor Review* (March 1953). pp. 261-66.

tion or an affirmation of the right of the locals to adopt such clauses in their agreements with management. In fact, a few union constitutions require the inclusion of arbitration machinery before approval of the agreement can be secured from the international. For example, the constitution of the United Brewery, Flour, Cereal, Soft Drink and Distillery Workers of America contains such a requirement.[4]

Within a relatively brief span of twenty years, there has been a change from almost no provision for grievance arbitration to almost invariable provision for this process. This reflects the extent of experience gained by the parties in labor relations in the past twenty years. The existence of these provisions and, more important, the degree to which they have been used for settling grievances have had a profound impact upon managements and unions. This impact relates not only to their relationships with each other but also to the way each party conducts itself on a daily basis.

It would be a mistake to appraise the influence of the arbitration process only in terms of a particular case or issue. Of course a given case may be of considerable moment to one or both of the parties, and the terms of its settlement by an arbitrator may assume great importance. But of equal if not greater importance is the role of arbitration where no case is involved, where the referral to a neutral seldom occurs. Once the parties have committed themselves to voluntary arbitration as the final step in resolving grievances under an agreement, there is increased pressure for settlement at an earlier stage.

For example, words used and documents introduced at the bargaining table may be subjected to censorship lest they be used as evidence in a subsequent arbitration. Clauses in a labor agreement are worded with basic concern not only for what the parties themselves intend by the language but also for the construction and interpretation that might be placed upon the clause by an outsider. Personnel practices of a company, such as the maintenance of meticulous disciplinary records, performance records and the like, may be conditioned by a judgment as to what the arbitrator will require for proof. As we have seen in Chapters 7 and 21, some companies have adopted elaborate programs for measuring employee ability or have decided that a foreman should be empowered only to suspend but never discharge an employee on the spot because of the criteria adopted by arbitrators.

[4] In some instances these union requirements involved new contract term arbitration as well as grievance arbitration.

A union may feel compelled to participate directly in the writing of an employee grievance to be certain that poor phrasing will not limit the avenues of argument and contract reference in the event of arbitration. In fact, several local unions require that all written grievances be approved by their attorneys before they are submitted to management. The net effect is that a grievance signed by a foundry laborer often reads like a formal, legal document, with such precautionary phrases as "including, but not limited to, violations of Articles IX, XIV, and XX of the Agreement and including disregard for practice heretofore established as an integral part of relationship rights and obligations."

Oftentimes the very way in which parties settle grievances is determined by their best guess as to how an arbitrator might dispose of the case. From the standpoint of a unionized management it is no longer enough to conduct itself only with regard to how the union might react. It must be equally mindful of how an outside neutral might judge its actions.

These few illustrations will serve to emphasize the principal concern of this and the following chapter. We are more interested in how the arbitration process has affected directly and indirectly the behavior and relationship of unions and managements than in the history and the mechanics of the process. The latter subjects will be examined only to the degree necessary for an understanding of the later sections. The literature in the field has been preoccupied primarily with the process per se. In fact, the literature has been so vast within recent years that one might wonder whether anything new or valuable can possibly be said about labor arbitration.[5] However, in this absorption with procedures, some of the salutary as well as some of the harmful effects of arbitration on the daily conduct of labor relations have been neglected.

In this chapter four principal subjects are examined: (1) the history and development of grievance arbitration, (2) arbitration procedures, (3) the scope of the arbitrator's authority, and (4) the significance and determinants of the volume of grievance arbitration.

With this background, Chapter 26 will consider several interesting

---

[5] An *Arbitration Bibliography* published by the American Arbitration Association in 1954 lists almost 600 books, monographs, and articles on the subject of labor arbitration. In addition the New York State School of Industrial and Labor Relations at Cornell University has published an excellent bibliography, *Dispute Settlements by Third Parties*, prepared by Vernon H. Jensen and Harold G. Ross (1955).

case experiences in arbitration as well as some of the more important and seldom emphasized problem areas in the field.

History and Development of Grievance Arbitration

The concept of arbitration is not new in labor relations. But historically it was used primarily as a substitute for the strike in resolving the terms of a new agreement. In the 1880's the Knights of Labor, troubled by strike failures in the depression period 1875 to 1879, concluded that strike action was anachronistic and sought to substitute arbitration as a national policy.[6]

As noted above, until the late 1930's there were only a few voluntary arrangements for the arbitration of grievances. The notable ones were in the printing, shoe, apparel, and coal industries, and even these arrangements undoubtedly had their genesis in a desire by the parties to resolve contract disputes without resort to strike. Because the parties failed to distinguish between disputes over the terms of a new contract and grievances arising under a contract, the latter also fell within the scope of the arbitrator's authority.

As early as June 2, 1886, the Commonwealth of Massachusetts created a Board of Arbitration and invited labor and management to use its services to resolve disputes. Since at that time the formal agreement was relatively unknown, the "disputes" referred to the Board were not only of a grievance nature but also on such basic matters as wages, hours, and working conditions. This Board, the first in the United States with authority to hear and decide disputes, was intended primarily to settle the many piece-rate problems that plagued the shoe industry.

In 1900 the American Newspaper Publishers' Association entered into an arbitration agreement with the International Typographical Union, and in 1902 a similar agreement was made with the Printing Pressmen's Union. The Pressmen's agreement has been renewed periodically since that date. These agreements initially covered both new contract arbitration and grievance arbitration.

---

[6] There is some question whether what the Knights meant by "arbitration" was really arbitration. A local contemplating a strike had to select an "arbitration committee" to settle the dispute. If unsuccessful, the dispute went to a district "arbitration committee," then to an inter-district committee, and finally to the general executive board. Only after this procedure was exhausted could a strike be authorized. In effect, these were appellate negotiating committees. See N. J. Ware, *The Labor Movement in the United States 1860-1895* (1929), pp. 121-22.

What is described as the "oldest, permanent, industry-wide grievance arbitration machinery in the country" is the Anthracite Board of Conciliation, which was established in 1903. The Board consists of industry and union representatives who try to resolve disputes arising under the agreement. Its principal function is to hold hearings, collect evidence, and submit the dispute to the outside umpire. The umpire does not attend the hearings; the testimony and briefs are mailed to him by the Conciliation Board.[7] The umpire's functions are described as follows:

(1) He decides grievances which arise in relation to the industry agreement, using as literal an interpretation as possible. (2) He decides grievances arising under the written agreements. (3) He decides grievances not covered by the industry-wide or written local agreements but relating to the preservation of established practices at each colliery.[8]

In the first 25 years of its operation, the Board handled 2,276 grievances. Of this total, 1,123 were settled without adjudication, 273 were decided by the Board, and 880 had to be decided by the umpire. In the next 23 years (through 1951), 4,277 were handled. Of these, 1,850 were withdrawn or adjusted. It is interesting that only 79 were settled at the Board level. The umpire decided 2,348.[9]

In the apparel industry three historic adoptions of grievance arbitration deserve mention. The first is the agreement signed between the Chicago Joint Board of the Amalgamated Clothing Workers and Hart, Schaffner and Marx in 1911. This brief document, which ended the strike of 1910, provided for the appointment of an arbitration committee of three members, one member to be selected by the employees, a second by the company, and the third by the designees of the parties. Clarence Darrow was named by the local unions and Carl Meyer by the company. For a period these two men worked alone without naming a neutral, and their initial decisions were of considerable significance. However, work stoppages continued, and the arbitrators became swamped with unresolved complaints. Most of the issues involved piecework prices. Consequently in 1912 a separate permanent board, known as the Trade Board, was created to adjust and fix piece rates and to handle other complaints. Its chairman was

[7] Stanley Young, "Fifty Years of Grievance Arbitration: the Anthracite Experience," *Labor Law Journal* (October 1957), pp. 705-13.
[8] The same, p. 710.
[9] Thomas E. Larkin, "Fifty Years of Handling Labor Disputes," *Coal Mine Modernization* (1953), American Mining Congress. (Reprint).

James Mullenbach. The decisions of the Trade Board could be appealed to the Board of Arbitration, which had selected J. E. Williams as chairman.[10]

The second pioneering effort in grievance arbitration in the apparel industry involved the International Ladies' Garment Workers Union and the New York Cloak and Suit Manufacturers' Protective Association. In 1910 an agreement, which was intended to be a permanent "treaty of peace," was signed. It provided for the establishment of a permanent Board of Arbitration, whose decisions were to be final and binding. Louis D. Brandeis became the first chairman. This Board not only acted on important grievances, but it also decided policy questions affecting the industry.[11]

The third historic adoption of the impartial chairman plan was in the very first collective agreement negotiated in 1915 between the New York millinery industry and the United Hatters, Cap and Millinery Workers Union. The first chairman was Joseph Barondess, who was soon succeeded by Dr. Paul Abelson.

Dr. Abelson continued in this post until 1938, although there was a lapse in the impartial chairman program from 1921 to 1932.[12] From the start, piece-rate questions and dismissal cases were the dominant issues decided by the chairman. It is interesting that one-third of the complaints submitted to the chairman came from employers through their association. Most of these involved the right to discharge an employee. Under the agreement an employer could not discharge a worker without first proving to the union, and if it disagreed, to the chairman, that there was just cause.

In many respects the arbitration process used in these classic illustrations bears only slight resemblance to the process we know today. The refinements have been considerable. But these were significant beginnings and provided a useful background for the extension of the process in later years.

[10] Amalgamated Clothing Workers of America, Chicago Joint Board, *The Clothing Workers of Chicago, 1910-1922* (1922), Chapter III, pp. 49-71.

[11] Louis Levine, *The Women's Garment Workers* (1924), pp. 200-01.

[12] In the 1919 convention of the union a resolution "to encourage a system of collective bargaining based on collective agreements between our local unions and the respective manufacturers' associations" was defeated. The views of President Zaritsky, a strong advocate of association bargaining and arbitration, did not prevail over those who felt the arbitration procedure forced employers to organize. In 1921 the New York agreement was allowed to lapse, and with it the impartial chairman setup lapsed also. It was not until 1932 that Zaritsky was successful in reviving collective dealing and the office of the chairman. Donald B. Robinson, *Spotlight on a Union* (1948), pp. 234-41.

In the period of the New Deal the revitalized United States Conciliation Service conducted an extensive campaign to include in agreements provisions for the voluntary arbitration of grievances arising under the agreement. The gradual acceptance by the parties of the point of view that, at least for grievance disputes, arbitration was preferable to the use of economic strength led the American Arbitration Association to establish its Industrial Arbitration Tribunal in 1937. Before then, this nonprofit, private association had devoted its efforts almost entirely to the promotion of commercial arbitration.

We have noted that in the relatively brief span of 25 years grievance arbitration has become almost universally accepted in American labor relations. In 1959 more than 90 per cent of labor contracts negotiated provide for it. There are a number of reasons for this phenomenal growth.

(1) Much of this period involved intense organizational activity. Unions were loathe to see their energies and resources dissipated on a strike to support the grievance of one employee who was disciplined or a small group of employees who were dissatisfied with a new standard. Furthermore, the organizational growth involved employees in mass-production industries; their numbers alone, their newness to unionism, and oftentimes their pent-up resentments led them to hasty and costly walkouts as a way of prosecuting a grievance. The new union leadership very early saw the advantages of peaceful settlement of most grievances by the final and binding decision of a neutral.

Acceptance of the arbitration principle represented an adjustment by managements to the union point of view. At the outset management was reluctant to accept arbitration of grievances largely because it meant giving the union status. It was only when unions had won status that employer opposition to arbitration was relaxed. In addition, managements found themselves harassed by quickie and, at that time, legal strikes. They came to realize that it would be well to grant a limited voluntary arbitration clause in exchange for a no-strike clause during the life of the agreement.

(2) The evolution from the organizational stage to the contract development stage gave added impetus to the acceptance of arbitration. The parties struggled to find ways to get along with one another. They also learned that there were many parts of the agreement that

could not be reduced to finite terms. Growth in the use of arbitration went hand-in-hand with the solution of wildcat strike problems described in Chapter 22.

(3) Public policy in the form of legal and moral persuasion played an important role. The National War Labor Board in the period 1942 to 1945, by its direct or indirect influence, caused the adoption of arbitration clauses for the first time in thousands of contracts. On many occasions the NWLB by directive order included arbitration provisions in agreements. In a policy statement of July 1, 1943, the Board stated that a grievance procedure should provide for the "final and binding settlement of all grievances not otherwise resolved. For this purpose provisions should be made for the settlement of grievances by an arbitrator, impartial chairman or umpire. . . ."[13]

The effects of the educational work being carried on by the American Arbitration Association and the U. S. Conciliation Service were also being felt. In the four years 1937 to 1941, after the Association volunteered its services in this field, it developed a panel of public-spirited arbitrators in almost 1,600 cities and handled more than 700 labor arbitration cases, most of them grievance arbitrations. The wartime no-strike pledges, which were observed with commendable faith by nearly all unions, stimulated interest in machinery for the adjudication of the day-to-day grievances that the parties themselves could not resolve. Finally, the experience of the railroads and their various unions under the amended 1934 Railway Labor Act, which set up the National Railroad Adjustment Board for the settlement of grievances, commanded the attention and interest of other segments of the economy that were new to unionization.[14]

The almost complete acceptance of the principle of voluntary

[13] National War Labor Board, *Termination Report* (1943), Vol. 1, p. 66.

[14] Although the Railway Labor Act of 1926 provided for a National Adjustment Board in addition to system boards of adjustment, it was never established because of carrier opposition. The 1934 amendment in effect created the only permanent agency engaged in compulsory arbitration in the United States. Either party may seek its services for final settlement of grievance disputes involving interpretation and application of existing agreements. The Board consists of 36 members, 18 selected from the railroad unions and 18 from the carriers. The Board members sit in four divisions each having jurisdiction over certain types of employees. They hear grievance cases referred to them, and, if they are evenly divided on a given case, an outside neutral selected by them or appointed by the National Mediation Board may join the regular members to decide the case. The experience under the system boards of adjustment will be discussed in Chapter 26.

arbitration in union and management circles was highlighted in the President's Labor-Management Conference called by President Truman in the fall of 1945. The subcommittee of leading business executives and labor leaders assigned to the subject of conciliation and arbitration was the only one of six subcommittees able to reach unanimous agreement. It reported to the full conference as follows:

The parties should provide by mutual agreement for the final determination of any unsettled grievances or disputes involving the interpretation or application of the agreement by an impartial chairman, umpire, arbitrator, or board. In this connection the agreement should provide:

(a) A definite and mutually agreed-upon procedure of selecting the impartial chairman, umpire, arbitrator, or board;

(b) That the impartial chairman, umpire, arbitrator or board should have no power to add to, subtract from, change, or modify any provision of the agreement, but should be authorized only to interpret the existing provisions of the agreement and apply them to the specific facts of the grievance or dispute;

(c) That reference of a grievance or dispute to an impartial chairman, umpire, arbitrator, or board should be reserved as the final step in the procedure and should not be resorted to unless the settlement procedures of the earlier steps have been exhausted;

(d) That the decision of the impartial chairman, umpire, arbitrator, or board should be accepted by both parties as final and binding;

(e) That the cost of such impartial chairman, umpire, arbitrator, or board should be shared equally by both parties . . .

Nothing in this report is intended in any way to recommend compulsory arbitration, that is, arbitration not voluntarily agreed to by the parties.

This historic document was used extensively in the years immediately following by managements or by unions to persuade the other party to agree to the inclusion of arbitration provisions in the agreement.

With rare exceptions the acceptance of grievance arbitration has ceased to be an important issue in negotiations. With this widespread acceptance have come other developments. In 1946 the Bureau of National Affairs published its first volume of *Labor Arbitration Reports* designed as a "systematic attempt . . . to collect and classify awards handed down by arbitrators." By 1960 thirty-three such volumes had been published and, together with other similar services, such as those of Prentice-Hall and the Commerce Clearing

House, had become an indispensable part of management and union libraries. From these selected and reported decisions, parties in negotiations could learn what seemed to be the current judgment of the neutrals on a given subject, given certain contract language. They would then try to formulate language accordingly to protect their own self-interests. Or the published awards might be used by the parties to determine how a given arbitrator, under consideration for selection, was disposed to handle a certain problem. Sometimes the arbitrator being considered was rated by reference to these volumes on the basis of how many times he had ruled for the union and how many times for the company. Further, these volumes have come to be used as standard references in the citation of precedent decisions in support of one party or the other. Finally, many companies and unions use the published cases as a part of their training programs for foremen and shop stewards.

An equally significant development is the growth of arbitration as a part-time or full-time profession for specialists in the field of labor relations.[15] In 1948 a professional society, the National Academy of Arbitrators, was formed to permit an exchange of views on problems in the field. There are now dozens of persons in the United States whose sole activity is the arbitration of labor disputes, and there are many hundreds who engage in this work along with their work as academicians. Although there are many thousands of self-designated arbitrators throughout the United States, the professional competition is more apparent than real. The bulk of the work is still being shared by a relatively few persons, most of whom acquired their experience through War Labor Board service during World War II and the Wage Stabilization Board during the Korean crisis. There is some reason to believe that the parties, because of their sometimes logical, sometimes capricious method of selecting and discarding arbitrators, are actually exhausting the supply of available men. It may be that unions and companies will have to give serious consideration in the near future to ways in which they can help train new men of competence and acceptability.

Although grievance arbitration is now the accepted practice on the American industrial scene, there are still a few relationships in

[15] There had been a few professionals earlier, such as James Mullenbach, Paul Abelson, Walter Millis, Charles P. Neal, and William Leiserson. George W. Taylor of the University of Pennsylvania has served as a professional arbitrator for thirty years.

which one or both of the parties have resisted the trend. For example, arbitration has not been widely adopted in building construction, and even where it has, it is seldom used. There are many reasons for this. In this industry job duration is too short, and attachment to a given employer is often too brief to make arbitration worthwhile. On-the-job labor relations are in the hands of operating people exclusively. If a problem arises that cannot be settled, it goes to an international representative and the secretary of a contractors' association. Their remoteness from the specific situation makes chances of successful mediation very good. Furthermore, in the building trades industry there are so many informal ways of bringing pressure that quick settlements are reached. In fact under many building construction agreements there is not even a grievance process of the type described in Chapter 24.

However, in the larger construction companies with a semi-permanent work force and with a labor relations staff, there is a grievance process and, although there is seldom an advance commitment to arbitrate with a neutral, there may be ad hoc referrals. It is also of interest that there seems to be a geographic difference in the use of arbitration in this industry. There is more grievance arbitration on the West Coast, where the construction industry is newer and has picked up the current labor relations mores.

A large multiplant automobile parts company has no arbitration procedure in one of its plants under a UAW agreement. This company followed a vigorous management philosophy designed to keep the union's influence under control. Yet while it has displayed extreme toughness and reliance on principle in dealing with any possible union encroachments on managerial prerogatives, this same company often has gone beyond what it was required to do in sharing the gains of productivity and in stabilizing employment.

Another auto parts company, also organized by the UAW, is proud of the fact that it does not have arbitration and emphasizes that it doesn't want it. The explanation is "We don't like it because we could lose control over our operations. We may be accused of giving in too much, but we manage to settle our disputes by ourselves." A careful analysis shows that this company has conceded many things to the union, and in its own words, "We've let the union get away with these things for a long time although we probably could knock them out if we took a strike." It is probable that its dependence on automobile companies as customers explains its virtual "peace-at-any-price" philosophy. Economically, it cannot risk a strike over unresolved grievances.

A third company in the same industry and organized by the same union was very much opposed to arbitration. Although no clear explanation was given, there was distrust and fear of the union on the part of top management. Even the middle and lower levels of management were convinced that the union was an evil influence and tried to chisel on the agreement. The local union was also firmly convinced that management was trying to undermine the agreement. Without an arbitration clause and with freedom to strike over unresolved grievances, the locals were militant and learned that pressure tactics would pay off. The company had lost a sizable contract because of a strike and was afraid to take another one. These few illustrations of management opposition to arbitration seem to have one common characteristic: while the company has held firmly to the principle that no outsider is to be allowed to dictate a grievance decision, it has not been firm about yielding on a grievance of dubious merit or risking a strike on the issue.

In some instances it is the union that has taken the initiative in opposing arbitration, with or without management's assent. An articulate spokesman in opposition to an arbitration clause in the contract is James Hoffa, now president of the Teamsters' Union. Speaking of the Central Conference of Teamsters' Agreement, which permits grievance arbitration only when it is voted by the joint employer-union committee, Hoffa observed that since 1938 there had been no arbitration, that there had been fewer strikes in trucking than in any other American industry, and that from 85 to 95 per cent of the cases on the Chicago docket had been settled by the Central States Council. More than 99 per cent of the grievances were worked out without resort to work stoppages or any outside arbitration.[16]

In Hoffa's words: "Even if it takes one or two hours or longer to work out a settlement among ourselves we are better off, knowing the business as we do from both sides, than to submit a grievance to some third party who attempts to please both sides and actually pleases nobody. In my opinion, the best method of settling griev-

[16] It is significant that Hoffa created this Central States structure. When local autonomy prevailed, it was customary to strike when a grievance could not be resolved.

ances is to leave open the end for final settlement and, if we cannot mutually agree, either for the employer to lock out the union or for the union to strike the employer. If we don't come out with a completely satisfactory settlement we come out with a settlement both sides can live with and one which doesn't change the terms of the contract." Mr. Hoffa's viewpoint has been conditioned, at least in part, by unfortunate arbitration experiences. He emphasizes the predatory concern of arbitrators when he says, ". . . we hire a third party at $100 a day. He goes out to make a decision to please me so I will use him the next time and tries to decide halfway for the employer so he will hire him the next time too. We have had that experience and I don't think we want it again." Hoffa tells of having spent $3,000 for an arbitration, and when the award was received "nobody understood it, and it wasn't even on the subject we were arguing about; we finally had to settle it by ourselves."

The distrust of arbitration was echoed by a management spokesman at the National Forum on Trucking Industrial Relations, who said:

> There was a very decided feeling on both sides that in going to arbitration we were expecting someone who was not familiar with the trucking industry to decide questions which were extremely costly to members of the industry. As a result, there was a very decided backward trend in taking questions to arbitration. In many respects, it was a means of emphasizing the necessity for settling your problems without going to that final step. I think the psychological effect was extremely good.

Negative attitudes among union leaders, however, do not always originate with unsatisfactory experience with arbitration. More often than not union resistance to grievance arbitration stems from a realization that it can probably extract more generous settlements from a management subjected to a strike threat or strike action than it can from an arbitrator who must be convinced of the merits of a grievance. It is a victory of power tactics over reason. A large automobile parts plant reports that one of its locals refused to accept the master agreement negotiated between its other plants and the UAW. Traditionally the workers went out on strike whenever they felt that they could not get satisfaction through the grievance procedure. Although a War Labor Board directive provided for compulsory arbitration of grievances, the contract clause adopted stated "Either party may go to arbitration." The union construed this as meaning that it had the right to strike if it did not wish to join in arbitration referral. The arbitration clause itself was finally submitted to arbitration, and the union was upheld in its position.

In still another company the management's major criticism of the contract was its failure to provide for arbitration as the last step in the grievance procedure. Although it felt that most differences with the union could be settled without resort to arbitration, it believed that such a provision might enable the company to demonstrate to the union the weakness of some of the cases carried beyond the first steps of the grievance procedure. One of the automobile manufacturing companies has been unable to persuade its local unions to arbitrate grievances, but it has not considered the threat of strikes over grievances serious enough to warrant making an issue of this subject in negotiations. In the automobile tool and die industry reliance on pressure tactics prevails over arbitration as a way of resolving grievances.

In summary, while there are notable exceptions attributable largely to tradition and conditioned behavior, grievance arbitration is a process now widely accepted in American labor-management relationships. Moreover, it is a much-used machinery, although there is considerable variation in its use as we shall see. Probably well over 100,000 grievance issues are settled by this process each year in American industry. This is a substantial increase over earlier years, but the increase is attributable largely to the inclusion of arbitration machinery in more labor agreements. For a particular company and union, the number of referrals may decrease as their relationship experience grows.

Arbitration Procedures

As stated at the beginning of this chapter, the mechanics of the arbitration process are not our principal concern. There are relatively few problems now confronting managements and unions in setting up arbitration machinery. They must decide three basic questions:

(1) Do they want a permanent arbitrator or umpire for the life of the agreement, or do they want to select the arbitrator on a case-by-case basis? A number of large companies and associations have pre-

ferred the permanent arbitrator or umpire arrangement, believing it to be the best way to insure reasonable uniformity in decision-making and to have an arbitrator who is familiar with the problems and operations involved. General Motors, Ford Motor Company, Chrysler, United States Steel Corporation, Jones & Laughlin, Goodyear Tire and Rubber Company, B. F. Goodrich, the hosiery, and the various local needle trades associations have all had the impartial chairman or umpire system for many years.[17]

It is perhaps less well known that many small companies have adopted the permanent arbitrator concept. The most recent trend is to designate three neutrals for the life of the contract, who hear cases on a rotation basis if they are available. By this method the smaller companies can achieve many benefits of the permanent system and insure prompt handling of cases without the cost of a retainer fee.[18]

The *ad hoc* approach is still the most prevalent, and even such very large companies as General Electric and Westinghouse select arbitrators on a case-by-case basis. One reason for preferring this system is that an arbitrator can be selected on the basis of the type of case to be heard, an engineer for a standards case, a lawyer for a contract interpretation issue, etc. Some people also believe that *ad hoc* arbitration and the difficulty of putting the machinery in motion will serve to discourage needless arbitration, while permanent umpire systems make arbitration too readily available. There is little basis in fact for this theory. The type of machinery used is seldom an important determinant of the arbitration rate. Finally, those who prefer the *ad hoc* approach argue that there is less likelihood of compromise verdicts or temptation for the arbitrator to mediate when he knows he is being called in to handle only one given case.[19]

[17] The term "permanent arbitrator" is often a misnomer. For example, the 1959 agreement between the International Harvester Company and the UAW provides for a "Permanent Arbitrator to serve until the termination of this contract, provided he continues to be acceptable to the union and the company." The GM-UAW three-year contract in 1955 specified that the impartial umpire shall serve for one year provided he continues to be acceptable to both parties. Some "permanent" arbitrators have found their tenure to be very impermanent.

[18] For an excellent description of the operation of the particular impartial chairmanship system in the hosiery industry, see Thomas Kennedy, *Effective Labor Arbitration* (1948).

[19] This argument loses its significance unless there is an explicit provision that no arbitrator may hear more than one case except by mutual agreement. Without such a provision, the union might seek to have several cases heard by an arbitrator selected on an *ad hoc* basis. Arbitrators generally have supported unions on this point.

Of some interest is the still limited, but growing, practice of parties to set up two separate systems of arbitration, particularly where a standards program is in effect. An illustrative experience is that of a large tannery and its union that had a permanent arbitrator for many years to whom all unresolved grievances, including many standards questions, were referred. At first the arbitrator went through the meaningless gesture of conducting a hearing, then designating an outside time-study engineer to make a study of the disputed standard; his report was given to the parties for comment, and finally the permanent arbitrator would give his decision. This unwieldy series of steps proved costly and time-consuming. Under the current agreement the parties have adopted two separate arbitration clauses, one for a permanent arbitrator to decide all nonstandards issues and the other for a permanent industrial engineering firm to decide all standards issues. This form of accommodation of the arbitration process is likely to become more widespread.

(2) Should the issues be resolved by a single arbitrator or by a three-man Board of Arbitration, two members of which are designated by the parties? There is some slight evidence to indicate that the use of a board, which was probably the prevailing form in the early days of grievance arbitration and is still in widespread use, is less popular.[20] Its proponents have widely divergent reasons for urging a board. Some view it as a way of keeping an eye on the arbitrator to be certain that he does not go far afield in his reasoning or his *dicta* or to insure that technical problems of company operation will be understood accurately by him in his deliberations. Other advocates look to the board as a way of permitting mediation and of producing a final settlement that will be within the range of the expectancy of the parties.

It would probably be well, however, for unions and managements to review the efficacy of the arbitration board arrangement. Sometimes it results in absurdities, as in the case of several companies where the principal union and company spokesmen at the hearing are also board members and participate as "judges." This means inevitably that the executive sessions of the board are often nothing more than a rehearing of the case. The highly partisan positions of

[20] No statistical information is available to prove this trend. In a survey made by the American Arbitration Association in 1957 it was found that during the prior year 81.6 per cent of all of its cases were decided by a single arbitrator.

most company and union designees mean that they are of little help in the deliberations, and many neutrals now go through the motions of a board meeting, then withdraw and send a draft of their proposed ruling to the other board members.

The necessity under many contracts of securing a majority vote often forces the neutral to compromise his own convictions. A large steel company for many years had a Board of Arbitration, which was finally abolished in 1951. The union was agreeable to this change. There had been several cases in which the union thought that the neutral was prepared to support its case at the start of deliberations, but he then turned down the grievances because the company board member was so persuasive. The company had also become aware of several defects in the board system. It found that in the hearings management was making inferior presentation of its cases, secure in its belief that any acts of omission would be taken care of by its representative on the board. The complaint was also made that the deliberations of the tripartite board frequently involved elements of negotiation and mediation. Since the abolition of the board, the arbitration process has become more decision-making and less mediative in nature. Not all management officials, however, agreed with the 1951 action. One key official said that he still preferred the tripartite board because it prevented risky dicta in the opinion rendered by the neutral; the implications of what the neutral said could be pointed out to him and revisions effected before the opinion was released. In this official's words, "the company can afford to lose cases, but it can't afford to have some of the things said that are said." He preferred that the board be retained but that the partisan members be denied a vote. This compromise arrangement is used by a number of companies.

(3) How is the arbitrator to be chosen? When it is decided that the permanent arbitrator system will be used, whether on the basis of a single arbitrator or a board chairman, the parties in nearly every instance select the neutral by agreement. In fact one of the early reasons given for having a permanent arbitrator was to avoid the difficulty of having to select a man for each individual case. One company reported that before it had an umpire appointed by the War Labor Board it spent more time trying to find a satisfactory arbitrator than it did in settling the case.

However, the problem of selection even in *ad hoc* cases has largely disappeared. Most agreements now provide that if the parties themselves cannot agree on an arbitrator they will seek the services of an appointing agency. Usually either the American Arbitration Association or the Federal Mediation and Conciliation Service is designated, although occasionally a local judge is asked to make the appointment.[21] The two services referred to actually do not make the appointment in most cases. Instead they select from their panels of private arbitrators the names of eight or nine neutrals, and the list is sent separately to the union and to the company. By ranking in the order of each party's preference a mutually acceptable arbitrator is chosen and then appointed. In effect the selection is by agreement. Very seldom is it necessary for the Arbitration Association or the Conciliation Service to make an administrative appointment because of inability to find one mutually acceptable person on several lists. Many states have established Boards of Arbitration that may be designated by the parties.

Scope of the Arbitrator's Authority

Although the principle of grievance arbitration has gained remarkable currency, there is still grave concern over the extent to which the outsider is allowed to resolve disputes between the parties. Only a very few agreements provide that "any and all disputes which may arise during the life of the agreement" may be appealed to arbitration by one or the other of the parties. The most commonly-accepted clause is of the type recommended by the President's Labor-Management Conference in 1945, the arbitration only of grievances involving the interpretation and application of the terms of the agreement. Accompanying this clause is standard language to the effect that the arbitrator shall have no authority to add to, subtract from, or amend any provision in the agreement. As a matter of principle, neither a company nor a union wants an outsider to tamper with the basic terms of the agreement.

Some parties, however, have found that the usual protective

---

[21] The American Arbitration Association is being used to an increasing extent because it not only helps select the arbitrator but also administers the hearing according to a number of well-tried rules. Illustrative of these rules are the following: if either party plans to use a lawyer, notice must be given in advance of the hearing; and the arbitrator must render his decision no later than thirty days after the proceedings are closed.

clauses are inadequate restraints. As Chapter 10 indicates, many companies were understandably dismayed, for example, when they were told by an arbitrator that, notwithstanding a management rights clause and complete contract silence on the question of subcontracting, the recognition clause could be interpreted as a foreclosure of the company's freedom to subcontract work.[22]

It must be remembered that an arbitrator under these scope-of-authority provisions often has the right to interpret his own authority. Sometimes the course of least resistance is chosen because in deciding arbitrability most of the merits of the grievance must be heard. Even the argument advanced by companies that a given issue is not arbitrable may not be successful, unless it is based on very specific contract language barring the subject from consideration by an arbitrator. The generally prevailing view among arbitrators is that a union is entitled to be heard if it can establish a *prima facie* case that the issue somehow involves interpretation of the agreement. Moreover, the burden is on the company to prove nonarbitrability. Under these circumstances it is not too difficult for a union to hurdle the nonarbitrability obstacle.[23]

The inherent risk in the arbitration process of having the neutral legislate in addition to interpreting and applying the terms of the agreement will be discussed in Chapter 26. This section explores some of the specific restrictions placed on the neutral's authority over and above the broader mandates of the type mentioned in the 1945 Labor Management Conference report.

In three large automobile companies the umpire is barred from ruling on any disputes involving production standards used in their measured daywork system. In some, issues involving health and safety and rates on new jobs are also specifically removed from arbitration review. From the time the umpire systems were created in these companies it was argued that these were matters for management to decide. Although the companies were willing to discuss

[22] The type of clause adopted may make a difference in the relationship between the parties. The parties should think through carefully how they want to use the process. A very restrictive clause may tend to create a legalistic relationship.

[23] The view of many managements that arbitrators seldom deny arbitrability is undoubtedly exaggerated. According to Benjamin Aaron, a quick review of the first thirty Bureau of National Affairs volumes disclosed 57 decisions in which arbitrators found the issues presented were not arbitrable. Bureau of National Affairs, "On First Looking Into the Lincoln Mills Decision," *Arbitration and the Law* (1959). The Supreme Court decision in 1960 in Warrior & Gulf Navigation Co. increases the scope of arbitrators' authority.

such matters with the union in the grievance procedure, they were reluctant to empower an outsider to judge management's decisions. Originally the UAW protested this position of the company. In several contract negotiations in the 1940's the union tried to have the excluded items covered under umpire systems. More recently the union's views have changed.

The present views of the parties concerning the exclusion of standards, that permits the union to strike on unresolved complaints, are of interest. An international union spokesman in 1958 emphasized that it was healthier to keep such issues as standards and health and safety out of arbitration. Revealing a change in union position, he said:

> A third party shouldn't settle these things, because in all probability he would foul up both parties. When you have arbitration as the terminal step, there is a tendency to let the arbitrator decide these matters with the result that the parties don't face up to their responsibilities. The local unions, if they could go to arbitration, would be likely to take the attitude "we might as well try for it," even if they knew they had little or no chance.

The officials in at least one of the three companies now seem to have some doubts about the restriction on the umpire's authority. Some company spokesmen said they would definitely like to arbitrate production standards and health and safety issues and get rid of the strike threat. There appear to be several basic reasons for the change in their thinking. First, they have found that a strikeable issue is often used by the local union as a vehicle for nonstrikeable issues. So-called "standards disputes" are used as a pressure device to win other issues. Second, union strategy has also been perfected to the point that when the strike stage is reached on an unsettled standards complaint, the union usually broadens the strikeable issue to include health and safety matters as well. It is the company's belief that this is done by the union for public relations reasons. The public is led to believe that the union is striking to protect the employees from hazardous working conditions. Third, they say it has been difficult to discuss standards disputes in an intelligent way with the union. Its industrial engineers are baffled by the opportunistic approach of the union. One union leader once told the company, "You set standards any way you want, and we'll dispute them any way we want." Fourth, it is the opinion of some management officials that they have had to make too many concessions on standards in the face of strike threats. Finally, the distinction between health and safety and mere inconvenience is so nebulous that in effect it means that the union is able to strike over working conditions during the term of the agreement.[24]

These experiences and doubts, even though they are not fully shared by all officials of this and other automobile companies, illustrate the dilemmas for management when disputes over certain subjects are excluded from arbitration review. If their exclusion has the effect of making them strikeable issues and if union power tactics prevail, a company may find itself giving in to an unwarranted extent. Most companies are willing to arbitrate standards. One large food company said that it would be willing to give a 10-cents-per-hour increase to get rid of the restriction it had once insisted on—that is, no arbitration of standards. It had concluded that it would probably fare much better at the hands of the arbitrator than it would under a system that resolved standards issues by pressure tactics.

Not all contractual provisions excluding certain issues from arbitration involve a choice between arbitration and possible strike. Some companies have been able to incorporate in contract clauses an explicit ban on arbitration review of certain actions without in any way lessening the import of the no-strike provision. For example, some companies have escaped the obligation to arbitrate their promotional decisions when a senior employee has been by-passed in favor of a junior employee on grounds of ability. This has been accomplished by insisting that the management's judgment as to relative ability be final and not subject to review by an arbitrator. The only reviewable question is whether it gave reasonable consideration to the criterion of seniority.[25]

Still another illustration is those few agreements in which the arbitrator is denied the power to modify disciplinary penalties; he

---

[24] See also Chapter 18, "Measured Daywork," for further discussion of this problem.

[25] What constitutes "reasonable consideration," of course, may be interpreted by an arbitrator in such a way as to admit the review of ability indirectly. Special consideration must also be given by management to the way in which it exercises its retained and unreviewable rights under a clause such as this. The mere existence of a review avenue may lessen the prospects of actual arbitration. In one case a company's by-passing of a senior employee under a clause such as this, for what the union considered capricious reasons, led to a six months' stalemate in subsequent negotiations over a union demand that seniority be the primary factor in determining promotions.

may only determine the guilt or innocence of the employee disciplined. One of the largest steel companies has this type of clause, and it is judged by management to be advantageous for several reasons. For one thing it allows the company to keep penalties realistic and at the same time keep down the number of grievances. The scope for challenging disciplinary action is reduced. The company recognizes that in occasional cases the arbitrator may reinstate an employee where he might otherwise have modified the penalty.

An airline company, following the pattern of others in the industry, had a similar arrangement in its contract for a number of years. After several arbitration cases it found that the restrictions on the arbitrator's authority produced results contrary to good labor and employee relations. In one case two employees were discharged for going into a swampy area with a company jeep to recover items that had blown off the runway area. The jeep became immersed in the mud and sand, and some damage was caused when the two men tried to extricate it. The company was convinced that the employees, both young men, were jeep-jockeys who went into the swamp area only to see what the jeep could do, but this new contention was not sustained by the arbitrator. He found that at most the men were guilty of very poor judgment and deserved some punishment. However, under the contract clause the arbitrator had to choose between reinstatement with full back pay or discharge; he was not allowed to modify the company penalty. He decided reluctantly that discharge was too extreme a penalty under the circumstances. The result was that two men of relatively junior status, having been found guilty of poor judgment and deserving of some penalty, were reinstated with more than six months' back pay. The settlement was almost a reward for misbehavior because neither of the men had worked in the interim. No one except the miscreants was happy with the outcome. Here again is a case in which the desire to restrict review authority must be weighed against the possible consequences.

Other examples might be given of attempts to restrict arbitration authority once the principle of grievance arbitration is accepted. They would only support the conclusion that the short-run successes from management's standpoint often prove to be bitter pills in the long run. If such restrictions are adopted without any awareness of their full implications, management has little right to hold the arbitration process responsible for its later problems.

Determinants of Grievance Arbitration Rates

Whether labor relations are good or poor in a given situation cannot be judged by numbers alone. Preoccupation with numbers has been a weakness in many analyses of the grievance procedure and the arbitration process. Extensive investigations reveal a considerable variation from company to company, and even from plant to plant within the same company, in the number of unresolved grievances that are referred to arbitration. It is important to know why this variation exists, and what its significance is for labor relations. The latter point will be explored in Chapter 26.

A distinction should be made between the number of cases on the arbitration docket and the number actually heard and decided by the outside neutral. Very often a case that remains unresolved in the last step of the grievance procedure short of arbitration is referred to arbitration by the union, and at the last minute a settlement is reached. There are several possible reasons for this disparity between the number of referrals and the number of actual decisions.

(1) It may be a defect in the arbitration machinery itself. If a union is required to put a case on the arbitration agenda within a specified time after the decision in the last prior step and if there is no prescribed sequence for hearing the pending cases, it is very probable that a backlog will develop. Either the union will make an automatic referral to protect an employee's interests or to postpone a withdrawal of the case, or it may deliberately build up a backlog in the interest of "horse-trading." A backlog of some magnitude, involving cumulative monetary claims on the company, is often a persuasive weapon for wresting concessions in borderline cases or for bargaining in basic contract negotiations.

In a large rubber company no orderly system was established for hearing cases. As a consequence, cases that had been processed through the grievance procedure as long as two or three years earlier, remained on the arbitration agenda, while new cases or the politically expedient cases were heard by the umpire. After several years' harassment on this point the company insisted that a docketing arrangement be adopted in the contract. It had the support of the international union in its effort because it too was troubled by subversion of the arbitration process by the local union. As a result of the company's successful effort most of the old cases were dropped by the union without prejudice as to principle. The cases referred to arbitration are now current, and a new case can be heard in a month.[26] Another large rubber company found itself flooded with a backlog of several hundred cases because it was unable to sell the union on a docketing system. The knowledge that once such a system is put into effect, it will transfer pressure to the union either to withdraw cases or to submit them promptly to arbitration has prevented the union from facing up to the problem.

A paper company reported that under its contract the union can keep a grievance arbitrable indefinitely as long as it appeals within thirty days. This "dormant filing" of fourth-step referrals to arbitration enables the union to avoid responsibility for deciding to accept a management answer. All cases are automatically referred to arbitration; in fact, so automatic has the habit become, that in a few cases the union filed for arbitration grievances that the company had granted in the fourth step. Yet in this relationship the actual number of cases heard and decided by the arbitrator is relatively few. What the company described as "more of an annoyance than a problem" is the accumulation of potentially arbitrable cases which are disposed of by contract negotiations or grievance horse-trading.

(2) The actual arbitration decisions may be substantially fewer than arbitration referrals because of the adoption by the parties of *supra* grievance machinery steps, sometimes labeled Step $3\frac{1}{2}$ or $4\frac{1}{2}$, of the type referred to in Chapter 24.

(3) The imminence of an arbitration hearing itself, accompanied by the uncertainties felt by both parties concerning the outcome of a neutral's examination, sometimes results in a last-minute settlement. The merits of a docketed case may appear less persuasive as the day of the hearing approaches. In this respect the arbitration experience is not unlike last minute out-of-court settlements in civil cases. An extreme case is that of a Boston arbitrator who flew to Los Angeles to hear a discharge case, was asked to wait in his hotel room for a short time while the parties conferred, and then one hour later was advised by the parties that they had settled the grievance and he was free to return to Boston. One union lawyer has commented that he

---

[26] Customarily when a formal docketing system is used, the parties provide that discharge or layoff cases that would cause hardship to employees or cumulative liability to the employer are given priority over other pending cases.

always impresses his clients with the fact that arbitration is "a good, but a risky and dangerous process" in the hope that they will be receptive to suggested settlement even on the day of the scheduled arbitration hearing.

(4) A surprising number of cases will be settled in the course of the hearing itself. This is the case especially when attorneys are the leading spokesmen or when "home office" people or an international union representative, in effect, are hearing the true facts of the case for the first time with the arbitrator. It is understandable, but unfortunate, that facts favorable to one's position will be disclosed to a spokesman, while those less savory will be concealed or glossed over before the hearing. The employee who overlooks the verbal warnings that he was given or the foreman who fails to mention that he always sought volunteers for overtime work may cause a case to go to arbitration that might never have been submitted had the entire story been known. This type of concealment should suggest an intra-company or intra-union problem. But, apart from this, it is always a dramatic contribution to good labor relations when a party to an arbitration proceeding has the objectivity to admit embarrassment and withdraw a case, the complexion of which has changed abruptly in the course of the hearing. This is far better than trying to bludgeon through to an inevitable adverse verdict. For these reasons, the number of cases heard and decided by an arbitrator may fall far short of those placed on the arbitration docket.

The determinants of the grievance arbitration rate are similar in many respects to the determinants of the grievance rate discussed in Chapter 23, but there are enough differences to warrant a separate discussion. It was observed in Chapter 23 that as a general rule, where the grievance rate is low, one may expect to find a friendly relationship between the parties, although the harmony may be for poor reasons. However, low grievance rates do not necessarily indicate good relations or conditions, any more than high grievance rates necessarily mean bad relations. The same general observations apply in judging the significance of arbitration rate variation. In the automobile industry one of the largest companies had an annual arbitration rate of approximately 1 per 3,500 bargaining-unit employees, while another company until recently had an annual rate of 1 per 233 employees. Yet at the time there was no reason to conclude that the labor relations were worse in the latter company with an arbitration incidence rate more than 15 times higher than in the former company. The experience of these companies will be studied in some detail in Chapter 26.

Among the principal determinants of the arbitration rate, which may assist in understanding variations in the rate from company to company, plant to plant, or from one period of time to another, are the following: (1) the attitudes of the parties in labor relations, (2) the provisions of the collective bargaining agreement, (3) operation of the grievance procedure, (4) leadership qualities of management and union, and (5) the influence of arbitrators.

Attitudes of the Parties in Labor Relations

If a relationship is characterized by tension and suspicion and an unwillingness to yield anything, there is more likely to be a fairly high rate of arbitration. This attitude militates against settlement of a problem in the early stages of the grievance process.

To illustrate, in an agreement between a textile company and its union there is the usual clause providing that payment for an un-worked holiday is made if the employee worked the last scheduled work day before and the first scheduled day after the holiday. The clause is unusual, however, in that it makes no allowance for excusable absences. A situation arose involving a long-service employee, who worked the day before Thanksgiving. His father was burned to death on Thanksgiving night, and naturally the employee did not work on Friday. The company refused to give him holiday pay, although it acknowledged that this was a hardship case. The union filed a grievance claiming that the intent of the clause was to prevent unjustified absenteeism before or after a holiday and that consideration should be given to legitimate reasons for absence. The company remained adamant, fearing that making an exception in this case would create a precedent that the union would use in future cases. It distrusted union assurances that a settlement would be considered without precedent value. The case went to arbitration, and the union claim was denied.

Another textile management with exactly the same type of clause said that its relationship with the union was such that it would never allow a case like this to go to arbitration. Over the years on its own initiative it had granted holiday pay when it was satisfied that the employee had a good reason for absence. It commented that "the union had never tried to take advantage of the company's voluntary action."

Where management constantly resists the union and takes a negative attitude toward it, there is likely to be a higher arbitration rate. Sometimes this applies even on a broad geographic scale. The influence of a strong manufacturers' association and several large law firms has resulted in an unusually high arbitration rate in one New England state. Frequent resort to arbitration is considered healthy evidence of resistance to the union all the way. It is interesting that in this state one also finds a high percentage of appeals of arbitration decisions to the courts for one reason or another. The attitude is reflected also in the arbitration clauses in the agreements. As a result, there is an ambivalence in the approach toward arbitration. Some contract arbitration provisions are designed for the chief purpose of restricting referrals to arbitration. Yet in practice the parties to such an agreement are likely to have a high arbitration rate.[27]

The legalistic approach cannot be divorced from the stage of development of a relationship. Insistence by the company that the letter of the contract be observed may cause a high rate of arbitration in the early stages. But once the new union understands that the company will take a firm stand in the grievance procedure and that grievances of doubtful merit are likely to be denied by an arbitrator, the rate of referrals usually decreases. This was the experience in the General Motors Corporation, for example. On the other hand, a company that won't yield even when it is clearly in the wrong will soon have enough arbitration reverses to cause it to review its policy.

---

[27] For example, an agreement of a metal fabricating company with the UAW, in addition to having explicit time limits for arbitration referral, a clear definition of the arbitrator's authority, and other less usual requirements, provides that if either party raises the question of arbitrability, this issue will be decided first. If either party disagrees with the decision on arbitrability, such party is to notify the other within 5 days and then application may be made "to the Superior Court . . . if said Court is in session, or to a Judge thereof if said Court is in recess, for a final decision on the question of arbitrability, and that the decision of such Court or Judge shall be final as to the question determined and that it shall bind the arbitrator in rendering the award." Under this agreement arbitrability is a frequent threshold issue, and the appeal to the Superior Court is not uncommon.

Contents of the Collective Bargaining Agreement

Very often in the interest of achieving settlements the parties may purposely resort to ambiguous phrases in the agreement. There is no real meeting of minds, and each party tacitly recognizes that if difficulties arise, an arbitrator will probably have to clarify and, euphemistically, to interpret the contract. In the chapters on subcontracting and work scheduling illustrations of this practice are given. Actually what the parties have done is to leave a void in the contract, camouflaged by some meaningless language, with the full expectation that an arbitrator will some day legislate for them.

This cause for arbitration referral is more frequent than one might expect, and it occurs with parties who would be shocked at the suggestion that basic contract terms be submitted to an outsider. It is often the awards in situations like this, that, when examined out of context, give rise to the claim that arbitrators are too quick to arrogate authority. Perhaps arbitrators err in their readiness to legislate under the guise of interpreting the agreement. Some arbitrators confronted with this problem decide wisely to refer the issue to the parties for further bargaining, occasionally doffing the arbitrator's cap for that of a mediator. If a decision is required by the parties, these same few arbitrators will label the process what it is, namely, the fixing of a basic contract term.

However, problems created by contract language do not arise solely because of faulty draftsmanship by the parties. A more important explanation of the frequency of arbitration is the inherent nature of a labor agreement. Some matters covered by an agreement lend themselves to precise, definitive language. For example, the terms of a union-shop provision can be expressed in explicit, unambiguous language, and problems of interpretation seldom arise. But many subjects by their very nature can be handled only by general propositions.

In an excellent discussion of this aspect of the labor agreement, the late veteran arbitrator Harry Shulman said:

> . . . Precisely because general propositions do not decide concrete cases (as Justice Holmes said), the parties may well agree on the general propositions. . . . Many illustrations can be cited. Negotiators can readily agree that the employer should have the power to discipline for cause. But they would probably negotiate for years without reach-

ing agreement on all matters that should or should not constitute proper cause and what specific penalties should be appropriate in the diverse circumstances. Negotiators can generally agree that "merit and ability" should be a factor, perhaps the paramount factor, in promotions. But they are likely to leave the agreement with quite different notions of what is meant by "merit" and by "ability" and how the factors are to be established.[28]

Where an incentive system exists, the contract may provide only that the standards established shall be "fair and equitable."

All of these phrases, necessarily imprecise, require the exercise of daily administrative judgment by management. These judgments in turn may be based on subjective considerations. It is easy to understand why these elements in an agreement are the most frequent source of grievances even in a company with sound administrative procedures and policies. Similarly if the agreement relies heavily on general propositions, there is a greater likelihood that management judgments will be tested by an outside arbitrator. It is harder for a union to take a strong position against an employee grievance when the issue involves a choice between two seemingly reasonable but conflicting judgments. It is difficult, for example, to prove that an employee's action was for "just cause" or that he is more "able" than another employee.

Probably the greatest influence of the arbitration process over the years has been in the formulation of criteria for applying these judgment clauses. This is the case especially if the process provides for a permanent umpire, whose tenure and consistency of rulings create a body of precedent cases. Many companies and unions prepare special summaries of cases to help foremen and department heads understand how the general proposition is to be applied to the concrete case. For example, the Ford Motor Company's Umpire Proceedings Section has prepared a digest of "Umpire Decisions on Discipline" with the cover-notation ". . . to be used as a guide in the imposition of disciplinary penalties." It is evident that constructive use of the arbitration process over the years may eliminate the need for referral of many judgment cases. However, as will be seen later, other determinants of the grievance arbitration rate often prevent

[28] Harry Shulman, "The Role of Arbitration in the Collective Bargaining Process," Institute of Industrial Relations, University of California, *Collective Bargaining and Arbitration* (1949).

this result. The optimistic statement "a good arbitrator will eventually work himself out of a job" does not take into account the many determinants involved.

It would be wrong to infer from the above comments that it is desirable for a company and a union to reduce the arbitration potential by creating, in the words of Shulman, "a perfectly meaningful agreement—a thing of beauty to please the eye of the most exacting legal draftsmen." Some lawyers, unsophisticated in labor relations, have done a great disservice to their clients by trying to do this very thing. One company unthinkingly accepted the advice of counsel and insisted that the union negotiate a complete set of disciplinary rules and a fixed formula of penalties. It has regretted having done this ever since. The company failed to anticipate every type of misbehavior that might occur. The union, having entered into this elaborate agreement with reluctance, now contends that no employee may be disciplined unless it is for violation of a rule specified in the agreement. Another consequence is that management gave up its basic responsibility to exercise initial judgment in an area where case-by-case judgment is vital. The plant manager says bluntly, "I'd a damned sight rather see my foremen develop by having to make decisions and then even have those decisions overturned by an arbitrator than to prevent them from making any decisions."

Operation of the Grievance Procedure

This has already been discussed in Chapters 23 and 24 on grievance adjustments and needs only to be mentioned as a determinant of arbitration usage. It is obvious that if the parties make full and effective use of the formal as well as the informal screening steps prior to arbitration, the number of cases decided by a neutral will be low.

Management and Union Leadership Qualities

The rate of arbitration in a given plant or company may be attributable to the presence or lack of strong leadership. What is most impressive is that a high volume or a low volume may indicate either effective management or union leadership or weak leadership on the part of one or the other of the parties. In some situations top management assumes that something is wrong with the caliber of administrative heads if many cases are carried to arbitration; the department head who has the fewest arbitrations is judged the most successful. This short-sighted rating system often results in settlements favorable to the union that an outsider might not have granted. Sometimes the pressure to settle is a direct outgrowth of top management's intervention in the so-called pre-arbitration screening step. A local management might be convinced of its position only to have a central office representative move in at the last minute with the philosophy that if "pennies and not principle are involved, grant the grievance and avoid the arbitration." If this attitude is carried to an extreme, it may force the company to reverse its position eventually by incurring many arbitrations for the primary purpose of undoing bad habits.

Weakness of managerial leadership, which reduces the volume of arbitration at the expense of unwise grievance settlements, may also increase arbitration referrals. Some companies have found that the unwillingness of its representatives to face up to decision-making responsibilities results in the referral of even weak cases to arbitration. Occasionally this is a function of a poor line and staff relationship. One company, which was losing more than two-thirds of the verdicts in arbitration, found that weak cases were being forced to arbitration by operating heads, who insisted on "giving them nothing unless absolutely necessary" over the vigorous, but ineffective, objections of the subordinate industrial relations staff. Some unions, hard pressed financially and embarrassed politically in defending the arbitration process under these circumstances, are inclined to feel that revival of the right to strike is more desirable than being "arbitrated to death treasurywise."

Weak union leadership may also account for either high or low utilization of the arbitration machinery. If the union is weak in the sense that its leadership is unwilling to sacrifice expenditure of union money for arbitration or is willing to make "deals" with management, the arbitration rate may be low. Far more common, is the weakness of the politically conscious leader, from the level of shop steward to that of the international staff representative, who would prefer to transfer the blame for an adverse verdict than to exercise true leadership and tell an employee that he had no case.

One union leader was honest and forthright in saying, "Why should I tell a man voting for me that he was wrong. Let the arbitrator tell him, and I can be a hero by denouncing the arbitrator for not knowing what he was talking about." There are few active arbitrators who have not had the experience of hearing a case and then having a union spokesman approach him discreetly afterward and say, in effect, "I know this case was a lemon, but what could I do?" Some union leaders, after an eloquent plea on behalf of an allegedly victimized employee, will even go so far as to warn the arbitrator minutes later that the aggrieved "deserves to be put in his place." Translated this often means: "He is the leader of a rival group within the union out to get me, but for political reasons I had to put on a good show."

The arbitrator and the process of arbitration thus may easily become as much a political foil as a source of justice. It is amusing, and even reassuring, to hear union leaders complain that cases they expected to lose were won because the arbitrator was naive enough to be guided by the merits. It is true that an arbitrator with an awareness of labor relations will be sophisticated enough to understand that the political grievance will, and rightfully should, be presented to him. But indiscriminate exploiting of arbitration by an elected union officer to escape leadership responsibility may become anathema to the arbitrator and result in decisions unduly prejudicial to the union.

Influence of Arbitrators

Unthinkingly the arbitrator himself may encourage practices that promote arbitration. This is particularly likely when the parties have a permanent umpire from the start who tends to do their work for them. With the wisdom of hindsight, a very large automobile company and its union now both acknowledge that encouragement of free employee expression through grievances and the easy access to arbitration may have been helpful in the early days of mutual distrust; but both feel that their first umpire may have encouraged undue reliance on the arbitration process. It is surprising how often a party to a labor relationship will yield its responsibilites to an outsider. When this happens, the outside neutral must remind himself that the basic responsibility for the conduct of labor relations rests with the parties themselves.

The cost of arbitration sometimes influences the frequency of its use. If the arbitrator's fee or the umpire's retainer is low, arbitration may be encouraged. One large rubber company and its union found that its financial arrangement with the permanent arbitrator encouraged referrals. If he heard one case a day, he was paid $100 for the case, two a day, $90 a case, and so on to six or more cases a day at $60 a case. Under this system the union usually saw to it that six or more cases were docketed each hearing day. On the other hand, if the cost is very high, arbitration will be discouraged. The Industrial Union Department of the AFL-CIO called a conference in 1959 with representatives of various appointing agencies to complain of the fee-charging practices of some arbitrators. It objected chiefly to the excessive "thinking time" charged for by arbitrators. The IUD has said that resentment of local unions may mount to the point where they will seek to eliminate arbitration and the no-strike clause.

The variation in arbitration rates will be illustrated by several case experiences in Chapter 26. In addition, the significance of the process in the bargaining relationship will be discussed at some length.

26 / *Arbitration and the Bargaining Relationship*

THE PHENOMENAL CHANGE during the past twenty years from almost no arbitration to almost invariable arbitration has had a profound effect on the relationship between unions and management. The parties behave differently when they are committed to referring unresolved grievances to an outside neutral, whose decision is final and binding. In both the negotiation and the administration of the agreement they must be constantly alert to the possibility that a contract will be reviewed by an outsider.

In the words of an industrial relations director with many years of experience in a rubber footwear company: "When we first adopted grievance arbitration, we didn't give much thought to what it would mean to us. It was just one of those developments that everyone was going along with during the war years. It didn't take us long, though, to discover that we had to think through many problems and policies. For the first time in our dealing with the union we had to bring in a lawyer to check the agreement. We discovered that the practices being followed by our foremen were becoming a Frankenstein because of the weight being given to them by the arbitrator. Decisions we used to make day-in and day-out after a few minutes' deliberation we now make only after lengthy deliberation. Most important, we had to face up to a basic policy question: How did we want to use this arbitration machinery? Where we had a 'gut feeling' that we were right in what we did, but intellectually we weren't quite sure, should we let the grievance go to arbitration? Or should we resolve our doubts in favor of the union?"

The purpose of the present chapter is to develop some insights into the role of grievance arbitration in the bargaining relationship. This will be done under two basic headings: (1) an analysis of various experiences with arbitration, and (2) a review of some of the preoccupying problems and considerations in the use of this terminal step

772

of the grievance process. In these discussions the ways in which the arbitration process affects the bargaining relationship will be our principal concern.

Experience with Grievance Arbitration

It has been pointed out in the preceding chapter that firms with the highest rate of arbitration do not necessarily have poor labor relations, and firms with little or no arbitration do not necessarily have good labor relations. In fact, some of the determinants of the volume of arbitration are quite independent of employer-employee relations. In general, where there is a friendly relationship, one may expect to find a low rate of arbitration. But it would be naive to assume, as so many analysts have, that frequent arbitration means a poor relationship or that infrequent resort to arbitration suggests a state of true harmony. Logically one would expect that as relationships developed, as the stability of contract terms is achieved through interpretations worked out in grievance adjustment or arbitration, the volume of grievance arbitrations would decrease. It is true that this often happens. But some parties, whose basic definition of rights and obligations, as expressed in the agreement, has been stabilized over the years, have a continuing high arbitration rate.

Sometimes a company and union with a long-run downward trend in the arbitration rate have short-run periodic bulges in the incidence rate. For example, a drastic innovation, such as the introduction of an incentive system for the first time, may cause a flurry of arbitration referrals. One company that had undergone a long economic strike had a 100-per-cent increase in arbitration following the strike, but the entire increase was attributable to the arbitration of disciplinary actions that arose as a result of alleged improper behavior by employees on the picket line during the strike.

In some situations, it is not the total volume that is significant. It is rather the type of grievance or issue. For example, a leather company over the past twenty years has experienced an over-all reduction in grievances going to arbitration. Seldom do disciplinary, equal-division-of-overtime, seniority, and other similar grievances go beyond the second or third step of the grievance procedure. Yet the referral of issues involving production standards is as high today as it was twenty years ago. An aircraft engine company and a UAW local have seen a steady, gradual decline in the rate of arbitration refer-rals. But just as important as the decline is the fact that most of the cases arbitrated in the past eight years involve promotions and dis-ciplinary actions for absenteeism. This phenomenon is explained by a sick leave clause which tends to encourage absenteeism and by a promotion clause which has been administered inconsistently.

It is disturbing that so few companies have learned how to analyze intelligently their experience with arbitration. Among practitioners and scholars there has been an unrealistic preoccupation with num-bers. The president of one company praised his company's conduct of labor relations because in more than ten years not one case had been referred to an outsider. Two years after this public boast as a member of a panel on the subject "Labor Peace: Why and How?," this same president was faced with a union strike over management's demand that it be allowed to exercise certain prerogatives in the in-terests of competitive efficiency.

Another executive, disturbed by the high volume of arbitration, announced summarily that "this business of letting some professor decide what we're supposed to do has got to stop." His subordinates construed this as a mandate to settle grievances at all costs rather than allow them to go to arbitration. A plant manager observed, "We're being blamed for the arbitrations, not the union. It goes against our grain, and it puts the supervisors on the spot, but if we're not supposed to arbitrate, we won't."

In each of these illustrations, the policy adopted by management was attributable to its concern with numbers alone. It was not the product of a considered analysis of why the volume of arbitration was low or high. Satisfaction with low volume blinded one management to the fact that it was the product of concessions to the union at the expense of efficiency and managerial flexibility. The wisdom and success of management in labor relations is seldom measurable by statistics alone.

It is difficult to classify experiences of companies with arbitration. Experience has a rate dimension, a time dimension, an issue-fre-quency dimension, or a combination of any of these three. In the selected experiences described below no attempt will be made to follow an orderly system of classification. Each experience or set of experiences has been chosen because it reflects directly or by contrast some of the considerations mentioned above. Furthermore, they illustrate some of the determinants of arbitration rates discussed in Chapter 25. While the typical trend in the volume of arbitration, i.e., high rate initially and low rate subsequently in the relationships, will be illustrated, the abnormally high- or low-volume situations will command special attention.

What may be considered the expected trend in arbitration is the experience of one of the large meat packing companies. In the 13-year period, 1943 to 1955 inclusive, this company had 223 arbitration cases under its agreements with the United Packinghouse Workers' Union, the Amalgamated Meat Cutters, and an independent brotherhood. Of this total, 191 or 86 per cent occurred in the first seven years. In 1950 there were 12 cases. Since that year the total has never exceeded five per year, and in one year (1953) no arbitration decisions were rendered.

This consistent downward trend in reliance on the arbitration machinery undoubtedly reflects the adjustment process in the relationship between the parties. A growing capacity for working with each other enabled both parties to resolve more grievances in the earlier steps of the grievance procedure. Furthermore, in this company, as in so many others that have experienced a downward trend in arbitration volume, it meant that when the union became established, the employees themselves developed a better understanding of their rights and obligations. Both the company and the union learned to do a better job of screening grievances of dubious merit. In addition, the problem areas in the contract-development stage of the relationship were gradually corrected, either by the parties themselves or by the initial heavy volume of umpire decisions, many of which created policy guides and supplied a framework of interpretation for the contract.

Evidence in support of this is found in an analysis of the cases by issues. Almost 47 per cent of all the cases involved wage-rate questions, particularly intraplant and interplant inequity claims. Over the years the stabilization of the internal wage structure and the tendency to equalize rates among various plants on like operations removed this as an area of contention. Today very few grievances involve wage rates. The second largest group of cases, approximately 20 per cent of the total, involved questions of discipline. About half of these were strike discharge cases and created a non-recurring bulge of the type described above.

To complete the arbitration profile of this company, it is interesting to note that although about half of the organized employees are under the CIO master agreement, they account for well over half of the total cases. Of 25 CIO organized plants only 4 have never had an arbitration, but as many as 18 of the 29 plants under agreements with the AFL or the independent union have never carried a case to arbitration. While local management variation may explain part of this disparity, the differences in union attitude are the predominant cause of this pattern. The CIO union was more inclined to bring grievances to arbitration because of its deference, perhaps excessive at times, to the observance of democratic processes within the union. As so many companies dealing with both AFL and CIO unions have found, the two have had somewhat different conceptions of their obligation to the rank and file. The CIO unions have been more inclined to process grievances and to use arbitration even when the merits were highly dubious. There is no indication from the record that the CIO approach pays off.

If a similar analysis were made of a large number of company arbitration experiences, it is likely that a trend of this type would be found in the majority of situations. Generally a low arbitration rate goes hand-in-hand with good labor relations. A subsidiary of a large steel company, which had a high rate of grievance arbitration in its early relationship with the union, embarked on a deliberate program to reduce the volume. Its review of grievances became more painstaking, and it adopted a rough guide called the "80–20 rule" for arbitration. The grievance review board works on the principle that a grievance should not go to arbitration unless the company has at least an 80–20 chance of winning. In recent years it has been winning 90 per cent of the cases. Several of the plants that had no arbitration cases pending in 1958 were ones in which the union had never won a case. This review board's policy does not mean that the review, which comes after the foreman gives his answer, results in an overturn of the foreman's decision. Rather, the foremen themselves are trained to apply the 80–20 guide.

This experience highlights another important lesson for managements. If weak cases—from management's standpoint—are allowed to go to arbitration, the win record is more likely to favor the union.

This, in turn, encourages the union to use the process and results in a high rate. Another company reports that in its ten years' experience with the union, it has never really lost a case in arbitration. Of 13 cases decided by an arbitrator, the company won 11 cases outright, and 2 were partially won.

A comparison of the arbitration experience of three of our largest automobile manufacturing companies reveals within a single industry excellent illustrations of three types of experience: the consistently high arbitration rate experience, the orthodox downward trend pattern, and the consistently low arbitration rate experience. Each of these companies is organized by the UAW and has a master agreement covering a number of geographically-separated plants; each has had arbitration experience under the single umpire system for at least 15 years. Yet in spite of these common characteristics, their experience with arbitration is markedly different.

COMPANY A. This case illustrates the high arbitration rate experience. Its first umpire, who was chosen when the arbitration clause was put into the contract in 1943, remained with the parties for 11 years. In the early years the arbitration rate was quite high, as might be expected. The parties were new in their contractual relationship, and union recognition had been achieved in 1941 only after a lengthy and militant campaign. The record of wildcat strikes was very high in the early years. Over the years, in spite of thousands of decisions and the daily resolution of grievances by the parties, the arbitration rate continued to climb. In 1950 a second umpire was chosen to relieve the overtaxed initial umpire; in 1952 a third was added.[1] In 1958 four umpires were used. In 1955 a total of more than 1,880 cases were appealed to the umpire, about 1,200 of which were settled by the parties and 650 of which had to be decided by one of the umpires. The rate of appeals and the number of decisions continued at a high level in 1956 and 1957.

Both the union and management became concerned with this phenomenally high arbitration rate. The union complained of the expense entailed in handling this number of cases, not only in terms of the umpire machinery cost but also in terms of the staff require-

[1] The original umpire died in 1954. At the time of his death there were 405 cases that he had heard that he had not yet decided. This created a serious problem for the parties, which was met by a series of conferences where they disposed of most of the cases by compromises. Only a few dozen were left to be reheard by the other umpires.

ments. It was troubled also by the high proportion of decisions that were adverse to the union, suggesting that too many cases were being referred to arbitration that had little or no merit. For example, in the period January through July 1956 the umpires rendered 282 decisions. Forty-six were decided favorably for the union, 28 were construed as partial grants of the union grievance claim, but 208 decisions represented outright denials of the grievance. In spite of the expense consideration and the high union loss record, the union spokesmen in 1956 still felt they would prefer to have this high volume situation than the one that exists in Companies B and C, described below. They considered the resort to arbitration as a healthy escape-valve.

This did not lead the union to an attitude of indifference, however. Over the years it attempted several corrective measures with varying degrees of success. At one time the international staff representative from UAW headquarters met with local management representatives trying to settle grievances that had been referred to the umpire, but he discovered that this practice only encouraged more grievances because the members began to rely on him to "pull something out of the hat" for them. In the union publications to the employees of this company, losses of the cases going to the umpire were highlighted deliberately in a further attempt to discourage locals from appealing weak grievances. The UAW staff representative assigned full time to the umpire proceedings maintained in his office a large blackboard chart showing the number of grievances going to the umpire from each location. Originally it was intended to dramatize to the visitors from the high-volume arbitration locals how excessive their referrals had been. Unfortunately this minor psychological device boomeranged. Local union officers from plants with little or no arbitration, seeing the impressively high totals of other locals, were made to feel that they had not been militant enough.

Management also tried to cope with this abnormally high rate of arbitration, although it agreed with the union that the rate was not symptomatic of unfriendly labor relations. The general climate of labor relations, management claimed, was as friendly as in the plants of its two principal competitors, where arbitration was used sparingly. The principal activity by the company was a more systematic and careful screening of cases after their referral to the umpire and before the actual hearings. Prior to 1956, when a case of dubious merit was received by the umpire proceedings department, it would be discussed with the plant industrial relations manager to see if it could be settled or compromised in a group of cases. However, this screening approach was discontinued because the company felt that the union was exploiting the pre-arbitration settlement efforts.

There are several possible causes for this unusual arbitration experience. No single factor provides the explanation; instead the experience is a product of the total complex of this relationship.

(1) There is reason to believe that the original umpire nurtured in the parties a philosophy of arbitration that encouraged extensive use of the process. He looked upon the grievance and arbitration procedure as a good safety valve, one that should be used freely and readily. In the uncertain and uneasy early days of the relationship he became a crutch to both parties, someone they could rely upon when the going got rough. The personality and competence of the umpire exaggerated the efficacy of the arbitration process in the minds of the parties. In another respect, his approach to arbitration probably contributed to the long-run high incidence rate. It was his practice to answer the immediate problem and to avoid the development of policies that could be used as precedents. Wisdom of hindsight now prompts the parties at least to ask themselves whether this type of umpire, who served so appropriately in the initial years, might not have lessened their capacity to work out their own problems.

(2) The tradition of democratic expression and individualism among employees in the local unions of this company is very high. Centralized control over the locals by the UAW International Headquarters is to be found to a lesser degree here than in the case of locals in Company B, for example. Very often the most vocal anti-administration sentiments within the UAW originate with these locals. Thus, the ability of the international to control the arbitration proclivities of the locals was limited.

(3) Until recent years the central and division labor relations staffs within the company were able to exercise only limited control over local plant managements. This situation appears to be changing. It has been reported that these top staff representatives have come from a position where they had virtually no influence to one in which they now have a significant influence.

(4) The frequency of arbitrations varies considerably from plant

to plant, and a breakdown of the total in a given plant by types of issues suggests that the continuance of local problem areas may account for part of the volume. The great majority of the cases appealed to the umpire since 1953 in one of the large assembly plants were disciplinary cases. They involved complaints against a worker for "loitering," the company method of getting at the problem of failure to meet standards. In another plant, the issue of foremen working was the most frequent in cases taken to arbitration, and, significantly, the union was winning many of the umpire decisions.

(5) Finally, Company A had the job during this period of tightening measured daywork standards. Although standards were not arbitrable, the irritations caused by this effort stimulated other grievances.

The continuing high-volume arbitration pattern became one of the most preoccupying concerns of the parties. The number of appeals was so great that the cases could not be screened properly. The problem of numbers alone was such that the union found it might withdraw a grievance in pre-hearing discussions only to discover that a like grievance slipped by, went to the umpire, and was granted.

The need for four umpires resulted occasionally in inconsistent decisions. Moreover, the complaint was made that so many cases were heard by a single umpire (one turned out 100 decisions in one week) that he could not give adequate thought and attention to the opinion and award. On the other hand, one division manager felt that the multiple setup helped eliminate many cases from the docket. He said that the fact that a different arbitrator might be hearing cases, one who was less familiar with the history and background of the division, led both parties to try to settle rather than undergo the greater uncertainty of decision at the hands of a new umpire.

This case history changed abruptly from one of high volume arbitration to low volume arbitration in 1958-59. The reason for the special efforts to reverse the trend is important. The parties found that their four umpires were hearing so many cases that inconsistencies in decisions were becoming more frequent. In brief the volume of arbitration began to create more problems than it settled.

In 1958 two measures were taken by the union to correct the high-volume situation: First, the UAW department for this company proposed a substantial increase in dues to be allocated for arbitration costs. In this way it was able to single out those locals that were most responsible for the high number of arbitration referrals.

Second, it developed a special intra-union screening procedure. Whenever a case was referred to an umpire by a local, an international union staff member was assigned to assess the merits of the complaint. If he had doubts, they were noted on the complaint and returned to the local union. If the local union persisted in referring these "doubtful" cases to an umpire, its request would be honored by the international. But the procedure gave the international valuable ammunition. In the likely event that these complaints were rejected by the umpire, the international staff representative could then go before a local and point out that the referrals had been of no avail and had been against the advice of the national union. As one top union executive said, "we have never tipped off an umpire to how we felt about a grievance, but up to now we haven't been let down. The umpires have denied grievances we felt should never have been carried to arbitration in the first place."

The result of these special efforts is that the traditional high backlog of pending arbitrations in this company is a thing of the past. In May 1959 the cases to be heard and decided by the umpires numbered less than 50. These parties have gone from an extremely high level of arbitration to a low level without any apparent change in their basic labor relations. The motivation for the change was not that the parties felt that the high volume was symptomatic of poor relations. It was primarily because they feared that a good relationship might be transformed into a poor one because of the capriciousness inherent in too many decisions by too many neutrals. In addition, the high cost became critical to the union, whose dues-income dropped sharply in the 1958 recession.

COMPANY B. Another large automobile manufacturing company has experienced the expected normal trend in arbitration volume. The number of cases decided by arbitration has declined steadily over the years. In the 1940's, the umpire was deciding 175 to 200 cases each year. By 1951 this figure had dropped to 57. In 1955 only 22 cases out of 100,000 written grievances for the entire company went to the umpire.

As in the case of the meat packing company described above, there

IMPACT OF COLLECTIVE BARGAINING

is reason to believe that the downward trend represented a natural consequence of the adjustment process in labor-management relations. This is illustrated by the history of umpire cases on the subject of discipline for work stoppages, slowdowns, or other interferences with production. In 1940 there were 11 such cases; during World War II there were 35 cases. But since then there have been practically no cases in this area. The company's firm policy from the outset in coping with illegal work stoppages, the endorsement of its policy by umpires (who under the terms of the early agreements were permitted only to judge the guilt or innocence of the alleged offender, not the degree of penalty assigned), and the gradual recognition by employees and union leaders alike of the serious consequences, all served to eliminate this problem area.

Why have this company and the UAW been able to avoid the experiences of Company A? Again the reasons must be stated in tentative terms. (1) Very early in the relationship this company adopted firm, carefully considered policies in handling labor relations. It construed arbitration as a judicial process, something essential in certain circumstances but to be avoided if at all possible. Even today the top spokesmen for this company speak of "litigating" whenever they refer to umpire proceedings. The notion of arbitration that implied an informal semi-mediative activity, was never entertained by this company. It always felt that arbitration was most useful as a way of confirming and strengthening company policies rather than as an arena in which to formulate policies. Its keen sense of "management's inherent responsibilities" led it to restrict the authority of the umpire from the outset. Its slight relaxation in this regard over the years has probably been only because the company felt secure that its policies and practices were well established and recognized. A labor relations specialist, commenting on the vastly different experiences between Companies A and B up to 1959, states that in the former company the initial question was "Why is this grievance good?," while in the latter company it was, "Why is this grievance no good?"

(2) The central personnel office of this company exercised more influence over local plant managements insofar as umpire proceedings were concerned than did the central office in Company A. Half of the eleven men on the staff of the corporate labor relations section were engaged in umpire work. It should not be inferred that the influence was of a formal control nature. On the contrary, it was

highly informal. Local plant labor relations staff were imbued with the company attitude described above, and the typical plant personnel manager usually spent 30 days at the time of his selection in the central office, most of it being on the umpire circuit. Thus, he developed a close personal relationship with the central staff people.

(3) Both the union and the company have developed an effective procedure for the screening of cases after their referral to arbitration but prior to actual hearing. It was estimated that as many as a thousand cases may reach the umpire's docket each year, i.e., cases which have gone through the third and last formal grievance step short of arbitration. But nearly all of these are disposed of by the informal screening device, either by settlement or referral back to earlier grievance steps. The international union people go to the locations involved, review the cases, and try to work out settlements. Similarly several from the central staff of the company go to the plants and work over the docketed grievances that are left. The company claimed that these screening committees as early as 1952 were "largely responsible for the appreciable drop in the number of cases which the umpire is called upon to hear."

It is reasonable to ask why the screening procedures in this company had a salutary effect, while those tried originally in Company A did not. The answer undoubtedly is in the differences in union orientation and, to a lesser extent, in management's use of the screening process. In this company the union locals were more responsive to the union department set up to handle the affairs involving this company. The top union leaders came from locals of the company, and the locals are more inclined to abide by the judgment of the international staff representatives. In Company A the opposite situation prevailed. Its union locals were organized later and prided themselves on relative independence from the dictates of the international. Variations in management policy also account for part of the difference in the effectiveness of screening. Company B policy has always been one of deliberate firmness. Company A has often placed the desire for settlement ahead of the objective of being "firm, but fair."

Company B made no claim that its gradually-achieved low umpire rate was proof of good labor relations. On the contrary, it warned against using either the grievance or the arbitration rate as a guide. It pointed to the fact that its rate of arbitration varied considerably from one plant to another apparently uninfluenced by the state of labor relations in the individual plants. There was also no reason to believe its current low rate had been at the cost of the company's giving in excessively or of the union's dropping of meritorious grievances. The low rate in this automobile company has been achieved, in part, by the union's growing reluctance to take weak cases to arbitration, an attitude which the union has only recently felt in Company A.

COMPANY C. This third automobile company introduced an umpire system in 1943, and it has had the services of the same umpire since that time. Given the number of covered employees, which has ranged from 80,000 to 140,000 in this period, the arbitration rate has been consistently very low. This company, with approximately the same number of employees as Company A, is at the other end of the spectrum. In 15 years it has averaged only 23 decisions per year, and in 1957 only 12 decisions were made; whereas in Company A the umpires issued 6,500 decisions in the same period, or an annual average of almost 435 a year. In Company B, 7 different umpires issued 1,761 decisions from 1940 to 1959, or an average of 93 a year. Yet labor relations in Company C have been characterized by more tension and irritation than in either of the other two companies.

In explaining the low arbitration rate, the umpire points to a number of procedural advantages.[2] For example, he considers a change in the method of compensating the chairman as having an impact on the number of cases referred to him.[3] In the first one-year contract a "guarantee" of fifty cases was given, for which he would receive a per-case fee. In 1947, at his request, this guarantee was eliminated on the grounds that the former payment might have the effect of keeping the case load at or near the guarantee. However, there is no statistical evidence for the period before 1947 to show that it did in fact encourage this tendency.

In addition, the pre-Appeal Board screening procedures are offered as an explanation for the low rate. This is a union not a com-

[2] David A. Wolff, Louis A. Crane, and Howard A. Cole, "The Chrysler-UAW Umpire System," Bureau of National Affairs, The Arbitrator and the Parties (1958), pp. 111-48.
[3] The term "chairman" is used here because the neutral is chairman of a 4-man appeal board, 2 members being from the company and 2 from the union. However, in effect he is an umpire since the cases are settled by his decision and not by a majority vote of the board.

pany procedure because "the burden of deciding on appeals almost always rests with the union." The union screening committee is composed of local union presidents, who meet periodically, with international union representatives present in an advisory, nonvoting capacity. The merits of the grievance are evaluated, and many grievances are eliminated at this step.

The Appeal Board, which antedated the umpire step, provides another screening opportunity; in recent years over 90 per cent of all cases referred to the Board without the presence of the impartial chairman have been disposed of by parties themselves at that level. The Board proceeds with an examination of each case as if it were being arbitrated. For example, "all evidentiary matter, including the written statements of witnesses, is placed on the table. Every pertinent section of the agreement is cited and its meaning explored." Given this pre-arbitration step, the arbitration hearings themselves are very much like appellate proceedings. Only the Appeal Board members appear before the chairman. Witnesses never appear; instead their written statements are filed. A "closed" session rule applies. Finally the parties have developed what is described as a "declaratory judgment" procedure. Either party may file an issue involving interpretation or application of the agreement without its having originated in the form of a specific grievance. This is said to be an effective means of "heading off trouble" and avoiding a multiplicity of grievances.

While the umpire in this company is careful to say that "each system of arbitration must reflect the concepts of the parties it services," he suggests that the system of Company C merits thoughtful consideration by others. Yet by almost any objective standard, the labor-management relationship in this company has been characterized by tension. The record of walkouts has been high, and the atmosphere between company and union is rated as unfriendly by competent observers. One might wonder why the relatively poor labor relations have not affected the arbitration machinery in this company. The fact is that the arbitration process has been conducted in a rarefied atmosphere, not easily accessible to the rank-and-file worker. For this reason it remains unaffected by the poor relationship between the parties. Also for this reason it may not be able to help improve the relationship.

The arbitration procedure in Company C bears little or no resemblance to the "safety valve" approach to arbitration found over many years in Company A; nor is it similar to the more orthodox approach of Company B. It may well be that the system discourages use of arbitration in all but the "key, critical issue" cases, thus explaining the continuing low rate of arbitration. Because labor relations seem to be poorest in this company with the lowest incidence of arbitration, some speculation is in order. Is the apparent excessive misuse of arbitration until 1959 in Company A to be preferred to the stated goal of minimal use in Company C? Does frequent use provide a catharsis for emotions that is superior to the contrived efforts of parties to "settle differences for themselves"? Or is the semi-planned, semi-natural evolution of the type found in Company B the one that warrants emulation?

These questions cannot be answered easily. But careful consideration in the light of the three disparate situations in this one industry should discredit some of the superficial conclusions often reached about the significance of frequency of arbitration. The patterns of average, relatively high, and relatively low volume of arbitration, can be found in a variety of situations. The experiences of the three automobile companies are not unique. While some of the reasons developed in the discussion of these three companies apply also to other situations, it is likely that other high- or low-arbitration patterns are for reasons quite different from those in Companies A, B, and C.

In the experiences described above there have been no clear cases of the abnormally high arbitration rate that indicates a complete breakdown of the arbitration process. Nor have cases been given to illustrate low arbitration because of either management default or union weakness. Some experiences in each of these categories are to be found.

A large farm equipment manufacturing company in a drive to improve efficiency found itself almost buried in an avalanche of grievances awaiting arbitration. As part of its aggressive policy the company made a wholesale reaudit of jobs and tightened standards on many jobs. This led to a flood of grievances of such a nature that the union could not agree to accept the company's grievance answers. In addition, for a period of time there was no arbitrator, the parties having failed to agree on one. As a consequence, 8,000 cases were on the arbitration docket, the vast majority of which involved incentive rates and production standards. In the spring of 1955 the vice president of the international union warned the company that contract negotiations could not begin until all the grievances were settled. A formula was negotiated to help resolve the cases. While most were settled, the problem of grievance appeals and arbitration cases continued to bother the parties. In 1957 the company staff representatives embarked on a planned tour of its plants in a concerted drive to settle the grievances.

In a number of companies the overwhelming volume of arbitration referrals is less serious than it might appear. It seldom represents the number of cases that are likely to be heard. Flooding the arbitration system, as explained in the preceding chapter, is often part of union bargaining strategy. Some companies report that they have hundreds of cases awaiting arbitration, many of which are as much as two or three years old. They seem relatively unconcerned about this situation, saying that neither they nor the unions expect these cases ever to go to arbitration. One textile company industrial relations director made a practice of postponing as long as possible the hearing of cases referred to arbitration. When thirty or forty cases had accumulated, the number seemed so formidable that in his opinion both parties were more disposed to settle them. He said, "we hold periodic bargain days, each of us giving a little. What it costs us in retroactive pay in some cases is more than offset by the avoidance of lawyers' and arbitrators' fees."

Low arbitration, on the other hand, may have very serious implications for management in the long run if it results from managerial expediency and default. The plant of one steel company in which there have been almost no arbitrations for many years admitted that it was probably because the union could get anything it wanted without arbitration. It was found that management had been lax, and incentive standards were very loose. The chief union committeeman was a master at slowdowns, wildcats, and pressure tactics, and the union had even acquired the right to schedule the men. In brief no arbitrator could possibly have been as lenient as the company seems to have been.[4] Another company for many years took pride in the absence of arbitration and the infrequency of grievances carried be-

---

[4] The risks of faulty interpretation of a low arbitration rate are illustrated by the fact that this plant was given serious consideration by the National Planning Association for inclusion in its study of *Causes of Industrial Peace* (1955).

788 IMPACT OF COLLECTIVE BARGAINING

yond the second step. After eight years of this apparently happy relationship the company found it was no longer competitive. Its efficiency had suffered because of loose incentive rates, and it had reached the point where discipline was imposed only if the union steward concurred in the judgment of the foreman. A more than three months' strike occurred when management insisted on contractual changes that would erase the practices developed over the years.

Sometimes management avoids arbitration, even though its chances of winning are high, because the grievance at hand involves "only a few cents or dollars," whereas the referral to arbitration might cost several hundreds of dollars. This policy, when pursued long and often enough, has proved far more costly to companies than they realize. The demoralized incentive systems described in Chapter 17 have been caused in part by this myopic position of management.

A low volume of arbitration may be found in companies with weak, nonmilitant unions. It is noteworthy that companies that have experienced a long showdown strike and have emerged relatively victorious usually have a sharp decrease in arbitration cases. Presumably the union is weakened and chastened. For example, an electrical manufacturing concern had a high arbitration rate after World War II. A fourteen-week strike occurred in 1950, which altered drastically the relationship between the parties. In the company's judgment the strike showed the union "that the company could be pushed only so far." The company as of 1957 had not had a written grievance for three years and had no arbitration case since the time of the strike seven years earlier.

Finally, low arbitration rates in some companies may reflect acts of omission by the company. This is particularly true when the volume is analyzed by type of issue. For example, in a large shoe company there are many grievance arbitrations on the subject of piece rates, but none on the subject of disciplinary cases. The answer is that the company seldom disciplines anyone. In a grain processing firm the boast was made that there had never been a grievance or arbitration over the question of seniority *versus* ability under the promotion clause. This was followed by the comment, "of course, we nearly always promote on the basis of seniority. That way we can stay out of trouble."

In each of these illustrations of very high and very low arbitration rates there is evidence of some defect in labor relations. One cannot explain these arbitration experiences without understanding the entire complex of each particular relationship.

The experience of the railroad industry warrants special attention. In Chapter 25 the machinery established by law for final adjustment of grievance disputes in this industry was described briefly. In the 24-year period 1935 through 1958 more than 50,000 cases were docketed with the Railroad Adjustment Board. In the same period 45,397 were disposed of in the following way: 11,281 were decided by the Boards without a referee, 17,764 with a referee, and 16,352 were withdrawn. The arbitration rate in this industry for many years has been very high. For the period 1950 through 1958 the rate of new cases docketed averaged more than 2,000 a year, and at the beginning of 1958 there were more than 4,000 cases open and on hand.

The backlog became so great in at least one division (the first, which covers train and yard service employees) that it was years behind schedule in handling cases. Not infrequently a grievance filed on the local property of a carrier would not be decided by the Adjustment Board until three to five years later.

In 1949 two supplemental boards were established to help the First Division cope with the mounting backlog. In 1952 the unions decided that these additional boards were unnecessary and served notice to the carriers of their desire to terminate them. During their brief tenure the supplemental boards disposed of 456 cases. The First Division case load was reduced also by the growing practice of referring cases to special adjustment boards set up by some of the parties to avoid the long delay. In the year ending June 30, 1951, only 2 such special boards were used, disposing of 123 cases. In the year ending June 30, 1958, 71 special boards were created and handled more than 1,400 cases.[5] In spite of these efforts by the parties to develop arrangements to meet the partial breakdown in the adjustment machinery, the referral volume, backlog, and delay continue to be a serious problem.

Other statistical information concerning this arbitration experience is equally interesting. An analysis made some years ago revealed that 16 railroads of the United States with one-third of the employees

[5] Seventeenth to Twenty-Fourth *Annual Reports of the National Mediation Board,* including Report of the National Railroad Adjustment Board.

accounted for 75 per cent of the total awards of the First Division.[6] It was found that approximately two-thirds of all decisions have been in favor of the railroad unions. The figure would probably be higher if it were not for the acknowledged fact that many unions deliberately bring cases which they know they cannot win. They do this to avoid having too favorable a record of victories lest the proportion of union wins discredit the machinery.

The explanations for this unique situation, including the phenomena of high referrals and backlogs, are elusive. The best available study cites among other things the lack of sound judicial procedures in the Adjustment Board's operation. For example, the Board may deny interested parties due notice to be heard, or it may base its decision on hearsay evidence. The First Division does not accompany its decisions with an opinion, yet there is great devotion to precedent. Another defect is inherent in the governing law itself. Judicial review may be sought only by the winning party in its effort to enforce the award. This leaves the losing party with little redress except to refuse to abide by an Adjustment Board verdict. On the other hand, such a negative position on the part of the loser is frequently upheld by the courts. Because of these faulty procedures, the courts have sustained Railroad Adjustment Board decisions in only one-third of the enforcement suits initiated.

The explanation, however, must go beyond the procedural and legal shortcomings. It is obvious that many carriers and their unions have stopped using effectively the pre-Adjustment Board grievance steps. The unions may feel that they stand a good chance of winning weak or borderline cases at the Board level. Experience justifies this expectation. The carriers may be indifferent, recognizing that even an adverse decision will be delayed several years.

One wonders what effect the long delay in this and other situations has on the individual employee whose grievance is being processed so slowly. It has been found that during the initial months after the complaint has been filed, the employee or group of employees inquire frequently about, and maintain a lively interest in, the status of the case. After repeated explanations by harassed union officers that

---

[6] Herbert R. Northrup, and Mark L. Kahn, "Railroad Grievance Machinery: A Critical Analysis," *Industrial and Labor Relations Review* (April 1952), pp. 365-82; (July 1952), pp. 540-59. A 1945 report prepared by E. J. Connors for the President on conditions of the First Division of the NRAB showed that a significant majority of the cases came from western railroads. This geographic concentration did not exist in 1958.

"this is the way the system works," the employees gradually become resigned to the delay. It has been said that many employees forget all about the grievance, and when a final verdict is issued a year or two later, it comes as an unexpected surprise. There have been half-hearted attempts by the parties to improve the process, but they have been ineffective. In an industry as tradition-bound as are the railroads it is probably not surprising that the desire to continue living with an inferior procedure prevails over a desire to try something new.[7]

Considerations and Problems in Grievance Arbitration

Some of the problems involving the mechanics of the arbitration procedure were discussed in Chapter 25, and, as we have already noted, the way these problems are handled may affect the bargaining relationship. In this section these additional matters will be covered: (1) the nature of grievance arbitration, (2) the arrogation of authority by the arbitrator, (3) the dangers of *dicta,* (4) the risks of winning, and (5) the role of precedent in arbitration.

Nature of Grievance Arbitration

A company and union should give very careful thought to how they want the grievance arbitration process to function. Do they want it to be a judicial process, with a fairly high degree of formality and with the arbitrator serving as a judge and ruling on the basis of the evidence before him? In this event do they want to keep out of the process those issues that are not within the scope of the "interpretation or application of the terms of the agreement"? Or do the parties want the process to be of a more informal nature, with an outsider serving as a catalytic agent and helping them resolve their difficulties by whatever means are at his command? These are not at all clear-cut distinctions. In the former conception of the process

[7] The airline industry and its unions, although covered by the Railway Labor Act, have avoided coverage under the Railroad Adjustment Board. Both parties prefer to establish their own arbitration procedures. Customarily in the airline industry there are four-man System Boards of Adjustment set up under each contract. When these Boards, consisting of two representatives from each party, cannot resolve a grievance, an outside neutral is selected to join the Board as chairman. The neutral may be designated by the National Mediation Board if the parties cannot agree on a selection.

the arbitrator's authority is likely to be carefully and narrowly de-fined in the contract. In the latter, the implementing clause is more likely to be liberal in delegating authority to the outsider.

Almost ten years ago there developed among professional arbitra-tors an interesting debate over a desirable philosophy of grievance arbitration. The discussions on this subject were provoked in 1949 by a thoughtful article prepared by George W. Taylor, a pioneer in the arbitration profession, for the second annual meeting of the National Academy of Arbitrators.[8] Taylor started with the thesis that it is erroneous to believe that a sharp line of distinction can be drawn between agreement making and agreement administration, given the skeletal nature of the labor contract. Therefore, in the grievance procedure and in arbitration, which he viewed as part of the procedure and as an extension of the collective bargaining process, some elements of agreement making must exist.

In procedures calling for a permanent impartial chairman, the arbitration form deemed preferable by Taylor, the essential function of the chairman is to bring about a meeting of minds if possible. This, in turn, means inevitably that the chairman must serve and function as a special kind of mediator, holding in reserve his power to decide, either by effectuating his own judgment or by joining with one of the partisan board members. But mediation in an effort to secure agreement should be the first step. Taylor rejects the so-called "legalistic" school of arbitration, which looks upon the process as something apart from the grievance procedure and which limits the neutral's authority to decision making. He argues that any arbitrator should be expected to do some mediating because his outside, fresh, nonpartisan approach may inspire agreement, which is far better than forcing a decision upon the parties.

A contrary position has been taken by many other arbitrators. Management spokesmen and, to a lesser extent, some union spoke-men have taken issue with Taylor's suggested fusion of the mediative and arbitration functions. One of the most forceful statements was made by the late J. Noble Braden, long-time vice president of the American Arbitration Association:

The position of the American Arbitration Association is well known. From the beginning of its work, it followed the historical and legal

[8] George W. Taylor, "Effectuating the Labor Contract through Arbitration," Bureau of National Affairs, *The Profession of Labor Arbitration* (1957), pp. 20-42.

standard that arbitration is a quasi-judicial proceeding based upon the fundamental principles of arbitration law; and that when a matter is submitted to arbitration, it is presumed that the good offices of conciliation and mediation have been exhausted and that the parties in dispute desire to have a just decision based upon the facts and evidence.[9]

A number of critics of the Taylor viewpoint argue that it is essential for the effective growth of parties in a labor relationship to do their own legislating and, painful as the consequences may be, to rely on arbitration only for a clearcut decision on the merits of a case. They fear that the mediative step is one that most impartial chairmen would misuse, holding the threat of an adverse decision over the parties' heads to force an undesirable compromise agreement.

Most managements have indicated a strong preference for the so-called judicial approach. For example, in two of the three automobile companies whose experiences were described above, management had very definite ideas about what it wanted. It insisted that the umpire serve as a jurist. In the third automobile company, for reasons given in the discussion of its high volume of arbitration, conscious policy on this question did not exist. The parties drifted into a process which for many years was semi-mediative, semi-judicial in nature.

Although there is no statistical evidence on the subject, there are enough known situations to warrant the conclusion that the informal, mediative-judicial approach tends to encourage referrals to arbitration. Furthermore, it is more likely to occur where there is an impartial chairman for a company or an industry. His continued relationship with the parties leads to informality, and he often resolves policy issues in the course of casual conversation with company and union representatives. One arbitrator, whose stated views endorsed the strict judicial approach, realized that in five successive visits to a company and union he had resolved eight cases, all by informal mediation. He and the parties had drifted away from the judicial process.

Still another reason why the impartial chairman structure is identified with the Taylor philosophy is to be found in the needle trades, for example. The functions and authority of the umpire in the New

[9] J. Noble Braden, "The Function of the Arbitrator in Labor-Management Disputes," *The Arbitration Journal*, Vol. 4, No. 1 (1949), p. 35.

York dress industry are broad, and his approach is often highly informal. The explanation lies in the size of the enterprises within the
association which was set up for bargaining purposes. The units were
small, and few of them were able to have their own piece-rate expert.
In effect the office of the impartial chairman became an administrative mechanism; he was called upon to set hundreds of piece rates.
Frequently he set the rates for new styles without management's
having attempted to set the rates in the first instance.[10]

From the standpoint of the parties, that arbitration philosophy is
best which serves them well, given the traditions and background of
their relationship. In a field such as this, it has already become evident that generalizations on what is theoretically "best" are often
dangerous. Discussion and arguments among arbitrators as to the nature of the process are healthy and stimulating. But the preferred
philosophy of an arbitrator should not be imposed unthinkingly
upon the parties he serves. George Taylor has made this point effectively:

> Arbitration doesn't belong exclusively to the arbitrators. On the con-
> trary, voluntary arbitration is inherently a collective bargaining device
> under the control of labor and management. Theirs is the primary
> task of developing the arbitration process along with their more direct
> collective bargaining. . . . It follows that varying types of arbitration
> should be recognized as necessary and proper.

Arrogation of Authority

Although the vast majority of agreements define the authority of
the arbitrator by limiting him to the interpretation and application
of the contract provisions and by denying him the right to add to,
subtract from, or modify the terms of the agreement, unions and
companies are concerned because many arbitrators enlarge upon
their authority unwarrantedly. Management is more often the com-
plainant in this indictment of the process. Three explanations may
be given for the problem, apart from the infrequent capricious behavior of neutrals themselves.

(1) The parties may think that they have negotiated a clause that
gives them adequate protection as to rights or as to obligations, but
the language is imprecise. For example, one firm after buying out a

---

[10] This is true also in the men's clothing and millinery industries, as was noted in the
historical description in Chapter 24.

predecessor company agreed with the union that "employee service with predecessor companies would be treated as service with the company for the purpose of vacation." Some people who had not worked for the immediate predecessor but who had worked for a more distant predecessor were subsequently employed. After six months they claimed two weeks' vacation with pay on the ground that twenty years ago they had worked for one of the predecessor companies for a total of five years. An arbitrator upheld their claim because of the contract language.

A union may complain that an arbitrator is unfair in permitting a company to restudy an entire job under an incentive system when the change affects only a few elements of the job. Yet these awards are made invariably under language which provides that when there are changes in methods, materials, or process, "the job" shall be restudied for the purpose of establishing a new standard.

Some companies, without fully realizing it, have given the arbitrator authority to review management decisions on matters that they thought were entirely within management's discretion. This is usually due to a misuse of contract language. It is surprising, for example, that managements have not insisted more vigorously on retention of the right to determine employee ability, leaving to arbitration only the question whether management's judgment was derived fairly and after appropriate examination of the records. While this may have been the intent, as evidenced by company allegations in specific cases, it was not expressly stated in the contract. Understandably the arbitrator felt free to substitute his judgment for that of management in appraising employee ability.

If the parties expect an outside neutral to be judicial in his definition of authority and in his resolution of a case, they must first seek to describe by the terms of the contract as explicitly as possible their own agreed set of rights and obligations. The more nebulous the agreement, the more probable will be the arbitrator's intrusion upon what one or the other of the parties considers to be its prerogatives.

(2) Very often the presumed arrogation of authority by the arbitrator, at least insofar as management is concerned, rests in the inadequacy of the "management clause" or in the absence of an "exclusion clause." Some management rights clauses state unequivocally that unless the agreement specifically and explicitly forecloses or otherwise modifies the company's right to exercise a certain judgment,

such judgment shall not be reviewable by any other person. Under such clauses the arbitrator is more likely to feel restrained. Similarly, some agreements provide by an "exclusion clause" that nothing expressly stated as an obligation or right within the agreement will be recognized during the life of the agreement as admissible for negotiation or arbitration. This type of clause very often inhibits an arbitrator from substituting broad considerations of justice, as he sees them, in such cases as subcontracting and promotion from within.

(3) The complaint may occur when the issue to be arbitrated is not defined by the parties themselves but is left to the arbitrator to determine. Very often the neutral has at least two preliminary decisions to make before he even concerns himself with the merits of an issue, both of which decisions involve self-determination of his own authority. Presented with conflicting views, he may be called upon to decide what is the issue to be arbitrated and then whether the issue is arbitrable under the agreement.

Some companies and unions have developed a step 3¾ in the grievance procedure to meet this problem. They agree that when a grievance is to be referred to arbitration, they will first try to stipulate the issue, thereby establishing the precise question to be decided by the neutral. This *supra*-contract step has a purpose that goes beyond the control over the arbitrator's jurisdiction. The very process of defining the exact issue to be arbitrated sometimes helps to resolve the issue. It has been found that a union or a company may recognize for the first time weaknesses in its case if it is forced to bargain on the stipulation of issue. For example, one local union which was prone to refer all politically-sensitive grievances to arbitration soon found that the process of "stipulating the issue" dramatized the absurdity of its case, resulting in the withdrawal of many cases at Step 3¾.

Some arbitrators at the start of a hearing will try to secure a stipulation of the issue and will engage in pre-arbitration mediative efforts to achieve this goal. They thus protect themselves by having their authority defined. In addition they are in a far better position to conduct the hearing on the merits. They will have a better basis for deciding what evidence is relevant and admissible.

On the other hand, some arbitrators deplore the apparent legalistic trend implicit in this preliminary step. Interestingly, they are the same arbitrators who view the arbitration process as a flexible extension of the collecti'e bargaining process rather than as a semi-judicial step in adjudicating grievances.

Yet the attempt by the parties to determine what is the issue to be decided is a logical bargaining step antecedent to a hearing on the merits. The mental exercise of phrasing the issue may be arduous and time-consuming, but it is one way of preventing an undesired arrogation of authority by the neutral. It also has the unexpected side effect of stripping it of its emotional aspects, which may have prevented its resolution by the parties themselves. It is fair to say that the parties at least have an obligation to know what they are arguing about. Too many parties who have developed the "arbitration habit" are unable to pinpoint the question they want to have arbitrated.

Dangers of Dicta

Most arbitrators accompany their awards with an opinion, the essential purpose of which is to explain how and why they reached their decision. These opinions are often very helpful and are credited by unions and companies with solving similar problems in the future. Sometimes an arbitrator is chosen because of his ability to write cogently and to the point. The observation has been made by both parties in many relationships that, while they have experienced defeats at the hands of a certain arbitrator, they have been made to understand through his opinion why they lost and feel that he gave a fair consideration to their arguments. Constructive policies may evolve from a series of well-stated opinions, a matter which will be discussed more fully under the heading of the role of precedent in arbitration.

But the *dicta* of opinions occasionally do more harm than good. One company criticized the tendency of arbitrators to put too much gratuitous advice into their opinions. It has been said that in the process of deciding a specific problem the arbitrator, by the wording of his opinion, may generate new grievances. A common complaint is that arbitrators anxious to please both parties will give the decision to one party and the language to the other party. An illustration is a nine-page opinion denouncing the employees involved in a disciplinary action and ending with the words, "but the company might very well extend clemency."

The risks inherent in an opinion that gives too much advice are illustrated by the following case involving a promotion grievance. Under a promotion clause which provided that the company was to consider seniority and ability but that the final determination of ability resided exclusively with management, an arbitrator was designated to hear the complaint of a bypassed senior employee. The arbitrator held for the company, but in his opinion he indulged in these *dicta*, that the present clause was a poor one because, he felt, managements were capable of erroneous judgments as to employee ability. He chided the union leadership for having negotiated such a weak clause and proposed a promotion clause, which he urged the parties to consider carefully in their next negotiations. This unsought advice created considerable irritation for the parties. A vocal minority in the union cited the opinion as evidence that the present leadership was inadequate. But the most interesting consequence was its effect on management's promotion decisions during the remaining life of the contract. The company deliberately avoided promoting anyone other than the senior man because it hoped to erase the memory of this opinion before the next negotiations. Its efforts failed. Included in the union's bargaining demands was the precise clause recommended by the arbitrator. At the bargaining table the union pointed out that an arbitrator of the company's own choice had urged such a clause and that it was unbecoming for the company under these circumstances to resist its adoption. The company reported, "We didn't give in to the union, but we had to buy off the request by granting other concessions."

A somewhat similar case is that of the arbitrator who was called upon to decide 12 job evaluation cases. In the course of the hearing he was given the names of more than 30 reference jobs to be used in testing the factor ratings for the disputed jobs. He then inspected both the disputed and the reference jobs. In his opinion he volunteered the view that at least 8 of the 30 agreed-upon reference jobs were improperly evaluated and that he was not going to use them in deciding the merits of the issues before him. Unfortunately, he neglected to say whether the 8 were evaluated too high or too low. All 8 were carried to arbitration in a new proceeding started because of his *dicta*, and a new arbitrator dismissed all of them. An embittered local union recording secretary commented: "It cost our treasury more than $3,000 just because he (the first arbitrator) had to shoot off his mouth."

Sometimes it is the cautious *dicta* that create problems. In a large automobile company, whose experience has been cited above, the lack of policy developed through arbitration explained in part the continuing high volume of arbitration for so many years. This absence of policy guideposts was attributable in part to the permanent arbitrator's practice of adding at the end of his opinion a statement that the award was not to serve as a precedent and was designed only to meet the specific problem at hand.

Risks of Winning

It might be expected that a union or a company invariably hopes to win its case before an arbitrator. This is not always true. More often than one might imagine the spokesman for one or the other of the parties enters the arbitration hearing with the tacit hope that he will lose his case. Normally the arbitrator is not privy to these thoughts, although he may suspect the attitude when a case is presented halfheartedly. But even this is a questionable clue. Sometimes an indifferent presentation means nothing more than a strong conviction that the case cannot possibly be lost on its merits. Conversely, the secret desire to lose may impel a spokesman to prosecute his case with unusual vigor lest he be accused later by disgruntled associates of having deliberately thrown the case. In a very few instances the arbitrator will be advised just before or after the hearing that it is hoped he will cooperate by bringing in an adverse verdict. Such an overt tip-off entails too many risks to be used frequently.

What circumstances give rise to a desire to lose? The three most usual explanations are the following: internal union politics, staff-line conflicts within management, and possible adverse effect of a victory on future bargaining. Other more isolated explanations may exist, but they do not account for more than a fraction of the total of such cases. For example, one company, which has had the same permanent arbitrator for many years and whose record of wins averaged better than 95 per cent, became aware that the local union executive board was under considerable pressure to drop the arbitrator and replace him with a new man. It adopted a deliberate policy of permitting weak cases to go to arbitration which it normally would have settled by granting the claims in the earlier grievance steps. It took special pains to put on the agenda cases that it wanted to lose. By this strategy the proportion of union victories increased, and the campaign to get rid of the permanent arbitrator diminished.

(1) Internal union politics and administrative problems account for a substantial number of cases where the risk of winning is deemed high. Many local union by-laws require that the union grievance committee report to the full membership its recommendations on unresolved grievances after the last step preceding arbitration. It may recommend arbitration or dropping of the grievance. If the latter is suggested, often the membership will reverse the committee recommendation and vote to refer the matter to arbitration. In one situation it was found that 50 per cent of the cases that went to arbitration were referred over the objection of the committee. Under these circumstances, a union leader may hope for a decision adverse to the union, believing that a "favorable" decision will undermine the grievance committee and negate its effectiveness in the long run.[11]

Still another recurrent situation is the emergence within the union of a rival political faction bent on discrediting the judgment of the current leadership. Its most fertile political argument is that grievances are not being pursued with thoroughness, that the present leaders give in two readily to management. Illustrative is the case of a local union whose president argued strongly against the referral of six cases to arbitration; he was convinced that not one of the cases had merit. His executive board, sensing its vulnerability to attack by a strong steward in whose department the cases arose, overruled the president. All six grievances were dismissed by the arbitrator, who incidentally knew nothing of the internal union problem. Later he was advised by both union and company representatives that the loss of these cases probably prevented a change in leadership and the introduction of a destructive militancy in the relationship.

There is probably no experienced arbitrator who has not been told at one time or another by the union leadership that the loss of its grievance was welcomed and that an unexpected victory would

---

[11] In a local textile union, the bylaws provided that only those employees affected by the grievance were entitled to vote on whether or not the grievance should be carried to arbitration. Under this rule arbitration referrals were frequent even though the union leadership was often opposed to referral.

have done untold damage not only to the stability of leadership but also to the union-management relationship. A permanent arbitrator who has been with the parties for a sustained period is likely to be more alert to the internal union political and administrative problems. It is disturbing that some arbitrators, as a consequence, decide a case on the basis of political considerations rather than its merits.

(2) The risk of winning or the desire to lose is found in management circles as well, particularly where there is a conflict of viewpoint between staff and line. Many top executives undoubtedly would be shocked to know how often their company spokesmen in arbitration proceedings say suggestively to the arbitrator on the side: "I'm sorry to be bringing a case like this to you. I told the department head he was wrong, but he won't accept my judgment." Translated this means, "I don't want to win this case."

One industrial relations director commented that he has found that the only way he can educate the foremen effectively in sound disciplinary procedures, in careful appraisal of employee ability, or in the policy of equal distribution of overtime is to let them be stung a few times by an adverse arbitration ruling. In these instances, arbitration is viewed as a painful but valuable educational device.

(3) Because of the nature of the collective bargaining agreement and the strategic moves that characterize the bargaining process, the pleasant taste of victory in a given case may be more than offset by unpleasant, long-run consequences. When this happens, a defeat at the hands of the arbitrator may be hoped for. Sometimes a right or obligation under the agreement is expressed ambiguously for deliberate reasons. Neither party is prepared to adopt specific language, preferring to leave the matter flexible. If a grievance arises and is allowed to go to arbitration, a favorable verdict may force the other party to make this a substantive issue in the next negotiations. One company for many years had used a merit rating program to appraise employee ability. It had been accepted as a fair test by the union, and few grievances developed. However, in one promotion case a disgruntled senior employee forced a case to arbitration. While the company felt that its case was strong, it feared that a victory might highlight the influence of the merit rating system and make it a subject of attack in the negotiation of a new agreement. It preferred to lose the case by relying on tests other than the merit system in presenting its evidence to the arbitrator.

Role of Precedent in Arbitration

Precedents in arbitration are of two types. Type one includes the previous rulings on similar issues involving the two parties, type two, the decisions in similar cases involving other parties and, more often than not, other contract language.

With respect to the first definition of precedent decisions there is little doubt of their value. Both unions and managements want consistency in ruling on like issues under the same contract language. Well-reasoned opinions, therefore, are helpful in determining the applicability of one decision to a succeeding case. In the experience, described earlier, of Company A in the automobile industry, a principal complaint by both parties was the failure of the original umpire to develop policy by precedent.[12]

It was also noted that the lack of reasoned opinions in prior awards caused difficulties in the First Division of the Railroad Adjustment Board. An Emergency Board created under the Railway Labor Act reported to the President that the principal cause of the large number of undisposed claims before the First Division was its failure to write opinions. "The result was the accumulation of a vast number of awards of no precedential value and of no assistance in the application of rules purported to be interpreted by the awards."[13]

Arbitrator Herbert Blumer in a case involving Inland Steel Company was asked by the union to give an opinion on whether an arbitrator's decision must be accepted by the parties as binding for all similar cases. He replied as follows:

> In the judgment of this Arbitrator, aside from certain conditions which will be shortly specified, it is only fair and reasonable to expect an arbitrator's decision to apply to subsequent cases of the same nature. Otherwise, a distinct injustice would be done. There would be an unwarranted financial expenditure in having to carry each case to arbitration—an expenditure that would bear heavily on the party least able to stand it. Further, the refusal to apply the arbitrator's decision

---

[12] It will be remembered that in this company the volume of arbitrations became so great that inconsistent awards were received from its four umpires. Although the parties felt that their relationship was generally good, they feared that the inconsistencies might be harmful. This motivated them to cut back use of the arbitration process.

The importance of and concern with the precedent value of arbitration is recognized by the United Steelworkers of America. See *Steelworkers Handbook on Arbitration Decisions* (1960).

[13] *Report to the President of Emergency Board No. 47* (July 30, 1947).

to similar cases leaves unsolved and unsettled the general problem covered by the decision. The parties have a legitimate right to expect the decision to clarify and stabilize their relations. . . .[14]

In many ways the precedence value of an arbitrator's award is greatest in helping the parties settle similar grievances without resort to arbitration.

The second concept of precedent conforms with the legal doctrine of *stare decisis*. In the early days of grievance arbitration it was expected confidently by many practitioners that there would emerge gradually a large number of printed opinions and decisions that would form a "common law." An arbitrator in a given case could govern his ruling by the common law that had developed from a number of decisions by other arbitrators.

This has failed to occur, and probably it should not occur. The variables that affect an arbitrator's judgment in one case may be so numerous that his finding may leave little applicability to another situation with a different set of variables. Many partisan lawyers delight in what might be labeled "numerical persuasion by precedent," and their briefs consist largely of citations of as many precedent decisions as they can find. Some arbitrators acknowledge this with the tongue-in-cheek statement, "The various precedent decisions cited by both parties have been read with interest" and then proceed to judge the merits of the case before them with little or no regard to *stare decisis*. A few, unfortunately, are unduly impressed by citations which seem to indicate a prevailing view among arbitrators and make their decision without enough regard to the facts, rules, and practices in the particular case.

The variables from one relationship to another, which make reliance on precedent unwise, also create a deterrent to its use. Because situations and arbitrators differ, it is possible to find countless rulings favoring either side of a given controversy. For example, on the subjects of subcontracting or the voluntary *versus* the compulsory nature of overtime one can find as many different decisions as there are possible points of view. This militates against the evolution of a "common law" in labor arbitration. One union leader commented, "My own feeling is that we would be better off with more of the catch-as-catch-can, higgling and haggling, unscientific, unpredictable

[14] As quoted by Frank Elkouri, "The Precedential Force of Labor Arbitration Awards." *Labor Law Journal* (December 1950), p. 1184.

approach. I think it is regrettable that arbitrators read each other's decisions. The very fact that they do so implies that what happens in one plant has relevance for another, and it seems to me that industrial relations cannot help but be deteriorated (because less differentiated) by this process."

There are advocates of a contrary point of view. One scholar has concluded that "predictability may well have a tempering effect upon business representatives and industrial peace based upon due process."[15] One arbitrator even held against one of the parties in a case he had heard on the ground that even though the contract was ambiguous, the losing party should have known what the prevailing view on the issue was among arbitrators. But these advocates for *stare decisis* are in the minority. There is much to be gained if arbitrators read each other's decisions, notwithstanding the union view stated above. But the gain is in stimulating analytical ability, in being prodded to think about new dimensions of a problem. If the study of decisions is to find one that can be followed in another case, or, worse still, to find an arbitration consensus by the test of numbers, it would be better to leave the decisions of colleagues unread.[16]

Summary and Conclusions

Within the past twenty years grievance arbitration machinery has become an essential part of the labor agreement in American industry. It is a way of insuring freedom from the disruptive effects of strikes and walkouts during the life of the agreement. Where properly used, grievance arbitration is a valuable tool in the administration of the agreement.

The extent to which arbitration is relied upon varies from plant to plant and company to company. The variation is not necessarily correlated with the degree of friendliness in the parties' relationship,

[15] Edgar A. Jones, "Labor Arbitration and *Stare Decisis*," *U.C.L.A. Law Review* (June 1957), pp. 657-61.
[16] For additional references on this subject see: John W. Taylor, Theodore Kheel, and Aaron Levenstein, "Reporting of Labor Arbitration," *The Arbitration Journal*, Vol. 1, No. 4 (1946), pp. 420-28; Editorial, "Creeping Legalism in Labor Arbitration," *The Arbitration Journal*, Vol. 13, No. 3 (1958), p. 129; and Archibald Cox, "The Place of Law in Labor Arbitration," Bureau of National Affairs, *The Profession of Arbitration* (1957), p. 83.

although one usually will find less reliance on the machinery where the relationship is good. Too little use of arbitration, if it results from unwise yielding on grievances by either party, may be more harmful in the long run than excessive arbitration. There is evidence to show that in the contract-formulation stage of a relationship, arbitration is used frequently. As stability in contract terms and their meaning develops over the years and as parties learn how to work together, the arbitration rate tends to decrease.

While problems relating to the mechanics of grievance arbitration have largely disappeared, there remain many serious questions as to the philosophy of grievance arbitration in labor relations. In too many instances remissness of management and union in facing up to their responsibilities has meant that the parties are serving the arbitration process rather than vice versa. More often than not critics of the process have failed to think through carefully what role they want this machinery to play in the conduct of their daily labor relations affairs. Grievance arbitration should not be expected to do the work of the parties. At a minimum a company should decide what grievance subjects it is willing to refer to a neutral and under what circumstances a grievance should be allowed to go to arbitration. The wise management will also be alert to the lessons to be learned from arbitration experience. It may discover contract clauses that need to be modified or administrative weaknesses that require corrective measures.

Few managements today doubt the basic efficacy of the grievance arbitration process. Its impact on the bargaining relationship is considerable, and it is the consensus that its net effect has been salutary. In spite of the many unresolved problems, it is remarkable that within the relatively short span of twenty years this machinery by and large has acquired its proper place in the government of labor relations by agreement.

A grievance arbitration process designed by the parties is peculiar to the American system of industrial relations. Nearly all managements and unions prefer it to the alternatives—the use of economic strength to resolve unsettled grievances or the creation of special labor courts by law. The late Harry Shulman, one of the deans of the arbitration profession, reflected the views of many parties when he said that the arbitration process was one that could be "ever consciously directed—not merely to the redress of past wrongs—but to the maintenance and improvement of the parties' present and future collaboration. . . . Its authority comes not from above but from their own specific consent. They can shape it and reshape it."[17]

Out of this constant shaping and reshaping of the process there may emerge in the future a new role for neutrals, a role created by the parties themselves. While many neutrals will continue to decide grievances, a few may be called upon to serve in a consultative capacity, meeting regularly with top management and union representatives on a continuing basis. Their purpose will be not to make decisions, but rather to assist the parties in an objective discussion of a broad range of problems affecting their relationship. There is already some evidence that this use of neutrals is being considered by companies and unions in critical bargaining relationships. In a few cases the implementing machinery has been established. It is the hope that such consultation, with the neutral serving as a catalytic agent, will prevent any serious breakdowns in the relationship. This development, which cannot be considered a trend, is an extension of the role of the neutral growing out of the experience with grievance arbitration over the past twenty years.

[17] Harry Shulman, "The Role of Arbitration in the Collective Bargaining Process," Institute of Industrial Relations, University of California, *Collective Bargaining and Arbitration* (1949), p. 24.

27 / *Problems and Policies in High-Cost Plants*

HIGH-COST PLANTS or plants which for other reasons (such as unreliability in making deliveries) have difficulty in meeting competition, present special problems for both management and employees. Management must consider whether the prospects of reducing costs are sufficiently good to make continued operation of the plant worth while; the employees and the unions must consider whether the effect of high costs on their employment security or on their ability to win wage increases is a serious matter.[1] In order that a high-cost plant may be worth operating, it is not necessary that there be good prospects of bringing costs down to the average in the company or the industry; it is necessary, however, that the continued operation of the plant promise as high a return as could be expected from alternative uses of the capital.[2]

Impact of High-Cost Plants on Industrial Relations

The decision as to whether a plant is worth operating may depend on the expected reaction of the employees and their unions toward efforts to cut costs. The range of reactions of unions to such efforts is exceedingly broad. Some unions may be indifferent as to whether or not a high-cost plant or enterprise survives; other unions may be intensely interested in the survival of the plant. When labor costs are high, other costs are often high also. Furthermore, high labor costs may be associated with other deficiencies, such as inefficient manage-

[1] On these matters there may be a difference of view between the employees and the union as an organization. These differences will be discussed below. In some cases the employees are more interested than their unions in the problems of high-cost plants; in other instances, it is the unions that are more interested.

[2] Whether or not a high-cost plant should be operated indefinitely depends on how much might be realized from a sale of the plant (presumably to buyers who would have other uses for the land and perhaps the buildings) or on the cost of moving the equipment in the plant to a new location where operating conditions would be more favorable.

ment, poor product design, or poor marketing plans. Such conditions affect the union's view of what might be accomplished by a reduction in labor costs.

It is obvious that higher-than-average labor costs have important effects on union-management relations—causing them to deteriorate if the union sees no problem to be concerned about and leading to cooperative relations where union and management regard high costs as a common problem.

This chapter is concerned primarily with managements' efforts to deal with the problems of high labor costs and with the reaction of unions to these efforts. As a basis for this discussion there will be a brief analysis of the reasons for high labor costs and of managements' reasons for taking steps to correct such costs.

Reasons for High Labor Costs

In the plants covered by this inquiry the following reasons for high labor costs have been most frequent, not necessarily in this order: (1) poor management, (2) the weak position of the employer in relation to his customers, (3) an unusually powerful and militant union with a short-sighted view of its interests, (4) incentive systems of wage payment, (5) World War II, and (6) acute labor shortages.

There is likely to be a combination of several causes of high labor costs in any one situation, and it may be difficult or impossible to ascertain which are the fundamental ones. For example, employers who are in a weak bargaining position in relation to customers will have high labor costs if they are led to practice a policy of appeasement toward the union. The policy of appeasement, in turn, encourages the union to be tough and militant and to threaten direct action to impose restrictions on management. In other cases, a tough and militant union may itself be an independent cause of high labor costs. Hence, when one finds a company in a weak bargaining position in relation to its customers and confronted by an aggressive and militant trade union, one may not be sure whether the weak bargaining position of the employer produced the tough and militant union or whether these are two independent sources of high labor costs.

Other examples showing the difficulty of ascertaining the original causes of high labor costs readily come to mind. An incentive system with loose standards, a tough militant union, and a weak management may be found together. Each of these conditions may be an independent cause of high labor costs, or one or more of the conditions may be responsible for the others. Incentive systems tend to create aggressive, militant unions, particularly when the incentive system is operated by a weak management. Hence, the aggressive union, though an important secondary cause of high labor costs, may not be an original cause.

A brief examination of some of the fundamental causes of high labor costs is in order.

Poor Management

Some managements are bound to be better than others, but why do poor managements sometimes survive for many years? There are many efficient owner-operated companies, but any management that is more or less sheltered from competition and is not accountable to others is likely in the course of time to become inefficient. An owner-operated company may have high costs simply because the founder is an inventor, an engineer, or a scientist who is excellent at developing new products and processes but poor at business administration. Some owner-operated companies are efficient so long as they are being managed by the founder, but the second or third generation owners may be poor managers. But if the company is protected from competition in some degree by patents, a trade name, or simply an excellent reputation, the high costs of the enterprise may not cause serious difficulty for some years. Owners of concerns making only low profits may live comfortably for a long time by not reinvesting earnings or even by distributing part of depreciation allowances. But when replacement of equipment can no longer be postponed, the firm finds itself in financial difficulties.

A company engaged in making flexible packaging and doing color printing on cellophane, polyethylene, and other materials by processes which it controlled was sufficiently profitable to do well under the management of an owner president who was poor at dealing with unions and subordinates and who imposed many unnecessary costs on the enterprise by unwise concessions to the unions. The manufacturer of a well-regarded brand of tableware operated in the face of slowly growing restraints and restrictions imposed by the union on a second and third generation management that was more interested in recreation than in the business. Many family-owned companies grew up in the automotive parts industry when automobile manufacturers were numerous and when "manufacturing" a car consisted largely of buying parts and putting them together. In its early days the automotive parts industry was profitable, and companies could make money even though they were not particularly well run. As automobile manufacturing became concentrated in the hands of a few large makers, who buy parts only when the supplier will sell them for less than it would cost the buyer to make them, many parts manufacturers found themselves badly handicapped by the loose shop practices and high labor costs that grew up when profits were large.

Bad management in a company often coexists with resourceful and efficient management in many individual departments. An organization of any size is almost certain to have a considerable sprinkling of efficient employees. These good men often struggle heroically to offset the mistakes of the poor managers. The immediate obligation of management is to get out production and to meet production schedules. When company policy handicaps management in meeting schedules, all manner of stratagems are developed to meet the problem. For example, if it is company policy to yield to economic pressure from the union (or if company policy on this point is uncertain), there will probably be many special deals worked out between middle and front line management on the one hand and the union on the other hand. Managers often work out ingenious arrangements by which union obstruction to production is limited, and management gives up a minimum amount of control.

Bad management may take so many forms that it is hardly worth while to try to describe them. A common fault of owner management springs from the practice of managing by ad hoc decisions instead of by carefully considered policies. Owner managers, because of the very independence of their positions, are likely to undermine subordinates by going over their heads, dealing directly with the union, and revising decisions made by the subordinates. Once a union finds that a top management is willing to bypass and reverse subordinates, it becomes unwilling to accept unfavorable decisions from subordinates and insists on taking all issues to top management.

Middle or front line management may make special deals with the union in order to prevent appeals to the top.

A great weakness of owner management is the absence of someone to challenge the owner or his decisions. Hence, management is likely to reflect his whims, prejudices, and preferences. A conspicuous example of personal management was that of the late Henry Ford. Another company, one specializing in printing labels and packaging, had poor industrial relations largely because it was dominated by the owner president, who was the principal developer of the process controlled and used by the company. His special interest in the printing process led him to make favorites of the printing press operators, who were members of the Printing Pressmen's Union. This was regarded by the members of the union as a sign of weakness, and they were encouraged to seek special favors. As a result, presses were overmanned, and the company was not permitted to make changes in rates and production standards except when there were "substantial" changes in equipment and methods. Through threat of stoppages, the union set overtime rules, shift arrangements, and other regulations in the press department.

A common weakness of poorly managed, high-cost companies is a lack of adequate staff. Industrial relations are likely to be considerably affected by whether or not a company has an industrial engineering staff and if so, whether the industrial engineering department is large enough for the particular enterprise or the plant. The absence of an adequately staffed industrial engineering department is likely to mean that production standards or piece rates are bargained, and the bargaining tends to produce wrangling and ill feeling. Furthermore, the bargaining of production standards or piece rates helps aggressive and militant factions to gain control of the union, which in turn leads to bad relations with management.

In some companies labor costs may be high because industrial relations policy is subordinated to sales policy, with the result that the management pursues a policy of peace at any price. The subordination of labor policy to sales policy may occur for several reasons. It may be the result of the weak bargaining position of the enterprise in relation to its customers—a matter that will be discussed below. It may be a result simply of the fact that the concern is making large profits and prefers to incur increases in labor costs rather than lose highly profitable business. Later when demand subsides and profits shrink, high costs may be a great burden. Many managements have failed to notice how quickly small increases in labor costs add up to substantial disadvantages. Subordination of labor policy to sales policy may result from the fact that the company is having trouble keeping up with the demand from customers and does not wish to fall further behind on its delivery schedule. It may result from the fact that the enterprise is engaged in a contest for a larger share of the market and does not want to be hampered by interruptions to production. It may result from the fact that the enterprise is in a weak market position and that it does not wish to weaken its position still further by being an unreliable source of supply. This was a principal reason for the fear of strikes of one of the less successful automobile companies, which went to considerable extremes in pursuing a policy of appeasement. Finally labor policy may be dominated by sales policy often because top executives had their careers in selling, are more interested in selling than in labor policy, and do not appreciate the long-run cost of subordinating labor policy to sales policy.

Bad management of industrial relations may result from inexperience in dealing with unions. A company making material for the electrical industry is an example. For six years after the unions came in (from 1936 to 1942) industrial relations were handled by the vice president in charge of manufacturing. There was no personnel or industrial relations department. The vice president believed that the company would be better off if it made private deals with the international representatives of the union. The private deals included "secret" union-shop agreements, which the company vice president kept in his safe. The plant managers never saw the contracts and were dependent on the vice president for their knowledge of the contents.

For a while the unions responded to the "private deal" approach by being moderate in their demands. But eventually the unions got tough, and the management responded by adopting a tough policy toward the unions. A wildcat strike during the war led the government to persuade the company to create an industrial relations department. After several years of tough policy on both sides there was a strike of three and a half months. This led the company (under advice from an outside so-called "expert") to adopt a policy of appeasement, which the unions took advantage of to insist on loose production standards, to perpetuate inequities in the wage rate structure, and to modify the interpretation of the seniority clause to compel management to base a larger proportion of promotions on seniority. A second strike, for five and a half months in 1952, was necessary to enable the company to put its house more or less in order.

Weak managements sometimes complicate their own problems by making it difficult for the international officers of the union to persuade the local to consider the long-run interests of its members. An international vice president of the United Automobile Workers criticized many companies (especially small ones) for yielding too readily to local union pressure. He pointed out that he could do little against excessive demands by the local when the employer undermined his position by granting the demands. The same complaint was made by the president of a large UAW local with branches in many small plants. He pointed out that it is advantageous to a union officer who wishes to protect the long-run interests of the members to deal with a strong management.

Employer-Customer Bargaining Position

It was pointed out above that the domination of labor policy by sales policy may result from a weak bargaining position of the enterprise in relation to its customers. In some industries, such as automotive parts, most of the output of some companies goes to one, two, or possibly three customers. These customers may not stock parts but insist on an uninterrupted flow from the supplier. If the latter fails to make deliveries on schedule, the customer will transfer his business elsewhere. Eventually the customers are likely to bring back most of their business but probably not all of it. In the automotive parts and the rubber industries there are many examples in recent years of managements pursuing a policy of appeasement because of fear that a strike would cause them to lose all or part of the business of important customers.

Militancy and Power of the Union

High labor costs may result from the fact that the employer is no match for a strong and militant union that bases its policies on the short-run interests of its members.

Where unions do not have the industry more or less completely organized, they may create high costs in the union part of the industry simply by compelling union employers to pay higher wages than nonunion employers do. The shrinkage of employment in the union parts of the cotton textile industry and the hosiery industry was due partly to the difference in labor costs between union and nonunion plants, aggravated by the fact that the nonunion mills, being newer than the union ones, had more efficient equipment. Even when a union has an industry quite completely organized, there may be considerable variation in the effect of the different locals on costs in the different plants. This is the case especially of the locals in recently-organized national unions that bargain more or less independently of the national union. Some of these locals are stronger and more aggressive than others, and some take a shorter-run view of the interests of the members than is taken by other locals; some deal with stronger employers than others. In the rubber industry the union tends to enforce a higher wage scale for making rubber footwear and mechanical rubber goods against the "Big Four" than against their specialist competitors.

In some industries the result of such policies has been that the stiffest conditions were imposed on employers in the weakest competitive condition—a sort of ability-to-pay in reverse determination of wages and working conditions. This has been true in the automobile industry, where General Motors, the strongest company, has negotiated contracts that are most favorable to the employer. Even where the national union substantially controls the negotiation of the contract and, therefore, its written terms, administration of the contract may be largely in the hands of the local union—and administration invariably has important effects on costs.[3] Managements generally have failed to notice how quickly small increases in costs add up to important cost disadvantages. Finally, some plants may have high labor costs because they have been organized by a union from another industry that insists that they pay its wage scale. For example, two plants making paper containers have been made almost noncompetitive since the steelworkers, who organized them,

[3] When negotiations between employers and local unions are controlled in some way by the national union (through the requirement that agreements meet minimum standards, through the requirement that agreements be approved by the national union, or through participation of national officers or representatives of the union in local negotiation), the terms of agreements may be kept more or less uniform.

have thus far insisted on keeping the same rates that the union gets in metal container plants. The paper container plants organized by other unions pay 25 cents to 50 cents an hour less than the steelworkers require. Employment in one of the plants has dropped from 800 to 250 in a five-year period, and men with 13 years' seniority have been laid off. It is certain that one of the two plants will have to be closed, and there is a good possibility that the other will also. These are among the exceptional cases in which the national union takes a tougher stand than the locals. The locals would be willing to make concessions, but the national, which negotiates a master agreement covering both metal container and paper container plants, is unwilling to accept less in plants making paper containers than in those making metal ones.

Why are some local unions tougher and more militant than others? Many of the tough and militant locals are little influenced by the national union. The nationals generally encourage locals to take a long-run view of their interests—that is, to consider the effect of their demands on the employer's ability to compete and, therefore, on the job security of the members. Hence, as a rule (although not invariably) national influence is in the direction of moderation. One militant local in an axle plant belonged to an independent national, not affiliated with the AFL-CIO, which exercised little control over its locals. A few of the toughest locals in the UAW feel quite independent of the national union because they are older than the national and helped found it.

Some locals may be militant because they are under the influence of leaders who believe in militancy, who believe that the function of a union is to prepare the workers for the class struggle or who believe that a union must be militant to retain the interest of the members. Some unions may be militant because working conditions are difficult and arouse the workers' resentment. Instability of employment may be such a condition, especially if production schedules are not carefully planned. Some unions are tough and militant because workers are paid under a piece-rate or bonus plan so that there are frequent opportunities to bargain over rates as jobs are changed or as new jobs are established. Unless the management is firm in discussing rates in factual and technical terms, and unless it stands steadfast in the face of threats of direct action, it virtually invites the union to become militant in order to force favorable settlements from management. Some unions are tough because the managements are tough, difficult, and arbitrary so that the unions must be too in order to win cases for their members. Finally, a union may be tough and militant because the management is weak and yields readily to union pressure. Indeed, weak managements are a cause of tough, aggressive unions no less than are strong managements. The reason is obvious. When management is weak, the union quickly learns that it pays to be tough. This matter is discussed in Chapter 22 dealing with the use of pressure tactics by unions.

Tough, aggressive locals, as has already been indicated, may impose high costs on employers through the terms of the union-management contract, the administration of the contract, or both. Some locals take pride in getting more than the so-called "pattern." In a Michigan automotive parts plant the slogan of the local was "A—B— leads General Motors." The differences in the wages, production standards, work loads, and other conditions between union and nonunion plants are frequently substantial—as the experience of the cotton textile and the hosiery industries shows. It is usually difficult, however, for one local to impose contractual terms on an employer that are materially different than other locals are accepting from other employers. Hence, among union plants in the same industry the biggest differences in costs are likely to result from differences in the administration of contracts.

Opportunity for large differences among union plants arises if incentive methods of wage payment are used and if the union is successful in bargaining rates and perhaps in pegging production. In an axle manufacturing plant there was a shop committee of five spending full time at company expense handling (or stirring up) grievances. The committee bargained individual rates, and the union pegged production at $2.74 an hour. Most workers made their quotas in six hours. In another plant manufacturing electrical goods, the unions took advantage of the fact that the employer had only five or six customers who were intolerant of delays on deliveries and used slowdowns and wildcat strikes to force hourly earnings up to $3.50 and $4.00 an hour. Women on light assembly work were earning more than tool and die-makers.

Since weak managements and tough, aggressive unions go together, as has been pointed out earlier in the chapter, it is often uncertain whether these two sources of high labor costs are each an original cause or whether one is the result of the other. A maker of automobiles had an incentive system with loose standards which permitted high hourly earnings for low production. Rest, preparation, and clean-up periods amounted to 43 minutes a day in comparison with 24 minutes in the plants of the company's principal competitors. There was a low ratio of supervisory to production employees but a high ratio of union stewards or representatives—one for every 25.1 employees. These people were paid by the company for time spent on union business. Grievances were not reduced to writing until the final appeal stage, so management could not keep track of grievances. The seniority system provided for plant-wide bumping. This produced an enormous internal plant turnover which, in a three-month period in 1953, cost the company three-quarters of a million dollars.

In most departments the union stewards were really in control. The problems of the foremen were aggravated by the fact that they could not count on top management to back them up. If the steward contacted the company's president or chairman about a grievance, the higher official frequently reversed the foreman. The result was that the stewards, not the foremen, were the "managers" of most departments. It was the stewards who interpreted the contract, and their interpretation was "the law." Lax administration and the need to find ways of getting production out in the face of a strong union led to private deals between supervisors and stewards. Seniority rights could be bought and sold.

It is evident that in the above case both the union and the management were responsible for high labor costs and that each tended to re-enforce the other—the tough union made the management weaker, and the weak management made the union tougher.

Incentive Systems

There is some question whether incentive systems should be classified as an original cause of high labor costs since an efficient management dealing with a union not more than normally militant under more or less normal circumstances can usually prevent incentives from producing high costs. But an incentive system is often a principal cause for a union's becoming militant since the opportunity to bargain rates rewards militancy. Furthermore, in tight labor markets an incentive system may be the deciding influence that prevents a reasonably efficient management from keeping costs under control. Hence, although incentive systems are perhaps a secondary and aggravating cause of high costs more often than an original one, they are an original cause in some cases.

The essential reason why incentive systems produce high labor costs is that production standards become loose. In some cases loose standards cause the workers to limit their hourly earnings, but it is nevertheless true that the employer is paying a high price for a given amount of output. In addition the output of the plant is limited, and the overhead per unit of product tends to rise. In other cases loose standards lead to high hourly earnings. The various ways in which production standards become loose were discussed in Chapter 17.

Production standards become loose chiefly through becoming out of date. Various small changes in equipment, methods, and materials are made. Each change may be so small that management does not bother to reset the standard—especially since resetting might lead to considerable argument. Some union-management contracts forbid retiming jobs unless the changes in method will alter the time by a certain minimum percentage. But a succession of changes in method for which adjustments are not made will soon produce a very loose standard. Loose production standards may be the result of great prosperity, which the management was willing to share with the workers by setting easy standards, or the result of a tight labor market, in which the management uses loose standards to attract help; or they may be simply the result of a militant union policy of challenging new standards and new rates.

World War II

The war introduced inefficiencies in many plants that lasted for years after its end. There are four principal ways, other than by helping to raise wages and employee benefits, in which the war raised labor costs in some plants: (1) by encouraging management to tolerate make-work practices; (2) by encouraging management to adopt a policy of appeasement toward unions; (3) by encouraging the development of loose production standards; and (4) by helping to break down personnel practices—introducing poor timekeeping, long coffee breaks, or absenteeism. Cost-plus contracts encouraged the hoarding of labor by union and nonunion plants alike, and hoarding led managements to tolerate make-work practices that they would ordinarily have strongly resisted.[4] The war led many managements to pursue a policy of appeasement in order to avoid interruptions to production. Some managements did it because they did not wish to cut off badly-needed war supplies; some managements yielded to pressure tactics of unions in response to short-sighted and ill-advised pressure from labor officers from the armed services; a few managements practiced appeasement for patriotic reasons—because they had the mistaken idea that patriotism required them to avoid interruptions of production.

The policy of appeasement encouraged unions to try to get their way by wildcat strikes and other forms of direct action—slowdowns, planned absenteeism, union meetings in the shop on company time, or refusal to observe management's directives. In some plants, therefore, the war had the indirect effect of causing unions to be tough and unruly and thus a prolonged source of high labor costs.

This effect is illustrated by a manufacturer of batteries, which pursued a policy of super-patriotism during the war. The union, under the influence of a labor attorney, became exceedingly technical and legalistic with a considerable staff doing nothing but working on grievances—either stirring them up or arguing them with management. This state of affairs was changed by a strike of 14 weeks' duration in 1950, which was also followed by important changes in management policies. The policy of appeasement was bad for the morale of management and often led the supervisors immediately responsible for production to wonder "What's the use?" In another plant in the Middle West the manager told the union committee after the union had won a strike at the end of the war: "You guys have shown you can run the plant. You had better do it wisely, because if you don't, you won't have any jobs left."

The war had a strong tendency to produce high labor costs in plants that had incentive systems of wage payment, since it tended to produce loose standards and high piece rates. Unions were encouraged by the acute labor shortages and by the demand for quick

---

[4] Fear of the effect of cost-plus contracts on management efficiency led a few far-sighted companies to refuse to accept cost-plus contracts. As the management of one company put it: "The most valuable asset we have is the efficiency of our management. We were not willing to sacrifice this asset in order to make a few more dollars during the war."

deliveries to insist on bargaining over standards and rates, and they frequently drove hard bargains. In a plant making transmissions for tanks the union established the practice that no standard would be put into effect without the approval of the union steward. Employers, disregarding their long-run interests, were often not averse to loose standards since high earnings were a way of attracting and holding labor in a tight labor market. The wage stabilization policy made for loose standards and high piece rates because both were ways of evading wage stabilization.

Acute Labor Shortages

Extreme labor shortages tend to produce high labor costs because they encourage local unions to become arbitrary and militant, and they often lead managements to pursue a policy of appeasement. A maker of automobile parts attributes his difficulties largely to the fact that his plant was located in an area where the Atomic Energy Commission was building a large installation. Any employee who was dissatisfied could get a job on the atomic energy project. Conditions were aggravated by the fact that the management of the automotive parts plant was inexperienced in dealing with unions, that virtually all of the output of the plant was for one exacting customer who made trouble at the slightest delay in deliveries, and that the local union had little or no guidance or leadership from the international union. From 1948 to 1952 there were 28 major work stoppages and many minor incidents. The local union was encouraged to be aggressive by the fact that workers were paid under an incentive system. The local union wanted to bargain production standards on every new job and on every job change. Most of the grievances and wildcats related to the establishment of wage incentive standards.

Origin of Managements' Interest in Labor Costs

What eventually leads managements in companies where high labor costs have been tolerated to try to do something about the matter? The change may come about in several ways. In some cases the conditions that led management to acquiesce in high labor costs or to pursue a policy of appeasement toward the union (the war or an acute labor shortage) may have ended. In some cases the attack on high labor costs may have come because the upward creep of costs has finally made the plant so noncompetitive that action *must* be taken. In still other cases the change of policy may be associated with a change in management, or at least in key people in the management. These may result from normal retirements, or high labor costs and other difficulties may lead the owners to change managers. Sometimes the attack on high labor costs has come after the plant has been bought by a large company, and new managers have been installed for the purpose of changing labor policies.[5] Finally, the interest of a company in constructing new low-cost capacity may lead the management to accept strikes in its high-cost plants to get rid of uneconomic working rules or loose standards of production. Thus a manufacturer of window glass waited until a new low-cost plant had been built and put in operation before accepting a long and expensive strike against obsolete and uneconomic practices (particularly expensive rules for handling shrinkages of employment) in one of its older plants.

CHANGING STANDARDS OF PRODUCTION AND WAGE PAYMENT SYSTEMS. In the automobile and automotive parts business, where there were acute labor shortages during the war and during much of the postwar boom period and where many local unions were militant, standards of production and incentive systems have been frequent causes of high labor costs. This matter is discussed in Chapter 17. In some cases incentives were abolished and replaced by measured daywork; in other cases incentives were kept, but jobs were restudied, and new standards set. Abolishing incentives sometimes meant cuts in hourly earnings for some workers. In one automobile plant eliminating incentives in the postwar period meant cuts of 30 to 60 cents in hourly earnings. Later, stiffer standards under measured daywork resulted in fewer jobs, and the company had 13 days of wildcat strikes in protest against the elimination of 1,800 workers. The company compromised the dispute by agreeing to take back 250 of them.

[5] One large company conditioned its purchase upon the willingness of the union to consent to changes in the labor-management agreement that eliminated make-work practices and other causes of high labor costs. Since the purchase by the larger company was necessary to assure continuance of operations in the plant, the local union reluctantly consented to the changes.

The new owner of an automotive parts plant estimated that in order to be competitive with General Motors, it would need to abolish incentives and put in day rates that would reduce average hourly earnings in the plant by about 33 per cent. This was a bigger cut than the union leaders felt able to sell to the membership, in spite of the fact that the members were worried about the future of the plant and were willing to make concessions to preserve their jobs. A settlement was reached which provided that piece rates would be retained but would be cut for the time being an average of 15 per cent. All jobs were to be restudied to establish permanent rates.

Another automotive parts manufacturer, confronted with pegged production under an incentive system, decided that the only way to stop the men from limiting output and, in particular, to stop an aggressive shop committee from seeing that the men limited output, was to abolish the incentive system. The management had to take a long strike, but it succeeded in eliminating the incentive plan and in getting the men to relax output restrictions. Some companies have been able to get away from costly incentive systems and various restrictions that have grown up in old plants only by building new plants and moving some work to them.

The high costs of loose incentive systems or standards of production have sometimes led management and the union to agree on a plan of cooperation in getting rid of the traditional incentive plans and giving the men a chance to improve their earnings by promoting efficiency. These plans are discussed in Chapter 28.

OTHER CHANGES IN UNION-MANAGEMENT AGREEMENTS. High labor costs often stem from union contracts that impose high operating costs. Two of the smaller automobile manufacturers negotiated changes in bumping rights to reduce high costs imposed by plant-wide seniority. An automobile parts manufacturer, in addition to negotiating a cut of 15 per cent in piece rates, induced the union to agree to the cancellation of costly side agreements that had been made in the various departments between the supervisors and the union steward or the workers. A manufacturer of flexible containers was handicapped by agreements providing for excessive crews on presses and other equipment. Some agreements regulating crew sizes were verbal understandings. In 1955 the management reached an agreement with one of the unions that no precedents, customs, conditions, practices, or agreements should be permitted in any way to modify the written agreement. The disallowance of side deals has given management an opportunity to tackle the problem of excessive crews on some equipment.

CHANGES IN ADMINISTRATION OF THE UNION-MANAGEMENT CONTRACT. Attacks on the problem of high labor costs may involve changes in the administration of the union-management contract—sometimes radical changes. The reason, of course, is that the decision to attack the problem of high labor costs is itself a major policy change that involves many changes in administrative methods. Where high labor costs have been tolerated, it is usually because labor policy has been subordinated to other policies, and management has tended to appease the unions. In such cases an attack on high labor costs cannot be made without abandoning the policy of appeasement. Changes in the administration of the labor contract for the purpose of reducing high labor costs ordinarily involve a series of specific steps, such as (1) changes in personnel at various levels of management, demonstrating to intermediate and front-line supervision that company labor policy is being changed fundamentally; (2) creation of additional jobs, especially ones providing new functions, such as training jobs; (3) increasing the size of the supervisory staff to much higher ratios than formerly; and (4) training supervisory personnel.

Occasionally one or two changes in top management may be all that is needed to bring about a radical change in labor policies—a shift from arbitrary, unpredictable, personal management to orderly management based on established policies. But such changes are essential because management cannot fail to make a strong fight against high labor costs without the acquiescence of the men at the top. But how is top management going to convince intermediate and front-line management that company policy has changed, especially after top management has failed to back up foremen and department heads? Nothing short of a demonstration of top management's willingness to stand fast in the face of slowdowns, wildcats, and other direct pressure is likely to be convincing.

The attack on high labor costs often involves the establishment of industrial engineering or time-study departments and the setting of new production standards. Or it may mean setting up an industrial

relations department to help in the development of new labor policies or training programs. In other cases existing departments, such
as in industrial engineering, have been increased in size.

A change in industrial relations policies for the purpose of attacking high labor costs may be accompanied by training programs either
for most of management or for front-line supervision. In the case
of a plant manufacturing flexible packaging, which was sold by the
owner president to a large container manufacturer, few of the executives were changed, but the well-established labor policies of the
new owners replaced those of the owner president. An industrial relations manager and a manager for industrial engineering from the
organization of the new owner were transferred to the plant. With
the former owner president out of the picture, it was expected that
the men from the new owner's organization would be able to win
acceptance for his labor relations philosophy of accepting unions,
but insisting on freedom to run the plant in an efficient fashion.

Where foremen have been shorn of most of their authority and
where their position has been made insecure by failure of higher
management to back them up consistently, a thorough program to
develop qualities of leadership may be needed to restore their morale. In a plant where the position of the foremen had seriously deteriorated as a result of the terms of the agreement with the union
and of failure of top management to back up the foremen, a ten-
week training program for supervisors was instituted. In small con-
ference-type meetings limited to twenty-five the new contract, which
restored some rights to management, was examined section by section. Of course, such a training program is useless unless management is willing to support its foremen by refusing to overrule them
without good reason and by refusing to yield to direct pressure tactics from the union.

Union Reaction to Efforts to Reduce Labor Costs

The reactions of unions, both national and local, to the efforts of
managements to reduce labor costs vary from strong opposition to
enthusiastic cooperation. The reaction of unions depends in the
main upon (1) whether or not the union is interested in the survival
of the plant or enterprise; (2) whether or not the union believes that

a reduction in labor costs would affect the survival of the plant or enterprise; and (3) the nature of the steps that management proposes to take to cut labor costs.

Sometimes unions have little interest in the survival of a plant because the failure or decline of one concern simply gives new concerns a chance to spring up and other old ones to grow. Unions are dealing at all times with enterprises that are competing more or less vigorously with each other, and unions cannot afford as a general rule to take a special interest in helping the less successful competitors survive. The jobs that the union members lose when some concerns fail, they gain in others. Under these circumstances, the union may be either indifferent or opposed to the efforts of management to reduce costs.

There are, however, many instances in which a union wants to save jobs even though it finds it difficult to accept the required sacrifice. One type of situation is when union plants are being driven out of business by nonunion plants. Another is when the union plant is more or less isolated, especially if it is fairly large. Its closing would create a group of disgruntled workers, who would blame the union for the loss of their jobs and might become the nucleus for a nonunion labor market. There have been such cases in the needle trades. To prevent the growth of the nonunion part of the industry unions are sometimes willing to give managements substantial help in reducing costs.

Unions are likely to be skeptical of management's claim that a reduction in labor costs is needed to help the plant or enterprise survive. They have heard managements in wage negotiations argue time and again that they could not afford to meet certain demands, and yet when the demands have been conceded, the enterprises have met them. Consequently, even when the inability-to-pay argument is valid and the management must have relief, the union may not realize it. For this reason, as we shall see, management may have to prove its sincerity by taking a strike.

Sometimes national and local unions may disagree over the advisability of helping a management cut costs. The national union may see more clearly than its local the threat of nonunion competition and be willing to make concessions that the local will not make. On the other hand, the national may prefer to lose control of a plant or see an employer go out of business rather than have the local make concessions that may be used as precedents against the union by other employers.

The reaction of the union to management's efforts to reduce costs depends on how good management's proposals are and the cost that they impose on the workers. Under some conditions there may be little or no cost whatsoever. Costs may be cut by dispensing with unnecessary jobs, and the reduction in the work force may be achieved by not replacing men who quit. In other cases, where loose piece rates or standards have produced exorbitant earnings, the cut in costs may require that the workers take substantial reductions in their pay. In such cases the opposition of the workers may be intense.

Putting Over the Program of Labor Cost Reduction

The methods used to put over a program for reducing high labor costs depend in the main on the reaction of the employees or the union to the problems of the employer; the relative strength of the union and the employer; and the established relationship between the union and the employer. Persuasion may be enough, or the employer may be so weak that persuasion is the only feasible method. In other cases other methods may be necessary. In general, the methods of putting into operation programs for reducing labor costs fall into six classes:

1. Education and persuasion—placing the facts before the union members and their families so that the union is convinced that its interests are served by making concessions.
2. Bringing the national union into the negotiations with the expectation that the national will attach more weight to the long-run interests of the members than does the local union.
3. Submitting the issue to arbitration.
4. Shutting down the plant or accepting long and expensive strikes to force acceptance of management's program.
5. Moving the work to other plants.
6. Establishing formal union-management cooperation to reduce costs and raise productivity.

Education and Persuasion

An educational approach was used successfully by a large maker of heavy lifting apparatus. Although the company had about half the market, it was having a hard time meeting the keen competition offered by its many rivals. In view of the fact that costs could be cut adequately only if employees accepted fairly stiff sacrifices, it may seem strange that the educational approach was successful. In this case, however, the management gave weight to its arguments by pointing out that unless costs were cut, the work would have to be moved.

The cause of the difficulty seems to have been the incentive system and the lax management that it encouraged. In 1943 the company had agreed not to change rates unless the method of doing the job were changed, but improvements in materials and tools were not considered changes in method. Management had tolerated lax time keeping. Employees were quitting 10 to 30 minutes early at the end of each shift, and in some departments they were taking rest periods of 10 to 15 minutes each hour.

A study of the company's costs and markets led management to conclude that the company would save money by abandoning its two plants in the East and building a single modern plant in the Middle West. Before making this move top management decided to find out whether the employees would accept a cost-reduction program in order to save their jobs. At one of the plants the company called a meeting of employees and their wives, at which the president outlined the alternatives open to the company and told the assembled employees that a cost reduction program was necessary or the company would be forced to move. A similar meeting, addressed by the president, was held later the same day for employees of the other plant and their wives.

The international union quickly took over the negotiations for a cost reduction program. The international opposed the efforts of the company to reduce its costs, adopting a policy quite different from the policy of national unions in many such cases. The management realized that it could change the attitude of the union only by convincing the rank and file that the company intended to move the work unless costs were reduced. The personnel manager, who was highly respected by the employees, talked directly with the people in the plants over a period of six weeks and provided the foremen and supervisors with the information they needed to discuss company problems with their people. Finally, after six weeks the local union officers, convinced that the management meant business, took the negotiations away from the international officers and worked out a compromise that was acceptable to the company. The union agreed that the old incentive plan should be replaced, that the company should have the right to set new standards on all jobs, using a Methods-Time-Measurement standard setting approach, and that a new job evaluation system proposed by the company should be introduced.

National Union Participation

The national union usually is better able than the local to appraise the competitive position of a plant. The reasons are obvious. The national is better able to see the condition of the industry as a whole, and its officers are less influenced than are the local officers by local political pressures. Hence, when a management seeks to induce a local union to make substantial concessions in order to make a plant competitive, it may try to get help from the national union. Especially in cases where incentive rates have been allowed to become loose so that cutting costs may involve substantial reductions in the earnings of workers, the influence of the national union may be needed.

As a general rule, nationals must operate through influence rather than authority, although they usually have an effective veto on decisions of locals to strike. The influence of national officers with locals varies greatly depending on the age and history of the union and the market conditions under which bargaining with employers occurs. As unions grow older, there is a tendency for power and influence to gravitate into the hands of the national. Hence, among many of the older unions in the AFL-CIO, nationals are in the habit of exercising considerable influence and authority over locals. When these older unions have established locals in recent years, they have trained the locals from the start to look for considerable guidance from the national.

Quite different, however, are the conditions in many of the new national unions. To begin with, there has not been time for the new nationals to establish much control over the locals. Furthermore, many of the locals were not organized by representatives of the national union; they were grass roots organizations started by the members themselves without outside help. Such locals often have a tradition of independence, in which they take pride. Finally, some of the locals in the new national unions are older than the national itself and helped to start the national. This history adds to their feeling of independence.[6] Whether or not a national union eventually establishes considerable control over locals depends largely on whether the members of the several locals work for employers who compete with one another in regional or national markets or for employers who compete very little with each other.[7]

Sometimes a national officer has unusual influence with a local because he has guided it through difficult strikes or because he worked in the plant and helped to found it. Such in part was the source of the influence of a vice president of the UAW, with a local in a large high-cost plant that was losing many millions a year. When approached by the management, he satisfied himself that the company's costs were far too high. He negotiated an agreement that provided major concessions to meet the company's needs, though it protected the employees by providing that as rising efficiency reduced the need for men, the work force would be reduced by not replacing employees who quit rather than by making layoffs. At a mass meeting held to explain the agreement to the workers there was strong opposition and a spirited speech against the agreement, but the vice president, because of his warm relationship with the workers in the plant, was able to convince them that if the agreement were rejected, the plant would probably be closed.

But international union officers in trying to interest members of local unions in the future of their jobs occasionally meet amazing indifference. Such was the experience of an influential vice president of the UAW, who sought to interest the employees of one of the smaller automobile companies in the threat to their security resulting from the precarious condition of their company. The vice president met for three or four hours with the executive board of one of the locals and then with the board of another local. He told them about the danger to their jobs, but he found definite bitterness toward management—bitterness that he could not understand because he said that management had been if anything too reasonable

[6] One large local in the UAW, which is several years older than the national and which helped found the national, does not permit the national representative to speak up in negotiations with the employer except with the consent of the local bargaining committee.

[7] For a discussion of the influence of the market on concentration of authority in the hands of nationals see Lloyd Ulman, *The Rise of the National Trade Union* (1955), pp. 175-81.

toward the union. When a company has been in business for many years and is by far the largest employer in the town, many of the employees find it hard to understand that the position of the company is not secure.

The attitude of national unions toward correction of high-cost conditions depends on their assessment of the total situation, but one important consideration must be noted. If costs can be reduced without threatening national union wage standards, the union's assistance is much more probable than when such a threat is involved. In fact, a local union may be more willing to accept a modified pattern wage increase than the national union. The character and impact of the cost-reduction program is an important influence on both national and local union attitude.

Submission to Arbitration

The concessions required to make a plant competitive may be so large that no union officer is willing to take the responsibility for making them. Particularly so-called "democratic unions," in which rank and file influence is strong are often incapable of negotiating agreements that put the long-run interests of the members ahead of the short-run. But even "democratic" unions may be willing to submit to arbitration issues which they are not willing to take the responsibility for settling. An example is the arbitration in the hosiery industry early in 1950. Wage rates in the northern, union mills had always been considerably above rates in the southern, non-union mills, and the union had made little progress in gaining members in the south. At various times the union had made concessions in an attempt to reduce the disadvantages of the union mills.[8] The pressures from the rank and file for wage increases were always considerable, and the ability of the union employers to resist the union

___

[8] Late in 1929 the union agreed to permit employers to "double" one-fourth of their knitting machines (that is, to operate two knitting machines with one knitter and a helper) and conceded a number of reductions on individual piece rates. In the summer of 1930 the union, after a close referendum vote, made piece rate reductions averaging about 15 per cent and enlarged the right of employers to double knitting machines. In September 1931 the union accepted a reduction in piece rates of 30 to 40 per cent. This reduction was so large that the nonunion mills did not dare meet it. Union mills were able to increase their share of the business, and the union was able to organize some nonunion mills, temporarily increasing union organization to about 70 per cent of the workers in the industry. Sumner H. Slichter, *Union Policies and Industrial Management* (1941), pp. 355-56.

demands was low. As a result labor costs in union mills continued to be substantially above costs in nonunion mills, and the volume of business done by the union mills steadily declined. In 1938 an arbitration made important cuts in piece rates and changes in the piece rate system that encouraged employers to install up-to-date equipment.[9] In the spring of 1950 the union share of the business having fallen very low, another general wage arbitration was held, and various reductions were made in wage rates estimated to cut the labor cost of hosiery in union mills by about 50 cents a dozen. Unfortunately, the cuts were largely restored a few months later in a second arbitration soon after the outbreak of the Korean War. The advantages given nonunion employers as a result of the short-sighted policies of the union and the weakness of the union employers have virtually destroyed the unionized parts of the full-fashioned hosiery business.

Another example of the use of arbitration to handle issues for which the union is unwilling to assume responsibility is in the northern cotton textile industry. Various disadvantages that this industry suffered, including high labor costs, had led to a shift of business to nonunion mills in the South, where the equipment was more modern, the wages and fringe benefits were lower, and the work loads (number of machines handled by a worker) were larger. By June 1951 the position of the remaining northern mills had become more serious than ever—partly as a result of wage increases conceded by northern employers only three or four months earlier. The concessions included an escalator clause, under which wages were adjusted to changes in the consumer price index every three months.

In the spring of 1951 a strike against southern mills failed to narrow the North-South differential. Hence, early in 1952 the wage schedule in the northern mills was put in arbitration, and in a notable decision it was cut by a small amount. But reducing the northern wage scale could not eliminate the substantial differences in labor cost resulting from considerably larger work loads in the South. The union officers were unwilling to negotiate increases in work loads in the northern mills in the face of strong opposition from the rank and file. The work load issue was submitted to arbitration, and between 1952 and 1954 there were no less than 160 arbitrations over work loads, almost all of which were won by the employers. In some of

[9] The same, p. 358.

these arbitration cases the union representatives and the employer had reached an agreement, but because of a factional fight within the union, the union officers were unwilling to take responsibility for accepting larger work loads. An important change was made in textile contracts in 1955 as the result of a strike. The new agreement permitted the manufacturer to set work loads that could not be challenged for six months, a longer period than many style fabrics are in production.

In 1959 a manufacturer of flat glass took a strike of about four months in an attempt to eliminate loose standards and restrictive rules. The union officers could not negotiate a settlement because union rules provided that every member of the negotiating committee must agree to a settlement, and two members out of more than forty held out. The issues were finally submitted to arbitration. The arbitrators made important changes in the union-management contract to help the company reduce its costs. They gave the company the right to eliminate job bidding and observance of seniority in making most temporary job assignments; they gave the company the right to make the initial determination of whether or not to put a job on incentives, subject to the right of the union to challenge management's decision through the regular grievance procedure; they gave management the right to set production speeds, subject to the union's right to appeal to arbitration.

Long Strike or Shutdown

Accepting a long strike or shutting down the plant are other ways of eliminating high labor costs. Convincing the members of a local union that they should sacrifice pay or cherished working rules or that they should step up their pace of work in order to enable their employer to meet competition is often accomplished only with great difficulty. Unfortunately the tactics customarily used by employers in negotiations increase the difficulty. Again and again workers have been told that the company cannot afford to pay higher wages, and yet higher wages have been granted, and the plant has gone on operating. Consequently, when it is really true that the plant must have a reduction in its costs, the negotiating process may break down. The officers of the union may be unwilling to take the political risks of making concessions, and the management may have to take a strike in order to convince the union that costs must be cut.

At a high-cost smelter in Montana the management recently took a wildcat strike of about a month over a reduction in the size of the crew. The payroll was cut in half, but, owing to new equipment and better efficiency, output of the plant remained about the same. The national union (the Mine, Mill, and Smelter Workers) knew that cutting the staff was necessary for the survival of the plant, which was one of many owned by the company. Hence, the national union did not encourage resistance by the local. On the other hand, the national made no effort to convince the local that high costs were threatening the jobs of its members. Consequently the company had to force a strike on the workers both to continue its operation and to save some of the workers' jobs.

A plant making electrical products, in which costs had climbed very high because of company policy during the war and because of the union's legalistic approach to labor relations (under the influence of a labor attorney who negotiated for the union), took a fourteen-week strike in 1950. The principal issues in the strike related to the company's pension plan, but the strike became the occasion for radical changes in the company's labor policies. The company won a complete victory. The influence of the labor attorney in the affairs of the local union was effectively destroyed, and the local union president, who developed into an industrial statesman, emerged as the real union leader. The company won the right to put into effect unilaterally a job evaluation plan, but management decided to work out the plan jointly with the union. The company also proposed a joint study of wage incentive problems.

The long strike was followed by important changes in management. Responsibility both for negotiations and for administration of the contract was transferred from corporate officers at national headquarters to plant men who had close and friendly relations with many of the workers and who were familiar with operating problems. The union was also asked to gather information concerning the wages paid by the company's competitors. These changes led to great increases in labor efficiency. Restrictions on output were eliminated, and the incentive plan was extended. The earnings of the workers in this plant are considerably higher than those of employees in competing plants. But productivity is now high, labor relations are good, and the plant is able to hold its own in competition.

Another manufacturer of electrical products that had practiced a policy of appeasement for five years from 1946 to 1951 took a strike of five and a half months in three plants in 1951–52 in order to restore the authority of management. Five plants in which the employees were represented by other unions were not affected. The management succeeded, by successfully resisting the strike, in introducing a policy of "arm's length selling"—to use its own expression. By this it means that the management does not let the union push it around, but at the same time it does not get into conflict by imposing the contract arbitrarily. It tries to win the union's acceptance of changes by explaining the reasons for its action.

In a plant making glassware a strike lasting from Labor Day to November 29 in 1956 was necessary to re-establish the right of management to run the plant—a right that it had not had for many years. A multiplant company acquired the plant, which had been a family-owned concern for many years, and put in a new management. The old management had been handicapped because it did not negotiate the contract; negotiations were handled on an industry-wide basis by the officers of an employers' association. But the old management had also been easygoing and tradition-bound. It tolerated the setting of crew sizes by tradition and did not insist on changes when automatic equipment was introduced. It also tolerated oral side agreements in the various departments regulating a multitude of practices, such as crew sizes or sharing of overtime. To meet its local problems in one plant, the company withdrew from the association and negotiated on a local basis. Negotiations in this plant broke down, and a strike followed. At the time of the strike there were over a hundred costly side agreements.

About a year before the strike the top management of the company had a conference with the national president and other officers of the union in an attempt to arouse their interest in the employment prospects of their members in the plant. But no impression was made. To the heads of this old, stable, and conservative union, used to doing things in certain ways, giving up traditional rules was inconceivable. The union preferred to face certain defeat in a long and costly strike to taking the responsibility for making concessions. The strike was bound to be settled mostly on management's terms partly because this was only one of many plants operated by the company, but in the main because only on terms that permitted efficient production was management willing to keep the plant in operation.

A strike lasting nine weeks in the fall of 1955 was necessary to enable a manufacturer of automobile parts to get rid of some conditions making for high labor costs. The management wanted to substitute measured daywork for an incentive system, under which output was being pegged at low rates, and to get rid of a full-time union committee of five that was paid by the company and that spent all the time on the floor of the shop doing whatever the committee members desired. The company was only partially successful in gaining its objectives. The incentive system was abolished, but work standards were not established—though there was tacit agreement that production would be maintained or improved. The union did not accept as much of a spread in hourly rates as the management wanted. The full-time committee of five was not abolished, but restrictions were placed on its activities.

No longer are members of the committee allowed to roam freely around the shop. Before a committeeman is allowed in any department, his presence must be requested by an employee, or the foreman must authorize his presence. The labor cost problems in this plant are only partially solved.

When an important customer insists that there be no further interruption of deliveries, a management that accepts a strike against its cost-reducing program may have to capitulate to the union. This was the experience of a manufacturer of special automotive equipment. The principal problem was runaway incentive rates—largely the result of loose administration during the war. The management first tried the educational approach. Management's first proposal for a revision of incentive rates was voted down by the rank and file of the union. Six months later the management raised the problem with an international vice president of the union. At meetings with the shop stewards, representatives of management and the union explained the competitive problems of the company. The shop committee agreed that a firm of consulting engineers be brought in to survey the problem and set new standards. Union time-study men, selected jointly by the union and the company, were trained to handle grievances over standards with the company time-study man.

The cost-reducing program, even after its acceptance, continued to meet strong opposition within the union. When the re-setting of standards was about three-fourths completed, union elections resulted in almost complete replacement of the old shop committee with a committee opposed to the program. Resistance was centered in the departments where earnings under the runaway incentive plan were unusually high. The ferment finally resulted in a three-week strike in October 1956, nominally over a discharge case. The international union advised the company to take a firm stand, but the company's principal customer, one of the "big three" automobile makers, insisted that production be resumed, and the company was forced to yield on the strike. The union committee is now trying to bargain standards.

Sometimes the management, instead of insisting on conditions that lead the union to strike, takes the initiative by closing the plant and announcing the conditions on which the plant will re-open. Shutting down the plant has two principal advantages over forcing a strike on the union. One is that it brings home to the individual union member the fact that his job is at stake. If the union initiates a strike, many members may think that preserving former conditions is a matter merely of winning the strike. A second advantage of shutting down the plant is that it tends to awaken the community to the fact that a number of jobs in the town are at stake. As a result the community may take an interest in the problem of the company. A foundry in a small midwestern town had a complicated incentive system, under which earnings crept up during the war and the postwar years until the workers were getting 62 cents more an hour than a principal competitor was paying in a foundry only 26 miles away. A study by an outside consultant brought in by the company indicated that standards were about 25 per cent too loose.

The company informed the local union that a correction of standards and rates was absolutely necessary. The local scoffed at the idea. It held the mistaken belief that the foundry was a big money maker for the company. The company was unable to get the international interested in the case. The management reports that in this case the international union neither helped the company nor hindered it. Before the contract expired, the company warned its customers that there would probably be a shutdown, and when the contract expired, the company told the union the terms on which it was willing to continue operating the plant. These terms included the abolition of the incentive system, the hiring of a neutral outside firm to set work standards, and a wage cut of 62 cents an hour. When the union rejected the company's terms, the executive committee of the company voted to close the plant.

The merchants and professional men of the community immediately formed a committee to see how the plant could be kept open. A series of public meetings revealed that the employees were not in agreement with the union leaders on this issue. The plant management entered into a tripartite agreement with the union and the citizens' committee, in which they agreed to ask top management to open the foundry on management's original terms. The management consented.

Moving Work to Other Plants

Sometimes the best solution to the problem of high labor costs is to move the work to other plants. This course may be taken if making the plant competitive would require greater sacrifices than the employees would be expected to make, if the company is too weak to win a strike over the issue of reducing costs, or if the management is aggressive and not disposed to spend time trying to persuade employees to make concessions, or for other reasons.

An interesting example of this method is found in a multiplant company that had excellent relations with its national union. But the local union in one of its large plants (a mattress factory) was dominated by socialists, who enforce an egalitarian philosophy. The local took pride in limiting production and fined members who earned "too much." Earnings of incentive workers were not more than 60 per cent of earnings of incentive workers in other plants. As management gradually transferred work from this plant to others, the work force fell from 3,000 to about 650. The management told the national union what it was doing, and the national warned the local union. The local paid no attention until employment had dropped quite drastically. At this time it approached management, but the company said "We've made our decision."

A manufacturer of refrigerators who had been plagued by restrictive practices and wildcat strikes finally decided that conditions had become so bad that much of the work would have to be moved to a different plant of the company where another union represented the employees. The union in the first plant had always said that it would strike if any part of the work were moved. The union did strike, but to the surprise and dismay of the leaders the company showed no interest in negotiating with them. The work remained moved, and efficiency in the plant that had lost much of its work improved substantially.[10]

One of the smaller automobile companies moved work because the enterprise was too weak to risk a fight over the reduction of labor costs. Shortly after this company was merged with another automobile manufacturer, an international vice president of the UAW negotiated an agreement correcting many causes of high labor costs. At a mass meeting of 2,800 employees held to ratify the agreement opponents of the agreement took over and accused the international of selling them out. The mass meeting overwhelmingly rejected the proposed agreement. As a result the company moved the work to another plant. The leaders of the opposition group went immediately to the international vice president to see what could be done, but it was then too late.

A maker of automotive parts and other metal products is an example of a strongly managed company with a "no-nonsense" approach to industrial relations, which is ready to move work on short notice to eliminate noncompetitive labor costs. Twice in the postwar period this company has moved work in order to keep an operation competitive. The management has adopted the policy that it is not going to stop growing because of lack of cooperation from its employees. If the employees will not cooperate, the company will move the work elsewhere. The company at one time made axles in one of its Ohio plants. It could not get production from a work force that limited output to about five hours' work a day. It built a new plant in Indiana and moved the axle work to this plant. The new plant has been enlarged three times in five years.

Another plant of the company in Pennsylvania began losing business in about 1951 or 1952 through lax standards. The personnel manager, who was a former union man, called in the local union officials and gave them a strong talk on low productivity. The lectures were repeated by the plant manager and by the director of industrial

[10] This experience is of interest in view of the numerous recent cases in which unions have claimed that the recognition clause in a trade agreement precludes an employer from moving work outside the plant. Employers have always moved work both in and out of plants, and no reasonable construction of the general terms of trade agreements supports the view that the recognition of a bargaining agent restricts the employer's freedom to move work in or out of the plant.

relations from the company's general office. The management prepared charts on film showing by power consumption in different
hours of the day the pattern of slack effort. After the failure of these
efforts to interest the local union in the revision of standards, the top
management built a second and more modern plant in Indiana, in-
tending to abandon the first one. No threats or "predictions" were
made about what would happen if efficiency in the old plant were
not increased, but the union knew that the new plant was being
built.

When the new plant started operating, the union committee in the
old plant tried to bargain rates. The management refused, announcing that it intended to abandon the plant unless the work standards
were brought up to a proper level. The union agreed after several
weeks of negotiation to a complete re-timing of jobs in the plant.
Then the company put on a campaign to sell more of its product and
now needs both plants. But it was necessary to start production in
the new plant before the union in the old plant was willing to consent to the re-setting of standards.

Formal Union-Management Cooperation

Various causes lead to union-management cooperation. Among
them is the desire of employees in high-cost plants to save their jobs
by helping the employer cut costs. The practice of formal union-
management cooperation is so important and involves so many problems that the entire next chapter is devoted to it. Chapter 28 discusses, among other things, formal union-management cooperation as
a method of dealing with the problems of high-cost plants.

Summary

Unions and managements in high-cost plants face the most difficult
problem in collective bargaining in present day industry and highlight bargaining's limited capacity for dealing with problems—especially those related to the long-run interests of managements and
unions. The experience of high-cost plants shows the tendency of
both unions and management to put their short-run interests ahead
of long-run interests. It reveals the danger to management (and indirectly to the employees) of putting "good" but shortsighted indus-

trial relations ahead of a sound labor contract and appropriate contract administration.

The problems of high-cost plants show the danger of letting conditions deteriorate. Taking away something that has once been given to the employees is both difficult and costly. Hence management can usually afford long and expensive strikes rather than make concessions that will later have to be taken back. And yet so weak are many managements and so much dominated by the sales department and by the short-run point of view that managements again and again make concessions that later have forced the enterprise to go through long and expensive strikes and, in some cases, have destroyed the business itself.

28 / Union-Management Cooperation

ARRANGEMENTS BY WHICH employees and managements can pursue their common interests are conspicuously lacking in modern industry. There is good reason for this. Nearly all enterprises in modern industry belong to the suppliers of capital and are operated by hired employees who are free to leave when they see fit, and who, therefore, have only a limited interest in the success of the firm. If things do not go well, the employee may always look for a better job elsewhere.

Conditions and institutions are gradually developing, however, that tie employees to the firm and thus create common interests between employees and managements. These conditions include pension plans, vacations, and other benefits related to length of service, systems of promotion in which experience and familiarity with the work are important. Most important of all is the institution of collective bargaining and its related institutions—particularly seniority rules and various other rights and privileges that depend upon length of service. Hence, unions unintentionally create stronger common interests between employees and employers. More than ever in a unionized enterprise the interests of the employees depend on the success of the firm.

With the interests that employees and managements have in common steadily growing in importance, arrangements for advancing these common interests may be expected to develop. Their failure to develop extensively up to now is a normal example of cultural lag. But there are various specific obstacles to the development of formal union-management cooperation which should be noted.[1] Some of

[1] These cases of more or less general cooperation in production are to be distinguished from specific and limited cooperation for special purposes—to promote public acceptance of the product of the industry, to get duties raised against supplies from abroad, to promote safety, or to provide training for apprentices and journeymen.

these obstacles to union-management cooperation originate with unions, others with management. An interest in union-management cooperation means that unions must abandon some of their strongly entrenched attitudes. Most unions take the position that employees are not getting a fair share of the fruits of production. They also usually take it for granted that the employer can afford to pay more and do not believe that he needs help in getting adequate production or income. Unions have learned that they must usually fight hard (or be willing to fight hard) to gain important concessions from employers. The idea of working in cooperation with someone whom they must also be prepared to oppose does not occur to them. If they were to consider the idea, they would probably reject it on the ground that a proposal for cooperation would be regarded by the employer as a sign of weakness and would weaken the bargaining position of the union. Unions have frequently argued against union-management cooperation on the grounds that it would diminish the effectiveness of the unions by undermining the militant spirit of its members.

Several principal conditions impede the development of management's interest in union-management cooperation; for example (1) managements underestimate what workers can contribute; (2) managements fear loss of prestige and authority and want the sole voice in determining how operations shall be conducted; and (3) some managements fear that giving unions a voice (even if only an advisory one) in making decisions now exclusively made by management would build up the prestige and strength of the union.

Growth of Formal Plans of Cooperation

War emphasizes the important common interest that employees and managements have in more production. Hence, both World War I and World War II led to the establishment of some schemes of formal cooperation in England; and during World War II such schemes were established in the United States and Canada—in considerable measure as a result of government encouragement. World War I brought ambitious attempts in England to establish lasting cooperation between unions and managements through the government-sponsored Whitley Councils. But neither the Councils nor the joint committees that grew out of World War I survived for long in most industries. Many of the joint consultative arrangements that were established in Britain in World War II continue to exist on paper, but by and large they are inactive.[2]

In Canada a notable plan for formal union-management cooperation was established in 1925 in the mechanical and maintenance-of-way departments of the Canadian National Railways. Late in the war Canada established the Industrial Production Co-operation Board to promote the formation of labor-management production committees.[3] In 1947 the work of encouraging joint consultation was transferred to the Department of Labour, and a Labour-Management Cooperative Service was established in the department. There is a slowly growing number of cases of formal union-management cooperation scattered throughout Canadian industry.

In the United States several thousand joint committees to promote production were established during World War II, but many never functioned, only several hundred made a significant contribution, and a large proportion of these petered out after the war.[4] Far more significant were the plans of formal union-management cooperation established on the Baltimore and Ohio Railroad in 1924, on the Canadian National Railways, in the Naumkeag Steam Spinning Company, and later by the United Steelworkers and in the Tennessee Valley Authority. There were also abortive efforts to establish union-management cooperation in the mechanical departments of several other railways—the Chesapeake and Ohio, the Chicago and North Western, and the Chicago, Milwaukee, St. Paul, and Pacific.[5] In recent years there have been a number of cases of union-management cooperation in the needle trades, and in the automobile and automotive parts industries. There has also been an important development in union-management cooperation under the Scanlon Plan, described below. Profit-sharing plans and various plant-wide incen-

[2] Sir Charles Renold, "Joint Consultation over Thirty Years" and Helen Baker, "Joint Consultation in England—an American's Comments," *Journal of the Institute of Personnel Management* (March-April 1951).
[3] Department of Labour, Ottawa, *Labour-Management Cooperation through Joint Consultation* (1958), pp. 10-11.
[4] For an account of the American experience, see Dorothea de Schweinitz, *Labor and Management in Common Enterprise* (1949).
[5] For an account of experience with union-management cooperation in the early years on the Baltimore and Ohio and the Canadian National, in the Naumkeag Steam Spinning Company, and in the needle trades, see Sumner H. Slichter, *Union Policies and Industrial Management* (1941) pp. 393-554.

tive plans have also been used effectively in developing cooperative arrangements.

Reasons for Adoption of Formal Cooperation Plans

Sometimes the initiative in establishing schemes of union-management cooperation comes from the unions (as in the case of the Baltimore and Ohio Railroad); sometimes it comes from management (as in the case of the Canadian National). In some cases it is impossible to determine which party is responsible since both recognized the need more or less simultaneously, and decisions on appropriate action were the result of suggestions by both union and management.

Usually general schemes of union-management cooperation are set up because the employer is having trouble in holding his own in competition, and both his business and the jobs of his employees are jeopardized. Such a situation may lead either the union or management to propose a plan of formal cooperation.[6] But there are many other situations in which management and unions see that they have a common interest. Some plans for union-management cooperation are intended to help get rid of badly working incentive plans. The plan may be a substitute for an incentive system that has broken down. In other cases, schemes for union-management cooperation may be adopted because day workers need an incentive to be more efficient, and because either the union or the management or both are opposed to conventional incentive plans. In one case a plan of cooperation involving a plant-wide bonus was adopted because the employees, who were on straight daywork, asked for an opportunity to raise their earnings through increased efficiency. In another case, formal union-management cooperation was adopted because the plant (a printing plant), which had been a captive operation producing for an assured market, had been sold and faced the problem of surviving in a competitive market. In some cases a formal plan of cooperation has been adopted because union and management were seeking ways of improving their relations generally. Finally, some highly successful companies have adopted such plans because they promote better management and more efficient operations. It seems

[6] Management may propose a wage cut, and the union may respond with a proposal that wages be kept the same but that the two sides try to work out a plan for cutting labor costs.

surprising that more widespread adoption has not resulted for this last reason. Not infrequently, formal union-management cooperation is established for a combination of reasons, as in the case of a company that wanted to get rid of a badly operating incentive system and at the same time to reduce the gap between its labor costs and the costs of its competitors.

Types of Union-Management Cooperation

Three types of procedure are used in effecting cooperation between unions and managements. One is for union and management jointly to hire outside experts to study a plant or a company and recommend a program of action, which may or may not be adopted. A second type is for the union itself to provide expert help for the employer through its national representatives, business agents, or technical experts. For example, some unions (the International Ladies' Garment Workers and the Amalgamated Clothing Workers) have industrial engineering departments to help their representatives handle rate problems. These engineering departments from time to time have been diverted from their usual activities to help employers who were in trouble and whom the union wished to save. National representatives and business agents who are skilled in the technology of the industry and in rate setting also have been used by the unions in the needle trades and others (the hosiery workers, the teamsters, and the automobile workers) to help employers cut costs and increase output. Sometimes a business agent or a national representative decides on his own responsibility to help an employer improve the management of his plant. A third procedure is for the union and the employer to organize a joint system of committees to encourage workers to make suggestions for improving operations and to consider the suggestions that are made. The plan may or may not be linked with wage incentives designed to encourage employees to increase plant productivity.

The first two types of union-management cooperation are intended to be temporary—the outside technicians or the union representatives withdraw after having helped the employer overcome his difficulties. The internal committees set up under the third procedure are intended to be continuing and to become an integral part of the plant organization.

The several types of union-management cooperation have very different implications for the life of the union. Neither of the first two types requires participation by the rank and file members of the union. The third type, however, depends on their participation and requires that the union members identify their interests and prospects with the success of the employer. Some unions, dominated by conventional attitudes toward employers, are unwilling to see their members develop a strong feeling of common interest with the employer. Some object to the development of a sense of common interest even where it exists and even where failure of the employer to hold his own in competition will mean the loss of attractive jobs for the employees. The first two types of union-management cooperation may be practiced by unions that are opposed to the third type.

Employment of Outside Experts

Unions are not inclined to spend money to help solve the employer's business problems—even though the jobs of their members may be at stake. But they may encourage the employer to engage outside consultants, and if the union leaders are fearful about the employer's ability to survive, they may help persuade the rank and file to accept the recommendations of the experts. This task may be an unpleasant one and may involve political risks for the union officers, particularly local officers. Unions occasionally join with the employer in paying the cost of bringing in industrial engineers to study rates, production standards, or production methods and costs in general, and to make recommendations. Ordinarily unions expect the employer to pay the costs of studies of standards and rates, but they may be willing to share the cost if they fear that the employer's experts will insist on too drastic change.

Expert Help by Union Business Agents and Technicians

Technical help to employers through business agents or technicians has been given most frequently in the needle trades, where there are many small, poorly managed companies and where the existence of piecework often means that workers' earnings depend on the quality of the management; in the automobile and automotive parts industries, where there have been important plants or companies that the union has desired to save; and in the hosiery industry, where union wage policy was gradually destroying the ability of union plants to meet nonunion competition.

The most common reason for the extension of expert help by union business agents and technicians is to save the jobs of union members, as when the Amalgamated Clothing Workers cooperated with various firms in the high-cost Chicago clothing market to help them meet competition from newer, low-cost markets, and when the UAW helped Willys-Overland change its wage payment system to get its costs down. But there are also special reasons for the union's giving expert help. In some cases it is to assist the employees to earn a decent wage. Under the piecework method of payment in the women's and men's garment industries, piece rates that add up to an average labor cost for the product may not yield satisfactory earnings if the scheduling of the work, the improper allocation of the work force, or improper subdivision of the garment into operations means that part of the work force is idle at times. Special help from the union is often necessary in the needle trades immediately after the union has organized a shop. In order to induce the workers to join the union, the organizers promise them wage increases. But if the enterprise has been below average in efficiency (as is true of many isolated firms outside the principal clothing markets), wage increases would make the shop noncompetitive and force it out of business. Its workers then would turn against the union and become the nucleus of a nonunion labor market. By helping increase the efficiency of the plant, the union can gain its members the promised wage increase without raising the employer's labor costs.

Particularly if a shop is organized as part of a campaign to organize an entire market, it is important to the union that the newly organized shop survive. When the ILGWU recently organized two new entrants into the Toronto sportswear industry, which was mostly unorganized, the local union business agent requested help for the newly-organized companies from the union's engineering department. Considerable help was given (in improving supervision of production, plant layout, and inventory and cost controls), and the employers, awakened to their shortcomings, wanted more help than the engineering department felt disposed to give. The latter said that it was not its business to manage companies.

The foregoing discussion of the reasons why unions give expert help to employers sheds light on the important question of what employers the union decides to help. Obviously it cannot help all employers. In industries such as the men's or women's garment industries, where a large proportion of the employers are in the red and where the mortality among business firms is high, the union cannot even help all firms that badly need assistance. Hence, it may lay itself open to a charge of favoritism.

As a matter of fact, the charge of favoritism does not seem to arise. Part of the reason is that most employers do not like to have unions interfere in their operations even to improve efficiency. Furthermore, unless there is a special reason for so doing, unions do not give help. Even saving the jobs of the union members by helping the employer meet competition is not enough reason for a union to help an employer cut his costs or raise the efficiency of his operations. Usually a union is not particularly disturbed if a firm is compelled to go out of business, since the loss of employment in one union plant often means an expansion of employment in another union plant.

The principal circumstances under which the competitive troubles of a union plant are of concern to the union are: when the business lost by the union plant goes largely to nonunion enterprises, and when the shutdown of the union plant would cause the workers to turn against the union and become the nucleus for a nonunion labor force. As was pointed out above, this danger is greatest when the union plant is one of the largest in town so that, in the event of its shutdown, its employees would have trouble in finding jobs in other union plants.

Unions deal with employers through business agents and other line officers—national representatives, national vice presidents, and, in a few critical cases, the national president. The few industrial engineering departments of unions are service departments that help the union line officers. They act only at the request of the business agent or some other line officer. They do not act on the employer's request and do not take his side against the business agent—even though they may agree with the employer. The union engineer may perhaps privately tell the business agent or the union committee that he thinks that the employer is right, but he will not do this in the presence of the employer, and he will not undermine the position taken by the union line officers, even though he is very much opposed to it. A national line officer (a vice president or national representative), being a line officer rather than a staff employee, has greater freedom than the union industrial engineer in dealing with local business agents, bargaining committees, or members. The national line officer may fight hard and publicly to get the local leaders to accept his point of view.[7]

The kind of cost-cutting help that union business agents and technical experts give may be divided into technical and political help. Technical help means help on all aspects of shop management that industrial engineers, accountants, and management consultants usually give. Only a limited number of local business agents are good at giving such help, but each of the two principal needle trades unions has a number of keen business agents, who have carefully observed methods in many shops and who are skilled at analyzing operations, detecting weaknesses, and suggesting improvements. Some national representatives of unions and vice presidents are also competent to do this. The engineering departments of unions are, of course, skilled in management methods, but the head of a union engineering department said: "The union does not pretend to know more about management than the employers do, except where it encounters very poor management."

Much of the union's help may be political—convincing the employees in the plant that their own security requires them to accept certain changes and assuring them that reasonable protection is given to their interests. In the men's clothing industry the union finds that newly-organized firms are frequently overstaffed, with too many workers on daywork, and that the earnings of pieceworkers are too low. Part of the union's problem is to find ways of reducing excess staff as efficiency improves. Sometimes this can be done by not replacing those who resign.

At an automobile plant in Toledo the main problem of the union was to sell the cost-reduction programs to the workers. It was proposed to eliminate the incentive system, under which production had been pegged at a fairly low rate by a militant local, and install measured daywork, with production set by an unbiased firm selected by the company and approved by the union leadership. There was an understanding with the company that the gain in efficiency would not produce layoffs—that work would be brought in, that workers

[7] The head of the industrial engineering department of a union said: "We are consultants to the *union* . . . we supply it with facts. . . . We don't tell the employer what our findings are. Often business agents ask us to come up with certain answers, but we insist on presenting honest results to him."

quitting would not be replaced, and that workers would be put on painting and maintenance in order to avoid layoffs. Stamping work and the manufacturing of cushions were brought in, and the changes were spread over eighteen months. The principal problem was to get the workers to accept the proposed program. The plant was shut down so that all employees could attend a mass meeting that lasted for five hours. There were three votes on three proposals: (1) the shift from incentives to daywork, (2) the increase in production, and (3) the understanding that there would be no layoffs. There was some outspoken opposition from the rank and file. The final speech was made by the international vice president in charge of the area, a former employee of the company who had many close ties with the employees. He told the people frankly that the company would abandon the plant unless operating costs were brought down. The employees voted to accept the program.

Unions sometimes predicate their willingness to help a company reduce costs on the company's willingness to eliminate unneeded supervisory personnel or to invest in additional equipment. Small family-owned companies after a generation or two may become cluttered up with members of the family who lack administrative skills and who may not be doing useful work. Companies that have been having financial difficulties are likely to have curtailed their investment programs and to need new equipment. Of course the companies may lack the funds to buy equipment—though depreciation allowances can be a source of funds even for companies that are losing money. When the UAW agreed to help a manufacturer of electrical apparatus reduce costs, part of the deal was that the company would spend about $2 million on new equipment.

Many conditions determine to what extent union business agents or technicians can help a company reduce its costs. For example, it is easier for union officers to help a company that is in trouble because the employees have pegged production than it is to help a company that is in trouble because weak management and the absence of pegged production have allowed great differences in individual earnings to develop. In the first type of case the union needs to persuade its members to increase their output, but it does not need to persuade them to accept reductions in their earnings; in the second type of case the union must induce some workers to accept reductions in earnings, or it must establish two rates on some jobs—a permanent rate lower than the previous rate and a temporary rate (a so-called "red circle" rate) available only to holders of the job at the previous excessively high rate.

Employee Participation Type of Plan

An important type of plan for union-management cooperation provides for employee participation.

THE GENERAL NATURE OF EMPLOYEE PARTICIPATION PLANS. Employee participation plans of union-management cooperation fall into two principal groups: (1) nonincentive plans, such as those of the Baltimore and Ohio Railroad, the Canadian National Railways, and the Tennessee Valley Authority, and (2) incentive plans, of which the Scanlon Plan (to be discussed below) is the principal example. For convenience the Baltimore and Ohio, the Canadian National, and the TVA plans will be referred to simply as employee participation plans; others will be given a specific title, such as the Scanlon Plan.

The cooperative plans on the B and O, the Canadian National, and the TVA are essentially the same in structure and methods of operation and represent fundamentally the ideas of Otto S. Beyer, Jr., who played an important role in the establishment of each plan and who was a thinker of courage and imagination. The plans presuppose substantially the same state of union-management relations and the same labor-management philosophy. All of them operate through joint union-management committees that encourage, collect, and pass on suggestions. The structure of these committees varies from one enterprise to another, but the committee structure parallels roughly the structure of the business. There are committees in departments or plants, or both, and an over-all committee for the enterprise as a whole.

The original idea behind the union-management cooperative plans on the B and O and the Canadian National was that the suggestions would come almost entirely from the rank-and-file employees rather than from supervisors. Supervisors, because of their position in management, were assumed to be able either to put their ideas into practice or to bring them to the attention of management. But a change has occurred in both the above plans. The supervisors are now expected to bring suggestions before the committees. The result has been a change in the fundamental nature of the union-management cooperative meetings. These meetings have become management conferences, at which rank and file representatives sit and participate in a discussion of management's reports and suggestions. The result has been to add to the interest in and the importance of the meetings. In the case of the TVA, it was from the start contemplated that supervisors would make suggestions, so that the transformation that has occurred in the B and O and Canadian National plans has not occurred in the TVA plan. In the TVA there has always been full participation by both management and rank and file.

Although the three plans mentioned above have the same fundamental structure and method of operation, the way in which a plan actually operates and the results achieved depend on conditions that vary with the enterprise and over time. These determinants depend on the economic condition of the enterprise and the industry, on personalities, and above all on the policies of unions and management. For example, the TVA plan is in general in an expanding enterprise, whereas employment on the B and O and the Canadian National has been dropping rapidly.

EXPERIENCE OF THE BALTIMORE AND OHIO. The plan of union-management cooperation on the Baltimore and Ohio is confined to the mechanical department and involves the shopcraft unions—the boilermakers, machinists, electricians, sheet metal workers, carmen, firemen, and oilers. It has not spread outside this department, although there was a brief attempt more than thirty years ago to extend it to the running crafts.

Committees for union-management cooperation on the B and O are on two levels—shop or plant committees in the several shops, roundhouses, and car yards, and the system-wide committee. The shop or plant committees consist of a union representative from each department and the principal line and staff people in management—the shop or plant superintendent or manager, the shop engineer, the head of stores, and the safety inspector, if there is one. Usually two or three foremen, who are rotated after a time, serve on the committee. The shop or plant committees usually meet once a month—although in the early days of the cooperative plan on the Baltimore and Ohio the shop committees met every two weeks. The meetings

are held on company time. Minutes are kept, and those whose suggestions are rejected are given an explanation. The system-wide committee on the Baltimore and Ohio consists on the management side
of the general superintendent of motive power and about 24 or more
members of his staff and operating assistants, and on the union side
of the general chairmen, and in some cases the vice chairmen, of
the shopcraft unions—usually 6 or 7 union representatives. The system-wide committee considers matters referred to it by the shop or
plant committees and also matters of company-wide interest brought
before the committee by the members, particularly the superintendent of motive power. For the general superintendent the committee
serves as an agency of communication for giving information about
his plans and getting the benefit of the thinking of committee members on any question that he or his staff wishes to bring up.

The cooperative plan on the B and O was started in 1930. The
initiative was taken by the unions, especially the machinists' union.
In fact the unions approached without success two other railroads
before persuading the B and O to try the experiment. The shopcraft
unions had several reasons for proposing union-management cooperation. The leaders were convinced that there were many wasteful
practices around railroad shops and that if these could be eliminated,
the unions would have a strong basis for claiming a wage increase.[8]
The unions were also anxious to bring back into the shops much of
the repair work that the railroad managements were contracting out.
Finally, after their defeat in the shopcraft strike of 1922, the unions
were eager to gain some of the prestige and status that union-management cooperation would bring them. The Baltimore and Ohio
management was interested, among other things, in improving its
relations with the shopcraft unions. Daniel Willard, the president of the railroad, whose deep personal interest in the cooperative
plan had much to do with its early success, insisted that it be tried
out first in the company's problem shop, Glenwood, near Pittsburgh,
where union-management relations were particularly bad.

The original intention was that the workers should receive some

---

[8] When the railroad managements demanded (and got) reductions in the wages of
shopcraft workers in 1920 and 1922, the unions had argued that the elimination of
waste would make wage cuts unnecessary. The unions were greatly influenced by the
earlier arguments of Louis D. Brandeis against rate increases. In 1911 and 1914 Brandeis
had argued that more efficient operation of the railroads would make traffic rate increases
unnecessary.

kind of reward for their contribution to greater efficiency and lower costs. This proved to be impractical except temporarily. Everyone was opposed to paying individuals for suggestions. Some of the union leaders thought that employees might be rewarded by giving them wage increases earlier than those given to men on other roads, but, after an attempt to do this in 1926, the idea was abandoned. The union men on other railroads resented the union's doing less for them than for workers on the B and O, and the management felt that it was being penalized for setting up the scheme of union-management cooperation.[9]

Union-management cooperation on the B and O has been operating under conditions of sharply decreasing employment. The drop in shopcraft employment became severe during the great depression of the thirties. There was a brief respite during World War II, but after the war the growing use of diesels and shrinking traffic continued the downward trend in employment. Many roundhouses and small shops were abandoned as divisions were lengthened and repair and maintenance work was concentrated.

The drop in employment profoundly affected the operation of the union-management cooperative plan. In the first place, it greatly reduced the number of suggestions. In the first fifteen years of the B and O plan there were 30,904 suggestions; in the next sixteen years, 10,247 suggestions; and in the 39 months ending June 3, 1959, 861 suggestions. Second, falling employment has changed the nature of the suggestions. Today nearly all those received in the B and O are "housekeeping" suggestions—they relate to conditions of work rather than to methods of production. But labor-saving suggestions have not disappeared entirely. A useful one was the development of a test control panel for testing various electrical controls on Alco 1600 and 2000-hp freight and passenger diesels. With this panel, developed by two electricians, control equipment may be checked under actual operating conditions. When it is installed in locomotives, only minor adjustments are required. Previously, if the controls were not func-

---

[9] The Baltimore and Ohio was the first road in trunk line territory to be approached for a wage increase in 1926 and the first to grant an increase. In the same year the management of the Canadian National wanted to reward its shopmen for their cooperative effort by giving them 2 cents an hour more than the Canadian Pacific paid, but both the management and the union on the Canadian Pacific objected. For a brief discussion of early efforts to reward employees under schemes of union-management cooperation of the B and O type, see Slichter, *Union Policies and Industrial Management*, pp. 450-52.

tioning properly, the equipment had to be removed for additional repairs. Another electrician developed a tester for solenoids. With this device it is possible to check the operation of electrically-operated valves before they are installed in the locomotive. Like the other test panel, this tester simulates actual operating conditions.

A movable jack arrangement for supporting truck frames while machining truck "jaws" was suggested by a machinist at Glenwood. Before this system was developed, the men had to block up the three corners of a diesel truck frame while the work was done. The new jack has made possible greater and more flexible movement of parts while machining of work is actually in progress. But it remains true that most suggestions that come from the rank and file are housekeeping suggestions.[10]

The most important change in the union-management cooperative plan on the B and O is in the fundamental nature of the plan itself. As the number of labor-saving suggestions from the rank and file diminished, the able and imaginative chief of motive power of the railroad has turned the system meetings into a method of communication with employees. Thus, union-management cooperation on the B and O has been transformed from a scheme by which the workers contribute to better production methods to a scheme of communication—two-way communication, but in the main communication from the superintendent of motive power to his staff and to the union general chairman.

In order to improve the union-management system committee as a method of communication, the chief of motive power and equipment has greatly enlarged management representation at the quar-

[10] There were no suggestions received at the national level on the B and O in 1958, although three system-wide meetings attended by over 20 management representatives and 6 or 7 union representatives were held. The number of suggestions at the national level in recent years was as follows:

1942	48	1951	22
1943	144	1952	11
1944	40	1953	31
1945	51	1954	24
1946	27	1955	17
1947	46	1956	34
1948	27	1957	52
1949	24	1958	0
1950	22		

In considering the small number of suggestions, allowance must be made for the fact that most of the suggestions cost the railroad money because they relate to working conditions and housekeeping rather than to methods of work.

terly system-wide meeting. Representation on the labor side remains unchanged, with the general chairman, and in some cases the vice general chairman, representing the crafts (about 7 representatives in all), but the number of management representatives has been increased to 24, 26, or 28. In addition to the general superintendent of motive power and equipment, various shop superintendents sat on the committee as did the chief engineer of motive power and equipment, the electrical engineer, various regional car builders, training and methods engineers, and other management representatives from the mechanical department.

The superintendent of motive power extols the union-management cooperative plan as a means for developing a thinking and adaptable work force that can handle work at less cost than outside contractors. "The need on the railroads today," says the general superintendent, "is to get people to adapt themselves to new situations." The system committee meetings give management a chance to call attention to a wide variety of problems and plans. Improper work or inspection comes in for discussion. At a B and O meeting in July 1956 it was pointed out that in May there had been 34 passenger train delays due to mechanical trouble. In June there had been 22, which was some improvement, but there was still need for more improvement. At the same meeting it was pointed out that the road was having a great many delays to both passenger and freight trains due to improper inspection and hotboxes. It was concluded that instructions on treating boxes were not being followed, and a hotbox committee to look into the matter was formed.

EXPERIENCE OF THE CANADIAN NATIONAL: MECHANICAL DEPARTMENT. There are two schemes of union-management cooperation on the Canadian National—one in the mechanical department and one in the maintenance-of-way department. The plan in the mechanical department was started in 1924 at the initiative of the president of the railroad, Sir Henry Thornton. In fact, considerable argument at a two-day convention of supporters of the plan within the shopcraft unions (including leaders from the United States) was necessary in order to persuade the shopcrafts federation to go along.[11] Sir Henry

---

[11] Some of the union men from the eastern region felt that it was contrary to good trade union principles for unions to try to encourage efficiency. Later some of the leaders who opposed the plan became its strongest supporters.

knew that the newly organized national railway was bound to operate at a deficit (at least for some years), and he was anxious to make as good a record as possible. He knew the importance of good labor-management relations to a publicly-owned enterprise, and he wanted the cooperation of the unions in keeping the personnel policies of the enterprise free of politics.

The union-management cooperative plan on the Canadian National has roughly the same organization and structure as that on the Baltimore and Ohio except that the Canadian National plan has regional committees as well as local committees and a system-wide committee. The regional committees are composed of the regional officers of the shopcrafts federation. The management representatives are the heads of the principal shops, and the general superintendent of motive power for the region is chairman. Management's representatives on the system-wide committee are the regional superintendents of motive power, and the union representatives are the regional officers of the shopcrafts federation plus the national officers. The regional committees on the Canadian National meet four times a year, and the system-wide committee once a year. The annual meeting of the system-wide committee lasts all day and, besides discussing matters referred to it by the regional committees and items brought up by members, it receives reports on topics of interest to the employees, such as traffic department problems, the apprentice training program, safety, first aid, fire prevention, and other matters. These reports are given by the officers in charge of the several activities.

The union-management cooperative plan on the Canadian National has had to operate in the face of sharply dropping employment and the closing of many shops and roundhouses. The results have been similar to those on the B and O—the number of suggestions has dropped, their nature has changed, and in addition there has been a marked shift in the sources of suggestions.

Up to the end of 1957, 44,290 suggestions had been turned in to the union-management cooperative plan on the Canadian National. In recent years the number of suggestions has dropped to less than a thousand a year—less than half the number in early years. In 1957 the number was 880. In times of shrinking employment workers show little interest in making labor-saving suggestions. In the four years 1954 through 1957 suggestions for new devices and shop methods and practices were only 3.1 per cent of total suggestions; up until 1953, 14.4 per cent of all suggestions fell in these categories.[12] In the period 1954 through 1957 a large portion of the suggestions related to the condition of shops and grounds and to lunch rooms, lockers, and garages. The most numerous kind of suggestion in the mechanical department is of the housekeeping type—relating to buildings, grounds, lunchrooms, lockers, and garages. Up through 1953, 24.4 per cent of total suggestions were of this sort, and in the four years 1954 through 1957 the proportion rose to 25.9 per cent—over 8 times as large as the number of labor-saving suggestions. Suggestions relating to safety, an important type of suggestion, are also numerous— 17.9 per cent of all suggestions from 1926 through 1957 pertained to safety. At the beginning of the union-management cooperative plan on the Canadian National virtually all suggestions came from the employees, but as the disposition of employees to make suggestions has declined, suggestions from management have become relatively more important. In 1957 more than half of the suggestions came from management—460 out of 880. In other words, the Canadian National plan of cooperation has gone through the same transformation as has the B and O plan. Instead of an arrangement whereby the rank and file brought their ideas to the attention of management, it has become a business conference, in which supervisors and rank and file submit their ideas to the group and under which the rank and file have a chance to criticize the suggestions of management.

As a result of occasional difficulties among unions and between unions and management, employee representatives (or the representatives of certain unions) sometimes refuse to attend local cooperative committee meetings. In the latter half of 1954 worker dissatisfaction with policies of management led to the refusal of union representatives on the local committees in the Atlantic region to attend meetings. Other refusals in the Atlantic region occurred in 1958. The drastic reductions in force have contributed to a decline of interest in the union-management cooperation plan by causing suggestions at many small points to dry up. New suggestions sometimes averaged less than one a meeting. For example, in the year 1957 there were 208 meetings in the western region, at which only 166 suggestions were received.

[12] The data on suggestions for manufacturing materials in the shops (which might be expected to increase during periods of falling employment) are lumped with the data on suggestions for developing new devices.

A proposal was made at the system meeting in 1955 by the workers and management of the western region that the objectives and activities of the movement be re-examined, the constitution re-written, and the aims set forth more clearly with a view to broadening the scope of the cooperative movement. The president of the Canadian National System Federation, who was the principal spokesman for the men, said that the union representatives had felt for some time that something had been lacking in the cooperative movement—though he couldn't identify it. He pointed particularly to the need for injecting more life into the meetings at the small points.

Between 1955 and 1958 meetings were held between representatives of the system federation and the management to draft a new constitution for the cooperative plan. The draft, presented at the system meeting in 1958, redefined the objectives of the cooperative movement, proposed consolidating the large number of small local committees (approximately 68) meeting monthly into 14 district committees that would meet quarterly, and recommended the preparation of a program of instruction so that all concerned would understand the plan. Under the new constitution there would remain 8 shop committees meeting monthly in the larger shops, 14 district committees meeting quarterly, and 2 shop committees meeting quarterly. The regional and system-wide committees were to remain unchanged. Although the new constitution was agreed on in all its essential features at the system meeting in 1958, the constitution had not been adopted by the annual system meeting of 1959. The delay was due to a difference of opinion between the management and the shopcraft unions over the participation of the Canadian Brotherhood of Railway Employees (an independent union) in the cooperative plan. This union wants to participate, and the management is willing to have it. The other shopcraft unions, which have some jurisdictional differences with the Brotherhood, are opposed to its inclusion. The new constitution of the cooperative plan cannot be implemented until agreement is reached on who is to participate.

EXPERIENCE OF THE CANADIAN NATIONAL: MAINTENANCE-OF-WAY DEPARTMENT. The first system-wide meeting of the union-management cooperative plan in the maintenance-of-way department of the Canadian National was held on January 26, 1930. The outstanding success of the cooperative plan in its early years in the mechanical department had much to do with the decision of the maintenance-of-waymen's union and the management to try the plan in the maintenance-of-way department. From the very outset the plan in this department was a conspicuous success.

The scattered nature of employment in the maintenance-of-way work led to division committees' being made the basic unit of operation. In 1958 there were 38 of these. Since attendance at meetings requires considerable travel, the division committees meet only four times a year. As in the case of the mechanical department, there are joint regional committees and a system-wide committee; each regional committee is headed by the chief engineer of the region, the system-wide committee by the chief engineer of the system. Both the regional committees and the system committee meet once a year.

A principal reason why the union-management cooperative program in the maintenance-of-way department has been such an outstanding success is that the work is scattered so that there is only limited contact between the men on the job and their superiors. Hence, the meetings have served an important need. The men had many ideas for improving tools and equipment that they had not had a chance to communicate to higher management and many suggestions for improving conditions in bunkhouses and on work trains. For example, it turned out that the railroad was buying several brands of shovels in order to distribute the business among shippers, although the men had a definite preference for a particular brand. Higher management had brought to its attention many poor working and living conditions about which it had not known.

The creation of this much-needed channel for communication between workers and management has been excellent for morale. Employee interest has remained high in most places in spite of the large drop in employment. The reason probably is that the scattered nature of the work creates a great need for the meetings.[13] Evidence of the success of the union-management cooperative plan in the

[13] The maintenance-of-waymen's union attitude toward the plan on the Canadian National was given by Mr. C. Smith, then general chairman (now an international vice president of the union), at the system cooperative meeting in 1956. Mr. Smith said: "We do not always see eye-to-eye with management . . . but I do feel the Cooperative Meetings, not only at System level, but also at Regional and Divisional level, have played no small part in preserving the mutual respect which labour and management have for each other in the interests of the industry as a whole."

maintenance-of-way department is found in the decision of the Brotherhood of Railway Signalmen to join. In 1959 the signalmen were represented for the first time at the system union-management cooperative meeting.

From 1929 to the end of 1952, 32,270 suggestions had been made. In recent years the number of suggestions has been falling off—in 1952 there were 1,113 new items; in 1954, 394 items; in 1955, 420; in 1956, 656; and in 1957, 542. The maintenance-of-way cooperative movement has produced a fairly high proportion of suggestions for improving tools, appliances, and work equipment and improving methods of doing the work. In 1952, 35.5 per cent of all suggestions (397 out of 1,113) fell in these categories; in 1957, 46.6 per cent (253 out of 542). Strangely enough, suggestions relating to housing conditions are less numerous than those relating to better methods of doing the work—264 in 1952 and 130 in 1957.

One of the most interesting recent developments in the union-management cooperative program in the maintenance-of-way department has been a plan for training employees. It began with the training of bridge and building foremen, who are members of the union and who are the key men in the maintenance-of-way force. The union has given strong support to this program, especially in the western region. At the annual cooperative committee meeting in 1957 it was reported that when the current class of foremen will have completed the training, 83 men (all in the West) will have finished the course. Arrangements were being made to extend the course to other regions. It was hoped that some foremen would continue their studies after completing the course. The International Correspondence School has prepared a special course for bridge and building foremen, and the maintenance-of-waymen's union has offered to refund one-fourth of the cost of the ICS course upon completion.

In both the mechanical and the maintenance-of-way departments the annual meeting is an impressive event. It ordinarily lasts all day —sometimes a day and a half. In addition to the regular members of the committees, there are technical observers from management or the union. Some of the observers give reports or addresses. At the 1959 maintenance-of-way meeting there were 18 management observers ranging from the vice president in charge of operations to assistant engineers. Reports and reviews of all principal personnel activities are given so that the meetings amount to a comprehensive annual stocktaking and discussion of the personnel activities of the road.

EXPERIENCE OF THE TENNESSEE VALLEY AUTHORITY. Union participation in the cooperative plan in the Tennessee Valley Authority was the outgrowth of efforts of local union leaders to win status and recognition for their unions in this public enterprise. Two men played key roles in this effort—Samuel Roper, general organizer of the plumbers' union and president of the Tennessee Valley Trades and Labor Council from 1937 to 1957, and Gordon Freeman, then business representative of the electricians' union and today international president of that union. Since the enterprise is a government one, Roper and Freeman were of the view that the union had to find substitutes for strikes and the closed or union shop. This they did by developing a policy of cooperation between management and the unions in the Tennessee Valley Trades and Labor Council. There is joint determination of prevailing wage rates (the Authority pays "prevailing" wages), joint safety committees, and joint apprenticeship committees. The union-management cooperative committees are a part of this joint program. Their origin is definitely attributable to the unions—or to individual union leaders. Many representatives of management were opposed to giving unions the recognition that the joint program gave them.[14]

The committee structure in TVA is similar to that on the B and O and the Canadian National—joint plant committees (25 in all) and a central joint cooperative committee cover the entire TVA operation. The union members of the plant committees are job stewards. The central joint cooperative committee is composed of the union representatives on the Tennessee Trades and Labor Council and top representatives of management from personnel, industrial relations, and operations.

The cooperative program in TVA has some unique methods of operation. For example, each plant committee has two co-chairmen, one from management and one from the employees, and a secretary. These three plan the agenda for each meeting. The local committees

---

[14] The program of the local union leaders in the TVA also met passive opposition from the international unions. The international presidents felt unable to endorse a program that fell short of the traditional methods of unions. But the local leaders did succeed in preventing active interference from the national organizations.

have sponsored programs to give employees a better understanding of all phases of TVA. They have also developed arrangements to exchange information among themselves. Beginning in 1946 they have held once a year a valley-wide meeting of all local committee officers and the Central Joint Cooperative Committee. At this meeting the several committees report on the suggestions that they consider their best ones for the year.

The TVA cooperative committees operate under very different conditions from those of the B and O and the Canadian National. First, the TVA is a much smaller enterprise with only between 6,000 and 7,000 employees. Second, the TVA until the last few years has had expanding employment in contrast to shrinking employment on the two railroads. Third, the union-management cooperation plan in the TVA has from the very start received suggestions from management as well as from the rank and file. This is an important feature. The practice of receiving suggestions from management improves the opportunity of the rank and file to discuss the suggestions and to suggest ways to improve them. Bringing the ideas of supervisors before the rank and file and other supervisors for discussion adds to the interest and significance of the meetings. They become management conferences with worker participation.

As a result of these differences the TVA plan has a remarkable record. The number of suggestions has increased instead of diminishing with the passage of time—rising from 184 in the fiscal year 1943 to 425 in 1956, 1,436 in 1955, and 1,885 in 1958. The number of suggestions in relation to the size of the labor force has been remarkably high, and in recent years it has been growing. It was 14 per 100 employees in the fiscal year 1948, 14 also in fiscal 1955, 19 in 1956, 32 in 1957, and 31 in 1958. The proportion of labor-saving suggestions (ways of doing the job better, quicker, or cheaper) is high and rising and represents a substantial proportion of all suggestions. In 1945–46 labor-saving suggestions were 38.1 per cent of the total; in 1952–53, 64.4 per cent; and in 1957–58, 66.0 per cent.

The outstanding success of union-management cooperation in the TVA is the result of two underlying conditions: first, the wholehearted acceptance of the philosophy of cooperation by both management and unions, and second, the development of unique management methods. The acceptance of the philosophy was aided by the desire of the unions to win recognition and status in a government enterprise, which could not grant the closed or union shop. The development of unique management methods reflects the interest of an alert and imaginative management in making the cooperative philosophy work. These methods include the monthly bulletin, *Teamwork,* published to promote the work of the local committees, and a *Manual for Cooperative Committee Members.* The central committee in its publications and "communications" recognizes local committees that have done particularly good work. Recognition of individual authors of suggestions is left to the local committees.[15]

Results of Plans of the Scanlon Type

The so-called Scanlon Plan of employee-management cooperation is similar in organization and method of operation to the B and O, Canadian National, and TVA type of plan and presupposes the same philosophy of industrial relations on the part of unions and employers. The Scanlon Plan is like the other plans in that it relies to a large extent on the participation of rank and file employees. But the Scanlon Plan is also like the TVA plan and like the plans of the two railroads in their later development in that it relies on participation by supervisory personnel as well as the workers. In other words, everyone gets a chance to criticize everyone else's suggestions whether the suggestions come from management or workers. But there are two principal differences between the Scanlon Plan and the other employee participation plans. In the first place, the Scanlon Plan provides a direct incentive for employees to make cost-saving suggestions. It is part of the present philosophy of the B and O that there be no direct incentives. Second, there are differences in the committee systems of the Scanlon Plan and the other plans. Whereas plans of the B and O type provide for a committee in each shop or plant, the Scanlon Plan usually provides for a committee of two, an employee representative and a management representative, in each department. The department representatives and others, in turn, help make up a plant committee (usually called the screening committee) to pass on suggestions that are beyond the authority of the department committees.

The Scanlon Plan was first developed by Joseph Scanlon in about 1937 to help reduce costs in a steel mill where he was a union

---

[15] An early description of the spirit of TVA labor-management relations is given in David E. Lilienthal, *TVA: Democracy on the March* (1944), Chap. 10.

representative. The success of the plan led the steelworkers' union to move Mr. Scanlon to national headquarters, where he helped install his plan in a number of plants where the United Steelworkers was the bargaining agent. Later he moved to the Massachusetts Institute of Technology and continued his work of helping interested employers and unions install the plan. Although the Scanlon Plan works best in plants where there is a union to stimulate participation among the employees, the plan has been installed in a few nonunion firms.

The incentive to make cost-reducing suggestions under the Scanlon Plan is a plant-wide one because it is part of the philosophy of the plan that efficiency depends on effective cooperation throughout the organization. Hence, it is the aim of the incentive to produce teamwork. The plan is significant because it shows the very great effect of teamwork on productivity and efficiency. The incentive toward teamwork is provided most commonly by giving the employees a large share (usually three-fourths) of the savings in labor costs. The savings are measured by ascertaining the extent to which the ratio of payroll to sales value of production is reduced below the previous normal ratio.[16] Thus there is no incentive for part of the work force to try to gain at the expense of the others. The Scanlon Plan usually covers supervisory personnel (including plant managers) as well as the rank and file workers. In computing the ratio of payroll to sales, the supervisory payrolls are included, and the supervisors share in whatever bonus is earned. This rule has not been adhered to in all cases, but it is the one preferred by Mr. Scanlon.

The Scanlon Plan does not work automatically, and whether it is successful or not depends upon circumstances. Certainly the success of the plan requires acceptance of its philosophy by both management and employees—a belief that cooperation is the way to get lower costs and a desire to try it. The plan also presupposes a considerable degree of mutual confidence between workers and management. The actual results of the plan vary considerably from case to case, but the plan has demonstrated its ability to produce the following results:

[10] Suppose that the normal ratio is found to be 35 per cent, which means that if a plant were selling $1 million of goods a year, payrolls would normally be $350,000. If the workers, by improving their efficiency, were able to produce $1 million of goods for a payroll cost of $310,000, three-fourths of the saving of $40,000, or $30,000, would

(1) A large number of technical suggestions both from rank-and-file workers and from supervisors designed to save labor and, therefore, to reduce the ratio of labor cost to sales revenue. Certainly the Scanlon Plan has demonstrated that most employers have been getting merely physical effort from workers when they might have gotten ideas as well. And the Scanlon Plan has shown that supervisors respond to the opportunity to earn a bonus by being imaginative and making suggestions.

(2) Willingness of workers to accept technological change and to help management make new equipment and methods work—since more productive and smoothly operating equipment helps to reduce the ratio of payrolls to sales income. Some material-handling equipment that had been installed in a plant prior to the Scanlon Plan had failed to work satisfactorily because of lack of employee cooperation but was readily accepted and was used effectively after adoption of the plan.

(3) A better pace of work and an avoidance of lost time. Since lower labor costs mean higher earnings for the workers, the Scanlon Plan gradually builds up a public opinion in the plant that is hostile to loafing. Under the Scanlon Plan people who have previously been happy to stand around doing nothing resent waiting for work. In one case a union representative criticized the management for recalling employees who were not needed and who could not be used effectively. In some plants the rise in efficiency has been particularly marked among that portion of the work force, such as maintenance workers and tool room employees, that previously had been on straight time pay and that had had no special interest in being efficient. The janitorial and watchman force in one plant was cut from 33 to 14 without the elimination of a single service. In the same plant the increased output of the tool room meant that there was little need to purchase tools from the outside. Furthermore, this increase in efficiency led the management to purchase new equipment and to return subcontracted work to the tool room.

(4) Greater interest in the quality of workmanship—since spoiled work cannot be sold and tends, therefore, to raise the ratio of labor cost to sales value of production. One plant reports a cut in the cost of its inspection department of 67 per cent—in spite of an increase in the output of the plant.

(5) Willingness of the workers to help each other and to share

knowledge of short cuts. Nowhere does the spirit of teamwork show itself more plainly than in the help given by experienced workers to new workers or by fast workers to slow workers—since a slow worker tends to diminish the earnings of all employees. In plants where individual or group piece rates prevail, experienced workers do not like to lose earning opportunities by helping new workers.

(6) More flexible administration of the union-management agreement. Under the Scanlon Plan every worker benefits from having each job done by the person most competent to do it. Hence, the plan discourages attempts by the union to impose rigid and narrow interpretation of seniority rules in making promotions and other job assignments. The management gains freedom in making transfers and promotions and in recalling men after layoffs. A company that has an agreement to permit calling back workers with specific skills regardless of seniority, reports that this operates smoothly under the Scanlon Plan. The union is not disposed to question management's judgment that a certain worker's special skill is needed. In another plant the interest in over-all costs led the machinists' union to give up jurisdiction over the work of cleaning the screens in air conditioning units so that it could be done by lower-paid production workers.

(7) Effort by workers to avoid overtime instead of trying to create it, since overtime tends to raise the ratio of payrolls to sales.

(8) A changed attitude by employees toward supervisors and management in general, marked in particular by a demand for more efficient management, and a disposition to be critical of its shortcomings. The effect of a demand for more efficient management on operations can be very great. No longer is the easygoing supervisor the best liked and the most popular. The Scanlon Plan encourages employees to demand supervisors who are good at planning operations in advance, having material on hand when it is needed, and keeping machines in repair.

(9) An awareness of the problems of the enterprise in making sales and meeting competition. Until a plant is operating at full capacity, an increase in output usually increases income more than labor costs. Hence, the Scanlon Plan promotes worker interest in the company's success in making sales. Price cuts to increase sales tend to raise the ratio and to reduce the bonus of the employees. The facts about sales and costs are presented to the screening committee

IMPACT OF COLLECTIVE BARGAINING

each month. The members of the committee thus gain first-hand information about the competitive successes and failures of the company and follow the course of sales from month to month. The Scanlon Plan is well adapted to the selling problems of job shops. One such shop bids on work that may require several thousand hours per job. Before the management submits a bid, it goes over its estimates and its plans with the workers. The men may suggest additional ideas on how to do the job. In some cases they ask management to put in a lower bid for the job.

(10) A better climate for contract negotiations. It is not the purpose of the Scanlon Plan to influence contract negotiations, but it does have this effect. It does not eliminate hard bargaining because it does not weaken the interest of the employees in higher wages. But the Scanlon Plan makes for more realistic and more informed bargaining. The monthly meetings of the screening committee give the union representatives the essential facts about the company's condition and the nature of the competition it faces. This knowledge on the part of unions does not eliminate differences of view between unions and management over wages and other matters, but it does enable the employees to take a broader and more balanced view of their interests. As a result, agreement is facilitated. A company reported that in its last negotiations under the Scanlon Plan agreement was reached after five meetings held within one month. Before the Scanlon Plan dozens of meetings spread over several months were required to produce agreement.

Problems of the Scanlon Type Plan

The success of the Scanlon Plan depends upon the interest of the employees and the management in making it work. Unless each side has faith in the honesty and sincerity of the other party, it will not work. Mr. Scanlon, his associates, and successors have seen this plainly and have been unwilling to start the plan in any plant unless they are convinced that the parties are ready to deal squarely with the many problems that are bound to arise. Among the questions that arise are the following:

(1) Does each employee feel a responsibility for the costs of the plant? When each of several hundred employees shares in a bonus, regardless of whether or not he helps earn it, there are bound to be some loafers and "free riders." This raises the question of what is

the maximum size of group in which the plan is practical. Nearly all of the plants in which the plan has been established have been fairly small—1,000 employees or less. However, it has been applied in one large company. When the Scanlon Plan was introduced in 1950, this company had 2,900 employees. By May 1957 it had 7,200 employees. Within the company there are three divisions all under one measurement. There is a screening committee in each division and also an over-all screening committee. A difficulty arose from the fact that some of the divisions were able to make a much better record than others. The employees had great trouble in making a bonus until one problem division was discontinued.

The union in this company says that it does not police employee effort, but that the workers do needle each other to increase efficiency. Experience does not yet indicate what is the maximum size of the group that can be brought under a group measurement and bonus arrangement or how the Scanlon Plan can be applied best to large companies. A company in the Middle West has 1,200 employees in two plants located near each other and operates successfully with one measurement and one screening committee—partly because management has a strong interest in making the plan work.

(2) What responsibility should unions take in dealing with loafers? As a rule, unions under the Scanlon Plan take no official action against loafers—though they do not protect them. But plant opinion is almost certain to be unfriendly to loafers. If the workers in the shop are interested in earning a bonus, they exert the same social pressures on loafers that they use in controlling speeders under conventional shop arrangements.

(3) Is it possible to measure satisfactorily the performance of the plan to be used in computing the bonus? The most usual basis is the ratio of payrolls (including supervisory, technical, and white collar payrolls) to sales value of production, but this measure of performance sometimes raises problems. One is whether the Scanlon Plan should extend to technical and white collar employees or be limited to so-called production workers. Inclusion of the technical and white collar employees causes the ratio to rise rapidly in years of poor business and prevents production employees from earning a bonus in those years. A second problem is to find a period that is normal—that does not represent either abnormally high or abnormally low labor costs. A third arises from the frequent variation in

product-mix. If some products have high labor content and others low labor content and the product-mix changes frequently, erratic fluctuations in bonus can occur. Ideally, changes in the bonus should reflect changes in worker performance. In some production situations it is difficult to devise a satisfactory measurement to reflect such changes.

(4) Can changes in the ratio be agreed upon amicably when changed conditions warrant a new ratio? There are many changes that may justify raising or lowering the ratio. A wage increase (or decrease) may call for a change in the ratio provided it is not followed by offsetting price changes. A change in the product of the plant or in the relative importance of different products may make a change in the ratio desirable. Changing market conditions and competition requiring the company to use cheaper materials may raise the ratio of labor costs to sales. So also may the addition of an engineering and research department with a substantial payroll.

Reaching agreement on a new ratio could be difficult if the two parties lacked confidence in each other's fairness and good faith. Sometimes experiment is needed to arrive at a satisfactory ratio. A company that was making important changes in its product, requiring the training of new workers, raised the ratio from 18 per cent to 20 per cent for six months. After the training period the ratio was established at 19 per cent.

(5) Are the employees willing and able to suggest new and more efficient methods of production? The Scanlon Plan has a far greater capacity to evoke suggestions than does the conventional suggestion system. Under the Scanlon Plan suggestion-making is usually approved by most of the work force because it usually helps raise their earnings. Conventional suggestion systems, on the contrary, encounter the hostility of a large part of the workers, who resent the attempts of the few ablest ones to get ahead and who sometimes fear that suggestions will throw some of them out of work. Under the Scanlon Plan the employees learn how cost-saving suggestions can promote job security by helping the company meet competition and by bringing work into the plant. Hence the plan tends to create an atmosphere that is conducive to the making of suggestions. Occasionally, however, employees lack the technical background that enables them to make good suggestions, or their interest in making suggestions for some reason may be low. Such was the case among

the employees of a small manufacturer of ceramic ware.[17] The employees were women with limited technical background, and management was unwilling to drop authoritarian attitudes and to try to encourage their participation in improving processes.

The number of suggestions actually made may exceed the number reported; some are made directly to foremen and are put into effect without report. Some workers institute changes of their own that they would not have made previously. Some ideas cannot be put readily into written form. One toolmaker developed a perfect die for a new product and did it without drawings. When asked why he had not made a suggestion, he replied: "How could I? What was I to suggest? That the draftsmen be fired?"

(6) Is management willing to accept the new role that falls to it when the problems of production are regarded as the common concern of employees and supervision? The more successful the Scanlon Plan in causing employees to identify their welfare with that of the company, the greater is the adjustment that foremen and other supervisors must make. The employees may be quite free about making suggestions. Some suggestions may cause the foremen to appear stupid. And when workers begin to suggest how the work could be done better, some foremen may feel "I am no longer a boss." This problem may require that foremen be taught new methods of management. One company has made clear that it expects the foremen to consult with the workers. If there is a production problem, the first question asked by higher management is: "Have you taken it up with the men?" At some companies the foremen now ask for suggestions.

Since the size of the bonus depends on the efficiency of management, supervisors must expect that failure of the employees to earn a satisfactory bonus will provoke a critical review of management's work.

(7) How does the Scanlon Plan work in periods of recession? Does the inability of employees to earn a bonus plus the fear of losing their jobs cause a great drop in the number of suggestions and a general breakdown of the Scanlon Plan?

Recessions present difficulties for both management and employees. Some managements have tried to protect employee morale

[17] Thomas Q. Gilson, and Myron J. Lefcowitz, "A Plant-Wide Productivity Bonus in a Small Factory," *Industrial and Labor Relations Review* (January 1957).

by refusing to lay off all unneeded employees. The effect of recessions on the behavior of unions under the Scanlon Plan cannot be predicted. In some plants recession has caused the drying up of suggestions without producing much effect on the willingness of employees to work effectively. Employees have also been unwilling to make suggestions that might reduce employment, but they have been willing to maintain efficiency. In other cases the recession of 1958 was actually accompanied by a substantial increase in the number of suggestions. Employees were trying to help the employer meet competition. The failure of the Scanlon Plan to produce bonus earnings during recession does not seem to have been important—employees attribute that condition to the recession rather than to the plan.

The following cases show the different experiences of several employers with the Scanlon Plan during the recession of 1958. A maker of automotive equipment was forced to reduce his labor force from 750 in November 1957 to 488 early in January 1958 and later to 250. No bonus was earned from January 1958 through July 1958. The management does not think that workers tended to nurse jobs during the recession—beyond the natural tendency of men to slow down somewhat when there is not a lot of work ahead. There was some complaining about the lack of a bonus, but the attitude of the workers was affected by their knowledge of general economic conditions. They blamed these conditions rather than the Scanlon Plan for the lack of a bonus; in fact, those who were still working were pleased to have jobs. There was a large drop in the number of suggestions. In the period October 1, 1956, to June 30, 1957, there were 216 suggestions; in the corresponding period in 1957–58 there were 71 suggestions. In March 1958 there were only 2, in April 1958 only 3, and in May and June 1958 only one each. But in July, with some pick-up in business, there were 12. There were 8 excellent suggestions in the screw machine department. This was the first department to pick up because it is a department that does contract work from the outside. In spite of the recession, the drop in the number of suggestions, and a 7-cent wage increase in October 1957 the payroll cost of the product per unit dropped 8 per cent in the second year of the Scanlon Plan, from October 1, 1957, to September 30, 1958. In the first year (October 1, 1956, to September 30, 1957) the payroll cost per unit of output dropped by 9 per cent.

Quite different was the experience of a manufacturer of containers, which during 1958 laid off 41 per cent of its work force.
This company had paid no bonus for several months, and prior to
that had had only a small bonus of 1.5 per cent to 2 per cent for
several months. And yet in the eleven months ending September
1958 the company received 528 suggestions—far more than in any
previous year and one-third as many as the company had received
in six years of the Scanlon Plan. To the employees in this company
the Scanlon Plan was a way by which they fought to get work and
to protect their jobs. The desire for job security, not the expectation
of earning a bonus, was what stimulated these men to make so many
suggestions.

Still different was the experience of a company making consumer goods. In the recession of 1957–58 the company cut its work
force from 1,000 to 770. The layoffs did not occur until late in the
recession—May and June 1958. Suggestions in the year 1957–58 were
more numerous than in the previous year, but not as numerous as
two years earlier. Changes in product and processes were made in
1957–58, giving the employees an opportunity to make suggestions.
They were stimulated to do this by a growing realization of the stiff
competition confronting the company. Some suggestions were made
through the cooperative plan that had no direct effect on the
bonus—though they may help the company compete. For example,
workers in the maintenance department suggested improvements in
the operation of the company's boilers that resulted in savings on
fuel oil. This saving, however, did not affect the bonus.

The bonus for the year ending July 31, 1958, averaged about 13
per cent. In the previous year it was 15.1 per cent, in the year before
that, 19 per cent, and in the first year a little more than 15 per cent.
It is impossible to say how much the drop in the bonus was due to
the recession—a representative of management attributed it to the
change in the product-mix rather than to the recession. The office
force in this company is not under the Scanlon Plan. The recession
does not seem to have caused a slackening of pace. There is a good
deal of policing of the speed of work among the work force—though
the people do not talk about it.[18]

(8) What wage structure shall be substituted under the Scanlon

[18] The management says that there are a few people whose production is lower than
it should be but "not nearly so many as under individual bonus rates before the
Scanlon Plan was put in."

Plan for the previously existing wage structure? When the Scanlon Plan is introduced into plants where payment is by the hour, there are usually no serious problems of wage adjustment. Quite different is the situation when the Scanlon Plan is installed in plants that have individual or group piece rates or bonus plans. Piece rates and bonuses are usually discontinued when the Scanlon Plan is introduced. But if incentive workers are put on standard hourly rates, many employees are almost certain to have their earnings drastically cut. The alternative would be to base day rates on the highest piece rate or bonus earnings—which no plant can afford.

The method of dealing with the problem depends on circumstances—such as the need of the company for a reduction in costs, the proportion of piece rates and standards that are loose, and the rate of turnover among the workers. A common way of handling the problem is by establishing so-called "red circle" rates. These are transitional rates that are paid to former piece or bonus workers as long as they continue to hold their previous jobs. The red circle rates are higher than the rates that are permanently established on the new jobs. Hence they are higher than the rates paid newly-hired employees. Their use results in the payment of two different rates for the same operations. Red circle rates, therefore, may be a source of friction among employees, but they may also be a way of reducing or eliminating the opposition of some employees to the Scanlon Plan.

When red circle rates are established in connection with the introduction of the Scanlon Plan, they usually are not individual rates but uniform rates applying to all former piece or bonus workers performing a given operation. Since they are based on the average earnings of the former piece or bonus workers, they decrease the earnings of some workers and increase the earnings of others. Red circle rates are normally wiped out by not applying negotiated wage increases to them.

A few unions are strongly opposed to prolonging the inequities of the former piecework or bonus system and will have nothing to do with red circle rates. One union reasoned that since the high earnings of some workers were causing trouble, it would be desirable to start the Scanlon Plan with reasonable rates for each job—even if this meant large wage reductions for some workers. Hence the union rejected the company's proposal that the problem be handled by establishing red circle rates. The plant is one in which labor turnover is low, so that the elimination of the red circle rates would have been a slow process. The high earners in the plant under the incentive system were semi-skilled production workers, who were making more than skilled tool and die workers. The union members felt that there was no need to prolong the inequities of the wage structure.

Effect of the Scanlon Plan Upon the Administration
of Union-Management Contracts

All plans of union-management cooperation are based on the theory that formal cooperation to promote efficiency will not affect the assertion of rights by either party under the union-management contract. And yet some unions oppose formal cooperation partly on the ground that it may soften the willingness of the members and the local leaders to stand up for the rights of the union members. Some unions have tried to protect themselves against this danger by providing that officers concerned with handling grievances and administering the agreement may not serve on cooperative committees. Thus in some of the Scanlon Plan plants members of grievance committees or bargaining committees do not serve on the screening committees. It is a rule that matters involving the interpretation of the union-management contract are not discussed at cooperative committee meetings. In some plants it is the custom for the chairman of the grievance committee to attend the cooperative committee meetings as an observer for the purpose of seeing that the cooperative committee does not exceed its jurisdiction.

Keeping the personnel of the cooperative or screening committee separate from the personnel of the bargaining or grievance committee has proved to be impracticable in many plants because the local union has only a certain number of leaders, and the real leaders of the union are needed on each committee. In a plant of about 700 employees making automotive parts complete separation of the bargaining committee and the screening committee was abandoned after a year. The executive of a company in which the Scanlon Plan has been a marked success thinks that the leaders of the union ought to be on both the bargaining committee and the screening committee because screening committee members learn about the economic condition of the company.

Union-management cooperation has affected the administration of agreements in some plants by making both unions and managements more disposed to take account of the problems of the other. Thus, the personnel manager in a plant of several hundred employees making automotive parts has been strict in enforcing a plant-wide seniority rule for layoffs because he believes that the union has earned this consideration. Some foremen were naturally reluctant to lose some of their best people, but if seniority required it, the employees had to be laid off. In one case a company was having trouble with a part that it was molding; something was eating the mold. The management put the operation in the hands of a research worker who was outside the jurisdiction of the union. The worker on the job was transferred to another operation. A strict interpretation of the agreement would have required that the management keep the skilled craftsman on the job doing nothing while the researcher did his work. Since workers were being laid off the union might have insisted on a make-work interpretation of the agreement. In the days before the Scanlon Plan, when company engineers ran machines in order to learn how to improve them, the position of the union had been: "Throw the parts away or have one of our men stand idle."

The contract between one company and a union provided for a lunch period from 12 to 12:30. The union consented to the lunch period for certain machinists being moved to 1 to 1:30 without the men being paid time and a half for working outside of standard hours. By working from 12 to 12:30 the machinists were able to make repairs on equipment that was in use at other times. Of course, had the machinists been paid time and a half for work done between 1 and 1:30, the bonus available for distribution to the employees would have been correspondingly reduced.

The Scanlon Plan makes for a great reduction in the number of grievances and for more informality in settling them. Generally written grievances disappear. The management of a maker of automotive parts reports that it never has grievances. And although workers are not ordinarily discouraged under the Scanlon Plan from asserting their rights under the agreement, the union committee sometimes puts the interests of the whole group ahead of those of an individual—as when the committee seeks to dissuade a man from using his seniority to bid for a job for which he is not well qualified.

The Scanlon Plan constitutes a contribution to the art of management of first importance because it demonstrates in terms of production and costs the effectiveness of a strong interest in teamwork and because it provides an effective means of creating teamwork, at least when the number of workers involved is 1,000 or less.

Construction Industry Joint Conference

A venture of great promise in union-management cooperation is the establishment in the construction industry of "The Construction Industry Joint Conference." Announcement of this venture was made on April 7, 1959.

The objective of the Conference is to promote the welfare of the building and construction industry in the public interest. It is designed to preserve and to promote the contract system by promoting improved performance and productivity by contractors and by workers.

The Conference provides a continuing forum in which labor-management and industry problems (not subject to existing machinery) can be discussed regularly and every effort made to reach constructive and equitable solutions. It is contemplated that mutually agreed upon methods will be devised to insure uninterrupted continuity of work on all projects and contracts. This conference does not affect the continued operation of the National Joint Board for the Settlement of Jurisdictional Disputes in the building and construction industry or any other existing machinery jointly established by the national unions and national contractor organizations.

The Construction Industry Joint Conference undertakes to:

(1) Provide for the need to present more effectively to private owners and government procurement agencies the advantages of the contract system.

(2) Consider the special problems and practices of particular localities where the pooled attention and assistance of national organizations of contractors and national unions may be used to improve conditions.

(3) Consider the need for a continuing and systematic study of a wide range of problems which confront the building and construction industry, in the promotion of the contract system.

The Construction Industry Joint Conference promotes and encourages the establishment of corresponding local joint conferences in local communities and metropolitan areas. It is composed of general presidents (or their representatives) of national unions and representatives of participating national contractors' associations. The Conference functions through periodic meetings and through frequent meetings of a Joint Administrative Committee set up to administer policies established by the Conference, to gather facts, and to make reports as assigned. This committee is composed of an equal number of representatives of national unions and of participating national contractors' associations. One-half the representatives of the national contractors' associations are drawn from general contractors' associations and one-half from specialty contractors' associations. An impartial chairman, appointed by the Joint Administrative Committee, is provided to facilitate the work of the committee and its subcommittees.

29 / Line and Staff Cooperation and the Position of Foremen

OF FOUR MAJOR SECTIONS in this chapter the first discusses management's labor relations function. It indicates the organizational characteristics that appear to have contributed to relative success in handling labor relations and thus provides background for discussion of line and staff objectives and problems. A second section, on line and staff organization, briefly considers the influence of unions on organizational structure. The third section, on line and staff cooperation, is devoted to a major objective of labor relations policies—achieving appropriate balance. A final section, on the position of foremen, analyzes the conditions that contribute to effective leadership at the level of first-line supervision.

Management's Labor Relations Function

The term "labor relations," while frequently restricted in meaning to union-management relations, is used in a broader sense in this chapter. The intention here is to include personnel policies and practices as well. To a considerable extent personnel policies are integrated with, and inseparable from, union-management relations. In part, however, personnel policies go beyond, and are independent of, union relations. While emphasis here is on union-management relations, this in no way implies that aspects of employee relations that are touched upon only superficially or not at all are not important. In most companies union and personnel responsibilities quite properly.are under unified direction.

Our study of a fairly large number of companies includes those with relatively good and those with poor union-management relationships. In point of fact, whether companies were surveyed by area or by industry, contrasts in the quality of labor relations were obvious. Some of the most interesting differences were between leading companies in major industries.

Companies that had achieved relative success in labor relations tended to give clear evidence of management by policy, effective administration at the worker level, and management initiative in labor relations. Policies were well developed, although individual aspects of the policy were not inflexible. The firing line was downstairs and not upstairs. There was effective administration at the lower levels, and a high degree of management initiative in labor relations also existed. Both policy formulation and administration were dynamic. Problems were carefully analyzed and appropriate action taken. The higher levels of management portrayed a situation similar to that at lower levels. There was honest communication. The first section elaborates in general terms these characteristics, which appeared to mark relative success.

The importance of management by policy was emphasized in Chapter 2. Companies with well-developed policies showed that labor relations were of vital concern to top management. Of particular importance was the formulation of long-range policies to minimize crisis consideration of policy and action. Such companies also did not overemphasize those matters that could readily be tagged by an immediate cost figure nor union relations as distinct from employee relations.

Policy considerations may be broken down into (1) basic policies, (2) general policies, (3) implementing policies, and (4) procedural policies. Brief consideration will be given to each of these four aspects of policy. Basic policy is of primary importance but inevitably broad in character. Two elements of basic policy will serve for illustration, a firm but fair attitude toward unions and employees, and a human relations approach to employees.

Almost every company stated that it had a policy of being firm but fair. The questions began to arise when various company officials were asked how both firmness and fairness were carried out. What general policies and implementing policies were included under each description? How was firmness implemented in negotiation? How was it implemented in administration? How had fairness been implemented? This basic policy appeared in some companies to be largely an empty slogan and in others a real guide. Almost every company maintained that it treated employees as human beings, encouraged employee suggestions, consulted with employees, and in other ways was forward looking in its employee relations. Again this basic policy appeared to be largely an empty slogan in some cases and a real guide in others.

One of the most interesting aspects of our study was to observe the dramatic changes that had taken place with shifts in basic policies. One company had a long record of poor union and employee relations. The president had never really accepted the union, and both negotiation and administration were replete with friction and difficulties. An able personnel manager was submerged in conflict he could not control. A change in presidents, plus the frustration for both parties of a fairly long strike, ushered in a period of an entirely new relationship. Many particular improvements were made in subsequent years. Many of these changes came from suggestions from the personnel manager, who now had an opportunity to lead. None of them were feasible so long as a "fight-the-union" basic policy remained.

A second case involved a change in presidents but was brought to a head by an opportunity to expand. The new president felt that it was unwise to plan a large investment unless reasonable relations with the union could be established. Again the company stopped fighting the union and reached a general understanding with a top union official. A period of great improvement followed. Wildcats were stopped, plant capacity was doubled, production standards were revised, and sensible deviations from the contract were allowed. In a third example a company with a good management policy took over a purchased plant and inherited a long record of poor relations with a local of the teamsters. The new management achieved steady improvement in worker efficiency and labor relations. Cooperation with union officials was established in such personnel activities as annual employee attitude surveys.

The above companies showed firmness in improving efficiency, fairness in negotiation and administration of contracts, and a strengthening of employee relations. Other instances could be cited where changes in top management officials, in corporate ownership, and in economic or other circumstances brought marked changes in basic policies and subsequent dramatic improvement in union and employee relations.

General policies, integrated with basic policies, are required for each substantive aspect of union and employee relations. Some such policies are embodied in a union contract, such as provisions with respect to discipline, production standards, layoffs, and promotions. Many chapters in this book discuss the substance of general policies. General policies in turn commonly require supplementation and implementation.

Supplementation and implementation can go to considerable length. Discipline for just cause is implemented, for example, by a system of progressive discipline. The question then becomes, how thoroughly have various phases of the progressive discipline system been thought out? One can ask, "How do you discipline for failure to meet production standards?" An answer may indicate that a great deal of attention and thought has been given to this phase of discipline, or it may indicate a lack of policy. The significant fact is that basic policies require both general and implementing policies at the operating level. Companies were found to vary considerably in the degree to which they had thought out implementing policies.

Procedural policies have been separated out for two reasons. The first reason is that the implementation of substantive policies has important procedural aspects. For example, written warnings are a common part of disciplinary policy. What are the procedural checks and balances on issuing written warnings? Are such warnings an empty gesture to please higher management or are they followed up? Procedural controls are important in implementing substantive policies, and deserve emphasis. The second reason for singling out procedural policies is that some procedures are in themselves organizational objectives. For example, most companies have a policy of settling grievances to the greatest possible extent at the first (or lower) steps in the grievance procedure. In some companies this procedural policy is itself implemented in various ways, in other companies it is not. Administrative objectives of a procedural character require thoughtful and many-sided implementation.

One result of the field work was to discover companies that had developed labor relations in depth in terms of both policy and staff. A good deal was learned about labor relations policy by discussing grievance settlements and employee relations with lower labor relations representatives who were close to the operating level. The understanding shown by such people in some companies was extremely encouraging. It was not because they could turn to a policy manual and find some pertinent words, though this was helpful, but because they showed real perspective and understanding of the problems. It did not take long to discover through this type of discussion, ranging over a variety of specific subjects, whether or not a company really had definite policies. If answers were easily and readily given—this is the policy, this is how it is implemented, here are some cases, and these are our problems—the typical result was an interesting and instructive discussion. A staff representative's desire to discuss problems and imperfections indicated that labor relations in that company had a dynamic quality.

The above indicates the close connection between policy and administration. Policy is to be judged primarily not by what is on paper but by action. Policy and administration merge in a host of particular decisions and actions. If policies could be made highly objective, decisions and actions could be substantially mechanical, and line (or staff) could carry out policies with no particular difficulty. In some phases of labor relations this degree of objectivity can be approximated. The pension area, for example, has few grievances and few difficulties in administration. Once a pension plan has been worked out, the answers to most questions are specifically given in the plan. Other benefit provisions, with some exceptions, are reasonably objective in character. The point, however, is that in many important phases of labor relations even approximate mechanical statements of policies and ready-made answers are impossible. As discussed in the grievance chapters, these are the areas where management may be challenged on the reasonableness of its decisions. Policies in these areas can be aids to, but not substitutes for, good judgment. How can the function of labor relations be defined with respect to this large number of particular decisions and actions?

There appear to be two related administrative considerations in the above question. One objective is to avoid extreme decisions that can set unwanted precedents or lead to reversals that weaken or destroy policy. The second objective is to influence the quality of the decisions that are made to carry out the positive spirit and intent of a particular policy. To make "good" decisions in the light of the applicable policies is the heart of the administrative challenge in labor relations.

The administrative task may be illustrated by reporting a discussion with a divisional director of labor relations in a large company.

There were about fifteen plants within this division, all operating under a master contract with one union. Labor relations in the entire division were good, but some plants had no significant problems, some plants had modest problems, and some were described as problem plants. A problem plant in this division, however, would have been regarded as a satisfactory plant in another division of the company where the level of labor relations was much poorer.

The divisional director said that his administrative responsibilities required him to exercise a restraining influence in some plants to prevent local management from being too tough or from taking improper advantage of its position; in other plants his job was to stiffen the back of local management if it tended to take the easy way out under pressure. This dual role with respect to different types of plants appears eminently appropriate but indicates the complexity of the problem of guiding the quality of the decisions that are being made and the difficulty of defining staff responsibility.

Carrying the analysis to particular plants brought out differences (1) in the labor relations climate of different communities, (2) in the abilities of plant managers and plant personnel directors, (3) in local union leadership and the character of local unions, (4) in the historical background of union-management relations, and (5) in production situations and production problems with their consequent effect on labor relations.

While certain reviews and report procedures were standard practice for all plants, the divisional director and his staff deliberately functioned in different ways in different plants. In some they exercised a very minimum of supervision; in others, very detailed supervision. In one plant the division was pulling back, as they felt that they had been supervising the plant too closely, in part because of its close geographical proximity. Some plant personnel directors were quite weak in relation to their plant managers, while others dictated labor relations in their plants. Implementation of policies varied in different plants in part by deliberate choice and in part because of the peculiarities of the history of particular plants.

While this interesting example could be spelled out in greater detail, it serves to illustrate how difficult it is to formulate operational policies, to translate them into action, and to generalize as to the control function labor relations should perform. In some plants temporary policies were in effect for particular reasons. In some plants certain policies were judged appropriate that would not have been used in other plants. Appraisal, judgment, and trial and error, as well as more basic principles, constitute the art of labor relations. It is against this type of background that organizational problems must be considered.

Some companies showed much more initiative in labor relations than others. This initiative was shown in policy formation, in negotiation, in personnel programs, and in administration. There were obvious differences in preparation for negotiation, in the knowledge of what went on in the plants, in the extent of policy at the operating level, in the amount of analysis of how policies were working, and, perhaps primarily, in the willingness to tackle problems and the vigor of the drive to make progress. Some companies appeared to ride along without taking any action, while others were in the midst of dynamic programs. Some companies had limited vision of their labor relations problems and opportunities, others were continuously searching for new ideas, new policies, and new procedures. Recognition should be given, however, to the general improvement in labor relations administration over the past twenty or so years. Companies are doing a labor relations job today that would have been amazing some years ago, and the number of competent labor relations men of various ranks has increased enormously.

Line and Staff Organization

It would be possible from the material gathered for this study to analyze directly some line and staff differences within various companies. There are companies in which the line takes nearly all the initiative in labor relations at practically all levels within the organization. In others primary responsibility at all levels rests with the staff, although nominally they operate under the principle of delegated authority. In a very small number of companies the concept of delegation has been dropped; the staff is responsible for personnel and labor relations, including the negotiation and administration of contracts.[1]

[1] Organizational patterns and variations have been well portrayed by Charles A. Myers and John G. Turnbull, "Line and Staff in Industrial Relations," *Harvard Business Review* (July-August 1956), pp. 113-24. To their five types of methods of administering the industrial relations function a sixth should perhaps be added to

The crucial problem, however, appears to be one of obtaining adequate line and staff cooperation. Organizational difficulties seem to
stem in major part from lack of cooperation and coordination; success in this area appears to result more from the achievement of cooperation than from any particular mixture of authority and responsibility. All companies face a problem in achieving cooperation.
While it is necessary to divide authority for particular kinds of decisions,[2] joint responsibility remains, since no kind of mechanical separation of authority is completely successful.

Before turning to the subject of line and staff cooperation, however, some comments on line and staff organization are warranted. In
the first place, a significant number of companies were drawing back
from what was regarded as overdependence upon staff. Apparently
many companies, when they were first confronted with strong unions,
created labor relations staffs and gave to them considerable authority
and responsibility, either formally or informally, and to a corresponding degree effectively removed labor relations decisions from
the line. Authority and responsibility were also shifted upward
within the organizations to obtain consistency in action, particularly
since guiding policies had not yet evolved.

This kind of organizational change, thus, was initially a response
to strong and militant industrial unionism. Where a single industrial
union obtained bargaining rights in a number of plants, with similar
contracts or a master contract, it can be argued that no other response by management would have been adequate. Line executives
were in no position to spend the time and thought necessary to handle the problem in all of its ramifications.

As time has gone on, union-management relations have improved,
particularly with respect to the administration of contracts. Organizational hostilities have declined, contract clauses have become more
permanent, and considerable accommodation has resulted. With the

---

allow for the rare cases in which the concept of delegation has been dropped and staff
is responsible for specified personnel and labor relations functions. Two large companies that operate under this pattern came to our attention. In fact these companies
operate in substantially the same way as do others with strong labor relations and
personnel staff departments operating under delegated authority. The major distinction of moment to our knowledge is the right, sometimes exercised, to take over temporarily complete control of labor relations in a plant that is not operating to the
satisfaction of the head of the corporate staff department.

[2] The suggestions on this point by Myers and Turnbull are significant. The same,
pp. 122-23.

development of policy and the stabilization of contract administration, it has become possible to move away from the concentration of authority and responsibility in the labor relations staff. The current trend is toward more decentralization in administration and more line responsibility. A key question arises over the position of first-line supervision in this revised picture. Many companies want to "strengthen the foreman" in the organizational pattern. With some companies this appears to have been primarily an empty slogan, but with others it has brought real though complex change. This problem will be discussed below.

Other moves in the direction of decentralization and strengthening line management have been discovered. Division line managements and plant managers have been participating more actively in labor relations. For example, a corporate labor relations director reported that his company had changed its organizational structure by moving toward decentralization, but he added that actually, however, it hadn't meant much as "we have to keep control over what happens." But in spite of qualifications there has been a significant move toward decentralization in many companies that goes hand in hand with added line responsibility and participation in labor relations.

In the second place, some companies have never set up an adequate labor relations staff. This lack is most conspicuous in industries consisting primarily of many small companies, but it is also to be found in companies of various sizes too much dominated by a production or sales point of view. To some extent industries with many small companies have delegated responsibility for labor relations to associations. The influence of industry associations in the negotiation and administration of contracts is clearly very variable. Without attempting to develop the subject at length, the most feasible method of upgrading the labor relations function in many situations appears to be to develop further the role of the association. But, regardless of size, companies require an organization in which labor relations objectives can be balanced with sales and production requirements.

The adequate development of labor relations in the small company presents special problems. In such companies it is not feasible to have a highly specialized staff. On the other hand, labor and personnel relations can be made the special responsibility of a particular executive. There are advantages and disadvantages in the use of consultants, but some consultants have provided constructive service to small companies. The small company also has advantages in the close personal relationships that can be maintained within the organization. The attitude and ability of the chief executive is, of course, of particular significance in a small organization.

Third, it should be noted that the role of the corporate labor relations and personnel staff varies considerably among multiplant companies. Companies that produce one or several related products in a number of plants, all organized by one or two unions, frequently operating under one or more master contracts, typically have a strong central labor relations staff. Companies producing diversified products in scattered plants and dealing with various unions on a plant basis may or may not have a strong corporate staff. The corporate staff in these latter situations may be primarily advisory and exercise very little control over divisions and plants. In a few such large companies the corporate labor relations function appears to be inadequately developed, but most such variations reflect differences in labor relations and product environments.

Fourth, brief mention should be made of differences in line and staff emphasis with respect to various groups of employees. The strong labor relations staff has developed predominantly with respect to production and maintenance employees. When technical and engineering employees were organized, some companies turned the labor relations function over to the already existing staff, with somewhat unfortunate results. Such staff individuals were too much oriented to the attitudes of production unions to deal appropriately with engineering unions. Somewhat the same thing has happened with organized office workers. As a result at least a few companies have strengthened line control of labor relations with respect to technical and office workers. This is not intended as a general criticism of staff activity with respect to technical and office employees but to note divergent experiences. A few companies at least feel that greater emphasis on line responsibility is called for in labor relations with technical and office employees than with production and maintenance employees.

Finally, note must be taken of the importance in both large and small companies of key individuals in both line and staff capacities. Shifting such individuals at or near the top of the management group brings out most clearly their conscious or unconscious determination of policies. Changes in ownership of particular plants demonstrate the same point. While a "great man" theory of labor relations cannot be the whole story, the fact should not be overlooked that the character of labor relations and the existing organizational structure in particular companies, divisions, and plants is extremely dependent on the particular abilities of the key men within the organizations in question.

Line and Staff Cooperation

The importance of teamwork among all officials involved in labor relations was evidenced early in our survey. The same emphasis is found in an excellent study by the National Industrial Conference Board, *Improving Staff and Line Relations*,[3] based on an intensive two-year investigation in seventy-eight companies. The introduction states in part:

> If staff and line are to work effectively together, all available evidence demonstrates that each must understand and sympathize with what the other is trying to do. More than this, both line and staff need to *help* one another accomplish their respective tasks. This acceptance and teamwork rarely emerge when staff and line are continually treading on one another's toes, bickering about their rights of eminent domain, or operating surreptitiously to establish a beachhead in the other's territory.[4]

The concept of mutual help, in contrast to that which sees the staff existing only to help the line, deserves emphasis. Mutual help implies that the staff has some functions to carry out that require help from the line. In the words of the NICB study, "In the modern business enterprise, many of the vital administrative activities are entrusted to staff."[5] For example, the industrial engineering staff commonly has primary responsibility and delegated authority to establish production standards. They cannot, however, do an effective job without both understanding and help from the line. It is quite possible and not unusual to lose control of production standards on the factory floor.

The general dimensions of the problem of lack of cooperation can

---

[3] National Industrial Conference Board, Studies in Personnel Policy, No. 153 (1956).
[4] The same, p. 9.
[5] The same.

be briefly illustrated from our study. Lack of cooperation was found within plants, among plants within a single division of a company, among divisions of a company, and at the corporate level. At all levels lack of a coordinated approach created inconsistencies in policy interpretation and application.

Within some plants friction was obvious. A common organizational pattern involved a plant manager and plant industrial relations director at one level and a labor relations supervisor and foremen at the worker level. Friction at times exi.:ed between line and staff, and at times between the higher and the lower teams. Consider very briefly an example of each type. In one plant the line and staff representatives were at odds over "foremen working." The contract provided that foremen should work only in emergencies and to train other workers. The plant manager could not emotionally accept this concept. In his eyes a good foreman stepped in and helped out in any kind of production difficulty. The staff representatives accepted the contract provision as stating appropriate foreman activity. This divided attitude created inconsistent practice and built up over time into a large grievance area. Considerable cost was involved in settling grievances, and the foremen were caught in the middle of line and staff attitudes. A major union-management problem was created by a difference of point of view within management.

In a second plant the labor relations supervisor and the foremen applied more strict standards of discipline and stricter interpretation of other sections of the contract than did the higher officials. In this setting, a high proportion of lower decisions became grievances, and most grievances were appealed to the top team with many modifications and reversals. There were many grievances, and union-management friction was created because of different points of view within management. Actually both of these examples were more complex than the brief statements imply, but they are accurate on essentials and can serve as illustrations.

Friction at the divisional level between labor relations and production can virtually nullify what can otherwise be a very important link in labor relations administration. Within one division in one company, the plant labor relations people finally stopped communicating with the division labor relations director. No effective support could be achieved through this channel, and such communication was resented by the plant managers.

This is a very interesting case. The quality of labor relations in all plants in this division, operating under the same master contract, was consistently poorer over a period of years than in the plants in other divisions. Many particular causes of poor labor relations were found in each plant within the division. It might be argued that all plants in this division had been unlucky enough to run into a series of particularly difficult problems. Such an analysis, however, would be of doubtful validity primarily because routine labor relations problems had become major problems in all of these plants. There appeared to be only one basic explanation. Serious differences of opinion at the divisional level between line and staff had created not only a lack of a consistent policy but attempts to practice different policies. Union-management relations had so deteriorated that all the plants had extremely high grievance rates.

The same kind of difficulty in varying degrees can exist at the corporate level. Inconsistent points of view among production, sales, and labor relations officials can lead to conflicting decisions in the interpretation of policy. In fact differences in point of view can frustrate the effective formulation and application of labor relations policy. One of the important problems in a company organization is to recognize subtle differences in emphasis. Pressure to maintain production and refrain from causing trouble can weaken the application of labor relations policies without open argument over policy as such. A production-oriented staff, a labor relations-oriented line, and mechanisms for coordinating the two will be discussed below.

A Production-Oriented Staff

Companies are critized for allowing staff to take over line authority, on the general theory that basic responsibility for results must inevitably rest with the line. However, there is the added implication that the labor relations staff tends to "give in" to unions and employees because the primary task of labor relations is to maintain harmony.

There are labor relations situations that appear to fit this pattern. The production people have uppermost in their minds maintaining production schedules, quality, and efficiency. Labor relations can, under some conditions, be viewed as interfering with these objectives; thus viewed, labor relations blocks the road to adequate discipline: "You can't fire anyone around this place." If the lower line tries to deny a particular grievance, they are not backed up, and their position is modified or reversed by higher staff. "They want efficiency, but labor relations won't allow any promotions except on seniority." "You're supposed to run this place without ever making anyone unhappy so you won't have any grievances." Such is the criticism portraying labor relations as being preoccupied with peace and harmony to the detriment of practical production considerations.

The implications of the above line of criticism have never been generally valid, and with time and experience the labor relations staff has tended to become more interested in a strong line management. Consequently it has encouraged in particular the development of a skilled and strengthened group of foremen and other first-line supervisors. Training first-line supervision has become a major organizational objective in most companies, usually at the insistence of the personnel and labor relations staffs. Foremen have been given some additional authority as well as added organizational support and assistance. The problem is complex and is discussed in the final section of this chapter.

Policies and decisions that are consistent with the production requirements of the organization are clearly necessary, a point that will be elaborated in the final section of this chapter. An experienced staff strives to develop such policies and decisions. Neither labor relations nor industrial engineering, though they both have important responsibilities, can run the shop, and no one is more aware of this fact than the staff members.

Criticism of labor relations staffs for lack of interest in efficiency is rarely valid. Actually staff employees, by suggesting policies and by striving for reasonably consistent application of policy, are commonly giving more thought to the goal of long-term efficiency than is the line. It was mentioned earlier that a division vice-president stated the labor relations job as sometimes to "stiffen the back" of the line, and at other times to "restrain the line." Many examples of these twin objectives could be cited, but only a few will be explored briefly to show their relation to the long-term efficiency of the organization.

At the time of one interview with a divisional vice-president in charge of labor relations, an important wildcat was in its third day at a major plant, and pressures for production were building up. The company followed a policy of disciplining for wildcats and of not discussing a grievance during a wildcat. The task of the labor relations director in holding to these two policies was an almost impossible one, and in fact what was believed to be a small compromise with policy was ultimately made.

Company and plant officials had been conferring on the problem for three days. At first the plant manager felt that production was so important that the company should make an exception and discuss the grievance; he later appeared to feel that it would be better just to let the union know that a satisfactory settlement could be worked out if they would go back on the job; and, finally, his position was that he felt confident that they would go back to work if he could promise that there would be no discipline. The division production management appeared to be ready to agree to the no-discipline approach. The labor relations divisional manager finally compromised and agreed that no disciplinary action beyond a written warning would be taken and that this fact could be communicated to one top local union official who could be trusted not to tell anyone else. The division labor relations director had personally dealt with the union official involved and had confidence in his discretion, but he would have preferred to hold out with no commitments, actual or implied. He commented that if he owned a company outright, he would never be his own labor relations director. He would want someone to check him.

Time after time labor relations officials recounted instances where they felt that the line, under pressure for production and quick resolution of problems, wanted to make concessions detrimental to long-term efficiency, to get the question resolved quickly and not interfere with production.

Just as interesting are situations where the line is tempted to take advantage of a particular situation. In one company a particular plant was regularly exceeding production schedules. The plant manager always started the production lines above the scheduled and engineered level. Frequently neither the workers nor the union objected. If, as happened from time to time, the union and workers put up a fairly stiff objection to the work pace, he cut the lines back to the engineered level. The vice-president of the company for production shrugged the problem off with the comment that at least that was the kind of one they could live with for the time being. But the question is how long they will be able to report that they do not have a militant local at that plant.

The director of industrial engineering of one large company reported that a serious strike over "speed-up" had been very fortuitous from the point of view of the industrial engineering department. The strike accomplished what industrial engineering had tried to do for years, that is, to obtain more than lip service to the policy of playing fair with the workers on the engineered standards. The line management had practiced all sorts of tricks on line speeds, product-mix, machine speeds, adding operations, and so forth, to get added product without changing standards or manning. It had taken a strike to establish the staff position.

Staff action that restrains the line in the interest of good labor relations interferes more with efficiency than does action to strengthen the line. Some labor relations policies do give security to employees with some limitations on efficiency. Reasonable efficiency can usually be maintained, however, either by appropriate administration or by creating new policies if one avenue of action is legitimately changed. The interesting point, for example, about good administration of discipline is that neither arbitrary nor wholesale disciplinary action need be taken if an effective disciplinary policy is operating.

Labor relations in its appropriate sphere does not harm industrial efficiency in the long run. There are exceptions, however. A question was raised recently as to whether or not a certain labor relations consultant was still taking money from employers to run their plants. There are at least three instances where this consultant has been the prime mover in making concessions that greatly weakened the competitive position of the companies involved and led ultimately to serious union-management difficulties.

The director of personnel and labor relations in one corporation some years ago pursued a policy that still hampers labor relations in the company. This director, in good technical staff fashion, used to "sell" the president of the company on a particular labor relations or personnel policy. The president would then order the policy or program put into effect by a certain date. This was referred to as the "bingo board" since, at the end of the year, the plants and divisions were scored on the basis of their success in getting these policies and programs into effect on schedule. No consideration was given to differences in local needs and problems. For example, a new job evaluation plan was ordered to be adopted in one division at a very unfortunate time. Their plants were in close geographical proximity, and they negotiated chiefly with one union. A new international representative had been shifted into this territory, and under his influence a new group of local officials had been elected. As a result of the new leadership relations between the company and union deteriorated substantially. This episode proved to be the one bad spot in a long history of good relations.

The job evaluation order came just prior to contract negotiation, and because of the deadline date for putting it into effect it had to be incorporated into the company proposals for negotiation. The division labor relations director and the production manager were very reluctant to introduce a major controversial issue into a negotiation that was going to be difficult at best. However, they received no sympathetic understanding at the corporate level. They did not, as a matter of fact, make an issue of evaluation in the negotiations. A strike was called, and the conciliation representative advised the company to make no additional concessions because the strike was inevitable. During the strike the controversial international representative was moved out of the area by the union. The new international representative worked with the local union and ended the strike without an agreement, an unusual union action. In the improved atmosphere an agreement satisfactory to both parties was reached. Months later, with greatly improved relations and with a closed contract, the company proposed a discussion of job evaluation. With no compulsion on either side since the contract was closed, the parties worked out and applied a job evaluation program, but the division was in disfavor because it was late in accomplishing this. In another division the same evaluation plan was put in against the best judgment of the division. They felt that the particular plan was poorly suited to their job structure. This judgment proved sound, and the plan has continued to be an administrative headache.

The net result of such actions in this company was a total lack of confidence in corporate labor relations. In time the divisions rebelled and the company today, under new management, faces a difficult and possibly expensive task in resolving the wide differences in labor relations policy that had developed among the divisions.

Where individuals and policies in labor relations have been unsuccessful, it has usually been due to essentially poor labor relations. However, there is generally too a lack of appreciation of production requirements and of the production point of view. Sometimes individuals in labor relations take a textbook type of approach in formulating a program but fail to assess its accomplishments realistically. A foreman training program, for example, can be good on paper but fall far short of its objectives in actual operations. Merit rating plans can become a meaningless or harmful kind of ritual. Suggestion plans that are apparently successful may actually accomplish little. Labor relations policies and practices must make sense from an operational point of view, and production officials check and balance the labor relations staff. Increasingly, however, labor relations staff is less subject to legitimate criticism on this point, and it is the line management that frequently follows the path of least resistance.

A Labor Relations-Oriented Line

As has been pointed out, production executives find it difficult not to make small concessions in the face of pressure. Continuous conditioning over the years to get out the production and keep plants on schedule makes them particularly likely to give in to keep the plants rolling. On the other hand, they may take advantage of a weak union or group of employees and thus build resentment and trouble for the future. Experience over the years has demonstrated the weaknesses of these positions, and production executives appreciate increasingly the importance of establishing labor relations policies and holding to them.

A production man's idea of being practical is often to give nothing he doesn't have to, but to give if pushed. One vice-president for production in a medium-sized company with several plants operated openly in this fashion. His policy was never to yield on anything unless a grievance was filed. When a grievance was filed, the first answer was always "no." If there was too much reaction to the denial, then the vice-president stepped in at the appeal stage and settled the grievance by some type of concession. Superficially good labor relations existed in the company, but lower level supervision and the industrial relations director, who reported to the vice-president of production, worked in a frustrating and increasingly deteriorating labor relations environment. The president of the company stayed out of labor relations administration, leaving the direction of this area entirely to the vice-president for production.

A labor relations-oriented line means essentially that the line appreciates the importance of a labor relations policy and a reasonably consistent application of such policy. Various instances could be cited where line officials formulate and practice very good labor relations policies. One machinery company has outstanding labor relations and personnel policies. In this case the president has formulated these policies and guides their administration. In another company the executive vice-president has been the key figure in developing and practicing balanced policies. In still another company two brothers share the top management, and one brother, responsible primarily for manufacturing, has developed very good labor relations. In none of these companies is there a personnel executive of stature or significance.

In other companies the key person has been a labor relations or personnel executive who has had cooperation from line executives, and, in turn, has worked effectively with the line. In larger companies, whatever their organizational structure, differences in the effectiveness of practiced policy are related to the understanding of labor relations on the part of top line officials. Several companies have had improved labor relations after a change in division general managers and higher officials. Labor relations in particular plants are clearly affected by the perception of plant managers and change when the managers are changed. While the ability of the director of labor relations is also important, a good director cannot operate effectively without the cooperation of the top line officials.

Mechanisms for Coordinating Line and Staff

Several procedures appear in particular cases to have contributed to a coordinated approach to labor relations. Staff and line must act as a check and balance system for a unified approach to labor relations. While no specific mechanism is advocated for a particular situation, the following will be discussed: (1) increased decentralization of administration, (2) joint line and staff consideration of grievances, (3) labor relations policy and administration committees, and (4) foreman training.

INCREASED DECENTRALIZATION OF ADMINISTRATION. Such a move en-courages detailed policy development and cooperation between line and staff. There are so many intermingled considerations in decentralizing that they cannot be developed here at great length. Perhaps the most important objectives are to build a strong foreman group and to give initial answers on grievances that management will back up. Usually, though not always, this involves discussing policies in detail to get them down to the lowest operating level.

In multiplant companies, if the plant personnel director's responsibility is upgraded and if the final step of the grievance procedure prior to arbitration is taken in the plant, cooperation will be strengthened. A number of companies, partly consciously and partly unconsciously, have upgraded the plant personnel director's responsibility. The vice-president in charge of labor relations in one large company, which is doing an excellent job in this area, related the company's experience with plant personnel directors. At first, when the labor relations responsibility developed beyond the stage of employment clerk, the plant managers tended to resent personnel directors, and they put weak men in the position. As time went on, particularly because of the pressures of the war, the plant managers began to appreciate the importance of the labor relations job. They began to want strong labor relations assistance and gradually moved in that direction. Eventually, in the opinion of this vice-president, the company developed strong plant teams of plant managers and plant personnel directors. These plant teams became of key importance in the administration of labor relations. Throughout our study good labor relations appeared quite commonly to be associated with strong and able plant personnel directors. The balance of power between plant manager and plant personnel director varied (a point that will be considered later), but making this level a key one in corporate administration encourages cooperation, and tends to make policy effective at the plant level.

Putting the last effective company grievance answer in the plant also encourages cooperation. If divisional or corporate labor relations takes over all grievance decisions prior to arbitration, the grievance process can change subtly in character. Above the plant level, the grievance loses some of its operating problem aspect, becomes somewhat artificial, and is more formally embedded in contract and other technical language. Several companies consequently were in process of shifting the final grievance decision back to the plant. In one large plant, itself a division of a company, labor relations appeared definitely to be functioning better with this third-step decision back in the plant. Both the plant manager and the plant personnel director became more sincerely concerned in decisions and their repercussions. In other companies such statements were made as: "We're decentralizing our corporate labor relations responsibilities"; "we're arbitrating now in the plants"; and "we're spending more and more time in the field." Again, however, this is decentralization within a unified policy framework. Also it must be said that at times divisional and corporate intervention is helpful.[6]

Decentralization of labor relations administration makes it necessary to consider at all levels how to make decentralization effective. It forces consideration of substantive policies to see if they are the best guides that can be established. It forces an understanding among the people involved of what a written policy means. It forces analysis of how policies are actually working. It forces an attempt to define standard practice and variations from standard. Decentralization in administration does not guarantee cooperation between line and staff, but it appears to encourage it as an essential ingredient for making decentralization work. While this discussion has been primarily in terms of large organizations, the more complex setting only emphasizes the fact that pushing down the point where the effective decision is made, if it is to work within a framework of policy, necessitates close cooperation at all levels between line and staff.

JOINT LINE AND STAFF CONSIDERATION OF GRIEVANCES. Some grievance machinery permits management above the foreman level to act without staff representation. Some machinery calls for staff representatives to act officially without line representation. Some machinery has official representation of both line and staff. In one large company in the third step, instead of the plant personnel director acting alone (with staff and line from lower levels), a change was made to action by the plant manager (or his representative) and the plant personnel director. Almost universally throughout the plants that were visited this change was reported to have improved staff and line

[6] This is the case where resolution requires individuals less involved in local conflict. Many multiplant companies favor removing the step prior to arbitration from the plant environment, but this procedure can be quite harmful if real answers appear to come only from this level.

relationships and the effectiveness of management in handling grievances. There is no statistical evidence that joint representation in the
grievance procedure works better than line or staff acting alone. In
a few situations joint action has tended to get away from a "one-man
show" at the top and has encouraged cooperation at lower levels. In
one plant that was studied fairly closely there was a marked increase
in cooperation and understanding at all levels. Informal cooperation
may achieve the same results, but official joint representation insures
continuous joint knowledge and participation.

LABOR RELATIONS POLICY AND ADMINISTRATION COMMITTEES. Some
companies operate at the plant and corporate level with labor relations committees and some without such committees. There is always a temptation when arguing for increased cooperation in some
phase of business to suggest just one more committee. Sometimes
companies operate very effectively in labor relations by relying on informal consultation and feel no need for a committee. A committee
may, however, do at least two things. It may insure more balanced
consultation on important points, and it may emphasize policy considerations more thoroughly than does consultation on a specific
problem.

At the corporate level in one company, plant managers had the
option of consulting with their respective line vice-presidents, the
corporate personnel director, or at times the treasurer. While this
may be criticized as poor organization, it was more than that. At the
expense of consistency, it did give the plant manager some flexibility.
The views of these various men were known to differ on particular
points and, depending on the answer the plant manager desired, he
had a better chance of securing it by consulting with different individuals on different problems at different times. By creating a corporate committee and channeling routine labor relations communication through the corporate personnel director, a distinct improvement in policy understanding was achieved as well as a clarification
of administrative procedure. The committee ironed out inconsistency in corporate policies.

In a second company a top group functioned as a committee, although it was never formally so constituted. The division vice-presidents with the executive vice-president and personnel director began,
under the direction of the executive vice-president, as the negotiat-

ing team for the master contract. This led to a continuing relation-ship to discuss and decide on policy and major administrative de-cisions. After several years the executive vice-president became presi-dent, and the personnel director took over leadership of the group on labor relations matters. The labor relations director gradually assumed greater responsibility, particularly as new men were made division vice-presidents. While the organization has a good backlog of common understanding, there is now a question whether a formal committee should be set up to recreate the degree of mutual under-standing that originally existed.

At the plant level in all companies, at the corporate level in small and medium-sized companies, and even to some extent in large com-panies, labor relations policies and decisions are often dominated by one man. In one fairly large company labor relations actions are clearly dominated by the vice-president in charge of labor relations. The president of the company, after a number of years in which he personally directed labor relations, delegated the responsibility com-pletely to the director of labor relations. While the vice-president for labor relations theoretically holds a staff position in the company, he does not operate in that fashion. Appeal up the line by operating people means continuous support of the director of labor relations by the president. Labor relations in this particular company would be regarded as above average. The director of labor relations is un-questionably capable. If, however, a labor relations committee were charged with the task of reaching agreement on policy matters and important administrative decisions, subject to appeal to the presi-dent, there is good reason to believe that internal friction within management would be reduced.

In many plants labor relations decisions are dominated by one man. In some instances this is a line executive, and in some instances a staff executive. In some cases labor relations appear good, and in some poor. Where labor relations are good, it is difficult to argue about the organizational structure, regardless of its nature. In one company with a large number of plants one plant is frequently singled out as having ideal labor relations. The director of labor re-lations is cited as most directly responsible for this. He has been in the plant for many years and knows all the employees by name. The plant manager spends no time on labor relations because he does not need to. Labor efficiency is good, and grievances are almost unknown.

In another plant of a different company, the plant manager domi-nates labor relations and has dramatically improved both efficiency and labor relations by his manner of dealing with the local union and the employees. If labor relations are relatively poor, then the temptation is strong to criticize organizational structure. If dominated by line, then one can say a stronger labor relations director is needed to assist the manager in a field in which he is weak. If dominated by staff, then the staff man can be criticized for assuming line authority, as well as for being inefficient in his work.

While organizational structure can be varied legitimately accord-ing to the relative abilities of individuals, a joint approach, facili-tated by a commttee arrangement, frequently seems to give balance to policy and administration. Whether labor relations are good or bad, domination by one man raises questions of permanence, sta-bility, organizational efficiency, and internal friction.[7]

The question can be raised whether a special labor relations committee is needed. Cannot an executive committee at the corpor-ate level or a general administrative committee at the plant level serve? In some companies this arrangement appears to work satisfac-torily. A special committee may, however, work better. Many times questions do not seem important enough to voice at the general com-mittee level, though they could advantageously be discussed in a more limited committee. Access to a general committee may be a type of rubber stamping. An arrangement that seemed to work well in one company was a lower level committee that advised the per-sonnel director. Depending on the reaction of this committee to pro-posals, the personnel director would either act through delegated au-thority or voice the question at the executive committee level.

No particular administrative arrangement would be appropriate for all companies. It is suggested, however, that special labor rela-tions committees often can be effective in building cooperation in policy formation and in administration.

FOREMAN TRAINING. Since foreman training is discussed in the con-cluding section of the chapter, there will be only brief reference here

---

[7] Very close study of "one-man shows" would be necessary to determine how they actually operate internally. Some might reflect very superior administrative ability, not necessarily "domination," and some might show only superficial effectiveness. The nature of our study did not allow the kind of close study that is required to appraise these situations.

to its potential scope and significance. Conferences with first line and other levels of supervision can do more than impart knowledge and teach administrative skills. Such conferences can serve in the development of, and agreement upon, labor relations policy. For this reason many companies have given up use of the word "training." Training is too narrow a concept to cover adequately the use of conferences as an integral part of running a plant or company. Discussing the problems, past accomplishments, and objectives of the plant or company with foremen as a staff activity (decisions are not made in such meetings) can develop mutual understanding between line and staff. The major defect of many training programs is that they are too much of a "sideshow." To secure cooperation, emphasis should be on two-way communication and participation as well as on education and training.

Position of Foremen

This section will discuss (1) top management's view of the foreman's job, (2) a foreman's view of his job, (3) an example of foreman problems and steps toward their correction, (4) some simple labor relations objectives, (5) strengthening the foreman, and (6) foreman training.

Top Management's View of the Foreman's Job

There is no question that top management usually has a broad concept of the foreman's importance and his responsibility. This is evidenced by various slogans, such as, "the foreman is management's first line representative," and "to the worker the foreman is the company." It is evidenced too by discussion of the crucial importance of foreman behavior toward employees in maintaining efficient production, good union relations, and good employee morale. Finally, it is at times evidenced by a detailed analysis and description of the foreman's responsibilities and authority.

One company, for example, has a four-page printed statement of the foreman's responsibility, which occupies a strategic introductory spot in the supervisor's manual. This covers seven major divisions of responsibility, of which personnel and labor relations is only one. In addition to labor relations are responsibilities for quality standards, cost functions, production schedules, effective use of machines and equipment, utilizing service departments, and contributing to the development of the company. All of these functions are broken down into various specific statements of responsibility. Within the area of personnel and labor relations there are various responsibilities covering manpower analysis, requisitioning employees, accepting or rejecting employees, induction, training, assigning work, applying the labor agreement, improving job performance, promotion, demotion, preventing grievances, handling complaints and grievances, counseling with employees, warning and disciplining employees, assisting in layoff, control of time worked, safety and health, plant security, fire protection, informing and assisting employees in various ways, and consulting with other line personnel and with staff. All together there are sixteen major categories within the personnel and labor relations area and over fifty specific responsibilities. In all areas, including labor relations, there are about one hundred kinds of responsibility, some being quite narrow and some quite broad.

At the beginning of this responsibility statement there are words to the effect that foremen have the authority necessary to fulfill the responsibilities. Actually the foremen have unrestricted authority on very few of these responsibilities. In some areas their authority is so limited as to be almost nonexistent. In others it is adequate. The fact that the foreman's authority is restricted in many respects does not diminish the importance of the management functions involved, nor does limited authority mean that the foreman does not play a strategic role in carrying out most of these functions.

A detailed listing of foreman responsibilities highlights the broad range of management activities that are carried out, whether effectively or not, at the worker level. In each of these, the foremen have an important role to play. All such written statements tend to emphasize the positive aspects of responsibility and to minimize the limitations on authority. This is understandable from top management's point of view.

The Foreman's View of His Job

How a foreman views his job depends on how top management acts toward him. His position is a frustrating one if he is unreasonably and uncritically held responsible for results. In one unpublished detailed study of a limited number of foremen in several companies, cases were reported where foremen were in exactly this situation. Top managment wanted "no excuses" and "no stories"; they wanted results. In such situations there is an amazing variety of ways in which higher management can second-guess the foreman. Anything that didn't work to the satisfaction of higher management is clearly wrong, and the foreman should have known enough to act differently.

Inevitably under such circumstances foremen tend to cover up and protect themselves in various ways, primarily by not assuming responsibility. If it is possible, they let things ride and do nothing. If workers on a job are supposed under the production standard to "take six passes" at a product, but it is difficult to determine later whether they took three or six passes, why should a foreman get himself into difficulties by interfering with what the workers are doing? He "identifies with the workers" in such situations, in the words of the sociologists. If a situation demands action, the foreman "passes the buck." He consults people in top management until he finds someone who will tell him what to do and consequently relieve him of responsibility. "We have a bunch of weak foremen in this plant; they badly need more training; they always run to someone to get the answer."

There are devious ways to avoid responsibility. In one plant, where foremen were driven hard on their departments' performance, the foremen did everything they could to make a good showing on paper. They protected their loose standards from discovery; they fought to get looser standards; they devised but did not report shortcuts in production; and they cheated in reporting production. Those who did well on paper were regarded as the best foremen. Some achieved some really loose standards, which gave them a high departmental performance rating.

In any particular situation the foreman must make the decision whether or not to consult with higher management. If he is to be judged uncritically by the results, acting without consulting would be very risky. In such an environment foremen are very conscious of the consequences of not consulting because the action taken, judged with the advantage of hindsight, may prove to have been the wrong one. As a result foremen are likely to be afraid to assume responsibility. It is less disquieting to be criticized for consulting too often than to run the risks involved in acting independently.

Insult is added to injury when the foreman, who himself is being judged uncritically by results, at the same time is being told to "treat the worker as a human being; suggest, don't order; listen to the worker's story; put yourself in the worker's position; lead, don't drive; always get the facts before you act; etc." This kind of double standard can indeed be painful.

To the degree that the above attitudes prevail, foremen are likely to feel that their authority is severely restricted relative to their announced responsibilities. Even under favorable conditions, foremen almost inevitably view their job in narrower terms than does top management. If their attitude is also injured by uncritical appraisal of their performance, the foremen may feel and act very much, as unions sometimes describe them, as "errand boys" and "men with flashlights in their pockets."

An Example of Foreman Problems

To illustrate foreman problems a fairly detailed account will be given of the situation in one plant. Many of the conditions found there are general in character, though some are necessarily peculiar to this plant. The plant is only five years old, and most of its specific problems are closely related to this fact. It is, however, part of a company that has good labor relations and well-developed management policies. The local union, composed of many young employees and with inexperienced local officers, is also part of a well-established and well-led international union.

Attention will be given to management problems at the foreman level. The union side of the problem will not be discussed, but one fact that contributed to the plant problem was the very small amount of assistance sought and received by the local union from the regional and international officials. The local union president, who was just under twenty-five years of age, appeared to be associated through his father with a faction that was at odds with the regional office. He wanted nothing to do with the regional office, and the feeling was reciprocal. Whatever the reason, local union officials neither sought nor received assistance, apart from formal relations, and tended to buck the international representatives when they came into the plant on negotiation and top-stage grievances. The local definitely was not controlled or guided by the international.

There were also factions within the local union, and the president was not in a secure position. During the five-year history of the plant he had been voted out for one term and had regained the presidency after a lapse of a year.

The management analysis as here presented is through the eyes primarily of two men, the training director and the second-step grievance supervisor. Both men reported to the plant industrial relations director. An attempt to correct problems began with the replacement of the first industrial relations director by a new director. The new industrial relations director had been in the plant just under one year at the time of the interviews.

Top line management in the plant can best be described as passive to negative with respect to labor relations. The plant manager appeared uninterested in labor relations, though cooperation began under the second industrial relations director.

The problems of the foremen can be appreciated only in the light of today's complex technological and organizational requirements and should not be considered in terms of labor relations alone. These foremen were surrounded by specialists, and the technology in the plant was so complex that their understanding of the machines could be only superficial. Interestingly enough, the staff people in machine design were fast becoming key operating people, called down to the factory floor frequently since they alone understood the more complex machines. Quality control had its specialists and systems. Maintenance had special operating responsibilities, and production control set the schedules. Industrial engineering set standards, the comptroller handled budgets, and inspection operated independently. The line, with the foremen taking the lead, "got out the production" and "maintained quality" in this complex operation.

Complex technology and organization are of course remarkable engines of efficiency, but if one thing goes wrong, problems multiply in all directions. The point need not be developed, but to have foremen who can make key decisions in all the various areas, with staff specialists restricted to advice only, is clearly not operationally possible. In the words of the NICB study, "In the modern business enterprise, many of the vital administrative activities are entrusted to staff."

A first evidence of the foreman problem may be seen in terms of turnover. At the time of the interviews there were somewhat fewer than 300 foremen. Foreman mortality had been in excess of 100 during the previous year. About 70 men were currently trainee-foremen, being engaged in a work and classroom training program lasting about six months. The class instruction of over 100 hours involved personnel, union relations, tools, machines, equipment, costs, and some additional subjects. There were 32 units of study, well-prepared and worked out, in this introductory training. Tests were given to check comprehension. Regular training continued for all foremen under a one-hour-a-week regular personnel development program.

Foremen were hired both from outside and from inside the plant. There were two schools of thought on this subject. At that time the plant was concentrating on hiring from inside, having had a run of bad luck with outside hiring. In spite of preliminary screening, with only about one out of ten of those passed being hired, a high proportion had quit or not made the grade.

The job was regarded as a pressure job because of the fast tempo of production in a complex process. The training director felt that, disregarding the special problems existing in the plant, only a small proportion of men have the kind of personality that could adapt to production conditions.

The grievance rate was very high. Grievances ranged over many subjects with "runs" on particular subjects from time to time. Grievances had little relation to the contract. Almost every grievance that was denied at step one (foreman) was appealed to step two (labor relations supervisor). Grievances denied at step two were appealed to step three (plant labor relations director and union grievance committee).

At step three many step-two denials were reversed or modified. Step three was the crucial one on all types of grievances. Foremen did not know where they stood in many grievance areas. Disciplinary actions regularly did not stand up. Pressure tactics were common, both slowdowns and wildcats. Frequently foremen found out what happened to grievances only through the worker involved. Certain "payoff" types of grievances, such as foremen working, improper call-in, and improper overtime assignment, were an important and somewhat amusing source of income for many employees.

There can be little doubt about the attitude of the foremen. The training director knew them very well. He got acquainted with them as trainee-foremen, he saw them in regular foremen training meetings, they talked with him privately, and they talked with him when they quit. They felt keenly that they were not backed up or supported and that the union was "running the shop." They had no confidence in the plant personnel director, with whom they had little contact. They were subjected to a great deal of pressure by their line superiors, but received little or no understanding from them. Reasons were regarded as excuses and were signs of weakness. While the foremen all felt that their pay and benefits were very good, the rewards were not enough in view of the rat race they were in.

What was the position of the training director? He had only limited confidence in the first plant industrial relations director. He communicated in general terms with the director but never specifically concerning any foreman by name. Communicating with his superior on foremen attitudes did no good, since it resulted in no change in the content of foremen training or plant practices.

The training director's judgment was never sought in connection with trainee-foremen. Doing well in the class part of the trainee-foreman program had no bearing on the man's pay or status. Trainee-foremen were made foremen or dismissed on the judgment of line superiors without any consultation with the training director. Also the director pleaded with his superior that certain trainee-foremen be removed from the group because of lack of ability and because of performances and attitudes that fostered disrespect for the program. This proved ineffective.

The regular foreman-development program was potentially valuable. The content was selected from prepared materials from headquarters by a committee that included the plant personnel director and the plant manager. This material was then gone over in a session with top management in order to adapt it to plant problems. It was then given to lower line officials. The material selected was the most innocuous possible and was in fact never adapted to plant conditions.

The training director went through the ritual of regular foreman conferences, carefully avoiding all of the real problems in the plant. Much of the material was interesting, and some was helpful. Some material was adding insult to injury. It was impossible to get ma-

terial that didn't at times fly in the face of practice. With superior
training facilities, excellent basic materials, and a well-educated
training staff, foremen were indoctrinated in their important responsibilities, which inevitably added to their resentment of actual conditions.

The labor relations supervisor was in a position similar to that of
the training director. In important respects he found it impossible
to exert any influence. He continued to advise foremen in accordance with his view of company policy and the union contract, but
he found it impossible to adjust his actions at the second step of the
grievance procedure to conform with actions at the third step. Inconsistencies at the third step offered no policy guides. In order to get
along with the foremen he stopped discussing problems with the
plant industrial relations director. He did the best job he could,
but he had no chance to build respect for first- and second-step decisions in the grievance procedure.

When a new plant industrial relations director took over that
position, the whole character of labor relations began to change.
Interestingly enough, one of the first things the new industrial relations director did was spend a good deal of time in the factory getting
acquainted with the foremen and listening to them. Gradually they
began to speak frankly with him. An immediate difficulty for the
foremen was control of work time. Absenteeism was high, and employee time off the job was far in excess of allowed time. The cafeteria was jammed at all hours of the day. An analysis indicated that
the average time off the job for those working was a little over an
hour a day. To settle this issue quickly, the cafeteria was locked
except for regular lunch periods.

This action brought a storm of protests. The cafeteria was reopened after a discussion with the union, in which the rules for time
off the job were re-established, and notice was given that discipline
would follow infraction of the rules. The problem was quickly
brought under control.

A quite mechanical disciplinary policy for absenteeism was worked
out. Stated penalties for varying amounts of absenteeism were applied almost regardless of the reasons for absence from work, and
the problem quickly declined. This policy was not intended to be
permanent, but was regarded as necessary for the time being.

A major change took place at the third step of the grievance procedure. Second-step denials were upheld unless there were very strong reasons for modification. A significant number of denials involved a refusal to recognize as grievances under the contract many complaints that had been carried to the third step. The crucial decision on "routine grievances" was pushed back to the second step. The grievance rate began to drop. Most denials stood little chance of reversal or modification because of established precedents under a permanent arbitration system.

Discipline on a wildcat, substantially upheld in arbitration, created a major turning point in the character of contract administration, as far as could be determined. This had taken place in the recent past, and more time was required to assess the results. At the time of the study there were very generally improved employee attitudes and work performance. On the union side the international was beginning to play a more important role.

The morale of the training director was greatly improved. Through discussion with the industrial relations director and plant manager, trainee-foremen performing poorly in the class phase of the introductory program could be taken out of the program. One man had been removed, and the training program immediately began to be taken more seriously. There was still a long way to go in improving the regular foreman-development program, but the problems were now recognized, and the plant manager was working with the plant industrial relations director in suggesting adaptations of material to meet plant problems.

The industrial relations supervisor was now very happy that he had not yielded in the earlier period and that second-step decisions were reasonably consistent. There were policy problems that needed to be worked out, but there was now opportunity to do so through both line and staff. One move had been made in the discipline area. Foremen were instructed on discipline in terms of a "minimum" and "maximum" penalty. They now had both discretion and support in discipline, and this was made clear throughout the plant. However, some foremen had given up on discipline, while at the same time it was feared that some were beginning to be too strict. There was also the question of what other decisions could be pushed back to the foremen.

It is very interesting that in this plant serious problems had never developed in the production standard area. Industrial engineering staff, foremen, and a union time-study steward had throughout worked harmoniously in this area with very few grievances. This was during a period of extensive technological change.

Clearly a "team approach" was beginning to take shape under the leadership of the new industrial relations director. The director had found no difficulty in working with the plant manager. The latter was still predominantly preoccupied with production problems, and there was an open question as to whether he would participate in third-step grievance meetings, but his interest and participation in labor relations had increased. There had been no major shifts in line and staff responsibilities, but the introduction of "management by policy" had clearly begun. In one sense this is a simple case because corporate policies already existed both in addition to and under a master contract. There was no question, however, that the status and significance of foremen changed dramatically in the changed environment.

Labor Relations Objectives

Much of labor relations administration can be put in terms of two simply stated procedural objectives: (1) preventing grievances, and (2) resolving routine grievances at the lower steps of the grievance machinery. The accomplishment of these two objectives has many ramifications, which will be only briefly indicated.

If grievances are to be prevented or resolved as "oral complaints," foremen must be able to determine within tolerable limits what will happen if a formal grievance is brought. To make this determination normally requires service from the staff, either the labor relations staff or some other. Obtaining assistance in the absence of a formal grievance is frequently a key consideration. If staff people are too busy to perform service at the request of a foreman, then the foreman has little influence. If it takes a formal grievance to "get action," then formal grievances are inevitable.

The ability of foremen to do something about a problem appears to be far more important than the extent of their formal authority. Language governing the first grievance step in the contract frequently requires that employees discuss grievances with the foreman before going to the union steward. But language is not crucial because employees in fact have a choice of raising problems with the steward or the foreman. The worker may make a suggestion to the foreman, may orally complain, or may formally grieve. If foremen can be and are responsive to minor suggestions and complaints, and can carry through to investigation and action, formal grievances are much less necessary. It appears, however, that quite frequently formal grievances get far more serious attention than do informal complaints. In such situations the union representative is more important than the foreman, and formal grievances are encouraged.

Resolving routine formal grievances at the lower steps of the grievance procedure is in good part a question of getting the right answer the first time. This, of course, relates to the first point. If, at the foreman level, and at an oral stage, a foreman takes a position unsatisfactory to the employee, the foreman needs to have organizational support for the position he takes. Consultation and investigation can provide the basis for this support.

One multiplant company had a very elaborate review of grievance answers by its foremen. These answers went to a corporate labor relations review board consisting of a chairman with extensive labor relations experience, a labor relations corporate lawyer, and an industrial engineer who reported to labor relations. This board had available elaborate data on grievance dispositions and arbitration decisions. The objective of the board in reviewing foremen answers was not primarily to check the answer in the immediate case. In extreme cases, if an answer was felt to be quite wide of the mark, the committee would communicate back through the plant manager, suggesting immediate reconsideration at the foreman level. For the most part the review was operated as an educational process designed to maintain high standards in first-step answers.

This procedure over a number of years brought a real change in union attitude toward first-step decisions. At one time the union had demanded elimination of the foreman step as being a waste of time and energy. Later this was not the case as there had been a growing appreciation that grievances were more open to discussion at this step than they were later. Positions taken at the first step were likely to hold through all steps, including arbitration. It should also be mentioned that the grievance procedure in this company made some distinctions regarding the step at which different kinds of grievances were to be first filed.

Many grievances in all companies go beyond the foreman level. In several companies a large proportion of grievances are settled at the second step. The step at which different types of grievances are settled was developed in Chapter 24. For purposes of this chapter it needs only to be noted that matters that are not resolved by foremen without a formal grievance are frequently carried to the second step. A high proportion of cases will still be resolved in accord with the answer at the first step.

Getting right answers the first time—answers on which the company is ready to stand—and giving to foremen an opportunity to "get action" in response to their own requests in the absence of formal grievances, creates a basic situation in which foremen are important. They then have a position of leadership that is not restricted to the scope of their "unfettered" authority. Accomplishing these simple objectives reasonably well hinges upon the quality and character of the entire labor relations activity of a company.

Strengthening the Foremen

A number of companies have carried through a program for strengthening the position of foremen. Where this has been successful, far more than the foremen have been involved. In effect an entire new look has been taken at the administration of labor relations within a company. Frequently a key step was to control union pressure tactics. This in turn required an improved grievance procedure. Improving the grievance procedure meant rethinking various areas and phases of policy. Carrying out revised policy gave impetus to foreman training.

To exaggerate somewhat, there is no foreman problem as such. If foremen are having major difficulties, as indicated earlier, this is symptomatic of more deeply-seated labor relations problems. "Strengthening the foremen" fundamentally means creating a labor relations environment in which foremen can operate effectively. This does not necessarily involve a marked increase in the foremen's decision-making authority.

A strong case can be made for giving foremen the key decisions on discipline. Their actions can be reviewed within a broader frame of reference in this area, rather than with respect to individual disciplinary decisions. Foremen normally train employees. They make decisions on employee transfers within their departments. They may or may not make decisions on hiring, layoff, and promotion. They participate in the decisions they do not make. Their judgment is

important in setting production standards. If they do not make decisions with respect to hiring, layoff, and promotion, their judgment
on the relative abilities of employees is normally accepted.

It is hard to say just what decisions foremen should make. The
opportunity for a wider range of foremen decisions appears greater
in some circumstances than in others. Where foremen are given the
authority to make decisions, it should be clear that they are given
the right to be wrong in particular cases. But foremen can operate
without "unfettered" authority so long as they have a real opportunity to influence decisions in the light of their knowledge of men and
operating conditions.

Having a strong foreman group is an essential part of a good
labor relations program, but emphasis on unfettered authority appears in part misdirected. It is doubtful whether expanded authority
is the key consideration. Some companies who undertake to
strengthen their foremen appear to do so without adequate analysis
of their basic labor relations weaknesses. More important, where
companies have in fact strengthened their foremen, it has meant
creating a total labor relations environment that gave foremen an
opportunity to perform more effectively. The authority of foremen
has been slightly increased, but the more crucial changes were the
development and application of policies along with frank and open
communication within the plant or company.

Foreman Training

Our material does not lend itself to a detailed appraisal of foreman training. One point in particular should be made, however.
Foreman training is most effective where it is reasonably well integrated with the actual operation of the business. This, of course, is
simply an additional illustration of the teamwork dimension of labor
relations.

A situation was discussed above in which there was little resemblance between what was presented in the foreman training sessions
and what happened in the plant. Other examples could be cited. In
two plants of one company, the only two plants of this particular
company that were studied, an intensive foreman training program
appeared to be quite off the track. In this case two hours a week
were spent in training with each foreman. Very well prepared material came down from headquarters. Again it was expected that this

material would be adapted to plant conditions, but this was not done. The plant manager gave lip service to the concept of training, but it in no way influenced operations within the plant. The plant industrial relations director was unable to change this situation, and the training director was definitely unhappy about it. Continuous contrasts between what was said and implied in training and what happened in the plant were brought to the training director's attention, although usually in off-the-record private conversations.

On the other hand, conferences with supervisors can be an integrating influence. They can be used to discuss (1) information pertaining to the company's activities, (2) the provisions of the union contract, (3) company policies, and (4) plant problems. It is far better to give out information where there is an opportunity for questions and discussion than to communicate it in written form. The union contract and company policies can be discussed in terms of hypothetical and actual case situations thus laying the groundwork for better understanding of the meaning of the policy. A fruitful use of conferences is to explore alternative approaches to problems, which in turn can be considered for adoption.

In all of these ways conferences are a device that helps in the operation of the business. They are not "training" in the ordinary use of the word. The emphasis is not on imparting knowledge in an academic sense or on teaching skills. The emphasis is on reaching an understanding with respect to the interpretation and application of policies and on devising solutions for problems.

Foreman training can also be used to teach administrative skills. Procedures and techniques can be taught, as, for example, work simplification and setting standards. Human relations skills can be explored—how to handle grievances or how to give orders. These uses of foreman conferences raise complex problems, though clearly they have contributed in particular instances. An important problem in human relations concerns the attitudes and actions of superiors toward foremen. If foremen are expected to coach and assist employees, they most certainly must be treated with at least an equal degree of respect.

Foreman training is now widely practiced by both large and small companies. To what extent this activity is mere window dressing is something of an open question. After devoting considerable thought to the question "what have you accomplished by foreman training?," one training director finally came up with the fact that he had gotten improved parking facilities for the foremen. Not that that wasn't an accomplishment under today's circumstances. It was, nevertheless, a rather startling reply, and after considerable discussion he failed to enlarge upon it as an answer to the original question. On the other hand, many companies appear to be making effective use of foreman conferences. Success seems to depend on avoiding side shows and placing sincere reliance on conferences with supervisors to assist in achieving unified labor relations policy and action.

30 / Negotiation of Union-Management Contracts

THE SUCCESS OF THE PARTIES in reaching agreement depends mainly on an understanding of each other and each other's problems, but negotiations that are well planned and well conducted help bring about a meeting of minds. Our concern in this chapter is with the process of negotiation itself and its bearing on the success of the parties in reaching agreements.[1]

The nominal purposes of negotiations are two-fold: (1) to reconcile differences between the two sides, and (2) to work out ways of advancing interests that the two have in common. The first of these purposes attracts the more attention, but the second is of great importance. Indeed, most of the matters that come before negotiators involve a mixture of conflicting as well as common interests. Furthermore, the objectives of negotiations are not simply to advance the interests of each side. Negotiations are conducted on each side by men who have more or less distinctive purposes of their own. The two sides are not monolithic. The individual union representatives are officers and often aspirants for higher office, with supporters and opponents within the union and sometimes rivals in other unions. Various representatives of management have differing philosophies and different views of their own interests and the interests of various parts of the company. When an association of employers bargains with a union, there are likely to be sharp differences of interest among members of the association.[2] Hence, there must be reconciled differences *within* groups as well as *between* groups.

The organization and methods of negotiation are sometimes a

---

[1] The ambiguous term "bargaining power" will not be discussed here but will be taken to mean the ability to induce the other side to make concessions that *it would not otherwise make*. It means more than the mere fact of obtaining concessions.

[2] Some members are better able to take a strike than others; some are affected severely by certain union rules that are not burdensome to other members.

matter of custom and sometimes one of formal rules. The formal rules may be found in company policies, in union constitutions and bylaws, and occasionally in special agreements. The employer and the union, for example, may agree on ground rules that are intended to save time and to make for more orderly negotiations. Occasionally these agreed-on procedures are fairly elaborate, as illustrated by the bargaining procedures contract negotiated in June 1958 between the Simmons Company and the Upholsterers' International Union of North America as agent for six of its locals. This agreement sets forth in detail how the parties are to conduct their negotiations for a multiplant contract and local plant supplements.

Union Representation in Negotiations

The representation of employees and management in collective bargaining takes an almost indefinite variety of forms. The simplest case of employee representation is that of a local union dealing with an employer. Even this is handled in various ways. Representation is usually by a business agent or a bargaining committee. Business agents who are in a strong position locally may handle the negotiations themselves and may not submit the result to ratification by the rank and file—indeed, some business agents would refuse to negotiate without the authority to make a binding settlement. Other business agents negotiate subject to the approval of the rank and file, which is expected as a matter of course. Some local unions negotiate through specially-elected bargaining committees that report to the membership. The men on the bargaining committee are likely to be the active leaders in the union.

Many unions use lawyers in several ways in their negotiations. Sometimes they are used as advisers to the regular union negotiators; sometimes the lawyers assume the principal burden of negotiating. Two general types of lawyers represent unions. One tries to dominate the local union and to make it dependent on him, frequently by persuading the union to take extreme positions so that it is in constant trouble with the employer. A second type of lawyer may be described as the constructive type. He is a true expert in industrial relations and interested in negotiating the kind of labor-management contract that will benefit both the union and the employer. There is an increasing number of this latter type who are devoted to the trade union movement and are of great assistance to many local unions that for one reason or another receive little guidance from their national unions.

Most national unions, especially the older ones, exercise some control over the freedom of local unions to involve themselves in the hazards and costs of strikes. In its milder form this control involves refusal of the national to support strikes financially unless its prior approval has been obtained. The stricter degree of control requires the national approval for a strike. Before a national either agrees to share in the cost of the strike or to permit the local to conduct a strike, the national is likely to try to settle the dispute through the intervention of a national vice-president or international representative. Although national intervention sometimes undermines real bargaining by the local union representatives, more often than not the international representative provides constructive leadership and guidance that may be lacking or limited in perspective at the local level.[3]

---

[3] The following is a vivid account of how an international representative works with local union negotiators, as given by an international representative of one of the older AFL unions:

Suppose wage negotiations are to start on Monday. The international representative, if he is conscientious, and he usually is, comes to town early, maybe on Friday or Saturday and contacts the local activators to find out just what the local members want. The international man talks the situation over with the local activators, and later with the president and negotiating committee of the local union.

The local people tell the international representative, "we want 35¢." He mutters under his breath "it's a nickel this year," but instead of blowing his top, he asks, "Is that all! Where's the rest of your demands?" So they give him their list, which might run from the top of the table to the floor. He does not squelch them. The international representative has the instinct to feel the reactions of people before they are aware of them themselves. It is not facts that he deals with. He has to deal with the political situation. People like Boulware think collective bargaining is looking at the facts and deciding what is right. Hah! they miss the boat.

Maybe there is a stranger in the meeting that the international representative has never seen before. The international representative figures he is a new committee member or activator and keeps a watch on him to size him up. The stranger might say he wants all of the local union's demands. "Ah hah," says the international representative to himself, "a radical." But he has to find out if he is serious or a blowhard. If he is serious, and if he is competent as well, it is dangerous. The only thing to do is to have him made a foreman or put him on the international staff.

The international representative tries to bring in what other plants have got. For instance, it might be a nickel. He treats what the others have got as a "good agreement" and builds it up, so by the time they enter negotiations, they all know what they want. But he does not chop down their demands. Let the employer do that. Why should we (the union) tell the people what *not* to ask for? It is dangerous and the employer will do it for us anyway. Let the employer do it.

When a union negotiates a master contract covering several plants of a multiplant company, the union is usually represented by a negotiating committee of representatives from each plant, though actual negotiations may be conducted by a small part of the committee or by several subcommittees. Negotiations covering 15 or 20 plants usually mean a very large negotiating group. If the union committee has representatives from each plant, management is likely to want to have representatives from each plant. In negotiating the master contract in one large multiplant company, the United Steelworkers have about 45 representatives and management a few less. In negotiations with two other large companies, the steelworkers start off with 75 to 100 people on the committee. In the flat glass industry the union sent a large committee to bargain with the two major companies. In one automobile negotiation in 1959 the union committee had 17 members, of whom 11 were hourly-paid employees and the others full-time representatives of the union.

If negotiations are to be conducted reasonably, there must be unified leadership among the negotiators who speak for the union and accept or reject company propositions. In an important negotiation in 1955 there was divided leadership in the union committee. The members of the committee could not agree to accept anything the company offered, and a strike resulted. Only with great difficulty and with the help of an outside conciliator was agreement finally reached.

Large committees have both advantages and disadvantages. The

The prime function of the international representative is to crystallize the local situation in his own mind, to anticipate and reveal the feelings of the local union almost before the union itself does. The international man must be sensitive and alert to the local political situation. He must recognize the radicals and determine whether they are competent and seriously militant. But seriously, the international representative must skillfully determine and reveal the local situation to the local union in the light of the situation in the rest of the industry.

If they all leave the negotiations with the feeling that it is not too hot a settlement but it is O.K., what else do you want. You made a settlement the men will work under for another year or two, and that is what you are after. The leadership of a union is interested in a wage settlement—the best wage settlement possible in the light of the local and industry-wide situation. Actually the union leaders are interested in a settlement and that is all. The personnel officer and the union spokesmen are the only ones with the same interests—the need for a settlement. In each group (union and management), there are major differences of opinion, but the union leaders and the personnel people have the same opinion, the need for a settlement. The union comes to the bargaining table committee to get a settlement at almost any cost. A settlement means members, keeping the old ones and getting new ones, dues and the flow of funds to the union, and, specifically, my job.

advantages involve the educational and democratic value of keeping reasonably large numbers of representatives closely informed on the content of negotiation and of securing some degree of participation by them. The major disadvantage is the difficulty of conducting negotiations with large groups. In many situations negotiations begin with large committees on each side, but bargaining teams are reduced after an initial exploration of issues. If teams are not reduced, settlement is likely to take place in informal meetings of key individuals outside of the formal meetings. In some cases small committees conduct the negotiations in the presence of larger groups in a sort of fish-bowl atmosphere. Also negotiations may take place in small committees that continuously report to larger groups. Unions with strong democratic traditions have difficulties in devising representative mechanisms that are not a stumbling block in achieving settlements. Some managements welcome large committees on the ground that representation from every plant gives the company a better chance to spread information about the company and about the management's viewpoint.[4] If the union has a large committee, some managements want a large committee also. Managements say that they want someone present from each plant who has first-hand information of any local conditions that the union negotiators may bring up.

Although arrangements for handling negotiations differ from union to union and industry to industry, the following illustrates the basic steel organization for multiplant negotiations. The union has a wage policy committee of about 170 set up by the convention. Each of the 29 districts of the union is represented on the committee, which is given power by the convention to make and ratify agreements. To prepare for wage bargaining the officers of the union convene the committee. Resolutions and suggestions come from locals throughout the country to the committee, which coordinates and condenses them into a coherent wage policy. This policy is expressed in general terms, such as a "substantial wage increase" or "a general wage increase," with other general statements concerning fringe benefits. In 1959, the union and the 12 largest steel companies set up a negotiating committee of 8.

---

[4] Some companies point out that large negotiating committees expedite negotiations since the unions are unwilling to foot bills for a large number of representatives for a long period of time.

Management Representation in Negotiations

Management may be represented in negotiations by operating officers, employers' associations, lawyers or industrial relations consultants, industrial relations staffs, or combinations thereof.

Representation by Operating Officers

This was the original method of representation, and it is still frequently used, especially in companies too small to have industrial relations departments. Negotiations by operating officers help keep the terms of labor-management agreements properly related to operating conditions and problems. This method has the great disadvantage that operating men can ill afford to take time from their jobs to engage in bargaining, and they are not necessarily capable bargainers. Nothing is more likely to produce bad bargains for employers than impatience on the part of management representatives to get back to their regular jobs. A labor relations staff is selected partly to obtain individuals skilled in the art of negotiation.

Representation through Associations of Employers

The association may be quite informal, consisting of little more than a bargaining committee (as when contractors in small communities negotiate with unions), or it may be a formal organization with dues and a professional staff. There are two general types of association—specialized organizations confined to employers in a given industry, such as the associations in the construction industry, the printing trades, the tool and die industry, the coal industry, and general associations covering plants in various industries throughout a city or area. Especially in industries where there are numbers of small competing employers, the competitive equality made possible by bargains between associations of employers and unions is important alike to the employers and their employees. General associations covering a variety of industries, such as the Associated Industries of Cleveland, and the San Francisco Employers Council, can be invaluable to their members. The Cleveland association makes regular surveys of the provisions of union-management contracts in the city, so that it is prepared to inform its members on prevailing rates of pay, and what are customary contract provisions with respect to vacations, pensions, sick benefit plans, and the like. It also knows whether a union that is negotiating with Plant A is considering a strike against Plant B. The Cleveland association, in addition to giving information and advice, also helps conduct negotiations for members—an important service to many employers too small to maintain specialized industrial relations departments. In 1956, for example, it negotiated 25 contracts with the United Automobile Workers and helped in the negotiation of 10 or 12 more.

Representation through Lawyers and Industrial Relations Consultants

Some companies, finding themselves suddenly organized and without an industrial relations staff (or a staff experienced in labor law), turn to lawyers for representation. Some of the lawyers are tough and sharp, but they are employed to fight the union, not to develop good relations with it. As management and unions learn how to get along together, the demand for representation through anti-union lawyers seems to be diminishing. But many employers who are too small to have their own industrial relations departments and who do not have the services of an employers' association use labor consultant services or attorneys who do not specialize in fighting unions. There are today a considerable number of law firms and labor consultants well qualified either to advise employers during negotiations or to take on the responsibility of negotiating for them.

Representation through Industrial Relations Staffs

In the largest companies there is a strong tendency for the responsibility for conducting negotiations to be assigned to the director of industrial relations and his staff. In large companies it is recognized that handling industrial relations is sufficiently important to call for a man of stature who is well qualified to negotiate for the company. The practice of handling negotiations through the industrial relations staff is steadily spreading to companies of medium size. In a large company the negotiating team is likely to include such members of the industrial relations staff as are needed, plus some one from finance and the legal department, and some representation from operations. The addition of a representative from the legal department is important because with the growth of arbitration, management (as well as the union) wants to be sure that the language finally adopted means precisely what it is intended to mean.

Representation through Plant Managers
and the Industrial Relations Staff

Some companies follow the policy of building up the importance of the plant managers by giving them the responsibility of conducting negotiations with unions. The managers are assisted by the industrial relations staff. The practice of concentrating responsibility for negotiations in plant managers is usually found in multiplant companies where the plants are numerous and small and where separate local agreements are made for each plant. In one large company with many small plants a representative from the national industrial relations staff of the company regularly sits with the manager during negotiations.

There is reason to believe that the efforts of some multiplant companies to transfer negotiations to plant managers are not entirely successful. Some managers enjoy negotiating, but many do not, and even those that like to negotiate find themselves handicapped by the fact that the union committee has far more time for negotiating than the manager can take from running the plant. Hence, if the plant is large enough to have an industrial relations department, this department is likely sooner or later to take over negotiations. Of course most important is not who represents the company, but whether a wise position is taken by the company representatives with respect to the several interests of the firm. These problems were dis cussed in Chapter 29.

Technical and Special Issues in Representation

With the extension of negotiations to such matters as pensions and health and welfare funds, both unions and employers have made greater use of technical advisers in negotiations. A company may bring its economist into negotiations for a day or two in order to answer the economists of the union. A few of the larger unions have established pension departments, health and welfare departments, or social security departments that can furnish technical aid; outside sources, such as insurance underwriters and consulting actuarial firms, are used by both unions and employers. On technical matters much of the real negotiating may be handled by the technicians.

Subcommittees may be created during negotiations to handle special problems. In the negotiations with one of the Big Three in the automobile industry in 1958 subcommittees were set up to work on seniority problems, problems of the skilled crafts, and the particular problems connected with one of the special operations of the company.

Liaison Between Negotiators and Administrators

Whether a union-management contract is practical and well thought-out is likely to depend in considerable measure on whether the men who negotiate it are in close touch with operating conditions. It is not essential that the negotiators be operating men, but it is important that there be good teamwork between the men who make the agreement and those who must operate under it. The problem of proper liaison arises when negotiations are conducted by a lawyer or by employers' associations, when national union representatives enter the negotiations, and even when responsibility for negotiations within a company is turned over to the industrial relations staff.

A large company complains that it must negotiate its agreement with the central staff of the steelworkers, who have nothing to do with the administration of the agreement. There are 16 district directors of the union who oversee the activities of the locals under the agreement, but they are not present at the negotiations. In addition, the district directors are responsible for the activity of many other locals in other industries. The company has no one to whom it can go in the administration of the contract who has participated in the negotiations and who understands what changes were made in the contract and why they were made.

In part of the aluminum industry it had been the custom for the negotiations between the steelworkers' union and an aluminum company to be taken over at the last stage by the top national officers of the union. A leading producer in 1956 took a short strike in order to prevent the negotiations from being taken over (as in years past) by union leaders who do not participate in the administration of the contract. The company hopes in the future to continue to make its settlements with the leaders of the aluminum workers in the steel-workers' union.

The UAW, on the other hand, tends to establish company conference units that are helpful to both the union and the company in developing liaison between negotiation and administration. Both unions and companies need to recognize the importance of the connection between negotiation and administration. In at least some cases there are structural weaknesses on both sides in this connection.

The Unit of Bargaining

Our purpose here is not to explore the effect of the unit of bargaining (the plant, the multiplant firm, or the multifirm group) on the relative bargaining power of the employers and the union,[5] but rather its effect on the problem of negotiating workable agreements. The broader the bargaining unit, the greater is the problem of maintaining unity and of agreeing on a position vis-à-vis the other party.

Few general rules can be laid down as to what determines the preference of employers or unions for different bargaining units. Sometimes different unions dealing with the same company have different preferences, for example, the United Steelworkers and the International Association of Machinists in dealing with the large can manufacturers. The steelworkers have obtained master agreements covering a number of plants; the machinists prefer to negotiate separate agreements for each plant. If the employers turn out a more or less standard product and if labor costs are important and competition is keen, the pressure is likely to be strong among both employers and employees for area-wide or industry-wide contracts. Roughly equal competitive conditions in terms of the labor contract are thus established. There are many such area-wide contracts in American industry but few industry-wide contracts. Furthermore, the tendency of a large part of industry to produce differentiated products and of each enterprise to develop its own methods of production plus the tendency for one large company to pay about what its principal com-

[5] In the case of multifirm bargaining the results depend, among other things, on the degree of solidarity among employers and on whether the position taken by the employers is more or less dictated by the low-cost firms or by the high-cost firms. Unions in bargaining with groups of employers try to divide them, so that much so-called industry-wide bargaining is such in name only.

petitors pay diminishes the pressure for industry-wide or area-wide contracts.

Multienterprise bargaining increases the problem of maintaining adequate liaison between those who negotiate the agreement and those who work under it. The task increases in difficulty as the number of plants or enterprises increases.[6] When bargaining is for a number of plants or enterprises, the special problems of particular enterprises, plants, or local unions may receive little attention. A manufacturer of glass tableware withdrew from an industry-wide bargaining arrangement because other employers were not interested in its special problems. In this industry the national agreement failed to cover day-to-day problems and was described by the leading employer as an "umbrella for the inefficient." Industry-wide bargaining among the railroads has handicapped managements in bargaining for rules changes since rules that are burdensome to some roads are not burdensome to others. Some unions oppose industry-wide bargaining on the ground that it holds back the strongest locals of the union from pushing for better conditions. Also various unions prefer the tactical advantage of bargaining company by company and selecting different companies as pattern setters under different circumstances and at different times.

There are sharp differences within the ranks of employers and unions in their preferences for multiplant as opposed to individual-plant agreements. Some unions have a strong preference for multi-enterprise, or at least company-wide, agreements; others prefer individual plant agreements. The same differences exist among employers. In general, however, the proportion of unions preferring multiplant or multienterprise agreements is greater than the proportion of employers with this preference. From the union standpoint company-wide agreements have the advantage of enabling the union to get the same terms for its members in all plants, thus avoiding charges that the workers in some plants are being favored over those in other plants. From the standpoint of management, company-wide agreements have the advantage of simplicity (the same rules apply in all plants), and they prevent the union from whipsawing the company by using the settlement with one plant to get a still better settlement for the employees in other plants. Regardless of the position

---

[6] On the other hand, the opportunity to compare results in different plants or different enterprises is often quite illuminating.

taken by a company with respect to individual-plant or company-wide agreements pertaining to operations, virtually all concerns prefer company-wide pension schemes. The negotiation of such pension schemes on a company-wide basis has tended to bring into common meetings representatives from all plants of the company and thus indirectly to lay the foundation for company-wide agreements pertaining to operations.

Company-wide agreements (as well as industry-wide agreements) have the disadvantage from the standpoint of labor of preventing the strongest local unions from moving ahead as rapidly as they might. This is the reason why the machinists' union has preferred plant-by-plant agreements in the metal container industry. Company-wide agreements have the danger from the standpoint of management that they lack flexibility and impose conditions uniformly throughout operations where variation of working rules is required. A manufacturer of flat glassware that is now committed to company-wide bargaining would prefer plant-by-plant bargaining because it fears that company-wide bargaining will lead to the spread of wasteful rules and wage payment systems from old plants of the company to new plants. Company-wide agreements make it easier for the union to tie up all of the company's operations by a strike. Company-wide agreements may be inappropriate and subject the company to important competitive disadvantages in case the different plants of the company make different products and sell under very different competitive conditions. In late 1958 and early 1959 an auto parts company went through a long strike to replace a company-wide agreement with the UAW with plant-by-plant agreements. The company makes a considerable variety of products, and its several plants compete with different rivals and under different conditions.

Setting up machinery for company-wide or area-wide bargaining may involve political problems for the union. An illustration is furnished by thirteen locals of the Amalgamated Association of Meat Cutters and Butcher Workmen that negotiates with a New England chain store. The locals have set up a Food Council of delegates, chiefly business agents and presidents, selected by the various local executive boards. The larger locals have more representation on the council than the smaller locals—the Boston local, the largest, has three representatives. The council selects a negotiating committee of thirteen—one from each local. Use of the thirteen-man committee was prompted by the fear of each local that its interests would not be protected if it did not have a man present at the negotiations. The thirteen-man committee proved cumbersome, and with the development of greater cooperation and unanimity among the locals, the actual work of negotiating was delegated to a smaller group of five or six of the thirteen. The smaller group may not consummate a settlement of its own but must report for approval to the full thirteen-man committee. Each of the contracting locals agrees to make no separate agreement with the company once the Food Council's negotiating committee has signed the contract.

It is difficult to summarize what is the trend with respect to the unit of negotiation. It is perhaps true that in the long run the tendency is for the unit to become larger. But in a few instances there has been movement away from company-wide bargaining units. A related and important question is what bargaining issues are appropriate for negotiation in the company-wide master contract and what issues should be left to local determination in local supplements. In practice there is clear variation in the way managements and unions have defined the scope of central and local bargaining.

Preparation for Negotiations

Preparation for negotiations ordinarily involves consideration of two principal matters: (1) the general position that the union or the company will take in negotiations, and (2) the specific contract changes that the union or the company intends to make.

General Positions of the Parties

Unions and employers need to be making continuous studies of changes in wages, markets, technology, and of industrial trends generally in order to decide what changes are needed in the labor-management contract. As a basis for determining the approximate size of the package that would be appropriate, companies and unions participate in local, regional, or national surveys of changes in wages and employee benefits and draw on materials issued by the U. S. Bureau of Labor Statistics and various employer associations, such as the American Newspaper Publishers' Association, the Associated Industries of Cleveland, the San Francisco Employers' Council, the

Glass Container Manufacturers' Association, the National Metal Trades Association, the wage settlement reports of the National Industrial Conference Board, the Bureau of National Affairs, and others. The data are fairly abundant but scattered and often quite incomplete, especially with respect to employee benefits. A good regular statistical picture of wages in the United States is lacking. A few large companies regularly exchange information on the earnings of their employees.

From time to time special advance studies are made of problems of particular interest to the employer or to the union that are expected to enter into negotiations. The airline pilots have studied the probable manning requirements of jet planes and the effect of jets on employment opportunities. The International Ladies' Garment Workers Union, from its knowledge of the structure of the industry, has tried to develop labor-management contracts that would impose the union's wage scale. One of the most noteworthy studies is that made by Professor William Haber of the University of Michigan and associated economists of employment trends in railroad maintenance-of-way work. This study was done in 1956-57 for the Brotherhood of Maintenance of Way Employees and was paid for by the union. The title of the work is *Maintenance of Way Work on United States Railroads,* and the circumstances that led the union to arrange for the study are explained at length in Chapter 12, "Union Policies Toward Technological Change." The union has published the study to make it available to managements. It is intended to serve as the basis for a bargaining program for the union, although the recommendations in the study are the author's. The study points out that the absence of increase in railroad mileage and steady progress in technology must be expected to decrease more or less steadily the number of jobs in maintenance-of-way work. The study asks "What should be union policy in face of the anticipated decrease in the number of jobs?" In particular, the study asks whether the union should seek to compensate for decreasing employment opportunities by striving for a reduction in the hours of work. The authors reach the conclusion that merely reducing hours in order to create more jobs would not solve the problem; it would simply cause the problem to take a different form.

Other notable examples of advance preparation and forward planning are the special separate studies made by the UAW and the Ford

Motor Company of the so-called guaranteed annual wage prior to the negotiations of 1955. The union published and put in circulation for discussion among its members and among employers a carefully developed and detailed plan for a guaranteed annual wage. The Ford Motor Company alerted by the union to the fact that demands for some sort of guarantee would be presented and would probably be a strike issue and fearful that the company might find itself forced to adopt the union approach, set up a study group to explore the problem. The company study group was established more than a year before negotiations over the new contract began. The Board of Directors laid down three major requirements.[7] At an appropriate time in negotiations the Ford company representatives brought forth their carefully prepared plan of supplemental unemployment compensation, which was accepted with only minor modifications.

The International Longshoremen's and Warehousemen's Union and the Pacific Maritime Association have developed an agreement to guide their further negotiation of methods of sharing the savings from more efficient ways of handling cargo. This applies particularly, but not exclusively, to "containerization" (the handling of cargo in large containers). The two parties agreed on the desirability of reducing cargo handling costs in order to attract business back to the ports. They also agreed on the desirability of preserving the present registered force of longshoremen as the basic work force in the industry and to share with that work force a portion of the net labor cost saving to be achieved by mechanical innovations, removal of restrictions, and other means.

Most unions and companies before going into negotiations survey their situation and plan their position, but there is still surprising lack of preparation in some cases. In March 1957 a company called up its employers' association in a large Middle Western city and asked that a representative come out to help with negotiations. The

---

[7] The three points were: (1) It should not shackle management's freedom to manage; (2) it should have a definitely determinable cost with a definitely limited liability; (3) it should not offer unemployment benefits so great as to remove the incentive to work.

It has also been pointed out that the plan was designed to accomplish the other purposes, namely (1) to provide a means of supplementing benefits to laid-off Ford employees under state unemployment compensation, and (2) to minimize the danger of available funds being exhausted by payment to low-seniority employees to the detriment of high-seniority employees, who might subsequently be laid off. James F. Bird and Grace Gluck, "Ford's Unemployment Supplements," National Industrial Conference Board, *Management Record* (July 1955), p. 266.

company requested that the representative arrive not later than 2:00 P.M., as negotiations were to begin at 3:00 P.M.

Specific Union Proposals for Change

In the 1948 General Motors negotiations the union proposed deletion or changes in 132 paragraphs, leaving only 32 minor paragraphs unchanged, and in 1950 the union asked changes in 40 per cent of the 152 paragraphs. In the 1959 steel negotiations the union asked for over 250 changes. The large number of proposed changes do not mean that the union thought the contract was worthless. Someone in almost every local is likely to want to have certain language changed. It is easier for the union to pass on the proposals to the employer than to assume the onus of rejecting them.

Unions have different ways of selecting their demands. Local union bargaining committees may receive instructions from the local meeting. It is often easier to approve a proposal that some member or group wants to make than to alienate some members of the union by refusing to include their pet idea. Consequently there may be little connection between the nominal demands of the union and the proposals for which the negotiators seriously bargain. But the negotiators have a good idea of what the members really want. Rank and file influence is shown by the large number of wage settlements that have taken the form of straight cents-per-hour increases in contrast with percentage increases. It is shown also by the rapid spread of health and welfare funds, when a desire for this protection developed in the postwar years.

In the case of multiplant bargaining the various locals are given an opportunity to submit proposals. The result is likely to be the long lists of demands already referred to. The employees in each plant (or some groups of employees) are likely to want certain changes in the labor-management contract. But in multiplant bargaining, as well as local bargaining, the proposals on which the union negotiators really concentrate are determined largely by a few leaders of the union in the light of their knowledge of the desires of the rank and file. In the case of prominent national agreements, such as in steel and automobiles, the influence of the leaders is particularly outstanding. The rank and file may find themselves proposing something, such as supplemental unemployment compensation, that they had not thought of, or they may find themselves suddenly demanding the sharing of profits only a few years after their leaders had strongly denounced profit sharing.

National unions exercise varying degrees of control over the proposals made by local unions. For example, the Upholsterers' International Union has established minimum standards which it expects its local unions to obtain. Locals that do not negotiate the minimum standards are required to give an explanation to the national. Various degrees of such influence and control are to be found.

As a matter of historical curiosity, the rather formal arrangements for proposing changes in the contract that prevailed for many years in the national collective bargaining in the flint glass industry should be mentioned. The agreement was negotiated each year in August at Atlantic City. The national constitution of the American flint glass workers' union provided that proposals for changes in the agreement must be considered by the local unions in January. Any changes recommended by a local were sent to the national secretary in February. He sent the collected proposals to the trade in March, and the various locals voted approval or disapproval. The result of the vote was announced in May, and the secretary sent the proposed changes to the manufacturers' association that month. The union held a convention early in July, at which a final position was taken on proposed changes in the agreement. Negotiations began late in July or early in August, and propositions were taken up one by one—first a proposition from the union, next one from the employers.

A recession produces special demands of temporary significance, such as the one made on one of the Big Three automobile makers in 1958 that overtime be limited to two hours a day and eight hours on Saturday. This demand stayed on the table for several months. A recession also makes unions sensitive to the contracting out of work, and demands for restrictions on contracting out were numerous in 1958 and 1959. But in spite of the recession some companies succeeded in broadening their right to contract out work.

Specific Company Proposals for Change

Management must be prepared to answer the union demand for changes in the contract. In addition, the management is sure to find that some parts of the contract have been giving trouble and must be prepared to propose specific and carefully considered changes that would relieve the difficulties. One of the Big Three automobile manufacturers found that 60 per cent of the grievance case load was generated by five sections in the agreement—those dealing with (1) foreman working, (2) overtime, (3) rates and classifications, (4) discipline, and (5) promotion. Another automobile company is not content to study only those parts of the contract that are causing problems. That company, among others, studies how *all* parts of the contract are working and says that it learns as much from studying the parts that are working well as from those that are causing trouble.

Various steps are taken by different managements to prepare company proposals for improvements in the contract. A manufacturer of electronic equipment prepares management's proposals (1) by reviewing all grievances that have reached the third step in the grievance procedure during the last year (such grievances are likely to indicate ambiguity in the language of the agreement) and (2) by conferences between division industrial relations staffs and operating staffs on changes or special features needed in the agreement. For example, the rule governing management's right to work short time before invoking seniority needs to be different in some divisions of the company from others. An increasing number of managements keep systematic watch on how each section of the labor-management contract is working so that management at all times has a quite definite idea what changes are needed. A large maker of flat glassware maintains a "bargaining book." Two pages are devoted to each clause in the labor-management contract. On the left-hand page is the clause as it now stands; on the right-hand page is the clause as management would like to see it written. The help of operating men, including foremen, is sought in working out changes that would improve the agreement.

In an airplane manufacturing company where negotiations are conducted by the industrial relations staff, the industrial relations people meet with all levels of supervision to get suggestions and ideas for contract changes. A multiplant aluminum manufacturer whose industrial relations staff handles negotiations brings in the heads of the divisions for two or three weeks prior to negotiations. There is also a review of problems by plant industrial relations men, who are asked to indicate changes that they think should be made in the labor agreement.

A manufacturer of metal containers, which opened negotiations with the steelworkers about October 1, 1959, began meetings with the division industrial relations directors early in January of that year. From these directors the central industrial relations staff obtains a catalogue of provisions in the contract that have caused trouble—ambiguous language that needs improving, and local practices that should be changed or standardized.

In a company with many widely scattered, small plants, in which negotiations are handled by local plant managers, the local managers are guided in making proposals by a list of check points supplied by the national industrial relations staff of the company. Simultaneously a general review is made by the central office. When the proposals of local managements are completed, they are reviewed by the central industrial relations staff.

Another management is assisted in preparing its case by the activity reports on industrial relations that each plant submits to central personnel each month. These reports are not statistical summaries but are reports on significant developments. They are useful in helping the company anticipate what it is going to hear from the union. These reports enable the negotiators to have material on hand to answer the other side promptly.

In general one may say that there is a close connection between the quality of the administration of the union-management contract and the quality of the preparation for negotiations. Good administration by a management (or a union) means that the management or union is well informed and is able to take an intelligent position in negotiation. Managements should bear in mind that the opportunity given by negotiations to answer questions raised by the union is an extremely valuable one. No information registers quite so strongly as that given in response to a specific question or objection raised by the other party.

Recession affects the choice of proposals by management as well as by unions. Thus, the competitive pressures accentuated by the recession of 1958 led a few companies to insist on breaking away from company-wide contracts and to take strikes in order to win separate plant contracts.

A large milk processor and distributor, which makes many local agreements negotiated by plant managers, does a large part of its preparation after the first session with the union. Management at the first session makes no proposals or suggestions and does not argue over issues. It tries to find out what the union wants and why. Meetings are adjourned for one to four weeks while the central industrial relations staff and the local management review the discussion at the first session, determine the essential issues, and decide what the company should do.

Methods of Negotiation

Negotiations are becoming more orderly and businesslike, although they leave much to be desired. The union and management delegations are frequently headed by men who have served before as chairman and who have learned the need for order. There is general agreement that profanity is less frequently used, and some managements have made it clear that their representatives will promptly leave the meeting if abusive language is used.

Agreements that the two sides will refrain from publicity during negotiations are becoming increasingly common and appear to be closely observed. With large committees there may be some speaking to the gallery, at least during the early stages of negotiation, even though it does no good without publicity. Indeed, with a large committee of forty or more members, time may be allowed to permit the local representatives to present their views. But then serious negotiations must be undertaken by a small group of union and management people.

The teamsters in negotiating with one association wanted to hold closed sessions, with only one or two people on each side rather than with a full union committee as the association preferred. The teamsters wanted commitments for future years without making these commitments known to anyone but the negotiators. In the judgment of the employers, the union did not want active interest and participation by members.

This association has taken a firm stand against this kind of negotiation, and its members expect to know what is going on. Furthermore, they feel secret and unwritten agreements create a suspicion of dishonesty and sellouts. Finally, secret negotiations conflict with the policy of the association of encouraging interest and participation by its members in its affairs.

Particularly in the case of critical national negotiations involving issues that relate to public policy or that have pattern-setting consequences, the external pressures on the parties are likely to be very great. These pressures may come from other companies, unions, or the government. Under such circumstances, especially when an impasse develops in negotiations, the parties tend to feel strongly that public statements are necessary for support. An effective public relations program necessitates the oversimplification of issues and the use of slogans. The public statements make it harder to resolve the issues, and there is no easy answer to this dilemma. From the standpoint of the collective bargaining process, public commitments complicate enormously the problem of reaching a settlement.

Complete stenographic transcripts of negotiations have been made in a few cases (in the General Motors-UAW negotiations at one time, for example) but are now unusual. One union officer observed that it is bad enough to quarrel over the meaning of the contract without getting involved over arguments as to the meaning of the transcript. Stenographic records have other disadvantages. They discourage talking by some members of the committee, and they encourage formal speechmaking "for the record." Stenographic records retard the give-and-take of negotiations by forcing frequent recesses for "off the record" consultations and caucuses. But in one important negotiation both parties want a transcript and read agreed interpretations of the contract into the record. The contract is changed less frequently than the interpretations. Both parties approve the flexibility they have developed in modifying interpretations.

Negotiations are easier if the committee has definite proposals to work from. The usual procedure in negotiation is to put aside difficult issues and concentrate on items on which the parties are not far apart. All agreements on specific items, of course, are tentative—depending on acceptance of the agreement as a whole. By beginning with problems on which agreement can be obtained it is possible to establish a pattern of agreement. Success in disposing of a few of the easier issues puts the parties in the best possible mood for attacking the thorny problems.

Agreements gain in authority if they are ratified by some body considerably larger than the negotiating committee. When agreements are negotiated by a local union, submission to the membership for ratification is usual. In the case of a multiplant or multienterprise agreement, submission to the entire membership may be cumbersome and impracticable. Hence, it may be ratified by a representative body. In the steel industry and the rubber industry agreements are submitted to the wage policy committee of the union. Ordinarily a majority vote is enough for ratification, but occasionally the rule is different. The flat glass workers had great difficulty in settling a strike in the winter of 1959 because the union rule required unanimous approval, and two members of the committee refused to agree to the proposed settlement.

Important Recent Developments

The two most important developments in negotiations in recent years are (1) the growing willingness of employers to take the initiative in proposing changes in the contract and (2) the growing appeal to facts as a basis for defining and resolving issues and finding out what the parties really want.

During the early years of collective bargaining in many newly-organized plants virtually all proposals came from unions. Managements undertook to concede as little as possible. But some managements soon decided that the negative approach to bargaining hurt them in the eyes of the workers and gave workers a bad conception of management. The negative approach caused managements to appear to be against gains for the workers and gave unions a monopoly of favoring such gains. Hence, managements soon began to make proposals of their own, and some of the most important ones that have been considered in negotiations have originated with management. Thus, General Motors took the initiative in 1948 when it proposed the improvement factor. General Electric has adopted the policy of offering early in the negotiations about all that it expects to give. In 1958 the Big Three automobile manufacturers made a substantial offer early in the negotiations and conceded very little more. In the summer of 1956, when there were large wage increases in the paper industry, a prominent paper company agreed to re-open several months early on wages in return for the union's willingness to negotiate an entire new contract. The union was indignant over the company's best offer, but agreed to tell its members about the offer. The company felt that it could not trust the union to tell the story. By mail and the press it showed what the increases on specific jobs would be. Influenced apparently by the favorable reaction of the rank and file to the company publicity, the union leaders recommended acceptance of the company's offer, and it was accepted.

If negotiations are to be conducted on the basis of factual study and discussion of the various proposals, time should be given each side to study and reply to the proposals of the other. In a few cases arrangements have been made for the formal exchange of propositions. The exchange for years in the industry-wide collective bargaining in the flint glass industry has been mentioned. The written agreement governing collective bargaining between the Simmons Company and the Upholsterers' International Union provides for such an exchange. Article IV of the agreement stipulates that "all proposals regarding either the Master Multi-Plant Working Agreement or Local Plant Supplements shall be consolidated and presented in writing by the respective negotiating committee chairman to the other party within thirty days from the first notice by either party of desire to negotiate. . . ."

The appeal to facts gathered in special studies can substantially affect the outcome of negotiations. A manufacturer was confronted with a demand from the steelworkers that it adopt a job evaluation plan based on the cooperative wage study of the steel industry. The manufacturer knew that acceptance of this proposal would distort many relationships in its wage structure. By gathering facts showing the effects in specific cases the management was able to persuade the union to join with the company in working out a plan designed to meet the needs of this particular company.

A noteworthy example of use of facts to get the union to change its bargaining position is that by the flat glass manufacturers, who in 1955 got the union to modify its demand for a guaranteed annual wage or supplementary unemployment insurance plan. Late in 1954 the flat glass workers began to work up interest among the rank and file in the so-called "guaranteed annual wage"—later given the more realistic title of "supplementary unemployment benefit." In January 1955 the union officers began a tour and held mass meetings among employees to explain the plan to them.

One company did not want to remain silent in the face of the union campaign, but it also did not want to write to the employees at their homes because that might be interpreted as an effort to undermine their confidence in their leaders. The foremen, however, were receiving many questions about the so-called "guaranteed annual wage." Hence, the management decided to devote one of the regular weekly meetings with the foremen to the subject. The company also prepared a memorandum of five or six pages for the foremen and encouraged them to talk with the men about it.

In the negotiation with the union, a representative of the company took half a day to present the case against the guaranteed annual wage. He pointed out that nearly half of the 36 members of the union bargaining committee had never been laid off, and that virtually none of the others had been laid off during the past ten years. He asked what the supplementary unemployment benefits would mean to high-seniority men. The result was that the union bargaining committee was not willing to make a strike issue of the union demand, and a compromise was reached in which the union and the companies agreed to make a joint study. The final outcome was the acceptance of a security benefit plan that called for an individual savings account for each employee.

In contrast with the resourcefulness shown by the glass companies was the defeatism displayed by a steel fabricating company. The management decided in 1956 that it would be useless for the company to study the problem of supplementary unemployment benefits on the ground that whatever was done in basic steel would be forced on the company. Consequently, the company made no intensive study of the subject and negotiated on the basis of what happened in steel. The company's attitude was: "All our research would be obsolete, so we feel there is no sense in preparing."

Comments on Negotiations and Strikes

While, as previously stated, no attempt will be made to analyze the ambiguous and complex term "bargaining power," it must be recognized that negotiations take place under varying circumstances. Two extreme situations may be noted. In one division of a large company bargaining was on a plant basis. The division had about a dozen plants, practically identical in character and widely separated geographically, and dealt with various unions in these plants. The labor relations director explained that they had no "bad" contract clauses in these plants. They simply refused to agree to a clause that was not satisfactory to them. They had not had strikes in the plants, but, while their policies appeared constructive, it was perfectly clear that any plant union that struck would have been in a hopeless situation.

On the other hand, one large teamster negotiation was described as follows. The union sent telegrams to a large number of companies informing them that a master contract would be negotiated. At the appointed time and place the union presented the proposed contract. The union leader made a short speech to the effect that the sooner everyone signed up, the easier it would be for them. At least in this instance there appeared to have been little cohesion among employers and substantially no negotiation in the process of settlement. Industries with many small employers, highly competitive, and with diverse interests at times appear to be unable to develop effective associations for bargaining purposes.

There are, as the above examples indicate, some negotiations in which one or the other party is in a very strong position to dominate, but they are very few in number. In discussing the process of negotiation in most bargaining relationships it was quite clear that each party had the ability, in the event of a strike, to inflict serious loss upon both parties. This does not mean that in some abstract sense there was an equality of bargaining power, but only that neither party could undertake a strike lightly.

Granted a situation in which either party can inflict serious loss on the other party, it is far from easy to explain the course of negotiations in particular situations. Many times in the course of interviews, for example, a management official would point out undesirable features in a contract. The inevitable query was, "if it's so bad, why did you agree to it?" And the equally inevitable reply was, "why, we couldn't take a strike over that." It was quite fascinating to discover the multitude of reasons why companies could not take strikes. Their financial position was never quite right; it was either too weak or too strong. If it was too weak, it was impossible to survive a strike. If it was strong, a strike was simply unthinkable. For example, one company with 37 mutual consent clauses explained that it could not take strikes over small issues because of its very satisfactory profits. And, of course, there were a wide variety of ways in which companies could lose competitive standing. Consumer goods industries, raw material industries, machinery industries, pipe line industries—all industries and companies had their particular reasons for being vulnerable.

But is unwillingness to strike or to take a strike an adequate explanation for many questionable contract provisions? Various bargaining relationships may be reviewed in which strikes have been infrequent or non-existent and in which power differences do not appear marked, but where differences in contract terms and in attitudes of the parties toward each other have resulted from negotiations. There are many relationships in which there is little hostility. Year by year negotiations take place, and neither party considers seriously the prospect of a strike. Neither party is disturbed by the terms of the settlements. The needs of each party have been adequately met. There are also relationships that appear to be peaceful because questionable concessions have been made. In several quite prosperous companies peace appears to be based on questionable contract and economic concessions, as was the case also with some weaker companies. There are also degrees and patterns of hostility. There may be a pattern of questionable concessions or a sort of armed truce under which both parties appear to fare reasonably well.

A review of bargaining relationships in an industry or in a community shows variations in negotiation and in contract administration which to be sure have elements of difference in power positions, but in which power is not an adequate explanation. Differences in attitudes and policies, as well as bargaining power, explain the variations.

In most situations the process of negotiation appears to have improved with the growing experience of the parties. This does not mean that parties do not reach an impasse at times with a strike being the consequence. It does mean that parties are less likely to stumble into a strike. In the course of the study a substantial number of strikes were discussed. In a few cases they were the result of unskilled negotiation, particularly a poor appraisal of the disposition toward a strike by the other party. In one case, for example, a management proposed a wage reduction. The union took this proposal as a prelude to a "no-increase" settlement, and aroused membership opposition to a cut in order to have a victory in a no-increase settlement. But the employer was in earnest, and a strike resulted. A high official in the union said that he would never have gotten into that position if he had realized that the employer actually expected a wage cut. In another case an employer made a proposal purely to trade it off later. The union reacted violently against management's "trading horse," with the result that some top management officials refused to concede. The labor relations director commented that he had never before gotten himself into such a mess. It then required an effective mediation to get management to concede a completely arbitrary proposal.

Negotiations are conducted increasingly by experienced individuals. Neither party is likely to get "boxed" into a strike or allow a strike to take place without making an offer or concession which represents a position on which the party is prepared to take a long strike. Generally the parties realistically appraise each other's position, and an intelligent settlement is achieved.

Of course, there have been relations that deteriorated over a period of years and culminated in a serious strike. While it is not universally true, many such strikes in retrospect appear as turning points in union-management relations. A strike can have a definitely sobering effect on both parties. It is also not uncommon for such a strike to bring in its wake changes in leadership and in basic policies.

In labor relations a strike is usually regarded as a failure of collective bargaining. From the point of view of both the company and the union the costs of a strike generally exceed the short-run gains involved. Settlements once they are achieved commonly appear to the outside observer to be ones that reasonable men could have reached without the costs of the strike. In addition, the process of negotiation usually appears to function poorly in situations that involve strikes. In negotiations that result in strikes very commonly one or both parties enter the negotiation expecting a strike to take place. Instead of narrowing and resolving issues, the parties hold stubbornly to their positions, and a strike results. In some such cases tactics were designed to cast the other party in a poor light.

The intention is not to "whitewash" strikes, but to state that a strike, analyzed as part of a longer labor relations history, may take on quite a different aspect from the short-run view of an antagonistic and poorly-conducted negotiation. Not infrequently the real issues in a strike have been building up for some years, and the results may be reflected over many subsequent years. This statement appropriately should be documented by describing and analyzing a substantial number of strikes. A lengthy memorandum was prepared in connection with the study for this purpose. But the difficulties of significant but disguised analysis are extremely great, and detailed analysis will not be attempted. It must be stated, however, that the authors were considerably impressed by the number of instances in which serious strikes had been constructive turning points in particular histories of union-management relations. Some of these strikes, judged in their contemporary setting, had the earmarks of decidedly irrational warfare. For example, one can look back on a 1948 "go-for-broke" strike with a realization that it was rooted in developments dating from at least 1940 and that it brought new employer leadership and new union attitudes that resulted in a gradually changing character of the relationship in the next decade.

Issues in negotiation and the process of negotiation must be viewed broadly. Pattern-setting, pattern-following, changes in the economic and political climate, changes in the fortunes of particular industries and companies, changes in the general and particular climate of union-management relations all have their effects. The process of negotiations reflects many circumstances, not the least of which is the leadership qualities of the individuals involved. To separate process from substance, as this chapter attempts, is hazardous. But improving the process of negotiation should in itself be a conscious goal of the parties.

31 / *Emerging Characteristics of Collective Bargaining*

DURING THE LAST twenty years orderly industrial relations have been established gradually throughout most of American industry despite the tendency of many newly-established unions to use slowdowns and wildcat strikes and the tendency of many managements to practice appeasement.

Many new bargaining relationships started off without much understanding by either side of union-management contracts. Instead of handling all complaints through the grievance machinery provided in the agreement, unions used threats of economic pressure to get quick favorable action. Managements in many cases failed to stand up for their rights. This was true even in companies that in pre-union days had strongly opposed unions. Company operating executives or industrial relations executives did not want their records marred and their chances for advancement jeopardized by labor trouble. A stoppage of production would look bad in their record, so they made unwise contract and other concessions, many of which turned out to be quite expensive for the employer. The pressure for concession was increased by the war and by the large profits of the postwar boom, which made many managements extremely reluctant to lose production.

The problem of establishing orderly industrial relations was complicated by the internal political characteristics of unions. The burst of union membership between 1935 and 1945, a unique decade in the history of the labor movement in the United States, was essentially a grass roots phenomenon. The movement had a crusading spirit, challenged the traditional structure of unions, was opportunistic in character, and lacked experienced leadership. Industrial democracy was on the move, and this movement protesting management authority could not be expected to accept "responsible" unionism quickly. The grievance process and direct action reflected this

946

tradition of democracy, and an important continuing variable in union-management relationships is the internal political character-istics of particular unions. In many cases management has been forced to operate while subject to undisciplined and highly "demo-cratic" challenge. In other cases management has been confronted with extreme positions and pressures from highly disciplined and autocratic unions.

The practice of appeasement has some tendency to perpetuate it-self because once a management yields to threats, it gives the union an incentive to use threats. It is a fact of greatest importance in the in-dustrial relations history of the United States, however, that in most plants direct action by unions and appeasement by management are dying out. There are several reasons for this.

As unions have gained organizational stability and experience, as their objectives have been more adequately achieved, and as griev-ance and arbitration procedures have been established, pressure tac-tics have become less necessary. At the same time, experience has shown managements that the practice of appeasement soon becomes intolerably expensive. Managements wanting to abolish costly poli-cies and practices have often had to demonstrate their determination by accepting long and expensive strikes. Some of the important re-cent strikes (in International Harvester, Westinghouse, Eaton Man-ufacturing Company, Pittsburgh Plate Glass Company, and the steel industry in 1959) represented in considerable measure efforts by companies to regain operating efficiency lost through a process of gradual erosion.

What have been the developing characteristics of industrial rela-tions in American industry? They may be classified into five groups: (1) the narrowing of the scope of managerial discretion; (2) the de-velopment of management by policy; (3) the introduction of impor-tant changes in management structure; (4) diversity in the character and results of collective bargaining; and (5) the growth of adjust-ment in contract administration.

Narrowing Scope of Managerial Discretion

The scope of managerial discretion has been narrowed in two principal ways: by the terms of the union-management contract and by the administration of the union-management contract. The union-management contract limits managerial discretion in three principal ways:

1. By requiring that management follow rules for layoffs, transfers, promotions, retirements, assigning overtime, setting production standards and rates,

2. By requiring that management be "reasonable" or "fair" or that management act only with just cause, or after consultation with the union, or with the consent of the union,

3. By prohibiting certain types of conduct, such as excessive overtime.

Companies have differed greatly in the extent to which they have agreed to restrictions on management discretion. Some companies have always insisted on keeping adequate control of the shop. These companies, of which General Motors is an excellent example, study every proposal carefully to determine its probable effect on shop control. Some companies, for example, have insisted on retaining the right to assign workers; others, less interested in control of the shop, have bargained away the right to have employees work outside of classification. The rights of management have been restricted in various ways and degrees by seniority. While most seniority arrangements represent a constructive compromise, a few impose unreasonable burdens on management.

Limits to management's control of the shop depend very decidedly on the way the management administers the agreement. Administration is to a considerable degree a matter of action subject to challenge and response—the union challenging management's decisions and management defending its decisions. But different managements and unions assert their rights with varying degrees of frequency and reasonableness.

Because of differences in administrative practice and in interpretation, similar or identical contract clauses may lead to widely divergent results. The meaning of agreements cannot be determined by simply reading them. For example, there are many similarities among labor contracts in the basic steel industry. But there are variations in interpretation among plants of the same company, among divisions of the same company, and among companies. The gap between results and the language in the contract can be large and significant.

Variations in the results of identical contract clauses are particularly important when the obligation of management is simply to be reasonable. Thus, there are varying degrees of discipline, and the penalty imposed by management may be challenged on the ground that it is not appropriate to the offense. Likewise, production standards and incentive rates must presuppose a reasonable pace of work. Unions and managements, by the interest that they show in these matters and the vigor and determination with which they act, affect the quality of discipline and the speed of production lines. Hence, limits on managerial discretion may be greater than one would conclude from merely reading the contract.

Union influence on decision making may go beyond criticizing and protesting the decisions of management. In a few cases the union participates in making decisions. Management may, as a matter of practice, submit proposed decisions to the union for review and comment since the union officers may see aspects of the problem that escaped the attention of management. All of this means that the decision-making process has been broadened in many cases to include consultation. Consultation occurs in some instances simply as a matter of practice: management does not agree to consult, but in practice does consult. In other instances management may *agree* to consult before taking action, while retaining the right to make decisions subject to challenge as to their reasonableness or conformity with the agreement.[1] A few unions have succeeded in requiring that management act on certain matters only with the consent of the union. In those cases where the union has a veto, it is in an extremely strong bargaining position even on matters beyond the scope of the mutual consent clause.

Finally, restraints are imposed on management through arbitration provisions. Nine out of ten contracts today provide for arbitration—a big change from twenty years ago. Agreement to arbitrate means that management must be prepared to submit many decisions to the judgment of neutrals and to abide by the results. Arbitration also means that companies may find their discretion limited by their own past practices.

[1] The British trade union productivity team found little interest among American trade unionists in joint consultation. The British unionists said: "A fact we found surprising was unions' lack of interest in formal consultative machinery especially as many of them seem well qualified to make a contribution to plant efficiency through such machinery. The truth is that most unions do not expect or, we suspect, want to be consulted about the running of the plant. . . . There is nothing restrictive in this attitude, even if it is not cooperative. The job of managing is left to management." British Trades Union Congress, *Trade Unions and Productivity* (1950), p. 57.

950 IMPACT OF COLLECTIVE BARGAINING

The above discussion emphasizes primarily the way in which management's discretion has been limited. Far more difficult is to assess the significance and meaning of the actual limitations that have been imposed. One way in which management's discretion has been limited is by the increase in the number and variety of matters covered by the union-management contract. Another is the continuing process of contract interpretation and application. But the qualitative significance of these developments depends on value judgments. While there have been many positive gains to employees in the mutual development of policy, which limited management discretion implies, one qualitative aspect of this trend must be singled out for discussion.

Unions tend to favor policies that treat all employees alike. Managements also, to avoid challenge, seek objective criteria in the administration of policies. Under collective bargaining, decisions based on management's judgment of differences among employees or differences in circumstances tend to be limited.

Various illustrations of this tendency may be recalled: (1) The seniority principle sometimes has been carried to extreme limits. In many cases there are almost no exceptions to the application of seniority in promotion. This development is commonly by practice rather than by contract requirement. The simple principle appeals to union leaders; and the path of least resistance for management is to avoid making exceptions. Seniority also may be invoked in almost all temporary transfers. In one case the senior man had been asked whether he wanted to fill in for an absent employee on a particular job no less than sixteen times over a relatively short period. He had refused each time. On the seventeenth time the foreman forgot to ask, the employee grieved and was awarded pay. Past practice required that temporary vacancies be filled by a process of polling employees in the order of their seniority. (2) The merit principle has tended to disappear and to lose meaning. Where rate ranges exist, advancement to the maximum is more or less automatic. (3) The selective retirement principle is not used under bargained pension plans. In one case the possibility of selective retirement was raised within the management group. With less than two minutes' discussion management decided that it was impossible because it would cause grievances. (4) In discipline management has searched for and sometimes used automatic rules. Classification of reasons for discipline, with automatic and rigid penalties, has largely been given up, but it would never have been attempted except for the compulsion toward mechanical application of policy. There is a continuing reluctance to give weight to attendant circumstances because it is feared that exceptions weaken policy. In disciplining for absenteeism a number of companies use an automatic policy that makes no attempt to take into account the reasons for absence.

The trend away from the exercise of judgment by management in decisions of the types noted above cannot readily be labeled all "good" or all "bad." In the absence of unions the exercise of judgment by management was frequently abused, harmful to employee morale, and discriminatory in a true sense. But there are also drawbacks in removing substantially all rewards for superior performance. Not only is management deprived of ways of stimulating efficiency and obliged to accept practices involving excessive training or other costs, there are also questions of true equity in decisions affecting individuals and of a satisfying work environment for employees. Value judgments differ, but the easy way for unions, managements, and arbitrators must be seriously questioned. Effective and equitable management requires that many decisions be based on a judgment of men and circumstances. In a few instances, with improved union-management relations and a closer meeting of minds on basic principles, more flexibility has been accepted in the development and administration of contract provisions. This is an encouraging sign.

Development of Management by Policy

Collective bargaining seems to have greatly encouraged the development of management by policy. As stated in Chapter 29, companies that have been relatively successful in union-management relations gave evidence of following wise basic policies, of negotiating balanced general policies, of developing good implementing and procedural arrangements to make policy effective at the operating level, and of having considerable initiative in labor relations administration. The challenge that unions presented to management has, if viewed broadly, created superior and better-balanced management, even though some exceptions must be recognized.

One of the principal policy problems created by the rise of trade unions and collective bargaining is the introduction of competition within the firm between industrial relations and other policies, especially selling policies. Before the days of unions, such competition scarcely existed because management was free to subordinate industrial relations considerations to the interest of the enterprise in sales. But unions introduce the need for compromise. For example, to what extent should good industrial relations practices be sacrificed in order to avoid an interruption in sales or a temporary drop in output that would force a drop in sales? Should short-run profits be sacrificed in the interest of sound industrial relations, or should managements yield to economic pressure in order to avoid a short-run loss of profits? Companies that are in danger of losing important customers by failing to make deliveries on schedule find it difficult to pursue firm industrial relations policies and to insist on their rights under the union-management contract.

The need to compromise conflicting interests within the firm shows that collective bargaining tends to make exacting demands on management and to increase the need for wise and well-balanced executives and for effective collaboration in policy-making between operating officers and staff executives. Conditions are constantly changing, and the compromises between rival policies decided on today may not be suitable for tomorrow.

If one single statement were sought to describe the effect of unions on policy-making, it would be: "they have encouraged investigation and reflection." Some unions are in fact only a slight check on management; other unions run the shop. But whether the union influence is weak or strong, it always tends to force management to consider the probable consequences of its proposed decisions and to adjust those decisions accordingly.

Introduction of Important Changes in Management Structure

The need for expert administration of the many rules that come with union-management contracts and the problem of negotiating many technical supplements to the contracts has affected the structure of management. Specialists of various sorts are required to administer seniority rules, transfers, promotions, pensions, sick benefits, and other personnel practices that must be properly executed because the company is subject to grievances if it fails to meet its obligations. Not only are these specialists needed, but their work must be properly organized and supervised, and it must be coordinated with the work of the operating officers of the company. Hence, not only *staff*, but *staff organization*, is needed.

Twenty years ago there was very little staff in industrial relations. Today most large companies have lawyers, economists, statisticians, medical officers, social workers, psychologists, pension experts, insurance experts, and experienced personnel and labor relations officials and representatives. Smaller companies try to get the same kind of technical help by bringing in part-time consultants. The variety of staff organizations that has sprung up as a result of the need to deal with unions is very great. All of these organizations reflect the need for specialized knowledge to meet the wide variety of problems that arise in administering labor-management contracts.

The rise of unions has affected the operating organization as well as the staff. The degree of centralization or decentralization of management is affected by the presence of unions in the several plants of multiplant companies. It is hard to generalize about the effects of unions on line management. In most instances unions have tended to strengthen central management's control of certain basic labor policies that are applied in all its plants. In other instances unions have had the opposite effect—they have created so many difficult special problems that top management has given each plant the responsibility of making its own bargain. In still other cases the impact of unions is to strengthen the pressures for uniformity and centralization in certain matters and to reinforce the toleration of plant autonomy in others. The nature of the firm's product or product-mix seems to affect this decision, but is only one of the many influences determining the choice between centralized and decentralized management. The net effect of unions, however, is probably to increase the proportion of cases in which top management prefers uniform labor policies in its several plants.

It is not true, however, that management always gets the kind of unionism it is entitled to. Perhaps it does in some long-run and general sense, but unions vary in their own qualities and characteristics. Mutual interaction is not simply a process of union adjustment to management attitude and action. For example, reference was made at one point to a plant in which an aggressive and strong local union leader outlasted sixteen plant managers, and the plant was ultimately closed. Another plant comes to mind in which the local union leader unquestionably enjoyed fighting management. His bitterness toward management appeared to be exceeded only by his bitterness toward the international union. This management, the international union, and other local unions maintained satisfactory and constructive union-management relations. But it would be naive in the extreme to say that in this one plant management was getting the kind of union-management relations it deserved.

Diversity in Collective Bargaining

No matter what standards of comparison are used, there is great diversity in the character and results of collective bargaining. There are many differences in the economic and technological environment. Managements differ in attitudes and policies, and so do unions. Interest throughout this book has been in trends or patterns of development and in variation. Several chapters have been organized around the determinants of the various conditions described. Almost all chapters, however organized, have described and illustrated variations and have attempted to assist in understanding the differences that were found. A few concluding observations are warranted.

In the first place, the authors became increasingly conscious of the elements of individuality in each collective bargaining situation. The necessity to disguise identity and to organize material by topics inevitably resulted in giving up certain insights. Each union-management relationship had its particular history, its particular leadership, its particular economic and technological environment, and its particular problems. All of these many elements combined into an interrelated whole. While a very deliberate effort has been made to use illustrative material throughout the book, much of the richness of particular situations has been lost. Union-management relations are such, however, that an understanding of the many facets of variation can be achieved only in the light of very particular situations.

In the second place, generalizations that unions usually or always have this or that *particular* effect are highly hazardous. The sus-

picion exists that it would have been much easier to write a concluding chapter in a book on union-management relations if it had
not been preceded by three years of field work. The stubborn facts
of reality do not permit easy generalizations. To be sure, in *some*
economic and technological environments, associated with *some*
management and union policies and practices developed by *some*
management and union leaders worker productivity has fallen to
noncompetitive levels. In *some* situations it fell to low levels but has
been restored to competitive levels. In *some* situations the process of
restoration required a strike. In *some* situations worker productivity
has remained good over the entire history of the relationship. In
some situations management, left to its own devices, established an
unreasonably high work pace. To *some* degree union pressure has
encouraged technological change. What total effect have unions had
on worker efficiency and output per man-hour? For many (but not
all) purposes it seems more important to search for an understanding
of differences than to attempt generalizations.

In the third place, the results that flow from techniques, and the
manner in which many problems are met, depend upon the economic, the technological, and the labor relations environment. Various disciplines—economics, industrial engineering, sociology, psychology—contribute to an understanding of industrial relations problems. But labor relations also requires independent study. The
behavior of managements and unions—the institutional relationships
and the policies pursued—affects the results derived from such techniques as wage incentives, job evaluation, suggestion plans, and so
forth. Procedures such as the grievance procedure operate quite differently in different plants and companies. Responses to similar economic and technological problems are by no means uniform.

For example, as noted in the grievance chapter, the determinants
of grievance rates are many and varied, and far removed from any
absolute degree of justice and injustice with which management is
treating a group of employees. The determinants named are generalizations from various specific situations. They are helpful guides in
the analysis of individual union-management experiences but must
be made specific in each relationship. For example, one plant of a
large multiplant company comes to mind. The employment manager wanted an efficient plant. He associated efficiency with youth
and filled the plant with youngsters. There were 2,000 employees

with an average age of a little over 21 years. The union president was 24 years old. An important determinant of the grievance rate in that plant was obviously the employment policy that had been followed.

Wage incentive plans are based on the assumption that individual employees will respond to an opportunity to earn more money. But obviously this simple notion becomes submerged in a more complicated reality, a reality including particular management policies and practices and union policies and practices. For example, an American professor returning from Russia reports the widespread use of, and enthusiasm for, wage incentives in that country. Comparison of the operation of wage incentives in the United States and in Russia opens a fascinating area for speculation. While the comparison is no doubt complex in fact, in this instance management in Russia may, from various points of view, be operating in an environment decidedly more favorable to the use of incentives than does management in the United States. But to return to the main point, systems, techniques, procedures, and actions must be viewed in their particular environmental context to understand results, and any explanation of results must take account of determinants such as the policies and practices of the particular unions and managements.[2]

In the fourth place, one element of variation in union-management relations deserves repeated emphasis. While differences in the terms of union-management contracts are important, contract provisions are sometimes a poor clue to policy and practice in a plant. If a comparative study of seniority clauses and practices were made, for example, widespread differences would be found. Contract provisions that give management considerable latitude in departing from seniority would be found to remain in contracts because they have long since ceased to have meaning and hence are no issue between the parties. The ramifications of seniority are almost never fully portrayed even in local supplements. Parties differ in the degree to which they try to maintain consistency between contract terms and practice. The point need not be labored, but throughout this book only incidental attention has been paid to contract clauses. This was only partially a conscious decision. Much of the reality of labor rela-

[2] This point of view is ably developed in John T. Dunlop, *Industrial Relations Systems* (1958).

tions is in the implementation and interpretation of general clauses, principles, and rights.

Finally, variation in response to similar economic and technological environments is extremely interesting. Various firms in an industry, or closely comparable firms, or various plants within a company show significant differences in the character and results of collective bargaining, and it is often unrewarding to search for the explanation in external circumstances. Even working within the framework of the same general policies and procedures, differences in leadership qualities of management and union officials appear very important. Dramatic changes in the quality and character of union-management relations often result from changes in leadership. While it is desirable to search for other causes beyond variation in the ability and personality traits of individuals, the obvious importance of this variable in many comparisons should not be ignored.

Growth of Adjustment in Contract Administration

Emphasis in the previous section was on diversity in the character and results of collective bargaining. There also has been a growth in adjustment in day-to-day union-management relations, which is not inconsistent with continuing diversity. The notion was earlier introduced that in retrospect it is possible to discern over the last twenty or twenty-five years an organizing stage, a contract development stage, and a stage of adjustment in contract administration. Day-to-day conflict has declined as one stage has merged with and overlapped the next.

One dimension of adjustment has been the limited but significant growth of formal cooperation. Unions and collective bargaining can be more than instruments of protest, criticism, and protection. They can be instruments through which employees join with management in working out constructive schemes that require planning and that could not be created by competitive influences alone. An example is the cooperative effort to train skilled craftsmen. There have also been instances of unions joining with managements to study and expand markets. Of great significance to rank and file workers are the few instances of cooperative planning to introduce technological change. Joint action on the West Coast waterfront is a case in point.

A recent example is Armour and Company, where basic changes in manufacturing practices have required that a large part of the work force be taught new skills. In order to finance the retraining of the work force in new techniques, the company is creating a special fund and working jointly under a negotiated program. Unions play a vital role in some cooperative arrangements, such as the Scanlon Plan, that are built on planned employee participation.

Formal cooperation is not as significant, however, as the more general process of adjustment. Management has moved in the direction of concessions to unions, for example, by accepting a narrowing of managerial discretion, most obviously indicated by the expanded scope of labor contracts, by agreeing to extensive reliance on seniority, and by endorsing arbitration of grievances. Managements have also furthered the process of adjustment by the development of management by policy. Unions have made important concessions to the needs of management, for example, in the acceptance of job evaluation, progressive discipline, and discipline for wildcat strikes.

Adjustment of the goals and the policies of management and of unions has gone farther in the case of some issues than others. It has gone farthest in the following areas: (1) work-sharing and layoff systems, (2) formal or informal evaluation of particular job rates, (3) administration of the wide range of employee benefit plans and provisions, (4) systems of employee discipline, including the control of wildcats, (5) scheduling of work, (6) development and operation of the grievance procedure, and (7) acceptance of arbitration. Adjustment is less well developed in the following areas: (1) production standards and wage incentives, (2) promotion principles, (3) work assignment, and (4) subcontracting.

The process of adjustment is neither complete nor uniform. As certain conflict areas tend to become quite generally resolved, conflict may increase in other areas. Conflict over employee performance and subcontracting has intensified in recent years. Changes in business conditions and political considerations also have their influences on union-management relations.

Recognition must be given to the fact that, just as there are a limited number of highly cooperative union-management relationships, there are also a limited number of plants and companies in which conflict is quite intense. But the number in the latter category appears definitely to have declined over the years as the process of adjustment has moved forward. There are also some situations in which conflict is not intense but in which the terms of peace inadequately meet the long-run needs of one or both of the parties.

Adjustment in particular bargaining relationships implies more than a reduction of conflict. It is unquestionably true that managements can take advantage of weak unions and unions can take advantage of weak managements. Such situations may be peaceful, but they are not conducive to lasting peace. The term "good labor relations" must include within its meaning more than absence of conflict. Labor relations cannot be considered good if the absence of open conflict is due to the acceptance of inferior working conditions in a strong management-weak union situation. Nor can they be considered good if efficiency is impaired in a strong union-weak management combination. The selfish interests of each party must not override the reasonable interests of the other party or the common interests of both parties. A balanced relationship is, in fact, not likely to be characterized by unbroken peace. Both very low and very high grievance rates arouse suspicion. Even formal plans for union-management cooperation that are working well are not milk and honey affairs. Sharp differences of opinion arise, but the capacity exists to resolve differences in constructive fashion. To go further, at least some strikes have contributed to the process of adjustment.

To say that there has been growing adjustment in contract administration is not to overlook the amount of conflict still remaining with respect to manning, loose production standards, costly seniority extensions, and other rules and practices that unduly handicap efficiency. Management in many plants and for a period of several years has been restoring plant efficiency. It has been stated that this is an area of low adjustment. But removing the effects of excessive past concessions is quite consistent with the process of adjustment. Nor should the degree of conflict be exaggerated. Many union leaders have recognized the need for particular plants and companies to restore efficiency and have assisted in the process.

Some strikes have been required to eliminate costly practices. In these cases management went unsuccessfully year by year to the bargaining table with proposals to improve efficiency. A strike would have been required to gain concessions of this character, but rather than take a strike, management yielded on its demands. However, increasingly management has been willing to take a strike in the interest of the long-term welfare of the organization. In strikes of this character on which it is now possible to look back with a few years of perspective, it is frequently possible to conclude (to reverse a common expression) that both sides have won. Strikes frequently have brought significant management concessions to employees and unions. Strikes resulting from the failure of persuasion to achieve union and employee concessions do not mean collective bargaining has failed.

Nothing has been said on the question of conflict in negotiation over wages and the economic package. No conclusion is intended concerning the degree of adjustment with respect to the negotiation of economic demands, but there are some signs of a more realistic facing up to the problems involved. The conclusion is only that day-to-day contract administration reflects growing accommodation. This accommodation represents substantial progress compared with the state of affairs in 1940 or 1950.

Social Significance of the American System of Industrial Relations

The American practice of settling labor issues in the main by collective bargaining rather than by legislation has aroused little interest abroad. But the American collective bargaining system must be regarded as one of the most successful economic institutions in the country. In the great majority of plants it has produced rules and policies that are fair to both sides and that permit managements to conduct operations efficiently. Although there is wide variation in the results of bargaining, the concentration of settlements that are good compromises is large. And these compromises have been worked out with very little loss of time from strikes and lockouts.

An important result of the American system of collective bargaining is the sense of participation that it imparts to workers. The many local agreements or local supplementary agreements help create such a feeling. It is true that few workers participate directly in determining their working conditions and rate of pay, but they belong to organizations that do participate. Hence, the ordinary worker does not feel left out. He knows that important changes cannot occur in markets and technology without their effect on him being considered.

These are not the conditions that produce demands for radical changes or in which movements of dissent and protest flourish. Collective bargaining must be reckoned among the influences that make the American society stable and conservative. But there is concern that this stability and conservatism are achieved at the expense of the consumer. How to diminish the tendency of our economic institutions to produce rising prices is one of the great unsolved problems of the time. But the American system of industrial relations is characteristic of our free society. Free collective bargaining produces compromises which cannot be expected to meet fully all definitions of the public interest. Nevertheless, experience to date evidences a degree of social progress that few would have predicted twenty years ago.

Index

Aaron, Benjamin, 739n, 757n
Abelson, Paul, 744, 748n
Ability vs. seniority criterion. *See under*
Promotion policies and procedures
Absenteeism, 113, 118-19; disciplinary measures against, 637-40
Adjustment, system boards of, 743-46, 746n, 789-90, 791n, 802
Aeronautical Lodge v. *Campbell*, 138
Agency shops, 27, 27n
Air Line Pilots Association, 249, 380, 398, 607-8
Airline companies, work scheduling problems of, 213, 215, 216, 233-34
Amalgamated Clothing Workers, 29n, 36, 48, 48n, 53, 70, 291, 301, 355, 374, 383, 409, 463, 497n, 523-24, 743, 845, 847
Amalgamated Lithographers, 224
Amalgamated Meat Cutters and Butcher Workmen, 351, 701, 775, 929
American Airlines, 363, 475
American Arbitration Association, 652, 745, 746, 754, 756, 756n, 792
American Association of Industrial Relations Counselors, 561
American Bakery and Confectionery Workers, 394, 416
American Communications Association, 486
American Federation of Hosiery Workers, 470, 524
American Federation of Labor, 246, 247, 260, 287-88, 372, 408, 409, 667, 700, 701, 701n, 708, 776
American Federation of Labor-Congress of Industrial Organizations, 2-3, 30, 248, 771, 815, 828; Constitution, on jurisdiction, 248 248n

American Flint Glass Workers, 76n, 77, 263-64
American Management Association, 630
American Medical Association, 410, 411
American Newspaper Guild, 289, 313, 467, 469, 472, 473, 477, 604; severance pay plans, 474-75, 483, 486, 488
American Newspaper Publishers' Association, 742, 930
American Tobacco Company, 474
American Train Dispatchers' Association, 38n
Anderson, Odin W., 418, 418n
Anthracite Board of Conciliation, 743
Apprenticeship and training (*see also* Skilled workers), 59-103; apprenticeship as source of skilled workers, 68-69; Boilermakers' program, 86-88; construction industry, training in, 81, 82, 103; contests, 92-93, 93n; coordinators, use of, in training programs, 92, 92n; demobilization, effects on union policies, 77, 99-100; depression (1930's), effects on union policies, 75-77, 99; Electrical Workers' program, 82, 83, 95-98; expansion of training, prospects for, 102-3; glass industry's program during depression of 1930's, 76n; joint apprenticeship committees, 74-75; layoff, protection of apprentices against, 85; Machinist's program, 88-91; number of apprentices, influence of unions on, 81-82; number of apprentices in registered programs, 69, 69n, 102-3; Operating Engineers' program, 85-86; Plumbers and Steamfitters' program, 91-95; postwar changes in union policies on, 77-81; proportion of

963

work rules in, 350-51, 350n; Pacific Coast, use of overtime on, 242-43; regulation of sling loads, 318, 330; San Francisco waterfront, removal of restrictive working rules on, 319, 319n; wage rates, 243

McCaffree, Kenneth M., 613, 613n
McCauley, John S., 83n, 97n, 102n
"Machine seniority," 107, 115
McClellan Committee, 49
McConnell, John W., 372n, 373n
McCorry, Ann H., 172n
McDonald, David, 231
MacDonald, Robert M., 610n
MacGowan, C. F., 86n
McKersie, Robert B., 533n, 541n
McKiever, Margaret F., 402n, 408n, 409n, 411n, 414n
Maintenance-of-membership agreements, 27; proportion of contracts in 1946 and 1954, 33-34
Make-work rules and policies, 317-41, 350, 350n, 369; effects of, 337-38; elimination of, employers' efforts toward, 339-41; excessive crews, requirement of, 322-29; excessive relief time, requirement of, 330; factors limiting, 338-39; factors underlying union success in imposing, 336-37; less efficient work methods, enforcement of, 330; limits on amount of load, 318; limits on the number of machines operated, 321-22; loose production standards, enforcement of, 331; principal kinds of, 317-32; prohibition of use of modern equipment, 329-30; reasons for union interest in, 335-37; repeated work performance, requirement of, 320-21; restrictions on duties of workers, 318-19; unnecessary standby crews, requirement of, 331; unnecessary work, requirement of, 321; unnecessary workers, extent of the practice of hiring, 332-35
Management (see also Contracts; Grievances; Union-management cooperation): adjustment to the presence of the union, problems of, 13-14; administration of contracts, policies concerning, 14-20; collective bargaining, impact on, 946-61; competitive costs, success in achieving, 10-11; development of, by policy, 951-52; and discipline, uniformity in administer-

ing, 19; discussion of plans with the union, 22; and employees, communication with, 24-25; grievances, policy on, 713-20; impact of unions on, factors underlying, 6-7; interest of, in job evaluation, 560; interest of, in labor costs, 820-24; issues for, in industrial relations, 9-26; joint union-management action, 23-24; labor relations function of, 879-85; leadership, effect on grievance arbitration rates, 768-69; maintenance of established shop practices, policies toward, 17; policies toward unions, decisions influencing, 10-13; policy decisions implementing labor policies, 21-26; pressure tactics, effects on, 678-82; pressure tactics, policy toward use of, 15-16, 682-87; and production standards, 550-55; quality of, impact on labor costs, 809-13; reorganization of, to deal with unions, 20-21; representation of, in contract negotiations, 923-25; restraints imposed on, 947-51; role in negotiating and administering agreements, 11-12; scheduling problems of, 219-21; structural changes, 952-54; subordinate, support of decisions of, 20, 20n; supplementary agreements, policies toward, 17-19; support of union officers by, 22-23; union-management relations and pressure tactics, 665-68; and usurpation of authority by union representatives, 16-17; work assignment policies and practices, 254-55
Manufacturing industries, organization of workers in, 2
Manufacturing and service enterprises, work assignment and jurisdictional problems in, 262-66
Marine Engineers' Beneficial Association, 473
Massachusetts, Board of Arbitration created in, 742
Mathewson, S. B., 591n
Meany, George, 265
Measured daywork, 530-57, 606; administration of, 539-46; grievance procedure, 549; and production standards, 550-57; replacement of incentive by, 534-39; technology and method of pay, 530-34; term, defined, 490n; and use of union time-study representatives, 546-50